Contemporary
Literary Criticism

Guide to Gale Literary Criticism Series

When you need to review criticism of literary works, these are the Gale series to use:

If the author's death date is:

You should turn to:

After Dec. 31, 1959
(or author is still living)

CONTEMPORARY LITERARY CRITICISM

for example: Jorge Luis Borges, Anthony Burgess,
William Faulkner, Mary Gordon,
Ernest Hemingway, Iris Murdoch

1900 through 1959

TWENTIETH-CENTURY LITERARY CRITICISM

for example: Willa Cather, F. Scott Fitzgerald,
Henry James, Mark Twain, Virginia Woolf

1800 through 1899

NINETEENTH-CENTURY LITERATURE CRITICISM

for example: Fedor Dostoevski, Nathaniel Hawthorne,
George Sand, William Wordsworth

1400 through 1799

LITERATURE CRITICISM FROM 1400 TO 1800
(excluding Shakespeare)

for example: Anne Bradstreet, Daniel Defoe,
Alexander Pope, François Rabelais,
Jonathan Swift, Phillis Wheatley

SHAKESPEAREAN CRITICISM

Shakespeare's plays and poetry

Antiquity through 1399

CLASSICAL AND MEDIEVAL LITERATURE CRITICISM

for example: Dante, Homer, Plato, Sophocles, Vergil,
the Beowulf poet

(Volume 1 forthcoming)

Gale also publishes related criticism series:

CHILDREN'S LITERATURE REVIEW

This ongoing series covers authors of all eras. Presents criticism on
authors and author/illustrators who write for the preschool
through high school audience.

CONTEMPORARY ISSUES CRITICISM

This two-volume set presents criticism on contemporary authors
writing on current issues. Topics covered include the social sciences,
philosophy, economics, natural science, law, and related areas.

ISSN 0091-3421

Volume 41

Contemporary Literary Criticism

Excerpts from Criticism of the
Works of Today's Novelists, Poets,
Playwrights, Short Story Writers, Scriptwriters,
and Other Creative Writers

Daniel G. Marowski
Roger Matuz
EDITORS

Jane E. Neidhardt
Robyn V. Young
ASSOCIATE EDITORS

Gale Research Company
Book Tower
Detroit, Michigan 48226

STAFF

Daniel G. Marowski, Roger Matuz, *Editors*

Jane E. Neidhardt, Robyn V. Young, *Associate Editors*

Molly L. Norris, Sean R. Pollock, Jane C. Thacker, Debra A. Wells, *Senior Assistant Editors*

Kelly King Howes, Michele R. O'Connell, David Segal,
Thomas J. Votteler, Bruce Walker, *Assistant Editors*

Jean C. Stine, *Contributing Editor*

Melissa Reiff Hug, *Contributing Assistant Editor*

Lizbeth A. Purdy, *Production Supervisor*
Denise Michlewicz Broderick, *Production Coordinator*
Eric Berger, *Assistant Production Coordinator*
Kathleen M. Cook, Maureen Duffy, Sheila J. Nasea, *Editorial Assistants*

Linda M. Pugliese, *Manuscript Coordinator*
Donna Craft, *Assistant Manuscript Coordinator*
Jennifer E. Gale, Maureen A. Puhl, Rosetta Irene Simms, *Manuscript Assistants*

Victoria B. Cariappa, *Research Coordinator*
Maureen R. Richards, *Assistant Research Coordinator*
Daniel Kurt Gilbert, Kent Graham, Keith E. Schooley, Filomena Sgambati,
Vincenza G. Tranchida, Mary D. Wise, *Research Assistants*

Jeanne A. Gough, *Permissions Supervisor*
Janice M. Mach, *Permissions Coordinator, Text*
Patricia A. Seefelt, *Permissions Coordinator, Illustrations*
Susan D. Battista, Margaret A. Chamberlain, *Assistant Permissions Coordinators*
Sandra C. Davis, Kathy Grell, Josephine M. Keene,
Mary M. Matuz, *Senior Permissions Assistants*
H. Diane Cooper, Colleen M. Crane,
Mabel E. Schoening, *Permissions Assistants*
Eileen Baehr, Margaret A. Carson, Anita Williams, *Permissions Clerks*

Special thanks to Carolyn Bancroft
for her assistance on the Title Index

Frederick G. Ruffner, *Publisher*
Dedria Bryfonski, *Editorial Director*
Ellen T. Crowley, *Associate Editorial Director*
Christine Nasso, *Director, Literature Division*
Laurie Lanzen Harris, *Senior Editor, Literary Criticism Series*
Dennis Poupard, *Managing Editor, Literary Criticism Series*

Library of Congress Catalog Card Number 76-38938
ISBN 0-8103-4415-7
ISSN 0091-3421

Computerized photocomposition by
Typographics, Incorporated
Kansas City, Missouri

Printed in the United States

Contents

Preface

Literary criticism is, by definition, "the art of evaluating or analyzing with knowledge and propriety works of literature." The complexity and variety of the themes and forms of contemporary literature make the function of the critic especially important to today's reader. It is the critic who assists the reader in identifying significant new writers, recognizing trends in critical methods, mastering new terminology, and monitoring scholarly and popular sources of critical opinion.

Until the publication of the first volume of *Contemporary Literary Criticism (CLC)* in 1973, there existed no ongoing digest of current literary opinion. *CLC,* therefore, has fulfilled an essential need.

Scope of the Work

CLC presents significant passages from published criticism of works by today's creative writers. Each volume of *CLC* includes excerpted criticism on about 50 authors who are now living or who died after December 31, 1959. Almost 1,800 authors have been included since the series began publication. The majority of authors covered by *CLC* are living writers who continue to publish; therefore, an author frequently appears in more than one volume. There is, of course, no duplication of reprinted criticism.

Authors are selected for inclusion for a variety of reasons, among them the publication of a critically acclaimed new work, the reception of a major literary award, or the dramatization of a literary work as a movie or television screenplay. For example, the present volume includes John Ashbery, whose recent collection of verse, *A Wave,* won the Lenore Marshall/Nation Poetry Prize; Angela Carter, recipient of the James Tait Black Memorial Prize for her novel *Nights at the Circus;* and Sam Shepard, whose play *A Lie of the Mind* won the New York Drama Critics' Circle Award. Perhaps most importantly, authors who appear frequently on the syllabuses of high school and college literature classes are heavily represented in *CLC;* T. S. Eliot and Ernest Hemingway are examples of writers of this stature in the present volume. Attention is also given to several other groups of writers—authors of considerable public interest—about whose work criticism is often difficult to locate. These are the contributors to the well-loved but nonscholarly genres of mystery and science fiction, as well as literary and social critics whose insights are considered valuable and informative. Foreign writers and authors who represent particular ethnic groups in the United States are also featured in each volume.

Format of the Book

Altogether there are about 700 individual excerpts in each volume—with an average of about 14 excerpts per author—taken from hundreds of literary reviews, general magazines, scholarly journals, and monographs. Contemporary criticism is loosely defined as that which is relevant to the evaluation of the author under discussion; this includes criticism written at the beginning of an author's career as well as current commentary. Emphasis has been placed on expanding the sources for criticism by including an increasing number of scholarly and specialized periodicals. Students, teachers, librarians, and researchers frequently find that the generous excerpts and supplementary material provided by the editors supply them with all the information needed to write a term paper, analyze a poem, or lead a book discussion group. However, complete bibliographical citations facilitate the location of the original source as well as provide all of the information necessary for a term paper footnote or bibliography.

A *CLC* author entry consists of the following elements:

● The **author heading** cites the author's full name, followed by birth date, and death date when applicable. The portion of the name outside the parentheses denotes the form under which the author has most commonly published. If an author has written consistently under a pseudonym, the pseudonym will be listed in the author heading and the real name given on the first line of the biographical and critical introduction. Also located at the beginning of the introduction to the author entry are any important name variations under which an author has written. Uncertainty as to a birth or death date is indicated by question marks.

- A **portrait** of the author is included when available.

- A brief **biographical and critical introduction** to the author and his or her work precedes the excerpted criticism. However, *CLC* is not intended to be a definitive biographical source. Therefore, *cross-references* have been included to direct the reader to other useful sources published by the Gale Research Company: *Contemporary Authors* now includes detailed biographical and bibliographical sketches on nearly 86,000 authors; *Children's Literature Review* presents excerpted criticism on the works of authors of children's books; *Something about the Author* contains heavily illustrated biographical sketches on writers and illustrators who create books for children and young adults; *Contemporary Issues Criticism* presents excerpted commentary on the nonfiction works of authors who influence contemporary thought; *Dictionary of Literary Biography* provides original evaluations of authors important to literary history; *Contemporary Authors Autobiography Series* offers autobiographical essays by prominent writers; and the new *Something about the Author Autobiography Series* presents autobiographical essays by authors of interest to young readers. Previous volumes of *CLC* in which the author has been featured are also listed in the introduction.

- The **excerpted criticism** represents various kinds of critical writing—a particular essay may be normative, descriptive, interpretive, textual, appreciative, comparative, or generic. It may range in form from the brief review to the scholarly monograph. Essays are selected by the editors to reflect the spectrum of opinion about a specific work or about an author's literary career in general. The excerpts are presented chronologically, adding a useful perspective to the entry. All titles by the author featured in the entry are printed in boldface type, which enables the reader to easily identify the works being discussed.

- A complete **bibliographical citation** designed to help the user find the original essay or book follows each excerpt.

Other Features

- A list of **Authors Forthcoming in *CLC*** previews the authors to be researched for future volumes.

- An **Appendix** lists the sources from which material in the volume has been reprinted. Many other sources have also been consulted during the preparation of the volume.

- A **Cumulative Author Index** lists all the authors who have appeared in *Contemporary Literary Criticism, Twentieth-Century Literary Criticism, Nineteenth-Century Literature Criticism*, and *Literature Criticism from 1400 to 1800*, along with cross-references to other Gale series: *Children's Literature Review, Authors in the News, Contemporary Authors, Contemporary Authors Autobiography Series, Dictionary of Literary Biography, Something about the Author, Something about the Author Autobiography Series*, and *Yesterday's Authors of Books for Children*. Users will welcome this cumulated author index as a useful tool for locating an author within the various series. The index, which lists birth and death dates when available, will be particularly valuable for those authors who are identified with a certain period but whose death date causes them to be placed in another, or for those authors whose careers span two periods. For example, F. Scott Fitzgerald is found in *Twentieth-Century Literary Criticism*, yet a writer often associated with him, Ernest Hemingway, is found in *Contemporary Literary Criticism*.

- A **Cumulative Nationality Index** lists the authors included in *CLC* alphabetically by nationality, followed by the volume numbers in which they appear.

- Beginning with Volume 40, in response to suggestions from many users and librarians, a **Cumulative Title Index** has replaced the Cumulative Index to Critics. The Cumulative Title Index lists titles reviewed in *CLC* (novels, novellas, short stories, poems, dramas, essays, films, songs) in alphabetical order. Titles are followed by the corresponding volume and page numbers where they may be located; all titles reviewed in *CLC* from Volume 1 through the current volume are cited. In cases where the same title is used by different authors, the author's surname is given in parentheses after the title, e.g., *Collected Poems* (Berryman), *Collected Poems* (Eliot). For foreign titles, a cross-reference is given to the translated English title. Titles of novels, novellas, dramas, films, record albums, and poetry, short story, and essay collections are printed in italics, while all individual poems, short stories, essays, and songs are printed in roman type within quotation marks; when published separately (e.g., T.S. Eliot's poem *The Waste Land*), the title will also be printed in italics.

Acknowledgments

No work of this scope can be accomplished without the cooperation of many people. The editors especially wish to thank the copyright holders of the excerpted essays included in this volume, the permissions managers of many book and magazine publishing companies for assisting us in securing reprint rights, and the photographers and other individuals who provided portraits of the authors. We are grateful to the staffs of the Detroit Public Library, the Wayne State University Library, the University of Michigan Library, and the University of Detroit Library for making their resources available to us. We also wish to thank Anthony Bogucki for his assistance with copyright research.

Suggestions Are Welcome

The editors welcome the comments and suggestions of readers to expand the coverage and enhance the usefulness of the series.

Authors Forthcoming in *CLC*

To Be Included in Volume 42

James Baldwin (American novelist, essayist, and critic)—A prolific and popular author of such novels as *Go Tell It on the Mountain* and *Giovanni's Room*, Baldwin examines the state of black people in the United States in *The Price of the Ticket*, which features essays from his entire career.

Julian Barnes (English novelist, editor, and critic)—Barnes's novel *Flaubert's Parrot*, an insightful and humorous combination of fiction and criticism, has garnered considerable praise and has inspired renewed interest in his earlier novels, *Metroland* and *Before She Met Me*.

William S. Burroughs (American novelist and short story writer)—In his recent novels, *The Place of Dead Roads* and *Cities of the Red Night*, Burroughs continues to employ the experimental techniques that won him fame for such works as *Naked Lunch*.

Robertson Davies (Canadian novelist, dramatist, short story writer, and nonfiction writer)—An outstanding figure in Canadian letters, Davies has recently published *What's Bred in the Bone*, a novel that has furthered his reputation as an important contemporary author.

Harlan Ellison (American short story writer, novelist, scriptwriter, and nonfiction writer)—*An Edge in My Voice*, a collection of essays on nonfiction topics, displays the controversial moralistic approach that distinguishes Ellison's award-winning science fiction works.

Dick Francis (Welsh-born English novelist)—Francis is a popular and respected mystery author whose experiences as a jockey have influenced his novels centered in the world of horse racing. His recent novel, *Proof*, is a tale of murder and intrigue involving the wine and liquor industries.

Larry Kramer (American dramatist, novelist, and scriptwriter)—In his acclaimed play *The Normal Heart*, Kramer seeks to broaden public awareness of the physical and psychological effects of AIDS.

Harry Mulisch (Dutch novelist, short story writer, dramatist, poet, and essayist)—One of Holland's most acclaimed and popular authors, Mulisch has gained attention in the United States for his novel *The Assault*. This work examines four years in the life of a man whose family was unjustly executed by Nazi forces during World War II.

Dave Smith (American poet, novelist, and nonfiction writer)—Regarded as one of the most important poets to have emerged in the United States during the 1970s, Smith explores a wide range of themes in his verse. His recent collection, *The Roundhouse Voices: Selected and New Poems*, has received significant critical attention.

Walter Tevis (American novelist and short story writer)—Tevis is best known for his novels *The Hustler, The Man Who Fell to Earth*, and *The Color of Money*, each of which has been adapted into a critically acclaimed film.

Mario Vargas Llosa (Peruvian novelist, short story writer, and nonfiction writer)—Criticism on this leading contemporary Latin American writer will focus on *The War of the End of the World* and *The Real Life of Alejandro Mayta*, his latest novels.

Derek Walcott (West Indian poet and dramatist)—In his poetry Walcott explores themes related to his mixed heritage while evoking his life in the Caribbean islands. The publication of *Collected Poems, 1948-1984* has secured Walcott's position as an important and versatile poet.

John Betjeman (English poet and nonfiction writer)—Poet Laureate of England from 1972 until his death in 1984, Betjeman is best remembered for his literal, descriptive poetic style and his blend of humor and seriousness.

Rita Mae Brown (American novelist, poet, essayist, and scriptwriter)—Brown's fiction revolves around strong female characters who are distinguished by their humor and their determination to succeed. Her recent novels include *Sudden Death* and *High Hearts.*

Dennis Brutus (South African poet, essayist, and critic)—Brutus, who has lived in exile in England and the United States for over twenty years, is considered one of the most significant contemporary South African poets and is also well known for his participation in the anti-apartheid movement.

E. E. Cummings (American poet, novelist, essayist, and dramatist)—One of the most innovative poets of the twentieth century, Cummings experimented with typography, syntax, and punctuation while exploring such traditional themes as love, loss of innocence, and supremacy of the individual.

Zbigniew Herbert (Polish poet, dramatist, and essayist)—One of Poland's most important contemporary poets, Herbert often explores historical and political themes and centers on the conflict between ideals and reality. His recently translated works include *Report from the Besieged City,* a collection of verse, and *Barbarian in the Garden,* a volume of essays.

L. Ron Hubbard (American novelist, nonfiction writer, and short story writer)—Best known as the controversial author of *Dianetics* and the founder of the Church of Scientology, Hubbard was also a significant science fiction writer. His posthumously published fiction works include *The Enemy Within* and *An Alien Affair.*

Tama Janowitz (American short story writer, novelist, and journalist)—Janowitz became a literary celebrity with her short story collection *Slaves of New York,* in which she uses deadpan humor to chronicle the lives of bizarre characters who populate the art galleries, nightclubs, and restaurants of New York's Soho district.

Clarice Lispector (Ukrainian-born Brazilian novelist and short story writer)—Since Lispector's death in 1979, two of her works, *Family Ties* and *The Apple in the Dark,* have been reissued in English translation and two others, *The Foreign Legion* and *The Hour of the Star,* have been translated and published in the United States for the first time.

Nicholas Mosley (English novelist and nonfiction writer)—In his fiction, Mosley employs modernist narrative techniques to explore the underlying motives of human behavior. His recent novel, *Judith,* is the third of a projected six volumes detailing the lives of the characters in his complex work *Catastrophe Practice.*

Joe Orton (English dramatist, scriptwriter, and novelist)—Best remembered as the author of *What the Butler Saw* and other popular plays of the 1960s, Orton blended black humor, farce, and violence in his dramas to satirize archaic British moral standards.

Reynolds Price (American novelist, short story writer, essayist, poet, and dramatist)—A respected writer in several genres, Price is best known for his fiction, which is firmly rooted in the Southern tradition. Price's recent novel, *Kate Vaiden,* has been widely praised as his most accomplished work.

John Updike (American novelist, critic, and short story writer)—Updike is regarded as one of the most eminent authors in contemporary literature. His recent novel, *Roger's Version,* centers on the spiritual conflicts of two men, one of whom seeks to prove the existence of God through the use of computers.

(Kareen) Fleur Adcock

1934-

New Zealand-born English poet, editor, and translator.

Adcock is praised for her clear, precise language, her ironic wit, and her disciplined yet inventive style. Her poems are delivered in a restrained voice that is occasionally countered by surprising, sometimes nightmarish imagery, resulting in a compelling blend of the rational and the fantastic. Andrew Motion described this aspect of Adcock's work as a set of dichotomies "between high hopes and bad dreams, between fact and fantasy, between innocence and disillusionment, and between what can be observed and what can be imagined." Several critics have noted Adcock's penchant for traditional form as well as her pronounced awareness of her role and responsibilities as a poet.

Adcock's first volume to attract critical attention, *Tigers* (1967), describes the familiar objects, scenes, and relationships of domestic life. The poems in her next collection, *High Tide in the Garden* (1971), retain similar concerns while expanding the imaginative scope of her work by exploring such topics as dreams and nightmares, love and sex, and her bond with her children. *The Scenic Route* (1974) includes verse that focuses on an intimate personal realm as well as observations drawn from Adcock's travels through England, Ireland, Nepal, and other countries. In this volume, Adcock addresses her connection with New Zealand, where she was born and spent most of her childhood. Adcock's feelings about New Zealand also dominate *The Inner Harbour* (1979), in which she details the experiences of dreams, sickness, death, and self-knowledge. Reviewers of these volumes lauded Adcock's juxtaposition of her characteristically quiet, rational voice with startling images and noted a trend toward poetry more rooted in the emotions. In a review of *The Inner Harbour*, Peter Porter stated that "the progress of her work has been into a warmer world of the affections, and never away from a classical detachment of style, which has always been hers to deploy." Adcock's other publications include *Selected Poems* (1983) and a collection of poems that she translated, *The Virgin and the Nightingale: Medieval Latin Poems* (1983).

(See also *Contemporary Authors*, Vols. 25-28, rev. ed.; *Contemporary Authors New Revision Series*, Vol. 11; and *Dictionary of Literary Biography*, Vol. 40.)

Photograph by Marti Friedlander. Courtesy of Fleur Adcock

THE TIMES LITERARY SUPPLEMENT

Some of Miss Adcock's explorations of love relationships [in *Tigers*] have a tender and mild, and yet fairly shrewd quality (see **"The House"** and **"Parting is Such Sweet Sorrow"**) even if others (earlier work?) tend to shelve down too easily into vague and hazy romanticism. She makes a kind of suballegory out of the domestic context with occasional success, but is not a writer for the deeper matters, as some not-too-successful dream poems make clear. Perhaps the most rewarding verses in a readable if unsensational volume are those addressed in a casually whimsical and yet pleasantly balanced way to children and animals: **"Tigers"** itself, **"For Andrew"** and **"Think Before you Shoot"**.

"Fertile Desert," in The Times Literary Supplement, *No. 3420, September 14, 1967, p. 820.*

HOWARD SERGEANT

Although the New Zealand poet, Fleur Adcock, attempts a variety of themes in [*Tigers*] . . . , she is most successful in the poems which deal with intimate human relationships such as those existing between lovers, or between mother and child. For this particular genre, her disciplined (though not austere) style is extremely well adapted, since it enables her to maintain a tightrope sense of balance between sentimentality on one side and over-romanticized gesture on the other. In fact, now and then there is a touch of venom (as in **"Instructions to Vampires"** and **"Advice to a Discarded Lover"**) which may take by surprise the reader who has allowed himself to be led into a false state of security by Miss Adcock's deft command of language. In the mother-to-child genre she achieves her finest effects by narrowly averting the danger of whimsicality, as she does so faultlessly in **"For a Five-Year-Old"**.

Howard Sergeant, in a review of "Tigers," in English, *Vol. XVII, No. 97, Spring, 1968, p. 30.*

ALAN BROWNJOHN

Poets still tend to look for the same conclusions, but in different places now: Fleur Adcock's allegories and love parables are a case in point. *High Tide in the Garden* has a successful sequence, **"Gas"**, where material from nightmare is ordered with a nicely controlled sense of horror. But too often she pulls back, resting on secure or reassuring ground: the domestic poem of the Sixties is alive and well here, not menaced quite, perhaps, by **"Bogyman"**, or the faceless super ego of **"Clarendon Whatmough"**, or the doubts in the love poems—or even the 'savage tide' of the most promising poem, **"Being Blind"**. Refusing the fashionable postures is admirable, but an original, individual voice with something different to say—one feels it *could* happen—is only emerging occasionally so far. (p. 856)

Alan Brownjohn, "Different Guises," in New Statesman, *Vol. 81, No. 2100, June 18, 1971, pp. 854, 856.*

THE TIMES LITERARY SUPPLEMENT

Fleur Adcock's poems have a well-bred, genteel air about them, even though their point is often deliberately to ruffle this fastidious control by introducing elements of nightmare and fantasy which tend to undermine it. . . . Even so, one can't entirely avoid the suspicion that the odd glimpse into chaos is briefly admitted into these elegantly wrought poems [collected in *High Tide in the Garden*] in order to confirm that there is, after all, a bit more to Miss Adcock's world than the garden, sons and cats of whom she fondly speaks. The poems have an Eliotic trick of introducing the odd, fussily pedantic fact into their reflections ("a misty autumn Sunday, not unpopulated by birds"): and while this device for fending off direct feeling is meant to be faintly self-parodic—a way of keeping balance in public— it also seems to betray a genuine distance from experience:

> I write in praise of the solitary act:
> of not feeling a trespassing tongue
> forced into one's mouth, one's breath ʼ
> smothered, nipples crushed against the
> ribcage, and that metallic tingling
> in the chin set off by a certain odd nerve . . .

This is a self-conscious verbal pose, but something more as well, which the pose partly pokes fun at and partly protects. Several of the poems have a sort of running, parenthetical self-commentary woven through them, a series of judicious quibbling asides which can amount, in the end, to a slightly precious self-consciousness. . . .

"Jumping over the Cracks," in The Times Literary Supplement, *No. 3621, July 23, 1971, p. 855.*

DOUGLAS DUNN

Vigorous imagination galvanises an untranquil state of feelings in Fleur Adcock's second collection [*High Tide in the Garden*]. She invents "otherness" characters with whom she talks on the subjects of fear (**"Bogyman"**) and, in **"Clarendon Whatmough"**, the oppressions of righteousness. Both poems have sufficient directness to underplay the strain on the jaunty verse, especially in **"Clarendon Whatmough"** which is written in

the rhymed light verse of terror relying, as poetry of the grotesque often does, on the ironic antithesis of an important subject expressed in unlikely form. . . . To be absolutely successful, the poem would have had to carry a denser burden of shock and imagery. As it is, it relies too much on narrative and scene-setting; but it does at least demonstrate that Adcock is prepared to take risks with imagination. More evidence of this is immediate from **"Gas"**, a long and mysterious poem. Gas falls on a village; it deals death and duplication. People die or become two, then four, then eight . . . They long for "what death there is."

Whatever it is that's being said, **"Gas"** is a powerful poem that would have been less impressive had its mission been clearer. Her best poem is a great deal less ambitious than **"Gas."** Although calm and gently written, **"Country Station"** is a poem in which everything is right, the ambition is (as it should be) to match the mood and story of the recollection rather than be impressive. (pp. 74-5)

Douglas Dunn, "A Bridge in Minneapolis," in Encounter, *Vol. XXXVIII, No. 5, May, 1972, pp. 73-8.*

JOHN R. REED

[Fleur Adcock] is capable of rendering immediate experience both believable and significant to a reader, as in poems [in *High Tide in the Garden*] like **"On a Son Returned to New Zealand"** or **"Mornings After."** She is also willing to experiment, if not with language, at any rate with approach. **"Gas"** is an intriguing attempt to convey, in what resembles a science fiction atmosphere, the discovery of the inescapable flexibility of identity in a world deprived of meaning. After all, though, the poems only tease us. Chiefly they do not say anything we would be sorry not to have heard, and it is, I think, primarily because their language is not exciting enough. The poems are competent and interesting, but sometimes lapse into uncertain playfulness, as in **"Clarendon Whatmough"**, where the rhymes are neither good nor comic, or into the artificial profound, perhaps sufficiently represented by a line from **"Grandma"** which declares: "even the dead want to be loved for their own sake." In some cases, the poems are excessively simple, betraying any expectations of syntactical development. **"A Game"** is an example of this characteristic; but more ambitious poems, like **"A Surprise in the Peninsula"**, display the same weakness. I do not, however, wish to charge the poet with having failed to experiment with diction or metre, for I have the impression that these matters were not foremost in her mind when she wrote them. I suspect she was more concerned with the play of a refined sensibility on certain themes and situations. The craft, supposedly, comes automatically. (p. 49)

John R. Reed, "Magicians and Others," in Poetry, *Vol. CXXII, No. 1, April, 1973, pp. 47-55.*

COLIN FALCK

Fleur Adcock occasionally writes lines like 'My spine trickles with little white flames' which her poems would be better without, but there is a receptivity to life and an honesty of self-exposure in her verse which is not unattractive. The balance between what is presented—one always knows what is going on—and what is poetically made of it is sensitively maintained. In her new book *The Scenic Route* there are personal poems and also some travel poems which take in more of the outside world, and although they rarely gather themselves into anything significantly quotable they have a delicacy of rhythm and language which is far from common and the kind of serenity in the face of experience which can only come from having had some experience. More straightforward and understated than her earlier books, *The Scenic Route* may well be her best so far. (p. 68)

Colin Falck, "Coming Through," in The New Review, *Vol. 1, No. 9, December, 1974, pp. 66-8.*

JUDITH MOFFETT

In Fleur Adcock's thoughtful poems there is nothing otherworldly; her voice is wholly human and of a quality which might well pass with American readers as wholly British—pleasant, even, controlled, consistent in pitch—despite her New Zealand origins and present residence in Ireland. As a voice it hasn't much variety, but it's a tool of limited application expertly applied within its range. Emotion (however widely registered), even the tone of emotion, is trained to surfaces of calmness maintained in spite of heartsickness, grief, dread, the throwing of caution to the winds; such things are suggested or made spare statements of. (p. 166)

Only when describing a literal fever, an actual dream, does the atmosphere in her poems grow feverish or dreamlike. If this makes just a bit for monotone, the poems are so right as they are that it would be ungrateful to wish them otherwise.

In tone and subject-matter *The Scenic Route* puts me in mind both of Lowell's less desolate life studies of his forebears and of Elizabeth Bishop's *Questions of Travel*. A few of these poems pay homage to Adcock's great-grandparents, Irish emigrants to New Zealand a century ago; Adcock herself [travelled] "back" to her roots in Ireland for a visit in 1945. . . . Having acquired the habit, she continues traveling: to Italy, Holland, Nepal, New Zealand again. Travel produces poems which cherish the variable physical details of her world. And hers is a mostly cherishable world of daylight and exotic places, and of ordinary places and people rendered unique by being experienced; her physical details are daylit nature's and those of artisans. She gives the mud puddles and cesspools a level look but doesn't paddle about in them. (p. 167)

As a technician Adcock knows exactly what she's about. Her forms are often traditional, always deeply aware of tradition. Many of her poems are simply anecdotal, seem to have no metaphorical dimension at all, but are none the less genuinely poetry for that. Aware of the political tragedy in Northern Ireland, able to write about it, she doesn't let it bog her down. Like Fleur Adcock's other collections, *The Scenic Route* is a small book. If its poems can't be called exciting or startling, they are products of an authentic talent. (p. 168)

Judith Moffett, "Life More and Less Abundantly," in Poetry, *Vol. CXXVII, No. 3, December, 1975, pp. 164-75.*

ROGER GARFITT

[In *The Scenic Route,* Fleur Adcock lays aside the] effective rhetorical method that she had created, particularly in her erotic satires, . . . to work out of what Randall Jarrell called "the dailiness of life". . . . This is a personal and fragile renewal, dependent upon the civilised arbours of the English Home Counties where she has lived the last ten years, and Fleur Adcock sets it shrewdly against the more guarded attitudes she has to maintain on visits to Nepal and Northern Ireland. The collection's most interesting feature is that it carries over into a sequence of love poems this same tension between the civilised inheritance of disciplined mental values and the positive/negative potency of unreason. In "**Kilpeck**", in tracing the love's hesitancy she traces the cautious surrender of the Western mind to an instinctive force. . . . The hesitation is viewed ironically, but also with the sense that perhaps only out of this proper caution does the final surrender, in "**Folie à Deux**" and "**Over the Edge**", become positive. The moral discrimination is carried through into the delicacy of the verse movement: the sequence stands as a quiet but original achievement. (pp. 64-5)

Roger Garfitt, "The Languages of English," in Stand Magazine, *Vol. 17, No. 1, (1975-76), pp. 63-75.*

ANDREW MOTION

[The fourth and final section of Fleur Adcock's *The Inner Harbour*] contains a series of poems which discuss her attitude to New Zealand after a 13-year absence. But these do not cannibalise the past . . . : their rehearsal of childhood memories more often conveys detachment than nostalgia. While admitting that going back has made her 'for the first time an exile', she knows the appeal of her original home is less compelling than that of her adopted England. . . .

Such unillusioned self-knowledge is apparent in all her previous work, and *The Inner Harbour* develops it to a fine art. But this, paradoxically, is the book's weakness as well as its strength. What she calls 'The clogging multiplicity of things' is sometimes too absolutely ordered. It is almost as if she is shy of inexplicable or unruly elements in her own nature and what she sees around her. Poems about dreams and the subconscious, for example, move quickly away from troublesome abstract speculation and seek comfort in the realm of reliable objects. As one might expect, she is well aware of this reductive tendency. The best poem in the collection, "**The Ex-Queen among the Astronomers**", departs from her familiar documentary style to discuss the relative merits of sensuous and empirical attitudes to experience. Its passionate heroine and its 'men of science' are both concerned to bring 'the distant briefly close', but she achieves far greater success as a lover than they ever do by staring into 'huge lenses hung aloft to frame / the slow procession of the skies'. The point is not so much that Fleur Adcock feels she should be resigning her rational intelligence, but that she realises its limitations. And when these are most frankly confronted, her poems admit a sense of mystery which allows her to write more inclusively.

Andrew Motion, "Flogged," in New Statesman, *Vol. 97, No. 2516, June 8, 1979, p. 833.*

ALAN BROWNJOHN

There has been a quiet serendipity about Fleur Adcock's poetry in its more conventional moments: a casual, often very appealing, yet curiously unambitious assembling of sensations and observations. Then suddenly something angry, or nightmarish, or discomfiting leaps out—poems like "**Against Coupling**" in *High Tide in the Garden* or "**Feverish**" in *The Scenic Route*—and she seems almost another writer. The surprises in her new book, *The Inner Harbour,* are not only in mood or subject, but in form. If her most resonant and moving poems here are not the poems of returning to New Zealand in the title-sequence and elsewhere but the recollections of the dead in

"**Letter from Highgate Wood**" and the poignant observations of sickness in "**The Soho Hospital for Women**", the most unexpected and promising departures come in poems of a formal adroitness which she has rarely tried. It's there in "**A Way Out**" (a little reminiscent of Richard Wilbur in its lyrical excursions, but none the worse for it). . . . And it's certainly there in "**Proposal for a Survey**", which maps out "Poets' England" with a kind of Byronic impudence. . . . Pressing small, rather unlikely objects into ominous or intriguing service—here, rubber-seeds, a "carved spoon broken in its case", a "round baby sparrow/modelled in feather-coloured clay"—is one of her ways of lifting a fairly slow-paced lyricism into vividness. She does it well; but soaring higher in planned patterns of flight seems to be working out as well. (p. 49)

> *Alan Brownjohn, "A Change of Landscape," in* Encounter, *Vol. LIII, No. 2, August, 1979, pp. 45-51.*

PETER PORTER

Poets are supposed to get better and better, so that when they really do to report the fact seems little more than automatic praise. In Fleur Adcock's case, the progress of her work has been into a warmer world of the affections, and never away from a classical detachment of style, which has always been hers to deploy. *The Inner Harbour* is dominated by death: named deaths and the imagined sort, which raise such editorial dust.

> This is my laconic style.
> You praised it, as I praised your intricate pearled
> embroideries; these links laced us together,
> plain and purl across the ribs of the world. . . .

Many poets have happened on that rhyme and botched their sentences together to obtain it. Here it is natural and poignant at once. In "**The Soho Hospital for Women**," she puts the terrible facts down plainly enough, but the poem has a sort of lightheartedness which is not due just to her escaping the place this time. She makes a virtue of the helplessness of words—in fact, throughout the book, her poems seem to rest on the page with a special lenient grace. No matter how grim their message, they never apostrophise or buttonhole the reader.

> *Peter Porter, "Stuff That Dreams Are Made On," in* The Observer, *September 9, 1979, p. 37.*

TREVOR JAMES

The association between poetry and painful experience has been well noted by critics and practising poets alike. . . . Yet that association is fraught with problems: the difficulties of assimilating personal anguish into art, the issue of some personal privacy in something which is to be read by others and the tangle of complications which these and related factors cause in a finished creative work. In some measure this explains the disappointment I felt with reading the first two sections of [*The Inner Harbour*]: in "**Beginnings**" and "**Endings**" the elements of personal catharsis seemed obtrusive and often banal. "**Send-Off**" might have been the occasion of a poem but not in its own right, unless a momentarily condensed emotion is all that is required:

> Half an hour before my flight was called
> he walked across the airport bar towards me
> carrying what was left of our future
> together: two drinks on a tray.

Yet her strengths are also in this type of statement—when it is expanded and the reader's imagination given something to work with. That laconic, rather ironic style, epitomised by its reflective and disengaged qualities, acts as a superb controlling device for difficult emotions in the fuller context. Where in "**Send-Off**" it seems banal and mechanical, it is altogether different in so personal a piece as "**Poem Ended by a Death**":

> They will remove the tubes and drips and dressings
> which I censor from my dreams. They will, it is true,
> wash you; and they will put you into a box.
> After which whatever else they may do
> won't matter. This is my laconic style.

The success of such poetry however is also conditioned by the degree to which it absorbs the reader into it and demands identification. Even this poem still leaves the reader largely outside as it returns again to the writer, and we are left feeling that we have pried in someone else's diary. (pp. 194-95)

While Adcock would probably not claim to be a feminist propagandist she sees woman as being betrayed in many of the love poems. "**Off the Track**" is a fine example, but even there blame is not assigned to the man but shared. Betrayed by herself perhaps, by the difficulties of any relationship: these fundamental human issues are veiled by metaphors that incline toward allegory and then are terminated by the last stanza with the characteristic objectifying statement. In this case its effect is largely dependant upon the vivid contrast it affords. . . . Much more of the feminist camaraderie is demonstrated by the "**Soho Hospital for Women**". In this sustained piece she evinces a disciplined humane identification with the difficulties others have to endure. Yet she is not enslaved by the common denominator of gender; she retains a sense of self-identity which is yet humbled and qualified by the knowledge of others' sufferings. (pp. 195-96)

The issue of the 'self' and the theme of 'home' are important in her poetry, and a significant concern of New Zealand literary studies. Accidents of up-bringing locate Fleur Adcock as a New Zealander but her cultural orientation is clearly toward England. . . . Nonetheless New Zealand retains for her what someone (I think Kingsley Amis) defined as 'the affectionate, dimly melancholic appeal of a place one has done some growing-up in'.

The title poem "**Inner Harbour**" is clearly earthed in memories of the family boatshed at Paremata and suggests dimensions of discontent which led to disengagement from the close community and acceptance of the cultural expansiveness and occasional anonymity of London. There is reflection in all the final poems, inevitable nostalgia and analysis, but the verdict is clear. "**Instead of An Interview**" gives the comment which so many New Zealand poets and writers have in some way shared:

> the dreams I'd not bothered to remember—
> ingrained; ingrown; incestuous: like the country.
> (pp. 196-97)

It may not be popular with many New Zealanders that so fine a poet should seem to reject her roots, but I doubt whether it is a dismissal of New Zealand so much as a natural instinctive reflex of Adcock's personality. The movement into the self, into a dimension of personal, emotional and imaginative freedom, can be traced in her 'love' poems as well as in these particularly regional pieces. (p. 197)

Trevor James, ''Fleur Adcock and Alan Loney,'' in Landfall, *Vol. 34, No. 2, June, 1980, pp. 194-99.*

ANDREW MOTION

Most of Fleur Adcock's best poems have something to do with bed: she writes well about sex, very well about illness, and very well indeed about dreaming. **''Mornings After''**—from her third book, *High Tide In The Garden* (1971)—explains why this should be so. The poem is a conversational enquiry into the source and content of dreams, and in it, after remembering various nightmare visions, she wonders ''Do I, for hours of my innocent nights, / wallow content and charmed through verminous muck, / rollick in the embraces of such frights?'' If she does—and she cannot help but leave the question unanswered—she protests that ''I do not care to know''. In the interests of decency and stability, she advises herself to ''Replace the cover''. But while such glimpses into the unconscious might make her waking existence more painful, and undermine her sense of a respectable self, they also enormously enrich her poetry. Her imagination thrives on what threatens her peace of mind, and only when she is unguarded can these threats have their full creative effect. Hence the importance of bed: it is the place where the elegant, artful barriers that she builds from day to day are most easily overthrown. Passion and sickness are voluntary and involuntary ways of lessening—if not actually losing—self-control, and dreams themselves are direct dispatches from a side of the mind that cannot be manipulated or tidied up.

Adcock realized this discomfiting strength in her work at an early stage in her career. One of the first poems in her *Selected Poems*, **''Miss Hamilton in London''**, concentrates on a character whose daily experience is determinedly humdrum, but whose nights are hellish. . . . Poem after poem in the book rehearses similar or parallel dichotomies: between high hopes and bad dreams, between fact and fantasy, between innocence and disillusionment, and between what can be observed and what can be imagined. Not surprisingly, these tensions are reflected in the tone as well as the themes of her work. This is especially true of her early poems, where a slightly inflated romantic manner (her son in New Zealand is ''my green branch growing in a far plantation'') often negotiates with something much flatter and more throw-away (my ''laconic style'' she calls it in *The Inner Harbour*) which is distinctly reminiscent of the Movement in general and Larkin in particular. Chatty phrases are carefully positioned to act as brakes on her rhetoric and all that it stands for. . . . As her work develops, a refined version of this laconic style becomes customary, and in doing so it provides her with a poetic manner which is so well ventilated and unostentatious as hardly to seem like a manner at all. It frees her, in theory at least, from the restrictions on subject matter and attitude which often beset more highly wrought and recherché stylists. . . .

Adcock obviously evolved her flexible, all-purpose style to allow herself the widest possible range of response. . . . But the ostensible freedom of her language has none the less always been subject to certain traumatic constraints. There are several poems in the *Selected Poems* which (lightly but intently) admit that certain ideas and places have been so much discussed in the past that they are now virtually inaccessible as subjects. . . . In a poet for whom place, or the lack of it, is so important, the sense of being pre-empted is a serious disadvantage—and it helps to explain why her poems about the various trips she has made to her native New Zealand are not among her strongest. The subject, it is tempting to think, is simply too obvious for her—too candid in its demands for a response, and therefore too likely to prompt the over-articulation of thoughts and feelings. The poems from *The Scenic Route* about Ireland—which in familial terms seems to signify less to her than New Zealand—are more potent and emotionally complicated because they refer to subjects which take her by surprise. **''The Bullaun''**, typically, integrates lyrical elements with political speculations and geographical celebrations in such a way as to seem simultaneously skilfully managed and—so to speak—taken aback. . . .

For all its air of engrossed discovery, and of appearing to confront something not wholly explicable, [**''The Bullaun''**] ends by seeming to know what it means. In Adcock's most memorable work, though, her capacity to be surprised and at a loss is even more fully developed. The appropriately titled **''A Surprise in the Peninsula''**, for example, or **''The Ex-Queen among the Astronomers''**, or the new poem **''Blue Glass''** all demonstrate her formal controls, her cool tone, and her sharp eye for authenticating detail, and yet they apply these things to subjects and situations which are profoundly mysterious. In **''The Ex-Queen among the Astronomers''**, the enticingly odd and erotic narrative acquires a marvellous intensity by refusing to give more than the most tantalizingly reticent articulation of its theme:

> She plucks this one or that among
> the astronomers, and is become
> his canopy, his occultation;
> she sucks at earlobe, penis, tongue
>
> mouthing the tubes of flesh; her hair
> crackles, her eyes are comet-sparks.
> She brings the distant briefly close
> above his dreamy abstract stare.

This poem is a powerful instance of Adcock exploiting the murky unconscious mind with precisely those qualities—the wit, the control—she normally deploys to contain it. It is probably asking too much to wish that she wrote like this more often—and anyway, there are very rewarding pleasures to be gained from her less darkly imaginative work. Throughout her writing life, she has made a fine art from holding onto principles of orderliness and good clear sense; but she has made an even finer one from loosening her grip on them.

Andrew Motion, ''Under the Covers,'' in The Times Literary Supplement, *No. 4196, September 2, 1983, p. 922.*

JOHN LUCAS

'This is my laconic style,' Fleur Adcock says to a dead lover in the less-than-laconic **''Poem Ended by a Death''**. Most of her best poems preserve a decorum in the face of death, disease, pain. So do most of her worst. Reading through her *Selected Poems* you realise that the dividing line between containment and contentment is narrower than at first seems possible. She is a shapely poet, but the shapes often seem pre-determined; it is as though the experiences she sets out to record come prepacked, neatly ordered, consigned to the reader in exact measure. Even the tough-tender **''Soho Hospital for Women''** can turn from pitiless exactness to the statement that a first death from cancer 'is not for me to speak of'. Then why mention it? But running through her work is a wit that hones itself, coolly and deliberately, on rebarbative material. When this is successful, the result is a poem of unique value, and such poems occur with increased frequency as the volume goes on. The last 20 pages include her best work so far. (p. 25)

John Lucas, "Sight Lines," in New Statesman, *Vol. 107, No. 2756, January 13, 1984, pp. 24-5.*

JOHN MOLE

Towards the end of **"Mornings After"**—an early poem [included in *Selected Poems*] but entirely characteristic in its edgy, candid elegance—Fleur Adcock asks:

> And are the comic or harmless fantasies
> I wake with merely a deceiving guard,
> as one might put a Hans Andersen cover
> on a volume of the writings of De Sade?

This question, in various guises, remains the source of much of her best writing to date. She knows only too well that nothing, or nobody, she wakes with (least of all herself) is as harmless as may appear, and anyone who has read Hans Andersen at all carefully will certainly not be deceived into thinking that to use him as a cover for De Sade is to hide much in the way of pain and cruelty.

Like Robert Graves, whose combination of fastidious classicism and violent phantasmagoric effect has served her as a model, Fleur Adcock is caught in her own cool webs and has seen the spider. Part Alice, part Cat-goddess, the personality which emerges from her immaculately crafted poems is sensible and dangerous, attractively inquisitive but seldom less than puzzled to distraction. Her imagination works most effectively on a shifting ground between sleeping and waking where the landscape partakes of both and it is never clear which is illusion:

> I am not at all sure that this is the real world
>   but I am looking at it very closely.
> Is landscape serious? Are birds?

It is typical of Fleur Adcock to ask this question in a poem which has already looked at "the real world" with an exact attentiveness. She just can't quite trust the *evidence,* just as in her many poems of travel she cannot feel at home in any of the places she so vividly describes.

Coming back to England after a visit to her native New Zealand, she asks (again and again these *questions* in a poetry which is, on the surface, so secure in its accomplishment), "By going back to look, after thirteen years, / have I made myself for the first time an exile?" No. She hasn't. Exile is the condition of her art. "I merely opened a usual door / And found this", she writes in **"Unexpected Visit."** What she finds is "Not my kind of country" (what is?)—

>   there is no
> Horizon behind the trees, no sun as clock
> Or compass. I shall go
>
> And find, somewhere among the formal hedges
> Or hidden behind a trellis, a toolshed. There
> I can sit on a box and wait.

The last sentence is a fine example of Fleur Adcock's tense composure under the stress of disorientation. She will sit there making a poem out of the experience to carry her back through the door until the next dislocation returns her to the same (or nearly) spot.

The pleasures of her poetry are various: vivid observation of nature (particularly small animals which evoke a protective, unsentimental tenderness), the details of love-making recorded in its erotic particulars (her often anthologised **"Against Coupling"** is outflanked by the many poems which ignore its advice both in *Selected Poems* and in her set of translations from medieval Latin [*The Virgin and the Nightingale*], and her humorous observation of the literary and social scene. But it is her awareness of how at any moment she may be seized by a terrible strangeness that admits the most compelling note into her work. . . . (p. 48)

John Mole, "The Reflecting Glass," in Encounter, *Vol. LXII, No. 3, March, 1984, pp. 46-52.*

PETER BLAND

Fleur Adcock is New Zealand born but English both by choice and residence. As if clinging to a more personal sense of identity (after the confusions of changing a national one) she often uses the first person in her poems. . . . There are plenty of 'I am's' and 'I was': the persona (because the 'I' is as much a persona as any other literary invention) is that of a self-observing, feminine loner, talking quietly and intelligently about her place in the world (or her lack of a place) and addressing many of her poems to friends, relations, lovers, sons, etc. It's like reading someone's private letters. Sometimes the shared intimacy is fascinating (when interestingly 'intimate' things are happening), sometimes it's less so (because the reader can't always know the Alistairs, Marilyns, Jims, Megs, Andrews, Gregorys etc, that are part of her circle). (pp. 82-3)

Fleur Adcock's development has been in the use of an increasingly sophisticated and flexible speaking voice that can respond to a wide range of subject matter—particularly landscape. [Among the verse included in her *Selected Poems*], **"The Bullaun"** (set in Northern Ireland) and **"Script"** (set in New Zealand) are considerable achievements, balancing psychological insight and objective description with great skill. Yet the best of her New Zealand work, **"For Andrew", "For a Five-Year Old", "Incident", "I ride my High Bicycle",** are still as good— in their more direct and plain-spoken way—as anything else she's written. Later poems—**"The Ex-Queen among the Astronomers",** and **"Blue Glass",** show an ability to escape the 'I' and an occasional desire to dig down to more primal creative sources. Poems such as **"Incident", "Crab", "Influenza",** and **"Against Coupling",** have a spare tremulous poise that is uniquely hers, one which faces up to the impersonal in personal relationships. The classical 'object of love' is just that, and none the less human for it. Here, too, her coolness of tone (the speaking voice is *always* edged with formality) comes into its own. In the heat of the sexual encounter that slight chill works wonders. She has, at her best, what Frost calls 'a genuine metaphysical tremor'. (p. 84)

Peter Bland, "Slight Chill," in London Magazine, *n.s. Vol. 25, No. 7, October, 1985, pp. 82-4.*

Lisa Alther

1944-

American novelist.

Alther's first novel, *Kinflicks* (1976), drew critical acclaim for
its ironically humorous treatment of death, sex, and the search
for identity. The protagonist, Ginny Babcock, is a young woman
who has returned to her southern hometown after many years
during which she has attempted to find meaning in her life.
Ginny recalls her experimentation with a variety of lifestyles,
including lesbianism, communal living, and marriage, through
first-person narrative; the present, which focuses on Ginny's
feelings as she watches her mother approach death, is told in
the third person. These alternating points of view balance the
humor and seriousness and the light and dark atmospheres of
the novel. As John Leonard noted, "This is a very *funny* book . . .
about serious matters." As well as being a story of generational
miscommunication, *Kinflicks* also observes many social and
political changes which occurred during the 1960s and 1970s.

Original Sins (1981) also concentrates on sociological matters
of the past two decades, although in this novel Alther places
less emphasis on humor. She examines topical issues—civil
rights, women's liberation, radical politics, unionism, Vietnam, ecology, the sexual revolution—from the perspectives of
five socially disparate friends as they progress from childhood
to adulthood. Their rites of passage in a small southern town
and the adventures of three of the characters in New York
reflect the confusions and conflicts of a changing society. In
addition, Alther integrates into *Original Sins* an examination
of the bargaining, power plays, and double standards inherent
in personal relationships.

Other Women (1984) focuses on Caroline Kelly, another female
protagonist who has tried a number of different roles in her
quest to find herself. Unable to separate the world's problems
from her own, Caroline undergoes psychiatric therapy in an
effort to relieve her depression. The most important interaction
in this book is between Caroline and her female therapist; the
observations of doctor and patient are presented in alternate
chapters. Like Alther's previous novels, *Other Women* was
praised for its ironic social humor.

(See also *CLC*, Vol. 7; *Contemporary Authors*, Vols. 65-68;
and *Contemporary Authors New Revision Series*, Vol. 12.)

JOHN ALFRED AVANT

Original Sins is several novels in one bulky package. Following
a prologue set in 1955 with an Eden image—five youngsters
in their hideout in a weeping beech tree dreaming of the future—Lisa Alther gives us Southern rites of passage ironically
treated: pep rally, Sadie Hawkins dance, cheerleader clinic,
beauty pageant, minstrel show, some church services. After
her characters have graduated from high school or dropped out
to get married, she takes up a new structure and presents each
of her five major characters separately, at certain points in their
lives, bringing you up to date through flashbacks. This done,

Photograph by Kristin V. Rehder

she pursues the histories in the same order. In the epilogue,
one of the principals has died, the other four meet after the
funeral, while their five children look down on them from the
weeping beech tree, feeling superior.

The five characters, children of the New South, fit into familiar
scenarios. Emily and Sally Prince are privileged white girls
from the family that founded the cotton mill, the sustaining
industry of Newland, Tennessee. Raymond and Jed Tatro are
sons of a mill foreman, grandsons of coal miners in the nearby
Kentucky mountains. The obligatory black, Donny Tatro, a
distant, unacknowledged cousin of Raymond and Jed, is raised
by his grandmother who keeps house for the Princes.

The novel is a *Bildungsroman* times five, showing how The
Five (their childhood club name) learn that life is different
from what they were taught it would be. Alther's earlier work,
Kinflicks—a novel that seemed to be writing itself in your head
while you read—was picaresque, a woman's trip up the road
with deliriously funny, sexy encounters. Ginny Babcock, the
privileged white Southern heroine, wandered through the story
responding with a slightly dazed "Who, me?" double take to
the benign monsters, complex libidinous figures of both sexes,
who tried to make her and often succeeded. The tone was loose
and spontaneous except for the juxtaposed chapters that dealt
with the mother's slow hospital death. There Alther did use

19

her laborious accumulation of medical data to suggest age and pain and waste.

Yet *Kinflicks,* a long novel that went by like an evening's giddy dancing with occasional slow stretches, didn't completely satisfy. Alther was unable to make Ginny's coming to consciousness convincing. The novel just wound down, as though Ginny had nothing more to tell us until she'd thought a few things out. . . .

In *Original Sins,* the stories set forth a succession of easy ironies. When The Five go to a movie theater as children and Donny has to sit upstairs in the colored section, "The Star-Spangled Banner" is played before the movie starts. At a Plantation Ball held just before the civil rights bill is passed in 1964, the emcee pays homage to "our Southern way of life" while a white-jacketed Donny, hired to play the darky serving punch, stands resentfully. After Raymond has gone to visit his "hillbilly" grandparents, just about the only people he knows who seem in touch with their lives, he's back home with his own parents, who are watching "The Beverly Hillbillies." Northern male activists, who had been contemptuous of white Southerners in the late 1960s, are rejected for their sexist attitudes by female activists in the 1970s.

Alther tells us that everyone's conditioning is inadequate and that being Southern is a particular handicap: the original sin. They try to attain a state of redemption, and since they've started out flawed, it's hard, in most cases hopeless. The Eden theme, witty in its way, is limited to prologue and epilogue. In between is a turgid narrative, meant to have the epic sweep of an Edna Ferber novel, only the author has no idea how to bring it off. Alther is earnest and moribund, doggedly trying to work out what she thinks has to go into this novel: Tennessee valleys, cotton mill machinery, Upper West Side apartments, feminist consciousness-raising sessions, voter registration drives, Black Panther meetings and Southern race riots. The panorama is static; the scenes are friezes, illustrating what the characters have failed to learn and how unaware they'll be at the next stage.

Alther is naïvely didactic, explaining the meaning of everything, preparing us for every step. (p. 506)

In her eagerness to tell it all, Lisa Alther has forgotten everything she knew about unobtrusive prose. She throws us out of the novel again and again with glaring metaphors—"The fury drained away quickly, like air out of a bicycle tire"—and with sex/nature rhapsodies—"Afterward they lay in each other's arms and watched the long pale fingers of dawn gently stroke the night sky until the grey became engorged with crimson." It's hard to believe this is the same novelist who in *Kinflicks* could describe a hallucinogen-induced trip without fragmenting the narrative line, while writing a scene that advanced the plot. . . . (pp. 506-07)

When *Kinflicks* came out five years ago, I thought Alther, with her gift for action scenes and her light, sassy prose, might go on to write a female version of *The Unvanquished.* In his humorous tales, Faulkner knew how not to *seem* to take himself seriously. *Original Sins* keeps dumping on Southern values, then drawing up defensively against criticism Alther posits from outside the South. Thus, the novel is stiff, gaseous. Lisa Alther wants to be funny, but she feels the need to preach. Her sound and fury tell us nothing. (p. 507)

John Alfred Avant, "Bildungsroman Times Five," in The Nation, Vol. 232, No. 16, April 25, 1981, pp. 506-07.

PAUL GRAY

After writing a truly successful first novel, most authors feel obliged to try again. The odds are not encouraging. Fledgling novelists tend to pour everything they know or have experienced into their first efforts. . . . Then there is the problem of a pre-sold audience, its expectations buoyed by an impressive debut. What, this group itches to know, can the sophomore writer do for an encore?

The critical and commercial acclaim that greeted *Kinflicks* (1976) subjected Novelist Lisa Alther . . . to just that question. The answer: [In *Original Sins* she] does pretty much the same thing over again, except that she does more of it and better. *Kinflicks* followed a single heroine from her Tennessee upbringing through a series of wacky encounters up North with the countercultures of the '60s. *Original Sins* quintuples its predecessor, offering five main characters, all Southerners, who try to grow up in a region and a country that are changing even faster than they are. . . .

With commendable speed and economy, Alther divides these five young people into the three who will leave home and the two who must stay. After much comic fumbling and steamy negotiating, Jed takes Sally's virginity. She responds like any well-brought-up Southern girl in the early '60s: "She clung to his hand, seeking from his fingertips assurance that he still respected her, would protect her reputation, would eventually marry her, and would love her forever. That didn't seem like too much to ask." When her pregnancy finally occurs, Sally and Jed marry and concoct an earlier wedding date that the town's mythology can live with. Her father gives Jed a job in the mill.

Emily, Raymond and Donny wind up in New York, all seeking freedom from the constraints of the South and all baffled by the impersonality and rootlessness of the big city. They are easy touches for any groups that offer them companionship and forgiveness for the site of their births. . . .

As she cuts back and forth between the adventures and peregrinations of her characters, Alther constructs a broad social portrait of nearly two decades of American life. She covers civil rights, Viet Nam, women's lib, the sexual revolution, radical politics and back-to-earth movements. Raised in the comfortable stasis of a small Southern town, Alther's young people are woefully and often hilariously unprepared for what life in the '60s and early '70s throws their way. What is more, the tight little community they grew up in is being rattled into unrecognizability. Outside organizers have installed a union at the cotton mill, which has passed from the hands of the Prince family and is now owned by a distant conglomerate. Even stay-at-home Sally and her lug of a husband are ruffled by new-fangled ideas. Sally decides that she wants a career.

Original Sins is an old-fashioned novel in the best sense of the term. It propels singular, interesting characters through a panoramic plot. Alther takes risks that sometimes fail. She is willing to sacrifice plausibility for a comic effect, to put her characters through paces that occasionally seem dictated rather than inevitable. But such lapses are more than offset by the novel's page-turning verve and intelligence. Alther knows that no theory or ideology can account for the cussed complexities of daily life. As Emily, Raymond and the rest stumble from one ism to another, their author both mocks their blindness and applauds their determination to keep searching. She gives generously, both to her readers and to the children of her imagination.

20

Paul Gray, "Beating the Sophomore Jinx," in Time,
Vol. 117, No. 17, April 27, 1981, p. 71.

MARY CANTWELL

Lisa Alther's first novel, *Kinflicks,* started high and never came
down.

Ginny Babcock, *Kinflicks'* heroine, is a perennially displaced
person, a Southerner who looks for herself in teen-age sex,
post-adolescent bisexuality, marriage, motherhood, a woman's
college up North and a Vermont commune.... Ginny's past
is narrated in the first person, her present (she is home in
Tennessee with her dying mother) in the third. Miss Alther's
alternation of the two points of view adds up to an almost
flawless balance of light and dark, the skittery and the sad. It
is a balance that is entirely missing from *Original Sins.*

Except for the addition of several black characters, and the
substitution of New York's Upper West Side for Vermont,
Original Sins reads as if Miss Alther had been told to rewrite
Kinflicks, but to be serious this time. Once again the setting
is Tennessee, but instead of one Ginny Babcock we have five
representatives of the South.... Their tangled roots are deep
in the Southern past, and when they were children, the Five,
as Miss Alther calls them, were inseparable.

Miss Alther uses their lives—from childhood to their early
30's, through marriage, parenthood, Harlem, the civil rights
movement, lesbianism, feminism and good ol' boyism—to paint
a picture of the South. The result has all the spontaneity of a
paint-by-numbers landscape. In *Kinflicks* Miss Alther was following a logic known only to herself, which made her denouements a continual surprise; in *Original Sins* she telegraphs
her every punch. The situations about which she is so sober
now are the same ones about which she was once funny; what
she first said laughing, she is saying again with a straight face.
That Miss Alther's second novel is not successful is partly
because her first was: the parody, it seems, was published
before its target. (p. 9)

Bent on symmetry, Miss Alther ends her book where it began,
with five children sitting in a tree. One knew she would: there
is nothing unpredictable about *Original Sins.*

Having worked so brilliantly with one character, Ginny Babcock, Miss Alther should not be faulted for wanting to stretch
herself and work with five. Nor does one doubt either the
accuracy of her anecdotes or her knowledge of the terrain. But
why a writer who possesses a true comic genius, as Lisa Alther
does, would choose to smother it is unfathomable. (p. 38)

*Mary Cantwell, "Serious When Once She Was
Funny," in* The New York Times Book Review, *May
3, 1981, pp. 9, 38.*

MARK SHECHNER

In *Original Sins* Lisa Alther returns to the locale of her first
novel, *Kinflicks* . . . , to carry on what she began there, charting
the moral topography of her portion of the south—the industrial
valleys of eastern Tennessee that, by virtue of abundant coal,
cheap electricity from TVA, and non-union labor, had been
exploitable ground for capital investment from the north long
before most Americans ever heard of the new south, or what
its chambers of commerce sunnily call the Sunbelt. It is the
new south whose basic economic premises were already plain
enough half a century ago to arouse resistance among senti-
mentalists of the old south such as the 12 writers who collaborated in 1930 on the Agrarian manifesto, *I'll Take My Stand.*
Alther's novels are latter-day confirmations of the Agrarians'
bleak vision of an industrialized south. Torn by labor strife,
divided by racial animosity, beset by anomie, and uglified by
highway strip development, the new south is a mess.

Original Sins is anything but a sequel to *Kinflicks,* however;
it is more of a reprise, a regrouping of familiar elements under
radically different theses, as though Alther were dissatisfied
with her first efforts and desired to correct, possibly even atone
for, them. Newland, Tennessee, in *Original Sins,* is recognizably the Hullsport of *Kinflicks,* and several of the central characters are decidedly Hullsport types, seen this time with a less
charitable eye. *Kinflicks* is a broad social comedy verging on
farce, in which the social and sexual calamities that befall its
heroine, Ginny Babcock, are only Chaplinesque pratfalls, after
which she dusts off her baggy trousers, straightens her bowler,
and trots off in search of better calamities. The book is alternately ironic and rueful, and it is brilliantly detailed by a comic
imagination that thrives on disillusionment and is ever eager
to suffer the worst for the sheer fun of it. *Original Sins,* by
contrast, is a protest novel of a conventional sort, a compound
of outrage and doctrine. It is an all-out assault on the south
for its rigidly maintained double standards on matters of race,
sex, and class and for its failures to face up to its deficiencies.
(pp. 34-5)

It would be gratifying to report that in *Original Sins* Lisa Alther
has achieved a satisfactory integration of social ideas and social
observation. But for the most part she has not. Her rejection
of men is so complete that even their villainy comes right out
of central casting. All are dramatized social ideas, clichés or
close to it: the good ole boy, the misogynistic revolutionary,
the black victim who turns his rage against his wife. Having
designated a place for every man and deposited every man in
his place, the social redeemer in Alther has given the artist in
her no freedom to imagine men afresh. Every man is a robot
of inadequacy, who can do little but dramatize over and over
his crippled nature, usually through an insistent sexual or racial
bullying, until the lesson becomes as boring as it is routine.
(p. 35)

Jed, Raymond, Hank—the lot of Newland male society—are
cavalierly drawn cartoons who speak a hybrid argot that is half
Tennessee, half textbook.... The language of men fails everywhere despite Alther's efforts to spruce it up with a dena-
tured hillbillyism that is indistinguishable from the homoge-
nized mountain dew of "Hee Haw" and "Grand Ole Opry."
Alther's men speak a language of universal CB-isms—"with-
outen we," "we got us here," "it like to happen," "they's
jes plumb downright," "infernal new-fangled"—but to no
effect for what is dead at the heart cannot be brought to life
by any amount of canned regional flavor. Sally and Emily,
whom Alther truly cares about, speak standard, American-
heartland English precisely because Alther wants to bring the
utmost clarity to what they are experiencing and saying.

What life there is in *Original Sins* belongs to Sally and Emily,
and only in their sections does the book achieve anything like
the effervescence of *Kinflicks.* . . .

Lisa Alther is a writer of messy, rambunctious novels, whose
vitality is part and parcel of their messiness. But her exuberance
can pall, especially when her subject eludes her grasp and she
tries to make up for what she hasn't quite fathomed in sheer
doggedness. And since she hasn't quite fathomed men—no

small matter for a writer whose subject is the ubiquity of sexual grief—she finally has nothing to say about them that can't be found in any handbook of feminist protest. She wants to have it both ways with men: to see them as the enemy, not just of women but of love itself, and to portray them as victims, whose capacity for tenderness, sensuality, and patience has been impaired by economic disadvantage and working-class alienation. The system is to blame. But such a decidedly "liberal" position runs against the grain of her imagination, and she composes the inner lives of Jed, Raymond, and Donny—normally a device for evoking sympathy—only to show us that they are every bit as emotionally arid as they seem. Trying to make them three-dimensional, she merely heightens their one-dimensionality. (p. 36)

> Mark Schechner, "A Novel of the New South," in The New Republic, Vol. 184, No. 24, June 13, 1981, pp. 34-6.

CAROL RUMENS

[*Original Sins*] has a documentary flavour; at times it reads like a sensitive, scrupulously well-balanced social history of America from the 1950s to the 1970s. The reader is haunted by the thought that the central characters, with the exception, perhaps, of the obstinately individualistic Emily, exist chiefly in order to illustrate differently developing states of political consciousness, as their progress from childhood to maturity is traced in often absorbing but sometimes oppressive detail. . . .

Alther's disengagement may be one of the reasons why the writing does not quite "catch fire" but it has the virtue of keeping clear of easy solutions and of gently mocking those who seek them. Alther is as cool towards her radicals as to her rednecks. Raymond, Emily's fellow outsider, because disillusioned with the Civil Rights movement, returns south and is last seen humourlessly attempting rural self-sufficiency. Emily graduates uneasily from marriage to lesbianism, while Southern Belle Sally, the ex-cheerleader, takes up creative apple-carving and heads a TV ecology drive to turn Trash into Treasure. Jed, her husband, remains totally irredeemable; only a car-wreck can cure him, terminally, of his pathological machismo.

The description of the courting rituals of Sally and Jed, a mercilessly clear-sighted look at sexual role-playing has a touch of the high spirits (verging occasionally on hysteria) of Alther's earlier novel *Kinflicks*. . . . But on the whole, Alther packs a rather lighter satirical punch than in her previous book. It is almost as if she believed that the big political themes with which she is occupied really would go off with a bang if she handled them too playfully.

> Carol Rumens, "Staying Cool," in The Times Literary Supplement, No. 4082, June 26, 1981, p. 730.

CHRISTOPHER LEHMANN-HAUPT

Caroline Kelley, the heroine of Lisa Alther's new novel, *Other Women*, doesn't shoot the men who mistreat her. She switches to women first, and then . . . she goes into psychotherapy. There follows the detailed story of her treatment—what one might describe as a Wasp version of Judith Rossner's *August*. . . .

Miss Alther, whose earlier novels include *Kinflicks* and *Original Sins*, handles Caroline's story with considerable psycho-

logical acuity, skillfully anatomizing the sort of people who indulge in cosmic projection. But there are a couple of big problems with *Other Women*. First, it has a fatal tendency to overstate its case. . . .

Second, the dice are loaded. One of the more dramatic issues in the book is whether Caroline is going to end up homosexual or not. But the three men in her life are all unpleasant caricatures—several aspects of a single self-centered male chauvinist—while the women are both various and appealing.

It's true that Caroline's main struggle in the story involves learning to be alone. It's also true that the portrait of her therapist, Hannah Burke, is almost as good an advertisement for heterosexuality as Caroline's is for lesbianism. But in either case, the reader begins to feel manipulated after a while. As the novel progresses, its scenes feel less and less spontaneous and increasingly didactic.

Besides, Hannah, the therapist, eventually breaks the formality of the therapeutic relationship and begins to intrude herself in Caroline's private life. This may be a case of the author fulfilling what amounts to a universal urge to befriend one's therapist. But on paper it's unprofessional. Along with the novel's tendency to overdo its effects, it finally undermines our belief in the story. We end up wondering: Whoever heard of such a streamlined therapy? How could such a mixed-up person be straightened out in less than a year?

> Christopher Lehmann-Haupt, in a review of "Other Women," in The New York Times, December 10, 1984, p. C16.

CAROL STERNHELL

In *Other Women*, Lisa Alther does for counterculture lesbians what Judith Rossner [in *August*] did for the Upper West Side/East Hampton crowd—and I don't mean that as a compliment. One was annoying, but two is a definite trend; if the decade's gift to political discourse has been Reaganism, its contribution to literature may well be the therapy novel. Certainly the political philosophy and the literary form share a smug insularity that prefers self-absorption to social responsibility, individual solutions to collective problems, simple answers to impossible questions. The complexity of real life—career choice, political commitments, sexual preference—is reduced quite literally to diaper drama. . . .

At least in *August* the analysand was an 18-year-old airhead who had never done anything in her life but talk to shrinks. Her indifference to the world outside her therapist's office (and the boundaries of her own skull) was less upsetting because she herself was so vapid. To me, *Other Women*—with its appealing, intelligent heroine, a 35-year-old sometime radical in faded jeans and graying Afro—is much more disturbing. Far from being indifferent, Caroline Kelly, an emergency room nurse and former abortion rights activist, confuses the world's suffering with her own. . . . Her presenting symptom, when she enters therapy, is cosmic depression: "But what could anybody do about this ghastly world?" . . . When her motherly shrink, the uncannily insightful Hannah Burke, asks Caroline to name her most painful recent experience, she replies, "The Jonestown thing, I guess." Hannah, who has problems of her own, is understandably irritated: "These failed revolutionaries sometimes pissed her off, projecting their inner state onto the world and then insisting it constituted objective reality."

Actually, it's no wonder that Caroline is confused; "objective reality" in *Other Women* generally seems to mirror the state of her psyche. True, if she has a fight with her lover Diana she immediately thinks of Jonestown, or of the Argentine peasants "who raped that girl and sewed a human head inside her." On the other hand, if she and Hannah have a particularly productive session, the sun is likely to come out from behind a cloud; geese fly homeward and red tulips bloom. . . . By the last paragraph—after six remarkably effective months of therapy—"all the ice had melted. Summer was coming . . . the branches, swollen with new buds, were filled with chattering yellow evening grosbeaks, fresh back from more balmy lands, sporting their jaunty masks like revelers returning from a Caribbean carnival." Needless to say, Caroline, tired of split heads and smashed bones, will be working in the delivery room from now on.

Alther's characters have always tended to shed skins every few seasons, to metamorphose repeatedly, transposing themselves into new lives. In *Kinflicks,* her exuberant first novel, Ginny Babcock mutates from Hullsport High flag swinger to Ivy League grind to commune dweller . . . to polyester pantsuited housewife. The marvelous *Original Sins*—my favorite of Alther's books—follows a group of friends through their own transformations and the transformations of the '60s. Like her predecessors, Caroline Kelly has lived several lives by the time we meet her: bourgeois suburban wife and mother; "servant of humanity," working at the People's Free Clinic and living "with a dozen other people whose idea of a good meal was sautéed bamboo shoots"; rural lesbian feminist, suddenly aware that "capitalism wasn't the problem. Racism wasn't. Nationalism wasn't. Men were." . . . [As] she enters therapy Caroline is thinking of transforming again, into the proper (and wealthy) wife of Dr. Brian Stone. Even her appearance at Hannah Burke's office is a kind of desperate metamorphosis. "She'd tried all the standard bromides: consumerism, communism, feminism, and God; sex, work, alcohol, drugs, and true love. Each enchanted for a time, but ultimately failed to stave off the despair. The only bromide she hadn't tried was psychotherapy."

Psychotherapy works wonders, of course; the problem is the wonders seem terribly prosaic, and terribly pat. Where *August* was unconvincingly intricate, an impossibly neat psychological puzzle with no missing pieces, *Other Women*—which is structured exactly like *August*, with alternating chapters from the viewpoint of patient and shrink—offers therapeutic platitudes. The novel's central insight—"each of us is the author of her own moods"—would be equally appropriate in a Leo Buscaglia pop sermon, one of *Cosmo*'s "How Well Do You Know Yourself?" quizzes, or a fortune cookie. Basically, Caroline learns that she can choose happiness, that "the strength you've insisted on assigning to others is actually within yourself." She learns to see the flowers instead of the dead bugs. . . . I imagine these are sentiments much admired by est graduates, but in the real world they sound sappy.

To me, the most annoying thing about therapy novels as a genre is that they reduce *everything* to those scripts we learned as infants. When Hannah's son brings home a new woman, the therapist immediately thinks, "It was intriguing to try to figure out how each of Simon's girlfriends was similar to herself, since presumably that was why he picked them." Hannah's theories about sexual preference are just as reductive. . . .

Caroline's central fear is rejection; her central desire is to please; her central psychological truism, endlessly repeated and always in italics, is: "*I know what you want and you can't*

have it." Her parents, of course, were cold and remote, impossible to interest, impossible to please. . . . Hannah's task is to replay the script: "But rejection and abandonment were Caroline's inner ambience, probably shaped in those first months when Daddy went to war and Mummy went berserk with abandonment and terror. But consciously Caroline knew none of this. And telling her in so many words wouldn't work."

If this were just Caroline's "inner ambience," I think I'd buy it. The maddening thing about *Other Women* is that Hannah, and implicitly Alther, impose this narcissistic script on my whole generation. Those flower children "acting out their indignation in the streets" are World War II babies, "an entire generation sensitized as infants to loss and terror," children who take responsibility for all the world's ills. . . . Their political commitments are merely a diversion; an unhealthy avoidance of more important internal landscapes. . . .

It's hard to believe that Alther—the author of two politically and psychologically complex novels and a wonderfully astute observer of our perversely human condition—really means what she's saying here. And certainly some people do use the political arena (like any other) to act out their private dramas. But in *Other Women* political activism is *only* presented as an immature and irrelevant choice.

Carol Sternhell, "At Last, a Cure for Politics," in The Village Voice, Vol. XXIX, No. 51, December 18, 1984, p. 71.

ADRIAN OKTENBERG

Alther's third novel [*Other Women*] combines the manic comedy of *Kinflicks*, her first, with the depressive substance of *Original Sins,* her second, to produce her most challenging and successful work to date. Its topic is the psychotherapy of one woman undertaken with another, its theme is the achievement of adulthood in this childishly topsy-turvy world, its triumph is in its struggle to come to terms with things as they are and things as we would wish them to be.

Meet Caroline Kelley, emergency room nurse, on her initial visit to the office of Hannah Burke. Attractive, vivacious, tough and smart, she has come against her better judgment. What can anyone do for her that she can't do better for herself? More important, that she shouldn't be able to do? (p. 17)

Hannah Burke, sixtyish wearer of polyester, bridge-player, chain-smoker of Mores, diagnoses the problem in a British accent. And asks, "Why did you pick me?"

The odd coupledom of these two women produces one of the most reverberative relationships in recent fiction. Through it, the two examine everything they know about themselves, each other, and the world. Shaped by her early training . . . , Caroline's view is that "only an idiot wouldn't be depressed in a world like this." Hannah counters, "This world is like a diamond on black velvet." That the two views can coexist, even be reconciled, is the meaning of maturity. Nothing we know or feel is easy; but then ease is not the point.

But the novel is not as darkly introspective as I have made it sound. It is utterly unlike the self-indulgent egoism produced by many male writers who have recently chosen this theme. One of the explicit points of the book, in fact, is that men are permanently stunted, infantile. A reason for the novel's success is that it is not directed merely toward exploring the writer's psyche, personal problems or sexual history. Its consistent aim is outward, its intent is to connect with and respond to the kaleidoscope world, its variousness, its ultimate mystery. Its success is in the brilliance of its dialectic: Is the world a joke on us? Or we, on it? The dialectic is carried out by means of explicit jokes throughout and an uncompromising, implicit feminism.

All comedy is tragic; all tragedy is finally comic. That Lisa Alther understands this, and fuses the two, is one of her great gifts as a writer. *Other Women* is a gift to its reader and her best book to date. (pp. 17, 20)

Adrian Oktenberg, "Odd Couple?" in New Directions for Women, *Vol. 14, No. 1, January-February, 1985, pp. 17, 20.*

FRANCIS KING

Whenever some American confides in me that he or she is 'in' analysis, I shrink away as from a discussion of bowel-movements. When I have to read a novel in which the central character is 'in' analysis, my reaction is the same. In consequence, on reading the blurb of Lisa Alther's *Other Women*—which makes it sound as if it were the fictional equivalent of an updated *The Seventh Veil,* with a neurotic heroine eventually succeeding in healing herself by ferreting out the demons of her past—I did not feel encouraged. Yet I was wrong. Against all my expectations, this proved a fine novel. . . .

One of the strengths of the novel is that the author devotes almost as much attention to the therapist as to her patient. Hannah has herself suffered a series of tragedies in her life, sufficient to drive her to an analyst's couch: death of her mother when she was five; desertion by her father a year later; unhappy marriage to a working-class bully, who is killed in the war; death of two children from carbon monoxide poisoning from a faulty stove. It is because she can say 'Look, I have come through' that she is able to heal others. (p. 23)

Hannah's view of neurosis—which one takes also to be Ms Alther's view—is that it originates in The Pattern: that is, the bad emotional and behavioural habits which we pick up in childhood and which then cause us endless damage and distress until we manage to unlearn them. Thus Caroline, whose parents never seemed to have time for her, so intent were they on feeding the world's sick and bandaging its wounded, has ac-

quired the habit of soliciting attention, love and protection by herself doing good. A member of a 'caring' profession, she cares for (looks after) those around her, in the hope that in return they will care for (love) her. Hannah's task is to persuade her to abandon this Pattern, and so to grow up.

As Caroline goes back over her past, in order to learn its bitter lessons, so does Ms Alther. Whether Caroline is in the arms of her female housemate, succumbing to the wooing of a male doctor at the hospital at which she works, or having a one-night stand with a woman, a camp counsellor, picked up in a sauna, the scenes of love-making are all handled with explicit assurance. (pp. 23-4)

What I missed in this predominantly grave novel was the humour that made Ms Alther's first novel, *Kinflicks,* such a joy. There is one wonderfully comic chapter when Caroline takes her two sons to the parental home for Christmas. Inveterate do-gooders that they are, her father and mother have invited so many of their down-and-out or dotty protégés to Christmas dinner that she and the boys have to go short. Equally comic is the chapter in which Caroline attends an appalling party given by a Peugeot dealer and his wife—not used to the company of heterosexuals, still less to men making blatant passes at her, she suffers a growing discomfort. But, sadly, such passages are rare.

Inevitably, Caroline falls for her therapist; and though, contrary to my expectations, Hannah does not fall for her—I had feared an ending which would have the two women slowly melting into each other like two chocolate bars left out in the sun—a rapport extending beyond the consulting-room is established. The close is a happy one—few therapists can have had such instant success with a patient; but, like everything else that happens in the novel, it never seems forced. If Caroline has freed herself from the tyranny of The Pattern, that does not mean that from time to time it may not reassert itself; and though the two women are close at the moment of goodbye, they may well drift apart, now that their professional relationship is over. . . .

Love between women has rarely been treated with more sympathy, truth and tact. (p. 24)

Francis King, "Hannah and Caroline," in The Spectator, *Vol. 254, No. 8174, March 9, 1985, pp. 23-4.*

Reinaldo Arenas

1943-

Cuban novelist, poet, and short story writer.

Arenas's work is marked by his imaginative embellishment of history and reality and reflects the turbulent political atmosphere of his homeland. Although Arenas makes frequent use of surrealistic imagery, satire, and elements of the fantastic, his work is rooted in reality and evokes an undercurrent of powerful and sincere emotion. Before his self-exile from Cuba in 1980, Arenas built a strong international reputation. He now lives, teaches, and writes in the United States.

Arenas's first novel, *Celestino antes del alba* (1967), was critically acclaimed in Cuba and abroad. This work centers on a mentally retarded but imaginative boy who, like Arenas, grows up a member of a poor family in rural Cuba. Kessel Schwartz described the book as "a fantastic, anguished, and poetic novel which reveals the grotesque, brutal, and yet fantastic rural world as seen through [the boy's] interior monologue." In *El mundo alucinante (una novela de aventuras)* (1969; *Hallucinations*), Arenas again fuses reality and fantasy. This novel recounts the life of Fray Servando Teresa de Mier, a Mexican monk of the early nineteenth century who was persecuted for his assertion that Christianity existed in Mexico before the arrival of the Spanish. *Hallucinations* is a picaresque, multilayered work lauded for its inventive use of language, myth, and history. Cuban authorities detected in the book a satirical, antirevolutionary tone, and Arenas was not allowed to publish it in his own country; *Hallucinations* was eventually published in Mexico. Arenas's subsequent works of the 1970s, *Termina el desfile* (1972), a collection of short stories, and *El palacio de las blanquisimas mofetas* (1975), a sequel to *Celestino antes del alba* which depicts the adolescent protagonist's emergence into adulthood, were also published abroad.

The Castro regime held Arenas in disfavor throughout the 1970s because of his homosexuality and what was perceived as his antigovernment stance. During this period, he was jailed several times, threatened, and deprived of recognition as a writer. In 1980, Arenas was one of approximately 140,000 Cubans who left their country for the United States in the Mariel boatlift. Since his arrival, Arenas has gained increased recognition and has published several new works. *El Central (A Cuban Sugar Mill)* (1981) is a long poem based on Arenas's experiences while serving six months of forced labor in a sugar mill in western Cuba. The poem links the country's early colonial history of slavery and oppression with present-day conditions. *Otra vez el mar* (1982; *Farewell to the Sea: A Novel of Cuba)*, which Arenas rewrote twice from memory after his manuscripts were confiscated in Cuba, has received widespread critical acclaim. This two-part novel centers on a husband and wife who, with their eight-month-old baby, leave Havana for a short vacation at the seashore. The first section is written from the wife's perspective; it tells of her frustrated love for her husband and her confusion over his depressed state. The novel's second part, structured as a long, rambling poem, is narrated by the husband. Formerly an enthusiastic participant in the Cuban revolution, he is troubled by his alienation and disillusionment and by his homosexuality. Most critics agree that *Farewell to the Sea* is a powerfully written work with universal implica-

Photograph by Layle Silbert

tions. Jay Cantor observed that Arenas "is not interested in ordinary realistic drama. He wants to give the reader the secret history of the emotions, the sustaining victories of pleasure and the small dishonesties that callous the soul."

THE TIMES LITERARY SUPPLEMENT

Cuba is a country which, unlike most others in Latin America, has had a singularly fertile and imaginative literary tradition, and although the Cuban revolutionary authorities are more eager to encourage experimental writing by foreigners than by Cubans, Reinaldo Arenas's ***Celestino antes del alba*** is evidence that the limitations imposed on Cuban writers are not always excessively dour ones.

The novel depicts the vision that a retarded, hallucinated child has of a cruelly aggressive and arid rural environment in Cuba. The son of an unmarried mother, he is brought up in the household of his grudging and violent grandparents. The child cannot easily distinguish between fantasy and reality, and whenever the grandfather pursues him with an axe, he is able to fly off and escape into the clouds. At one point he is devoured by ants; on the next page he is safely in bed, having night-mares. . . .

In many ways the child's madness is an excuse for Reinaldo Arenas to indulge in a surrealist romp, a point easily made when the child blithely quotes Arab and Chinese poems which his retarded and provincial mind could scarcely have encountered. . . . [One] of the merits of this novel . . . is the lively and convincing manner in which the fantasies are sustained. But there is also a great deal of human and social significance in the child's pathetic longing for affection in so unsympathetic an environment.

Celestino antes del alba is a distinguished first novel in what has now become an eminent tradition of fantastic literature in Latin America, and it deserves the considerable publicity it has received in the Spanish-speaking world.

> *"Double Vision," in* The Times Literary Supplement, *No. 3557, April 30, 1970, p. 485.*

ANITA VAN VACTOR

The energy, playfulness, challenging extravagance of Reinaldo Arenas's writing asserts the freedom not to be intimidated by ideological versions of reality. The strength of his book [*Hallucinations*] lies in the completeness with which this young Cuban novelist succeeds in identifying personal and political liberation. His hero, Friar Servando, spends a lifetime escaping from prisons: he would rather save than risk his own skin, and his passion for survival nourishes and develops his dedication to the cause of freeing Mexico from the Spanish colonisers. There was a real Fray Servando Teresa de Mier in Mexico, nearly two centuries ago: in his heretical sermon on the apparition of Our Lady of Guadalupe, he claimed that the Apparition (and therefore Christianity) had come to Mexico long before the Spaniards, thus undermining any justification for their presence there. For this he was exiled and endlessly persecuted. Arenas incorporates passages from Servando's memoirs, but otherwise re-invents, having discovered that Servando existed more truly in his own imagination than in the dehumanised reports of history books.

The friar's adventures, as the title suggests, are hallucinatory, but not, as the blurb says, 'wildly improbable' except in a radically ironic sense. In vision, even in technique, Arenas shares a kindred spirit with Blake, especially the Blake of *America*. For both writers, prison *is* hallucination, a negative and melodramatic state of mind engendered by belief in the lurid frauds imposed by church and state, to enslave the weak. The hallucinated cannot imagine the possibility of liberation: it appears to them, if at all, in the form of the improbable, or the fantastic, of terror and diabolism. . . .

Arenas does run the risk of lapsing into mere whimsy or a flaunting schoolboy rebelliousness, but good judgment mostly saves him, and the skill to keep aloft by playing one style off against another. He knows how to turn an elevated manner in the direction of pomposity or of eloquence. At the Parisian soirées of Chateaubriand and Mme de Staël his tone is light, cynical, urbane; and he can work a colloquial vein either for slangy impudence or humble directness. (It's the colloquial range, full of puns and mocking flights of internal rhyme, that seems to suffer most in an otherwise convincing translation.) And although he's never pious or sentimental about human wretchedness, he knows how to speak out plainly in the voice of honest indignation. The presence of such a voice, in a writer

so skilful, is especially remarkable and moving in these days when stylistic ingenuity is normally cultivated as a defence against strong, open feeling. (p. 528)

> *Anita Van Vactor, "The Disasters of Conscience," in* The Listener, *Vol. 85, No. 2195, April 22, 1971, pp. 527-28.*

PUBLISHERS WEEKLY

[Arenas] writes, in this highly imaginative, fictionalized biography [*Hallucinations*], in both present and past tenses, in first and third persons, often switching within sentences. The subject is the life of Friar Servando Teresa de Mier, a Mexican cleric, who was condemned to a life of persecution because of his sermon casting doubt on the authenticity of the apparition of Our Lady of Guadalupe. His highly improbable, picaresque adventures in Europe, England, where he meets both Lady Hamilton and Virginia Woolf's "Orlando," in the U.S., where he becomes a cotton picker, and in Mexico, are related in a bewildering mixture of fact and fantasy. Arenas is an original and imaginative writer with a bizarre sense of comedy, yet it seems that his work is too deeply rooted in the ethos of Latin America to have much meaning or appeal north of the border.

> *A review of "Hallucinations," in* Publishers Weekly, *Vol. 199, No. 23, June 7, 1971, p. 50.*

HELEN R. LANE

To the gallery of enduring universal types, the Spanish literary tradition has contributed the *pícaro*, that roguish wanderer as untrappable as wind who outwits a wicked world that would enchain his very uvula. Reinaldo Arenas, a young Cuban author obviously taken with this figure of untrammeled freedom as Latin America's only hope of authentic liberation, has chosen as the hero of his *Hallucinations* an amazing real-life adventurer: Father Servando Teresa de Mier. . . .

Arenas calls his imaginary biography of Friar de Mier "simply a novel," but his impenitent amalgam of truth and invention, of historical fact and outrageous make-believe is also a philosophical black comedy. It is also a sweeping fresco of an age of unbelievable injustice, and an implicit call for more Third World *hombres formidables* of this friar's incredibly incorruptible stamp. (p. 4)

Hallucinations has been aptly named, for Arenas works in the sardonic nightmare tradition of Quevedo and Goya, and images of human cruelty as sharp as slivers of glass and as penetrating as a scream fill its pages. But this *pícaro* proceeds through a world of blood and bayonets and breaking bones with the equanimity of an armored tank. The unremittingly utopian Friar escapes one dreary prison after another, aided variously by his wits, an umbrella, "the juice of his finger nails," and pure poetic invention. He meets the onslaughts of rats and lice, a marriage-bent female, bloodthirsty inquisitors, a slaveship captain, and a plantation overseer in the cotton fields of the American Deep South with the same crusty soul-saving irony and skin-saving presence of mind.

He encounters on his travels not only cynical revolutionaries in the French capital and venal priests all over Western Christendom—but also such figures from a country of the mind as Virginia Woolf's hermaphroditic Orlando. In the end, the historian's fact and Arenas's fiction blend into a surrealist fantasy of sheer freedom versus sheer power that breaks every earth-bound canon of conventional fictionalized biography.

This is a wildly unpruned *ficción,* often as cluttered as a Churrigueresque Mexican cathedral and suffering on many pages from Latin logorrhea. It is definitely not a book for readers who get queasy at leaps of dream-logic and trapeze acts of the imagination.... This book is a very Spanish vision of the chaos of life itself, a sleep of reason where moral miracle and monstrousness cohabit, where humor is warp and horror woof, where even such irrepressible spirits as Father de Mier are doomed to become only echoes' bones. (pp. 4, 20)

The reader who lets himself be swept away by the force of Arenas's vision will find it not at all strange that the laws of the probable in this moral fable have no more bearing than in a medieval legend. Thanks to his verbal prodigies (at once savory and soaring) Friar Servando Teresa de Mier joins the roll of picaresque saints a lay age can light a candle to. *Hallucinations* becomes a spirited demonstration that, as Don Quixote told Sancho, "the high road is far better than the inns." (p. 20)

> Helen R. Lane, in a review of "Hallucinations," in
> The New York Times Book Review, *August 29, 1971,*
> *pp. 4, 20.*

ALAN SCHWARTZ

When Reinaldo Arenas published *Celestino antes del alba* in 1965, at the age of twenty-two, he was hailed by the Cuban Writers' Union as a major new talent. The following year, *El mundo alucinante* was published not in Cuba but in Mexico. The book was translated into French subsequently and was well-received in Europe. Now we have an excellent English translation [*Hallucinations*] by Gordon Brotherston, but the work has not yet been published in Cuba, and the reader can only wonder why.

With uncompromising faith in a politically independent future for his country, Friar Servando Teresa de Mier, the hero of this tale, is pursued through the New and Old World by the Inquisition, is imprisoned, tortured, assaulted sexually, starved and enslaved. After a series of preposterous escapes, he returns to his native Mexico, assists the revolution, and sees his political dream only imperfectly fulfilled by the republic of President Guadalupe Victoria....

A unique characteristic of this narrative is its technique: Incidents are reported from three different points of view to create the effect of a cubistic picture without losing the story line. Poems and citations from historical sources counterpoint the tale and create a see-saw between hallucination and history. The tour de force isn't completely successful, however, because the friar remains a two-dimensional idea, insufficiently fleshed.

Nevertheless, if one reads this book not as a novel, but as a romance in the tradition of *Candide* or *Rasselas,* the flaws in its ambitious technique are overshadowed by the madcap inventiveness, the acid satire, and the powerful writing....

But the question nags: Why not Cuban publication to date? Is this picaresque fantasy so damaging to Castro's government or have we simply an international example of "banned in Boston"? What political implications might cause difficulty for the writer in his native country? Perhaps it is the disillusionment suffered by the revolutionary utopian whose experiences make him suspect that political systems are based upon some kind of fraud and that the reward of idealism is persecution. There is a suggestion that even to the revolutionary leaders there comes a pragmatic realization that freedom, truth, and justice inspire fine rhetoric, but control is maintained with bread and circuses.

At the end of his life Servando doubts all political achievement including his own, and feels as the victim of an undefined swindle, "afraid that at the end of those vast enclosures there wouldn't be anyone waiting for him." This is an interesting man, faithful to his skepticism, and Señor Arenas has tried to know him in that extension of identity which is the magic of fiction; we can appreciate this slightly flawed enchantment for the fascinating adventure and allegory it sustains.

> Alan Schwartz, "A Cuban Romance," in Book
> World—Chicago Tribune, *September 5, 1971, p. 8.*

ANA ROCA AND REINALDO ARENAS

[Roca:] *Your writing might be described as open-ended. The reader has to participate in order to complete it. How do you manage that? Could you say something about your technique as a novelist, your ideas on the novel, and any similarities with other contemporary Latin American fiction?*

[Arenas:] A writer has to belong to his own era. We can't write eighteenth or nineteenth century novels, because we're living at the end of the twentieth. Like any other form of modern art, the contemporary novel must reflect the dynamism in which we live, to which we belong, and of which we are an integral part. We ourselves create that dynamism. So I don't think it's possible to write the stereotyped novel—a plot, a climax, a denouement—nowadays. Modern writers have to realize that, and this applies particularly to those of us who are island-dwellers, constantly surrounded by the sea, the breeze, and open spaces. To depict the essence of anything Cuban, we have to follow the example set by the island itself—where everything penetrates, everything is wide open—and that's the way my novels are.

Could you give an example?

In *Celestino Antes del Alba*—and even in *El Mundo Alucinante*—the dialogue is repeated and the scenes replayed from different angles.... I think a reader could pick up one of my novels and start reading it anywhere. They shouldn't be read for their storytelling qualities; they are participation vehicles. The reader, like the author, must become a part of the novel and the story.

What was your inspiration for the character of Celestino? Could you comment on literary influences?

Celestino is utterly alone. He is the child who, discovering the world, also discovers himself in the midst of the violence that surrounds him. Alone, he invents a character who is his friend—the friend all of us would like to have, who is essentially our own self. At the same time, it is the revolt of a poet who wants to create in a completely violent medium. In his attempt to write this endless poem on the tree trunks, on his parents and the whole family, the entire neighborhood, he covers the whole country. I'm not sure: perhaps in the midst of such violence—or let's say in this tragic backdrop for the novel—the influence of tragedians of all eras is apparent. At times the novel becomes a drama and the tragic element reaches a climax, and from then on it is tragic theater. So from that standpoint there may be other influences as well.

How did you come to write about the historical figure of Servando Teresa de Mier?

I was preparing a lecture on the Mexican novelist Juan Rulfo when I came across a reference that mentioned Fray Servando as the friar who had traveled all over Europe at the end of the eighteenth century, telling incredible adventure stories, serving time in one prison after another, and working for the independence of Mexico. I was anxious to learn more about him, and I found the first volume of his autobiography. I was so inspired by the character that I did a series of rewrites. I transposed his life into fiction, against a background of actual events, plus others that never happened. My aim was to portray this compelling personality as a part of the American myth, the New World myth: this figure, part raving madman and part sublime, a hero, an adventurer, and a perennial exile, who was Fray Servando. (p. 37)

*In the story called **"Con los Ojos Cerrados"** ("With Closed Eyes"), there is a quotation from Felisberto Hernández that says: "I don't think I should limit my writing to what I know—it should include the rest as well." What do you mean by that?*

"The rest" refers specifically to what cannot be seen and nevertheless is more important than anything that can be captured by a camera. Sleep, wakefulness, imagination, fear, hope, love. I am against what professors of literature call "realism." If true realism is to be applied to human beings, it is the exact opposite of the conventional realism we've grown accustomed to in the horrible works of the Spanish novelists Emilia Pardo Bazán and Benito Pérez Galdós. Recently, of course, people have stopped talking about realism. Now they refer to socialist realism, which is supposed to portray human beings as animals who work, eat, sleep, get up, go to bed . . . and mouth nothing but political and absolutely dogmatic ideas. We might say that socialist realism is really a caricature of realism.

But then what is true realism?

To me, true realism is fantasy, the fantastic, the eclectic. It knows no bounds, for otherwise it would no longer be realism. When I go to sleep, I don't cease to exist: I dream. And when I am silent, my imagination continues to function. . . .

Very often when I read your works I have the impression that I'm reading poetry. It seems to me that sometimes you're more poet than novelist, and that underneath the novelist there's a great poet.

I believe that everything should be tinged with poetry. When there's no poetry, nothing is of any consequence. . . .

In years to come, how would you like people to remember you as a writer?

I would like to be remembered not as a writer in the conventional sense of the word, but rather as a sort of goblin—as the personification of a mocking spirit. (p. 38)

> *Ana Roca and Reinaldo Arenas, in an interview in* Américas, *Vol. 33, No. 9, September, 1981, pp. 36-8.*

ORLANDO ROSSARDI

[In *Termina el Desfile*] Reinaldo Arenas presents a rich, balanced selection of his short stories, in which—as in almost all his works—the author makes a personal appearance to assure that the right conclusions are drawn. Outstanding among the collection is the lengthy story **"La Vieja Rosa"** ("Old Rose" . . .), which is an excellent model of narrative construction.

Arenas likes to relate his realities by first laying them bare, and then approaching them through situations created by the characters themselves. He throws out ideas, dreams, imaginations, and feelings "that cannot be touched"—in Arenas's words—"but that when named are reflected within and without man." The fact that he is making a statement does not stem the flow of the fantastic and poetic elements; his testimony is valid both as a document and a legitimate work of art. The fusion of both, and his aversion to the baroque, give the reader caught up in the Latin American novel "boom" the sensation of having discovered a book well achieved without bowing to the dictates of the day, and having experienced the pleasure of a work well written.

> *Orlando Rossardi, in a review of "Termina el desfile," in* Américas, *Vol. 34, No. 1, January-February, 1982, p. 63.*

JAMES BESCHTA

[*El Central*] is in keeping with the tradition of Latin American poetry. It is a poetry that is of and for the people, one that tells of suppression and class struggle. It is accessible to the common man because it is both about and for him; there is no elitism in this work. Also, there is a sense of immediacy and involvement that distinguishes it from American poetry.

This poem was written while Arenas was doing forced labor in 1970, in Castro's Cuba. It is a powerful protest and lamentation, a rebellion and a mourning of lost adolescence. But it is also, perhaps like all accounts of oppression, a history, a record of humanity's constant freedom-quest. In an imaginative approach, Arenas parallels historical characters and information involving the role of slaves in Cuban colonization with his own situation. The effect is insightful and dramatic as the poem builds, often through selective repetition, to a conclusion that is at once desperate and hopeful.

> *James Beschta, in a review of "El central (a Cuban Sugar Mill)," in* Kliatt Young Adult Paperback Book Guide, *Vol. XVIII, No. 6, September, 1984, p. 32.*

RICHARD COOPER

A reign of terror sparks great creative achievement as well as the debased servile idolization of despotism. [In *El Central*] Arenas portrays the brutal history of Cuba, groaning under successive masters. He has written not just a work of art, but a moral testimony against injustice.

"El Central" refers to the sugar mill which casts a shadow across Cuban history. Arenas harks back to the heritage of the Indians exterminated by the Spaniards and the legacy of slavery intimately bound together with the production of sugar, now devoted to the Soviet masters of "independent" Cuba. He grasps the similarity between the new despots and the Spanish conquistadors who subjugated the island in the name of their God and Country. "Hands enslaved in the name of the nation and its sacred principles . . ."

The Marxists constantly employ the metaphor of the Prussian philosopher of state omnipotence, G.W.F. Hegel who identifies Marxism with ". . . the cutting edge of history." Perhaps Arenas alludes to this vulgar catch phrase in the line "And violence rankles like the cutting blow of a machete-blade in the rainy season.'' As the Indians and blacks discovered with the conquistadors, being on the cutting edge of history is no pleasure. ''Thousands of repressive laws have been created. Over 150 concentration camps have been built. Some 50,000 people have been shot, more than a million have exiled, and the rest of the population has been enslaved. Does anyone deny us eternity?''

Arenas cannot be considered a political writer like Solzhenitsyn or Athol Fugard in South Africa. He writes out of moral and artistic integrity, which is enough to condemn him in communist eyes. His experience has been as a great teacher. The Marxists justify themselves in the name of history. Arenas retorts: ''To speak of history is to abandon momentarily our obligatory silence to say (without forgetting dates) what those who were suffering obligatory silence could not say. To say what is now useless. . . . Slave-hands extract gold, work sugar mills, build bridges, dig graves, construct highways; and now strangle people and applaud.''

The Leviathan state threatens culture, society, and the very lives of individuals. *El Central* utters the strangled cry of the oppressed. Who shall listen? (pp. 22-3)

> Richard Cooper, in a review of ''El Central,'' in San Francisco Review of Books, *May-June, 1985,* pp. 22-3.

KIRKUS REVIEWS

[*Farewell to the Sea*] provides a sense of the outrage felt by serious Cuban intellectuals (especially those who also are homosexual, doubly pariahs), plus a taste of the still flourishing baroque tradition in Cuban fiction personified by such masters as Lezama Lima and Cabrera Infante.

The novel is cloven in two. The initial part is a humid, bleak, horror-accumulating monologue, narrated by a young Cuban woman spending a few weeks at a beach cabin with her baby and deeply depressed poet-husband. Disillusion is a condensing fog over everything. . . . The husband's political depression, his complete alienation, ultimately plagues the young woman with a no-way-out despair.

But the husband isn't merely a poet: he's also homosexual; and the book's second half, which mostly is in verse (the husband's poetry . . .), is at once mythic fantasy, dark satire (a brilliant set piece in which a prancy queen negotiates the streets of the new puritanical Havana), and a litany of sadness and anger. As poetry, it doesn't quite match in intensity the wife's prose section, the oblique mirroring there being more powerfully bleak; and too much of it rains a dandruff of campy literary gesture—yet, together, the two disparate pieces pretty much complement each other.

By no means congenial, nor as intriguing finally as the book it most aspires to (Lezama Lima's masterpiece *Paradiso*), it's a work that still bears powerful witness to the continuing, adventurous elegance of Cuban writing. (pp. 956-57)

> A review of ''Farewell to the Sea,'' in Kirkus Reviews, *Vol. LIII, No. 18, September 15, 1985,* pp. 956-57.

LONNIE WEATHERBY

[In *Farewell to the Sea,* Arenas] has written a splenetic indictment of totalitarianism in general and his native country in particular. The novel's first part, an interior monologue, represents the memories and fantasies of a woman on vacation with her husband and infant son. Trapped in a repressive country, saddled with an uncommunicative husband and a child she feels no bond to, she is suicidally obsessed with the idea of escape. The ocean surrounding Cuba is symbolically both her liberator and her jailer. The second part is a series of cantos which provide an explanatory gloss on the phantasmagorical narrative of the first part. The novel is imaginatively conceived, but the hysterical, shrill tone vitiates its power.

> Lonnie Weatherby, in a review of ''Farewell to the Sea: A Novel of Cuba,'' in Library Journal, *Vol. 110, No. 15, September 15, 1985,* p. 90.

JAY CANTOR

Reinaldo Arenas, a Cuban writer, made his way to the United States as part of the Mariel exodus in 1980. But the rigors that implies are rarely directly realized in *Farewell to the Sea*. . . . Oppression here is a pounding, omnipresent but also somewhat abstract fact, like the sea of the title itself.

The scant story of Mr. Arenas's novel . . . is of a couple's week at the seaside. The husband has a brief affair with a boy staying with his mother in a cabin nearby. The boy commits suicide. The couple return to the city. The book's action takes only slightly longer in the novel's telling than it does here. The boy's personality is almost nonexistent, the motivation of the suicide unmentioned. The responses to the drowning are the work of a few pages. Mr. Arenas is not interested in ordinary realistic drama. He wants to give the reader the secret history of the emotions, the sustaining victories of pleasure and the small dishonesties that callous the soul.

The first third of the novel is a long monologue by the wife that unfolds during the week's vacation. Punctuated by her dreams and fantasies, this section is pervaded by the dreary monotony of life under Fidel Castro, the silence and separation between characters. The revolution declines in rhythm with the wife's recognition of the hollowness of her marriage. . . .

This appropriately unnamed wife's plaint is tightly strung along its theme—her longing for her husband. She speaks of the terror of the regime, under which ''the obligatory adoration of a single person . . . is raised to dizzying heights, and persecution and absolute enslavement are the order of the day.'' Yet she herself seems in thrall to Hector, her husband, and has few thoughts that are not formed by her adoration of his body, her yearning for him. Even her dreams of escape are dreams of love. ''Somewhere there must be more than this violence and loneliness, this stupidity, laziness, chaos, and stupor. . . . Somewhere someone is waiting for me.''

It could hardly be called ethically wrong—except by the same sort of mentality that leads to the jailing of writers in Cuba— that her political urgency here ends in the necessarily always unrequited refrain of a love song. It is part of Mr. Arenas's strength that he does not give his characters' unhappiness a simple political explanation. . . . It is the necessity of art to complain endlessly, to say—as if pointing to the sea—that beyond the confinement of the state there is another confinement, beyond this freedom there is another freedom, so large as to be unbearable. The book asks the questions of art, but one feels it could do it more artfully. For each point is repeated and after a while the wife's obsession feels like a limitation not of history, or the human condition, but of the author, who might have granted her a wider life, given her a name.

The last two-thirds of the novel, Hector's portion, which covers the same week at the beach, is almost entirely phantasmagorical, with long portions of poetry that sometimes show flashes of brilliance. One section is a wonderful refutation of Whitman's optimism, done in Whitman's style. But the poetry frequently gives the feeling of hysterical wordplay, of a mind maddened by slogans and enforced silence, clearing itself of static and lies before sleep. The poetry often fails, too, from a gauzy insubstantiality: "Remember, we are nothing but some passing terror, an angry/impotence, an insatiable, ephemeral flame."

Hector's personality, openly and honestly presented, can be unattractive, selfish, unfeeling. He uses as accusation toward others the very sorts of sexual politics that are used to condemn him. . . . His fantasies of monsters, mass executions and cruising are sometimes powerful in their perception of political degradation as physical degradation, but they are also often wearing in their length and repetitiveness.

One feels within the silence that surrounds these characters the power of the regime, of Mr. Castro's voice, which has perhaps monopolized and subverted the possibilities of speech, made itself the limit even of fantasy, causing Hector to turn within himself in a solipsism so extreme that it is almost a self-immolation. Maybe that is as close as he can come to power over his own life. But it would be awful to think that the regime need inevitably triumph over the demands of the novel, its possibilities for variety, for an involving verbal texture and for the imagination of others.

> *Jay Cantor, "Dreams of Escape, Dreams of Love,"* in The New York Times Book Review, *November 24, 1985, p. 31.*

ANTHONY DeCURTIS

A novel that casts post-revolutionary Cuba as hell on earth, *Farewell to the Sea* is simultaneously a desperate hymn of anti-Castro protest, a febrile gay-rights harangue and a heartbreakingly incisive portrait of a marriage rotted by its own repressed emotions. To render this sometimes horrifying, sometimes blackly hilarious tale of personal hypocrisy within political duplicity, Reinaldo Arenas employs a kind of magic surrealism, evoking a nightmarish dreamscape where James Joyce's stream-of-consciousness and William Burroughs's savaged consciousness find equal expression. The result is a stunning literary tour-de-force whose impact will be undeniable even to those who find Arenas's anti-communism obnoxious.

Like *Ulysses, Farewell* works imaginative wonders with minimal plot. A young couple leaves Havana for six days at the shore with their infant son and, freed from the distractions of their day-to-day existences, they find themselves confronted with the escape of long-suppressed hopes and dreams.

The gorgeous, wrenching internal narrative of the book's first half describes the woman's sexual frustration and the struggle between realization and denial of the grim terms of her marriage and life. The second half is a careening free-verse poem that details the husband's homosexual passion, his fury at his country's betrayal of its revolutionary promise and his howling dissatisfaction within "the depths of this hellish poem—which is life." (pp. 74-5)

Born of Arenas's "uncontrollable sense of wanting to speak," *Farewell to the Sea* will surely excite an array of urgent voices on the strength of its artistic achievement and controversial force. Like Allen Ginsberg in an earlier time, Reinaldo Arenas has put his shoulder to the wheel—the turning's just about to begin. (p. 75)

> *Anthony DeCurtis, in a review of "Farewell to the Sea," in* Saturday Review, *Vol. 11, No. 6, November-December, 1985, pp. 74-5.*

MICHAEL WOOD

Homosexuality is at the center of Reinaldo Arenas's *Farewell to the Sea,* a work as brilliant as it is troubling, but the prejudice here is internalized and put dramatically to work. It becomes homosexual self-hatred, the victim's endorsement of the tormentor's values, and more generally a figure for what Arenas sees Cuba as doing to itself. This novel, Arenas has said, depicts "the secret history of the Cuban people"—a claim that is no doubt too ambitious and definitely tendentious. The secret, Arenas suggests in an exuberant prose which plainly enjoys its own antics, is that the Cubans hate Castro and what has happened to them, that only time-servers and small tyrants are happy in that country, that resentment and suspicion and brutality and fear are the realities of contemporary Cuban life. . . . It is hard, as Herberto Padilla has said, to judge the work of dissidents: we either lionize the writer or get defensive about the accusations. What we must do, I think, is *listen;* and then try to tell how central or how marginal these protests are; how urgent or how self-serving.

The work has high literary as well as political ambitions; it seems conceived as a successor to Lezama Lima's *Paradiso,* as a Cuban cousin of Pound's *Cantos,* and it draws on bits of Joyce's *Ulysses.* It is part novel, part free-verse poem, full of parody and phantasmagoria, but also of carefully observed current scenes. It lives in the tortured consciousness of its two main characters, and also in its profuse spray of language, its harsh and mocking incantation of sorrows and pains. . . . The book may be too obsessive and too prolix to earn the authority of the works I've mentioned—although those adjectives describe entire patches of the *Cantos* well enough, so perhaps we shouldn't hurry to arrive at a judgment. Certainly *Farewell to the Sea* is a major work by a gifted writer, and Octavio Paz's "remarkable," on the dust jacket, seems tame, almost an irony.

Hector, a diffident, disaffected veteran of the final struggle against Batista, and his unnamed, loving, frustrated wife have taken a cabin by the sea for a week. Their eight-month-old baby is with them, they want to spend time away from the crowding and routine and hopelessness of life in Havana. The date is 1969. . . . What we read are the thoughts of these two people, in subtly interwoven times, arriving at the beach, driving back at the end of the week, remembering their past, experiencing present moments in the sea, at meals, in bed, walking, reading. We get first the wife's thoughts, in a long, sinuous interior monologue in which the passing days are marked but which is otherwise undivided. It is full of cramped memories, and violent, unsatisfying dreams—at one point she turns a scene from the *Iliad* into a wild sexual orgy, heroic phalluses everywhere. She has sudden, evanescent moments of happiness too, and her perceptions are captured in language of great beauty. . . .

But mainly she is lost, uncertain, anxious for a consolation she only half believes in. "Somewhere there must be more than this violence and loneliness, this stupidity, laziness, chaos, and stupor which are killing us.'' ''The terrible,'' she thinks in a memorable phrase, ''becomes merely monotonous.'' ''Real disaster never comes suddenly, because it's always happening.'' She understands though that her unhappiness has to do with her character and with Hector's indifference to her, and that in Cuba as elsewhere it is possible to blame public events for private griefs. (p. 36)

Neither Hector nor his wife believes in words—''There are no words, there are no words, there definitely are no words''—and yet words are all they have, the silent, mental spinning out of their loneliness. Hector is a poet—or was before he lost his hope or his will and stopped writing, and his part of the book, divided into six cantos to match his wife's six days, is a buzzing mixture of verse and prose, of rhetoric and self-scrutiny. Hector is an uneasy homosexual, vaguely kind to his wife, only unintentionally cruel, always absent, usually silent. . . . He plays happily with the child, sometimes getting overhistrionic in his diatribes against the Cuban situation. He has an encounter with a handsome boy met on the beach. . . . The boy later commits suicide by throwing himself from a cliff.

Hector has lyrical moments too, usually associated with the sea. . . . But mainly his thoughts are ''offensive and offended,'' as his wife thinks his speech is. She at least has the clarity of her unrequited love; he has only anguish and disgust and rage. He often sounds like a hysterical version of Eliot's Prufrock, or a stray from *The Waste Land,* which he both quotes and parodies. . . . He arraigns Whitman for his easy hope . . . but he also has more local, more particular complaints, bitterly listing what he calls the privileges of the present system in Cuba:

> Writing a book on cutting sugarcane
> and winning the National Poetry
> Prize;
> Writing a book of poetry and being
> sent to cut sugarcane for five
> years . . .

> Concentration camps exclusively for
> homosexuals . . .
> Song festivals without singers . . .
> The child as a field of police
> experimentation . . .
> Tamarind trees felled to plant
> tamarind trees;
> Betrayal of ourselves as the only
> means of survival . . .

(pp. 36-7)

How closely are we to associate Hector with Arenas? A delicate question, since Castro's regime, and perhaps some of Arenas's friends, think there is no question at all. Arenas, I would say, wants us to note the shrillness of Hector's thoughts, their whining tone, his self-pity, and his failure to distinguish, in itemizing his complaints, between hurt flesh and wounded vanity. Arenas wants us to see too that some of what Hector finds in Cuba are only what he grimly calls ''the era's standard adornments: bombs, shots, arguments, shouts, threats, torture, humiliation, fear, hunger''—not confined to Cuba, but then not banished from Cuba either. . . . In spite of Arenas's grandiose phrase about secret history, the book is not that; it is not a history at all, secret or otherwise, and not an indictment, but a novel, that is, an evocation of desperate, complex, individual, imagined lives.

Even so, we must ask . . . how this fiction relates to our facts, what order of truth it aims at. The point, it seems to me, is not that Hector must be right or wrong, but that he must be *heard;* and if he can't be heard, he is already halfway right, evidence for his own exorbitant case. Unhappiness needs a voice, is perhaps the least censorable of all conditions. It can be unjust in its accusations, but it can scarcely be unfelt. And if it is widely felt, then that in itself is a truth to be faced. (pp. 37-8)

Michael Wood, ''Broken Blossoms,'' in The New York Review of Books, *Vol. XXXIII, No. 5, March 27, 1986, pp. 34-8.*

John (Lawrence) Ashbery

1927-

American poet, critic, editor, novelist, dramatist, and translator.

A major contemporary American poet, Ashbery is regarded as a talented stylist whose work is difficult and demanding. He commonly creates long, flowing phrases in which he experiments with syntactical structure and perspective, resulting in poems that seem accessible yet elude interpretation. Roberta Berke commented: "In Ashbery's poems there are constant echoes of other secret dimensions, like chambers resounding behind hollow panels of an old mansion rumored to contain secret passages (which our guide emphatically denies exist). Ashbery both hunts for these secrets and tries to conceal them." Some critics fault Ashbery's work for obscurity and contend that it lacks thematic depth. However, many others regard him as an important and influential poet whose work represents a search for order while accommodating randomness, invention, and improvisation. Ashbery has won numerous honors: *Some Trees* (1956), his first book, was published in the Yale Series of Younger Poets and contains an introduction by W. H. Auden, whom Ashbery has acknowledged as an influence; *Self-Portrait in a Convex Mirror* (1975) won the Pulitzer Prize, the National Book Award, and the National Book Critics' Circle Award; and *A Wave* (1984) won the Lenore Marshall/Nation Poetry Prize. Ashbery also shared the 1985 Bollingen Prize in poetry with Fred Chappell.

Ashbery became interested in writing while a student at Harvard University. During the mid-1950s, Ashbery won a scholarship to study in France. He lived there for ten years, supporting himself by working as a poet and translator and by writing art criticism for the Paris edition of *The New York Herald Tribune*. Painting, which first attracted Ashbery when he was in his teens, has had a lasting influence on his poetry. He once stated: "I attempt to use words abstractly, as an artist uses paint." Early in his career, Ashbery was linked by critics to the "New York School" of poetry, which included Frank O'Hara and Kenneth Koch. Their work reveals the influence of such artistic movements as surrealism and abstract expressionism. Several critics have placed Ashbery in the American Romantic literary tradition that includes Walt Whitman and Wallace Stevens. Like the works of these poets, Ashbery's verse features long, rhythmical phrasings, an expansive range of subject matter, and extensive use of ordinary language and American idioms.

The publication of *Some Trees* brought Ashbery immediate recognition. The poems in this volume display his ability to write in various poetic forms and his penchant for creating odd juxtapositions of words and images. Ashbery's next major book, *The Tennis Court Oath* (1962), is generally considered one of his most difficult works. The collage technique he employed in several of these poems resulted in charges of obscurity—a complaint that critics have raised about several of Ashbery's works. *Rivers and Mountains* (1966) and *The Double Dream of Spring* (1970) were widely praised and are regarded as works in which Ashbery consolidated his talents. Many of the poems concern the theme of change and blend both objective and subjective perspectives. The poems also exhibit Ashbery's re-

curring, self-reflexive technique of examining the creative process of art. Several critics noted that in these works Ashbery is concerned with what should and should not be included in a poem; Harold Bloom, one of his most enthusiastic supporters, stated that for Ashbery, as for Stevens and Whitman, "poetry and materia poetica are the same thing." Ashbery's willingness to experiment with diverse poetic forms is evidenced in *Three Poems* (1972). This volume contains long prose poems written in the stream-of-consciousness technique. While these poems display a more restrained use of language than Ashbery's earlier work, they contain the subtle transformations of mood, tone, and image that characterize his verse.

Self-Portrait in a Convex Mirror is Ashbery's most celebrated book, and the long title work is considered a major contemporary poem. This poem is based on a painting by Francesco Parmigianino, an Italian Renaissance artist who painted a portrait of himself at work in his studio reflecting his observations while peering into a convex mirror. Like the painting, the poem offers a distorted and subjective view of reality, leading many critics to assert that this is Ashbery's representation of the human condition. Ashbery meditates on the painting and his personal life while creating images of himself at work on the poem. His next two collections, *Houseboat Days* (1977) and *As We Know* (1979), like *Self-Portrait in a Convex Mirror*, contain a long poem and a number of shorter poems written in various forms. Both works drew significant critical acclaim. "Litany," the long poem included in *As We Know,* offers another example of Ashbery's experimentation with form. The poem is made up of two columns of verse that represent, according to Ashbery, "simultaneous but independent monologues." With *Shadow Train* (1981), Ashbery abruptly adopted a shorter verse form, producing fifty sixteen-line poems that resemble sonnets. Although critics continued to acknowledge Ashbery's mastery of form, they debated the importance of this volume.

Like Ashbery's books of the late 1970s, *A Wave* contains poems in a number of forms, including the sonnet, the masque, haiku, and the long poem. The title poem is a meditation on love, death, and change that wavers between mysterious and ordinary images and emotions, personal and universal concerns, and objective and subjective reality. Several critics noted that this piece offers Ashbery's most successful recreation of peculiarly American idioms. According to Helen Vendler, "Ashbery's genius for a free and accurate American rendition of very elusive inner feelings, and especially for transitive states between feelings, satisfies our baffled search for intelligibility of experience."

Ashbery's other publications include a novel, *A Nest of Ninnies* (1969), on which he collaborated with James Schuyler, verse plays collected in *Three Plays* (1978), and *Selected Poems* (1985). He has also edited a number of books and magazines and contributed criticism on art and literature to various periodicals.

(See also *CLC,* Vols. 2, 3, 4, 6, 9, 13, 15, 25; *Contemporary Authors,* Vols. 5-8, rev. ed.; *Contemporary Authors New Revision Series,* Vol. 9; *Dictionary of Literary Biography,* Vol. 5; and *Dictionary of Literary Biography Yearbook: 1981.*)

DAVID ST. JOHN

It will surprise those readers who continue to insist upon the "difficulty" and "obscurity" of John Ashbery's poetry to find that his new collection, *A Wave,* contains the most direct and intimate writing of his career. Early on in *A Wave,* in the poem **"When the Sun Went Down,"** Ashbery bluntly announces what will be a recurring concern of the book:

> To have been loved once by someone—surely
> There is a permanent good in that,
> Even if we don't know all the circumstances
> Or it happened too long ago to make any difference.

The exhilarations and disappointments of love appear everywhere in these poems, along with great generosity and hopefulness. However difficult the eddy and flow of a life, there is, Ashbery says, the possibility "That we may live now with some / Curiosity and hope. Like pools that soon become part of the tide."

It's always a pleasure to watch Ashbery invoke a variety of forms, and *A Wave* is splendidly diverse. Certain passages tend to stand up right off the page, dressed in the beauty of their

pain, as in the title poem, **"A Wave,"** which begins with three spare, disturbingly dream-like and ominous lines:

> To pass through pain and not know it,
> A car door slamming in the night.
> To emerge on an invisible terrain.

"A Wave" is an extraordinary poem, standing with **"The Skaters,"** **"Self-Portrait In a Convex Mirror"** and **"Litany"** among Ashbery's major achievements. Some of its most lovely passages are about the writing of the poem itself, though the prime concern remains love. . . .

In this poem, and in this superb and heartbreaking collection, Ashbery offers us a poetry of consolation, a poetry which both guides and instructs us, insisting like a good parent upon our own individuality—a poetry quite like "the light, / From the lighthouse that protects as it pushes us away."

> *David St. John, in a review of "A Wave," in* Book World—The Washington Post, *May 20, 1984, p. 6.*

HELEN VENDLER

The figures traced in John Ashbery's rich new book have to do with death: in fact, *A Wave* has qualities of a last testament, The Angel of Death opens the book, appearing in a poem ["**At North Farm**"] at once so ordinary and so literary that we read it with a pure transparency of understanding:

> Hardly anything grows here,
> Yet the granaries are bursting with meal,
> The sacks of meal piled to the rafters.
> The streams run with sweetness, fattening fish;
> Birds darken the sky. Is it enough
> That the dish of milk is set out at night,
> That we think of him sometimes,
> Sometimes and always, with mixed feelings? . . .

No pleasure is sweeter in the ear than something new done to the old. Ashbery's deep literary dependencies escape cliché by the pure Americanness of his diction. A middle-aged American reads "Hardly anything grows here" with immediate recognition, a shock not possible any longer from the mention in a contemporary poem of "stubble plains" or "the barrenness / Of the fertile thing that can attain no more"—words used so memorably that they cannot be reused. Ashbery's gift for American plainness is his strongest weapon: "Hardly anything grows here" disarms us in its naked truth.

At the same time, in barren middle age one has seen too much; there is more experience than one can ever consume in recollection or perpetuate in art—the granaries are bursting with meal. That too, while Keatsian, is American in its "bursting with meal" (in Keats, what bursts are clouds, in tears). Ashbery's propitiatory dish of milk for the goblin (to keep him outside the house) is just unexpected enough, as folk naiveté, to throw us off balance (in this Keatsian, Stevensian context); it gives us death through the lens of the literary grotesque instead of through the lens of tragicomic fate (traveling furiously) or the lens of seasonal turn (vegetative barrenness, harvest plenty). Will it keep Death out of the house if we set milk out for him? (Milton: "The drudging Goblin sweat, / To earn his cream-bowl duly set.") Will it mollify the Goblin if we don't think badly of him? And yet, isn't there as well a hope that he will come and stop for us and give us what he has for us—the death notice, perhaps, in his hand? Emily

Dickinson, whose air of macabre comedy often resembles Ashbery's, would have read this poem with perfect comprehension.

A few pages later, Ashbery tells the "same" story over again, staged this time at the moment of receiving the death notice. Sick and shaken, one hears the bad news about one's future:

> It was as though I'd been left with the empty street
> A few seconds after the bus pulled out. A dollop of
>   afternoon wind.
> Others tell you to take your attention off it
> For awhile, refocus the picture. Plan to entertain,
> To get out. (Do people really talk that way?)

The awful thing is that people really do talk that way. To see the very coin of our conversation exposed in the palm of the poem is horrible, but mesmerizing.

Yet once again, Ashbery tells the "same" story. This time he enters it as he realizes the terrible shortness of time, and begins to count the beads of the past. . . . But there is no leisure to remember those Wordsworthian spots of time:

> . . . the wrecking ball bursts through the wall with the
>   bookshelves
> Scattering the works of famous authors as well as those
> Of more obscure ones, and books with no author. . . .

Ashbery does death justice: old structures die so that new structures of language may come into being. The wrecking ball lets in "Space, and an extraneous babble from the street / Confirming the new value the hollow core has again." The hollow core, the possibility of signification itself, is made by artists into a cultural construct (here, a library); the wrecking ball lets in a new influx of demotic speech, and a new generation will construct the library all over again around that perpetual hollow core. If Ashbery's poetry is made possible only by the wreckage of Romanticism and Modernism, then his own death and wreckage will empower a new poetry issuing from consciousness, "the light / From the lighthouse that protects as it pushes us away." The potential for culture is protected; the individual is cleared away. (I am translating Ashbery's delicacy into crudity, his narrative into observation.) . . .

Ashbery retells both death and life with American comic pragmatism and dead-pan pratfalls [as in **"More Pleasant Adventures"**]:

> The first year was like icing.
> Then the cake started to show through.

Reading Ashbery, one notices the idiom: when, exactly, did "show through" come into common speech in this sense? and "started," too, for that matter? The poem ends with the remark, "And paintings are one thing we never seem to run out of": when did "to run out of something" become our normal way of saying that the supply was exhausted? "What need for purists," says Ashbery, "when the demotic is built to last, / To outlast us?" His campaign (of course, not only his) to write down the matter of lyric in the idiom of America is a principled one. His eclectic borrowing from many past styles—an aesthetic some would like to call postmodern—creates a "variegated, polluted skyscraper to which all gazes are drawn," the style of our century, to which we are both condemned and entrusted, a "pleasure we cannot and will not escape."

I have been writing, up to now, about the first seventeen pages of Ashbery's book, simply to give the sense of a reader's first assenting page-turning. It is scarcely to the point, as we turn the pages, to ask what Ashbery "thinks about death." Of course he thinks the things anyone could, and many have, thought about it. The aesthetic interest is how he makes it new. The duty and pleasure of art is to invent a thousand and one ways of telling the same story (or painting the same Crucifixion, or varying *"Non piu andrai"*). Nobody wants a new lyric subject. We want the old subjects done over.

Ashbery's genius for a free and accurate American rendition of very elusive inner feelings, and especially for transitive states between feelings, satisfies our baffled search for intelligibility of experience. (p. 32)

Art, for Ashbery as for Keats, is meat and drink, plumping the hazel shell with a sweet kernel. And art is company: feeling with outrage our own mortality . . . , we turn to the poets who have felt the shock before us, and find them there on the other side. On the other hand, nobody stares truth, or art, in the face for long: psychic denial revises mortality, makes it recede, and disingenuously "speaks no longer / Of loss, but of brevity rather: short naps, keeping fit." The scorpion sting of that satiric close leaves its accusatory poison within us.

In this excellent collection there are things readers will be of two minds about. There is a long literary piece called **"Description of a Masque"** which invokes, for my taste, too many in-jokes. There are some attempts in the demotic (**"The Songs We Know Best"**) that seem to me uneasy in their use of slang. On the other hand, these pieces are only exaggerations (whether on the literary side or the populist side) of Ashbery's search for a renewed idiom. His rewriting of haiku into one line, and his several prose poems called **"Haibun"** (the poetic prose written by a haiku poet), suggest a restless investigation of form.

Ashbery's major piece in this book, giving its title to the collection, is the long poem (over six hundred lines long) **"A Wave,"** which as I read it is Ashbery's *Prelude*. A Wordsworthian poem of Whitmanesque lines, it ranges from childhood to death, and describes, in the largest sense, the *vie poétique*. (p. 33)

There seems to be a general belief among readers that to write about "poetry" is somehow not to write about "life." But "poetry" is the construction by consciousness of an apprehensible world. Every person constructs such a world, and lives in it. When the poets write about poesis, they are writing about what is done every day by everyone. . . . In recording and enacting the process by which we come to consciousness, form an identity, see our selfhood shadowed and illuminated by circumstance, and finally bid farewell to illusions of immortality, Ashbery reveals the nature of personal life in our era. To say that a poem is "about poetry" means, surely, that it is consciously about the way life makes up a world of meaning. . . .

The poets, by describing their act of self-making, call us to witness our own processes of soul-making. *A Wave,* the account of a contemporary American life from childhood to death, self-composed, calls us to see our own self-composing in it.

Of course, *A Wave* will eventually receive long commentaries, and I can give here only the briefest idea of its scope. It issues from "the dungeon of Better Living" and speaks in an imminently menaced environment. . . . It is Wordsworthian in its belief that "memory contains everything" and that an immense amount of discourse is needed to describe the sensations of life. The task of consciousness goes on, schooling the intelligence into a soul. Only a few (Arnold's "saving remnant") undertake this task with full wakefulness; they will live to see their work carried off in the impersonal wave of death. . . . (p. 34)

Throughout *A Wave,* the joyous interplay of experience and memory, memory and expression, is played out in the shadow of death. The poet questions whether it is worth writing his preludes in the light of extinction. . . . But the effort to recognize consciousness, and to give a musical expression to consciousness, is rewarded by the fullness and amplitude of the examined and constructed life. At the moment of execution,

> . . . When they finally come
> With much laborious jangling of
>   keys to unlock your cell
>
> You can tell them yourself what it is,
> Who you are, and how you happened
>   to turn out this way,
> And how they made you, for better
>   or for worse, what you are now,
>
> And how you seem to be, neither
>   humble nor proud, *frei aber einsam.*

"Free but lonely": Ashbery writes here, with irony, the epitaph for all the solitaries who have freely made their own souls, and know the souls they have made. The charm of Ashbery's urbane style—so various, so beautiful, so new—persists throughout this long poem, and will induce the rereadings the poem demands. It is a style that resists, in its glowing reflectiveness, the approaching darkness of the cimmerian moment. (pp. 34-5)

> Helen Vendler, *"Making It New,"* in The New York Times Book Review, *June 14, 1984, pp. 32-5.*

DOUGLAS CRASE

In 1960, during the ten years John Ashbery was living in France, there appeared in this country a 35-cent French thriller called *Murder in Montmartre.* The translator, having been paid by Dell Publishing Company to add some heavy breathing for the American market, signed himself "Jonas Berry"—but if you pronounce the name John Ashbery as they do in Paris and then phoneticize, you'll have a good idea who got the paycheck. Or one of the paychecks, anyway, since Jonas Berry's words had to be overhauled before publication by the pen of Lawrence G. Blochman. The reason, Blochman has explained, was simple. Some translators have trouble with the original French, but this Jonas Berry "just couldn't write English."

So the secret is out. A good thing, too, because in his new book of poems, *A Wave,* John Ashbery is not writing English again, and doing it with such authority you can't ignore what he really is writing—an American so roomy and sure that its appearance among us amounts to a national gift. "I guess I was trying to 'democratize' language" is the way Ashbery put it, referring in a recent interview to the prose-poem meditations in his *Three Poems* (1972). Now, in [*A Wave*] and especially in its long title poem, he has placed the vast prose vistas of *Three Poems* within the lyric measures he realized most explicitly in *Houseboat Days* (1977). In retrospect, it seems an inevitable triumph; and the trio of *Three Poems, Houseboat Days* and *A Wave* will probably be seen by his audience as the indispensable core of Ashbery's work.

Not everyone is a member of that audience. But someone approaching Ashbery's poetry for the first time, even for the

exasperated second time, will be generously greeted by *A Wave;* the poems in this volume are as lovingly addressed to the reader as any in our poetry since Walt Whitman offered to stop somewhere waiting for you. . . . The diction in **"Just Walking Around"** is pure enough for a hymn in common measure; but when Ashbery writes elsewhere of "gonzo" or "chroniqueurs," when he chooses at a critical juncture of the title poem to describe a moment as "cimmerian," then he is not exactly writing "plain American which cats and dogs can read"— to judge by Marianne Moore's prescription.

A more complete explanation would have to recognize how this poet writes not just in American, but in an ionized version that looses the poem from attachment to anyone or anywhere in particular. Ashbery is insouciant about place; he is prodigal with pronouns, profligate with tenses and extravagant with evasion and hyperbole. Who, what, where, why and when— they are spun off like freed electrons. The result is a poem that really is "ionized"—a poem seeking to combine. Did the poet ask you to "grant that we may see each other"? The poem likewise seeks to be completed in that meeting. The Ashbery reader must be not so much reader as communicant.

Much of Ashbery's work is available today in some dozen foreign languages. Readers in those languages are not likely to lust after a precise rendering of our vernacular, even if it could survive translation. More likely, they too are attracted by the translatable ionization of syntax and grammar that turns them into communicants. From *A Wave,* an example certain to find its translators soon is the beautiful if foreboding **"Rain Moving In."** . . . It is remarkable that a poem so periphrastic and evasive can be so frankly chilling at the same time. "The blackboard is erased in the attic"—a description of Ronald Reagan? Or that we are all, as a civilization, without memory? "Great fires / Arise"—nuclear attack? "The dial has been set"—it is long since programmed, and nothing we can do? Nothing, except bask in the bargain we've made with the very danger that is upon us—nuclear peril, or the pricey dollar? The approach of mortality? Maybe just the grim-looking weather. Hard to believe, on this evidence, that Ashbery is sometimes accused of writing frivolous verse; a poem that says we have made our danger our home will be recognized, throughout the NATO countries anyway, as engaged and political.

Or one may at least read it that way; as the poem's communicant you can find in it what you please. "I contain multitudes," enthused Whitman. "So much variation / In what is essentially a one-horse town," writes Ashbery, and it doesn't sound like he's complaining either. At a reading early in 1984, Ashbery told his audience how an idea in **"At North Farm"** had come from the Finnish folk epic the *Kalevala.* Helen Vendler has since pointed out the trace of Keats in that same poem [see excerpt above]. Yes, our culture is already crowded with literary goodies; but the poet of *A Wave,* though he acknowledges "the luck of speaking out / A little too late," seems to be pleasantly surprised at his luck. How nice to have awakened among all the treasures that are yours to rearrange when you live at the apex, spatially and temporally, of empire. . . . (pp. 146-47)

Critic Fredric Jameson, having done much to define postmodernism, now laments it as a "failure of the new," a sad admission that the consumer economy has rendered you and me "incapable of achieving aesthetic representations of our own current experience," our times. Instead, we combine off-the-shelf allusions (Keats and the *Kalevala* are good examples) in a pastiche of culture that equals no culture, as all colors together equal none. But before giving way to a verdict of despair in the case of *A Wave,* we ought to remember we are dealing with a poet here, and remember what a poet really does. Allusions to Keats and the *Kalevala* are not the pertinent evidence if a poet, as no-nonsense Dr. Johnson informs me in his dictionary, is "one who writes in measure." Period.

It sounds so old-fashioned, measure. What can it have to do with a poem like **"Rain Moving In"** . . .? No *abba* rhyme scheme, no iambic pentameter, but look—fourteen lines, and at lines eight and nine even a "step / Into disorder" to turn us into the sestet. The poem is a sonnet. Maybe it's in free verse, but it's a sonnet all the same. There are also two double sonnets, a tailed sonnet, even a heroic sonnet in this book. Given the teasing titles under which most of them appear, I suppose you could say these sonnets are themselves more proof of pastiche. The sonnet is rich pelf, for sure; its display in our nearly twenty-first-century times is arguably a "failure of the new," a sign of conspicuous cultural consumption. But only if you know it's there. In *A Wave,* Ashbery has reclaimed the form so thoroughly it took me much sleuthing to be sure of its presence; a lot of readers will never know it's there.

And who knows, maybe Ashbery doesn't know the form is there. All the better, because he is demonstrating in these poems how to choose the sonnet, say, as if you actually were innocent of its cultural price tag. Not so innocently chosen, perhaps, is his pantoum **"Variation on a Noel."** But he is radiantly fresh with the ballade, the Japanese haibun or the three-part ode—one of which, **"But What Is the Reader To Make of This?"** could be read as the sketch for his new title poem, or crib sheet for the project of his whole career:

> and the general life
> Is still many sizes too big, yet
> Has style, woven of things that never happened
> With those that did, so that a mood survives
> Where life and death never could.
>   Make it sweet again!

Sonnet, ode or "the general life"—the way a poet makes it sweet again is by writing like Dr. Johnson says, in measure. In *A Wave,* measure shows itself in the longish, lenitive lines that are Ashbery's special contribution to American poetry and a powerful influence on the work of younger poets. With their prosy cadence and many unaccented syllables, with their strong and frequently medial caesura (the pause within the line), his lines often evoke the French alexandrine—itself brought close to free verse in the works of Verlaine and Rimbaud. If Ashbery's truly is a free verse that beats to a distant alexandrine, then we have a new American measure. Lax and roomy, it would be just the thing to accommodate the poet's need to write in measure with Emerson's stern and just admonition that in America it is the meter-making argument and not the meter that makes the poem. Make a sonnet, say, from such a measure, and you've engaged not in pastiche, but in rejuvenation.

There are 802 of Ashbery's rejuvenating lines in **"A Wave,"** the title poem, which closes the book; and they are grouped in thirty stanzas, the same number as in the ballad for two voices that likewise closes *Houseboat Days.* So the invitation to compare this new poem with a ballad is hard to resist. The traditional ballad is fueled by a single dramatic tension which propels it and its characters toward climax and catastrophe. In **"A Wave,"** that climax is already over, presented in the first three lines of the poem as an accomplished fact; we are left with the poet to consider his emergence on what is called the

"invisible terrain" that comes after. We are also left with another 799 lines in which the ballad's regular rules of the road will be modified further. Is a ballad dramatic and impersonal? Then **"A Wave"** will be the opposite: an iterative, largely inconclusive analysis of private motivation and attainment. In fact, **"A Wave"** is nothing less than a dialogue of self and soul, what the poem itself calls "the subjective-versus-objective approach." Ashbery has admitted before to removing subtitles in order to make his work more mysterious. But if you label the stanzas of **"A Wave"** alternately as A and B you will discover that the poem blossoms without losing its mystery or going to seed. "Were we / Making sense?" asks the B voice. And in your newly labeled next stanza the A voice will offer not so much a considered response as an alternative testimony: "And the issue / Of making sense becomes such a far-off one. Isn't this 'sense'— / This little of my life that I can see . . .?"

The sense at issue here is very much the one that troubles the landscape of postmodernism: How are individuals to make sense of the "invisible terrain" of our own times? How can you image the world? In our culture, with grace and good works equally suspect, this has become the issue of personal salvation itself—certainly ever since Emerson reported to his journal on October 25, 1840, the famous dream in which an angel presented him with the world, and he ate it. Of course if you digested the world in 1840 you might treat yourself to a pretty grand salvation. All human incursions together were "so insignificant," as Emerson wrote in *Nature,* amounting to no more than "a little chipping, baking, patching, and washing, that in an impression so grand as that of the world on the human mind, they do not vary the result."

Well. Tell that to the reader at near twenty-first century who, if he or she eats the world, will have incorporated a resource-limited, environmentally compromised, politically bewitched little ball which can be made to go poof in an instant by one culturally arrested septuagenarian. Can it be good for your health to digest an image like that? In **"A Wave"** there is some disagreement. Voice B proposes that you just "come up with something to say, / Anything," because "The love that comes after will be richly satisfying, / Like rain on the desert." A is not so convinced and is beset by "the opposing view" that once you've put everything in your own words you will be locked in the tiny cell of the self, *"frei aber einsam,"* free but lonesome. Yet A and B aren't really arguing the point. And thus does **"A Wave"** perform its trick: as a discourse, it's so busy settling nothing that it keeps you occupied until long after you've started to image the "invisible terrain" of the present in the poem's new style.

The brave hearts of every generation must need to feel their times are new, and worth imaging in selves and souls. How much those feelings depend on the assurance that the planet has prospects beyond one's own lifetime is a matter we can only speculate on. Certainly there are millions throughout Europe and North America who believe they have been dispossessed of that assurance, and long to have it back. They do not all, not even most of them, read John Ashbery. But their longing helps explain further how his work has become a central event in poetry. In the face of factual dispossession, Ashbery has created a language that restores newness as you read, a language that is always cresting with potential like a wave. . . . No wonder his readers return Ashbery's affection. If you let him, he will restore you to a world we thought was lost, one where the times are justified in the spirit of the individual— you. (pp. 147-49)

Douglas Crase, *"Justified Times,"* in The Nation, *Vol. 239, No. 5, September 1, 1984, pp. 146-49.*

PETER STITT

The most common line one sees reviewers taking on the work of John Ashbery is that he is a stylist without thematic substance, that his wonderfully entertaining gestures take place in an intellectual vacuum. Certainly the style is there: enticing, seductive, playful, and taking many forms. Among the specific forms that have bred puzzlement in many critics is Ashbery's love for the discrete statement—a group of words, not always a sentence, that gives great pleasure in the reading yet leaves the reader wondering what it means. Take, for example, two of what he calls **"37 Haiku"** that appear on page 37 of *A Wave:* "You have original artworks hanging on the walls oh I said edit" and "A blue anchor grains of grit in a tall sky sewing."

As time goes by, however, and as readers learn more how to read Ashbery, the meaning is beginning to filter through. In fact, Ashbery's [*A Wave*] . . . shows considerable thematic depth and could be viewed almost as a primer on his thinking. For one thing, he attends here to the two oldest and most traditional themes of all poetry, love and death. Both these topics are everywhere in the book. . . . (pp. 635-36)

Ashbery *always* seems to undercut the seriousness of what he says, which doesn't mean he doesn't mean it; it only means that truth for him is indeterminate. Thus he always equivocates, as in this stanza on love from the poem **"They Like"**:

At a corner you meet the one who makes you glad, like
　a stranger
Off on some business. Come again soon. I will,
I will. Only this time let your serious proposals stick
　out
Into the bay a considerable distance, like piers.
　Remember
I am not the stranger I seem to be, only casual
And ruthless, but kind. Kind and strange. It isn't a
　warning.

The indeterminacy of the language in passages like this one reinforces the uncertainty of love itself. And when love is linked with death, it is most indeterminable of all.

Death and indeterminacy appear together elsewhere, as in what may be the best poem in the volume, **"At North Farm,"** . . . That this poem *is* about the coming of death, rather than some more obviously desirable character, is attested to by the bowl of milk, by the example of Ashbery's earlier poetry (where similar visitations are made), and by the fact that many of Ashbery's poems generally have an allegorical cast to them. Thus, although the terms are vague, and the characters never explicitly identified, the reader is able to narrow his interpretation of what seems so nebulous at first reading.

Far from being a stylist devoid of content, John Ashbery is actually a philosophical poet, as many poems in *A Wave* reveal. Like other everyday thinkers, Ashbery wonders about the meaning of life: how are we to understand what happens to us? The longest of the prose poems in this volume is called **"Description of a Masque."** The masque described is clearly a literary work rather than something that could be performed; it also has an allegorical cast to it (a chief character is named Mania). After several pages worth of action, Ashbery comments on what has been happening, both in the masque itself and in his description of it (Ashbery's poetry is always a meta-

poetry, after all, continually commenting upon itself). . . . (pp. 636-37)

Ashbery is also a philosophical poet in a special way: he instinctively reflects the understanding of the world given us by contemporary physics. Today's physicists know that their very observations of reality help to determine the nature of that reality. The world we perceive is a world that we subjectively create out of *a)* the process of our observations, and *b)* the "objective" materials supposedly out there. I say physicists *know* that this is the nature of the *actual reality* that surrounds us; we are not talking here about some impractical theory concocted by some Bishop Berkeley.

Thus when John Ashbery says that "our minds, parked in the sky over New York, / Are nonetheless responsible," he is telling the truth, the philosophical truth of the world we inhabit. This material is to be found everywhere in this book (especially in such poems as **"Cups with Broken Handles"** and **"Landscape"**), but it appears perhaps most affectingly in **"Down by the Station, Early in the Morning."** The poem begins by lamenting the gradual death of everything, how "It all wears out." After enumerating several examples, Ashbery continues:

Each is a base one might wish to touch once more

Before dying. There's the moment years ago in the
　station in Venice,
The dark rainy afternoon in fourth grade, and the shoes
　then,
Made of a dull crinkled brown leather that no longer
　exists.
And nothing does, until you name it, remembering, and
　even then
It may not have existed, or existed only as a result
Of the perceptual dysfunction you've been carrying
　around for years.

It is entirely typical of Ashbery to blame himself for this process. Because he instinctively knows that his perceptions help to create the reality he perceives, he feels responsible for, and therefore guilty about that, reality. Yet it is not the guilt that matters here, but rather the process discussed and what results from it. . . . The poem is magnificent in every way. In style, it has the usual Ashbery charm and humor, his brilliant inventiveness. In content it demonstrates in every line the interpenetration between the subjective and the objective that I have been discussing here. It is also a touching meditation upon death and degeneration. And, most important, this is a poem with deep and coherent meaning—not just an empty exercise in style. The time has come for John Ashbery to be understood—and recognized (by everyone, not just his coterie)—as the truly original, the truly meaningful poet that he is. (pp. 637-38)

Peter Stitt, "Objective Subjectivities," in The Georgia Review, *Vol. XXXVIII, No. 3, Fall, 1984, pp. 628-38.*

DENIS DONOGHUE

A Wave gathers about forty recent poems and prose-poems, and ends with the title-poem, a long meditation which readers may want to compare with Ashbery's **"Self-Portrait in a Convex Mirror"** and **"Fantasia on 'The Nut-Brown Maid.'"** The origin of **"A Wave"** may be the passage about dreams in **"Self-Portrait"**: 'They seemed strange because we couldn't actually see them . . .' As in **"Self-Portrait,"** Ashbery's style is loose-limbed, musing, discursive, unrhymed verse, the lines of varying length but mostly long, as of someone drowsing at twilight, murmuring to himself and enjoying the state of not being interrupted. His sentences are propelled by no duty other than that of steering the mind past lucidities it would rather not meet. Ashbery's poetry has always accepted the aspiration of music toward formal perfection which maintains an air of making sense without incurring the obligation of any particular meaning. He values 'the kind of rhythm that substitutes for "meaning"'. For him, long poems are spaces to move about in, like a big canvas for the painters he admires, site of many gestures which are not troubled by the fact that they are all the same. No analogy with drama is appropriate; or with oratory. What makes Ashbery's procedures distinctive is that while his common form is a monologue and might be maintained even if the speaker were on Mars and Earth did not exist, he doesn't claim any authority for its tone. Nothing of Yeats's rhetoric inhabits these poems. Ashbery doesn't command his experience. Nor does he submit to it. He prescribes the formal condition upon which he responds to whatever happens: a monologue in which conscientiousness keeps allowing for rival accounts of the same thing. But he doesn't claim that his procedure covers the case, or is at all adequate to its provocation. . . .

Ashbery is an aesthete of the provisional perception which 'belongs where it is going / Not where it is'. He is especially gifted in sensing states of feeling which don't claim to coincide with states of being: it is enough that the reader senses the process of musing and doesn't claim to apprehend the shapes it seems to take. No wonder Ashbery refers to the wind as 'something in which you lose yourself / And are not lost'. . . .

If Ashbery's poems are monologues or 'dialogues of one', much depends upon his ability to imagine attitudes alien to his own, and to speak them as if in his daily voice. **"A Wave"** bears comparison with **"Self-Portrait,"** but doesn't rise to its extraordinary mark: mainly because the work of art, Parmigianino's self-portrait, forces Ashbery to recognise ways of feeling, knowing and being which don't coincide with his own, and the recognition drives his common voice beyond itself. There are many passages in **"A Wave"** so winning that I am nearly willing to settle for its circumventions, its serpentine evasions. But in the end the force of everything in life it excludes or ignores makes one's pleasure a little ashamed of itself. It comes to this: there is nothing in **"A Wave"** which Ashbery's mind has much difficulty in taking as itself. The admission of rival sentiments comes to appear merely a nuance of the mind's habit. (p. 22)

Denis Donoghue, *"Making Sense," in* London Review of Books, *Vol. 6, No. 18, October 4 to October 17, 1984, pp. 22-3.*

PETER PORTER

Somerset Maugham once hijacked a critical put-down by using it as the title of his next book—'the mixture as before.' Admirers of John Ashbery will be pleased to know that *A Wave* has just this unrepentant tone: his old irresponsibility is back after the solemn divagations of *As We Know* and *Shadow Train.*

Ashbery has no need to stress his seriousness even to the solemn legislators of American literature—he is difficult enough, God knows. The quality which *A Wave* shares with *Self-Portrait in a Convex Mirror* and *Houseboat Days* (Ashbery's two most enjoyable collections) is cocksureness. An author's self-con-

fidence does wonders for his readers. When Ashbery goes truffling for exciting bits of syntax in his often unfollowable poems, we are led because we know we are going to enjoy ourselves too.

Ashbery is misunderstood by many of his admirers. He is not much like Stevens or indeed like any Modernist master. Robert Browning and the tradition of the 'garrulous-reflective' is more his style. Chiefly, he is himself, though he has said he looked to early Auden as an influence. From this clue one can build up a short catalogue of Ashbery's qualities: urbane, fond of personification, talkative, anecdotal even, willing to admit that language is only a system of symbols and that ideas are as real as things if words are to be their medium—in short, as far from William Carlos Williams as possible. But Ashbery is an innovator—the fuss Americans make about him has its reasons. . . .

Dreams and Surrealism have often been invoked by modern poets. Ashbery seldom seems to court unreason but he uses orthodox poetical techniques to dislocate consecutive sense. Why then does he please his readers? I think this is because we recognise something really new in him, some quality of imagination genuinely post-psychoanalysis, post-Structuralist, happily beyond Deconstruction. And it has the advantage of being cloaked in traditionally eloquent language. Perhaps it is time to stress his faults. He has a sniggering Cocteauesque side which is shown in *A Wave* by **"Description of a Masque,"** and his old fault of dangling woefully elongated lines across the page is still unpurged.

It is unfortunate that Ashbery tends to be regarded in this country as an example of American cultural hype by many home-bred critics, and hoisted as a revolutionary sign by their avant-garde opponents. Readers looking for a way in to his poetry should try the loose-limbed **"The Songs We Know Best."** . . . **"Just Walking Around"** is almost Ashbery's "Crossing the Bar," and there are plenty of other poems in *A Wave* which use warmth to relieve bafflement. Here, from one of his Haibun prose-poems is a statement which catches the essence of Ashbery's art—'I believe that the rain never drowned sweeter, more prosaic things than those we have here, now, and I believe this is going to have to be enough.'

Peter Porter, *"Cocksure Muse," in* The Observer, *October 21, 1984, p. 24.*

PETER HAINSWORTH

[Ashbery's recent volume of poems, *A Wave,* is] one of his best. Too much that he has written recently has been rather dull experiment. The quatrains of *Shadow Train* (1981) were all too often little more than lax five-finger exercises in superficially regular form, and *As we know* (1979) was dominated by the sixty pages of **"Litany"**, which, in spite of fascinating sections (particularly on literary criticism), suffered from the over-casual juxtaposition of the two monologues of which it was composed. Still, some of the shorter pieces in *As we know*— say **"Train Rising Out of the Sea"** or **"Late Echo"**—had pointed in a different direction. It is this which is now followed through in *A Wave* and reaches its high point in the long, absorbing poem which gives the collection its title.

In a way Ashbery has returned to the serious playfulness of *Houseboat Days* and earlier books, but, though there is much in *A Wave* that is jokey, seriousness has the edge. Not that anything previously said is recanted: everything is, rather, reaffirmed, but with a more open voicing of implications and consequences. Final truths that used to be recognized only to be postponed or displaced are now given prominence, with the result that as a whole *A Wave* contains more explicit and more moving writing than perhaps anything else that Ashbery has done.

Ashbery is a poet of mutability, for whom nothing is constant except change itself. His concerns are with the incompleteness, instability and fragmentariness of our lives, and the impossibility of getting whatever is going on into a perspective that is in any way accurate. That is not in itself a particularly original or distinctive line of thought. But European poets with a similar sense of the changefulness of things have commonly felt that unless it involves only the replacement of one order by another, change must be a threat, against which is to be set some image of stability—God, perhaps, or love which alters not, or the powerful rhyme. Ashbery has always taken the opposite, more American path, and tried to embrace change, as if the mistake were to resist it or to look for a human order in it. In a sense he is an Emersonian who sees life as something much larger and more eventful than any individual or collective understanding can cater for. But he is confident, like Emerson (whom he sometimes echoes), that things will take care of themselves and of us if we only let them. "We get lost in life, but life knows where we are" is a line from **"More Pleasant Adventures"** which sums up, with perhaps cosy sententiousness, that side of Ashbery which wants to surrender to the flow of things and believe that it is good. More frequently the dominating mood is a sophisticated New York hedonism that plays with images of contemporary America and with a soft-spoken, slightly mannered version of its language without assigning a definite value to any of the transient phantasmagoria. The visual and linguistic spectacle becomes enjoyable for its surprises, its sensual possibilities and the chances it offers of looking into an underlying void which Ashbery has always refused to see as terrifying.

What is disconcerting and—at least for enthusiasts—exhilarating about his work, is the absorption of the play of mutability into the substance of his verse. Ashbery is a radically mimetic artist who aims to reproduce experience as directly as possible, while making it plain that the gap between words and things is infinite: reality has always passed on, or at least is absent from what we are reading. There is disorientation involved in encountering a vertiginously shifting something that constantly implies that it is nothing, and this makes his work seem difficult, provoking suggestions that he deconstructs the image at the very moment of creating it. And of course the risk is that this kind of writing will get completely out of control. "I always answer the telephone", Ashbery said in a 1979 interview, "and I find it helps me with my work." In some Ashbery poems the person from Porlock has been allowed to interfere too much. But in his best work there is a brilliantly unpredictable shaping of the poem, which seems to spring directly from the flow of composition, much as the structure of a Japanese painting is supposed to do.

This shaping is a good deal more apparent in *A Wave* than in many other books, partly because the reflective element is so much more explicit. Take **"I See, Said the Blind Man, As He Put Down His Hammer and Saw"**, which opens with a characteristic roller-coaster ride:

> There is some charm in that old music
> He'd fall for when the night wind released it—
> Pleasant to be away; the stones fall back;

The hill of gloom in place over the roar
Of the kitchens but with remembrance like a bright
> patch
Of red in a bunch of laundry. But will the car
Ever pull away and spunky at all times he'd
Got the mission between the ladder
And the slices of bread someone had squirted astrology
> over
Until it took the form of a man, obtuse, out of pocket
Perhaps, probably standing there.

The prosiness is deceptive: it is really an undeclinable invitation to read the lines as if they had the meanings of normal discursive writing. And once drawn in, the reader is hurled from one undefined context to another, the disorientation being compounded by the repeated shifts of register. Drawing-room conversation in the opening line, a little poetry ("the hill of gloom"), more colourful suggestions of past violence ("a bright patch of red in a bunch of laundry"), linguistic desecration ("squirted astrology")—all flash by before we can reach the man we can stop and look at. Earlier Ashbery might well have gone on into further metamorphoses or left us there to make the best of what is in fact a richly compressed symbology. But the Ashbery of *A Wave* is insistent that we should think about the image that has just come into focus. "Can't you see how we need these far-from-restful pauses?" he now asks in the opening of the second section, and in the remainder of the poem he expands on the implications of this, its middle line and its turning point. The blind man has seen, but only a little and only for a moment. Thought, even ironic awareness, cannot be a barrier against the enormous, impenetrable forces for change which will eventually put an end to each of us and are already at work even as we read and think:

> The armor
> Of these thoughts laughs at itself
> Yet the distances are always growing
> With everything between, in between.

It is an elegiac, even sombre close to a poem that began flippantly. And this darker note sounds through a good deal of the collection. As serious hedonists have always known, to continue to take things as they come and to find pleasure in them when endings are in sight demands disciplined awareness, not resignation or a desperate resorting to transcendence. . . .

In the end it is the present which is still the issue. **"Rain Moving In"** makes a readily graspable statement of how most readers of poetry must be situated with respect to their origins and their final resting-places. . . . But in other poems there is a more breathtaking evocation of a sustaining void that has to be seen even in the midst of destruction. . . .

A Wave is a rich collection which approaches its central concerns from a variety of angles. Haiku or pseudo-haiku accent the orientalizing aspect of Ashbery's imagination. But then a series of jokey prose pieces, which Ashbery calls "haibun", play off prose against haiku. Other prose pieces are even more flagrantly unpoetic, especially the narrative **"Description of a Masque"**, which spreads its pantomimic representation of metamorphosis over twelve somewhat loose pages.

Lastly there is the title poem. "A Wave" is a complex orchestration of the theme of mutability. Its flow absorbs much of the sea of experience and what it calls "the ocean of language", but most important is the wave of love that rises and falls at the climax of the poem in a magnificent twenty-seven-line verse period. That is near the end of the second of three parts into which the poem falls, and which look in turn towards the past, the present and the future while recognizing always that there is really only the one image of time, the flux of the poem itself. The opening is a disturbing image of forgetfulness:

> To pass through pain and not know it,
> A car door slamming in the night.
> To emerge on an invisible terrain.

This will subsequently expand into an Eliotesque representation of a forgetful society imprisoned in "the dungeon of Better Living". But such images of forgetting are criss-crossed with other images of repetition and remembering, which eventually turn, via the moment of love, towards definitive conclusions. . . .

In "A Wave" Ashbery re-makes the strangeness of experience on a large scale and simultaneously invites the reader to look at it without evasion. The blind man will not see everything perhaps, but he may contemplate the experience as it is occurring in the poem. This opening into contemplation is as restorative an effect as any that poetry can bring about. For it to work only attention and awareness are needed. As always Ashbery is an available, even popular poet.

> *Peter Hainsworth, "Change Unchanging," in* The Times Literary Supplement, *No. 4264, December 21, 1984, p. 1466.*

JOHN HOLLANDER

The Lenore Marshall Prize this year has been awarded to John Ashbery's *A Wave*. . . . [This volume] marks that high level of accomplishment and imaginative power that could be glimpsed in his first collection, *Some Trees,* which won the Yale Younger Poets Award in 1956. In poems like **"Some Trees," "The Mythological Poet," "The Picture of Little J. A. in a Prospect of Flowers"** and others, he looked far beyond the fashionable late modernism of their literary moment, and in those like **"The Instruction Manual"** he constructed a paradigm for many of his later poems. His protagonists, coping with the tasks of daily life, are, throughout his work, bearers of our last remaining hope for centrality, the heroic consciousness. Ashbery is thus a poet like Whitman and Stevens, although even his most appreciative critics have taken insufficient notice of this remarkably original poet's relation to W. H. Auden.

Like many important poets, Ashbery has been misunderstood by many of his admirers, who consider him as part of a poetic movement (there are no true poetic movements, only literary associations), the so-called "New York School"; who admire his affiliations with the New York art world; and who don't always distinguish between poetic density and the difficulties it produces.

A reader previously unacquainted with Ashbery's central work may trace its development from many of the poems in *Some Trees* through **"A Last World"** in his second book, *The Tennis Court Oath* (1962), through **"Clepsydra," "The Skaters"** and the title poem of *Rivers and Mountains* (1966), on through **"Soonest Mended"** and **"Fragment"** in the 1970 volume, *The Double Dream of Spring.* Here he establishes his characteristic mode in the long, apparently discursive poem, further developed in his prose meditations in *Three Poems* (1972); the title poem of *Self-Portrait in a Convex Mirror* (1975) as well as the magnificent, somewhat shorter **"Grand Galop"** in the same volume; **"Fantasia on 'The Nut-Brown Maid'"** in *Houseboat*

Days (1977); and the splendid **"A Wave,"** which gives its name to the current prize-winning collection.

In one sense, these are all love poems; in another, they are about work and about the major quests of modernity—the getting through the phases of one's life as if they were at once the labors of Hercules and the sequential clues of a children's treasure hunt. They are immensely serious meditations on the nature of maturity, on the ramifications of that central tragic pattern of learning that shapes all but the dullest of lives ("If I only knew then what I did later . . ."). **"A Wave"** is characteristic of Ashbery's diction in its complex, periodic expository style (as well as, from time to time, its undramatically colloquial one), a poetic way of walking through a contemplative course and suddenly turning a corner onto a wildly metaphoric formulation. It is full of the catalogues of objects and moments celebrated elsewhere in his work. . . . (pp. 386-87)

This volume also breaks new ground for Ashbery in **"Description of a Masque,"** an exuberant prose poem which resembles the court masques of Ben Jonson. And the intense yet exquisite shorter poem of a kind exemplified in the poet's previous work by **"Tapestry"** and **"Wet Casements"** is represented by [**"Trefoil"** and **"Down by the Station, Early in the Morning"**]. . . . (p. 387)

It is fitting that the Lenore Marshall Prize has been awarded to so central an American poet at the height of his technical and conceptual strength. (p. 388)

> *John Hollander, "The Lenore Marshall Prize," in* The Nation, *Vol. 241, No. 12, October 19, 1985, pp. 386-88.*

MICHIKO KAKUTANI

"The words are only speculation / (From the Latin speculum, mirror)," writes John Ashbery. "They seek and cannot find the meaning of the music. / We see only postures of the dream." The lines are from Mr. Ashbery's dazzling masterwork **"Self-Portrait in a Convex Mirror,"** and like so much of his verse, they address not only the situation at hand in a given poem, but also the overall condition of his art—his relation, as a poet, to the reality around him. In this case, the lines also uncannily describe the effect of reading Mr. Ashbery's poetry—an effect not unlike that produced by listening to a piece of avant-garde music. Certainly his elliptical work frequently defies conventional attempts to impute meaning—most are vague about time, place and characters, as though external reality were quite beside the point; many constantly shift point of view, as though the idea of fixed character, too, were outmoded. And yet its meditative, allusive beauty retains a powerful ability to entrance, goading the reader to re-examine his own relationship to the world. . . .

Although there are some significant omissions—for some reason, such notable works as **"Civilisation and its Discontents," "Evening in the Country," "Fragment"** and **"The Sun"** do not appear—[*Selected Poems*] still offers an ample selection of his work, a selection that attests to both his maturation as a poet, and his ongoing interest in investigating the formal possibilities of his art.

It's clear, reading this volume, that that urge to explore uncharted regions has occasionally led Mr. Ashbery to dead ends. Following his brilliant debut with *Some Trees* (1956)—a book of exquisite, lapidary poems, indebted in tone, imagery and esthetic theory to Wallace Stevens—he began writing a series of dense, abstract poems, poems so hermetic and self-referential as to preclude almost any sort of intelligent response. Apparently Mr. Ashbery was interested, during the period of *The Tennis Court Oath* (1962), in trying to shatter old-fashioned syntax, in much the way that the Abstract-Expressionist painters were attempting to subvert traditional expectations, but the result, in many of these disjunctive poems, often seemed simple obscurity and pretension. . . .

A similar problem exists with portions of *Three Poems* (1972), a set of nearly inpenetrable prose poems that have the effect of making English feel like a foreign language; and occasional poems in *Houseboat Days* (1977), *As We Know* (1980) and *A Wave* (1984) that tend to fold up into themselves, like flimsy origami constructions. Besides heightening Mr. Ashbery's already cerebral tendencies—even his more accessible poems cloak emotions like love, anger and desire in layers of chilly artifice—these elusive works speak to a certain solipsism. They announce that they do not really need readers, that their internal logic, however mysterious to an outsider, is entirely self-sufficient.

Yet at his best—and this collection is filled with such examples, including **"Clepsydra" "Soonest Mended," "Self Portrait," "Syringa"** and a section from that wonderful long poem **"The Skaters"**—Mr. Ashbery remains one of his generation's most gifted and eloquent poets. Like his mentor Wallace Stevens, he writes persuasively—and movingly—of the poetic process, of the attempts of the artist to wring order out of chaos. And like Stevens, too, he writes with enormous subtlety, about the ambiguities of the self, our attempts to mediate between what we are, what we perceive ourselves to be, and what the world, beyond, sees us to be.

Mr. Ashbery's greatest subject, though, is time—and flux, and he chronicles its constant ebb and flow in impressionistic detail, meditating upon the moment-to-moment shifts in emotional weather that it engenders, the "comings and goings," the human "mutterings, splatterings" that pass in its wake. For Mr. Ashbery, time is "an emulsion" in which we must, of necessity, live. But if it makes for a sense of precariousness—"the sands are frantic / In the hourglass"—it is also redemptive, for it holds forth the possibility of change, of remaking "that too-familiar image / Lurking in the glass / Each morning, at the edge of the mirror." . . .

Such lines, at once, ratify Mr. Ashbery's overall achievement, and attest to the existence, beneath the sometimes too glittering surface of his work, of a rich and humane vision.

> *Michiko Kakutani, "With Poetic License," in* The New York Times, *December 7, 1985, p. 18.*

JAMES FENTON

There is a great deal of distress in poetry, much of it got up in some esthetic disguise. Among the advocate-critics of John Ashbery one notices a trick of rhetoric whereby conventional blame-words have turned surreptitiously into praise: "banal," "prosaic," "trivial," "diffuse," "opaque," "meaningless"—the list is infinite. . . .

But are we to blame Mr. Ashbery for what the critics write about him? Well, why not? It might make for a festive kind of revenge. After all, there were times during my reading of this *Selected Poems* (a gathering from 30 years' work) when I actually thought I was going to burst into tears of boredom. . . . But I was approaching the book under a certain misconception,

that it was asking to be, well, *read*. Mr. Ashbery doesn't share that view: "I think I'm just accepting the universal fact that really nobody sits down—I mean maybe there are some people, poetry freaks—and reads a book of poems from beginning to end," he said in an interview in 1981. . . .

On the one hand we have the poet as he presents himself to the interviewer and at times in the poems—easygoing, antididactic, aware of the haphazard nature of life and consciousness, undemanding of our attention. On the other hand, in sharp contrast, we have the exorbitantly demanding poet, asking of the reader impossible feats of attention, taxing our patience, yielding only a minimum of reward, parsimonious with clarity, hedged about with obscurity and nevertheless always hinting at a profundity of philosophical insight which is designed to make a nonphilosopher uneasy. The entirely permissive poet and the overbearing ego at one and the same time. It is a highly complex performance.

"The critics always get everything wrong," Mr. Ashbery remarked in the interview just quoted. Yet one feels that the work is designed precisely in order to insure that they will not get it right. There *is* no "getting it right." . . . I shall be stopped at the gates if I try to penetrate an Ashbery poem. Look! The camera has already been activated and the dogs let loose in the grounds. Let's just scramble back over the electric fence.

It is interesting that Mr. Ashbery sees himself as representing an antididactic tradition, and that when he talks of his following in England he sees them as something of an oppressed group, people who are unpublished or, if published, ignored. He sees English poetry as dominated by Philip Larkin or Ted Hughes, by a "blood and stone" mentality. He sees enmity between England and America, with English establishment poets having a sense that "poetry should be moral, that it should be didactic and should . . . make sense. Make sense in the traditional sense of making sense."

In fact, one way or another, our great heroes in England have always been Americans. Until recently, that is, when America seemed to run short of heroes. We always used American poetry as a rebuke to our own. We thought our American cousins much more eminent than we were. And our bitterest arguments were really over the question, which of our American cousins are the most eminent? Who is the First Born?

Sometimes, of course, this sense of belonging to an eminent family whose ideals we could not meet became oppressive. I remember very well the *Selected Poems* Mr. Ashbery published in England in 1967, which was dominated by one long item, **"The Skaters."** This was obviously the work of the black sheep of the family. Its poetic was entirely destructive. Not only did it not make any sense, it wasn't intended to do so. The whole thing felt like a hoax, a mockery of the reader and the critic. And this seemed terrific. Mr. Ashbery had eliminated sense, and there is a powerful yearning in England to be rid of the burden of sense. It is partly infantile—let us return to the nonsense of childhood. It also gets a response from that side of adolescence that yearns for an orgy of iconoclasm. Down with the eminent ancestors. Let us pull their portraits off the walls.

I still enjoy **"The Skaters,"** (the version in this collection is abridged) although I treasure mainly its moments of absurd clarity. And I very much admire that didactic poem **"Self-Portrait in a Convex Mirror."** . . .

But John Ashbery as a rallying cry? John Ashbery as a rebuke to our native shortcomings? Pages and pages of John Ashbery? Even if I follow his advice—put the book down, go and see a friend, get drunk, see a film, have another go—no, there is not enough nutrition in this diet. . . .

What I see now, where once I saw a relaxed and exquisite mockery, is an esthetic loneliness, like the loneliness of secret work. I see a joke turn sour on the features, like one played once too often, with a little too much violence, like a joke that is meant to hurt. This vaunted depiction of consciousness, of experience, this excursus into the meaning of meaningless, this way of nattering on the whole night, this derogation of sense: none of this helps with the question—what shall I do with my gift? I don't believe in this ontology—or lack of it. I don't believe in this esthetic. I still respect the talent, but not the resort to the sad shadows.

*James Fenton, "Getting Rid of the Burden of Sense,"
in* The New York Times Book Review, *December
29, 1985, p. 10.*

Thea (Beatrice May) Astley

1925-

Australian novelist and short story writer.

An established author in her native Australia, Astley is beginning to gain recognition in the United States. She has won respect for her well-crafted novels and is especially noted for her perceptive prose, which is a mixture of poetic extravagance and biting realism. A prevalent theme in Astley's works, as expressed by Arthur Ashworth, is "the sterility in human relationships." In her novels, Astley often uses a small-town setting and derives tension from the inhabitants' petty cruelties toward each other. Religion, another important element in many of Astley's works, is invariably portrayed as having a crippling effect on individuals.

Astley's first two novels, *Girl with a Monkey* (1958) and *A Descant for Gossips* (1960), examine the limitations inherent in rural life. The thematic concerns in *The Slow Natives* (1965) include family relationships, adolescent rebellion, and religion. In this novel, the young protagonist seeks his identity beyond the dismal confines of his parents' lives. Astley's cynicism toward religion is apparent in *A Boat Load of Home Folk* (1968), in which a priest commits suicide after being caught in a sexual act with a young boy. Religious undertones are also present in *The Acolyte* (1972), which examines a young man's fanatical submission to an egotistical musical genius.

Social injustice and revenge are Astley's major concerns in *A Kindness Cup* (1974). Based on a true incident, the book relates a rural teacher's attempt to bring to justice a group of vigilantes responsible for the death of an aboriginal girl twenty years earlier. Returning to the small-town milieu in *An Item from the Late News* (1982), Astley dramatizes the effects of intolerance and bigotry on outsiders and nonconformists. Astley's recent novel, *The Beachmasters* (1985), recounts the efforts of the natives of the fictitious island of Kristi to stage a revolution and gain their freedom. Sally Dawson described Astley's prose in this novel as "mature, enquiring, and often verbally stunning."

(See also *Contemporary Authors*, Vols. 65-68 and *Contemporary Authors New Revision Series*, Vol. 11.)

Courtesy of Thea Astley

language is sometimes extravagant, and now and then reveals too strong an influence of Joyce, but she is never dull; her phrases and imagery are often extremely perceptive, and she has an extraordinary facility with words. Her faults are the faults of enthusiasm—which to my mind is more creditable than otherwise in a young writer. *Girl With A Monkey* shows Miss Astley struggling towards a style which will be totally her own; her next novel will undoubtedly achieve it.

> *Laurence Collinson, in a review of "Girl with a Monkey," in* Overland, *No. 15, July, 1959, p. 48.*

LAURENCE COLLINSON

[Thea Astley's *Girl With A Monkey*] is not a "great" novel, as most of the other reviewers have been at pains to point out, but it is an excellent first novel, written with originality and gusto. Its theme is the relationship between a young schoolteacher and a laborer in a North Queensland town; and although the "We come from different worlds" idea is no new one, it becomes unorthodox here because of the humorously ironic treatment of the girl, and the detachment with which she, as narrator, observes her proletarian "lover" whom for once we recognise as a human being rather than a sentimentalised projection of an author's political outlook. Miss Astley has no fear of letting her temperament shine through her prose: her

R. G. GEERING

Thea Astley's first book, *Girl With a Monkey,* was a fresh and sensitively written story of a young woman school-teacher about to leave a small north Queensland town to escape from a frustrating love affair. *A Descant For Gossips,* her second novel, has a similar setting . . . , but is a longer and a more ambitious book. It dramatises the power of scandalmongering by showing its effects on three characters—a lonely, unloved thirteen-year-old girl, Vinny Lalor, and two of her teachers, Helen Striebel and Robert Moller, who extend to her some sympathy and affection.

Helen, a widow in her early thirties, and Robert, aged forty-seven, whose wife is an incurable invalid, become lovers; their secret is soon discovered and eagerly worked on by the local character-assassins. . . . The behaviour of the adult world is paralleled by the equally malicious joy of the schoolchildren in driving Vinny to desperation by teasing her into believing that an innocent, romantic interlude with a young boy will result in her having a baby. Our attention alternates between Vinny and the middle-aged lovers, but the book hangs together because the fortunes of these three characters, whether they are aware of the fact or not, are interdependent, and often run parallel.

Miss Astley writes about smalltown life as only one who has experienced it can. Her values are humane and just, and the reader in his turn knows exactly where he stands. She shows up this life with all its snobberies, petty jealousies and hatreds, its narrowness and its ghoulish glee in vilification. Not only has she a sharp eye for hypocrisy and nastiness, but she also wins sympathy for her lovers—they have offended society, but they are better in every way than their self-righteous judges. An air of sadness and a feeling for the mutability of all human relationships hang over their stolen pleasures, so that the reader feels little hope for their future as they part at the end of the book. Understanding and sympathy are present, too, in the picture of the vulnerable, love-starved child.

Nevertheless, the main strength of the book is in its satire. The Talbots, and, indeed, all the upper crust are unsparingly treated. . . . (p. 53)

Miss Astley often writes in a highly charged, poetic style abounding in images. She is capable of sharp visual effects in description; but she can also lapse into such ponderous atrocities as: "Connivance and the acid testing of propinquity had both failed to achieve for him a tolerance of situation, a docility of all the factors that seemed to work unendingly towards his and Helen's eternal separation". . . . A poet's love of words leads occasionally to the search for the unusual, and to some strange coinages. . . . When we read that a car roared "extrovertedly" . . . and a saxophone "whimpered up to orgastic heights" . . . , our reaction is most likely to be irritation at over-writing, and surprise that such stylistic blemishes should occur in a book which is, for the most part, well written.

There is, likewise, some over-emphasis in the handling of events in the final stages of the story, which gives the ending a melodramatic twist. Vinny's fear and despair are real enough. Was there any need to insist on such a concatenation of events to underline the tragedy and bring the girl to suicide? Helen makes a mistake about the time of the train's departure, so that Vinny comes to the hotel as arranged, only to find Helen has suddenly gone for ever; Vinny finds the cast-off present (and it is hard to believe that such a person as Helen, either deliberately or accidentally, would have left it behind); and this sorry business is conducted under the eyes of Allie, the pregnant housemaid, who is a frightening embodiment of Vinny's deepest fears.

When all has been said, however, this novel has great merit. Miss Astley is a most welcome addition to the ranks of our contemporary novelists. . . . (pp. 53-4)

> R. G. Geering, "School for Scandal," in Southerly,
> Vol. 21, No. 2, 1961, pp. 53-4.

J. F. BURROWS

[The world of *The Well-Dressed Explorer*] is a localized and particular world, where local colour is more than a slap-dash coat of local paint. It is an uneventful world whose sharp-eyed observer is ever alert for any "scrawls of dirt charitably passing off vagueness as cosiness", any small social pretensions or mean little rationalizations, any unwarranted claim to comfort and security. It is a world indeed where outward incident is examined only as a means of revealing the inner life of those concerned. It is a world of high—and as yet unsubstantiated—literary aspirations.

Miss Astley's previous novels are *Girl with a Monkey* (1958) and *Descant for Gossips* (1960). In both of them she elects to view her world wholly or in large part from the standpoint of a teacher in a country town. (p. 278)

There is a sense in which such a protagonist is well qualified as a satirical observer of the tiny world in which he finds himself. Coming from outside, his position is naturally one of detachment. Representing intellectual attitudes more sophisticated than those he will commonly encounter, his Olympianism is further reinforced. His position is nevertheless most delicate, for he has every encouragement to become an intellectual snob of the shoddiest kind. If he succumbs he has no chance of facing seriously the problems which the townsfolk pose for the would-be satirist. How can they possibly *choose* to live here? Do they *really* believe that this is the centre of the universe? The observer need not come to share this provincial creed—indeed, if he were to do so, his satire would die unborn. But if his satire is to be of any real depth or substance, he needs to come much closer to an understanding of these mysteries and to an honest recognition of them as genuine rites than (with few and minor reservations) these two novels display. What he needs, in short, is charity: not the charity which weakly forgives, but that which seeks patiently to understand.

In *Girl with a Monkey,* Elsie Ford is permitted French, Latin, and German allusions. When her friend and colleague Laura is so rash as to risk a Latin phrase, it is made clear that these privileges are restricted to protagonists. Any imitation by the townsfolk is, of course, doomed from the first. In *Descant for Gossips,* Helen Striebel is one of only three "real" music-lovers in the town. Another is Alec Talbot, but "Helen had ceased to discuss music with the Talbots when she discovered that they used it merely as a dividing-line between themselves and the hicks." Yet the novel itself makes it clear that, beyond her willingness to patronize the less aspiring of the hicks, this charge can be as justly levelled at the admired Helen as at the deplored Alec Talbot. . . . (pp. 278-79)

Given such observers as these, one would hardly expect the life of the "hicks" to be examined with much sympathy or imagination. Taking them in isolation, one might indeed see Elsie and Helen as ironical portraits, characters whose bent for shallow satire is itself satirically observed. The inappropriateness of such an interpretation, and the full extent of Miss Astley's failure to base her satire firmly in the life of her country towns, are both made manifest in the sentimentality of her occasional sympathetic portraits. By displaying such unaspiring hicks as Szamos, the milk-bar proprietor, in a sympathetic light, Miss Astley seems to be seeking a positive standard of reference by which the inhumanity of his neighbours can be judged. Unfortunately the humanity of Szamos is the vague and sentimental benevolence of Nino Culotta.

The examination of these particular weaknesses in the earlier novels is warranted by their recurrence at the heart of *The Well-Dressed Explorer,* even though, in turning to the satirical biography of a journalist, Miss Astley is freed from the more obvious temptations of her country teachers.

In this most recent novel, Miss Astley's eye for detail is as keen as ever. (p. 279)

The minor characters of the novel are also brought before us with uncommon force. And to the extent that the novel is a rogues' gallery of snapshots, Miss Astley has the same success with these journalists and party-goers as with the headmasters and rural dignitaries of the earlier novels.

The wonder—and the pity—is that these talents are not more serviceable in the portrayal of the major characters. Alice Brewster is admired but not explored. Faced with this odd mixture of emotional endorsement and dramatic incomprehension, one comes to recognize that no real data will be furnished. Despite Miss Astley's claims for her, the *dramatized* Alice is no more than the type of long-suffering wives. Her daughter Jeannie tends rather to disrupt the novel. Jeannie the character, emanation of her father, and Jeannie the observer, reporter on her father, are juxtaposed with a confusion that never becomes complexity.

But the centre of the novel is George Brewster, the sentimental egotist, the emotional cannibal. Here, as never before, Miss Astley aspires to the ambivalence that distinguishes satire from mere scorn. Clearly we are expected to attain a wry affection for an amiable, well-meaning, and self-pitying monster. He is monster enough . . . , as when, in the midst of a continuing affair with one woman, he relieves his conscience at the expense of his wife's feelings by confessing to another quite transitory infidelity of which his wife could never have learnt. Conversely, he is amiable and well-meaning enough, as in his inability to bear malice or to seek mean victories. The trouble is that these two—and other—aspects of Brewster's character do not coalesce. In a review of the novel . . . , Sidney J. Baker found that the character was united by the long tracts of "poetic prose" with which the novel begins. Clearly there is an attempt of this kind. On a psychological level, the posturing role-playing George of adulthood is foreshadowed by the boy's practising of phrases and gestures to flatter his masters. On a "poetic" level, there is the recurrent imagery of leaf and tree to suggest that George's later affairs are a striving to recapture his first love, Nita, and through her the lost world of his childhood. But there is much of George that is not foreshadowed; and after being overworked early in the novel, the imagery referred to and the attitudes it implies vanish until George's dying dream. The George of the central part of the novel therefore remains an uneasy union of sentimentally-observed virtues and scornfully-observed follies and vices. And if George's character fails, the trivialities that so pervade the texture of the novel are no longer significant.

If in the long run this novel, like its predecessors, wavers into incoherence it seems to be because these "flickering glances", these "spots of wild light", are no substitute for a steady and informing radiance. (pp. 279-80)

> *J. F. Burrows, "Chalk and Cheese," in* Southerly,
> *Vol. 23, No. 4, 1963, pp. 276-80.*

ARTHUR ASHWORTH

[*The Slow Natives*] is set in suburban Brisbane, in country towns in Queensland and the beaches of the Gold Coast. The theme of sterility in human relationships, important in all [of Thea Astley's] novels, is a primary one again here. It is given a twist by being linked in one of the novel's sequences with the teen-age situation.

The central characters are the Leversons. Bernard and Iris Leverson are summed up with cruel perception by their fourteen-year-old son, Keith. The conversations of teenagers about their parents illustrate the new generation sitting in judgment on its elders, who are the slow natives, the black stuff between elephants' toes. (p. 63)

The relationships of the three members of the Leverson family form the central issue of a rather complex plot, and give unity to the various parts of the novel. Bernard in middle-age has lost interest in life, caught in what he calls "this rolling dullness in human relationships." He is fond of his son Keith, but has lost contact with him; communications have broken down. Iris is an uninteresting, not very bright woman whose life and home are run according to the notions of glossy women's magazines of the more sophisticated type. She engages in a love-affair with a married man of their suburban circle, the sort of affair which is born of boredom rather than passion. Knowledge of this drives Keith, already an impossible teenager, to his final acts of delinquency. Keith suffers from the lack of any display of strength on the part of his father which he can respect enough to revolt against. His behaviour is designed to punish his parents. His father's apparent weakness hurts him most, and he tries to sting Bernard into an attitude of authority. . . . The need for punishment, for a strong figure of authority is thus presented as the main motivation for Keith's behaviour. (pp. 63-4)

Keith's periodical departures from home lead him to Leo Varga's beach shack, furnished with radiogram, records, polished floors with cushions, surf-boards in a shed outside—a trap for maladjusted teenage boys. If Leo Varga's character is drawn without sympathy and real penetration of motives, it is nevertheless a sharp and detailed portrait of a certain type of athletic homosexual. Boys like Keith are his prey. These sequences are presented in a brassy, jerky, impressionistic style, brittle as the jazz tunes that play always in the background. Keith's final rejection of Leo leads to his flight from Brisbane where he meets up with Chookie, also in flight . . . , and by a series of hitched rides they reach Surfers Paradise. Keith is clever, smart, self-pitying, selfish, lacking in emotional capacity. Chookie is ignorant, illiterate, crude, but capable of understanding and pity. The two boys form an interesting contrast. There is another brilliantly created scene in a cabaret crowded with young people in Surfers Paradise, before the two steal a fast car and drive towards the inevitable crash.

The ending of the book doesn't come off. The underground religious theme, which has been hinted at in the introduction of religious imagery from time to time, moves into a dominant place. The accident shocks Bernard and Iris back to life. Chookie is dead, Keith has lost a leg. Chookie's death is tragic, Keith has not the stature to be tragic. And here the technique falters and the author resorts to contrived melodrama in the confusion as to which boy is dead, and to sentimentality in the presentation of Bernard's state of mind. (p. 65)

The whole structure of the book is betrayed by this ending. It comes like a burst of organ music at the fade-out of a film, where nothing has been solved and the characters are illuminated in a technicolour glow of sentimentality. A miracle cannot be dragged in to resolve a plot in this fashion, even such a doubtful miracle as Bernard's conversion from boredom.

If one can get over the ending, the virtues of this novel are apparent: the creation of real people in real settings, the subtle exploration of anguish and despair behind the facade of personality, the astringent analysis of emotional inadequacy in human relationships. Since these are not minor virtues, it is a pity that the failure in construction is a major one also. [*The Slow Natives*] is much more ambitious than *The Well Dressed Explorer,* but it lacks the integration of that novel. (pp. 65-6)

*Arthur Ashworth, in a review of "The Slow Natives,"
in* Southerly, *Vol. 26, No. 1, 1966, pp. 62-6.*

L. J. CLANCY

Miss Astley has a reputation which I find difficult to understand, and her latest novel, clumsily entitled *A Boat Load of Home Folk,* does nothing to solve the puzzle. The novel concerns a small group of passengers who call at a port on an island in the Pacific. There are occasional flashbacks but most of the action takes place in the twenty-four hours following 7 a.m. on 10 December, where the tensions between the characters finally erupt while a symbolic hurricane rages destructively over the island.

The characters are a sorry lot. Consider this group of people: a priest who is found making love to a native boy; a disenchanted middle-aged couple who are incessantly unfaithful to one another; a sixty-two year old woman with a heavily painted face who is seeking a lover; and her maiden companion who is disappointed when a native boy who has been following her refuses to rape her but merely takes her watch. Clearly, it is difficult to be anything but satirical about people like these and Miss Astley is unsparing in her observation.

The opening image in the novel, an image which is discarded but then returned to three times in the last chapter, is that of a postcard, and this accurately suggests the detachment and impersonality of the author. One by one she takes her characters apart mercilessly by the selection of the most squalid physical details. Of Miss Paradise, for instance, she observes the painted face which 'had broken up suddenly into smudged areas of tears like a grief-stricken map whose boundaries had been changed by war'. . . . It is not so much the physical detail itself but the relish which the author shows, the eagerness with which she seizes on the more unsavory features of the natural processes of the body, that makes this sort of comment disturbing.

Moreover, there is in the images employed a continual endeavour to impersonalize the characters, to reduce them to the status of entomological curiosities. Miss Astley's talent seems to be for the miniscule: sharpness of observation, a gift for the cutting remark—there is no doubt that she possesses these qualities but when it comes to putting them at the service of an organized work of art she seems at a loss.

This comes out most clearly perhaps in her treatment of the neuroses that Catholicism may bring with it. . . . Miss Astley has been deeply affected by her Catholic upbringing but her attempts to convert this experience into the stuff of which novels are made reveal several inadequacies. *A Boat Load of Home Folk* reads in some parts like a speeded-up Graham Greene novel. Greene's influence is, in fact, apparent everywhere. The novel remarks somewhere of its main character Stevenson that 'He was obedient to doom,' and the general submissiveness that this remark suggests extends to most of the characters. It is this numbness, this self-indulgent acceptance of failure, that is the worst and most stiflingly degenerate hangover from Greene and the quality that most vitiates the novel's force by contributing even to a general enervation of

the prose in several places. Sentences such as: Stevenson 'felt, looking across at Miss Trumper, an almost-love that, now he was older, came with a gush for the unlovely or the unendurable even', and 'I like this place in a queer sort of way, the way one gets to love one's disease, the eating enemy-friend to whom one is host', sound uncannily like Scobie speaking in *The Heart of the Matter.* But where Greene prepares the reader, with great care and sensitivity, for the ultimate collapse of Scobie's character, Thea Astley simply confronts the reader with such a collapse. After all, Scobie took almost the whole of *The Heart of the Matter* to kill himself; in this novel Father Lake takes only one chapter to crumple from disenchantment with his vocation to attempting homosexual relations with a native servant boy.

Miss Astley, then, remains an exasperating novelist. She has possibly the sharpest eye, and most biting tongue of almost any contemporary Australian novelist, but none of her novels stands as a fully achieved work of art in itself. . . . Miss Astley's penchant is for satire, yet she is caught up on the horns of a dilemma. The neuroses that Catholicism can lead to are what most inspire her imagination yet she is unable either to control her presentation of them or to make it dramatically credible. (pp. 416-18)

L. J. Clancy, in a review of "A Boat Load of Home Folk," in Meanjin, *Vol. XXVIII, No. 3, September, 1969, pp. 416-18.*

DAVID GILBEY

A Kindness Cup, described as a "cautionary tale" is a bitter, cynical book based on an actual incident at The Leap, Queensland in the second half of the last century: a young aboriginal girl, Kowaha, clutching her baby while being pursued by a posse of white vigilantes, leaped to her death off a scarp of rock. However, as in most of Thea Astley's work, the main focus of the book is not on the events themselves but on how they are perceived and orchestrated.

The reader's view is complicated and many-sided; a dramatic replay of this incident is preceded by vignettes of town and school life at the Taws, and interwoven into an account of the subsequent official Inquiry. These details are recalled in fragments by the schoolteacher Tom Dorahy during a reunion week. . . . The various strands of the novel interlock in several narrative and dramatic movements—the dispersal of the blacks at Mandarana leading up to the fatal leap; the trial of the "vigilantes" culminating in their acquittal and Dorahy's dismal attempts to set things right during the reunion. Appropriately, the climaxes are cumulatively crushing for Dorahy as each is a more agonizing personal failure than the last. It is his perspective that is the novel's focus and though its self-critical anguish is perceived ironically, the novel is a pessimistic view of Australian social attitudes and life in general.

A variation on the typical Astley hero, Tom Dorahy is now a weak old man with "tired blood" . . . bent on revealing, even after twenty years, the injustice and cruelty involved in the central incident. . . . (p. 442)

In his role as a teacher, as a witness at the trial, as an avenger, Dorahy is a great pretender. He is "educated" and can therefore make clever, allusive observations intended to establish his own superiority, but these are largely wasted on his pupils and the townspeople. . . . He plays witty verbal games of innuendo and insinuation that fail because others won't "play" and take his implied meanings. Thus his gibes at Buckmaster (sic) and Sweetman (sic) are hidden beneath polite communication. Dorahy can only seethe helplessly when they don't take his "bait" but prefer the polite way out he has offered them. He devises strategies and plans that mostly backfire, such as when, at the height of the reunion festivities he tries to confront the instigators with their "victim" Charlie Lunt, who is unwilling to be thus sacrificed but ends up being killed by hired thugs while in the background the concert is in full swing. Dorahy is too clever for his own good since he embellishes his imprisonment and helplessness. Even two central and extended images, the Rape of Lucrece (paralleling Kowaha's leap) and "a cup o' kindness" (ironically undercutting the sentiments in "Auld Lang Syne"), dramatic as they are, underline Dorahy's ineffectuality. He lives out his lifetime of self-conscious defeat and personal ignominy in beaten (in this case "up") helplessness.

Set against Dorahy, the other characters seem insubstantial since we don't get them much from "inside". They are presented to us partly through Dorahy, largely in terms of social or moral stereotypes, and their roles given unpleasant or ugly overtones. . . . (p. 443)

Miss Astley's satirical epitomizing is deft and cruel, using characters' weaknesses, failures and roles as a frequent source of imagery. Significantly, few escape their roles even when the role is developed beyond first impressions. Boyd, for example, is an articulate fence-sitter who finally makes a protest which becomes rhetorical, or Lunt like a suffering Christ . . . or Saint . . . refuses to make a protest, succumbing to his fate.

Perhaps Dorahy himself doesn't ever escape the role of misguided avenger. In this regard characterization in the novel is not subtle since distinctions are made by analogy and metaphor, which, if a sharper method, is much more brutal than description or exposition. Dorahy's dominating consciousness therefore seems not so much analytical as imagist. The irony in his perceiving others in terms of roles, images and labels that are distant from him is that he becomes tarred with the same brush—his mind is created for us by the images he uses of others.

A Kindness Cup is written in a less tortured style than *The Acolyte,* although the distinctive Astlean flourish still draws attention to itself by angular, odd, or ugly phrases. Mostly this syntactical awkwardness is dramatic, revealing the mind of the character who is using it. . . . (pp. 443-44)

Many of the scenes are superbly written—Buckmaster arguing with his wife . . . ; the dispersal of the blacks and Kowaha's leap . . . ; the burning of Boyd's printery . . . , and the final reunion week concert. In this last, Astley's talent for social comedy focuses on the clichéd, maudlin sentimentality enforced by the organizers (once the vigilantes but now the acme of respectability) and expected by the audience. While the choruses of "Auld Lang Syne" reach a crescendo inside, Dorahy, Boyd and Lunt are brutally attacked by a "hate-pack", questioning Dorahy's earlier, more comfortable view "the blows dealt in metaphor were deadlier than the thwack of flesh on flesh". . . . It is Lunt's statement "There's no purpose" . . . that is finally and firmly illustrated by *A Kindness Cup.* The characters in The Taws are after all representative Australians. (p. 444)

David Gilbey, "New Modes in Fiction," in Southerly, *Vol. 35, No. 4, December, 1976, pp. 442-59.*

ELIZABETH WEBBY

Although Thea Astley's publishers make no rash claims about discontinuous narratives, the full title of her collection is *Hunting the Wild Pineapple and other related stories*. . . . Astley has a central character, Leverson, who, although in no way a type or an author-surrogate—he is a failed hotel manager minus one leg lost in a car accident—appears in nearly all the stories but lives in none. Leverson's narrative voice is often reminiscent of Hal Porter's. Perhaps, as Porter once nearly lost a leg in a car accident and was a hotel manager, some sort of literary in-joke is intended—North Queensland as it would look to Porter if he ever went there? And if [Frank] Moorhouse and [Michael] Wilding can appear in each other's stories, why can't Porter appear in Astley's? The problem . . . is that although Leverson is a constant character he is not central to all stories in the way that the narrators of Moorhouse's later collections are. So there are clumsy constructions of the 'I always seem to be explaining how I got where' . . . type. At times Astley has also to resort to the sort of nineteenth-century framing device which Lawson is praised for discarding. One example of this occurs in an otherwise excellent story, **"Ladies Need Only Apply"**, supposedly told by Leverson who hears it from someone else. Actually the point of view is that of the central character, a middle-aged lady school teacher on leave in North Queensland who becomes enmeshed with Leo, an m.c.p. alternative-life-styler with some of the horrible fascination of Christina Stead's Sam Pollit. Leo and the North Queensland climate combine inexorably to force Miss Klein down into the mud, humbly begging for his attention, 'naked, glistening silver with lust and rain'.

In **"Ladies Need Only Apply"** the peculiarities of life in North Queensland are used dramatically as well as scenically. Other stories may have more engaging characters, such as the Fixer with his yards of bad verse, or more comic episodes, such as the actual hunting of the wild pineapple. But they remain at the anecdotal level rather than cohering into fictional wholes. So, while there is much to laugh and wonder at in *Hunting the Wild Pineapple,* it does demonstrate the dangers as well as the delights of regionalism. Astley's writing seems to have taken on too much of the casualness and purposeless fecundity of the North. (pp. 129-30)

Elizabeth Webby, "The Long March of Short Fiction: A Seventies Retrospective," in Meanjin, *Vol. 39, No. 1, April, 1980, pp. 127-33.*

JUDITH H. McDOWELL

First published in Sydney in 1972, Thea Astley's funny, bitter novel *The Acolyte* has been reprinted—wise and welcome testimony to the growing acceptance of Astley's role as one of the major novelists currently writing in Australia. Astley's achievement so far has been impressive, and this book illustrates one of the main reasons why: her ability to render scenes and characters with scrupulous honesty and in dazzling detail.

The acolyte of the novel is Paul Vesper, the narrator, who early in his life falls under the spell of the "great man," the blind pianist and composer Jack Holberg. Vesper, a self-confessed under-achiever, sacrifices everything in his dedication to Holberg, including his fiancée and his dignity, as he eventually leaves his engineering job to devote his time to Holberg's needs, moving into Holberg's glass mansion in the country. . . .

All the characters are credible and depicted in revealing detail. The narrator Vesper is a precious intellectual with a torrential vocabulary; he leads a rather sterile life working for his demanding genius and, having little talent for the art to which he devotes this life, longs vaguely for some aboriginal edenic beach village to which he never goes. The sisters Hilda and Ilse, the Teutonic "goose-girls," one of whom marries Holberg and the other bears his child, are united in their victim natures; hopelessly devoted to the genius, they dwindle—one mentally, one physically—into mere shells of women under the genius's cruel indifference to either. The only one who stands up well in the face of the genius's demands is Aunt Sadie, a marvelous and outrageous slip of an old woman who wears, among other outlandish things, a cowgirl costume, swills booze, plays the horses and frequently has a bash at the vibes with a jazz group called the Jimjams. The genius himself comes vividly alive for the reader; the "great man" is truly admirable for his amazing achievements, but also both pathetic in his affliction and insufferable in his egocentrism.

Finally, in what is perhaps the only possible conclusion to this devastatingly incisive exposé of an obsessive life-style, Vesper, reaching what he labels as his "revolutionary climacteric," realizes what a cross Holberg has been for him to bear and sees himself as a servitor sucked dry of youth, like the other devotees, a nothing except insofar as he ministers. And for what purpose? . . . All that is left, finally, for Vesper is a gesture, and in the book's final scene, which is both funny and serious, the acolyte illustrates the slightly proverbial truth that the only way one may be able to get out of glass houses is by throwing stones.

> *Judith H. McDowell, in a review of "The Acolyte,"
> in* World Literature Today, *Vol. 55, No. 4, Autumn,
> 1981, p. 724.*

KERRYN GOLDSWORTHY

[Thea Astley's writing is] full of ambiguous dualities, ironic reversals and polar extremes. (p. 478)

'Disaster', says the narrator of *The Acolyte,* 'comes out of the most sheltered places', and from the calculated ambiguity of his creator's syntax it isn't possible to tell whether he means *even* the most sheltered places or *only* the most sheltered places. Circumstances in Astley's narratives gather themselves, from random unremarkable beginnings, about a central knot of disaster like the whorl at the heart of a marble; as the story progresses you can see some kind of explosion or disintegration coming more and more clearly and inevitably. For a writer so relentlessly witty from sentence to sentence, she writes novels whose overall shape bears a remarkable resemblance to that of tragedy in their slow inexorable slide past the point where the audience catches on, says 'Oh, no!'—and can do nothing except keep watching till there's nothing left to wait for.

Actually if Astley were to turn her hand in a moment of what would for her be eccentricity to the writing of detective novels, horror stories and other thrillers, she would probably make a lot of money. Her gift for the creation of an atmosphere of unease which progresses through suspense to menace is apparent even in her extraordinary first novel *Girl With a Monkey,* in which the reader's sympathy and growing concern for the central character is expertly manipulated right to the end. Just as we feel that disaster has been averted, there comes a piece of dialogue more violent in its effect on the reader than any

punch-up; it elicits a massive shift in reader sympathy and makes the meaning of the novel's title finally, entirely clear.

After this psychic violence at the end of her first novel, however, there's almost always climactic physical violence of one kind or another in her subsequent books, whether it's the large-scale mayhem of the hurricane in *A Boat Load of Home Folk* and the massacre in *A Kindness Cup,* or the mutilation and/or death of various characters in *A Descant for Gossips, The Slow Natives, The Acolyte,* and *An Item From the Late News.* There's something almost Gothic about Astley's imagination, and in this her writing is reminiscent of short stories by women writers of the American South. Flannery O'Connor, in her relentless retributions, and Eudora Welty, in her knowledge of small-town life and her delight in the physical texture of any given day, are the two names which spring most readily to mind.

Another comparison which repeatedly suggests itself to me is with Muriel Spark. . . . Like Spark, Astley sets up such a mesh of ironies, stretched between author, characters and reader, that it's often impossible to tell just where the authorial irony is located. . . . (pp. 478-80)

In her fiction Astley can (and, repeatedly, does) turn a horribly ruthless eye on human specimens of both sexes, but while her demolition of her female characters' characters is usually of the flip throwaway variety—the disposable insult is a form she has under total control—her male characters expose themselves by their own behaviour. (p. 480)

My favourite in this particular portrait gallery is the passage in *A Boat Load of Home Folk* in which an ill-assortment of hurricane refugees, sheltering in a relatively undamaged house and trying to get a little sleep, is woken in the small hours by the complaints of one of their number; Gerald Seabrook is hungry, so he nags till the women wake up, get up, and find and cook some food. He is served along with the others a plate of the cardboard pieces from a torn-up Weeties packet, disguised by white sauce, cheese, salt and pepper, at the hands of the enraged Miss Paradise. . . . (p. 481)

Maybe this isn't surprising in a writer who seems suspended—rather than torn—between a kind of stern high-mindedness about human behaviour and what seems like a wholehearted delight in the sensual qualities of the physical world. And for Astley oppositions of this kind seem separated by the most delicate of lines; her fiction is largely about the ease with which some positive quality or experience can become its own dark shadow. The control and authority so fatally absent in *The Slow Natives* can easily become the force and brutality so appallingly present in *A Kindness Cup;* the lush beauty of the Queensland rainforest melts into the lush materialistic hideousness of its denizens' backyard barbecues.

This aspect of Astley's fiction—the sense of duality and concomitant ambiguity which seems to me to characterise her writing in all kinds of different ways—is encapsulated in the use she makes of the word 'acolyte'. Many writers wear an invisible charm bracelet, dangling special words which have become for them the repositories of meanings far beyond their value in ordinary verbal currency—words that emit, from within the context of each writer's work, a kind of semiotic radiance. The word 'acolyte' is one such for Astley; it turns up again and again in her fiction, sometimes to suggest the nature of the power relationship between one character and another and sometimes to suggest the ritualistic quality of the scene in which it occurs. More importantly, however, it's sometimes a term of approval and sometimes a term of abuse; the role of acolyte is often played out uncomfortably close to the fulcrum of Astley's moral seesaw.

Individual characters wander in and out of the acolyte role but many—most, in fact—of her main characters are permanently locked into the role of outsider. In a statement made in 1972 Astley said,

> My main interest . . . is the misfit. Not the spectacular outsider, but the seedy little non-grandiose non-fitter who lives in his own mini-hell. . . . [My] novels have always been . . . a plea for charity—in the Pauline sense, of course—to be accorded to those not ruthless enough or grand enough to be gigantic tragic figures, but which, in their own way, record the same *via crucis.*

Her recent work has gone beyond this particular version of the outsider; Wafer in *An Item From the Late News* is what Astley would probably be vastly amused to see called a charismatic figure, a long way from the unpopular, unattractive, doomed child Vinny Lalor in *A Descant for Gossips*—but their respective fates are very similar indeed, not only in the physical awfulness of what happens to them but also in the reasons why it happens. (p. 482)

It will be interesting to see what Astley does next; her last two books have been respectively the lightest-hearted and the grimmest of all that she's written. *Hunting the Wild Pineapple* has some outrageously funny moments . . . , while *An Item From the Late News* is not only graver in tone, more preoccupied with the nature of evil, than any of her previous writing; it doesn't even have the witty narrator who, unhappy or not, saves a lot of *The Acolyte* from being excessively grim. On the contrary, the narrator of *An Item From the Late News* is a fairly humourless, fairly neurotic character the use of whom to tell the tale was a brave, and must have been a difficult, thing to do. The story **"Travelling Even Farther North"** . . . , in which the narrator gives up trying to eat her plastic chips and smokes them instead while quoting snatches of English, French and German poetry to herself as she watches the passing parade, suggests that Astley has taken off at some surreal tangent to what most of us sadly acknowledge as the real world. (p. 484)

> *Kerryn Goldsworthy, "Thea Astley's Writing: Magnetic North," in* Meanjin, *Vol. 42, No. 4, December, 1983, pp. 478-85.*

A. L. McLEOD

Nine fictions in the past 25 years have earned for Thea Astley a certain fame in Australia, at least: her scouring irony and penetration of the national myths, particularly as they are reflected in small-town life and personal relationships, have been cautiously accepted by most of her readers. Although she writes of her fictional Queensland outback town of Allbut as "a no-hope landscape, the bummer's Eden," where "the grossness is horribly apparent," one detects a certain fondness for the myriad towns of which Allbut is merely an example. But her style is an odd admixture of mannered phrases, aphoristic statements, and demotic clichés juxtaposed with passages of poetic beauty and incisive realism, especially in the dialogue of "the bush." Many readers will find the Australian slang unfamiliar and hence the characterization and dialogue deficient. But then, as one of her characters observes, "This country pays little tribute to elegance. Even of expression." A study in small-

town brutality towards outsiders, [*An Item from the Late News*] has elements that remind one of both Shirley Jackson's "The Lottery" and Steinbeck's *The Pearl* and illustrates most poignantly the author's observation: "There is only one perfect shelter: indifference." Astley is an accomplished and important writer of fictions. (pp. 810-11)

> *A. L. McLeod, in a review of "An Item from the Late News," in* Choice, *Vol. 22, No. 6, February, 1985, pp. 810-11.*

SALLY DAWSON

From *Girl with a Monkey* (1958) onwards, the celebrated Australian writer Thea Astley has directed her satirical, sometimes moralistic gaze at the pettiness and violence of small-town philistinism. *An Item from the Late News* tells the story of Wafer, a bomb-age baby, haunted in adult life by the vision of his father being blown apart before his eyes (and of all those other victims of bombs, past or to come), who seeks peace and shelter in the country that is itself the "perfect bomb shelter"—Australia. But the offensively male inhabitants of Allbut, the town he settles on for his retreat, do not welcome tolerance (Wafer befriends all manner of outcasts) and equivocal delicacy in their hard-hitting, beer-swilling community.

We have seen this kind of community before in Astley's work: like Patrick White's Sarsaparilla, though without its sustaining vitality, it is a place of small minds, narrow prejudices and decayed prosperity. Her tone ranging from irony to righteous indignation, Astley systematically strips off the layers of respectability to reveal sinister undercurrents—the animality that underlies tough masculinity, the terrible weakness that disguises itself as decency and solidarity. Debunking the old mateship myth, she lays bare a society where "women are never quite adults" and where most of the men are never quite human.

The story is told by Gabby. . . . It is Gabby's artistic consciousness which allows her access to unseen events and unconfessed thoughts. This is just acceptable, since what is lacking in verisimilitude is made up for in inventiveness, but like most of the characters, Gabby suffers by being essentially unrecognizable as a person. Astley is very good at the revealing cameo of a minor eccentric or fanatic, but her major characters fail because unsupportable forces on them myths they cannot support. . . . [Both Wafer] and Moon, his counterpart, take on Christlike/Devilish overtones. But these characters do not possess the inner resources that make, say, Randolph Stow's Diviner in *Tourmaline* both fearful and affecting. Given to such statements as "I was conceived . . . behind the point where two seas meet", Wafer is impossible to imagine.

The narrative, experimental and blinding, promotes an essentially unreal world where only words have much significance. Although the preoccupation with human frailties and prejudices remains, *Beachmasters* shows Astley's talent blossoming into a more expressive and imaginative medium. Mature, enquiring and often verbally stunning, this latest novel centres on the pathetic grab for independence by the natives of the tiny (fictional) island of Kristi. The novel is not essentially political—despite a certain topicality—except in so far as it chips away at the old myths of patriotism and colonialism. Familiar ground this may be, but Astley's approach is inward and intimate. In the struggle for national identity, she says, no one, however decent or innocent, can remain neutral. The real struggle is a personal one, as in the case of the young *hapkas* (half-caste) Gavi Salway, "the boy always on the wavering perimeters of discovery'' whose own identity is formed and proved along with that of the island. Ironically, the puny revolution will reveal many a deficient soul, puncture many a self-deception, colonial and native, and not even the wry charismatic chief, Tommy Narota himself, will escape unscathed. . . .

Most impressive throughout is Astley's delicate treading of the fine line between poignancy and absurdity—nowhere more effectively than in the glorious anti-climax of the moment of secession.

The story is vigorously sustained through a series of interacting scenes, but the real vitality comes from the language of the ''triple-tongued'' island itself where English, French and pidjin (Seaspeak) fuse and confuse. The ambiguities of a situation where pidjin can be a colonial insult or a mark of belonging are explored with ingenuity and humour, and the whole is punctuated by Seaspeak refrains . . . , drifting elegiacally through the narrative. In all respects a more satisfying novel than its predecessor, *Beachmasters* shows Thea Astley at her subtle, illuminating best.

Sally Dawson, ''Myth-Chipping,'' in The Times Literary Supplement, *No. 4311, November 15, 1985, p. 1295.*

Madison Smartt Bell

1957-

American novelist and short story writer.

In his novels Bell depicts the sordid New York underworld of drugs and violence. Concerned with the sociological motivations for his characters' actions, Bell's purpose, according to David Montrose, is to "anatomize the circumstances that create violent deeds instead of simply providing details of those deeds." While Bell has been faulted for using contrived literary devices and trendy subject matter, he is often praised for his strong characterizations and for the authenticity of his characters' street vernacular.

Bell's first novel, *The Washington Square Ensemble* (1983), is a fast-paced and occasionally violent portrait of the New York City heroin trade. Resembling a jazz composition in its stream-of-consciousness narration by five alternating voices, the novel chronicles twenty-four hours in the lives of drug dealer Johnny B. Goode and his companions. Bell's narrative digressions expand the novel's scope to include extended insights into each character's personal history. His second novel, *Waiting for the End of the World* (1985), concerns a group of social misfits plotting to destroy Times Square with a homemade nuclear device. As in *The Washington Square Ensemble*, Bell interweaves sketches about the backgrounds of his characters to explain their violent behavior. Meg Wolitzer noted that "Mr. Bell has a keen eye and his panoramic observations about the city are often lyrical and moving."

(See also *Contemporary Authors,* Vol. 111.)

Photograph by Andrew French. Courtesy of Madison Smartt Bell

IVAN GOLD

Johnny B. [Goode, central figure of *The Washington Square Ensemble,*] deals all manner of substances for use and abuse at the foot of Fifth Avenue, in New York's Washington Square Park. He has no clear idea of how the mob (whichever family it is) manages to get the stuff in from Turkey (or wherever they get it from) and cares less. His priorities are earning enough to continue the upkeep on his Park Avenue apartment, avoiding the law and riding herd on his peculiar three-man sales force, whose own first-person accounts of life in the park interlard Johnny's to create the surface of *The Washington Square Ensemble.*

These intimates are Yusuf Ali, an enormous American Muslim, abstemious where drugs are concerned, but given to long, soporific citations from the Koran; Santa Barbara, a Puerto Rican from Hoboken so involved with voodoo that one or two chickens will lose their heads during the course of the day he (in an eloquent pidgin) describes; and Holy Mother (named, like the rest, by Johnny B., who has a gift for this sort of thing), of Italian descent like Johnny himself, once a hitman for the Gallo brothers, now a hopeless junkie who will die of his habit, a needle protruding from a vein in his neck. Holy Mother was incarcerated in Attica when it blew, and his account of the

prison riot and its aftermath provides what may be the book's most gripping scenes.

Then there is Porco Miserio, not part of the charmed inner circle (well on the outs with all of them, in fact) yet in some murky manner Johnny B.'s alter ego. He is an unregenerate juicehead who can often be found on the Bowery, yet retains the ability to blow a sweet jazz saxophone after consuming however many quarts of whiskey. He also commands a felicitous prose style, albeit one not easily distinguishable from Holy Mother's or Johnny B.'s. (pp. 7, 24)

The Washington Square Ensemble has all the faults of a first novel (the last 50 pages almost undo it, as the author struggles for an ending) and some of the virtues of a fourth: Perhaps it takes the fresh vision of a 25-year-old Tennesseean like Madison Smartt Bell to render New York's druggy, seamy side, to give the flavor of a meal taken in a Ukrainian restaurant on Second Avenue, describe the view of the city through a hangover from the Williamsburg Bridge at dawn, convey the abject fear you too might feel crouched in a dark Brooklyn basement with Joey Gallo about to appear at the top of the stairs. (p. 24)

Ivan Gold, "Addiction Fiction," in The New York Times Book Review, *February 20, 1983, pp. 7, 24-5.*

THOMAS RUFFEN

This tough-edged, streetwise novel [*The Washington Square Ensemble*] is a flawed yet brilliant first book. Bell has that rarest of literary gifts: the ability to make word into flesh, to delineate compelling, vivid characters who bring to life the stark, harrowing world of tenements, derelict bars, shadowy alleyways, and inner-city parks where deviant behavior is the norm. . . .

The story itself is no more than a few violent incidents in a long lifetime of violence, but the digressions, narrated in sociopathic streams of consciousness, provide fascinating glimpses into the fabric of lawlessness and urban decay.

Bell has a remarkable ear for the street vernacular of many divergent voices. His dope-dealers take turns narrating the events of taut, suspenseful hours leading to the denouement. Along the way, they veer into tangents of memory, fits of existential rage, and into their own private nightmares. . . .

The police tell their story too, in vignettes of world-weary inability to cope with the underside of life.

The Washington Square Ensemble is a captivating account of malice, danger and exhilarating insanity; thoroughly entertaining, but not for the squeamish. The author attempts too much, yet nearly pulls it off. Certain character motivations and somewhat contrived events stretch believability to the snapping point, but the reader is constantly rewarded by the dark poetry of a raw talent who orchestrates a mad symphony of contemporary outlaws.

> Thomas Ruffen, "A Crowd of Toughs in the Underbelly," in Los Angeles Times Book Review, February 27, 1983, p. 3.

KEN KALFUS

While Bell doesn't quite glorify [drug dealers in *The Washington Square Ensemble*], New Yorkers who use the park for purposes other than purchasing drugs are likely to feel that he credits his pushers with more humanity and reasonableness than they possess.

Johnny B. is the drug dealers' fast-talking boss. He has given each of his "retailers" names—Yusuf Ali, Holy Mother, Santa Barbara—thereby grabbing each of them "by the short hairs of the soul." The retailers, along with Johnny B. and his erstwhile friend and customer Porco Miserio, take turns telling their stories. . . .

Bell's dust-jacket pose complements the toughness of his characters. Yusuf Ali, before his conversion to Islam, skinned and ate rats in his cellar in the South Bronx. Holy Mother is a former Mafia hit man and a survivor and unconvincing historian of the Attica prison riot. As part of his initiation into the secrets of black magic, Santa Barbara drinks blood from the neck of a chicken moments after its head has been torn off. Washington Square Park isn't a park; it's a sideshow, complete with geek.

Telling a story from more than one point of view is a difficult trick, and Bell almost brings it off. He has created five distinct and consistent voices; well, nearly distinct, but most writers struggle to find *one* voice. The book has the feel of a modern jazz composition: the "ensemble" jams to one theme, but each player gets a solo.

Unfortunately, making such lowlifes interesting is an even harder trick. A rap and a life history isn't enough to animate them,

or to inform us about the world as seen from the bottom of Fifth Avenue. Except for Johnny B., who is on stage the least, Bell's underworld characters are extravagantly crazy, and their craziness tells us little that is important or true. *The Washington Square Ensemble* is a hallucinogenic novel, but not quite a mind-expanding one. (p. 407)

> Ken Kalfus, "Toughing It Out," in The Nation, Vol. 236, No. 13, April 2, 1983, pp. 406-08.

MARY FURNESS

The Washington Square "ensemble" is a heroin-pushing gang, although its leader prefers to dub his wares "pharmaceuticals"; he is a cool, clear-thinking criminal who likes to keep himself, his pockets and his veins clean. He also likes naming things. . . . Having hit on "Lemon Peel" as a good name for an old negro with yellow stains on his beard he reflects that "when I've called him that enough times to enough people that will be his name, because that is the way the world works, and what you call a thing is what it is."

All the characters [in *The Washington Square Ensemble*] are philosophers in their own ways. Three of them work for Johnny and all have been named by him. . . . The action of the book lasts a mere twenty-four hours, but enough happens, both in the past and in the present, enough is talked about and thought and noticed, for a much longer time-span.

Each of the characters talks in turn, in his own language (this takes some getting used to, but the initial suspicion that it is a clever trick which will fail to conceal some fundamental flaw in the structure is quickly dispelled). They tell us about how they came to be what they are, and these stories within stories are so absorbing—Holy Mother's experiences in Attica State Penitentiary, for example—that it's easy to forget there is a main thread. Then the past catches up with the present, the separate characters and strands knit themselves together.

Madison Smartt Bell's language is American at its best; lively and expressive, but always lucid and never merely distracting. His subject matter is more Chandlerian than Woolfish, but he is a master of demotic stream-of-consciousness and the descriptive commentary. . . .

The novel brilliantly evokes a world of violence, depravity and despair without inducing a lowering of the spirits. As it unfolds, the ensemble, tough and inured to the seamiest side of life, reveal themselves to have higher feelings and loyalties that are manifested in quiet, almost unnoticeable actions. Moments of tension turn almost imperceptibly into cool and sustained triumphs, like one of the passages of jazz which the author describes so well.

> Mary Furness, "Do-be-do-be-do," in The Times Literary Supplement, No. 4195, August 26, 1983, p. 915.

KIRKUS REVIEWS

Bell, in his debut novel, *The Washington Square Ensemble* (1983), proved himself a sharp writer of urban darks and depths. He's gone a touch more commercial now [in *Waiting for the End of the World*], fashionably apocalyptic, with a semi-thriller about psychos organized into an anarchist band that intends to blow up New York with a homemade atomic weapon. But what remains most (if too rarely) stirring is Bell's gritty-city blues. The suspense, however, is woodenly inevitable and gothic and clichéd (subway tunnel denouements, etc.).

A rich ex-student radical-turned-clinical psychologist, Simon Rohnstock, is the evil genius to a bunch of misfits (Vietnam-, ghetto-, or mental-hospital-grads) whose rage he parlays into a devil's brew of destructiveness. But a Brooklyn photographer (and epileptic) named Larkin, nominally one of Simon's maniacs, is the only holder-back. An anti-hero of the old school, Larkin licks the gutter with his tongue but still has enough existential responsibility to ultimately destroy the plot and save the city. Bell relies far too much on diversionary gimmicks—case-like histories of each character, a summer month's worth of headline stories from the N.Y. *Post*—when he isn't straining Larkin's psyche through a net of agonized prose. . . .

[The novel is more] water than wine. . . . The mean-streets, wacko side of New York is stark and menacing in Bell's simulacrum of them, but the book is too quick to jump out of the way of its own obviousness, thus never grabbing hold of its essential narrative. Talented writer, nervous book.

> *A review of "Waiting for the End of the World," in* Kirkus Reviews, *Vol. LIII, No. 12, June 15, 1985, p. 538.*

MEG WOLITZER

[*Waiting for the End of the World*] digs deep into the underside of New York City and comes up with a vision of urban life that is by turns dizzying, real and exaggerated. Clarence Larkin, a photographer working for a doctor at Bellevue Hospital, falls in with a gang of terrorists and drifts through the seedy world around him. As in Dante's version, this hell is stratified and the reader is treated to a series of startling looks at unimaginable lives.

In one scene, we see four men sitting in an apartment, calmly comparing souvenirs of conquest. "Hutton pulled a plastic sandwich bag from his field jacket and shook two yellowish ears onto the coffee table in front of him. . . . 'Those are real cop ears,' Hutton said. 'Fresh ones.'" The tone of this section is deliberately without affect, and that seems to be the most shocking thing about it; terrorism, we are told, has become an inherent part of city life, as ordinary and constant as any of our daily rituals. Unfortunately, the flatness of the prose keeps the reader from becoming involved.

Much more effective are the descriptions of the terrorists' childhoods, which bring to mind the middle-class histories of some members of the Weather Underground. It is fascinating, in art and life, to see how someone might grow up into such a desperate character—how, in effect, someone might get from *here* to *there*. . . .

It is curious that in a novel about violence the most powerful moments are those that are not violent at all. Mr. Bell has a keen eye and his panoramic observations about the city are often lyrical and moving: "The sun was jammed into the Manhattan skyline as if caught in a row of broken teeth, and to Larkin the earth appeared to be tilted. . . . Down on the Manhattan and Brooklyn bridges the lamps were snapping alight like beads dropping onto a string."

Madison Smartt Bell's first novel, *The Washington Square Ensemble,* was concerned with the world of street drugs and

half-lives, and now the author has returned to even more sordid territory. Lyricism and terrorism do not mix well here, and the novel never quite reconciles itself to this problem. The reader is left with a very bleak but sometimes memorable vision of a world out of control.

> *Meg Wolitzer, "Layers of Hell in the City," in* The New York Times Book Review, *August 18, 1985, p. 18.*

DAVID REMNICK

Bell's first novel, *The Washington Square Ensemble* was set mainly among the seemier strata of Greenwich Village, and now [in *Waiting for the End of the World*] he has crossed the teetering Williamsburg Bridge to a similar Brooklyn. His Brooklyn is not the increasingly prosperous frontiers of Park Slope and Brooklyn Heights, but the crumbling margins, the neighborhoods that are far too desolate and old, even for slummers and other pretenders. . . .

His protagonist is Larkin, a deeply confused and deluded refugee from the middle-class who lives from day to day, nightmare to nightmare. He is a failed pianist, a drunk, an epileptic, a character at once nasty and sympathetic. As he stumbles along the streets, past burned out warehouses and exhausted tenements, he is witness to a myriad of inexplicable events. And because of his ratty condition, he is hardly noticed. (p. 3)

Events grow more inexplicable, more terrifying as the story develops. Larkin hooks up with some equally disturbed partners: David Hutton, a Vietnam veteran, Charles Mercer, an ex-cocaine runner, Ruben Carrera, a fatherless child and victim of a lunatic mother and Simon Rohnstock, a sour child of privilege, pathetic revolutionary and the ring-leader of this mad "cell." After executing a series of "warm-up" murders, their scheme is to plant an atomic bomb made of stolen plutonium in the catacombs under Times Square. The novel moves toward the success or failure of that mission with terrific power; the plausibility of the plan gives the novel its engine.

The less successful aspects of *Waiting for the End of the World* are in the plan of the novel itself. After a dramatic prologue that describes the theft of the plutonium, Bell lingers over Larkin, his strangeness, his world, his invisibility. Here is some of the strongest writing in the book. The portrait of Larkin's desolation is powerful and deeply felt. But as he moves on, Bell can be too self-conscious, his structures and intentions too naked. A long chapter on the "cell" is written in the fashion of interwoven sketches. The intention, it seems, is to create a dossier, a compendium of motives that will somehow explain the cell's apocalyptic mission. But the form Bell chooses here feels too deliberate and "written" and the motives themselves too "created."

Bell also relies too much on the *New York Post*. Strangely, and perhaps sadly, that tabloid—"HEADLESS MAN IN TOPLESS BAR"—has been mined endlessly in recent years. The shock appeal is long gone. Bell devotes a whole chapter to "The State of the Earth According to the New York Post" and the effect is, once more, too self-conscious, too much of an interruption and "idea," not enough a true part of the novel.

Bell struggles with his voice at times, relying excessively on a stilted irony. The prose is sometimes clogged with similes, redundancies and the occasional mistake: "In the passenger seat was Billy Morris, older and heavier than Henderson and far less trim.'' Or ''Rita Jenrette, ex-wife of a discredited US senator . . .'' (Mr. Jenrette was a congressman.) There are passages here of real brilliance; the descriptions of Brooklyn and Larkin are full of fire. But the lapses hurt. In general, Bell's best, most controlled writing so far, has appeared in short stories such as **''The Naked Lady,''** which was published in *Best American Short Stories 1984.*

But ambition can sometimes carry a work, and ambition certainly makes *Waiting for the End of the World* well worth reading. (pp. 3-4)

> *David Remnick, ''The Bomb beneath Times Square,'' in* Book World—The Washington Post, *September 1, 1985, pp. 3-4.*

DAVID MONTROSE

[With *Waiting for the End of the World*] Madison Smartt Bell has obviously sought to produce a latter-day version of Dostoevsky's *The Possessed,* albeit on a smaller and far less complex scale. Larkin is his equivalent of Stavrogin; Simon Rohnstock, the organizer of the cell, corresponds to Verkhovensky. As in his first novel, *The Washington Square Ensemble,* plot is conspicuously subordinate to character and atmospherics. In that book, narration was shared among the novel's five exotic principals, and the resulting interplay of vigorously discrete voices communicated rich impressions of personalities and locations. *Waiting for the End of the World* is told by an omniscient narrator, and the difference is considerable. For one thing, the recounting voice is rather flat and colourless, nowhere more so than in the sixty pages which document the life-

histories of the cell-members, charting their gradual convergence. . . .

Where the novel differs most significantly from its predecessor, though, is in its mediocre characterization. Bell devotes a substantial amount of space to Larkin's disordered state of mind without ever achieving much in the way of psychological penetration: he does not come alive as either the spiritual bankrupt who welcomes the prospect of Armageddon or, latterly, as the redeemed man who rids the Bowery bums of the devil he has inadvertently brought into their midst (the strangler who preys on them) and thwarts the cell's designs. As for Rohnstock: the reader obtains little sense of the presumed ardour that has induced him to dedicate most of his adulthood to preparing for active engagement in the ''revolutionary struggle''. Apparently intended to be cold, ruthless and masterful, he leaves an impression of mere bloodlessness. In consequence, his dealings with the rest of the cell are rendered implausible. Apart from Larkin—who is involved for reasons of his own—their paramount loyalty is not to an ideal but to Rohnstock himself. And his dominance rests on a purely notional attribute, his charismatic personality.

Bell's concentration on character denotes serious intent: his aim is to anatomize the circumstances that create violent deeds instead of simply providing details of those deeds. Execution, however, not intent, is what counts: a poor serious novel, like this one, is still a poor novel.

> *David Montrose, ''Skid-Row Subversives,'' in* The Times Literary Supplement, *No. 4312, November 22, 1985, p. 1310.*

John (Gerard) Braine

1922-1986

English novelist, dramatist, scriptwriter, and journalist.

With the overwhelming critical and popular success of his first novel, *Room at the Top* (1957), Braine was hailed as one of the most notable young British authors of the 1950s. He is often associated with the ''Angry Young Men,'' a group of British writers whose literary output reflected the heightened social consciousness of post-World War II England. The works of authors affiliated with this group, including Kingsley Amis, John Osborne, and Alan Sillitoe, typically feature young, disillusioned characters who strike out against social inequities that are attributed to England's rigid class structure. The protagonist of *Room at the Top*, Joe Lampton, breaks away from his working-class background and gains the respectability he seeks by marrying his wealthy employer's daughter. At the novel's end, however, having rejected the woman he truly loved and sacrificed his humanity for power and materialistic gain, Lampton becomes bitterly dissatisfied with his newly-acquired social status. In its sequel, *Life at the Top* (1962), Braine further details Lampton's disillusionment with his social position and his attempts to lead a life based on conventional family values. These works, like all of Braine's fiction, are written in a clear, journalistic prose style which heightens the chilling realism of his plots. *Room at the Top* and *Life at the Top* were adapted for film.

While none of Braine's subsequent works have elicited the praise that was accorded *Room at the Top,* most of his later novels have gained moderate critical and popular attention. In addition to their shrewd social observations, many of these works feature recurring themes. Catholicism, for example, provides the moral framework for *The Jealous God* (1965) and *The Crying Game* (1968). *The Jealous God* concerns a man who suffers emotional anguish because his Catholic faith forbids him to marry the divorced woman he loves, and *The Crying Game* (1968) focuses on a Catholic journalist who becomes involved in an immoral lifestyle but eventually returns to his earlier values. Adultery is another prevalent subject in Braine's work. In *Stay with Me till Morning* (1970), the protagonist discovers his wife's infidelity and subsequently engages in several affairs; he eventually leaves home but returns after suffering a heart attack. The husband in *Waiting for Sheila* (1976) is aware of his wife's philandering yet chooses to ignore her trysts. *One and Last Love* (1981) concerns a man and a woman who seek happiness with each other outside of their unfulfilling marriages.

Braine has recently written sequels to two of his works. *The Two of Us* (1984), which continues the story introduced in *Stay with Me till Morning,* was praised for its accurate evocation of the Yorkshire landscape and society. *These Golden Days* (1985), which features an aging writer who has never repeated the remarkable success of his first novel, portrays the romance begun in *One and Last Love.* Critics noted similarities between Braine's career and that of the protagonist of *These Golden Days.* Braine is also the author of the espionage novels *The Pious Agent* (1975) and *Finger of Fire* (1977) and a biography of British author J. B. Priestley.

© *Jerry Bauer*

(See also *CLC,* Vols. 1, 3; *Contemporary Authors,* Vols. 1-4, rev. ed.; *Contemporary Authors New Revision Series,* Vol. 1; and *Dictionary of Literary Biography,* Vol. 15.)

WHITNEY BALLIETT

Most first novels are hot-faced attempts to kick off the clodhoppers of adolescence, which is the sort of struggle best finished within the bosom of the family. But Mr. Braine already knows just how much prodding the priceless luck of his own creativity can take. There is no rheumy poetic prose in his [*Room at the Top*]. There is very little sound from the ropes and pulleys that get characters into rooms, seated, their knees crossed, and their cigarettes lit. His flashbacks and descriptions do not intrude like misplaced whales. Mr. Braine is also at home with a knowledge that most novelists never even dream of—the indispensable lubricating powers of humor. His subject matter—a young, lowborn English accountant, Joe Lampton, who gains the world and loses his soul—is squarely in the line of the great English social novels. Although Mr. Braine deals largely with his own generation, he unfailingly regards it with a buoyant detachment that would be remarkable in a writer three times his age. Where Dickens, for one, often tended, because of personal difficulties, to view the social struggles around him with a myopic and nervous sentimentality, Mr. Braine, like E. M. Forster, calmly dons corrective bifocals on the first page and never takes them off. He is fully aware that the slow, tangled process of a lower class pushing upward, like bubbles in a swamp, is in reality a series of shamelessly materialistic maneuvers. At the same time, he is aware that all oneupmanship, no matter how cruel, is inevitably funny and, as a result, deserving of mercy. When the angles of his vision are miraculously brought together in the last chapter, the effect is of classical tragedy, inside out: Joe Lampton, whose only nobility is honesty, is destroyed by self-knowledge. But the dominant tone of the book, which is written in a deft, almost journalistic prose, full of the sort of bounding images that no present writer in English can escape thanking Dickens for, is a loping nuttiness that comes out time and again. . . . (p. 186)

Lampton, the narrator, resembles someone who has just been for a brisk, cold walk in the woods and has settled comfortably down, scarlet-cheeked and tingling, to a fire and a drink. He is also, like Holden Caulfield, the hero of J. D. Salinger's *Catcher in the Rye,* one of the few appealing heroes in contemporary fiction, which already has its share of Queegs and Snopeses. He is twenty-five, handsome, fair-haired, and an expert accountant when he takes a job in the municipal government of Warley, a small, slightly industrialized town set pleasantly on the moors of northern England. He has come from Dufton, a sluggish, gloomy town, the only child of lower-middle-class parents, both killed six years before in the Second World War. (Mr. Braine neatly skirts a hazard that even James was guilty of; he carefully fills in the background of his major figures, lest they float meaninglessly around, fragments of virtue or evil, in the no man's land between author and reader.) He brings with him, in addition to a few clothes and eight hundred pounds in savings, a couple of ironclad hopes: that there will be no Zombies in Warley, and that, as a result, he will have an excellent chance of making his fortune, quite possibly by marrying it. (A Zombie, to Lampton, is anyone who, in a small-town way, is pompous, stupid, dull, greedy, and so forth.) If he succeeds, it will be a stunning victory over the Lampton-Lufford Report on Love, an ingenious system of social classification invented in Dufton by Lampton and Charles Lufford, his best friend, as a safety valve for their frustrations. The report grades men and women according to their earning powers and their correlated sexual energies. It is a first-rate instance of Mr. Braine's peculiar prankishness. . . . (pp. 186, 188)

Shortly after his arrival in Warley, . . . Lampton meets Susan Brown. . . . Susan turns out to be a Grade Two girl, whose father, a local magnate, is worth easily a hundred thousand pounds. Lampton courts her industriously despite the social odds, her inexperience and hesitancy as a lover, and her use of such words as "squiffy" and "squoo." In the meantime, treading water, he acquires a mistress, Alice Aisgill, an attractive but rapidly fading woman, unhappily married and nine years his senior. (Mr. Braine handles their affair—particularly four days in a cottage by the sea—with delicate and touching realism.) Lampton precariously balances his ambitions against his lust until, as such things will, the situation becomes almost ungovernable. He is rescued by his own folly. Mr. Brown, Susan's father, collars him and—part fairy godfather, part ogre—tells him he must marry Susan because she is pregnant (Lampton has finally stilled her fears), gives him his blessing because he regards him as a plucky youth, and sets him up in business,

starting at a thousand pounds a year. The alternative, Brown suggests, is Lampton's departure from Warley. Lampton decides immediately and with his eyes wide open. He gives up Alice, whom he realizes he has genuinely grown to love, as quickly and painlessly as if he were extracting a baby tooth. The aftereffects take up the last, and longest, chapter, in which Mr. Braine abruptly drops his comic mask to deliver a masterpiece of nightmarish horror. After their final meeting, Alice gets into her car and drives straight into a stone wall, dying a slow and terrible death. Lampton promptly goes on a monumental bender, in which he makes love to a chippy in an empty lot and gets into a fight in a back alley. He is rescued by two friends of Susan, who hustle him, bleeding and filthy, into their car. The end of their conversation, which is the end of the book, is indelibly poignant and damning. In its last sentence, just eight words long, Mr. Braine suddenly and masterfully translates his story of small-town mishaps into a horrible universal truth. . . . (pp. 188-89)

Ten years later—the entire book is a recollection of Lampton's early days in Warley—he knows dully that he, too, is dead. He has, in fact, become a Successful Zombie, who no longer feels, sees, perceives, or cares. . . . He has not fooled himself for a second. That, precisely, is why, contrary to all schoolbook morality, one cherishes him. (p. 189)

Whitney Balliett, "The Successful Zombie and the Grade Two Girl," in The New Yorker, *Vol. XXXIII, No. 36, November 2, 1957, pp. 186, 188-89.*

THE TIMES LITERARY SUPPLEMENT

Room at the Top was a sustained and most competent piece of story-telling, all-of-a-piece and written in a consistent and compelling style wholly suited to its subject. It was an immensely successful book about Success, and in [*The Vodi*] Mr. Braine has perhaps been over-anxious not to repeat himself. . . . [He] seems to have decided, not quite justifiably, that the only possible subject for his next book must be—Failure.

The hero, Dick Corvey, is a patient in a tuberculosis sanatorium, allergic to antibiotics, likely—and even willing—to die. His will to live is restored by an affair with a pretty nurse; meanwhile, his unsuccessful career until early middle-age is related in a series of flashbacks. He has been haunted throughout his life by a childhood fantasy of Evil: a race of malevolent beings known as the Vodi, ruled by a hideous ogress called Nelly. He recovers from his illness, and the Vodi seem to be exorcized; then the nurse, who has half-reciprocated his affection, decides to marry her rich careerist lover after all. A tragic ending seems inevitable: the loss of Dick's regained will to live, his relapse and death. He decides, however, to compound with his destiny (or the Vodi), and to accept a second-best solution: an affair with a less attractive nurse and, when he is discharged as cured, a job as a male nurse in the sanatorium. Here it might have been better to leave him; but Mr. Braine, having decided to write a novel about failure, cannot bear that the failure shall be complete, and the bitch-goddess beckons once again. The ending, though feasible enough, seems slightly contrived and rather perfunctory.

This book has not the drive and confidence of its predecessor, but is in some respects a more interesting novel. The idea of the Vodi was a good one in itself, but Mr. Braine's treatment of it is lacking in the imaginative intensity required to make such fantasies convincing; he is better at social observation, and here, as in *Room at the Top,* this is often brilliant, if sometimes rather baffling. . . . His chief danger is a certain over-facility, which, at times, degenerates into the slickness of a strip-cartoon; at his best, however, he is an honest and intelligent observer of the social scene.

"Combating Malevolence," in The Times Literary Supplement, No. 3012, November 20, 1959, p. 673.

GRANVILLE HICKS

John Braine's reputation as one of England's Angry Young Men rests primarily on his first novel, **Room at the Top,** which was published in 1957 and was made into what I have been told is an excellent moving picture. The novel's hero, Joe Lampton, is a young proletarian who hates his working-class background and is determined to lay hold of the good things of this life. The desire to get ahead economically and socially is a common ambition and is in many quarters regarded as a worthy one. More than half a century ago, for instance, Horatio Alger made a fortune by exploiting the theme. Braine's treatment, moreover, is a little like Alger's in that Joe achieves his ambition not by hard work nor even by ruthlessness, but by being lucky enough to attract the attention of a rich man. But whereas the typical Alger hero does this by saving the rich man's daughter from runaway horses or some other menace, Joe does it by getting the rich man's daughter pregnant.

There is another difference: Alger leaves us with the assurance that his hero is going to live happily ever after, but at the end of **Room at the Top** we know very well that Joe is bound to have a miserable time. **Life at the Top** . . . describes his miseries. Ten years after the end of the earlier book, Joe has what looks like a good job, a large house in the best part of the city, two cars, and many of the other luxuries he had dreamed of. But his father-in-law dominates not only his economic life but also his political life and to a great extent his domestic life, and his mother-in-law never leaves him unaware of his vulgar origins. His wife, Susan, is beautiful, and often they find one another desirable; but they bicker constantly, and sometimes there are serious quarrels. His son has been sent, on the grandparents' insistence, to the right kind of preparatory school, and Joe feels that Harry has been completely alienated from him. He has only one solace, his four-year-old daughter, Barbara, whom he adores in a fashion verging on the maudlin.

If this summary reminds readers of stories they have encountered in the women's magazines, they are not so far wrong as I could wish. The man—or woman—who is handsomely endowed with material possessions and yet is unhappy is one of the stock characters of contemporary popular fiction. Of course, this cliché, like all clichés, bears a certain relation to reality; there are, as we say, people like that, lots of them. But the popular fiction writer achieves only a superficial verisimilitude, never tells us anything more about such people than we already know, never comes anywhere near to the heart of the matter. And I am afraid that much the same can be said of Braine.

Joe tells the story himself, as he did in **Room at the Top,** and he lets us know what he is feeling. Often he indulges in self-reproach. (p. 20)

Self-reproach yields easily to self-pity. At the outset he tells us: "I felt weighed down by things, all the material possessions which had accumulated during ten years of marriage." At the end he says: "Looking back, I saw nothing but struggle: struggle to reach Dufton Grammar School, struggle to pass my matriculation, struggle to become a clerk in the Treasurer's at

Dufton, struggle to marry Susan and the long struggle, which only since summer I've known to be so, of marriage itself." "I've had to sweat for everything I've got," he tells his mother-in-law, and apparently he believes it. (pp. 20-1)

In the months that the novel describes—the crucial period in Joe's marriage—there are business and political complications, adultery on his part and adultery on Susan's, a series of crises. There is even a crisis in his relationship with his daughter, which, since it is about the only surprise the book affords, I won't go into. But in the end it turns out that Joe has grown up, and if Braine doesn't have nerve enough to provide a conventional happy ending, he comes up with what will do, in these uncertain times, as a reasonable substitute. "With no warning," Joe reports in the closing sentences, "through no conscious effort, I was happy, happier than I had been since childhood. It could not last, it was already evaporating as I began to be grateful for it; but I knew it would come again."

Joe Lampton, it is clear, does not understand himself; and if Braine has any deeper insight, he has not found a way in his handling of the first-person narrative to reveal it. As a document the book has some interest, for it shows that a confusion of values that we tend to think of as peculiarly American can be found in contemporary England; indeed, except for superficial matters, life over there seems very much like life over here. What is depressing is that Braine appears to believe that he has risen above the confusion, when he is as much its victim as any slick novelist you can name. In my self-interview . . . I named John Braine as one of the English writers worth watching; I may as well say here and now that I was wrong. (p. 21)

Granville Hicks, "Too Much and Not Enough," in Saturday Review, Vol. XLV, No. 40, October 6, 1962, pp. 20-1.

PETER BUITENHUIS

[In **The Jealous God**] Mr. Braine shows that he is capable of making a journey beyond the reaches of his own immediate experience, which is the hallmark of a developing novelist. **The Jealous God** is set firmly in the familiar English North Country but the main character is a 30-year-old Roman Catholic schoolteacher, Vincent Dunvargan, descendant of an Irish immigrant family that still keeps up the ties of blood. . . .

He meets and falls in love with the beautiful Laura, a non-Catholic. It is not until he is deeply involved with her that he finds out that she is a divorcée and thus, in the eyes of the church, still married. . . . He vacillates back and forth between her bed and his religious scruples until the final, somewhat contrived and melodramatic resolution.

The most notable and successful aspect of the novel is its sense of the family group. In typically English fashion, the various sons and their families and the surviving grandparent live in or around the same town; their lives overlap emotionally as well as physically. This situation infinitely complicates the moral problem that Vincent faces. The all-embracing family context is admirably represented by Mr. Braine in a number of scenes in houses, clubs and pubs. There are savage confrontations and bitter recognitions, accusations and regrets. The reader gets the impression of life lived on every side which, as Henry James pointed out, is the chief function of the novel.

Mr. Braine himself, somewhat surprisingly, refers to James in a comment on one of the scenes. An untidy quarrel quiets down until it becomes, in Vincent's eyes, "if not exactly drawing-room comedy, a scene from a novel by Henry James, civilized and complex, the nastiness and rawness kept under fur wraps.'' Not much in this novel is kept under wraps, but Mr. Braine has learnt from the Old Master how to control and order his narrative through the central consciousness of his hero, as well as through the precision of his style. The structure of the novel, too, is largely scenic. The conflicts are objectified and dramatized; they are seldom discussed in the abstract and even more rarely meditated upon by Vincent himself.

This virtue is in fact carried to a fault. It is true that Vincent is supposed to be incapable of feeling enough, is even accused by Laura of not being a real person at all. Actually he is too often a spectator, infuriatingly passive at times when his situation calls for decision. If Mr. Braine had gone into his consciousness further, his reader would at least be able to understand why Vincent is a sort of mute, inglorious Hamlet. It may be that, although venturing into Greene pastures, Mr. Braine felt himself ill-equipped to make a deep analysis of the Catholic conscience. . . .

Despite the hollowness at the core, however, the flesh of the novel is solid. Mr. Braine has an eye for human and other detail which, although at times starry-eyed, is perceptive and persuasive.

Peter Buitenhuis, ''Vincent and Laura,'' in The New York Times Book Review, *March 7, 1965, p. 4.*

CLIVE JORDAN

It's odd that new novels by John Braine and Colin Wilson should raise the spectres of the Angry Young Men from graveyards of dead newsprint, just as we drift backwards into conservatism. Jimmy Porter, Jim Dixon, Joe Lampton . . . how remote all those determinedly post-Orwell proletarian cult-figures from the later 1950s sound.

And yet they served their turn. Round about the time the last clarion-calls of imperialism crackled through the rusty field-telephones of Suez, it was obvious that something had to change. The journalists and media-men put their heads together and came up with one of the answers: the Angry Young Men. Like Harold Wilson's 1970 majority, they never really existed except in the mass media. Osborne, Amis, Wain, Braine, Colin Wilson—it wasn't long before, like the Beatles, they turned out to be playing different tunes. But what they did have in common—no-nonsense, anti-traditional, anti-aristocratic, vigorously sexy—people wanted. Having helped to define a mood, the Angry Young Men were made to express it.

It's possible that John Braine's *Stay With Me Till Morning* [published in the United States as *The View from Tower Hill*] still expresses the mood of his generation in the 1970s. There's not much left in this sixth novel of the go-getting ruthlessness that made Joe Lampton seem so 'modern' in *Room at the Top*. And Braine's early support for Labour has turned into ferocious, reactionary conservatism. *Stay With Me Till Morning* belongs to the dogbitten middle years—disillusioned, backward-looking, pragmatic in human relationships. (pp. 920-21)

The style, like the subject-matter, might be described as 'Northern Materialism'. Braine puts his words together solidly, bluntly, with no charm and precious little distinction. He describes heavy petting with the same leaden neutrality as the furniture or the new car. He's still fascinated by the marks of status—the brand of perfume, type of car, newspaper—but as keys to character these status-symbols strike me as only a shade deeper

than the flashy automatic cataloguing of Ian Fleming. The most interesting element in the new book is Clive Lendrick's flight from 'materialism' into 'art'. This messy attempt to define freedom hints at deep dissatisfactions behind Braine's cantankerous public face: animals in traps tend to roar loudest. (p. 921)

Clive Jordan, ''Dogbitten,'' in New Statesman, *Vol. 79, No. 2050, June 26, 1970, pp. 920-21.*

NORA SAYRE

The View From Tower Hill has no ambitious manipulators, and the view of women is thoroughly humane—if their skulls are empty, so are the men's. Mr. Braine seems to be saying that money is dull and that sex can be upsetting. Clive and Robin Lendrick are a decent, amiable couple; snug in the provinces, they have always lived ''according to plan,'' have ''kept to the rules,'' appreciating their ''solid prosperity.'' After 20 years of marriage, both dread change and yet begin to itch for it. They have their first affairs. . . .

Throughout, sex is compulsive, rather than expansive; relief matters more than passion. Neither husband nor wife seems especially stung by the other's freelancing—until their marriage nearly collapses, and Robin discovers that she can't marry her lover and Clive realizes that he'd hate to marry his. He has a convenient heart attack, which requires him to return to his wife, although he continues to see Ruth. It's all quite comfortable. . . .

This is a puzzling book; one can't quite tell what's intended. Parts of it read like a repudiation of *Room at the Top*. But is it meant to be a moral novel—a quiet indictment of squaredom and the headless accumulation of goods? Perhaps it was designed as a plain documentary—which stresses that life can be as violent and as messy for the cautious as for the reckless. Or it may mean that conventional creatures shouldn't lurch outside their fences. Still, it's useful to have to remember that such traditional persons weren't invented by Nixon, and that the seventies are painful for them. Admittedly, they seem rather remote—perhaps because they're constantly ignored: especially in fiction. But their vulnerability and distress are reminders that urban coolness and carelessness are forms of self-protection, rather than freedom.

Nora Sayre, ''Braine in Bed, Drury on Mars, Jones in Paris, Buechner in Dixie: 'The View from Tower Hill','' in The New York Times Book Review, *February 14, 1971, p. 6.*

PAUL THEROUX

In one of the bibulous little tutorials in [*The Queen of a Distant Country*], about an older woman's influence on a young writer, the woman says apropos his fiction, ''Do not ever let me catch you thinking.'' Tom Metfield ignores some of her advice, but to judge from *The Queen of a Distant Country*, which he narrates, he has taken this bit of wisdom to heart. There is no evidence of thinking anywhere in it, only many passages of smug reflection about the cozy agony of being a successful writer. . . .

Tom is unschooled, uncouth and from a humble home in darkest Yorkshire, but he spends enough time scratching in the branch library to get the itch to write. . . .

Tom is a precocious writer, but admits to being rather backward sexually, and it is probably the curse of the branch library that causes him to fumble his first attempt at love with Cora. "I found a Petrarchan sonnet assembling itself in my head," he writes, "at the moment I entered her." The girl conceives, aborts, and drops out of his life, a disappearing-act repeated more than once in this novel, which is long on self-cherishing narration, but short on everything else, including the qualities Tom says he admires most in fiction; plot, character and "color."

So short, in fact, that a potentially interesting character like Miranda . . . is prevented from meeting our gaze for most of the way. She drinks; she chirps her advice, and we get glimpses of her utterly sordid existence, but invariably Tom's—or rather, Mr. Braine's—lip-smacking style puts her into total eclipse as he goes on to add new meanings to the word triteness.

Throughout, Tom mentions his first novel, gives us a rundown on its theme and message and praises it to the skies. But you don't have to be Laurence Harvey to deduce that Tom is talking about **Room at the Top** and that this present novel is nothing less than a cry from the heart of Mr. Braine in search of a character he, manifestly, has not yet found. To write a widely-acclaimed novel is a good thing; to write about acclamation in this tedious way is bad manners.

> *Paul Theroux, "Close Friends, Woman's Influence, Vegetarians, Femme Fatale," in* The New York Times Book Review, *May 27, 1973, p. 16.*

VICTORIA GLENDINNING

The Pious Agent is a spy story set in [Mr Braine's] own home territory of Woking and district. It is based on the statistic that there is an annual total in England of about 500 undetected murders, and on the fact that since 1961 no Soviet agent has been brought to trial in this country. Mr Braine deduces or imagines a secret service department whose task it is to bump off Russian spies on the quiet. The organisation takes its code-names from C. S. Lewis's Narnia books, which adds a little tone. The hero is killer-agent Xavier Aloysius Flynn, who combines murderous patriotism, devout Catholicism and enthusiastic sexuality with no conflicts, thanks to repeated Acts of Contrition. There is also a nice character called the Disposer, who deals with the corpses in a donnishly disapproving way.

Mr Braine, like Flynn, does a good professional job, and springs some genuinely surprising surprises. But there is rather a lot of completely unfunctional matter in the way of sub-Bond sartorial detail; and what is much odder is that he seems to have developed an obsession for floor-coverings—no one enters a room without our attention being drawn to the deep-pile Axminsters (these seem very popular), the red Turkey, or some old lino of which Flynn is particularly fond. It's a good read, however, of a routinely competent kind; and Mr Braine conveys vividly a Britain crawling with hostile elements, which include a leftist industrial sabotage group called FIST. Slight paranoia makes for good thrillers. (pp. 782-83)

> *Victoria Glendinning, "Seeing Red," in* New Statesman, *Vol. 89, No. 2308, June 13, 1975, pp. 782-83.*

NEWGATE CALLENDAR

In one respect, **The Pious Agent** is almost a caricature of the genre. Braine, one feels, has read everything of such writers as Deighton and le Carré, and then has applied their formulae to this book. There are no surprises in **The Pious Agent**. Quite the contrary: everything is predictable, and this especially ap-

plies to the ending. One has read it so many times before, and looks forward to reading it so many times in the future.

What saves **The Pious Agent** is its style. Braine is a smooth, sophisticated writer. He can take his killer agent—a stereotype by now—and make him talk and act like a real human being. Nor are his Russians caricatures. There are a few things, however, that do not come off. The memo device (or is it a phone call? no matter) that starts the book and that is used here and there later on, is hard to take. . . . Anyway, derivative and eclectic as **The Pious Agent** is, it nevertheless is an exciting and stimulating read. (pp. 62-3)

> *Newgate Callendar, in a review of "The Pious Agent," in* The New York Times Book Review, *May 2, 1976, pp. 62-3.*

FERDINAND MOUNT

[In **Waiting for Sheila,** the] terrain is unmistakable. We are in Joe Lampton country, in a world of unnecessary unpleasantness where power and sex are the only two currencies. Jim Seathwaite, general manager of Droylsden's department store, getting quietly drunk by himself amid his consumer durables in Sugar Hill, a Surrey commuter town, conducts a probe into his sexual past to uncover and operate on some deep-lying wound. Why is he waiting alone in his desirable residence for Sheila his desirable wife? How has he come to be where and what he is? At each turn of the plot the scalpel goes a little deeper. The wound is exposed, cauterized and roughly stitched up again. Patient discharged, not cured.

This is John Braine's first straight novel since his manual, **Writing a Novel.** It is a first-class working model of his own method. Like Jim Seathwaite's consumer durables, everything is of sound quality: plot, relationships and, notably, the celebration of sex—a lyrical interruption in the otherwise dour tone of the narrative. The characters are solid, consistent (with the exception of Henry, the elderly solicitor who we are told on page 104 is immaculate and unemotional, but turns up in person on page 146, drunk, dishevelled and maudlin). Like all Mr Braine's work, the book is dotted with sharp observations and sudden pleasures.

Yet there is something lowering about the overall effect. Is this because life in Sugar Hill and Droylsden's is bound to be a depleted kind of life, just as Jim's sad fumbles and glimpses of French knickers are a depleted kind of sex? . . . Jim Seathwaite's unhappiness has the kind of traumatic origin you would expect it to have. The revelation surprises the reader, but the surprise is to do with recognizing not so much a previously unexamined reality as a classifiable type of fiction. In his manual, Mr Braine advises would-be novelists to aim to produce not a best-seller but a "publishable" novel. Mr Braine's talent is so abundant, his skills now in such full bloom that it is tempting to hope that one day soon he will write an "unpublishable" book for a change, 700 pages long, rampantly self-indulgent, violently inconsequential—and irresistible.

> *Ferdinand Mount, "The Durable Consumer," in* The Times Literary Supplement, *No. 3873, June 4, 1976, p. 665.*

ROSALIND WADE

John Braine's talents [in **Waiting for Sheila**] are rooted in the most explicit approach to the sexual experiences of his characters, about which he contrives to generate a kind of steamy excitement. When we first meet Jim Seathwaite, the affluent manager of a Surrey department store, he is snugly ensconced in his luxury villa awaiting the return of his attractive wife, Sheila. It soon becomes clear that despite his apparent self-sufficiency, Jim's reliance on Sheila borders on the pathological. The scope of the novel is to explain, by means of numerous flashbacks, the origin of his dependence.

Beginning with Jim Seathwaite's boyhood in dreary Droylesdon, he is presented as a bright lad, though blighted early by the half-understood affair between his mother and uncle. With the untimely death of Jim's father, Mrs. Seathwaite is free to indulge her nymphomaniac tendencies, the realisation of which scars Jim to an extent she is incapable of understanding. Mrs. Seathwaite emerges as a woman frightening in her hedonistic sensuality, and it is not surprising that Jim makes a bold attempt to seek release from the buried nightmare through a series of casual entanglements. Unfortunately, periods of sexual incompetence convince him that he is impotent. And so he might have remained, but for the emergence into his life of Sheila, his boss's mistress and secretary. Sheila is a woman capable of powerful tenderness. She also nourishes an iron determination to achieve married status. Rather surprisingly, she cares enough about Jim to coax back confidence in his manhood, so that he becomes the father of two children. Inevitably, he finds himself completely dependent on her willingness to maintain him as a normally functioning male, despite her determination to bestow her favours as and when she pleases. And so the novel ends as it begins, with Jim waiting uncomplainingly for Sheila to return from one of her nocturnal 'outings.'

This absorbing if frequently squalid sequence of events is brusquely unfolded, sometimes with crudity but always with humour and commonsense. And if in the final pages no solution is offered to Jim's dilemma this is no reproach to the author; rather the reverse, for Jim Seathwaite is seen as a man permanently maimed by his wounding childhood experiences. (pp. 214-15)

Rosalind Wade, in a review of "Waiting for Sheila," in Contemporary Review, *Vol. 229, No. 1329, October, 1976, pp. 214-15.*

MAURICE RICHARDSON

[*Finger of Fire* is the second] instalment of Braine's Bonded Brainchild, Xavier Flynn.... His department is more deeply penetrated than ever by the KGB.... But he soldiers on in London and Los Angeles frustrating FIST, a new international organisation of diabolist fellow travellers threatening to burn up Piccadilly Circus by laser beam. Enough torture to fill Foxe's *Book of Martyrs.* Veiled identities all over the place and a story-line like St Vitus dancing the polka, Lesbians a speciality. Curiosities are all very well, but Braine must control these brainstorms of his if he is to remain readable.

Maurice Richardson, "Crime Ration," in The Observer, *June 12, 1977, p. 24.*

JAMES BROCKWAY

I have been puzzled to find out whether [*Finger of Fire*] is so bad and boring because John Braine knows they *have* to be to sell, whether it is because he has simply botched the job, or whether his book is intended as a parody of the boring traditions of the spy novel—all blood, bullets and ballistics and ads for cars, cognac and cigars.... Clear all this away, and prayer-muttering, RC, Irish hero-spy Xavier Flynn's occasional outbursts of 'Goddamit, if only I could kill someone' or 'I think that I should kill someone' (accompanied by an Irish grin), and one might find some sort of story somewhere, I suspect, although by page 135, where I gave up, I was thinking what Flynn actually says on this page: 'I don't know and I don't care'. Millions, however, do, and a sizeable proportion of those millions will buy this book and stick it on their shelf like other religious people who used to buy plaster Virgin Marys to decorate their homes.

I know I must not say anything more about *Finger of Fire,* except to express the hope that the pain spreading from Flynn's arm to his chest in the last passage of this novel will reverse direction, and prove to be acute cardiac trouble, causing death to strike swiftly and soon. (p. 63)

James Brockway, "Memento Mori," in Books and Bookmen, *Vol. 23, No. 2, November, 1977, pp. 62-3.*

PETER KEMP

[In Braine's books, sexual] performance is a subject of obsessive concern: being outclassed at it drives one man to suicide in *The Jealous God,* while the shortcomings of another provoke a flurry of macho tattle in [*One and Last Love*].... There is a pervasive air of sexual and artistic narcissism—as ... *One and Last Love,* emphatically shows.

Its hero-narrator, Harnforth, a fifty-six-year-old novelist from Yorkshire, represents Braine's concept of the artist—an amalgam of he-man, money-box and seer, held together by a thick cable of self-satisfaction. Aping Hemingway, he announces he is going to "tell the truth" and "tell it straight": he will be "setting down honestly a real love story". In so far as the emotion concerned is self-love, he is accurate. *One and Last Love* documents unswervingly a man's doting infatuation with himself....

"If you can't see sex with a certain wonder, it's better not to write about it at all", Braine sternly declared in *Writing a Novel.* True to this, a more high-minded note sometimes intrudes into his novel's documented rompings: "we make love to each other as the people we are and not as bodies". Fellatio becomes "sacred", and men in a strip-club watching "a naked girl writhing on a divan with a life-sized black dummy with a ten-inch phallus" are really "worshipping".

For all this sporadic sexual sanctimoniousness, the book gravitates more often towards the earthy. Most of the women Harnforth comes in contact with aren't much more than mobile mammaries. All that stands out about them is their breasts.... And the characters are further ballasted against any tendency to drift off into the empyrean by those bundles of brand names that are Braine's stock-in-trade as a novelist. Male fantasy merges into mail-order catalogue as ... he starts scattering the labels. Sulka's, given an appreciative mention as long ago as *Room at the Top,* is still being patronized. Axminster proves widely serviceable: "dark red" in Harnforth's love-nest, "warm blue" in a story he plans, "blue-green-and-white" in his home. His clothes have tags all over them—from his Viyella shirt down to his Bally shoes. Braggi is his favourite toiletry. And there is a splendid moment when we see him making an entrance at a Hampstead *soirée:* "I hand my Burberry to the maid at the door" ("If one of your characters owns a Burberry",

Braine explained in *Writing a Novel,* "it instantly imparts information about him").

In this novel, Harnforth . . . attracts recognition like a magnet. As he dines at the Gay Hussar, "Michael Foot passes my table and nods briefly at me". And outside the circle of "my friends of the *gens du monde*", tribute is even headier: a young man pours out fulsome appreciation in a Fleet Street pub; a German porno-*artiste* pleasingly displays her knowledge of his work.

Despite all the applause, however, there's a crater at the centre of the novel where Harnforth's creativity should be. Nothing he says or does suggests he is remotely literary; and much suggests the opposite. His supposedly sensitive incursions into poetic quotation, for example, often come to grief. He mangles the opening line of Hadrian's poem to his soul, "Animula vagula blandula", into "Anima blandula, vagula", and non-sensically garbles Ovid's line from the last moments of *Dr Faustus,* "lente, lente currite, noctis equi", into "Lente, lente, curres nocte". *One and Last Love*—its title itself a misquotation—is a strange production: a Portrait of the Artist, without the Artist. Despite the fawning commentary—"Your brain's racing away"—its hero never shows the slightest sign of literary responsiveness or skill. Novelists, Braine portentously declared in *Writing a Novel,* are "not . . . quite human". But Harnforth is as distant from real talent as he is from real life.

Peter Kemp, "Spilling the Secrets of Success," in The Times Literary Supplement, No. 4082, June 26, 1981, p. 719.

JOHN NAUGHTON

Strange what age does to writers. And success. In John Braine's case, it's beginning to look as if it is wearing him smooth, like a doorstep weathered by dripping water. At any rate [*One and Last Love*] is mellow and relaxed, self-celebratory in a quiet way, hovering on a knife-edge just this side of sentimentality.

It's about a writer, a successful middle-aged one, well into his second marriage and suddenly conscious that, as Samuel Johnson put it, such arrangements represent the triumph of hope over experience. But, since he loves his kids and basks in their affection, he doesn't rock the marital boat.

So . . . he takes a mistress? Not quite: he falls in love, just like people used to do before the war. The lady is, like him, a middle-aged writer, though apparently less successful. And they have a quiet affair, conducted through regular, leisurely afternoons in bed in a borrowed flat off Shaftesbury Avenue. The two lovers whisper quiet nothings to one another, but without any detectable irony, after which they part, and return amiably to their respective ménages for the evening.

In these hardbitten times, it is all most disconcerting. Not a trace of angst anywhere. Not a glimmer of biting sarcasm, or bluff Yorkshire wit. Not a single crack about North of Watford. Just a simple story of everyday love in Soho. It's filled in with a wealth of circumstantial detail—mainly about the physical trappings of success—Rolex watches, Lowry paintings, lunches in the Gay Hussar (complete with references to its real-life clientele), the Granada Ghia. And it's redolent with a sense of the enjoyment which London gives to many of its citizens, especially those who are not slaves to a desk.

What, one wonders, is up with Mr Braine? Is he losing his marbles? Has he forgotten his trademark—the sharpness which first lifted him on to the bestseller lists and later sustained

outbursts of rightist choler? What will they think up at t'Mill? Who cares: everyone has a right to at least one burst of sentiment.

John Naughton, "Mellow Braine," in The Listener, Vol. 106, No. 2718, July 2, 1981, p. 25.

PATRICK SKENE CATLING

John Braine writes with solid competence about bourgeois sin in the West Riding of Yorkshire in 1969. *The Two of Us* is the sort of well-made meticulously realistic social melodrama that Arnold Bennett might write if he were still at it today. A Charbury woollen mill supports the conventional wickedness (adultery, gambling) of two brothers of the firm's founding family and of some of their friends and neighbours. The mill makes high-grade Yorkshire worsted, and Braine makes high-grade Yorkshire dishonesty. He makes it entirely honestly and gives good value for money. The sets, characters, costumes and props are convincing, and they are disposed with a firm hand and moral consistency. The plot moves along with fatalistic inevitability, yet there may well be moments when the reader will wonder what is going to happen next.

Braine is a keen observer, and an apparently tireless recorder, of the material indicators of class and wealth in a small, prosperous manufacturing town in the North. He describes in detail the landscapes, the houses (exteriors and interiors, with furniture and fittings, fabrics and colours) and the people and their clothes, and specifies their cars, menus and brands of drinks, cigarettes and cigarette lighters. One gets to know what life in Charbury is really like, if you are one of the upwardly mobile swingers who appreciate what it means to indulge in a little *cinq à sept* in suburban Mirraton on Wednesdays. They call it *cinq à sept;* but it is obviously only a bit of ordinary slap and tickle, because Mirraton is not what it was.˙. . . Oh, dear. I'm afraid it is impossible to promise that this book will please *everybody* in the West Riding. Braine may not be a snob, but most of the people he writes about seem to be snobs. Perhaps that is the novel's message: most people are snobs, even in Yorkshire. (p. 29)

Patrick Skene Catling, "Revelations," in The Spectator, Vol. 252, No. 8126, April 7, 1984, pp. 28-9.

ROSALIND WADE

The Two of Us, is a sequel to *Stay with Me Til Morning,* and it is interesting to speculate how often a second instalment of a novel comes across satisfactorily. The problem is that the reader who comes freshly to the sequence is vaguely aware of having missed out on some vital clues.

So it is with *The Two of Us.* A nagging certainty lingers that the nerve-shattering affair between Robin Lendrick and Stephen Belgard, the strains of which for Robin's husband, Clive, in *Stay with Me Til Morning* resulted in a heart attack, was stronger stuff than we are offered in *The Two of Us.* It can be fascinating to view the participants in a major domestic drama some time after the event. And yet, in this case, the persistent and often tedious pursuit of love seems to be of very secondary importance.

The characters are doughty Yorkshire men and women, set against a background of J. B. Priestley country which John Braine also knows so well. Industrious managers and company promoters' wives discontented with themselves and their surroundings are presented in lengthy dialogues and thought sequences. Sometimes, it is difficult to keep their identities clearly in mind, yet in their limited way they are convincing, and the continued domination of t'mill, from which for centuries the nation has derived much of its wealth, is not to be belittled or ignored. Tasteless interior decor, heavy meals and indifference to international politics or the activities of the Arts Council do not detract from the power of a Yorkshire community. So at any rate admits Stephen Belgard, now a successful TV writer, returning in search of his 'roots' to the moors after a brief session in well-heeled Surrey. Inevitably, he and Robin resume their relationship. The reunion has a bitter-sweet quality and cannot be expected to last, since Stephen now has a wife and baby son.

The activities of the Lendricks' daughter, the curiously named Petronella, provide a sub-plot, although the rebellious teenager is not very convincing and merely provides yet another stereotype for the adolescent portrait gallery. Yet despite some misgivings and reservations there is much to enjoy and admire in *The Two of Us* with its more measured and objective view of the John Braine scene. It would be unfair to admit that we are still hoping for a return to the brash self-confidence of his first novel, *Room at the Top* which, during the early fifties, like John Osborne's *Look Back in Anger* and Kingsley Amis' *Lucky Jim* became part of the mind's furniture.

Rosalind Wade, in a review of "The Two of Us," in Contemporary Review, *Vol. 245, No. 1422, July, 1984, p. 45.*

FRANCIS KING

It is presumptuous of a reviewer to assume that, if a novel is written in the first person, then the narrator must be identified with its author. But in the case of *These Golden Days*, a sequel to his *One and Last Love,* John Braine seems deliberately to invite that presumption. . . .

Tim's first novel, a best-seller, appears, from his account of it, to be identical with Mr Braine's first novel, *Room at the Top,* also a best-seller. When Tim records the real-life events on which he based his novel—the older woman was far older, he himself came from the middle, not the working class, the death in a car accident was in fact his mother's—one is tempted to assume that these are real-life events in Mr Braine's story too. Perhaps, therefore, since Tim Harnforth and John Braine so often seem to be one and the same person, the most convenient way in which to refer to the narrator of this book will be as 'Jim'. (p. 32)

Jim's narrative ebbs and flows between the uncertainty of his past and the certainty of his new life with Vivien. In the past are his parents, the Irish mother who adores him, and the English father, a retiring schoolmaster, who seems always to feel constraint in the company of his clever, tough, thrusting son. There are relatives, each delineated with affection and humour. There are the two wives. . . . There are the children,

cruelly lost to him. In the present, there is, above all else, Vivien, who visits him whenever she can and who even goes away on holiday with him. There are also the friendly Hampstead neighbours, met over drinks or cups of coffee, and the local tradespeople. . . .

There is something both poignant and cheering in this story of how, as in a Victorian novel—and, after all, most of us would probably prefer to live a Victorian love-story than a modern one—a man in late middle age, washed up financially, creatively and emotionally, is redeemed by the love of a good woman. Admittedly, as when one is reading a Victorian novel, one has the vertiginous sensation that the whole edifice may at any moment disintegrate like something spun out of sugar; but that threat, though constantly present, is miraculously never realised.

As in all Mr Braine's novels, characters are often, in part at least, defined by the brands of goods that they use. This device, often derided by others, seems to me perfectly legitimate—Jim and Vivien, drinking Liebfraumilch with their joint of lamb are clearly people of a different kind from their Hampstead friend who lights her Gauloise cigarette with a gold Cartier lighter. As in all of Mr Braine's novels, too, sudden, surprising insights intermittently shoot up, like thorn bushes, from the otherwise level common of his prose—faces are as much a matter of fashion and choice as are clothes; it was the invention of the washing-machine that caused the disappearance of the detachable collar as an item of daily wear.

Whether we call him John, Tim or Jim, the character at the centre of this small, moving book strikes one, for all his occasional small vanities and self-deceptions, as essentially brave, decent and honourable. What, in effect, he is saying is 'Look, I have come through!', and one is glad that he can both say that and say it so persuasively. (p. 33)

Francis King, "So Far a Happy Ending," in The Spectator, *Vol. 255, No. 8204, October 5, 1985, pp. 32-3.*

MARGARET WALTERS

[*These Golden Days*] sets out to celebrate a fresh start in life, but its tone is embarrassingly personal. His writer-hero feels that, at 60, he's finally finding what he really wants: 'no mess, no disorder, no dirt.' He expatiates on the pleasures of the simple life in Hampstead village—clean underwear, oranges and cheese for breakfast, a trip to the coffee shop where a reader recognises and congratulates him, an undemanding love affair. But the real energy in the novel is in his bitter and obsessive outbursts against his former wife, and his pining for the big house he lost in the divorce settlement. The earnest claims to happiness sound a little implausible: the 'golden days' are overshadowed by the unassimilated past.

Margaret Walters, "Bombs and Blarney," in The Observer, *October 6, 1985, p. 25.*

Charles Bukowski

1920-

German-born American poet, novelist, and short story writer.

A prolific "underground" writer and a cult figure, Bukowski depicts the sordid urban environments of the socially downtrodden in his poetry and prose. Because he relies on emotion and imagination rather than intellect to inform his work and uses simple, direct language, violent and sexual imagery, and loose poetic structures, Bukowski is often considered anti-literary. While some critics find Bukowski's subject matter and style vulgar and offensive, others claim that by assuming an exaggerated masculine pose in which sexual bravado, alcohol abuse, and violence are routine, Bukowski is satirizing the machismo attitude. Bukowski's voice is strongly autobiographical and possesses, according to Thomas Broderick, a "rare humor that arises out of misery, pain, failure, and the inability to do anything about them." While critics have cited the Beats and modern confessionalists as influences on Bukowski's style, most consider his poetry unclassifiable.

Bukowski's verse is significant, according to John William Corrington, as a "poetry of surface." Corrington contends that Bukowski's poetry is concerned with "the color, texture and rhythm of modern life" and is not obscured by lofty ideals or theory. Bukowski's early poetry included in *Flower, Fist, and Bestial Wail* (1959), *Longshot Poems for Broke Players* (1961), and *Run with the Hunted* (1962) displays the major themes and interests he has explored throughout his career. These include a love of music and art, sexual adventurism and experimentation, and the abandonment and despair often experienced by the underemployed and socially rejected. *It Catches My Heart in Its Hands: New and Selected Poems, 1955-1963* (1963) and *Crucifix in a Deathhand: New Poems, 1963-1965* (1965) are among Bukowski's best-known works. With his recent collection, *War All the Time: Poems, 1981-1984* (1985), Bukowski's verse has become somewhat more subdued, but in his review of this volume, Kenneth Funsten maintained that Bukowski's altered style has not diminished the vitality and authenticity of his work.

Bukowski is best known as a poet, but his novels have also attracted critical attention. *Post Office* (1971), *Factotum* (1975), and *Ham on Rye* (1982) are autobiographical tales featuring the tragicomic adventures of a roguish character named Henry Chinaski, who lives in the same urban flophouses depicted in Bukowski's poetry. These novels are characterized by their energy, humor, and incisive observations. Bukowski has also written several collections of short stories, including *Erections, Ejaculations, Exhibitions, and General Tales of Ordinary Madness* (1972), *South of No North* (1973), and *Hot Water Music* (1983). Like his poems and novels, these stories explore themes of sexual promiscuity and urban depravity.

(See also *CLC*, Vols. 2, 5, 9; *Contemporary Authors*, Vols. 17-20, rev. ed.; and *Dictionary of Literary Biography*, Vol. 5.)

© M. Montfort

R. R. CUSCADEN

All of Bukowski's major interests and themes are in evidence in his first book, *Flower, Fist and Bestial Wail;* indeed, they are defined in the volume's title. These early poems are not equally successful; too much reliance is placed upon a dated surrealistic technique and in neglecting the use of the first person singular Bukowski fails to employ a strength which gives unity to his later work. Nevertheless, everything is here: the obsession with music (his three books mention Bach, Hugo Wolf, Borodin, Brahms, Chopin, Berlioz, Beethoven) and art (Carot, Daumier, Orozco, Van Gogh), and, most importantly, the sense of a desolate, abandoned world.

In his poem in the first volume entitled **"I Cannot Stand Tears,"** the poet, always the non-participant, watches "several hundred fools / around the goose who broke his leg / trying to decide / what to do." A guard walks up, "pulled out his cannon / and the issue was finished." The details here are interesting. The crowd is composed of "fools", the goose implies the golden egg (poetry?), the (perhaps inevitable) guard has not merely a gun but a "cannon". And the issue is especially finished for the poet: "I folded my canvas / and went further down the road: / and bastards had ruined / my landscape." (p. 63)

A key poem in this first book is **"The Paper on the Floor."** The poet meditates on the enforced soap-opera quality of most lives: "The explanation usually comes in the morning / over the breakfast table," and the overwhelming "nothing nothing nothing nothing" of it all "pushes at the back of my eyes / and pulls my nerves taut-thin from toe to hair-line."

Can life grant only bogus emotions, manufactured experiences? "Very well," Bukowski says in **"The Twins"** (a moving poem about his father's death), but, if so: "grant us this moment: standing before a mirror / in my dead father's suit / waiting also / to die." Grant us, in other words, even occasional moments of meaning. Grant us, at least, the compensatory joy of being ignored. (pp. 63-4)

His second volume, *Longshot Poems for Broke Players*, presents a more specific vision and definition of our curious world, as in the poem **"Where the Hell Would Chopin Be"**: "indented most severely in my mind: the working secret / of a universe shot with flares and rockets, / monkeys jammed / with meteoritic registers of love in space." This is, of course, a kind of protest poetry, but Bukowski's protest is hardly political in the way that much of the poetry of Spender and Auden was during the thirties. Nor is it anti-political as much as it is non-political. This, it seems to me, is because Bukowski visualizes the political approach as impotent, as he indicates in **"Poem for Personnel Managers"**: "the world rocks down against us / and we / throw out arms / and we / throw out our legs / like the death kiss of the centipede: / / but they kindly snap our backs / and call our poison 'politics'."

There is a good deal of Jeffers-like pessimism in these poems and Bukowski himself admits this indebtedness: "If I have a god it is Robinson Jeffers, although I realize that I don't write as he does." (p. 64)

Bukowski rarely gives in completely to utter, hopeless despair, and this, not the variance in style and technique, marks the essential difference between him and Jeffers. The despair of Bukowski exists just because he continually hopes; Jeffers' despair is the result of no hope at all. "I want trumpets and crowing, . . . I want the whir and tang of a simple living orange / in a simple living tree" Bukowski writes in **"Bring Down the Beams."** But, as he makes clear in the same poem, art—especially the Wednesday sonnet and the Sunday painting—is no substitute for life: ". . . we sit and piddle with charcoal / and talk about Picasso / and make collages: we are getting ready / to do nothing unusual, / and I alone am hungry / as I think about the sun clanging against the earth / and all the bones moving / but ours."

Too often, he feels, the world of art and letters is little more than a morass of gossip and back-biting, as in **"Letter from the North"**: "my friend writes of rejection and editors / and how he has visited K. or R. or W. / . . . write me, he says, / I got the blues. / / write you? about what, my friend? / I'm only interested in / poetry."

Run with the Hunted, his most recently published volume of poems (the title, with its compassionate avowal of siding with those on the "wrong", or Algren side of the street, is significant), finds Bukowski far more mellow, far more mature, than in his first two books. It is not too much, even, to term these poems "late". In any case, his awareness of the world's patently obvious absurdities is here stated without what was previously a sort of surprise; he here looks around at a world grown familiar, and comments thereupon in an almost bemused fashion. There is an enlarged and personal vision of subtle horrors in **"The Priest and the Matador"** . . . , in which as always there is the awareness of estrangement, the concern

with the failure of response. Although he has not given up hope that response might exist we read in **"Wrong Number"**: "carefully, I call voices on the phone, / measuring their sounds for humanity and laughter; / somewhere I am cut off, contact fails."

Without ceasing to fight, his course of action is now less direct; at times, perhaps, a bit more resigned. In **"Sundays Kill More Men than Bombs,"** a narrative of his divorce, he writes: "but that morning when she left / about 8 o'clock she looked / the same as ever, maybe even better. / I didn't even bother to shave; / I called in sick and went down / to the corner bar."

Bukowski is a poet of the permanent opposition. He opposes "the ruin" on a basis of personal anarchy which must attempt the impossible and create its own order. There is nothing about him of the "dumb ox" and he is certainly not a man without art. . . . In the best of his work may be found that quality of courage which, as Michael Roberts wrote, occurs "beyond the inhuman pattern" and persists in "men / broken, ephemeral, undismayed." (pp. 64-5)

R. R. Cuscaden, "Charles Bukowski: Poet in a Ruined Landscape," in The Outsider, *Vol. 1, No. 3, Spring, 1963, pp. 62-5.*

JOHN WILLIAM CORRINGTON

The recent publication of Charles Bukowski's selected poems [*It Catches My Heart in Its Hands*] marks a kind of watershed in the career of one of the West Coast's most striking poets. . . .

As those who know his poetry will testify, Bukowski's poems go well enough one by one. But there is no substitute for reading a man's work in bulk. . . .

Faced with several score of Bukowski's best poems, the illusion of ignorance or perverse and directionless crudity dissolves like a tar-doll in August sun. Individual poems merge to form together a body of work unrivalled in kind and very nearly unequalled in quality by Bukowski's contemporaries.

Perhaps the most crucial failure of Bukowski's critics is their general blindness to the sort of thing represented by his poetry. It is a vain error to damn oranges because they do not taste like apples—and it is equally profitless to decry what I call a "poetry of surfaces" because it fails to investigate and re-create the depths of human experience.

The phrase "poetry of surface" is not mine. So far as I know, Eliot coined it in an early discussion of Jonson's poetry. It distinguishes between the sort of "vertical" poetry—like *The Waste Land*—which probes the psychological, moral, religious and sociological center of man, and a "horizontal" poetry which concerns itself rather with delineating man in terms of his more visible, more immediate, more physical surroundings. This "horizontal" poetry makes little use of metaphysics. Rather than attempting an X-ray of man's moral skeleton, his spiritual viscera, this kind of poetry contents itself with the flesh, the surface of the human condition. (p. 123)

Now in Bukowski's poetry, this concern for surface—for the color, texture and rhythm of modern life—reveals itself both in what he writes and in what he does not write. On the positive side, it underlies his attention to detail, his consistent presentation of physical minutia of seeming inconsequence:

> . . . and the cat kept looking at me
> and crawling in the pantry
> amongst the clanking dishes
> with flowers and vines painted on them . . .
> ("**Love Is a Piece of Paper Torn to Bits**")

The cat and dishes alone would suffice, but Bukowski adds flowers and vines as much from a kind of fidelity to the physical verities as because of the implications carried by flowers and vines in a poem about a collapsing marriage.

Again, in a long poem describing himself and others as the human refuse thrown up by depression and industrial society, "**Poem for Personnel Managers,**" this concern with surface is manifested not by what Bukowski chooses to add to his portrait of hopeless men, but by his pointed avoidance of what might be called the "social implications" of the situation:

> we are shot through with carrot tops
> and poppy seed and tilted grammar;
> we waste days like mad blackbirds
> and pray for alcoholic nights.
> our silk-sick human smiles wrap around
> us like somebody else's confetti:
> we do not even belong to the Party. . . .

"We smoke, dead as fog," Bukowski writes. And his vision of suffering is not adulterated with the academic jargon that, in the face of human agony, seems itself a part of the brutal instrumentality it describes. There is no withdrawal in Bukowski's work. All his poems have the memorable and terrible immediacy of the news broadcast from the scene of the *Hindenberg* crash. There is nothing of the sublimated social-worker or psychiatrist in him, and the endless gabble of the professional injustice-collector is totally absent from his work. In remaining on the surface—staying with sure and certain phenomena, a series of significant acts, events, actors and victims, Bukowski avoids the pitfalls of "motivation" and "meaning." He remains in control of the indisputable, the unquestionable—and leaves the jungle of social and political and moral purpose and counter-purpose to those who find such abstract projections more significant than life itself.

A few weeks ago, Bukowski's work came up in the course of a conversation in Houston. A young woman shivered at the mention of his name. "Bukowski? He's a savage," she said vehemently. "Nothing but a savage." The word "savage" properly applied to Bukowski's poetry may help solve the puzzle of his sensibility and the academic resistance to it.

With the growth of the pseudo-civilized as contemporary norm, "savage"—like "barbarian"—has become a pejorative rather than simply a term descriptive of certain attitudes, convictions, and responses. . . . But pejoration aside, Bukowski stands nearer the world-view, say, of Chief Joseph of the Nez Perce than that of Henry Adams or Bernard Berenson. Bukowski's world, scored and grooved by the impersonal instruments of civilized industrial society, by 20th-century knowledge and experience, remains essentially a world in which meditation and analysis have little part. There is act and observation. . . . That middle stage between act and art, the stage at which one presumes a kind of intellectual gathering and synthesis antecedent to the shaping of image and metaphor, simply does not exist in Bukowski's poetry. Act moves into image directly; feeling is articulated as figure and intellection is minimal. As the savage

projects his world in terms of myth, with sight, sound—the natural order of phenomena—as its keystones, so Bukowski remains focused upon the concrete. If there is symbolic value in the work, the reader is spared a kind of burdensome awareness of that symbolism on the part of the writer. Thus, for example, in "**The Tragedy of the Leaves**,"

> I awakened to dryness and the ferns were dead,
> the potted plants yellow as corn;
> my woman was gone
> and the empty bottles like bled corpses
> surrounded me with their uselessness;
> the sun was still good, though,
> and my landlady's note cracked in fine and
> undemanding yellowness; what was needed now
> was a good comedian, ancient style, a jester
> with jokes upon absurd pain; pain is absurd
> because it exists, nothing more;
> I shaved carefully with an old razor
> the man who had once been young and
> said to have genius; but
> that's the tragedy of the leaves,
> the dead ferns, the dead plants;
> and I walked into the dark hall
> where the landlady stood
> execrating and final,
> sending me to hell,
> waving her fat sweaty arms
> and screaming
> screaming for rent
> because the world had failed us
> both.

It would be folly to try to read such a poem as simple description. But it would be equally foolish to suggest that the poem's surface is, as it were, simply an excuse for its symbolic significance. Symbol rises from event; a kind of 20th-century mythos stands like shadow over and above the specifics of Bukowski's dark hallway. Bukowski's poem is symbolic as all great work is symbolic: the verity of its surface is so nearly absolute that the situation it specifies produces the overtones of a world much vaster than that of the landlady's dark hall.

There is a kind of poetry in which one finds what may be called a resident ideational content. The greater bulk of Wallace Stevens' poetry is of this kind. However opaque the surface of "Disillusionment of Ten O'Clock," a careful reading and a comparison with section VI of "Six Significant Landscapes," quickly shows that Stevens has an idea, a theory in mind, and that, despite the difficulties, he is attempting to transmit that theory through the agency of his verse. Such work presents, as it were, a series of problems to be solved, issues to be clarified, metaphoric complexes to be explicated. This kind of poetry is the proper subject of criticism.

But there is another sort of poetry which, rather than containing ideas, projects a kind of structured emotional and imaginative form. In combination with the sensibility of a reader, this kind of poetry produces ideas not resident in it. An individual poem of this kind serves as a kind of trigger: it sets off a wave of responses in a given reader, and the resultant idea-emotion complex is, in Wordsworth's phrase, "half-created" by the reader—not simply dredged out of the poem's verbalization. Some of Bukowski's poems are of this sort. What, precisely, in terms of idea, are we to make from this:

> the blossoms shake
> sudden water
> down my sleeve,
> sudden water

cool and clean
as snow—
as the stem-sharp
swords
go in
against your breast
and the sweet wild
rocks
leap over
and lock us in.
                    (**"I Taste the Ashes of Your Death"**)

A poem of this kind, I think, is ample proof that however little thought Bukowski may give to his writing, he has mastered the literary lessons of the past century. In the tradition of Mallarmé and Lorca, he is capable of producing a poetry of pure emotion in which idea, information, the narrative or anecdotal, is held to a minimum. "The Ultimate Poem," Wallace Stevens has stated in one of his titles, "Is Abstract."

I have not meant to suggest that Charles Bukowski's poetry represents something new or even something basically superior in modern American poetry. Nor have I intended to intimate that sublimation of the intellectual is a value in itself. What I do wish to suggest is that Bukowski's work represents a renewal of interest in the poet as something other than thinker and civilized representative of the University Establishment. It is worth recalling that those poets who have most endured have rarely written the kind of geometric thing we find in contemporary "academic verse." Whatever uses we may find for poetry, the honing of the mind is not properly among them. Thus, in a sense, poetry remains—or should remain—the savage child of the arts. That poetry which fails to stir, which loses its appeal as a sensuous activity, fails, it seems to me, as poetry. Bukowski, standing in a mixed tradition of Whitman and Mallarmé, Jeffers and Lorca, brings back this evocative quality to modern verse. Compared to the work of most of his contemporaries, his poetry relies on the image and its emotional connotations much more than on the idea and its rational concomitants. . . . (pp. 124-28)

It is precisely Bukowski's refusal to become trapped in the cerebral that marks the savage quality, the surface dynamism of his poetry. Whether one chooses to see all this as a reaction to the closely-reasoned and imaginatively-sterile work of the academics, or—in a larger and less pointed context—as a predictable and timely revitalization of modern American poetry, Bukowski's work remains a significant force offsetting a recognized and widely-lamented atrophy that has, for much of this century, rendered poetry a "sullen art," a series of super-conundrums, a game of the mind or a cultural ritual performed alone. Bukowski's increasing popularity seems to indicate that possibly it is not that people have abandoned poetry, but that poetry has tended to lose its audience by eschewing that savage vitality, that splendid surface that so long distinguished it from fiction or history or philosophy. Lacking imaginative and emotional immediacy, poetry cannot compete. But those poets who have worked more nearly as warlocks than as logicians still find a considerable readership: Dylan Thomas, e. e. cummings, and others. Bukowski, I believe, belongs in this company.

If it is argued that Bukowski lacks depth, one might do well to paraphrase Aristotle: "There is a degree of profundity suitable to every discipline. The wise man does not ask of an art-form that which is not proper to it." If depth is the ultimate criterion of literary value, then Shakespeare fades before Descartes; Coleridge before Kant. But if emotional and imaginative

excitement is an acceptable purpose, the poetry of Charles Bukowski is unusually successful, and his surfaces are as valuable in their savage way as are the civilized depths of T. S. Eliot. (pp. 128-29)

John William Corrington, "Charles Bukowski and the Savage Surfaces," in Northwest Review, *Vol. 6, No. 4, Fall, 1963, pp. 123-29.*

CARL MORSE

Charles Bukowski is a loner grimly preoccupied with death and the pall of absurdity it casts on life. "Regard me," he says [in a poem from *It Catches My Heart in Its Hands*], "as the one who picked the meat from the bones and shot craps with God as the poison coronets floated the air." His is a world of "swarm and explosion" where "youth" is "fenced in / stabbed and shaven / taught words / propped up / to die"—a world in which "you and I ain't living well / or enough." This world is centered on rented rooms, demonic landladies, beer dames, the track, one's own soul, and poems. Most of the latter are sparely written narrative accounts of combinations of the former.

When bad, the poems are merely protest, which—no matter how justified or vigorous—is not by itself poetry. They are, however, superior protest and a lot of fun to read when cut by some of Bukowski's delicious humor or by one of his infrequent moments of calm and detachment. His comedy is superb in lines like: ". . . when I took her home / she said / Big Red was the best horse / she'd ever seen— / until I stripped down." (p. 11)

The detached moments come in lines like: "the sea waits / as the land waits / amused and perfect." And there is one entirely tranquil poem called **"Counsel,"** which is full of sensible advice like: "Engage not in small arguments / of hand or voice / unless your foe seeks the life of your body / or the life of your soul; then, / kill, if necessary."

The really good poems, however, are those in which story is raised to the level of fable. These include **"I Cannot Stand Tears"** ("there were several hundred fools / around the goose who broke his leg . . ."), **"Love Is a Piece of Paper Torn to Bits," "The Race,"** and **"A Farewell Thing While Breathing."** The first, especially, continues to reverberate with each reading. All of Bukowski's bad stuff, of which there is plenty, is worth ignoring for the sake of these. (pp. 11-12)

Carl Morse, in a review of "It Catches My Heart in Its Hands," in The Village Voice, *Vol. IX, No. 23, March 26, 1964, pp. 11-12.*

DABNEY STUART

Whether or not one likes the poems [in *It Catches My Heart in Its Hands*], it is difficult to be indifferent to them. They are energetic, tough, and unnerving. Written out of a driving necessity for expression, they become a battleground on which Bukowski fights for his life, and sanity. Against his enemies, who are grimly, irresponsibly powerful, his words and wit and sour bitterness are fragile weapons. The effort, consequently, is last ditch.

It is also disturbingly ironic. Auden wrote in his tribute to Yeats, "Poetry makes nothing happen." Bukowski is intensely aware of this, laments it because in the world he inhabits it reduces the poet to an ineffectual isolation. Sometimes he almost whines. The implication that continually intrudes itself into his work is that he would like nothing better than to cure the sores he unscabs, yet he realizes, perhaps correctly, that they are incurable. It is an ultimately frustrating situation; yet the poet has one thing he can control and vitalize: language. Auden also wrote that poetry "is a way of happening"; the coin that Bukowski flips seldom lands this side up, though William Corrington's statement (in his introduction) that Bukowski's poems are "the spoken voice nailed to paper" is true. It is also misleading (as are many of his other observations)—two hundred million people don't all speak the same way—and it does not necessarily mean, as he claims it does, that Bukowski's poems are art. About the world Bukowski seems forced to say *che sarà, sarà;* to say that about language is a capitulation of another sort, unwise, uncreative. The American language, as Bukowski hears it, can be nailed to paper rather easily. But to give it form or, better still, discover a form in it, is another thing. That Bukowski is, as William Carlos Williams was, trying to do this is not apparent to me. Moreover, the challenge of mirroring *in language* itself (not merely stating) the appalling ironies and overwhelming complexity of our lives has been met more squarely and successfully by Robert Lowell (in *Life Studies*), W. D. Snodgrass (in *Heart's Needle*), and Anne Sexton (in *All My Pretty Ones*).

If Bukowski has arrived at the door to something great, he has knocked very lightly for entrance. All of us would like to hear what is significant and enduring about our tongue; it might lead us to a nobility our present masquerades so poignantly reveal we long for. There is always the terrifying thought that our language is itself at fault, but this is a grievous abdication of responsibility for what we are, after all, the makers of, and no living poet who cares as much as Bukowski seems to would submit to it. Escapists don't write great poetry. (pp. 263-64)

Dabney Stuart, "Seven Poets and a Playwright," in Poetry, Vol. CIV, No. 4, July, 1964, pp. 258-64.

KENNETH REXROTH

Charles Bukowski suffers from too good a press—a small but loudly enthusiastic claque. . . . However, if you put aside his volunteer public-relations experts, he turns out to be a substantial writer.

I suppose the academicians would call him the most recent representative of naturalism and anti-literary revolt. . . .

No Establishment is likely ever to recruit Bukowski. He belongs in the small company of poets of real, not literary, alienation, that includes Herman Spector, Kenneth Fearing, Kenneth Patchen and a large number of Bohemian fugitives unknown to fame. His special virtue is that he is so much less sentimental than most of his colleagues.

Yet there is nothing outrageous about his poetry [in *It Catches My Heart in Its Hands*]. It is simple, casual, honest, uncooked. He writes about what he knows—rerolling cigarette butts, cashing in the neighbor's milk bottles to get two-bits for the morning visit to the bookmaker, the horse that came in and the hundred-dollar call girl that came in with it, the ragged hitch-hiker on the road to nowhere, the poignant, natural real scene around him where the last ride set him down.

Bukowski is what he is, and he is not likely to be found applying for a job with the picture magazines as an Image of Revolt. Unlike the Beats, he will never become an allowed clown; he is too old now, and too wise, and too quiet.

Kenneth Rexroth, "There's Poetry in a Ragged Hitch-Hiker," in The New York Times Book Review, July 5, 1964, p. 5.

FRED COGSWELL

Both as a significant aspect of one means of arriving at personal integrity in the modern world and as a collection of poetry, *Crucifix in a Death Hand* is one of the most striking books that I have read in a long time. . . . Bukowski is an example of Blake's 'just man' condemned to rage 'in the wilds' that the modern world must possess to any person of genuine integrity. He represents a very rare type, a man so insulated by his own temperament against the shams of his time that he is completely uninterested in attempts to redeem a fallen humanity through study of the past, myths, or ideology. He regrets the rarity of men and women with whom a genuine communion is possible, and he yearns in the hideous shadows of mechanization and standardization for a beauty that is akin to the clouds, the plants, the animals. Such a beauty he finds in words, and the making of poems. (pp. 69-70)

Bukowski's is essentially the existentialist's answer to the problem of existence. To arrive at a well-defined sense of one's own identity and from this security to look at the shadowy world that surrounds one without illusion and as far as possible without emotion. It is a good answer, and although Bukowski finds it difficult he essentially succeeds. (p. 70)

Fred Cogswell, "Two Ways of Dealing with the Exterior," in The Fiddlehead, No. 67, Winter, 1966, pp. 69-71.

ALICIA OSTRIKER

In his fourteenth book [*At Terror Street and Agony Way*], Bukowski remains the Bad Boy. His style is loose and humorously tough-guy. His themes are, for example, boxing, beer-drinking . . . , horse racing. He is a good old-fashioned likeable male chauvinist, meaning that the women in his work are an anonymous "x-wife" and several other props to use and/or put down, a dirty business at best:

 it's unfortunate, and simply not the style, but
 I don't care: girls remind me of hair in the sink,
 girls remind me of intestines and bladders and
 excretory movements;

but that the real world is a world of men and meditation, yearning for the companionship of the not impossible he:

 a living man, truly alive,
 say when he brings his hands down
 from lighting a cigarette
 you see his eyes
 like the eyes of a tiger staring past
 into the wind.

Inevitably, Bukowski's world has been a world of loners, taking punches. Bukowski takes them well. He writes wryly, spryly, about failure, to a smell of transient furnished rooms, grubby streets, brutality in many states, thoughts of great and dead poets and composers and the Spanish Civil War. . . . [He] writes most substantially when he hangs his poems upon anecdotes. **"I Wanted to Overthrow the Government But All I Brought Down Was Somebody's Wife"** and **"Shot of Red-Eye"** are two comically tragic tall tales interlocking bawdry and the class struggle, bluntly ironic about both. . . . **"The**

Weather is Hot on the Back of My Watch," a powerful Faulknerian meditation on violence in the American grain—a Texas crow-shoot, and the half-dead crows clubbed to death by a hundred farmers—has an almost metaphysical grip and concision. But even at his slightest, for example **"Brewed and Filled By . . ."** which spins from contemplation of "my beercan hand," he's pretty good. (pp. 220-21)

Alicia Ostriker, "Other Times, Other Voices," in Partisan Review, *Vol. XXXVIII, No. 2, 1971, pp. 218-26.*

THE TIMES LITERARY SUPPLEMENT

Like all the best picaresque, Charles Bukowski's first novel [*Post Office*] has the air of negligently re-worked autobiography. Henry Chinaski, anti-hero and bastard extraordinary, works in the Post Office, a life of monotony and brutalizing physical exertion, harassed by bullneck superiors and a squawking citizenry. An unrepentant drunk and outrageously successful gambler, Chinaski moves with Napoleonic timing from race-track to race-track and bed to bed. There's something unreflecting, to say the least, in his dealings with the other sex ("I finished her off, zipped my fly, picked up my mail pouch and walked out leaving her staring quietly at the ceiling"), but karma is lurking under the bed-springs in the shape of a Texan nymphomaniac, whom everybody except Chinaski thinks he is marrying for her money. . . .

Their marriage over, his wife preferring a Turk from her office, Chinaski winds up in the Post Office again, on a twelve-year stretch.

There is genuine melancholy in the tale, increased not diminished by the cocky monotone Chinaski uses to recount the death of an alcoholic girl-friend or the washed-up history of a southpaw welterweight. It is a brave, vivacious book but it lacks the connexions which might have made it an outstanding one. Mr Bukowski's loser's string of anecdotes, convulsively funny and also sad, is unflagging entertainment but in the end doesn't add up to more than the sum of its parts, somehow missing the novelist's alchemy.

"Postman's Knock," in The Times Literary Supplement, *No. 3761, April 5, 1974, p. 375.*

VALENTINE CUNNINGHAM

Jean Genet thinks Charles Bukowski is the best poet in America. The photograph of Bukowski's face, pitted and rutted, lumpy and knotted, a corrugated dereliction of an industrial landscape, looks just the part of Genet's favourite American poet. . . . And *Post Office*—comic, raunchy, foul-mouthed, rambling, wittily unsentimental about its narrator, Henry Chinaski's, grisly depravities—fits the face. It will certainly also fit quite snugly on the shelf next to my copy of Bukowski's *Erections, Ejaculations, Exhibitions and General Tales of Madness. Post Office* may be sixty-year-old Bukowski's first novel, but its brief is the same as his hundreds of shorts, familiar to perusers of American underground papers under titles like **"The Fuck Machine"**, **"Ten Jack-Offs"**, **"My Big-Assed Mother"**, **"All the Pussy We Want"**, **"Cunt and Kant and a Happy Home"**, **"Great Poets Die in Steaming Pots of Shit"**, **"The Big Pot Game"**, **"Notes of a Potential Suicide"**. He's a bit old, you may be thinking, for this kind of thing.

And there's lots of it in *Post Office*. Postman Chinaski is a close relation of ex-postman Bukowski ("threw some water on my face, combed my hair. If I could only comb that face, I thought, but I can't"), and, like his author, obsessed by "asses" and "ass". He really gets through the "shack-jobs", Betty, Joyce, Mary-Lou, Fay, and all the rest. And he checks women out by their asses. Betty's "warm tail" is just the job after a hard day in the mailvan. . . . Not that Chinaski's own backside doesn't also on occasion concern him. "Then I felt something jamming its way into my crotch. It moved way up there, I looked around and there was a German Shepherd, full-grown, with his nose half-way up my ass. With one snap of his jaws he could rip off my balls." . . . It's clearly a dog's life in the Post Office, badgered and pestered by rules, superintendents and a fawned-on public. No wonder Chinaski is on the drink, particularly the fifths of whisky that are the eventual death of Betty, those snorts by the bottle-full devotedly alluded to as they exude from his own sweaty pores ("The whiskey and beer ran out of me, fountained from the armpits": there's a good deal of BO in this novel). No wonder, either, that he goes crazy and believes everybody he meets is mad, particularly in the sorting-rooms. And if they're not crazed, Butchner (who keeps up a quiet undertow of filthy talk about every girl drifting by) and Janko (who bawls out his fantasies to all the world: "HEY, HANK! I REALLY CAUGHT A HEAD JOB TODAY") are managing a fine imitation of being seriously disturbed. Like Bukowski's fictions, the Post Office is no place for the sensitive. Slack-bottomed Robby, the Catholic from Fay's writer's workshop, is, she insists, "TOO SENSITIVE TO WORK AT THE POST OFFICE". Only loonies and losers, it appears, can stick at "sticking the mail". And losers don't come any more losingly than Chinaski, despite his boastful prowess with the geegees. . . .

Does he, though, have to be quite so nasty? He slaps his women about, he's a sexist rotter, not averse even to a spot of doorstep rape ("'Rape! Rape! I'm being raped!' She was right.") He is pronouncedly sympathetic to assholes. When Joyce turns down the snails he's cooked because "They all have tiny little *assholes*", he stands vehemently up for them. . . . It's a sympathy rooted in his being so obviously one himself. But it's a sympathy that, despite one's outrage, Bukowski makes the reader share. Pressed in by Post Office bureaucrats, their mean-minded regulations and their heaps of paperwork, the misfit looks frequently like an angel of light. His refusal to play respectability ball with the cajoling, abusive, never-take-no-for-an-answer loops who own the mailboxes he attends . . . can make even this ribald mess of a wretch seem a shining haven of sanity in the prevailing Los Angeles grimnesses.

Valentine Cunningham, "Male Order," in The Times Literary Supplement, *No. 4030, June 20, 1980, p. 706.*

GALEN STRAWSON

Charles Bukowski's Henry Chinaski [the protagonist of *Factotum*] is not a factotum in the usual sense of the word—he's not what the employers at one of the factories he works in call "the extra ball-bearing", the guy who "sees that . . . wastebaskets never overflow. . . ." He's a factotum because he does a hundred different jobs in a hundred different establishments, all over war-time America but mostly in Los Angeles, never lasting more than a few weeks before being sacked.

Chinaski is a stylist. An improvident, lovely rogue, if he's not getting the sack and severance cheque that goes with it, not in bed with a woman, not drunk or purblind, not playing the horses, then he's writing short stories and printing them out by hand (he can't keep typewriters out of pawnshops) and sending them to magazines. On the run, he reads Henry Miller on the Greyhound bus all the way from Los Angeles to Miami: "He was good when he was good and vice versa." (But does that mean he was good all the time or that he was also bad when he was bad?) . . .

Bukowski's is an American style familiar enough from other writers: bathetic, bone-lazy-laconic; free with the tough and designedly *malgré soi* touching understatement; and harder than it looks, perhaps, until you get the hang of it—"Tommy drank, we both drank. His conversation was O.K." It's Kerouac mixed with Chandler, Chandler down on himself for long-windedness, Kerouac agreeably divested of his overpowering sentimentality about being down and out. Sometimes it seems just too mannered in its bluntness. But it's also funny and sharp, observant, clever with details, and honest. . . . Only occasionally does he lapse into feebleness. . . .

Chinaski enjoys a hedonistic interlude at the expense of a mean and rich old man and his gaggle of broads; he forms a liaison that borders on something like love with an older woman, hard-drinking pot-bellied Jan. But it's the endless string of jobs, the tragicomedies of application and dismissal over and over again, the absurd particularities of neon-light factories and brake-shoe distribution companies, that are the vertebrae of a tale that otherwise has little shape, being a tale about a life that itself has little shape.

If there is any other theme in this novel by the author of *All the Assholes in the World and Mine,* it is Chinaski's increasing concern with bottoms, and with people not wiping their bottoms properly. Cleaning out the women's restrooms at the Times Building in LA (applying for a job as a reporter, he makes it as a janitor), he is "conscientious with the ass-wipe" (the lavatory paper) and moved to reflect that "even the most horrible human being on earth deserves to wipe his ass". . . .

Is it an impartial concern for all-revealing *verismo* that leads Bukowski into these and other cloacal details? He misses out too much else that's a necessary and routine part of daily life for the suggestion to hold water. It's just Chinaski's thing. He's not any less attractive for it, and, *verismo* or no, *il est dans le vrai.* That's where we leave him, unemployed and abandoned by Jan, glum in the willy-nilly proof of his love for her—unable to get it up for a demented stripper.

Galen Strawson, "Bottoming Out," in The Times Literary Supplement, *No. 4092, September 4, 1981, p. 1000.*

PETER SCHJELDAHL

Charles Bukowski's 35th book in 21 years [*Dangling in the Tournefortia*] is a volume of 107 recent poems that continue the unlikely saga of an intensely (and confessedly) unappealing man's capacity to find himself interesting. And to *be* interesting, I hasten a little incredulously to add. Low-life bard of Los Angeles, Mr. Bukowski has nothing new for us here, simply more and still more accounts in free verse of his follies with alcohol and women and of fellow losers hitting bottom and somehow discovering new ways to continue falling. Page after page, the poet contemplates the worst about himself and others

with a sort of awful buoyancy, not complacent exactly but seemingly indifferent to values beyond the sheer dumb ongoingness of the human organism. How can I possibly enjoy this stuff so much?

Mr. Bukowski writes well, for one thing, with ear-pleasing cadences, wit and perfect clarity, which are all the more beguiling for issuing from a stumblebum persona. His grace with words gives a comic gleam to even his meanest revelations. But his power goes at least slightly beyond his skills as an entertainer. There is real poignance to the people encountered in his work—the masochistic or embittered female marks, the impotent or threatening male rivals. This poignance is strangely enhanced by being ostensibly unfelt by the poet, who nonetheless takes pains to be sharp and persuasive in his characterizations. He has the "hard-boiled" writer's trick of making the reader care more by appearing to care less.

Is it possible to admire a writer for allowing us to feel superior to him? Some such perverse transaction seems afoot here. Or perhaps it is simply a craving for "truth" that hooks some of us. Any truth, however grotesque, is better than no truth, and its unveiling makes us happy. It may even be that we are readiest to believe the grotesque: Why would anyone say those things if they weren't true? Whatever the facts in his case, Mr. Bukowski is an exceedingly wily clown, and our literary circus would be poorer without him. (p. 13)

Peter Schjeldahl, "Lines from L.A. and N.Y.," in The New York Times Book Review, *January 17, 1982, pp. 13, 16.*

KEN TUCKER

Dangling in the Tournefortia is Bukowski's most self-indulgent collection ever, but with a compulsive autobiographer like this, that's not necessarily an insult. . . . [The] poems in *Dangling* obsess upon the plight of the honest writer, the poor bastard who doesn't sell out, who resists the blandishments of cult celebrity. Just as Virginia Woolf's letters describe a daily procession to a room of her own, so do Bukowski's poems set down a ceremonial creative pattern: Bukowski wakes up, vomits, drinks, writes, drinks, fucks, drinks, and falls asleep. " . . . it was 11 a.m. and I was puking / trying to get a can of ale down / the whore in the bed next to me / in her torn slip / mumbling about her children in / Atlanta. . . ."

Very quickly, Bukowski's pervasive first-person-singular becomes a pathetic boor who nonetheless makes the right sort of connections between his art and his life: "I can't / write / and / I can't / come / either . . ." With depressing regularity, the character Bukowski has made of himself overwhelms his powers of invention. Certainly, his best poems have virtues: a crisp, hard voice; an excellent ear and eye for measuring out the lengths of lines; and an avoidance of metaphor where a lively anecdote will do the same dramatic work. When he's hot, such honest instincts compel Bukowski to explode the pretentious myth of the tortured artist: "Winthrop asks, 'How's your poetry coming / Buck?' / I tell him that I rip off 6 or 8 / every couple of nights. . . ." And *Dangling in the Tournefortia* is a record of Bukowski's middle-aged life now that both his obscurity and his fame have reached their peaks ("how marvelous to be me without / trying. / it looks on tv / as if I knew exactly what I / was doing").

But Bukowski's sleazy contempt for all women and any man who can't drink him under the lectern is genuinely hateful. I suppose that a contemporary poet who can inspire rage and frustration in his readers is automatically superior to prissy, affectless modern masters like Stanley Kunitz and Mark Strand, but—and this is a question Bukowski himself ponders throughout this book—how much superior? (pp. 42-3)

Ken Tucker, in a review of "Dangling in the Tournefortia," in The Village Voice, *Vol. XXVII, No. 12, March 23, 1982, pp. 42-3.*

BEN REUVEN

Charles Bukowski is the laureate of the Los Angeles literary underground, an eccentric who sees the world with a clarity of vision possessed only by artists and madmen. His work is full of passion, lust and raw humor; if he were only a bit more lyrical, a bit more celebratory, Bukowski might have been hailed as another Henry Miller. But he makes no such easy compromises. As he demonstrates once again in *Ham on Rye* . . ., Bukowski's real gift is for unvarnished and unrelenting truth telling.

Ham on Rye is Bukowski's 37th book, but his prose has never been more vigorous or more powerful. Here we follow the familiar figure of Henry Chinaski, the author's autobiographical alter ego, through childhood, adolescence and early manhood in Depression-era and wartime Los Angeles. These first-person reminiscences are taut, vivid, intense, sometimes poignant, often hilarious: Henry's zealous grandmother attempts to exorcise a bad case of acne by stabbing him with a crucifix after the doctor's electric needle has failed. His embittered father bemoans Uncle John's thwarted counterfeiting enterprise only because it was so modest. ("Dimes! Jesus Christ, what kind of ambition is that?") And Henry's voluptuous junior-high teacher seeks to soothe her young charges but succeeds only in arousing them, to catastrophic effect.

What emerges from *Ham on Rye* is Bukowski's vision of growing up as an ordeal of little brutalities that make us or break us while we are still too frail and too ignorant to do anything about it. For Chinaski—that is, for Bukowski—the only escape was the cool, quiet reading room of the Los Angeles Public Library. . . . *Ham on Rye* might be subtitled "The Making of a Writer"—Chinaski/Bukowski finds solace and salvation only on Skid Row, where he begins to make sense of his life, with the aid of a pinball machine and a portable typewriter.

Ben Reuven, in a review of "Ham on Rye," in Los Angeles Times Book Review, *October 3, 1982, p. 6.*

WILLIAM LOGAN

Bukowski writes of a class that receives little poetic attention. His gritty, lumpen-proletariat antagonism is alienating; but it is sociology, not pathology. Bukowski doesn't like his fans— he hardly likes anybody ("I lost my enthusiasm for / the masses at the age / of 4"). If he's pleased by his late success and the wealth it has brought, it has made his poetry no less bleak. The repetitive subjects around which these snapped-off bits of prose [in *Dangling in the Tournefortia*] orbit are women (mostly unhappy, or unhappy with him), alcohol, and horse racing. Only occasionally do his bitter anecdotes lapse into something recognizably poetic in effect: "never again will I see all of your beauty sleeping, wide- / legged, immune to me: we've all been cheated." Mostly it's one sorry story after another, sometimes spreading from one poem into another.

Like most tough guys, Bukowski's a sentimentalist, and dozens of these poems are soiled by their own bathos ("she is sad. her walls cover her. she is alone. / I want to know her name."). It is easy to dismiss such anti-poetry, badly structured, vain, and misanthropic. But after periods of intellectual self-castigation, when this poetry is overrated, one might fight against underrating it. It is hopelessly flawed; but in an unemotive time it is a severe reminder that the best poetry stays close to strong emotion, to lives as they are lived. Life here has almost entirely mastered art.

William Logan, "Life Mastering Art," in The Times Literary Supplement, *No. 4153, November 12, 1982, p. 1251.*

DAVID MONTROSE

Bukowski, like Henry Miller, turns life directly into art: his novels, stories, and copious poems are usually autobiographical instalments minimally disguised by the adoption of a persona ("Henry Chinaski"), with easily penetrable name-changes for other characters. Sometimes, even this thin mask of fictionality is dropped. But if Bukowski's lowlife Los Angeles—a world of bottom jobs and booze, gambling and petty crime, whores amateur and professional—is reminiscent of Miller's Paris, the prose, though not the vocabulary, is plainer, closer to that of Sherwood Anderson's first stories.

Devotees have long detected evidence of decline in Bukowski's work: the deterioration in his novels since the promising *Post Office;* the falling ratio of hits to misses in his always uneven poetry. Above all, they point to the infrequency with which Bukowski now publishes the inimitable stories that were his trademark. This novel [*Ham on Rye*]—his most ambitious and substantial to date—will come as a welcome surprise. Particularly striking is Bukowski's uncharacteristic restraint: the prose is hard and exact, the writer's impulse towards egocentricity repressed. Bukowski's previous novels—*Post Office, Factotum,* and *Women*—documented Henry Chinaski's adult life; *Ham on Rye* covers the missing years, stretching episodically from Henry's infancy during the early 1920s to 1941 and the bombing of Pearl Harbour.

The opening chapters—unsentimental memoranda of childhood recalling Hemingway's Nick Adams stories—are dominated by Henry's tyrannical father. Obsessed with ambition, Chinaski Snr has convinced himself that he is rich and successful. He forbids Henry to play with other children in the district: "'They are bad children,' said my father, 'their parents are poor.'" . . .

The novel widens when Henry begins school; his father recedes from the foreground. At school, Henry is a loner, unpopular and bullied. An attempt to stick up for himself backfires: reported to his parents by the principal, he receives a beating— the first of many—from his father. . . . This sense of estrangement intensifies with adolescence. Henry's father insists that he attend a high school miles outside the district because "the rich kids" go there. . . . He finds consolation in the thrill of words: literature, writing stories. But he can never shake off the outsider's paranoid suspicion that others—especially the boys who get the girls—are privy to some secret knowledge, denied him, which enables them to make their way in the world.

After high school, Henry is briefly a department store stockboy, then a college student. Eventually thrown out of his parents' house, he arrives at his real beginning, the kind of life about which Bukowski's followers are accustomed to reading: the round of cheap rooms and seedy bars that, along with race-tracks, comprise the settings for nearly all Bukowski's prose and poetry. He submits stories to magazines, accumulates rejection slips.

Although *Ham on Rye* surpasses expectations, Bukowski—a fine practitioner of the short story—has not yet mastered the novel. *Ham on Rye* avoids the shapeless rambling that so marred *Factotum* and *Women,* but, in the process, loses some of the author's characteristic vividness, energy, and humour. Even so, there is much to applaud in the novel, not least the freshness of its raw material. Prolific and autobiographical, Bukowski has been prone to repetition, using certain experiences twice, three times. His early years, though, are virgin territory largely untranslated into poetry or prose, an old dog's new tricks.

David Montrose, "Virgin Territory," in The Times Literary Supplement, *No. 4157, December 3, 1982, p. 1344.*

STEPHEN KESSLER

One of Bukowski's central themes is human violence, domestic and otherwise—a violence with roots in his own brutalized childhood. His pitilessly honest treatment of this reality has provoked hostile reactions from genteel and politically rigid sectors of the public. As a lifelong tough guy and terminal alcoholic, Bukowski's persona—both in his writings and live readings—has always had a calmly murderous assertiveness. . . .

Anyone who takes the trouble to read Bukowski closely can see that his persona is just that: a mask to cover his "big, soft baby's ass" of a heart. He is a soulful poet whose art is an ongoing testimony to perseverance. It's not the drinking and fucking and gambling and fighting and shitting that make his books valuable, but the meticulous attention to the most mundane experience, the crusty compassion for his fellow losers, the implicit conviction that by frankly telling the unglamorous facts of hopelessness some stamina and courage can be cultivated.

Without trying to make himself look good, much less heroic, Bukowski writes with a nothing-to-lose truthfulness which sets him apart from most other "autobiographical" novelists and poets. Hemingway's romantic relationship with his own machismo looks strained compared to Bukowski's stoicism; Henry Miller's moralistic / philosophical attack on social and literary conventions seems transcendentally naive beside Bukowski's below-good-and-evil outlook. Firmly in the American tradition of the maverick, Bukowski writes with no apologies from the frayed edge of society, beyond or beneath respectability, revealing nasty and alarming underviews.

Civilization, as Bukowski knows it, is a lost cause; politics is an absurd charade; work is a cruel joke. People are insufferably pretentious. Drinking, listening to classical music, typing and playing the horses are somewhat helpful treatments for rampant misery.

This picture would be grim if it weren't for the humor and depth of his perception. "The problem was," he writes in his new novel *Ham on Rye,* a relentless account of coming up in the Depression, "you had to keep choosing between one evil and another, and no matter what you chose, they sliced a little bit more off you until there was nothing left. At the age of 25 most people were finished. A whole god-damned nation of assholes driving automobiles, eating, having babies, doing ev-

erything in the worst way possible, like voting for the presidential candidate who reminded them most of themselves."

While as a work of fiction *Ham on Rye* may not have quite the richness of character or sustained narrative drive of his 1978 masterpiece, *Women,* it's an essential document for understanding the origins of Bukowski/Chinaski's world view. "The first thing I remember is being under something"—an opening line with a resonance that won't quit because all his life (until his recent international acclaim) that's exactly where he's been.

Beaten repeatedly with a razor strop by a frustrated, usually unemployed father; stuck outside the social mainstream from elementary school on; cursed with a bewilderingly atrocious case of boils as an adolescent, Henry Chinaski's incomprehension is limitless. . . .

The fist fights which punctuate *Ham on Rye* (like Holden Caulfield's pathetic phone calls in *Catcher in the Rye,* the echo of whose title I'm sure is no coincidence) are Henry's main means of communicating with his contemporaries. The kid's father is so inexpressibly brutal, so totally lost in his own pathological unhappiness, it's a miracle the child survives at all. . . .

A desperately miserable person tormented by his own mediocrity and taking it out on his son, Chinaski's old man must have plenty in common not only with other ordinary slobs who suffered through the Depression but with innumerable men today who find themselves "under something." By writing this terrible tale in a tone of understated but unmistakable mercy—a forgiveness of "all the fathers" who've lost control—Bukowski makes peace with his hateful forebear as well as with their common predicament: poverty.

For all the sadness and sordidness of his story, Bukowski gives us a courageous account of a human heart keeping itself responsive against all odds. Without ever suggesting that he's "right" about anything, his clarity of vision, the clean evocative simplicity of his prose, his resilience in the face of fear and suffering all make him singularly readable and real compared to numerous lesser authors of greater repute among the literati.

Though what he has to say may be hard to stomach, Bukowski is living proof of the healing and redemptive powers of art. His books are read, his style is imitated, his voice is listened to because he has something important to offer: it has to do with endurance. "Words weren't dull, words were things that could make your mind hum. If you read them and let yourself feel the magic, you could live without pain, with hope, no matter what happened to you."

Stephen Kessler, "A Life of Crusty Compassion: 'Ham on Rye'," in San Francisco Review of Books, *January-February, 1983, p. 11.*

THOMAS BRODERICK

If Mailer, Vonnegut, and Irving are taken seriously in this country, then Bukowski deserves the Nobel. For some strange reason, the academics have left him alone. He should be grist for them, but they never mention his name. . . . If the academics were to bother with him, they would praise him for all the wrong reasons. At his best, he writes as pure a line of American prose as Williams, Crane, Hemingway or Selby. He has the ear for it and it seems to flow easily. . . . His construction of American life is equally as pure. It is how Williams would have presented America had he been raised in Los Angeles in the wrong neighborhood. Bukowski's America is one of unremitting cruelty: parents towards children, kids against kids, teachers against students, students against teachers, bosses against employees, men against women, the rich against the poor, classes against classes, on and on. His character, Henry Chinaski (whose childhood is presented in [*Ham on Rye*]) is the victim of it all; at the same time, he is also the victimizer. As Williams wrote, "The pure products of America go crazy." Bukowski creates the pure products, each carefully delineated according to social caste, money, looks, athletic ability, academic achievement, etc. All gone mad, but in very specific ways. And just as mad, as I say, is Chinaski: a mean, cruel son of a bitch, who also happens to be a sentimentalist. This is Bukowski's portrait of Chinaski-artist as a young man. And as in his other novels about Chinaski, the fact that he is a writer (in this case, a budding writer) does not dilute his essential depravity. In this novel we get to see *why* Chinaski became the brute that he is, but the why does not make him any less unlikable. . . . Amid all this, Bukowski is one of the funniest writers in America. It is the humor of Céline, but it is that rare humor that arises out of misery, pain, failure, and the inability to do anything about them.

Thomas Broderick, in a review of "Ham on Rye," in The Review of Contemporary Fiction, *Vol. 3, No. 3, Fall, 1983, p. 223.*

MICHAEL F. HARPER

Ernest Hemingway and Henry Miller are alive and ill and living in a rented room in East Hollywood—or so one might think after reading [*Hot Water Music,* Bukowski's] collection of 36 short stories. Sordid, obscene and violent, Bukowski's Los Angeles is more like Miller's Paris than Hemingway's, but our guide through this underworld responds to Hemingway's laconic stoicism, not Miller's apocalyptic rhapsodies.

Bukowski's narrators, who are sometimes "underground" writers like their creator, live in a world of cheap hotels "filled with prostitutes, winos, pickpockets, second-story men, dishwashers, muggers, stranglers and rapists." The inhabitants of this world are all losers, because "life" is a game where the odds are stacked against you. . . .

Lives of quiet desperation explode in apparently random and unmotivated acts of bizarre violence. A jealous wife shatters her husband's dreams with a revolver; a drunken woman takes a matchbook and tries to turn herself into Joan of Arc at the stake; a bank manager gets drunk and molests children; a man facing unemployment conquers his impotence by raping a neighbor in an apartment elevator; an ex-stripper sexually mutilates the man she is ostensibly seducing; a small-time gambler who reads Camus impulsively slits a stranger's throat and steals his matches. Most of the dialogue is unquotable in these pages, and story after story describes murderous impulses born of frustrations for which there is no cure.

"No cure"—that is the key to Bukowski's bleak vision, and it is in this fatalism that he most resembles Hemingway. In the final analysis, the horror of the lives Bukowski describes is not, in his view, the product of any particular social or political system, and hence it cannot be eradicated by social and political change. Human life is horrible, Bukowski implies, because of all the ills that flesh is heir to, and social decay is simply an extension of the biological order making men and women susceptible to hemorrhoids and halitosis, vulnerable to

attacks by hot lead, cold steel and sharp teeth. In short, the ultimate realities in Bukowski's world, as in Hemingway's, are flesh and the death that will eventually overtake it. . . .

The Bukowski hero is the man or woman with the courage to face this fact squarely, to recognize that death makes nonsense of all pretensions to beauty, tenderness, love and delicacy, to accept that all humane ideals are sentimental lies which are dangerous because they offer only cruelly false hope.

All you can do is take whatever comfort you can find (booze, or another warm, decaying body) wherever you can find it (usually a dirty, ill-lighted place). . . .

If all this strikes you as the ultimate wisdom, then Charles Bukowski will seem a very profound writer. There is certainly a raw power in these stories, but Bukowski's hard-boiled fatalism seems to me the flip side of the humanism he denies and therefore just as false as the sentimentality he ridicules. The things he writes of are undoubtedly "true," in the sense that they have their counterparts in "real life," and a virtue of his work is to give a voice to the kind of people usually excluded from "literature"; but in condemning as phony any idea or feeling that is alien to his chosen milieu, Bukowski mistakes a partial truth for the whole.

However "unromantic" they may seem, these stories are imbued with the perverse romanticism of adolescent disillusionment. Having discovered that the world is not heaven, he insists on seeing it as hell. Hemingway would be proud of his pupil.

Michael F. Harper, "A Sordid, Obscene, Violent Underground Los Angeles," in Los Angeles Times Book Review, *December 11, 1983, p. 2.*

GERALD LOCKLIN

Anyone who approaches . . . [*Hot Water Music*] as the autobiography of Charles Bukowski will be creating problems for himself. There *is* a level of autobiography to Bukowski's novels and to many of his poems and to some of his stories, but he is also much more apt in his stories than in his novels to invent. This volume demands a sensitivity to nightmare, hyperbole, repressed fears, wish-fulfillment, tall tales, jokes, grand guignol. The works are not that far, in other words, from what are arguably the origins of American variants of the genre in the works of Poe.

In "**You Kissed Lilly,**" for instance, a fifty-year-old woman shoots her fifty-six-year-old husband twice in the chest in his sleep out of jealousy over a five-years-past infidelity. He awakes and shoots her in both thighs. He tries to throw the gun through a window; it smashes the glass but falls back into the room. She picks it up, makes him crawl, blows away his lower lip and jaw. She smashes a different window with his shoe, which does fall through the window. Then she shoots herself in the chest. He is still making noises when the police arrive. They decry the messiness of domestic quarrels. At her own place Lilly is masturbating to a Marlon Brando movie.

Black humor? Freudian? Sure. And yet most murders, we keep hearing, *are* kept in the family. (pp. 158-59)

Americans often wonder out loud at Bukowski's popularity in Europe, and yet is it any wonder that his flouting of the conventions and proprieties of a "bourgeois" literature would appeal to a generation weaned on Barthes, Foucault, Derrida, Lacan? Where but in the English-speaking countries could manners become elevated to such a powerful aesthetic criterion in the first place? In his present oxymoronic status as the world's richest and most famous "underground" writer, Bukowski is free to pull out all the stops and, in the course of this volume, he leaves few untugged. (p. 159)

*Gerald Locklin, in a review of "Hot Water Music,"
in* Studies in Short Fiction, *Vol. XXI, No. 2, Spring,
1984, pp. 158-59.*

DAVID MONTROSE

Although not an exclusively autobiographical writer, the prolific Charles Bukowski has always drawn heavily on personal experience for his poems, stories, and novels; certainly, the presence of Bukowski himself, usually in the transparent disguise of "Henry Chinaski", has normally been a feature of his better work. Fortunately, an eventfully misspent adulthood supplied a fund of experience rich in potential. Bukowski's uses of it were, admittedly, wildly uneven in quality, but, at his best, notably in various early stories, he reproduced the squalor and violence of low-life L.A. with the dirtiest of dirty realism. . . . But, by the mid-1970s, this source had worn thin. That the new material available—Bukowski's career as a minor literary celebrity—carried much less substance was strikingly illustrated by his third novel, **Women,** a fragmentary account of his life since 1970 that was little more than a self-aggrandizing catalogue of interchangeable sexual encounters. Small wonder that Bukowski's last novel, **Ham on Rye,** cast back to a largely unutilized source: his childhood and youth.

Hot Water Music, Bukowski's first collection of stories for over ten years, evinces a similar circumspection only in **"Some Mother"**, an uninspired tale of adolescent curiosity concerning the mysteries of the female body. Bukowski/Chinaski appears in less than half of these thirty-six stories. A number of others, though, are Chinaski vehicles in all but the protagonists' names. The collection mainly comprises further reworkings of Bukowski's older material and further reminders that the newer is, by comparison, infertile stuff. Even allowing for a sense of *déjà lu,* what is immediately apparent about the former is their tiredness. Two stories, for instance, deal with incidents following the funeral of Bukowski's father: events which, in several poems, he has used to good effect. Here, though, they receive perfunctory treatment. Similarly ill-handled are **"It's a Dirty World"**, **"Beer at the Corner Bar"**, and **"Home Run"**, where familiar scenes on the wild side are depicted with little of Bukowski's once-customary verve. **"Fooling Marie"** shows something like his old spirit, but its content—a gambler is robbed in a motel room by a woman who has picked him up at the racetrack—comes right from the bottom of the barrel. The stories based on Bukowski's more recent experiences frequently resemble postscripts to **Women.** **"Not Quite Bernadette"**, though, is an entertaining shaggy dog story, while **"Scum Grief"** also amuses. . . .

The non-autobiographical stories—or, at least, those not obviously autobiographical—tend towards fatal inconsequentiality. In **"Less Delicate than the Locust"**, for example, two painters and their girlfriends visit an expensive restaurant; they get drunk, create a disturbance, and leave without paying the bill. The End. The principal exceptions are **"Turkeyneck Morning"**, a brief episode from a lousy marriage, and, in particular, **"Broken Merchandise"**, which concerns a middle-aged nobody with a nagging boss at work and a nagging wife at home, who vents his frustrations on two young trouble-makers who cut him up on the freeway. Though by no means

one of Bukowski's very best, it is the kind of story with which he has always compensated for his regular misfires. In **Hot Water Music,** though, the misfires occur far too often even by his erratic standards, the compensations too rarely and too meagrely.

David Montrose, "A Bit on the Wild Side," in The
Times Literary Supplement, *No. 4231, May 4, 1984,
p. 486.*

KENNETH FUNSTEN

By his own standards, *War All the Time: Poems, 1981-1984* is as good as Bukowski gets: looser, simpler, more human and less holy than ever. But for readers desiring that shoddy, sagging American underbelly Bukowski made so famous, *War All the Time* may be disappointing.

Chinaski, Bukowski's *persona* in the poems and stories, is no longer a desperate bum living on the edge. He owns a home, has his own driveway and garage. This is important: not even his car is "on the streets" anymore!

Bukowski's geographies now consist of his neighbors—staunch, middle-class types—his BMW and its pulsing radio, his telephone, mailbox and typewriter. Near book's end, one poem portrays Chinaski watching a group of children ice-skating in a mall while he waits for a woman friend. The children are all color and movement:

> I like it, very much, but then I think
> as they get older they will stop skating, they will
> stop singing, painting, dancing,
> their interests will shift to
> survival,
> the grace and the gamble will disappear.
> but let's not feel too bad:
> this happens to animals too:
> they play so long
> then
> stop . . .
>
> then I see Linda, it appears that she has
> found something that
> pleases her, she rushes toward my table, she
> waves,
> laughing.
> I stand up, wave, smile,
> things seem very happy
> as down below us they whirl and
> glide.

The adult woman from whom the children's "grace and gamble" should have disappeared but have not refutes Chinaski's sad generalization, Bukowski's own past pessimism. The poet concedes a defeat at the hands of happiness—and a victory for his present experience.

We may be hard put to find the fighting in *War All the Time,* but the peace in these new poems is as authentic as the war ever was in the old ones.

*Kenneth Funsten, " 'The Grace and the Gamble Will
Disappear, but Let's Not Feel Too Bad . . .'," in*
Los Angeles Times Book Review, *March 17, 1985,
p. 4.*

JULIAN SMITH

Bukowski's opposition to the status quo is signaled by his language. The tough-drunk persona created in the writing is intimately linked to the way in which his fictions operate, and he shows enormous resource in working a subversive content on the linguistic level. We term "postmodern" those writers who have learned from modernism, and then added extra-stylistic components. While Bukowski had to erase other voices from his work (Céline, John Fante), he rewrote Hemingway with postmodern laughter, forming an utterly distinctive writing—allusive, anarchic and miraculously entertaining. (p. 56)

In common with many other writers (Ginsberg, Burroughs, Snyder), Bukowski published in underground newspapers of the 1960s and 1970s; he became a prolific contributor to his local papers, *Open City* and *L.A. Free Press,* and his fiction took its place alongside coverage of student unrest, the New Left, black power, civic and police corruption, the draft resistance, drug information, and adverts for sexual contacts and services.

Exploiting this popular platform for his writing, Bukowski's uninhibited mixture of fiction and opinion is almost impossible to read without explosive laughter on virtually every page. This is partly the result of subject matter in [*Notes of a Dirty Old Man*]: a winged baseball hero brought down to earth by women and drink; sex with a three-hundred-pound whore; the last days of Neal Cassady; boxing and racing; revolution and literature; a man who wakes to find his skin turned gold with green polka dots (recalling Kafka's *Metamorphosis*); drunkenly mistaken anal intercourse; demonology; and a grossly superb cast list of comically inept muggers, murderers, gangsters, misogynists, bums and whores, rapacious landladies, struggling writers, misunderstood geniuses, day laborers, perverts and other social oddballs.

This satiric critique of capitalism, bourgeois morality and conventional culture is accompanied by a deliberately disorderly syntax, a "spontaneous" typewriterese that creates its effect by a radical difference from smoother, more literary writing. . . . (pp. 56-7)

The tools in his craftsman's bag are used to create an impression of artless spontaneity. How is this textual illusion obtained? By the use of the first-person singular; a vigorous street language with no recourse to dictionaries, complex words or intellectual concepts; by the use of first names or real names as though the reader were an acquaintance; by the cultivation of a no-bullshit approach, as though the speaker were too busy telling the truth to dilute it with high cultural values; and most effectively by jokes and asides to the reader. . . .

Bukowski flavors the lexical stew of *Notes* with misspellings, ungrammatical constructions, sentences with no verbs, repetitions, split infinitives, much slang and swearing, sexual innuendo and other linguistic ambiguities that enable him to splice sexuality, violence, nastiness and humor. By deliberately leaving in the text the sort of grammatical confusions common in speech but usually suppressed in written English, Bukowski is indicating that he wants to align writing with *spoken* rather than *written* conventions. . . .

Surface indications to the contrary, Bukowski's fiction addresses itself to literate readers capable of appreciating the enormous number of irreverent references to writers, composers, painters and philosophers, and its slangy departures from polite literary expression. Which is why his writing goes down

so well with university audiences, even though his humor subverts their educational values.

From John Fante, Bukowski took the idea that the streets of Los Angeles (not Hollywood) represented a viable fictional world; from Céline, an attitude of misanthropic extremism. But Ernest Hemingway, the most accessible modernist, provided Bukowski with a macho role model, an existential material, and an experimental style already pushed in the direction of American "speech." The aficionado of the L.A. Public Library pushed the stripped-down, denotative (classic) style of Hemingway into play, parody, and laughter. Bukowski echoed the aesthetics of the prose technician. . . . (p. 57)

Hemingway (perhaps one should say *Ham*ingway) stressed simplicity of expression and small, "honest" words (instead of abstractions) and action to keep the existential void at bay. As Hugh Kenner says, Hemingway's "bullfights and lion hunts were aesthetic gestures"; the Bukowski hero parallels this by going to the racetrack. This allows for a flippant treatment of existential states—exaltation and despair, hysteria and boredom. Hemingway's regard for the authenticity of words and feelings seeps through onto the Bukowski page. But Bukowski's humor makes the page more divided, fecund, ambiguous, and harder to pin down ideologically than other writers (say, Mailer) who recycle Hemingway's male mythology. (pp. 57-8)

The function of his humor is sometimes to subvert cant, whole attitudes (e.g., sexism) that his stories, on another level, exploit. Sexual stereotypes—women as "all ass and breast," rapacious and available, a poor companion for the male compared to barroom buddies—hold sway throughout American fiction. At his best, Bukowski animates his stereotypes with great panache, investing "ideological unsoundness" with a liberating humor. A remarkable cultural allusiveness sends up machismo as well as alluding to and invoking it: "'Let's go out there and tell them to jam that horn up their ass,' said the kid, influenced by the Bukowski myth (I am really a coward) and the Hemingway thing and Humphrey B. and Eliot with his panties rolled.well.I puffed on my cigar.the horn went on."

Several Bukowski stories include fantasy dialogue with Hemingway's shade: **"The Killers"** parallels Hemingway's story of the same name; the opening of **"Stop Staring at My Tits, Mister"** parodies Hemingway in a crudely sexist mood; a rat-bearded professor bears a distinct resemblance in **"Would You Suggest Writing As a Career?"**; as a coup de grace, Henry Chinaski knocks out the aging Papa in **"Class"** ("You met a pretty good man, Mr. Hemingway").

The Hemingway legacy survives most vitally in the creation of a persona sometimes called "Bukowski" or "Henry Chinaski," what Barthes calls "a paper-author: his life is no longer the origin of his fictions but a fiction contributing to his work." Bukowski's artifice disguised as autobiography enables **"Too Sensitive"** to double-bluff the reader by ending on this note: "Meanwhile, I write about myself and drink too much. but you know that."

The intrusions of the author/narrator into the text are integral to many Bukowski stories, not merely winking to the reader but pointing up the text's artificial, fictive status. A playfulness clearly places Bukowski in the same camp as the postmoderns: "So, reader, let's forget Mad Jimmy for a minute and get into Arthur—which is no big problem—what I mean is also the way I write: I can jump around and you can come right along it won't matter a bit, you'll see."

Surrealism and existentialism enjoyed a delayed vogue in the American avant-garde of the 1950s and 1960s (Beat writers revived Artaud and Céline as major influences; *The City Lights Journal* made available the work of Michaux, Prévert, Genet, Artaud). While a rhythmic, semi-surreal language is sometimes evident, employing an illogical, dreamlike syntax ("but death was really boredom, death was really boredom, and even the tigers and ants would never know how and the peach would someday scream"), surrealism and existentialism's influence on Bukowski's fiction is most productive when reinvented, transmuted.

"The Gut-Wrenching Machine" is a comic commentary on authenticity, a concept crucial in existentialism's mythology. Criminals and tyrants supposedly live more authentically (that is, unhampered by moral codes, external authorities) than the solid, law-abiding citizen. Danforth and Bagley operate a wringer, turning out sufficiently pliable human material by squeezing the guts out, fitting their clients for "normal" life, the materialism of bourgeois society: "The ones labeled 'married with family' or 'over 40' lost their guts easiest."

Surrealism survives in Bukowski's bizarre characterization, the incorporation of fantastic events into a matter-of-fact narrative ("**The Fuck Machine**," "**Six Inches**"), always accompanied by quick-fire dialogue, endless one-liners, and a surrealism of the everyday; characters take onanistic photographs, fuck the phone, and fold complaining women into walls. Sexual explicitness is constantly undermined by grotesque details. With unexpected language reversals, deliberate anticlimaxes, and punchlines, Bukowski's stories point up their essential hero— the irreverent writer struggling with both the world and the word.

Self-referential stories about: being a writer on the reading circuit ("**Would You Suggest Writing As a Career?**"); a writer afflicted by minor fame ("**Great Poets Die in Steaming Pots of Shit**"); a writer continually interrupted in his attempts to complete a luridly improbable story ("**Twelve Flying Monkeys Who Won't Copulate Properly**"). (pp. 58-9)

The frisson provided by cultural reference and tough-guy language is typically irreverent, disruptive, avant-garde; for Bukowski, the pleasure of the text is always laughter. (p. 59)

Julian Smith, "Charles Bukowski and the Avant-Garde," in The Review of Contemporary Fiction, *Vol. 5, No. 3, Fall, 1985, pp. 56-9.*

John (Milton) Cage (Jr.)
1912-

American composer, essayist, poet, and nonfiction writer.

An influential and controversial figure in American music and a catalyst of avant-garde movements in several art forms, Cage is also an innovative author of prose and poetry. In his writings, Cage discards conventional linguistic structures in favor of his own syntactic guidelines, which are often governed by chance operations derived from the ancient Chinese text *I Ching*. This method emphasizes Cage's belief that chance is a controlling force in both art and life. Although some critics claim that Cage intends to subvert traditional artistic principles, others insist that he seeks to extend the possibilities of art through use of mixed-media and multigeneric forms. These forms, first employed in his musical compositions, are reflected in Cage's writings by his experimentation with typography and his blending of prose and poetry, polemic and playful creativeness.

Cage's pioneering efforts with ambient, electronic, and recorded sounds and his invention of the prepared piano have earned him a prominent position among contemporary composers. His musical compositions range from four minutes and thirty-three seconds of silence in the piece *4'33"* (1952) to the combined sound of seven harpsichords, fifty-two tape machines, fifty-nine power amplifiers and loudspeakers, and 208 computer-generated tapes in *HPSCHD* (1967). In creating atonal compositions, Cage explores the musical possibilities of rhythm without harmony. Cage's interest in rhythm led to his development of the prepared piano—an instrument devised by placing miscellaneous objects between the strings of a piano to produce percussive effects that can be varied by altering the placement of the objects. *Sonnets and Interludes* (1946) is his major piece for prepared piano. Cage's other compositions include *Imaginary Landscape, No. 1* (1939), which is considered the first musical piece intended for performance on electronic devices, and *Music and Changes* (1951), in which he employs the chance method of determining note sequences that he derived from the *I Ching*.

Cage's first book, *Silence: Selected Lectures and Writings* (1961), introduced his experiments with syntactical structure and typography. The pieces collected in this volume focus on music in a form combining lecture and poetry. In his second book, *A Year from Monday: New Lectures and Writings* (1967), Cage expanded his inventive techniques while turning from music to sociological and political concerns. He continued to explore these themes in subsequent books, including *M: Writings, '67-'72* (1973), *Empty Words: Writings, '73-'78* (1979), and *X: Writings, '79-'82* (1984). Like Buckminster Fuller and Marshall McLuhan, whom he has acknowledged as influences on his social ideas, Cage envisions the formation of a global society united by technology. According to Cage, new art, like his own, in which one finds aesthetic value in the objects and events of daily life, will be fundamental to understanding and participating in society. Many of Cage's ideas, as well as anecdotes and observations, appear in his collections under the title "Diary: How to Improve the World (You Will Only Make Matters Worse)." Some critics point to a naive idealism and flawed reasoning as weaknesses in Cage's social, political, and artistic ideas. Others, however, find his work refreshingly op-

Photograph by Rex Rystedt. Courtesy of John Cage

timistic and important for suggesting new outlooks on the structure of thought and communication. In addition to social commentary, Cage's books feature his experiments with acrostic poetry, his application of chance operations to rework the creations of other authors, and his criticism of literature, music, and art. In discussing critical reaction to Cage's work, Richard Kostelanetz stated: "Even though his ideas usually attract more comment than commentary, more rejection than reflection, he is, to increasingly common opinion, clearly among the dozen seminal figures in the arts today."

(See also *Contemporary Authors*, Vols. 13-16, rev. ed. and *Contemporary Authors New Revision Series*, Vol. 9.)

BETTE RICHART

[Cage is] a necessary therapy, and since it is his book [*Silence*] and not his music that we are discussing here, unqualified alleluias are in order, for it is an enchanting book.

After Cummings, Stein, some of Eliot, and the birth and death of all the little mags . . . one shouldn't have to apologize for typography, but I must warn you not to be put off by eccentricity in that field, as I was till I began to see what Cage was doing. In the lecture **"Where Are We Going? And What Are We Doing?"** I started to see, as well as hear, the structure of the fugue; since I am a dedicated non-musician, the achievement is Mr. Cage's—and the printer's. . . .

Cage is a raconteur of the first order. One story he mentions again and again: the sound chamber which magnified the high tones of his nervous system, the low tones of his circulatory system. These sounds, so intimately important, are part of what he means by "silence"—a word he uses to include all sounds that are not "part of a musical intention." As he says, the world is teeming with them. It may be a long time before many people share his conclusion that "electrically controlled sound is music," but the principle of control is never absent from his considerations, and "the principle of form," he says, "will be our only constant connection with the past."

These lectures, given "not to surprise people, but out of a need for poetry," make the intent of modern art, or really contemporary art, very clear. From metal sculpture to Cage's own work, there is a common purpose: it is not to illuminate the darkness (a platitude which infuriates Mr. Cage) but to partake of darkness—after all, it is light enough, in Christian as well as in other mysticisms. . . .

In the famous lectures on Nothing and Something (the typography, in both instances, is a topography!), the problem of form is analyzed in a way that no one since Suzanne Langer has attempted. "Structure without life is dead," is a familiar conviction, though an important one. See what comes next, however: "But life without structure is unseen." Life without art is unseen; the thought of life without form is obscene, as if the bust of Homer in that marvel of Rembrandt's were suddenly to become a jelly-fish before one's very eyes. "Form is what interests everyone and fortunately it is wherever you are and there is no place where it isn't. Highest truth, that is."

One other interest which is reasonably universal is love, and naturally Mr. Cage has something to say about that too. "I remember loving sound before I ever took a music lesson. And so we make our lives by what we love." Perhaps form is the ultimate evidence of man's love of his work: in the curious cavern of time, some Leonardo invented the wheel, before a statue could even be dreamed of. I have always imagined him standing for a moment, alone with his isolating genius, admiring the beauty of that shape before starting it off on its journey down history. During such a moment of contemplation, a man shines with utter giving, and despite his buffoonery, it is in such a light that I see Mr. Cage. (p. 416)

Bette Richart, "A Modern Composer Lectures on Art," in Commonweal, *Vol. LXXV, No. 16, January 12, 1962, pp. 416-17.*

CALVIN TOMKINS

For several years now, John Cage's book *Silence* has been what Greenwich Village booksellers call an "underground best seller." Intense young loyalists of the New York art scene carry it reverently to happenings, thus demonstrating their awareness that Cage, America's reigning musical revolutionary, had initiated the happenings movement at Black Mountain College in 1952. . . .

It has been evident at any rate that Cage's influence extends well beyond the field of contemporary music, where his experiments with "found sound," electronic composition and chance methods have outraged traditionalists for 30 years. To those who have followed Cage's career, it will not be particularly surprising to learn that he now considers music merely "child's play." In [*A Year from Monday,* a] new collection of lectures, essays and other writings completed since *Silence* came out in 1961, he makes plain that he is less and less interested in composing music and more and more interested in improving society—an enterprise to which he devotes himself despite a cheerful premonition that he will only succeed in making matters worse. . . .

Like Buckminster Fuller and Marshall McLuhan, to whom he gives full and generous credit where credit is due, Cage foresees the electronic transformation of society, the global village, the disappearance of work, money, privacy, individualism, nationalism, war and other linear stigmata. The message is similar; the medium, however, is utterly unique. To read Fuller and McLuhan is to struggle with prose styles that, for all their neologisms and contortions of syntax, are still based on 19th-century linear models. Cage, on the other hand, has made it a point to compose most of his writings according to the same methods that he uses in his music, and since 1950 this has meant according to the methods of chance.

Take, for example, his **"Diary,"** three installments of which make up a large portion of the new book. Cage decided in advance that the diary would be a "mosaic of ideas, statements, words, and stories," and before writing in it each day he determined by means of chance operations (a rather elaborate procedure derived from the *I Ching,* the ancient Chinese book of oracles) how many parts of the mosaic he would employ, and how many words there would be in each, the total each day to equal or exceed 100 words.

Using . . . 12 different type faces, he let chance determine which type face would be used for which idea, statement, word or story, and also where the left-hand margins would fall. The result, which must have caused some typographer untold anguish, is a sort of open-ended prose poem, a verbal collage that proceeds according to its own highly disciplined illogic and whose effect, for this reader, is simultaneously witty, naive, irritating, oddly moving, self-indulgent, evangelistic, and as fresh and surprising as electric flowers in the global village square. It is also stamped at every point with the author's irresistible gaiety and lucid intelligence, a quality of mind that somehow holds together all the fragmentary workings of chance. . . .

Many of the ideas in the present volume will be familiar to students of *Silence*. The difference is mainly one of emphasis: a shifting from esthetic to social concerns, and a reiterated belief that the new art provides us with a key to the new life in tomorrow's electronic universe. The new art, in which great numbers will participate freely and without competitiveness, indicates ways in which "many centers can interpenetrate without obstructing one another." Daily life is what matters, provided one is truly awakened to its wonders. "What's marvelous is that the moon still rises even though we've changed our minds about whether or not we'll ever get there."

None of this, one can say, is especially profound or even strikingly original, and yet I have no doubt that it will be read like Scripture by the young. Read and enjoyed (which is more than can be said for McLuhan), and rightly so, because in Cage's case the medium, which happens to be print, is really the message. Tune into him at any point—statements (outrageous or otherwise), quotations from the books he's been reading (lately, Thoreau and Veblen), sermons (the meeting of East and West; the uses of anarchy), even the seemingly inconsequential, humorous, Zen-like stories that he drops at intervals into the more formal text in order, as he says, to provide "an occasion for changing one's mind"—and you find yourself traveling at high speed along the new electronic wavelength.

Calvin Tomkins, "Social Concern," in The New York Times Book Review, *January 21, 1968, p. 6.*

MICHAEL KIRBY

There is no question that John Cage is one of the key figures in contemporary art. This fact might make [*A Year From Monday*] worth reading, but it would not necessarily make it an important book. Talking with my friends who are artists, I often have the rather romantic idea that everything they say somehow explains their work; I am less interested in their writing. In writing it is too easy to hide, merely to tell the reader what you would like him to think. Theory need not match practice in art, and many artists contradict themselves when they write about their work. None of this is true of Cage, however. Although I have only met him once or twice, all evidence points to what I am tempted to call a *unique* congruency between his everyday life, on one hand, and his public presentations of music, lectures and writings, on the other. He seems without contradictions. There is nothing that must be interpreted. Surface manner may change with the situation, of course, but the same fundamental "rules" govern all of his life, which happens to include his art. This ontological consistency—"honesty" seems too limited a word because it indicates only moral choice—is one of the things that makes *A Year From Monday* an important book. Given Cage's position as innovator, intellectual and guru, his collection becomes a lucid example of the kind of thought that has had great influence on the *avant-garde*. (p. 362)

Cage is an inveterate innovator. He cannot let things be as they usually are or always have been. In this case he cannot merely present traditional printed prose. He is concerned with the processes of composing, speaking, and visually reading words. Whereas his earlier collection, *Silence* (1961), and the "Juilliard Lecture" (1952) in this volume tend to emphasize the organization of sounds in time, the concern of many of the pieces in the present collection is less "musical" and more "poetic" or "painterly": they are primarily designed for the eye. The transcript of a tape recording includes symbolic representation of breathing, swallowing, and the soft grunts and groans I call "vocalized thinking." Twelve different type faces are used in **"Diary: How to Improve the World (You Will Only Make Matters Worse) 1965,"** and the 1967 installment of the same title adds various shades of lightness and darkness of print. (The organization of lines on the page makes **"How to Improve the World"** look like a poem. Three such texts are included here, and more are promised; it seems as if it would become Cage's *Patterson*.) Even the most traditional piece in the volume, a letter written with no thought of publication, is given a slightly unusual visual life by being photographically reproduced in the original handwriting rather than being set in type.

Cage's writing does not tell us what to think as much as it makes us think in a particular way. He is as much concerned with the structure of his writing, and therefore the structure of thought, as he is with the particular ideas that are expressed verbally. . . . In creating most of the pieces in this book, Cage

began with an objective "plan for writing," in which variables such as the number of sections, the subject of each section, the number of words or lines of writing in the section, the amount of blank space and so forth, were determined by chance. (Most commonly, he used either a method of coin-flipping derived from the *I Ching* or the set of transparent plastic sheets he created in 1960 to produce his *Cartridge Music*.) If it seems as if the result should be arbitrary, formless and pointless, the opposite is true: each part is felt to be in its "proper" place. Everything fits.

I am intentionally not emphasizing the subject matter of the book: the many short stories that Cage scatters throughout as he did in *Silence;* the somewhat new social consciousness which he relates in part to Buckminster Fuller and Marshall McLuhan . . . ; the comments on artists such as Marcel Duchamp and Jasper Johns; the variety of other subjects upon which Cage touches. These small units out of which the larger mosaics of the articles and lectures are composed are almost always clear, compact, pointed and unemotional. Often they have the same impact and "resonance" as the large work of which they are a part: there is an unusual identity between the individual texts and their parts, between each article or lecture and the whole book. I cannot say that these separate units are unimportant. . . . But Mumon wrote of the thousands of roads that enter the great path through the gateless gate: Cage has many subjects but only a single unitary "content." "Each something is the celebration of a nothing which supports it," and it is finally the "content" or "message" of *A Year From Monday* that makes it an important book. In these days of tough-minded and tough-postured art, the use of the word "spiritual" is suspect, but it must be said that John Cage demonstrates in an unpretentious, subtle and forceful way the profound spiritual basis of *avant-garde* art, at a time when many people prefer to dismiss the most important works of our day by considering only the surface. (pp. 362, 364-65)

Michael Kirby, "Gate to the 'Avant-Garde'," in The American Scholar, *Vol. 37, No. 2, Spring, 1968, pp. 362, 364-65.*

ELLSWORTH SNYDER

Some of the writing [in *A Year From Monday*] is purely for information, such as the first of the **"Two Statements on Ives"** or **"Diary: Audience 1966"**; some for amusement and revelation, such as the little anecdotes that appear throughout the book; and a great deal of it, such as **"Mosaic,"** a review of the *Schoenberg Letters,* or **"Miró in the Third Person: 8 Statements,"** to show the same process in writing as Cage uses in composing. Some of the writing is obscure, none of it is dull. If greatness in writing is a matter of composing unforgettable lines, as Virgil Thomson maintains in speaking of Gertrude Stein, then Cage ranks high indeed. And like Stein, Cage is presenting common-sense ideas in poetic ways. . . . Cage's audacity in not stating his ideas in a straightforward, academic manner outrages some, but many find it refreshing. It is the ideas that count, and Cage's ideas grow while remaining philosophically consistent.

For Cage the distinction between what is art and what is life remains very small, if indeed there is one at all. He belongs to that international group of creative minds that wonder what art might be. (p. 482)

Conceptually, *Silence* and *A Year From Monday* are the same, but they are different too. The difference is twofold. First,

Cage has become more and more interested in global social concepts. "The question is: What are the things everyone needs regardless of likes and dislikes?". . . . "What's urgent is society. Not fixing it but changing it so it works." "What's needed is global planning . . ." . . . Second, whereas in *Silence* Cage was a student of Richard Buhlig, Henry Cowell, Guy Nearing, Arnold Schoenberg, and Daisetz Suzuki, in *A Year From Monday* he is a student of N. O. Brown, Marcel Duchamp, Buckminster Fuller, and Marshall McLuhan. . . . Of particular importance to him is observing that which is happening in life, intentioned or non-intentioned, as it is happening, without the intrusion of value judgments, because value judgments get in the way of what should be our proper business—that is, curiosity and awareness.

And *A Year From Monday* is a book for anyone who still has curiosity. (p. 483)

> *Ellsworth Snyder, in a review of "A Year from Monday: New Lectures and Writings," in* Notes: The Quarterly Journal of The Music Library Association, *Vol. 25, No. 3, March, 1969, pp. 482-83.*

RICHARD KOSTELANETZ

[*The essay excerpted below originally appeared in a different form in* The Denver Quarterly, *Winter, 1969.*]

John Cage is one of these rare figures whom, if he did not already exist, the philistines would need to invent; for not only are his ideas so original that they all but beg to be misunderstood and/or misinterpreted, but his is the sort of eccentricity that unenlightened minds can smugly dismiss without a glimmer of revelation. It is true that some of his activities generate first-level newspaper copy, as well as arouse suspicions of fraudulence; however, many retrospectively unquestioned "breakthroughs" in all contemporary arts at first struck even the sophisticated intelligence as suspect, while, beneath Cage's comedy and his propensity for unprecedented actions, are eminently serious purposes. What makes uncomprehending criticism more irrelevant, if not more pernicious, than even undiscriminating adulation is that Cage, very much like two of his own gurus, Marshall McLuhan and Norman O. Brown, is a fount of richly imaginative ideas that cannot be rejected or even accepted whole cloth. Even though these ideas usually attract more comment than commentary, more rejection than reflection, he is, to increasingly common opinion, clearly among the dozen seminal figures in the arts today. Quite simply, much of what he says is valuable and digestible, though much is also chaff. . . . *A Year from Monday,* a second collection of fugitive pieces, provides a propitious occasion for more comprehensive scrutiny; and let me start by saying that this book is rich in ideas relevant to all sorts of artistic, philosophical, and social endeavors. He is so emancipated from professional conventions that he is free to follow his imagination into any medium and risk innovative work in areas other than music. Though his ideas invite philistinism, even from the sophisticated, I doubt if any open-minded and intelligent person would not be challenged—surely irritated, perhaps persuaded to change his mind—in the course of perusing this compendium of provocative aphorisms, intellectual absurdities, and formulations so original they will doubtlessly make sense to some, nonsense to others. . . . His book is so fertile and various that one must dip in, pick out, and think about whatever strikes the mind, and that process itself informs the structure of these miscellaneous paragraphs. A further truth is that an assignment to write on

Cage brings out, for better and worse, one's courage for originality.

One must initially acknowledge Cage's indisputable originality in an age that suspects everything has already been done; for nearly all that he makes, whether in art or life, is riddled by idiosyncratic and imaginative touches. . . . His penchant for the unusual give his writing the quality of constant surprise; and, for this reason, much of it evades immediate comprehension, though his thought is not particularly complex. . . . In [*A Year from Monday*], the author of a revolution in music clearly wants to accomplish something similar for prose; and although the desired breakthrough still seems a few steps away, Cage is by now discernibly beyond literary conventions. . . . In his earlier collection of pieces, *Silence,* the more recent essays eschewed linear organization for the structure of random comments; and, in the new book, few collections of sentences are even as approximately linear as this paragraph. The discontinuous compositional style seems an appropriate vehicle for Cage's invariably unconventional thoughts, as well as an approximate literary analogy for his scrupulously discontinuous music, yet precisely because the style continually risks obscurity, it signifies that Cage is still more of an artist than a propagandist.

One radical artistic idea that Cage has pushed beyond its previous provinces is the work of art as *primarily* an aesthetic illustration. The illustrative point of *4'33"* (1952), which consists of four minutes and thirty-three seconds of David Tudor, an established musician, sitting silently at the piano, is that all the unintentional, random sounds framed within that auditorium and within that period of time can be considered "music," for "doing nothing," as the critic Jill Johnston notes, is clearly "distinct from expressing nothing." By investing a situation where music is expected with nothing but silence (and where, as in the original performance, the well-known performer three times moves his arms in ways that suggest the piece has three distinct movements), Cage implied that in the silence was "music" that could be heard; this polemical illustration is an example of "art by subtraction" to the point that negation produces addition—in Mies van der Rohe's felicitous phrase, "Less is more." . . . At the root of Cage's compositional principles is collage—the mixing of materials not normally heard together; but, because he is less interested in barbed juxtaposition than abundant mixtures, the result is less collage than something distinctly Cagean. That roughly explains why an experienced ear, though it may not have heard a particular piece or rendition before, can usually identify a certain unfamiliar piece as Cage's work and not another's. In *Theater Piece* (1960), he pursued an implication of *Music Walk* (1958) by suggesting that a plethora of physical actions could, by performer's choice, be substituted for randomly activated sound-generating procedures; and, since he has previously ruled that all sounds are music, this instruction eventually implied, by analogy, that "theater" could be said to exist as soon as the perceiver's mind wished to define it. "Theater takes place all the time, wherever one is," Cage wrote in *Silence,* "and art simply facilitates persuading one this is the case." Nonetheless, it is precisely in their realized inchoateness and, in Cage's phrase, "purposeful purposelessness," as well as extravagantly spectacular qualities, that his own recent theater pieces distinguish themselves from both ordinary life (merely the "model" for the art) and others' "happenings" theater. In retrospect, then, the primary significance of *4'33"* lies precisely in its inferences, which gave Cage and others "reason" or "permission" to create eventually a musical theater that is indeterminate not only in its composition but its performance, too—aleatory kinetic presentational structures that are chaotic in both structure and detail. What is most conspicuously lacking in *A Year from Monday* is an analogous path-breaking gesture that could command as much suggestive influence for literature as his earlier "musical" demonstrations. . . . Regrettably, Cage has not particularly developed his stunningly suggestive assertion in *Silence:* "I have nothing to say and I am saying it and that is poetry." Maybe such a radical printed literary work cannot exist—if I could conceive it, I might do it myself; but, in principle, I hesitate to make such blanket negative statements about the future of Cage, or literary art.

Adopting the musical notion of unashamedly artificial constraints to literary purposes, Cage posits unprecedented ground rules that serve to emancipate him from conventional ways of organizing and rendering words. An instance of this is "Indeterminacy" (1958), consisting of ninety funny stories, each of which, by self-imposed rule, will be a minute in length when read aloud. When Cage performs this piece on a . . . record of that title (1959), while David Tudor makes random noises in another room, "Indeterminacy" is very much about variations in prose tempo, as well as the random interactions between musical sounds and verbalized words. Here the form of the work expresses part of its ultimate content, as a performance illustrates (as opposed to explains) the piece's declarative title and Cage's aesthetic position; therefore, the ninety funny stories, which are pleasurable in themselves and comic to various degrees, are just the surface occasion for less obvious, but more substantial, concerns. Here, as in much else of Cage, the unperceptive spectator can be deceived into accepting the surface as all of the point—as silence is simply no sound, so stories are just anecdotes; but more significant meanings are invariably implied or inferred, by the piece, the spectator, or both. However, to put these stories into conventional print, as Cage does in *Silence,* destroys much of their primary effect (corrupting their original purpose even more than recordings of Cage's recent pieces betray, as fixed renditions, their scored indeterminacy); and, in the traditions of *printed* literature, ninety funny anecdotes within a larger frame comprise no innovation at all. Similarly, another performance piece, "Juilliard Lecture" (1952), published in the new book, is in its printed form all but unreadable, as is "Talk I" (1965), which, as Cage's headnote reveals, was not intended to be understood anyway.

The major essays in *A Year from Monday* comprise a three-part "Diary: How To Improve the World (You Will Only Make Matters Worse)," its sections subtitled respectively the years 1965, 1966, 1967; and, in composing what he characterizes as a "mosaic of ideas, statements, words, and stories," Cage posits a system of compositional constraints and indeterminate procedures (which also constrain his expression). . . . In practice, these constraining procedures induce an original style with its own distinct tone and particular rhythms. The "Diaries" are "poetry," not because they manipulate poetic conventions, but because they cannot be persuasively classified as anything else. However, as a form suitable primarily for miscellaneous insights and connections, prejudices, and gossip (usually to an excess), anecdotes and speculations, it is also a rather needlessly limited vehicle for verbal expression. Although it enables Cage to note unusual analogies, make one-line suggestions, relate one kind of position to another, and provide reviewers with numerous quotable gag lines (that are not representative of the text as a whole), this note-making format discourages the elaboration and development of thoughts, as well as granting Cage an easy escape from the necessity of pursuing the implications of his more radical ideas. On the other hand,

precisely in its disconnectedness, such prose demands that the reader make his own connections. Beyond that, the form here, unlike "Indeterminacy," suggests no conceptual content that I can perceive or infer (even though previous experience with both Cage and other avant-garde materials persuades me to add that I may well be missing the significance); therefore, the primary substance of these diaries lies not in the form but the quality of the commentary, which is inevitably erratic, instinctively radical, and often stimulating. Finally, as a literary form appropriate for random remarks, this compositional process represents a successful mating of man and his makings; nothing could be more suitable, if not congenial, to an artist on the move, as Cage . . . is most of the time, as distinguished from a contemplative thinker or a professional writer. Perhaps because Cage derived an expression appropriate in form to his personal style, *A Year from Monday* is a more readable, communicative, and artistically suggestive book than its predecessor. (pp. 193-99)

In the history of contemporary art, Cage functions as an antithetical catalyst, who leaps ahead so that others may move forward by steps. Late in the 1930's, he suggested prophetically that all noises, including those electronically produced, would enter the domain of serious music; and, by his own use of sounds unfamiliar to concert halls, he helped establish precedents for all contemporary electronic composition. Indeed, by making art out of materials not usually familiar to art, Cage, along with his friend Marcel Duchamp, also provided antithetical precedents for pop art, found objects, industrial sculpture, and much else; and Allan Kaprow, a sometime painter who originated (and christened) that performance art known as happenings, testifies that, although he personally does not subscribe to all of Cage's radical innovations, "he taught us to be free." In this respect, another implicit theme of *A Year from Monday* is that all kinds of criticism and all kinds of fiction, including critical fictions and fictitious criticism, can be put on pages, intermixed, and bound between hard covers. (p. 201)

The news in *A Year from Monday* is that Cage has recently been renouncing music for social philosophy; but, just as he abandoned concert music for a mixed-means theater that subsumes his music, so he regards his music, which has always been about *changing peoples' minds,* as a springboard into political thought. In retrospect, we can see how much politics has always been present in his music. First of all, his music implies the abolition of archaic structures, as does his politics; and both his music and his social thought suggest that new forms ought to be built from the most essential materials. . . . (p. 205)

In Cage's coherent web of related radical ideas, the major common theme is that, since great changes are still possible in both life and art, we should strive to achieve what has not already been done. . . . Although his bias is "not fixing [society] but changing it so it works," what *A Year from Monday* does not offer is a politics—advice on how the golden age will come—perhaps because Cage believes that widespread mind-change *precedes* social change, and he senses, not untenably, that technological development itself will accomplish most of the transformations. "Once we give our attention to the practice of not-being-governed, we notice that it is increasing." This sense that the world is getting better largely on its own momentum may strike some political people as slightly naïve; but Cage's professional life exemplifies its own kind of radical activism. As a man who frequently commands audiences, spreading a certain gospel, reprogramming the heads of those who learn to appreciate his ''music,'' offering images and proposals for a radically different future, exercising his almost Jesuitical persuasiveness—all at a time when most self-styled ''radicals'' offer merely negative criticisms—Cage is a harbinger-publicist for a new, necessary, comprehensive, unprecedented, unstructured, mixed-means revolution. (pp. 205-07)

Richard Kostelanetz, ''John Cage: Some Random Remarks,'' in John Cage, *edited by Richard Kostelanetz, Praeger Publishers, 1970, pp. 193-207.*

DONAL HENAHAN

In *Silence, A Year From Monday,* and now *M,* the latest installment in his diary series, we have the solid, seizable stuff of art, whether the anti-artist likes that or not: Cage caught. Throughout his career Cage has worked at being the outsider, the banana-peel strewer on the sidewalks of the Academy, the kid who says he doesn't want to be in the club. And it is clear that this has been more than a pose. But, with a genuine artist's instinct for the usable past, he comes in *M* to identify himself closely with one major figure in the American Lit Club whose talents dovetail with his own: Thoreau.

Like Thoreau, Cage is interested in wildness, anarchy, oriental mysticism, plainness and flabbergasting middle-brows. In *M* he takes a thoroughly Thoreauvian approach to thinking and writing: Despite any logical cohesion they seem to have in final form, Thoreau's essays are mosaics or collages, fashioned out of random notes and observations jotted down in journals. So are Cage's diaries, except that his entries do not cohere; they are Delphic bulletins that either make oracular sense or no sense at all.

So it is not strange that *M* (whose very title was picked by consulting I Ching, the Chinese book of changes) can be dipped into at any point, read forward or backward, without losing the flow. Visually and often poetically striking, the book is organized around words and names beginning with M, according to Cage's own quirkly rules, which readers of his *Notations* will recognize. Each observation, insight, witty aside or quotation (from Thoreau, Mao, Norman O. Brown, Buckminster Fuller, Cage) is set in its distinctive type face, and entries take their place in a sequence decided by I Ching. That may sound horrible, but only if you are the sort who is confused and annoyed at rummage sales.

Cage's reliance on I Ching is the kind of thing that infuriates his detractors. But what seems to be his fascination with irrationality is really something more: it is not chaos he wants but diversity, multiplicity, looser structures in life and art. (p. 34)

Cage is the ever reborn American Optimist, the neo-Rousseau believer in noble savages and quintessential human goodness. He runs wild in a universe that is nice enough to let him, and maybe that proves him right. There is an old-fashioned innocence about him, a Transcendentalism that, as in Thoreau, merges and blends with a genteel primitivism: Cage as Leatherstocking in fashionable blue denims, padding through harmless jungles, immune to tooth and claw and even to worry. ''If the situation is hopeless, we have nothing to worry about'' is one of those insights, more consoling at first glance than upon reflection.

Further exploring the rummage sale of his mind, we come upon: ''Imitation of nature in her manner of operation, tradi-

tionally the artist's function, is now what everybody has to do. Complicate your garden so it's surprisingly like uncultivated land.'' Pure Thoreau, that. Or, his reply to someone who says his thinking is full of holes: ''That's the way I make it.'' Pure Cage, that.

It would be easy to attack such stuff as wisecracks and copouts. ''Fame has advantages,'' Cage admits. ''Anything you do gets used. Society places no obstacles.''

And there is a good deal in *M* that will strike some readers as trivial or worse. Interrupting the diary at several points, for instance, are acrostic poems of a variety that Cage calls mesostics because they are read down the middle instead of across. They are based on names of friends and heroes (Mark Tobey and Marcel Duchamp) and mushrooms. One especially pretty example will show the technique:

> a utility aMong
>   swAllows
>   is theiR
>   musiC.
>   thEy produce it mid-air
> to avoid coLliding.

Here we see Cage organizing his thought in a way that tickles his puzzle-solver's fancy but which also shows that the need for form is not so foreign to him as some critics have imagined. In these mesostics he makes sure that ''a given letter capitalized does not occur among the letters between it and the preceding capitalized letter,'' a formally constricting scheme akin to serial technique in composing music and a reminder that Cage was, early on, a student of Schoenberg, this century's foremost musical logician.

Cage notes, however, that he would like increasingly to avoid the logic of syntax: ''As we move away from it, we demilitarize language . . . nonsense and silence are produced, familiar to lovers.'' But this mistrust of linear logic seems at odds with his famous adoration of machinery (nothing thinks more linearly than a computer) and his avowed faith in technology as our salvation. The diary series was begun in 1965 ''to celebrate the work of Buckminster Fuller,'' and it is still the Fuller brush that Cage trusts will sweep the world clean. Like Fuller, Cage understands the role machines have played in bringing us to our present terrorized and polluted state. But, rather like Robert McNamara taking over the job of pacifying Vietnam, Cage believes all will be solved by submitting the problem to more efficient machines. Whether by consulting I Ching or IBM, we will have Progress.

So, under the robes of the Zen priest, the dice-throwing shaman, the chaos-embracing composer and the poet of noble savagery, we have no trouble finding John Cage the apostle of know-how and benign technology. He is the American Optimist and Odd Fellow, quite at home in the local lodge, no matter that he looks like a self-made kook and mystic. He preaches artistic and social anarchy, but always with a cheerful humor and a practical man's concern for the society he must continue to live in, a concern he expresses with poetic pith in his Foreword's peroration:

> The party's nearly over. But the guests are going
> to stay: they have no place else to go. People
> who were invited are beginning to arrive. The
> house is a mess. We must all get together without saying a word and clean it up.

Billions of words have been spilled on the subject of over-population and environmental pollution, but it takes our American poet of irrationality to say it all so simply and so well. (pp. 34, 36-7)

Donal Henahan, "He Is the American Optimist," in The New York Times Book Review, *September 23, 1973, pp. 34, 36-7.*

ROGER SMALLEY

From the vantage point of *M,* his third volume of collected writings, the progressive bankruptcy of John Cage's thinking becomes startlingly apparent. His first book *Silence,* published in 1961 and containing writings of the previous two decades, was the inventory of a richly provocative mind. Here were many new ways of thinking about the nature of music (and its necessary opposite, silence) freshly and inventively expressed. Four simultaneously delivered lectures unequivocally communicated the thesis that we are continuously surrounded by a multiplicity of conflicting viewpoints and opinions; he explained the structure of his music in a talk put together according to the same principles as the music itself; a series of Zen-like anecdotes showed how it is possible to see art manifesting itself in aspects of life other than the purely 'aesthetic.' New uses of typography and layout brought these concepts onto and off the printed page with maximum clarity.

A Year from Monday followed in 1968 and contained the first three instalments of **"Diary: How to Improve The World (You Will Only Make Matters Worse)"**. . . . The subject matter of the diary is increasingly concerned with specifically political, economic and social issues in a way not previously encountered in Cage's writings. From the beginning of this project one could sense a dichotomy between the ideas themselves and the manner in which they are expressed, between the course of action which they implicitly call forth and the musical activities with which Cage has surrounded them. Implicit contradictions which become distressingly explicit in *M.* . . .

Cage continues to nibble tentatively at these themes in the four further instalments of his diary which make up the larger part of *M.* I read them with a steadily increasing sense of depression. If anyone feels they have something valuable to say on these subjects it doesn't seem unreasonable to ask that they write with clarity, directness and precision. This is scarcely material suitable for chance operations, typographical tricks, witty anecdotes or feeble paradoxes. Even more disturbing is the paucity of ideas which manage to filter through the pointless and artificial constraints placed on their expression. In the sixteen pages (each containing one narrow column of print) which constitute the first diary most of the genuine flashes of illumination are to be found in quotations or reported speech of writers such as McLuhan, Thoreau, Norman O. Brown, Gandhi, Buckminster Fuller and Nelson Goodman. Cage's own contributions are mostly restricted to what I would call (after half-truths) 'half-thoughts' ("It's useless to play lullabies for those who cannot get to sleep") or statements of an unfounded and unconvincing optimism: "We're leaving the Piscean age, entering the Aquarian one. We'll be living in a situation of overlap, interplay, global unity, universal understanding, collective peace and harmony." There is not a constructive word in this book about how humanity might make the transition from the world as it is now to the starry-eyed vision of the future envisaged in that quotation.

In addition to the diary, the book's principal contents comprise a **"Mushroom Book"** (which contains a few useful cooking hints for enthusiastic mycological gourmets), **"62 Mesostics re Merce Cunningham"** and **"Mureau"** in which the excellent and poetic statements of Cunningham on dance and Thoreau on music are syntactically dismembered so as to render them meaningless and set in over three hundred varieties of typeface.

The intolerance which I detect in my review is, I think, a product of the mounting frustration I felt as I conscienciously read on through every page of this long book in the unfulfilled hope of finding at least a few nuggets of useful information or enlightenment in its pages. . . .

"I have nothing to say and I am saying it," wrote Cage in his 1952 **"Lecture on Nothing."** Truly in *M* he has "nothing to say" and he spends two hundred and seventeen very tedious pages saying it. If he still *has* anything to say (and the short foreword to *M* permits one to hope that he has) then I think he now owes it to his readers (and listeners) to express it coherently. If not, perhaps Silence would be the best policy.

Roger Smalley, "Silence Was Golden," in The Spectator, *Vol. 231, No. 7586, November 17, 1973, p. 644.*

HANS KELLER

To the serious student of Cage—and there are many of them, whether they know it or not—[*Empty Words: Writings '73-'78*] will not altogether be news. For one thing, 'most of the material in this volume has previously appeared elsewhere', while for another, Cage is gradually running out of gas, with a paradoxical double result; while old gas is being re-used, he is now forced to use something else, too—not only 'empty words', but also, yes, a thought or two (at the outside).

Since there is, of spiritual necessity, less unity here than in the most heterogeneous anthology or symposium, any unifying review on the essence or character of what Cage has to say . . . would be as unfair as it remains tempting; it would be unfair but for the fact that Cage himself has found a way of unifying, not his vacuoles and occasional fillings, but their required recipients: he wants them to have that in common which, in his own view, his products have in common—an imaginative lack of learning.

It is in his dedication that he hands them their diploma, which singles them out, as his likes, for their contempt of diplomas: 'To the students in the school from which we'll never graduate.' This is really it: we have to pay him the compliment that he has achieved an 11-word self-characterisation which intimates what he has to give—and take away. He is over-conscious of its wisdom, but oblivious to its stupidity, which is almost willful. Let's spell it all out, then: craft is bad, mastery phoney, so you can't graduate about what matters; in fact, you can't graduate as a genius, a new mind. Agreed, you can't. But you can't convey your genius without acquiring the necessary craft, which can be graded, and in which you can therefore graduate, qualify. In short, Cage's half-truth would be all right so far as it goes if the other half weren't such a lie—the curse, this, of even the best half-truths.

What is it that blinds and, specifically, deafens Cage to the other half, to the significance of learning in general and musicianship in particular? Is it his genuinely revolutionary insight into the paralysing, indeed blinding effect of knowledge, prejudice, 'precedent' (as he calls it, the mortal enemy of 'discovery')—of the heavy burden of the past? No. Though insight may distort, it never blinds.... The answer, I'm afraid, is banal: it is John Cage's own inferiority feelings that deafen him to the attainments of the musical graduate; it's his awareness of his skill, of a musicianship he could only have developed on the basis of a higher degree of sheer musical talent, natural musicality, than he knows he possesses.

The evidence is all over the place.... In the late Thirties, Cage

> had two ways of composing: for piano or orchestral instruments I wrote twelve-tone music (I had studied with Adolph Weiss and Arnold Schoenberg); I also wrote music for percussion ensembles: pieces for three, four, or six players.

Isn't he revising history twice over? So long as Schoenberg was alive, we didn't hear about Cage's studies with him: Schoenberg would have denied them.

Whatever he did with Schoenberg, he never came to 'study' with him: though foreseeing penetratingly, a possible 'inventor', Schoenberg did not find Cage sufficiently musical for the job of a composer. Had Cage genuinely studied composition with him, he would soon have found out that Schoenberg never taught twelve tone technique at all—not even to the famous twelve-toners, Berg and Webern. But Cage's implication is that he learnt one of his 'two ways of composing' from Schoenberg: empty words indeed. What is significant is the anxious showing-off of a graduation that never happened and which, at the same time, is held in philosophical contempt. Cage's liberation from culture, from art itself, is as culture-ridden as are his public fantasies about his lessons with Schoenberg.

Yes, nowadays, we seem to need a microscope in order to perceive the over-lifesize symptoms of Cage's cultural mania, the passion with which he proves himself one of the boys, a member of the exclusive club of musical creativity's top organisers, structurers, secret serial scientists. (pp. 19-20)

> *Hans Keller, "Late Cage," in* The Spectator, *Vol. 244, No. 7929, June 26, 1980, pp. 19-20.*

EDWARD ROTHSTEIN

"It's useless to pretend to know mushrooms," says John Cage in *For the Birds.* "They escape your erudition." The more you know them—about telling, for example, a *Spathyema Foetida* from a *Collybia Platyphylla*—"the less sure you feel about identifying them." (p. 12)

At any rate, *For the Birds*—the latest textual addition to the Cage canon—adds significantly to our understanding of mushrooms and Mr. Cage. With its biographical detail, it is a complement to Richard Kostelanetz's *John Cage,* showing how the composer himself has grown in the musical wild. He developed when the laws of musical linearity—tonality and counterpoint—were wildly overrun. But he would have been stifled in the arid, harshly lit ground provided by his one-time teacher, Arnold Schoenberg.... Somewhere in the overgrowth and chaos Mr. Cage took root; by 1950 he was the free-growing alternative to the cemented determinism of advanced serial composition.

Mr. Cage explains the title of this book, using an aviarian metaphor rather than a toad-stoolian one: "I am for the birds, not for the cages in which people sometimes place them." He is "for the birds"—a lunatic, a charlatan, a clown—and he is "for the birds"—an advocate of that region of freedom where even his own name dissolves into air.

In previous books, Mr. Cage has also been concerned with breaking bonds. *Silence, A Year From Monday, M* and *Empty Words* relish their own eccentricities; lines and spaces and meanings are disrupted with as much gala zest as in Mr. Cage's music. *For the Birds,* though, is least "for the birds." Its margins are justified, binding Mr. Cage in 11 interviews with an energetic French philosopher, Daniel Charles.

The formal restraints were hard come by. The interviews took place in France in 1970; they were translated into French; the English tapes were lost; the French texts were translated back into English. In 1972 and 1980 Mr. Cage interjected footnotes and placed brackets around statements he didn't remember saying. There is a prefatory **"Sixty Answers to Thirty-three Questions From Daniel Charles"** in which Mr. Cage pastes, in graffiti style, gnomic, random answers to interview questions.

There is also conversation "against the ego," on "the will to disorder," on "the performer's revolt," on "revolution and synergy," on mycology, on subjects random and controlled. What is his objection to linearity, to meaning? Would he agree to conduct Beethoven's nine symphonies? ("I would agree if I could use enough musicians to conduct, in one single concert, all nine symphonies superimposed.") (pp. 12, 39)

And Mr. Cage has lots to say about mushrooms....

The mushroom is his icon; its whimsical freedom is everywhere. "Accepting chance," says the mycologist Mr. Cage, "makes prejudices, pre-conceived ideas, and previous ideas of order and organization disappear!" ...

But there is something about mushrooms that defies Mr. Cage's flights of Zen fancy. He admits of "chance" operations: "It's only if I act like that with mushrooms that it can kill me." He would not, then, use the *I Ching* to pick mushrooms; there are bounds on his activity, limits to his freedom.

Categories and laws, in fact, fill Mr. Cage's airy regions of freedom like the scientific Latin names for mushrooms he must learn. His musical dice throws involve as many complex operations as harmony and counterpoint; *HPSCHD* required computer calculations to set up the necessary bounds. (p. 39)

His political anarchy also has its rigidly ordered shadow. "The Maoist model," he writes in a 1972 footnote, "managed to free a quarter of humanity; that gives cause for thought. Today, without hesitation, I would say that, for the moment, Maoism is our greatest reason for optimism." This may not only be for the birds, but for the cages people are put within.

So Mr. Cage sets up cages while he destroys them. The music is not even as freely meaningless as he claims. Aside from such early works as the translucently beautiful sonatas for prepared piano, his works avidly take on literal meanings; the music is heard not as koan, but as rebellious gesture. The music is meant to uncage, to free from the grid of the past. But the result is the opposite. Its meaning is caged in that very gesture.

There is something exhilarating in the radical scope of Mr. Cage's play with freedom and law; his pronouncements—musical and literary—are wrought with captivating swagger, bluster, and charm. But given the state of our musical world, such attitudes are also a bit discouraging. For even now, as celebrations of Mr. Cage's 70th birthday begin, he remains less important as a composer than as a symptom, embodying fundamental gestures of this century's cultural beliefs: Natural law is devalued, social tradition is minimized, while rebellious gestures are given sense by the tradition they deny. The result is a classic modern trap, not avoided by Zen transcendence.

Mr. Cage's career, in fact, seems to provide a marker for the end of musical modernism, which now lies in as much disarray as the carcass of the musical tradition it once fed upon. (pp. 39-40)

> *Edward Rothstein, "Sounds and Mushrooms," in* The New York Times Book Review, *November 22, 1981, pp. 12, 39-40.*

RICHARD KOSTELANETZ

[*The essay excerpted below originally appeared in a slightly different form in* The New York Times Book Review, *December 2, 1979.*]

[*Empty Words*] contains expository essays on **"The Future of Music"** and **"How the Piano Came To Be Prepared,"** and these are of interest to followers of Cage's musical thinking. Another section, ostensibly about both the choreographer Merce Cunningham and food, illustrates Cage's genius for storytelling. However, most of this new book contains language constructions that must be called "poetry," partly because they are not prose, but mostly because they cannot be persuasively classified as anything else. Since these *poems* are radically unlike everything else in American writing today, it is scarcely surprising that they are rarely discussed by "poetry critics" and never mentioned in the current surveys of American literature.

Notwithstanding his advocacy of "chance" and artistic freedom, Cage is an artistic formalist, who invents alternative ways of *structuring* language. One device is the mesostic. Whereas the familiar acrostic has a word running down the left-hand margin of several lines, the mesostic has a recognizable word running down the middle. In Cagean practice, this vertical word is usually the name of a friend—Merce Cunningham, Jasper Johns, Norman O. Brown. Within this mesostic constraint, Cage makes concise statements. . . . (pp. 231-32)

The title piece of *Empty Words* is a four-part poem drawn from Henry David Thoreau's remarks about music and sound. What Cage did here is copy relevant passages out of Thoreau's books and then subject them to *I Ching*-aided chance processes that, in effect, scrambled and combined them, producing a nonsyntactic pastiche of Thoreau's language:

> speaksix round and longer than
>   the shelloppressed and
> now ten feet high heroTheclosely isor
>   have looked wellthat and spruces
>   the and a darker line below it

This stanza comes from the first page of the first part, which contains phrases, words, syllables, and letters (characters) from Thoreau. The second part of **"Empty Words"** contains just his words, syllables, and letters; the third part just syllables and letters; and the fourth part just letters.

"Empty Words" is less about Thoreau than about sound, or the sound of language about sound, compressed and recombined; reading it is not about assuaging our powers of literary understanding but about challenging and expanding them. This is rigorously Platonic poetry that takes initially spiritual liter-

ature and recomposes it into a yet more ethereal realm. In my opinion, **"Empty Words"** is better heard than read; for not only has Cage performed selections from it dozens of times around the world, but his reading of the entire work will soon appear as a fourteen-record set.

Scarcely contented with past poetic inventions, Cage has recently developed a series of conceptually ambitious schemes for extracting language from James Joyce's multilingual masterpiece, *Finnegans Wake*. In the initial scheme, Cage works from the beginning of Joyce's book to its end, taking out words that contain letters that fit into a mesostic structure based upon the name "James Joyce." . . . It is a measure of Cage's originality that nobody ever made poetry like this before—the method is, like so much of his work, at once sensible and nutty. To my mind, *Writing through Finnegans Wake* is interesting in part because it is so audaciously innovative; it succeeds in part because it recycles James Joyce. Hearing Cage read it aloud, with sensitive precision, is a special pleasure. (pp. 232-34)

Cage describes **"Empty Words"** as progressing, over its four parts, from literature to music, and it seems to me that both this work and its Joycean successor finally realize an identity between the two traditional arts. "Text-sound" is the epithet I use to define language works that cohere primarily in terms of sound, rather than syntax or semantics; and Cage, as a literary musician, is clearly a master of that domain. On the other hand, since both **"Empty Words"** and **"Writing through Finnegans Wake"** are language-based, they fit snugly into the great American tradition of poetry that realizes an eccentric innovation in the machinery of the art—a radical change not in meaning or in sensibility but in the materials indigenous to poetry: language, line, syntax, and meter. (In this sense, Cage's principal poetic precursors are Whitman, Cummings, and Gertrude Stein.) Considered in this way, Cage is not a literary curiosity but an exemplary American poet. (pp. 234-35)

> *Richard Kostelanetz, "Polyartist's Poetry," in his* The Old Poetries and the New, *The University of Michigan Press, 1981, pp. 231-35.*

SMALL PRESS REVIEW

[The publisher classifies *Themes and Variations*] as "poetry/music." If you know the work of Cage, one of the foremost figures of the Black Mountain experiments in art and culture, you know it is probably both and more. Cage opens a new chamber in the work he has created "out of a need for poetry." This is a poem, a score for oral performance, a typographic experiment, a musical composition in which the words are notes and the ideas, phrases, a series of mesostics determined by chance operations and combined with the traditional Japanese form of Renga. Root ideas fragment in musical phrases and rise again like apparitions. The text becomes a charged environment in which each "thing" of language appears with the spontaneity and originality of a new world. In his mesostics, Cage uses the names of fifteen men who have influenced him . . . , and he draws his content from 110 key precepts scattered through his books. The result is a startling recreation of his own intellectual and spiritual journey. The work establishes the almost personal connection between the work and poetics of our foremost experimental composer.

> *A review of "Themes and Variations," in* Small Press Review, *Vol. 15, No. 4, April, 1983, p. 8.*

GEORGE F. BUTTERICK

X is the latest Cage work to test our credulity. . . .

The title of *X* was derived by subjecting the alphabet to chance operations via the *I Ching,* his usual methodology, although in this case it may be less fortunate because too meaningful, intentional, traditional—"X" as in industrial or air force designations for "experimental"—and it has already served as title for at least two literary journals, not to mention the recent prominent L.A. band, as well as, more than two decades earlier, part of Malcolm Little's great sociopolitical argument. In any case, the collection consists of several types of "writing," as in Cage's previous volumes: his writing "through" other people's texts, using them as basis for chance rearrangements; entries from his continuing diary, **"How to Improve the World (You Will Only Make Matters Worse)"**; a nice set piece called **"James Joyce, Marcel Duchamp, Erik Satie"**; some poem-looking mesostics (an acrostic as spine or vertabrae amid the lines rather than at their beginnings); and a series of photographs that I will respond to with perhaps excessive enthusiasm. . . .

There is something essentially soft, amorphous about Cage that is charming and acceptable and nonsexist and agreeable, but ineffectual, so that he has to borrow struts from Fuller's technology or stalks from other temporary culture blossoms like Marshall McLuhan or Norman O. Brown to support his amorphous goodness. Somewhere along the line, Cage, Fuller, and other users of utopiates forgot what Freud, Heisenberg, and the masters of the Shaolin monastery remembered. Cage talks about "risk" in *A Year from Monday* (1967), but hardly convincingly: "But what's meant by risk? / Lose something? Property, life? / Principles? The way to lose our / principles is to examine them, to give / them an airing." Principles are relatively safe, however; the remark would have been more interesting if he had stayed with "property" and "life," and the best way to lose *them*. Perhaps he is a genius with a genial rather than a genuine mind.

There are lovely, endearing notions in his several statements of purpose, such as: "It is possible to imagine that the artists whose work we live with constitute not a vocabulary but an alphabet by means of which we spell our lives." Or again, he describes the work of Joyce, Duchamp, and Satie as having "resisted the march of understanding." Understanding, once it gets underway, *is* inexorable and proud and tends to crowd out discovery. Cage offers polymodal existence, and for this we embrace him (provided we don't crush him). He is basically a softie, a sentimentalist, with his own brand of wistfulness called "intelligent anarchy."

One of the pieces that might be singled out in *X* is the "alphabet"—more a theater script—called **"James Joyce, Marcel Duchamp, Erik Satie."** It is pretty breezy—light and airy—except for some borrowed moralizing about the need for conservation of energy resources through "use instead of ownership" and pieties like "good life for all men depends / on realizing it / for / each / single man from a to z"—nothing more profound or original than that. The body of the text consists of trills of fantasy, mostly fun, though sections are also schoolboyish. . . . Lots of silliness, vaudeville, improbable probabilities, it is one of the most enjoyable pieces in the collection. I wouldn't mind having it read to me (the capital letters of the mesostics are just an annoyance; cute, anybody might say). . . .

There is also the latest installment of Cage's ongoing diary, **"How to Improve the World,"** begun again after the silence of the late Sixties. Among its highlights are interspersed anecdotes concerning Merce Cunningham's Aunt Sadie. . . . Other anecdotes are from Cage's own family stock, as in previous volumes, and, incongruously, there are a number of sections concerning Puerto Rican politics, all in a lovely ripple of varying typefaces and all entries somewhat fuller than when the diary was launched in *A Year from Monday.* (p. 6)

There is always the temptation to misjudge Cage as a simpleton. Imagine paying a heartfelt tribute to a friend in these words, especially if you're a major cultural figure:

> iT
> is A long time
> i don't Know how long
> sInce
> we were in a room toGether   now i hear
> that yoU are dead . . .

No thanks; it almost wasn't worth the dying. His elegies, as in previous collections, are shallow, sentimental, and linguistically without interest to most poets (it's a busy world). They can be skipped unheeded, though curiously the one for composer Ben Weber ends rather intentionally and (perhaps because of it?) attractively. Still, one of Cage's purposes has always been to bring impatience to a boil.

Cage has been a genius in his time, a miracle of plenty in the land of steady habits. There seems no need to press him, even with savage indifference. Any quarrel isn't really with Cage, but with those who seek to raise him up as a poet, who turn their faces from the possibility that writing which is not prose is not automatically poetry. Poets will find of interest that Cage has added Pound to his travels, by including a mesostic composed of lines from Pound similar to his use of Joyce and Thoreau called **"Writing Through the Cantos"** (no doubt there's a pun on riding), and will also find of interest that he mentions "the poet Louis Zukofsky" (whereas in every other case he simply mentions the name without the profession).

Cage makes it easy for us. He suggests we don't have to understand him. He never understood Duchamp, after all, and Duchamp was a friend and inspiration. . . . And when Cage went on to say, "I preferred simply to be near him. I love him and for me more than any other artist of this century he is the one who changed my life . . ." I felt lifted right off the hook. One need only love Cage, if and when we do. (pp. 6-7)

Cage excites possibilities because of one thing—he understood the principle of boldness in art: it's art if you call it so. Now, why the Princess of Grace comes to *his* performances with fur under each chin, and not yours, gentle artist, is the history of art in our time.

If there is anything tiresome in the collection, and naggingly doctrinaire, it is his familiar principle of indeterminacy. What troubles one is the exclusivity Cage continues to give "chance operations" (how easy it is to be snappish when dealing with an optimist!). His chance is a lot like atheism—an absolutist position to deny an absolute. It is merely the substitution of one clockwork for another. The trouble with Cage is you can't fail. It's Betty Crocker. His system is as mechanistic as a WWII encoder, all ratchets and slots. It's the safety of his method that's constrictive. His *I Ching* lacks the conviction of Russian roulette or the immediacy of the weather. Is it enough to replace cause with effect? With standards like "noise" or "silence," you can't lose. The chance I like is where language, a sentence, takes a leap off, waving and kicking, into the abyss, and comes up with a grin between its teeth. True chance has more than a base of sixty-four for permutations, just as there are considerably more or less than twenty-four hours in a day. Every time we write we choose a construction almost infinite in its possibilities. It is one of the mysteries of language, that it can contain our vast souls.

The chief liability of the experimental mode is not disorientation but saturation. Repeat an experiment often enough and you've got predictability, a body of predictability, or science. In art, it is called a manner. Confirmation in science is achieved by producing identical results. In art, the results are monotony.

For the man Calvin Tomkins of *The New Yorker* has said has caused more disturbance or astonishment "than any other American" (*pace* John Wilkes Booth and Lee Harvey Oswald), there is not much disturbance in this book. But there is astonishment, grounds for astonishment, and a retinal crush of beauty. The real bonus are the photographs, which neither *A Year from Monday* nor *M* nor *Empty Words* could boast of, or perhaps needed. There are twelve "weathered images," taken under Cage's direction by Paul Barton, of ornamental "windows" on the Siegal-Cooper building on 6th Avenue between 18th and 19th Streets in Manhattan (around the corner from where Cage lives). Twelve windows to eternity, swept by light and streaked with color, that have everything one might want— falls and geysers, snow-tufted nests, alpine cradles, puffs of hair netted in drains, Belial's smoke, branches cracking each other, thumbed oil on tin, grandmother cobwebs, mildew on the march. What mirrors! The wicked stepmother's was nothing by comparison. Each reader has the sense, mirror of *my* soul. Each is an iridescent speculum within stone architrave framed in glazed brick, with mortar thick as cream and firm as icing made from scratch. Some stand on pediments, crushing them, like headstones. They are themselves framed by space, monuments to vision. They've obviously got weight, yet they float. They are animate, changing before the eye, imperceptibly at first, then with dizzying speed within their temporal frames, in a full range of a day's colors from gong copper to the soot of a tomb, the burnished back of a pocket watch to Maxfield Parrish purple loaming. Twelve eyeless windows, billows of marble, milky matter, meditative delights. The photographs alone increase our capacity for wonder. (p. 7)

George F. Butterick, "Rattling the Cage," in Exquisite Corpse, *Vol. 2, Nos. 5-7, May-July, 1984, pp. 6-7.*

DICK HIGGINS

Since most of [*X: Writings '79-'82*] is poetry, it seems high time to start describing Cage as a composer poet, not just as a composer who has somehow done a few poems: poetry seems as central to Cage's cosmos as music and, no doubt, there are many who prefer his poetry to the music.

But a cosmos is precisely what Cage focuses upon; he presents, in *X*, views of worlds—his own and those of artists who have been significant to him: Erik Satie, Marcel Duchamp, James

Joyce and, taking philosophy as the art of thinking, R. Buckminster Fuller and Daisetz T. Suzuki among others. If he presents a point of view, it is done by selection of quoted fragments rather than by commentary; although, since [his] earlier . . . books, the explanations that accompany each poetic text (these usually made by collage using chance operations or other randomizing systems) have become ever longer. In spite of his well-known desire to transcend the specifics and limitations of his own taste and intentions, presumably his main rationale for using chance, he seems to have developed a certain dread of being misunderstood, and the reader of *X* is therefore more apt to feel lead by Cage through the poems in the book than free to make of them what he or she will. The result is that this particular collection feels like an introduction to Cage's poetry, a grouping that will lead the reader to the earlier works. . . .

The two longest works, at fifty pages each, are **"Writing for the fourth time through Finnegans Wake"** and **"James Joyce, Marcel Duchamp, Erik Satie: an alphabet,"** both of them collections of mesostic stanzas, a form Cage has made uniquely his own. The mesostic is a poem in which there is some kind of text, called an "intextus," embedded visually within the lines of the main body of the piece; it was first brought to prominence by P. Optatianus Porphyrius in a series of panegyrics to Constantine the Great ca. 325 A.D., flourished in the Carolingian Renaissance of the ninth century, and again in the early Baroque (ca. 1585 to 1650), but has been more or less dormant since then. . . .

"James Joyce, Marcel Duchamp, Erik Satie: an alphabet," suggests a dream world in which those artists are all alive and in contact with Cage and such living friends as Robert Rauschenberg. Though not written by any randomizing system, it evokes the sounds and sense-patterns of the Joyce series. . . .

"Composition in retrospect" is a set of lyrical meditations on formal aspects of making art; it constitutes a poetics by example, since the intexti are: "METHOD, STRUCTURE, INTENTION, DISCIPLINE, NOTATION, INDETERMINACY, INTERPENETRATION, IMITATION, CIRCUMSTANCES." There is also a chance-composed text based on Thoreau's journals, **"Another song,"** which reads and feels like many pages in traditional modern verse, for example Robert Kelly, and a section of Cage's ongoing "Diary" series, a collection of impressions gathered daily—the complete "Diary" series should be collected between two covers some day. Neither of these pieces are mesostics, but there are a few other mesostics groups in *X*, **"B. W. 1916-1979"** (memories of the composer Ben Weber) and **"for her first exhibition with love"** (for Fanny Schoning), examples of Cage's most personal and intimate writing, gathered from among the perhaps hundreds of mesostics that Cage has composed for his friends and colleagues, few of them collected or published.

All in all, *X* is a welcome addition to the mushrooming corpus of Cage's poetry and . . . would make the best introduction to Cage's cosmology for those who have not, as yet, developed a taste for his music.

Dick Higgins, "Three Years' Texts," in The American Book Review, *Vol. 7, No. 4, May-June, 1985, p. 24.*

Morley (Edward) Callaghan

1903-

Canadian novelist, short story writer, journalist, dramatist, and autobiographer.

Once described by Edmund Wilson as "perhaps the most unjustly neglected novelist in the English-speaking world," Callaghan is best known for his allegorical fiction in which he infuses seemingly ordinary human relationships with complex moral, psychological, and religious significance. His prominent themes include redemption and salvation, the discrepancies between illusion and reality, and the conflict between materialism and spiritualism. Callaghan established a solid reputation during the 1930s as a significant new fiction writer, and his short stories were especially well received. In the 1940s, however, Callaghan ceased writing short fiction, concentrating instead on long, complex novels which generally met with slight critical favor. Callaghan's publications of the 1970s and 1980s renewed interest in his career, and he is now regarded as an important figure in twentieth-century Canadian literature.

One of many expatriate writers to travel to Paris during the 1920s, Callaghan associated with such literary celebrities as Ernest Hemingway and F. Scott Fitzgerald. Callaghan and Hemingway met while working as reporters on the *Toronto Star* in the early 1920s, and Hemingway recommended Callaghan's work to Ezra Pound, who aided in its initial exposure. Many of Callaghan's stories appeared in American magazines during the 1920s and 1930s. These works are characterized by his understated prose style and his focus on social outcasts. Many critics consider Callaghan's stories, some of which are collected in *A Native Argosy* (1929), *Now That April's Here and Other Stories* (1936), and *Morley Callaghan's Stories* (1959), to be his best work. One critic called the latter collection "one of the few achievements of Canadian prose, more powerful than any single Callaghan novel and more worthy of enduring than any single work of his better publicized peers: Anderson, Hemingway, and Fitzgerald." Many of Callaghan's previously uncollected stories appear in *The Lost and Found Stories of Morley Callaghan* (1986).

During the 1930s, influenced by Hemingway and Sherwood Anderson, Callaghan began to write spare, journalistic novels. Callaghan's prose, while remaining true to the genre's subdued, impassive style, exhibited greater lyricism and a profound sympathy for his characters, qualities which some critics attributed to his Catholicism. These novels take place during the 1930s and reflect an interest in the moral and spiritual effects of prevailing social conditions. Callaghan's first major novel, *Such Is My Beloved* (1934), is the story of a Roman Catholic priest whose awareness of the conflict between his spiritual convictions and his bourgeois status enables him to understand the two prostitutes he tries to reform. Redemption and salvation are again prominent themes in *They Shall Inherit the Earth* (1935), in which a man's guilt for allowing his malicious stepbrother to drown combines with the physical poverty he endures during the Depression. The illusive nature of appearances and the ambiguity of human motivations are examined in *More Joy in Heaven* (1937). In this novel, a prisoner who was rewarded with an early release for exemplary behavior becomes disillusioned with society and returns to crime.

Photograph by John Reeves

Callaghan departed from the style of his early novels during the 1950s, attempting to apply his characteristic themes in a form similar to that of the nineteenth-century novel. Racism is a prominent topic in *The Loved and the Lost* (1951), a novel for which Callaghan received the Governor General's Literary Award for fiction. In this work, a white girl's desire to associate with Montreal's black community distances her from both societies, resulting in harassment and her eventual murder by uncomprehending whites. A similar paradox pervades *The Many Coloured Coat* (1960), in which a public relations man's attempts to restore his damaged reputation result in deeper problems and disillusionment.

Critics detect in Callaghan's later publications a return to the moral vision and concise, unobtrusive style of his early work. *Close to the Sun Again* (1977) is the story of a former navy commander who attempts to come to terms with the materialistic, passionless life he has led. *No Man's Meat and The Enchanted Pimp* (1978) comprises two novellas. *No Man's Meat* was considered risqué at the time of its initial publication in 1931 due to its allusions to lesbianism and adultery but was described by Edmund Wilson as "a small masterpiece." *The Enchanted Pimp* revolves around a wealthy pimp who becomes obsessed with a benevolent prostitute. Callaghan rewrote the story as the novel *Our Lady of the Snows* (1985). *A Time for Judas* (1983), an unusual work for Callaghan, is a complex biblical-historical narrative about Judas Iscariot. Written in the colloquial manner of Callaghan's realistic parables, this novel focuses sympathetically on Judas's betrayal of Jesus Christ. Functioning simultaneously as a defense of Judas and as a treatise on the artist's responsibility to himself and others, the book abounds with allusions and parallels to modern times.

Critics have frequently debated the effectiveness of Callaghan's novels, focusing particularly on whether his understated prose style is an effective means of presenting moral conflicts and uncertainties. However, it is generally agreed that his fiction of the 1930s is his most important work. In addition to his fiction, Callaghan has written two plays, *Turn Home Again* (1939) and *Just Ask for George* (1939), and a book for young adults, *Luke Baldwin's Vow* (1948). In his autobiographical memoir, *That Summer in Paris* (1963), Callaghan discusses his experiences with various literary celebrities, including Hemingway and Fitzgerald, and the origins behind his own fiction.

(See also *CLC*, Vols. 3, 14 and *Contemporary Authors*, Vols. 9-12, rev. ed.)

HOWARD ENGEL

In his most recent book [*Close to the Sun Again*], Morley Callaghan has demonstrated that he is still a major force in Canadian writing. Some critics of *A Fine and Private Place*, his last novel, found it a glimpse of a diminished talent. While it may have had some sections that looked finger-smudged and worked over, it was a credible addition to his work. One can now see that it was not a gesture, a faltering attempt to keep his hand in; it was a book that promised that better work was to follow. *Close to the Sun Again* will make Callaghan-watchers jump for joy. It confirms the faith. In many ways, it's the Callaghan we've been waiting for. (p. 55)

Two things single out Callaghan from other writers. Callaghan's stories have always been moral parables with the lesson skilfully woven into a rich fabric of characters acting out their destinies against a busy urban landscape. He loves to show how men will act badly if given half a chance. The text of the moral lesson is just out of sight. His trademark is an almost biblical spareness. Further, he has an anarchic kink that makes you take a second look at this quiet, law-abiding, Rosedale septuagenarian. Like Eugene Shore, the writer in *A Fine and Private Place*, Callaghan is "a man who [delights] in criminals and sometimes [gets] them mixed up with saints. . ." In *More Joy in Heaven* he took a criminal named Kip Caley and showed us the morally ambivalent world of the rehabilitated crook. . . . [In most of his works], Callaghan is asking, "What if this ugly so-and-so really has the soul of a poet?" or "Supposing the fallen woman is right and the Church is wrong?"

In *Close to the Sun Again* we can find both parable and anarchy. "What is a man profited," asks the Gospel, "if he shall gain the whole world, and lose his own soul?" The man who gained the one and lost the other is Commander Ira Groome, late of the Royal Canadian Navy. In making the exchange—which is not shown in any overt Faustian way—Ira finds a kind of death-in-life, much like Coleridge's celebrated sailor, the Ancient Mariner. And only in the last pages of the book does the albatross fall from his neck. Ira has done as well for himself

in the boardrooms of multinational corporations as a man can. For thirty years he has cultivated his taste for the noiseless ride of a Rolls-Royce and the truly fine cigar. He also recognizes and achieves the finest in discreet bourgeois dalliance. On his return from South America to his native Toronto, he becomes head of the police commission, a respectable but not taxing position. You'd think it was the beginning of a gentle decline, but you'd be wrong. The end comes quickly. Touched by a memory of himself at the deathbed of his wife, and disturbed by the indifference of his son, Ira Groome begins to crack.

For years he has been holding people at arm's length because once, on a corvette during the war, he let life get too close. Like Icarus of Crete, he flew too close to the sun and melted the wax that held his wings. Like Icarus, he got a drenching. His response to this was never to fly again. Callaghan seems to be telling us that whatever the risks and whatever the cost, man must dare to fly in the face of the sun. If we don't risk our fragile wings, we're condemned to creep about on the ground like poor half-human things.

Callaghan watches his characters rather the way a zoologist studies a group of primates. He observes acutely and sets everything down in a notebook without much theorizing or comment. The narrator hovers above Ira Groome, giving us just as much information as we need to follow the story. . . . For all of the comparisons of Callaghan with his old sparring partner of his Paris days, Ernest Hemingway, it would have been much more useful all this time to compare the Canadian with Graham Greene, a writer he resembles far more. Hemingway's people are searching for courage under pressure and a kind of secular grace—objects less weighty than redemption and salvation, which are the recurring themes in both Callaghan and Greene. (pp. 56-7)

The convoy sections of [*Close to the Sun Again*] are as tightly drawn as a bowstring; the tension vibrates. It is some of the best writing about the sea I've read. I got the sense of men at the end of their resources, and of the "unplumbed, salt estranging sea" as rarely before.

Close to the Sun Again is a memorable and well-crafted book. . . . On the threshhold of his seventy-fifth birthday, Callaghan has written a book which is solid, mature, and wise. (pp. 57, 60)

> Howard Engel, "The Callaghan Novel We've Been Waiting For," in Saturday Night, Vol. 92, No. 9, November, 1977, pp. 57, 60.

D. J. DOOLEY

Evidently Callaghan's publishers are never going to forget Edmund Wilson's reference to him as the most unjustly neglected novelist in the English-speaking world; the statement appears on the dust jacket of [*Close to the Sun Again*]. Yet since the tribute was made Callaghan has done little to justify it. Instead, the list of critical complaints against him has become virtually a standard one: he is tough; he is often effective, especially in a short bout, but in a full fifteen-rounder his weaknesses become glaring, particularly his awkward style and his inability to devise and carry through a complicated fight plan. This novel, however, is short rather than long; it represents a return to the brief parable form in which Callaghan has had his greatest success. All of these parables contain traps for the unwary, and all of them contain puzzles and enigmas; *Close to the Sun Again* is no exception.

Most of it is relatively easy to decipher; it is a Robertson Davies type of story about a man named Ira Groome (frequently referred to as "the Commander") who is little more than his public personality. Completely dedicated to his work, he is utterly ruthless, because he suppresses all private feeling. His mistress, Carol Finley, can almost hear him say, "I hope you understand, old girl, there's nothing personal in this." Yet by the time he meets her he is on a pilgrimage, in search of the place where he can learn, and the person who can tell him, what went wrong with his life.

On her deathbed his wife Julia asks him why he became a stranger after they married. Her question destroys his picture of himself as the considerate husband of an alcoholic wife, and forces him to face what he has become. . . .

Even if it relies rather heavily on coincidence, the naval part of the story is convincingly told. It describes the rescue of a pretty girl of twenty, Gina Bixby, and a red-haired man of forty, Jethroe Chone. Both of them are near death from exposure—Jethroe especially, because he has given the girl most of his clothing. Yet when the girl recovers she speaks of the man with contempt. . . . In their conversations, Gina gives Ira an insight into the world of gambling and crime with which her father is familiar. Only a wartime voyage to England seemed to offer Gina an escape from a gangster named Marty Rosso, and Jethroe was told to take her there. Two nights before they sailed, however, he raped her; so Ira learned the reason for her revulsion against Jethroe, and became aware of her quiet determination to see that Jethroe paid the full price for his betrayal when they got to England.

In the subsequent action, the corvette is torpedoed, and Ira finds Gina relying on him for warmth and comfort, while the wounded Jethroe glares at him from the other side of their life raft. But just when he thinks he understands the state of Gina's mind completely, one astonishing event takes her away from him, and he is left disillusioned and alone. His reflections on this event cause him to make his decision to avoid personal commitment. . . . So he becomes the Commander aloof on his bridge, the executive looking down from his office building on the crowded streets of São Paolo, the well-dressed man walking across City Hall Square who is separate from the crowd of skaters and doesn't even recognize a former shipmate. (p. 36)

So much is clear; yet by his very omissions, Callaghan perhaps suggests more. Early on there is mention of a wise old priest and a bad priest (a psychiatrist), and near the end there are references to Pascal and to a white leopard (as in Eliot's *Ash-Wednesday*); religious values are being invoked, but subtly rather than blatantly. Surely there is irony in the reference to Ira as "the Lord" in São Paolo. He becomes a rock, a pillar of strength—to men in power. He lives a life of dedication, as his acceptance of the Chairmanship of the Police Commission demonstrates; he does his best to keep his fellow citizens safe. Yet in all his activities, there is no charity. There is plenty of irony again, therefore, in his lecturing the Deputy Chief, Tom Frawlick, "like a stern, dispassionate old medieval pope talking to a monk from the provinces," on selfless, impersonal commitment to a cause:

> now Ira Groome was saying quietly and sternly that a man could find freedom in perfect service. Sometimes a man performed this service with an act of abnegation, a thing done for the sake of the restoration of harmony.

Such a bleak, dispassionate outlook is a parody of any genuine commitment of self. The Commander is a Pharisee, who seeks to have the letter of the law obeyed but desires to separate himself from the messy human scene.

Consequently, *Close to the Sun Again* gives us a better insight into Callaghan's peculiar religious vision than do most of his other novels. He has some affinities with Graham Greene, even though he has called the latter a Manichee. In Greene's *The Power and the Glory*, when the whisky priest is captured and put in jail he looks on it as a microcosm: "This place was very like the world: overcrowded with lust and crime and unhappy love, it stank to heaven. . . ." He tries to tell a pious woman disgusted by the goings-on around her that God so loved this messy world that He sent his Son into it. Similarly, Ira Groome has a vision of the world from which he is detached. . . . He does not really act upon this vision; in fact, throughout his career he forgets what he learned from a girl in Yucatan, when he was a young archaeologist: the world is "cruel and senseless, a nightmare, always was, and always will be, and all we can do is make something beautiful out of the nightmare."

Nearing death, he realizes that he has committed high treason against himself; as Callaghan shows it, his error was both intellectual and moral: "In college he had read Pascal; if you don't believe in God, if you haven't got the faith, then act as if you have, perform all the rituals of faith, and you will come to believe. That was all wrong. You ended up believing in the habits that took over your heart." He had turned his back on the perplexity and mystery of people; for him to become "the Lord in São Paolo" was to become an ironically limited and lonely and faithless man. One kind of faithlessness, then, is the subject of this interesting and provocative novel. (p. 37)

D. J. Dooley, "Parable of Faithlessness," in The Canadian Forum, *Vol. LVII, No. 677, December-January, 1977-78, pp. 36-7.*

E. L. BOBAK

The novella *No Man's Meat* has been virtually without an audience since its first printing in Paris [in 1931]. . . . In February 1932, Callaghan's work was reviewed by *The Canadian Forum* in a column called "Canadian Writers of Today." Though the reviewer, H. Steinhauer, indicated a knowledge of *Strange Fugitive* (1928), *A Native Argosy* (1929), and *It's Never Over* (1931), he did not appear to be aware of the existence of *No Man's Meat*. Steinhauer saw Callaghan as having "too great a fondness for melodrama" and described *Strange Fugitive* as "extravagant sensationalism." In such a climate of opinion, *No Man's Meat,* whose plot centres on lesbianism, was better consigned to the little presses of Paris, and thus to virtual oblivion in Canada.

Fifty years ought not to have elapsed between the first and second printings of the work, [reissued in *No Man's Meat & The Enchanted Pimp: Two Stories*], as it is one of the best things Callaghan has ever done. Its length, too short for a novel, too long to be a typical Callaghan short story, may have helped keep it in the limbo usually reserved for fiction of awkward length. Callaghan wrote two other longer novellas around the same time. *An Autumn Penitent* and *In His Own Country* were published as part of the short story collection *A Native Argosy* and have since been reprinted together. The three novellas share a lucidity of perception and structure that Callaghan loses in longer, more pretentious work like *The Many Coloured Coat* and *A Fine and Private Place.*

No Man's Meat concerns a married couple, Mr. and Mrs. Beddoes, who are spending the summer at their cottage in northern Ontario. The two have substituted a "steady calmness" for passion, though the "dark lake" and the "big rock" outside their cottage suggest that the "undisciplined impulses" have been suppressed rather than extinguished. (One of the few flaws in the story is the occasional heavy-handed use of Freudian symbols.) The couple are visited by an old friend, Jean Allen, who had left her husband to pursue an attraction for a young woman. Both husband and wife are attracted by Jean's exuberance and vivacity, but history repeats itself and it is Mrs. Beddoes who leaves her husband because she falls in love with Jean.

Wisely, only very minor changes have been made in the text. . . . Callaghan is at his best here, perceiving, suggesting, but saying little directly. He creates a balance between nuance and disclosure, between allusion to character and emotion and literal occurrence. (p. 793)

The title *No Man's Meat* is puzzling. It appears to take a coarse view of a situation which is handled in the work itself with understanding or at least, with dispassion.

The Enchanted Pimp is about a special sort of procurer, one who deals with "solid respectable" men who want "fine young women of their own kind," who will provide the illusion of "something secret, sweet and stolen." The pimp, Jay Dubuque, meets a special sort of prostitute, Ilona Tomory. Clad in a long mink coat, she exudes "gentle compassion," carefully choosing her clients from among those who most need an "angel-of-mercy-in-bed routine." Jay believes that "Such a woman should be a well-known celebrated personality. A great and famous whore. A fabulous whore to be looked at, talked about, fought over because she could create this illusion; she could make a man feel that no matter what he had done he could be excused and comforted." (The language sometimes balances on the fine line between absurdity and credibility.)

Jay's ambition is to get Ilona out of the cheap hotel from which she operates and make her available to "rich, lonely, distressed men." His plan fails, but it results in Ilona's involvement with a scholar of religions who describes making love to her as a "sacramental" experience. The scholar eventually deserts her in search of a new religion, but not before she has come to see him as a "soulsucker." Her grace lost, she resumes her former life and is murdered by a client. Jay takes care not to forget her and thus guards himself against becoming the "Caliban" she once had accused him of being.

The background characters are sketched with a firm hand, for example, Ilona's parents, . . . who seem both pathetic and majestic in their maintenance of their life of illusion. . . . Background details also are precisely chosen. Jay's respectable "white-painted remodelled house with the wrought-iron railing" scrupulously projects the image Jay wants to present of himself to the world. Like the professional he is, Callaghan never loses control of the material.

Nonetheless, there is a certain tiredness about some of the characters. We are offered yet another "literate and interesting bartender" in Silver, and yet another whore who knows the "truth" in the Cookie Lady. Silver, for example, who has "uptown admirers," tells Jay that "there's as much mystery in dirt and dung as there is in heaven." This sort of dialogue casts doubt on Silver's worth rather than proves it. Ilona herself might have become a stereotype had it not been for all the differentiating details that Callaghan gives her. Ilona not only

barely misses being the whore with the heart of gold, but she is also too reminiscent of another Callaghan character, Peggy Sanderson. Some of the slang expressions do not work in the way they should. *Joe-boy,* in the opening sentence of the work, though explicit, is dated. *Clown* and *buster* do not work anymore as terms of abuse.

For all that, shorter fiction is what Callaghan excels at, and this story about the power of illusion easily stands next to the author's other sensitively conceived and executed novellas. (pp. 794-95)

> *E. L. Bobak, in a review of "No Man's Meat & The Enchanted Pimp," in* The Dalhousie Review, *Vol. 58, No. 4, Winter, 1978-79, pp. 793-95.*

JUDITH KENDLE

Close to the Sun Again is the second of two novels published recently by Morley Callaghan after a silence of almost twelve years. Much thinner and less well realized than the earlier novel, *A Fine and Private Place* (1975), the work is nevertheless an interesting combination of familiar themes and technical innovation and one which bears closest comparison with the adult novels written after the Second World War: *The Loved and the Lost* (1951), *The Many Colored Coat* (1960), and *A Passion in Rome* (1961). It harks back in particular to an earlier theme, that of the redemptive power of insight and awareness, and in doing so raises an important question: is the author's vision genuinely a tragic one?

Audacity and self-puffery aside, the earlier novel, *A Fine and Private Place,* was and is a brilliant *tour de force,* a *roman à clef* which manages to combine a love story and two crimes of violent passion with important glosses on two of the author's finest novels, *Such is My Beloved* (1934) and *More Joy in Heaven* (1937), plus providing the key to interpretation of his later work. It is the latter that is relevant here. In large part an argument against analysis/interpretation in favour of that mystery/anarchy often equated with compassion and love, the novel suggests that there are no final answers to life, just questions, and that one can make anything one wants to out of it. (p. 141)

Ostensibly the story of the deathbed repentance of a man who had mistakenly turned his back upon his personal life, *Close to the Sun Again* suggests that even last minute revelations are redemptive and that insight, however painful, is salutary. Or does it? As the white leopard of the closing paragraph crosses the clearing, we are reminded of the fate of Icarus who flew too close to the sun and of the words of the doctor in the novel who had warned Ira earlier that if you get too close to people, they will devour you. Is this perhaps what has happened to the hero?

The truth would seem to be a little of both. Certainly there is no attempt to repudiate awareness. Long a favourite theme of the author and one that he has made explicit himself, the redemptive quest for insight and awareness has forced painful conclusions upon his heroes before. From the restoration of Jim McAlpine's "respect for his own insight which had always been his greatest strength" in *The Loved and the Lost,* through Harry Lane's rejection of justice in favour of mercy in *The Many Colored Coat,* to Sam Raymond's resolve in *A Passion in Rome* to "see the ends of the earth and judge them," Callaghan's later heroes have opted time and again for the kind of painful awareness that can "give width and depth to a man's whole life.'' Indeed, one of them, Harry Lane, wonders if ''unawareness'' isn't ''the greatest of sins.''

The nature of Ira's ''treason'' thus becomes clear. Unable to face either the complexities of Gina's nature or the vexed realities of her relationship with Jethroe Chone, he turns his back on the wildness and the yearning, and opts for one-dimensional explanation instead. And yet the novel is a cautionary tale. Unable ultimately to forget it, he is brought face to face with the ''terrible beauty'' again at the moment of his dying. It would seem that however dangerous personal experience and elusive understanding may be, for Callaghan at least, there is no alternative. Only awful recognition of the mystery makes the kind of ''absolution'' the hero is seeking possible, and sympathetic understanding is the goal. (pp. 141-42)

Although it seems on the face of it that Ira is doomed to either an empty life bereft of meaning or a painful one too close to the sun, the novel misses, I think, the grandeur of a tragic vision. Part of the difficulty lies in the writing itself. Relying as he does upon the flashback technique and a car crash in order to force his hero to review his life, the author at once strains our credulity—how *could* the hero have forgotten such riveting events for so long?—and resorts to the fickle hand of fact. In either case, he diminishes his hero. Snatching victory, as it were, from the jaws of death—Ira is plucked willynilly from the ''chilling emptyness (*sic*)'' of the ''terrible void''— Callaghan flirts dangerously with sentimentality just as he leaves virtually unexamined the implications of beauty born in excess. In truth his vision is more romantic than tragic, the cult of passion, truth, and wildness in opposition to dedicated service. And one wonders about the validity of such a choice.

Not that there aren't some very fine things here. The subtle sacking of Tom Frawlick, for example, is a master stroke, as is the etiology of a drunk in the person of Ira Groome. It must be admitted, however, that characterization in general in the novel is preposterous and weak, so that it is the large dose of adventure and narrative incident that ultimately carries the day. The work is, in fact, divided into two halves, and it is the latter that is the most compelling.

Even here there are flaws. The Yucatan experience is poorly integrated, as are the obscenities in the text. These last seem particularly gratuitous, a sop to shipboard realism perhaps. Again, there is an annoying habit of dropping pregnant hints only to leave them undeveloped . . . plus a preoccupation with the heroine's bare feet that almost amounts to a fetish. On the whole, however, the chapters here are much shorter and the writing (with the possible exception of Gina's story) refreshingly clean and crisp. Indeed, the author reveals himself to be an expert at action scenes and description, skills not normally associated with his work, and the story speeds swiftly and inexorably to its close. (pp. 142-43)

> *Judith Kendle, ''Tragic or Romantic Vision,'' in*
> Journal of Canadian Fiction, *No. 24, 1979, pp. 141-44.*

LOUIS K. MACKENDRICK

[The novellas collected in *No Man's Meat & The Enchanted Pimp*] have distinct parallels with some earlier Callaghan pieces, as well as being tales about loving and the consequences of impulse. Not unexpectedly, there is a considerable difference in the ease and maturity of their telling—one is reserved; the other splendidly profane—and in the reach of their social observations. Both have the sense of parable: characters are more typical than individual, and theses are worked out. (p. 124)

[*No Man's Meat*] anticipates the novel *A Broken Journey* (1932) in several ways: there are similarities in physical environment, the technique of symbolism, the real aimlessness of the characters' lives, the use of the vital outsider, and in the dissolution of the ideal-fed group through purely human circumstance. But it is ultimately the story's style which offsets its onetime forthright subject.

Teresa Beddoes and her husband—nameless as befits his coolly deracinated life—are orderly and calm, city folk in city dress whose summer home manifests their ''contented peacefulness'' and ''steady reasoned happiness.'' Their temperaments are virginal; their existence unflurried and shallow. They make nature the symbol of their days, constantly seeing parallels and correspondences with it rather than apprehending it directly without aesthetic or ethical signification. Their sensitivity is not participation; it is no accident that the story happens beside the flat reflecting surface of the leadingly named Echo Lake.

To this passive situation comes Jean Allen, a vigorous and travelled personality who represents a vicarious involvement in life to the Beddoes. . . . There is a sequence of painful incidents for which Callaghan's flat style is strangely proper, rendering the awkwardness, self-consciousness, and violation that follow the wager. His title is a vulgar joke: the stress is in the middle. Jean is at a crucial time in the changeover of her sexual orientation, and it is Teresa who is opened up into emotional living, who goes away with the so-called free spirit.

Callaghan splatters his story with obtrusive symbolism, even in the dialogue. The characters have difficulty being seen as people rather than as illustrations of a thesis or as emblematic of a condition; they recite rather than speak and often sound like texts. *No Man's Meat* is realist in intent but metaphorical in method, and it becomes mechanical in the placement and revelation of its details: straitened figures are moved about a chessboard. It is a laboratory story, a set piece in a set place, a test case of style, character, incident, and ornament: everything is carefully worked out, much as the Beddoes have reduced the landscape to safety and predictability.

The Enchanted Pimp, conversely, wallows in authentic life. The lovely title suggests all the vulgarity and mystery that Callaghan renders so well in the story. It is priorly echoed in *Such Is My Beloved* (1934): both are concerned with the problems of spiritual and physical loving, with the realities of urban street life, with appearance and the invasion of integrity, with forgiveness and the errors in redemption of society's lower strata.

The pimp is Edmund J. (''Jay'') Dubuque who, having discovered an affinity between respectable ladies needing extra cash and visiting conventioneers needing companionship, thrives elegantly in downtown Toronto as ''Convention Services.'' He is also a gambler, and has a strict sense of honour and obligation, his vulnerable *amour propre*. A deformed foot epitomizes his other side, the lapses from uprightness into the mentality of the mean streets. . . . [When] he discovers Ilona Tomory, a whore with a heart, with an air of both superiority and compassion, he carefully tries to orchestrate her appearance into polite society, an act of transmutation. (pp. 124-25)

Yet Ilona sees Jay as Caliban and tells him that he must see that people are no more than what they seem to be. This accords with the message from Ilona's onetime romance, scion of an uranium king: the kingdom of heaven is within. . . . Jay would see tangible and outward signs that pretense can succeed; he whores after a dream as the story addresses itself to the distinctions between reality and magic, between romance of the commonplace and prestidigitation. The motifs of mystery, romance, and performance are clear, as well as the primal contrast of seeming and being, all the distinction between flesh and spirit. (pp. 125-26)

Callaghan's themes are smoothly integrated in *The Enchanted Pimp,* and the story is fired by an admirable energy, sympathy, and absence of strain and stiltedness. Nothing is cryptic here. It is ironic and bittersweet, and the sense of life, in whatever social locale, is splendidly realized. Innocence is betrayed and pathos is discreetly present; moral directives abound, but not too blatantly. The symbols are natural and the characters have a dimension that makes the two fictions of this volume an interesting contrast. Yet *The Enchanted Pimp* is a particular success; there is a kind of alchemy in the subject and its realization. (p. 126)

> *Louis K. MacKendrick, in a review of "No Man's Meat & The Enchanted Pimp," in* The Fiddlehead, *No. 124, Winter, 1980, pp. 124-26.*

RON MILES

Despite Edmund Wilson's description of *No Man's Meat* as "a small masterpiece," readers may question the reprinting of this 1931 story with Morley Callaghan's most recent novella, *The Enchanted Pimp.* One good reason is that both fictions treat man's loss of woman. In *No Man's Meat,* a wife grown weary of her tidy life opts for non-conformity and the companionship of a glamorous female friend. This ending has been prepared by . . . the affinity between the women—revealed through bird imagery associated with both—in their need to fly beyond limiting relationships. But aside from its subject, made impressive by the original date of publication, *No Man's Meat* contains little that deserves Wilson's praise. Indeed, the dialogue is unconvincing (as in much of Callaghan's work) and the narration often disturbingly awkward. . . . *The Enchanted Pimp,* which constitutes the other four-fifths of the book, poses a complementary version of man's loss of woman. Edmund J. Dubuque, who procures affluent but temporarily embarrassed women for visiting professional men, loses the "gentle golden whore" Ilona Tomory when she ceases to be sufficiently nonconformist. Thus Callaghan twists the thematic premise of *No Man's Meat.* He also twists a clichéd plot device: the compassionate prostitute, so often used as a narrative end in itself, is merely the catalyst for the real narrative, the enchanting of a pimp by a whore far below his own commercial milieu. And above this milieu and narrative, as always in Callaghan, the real story hovers.

That story has to do with materialism and magic. The former is conveyed particularly through a motif of fur. Dubuque's first client prostitutes herself to make a payment on her fur coat; Dubuque himself longs for a fur hat when he is poor, and flaunts his expensive hat and fur-collared coat after becoming successful. Ilona's unique sensuousness is largely associated with her mink coat, which she leaves behind when fleeing to Mexico with Sills, the disgraced son of a wealthy family. . . . The fact that Ilona's coat is really an illusion, a shabby relic frequently taped underneath to preserve its facade of elegance, makes Callaghan's point about the limits of materialism, limits which stress the need for magic. Dubuque himself, recognizing

the need, has long been an amateur magician who regrets his inability to become professional. . . . A skeptic who knows that magic is merely illusion, he is reluctant to believe what he thinks he sees in Ilona. At one point she calls him Caliban, emphasizing both his vulgarity and his misuse of extra-material forces. But he comes to believe in her powers, in the "magnetic promise" associated with the coat she wears: his loss of her at the end is the loss of an object of belief.

Much of the preceding terminology, not to mention the concern with materialism and magic, encourages a religious interpretation. Other encouragements abound. . . . [The] central characters are all crippled or wounded: Dubuque has a right foot deformed by polio; at one point he is beaten by hired thugs; Ilona hurts her knee falling from a car when she first enters Dubuque's life; the second distinct stage in their relationship begins with another hurt knee, when Dubuque kicks Sills with his specially made (and heavy) shoe; Ilona's mother dies; and Ilona is ultimately murdered, standing, a knife in her back. Into this setting Callaghan introduces hints of world religions. . . . Most importantly, Callaghan gives Ilona—in Dubuque's eyes—Christ-like qualities. He has "an illumination" about her, sees her working "gentle benediction" among "the lame, the halt, and the blind," forgiving sins. . . . Even the image of her death approximates Christ's. After her death, Dubuque's sense of loss completes the pattern. Without an object for his faith, he is a lonely member of the economic middle class who cannot be comforted by his pseudo-respectability. (pp. 120-22)

This is not new ground for Morley Callaghan, and some readers of *The Enchanted Pimp* will wonder why he persists in reworking subjects he has treated before. One explanation is that he is still trying to get them right, and at least one reader believes he is getting there. This time around, there are complexities *and* economies that seemed lacking in such earlier books as *The Loved and the Lost.* There is more frankness at the same time as there is more human uncertainty in his treatment of a favorite theme, the flesh and the spirit. "If fucking can't be a religious thing," Ilona asks Dubuque, "what can be religious?" Out of context, this sounds comic, but Callaghan conveys its seriousness and much of its importance. The coexistence of fleshly and spiritual demands outlasts youth and even middle age. (p. 122)

> *Ron Miles, "A Religious Thing," in* Canadian Literature, *No. 84, Spring, 1980, pp. 120-22.*

MARGARET ATWOOD

When I first heard about Morley Callaghan's new novel, *A Time For Judas,* it sounded like one of the more bizarre literary productions of recent times. For one thing, the biblical reference in the title wasn't metaphorical, like those of previous Callaghan novels—the book really was about Judas! That meant "religious historical novel," and visions of *The Robe* and *Quo Vadis?* danced in my head, producing a cacophony of cognitive dissonance. For what was Morley Callaghan, he of the modest modern settings, he of the understated declarative sentences, doing in such lush surroundings? It would be like Grandma Moses painting naked women, and Rubenesque naked women at that. (p. 73)

Nobody has to be nice to Callaghan's book just because he's eighty. If the agnostically minded can get over their initial queasiness about the subject matter, they'll find it a ripping good yarn, told with skill and panache. It manages to avoid being *The Robe*. It contains theology that will make more than a few traditional hairs stand on end, but is not inconsistent with a careful reading of the Gospels. It makes clear the anti-establishment, populist roots of Christianity. And, beyond all this, it will undoubtedly be seen as a sort of key, the work by which earlier Callaghan books will have to be read.

Tackling material like this—not only historical but sacrosanct—requires a good deal of audacity and cunning. Callaghan knows that he's faced with the authenticity syndrome: that is, how do you get the reader to swallow the outrageous proposition that you're telling her a new, *but real*, version of historical events? He resorts to a variation on the manuscript-found-in-an-old-jar ploy, well known to readers of archaeological-adventure fiction. He invents an ''I,'' whom we assume to be Morley Callaghan and therefore ''real,'' who knows a man, also ''real,'' who always wanted to write. This man gets sick, goes to Rome, meets a scholar who shows him an old manuscript found in a well-described jar. This manuscript is so mind-boggling that the Vatican makes him destroy it, but not before the sick writer gets a good look. The scholar retires in heartbreak, his big chance gone up in flames. The sick writer writes a novel based on the manuscript, then dies. The ''I'' is left with the sick writer's novel, which he feels morally obliged to publish. This preamble covers the authorial bottom nicely, accounting for any little anachronisms, especially of diction, by putting the story at second remove. It also explains why the ''real'' manuscript is no longer around, and polishes off the witnesses. Necessary, though a bit creaky.

But when we get to the sick writer's novel, Callaghan hits his stride. He's picked a logical kind of witness through whom to tell the story: his narrator is Philo (check the etymology; this novel is about various forms of love, among other things), a Greek from Crete who, through various shenanigans, mostly sexual, ends up as a scribe to Pontius Pilate. He's rescued from a street brawl by a sophisticated and intelligent Jew named Judas Iscariot, who helps cure him of an acute respiratory illness by providing him with a warm and generous-hearted prostitute called Mary.... He's curious about the Jews and their cults, so keeps an eye on Judas's master, a strange fellow usually referred to as ''the Galilean.''

His position with Pilate gives him a ringside seat at the judging of Christ.... His great friend, the brigand Simon, turns out to be none other than one of the Two Thieves, which puts Philo at the foot of the cross at just the right moment. Most importantly, his acquaintance with Judas has continued so that, when the latter feels the need to unburden himself, Philo is the one he picks as listener.

At this point, *A Time For Judas* provides an engrossing set of answers to questions that must have puzzled more people than Callaghan. Why did Jesus have to be betrayed at all? He'd taught openly in the Temple, and had just paraded through Jerusalem; many must have known what he looked like and even where he was. Why did Judas do it? Thirty pieces of silver seem hardly adequate. If Jesus was supposed to know so much, why did he pick Judas to be an Apostle in the first place? And when the sop of bread was handed to Judas at the Last Supper with a clear explanation from Jesus of what it meant, why did everyone just sit there? Why didn't anyone stop Judas from going off to do the evil deed? Through Judas's confession to Philo, we learn all. (pp. 73-4)

[The book is] all pretty daring, ingenious, and even convincing; and, when you get over the initial shock, you realize that this

particular subject is right down Callaghan's alley. His interest in betrayals of various kinds and in scapegoats, innocents who are misunderstood and/or suffer for the good of all, has ample scope here. Then there are the conflicts between the letter and the spirit, between self-righteous respectability and *caritas,* between carnal and spiritual love. Callaghan's novels have often displayed underlying allegorical structures, and this tendency actually works better for him here—where the story is so close to allegory anyway—than it sometimes does in modern-dress versions. The book is rich in parallels, cross-allusions, mirror-image doubles. Sometimes it tiptoes along the edge of soppiness, as attempts to describe religious experiences frequently do, but Callaghan is more restrained than most, and by and large the qualities of his style—plain and formal, rather than ornate or colloquial—suit this material. Realism—psychological or otherwise—it isn't, nor is it intended to be. The story has the same sort of ritualized reality, the brightly coloured, enclosed clearness, of Mexican crèches. This too is part of Callaghan's point, both about the story of Judas and about the nature of story itself. In a story, one is a human being, yes, but one is also a role. *A Time For Judas* shows how the role can take over.

Those expecting a standard historical romance or a pious Christian homily like those given out as Sunday school prizes will of course be disappointed, as will those for whom Callaghan became a fly in amber some time ago. But for readers willing to step outside the boundaries of genre and preconception, *A Time For Judas* will prove rewarding. (p. 74)

> *Margaret Atwood, ''The Gospel According to Morley,'' in* Saturday Night, *Vol. 98, No. 10, October, 1983, pp. 73-4.*

MARK ABLEY

Callaghan's most recent novel, *A Time For Judas,* presents a view of the Gospel story that St. Paul would have found anathema. It suggests that Judas, alone among the dozen apostles, had the courage and intelligence to understand Jesus's need to be betrayed.... Callaghan's novel is, in part, an explanation and a defence of Judas's behaviour. Its theological heresy and its Biblical trappings should not, however, blind us to its essential consistency with Callaghan's earlier fiction. His Jesus, like his Matisse, offers people the happy acceptance of reality. And Jesus has enough spiritual power that his followers can, at least for a time, fulfill the longing felt by Father Dowling in *Such Is My Beloved*: ''to make each moment precious, to make the immediate eternal, or rather to see the eternal in the immediate.'' In *A Time For Judas* as in Callaghan's pre-war writing, a replenished sense of humanity is the basis, not the opposite, of transcendence.

In order to reach Judas's story, the reader must peel away a number of layers. Callaghan provides a foreword in which he claims to have received the manuscript of the novel from a dying TV producer and former monk by the name of Owen Spencer Davies; Davies had compiled the work from notes he took while studying an original Greek text (soon destroyed by the Vatican). This text was supposedly the writing of an erudite, sceptical scribe named Philo of Crete, who yearns to live in Rome but has found himself, without much enthusiasm, assigned to the administration of Pontius Pilate. Callaghan uses our familiarity with the events of Holy Week, as described by the four Evangelists, as a kind of translucent backdrop for Philo's version of these incidents. (p. 67)

Callaghan pays homage in his foreword to the tradition in which his fiction stands: Gnosticism.... Most importantly, perhaps, Callaghan follows the Gnostic tradition that Jesus and Mary Magdalene were lovers: "The Lord loved Mary more than all the disciples," reports the *Gospel According to Philip,* "and he kissed her on the mouth many times." The word requires the flesh. These Gnostic scriptures are often confused and contradictory (at least in their fragmentary form today), but clearly Callaghan finds many ideas in them that match his own beliefs and intuitions better than the dogmas of St. Paul.

Such matters might count for little were it not for Callaghan's continued mastery of narrative, his sweet inventiveness with plot. To put it bluntly, he remains one of the best story-tellers in Canada. Contrary to my expectations, the twists and turns of *A Time For Judas* are rarely predictable. And this, in turn, pays tribute to Callaghan's subtlety at creating character. Philo is sufficiently shifty, corrupt, curious and intelligent that his actions and reactions keep the reader continually alert. His turbulent life in Jerusalem provides a natural basis for new variations on Callaghan's perennial themes of love and treachery.... Judas is portrayed with comparable skill; he kills himself out of remorse not for having betrayed Jesus but for having confessed the secret truth to Philo, and demanded that Philo write it down. As in the *Gospel According to St. John,* much depends on the sacred power of the word. "It's the story," Judas insists to Philo, "only the story that lives...." But Jesus had demanded silence.

Compared to the central characters—Judas, Philo, Pilate, Mary Magdalene, and a bandit called Simon—Jesus is a distant figure. Other characters define themselves against him; he remains elusive. This is not necessarily a drawback, although it does seem a kind of challenge which Callaghan elected to avoid. For a full comprehension of Judas, we may need to know more than the author tells us about the complex love he shared with his friend and master. Once Judas has vanished from its pages, the book takes a long while to wind down.

But the main flaw in *A Time For Judas,* one which may not exactly come as a surprise to readers of Callaghan's postwar fiction, is linguistic. Philo's narrative has been "translated" into a colloquial, speedy English that suits the story well. Yet the exact register of language slides about alarmingly: "'Whom will I ask?' I said. 'Ask Mary.' 'My Mary, eh? Well, where is she?'" For a sceptic, Philo displays a distressing tendency to lapse into the easy warmth of adjectives.... Callaghan's language lets him down when Judas experiences a cosmic harmony that somehow links Jesus with the entire universe. At such a crucial point, one does not want to be reminded of the Maharishi Mahesh Yogi.

The novel is gripping to read, but I did not find it particularly memorable. And for that, its language may well be to blame. In a well-known section of *That Summer in Paris* Callaghan declared, "The words should be as transparent as glass, and every time a writer used a brilliant phrase to prove himself witty or clever he merely took the mind of the reader away from the object and directed it to himself." But that passage establishes a false dichotomy: transparency on the one hand, self-conscious cleverness on the other. The finest writers are sensitive to language not for its own sake, but because it enables them to explore regions of conscience, perception, and feeling that are beyond ordinary discourse. Now as ever, Callaghan's writing has tremendous virtues; now as ever, there are large areas of consciousness from which his work is barred. The saddest thing about *A Time for Judas* is that it remains *prosaic.*

Better prosaic than pretentious—yet to fulfil the author's ambition, the book needed a few sparks of poetry. By dealing with extraordinary subjects in cool, undistinguished words, *A Time For Judas* makes the Gospel story more accessible, and more diminutive. (pp. 67-9)

> Mark Abley, "Plain Man's Scripture," in Canadian Literature, *No. 103, Winter, 1984, pp. 66-9.*

L.T.R. McDONALD

Morley Callaghan's recent fiction is a sad postscript to a worthy career. Just when it seemed that Canada's first and best known modernist writer had retired to the limbo of earnest interviews and *ex cathedra* pronouncements in the Sunday supplements, he reasserted his presence as a creative writer with three new novels. *A Fine and Private Place* published in 1975 broke a silence of fourteen years. Only two years later, he gave us *Close to the Sun Again;* now he has added *A Time for Judas.*

These three novels add no new material to his canon, for there is nothing in them that we have not seen before. For the most part, they plagiarize his previous writing. What is remarkable about these works is Callaghan's obsessive determination to shape the terms of his literary reputation by summarizing, reworking, and interpreting what he understands to be his unique contribution to modern literature. Two of the three novels attempt to mask their blatantly narcissistic quality by disguising themselves as disinterested studies on the nature of fiction and the genius of the creative novelist.

A Fine and Private Place, for instance, is about a novelist, Eugene Shore, who seems to have written the same novels that Callaghan wrote. Shore's novels, like Callaghan's, have been dismissed by a "local" critic, who seems very much like Callaghan's idea of Northrop Frye, and praised by an "international" critic, whose credentials are similar to Edmund Wilson's. The novels of Eugene Shore and also Shore himself become the fanatical concern of Al Delaney, a recent graduate with a Ph.D. in English from the University of Toronto.... Adding to this confusion of the relationships among novelist, novel, and "life," is the fact that Callaghan's novelist has such a profound influence on the lives of Al and [his girlfriend] Lisa that they undergo personal struggles and transformations, whose patterns imitate the patterns of both Shore's and Callaghan's novels. The most important of these patterns illuminate three themes that Callaghan has identified in his own work: the criminal-saint; the rejection of reason (or socialized ego) in favour of intuition (or "natural" unconscious); and the appropriation of religion by art. By offering a critical account of how one of these themes is developed in each of the three new novels, I will attempt to give an evaluative overview of Callaghan's recent work.

Philosophically, the criminal-saint theme expresses Callaghan's lifelong opposition to Manichean dualism; psychologically, it enacts the Freudian metaphors which shape his structures—libidinal energy (man's "potential") encounters the reality principle and is diverted into either self-creative or self-destructive activity. Philosophical monism is suggested by fictional structures that equate the energy which inspires the saint with the energy that informs criminal behaviour. The criminal-saint, then, is an image of the ambivalence of life. Callaghan's texts argue that the division of this paradoxical whole into warring camps of flesh and spirit or of criminal *versus* saint, is a socially determined practice that falsifies reality. What is more, Callaghan asserts, society consistently and perversely responds to saintlike behaviour as if it were criminal behaviour. (pp. 147-48)

Shore's criminal-saints are, of course, none other than Callaghan's protagonists: Kip Caley in *More Joy in Heaven,* Father Dowling in *Such is My Beloved,* and Peggy Sanderson in *The Loved and the Lost.*

Callaghan's literary self-criticism in *A Fine and Private Place* locates the rebellious nature of Shore's protagonists in the consciousness of their creator; they are equated with (if not reduced to) projections of Shore's own rebellious posture. In other words, Shore/Callaghan is a writer who, by creating criminal-saints, opposes and inverts society's corrupt scale of values. He identifies with the true saints, those whose way of being is misinterpreted as criminal because it is at odds with the vested interests of bourgeois society. This logic leads inevitably to the self-canonizing declaration that the artist is the greatest criminal-saint of them all. It is also important to note that the criminal-saint, consistent with Callaghan's increasingly anti-rational bias, is sometimes referred to as a poetic "clown-criminal" because he or she is a person of great intuitive (as opposed to analytical) insight.

At least in part, Callaghan's mistrust of human reasoning powers can be accounted for by his desire to maintain the freedom of the individual as a "transcendental subject" who somehow escapes the determinisms of Darwin, Marx, and Freud. Much of Callaghan's fiction, beginning as early as 1935 with *They Shall Inherit the Earth,* should be read as an attempt to come to terms with the presence in his own fiction of these determinant structures, and also as a dialogue with Hemingway over the nihilist philosophy that they imply. . . . Because he situates the effects of these determinisms in the ego, and because he is concerned with the power of socio-economic forces to shape the individual's ego to society's life-denying ends, Callaghan turns for truth to intuitive impulses and insights—originating in the deepest recesses of consciousness, supposedly beyond the reach of social determinism, and untainted by the self-rationalizing activity of the ego. *Close to the Sun Again* is a novel that dramatizes this conflict in its juxtaposition of the discontents of civilization and a myth of human origins that embraces and glorifies residual traces of the pagan. (pp. 149-50)

Close to the Sun Again begins with Ira Groome's resigning as a top executive of the Brazilian Power Corporation. After seven years of protecting the corporation's interests in Sao Paulo, he recognizes that something is terribly wrong with his life. What is wrong, it turns out, is that Ira Groome is no longer capable of love, of deep emotional commitment. We follow Ira to Toronto, where he accepts the position of chairman of the police commission. In this section of the novel, Callaghan documents the emptiness of Ira's life, teasing us repeatedly with the question of how he became a man whose endings seem to contradict his beginnings. The last half of the novel is a psychological flashback that gives us all the answers.

The conversion of Ira Groome from a young man of the heart to a rich man of the head is accounted for by a single traumatic incident that takes place in the North Sea during the great war against fascism. Ira's corvette picks up some survivors from a torpedoed civilian ship. One of the survivors is Gina Bixby, the refined and educated daughter of a professional gambler. Another, Jethroe Chone, "a man of threatening, savage silences", is her bodyguard. Ira falls passionately in love with Gina, and she, apparently, with him. However, this union is not to be, for Gina cannot disentangle herself from a sado-masochistic relationship with Chone, who raped her just before they fled the States. She is not free to love Ira because she feels guilty that she might have enjoyed being raped.

The corvette is torpedoed, and all three end up in the same life-boat. Chone commits suicide by jumping into the sea, and Gina follows him, screaming, "Come back, you bastard". . . . Ira attempts to defuse these events; he applies his reason to them in order to reduce their power to disturb. . . . In attempting to "*understand* what had happened", Ira Groome misses the point. According to Callaghan's pseudo-psychological equations, the ego's "understanding" represses a profounder comprehension of why Gina pursued Chone. The true significance of the events surrounding Gina and Chone is revealed to him at the moment of death. . . . "Chone, who was dead now and never to be remembered, had all the passion." (pp. 151-53)

[The novel's] conclusion preaches primitivism in its most naked and unapologetic form. In fact, every incident in the book is a plea for us to abandon ourselves to the primitive. To cite but one instance, Ira Groome tells the story of how, as a young student of archaeology in Yucatan, he learned all he needed to know about the ancient Mayan culture—not by analyzing the unearthed artifacts, but by making love to an eighteen-year-old native girl. Truth, he insists, was in her bones and he absorbed it as their bodies fused.

We come to the highest kind of truth, in other words, through intuition, not through the disinterested exercise of the reason upon the concrete facts of existence. It follows, all three novels affirm, that we should turn inwards in search of the truth. We must concentrate our energies on mending our individual psyches, rather than on changing the material conditions of public life. The subjectivism of this ethic is, however, a disappointing contradiction of the objective portrayal of social conditions that supports the social activism of Father Dowling, Kip Caley, and Peggy Sanderson—the same three protagonists, it is worth noting, that Callaghan's reductive self-criticism abstracts into "Criminal-saints" in *A Fine and Private Place.* These protagonists are rendered passive exemplars of a subjectively bounded attitude towards life; their original revolutionary gestures are divested of any objective dimension by Callaghan's second thoughts about their significance.

Callaghan's most recent novel, *A Time for Judas,* observes itself in the act of re-telling the story of how Judas betrayed Christ. The text's self-awareness of its status as "story" is an intentional enactment of its theme: the celebration of fiction's privileged status *as fiction. A Time for Judas* is a story within a story within a story. The containing story is presented as a foreword in which the narrator, an authorial self-projection, explains how the manuscript that constitutes the novel proper came to be in his possession. This manuscript is the story of Christ's last days as recorded by Philo of Crete. (pp. 153-54)

The story within Philo's story is the "story" as subject. The great revelation of Philo's narrative history is that Christ's betrayal by Judas was literally a case of history imitating fiction; that is, Christ consciously manipulated his private and public history so that its perceived events would tell a story the way a story must be told. Christ's life, according to this novel, imitated his art. Callaghan shames the timidity of those theorizers who are content to claim for fiction the power of conferring value and meaning on life. In *A Time for Judas* Callaghan argues that *fiction is meaning,* for the "story" exists prior to the history that it determines. Thus the reason that Judas betrays Christ is because Christ persuades him to do so.

Philo's narrative dwells on neither Christ as god nor Christ as man, but on Christ as storyteller. (pp. 154-55)

[As] a god Jesus Christ need only invoke his omnipotent powers to fulfil the demands of any story. That he does not do so, but rather chooses to author his life with all the guile and cunning of a maker of stories, is the ultimate act of art's appropriation of the claims of religion. Christ *persuades* Judas to betray him, and by so doing establishes an equation between the omnipotent god and the omnipotent narrator. . . . (p. 155)

Callaghan's novel is as "enigmatic" about whether or not Christ did rise from the dead as are the stories of the Master himself. Christ's followers believe that he rose from the dead because, when they enter the tomb on the third day, his body is indeed gone. Philo's narrative, however, reveals that he and Simon's sons stole the body and buried it elsewhere as part of a plan to ransom it to the high priests. Whether Christ rose from this second grave, whether he literally rose from the dead, is of no consequence. Callaghan's metaphors consistently conflate the variant readings: Christ as god and Christ as maker of fictions. Christ's fiction is effectively fact, no matter how we read it. Put another way, the truest belief is the one which is derived from the most compelling fiction.

The tendentious quality of Callaghan's writing is nothing new; as far back as *A Passion in Rome* Callaghan began advancing the proposition that art, far from being the mere hand-maiden of belief, is the incarnation of belief itself. In the autobiographical *A Fine and Private Place,* his metaphors laboriously associate Eugene Shore with Jesus Christ. Both are scapegoats in the story that is life; hence Shore, who "sanctifies" his characters, is killed off by Callaghan with a barrage of Christ symbols. Both god and novelist enjoy privileged access to an anti-rational source of truth. Al Delaney finally discovers the metaphysical basis for the truth-claims of Shore/Callaghan's novels when he arrives at the following romantic aesthetic: the storyteller negates his ego, and a structure of permanent meaning that is immanent in the natural world is magically bodied forth from the unselfconscious imagination.

This aesthetic, stripped of its idealist pretensions to knowledge of the nature of being or reality (its ontologism), could usefully serve as an accurate assessment of the literary assumptions that animate Callaghan's pre-war novels. . . . But Callaghan's recent fiction, even while in the act of proclaiming this aesthetic of self-negation, shifts our attention away from the history his stories once told and directs it towards Callaghan's way of seeing that history. Whereas the message glorifies the power of the artist to negate himself so the world can speak through him, the writing glorifies Callaghan and effectively negates the world so he can speak through it.

What is more, Callaghan's discussions of literary criticism in *A Fine and Private Place* insist that Shore/Callaghan's novels are not to be analyzed with the falsifying tools of reason, but are to be appreciated solely for their magical effect on us— just as in *A Time for Judas* it is the aesthetic efficacy of Christ's story, not its accordance with historical reality, that justifies its claims on our credulity. Callaghan thereby seeks to disarm theorizing criticism of his writing by placing it beyond the reach of rational understanding. (pp. 155-57)

L.T.R. McDonald, "The Resurrection of Morley Callaghan," in Literary Criterion, *Vol. XIX, Nos. 3 & 4, 1984, pp. 147-57.*

GRAHAM CARR

In the overall scheme of Morley Callaghan's work, *A Time for Judas* represents both a continuation and a departure. It was Barry Cameron who once pointed out that Callaghan's best fiction was "parabolic" in form, and that assessment also seems well-suited to this latest novel. While the plot is reasonably compelling, and the central characters are engaging and complex, it is a moral issue—the issue of betrayal—which folds over everything. In these respects *A Time for Judas* is not far different from Callaghan's earlier work. Alongside the similarities, however, contrasts also appear. (p. 309)

[Perhaps] the most significant departure in *A Time for Judas* is its overt concern with aesthetic issues. References to the art of storytelling appear throughout the book, and are used to advocate Callaghan's artistic creed of simplicity. At various times he explains his decision to use colloquial language in the narrative, and announces his aversion to technical criticism. Yet all this is done in distractingly blatant terms, as though Callaghan cannot trust himself to earn the aesthetic confidence of his readers and so must simply demand it instead.

For all the cunning of its plot, for all the resilient promise of its themes, *A Time for Judas* is never completely satisfying. Ironically, it is on aesthetic grounds that the novel really disappoints. The prose is often limp and directionless—the second sentence, for example—and stumbles more than once over a discarded cliché. Furthermore, while a certain simplicity is undoubtedly achieved overall, the suspicion begins to nag that simplicity alone is not enough—that beneath the rich coating of famous characters and chewy themes, there is only hollowness. In particular, this superficiality is visible in Callaghan's handling of the historical element central to the book's structure. In the end, his lack of interest in the uniqueness of the past betrays the ostensible reality of the story.

The narrator and protagonist of *A Time for Judas* is a Greek scribe, Philo, who works for Pilate and the Romans in Jerusalem. Although basically uninterested in the activities of the Christians in the city, Philo makes the chance acquaintance of Judas Iscariot. When, shortly thereafter, Judas is ostracized for betraying Christ, he comes privately to Philo to pour forth his story. At the same time, another chance meeting brings Philo into contact with a criminal who is sentenced to die beside Christ. The day the sentence is carried out, Philo goes to Golgotha and witnesses the Crucifixion. Later, as a grudging participant in a bizarre caper to steal Christ's body, Philo ends up witnessing the Resurrection instead. The cumulative effect of these startling events serves to awaken Philo and gradually force him to contemplate the meaning of what has occurred.

What unifies these events at a thematic level are the issues of loyalty and betrayal. The archetypal betrayer is Judas, of course. Yet Callaghan's Judas is more sympathetic than contemptible. Insisting that he was chosen to betray Christ only because he was the most loyal disciple, Judas laments having been "Used by the Son of God, picked out to be the victim". . . . Judas' misfortune and Philo's experience are virtual opposites. Although notoriously petty and corrupt, Philo has always been preserved by the hands of a benevolent destiny. (pp. 309-10)

Significantly, *A Time for Judas* is not just one story, but a Chinese box of stories. A journalist, Owen Spencer Davies, has, through the interventions of others, happened upon a lost narrative by Philo of Crete. Davies then adapts it for modern readers. But Philo's own reconstruction of Judas' story is based on hurriedly scribbled notes of the disciple's "incoherent" ramblings; and Philo's synthesis of those notes is, by his own admission, further distanced by having been "strained through my memory".... These narrative permutations only scratch the surface of the issue, however, for the even deeper problem involves Philo's reliability as a narrator. He is, after all, a philanderer, a cheat, and a liar who claims to be "excited" by his criminality. With all these complications, any thought of reading the novel straight becomes uncertain.

Whether Callaghan intends that such structural ambiguities be read into the novel is another matter. Some elements of the book seem to warn against focusing on these issues of form. At one point Philo grumbles: "Too much poring over the meaning of the word, the meaning of the meaning, then the meaning behind the meaning".... Indeed, it is quite easy to construe this passage as Callaghan's swipe at the textual concerns of academic critics. What Callaghan seems to prefer is something much more straightforward and literal. Almost ad nauseam, characters in *A Time for Judas* extol the virtues of storytelling in the simplest, most credulous terms possible.... [Perhaps] the most important example is Christ's explanation that someone must betray him for the thoroughly unpretentious reason that "the story requires it".... (pp. 311-12)

Unfortunately, Callaghan's obsession with simplicity has its deleterious effects too. For example, at times it seems he has caught the banality of natural speech more closely than anything else. His predilection for melodramatic cliché is symptomatic of this.... [The] most abominable cliché of all involves that hackneyed ruse, "the discovered manuscript," which is supposed to put the novel on a realistic footing, but puts one in mind of a bad mystery instead.

Disconcerting, too, are the superficies in the novel's time-frame that pass for a sense of history. An awkward, anachronistic confusion is created by Callaghan's conjunction of twentieth-century ideas and speech with a first-century event and atmosphere. Two problems are involved here. The first is a stylistic question about the demands of realistic narrative. By failing to make the various material elements of the story—dress, names, etc.—conform to the temporal range of his characters' language, Callaghan has disrupted the realism of the novel. The impress of contemporaneity he seems intent on creating by having Philo and Judas sound modern remains uneven when every other material fact about them is recognizably archaic. This is not an argument against contemporary adaptations; it is only a critique of incomplete ones.

The second problem with the novel's time-frame is more philosophical. Despite its historical setting, despite the long Christian tradition on which it draws, and despite the temporal reference in its title, *A Time for Judas* is essentially ahistorical and thoroughly present-minded. Once again, language is at the centre of things. From one perspective, Callaghan has used colloquial speech to make the story relevant to contemporary readers. But language is also the vehicle of intellect. Therefore, because the language used in the novel is modern, so the thought patterns conveyed by the archaic characters in the novel must also be modern. Still, is this really a point of difficulty in understanding the work? If one accepts the assumption that humans have thought and acted in essentially the same way throughout history then, of course, there is no problem.... "In parable," writes Barry Cameron, "we ask for plausibility in terms of the realm of ideas invoked, not necessarily in terms of character and fictional event." The point, then, really concerns how deeply one wishes to go in defining intellectual plausibility. From a purely historical perspective, any notion that thought patterns have been universal in time is demonstrably false. The kind of historical sense which is developed in works like *A Time for Judas,* therefore, is one by which the past simply, and perversely, becomes an extension of the present.

By raising these points, however, I am not suggesting anything ruinous about the novel. In many ways, *A Time for Judas* is a delightful piece of writing, and my quibbles about its structure should not obscure the fact that the text remains both vivid and comprehensible. (pp. 312-13)

> Graham Carr, "Crucifiction," in Essays on Canadian Writing, No. 30, Winter, 1984-85, pp. 309-15.

ALBERTO MANGUEL

[The story of *Our Lady of the Snows,* a rewrite of Callaghan's novella *The Enchanted Pimp,*] is that of Dubuque's involvement with Ilona: a man with a deep knowledge of the streets dazzled by a woman on whom he cannot fix a label. Dubuque is a Toulouse Lautrec figure: club-footed, visionary (he sometimes has second sight), a pimp who reads the dictionary for pleasure, and who in a sentimental fit sends $200 to a destitute family in the neighbourhood. Ilona is a mystery: too graceful, too understanding to fit the common rough image of a whore—a kind of Florence Nightingale hooker....

[Ilona and Dubuque] are only samples of the host of lower Toronto characters that Morley Callaghan brings into his novel. In fact it is startling to realize that the book spans barely more than 200 pages. The characters, like crowds at rush hour, seem too numerous to remember, their lives too intricate, their histories flung too far back into the past. The wealth of detail is distracting. Though in parts it adds reality to the novel's world, it ultimately becomes irrelevant to the story itself. The many lives brought onto the page give the impression of belonging to several plots running their separate courses at the same time. Each seems to belong to a different story; together they compete loudly for the reader's attention. (p. 18)

[The traits of Callaghan's characters] reflect less a concern for reality than a belief in the romantic spirit of the streets, in men and women who redeem each other from the safeguard of their traditional roles in society. Ilona and Dubuque are roughed-up versions of the Sleeping Beauty and her rescuing Prince. *Our Lady of the Snows* is an urban fairy tale.

This romantic view of the world allows for certain scenes of trite sentimentality. At one point Ilona, pursued by an Irish wolfhound, falls to her knees by the closed garden gate while the beast, much like Androcles's lion, turns from savage to meek, wags his tail "and with an awkward, almost apologetic shake of his big body" comes "brushing against her, licking at her face." The scene ends with Ilona entering a church and lighting a candle, convinced that her life is not wrong "because she was as she was, because of what she could do for a man, because of a hidden wonder in her." The romantic heroine becomes a first-aid kit.

The blurb on the cover advises that the title comes from Kipling's celebrated 1897 poem on Canada that so infuriated Canadians and adds: "Yet Kipling would not be pleased by this strikingly contemporary tale.'' . . . [It] seems correct to surmise that Kipling would not have approved of *Our Lady of the Snows.* Not because of its ''strikingly contemporary'' features (few writers were more ''strikingly contemporary'' than Kipling) but because its structure lacks the tightness, the meticulous linking of parts that Kipling demanded of fiction.

The rambling narration, the impossibly romantic protagonists, become, however, at times coherent and appealing, and remind the reader of the crisp style that Callaghan began to explore in his very early *Strange Fugitive* (1928). Scenes such as the meeting between Dubuque and Ilona's parents (the gentle, wary father; the faded, aristocratic mother) show how wisely Callaghan can portray complex human relationships, making no judgements and allowing his characters to seek their own redemption. Unfortunately, *Our Lady of the Snows* has few passages of this excellence, and the novel's initial objective film-like quality wanes and quickly disappears. (p. 19)

Alberto Manguel, ''Harlot's Web,'' in Books in Canada, *Vol. 14, No. 4, May, 1985, pp. 18-19.*

JAMIE CONKLIN

George Woodcock once complained that Morley Callaghan's books tend to stereotype women, portraying them as either saints or whores. This was particularly evident in his 1983 novel *A Time for Judas* . . . , where Callaghan imagined Mary Magdalene as two separate women—one a whore, the other a woman of virtue. The most interesting feature of *Our Lady of the Snows,* his latest novel, is its attempt to fuse that dichotomy by creating a female character whose profane acts have a strong spiritual dimension. He has attempted to elaborate a moral perspective that casts light on the shadowy barrier between purity and profanity.

Our Lady of the Snows doesn't represent an entirely new direction for Callaghan, however; he is still writing moral fables about people living on the fringe of society: prostitutes, pimps, and the regulars at a downtown bar. These characters, however, have taken on a new complexity. . . .

[The prostitute] Ilona is neither saint nor harlot; rather, she is a compassionate woman who responds to her poverty with an act of desperation. When she becomes a whore, she continues to display her compassion, and the result is that she confounds the simple thinking of Jay Dubuque.

Moreover, in the course of the novel Ilona becomes a representation of all female stereotypes. The Bradley House, the hotel she works from, becomes a spawning ground for an outpouring of myths about her past. Gil Gilhooey, the bar's owner and a failed writer, finds renewed inspiration in her, and by the end of the novel he has decided to become her chronicler. At times, Ilona seems to be more of a story than a flesh-and-blood person. Callaghan uses this tension between the real Ilona and the fantasies she inspires to show how a woman's acts can be transformed into a narrative blending of fact and fiction.

Although some of the situations in the novel are implausible, *Our Lady of the Snows* will stand as one of Callaghan's finer works. His prose, which continues to display the carefully measured cadence of his earlier novels, is almost biblical in tone and remains an excellent vehicle for his moral vision.

Another reason for taking note of *Our Lady of the Snows* is because it affords a rare opportunity to observe Callaghan refining and reworking an earlier idea. *Our Lady* is a major rewrite of a novella published in 1978 [*The Enchanted Pimp*], which also featured Dubuque and Ilona. But in this early version, Ilona is destroyed by her inability to come to terms with the split between purity and profanity. In *Our Lady,* Callaghan credits Ilona with more subtlety and strength.

Jamie Conklin, ''Bridging the Gap between Pure and Profane,'' in Quill and Quire, *Vol. 51, No. 5, May, 1985, p. 31.*

JAMES C. MacDONALD

Although it is certainly refreshing to read a major collection by Callaghan, I find it disturbing to think that [the stories collected in *The Lost and Found Stories of Morley Callaghan*] were ''lost.'' A quick look, for instance, in David Latham's ''A Callaghan Log'' in the spring, 1980, issue of *The Journal of Canadian Studies* reveals the origins of 22 of the 26 titles. This minor gripe aside, most readers can take pleasure in writing that is compact, lucid, humane, and still provocative. . . .

Any attempt to define the writing according to Christian humanism, rhetorical structures, the historical setting of the Depression, or the influence of Darwin, Marx, and Freud is defeated by the complexities of human action that make Callaghan unique. In the context of the stories, a more fruitful approach may be to look at how his concerns inform his work.

In ''A Boy Grows Older,'' an out-of-work father, Mr. Sloane, lends his son money. Mrs. Sloane suspects that her husband is afraid of their son, Jim, but wants to stop the payments, which they cannot afford. After receiving the money again, Jim realizes how weak his father really is, but he also understands that they all want to have faith in each other, which circumstance inhibits. Through the testing imposed by external forces they cannot control, an awareness grows of the fragility of familial relationships, and although still tenuous, a new bond is formed to help them face the reality of their situation. . . .

Themes of loss, of fear, of poverty, and the possibility of betrayal govern this intimate story, but the understated feeling of a precious common humanity prevails. In a similar vein, **''A Little Beaded Bag,'' ''The Chiseller,'' ''This Man, My Father,''** and **''The Fiddler on Twenty-Third Street''** explore intricate family dependencies and the need to be truly aware, not only of oneself but also of those who one most values.

Although some stories (**''The New Kid,'' ''Loppy Phelan's Double Shoot,'' ''An Enemy of the People,'' Big Jules,''** and **''Lady in a Green Dress''**) dwell on the slight but persistent theme of the nature of memory, and some (**''Just Like Her Mother''** and **''The Thing That Happened to Uncle Adolphe''**) introduce an intriguing situation following the death of a parent, the majority of stories examine how individuals perversely desire others to conform to their own reality.

The title **''The Consuming Fire''** appropriately defines Julia Watson, who imposes herself on her husband even after he has left her. Thinking that she is doing it for his own good, Julia gets him a job worthy of his talent. He rejects it because it gives him a chance to say no to her excessive care and love. For the first time, she sees what she has done to people who liked her: "She was terrified because she saw she consumed them. She put her trembling hands over her face." Julia recognizes that she has lived through others, and the fear that overwhelms her is the fear of emptiness. (p. 32)

For Callaghan, the point of a story is the revelation of a significant moment of self-awareness. The difficulty of its discovery lies in acknowledging the danger inherent in seemingly inconsequential events and having the courage and honesty to transcend them. These stories brilliantly show the variety of ways human beings can respond to the challenge. (p. 33)

*James C. MacDonald, "The Lost and the Loved,"
in* Books in Canada, *Vol. 15, No. 3, April, 1986,
pp. 32-3.*

Don(ald Richard) Carpenter

1931-

American novelist, short story writer, and scriptwriter.

Carpenter's early fiction, written during the 1960s, explores the breakdown of society through plots that revolve around criminals, the mentally insane, and other social outcasts. In the 1970s, Carpenter began to set his novels in the world of Hollywood filmmaking to comment on decadence and alienation in contemporary society. Carpenter himself has worked as a scriptwriter, and critics have praised the accuracy with which he recreates the lives and lifestyles of those associated with the entertainment business. His prose is generally unadorned, and his narratives are noted for their direct and compelling approach.

Carpenter's first novel, *Hard Rain Falling* (1965), revolves around the friendship that develops between Jack Levitt, a white convict, and his black cellmate, Billy Lancing. Lancing is killed while protecting Levitt from other inmates. Carpenter contrasts the relationship between the two men with the meaningless existence Levitt experiences years later in the outside world. Martin Seymour-Smith praised *Hard Rain Falling* as "a first novel . . . of remarkable quality, written with authority, detachment and an almost uncanny, deadpan intelligence." Carpenter's next novel, *Blade of Light* (1966), deals with social outcasts of a different order. Protagonist Irwin Semple is a simpleminded, inarticulate creature who is goaded into committing murder by the machinations of the intellectually superior Harold Hunt. While Semple exemplifies physical ugliness, Hunt personifies the spiritual desolation often fostered by an indifferent society. *Getting Off* (1971), which chronicles a man's efforts to adjust to life after divorce, is a transitional work, linking Carpenter's social fiction and his later Hollywood tales. Like Carpenter's earlier work, this novel revolves around a failed, depressed, and unlikable character; like the Hollywood tales, the protagonist is involved in the entertainment industry, and Carpenter focuses on sex and violence in his depiction of contemporary life.

The True Life Story of Jody McKeegan (1974), *A Couple of Comedians* (1979), and *Turnaround* (1981), along with several of Carpenter's short stories set in Hollywood, were considered by Bruce Cook to be "about as good as anything written about the movie business in the last 40 years or so." *The True Life Story of Jody McKeegan* chronicles a small-town girl's efforts to realize her dream of becoming an actress; *A Couple of Comedians* follows the career of a comedy team reminiscent of Dean Martin and Jerry Lewis as they rise from obscurity to stardom; and *Turnaround* uses three central characters—a screenwriter, a director, and a producer—to give a behind-the-scenes look at the pressures of the movie industry. In a review of *A Couple of Comedians*, Cook claimed that Carpenter "is doing for present-day Hollywood what Daniel Defoe did for 18th-century London—charting its licit and illicit commerce, exploring its underside, revealing in precise detail how the place works."

Carpenter's two volumes of short fiction, *The Murder of the Frogs and Other Stories* (1968) and *The Class of '49* (1985), bring together his dual themes of the individual in society and

© 1986 Thomas Victor

Hollywood moviemaking. *The Murder of the Frogs* includes several portraits of the grim side of life as well as two Hollywood stories. *The Class of '49* consists of the long title piece, in which Carpenter presents a series of interrelated sketches about members of the 1949 graduating class of a Portland, Oregon, high school, and two stories, one of which combines autobiography with the story of a Hollywood actor who attempts to work outside the system.

(See also *Contemporary Authors*, Vols. 45-48 and *Contemporary Authors New Revision Series*, Vol. 1.)

DAVID R. SLAVITT

In certain ways, Don Carpenter's first novel *Hard Rain Falling* is a typical book of the Sixties, with all the modish ties neatly assembled. There's the black man and the white man joined in hieratic, homosexual union; there's imprisonment and freedom; there's the picaresque structure; there's the pool-shark sequence; there's even the setting in the Pacific Northwest, which is getting to be the new Mississippi. On the other hand, this is not that kind of book at all. Its originality, its ingenious daring, and its frank risk of sentiment are such that they condemn with considerable authority that whole, stylish tradition against which the book must stand.

The delicate business of *Hard Rain Falling* is the description of a moment of romantic love between two cell mates in San Quentin. That Mr. Carpenter does this, in spite of all our inhibitions, and also in spite of the exhibitions of so many novelists and playwrights, is remarkable, but even more remarkable is the way in which he has managed it. The cellmates are Billy Lancing, a Negro pool hustler and college student in for check forgery, and Jack Levitt, the white protagonist, a foundling and former juvenile delinquent, serving time for kidnapping.

They have been friends and the implication is quite clear that had they not been incarcerated together in an all-male jail, they would not have expressed their friendship in just this way. But they are, and they do. And Mr. Carpenter sees it romantically, which is a couple of more exits to Brooklyn than the BMT has yet thought of. "Not the sex," says the pool hustler. "That's not the connection. You and me, we're the connection," and it's true enough. Lancing saves Levitt from getting raped by one of the prison wolves, and Lancing gets himself killed doing it.

The book is uneven and untidy. If Carpenter were a less talented writer, his novel would almost certainly be better constructed. As it is, Carpenter has contrived a strategy where almost any old irrelevant thing contributes to his purpose. The apparent aimlessness of everything that Levitt does, either before or after prison, only confirms that the encounter in the prison is the one meaningful, noble moment in Levitt's entire life. It looks like a game of old maid: only that one card counts.

The trouble is that Carpenter gets interested in the blind cards. Levitt is innocent of kidnapping, but in jail because of a deal a district attorney offered: pleading guilty to kidnapping or getting hit with statutory rape (of which he is guilty). It is rich but distracting from what I take to be the main point of the book, the depiction of the homosexual love affair and the assertion that it is a love affair.

The skill, tact, and honesty that such an assertion requires are considerable. And the effect of the assertion is astringently healthy. Mr. Carpenter doesn't translate from the homosexual situation as Albee did in *Who's Afraid of Virginia Woolf?*, making one of the men a woman, nor does he make a sociological or apocalyptic metaphor out of it, as Baldwin does. Least of all, does he attempt to titillate or shock. But he earns for his hero the kind of respect that we accord only to Socrates. . . .

There are a great many books about making it, but rather few that ask what it is that is being made. Mr. Carpenter's debut is most auspicious. He is a serious writer.

> *David R. Slavitt, "Lowering the Bars," in* Book Week—The Sunday Herald Tribune, *January 30, 1966, p. 14.*

WEBSTER SCHOTT

Jack Levitt, the non-hero of Don Carpenter's first novel [*Hard Rain Falling*] makes two mistakes. The first is being born. The second is being born in 1930. Illegitimate, dumped in an orphanage by his motorcyclist mother, educated in West Coast poolrooms and bordellos, boxing rings and jails, he has a personality rigged for combat and calamity. His gifts belong in another age. His fists and low boiling point equip him for the era of Indian wars and great train robberies. The author's purpose is to document this anthropological error and recover meanings from it. He chills us with documentation but moralizes in the abstract, like an existentialist teaching Sunday school.

As befits a tough, smart kid growing up absurd, Jack Levitt winds up parking cars in San Francisco and wondering where his wife is sleeping. His story ends when he is 30, senescence for hard-core swingers. To carry it further would require another 300 pages of social disasters. In any case, Mr. Carpenter over-achieves in making an imaginative work of such casebook stuff. Endowing Jack Levitt with one life is enough. Almost.

It's a life of felonious America in gestation. . . . *Hard Rain Falling* is *Last Exit to Brooklyn* amended but unaltered by cries of affection under the heap of warped and busted souls.

The author's characters move in a socio-economic system programmed for their defeat and incapable of signaling to them what, if any, readjustments they can make for salvation. Only Sally (Jack's wife with the outhouse vocabulary) has staying power. Given the advantages of education, cunning and eroticism, she acquires all: Jack's child, a playboy third husband, a berth with her movie-actor first husband aboard a yacht at St. Tropez. Everyone else is identified as psychoculturally unfit and is subsequently discarded. . . .

Like the novel itself, the flaws of *Hard Rain Falling* are boldly executed. Mr. Carpenter misses an existentialist windfall with Jack. Learning what love is from [Negro cellmate] Billy Lancing's death, Jack confers his on Sally and receives love's counterfeit. Robbed of his child, impotently sweating violence, he fails to strike and save himself and the novel from casual disintegration. Not an anti-hero, but finally an ironic non-hero, Jack is psychically obsolete.

He cannot rise, even existentially, to confront his own humanity through the grand crime of murder, or the outraged resignation of suicide. A gelatinous victim, he is left staring at a glass of Irish whisky certain to start him dreaming again— as in his creator's ministerial off-moments—of "a freedom from connection, from fear, from trouble . . . from the loneliness of being alive." Jack precipitates no moral enlightenment. He is quietly emasculated by society. The novel reverts to fictional sociology, a sharp, hard chip off Farrell and Dreiser.

Let practitioners of Deep Think worry over the teleology of Jack Levitt. Mr. Carpenter must settle for less. He preserves the events of a life in prose polished flat. He writes about pool, boozing it up, smashing faces and furniture, and taking the ride to Q as if he were Hemingway describing Caporetto. A 34-year-old encyclopedist and former teacher of English who has spent only one middle-class night in jail, he sends us, nevertheless, an accusing information—the crime of growing up imprisoned by hopelessness. Everyone's guilty.

> *Webster Schott, "A Swinger and a Loser," in* The New York Times Book Review, *January 30, 1966, p. 4.*

MARTIN SEYMOUR-SMITH

Hard Rain Falling is a first novel . . . of remarkable quality, written with authority, detachment and an almost uncanny, deadpan intelligence. I have seldom come across a new novel in which such compelling readability coexists with such absolute seriousness of purpose and keenness of psychological insight.

The story is of two unusually gifted and intelligent victims of sexual irresponsibility and social injustice: Jack Levitt, foundling, and Billy Lancing, negro. At sixteen both are dangerous hoodlums, willing to do anything to obtain money. Jack is formidably tough; Billy is a brilliant pool-hall hustler who can take money off most experts without trying. Desperate as they both are, however, neither is without conscience or love: Mr Carpenter ironically traces their histories as they half drift, half will themselves, through gangsterdom, prison, marriage, divorce, self-sacrifice and a strange and painful sort of reformation.

The first part discovers the two in Portland, Oregon, as adolescents busily pursuing the engrossing business of getting money by any means possible. In the second part they meet, some years later, in San Quentin prison, in which both are incarcerated for crimes they did not commit. Here their relationship with each other, and their understanding of life, deepens, and an event occurs that is crucial for both of them. The final section of the novel is an ironic and tragic tailpiece, the full and shocking significance of which is unlikely to strike the reader until some time after he has put the book down.

With his first book Mr Carpenter has established himself as an ironist of immediate stature who knows how to hold the reader's attention without making concessions. The plight of his heroes is always the plight of criminals—but at the same time his skill lets us feel it as the plight of all intelligent and sensitive beings. This is an impressive achievement, and an important contribution to modern fiction. It has all the narrative expertise of a best-seller and all the fiercely rebellious sophistication of the articulate avant-garde, but by its acute psychological and sociological know-how it asserts itself as a wholly original creative work in its own right.

> *Martin Seymour-Smith, "Asphalt Jungle," in* The Spectator, *Vol. 217, No. 7206, August 5, 1966, p. 181.*

STANLEY REYNOLDS

Blade of Light is a novel that truly reads as if it were the work of two people, one a deadpan Nathanael Westian creator of claustrophobic settings and monstrous characters and the other a woman's magazine writer with a dirty mind and a penchant for advertising slogan prose. Naturally one knows that good writers can sometimes write very badly indeed, but the switches in style and tone are so complete in *Blade of Light* that one doubts if even the most astute of literary guessing game panelists could divine the work as the product of a lone hand. Yet there are three or four scenes in the novel that show a masterly hand at work. (p. 594)

> *Stanley Reynolds, "Guilt," in* New Statesman, *Vol. 74, No. 1912, November 3, 1967, pp. 593-94.*

ROBERT J. SHEA

Irwin Semple is one of the most repulsive protagonists in modern fiction. Hideous in aspect and disgusting in behavior, Semple has a ring of empty seats around him even in the most crowded movie theater. He is ill-coordinated, partly mad, ugly and ineffectual. (p. 16)

At the beginning [of *Blade of Light*], Semple, aged 35, is released from a mental hospital. The book thereafter alternates between two different time periods, one describing Semple's high school days and leading up to the crime which got him locked up at 17, the other dealing with his return to the world outside the mental hospital and leading toward his confrontation with his enemy, Harold Hunt. Harold is the man whose machinations caused Semple's crime; he is Semple's physical opposite—graceful, clean-cut, intelligent, a leader and just cruel enough to be attractive. But ultimately, Harold is just as isolated as Semple, cut off from other people by his total self-involvement.

Over and over, in fact, Carpenter shows us images of aloneness. (pp. 16, 18)

The book also dwells on ugliness. Carpenter piles on the details of Semple's hideousness with deliberate striving for a freakish effect.

Blade of Light is unrelievedly about isolation and ugliness—of the flesh and of the spirit. In Semple's final meeting with his antagonist Harold there is no communication, only misunderstanding and death. The book takes a hard look at realities which may be more a part of the human condition than most of us would care to admit. (p. 18)

> *Robert J. Shea, "Sick, Sick," in* Book World—The Washington Post, *February 4, 1968, pp. 16, 18.*

WEBSTER SCHOTT

Don Carpenter's second novel [*Blade of Light*] confirms judgment of powers shown in his first, *Hard Rain Falling*. He stands among new American novelists of the 1960's gifted with conscience and destined for literature.

Like his first novel, *Hard Rain Falling*, Carpenter's second picks up where Depression Naturalism left off, and turns on the passion of a forgotten tradition. The new configuration is our affluent welfare society, a society that protects its psychiatric losses but cannot secure them with love or bless them with health. Consequently a new outsider forages for hope in the urban jungle and digs up disasters. This is the outcast Carpenter touches and fills with the breath of sadness and a strange dignity.

Carpenter's micro-hero is a dimwit named Irwin Semple released after 18 years in an asylum for the criminally insane because no one knows what else to do with him. He has mastered the rules of institutional survival. He has relearned how to hold a pencil and make it trace letters. He has acquired the skill necessary to mop a floor. He's ready for the outside because others are in line to get inside.

Moving back and forward in time, picking up five or six characters from Semple's boyhood and life after release, Carpenter tells a story of torment, waste, human breakdown. Illegitimate, face running with sores, reared by a family of alcoholics and inheritor of all the liabilities of neglect, Semple is booted out of school and tortured in ways that small children perfect. He metamorphoses from pest at school to village idiot. Defending the last repository of self, his sexual integrity, he commits a stupid crime.

Semple's life after incarceration is Carpenter's guided tour of purgatory restructured as occupational rehabilitation. He stumbles through meaningless jobs, consumes entertainment to destroy time. His primitive lusts and hungers peter out in frustration. The second life collapses in shocking, uncalculated violence. Semple cannot cope with the brute force of events, the brute indifference of men.

Don Carpenter's plot pulls the plugs to pathos, surprise, sorrow. Semple continually reaches out for human contact to fill the vacuum within. Carpenter's visions of his longing drain the emotions.... Carpenter holds society failing. Thus his minor characters—all broken links to the other reality Semple seeks—pass from corollary roles to full but separate lives that collide with Semple and crush him.

Carpenter's narrative races. His environment glimmers with dull authenticity. His secondary characters compel recognition. But the success of **Blade of Light** rises from Carpenter's conception and delivery of Semple. He shows us one of man's ugliest children spawned by man's animalism. He discovers in Semple's fractured personality the thin blade of human light. He creates the listless misery of the psychophysical outcast's loveless isolation. And Carpenter commands the skill and feeling to make from such cold reality art that forces us to share his emotion of irreparable wrong. To read **Blade of Light** is to suffer at a distance a life shattered, a soul abandoned.

> *Webster Schott, "Lunatic at Large," in* The New York Times Book Review, *February 4, 1968, p. 4.*

JAMES R. FRAKES

[The earlier books **Hard Rain Falling** and **Blade of Light**] established the quality of Mr. Carpenter's unblinking and unshockable vision, but this new collection of 10 stories [**The Murder of the Frogs and Other Stories**] offers an almost total inventory of the shambles, right down to the last shattered bone and sliver of bloody gristle. From the first story, **"Road Show,"** ... to the final novella, **"One of Those Big-City Girls,"** with its painfully specific transformation of "milady's toilette" into an autopsy of menopausal vanity and decay—all is either dry rot or galloping mold.

Does it all sound unrelievedly grim? Well, it is, for the most part. **"Limbo,"** for example, in a little over six stark pages, makes a universal wasteland out of a carnival midway. Ambition, initiative and all the other anointed Kiwanis virtues yield, in **"Silver Lamé,"** to the saddest kind of unquenchable lust. If a bird sings anywhere, it's a mockingbird. If an elk appears, it gets gut-shot. Love is either a disease or a profession.

No, Mr. Carpenter offers no pretty little thoughts, no fake faith-restoratives—just hard solid craftsmanship and style, which may well be enough, if not to retard the lemming-rush, at least to make it worth your while to experience for a few hours his refusal to transcribe anything in bad faith. [**"The Murder of the Frogs"**], an account of a 12-year-old boy's devastating rites-of-passage summer at a Sierra Nevada lake, builds up a deceptive atmosphere of fresh air, cold water and healthy young girls. But when suddenly and quietly the reader is assailed by the scene in which young Walter skins alive over 200 frogs, it becomes clear that this harrowingly "human" act is at the heart of the whole collection....

> *James R. Frakes, "At the Slaughterhouse Door, Hope Is in Short Supply," in* The New York Times Book Review, *September 14, 1969, p. 4.*

JOYCE CAROL OATES

[In **The Murder of the Frogs and Other Stories,** Don Carpenter's West] is made up of atomized, unfriendly people whom nothing, not even sexual intimacy, can make human. Carpenter's settings are the High Sierras, the Oregon countryside, Hollywood and San Francisco, and the famous superficiality of Hollywood is matched by a soul-deadening world of lower-middle-class resort summers in such stories as **"The Murder of the Frogs,"** where people return yearly to an "evocation of the rough frontier Americans have a right to be proud of; a small lake, arrived at by traveling five miles over a rough dirt road, high in the Sierra Nevada Mountains ..." The story, which concerns itself with a twelve-year-old's initiation into love and betrayal, is not an especially original one but its density of facts, its sense of reality, is enough to make it harshly memorable.

One section of **The Murder of the Frogs** is called **"The Art of the Film"** and its focus, naturally enough, is upon two successful Hollywood men, one a seventy-year-old studio boss and the other a script writer, whose lives are strangely unfulfilled. **"One of Those Big-City Girls"** is a sensitive, patient, sympathetic treatment of that classic of literary figures, the aging "glamorous" woman who discovers that she prefers to be degraded to being loved. Carpenter's later stories, which open this collection, seem to me less successful because they are less ambitious; but he is a writer of high competence. (p. 5)

> *Joyce Carol Oates, "The Search for a Sense of Self," in* Book World—The Washington Post, *October 26, 1969, pp. 4-5.*

CHOICE

Carpenter has the integrity, compassion, and control of a fine short story writer. What makes him especially interesting is his ability to fasten the reader's attention to the narrative line, and to use this line as the basis of a singular economy—as almost the sole means to develop his characters and concentrate his impressions of Oregon and Hollywood. This is indeed a demanding task, and, in his earlier pieces [in **The Murder of the Frogs and Other Stories**], complexities of character sometimes give way to the simple forward movement. But in **"The Murder of the Frogs,"** where Carpenter allows himself more space and narrative variety, he develops a complex and engaging character. The economy of the story is still achieved through the narrative line, but much power is derived from suggestion, from what is left out.

> *A review of "The Murder of the Frogs and Other Stories," in* Choice, *Vol. 7, No. 2, April, 1970, p. 228.*

SANDRA RUOFF WATSON

Caught between a well-meaning but ineffectual mother and a promiscuous sister who dies from a botched abortion, 15-year-old Jody [the title character in **The True Life Story of Jody McKeegan**] decides to escape (she hopes) to stardom and success in Hollywood.... A contemporary nonheroine, Jody sustains bouts of loneliness and depression which she tries to combat through drugs and alcohol. Carpenter's prose is realistic and incisive, but he keeps introducing characters without fully developing them. Both setting and plot are uneven, the resolution anti-climactic. Jody comes to realize that "time was wasting and death was coming," but it is almost too late to save herself or this story from casual disintegration.

Sandra Ruoff Watson, in a review of "The True Life Story of Jody McKeegan," in Library Journal, Vol. 100, No. 1, January 1, 1975, p. 64.

THOMAS LeCLAIR

The True Life Story of Jody McKeegan reads as though Don Carpenter had a grudge against language. The novel is a West Coast *Sister Carrie,* but even Dreiser would wonder why Carpenter was in the writing business. Jody McKeegan rises from poverty in Portland and lands on her back in Hollywood. There she follows Carrie's rule of always trading up: from a bit player boyfriend to a producer-lover who gets her into his movie. Like Carrie, Jody is a natural actress and performs well in her first film. That's where the book stops, and thankfully so because it's an embarrassing mix of hard luck stories, anecdotes, and "how it's done" movie gossip.

Carpenter has little sense of shape (the story moves by naive accretion) and no compunctions about extended banality. He describes a movie in which "people do not differentiate between their acts . . . all have the same distant quality," presumably without recognizing that his characters have this same equal distance because his language fails to create the differences and perspective we associate with art, even with life. . . . If a book can be mute—wordless despite its pages of type— then *The True Life Story of Jody McKeegan* is that book, a novel that hums old Hollywood tunes and flashes Variety clippings. Even if they're true they're not nearly enough.

Thomas LeClair, "Police Deals, an Anti-Utopia, Some Old Hollywood," in The New York Times Book Review, February 9, 1975, p. 6.

RICHARD ELMAN

Plover plays radio in San Francisco. M.C. for a dial-in talk show, he's quick and glib with opinions, but heavy, brooding and shy about his feelings. Your little-better-than-average-male-chauvinist-pig, he is hip enough to drink Dos Equis beer, and tender enough with any woman who is not his wife. Most of his 14 years of marriage have been spent hulking over the TV at night with his bottle of Dos Equis in a San Francisco suburb, but Plover can't allow himself to imagine that Thalia wasn't having a good time. He hulks at the center of Don Carpenter's fourth book [*Getting Off*], somewhat disoriented and befuddled and angry for having been kicked out of the house, at last, by that somewhat drab female. In the midst of his own subdued melodrama he doesn't know how funny he could be.

Plover never quite says it, but he somehow manages to believe that Thalia has been ungrateful. Throughout most of the pages of *Getting Off* he goes about as if encased or lacquered inside a brittle, thinnish shell of depression which has dulled all his perceptions and feelings so that he cannot experience the hard knot of m.c.p. anger beneath. He smokes dope, but trips nowhere. . . .

Plover remains entirely self-righteous and condescending. He claims to understand why Thalia needs to go her own way. He doesn't want to cause a fuss, but comes home every so often to have his shirts laundered. Poor sad sack, he has reserved for himself a limbo of friends' sofas and girl friends, borrowed apartments and motel rooms as if he were atoning with a series of half-hearted shrugs for a sin in which he did not quite believe. All the while he seethes. The only way he will ever get off is to admit to his own rage. But when he does finally, he is nasty, slaps Thalia about, actually believing this could be his ticket home again. Confronted, at last, by his estranged wife's split lip and hurt eyes, it all comes home to Plover that Thalia is every bit as angry as he is. Reconciliation? He needs a divorce. . . .

If a lesser craftsman had taken on the dream trip of unreality and self-pity between separation and divorce, we might have been given polemic or lugubrious rhetorical melodrama; Don Carpenter is careful, disciplined and exacting. He says what he has to say once and simply, moves from scene to scene with the grace of a professional, never boasts or pretends to any more sex or violence than there is in the experience, manages to keep his tone reserved (a kind of perfect correlative for low key depression) and, at the most important moments, dramatizes effectively. (p. 6)

Getting Off is the kind of novel that one reads (if one has ever been divorced) with gratitude that an author has bothered to set down so much tight, painful stuff so fastidiously; but afterwards one has no real sense of having been guided beyond the specific experience to any richness of illumination. For one thing, Carpenter's prose is so low key and played down that it rarely deals in metaphor; it's simply a scenario for understated psychological depiction. Also, novels such as this have a peculiar tic, a necessity to document at every turn the character's whereabouts, hangouts and buddies on the San Francisco scene, and this literal-mindedness sometimes gets a bit tedious. The author writes only as the character perceives, and, since the character is a little depressed and not too smart, though hip, it's as if one were being conducted through hell by some lesser figure than Dante—for example, the late George Orwell. (pp. 6, 18)

Getting Off is extremely worthwhile to read because we seem to get to know Plover and his ragged friends, have heard him on the radio, or overheard him in bars. We've bumped into poor Thalia, too, once too often with her shopping cart in the supermarket. But Carpenter has done more than simply average out a lot of ordinary people's experience. He has found a way to dramatize that experience, according to its true proportions, has taken the pulse, as it were, of a certainly large segment of contemporary butchdom and tweaked its weaknesses and agonies while discovering along the way some occasionally terse middle-aged moments of ecstasy.

From the opening pages in which Plover wakes beside a suddenly unresponsive woman to discover that their married act is finally over, we are with him in his search for new lady friends, apartments, a life style. Carpenter is able to make you believe in some clean, fresh way that smoking too much dope and drinking too many beers is an anodyne for the instantaneous intimacies of Sausalito bars and he can make you feel that slightly fetid wet-wash mood that depressed housewifery can lend to any nice suburban household. He knows his subject and the painful terrain Plover is forced to inhabit, cut loose and adrift long after his prime to gab with besotted buddies and ache for home again. Carpenter stays with his character because he is a writer of integrity, even though this sometimes leads him into stretches of suppressed feeling that for any sensitive reader may pass for mere dullness. (p. 18)

Richard Elman, "Plover Was Angry and Didn't Know It," in The New York Times Book Review, May 16, 1977, pp. 6, 18.

ROBERT KEILY

The society described in Don Carpenter's latest novel [*A Couple of Comedians*] recalls E. M. Forster's declaration that *Babbitt* depicted a civilization that could "only work or amuse itself with rubbish." The two comedians of the title are a fictitious version of such Hollywood pairs as Bob Hope and Bing Crosby or Dean Martin and Jerry Lewis. No one expects a comic's life to be funny, but the maudlin, self-pitying, pointless carryings-on of the performers in this book almost make *Waiting for Godot* seem frothy.

During the years that David Ogilvie and Jim Larson have worked together, they have developed a unique bond, something more than kinship: Each sees himself, especially his public image, in terms of the other. Except for intense periods of work in Hollywood followed by intense periods of play in Las Vegas, the two men lead separate lives. During the rest of the year, one lives in semi-retirement in the mountains and the other wanders from entanglement to entanglement. . . . In seemingly unconscious parody of Mark Twain's boys on a lark or Hemingway's men on a spree, they run off to the hills, motels, mansions and fast-food stands of California in their unending quest for beautiful women and the perfect vanilla milkshake. Periodically they smoke pot, pop pills and cry uncontrollably.

A Couple of Comedians might have made for a better satire if Mr. Carpenter had not been so fond of his fools. By sentimentalizing them he increases the reader's disgust but loses his interest. An early scene in which the two friends bury David's grandfather without notifying the authorities bears an unfortunate resemblance to a similar episode in *The Grapes of Wrath*. Without developed characters or believable circumstance, the act appears arbitrary and the emotion it tries to convey cheap. (pp. 11, 33)

Robert Keily, "Three Novels," in The New York Times Book Review, January 6, 1980, pp. 10-11, 33.

RICHARD SCHICKEL

In *A Couple of Comedians*, Narrator David Ogilvie—gagman of the title team—makes a list, in descending order of status, of the Los Angeles hotels favored by showfolk. He does it perfectly, beginning with the Bel-Air, ending with the Montecito. This may seem a small felicity, but it is precisely the sort of thing that writers of parboiled Hollywood *romans à clef* usually get wrong or skip altogether in their haste to get to the casting couch and the boudoir.

Verisimilitude is only one of several virtues of Don Carpenter's shrewd and tightly written novel. *Comedians* contains just one star other than its central comics, and she is only a walk-on. It needs no more. The cast is perfect, and the comedy unfailingly original. There are no libidinous or abusive producers, no hysterically egomaniac directors, not even a failed novelist making a rich, bitter livelihood by writing for the screen. The author has been a novelist . . . ; he has also been a movie and

TV working stiff, and what he is offering here is an accurate, lightly ironic record of the laid-back camaraderie animating the movie business.

This does not mean that Ogilvie's account of how his straight man, Jim Larson, goes slightly bananas in the course of finishing a movie is a mere fever chart. The journey of another kind of odd couple dramatizes, poignantly and wittily, Elizabeth Hardwick's observation that performers tend to lead their lives "gregariously and without affections." There are lots of gorgeous scenes, including an incident of status panic in Schwab's drugstore with a lunchtime crowd of actors desperately vying with one another for the attention of a powerful producer, and a party where a White House staffer learns how power politics works when it leaves D.C. for L.A. Carpenter does these set pieces so well that he sometimes forgets to nail down Larson's character firmly enough.

But there may be art in these ellipses. Performers of Larson's type are often only shadows of the carefully tailored selves they project to the public. In private, filling the empty days between engagements, they try to find an intensity to match that of their onstage moments. There is a sweet emptiness about them, a vacancy that leaves by-standers fecklessly trying to connect the dots of their personalities.

There is bite here, but no bitterness. The overall, and lasting, effect makes *A Couple of Comedians* an unusually literate and oddly touching novel about performers going through the sound stages of life. (pp. 87-8)

Richard Schickel, "Laid-Back Camaraderie," in Time, Vol. 115, No. 4, January 28, 1980, pp. 87-8.

BRUCE COOK

Don Carpenter is in a perfect position to write about Hollywood. He's worked there. He knows it. He's of it but not in it. . . . Partly as a result of this, nobody around today writes as skillfully and authoritatively about the crazy world of movies and show biz as Don Carpenter. He is doing for present-day Hollywood what Daniel Defoe did for 18th-century London— charting its licit and illicit commerce, exploring its underside, revealing in precise detail how the place works. He began with a few fine stories in *The Murder of the Frogs*, continued with *The True Life Story of Jody McKeegan*, and now offers another chronicle of life in movieland with *A Couple of Comedians*.

The book is about just what it says. Carpenter presents the comedy team of Larson and Ogilvie not so much in full-length portrait as in a series of quick, candid snapshots. David Ogilvie is the narrator here. His partner, Jim Larson, is the straight man, singing songs and making with the patter as Ogilvie mugs ("ogles") and supplies the gag lines that bring down the house. Ogilvie also supplies whatever contact with reality the team maintains. After years of playing penny-ante clubs and trying to make it on television with a succession of flop shows, the two finally have hit big in the movies. Their schedule now calls for them to do a movie a year and a month-long stint at the "Golconda" in Las Vegas. Not exactly taxing—but still too much for Larson, who is just about ready to flip out as the book begins. What's his problem? The old success-at-last syndrome.

Will Larson go off the deep end or won't he? That's what serves *A Couple of Comedians* as a plot. Not much, I grant you, but somehow it is all Don Carpenter needs as he propels his two protagonists pell-mell from one bizarre adventure into the next wacky episode. . . .

A Couple of Comedians is not so much funny as it is Hollywood-freaky. All Carpenter does is present the place, the milieu, the state-of-mind as it really is. What might seem the most extreme burlesque turns out here to be no more than stark realism. The book offers as accurate a picture of life behind the scenes in show business today as anything I have read since—well, since *The True Life Story of Jody McKeegan.* By the way, Jody herself puts in an appearance here, suggesting that Carpenter has embarked upon a kind of Hollywood *Comédie Humaine,* complete with crossed destinies and reappearing characters. . . .

Carpenter covers so much ground so quickly that it is hard to believe the book is so short. I only wish it had been longer. However, by the time it winds down at last to its not altogether surprising conclusion in Las Vegas, the reader knows the people and their world so well that he can hardly claim to be unsatisfied. It is rich, rich food fed at a fast, fast pace.

> Bruce Cook, "Getting Their Act Together," in Book World—The Washington Post, *February 10, 1980, p. 7.*

JACK SULLIVAN

[Don Carpenter's *Turnaround*] is an unapologetic celebration of greed and perversity in the movie industry. Two kinds of people inhabit Carpenter's world, both of them wealthy. First, there are those who fight boredom with a strict schedule of "tennis, lunch, cocktails, extramarital affair, nap, cocktails, opera, dinner, drunk and to bed." These idle rich, who make periodic incursions into the movie industry, are a dull lot compared to the climbing rich, "the scumballs of Hollywood, with their outrageous manners, disgusting perversions, unruly egos and uncontrollable behavior." Carpenter's insidious novel invites us to observe this behavior—in scene after cocaine-permeated scene of political and sexual aggrandizement—with gloating, voyeuristic envy. . . .

Besides the conquests of his characters, Carpenter also traces, in authoritative detail, the "complex, serpentine flow of energy" and sheer luck that must go into the making of a movie if it is to avoid going into "turnaround," a horrible and fatal process of unravelling. Carpenter is expert at depicting the anxieties of movie makers who must ultimately "be scrutinized by large numbers of cold-blooded men who knew nothing about movies, only about money."

Carpenter is rather cold-blooded himself, but he is also rambunctious, inventive, and superbly entertaining. The makers of a movie that is "running scared" are described as looking in a meeting "like boys who had been caught torturing frogs"; a blocked writer is described as looking at the blank piece of paper in his typewriter and seeing "his fate written there." Two pages later, however, the struggling writer sells a script for $80,000—"Not a bad day's pay." Carpenter doesn't make his characters very likeable, but he does make them rich.

> Jack Sullivan, in a review of "Turnaround," in Book World—The Washington Post, *May 3, 1981, p. 4.*

THE NEW YORKER

[*Turnaround* is a] Hollywood morality tale in triptych. Mr. Carpenter, a former screenwriter and an admirable novelist, shows us a middle-aged production chief at the peak of his enormous power, a younger producer with a solid hit to his credit and a beckoning future, and an innocent young man who wants to write for the movies. There are also the women who figure in and somehow exemplify their lives. . . . Almost at once, Mr. Carpenter fills our cup to overflowing with sex, with drugs, with alcohol, with every sort of hangover, and this for a time seems to be what he has principally in mind. But then, by some crafty sleight of hand, the aging production chief, the younger producer, and the young writer stand fully alive before us in their weird and workaday world—stand eagerly awaiting their doom.

> A review of "Turnaround," in The New Yorker, *Vol. LVII, No. 23, July 27, 1981, p. 87.*

JEREMY LARNER

If *Turnaround* were a script, it would by now have gone into turnaround—meaning that the studio which financed it would have given up and declared itself willing to be bought out. For Don Carpenter has written the proverbial great Hollywood novel—and no one noticed. . . .

The problem with the great Hollywood novel is that it too is a Hollywood cliché. All these years we've been waiting to celebrate a book that would really show what bastards the bastards are; then we get such books and find them flat and predictable. The snotty among us have written that reality is no longer real; only surreal effects like Nathanael West's can capture the vulgarly exaggerated L.A. scene. But *Turnaround* is better than *The Day of the Locust* because it has more heart and less slop. And it knows more, it has more to tell us, because it is written with unassuming precision of detail.

Despite a few errors and improbabilities, one could learn from *Turnaround* how scripts get written, how movies get started, and the relation between the two. But more than that, *Turnaround* is written with love, not just of Hollywood, but of life and people as they are found there. If there is no dignity in the perpetual fight against turnaround, at least there is stupendous ingenuity. Show biz itself is a special kind of lie seeking against big odds to become truth—and it is in that seeking that Don Carpenter finds the high glee that animates his novel.

Carpenter doesn't glorify evil, but neither does he inflate thievery and exploitation into the end of Western civilization. We can see, from what he tells us, how bad movies are, and we are free to think what that means about the world that wants bad movies. But that is not Carpenter's subject. His subject is the efforts of characters on various rungs of the ladder to hang on, or climb higher, or step on someone else's hands—all of which he sees as human and worth recording. The characters and what they do are believable, not merely symptomatic. On every page we can cackle with the author . . .—yes, this is just what would happen, just how so-and-so would behave—and yes, even as the characters transcend our expectations and surprise us, yes, *this* is just how it has to be.

Carpenter's L.A. is, in its way, like the Paris of Balzac, where the scurrying is so intricate and the scheming so rich and hopeful that it is raised to the level of nobility. And of course it is corrupt. Any second-rater could tell us that. . . . But it takes a novelist to show us how Hollywood works in a way that is worthy of our sympathetic attention.

Carpenter's story is told strictly from the viewpoints of its three heroes. The naive hero is a young screenwriter, Jerry Rexford, who lives on the seamy side of town, the "B" Hollywood Carpenter knows so well. (pp. 36-7)

Among Jerry's friends is a man who clerks at a porno shop, who tells Jerry he will help him "crack Hollywood. You'll make it . . . because you know *me!*" After Jerry's failed efforts to send scripts through agents, it is indeed the porno clerk who produces the break-through contact, via a chain of odd contacts leading to the young hotshot producer, Rick Heidelberg. When Rick glances at Jerry's script, he sees at once it is something he can use. (p. 37)

Rick Heidelberg, the creator of that smash hit, *The Endless Unicorn,* is all calculation as he sets about the manipulations that will jockey him into his second hit or leave him out in the cold. Yet the quality of Rick's thinking, as Carpenter shows it, is original and creative—never mind that it is self-centered and sometimes silly. Carpenter catches the alertness and the appetite for taking chances, the precise skill at social measurement unknown to better men with fixed inner standards.

Heidelberg's friend and occasional opponent is the production head of a major studio, Alexander Hellstrom, a man of 50 who is preoccupied throughout the novel with a rich and stylish lady who fools him so badly that he is the last to see she is incorrigibly promiscuous. . . . Carpenter has a way of telling us about it that makes it seem neither clichéd nor offensive, but an attribute of a particular woman belonging to a particular wealthy set. (pp. 37-8)

[Carpenter] got involved in movies in the late 1960s, when he took his first script and managed to co-produce a fine, tough, little-known film, *Payday.* After that Carpenter went through 12 years in which he never got another script produced. It's noteworthy that in *Turnaround,* after introducing several dubious movie ideas, Carpenter allows Jerry Rexford to come up with two original gems. The fact that Carpenter serves them up in a novel is an indication not only of his allegiance but of the fate his best ideas would meet if they had to survive in the movie-making process he describes.

But even as his scripts were shot down by egos whose extra-movie needs they failed to fulfill, Carpenter began to write L.A. show-biz novels—*Jody McKeegan* and *A Couple of Comedians*—in which he mixed a geography of power with scenes from the down side of town, the region of the talents and semitalents who mill about the entrances, pushing to get in, yet capable of a touching empathy in their relations with one another. At first Carpenter was less sure of himself dealing with big shots than he was with the downtrodden. *Turnaround* achieves more completely what he has been trying to do right along: to show the Balzacian comedy of the parts interacting, of the rise from the bottom and the dip from the top.

In general, the novels that presume to expose Hollywood only mirror its own opinion of its importance. They speak in its terms if only to denounce those terms. Carpenter, with an easy, casual tone, gets the whole picture. He knows, finally, what the emperors of celluloid ice cream will never know, and he quotes it in his epigraph from Thoreau: "A man needs only to be turned around once with his eyes shut in this world to be lost." (p. 38)

    Jeremy Larner, "The New Hollywood," in The New Republic, *Vol. 185, No. 25, December 23, 1981, pp. 36-8.*

DAVID LEHMAN

The only unfortunate thing about *The Class of '49* is its title. You take one look at it and you immediately think: haven't I seen this movie somewhere before? And indeed this . . . novel by the San Francisco-based writer Don Carpenter reads as if it were made for the movies; it aspires to do for the high-school graduating class of 1949 what *Diner* and *American Graffiti* did for the guys and gals who came of age a decade or two later. But don't let that fool you; the novel's literary qualities are not to be quarreled with. Halfway through it, you're liable to wish that creative-writing instructors would teach their charges to write with such economy and apparent "absence of effort."

The Class of '49 consists of a succession of self-contained sketches that together imply a broad picture. The cast includes such familiar figures as the experienced girl who presides over the hero's sexual initiation; the couple who marry when she gets pregnant and then disappear into a grim workaday reality; the girl who has dedicated her whole life to becoming Rose Festival Queen; the gentlemanly lad who learns he has cancer. . . . But over it all hangs the premonitory shadow of the Korean War. "If we all joined up together, we could go through boot camp together," Jud says, with no more thought than he'd give to crashing a party or starting a brawl at the prom.

Carpenter's prose is all muscle and sinew. That's true, too, of the two separate stories included in the book. **"One Pocket,"** a well-done if somewhat forgettable pool-hall saga, takes us to the Air Force base at Biloxi, Miss., in 1952, when there were "forty thousand airmen and one hooker." **"Glitter: A Memory,"** by far the better story, gives us the tragicomic life of a Hollywood star named Felix Bilson, who never had the big breakthrough predicted for him. Felix's early success as a James Dean look-alike is followed by the dark period after his wife's murder. . . . Then, amazingly, Felix achieves his breakthrough: he successfully challenges the studio's seven-year "slave contract." This is fun; Carpenter knows his Hollywood. (pp. 100-01)

    David Lehman, "Those Were the Days, My Friend," in Newsweek, *Vol. CVI, No. 22, November 25, 1985, pp. 100-01.*

BRUCE COOK

[Don Carpenter is] one of the best-kept secrets in publishing today. A first-rate writer who is superior to many who are far better known, Carpenter now has a considerable body of work behind him. Although widely varied in tone and subject matter, his novels and stories have in common qualities of bone-honesty, wit, and intelligence that set them far apart from the run-of-the-mill academic and commercial fictions.

The Class of '49 is Don Carpenter's eighth book. Made up of two stories and the title work, it is one of those slippery items that is a little hard to classify. In shape, and even in substance, it seems a bit more like a collection of interrelated short stories. In short pieces of four or five pages or even less, Carpenter presents the members of the 1949 graduating class of Adams High in Portland, Ore. They check in and out of one another's stories; playing supporting roles until they get their star turn. A few even reappear in leading roles, giving some sense of unity to it all, lending an implication that this is almost a novel and these are its main characters. . . .

If *The Class of '49* has a protagonist, then it is [Tommy German]. Secretly intellectual in his inclinations, yet as wild as any of his macho buddies, he seems to anticipate those mad angels of the Beat Generation who were then just about ready to explode upon the scene. A kid like Tommy German wouldn't even be possible today: He was a rebel at a time when there was something real to rebel against.

Pool and billiards figure prominently in the best single piece in *The Class of '49,* **"Cooney on World Affairs."** In it, Blaze Cooney, a bright kid with a talent for the game gets a nasty introduction to the adult world when he finds out that winning isn't always in one's best interests. It seems that Don Carpenter himself knows his way around the pool table and has shot a game or two in his time. In **"One Pocket,"** he tells us his personal history as a pool shooter, and in the process a good deal more as he leads up to the Big Game of his life.

Carpenter has lived by his wits and his typewriter about every way a writer can. One of those ways was working in Hollywood. . . .

[Perhaps] the biggest blessing of Don Carpenter's Hollywood period was the wealth of material it gave him. There are stories in *The Murder of the Frogs,* and a rough Hollywood trilogy, *The True Life of Jody McKeegan, A Couple of Comedians* and *Turnaround,* which are together about as good as anything written about the movie business in the last 40 years or so.

To them we may add **"Glitter: A Memory,"** the final tale in this lopsided collection. Here he tells two stories—his own and that of Felix Bilson, an actor who got in trouble by bucking the system. Carpenter is at his reflective and recollective best, presenting it all with such a sense of truth that we are tempted to look for real names to substitute for those we are given in the story. He brings the two narrative threads together and ties them up nicely in a touching scene played out in, of all places, a go-go bar.

But Don Carpenter is full of surprises. The only real consistency he guarantees is the high quality of his work.

Bruce Cook, "Seriously, What Became of the Class of '49?" in The Detroit News, *January 12, 1986, p. 14B.*

Angela (Olive) Carter

1940-

English novelist, short story writer, nonfiction writer, script-writer, and author of children's books.

In her fiction, Carter combines elements of surrealism, myth, and eroticism with feminist and political observations. In several works, she employs science fiction motifs to create fantastical landscapes through which she examines contemporary issues. In *Nights at the Circus* (1984), for example, winner of the James Tait Black Memorial Prize, Carter offers a symbolic portrait of the female condition, placing her story amidst the bizarre characters of a traveling circus and focusing on the personal liberation of a six-foot-tall winged woman. Carter's work is distinguished by its display of unrestrained imagination, colorful imagery, and sensuous prose. Equally notable are the Dickensian eccentricities of her characters and her talent, as one critic noted, for "twining the macabre and unlikely with the possible." Although alternately praised and faulted for her extravagant Gothic approach, Carter is highly regarded as a writer of unique and imaginative fiction.

Carter's early novels, *Shadow Dance* (1966), *Several Perceptions* (1968), and *Love* (1971), introduce the Gothic elements in her work. Carter's vivid descriptions of Great Britain's counterculture create a surreal atmosphere in which strange incidents are commonplace. The protagonist of *Shadow Dance* is portrayed as the embodiment of the apathy and amorality of his generation. Acting on impulse, he disfigures his beautiful girlfriend and eventually commits murder. *Several Perceptions* concerns a suicidal young man and his encounters with various eccentric individuals. *Love,* a bleak story of the obsessive nature of love, centers on a young man whose suicidal wife and drug-abusing brother are dependent upon him.

Carter's feminist and philosophical concerns are woven into her fantasy novels. *The Magic Toyshop* (1967) depicts the sexual coming-of-age of a young woman who loses her parents and must live in a household of eccentric relatives. Although finding the plot implausible, John Wakeman commented: "The book succeeds, awkwardly but firmly welded together by the heat of its author's imagination. It leaves behind it a flavor pungent and unsettling, which owes as much to its imperfections as to its virtues." *Heroes and Villains* (1969) is a futuristic tale of Earth a century after atomic devastation has splintered its population into antagonistic factions. *The Infernal Desire Machines of Doctor Hoffman* (1972) recounts the efforts of the protagonist to restore reality in a world where machines give unconscious images concrete form. In *The Passion of New Eve* (1977), a fervent denunciation of sexism and machismo, a man experiences rape and other brutalizations after being surgically transformed into a beautiful woman. A number of the characters in *Nights at the Circus* are archetypes for female oppression and liberation. As Valentine Cunningham noted, "This troupe of ladies first endures, then throws off the demands of men. . . . Again and again they break down the brothel bars . . . [and] work out their own female salvation."

Carter's short stories have been collected in three volumes: *Fireworks: Nine Profane Pieces* (1974), *The Bloody Chamber and Other Stories* (1979), and *Black Venus* (1985). Each vol-

Fay Godwin's Photo Files

ume contains thematically linked stories, many derived from fables, fairy tales, and mythology. As Ellen Cronan Rose observed, Carter is both "an analyst of fairy tales and their cultural implications" and an "improviser, using the tales as a base for imaginative speculation." In her nonfiction work *The Sadeian Woman: An Exercise in Cultural History* (1979), Carter examines the causes and implications of the pornography promoted by the Marquis de Sade. *Nothing Sacred* (1982) is an anthology of Carter's feminist and political articles, and *Come unto These Yellow Sands* (1985) collects various scripts she has adapted from her fiction.

(See also *CLC*, Vol. 5; *Contemporary Authors*, Vols. 53-56; *Contemporary Authors New Revision Series*, Vol. 12; and *Dictionary of Literary Biography*, Vol. 14.)

ELIOT FREMONT-SMITH

[*Honeybuzzard*, published in Great Britain as *Shadow Dance*, is] promising, i.e., a disappointment. Like its title, it buzzes on the page, but not much in the mind. Perhaps that shouldn't be surprising: the author is a young English poet whose American publisher has the audacious command of language and care of its other writers to call her "certainly one of the most exciting finds of recent years." Chew that around for a while.

Honeybuzzard is a somewhat remote, comical nightmare. Its remoteness is due in part to its setting, a city in (my guess) Midlands England, and to the rootless, classless station of its characters—workingmen's sons and daughters who are trained for nothing and who wander around looking for niches for their souls from which they can securely peek out at the world. These people do exist; they are the displaced persons of post-Beatle England, and like all victims, they live surreal.

Take Honeybuzzard, who has no real name, wears Mod clothes, looks "lithe and slick as a stick of licorice" and does everything on calculated whim—calculated to put all ordinary values in reverse. Momentarily attached to a beautiful waif, he slashes her face with a knife. His charm comes from the single-minded energy with which he disarms shock by making it routine; it's not even a case of revolt—merely something to do while breathing. "I like—you know—to slip in and out of me," he says, lights shooting "off his shiny leather jacket in fusillades."

To his fascinated, guilt-ridden partner, Morris Gray—the two of them operate a junk store that occasional American tourists mistake for an antique shop—Honeybuzzard seems an appendage, a limb he doesn't know too well. . . .

Yet Honeybuzzard is all Morris really has. Edna, Morris's whining wife, wants only to suffer in compassion and be appreciated for it. Through headaches and tears, she knits Morris an unwanted sweater. He wonders if the feeble desire he feels for her comes from his making her cry. Approaching the bed, "he kicks aside the knitting which caught at his feet as if it were a little black dog, trying to protect its mistress from him." One needs obsessions; Morris's were not at home.

Eventually, Edna deserts him too; she finds a widower who needs her more. The widower's Finnish wife had killed herself over a monumental misunderstanding about who cut up Honeybuzzard's girl. But the worst was this: "No one could read the note she left because it was in Finnish and very badly spelt, too. They had to get the Finnish consul in the end. It was awful."

Incidents, then, so crude and trite that these words become indistinguishable—incidents that are for these people the sum of consciousness, feeling, life. It isn't tragic, it isn't even cruel; in the end, it isn't much of anything, sociology perhaps. One is touched, and Miss Carter does force an awareness of how shocking it is to be only touched. She writes a vivid, efficient prose, and she pins down moods like so many captured moths. Yet nothing is really pinned down; the moods disintegrate, the characters float away, the climax is a tiny, distant pop.

Was it meant to be more than this? It's hard to tell, which is a likely trouble with promising novels like *Honeybuzzard.* Yet Miss Carter's gifts are much in evidence; she should be urged to call again.

Eliot Fremont-Smith, "Shock Disarmed," in The New York Times, February 3, 1967, p. 29.

EDWARD M. POTOKER

In Angela Carter's slender first novel [*Honeybuzzard*] we meet a man called Morris, who has a face like an El Greco Christ and is well-intentioned but ineffectual. Though he feels pity for suffering fellow-beings, he can translate it into action only by lifting a drowning spider out of his bathtub. He is married to a beige Victorian woman who wishes that her husband were either good or bad; Morris is really neither. He longs to assert himself, to prove his uniqueness, and does so by ordering meringues for breakfast. His gums bleed constantly.

Honeybuzzard is Morris's friend and business partner, a kind of Gothic beatnik who likes to wear false noses, false ears, and plastic vampire teeth. . . . He is amoral and Satanic. He rules his world by cruelty and whim, and laughs at Morris's sense of pity. . . .

In selecting her central character and theme Miss Carter casts her lot with the familiar. Morris is the ineffectual, impotent scapegoat-victim who has appeared in so much postwar fiction. The outlook is the fashionable one of utter despair. Life, as the author views it, is brutal, cannibalistic, and doomed by depravity. Only imbeciles keep it alive, like Honeybuzzard's girl friend Emily, who happily forgets that the child she carries was begotten by a psychopath. As often happens with materials of this sort, the book suffers at times from a lack of restraint, as though the author were not quite sure if she had shocked us sufficiently to drive her point home.

On balance, however, Miss Carter is an exceptionally talented and imaginative writer. She has considerable powers of description, and her catalogues of Victoriana are one of the book's treasures. She sets a grotesque stage and peoples it with characters who are often extravagantly Gothic. She portrays life as a perpetual Witches' Sabbath. She sets up outrageous tensions between her people and suggests many layers of meaning. The reader is suspended between belief and disbelief, crying yes and no with an equal voice.

Edward M. Potoker, "A Gallery of Grotesques," in Saturday Review, Vol. L, No. 7, February 18, 1967, p. 36.

JOHN BOWEN

The characters in Angela Carter's first novel [*Honeybuzzard*] live in "the twilight zone," on the underside of respectable English life. . . . They live at odd hours in odd places, eat badly, drink when they can afford it. They have neither enduring talent, nor ambition; they live in the moment. They are grotesque. Even the more ordinary characters in this novel are grotesque, even the old waitress in the cafe, whom Morris believes to be one of those Struldbugs (of whom Swift wrote), who live forever. Indeed, she is "killed" by Honeybuzzard, and seems none the worse for it next day.

They are grotesque, these people, yet familiar. We may look inwards and find them in each of us. Honeybuzzard is childish, willful, selfish, irresponsible, cruel, capricious, impulsive, a killer. He is Hyde with Jekyll's face. He is the id. And Emily, who is narrow, ordered, lives by rules, and is obsessively clean, in the end turns murdering Honeybuzzard over to the law. Clearly she is the super-ego. Between them is poor Morris, not much of a person, with not much of a will, full of guilt and good intentions, an ego on the verge of disintegration.

American readers may find Miss Carter's characters familiar in another way. "Southern Gothic" is a label which has been slapped on the work of Tennessee Williams, Carson McCullers and Truman Capote, among others. I'm not sure of the extent to which the "Southern Gothic" writers actually took over the apparatus of the English Gothic novel, but I am sure enough of *their* influence on Miss Carter. She has taken the whole

Southern circus—mutilation and beauty and evil, hot weather and a dark luxuriance of bizarre images—and pitched her tent in Bristol. The result is a most entertaining piece of piracy, and a most accomplished novel.

John Bowen, "Grotesques," in The New York Times Book Review, February 19, 1967, p. 44.

IAN HAMILTON

Melanie is a simmering fifteen-year-old who dreams of phantom lovers and strikes naked, wanton poses before bathroom mirrors. Discovering her budding body, she embarks on 'a tranced voyage, exploring the whole of herself, clambering her own mountain ranges, penetrating the moist richness of her secret valleys, a physiological Cortez, da Gama or Mungo Park'. The adventures she actually experiences in *The Magic Toyshop* are odder than this, and less glumly recounted, but have just as evidently been loaned to her by an indulgent novelist. Suddenly orphaned, she is adopted by weird Uncle Philip, and it is in his toyshop that girlish fantasy gets down to detail.

Grinning Gothic detail, mostly, and piled on by Miss Carter with an unremittingly inventive hand. Uncle reigns, with monosyllabic violence, over a household of Irish redheads—his wife, struck dumb on her wedding day, and her two brothers, one of them a brilliant musician, the other an excellent painter. During the day, Philip makes toys, but at night he gets on with what really matters to him—his theatre of near-life-size puppets. Plunged into such company, what can Melanie do but suppress her genteel qualms, join up with the gentle, suffering redheads and, for her sake, finally play Leda to her uncle's puppet swan? After all, she has her young brother and sister to protect, and awakening to sex is awakening to responsibility.

The novel is dense with replicas of one kind or another. Besides the actual toys and puppets (and Miss Carter could play with these for hours) there are statues, masks, costumes, icons, allegorical paintings, and the characters themselves are, painstakingly, pictured in crude toy-like lumps and colours. Of course, we remember the opening scene at the wardrobe mirror and we register the point about appearance and reality. But this is a point which Miss Carter, with her great decorative skill, finds it all too easy to distend. There is a rambling, pleased effortlessness in the way she assembles her bizarre jigsaw and what ought to be rather terrifying (so the heroine's ever-widening eyes insist) too often turns out to seem just cosily peculiar and easily grown out of.

Ian Hamilton, "Comfortably Surreal," in The Listener, Vol. LXXVIII, No. 1998, July 13, 1967, p. 57.

THE NEW YORKER

Mrs. Carter, a really gifted writer, wastes her talent and her readers' time on [*The Magic Toyshop*] an ugly extravaganza about a fifteen-year-old girl, Melanie, who is left an orphan and penniless when her parents are killed in an airplane accident. Melanie and her serious young brother, Jonathon, and her baby sister, Victoria, have to leave their comfortable country home and go to London to live with their mother's brother, a vindictive eccentric whose smallest fault is his miserliness.... Melanie struggles to retain her sanity and her human sympathy in this queer household, which grows more violent with every day that passes. The ending is open to different interpretations, unless one is unkind enough to assume that the author simply ran out of tricks. (pp. 133-34)

A review of "The Magic Toyshop," in The New Yorker, Vol. XLIV, No. 1, February 24, 1968, pp. 133-34.

JOHN WAKEMAN

The heroine of [*The Magic Toyshop,* a] violent English fairy tale, is Melanie, who is 15. Her parents are away in America, but she has for company her younger brother and sister, the old housekeeper, and her mirror. Melanie is bewitched by her maturing body, her "newfound land," which she dresses and rehearses endlessly in imaginary roles, dreamily speculating about its sexual and marital prospects.

One hot midsummer night, Melanie puts on her mother's treasured wedding gown, and wears it out into the moonlit garden. This is *hubris,* and she is at first entranced and then terrified by the enormity of what she is doing. Locked out, she takes off the great dress and carries it up the apple tree to her bedroom window. It is an ordeal, a rite of passage, which leaves the gown blood-stained and ruined. Next morning comes the punishment: news that Melanie's parents have been killed. She breaks her mirror and buries the dress under the apple tree.

The three orphans are now consigned to their Uncle Philip's dreary cavern of a house in a seedy London suburb. . . .

The claustrophobic mood of the house is well conveyed, and so is its erosive effect upon Melanie's normally stable personality. Uncle Philip, when he appears, is a foul-mouthed sadist who cares only for his giant puppets, and tolerates people to the extent that they also become his puppets. Except for the anarchic [son] Finn, the family behaves like the dolls in "La Boutique Fantasque," coming to life only when Philip is asleep. . . .

Angela Carter is a poet as well as a novelist, and prolific of striking images which, however, she is inclined to work to death. Her character drawing shows the same impatient straining after impact, so that her minor people tend to be picturesque caricatures, reminiscent of "Under Milk Wood." Even Uncle Philip is only a paper tiger; Aunt Margaret, however, is thoroughly imagined; and Melanie herself is a solid, attractive personage, whose resigned, ambivalent relationship with Finn is one of the book's pleasures.

Beneath its contemporary surface, the novel shimmers with blurred echoes—from old tree myths, from Lewis Carroll, from "Giselle" and "Coppelia," Harlequin and Punch. It can be read as a paradigm of the war between the generations—or, more easily, as a simple fantasy. Even so, the plot is grossly implausible, and seems constantly to be taking directions that surprise the author as much as the reader.

All this is reprehensible and often irritating, and the reviewer should no doubt remonstrate. And yet the book succeeds, awkwardly but firmly welded together by the heat of its author's imagination. It leaves behind it a flavor, pungent and unsettling, which owes as much to its imperfections as to its virtues.

This is Angela Carter's second novel. The first was another dark fantasy called *Honeybuzzard*. She is still in her twenties and greatly talented and will no doubt write better books. But I would not have this one much different.

John Wakeman, "Dark Fantasy," in The New York Times Book Review, February 25, 1968, p. 38.

JOHN HEMMINGS

What is so intriguing about Miss Carter's writing is that so little in it betrays the hand of the woman novelist. *Several Perceptions* may remind one a little of the early Iris Murdoch, but has none of the caustic femininity of the Ednas, the Penelopes, the Marys and the Margarets of this world. One may, if one wishes, construe the book as a comment on our times, but to do so is to pass over nine-tenths of its charm. Having chosen to explore the mind of a young man, and to chart his exploration of the minds of an assorted group of elders and coevals of both sexes, Miss Carter has deliberately opted for imagination in place of observation, poetic symbolism instead of sociology. The mind, in Hume's image, is a 'kind of theatre' in which the players, strutting, declaiming and vanishing, figure the 'several perceptions' of the title. Joseph Harker, who is this theatre, describes himself as 'all over Paisley patterns: I'm colourful but mixed up.' Even if he's not meant to stand as an epitome of modern youth, he could do so.

Devoid of malice and private ambition, content to live in cheerless squalor, a Meursault with no Algerian sunshine to lull and bemuse him, he has the harshly uncompromising hostility to injustice that characterises the modern drop-out. His protest against the killing in Vietnam is at least original: he parcels up a rich turd and mails it to the White House with the brief injunction: 'EAT ME.' Other references to Lewis Carroll are dotted here and there, serving less as pointers than as the authentic trade-marks of surrealism. Joseph has a white cat whose name—though we're not told this—is no doubt Dinah. Ann Blossom, the prim, lame typist who befriends and scolds him, 'looked a little like Tenniel's Alice, severe and proper, but cropped and singularly lacking in charm'. Mrs Kyte's bedtime reading includes the Alice books but also *The Hunting of the Snark* and even *Sylvie and Bruno*. Mrs Boulder, the middle-aged tart (both these ladies are the mothers of friends of Joseph) emerges as the White Queen, and one can trace, with less assurance, other possible correspondences. All ends with a grand celebration party, when Alice becomes queen (Ann loses her limp), and the old fraud Sunny Bannister (the White Knight?) turns out to be after all what he always said he was, a virtuoso on the violin. *Several Perceptions* is a virtuoso work in itself: it probes its fundamental themes—love and betrayal, innocence and guilt—without ever lapsing into pretentiousness or portentousness.

John Hemmings, "Alice in Dropoutland," in The Listener, *Vol. LXXX, No. 2053, August 1, 1968, p. 152.*

THE TIMES LITERARY SUPPLEMENT

More and more, what might once have been described as the fiction of protest becomes the fiction of disgust, with angry, futile, bleeding images which disquiet the reader rather than harangue him. Here [in *Several Perceptions*], characteristic of the genre but also, since Miss Carter's fiercely expressionist style has begun to be recognized, very much *sui generis*, is the sort of "perception" which drives her hero to attempt suicide:

> Joseph had the chance of a fine education but threw it away; he had free choice on the self-service counter and voluntarily selected shit, old men dying, pus, and, worst of all, most dreaded of encounters, the sweet, blue gangrene. . . . Every minute of the lonely nights

was filled with dreams of fires quenched with blood and bloody beaks of birds of prey and bombs blossoming like roses with bloody petals over the Mekong Delta. . . .

Such a welter of sensation and depressive hallucination might have left no more than a fashionable whiff of despair, and indeed it is hard to draw any logical conclusion from Miss Carter's series of images or perceptions. But anyone who has found her previous strange novels, similarly filled with eccentric tramps and childhood nightmares, sticking uncomfortably in the memory will appreciate that however macabre and sensational the scene is, Miss Carter is not simply an image-maker. She splashes descriptions on to the page with extraordinary assurance and energy, but surrounds them with splendidly dismissive, witty little comments—rather as Miss Blossom, listening to Joseph's desperate questions, suddenly comes out with "Oh, shut your cakehole, do". Indeed, so circumstantial is much of the detail about Joseph's beatnik world that its allusions will be lost on readers a few years hence.

Not that Miss Carter seems a writer likely to worry about her future reputation. She has some of Miss Spark's demonic imagination and succinctness, and some of Miss Murdoch's fluent ability to get away with luridly sentimental costume scenes; at the moment the organization of a tenuous plot seems secondary to the fireworks of her style, but this novel suggests that she is narrowing her field to a few eccentric characters who can be believed in, even when their actions are not particularly pointful.

"Black Innocence," in The Times Literary Supplement, *No. 3466, August 1, 1968, p. 817.*

RICHARD BOSTON

Joseph, the protagonist of [*Several Perceptions*] is what would conventionally be called mad. Like his Biblical namesake, he is a dreamer, and early in the book he tries to kill himself. But his madness consists in an acute awareness of the madness of the world. He is obsessed with images of violence—Vietnam, Lee Harvey Oswald, Buddhist monks burning alive. . . .

The book (by the author of *Honeybuzzard* and *The Magic Toyshop*) is marred by some unconvincing dialogue and a good deal of overwriting. Bizarre similes and metaphors proliferate. ("Raptly he serenaded the tree, which dropped leaves on his head from time to time as if tossing contemptuous pennies. . . . Three small children . . . wore cheerful jerseys of blue and yellow wool and their sweet, shrill voices fizzed and sputtered like sherbet.") This sort of writing easily becomes wearisome.

The first three-quarters of the book gives a powerful account of the horror, the logic and the poetry of the schizophrenic's world. The end, however, is rather disappointing. Joseph has released the badger from its cage; it is Christmas time; there is a truce in Vietnam; an unsmiling lame girl who lives nearby laughs and is able to walk again; his cat has kittens; life renews itself, and Joseph seems to be adjusting to "normal" society.

Perhaps short of Joseph's successfully committing suicide, the novel had to have some such ending to round it off. One has no quarrel with Angela Carter's decision to end affirmatively. But after her early tough-mindedness, one had hoped for a more telling denouement than the Spirit of Christmas.

Richard Boston, "Logic in a Schizophrenic's World," in The New York Times Book Review, *March 2, 1969, p. 42.*

STUART HOOD

Angela Carter writes in the Gothic mode which, as she points out in one of the texts chosen as epigraph to [*Heroes and Villains*], is essentially a form of parody, a way of assailing clichés by exaggerating them to the limit of grotesqueness. The cliché she has chosen to exaggerate concerns the enmity between 'the professors' and 'the barbarians', who are bedizened, long-haired, ruthless, Id-dominated tribesmen living in the forest and raiding the embattled settlements where 'the soldiers' protect such guardians of culture as have survived a global holocaust. The forest is at times like that great wood which lies outside the glass wall of the Only State described by Zamyatin in *We* (to which Huxley and Orwell owed an explicit debt); sometimes it is more like Kipling's Wild Wet Wood. Marianne, 'the last rational woman in the world', elopes with a barbarian, meets the dangerous false clerk who has gone over to the barbarians, suffers pain, primitive passion and danger, survives the attacks of the 'Out People', a sub-race desperately disfigured by mutations, and emerges as a queen figure. This is a splendid adventure story and I know a number of teenagers who will read it avidly; but to deck it out with quotations from Jean-Luc Godard, Marvell, Leslie Fiedler and l'Abbé Prévost, as the author has done, is to make intellectual claims for the work which are not sustained.

> Stuart Hood, "Silly Woman," in The Listener, Vol. LXXXII, No. 2120, November 13, 1969, p. 674.

THE TIMES LITERARY SUPPLEMENT

The imaginary world of Angela Carter's [*Heroes and Villains*] is built of the blasted remnants of some vast catastrophe, but the form it takes has more to do with legend and a bookish view of the past than with a possible future. Small, enclosed settlements, inhabited by sombre-suited Professors who read books, are protected by Soldiers and kept going by Workers. Outside are the Barbarians, parasitical marauders, who live on plunder and organize themselves roughly but with considerable ritualistic dash. Farther out still, and barely to be distinguished from the wild beasts which have returned in quantities, are the Out People, freaks who may yet inherit the earth.

Marianne, the cool and easily bored daughter of a Professor, joins the gypsies, moving with Jewel, her brother's murderer, from the stillness of her ivory tower into the disorder of the Barbarians' life, temporarily based on a decaying mansion, from which bands of bedizened men set out to hunt beasts and Professors.

Seen, as it is initially, by Marianne, who "inspected these sights as if she were looking at colour illustrations in an ingenious book", this world is richly imagined, never whimsical and extraordinarily believable. . . .

The control of the material in the early chapters is formidable. The fantasy is made to work through the use of detail and the firmly established individuality of the characters. This only falters at that moment when Marianne, forced into marriage with Jewel and finding herself passionately attracted to him, is lost as the cool eye surveying the pop-up pictures before her. With this new focus, the relationship becomes something more familiar and yet less credible on its own terms, the attraction of an educated girl for the brutal stranger; and Jewel's newfound ability to parry such insults from her as, "You're not a human being at all, you're a metaphysical proposition", is one of the least satisfactory inventions of the novel. The occasional pretentiousness which creeps into the last part of the book is partly the result of Marianne's loss of detachment and the disintegration of the Barbarians' world once she has become part of it, but it does spoil what is in many ways a remarkably effective novel.

> "Facing the Past," in The Times Literary Supplement, No. 3534, November 20, 1969, p. 1329.

JOHN S. PHILLIPSON

"Bizarre" characters, said one reviewer of Miss Carter's first novel; a "fantastic world" said another of her second; "brilliant" said still another of her third. Assuredly the first two of these judgments apply to Miss Carter's latest fictional production [*Heroes and Villains*]. Whether one applies the third to it depends upon one's tastes in literature. I am willing to call it strikingly different, a kind of *tour de force* in sustained bizarre narrative. But brilliant? Maybe.

What Miss Carter gives us is described on the jacket as "surrealistic exotica—a genuinely Gothic novel." One is not sure what this strange fusion of twentieth and eighteenth-century literary and artistic phenomena means. Probably one would call it a sophisticated commentary on tomorrow's world, with nihilistic implications. . . .

[Structurally] this novel is weak: bizarre episodes follow each other swiftly and irrationally. We meet fantastic characters like the Doctor, F. R. Donally, Ph.D., who occupies a chapel where he plays upon a baroque out-of-tune organ and keeps chained to the wall a mentally retarded son, whom he beats regularly. . . .

We are never quite sure where this land is or even whether it exists. In it, God has long since been dead. On his back, Jewel [a Barbarian] has tattooed the temptation scene with Adam, Eve, and the snake, the last seemingly wrapped around Jewel's spinal cord. Is "his . . . landscape of ruin and forest" a kind of second (perverted) Eden? Jewel, the doctor remarks, "might become the Messiah of the Yahoos." (p. 211)

Presumably we are to regard all this as a satiric commentary on mankind. . . . "When I was a little girl," says [the heroine] toward the end of the book, "we played at heroes and villains but now I don't know which is which any more." One must trust appearances. This ironic comment seems to be Miss Carter's final dismissal of the world and its ways. (pp. 211-12)

> John S. Phillipson, in a review of "Heroes and Villains," in Best Sellers, Vol. 30, No. 11, September 1, 1970, pp. 211-12.

JOHN COLEMAN

Love is written to the hilt, bursting off with a compressed length of prose which might have enraptured M. Jourdain but scared the wits out of me. In other words, I find Miss Carter's style, however refreshingly studied as against the monosyllabic repetitions of much contemporary depiction of contemporary attic-dramas, a trifle above the matter to which she applies it.

The tale rotates poor, nutty Annabel and two brothers, Lee and Buzz, in a dance that can only end in tears before bedtime. Lee is the working-class thruster, university lad turned teacher, warmhearted welcomer of drifters like Annabel. Brother Buzz is a more complex case, hung-up about sex, and bad news whenever he appears. It's one of those fictions that get you just involved enough to ask angry questions of its participants. Why did you take on Annabel, Lee? Why did you take on the whole shoot, Miss Carter? But Miss Carter, allowing me the divorce of form and content, is a superb one with words, touching in the mad contexts and exchanges of her floaters with the eye of a painter, the ear of a poet. You need more, perhaps, to set up as a novelist too.

John Coleman, "*From Behind the Wall,*" *in* The Observer, *May 16, 1971, p. 33.*

ANITA VAN VACTOR

Love seems at first an oddly miscalculating, even silly tale about the ménage of three freaked-out hippy types, two brothers and a mad girl. A connoisseur of unreality, Annabel has the frigidity, the phoney charm, the manipulative powers, of a true schizophrenic. Her husband Lee smoothes his passage through the world by managing a large wardrobe of smiles (from which Annabel, having no smiles of her own, learns to borrow). He weeps constantly but ambiguously: are these tears the result of his sentimentality, or of his chronic eye disease? Malign, voyeuristic, Buzz feels and sees only through his camera: the others often wake up 'to find him perched on the end of the bed, clicking away'. Mixing the grim, the exotic, the farcical, Miss Carter traces the growth of a three-way symbiosis, a hermetic mythology decorated by Annabel's obsessive imagery and punctuated by her spectacular suicide attempts.

As a psychological novel, *Love* falls flat—onion layers of ritual histrionics when we are promised 'a Wagnerian maelstrom of emotions soon to suck them all down'. In her most embarrassingly sincere tone, Miss Carter (on the dust-jacket) describes her book as 'a tragedy of contemporary manners, a total analysis of a complex emotional situation, leaving nothing out and being as honest as possible'. This is a put-on. Miss Carter is really a *nouveau-romancier,* cleverly disguised as a naive English girl. Her deadpan manner may sound disturbingly obtuse if we are looking for psychological representations: its subversive intent becomes clear when we look at *Love* as collage, an assemblage of illusionist fragments on a flat surface— a work of pure presentation. Thus the 'Wagnerian maelstrom', with its suggestion of dimensionality, of tragic death, serves as a piece of décor, broken off from an official style of representation. In the same way, Miss Carter designates other moments as 'romantic' or 'expressionistic' or 'surreal'. *Love,* in fact, best describes itself, in the guise of some pornographic photographs which Annabel examines, fascinated, convinced that 'these indifferent arrangements of bizarre intersecting lines told a true story', which 'signified love'. Like pornography, *Love* inhabits that ambivalent territory between what we call 'love', on the one hand, and, on the other, pure design. The effect is elegant, disorienting, rather baneful and at times very amusing.

Anita Van Vactor, "*Unceasingly Thankful,*" *in* The Listener, *Vol. 85, No. 2199, May 20, 1971, p. 656.*

THE TIMES LITERARY SUPPLEMENT

Like the relationships it describes, [*Love*] by Angela Carter has an obsessive and extravagant quality. Admirers of, among others, *The Magic Toyshop* will recognize her preoccupation with the kind of people who find reality in fantasy. Again she is concerned with the darker side of sibling affection and the type of love that consumes.

This time her central character, Lee, is a pleasant, even ordinary, chap. A good-looking orphan, brought up with his brother by a puritanical, politically conscious aunt, he becomes a teacher, albeit one of the groovy modern type. But the two people who depend on him, his brother, Buzz, and Annabel, the thin, fey enigma he marries out of pity and puzzlement when Buzz is in Morocco, are, according to the rules of everyday society, unmistakably mad. They are more than mere drop-outs since both live in private worlds, the brother's decorated by daggers, dirt and hash, hers so negative and insubstantial that she rarely even moves. After living with her for three years Lee still feels that he is like a lone explorer in an unknown country without a map to guide him. Their intense triangle is first assembled, then sounded and finally dismantled, leaving a crystal-clear yet resonant note in the ears.

Miss Carter is extremely good at twining the macabre and unlikely with the possible. By ordinary accounting Annabel is an unconvincing creation, with her cataclysmic passivity from which she emerges only occasionally to commit some act of simple malice—she has her name tattooed over Lee's chest when she has recovered from a suicide attempt on discovering he has been unfaithful to her. There is a parallel with Iris Murdoch here, for many Murdochian forces of destruction are similarly fantastic and Angela Carter also has a taste for Gothick pads combined with an eye for *quartier* detail. . . .

Love is short but it is more than a long short story. In order to raise the temperature Miss Carter has not sacrificed the development of story or character. The writing may be lush but the narrative moves forward with a disciplined sense of purpose. Blows, beddings and death have struck by the end of the tale. Lee's room has changed from white, cool and spacious to gloomy and cavernous, cluttered with the furniture and trifles Annabel has bought or stolen. Lee is not released but he is explained, and Miss Carter should add to her reputation by this taut study of strangeness.

"*Private Lives,*" *in* The Times Literary Supplement, *No. 3616, June 18, 1971, p. 693.*

AUBERON WAUGH

No doubt some readers will have no patience with the exuberant ramifications of Miss Carter's imagination. For my own part, I can only testify that I read [*The Infernal Desire Machines of Doctor Hoffman*] enthralled, fascinated and bewitched. This column has not awarded a gold medal for some months now, but Miss Carter wins one for her sustained imagination, her originality and, most important of all, her clear, lucid English.

The hero, Desiderio, is a young man of Indian extraction. He works for the Minister, who personifies the forces of logic, reason, law and order, but also the excesses to which these properties are liable: pedantry, avarice and failure of the creative imagination. They are opposed by Dr Hoffman, who represents poetry, and the liberation of the spirit but also anarchy and the 'creative nihilism' of the rebel without a cause. War is declared, and Desiderio is sent to kill Hoffman, already infatuated by Hoffman's beautiful daughter, Albertina, who pops in and out of the narrative, generally disguised as a young man or a boy.

Sensibly the book now becomes a series of more or less unconnected episodes, like Gulliver, linked very loosely by the quest for Hoffman and the sexual tension of Desiderio's regard for Albertina. The battle-lines at this stage are drawn fairly clearly: reality versus freedom. But Miss Carter has no particular brief for either, and I was relieved to discover that her book contains no coherent ontological or existential argument. Like [*Alice's Adventures in Wonderland*] it merely asks a few questions in a pert way in the course of a rattling good fantasy narrative. Desiderio makes friends with a Count Dracula figure, representing death and negation, whose valet-catamite is, of course, Albertina in disguise. Together they visit a brothel (the House of Anonymity) where the girls are merely abstract expressions of perverted lust—the Madame, is, of course, Albertina. Next (after various adventures with the Determination Police) he joins some river folk and becomes engaged to their pubescent, nine-year-old daughter.

These river folk, who sing instead of talk, have no word in their language for 'to be,' although a complicated aria may hint at various shades of existence. Desiderio escapes when the river people threaten to eat him (Miss Carter does not dwell on the existential aspects of anthropophagy, which have surely been exhausted by W. S. Gilbert but she indulges herself at great length in the ontology of illusion: a magical peep-show which may or may not be done with mirrors, depending on which side one takes). (pp. 772-73)

Ontology takes a more scientific turn when characters and figments of Miss Carter's imagination are accorded 'reality' ratings, based on the proposition that a man who dreams he is a butterfly is, in fact, a man dreaming he is a butterfly rather than a butterfly which has woken up. Thus some centaurs who rape Albertina, very painfully and at great length, are sternly dismissed as being no more than emanations of her own desires.

Perhaps I have been unable to convey the joys of Miss Carter's book. She has one of the most robust imaginations I have ever encountered, but imagination is useless without the ability to share it. Her most conspicuous success is in realising that the fantastic, the bizarre and the illogical can only succeed in a narrative, if they are described objectively, as dead pan as possible. It is only when fantasy and reality become confused, as in the hallucinatory state, that the whole thing becomes a bore. Miss Carter's wild, popping eye never wavers. (p. 773)

Auberon Waugh, "The Surreal Thing," in The Spectator, *Vol. 228, No. 7508, May 20, 1972, pp. 772-73.*

VALENTINE CUNNINGHAM

Angela Carter's [*Infernal Desire Machines of Doctor Hoffman*] claims big things for itself with epigraphs from Wittgenstein and Alfred Jarry, but her extravagant ditching of the here and now for the fantastic nowhere and sometime does not quite seem to bring home the vigorously and constantly signalled insights into the nature of reality. Old Desiderio recounts Hoffman's long-past war against reality, his campaign against human reason, and attempts to liberate the world from time and space by means of eroto-energy. Desiderio's account is also a memorial to Albertina, Hoffman's daughter, with whom he regretfully never managed to expend any eroto-energy. Far from sharing his resistance to the 'flux of images' Hoffman bombarded the city with, the novel indulges in a flight of erotic fancy as it tracks Desiderio's flight from the Determination Police. Peep-shows; the dwarfish acrobats of desire; gothic scenarios and girls who turn to dead leaves in the night; a De Sade-like Count; a Swiftian episode with randy centaurs: the novel has little to offer but a flux of images.

Valentine Cunningham, "Country Coloureds," in The Listener, *Vol. 87, No. 2252, May 25, 1972, p. 693.*

GEORGE HAY

Doctor Hoffman is a demonstration of metaphysics, as distinct from being about metaphysics. The latter, that is, constitutes the bedrock rising out of which appears an extraordinary superstructure of dream landscapes, dazzling symbols and densely charged conversations. It is essential to insist that this is the order involved, otherwise we are left 'only' with a picaresque novel of outstanding originality. To take it as only this would be to miss the whole point, which is that life is about metaphysics, or it is about nothing. And it is this, that, with a few honourable exceptions, the New Wave has consistently evaded. Life, these writers have said, is not just about amassing dollars or breaking light-barriers. No more it is, but when it came to saying what it *was* about, the protagonists of the brave and the new retreated, at best into solipsism, at worst into giggles.

Miss Carter, now, starts off *in medias res* with a City whose Minister of Determination is locked in battle with the reality-subverting techniques of the sinister Doctor. Though this gives the chance for the deployment of some very evocative prose, no evasion of the subject is allowed. . . . If the whole [of the novel] ends in a somewhat dying fall, this is because the book's last page is prefigured and dictated by its first; of necessity, only the passage between chaos and order has flexibility, and hence, potential.

I have failed if I have given here the impression that the author achieves her philosophical validity at the expense of her characters. Not so. It is the very proof of her thesis that these characters, while expressing sundry philosophical viewpoints, lose thereby nothing of their quiddity. The Amerindian barge-master, the Bearded Lady, Mamie Buckskin, sharpshooter and connoisseur of equestriennes, the Alligator Man, the dreaded Doctor himself and his daughter, as beautiful and humourless as a theorem—it is *from* all these that the metaphysics emerge, rather than their depending as epiphenomena upon the metaphysics. I except here the incredible Count, and the hippolators, creatures of such density that in their case character and philosophy are one.

Let none say that in my admiration for Miss Carter's work I have departed from my thesis, which . . . is that science fiction is at base metaphysical, that the 'hardness' of physics is the more valid, not the less, for being firmly anchored on nothingness, and that the formlessness of much 'speculative fiction' is in exact measure with its refusal to admit that the numinous is *the exact*. Miss Carter has told us so, in the most astonishing and highly-charged prose (and I have said nothing of her use of Erotics!). But it is not true because she has told us so: she has told us so because it is true. (pp. 69-71)

George Hay, "Marionettes within Metaphysics," in Foundation, *No. 3, March, 1973, pp. 69-71.*

PADDY BEESLEY

The New York of Angela Carter's latest fantasy [*The Passion of New Eve*] is . . . mythic, futuristic and extreme. A horror city of pillage and rape, where the Blacks have burnt Grand Central Station and the women are in revolt, it is the jumping-off point for an English academic's transcontinental Marvel-comic trek through a landscape of symbols and significances. We get the symbols we deserve, as Miss Carter remarks in the opening chapter; and English Evelyn, hitherto content with a Garbo-like screen goddess as his main symbol of womanhood, discovers in a disintegrating America nastier and more threatening images which are, one assumes, mythic projections of contemporary sexual attitudes. Mama, castratrix of the phallocentric universe, who resexes Evelyn and prepares to impregnate him with his own seed; Zero, a Mansonish, woman-hating poet who rapes the new Eve(lyn); a gang of puritanical West Coast kids, toughly cleaning things up for God; and the movie-star herself, Tristessa, revealed as a man in drag, with whom Eve is forcibly mated (work that one out). If it all sounds jagged and cluttered in summary, then this is a good summary. Miss Carter leaves all plot on the escapes-and-captures level, shuns dialogue, and despite snatches of sharp phrasing, is prone to court silliness: what is offered as a harsh contemporary imagination comes across too often as exuberant zaniness.

Paddy Beesley, "Be Bad," in New Statesman, *Vol. 93, No. 2401, March 25, 1977, p. 407.*

PETER ACKROYD

Now that the conventional realistic novel has been embalmed with the sneer still on its face, certain 'modern' writers are veering wildly towards the grotesque, the fantastic and the merely silly. Surrealism is, after all, only realism with the ends cut off. Angela Carter's [*The Passion of New Eve*] doesn't quite resolve the dilemma which lurks here somewhere. Hers is a simple story of rape, castration and apocalypse. Novels of future shock are actually the easiest to write since they require only limited powers of observation and description—and, at this level, imagination is the cheapest commodity of all. Angela Carter's vision of New York must be the most lurid yet, surpassing even Doris Lessing in its horror: gangs of women-libbers blow up 'wedding shops' and send gift-parcels of 'well-honed razors' to new brides. That uneasy tone, perched somewhere between high seriousness and farce, unsettles the narrative as it leaps from one improbability to the next. And Angela Carter isn't quite sure where to land or, even, whether to land at all.

Nor is Evelyn who, 'reckless from grief,' has ambivalent feelings toward Leilah: 'she was as black as the source of shadow.' This languorous, sickly and polysyllabic manner swoons over itself throughout the book, and it can in turns be charming, repellent or merely obtrusive. Perhaps it has too much ground to cover. Evelyn mistreats Leilah terribly, but suffers a terrible revenge when he is abducted by a race of desert Amazons, taken to the futuristic city of Beulah, falls into the hands of a great 'Mother,' is transformed into a beautiful new Eve, escapes by a hair's breadth from being impregnated by his own semen, only to be raped by a 'non-verbal poet' aptly named Zero, and to discover that his favourite actress Tristessa is merely a man in drag. Someone, somewhere, might have made all of this interesting but Angela Carter has ruined her theme by shuffling it between pastiche and allegory. To say as the blurb does that she is investigating 'the nature of the mythology of sexuality' is like acclaiming Ken Russell as 'the musicologist and literary critic.'

The Passion of New Eve has, in fact, been culled from any number of B-films. It bristles with fantastic visual imagery; everything is a size too large or a shade too garish, with the result that bathos is never far away: "The garden in which Adam was born lies between my thighs,' responded Mother, all Mahler in her intonation." When the language is so gran-

diose and verbose it can only transmit fantasies and visions—and no novel can survive for long on such a meagre diet. The fact that Angela Carter has to work extremely hard for her major effects suggests that there is something old-fashioned and therefore whimsical about her manner. She is actually reverting to that ancient time when, as Eve Evelyn puts it, 'I have found a landscape that matches the landscape of my heart.' But straight Romanticism can no longer breathe within a straight novel, even one as apparently modish as this, and the effect is of languorous but cheap sentiment that doesn't have the substance to match its style. (pp. 23-4)

Peter Ackroyd, "Passion Fruit," in The Spectator, *Vol. 238, No. 7760, March 26, 1977, pp. 23-4.*

LORNA SAGE

Angela Carter's splendid new novel [*The Passion of New Eve*] has many images that will stick in your mind and grow there like crystals: the one that transfixed me was the ancient screen goddess in her desert retreat, whose hobby is making glass out of the sand and dropping hot globs of it into her swimming-pool where it solidifies into giant empty tears.

Miss Carter is, of course, sending up the frail and vulgar myths of Hollywood, but the uncompromising narcissism of the gesture, its perfect hollowness, gives it a weird integrity. Unlike most of our travesties, hers retains the magic the myth was (and is) all about. She's very special among English writers because she takes on the processes of myth-making and story-telling without puritan apologetics, and as a result her writing has the compulsive quality of a depraved fairytale.

This book combines the motif of the innocent abroad with a psychological excursion that gets closer and closer to home. By projecting contemporary America just a little way into the future (so that Harlem has a city wall and California secedes from the Union to have its own civil war) you arrive, with the English hero Evelyn, at a setting in which personalities disintegrate into their primitive elements, and re-form into monstrous hybrids. Not least of these is Evelyn himself, making his foredoomed way towards becoming the Eve of the title, and discovering painfully, hilariously ('They have made me into a *Playboy* centerfold') what it's like to be on the receiving end of male sexual fantasies.

What makes the plot go, however, is not the science fiction business about switching sex, but Miss Carter's expertise in finding (borrowing, stealing) images of fascination and repulsion that lead you on willy-nilly. . . .

The style is overripe, and mocks itself with adjectives like 'excoriated,' 'atrocious,' 'gratuitous,' 'synthetic.' Its tacky brilliance is thoroughly in keeping with the theme of a culture regressing into dreamy barbarism, returning to the nursery. The blandness of our symbols, Miss Carter thinks, is not their fault but ours—they still hold the key to our imaginative survival, if we can learn to play their game.

Lorna Sage, "Glass Menagerie," in The Observer, *March 27, 1977, p. 29.*

PATRICIA CRAIG

To supply the missing erotic quality at the narrative level is one of Angela Carter's objectives in *The Bloody Chamber*; but she is by no means dealing in gross clinical exposition. Each of the ten stories in this collection has a starting-point in a fairy tale or legend, but from this point it expands into a new, more elaborate and fanciful sexual allegory. 'Nothing,' as Angela Carter remarked in *The Sadeian Woman,* 'exercises such power over the imagination as the nature of sexual relationships.' The substance of the old tales can accommodate fresh varieties of meaning and reverberation, and although the imagery remains traditional its range of associations is easily extended. In Perrault, Andersen and Grimm the fundamental emotions of fear, relief, horror, triumph and so on are unambiguous, but the pattern of events is often more complex than it appears. The story of Little Red Riding Hood, for example, raises interesting questions about exactly what is embodied in whom, and Angela Carter (in **"The Werewolf"** and **"The Company of Wolves"**) with impressive economy draws out two alternative strands of meaning: only the sturdy figure of the child remains constant. Wise, and armed only with her father's hunting knife and her own integrity, she stands up to confront whatever is coming to her. In both cases she *is* the wolfsbane.

Angela Carter's themes are vampirism, lycanthropy, fear of corruption, the apprehension of malignity in natural forces; but in accordance with the somewhat ruthless optimism which underlines the therapeutic function of the prototypes, each ending signifies an action accomplished, a consummation effected, a fear dissolved. The snow child melts in the process of intercourse—an act preceded by a necessary pricking and bleeding, symbolically enacted by means of a rose with thorns. The overblown, androgynous rose, in fact, is the emblem most perfectly fashioned to express both sweetness and decadence: blood-red, blooming magically in the snow or nurtured on remnants of flesh discarded by a necrophagous queen. Bloodsucking and blood-letting have their metaphorical inverse in the innocuous blood of menstruation and defloration, and the psychological motif appertaining to each is superimposed endlessly upon the other: the slit throat, which represents the broken hymen, is itself represented by a necklace described as 'a bloody bandage of rubies' which brings us back to the 'jewel' of virginity. Hints, connections and associations proliferate, like the image of the bride in the bedroom filled with arum lilies, reflected to infinity in a wilderness of mirrors. Ms Carter's stories are too rich and heady for casual consumption; but they do provide, at a very high level, romantic nourishment for the imagination.

Patricia Craig, "Gory," in New Statesman, *Vol. 97, No. 2514, May 25, 1979, p. 762.*

SUSAN KENNEDY

[With the ten stories in *The Bloody Chamber*], each a polished artefact, Angela Carter extends her control over an area of the imagination on which she has already left her mark. Her retelling of European folk and fairy tales has the power, not only to cause us to think again, and deeply, about the mythic sources of our common cultural touchstones, but to plunge us into hackle-raising speculation about aspects of our human/animal nature. This she does by imaginative description that overwhelms us both by its precise observation of quotidian detail and by its ability to bend the mind to new channels, seeding it with a wealth of literary and cultural allusions that subtly enrich the telling.

The first and longest story in the collection, from which it takes its title, exemplifies her method. An innocent young music student is brought as the Marquis's fourth bride to his remote castle on the Breton coast, a collector's item to be ranged alongside his priceless jewels, his library of rare and salacious books, and to be enjoyed between business trips to New York. It is not just curiosity that opens the door to the horrors of the bloody chamber, it is the positive desire to be corrupted even while being repulsed by the manifestations of corruption: and this the voluptuousness of the description, the heavily-scented lilies, the Russian leather—the language, almost, of *Venus in Furs*—underline.

There is a risk (perhaps it is simply a failure of the reader's will) that too specific reference to objects of daily use and recognition will hold back the imagination. When we are told that someone is wearing a shirt from Turnbull and Asser we may want to cry, "But that's not my idea of him at all!"—and suspension of disbelief may falter. In most of these stories this is far from being the case—such details are the springboard for untramelled speculation. . . .

"The Tiger's Bride", a second version of Beauty and the Beast, achieves its brilliant effect by a reversal of the story's usual conclusion. Stripping away all the artificialities of his human mask—his hereditary palazzo, his treasure chest, his Mantegnas, his Cellini salt cellars—the Beast reveals the flesh and sinew of his true nature, pacing backwards and forwards on rank, wet straw; and is joined there by Beauty.

Three linked stories explore further the theme of man into animal, using as their vehicle variations of the werewolf legend. In one, Red Riding Hood becomes a wolf; in another the grandmother and the wolf are one and the same (barely two pages long, this last is a misleadingly simple concoction, deadly and witty in its savouring). **"Wolf-Alice",** the third in this group, for the first time makes believable the existence of those wolf-children that are discovered from time to time by the press. In all these stories it is startling how Angela Carter so sharply defines the animals she describes: the lupine scent, the rangy walk. . . .

"The Lady of the House of Love" recasts the tale of Sleeping Beauty. The queen of the vampires sits in her decaying ancestral castle, a Miss Haversham figure in her bridal gown though her beauty is unimpaired by time, playing her Tarot cards and cursing the destiny that forces her to consume her uncongenial diet. Onto this Carpathian stage bicycles a young English officer straight from the pages of Bram Stoker. His is the kiss that releases her to death: the rose she bequeaths him becomes a generation's blood that will soak the fields of Flanders. In such ways Angela Carter works on our imagination, undermining and reshaping its archetypes.

Susan Kennedy, "Man and Beast," in The Times Literary Supplement, *No. 4011, February 8, 1980, p. 146.*

ALAN FRIEDMAN

[An obsession] with sadistic power and masochistic sacrifice pervades *The Bloody Chamber,* a collection of tales by Angela Carter. She's a British novelist little known in this country though widely praised in her own, the author of more than half a dozen macabre novels and a polemical study of Sade entitled *The Sadeian Woman.* The 10 tales that make up the present volume are about werewolves and Puss in Boots, Beauty and the Beast, Count Dracula's daughter and other sympathetic victims. "She was pierced, not by one, but by a hundred spikes, this child of the land of the vampires who seemed so newly dead, so full of blood. . . . Oh, God!" Perhaps *The Bloody*

Chamber is the book that will make Angela Carter's reputation in America. But I doubt it.

Perhaps there are thousands of readers ready for the cutesy mannerisms and comical overwriting, the whipped passion as full of cold air as whipped butter with which she improvises her fairy tales and horror tales. "The perfume of the lilies weighed on my senses . . . there had awoken a certain queasy craving like the cravings of pregnant women for the taste of coal or chalk or tainted food, for the renewal of his caresses." Most of these stories have the kind of cloying cleverness we associate with precocious writers. Miss Carter's juvenilia?

To my recollection, none of her novels is composed—or decomposed—that way; they preserve, instead, a straightforward, almost innocent expression that enhances their frequently bizarre content. With no way of knowing when, or in what order, these tales were written, I can say only that her collection suddenly and decisively improves near the end. Several of the last stories are jewels, direct and intense. I had been thinking, while picking my way through the first hundred pages or so, that maybe we were too far along in history, too knowing nowadays, for the old fairy tale *frisson*. "The worst wolves are the ones that are hairy on the inside," she writes. And the best stories too, I thought as I read that. The trouble with the earlier stories in this volume is that they're hairy on the outside only. (p. 15)

Alan Friedman, *"Pleasure and Pain," in* The New York Times Book Review, *February 17, 1980, pp. 14-15.*

PATRICIA DUNCKER

Carter's tales [in *The Bloody Chamber*] are, supposedly, celebrations of erotic desire. But male sexuality has too long, too tenaciously been linked with power and possession, the capture, breaking and ownership of women. The explicitly erotic currents in her tales mirror these realities. Pornography, that is, the representation of overtly sexual material with the intention to arouse prurient, vicarious desire, uses the language of male sexuality. Even the women's equivalent of soft porn, romance novels and 'bodice-rippers', all conform to recognisably male fantasies of domination, submission and possession. Heterosexual feminists have not yet invented an alternative, anti-sexist language of the erotic. Carter envisages women's sensuality simply as a response to male arousal. She has no conception of women's sexuality as autonomous desire.

One of the deftest, most disturbing pieces in the book is her version of Snow-White, **"The Snow Child"**. Here Carter exposes the Oedipal conflict between Mother and Daughter: the snow maiden is the father's child, 'the child of his desire' who threatens to usurp the Mother's place. With one small touch Carter reveals the Mother as a sister to Sade's Juliette, the sexual terrorist, with a motif taken from the literature of pornography, 'she wore high, black shining boots with scarlet heels and spurs.' If the Mother ever fails the child in the fairy tales that child's life is always in jeopardy. In Carter's version the Mother offers up the child, as her sexuality blossoms in the rose, to the Father's lust, which destroys her. Carter removes the supposedly comforting denouement to the tale in which the mother is destroyed and the child successfully navigates the dangerous transition into sexual maturity. But she doesn't question the ideology implicit in the story, that the Mother and Daughter will—necessarily—become rivals for the Father's love and be prepared to countenance one another's

destruction. The division between Mother and Daughter, and between Sisters, is one of the cornerstones of patriarchy. The fact that so many of the tales suggest and endorse those old enmities is both sinister and predictable. Cinderella, Snow-White, Beauty and the Beast all argue the case for women, beware women. (p. 7)

The most successful narrative in Carter's collection is the most elaborate and expansive, the modern Bluebeard, **"The Bloody Chamber"**. This is a tour de force. The confessional voice of the tale is that of experience, the girl recalling her initiation into the adult world. Carter's story—and indeed all the earlier versions—are about women's masochistic complicity in male sexual aggression; and about husbands. [Charles Perrault, who transcribed the tale from the oral tradition in the late seventeenth century,] was in no doubt about this either. He draws the moral from the story; an admonition to nosey women who seek to know the truth about the men they marry. 'Curiosity is the most fleeting of pleasures; the moment it is satisfied, it ceases to exist and it always proves very, very expensive. It is easy to see that the events described in this story took place many years ago'. He then adds, embarrassed, 'no modern husband would dare to be half so terrible'. Carter's Bluebeard is simply a husband, he is given no other name. (p. 10)

Carter's **"Bloody Chamber"** uses all the iconography of the Gothic; the remote castle, the virgin at the mercy of the tormented hero-villain, the enclosed spaces, hidden atrocities, women voraciously, masochistically eager for the corruption of sexuality. All the pervading themes of pornography are there too; domination, control, humiliation, mutilation, possession through murder. All perpetrated on willing, eager victims. The marriage bargain becomes explicit, the bride as the bought woman, acting out the 'ritual from the brothel.' Carter's tale carefully creates the classical pornographic model of sexuality, which has a definite meaning and endorses a particular kind of fantasy, that of male sexual tyranny within a marriage that is grossly unequal; the child bride responsive to her husband's desire, ready to be 'impaled' among the lilies of death, the face with its 'promise of debauchery', a rare talent for corruption. Here is the sexual model which endorses the 'normal and natural sadism of the male, happily complemented by the normal and natural masochism of the female.' The husband of **"The Bloody Chamber"** is a connoisseur, a collector of pornography. When the child bride peers at the titles in his bookcase she finds the texts for the knowledge she reads in blood, a guide to her fate, *The Initiation, The Key to Mysteries, The Secret of Pandora's Box*, imaged in the Sultan's murdered wives.

But there are two other figures that Carter has created in her re-writing of the tale whose actions and presence alter the terms of the unequal conflict between husband and wife. In Perrault's original version the bride's sister Anne, about whom we are told nothing but her name, looks out from the tower as Bluebeard sharpens his cutlass in the courtyard, to proclaim the galloping arrival of the bride's two brothers. In Carter's version this figure becomes the blinded piano tuner, Jean-Yves, who loves the child bride not for her ambiguous beauty, the veil across corruption, but for her single gift of music. Only with the blinded boy who humbly serves her music can Carter envisage a marriage of equality for Bluebeard's bride. Men as invalids are constant figures in women's fiction; most remarkably in the writing of Charlotte Brontë: her heroes suffer on the point of her pen, she blinds them, maims them, drowns them. This is easy to understand; if a man is damaged and hurt a woman is released from the habitual sexual constraint forced upon her, she can take action, initiate contact, speak out, the power imbalance inherent in all heterosexual relationships, is levelled off. (pp. 10-11)

In the case of Bluebeard's bride it is as well that her lover cannot see her, for she carries the mark of her complicity and corruption forever, the complicity of women who have been made in man's image, who have desired to be possessed, who walk after the diva of Isolde, the model of Montmartre, the Romanian Countess, who meet the reward of that complicity in the bloody chamber.

It is not the brothers who arrive armed with muskets and rapiers to save Bluebeard's bride, but a figure who never appears in the fairy tales, the mother as travelling heroine. . . . Here Carter is transforming the sexual politics of the fairy tales in significant ways. The mother of Bluebeard's bride never deserts her child. She has the wisdom to give her child the freedom demanded by sexual maturity, the freedom denied to Sleeping Beauty by her royal parents when they seek to protect her from the fairy's curse, that her hand shall be pierced by a spindle. But the mother arrives with melodramatic timeliness, giving the lie to Papa Freud's Oedipal realities. . . . In fact, the bond between Mother and Daughter is never broken. Carter's tale, perhaps unwittingly, carries an uncompromisingly feminist message; for the women's revolution would seal up the door of the bloody chamber forever.

All Carter's books are either short novels or tales, fantastic narratives. *The Sadeian Woman* and her collected essays, *Nothing Sacred* (. . . 1982), are her only non-fictional work to date. Her style is as lavish and ornate as the detail on the architecture Puss-in-Boots finds easy to climb—'Nothing to it once you know how, rococo's no problem.' This is her great strength. Her re-writing, re-imagining of the fairy tales could have been more intriguing than it is, had she studied the ambivalent sexual language that is there in the original tales. Perrault's Red Riding Hood is—in French—designated by a masculine name, Le petit Chaperon rouge. At the moment when the ritual words are uttered—'draw the bolt and the latch will open'—she is the one who enters; the wolf wears the grandmother's clothes. In later versions the woodcutters find both Red Riding Hood and the grandmother safe in the womb of the wolf. These ambiguities are partially acknowledged in **"The Company of Wolves"**, but follow the sexual symbolism of Cinderella thrusting her foot into the envoy's slipper, of Bluebeard's wife penetrating the secret space of the bloody chamber. These currents are there too in Carter's tales. She cannot avoid them. And she could go much further than she does.

Carter chooses to inhabit a tiny room of her own in the house of fiction. For women, that space has always been paralysingly, cripplingly small. I think we need the 'multiplying ambiguities of an extended narrative'. To imagine ourselves whole. We cannot fit neatly into patterns or models as Cinderellas, ugly sisters, wicked step-mothers, fairy God-mothers, and still acknowledge our several existences, experienced or imagined. We need the space to carve out our own erotic identities, as free women. And then to rewrite the fairy tales—with a bolder hand. (pp. 11-12)

> *Patricia Duncker, "Re-Imagining the Fairy Tales:*
> *Angela Carter's Bloody Chambers," in* Literature
> and History, *Vol. 10, No. 1, Spring, 1984, pp. 3-14.*

ADAM MARS-JONES

Nights at the Circus doesn't so much start as break like a wave; the first third of Angela Carter's new novel is a glorious piece of work, a set-piece studded with set-pieces. The narrative has a splendid ripe momentum, and each descriptive touch contributes a pang of vividness.

The period is 1899; the central character is Fevvers, "The Cockney Venus", currently the toast of London as of most European capitals. Fevvers's fame is not earned merely by beauty; at close quarters, in fact, she looks "more like a dray mare than an angel". Her face, "broad and oval as a meat dish, had been thrown on a common wheel out of coarse clay". But she has wings, which may or may not be real; at all events, her trapeze act at the Alhambra is good enough for her to be pelted with bouquets night after night. A tour is looming with Colonel Kearney's circus, to St Petersburg, to Tokyo, and from there to America.

Before she leaves, she grants an interview to Jack Walser, a young and very sceptical American reporter; although she has given one vigorous performance already, earlier in the evening, she puts on another for his benefit. With corrections and embellishments from her foster-mother, now acting as her dresser, she tells the story of her life.

Hatched—brought up in a brothel—first flight—Madame Schreck's museum of female freaks—kidnapped—escape—first engagement at the circus. Fevvers tells her story with great relish and in extravagant detail. The voice belongs to Fevvers, but the point of view is the journalist Walser's, intrigued but basically unconvinced; the reader's complex nature, hungry for enchantment but also resistant to it, is beautifully served. . . .

A book like *Nights at the Circus* depends for its effects on a privileged relationship with a real world, a selective overlapping. If it is tied too closely to the actual, it will soon appear preposterous; if it strikes out too far on its own, it is likely to become empty and precious.

Angela Carter is on the whole very good at watching over her story's delicate status, at restricting (but not abolishing) its reference to a historical 1899. . . .

The balance between the earthbound and the merely windy, in any case, is a delicate one; but it is held throughout the book's first section. Some sentences are swollen with brilliant effects, but they never actually burst; the riches are never quite embarrassing.

The balance tips at the beginning of the second section, and never manages to return to equilibrium. If France has an intrinsic implausibility, how much more is Russia (where the story takes up) already a fiction? Russia's revolution, moreover, makes its nineteenth century seem absolutely distant, in a way that nineteenth century France does not.

The first pages of the second section, set in St Petersburg, show all the signs of a belated attack of nerves. The descriptions are erratic; some of them are subsequently attributed to Jack Walser, who has joined the Circus as a clown, sending bulletins back to London.

The point of view is confusing, and the sentences lose their sense of mission. . . .

Without Fevvers's voice and Walser's point of view the narrative falters. There were just as many impossibilities in the London section as there are in St Petersburg, but now they are presented directly rather than mediated through a character who may only be a charlatan or a freak. The various clairvoyant pigs, intellectual chimpanzees and depressive clowns of the circus don't exactly upstage Fevvers, but they certainly dilute her oddity in a way that does the book harm.

It's fair enough that Fevvers should have a rest after her stupendous performance in part one; but the entr'acte goes on indefinitely. . . .

By doing possible things impossibly well, the first third of the book achieves a major enchantment. The spell, though, is fragile, and depends on the novel neither quite corresponding with reality nor finally breaking with it, just as Fevvers must be neither proven fraud nor proven freak to be an extraordinary woman: "If she were indeed . . . a prodigy then—she was no longer a wonder."

This is the principle that is forgotten as the novel speeds off towards the orthodox strangeness of exotic places and prodigious events where other laws than the laws of projectiles are merrily violated and an impasto of impossibilities overlays the original teasing design: "it was the limitations of her act in themselves that made him briefly contemplate the unimaginable—that is, the absolute suspension of disbelief."

> Adam Mars-Jones, "From Wonders to Prodigies," in The Times Literary Supplement, No. 4252, September 28, 1984, p. 1083.

VALENTINE CUNNINGHAM

Angela Carter's fiction has always been written with a fallen angel's touch for the freaky and sinister, alleviated just a bit by a soiled fairy's relish for black but also puckish comic turns. Noticeably, though, this weaving of macabre spells hasn't always felt quite at home with Ms Carter's other more politicised self as the wryly leftish and feminist observer of the contemporary scene. But in [*Nights at the Circus*] . . . Ms Carter has at last hit on means of bringing together her various tastes and subjects. The result is a mistress-piece of sustained and weirdly wonderful Gothic that's both intensely amusing and also provocatively serious.

At the heart of all the stories, vignettes and recollections jostling for significance here is the story of a marvellous gigantic bird-woman, the fabled 1890s Cockney trapeze artiste Fevvers. Boozy, bawdy, demotically outspoken, and mythically endowed with a pair of great wings for flights above and out of the ordinary, this 'voluptuous stevedore' has an erotic mystique that quite bowls over the Californian journalist Walser, who has come across the globe in search of the astounding truth about her. Once admitted, in the novel's early parts, to the curious confidences of Fevvers and her anarchistic dresser Lizzie about Fevvers's rise to international circus repute from out of a sad sequence of houses of ill repute, Walser gets himself hired as a clown in order to stay close to his idol.

The subsequent riotous progress of Captain Kearney's circus—a Ludic Game he calls it—on its Grand Imperial Tour to St Petersburg and across Siberia takes up the rest of the book. And it's rivetingly gargantuan, an excited procession of the often overdone and always overwhelming sent crashing zanily about the world, a compelling fantastification crammed with freaks (not to mention the talking apes and an alphabetical pig) and with murderous and amorous pursuits. 'Processions that lack high stilts have nothing that catches the eye,' said Yeats. On Fevvers's bizarre journey to Byzantium the stilts are as high as Angela Carter can risk making them.

But like Dickens in *Hard Times* and Dostoevsky in *Crime and Punishment*, Ms Carter isn't using her troupe of entertainers merely to tickle the reader's fancy. Like theirs, her performers become the focus for harder questions. High-flying Fevvers, backed up by the time- and dimensions-twisting magic of Lizzie and the wondrous animal-taming musicianship of the Abyssinian Princess and her assistant the rescued waif Mignon, is made an allegory of woman as both wonder and worker of wonders. Fully taking on the patent risk of being supposed merely freakish, sticking together, acting sisterly, this troupe of ladies first endures, then throws off the demands of men, the brothel-creepers and the ring-masters. Men in this story try to keep women caged on the dark side of their most awful fantasies. They bruise and rape the females they desire and invent rituals to effect their own pleasing.

But Angela Carter's paradigmatic turn-of-the-century New Women are armed to resist these enslaving encroachments. Again and again they break down the brothel bars, chuck artfully concocted *bombes surprises* into their sadistic handlers' arrangements, work out their own female salvation. . . . Men who want their women only as freakshow stuff commonly go straitjacket mad. Even Walser turns into a gibbering shaman lost in the deeps of primitive Siberia.

This sexual comedy at any rate will not finish up as male writers have traditionally contrived to end their comic rites, in mere marriage and child-bed. Fevvers and Lizzie are put to us as twin Scheherazades, a pair of story-manipulating allies who are spinning out men's circus nights to their own profit, a couple of sexual revolutionaries taking over the male illusion game.

Rebarbative work. But this no-nonsense feminist takeover of the magical domains of story and illusion does still contrive to be likeable, not least because, persuasively, Angela Carter never allows her characters to be naïve about either the present solidarity or the future political prospects of women. Lizzie, for instance, keeps smuggling into Fevvers's warmer accounts some stern Marxised exhortations about the need for improved analysis of the class situation and the dangers of false consciousness. The novel also casts a cold eye on a couple of women who lock up women, one in a brothel-cum-freakshow, the other in a reformatory for husband murderers. What's more, Ms Carter ends up finding some accommodation for men: Walser will be kept on in Fevvers's good books if only as an amanuensis; sweetness might eventually come forth even from the hunkily aggressive circus Strong Man Samson.

This big, superlatively imagined novel may be an extravaganza, but it refuses to be as extravagantly hostile to men's doings and tellings as some of the less well-tempered women's books nowadays are. And it goes without saying that the Booker Prize judges want their heads and their critical standards examined for not putting this stunning novel on their shortlist.

> Valentine Cunningham, "High-Wire Fantasy," in The Observer, September 30, 1984, p. 20.

MICHAEL WOOD

The freedom to juggle with language, Angela Carter suggests, is a promise and perhaps an instrument of other freedoms. Certainly her own cheerful jokes bespeak a lively independence of hallowed prejudices. 'It's very tiring, not being alienated from your environment.' 'It won't be much *fun* after the Revolution, people say. (Yes, but it's not all that much fun, now.)'

St Petersburg, in [*Nights at the Circus*], is 'a city built of hubris, imagination and desire', and that, Carter says, is what cities, and lives, should be: crazy possibilities, even impossibilities, juggled into practice. . . .

[Carter] sets her *Nights at the Circus* in the last months of the 19th century and makes quite a bit of play with the timing, but insists that her narrative, 'as must by now be obvious', does not belong to 'authentic history'. It belongs instead to the history of hubris, imagination and desire, and a very disconcerting narrative it is. It disconcerts not so much by the lovingly-collected freaks it takes for characters, or by its capacious plot, always ready to welcome a new, stray story to its bosom, as by its very odd diction. It is a book full of echoes of other writers, Balzac, Blake, Sade, Baudelaire, Goethe, Mervyn Peake, Wallace Stevens and a host of forgotten describers of circuses, of Russia and of dear old smoky London, and for a while it seems lost in the throng. 'Lor' love you, sir,' it opens in stage Cockney, introducing us to Fevvers, the famous winged lady trapeze artist, toast of Europe and friend of Toulouse-Lautrec, a figure who has 'deformed the dreams' of an entire generation in Vienna. She is a sort of Zuleika Dobson of the music halls, a large, coarse, kindly woman, constantly downing eel pies and bacon sandwiches and champagne, and she unfolds her story for an initially sceptical American reporter called Jack Walser. . . .

Fevvers doesn't always speak like an extra in *My Fair Lady*. 'Like any young girl,' she says early in her tale, 'I was much possessed with the marvellous blossoming of my until then reticent and undemanding flesh.' And later: 'This clock was, you might say, the sign, or signifier of Ma Nelson's little private realm.' Her different dialects are deliberately, comically brought together at times—'This is some kind of heretical possibly Manichean version of neo-Platonic Rosicrucianism, thinks I to myself'—but the effect, although funny, doesn't explain the prose. It all sounds like parody, but of what? We need to understand that we have climbed, not into an imitation of some aspect of the turn-of-the-century, but into a self-mocking myth which at first, unlike Fevvers, has a little trouble getting off the ground. Things are clearer once we have been given Fevvers' past life, and the novel moves from London to St Petersburg and Siberia. (p. 16)

Michael Wood, "Stories of Black and White," in *London Review of Books*, *Vol. 6, No. 18, October 4 to October 17, 1984, pp. 16-17.*

CAROLYN BANKS

Much of today's fine prose is spare and lean, the literary equivalent of nouvelle cuisine. *Nights at the Circus,* while good as they come, is the opposite, a luscious and gooey dessert of a book, doled out in sinful proportions.

Consider, just for starters, the novel's heroine, Sophia Fevvers, a circus *aerialiste* who sports wings, friends, wings: "a polychromatic unfolding fully six feet across, spread of an eagle, a condor, an albatross fed to excess on the same diet that makes flamingoes pink." But that's not all. She's more than six feet tall with three-inch eyelashes, and eyes that burst open, "whoosh! like blue umbrellas."

Angela Carter—among Britain's most admired writers (*The Bloody Chamber* and *Fireworks* collect her brilliant, disturbing short fiction)—introduces Fevvers in her dressing room where "a hissing flute of bubbly stood beside her own elbow on the dressing-table, the still-crepitating bottle lodged negligently in the toilet jug, packed in ice that must have come from a fishmonger's for a shiny scale or two stayed trapped within the chunks. And this twice-used ice must surely be the source of the marine aroma—something fishy about the Cockney Venus—that underlay the hot, solid composite of perfume, sweat, greasepaint and raw, leaking gas that made you feel you breathed the air in Fevvers' dressing room in lumps."

Here American journalist Jack Walser has come to discover if Fevvers is fact or fiction. If the latter, he'll include her in his series of articles, "Great Humbugs of the World." Ah, but Walser wilts, falls in love, joins the circus, and thus, along with us, feels "the beginnings of a vertiginous sense of freedom."

As Fevvers admits, "it's been a picaresque life." We, like Walser, will trail Fevvers through Petersburg where, because of her, "the exhausted soul of Mother Russia stirred, a little," and deep into the Siberian wastes. First, however, Fevvers offers us her past. (p. 1)

[By] the book's end, we'd follow Fevvers anywhere. In fact, we may well have already. We are thoroughly ensorceled, we are hers. However odd and impossible the adventure she's narrated might seem when we attempt to recount it, under the spell of her voice, we believe it utterly. We hold our breath when a Grand Duke nearly melts her down to one-pint size and, when she breaks a wing in a train-wreck, we list to one side. We are, in short, wholly engaged, sympathy and senses.

This is because everything in this novel is intense and immediate even though it is set at "the fag end, the smouldering cigar-butt, of a nineteenth century which is just about to be ground out in the ashtray of history . . . eighteen hundred and ninety nine." Angela Carter is a conjurer as much as a stylist, placing images where we never dreamt they'd be placed, and indelibly, too.

Even the minor characters—the Princess, Mignon, the Strong Man, the clowns, the dancing tigers, and the penitent murderesses—seem major creations. We drool thinking of a book about any one of them.

When we have Fevvers—"her plumage rippled in the wind of wonder"—it is with a sense of having overindulged, though we would willingly again. *Nights at the Circus,* in fact, could make unrepentant gluttons of us all. (p. 13)

Carolyn Banks, "*Angela Carter's Flights of Fancy,*" *in* Book World—The Washington Post, *February 3, 1985, pp. 1, 13.*

GRACE INGOLDBY

Angela Carter's writing is . . . much easier to admire than to enjoy. Her latest collection of short stories, *Black Venus,* leaves one in no doubt whatsoever that she has language at her fingertips if not beneath her belt. The tired metaphor, the familiar phrase, dare one say the cliché, are outside the orbit of this distant angel who is brilliant when being colloquial and tilts each observation until it sheds a clearer, brighter light. The stories range from the Old World to the New, from kitchen comedy to a wolf child 'hairy as Magdalen in the wilderness' across to Shakespeare and on to Edgar Allan Poe. Carter alternately soars and pelts the reader with her prose; the murderess Lizzie Borden dreams, 'sleep opened within her a disorderly house', Black Venus dances in an apartment where 'night comes in on feet of fur', where the bulbous legs of armchairs 'grin and grimace cinquecento faces . . .' It is perhaps these last, the armchairs, which make the reader gasp for some relief. At times the prose reads with the breathless gush of a cookery writer praising egg whites, the mind drifts off . . . There is plenty here for the Carter connoisseur but nothing that bridges the distance between writer and reader to create commitment, involvement between the two; style has beaten content into submission to the detriment of both. (pp. 28-9)

Grace Ingoldby, "Putting on the Style," in New Statesman, *Vol. 110, No. 2847, October 18, 1985, pp. 28-9.*

LORNA SAGE

The stories in *Black Venus* are about everyday life among the mythic classes. Real people—Baudelaire's Creole mistress Jeanne Duval, Edgar Allan Poe and his mother, and Lizzie Borden, who unpicked her domestic problem with an axe—rub shoulders with entirely imaginary beings. But then of course these particular people are real only in quotation marks: in their different ways they made it into mythology, splendid inversions of nineteenth-century enterprise, and what Angela Carter is up to here is figuring out how they did it, or had it done to them. You could say she's doing a Samuel Smiles on infamy—there's a shocking and hilarious practicality about her decadents and exotics. Indeed the point is, partly, that they're less exotic and strange than we like to think. These are stories that make magic in order to break the spell of the past. . . .

The trick is to take the people out of the wax museum, set them in motion, subject them to surmise; and it works very nicely with Poe and Lizzie B, as well [as with Jeanne Duval]. On the other hand, some stories take airy creatures of "pure" fantasy and root them in the real. **"Overture and Incidental Music for A Midsummer Night's Dream"** follows the play's fairy plot, the mysterious background row between Titania and Oberon over that "lovely boy", and improvises a new and very funny play-within-the play. . . . Maliciously, Carter gives all the little people bad colds, and Puck a painful and permanent erection. However, this is all back-stage, and when the curtain rises everything (and everyone) will shrink to scale, mere moving wallpaper.

The underlying theme—naturally enough for such an addicted re-writer—is escape from tales ready-told: how to find, or make a narrative clue that will lead out of the labyrinth. In this sense, the stories in *Black Venus* are akin to those in *The Bloody Chamber*. There, though, it was grown-up Grimm and Anderson; here the source-stories are more difficult and diverse, and the argument with the past is carried out much more openly. As a result the tension (always there) between Angela Carter the magician and Angela Carter the moralist, between the con-

juring and the common sense, comes out into the open too. Admirers who like to think of her as all artifice, transgressions and transformations will find this collection uncomfortable, because there's no escaping the fact that Carter (as she has often said, indeed) thinks that the stories we tell ourselves, however bizarrely archetypal, grow out of—and into—particular realities. Which makes interrogating them a kind of duty as well as a pleasure.

Lorna Sage, "Breaking the Spell of the Past," in The Times Literary Supplement, *No. 4307, October 18, 1985, p. 1169.*

PAUL BAILEY

Angela Carter is very much around in *Black Venus,* as entertainer, social historian, schoolmarm, and defender of the misjudged and sorely treated. This is an invigorating book, written with beguiling style and gusto. The eight tales on display are distinctly cautionary in tone, setting little moral traps for the incautious reader. Only Angela Carter could introduce the Marquis de Sade into a narrative in which he seems to have no place whatsoever in order to make a point, and a joke, about the dark times he lived in. He appears, doing what came naturally to him, and exits, both in the same sentence.

The title takes a look at the travails of Baudelaire's Creole mistress, Jeanne Duval, and the manner in which she accommodated the poet. Sex for Charles is 'a performance worthy of the Comédie Française . . . a five-act drama with farcical interludes.' Angela Carter has always been bemused by the demands certain men make on what used to be known as 'fallen' women, and the laugh some of those women have on their humourless clients. According to her, Jeanne achieved a notable revenge, not to say poetic justice, when she went back to Martinique.

In **"The Cabinet of Edgar Allan Poe"** she narrowly avoids producing a psycho-pathological study by virtue of the skill with which she conjures up the death-in-life nature of Poe's art—an art born in childhood, in theatrical circumstances, full of nasty surprises. Her explication of what made Lizzie Borden tick, in **"The Fall River Axe Murders,"** is not nearly so persuasive—or, indeed, so emphatic. Ms Carter seems to be practising here a certain corrective discipline, albeit in a jolly fashion. A note of Miss Bossy-Boots enters the prose when she tells us just how many garments poor Lizzie had to put on and take off every day, or when she reminds us that the Victorians *stank.* Her attitude to Lizzie's family is cavalier. 'Passing judgment on people or characters in a book means making silhouettes of them,' wrote Cesare Pavese, and that's exactly what Angela Carter does in this—to my taste—morally dubious story.

Paul Bailey, "Vanishing Ireland," in The Observer, *November 24, 1985, p. 28.*

Robert (Edward) Duncan

1919-

(Born Edward Howard Duncan; has also written as Robert Edward Symmes) American poet, essayist, editor, dramatist, and author of children's books.

Duncan is considered to be an important contemporary American poet who has been linked at various times with the Black Mountain School, the San Francisco Renaissance, and the Beat movement. Many critics also note that his style of verse has affinities with Romanticism. Duncan's poetry combines his knowledge of such disciplines as history, mythology, mysticism, and literature with personal observations and emotions. The experimental form of Duncan's verse reflects his belief that composing a poem is a spontaneous act and that the poet need not revise nor formally structure his work. Duncan's poetic output, which he has termed a "collage," encompasses disparate themes through an ongoing creative process that he views as an extension of the vast tradition of poetry.

When his mother died shortly after his birth, Duncan was adopted by the Symmes, a couple whose deep immersion in mysticism and the occult informs the mythopoeic nature of his verse. Having decided at the age of eighteen to become a poet, Duncan was an active figure from the 1930s to the 1950s in the literary communities of San Francisco, the East Coast, and North Carolina's Black Mountain College. The poems in his earliest works, collected in *The First Decade: Selected Poems, 1940-1950* (1968) and *Derivations: Selected Poems, 1950-1956* (1968), concern homoerotic themes veiled in medieval allusions. Reflecting a myriad of influences, these poems display the wide range of Duncan's interests and learning.

For a brief time during the 1950s, Duncan taught at Black Mountain College. He is often associated with Black Mountain poets Charles Olson and Robert Creeley, the leading exponents of "projective" or "open field" verse. In this type of poetry, the poet's emotional and intellectual energy is transmitted directly and spontaneously, with lines determined by natural pauses for breathing. Duncan's first major volume, *The Opening of the Field* (1960), announces his use of Black Mountain aesthetic principles. The volume's opening poem, "Often I Am Permitted to Return to a Meadow," exemplifies Duncan's belief that the poet is a shamanistic figure deeply affected by the external world. This book also presents the first poems in a sequence entitled "The Structure of Rime," one of Duncan's several ongoing series of prose poems. Referred to by Duncan as "trance projections," this sequence is intended to convey poetic theory within the practice of composition.

In his next collection, *Roots and Branches* (1964), Duncan employs more elegant language in order to distance himself from mundane experience and to ennoble the art of poetry. The poems in *Bending the Bow* (1968) concern social and political issues of the 1960s. This volume contains the first of Duncan's "Passages," another open-ended sequence that differs from "The Structure of Rime" by its unhindered expanse of subject matter. In these poems, Duncan liberally intersperses quotes from and allusions to other sources as well as his own works. The overt political nature of *Bending the Bow* is evi-

denced in the poem "Up-Rising" ("Passage 25"), which attacks the United States government's involvement in Vietnam.

In his next major collection, *Ground Work: Before the War* (1984), Duncan again explores his topics through poetic sequences and collage patterns. The consistency of Duncan's verse led Geoffrey O'Brien to comment: "The single-mindedness of [Duncan's] life's work shows itself in the confident energy of every line; in an era when poets exercise their 'craft' and 'control' with defensive restraint, *Ground Work* exhilarates by its utterly uncautious raid on the sublime."

(See also *CLC*, Vols. 1, 2, 4, 7, 15; *Contemporary Authors*, Vols. 9-12, rev. ed.; and *Dictionary of Literary Biography*, Vols. 5, 16.)

DENNIS COOLEY

It is important to understand that for Duncan the organic form of his poetry suits the pastoral and ecological vision informing it. By breaking away from an assertive, interfering approach toward both artistic and natural creation, an organic poet is able to establish a close and respectful response to what is going on outside and inside himself. That is why Duncan speaks of ''a poetics not of paradigms and models but of individual variations and survivals, of the mutual affinities of organic beings and the evolution of living forms.''

The mimetic quality that Duncan mentions is not based on any fallacy of imitative form. He does not think the ragged shape of his poetry mirrors the chaos of the universe. For him, there is no chaos to imitate. In his cultivation of what more finicky minds see as disarray, he is recording the intricate harmony, *not* the confusions and misfittings, of a streaming, living nature as it continuously unfolds and as he is carried by it and in it (though that sense of reality hardly leads Duncan to indifference toward *society,* much less satisfaction with it). (p. 48)

As Duncan moves with the poem, wherever it takes him, many fissures appear in it because he leaps without premeditation from one part to another. (If he ''loses track,'' he simply stops and waits until the voice of the poem returns.) The poems do not consist of explicitly connected sections but of active snippets run elliptically together. Therefore, Duncan writes, ''We cannot afford to 'fill a gap.' As we learn what the force of a poem is, we learn that the gaps must be acknowledged where they are, in the music fold.'' . . . The junctures are functional in the poems, the apparently disparate pieces developing a rich give-and-take. Those myriad segments gain power and significance as they contrast with or correspond to others in the dynamic field of the poem. They reveal their resemblances and distinctions as they are drawn together and driven apart in a high energy exchange that, in Duncan's words, is not ''a synthesis, but a melee.'' Within a Duncan poem the logic of grammar and the laws of discursive thought are abandoned in favour of a compressed ideographic or associational logic. As a result, the adjacent particles are joined by leaps of the imagination rather than by rational explanations.

The individual parts of such complex networks can vary greatly in nature. Perhaps because of Rimbaud's influence Duncan's poems include blocks of prose as well as sections of ''open'' verse. . . . There is a good reason for that mixture of prose and poetry. A tapestry cannot be made from a single thread or even identical threads; it needs both a warp and a woof. Throughout Duncan's writing there is a constant emphasis on including as much human experience as possible, the documentary as well as the lyrical. For him (in theory at least), there can be no language or experience extrinsic to the life of a poem. . . . In the full extent of his polysemous work, Duncan moves between the sometimes mundane reality of ''prosaic'' and the special intensity of ''poetic'' phrasings. (The same holds for the mixture of language that sometimes occurs in his poems, such as **''The Fire,''** where he ranges from harsh, explosive sounds to a quiet, mellifluous ending.) (pp. 49-51)

Duncan composes collages, bringing his material into new complexes, including both rapid shifts in language and frequent insertions of ''prose'' passages.

The results of this method of composition often are unsettling since we cannot always immediately understand what arises in the field of the poem or how a particular passage relates to the rest of the poem. The shock that comes from such suddenness and uncertainty is central to Duncan's poetics. He insists that a jarring discord must enter his compositions to force us out of and beyond what we take for granted. Ultimately, Duncan hopes to provoke a reordering of habitual thinking by upsetting his readers. . . . (p. 51)

A reader can come to grips with Duncan's poetry only by abandoning himself to it, just as Duncan can compose it only by suspending his will and flowing with the currents of life around him. If the poet participates in the cosmic flux and the reader is carried away in the poem, they both enter its dance. . . . The ideal reader, susceptible to the poem, becomes an accomplice in it. For those who are ''alike in soul'' Duncan hopes, ''there may be a special green / and flowering of life in these words— / eager to be read, taken, yielded to.'' Words ''to win particular hearts, / to stir an abiding affection for this music, / as if a host of readers will join the Beloved / ready to dance with me.'' When that happens the poet and reader discover ''The *vis imaginativa* in which the things of men's souls and the things of the actual universe dance together, having concourse and melody.'' . . . That intense fusion occurs in a sacred round dance, a turning mandala receiving and delivering the numinous powers rushing into the material world.

The creative dance figures prominently in Duncan's poetry. It appears as ''a children's game / of ring a round of roses told'' in **''Often I am Permitted to Return to a Meadow,''** . . . and as a beautiful dreamlike ceremony of enraptured children circling in the simple, idyllic pasture depicted in **''A Poem Beginning with a Line by Pindar.''** . . . (pp. 51-2)

The poem that is the dance, like the evolving restless universe of which it is an expression, can never come to a final end. In organic poems, as in the natural world, the stirring energy that flows through all living forms cannot be arrested. That is why Duncan writes open-ended sequences of poems such as **''Passages''** and the **''Structure of Rime''** series, and why none of his poems is ever wholly isolated or complete in itself. Each poem participates in a continuous ''total design'' that is the poet's life work deriving from his relationship to a fluid world and the one Poem which he, like other visionaries, continues to write. In ''a poem larger than the book'' Duncan moves ''between an initiation and a terminus I cannot name.'' . . . All his writing has been an effort ''not to reach a conclusion but to keep our exposure to what we do not know.'' . . . Duncan, determined not to come to the conclusions he saw around him in the secure and limiting life of middle class respectability, has always tried to avoid a closed or settled world.

That resolution has led Duncan to break open individual compositions in various ways. He sometimes writes poems in which the title becomes the first line, according to the example of Marianne Moore, or others in which there is no terminal punctuation following the lead of Ezra Pound's early *Cantos,* such as *Canto 1* that ends ''So that:'', the unfinished expression and expectant punctuation indicating a sense of on-going existence that will not be brought to a full stop. For a similar reason, Duncan omits capitals at the beginnings of some poems and starts others with semi-colons, the visual form clearly implying that the poem is a continuation of some happening previous to it. The interminable poems register those parts of Duncan's life which he attends to from their inceptions to their disappearance. As his punctuation implies the poem begins in the midst of events and continues until he leaves or loses it, recognizing that he has been listening in on something that goes on whether or not he is tuned in to it, and knowing full well that, because he can touch but never hold the wave of fire as it sweeps through him, he can only catch glimpses of what is going on in the flickering succession of fragments that constitute one of his poems. Other visual oddities in Duncan's poems—incomplete parentheses, words broken over separate lines, and unorthodox syntax—serve much the same function as the unusual punctuation. The formal eccentricities are not meant to act simply as novelties, annoyances, ways of gaining special emphasis or meaning, or even means of dislocating readers. They are, finally, expressions of an ever-moving, asymmetrical universe. Because that existence is continuous, without beginning or end, so is the poetry that records it.

Though Duncan's conceptions of form stem mainly from his biological belief that a poem finds its own form as it naturally grows, he also describes his assemblages in terms of twentieth-century physics and music. Music, Duncan has read in Stravinsky's *Poetics of Music,* is formed by combining "fragments": "'Melody, *Mélodia* in Greek, is the intonation of the *melos,* which signifies a fragment, a part of a phrase.'" ... Conceiving of his compositions as musical phrasings, Duncan connects the poetic tradition in which he is writing to Stravinsky's views.... What Duncan finds especially significant in modern music is the fact that, in contrast to the earlier use of traditional scales, it enables the artist to include virtually all keys as part of a fuller, more complex harmony.... (pp. 53-4)

To let the poem assume its own structure and coherence suitable to the particular qualities of the experience that it carries is anything but capricious. It can be argued, however, that importing and imprinting rigid figures on the fluctuating current in nature and human life—commonly recommended as an artistic virtue, even necessity—is itself a willful assertion.

There are other reasons for writing open verse. The unusual visual shapes that emerge in organic literature indicate soundings for the poem as Duncan hears and records it. Superficially, the words might appear to be strewn haphazardly across the page. Actually, they are painstakingly noted. By laying out his words on the page in a particular though unpremeditated manner, he attempts to set a musical score that is supposed to help us through the poem with the proper pacing and emphasis. Scoring the poem (often on a typewriter) is meant to duplicate the poet's voice through the use of visual cues such as extra spaces between words, irregular margins, unexpected periods, and varying gaps between lines and stanzas. Since a poet's voice inevitably differs somewhat from everyone else's, it requires careful and sometimes detailed notation if a reader is going to catch his particular inflections in the poem. It is often hard to know in specific instances how effective such devices are, but they matter a great deal to Duncan. (pp. 55-6)

Duncan is convinced that form and content are inseparable. It is therefore crucial to see how adequately his poetics fit his vision. His fragmented, often incantatory, poems are full of interruptions, leaps, involutions, false starts, and retracings. In his compositions there are no studied or elegant turns of phrase. There are no calculated periodic sentences, epigrammatic statements, or deliberate parallelisms. And for good reason. Such niceties of expression, particularly when they appear in poetry, can imply that an author is in full control of a settled situation, that his outlook is secure, and that most of the answers are in. At its worst it offers little more than the reworking of conclusions already reached or the shining up of old homilies—conventional wisdom in traditional dress. That composed manner of writing derives largely from an assurance of consensus and an ear for effects. Tidy forms and self-conscious techniques suggest that creating poetry consists of studiously reshaping an experience *after* it has taken place. The conservative aesthetic emphasizes the poem as a lucid, detached, and finished *product.* (A refined style can, of course, indicate fear as well as complacence—a determination to hold the line against disturbing events.)

In contrast, Duncan's tangled, gnarled compositions catch ideas and images *during* the heat of their immediate formation. They exist in a continuous present because they are created on the spot, in *process,* stuffed with almost everything that occurs to him. Duncan finds tension in the moment-by-moment unfolding of the poem, an uneasiness that is apparent in the nervous shifts that are as striking in his speech as in his poetry. Acutely sensitive to what is happening in his mind and in the poem, he expresses himself in a fast-moving, elliptical and convoluted way. The language arises directly out of his immediate experience (including his impressive knowledge and intelligence) and meets it head on. He speaks his mind. Duncan's words are not chosen to serve as a discursive and generalized comment on events at some point of removal from them. The seemingly haphazard poems avoid the plain and studied manner suitable for clarifying and refining accepted truths. Instead, they are informed by a tortuous style appropriate to intense and uncertain groping. Duncan's poetry, like Pound's, registers "the defects inherent in a record of struggle," ... that virtually precludes ease and grace in writing. Such agitated outpourings clearly are out of line. The contorted, sometimes awkward, configurations they take on, "twisted out of shape, crippled / by angelic Syntax," ... reveal a powerful mind, free of dogma and certainty, and saturated with a natural and mental world that is almost bewilderingly mobile and complex. Because Duncan, no more than his reader, can know what is coming next in the poem, the effect of his writing depends more on surprise than fulfilled expectation. Duncan evidently has found a style that is right for him, however taxing it might be for some of his readers.

Duncan's poetry incorporates more than the shifting universe. It is also built out of a shared world of imagination. As a result, he does not see his work as a body of original poetry drawn out of his own unique personality but, like Shelley, as a particular manifestation of the one great poem all true poets cooperatively have built up since the beginning of time.... Duncan, finding the poetry of effects and personality superficial and dishonest, doesn't write *his* art but *The* Art. According to him, "Poems are for me only occasions of Poetry." ... He becomes a participant, not a personality, in the poem. To do otherwise, he thinks, would be to make poetry a matter of private property or copyright, simply another commodity peddled on the market.... (pp. 56-8)

Those who prefer poetry that is very personal and novel might object to Duncan's extensive use of other authors, especially when he goes to the extent of unabashedly relying on unaltered material to provide power and significance in his own work. As he sees it, his poetry *is* original—it "directs us to the point of origins." The point is essential in understanding Duncan's poetics. Modern readers have come to expect unique, individual voices in poetry. But Duncan doesn't conceive of his work as something written in a deliberately peculiar way. For him, it arises out of participation in a cosmic and communal life in which he virtually discards his private personality to follow and to be created by a collective tradition....

There are more important reasons for the inclusion of other writers. For one thing, the echoes serve to identify and maintain the poetic tradition as Duncan sees it. At the same time, the numerous quotations offer Duncan a way of acknowledging his indebtedness to other writers. More importantly, they give him the opportunity of bringing the past to bear on the present. However postmodern he is, Duncan, like Pound, believes (and often says he believes) that "All ages are contemporaneous."

What has been seen and said in the past again appears alive and immediate in Duncan's own time and writing. His poetry builds on those correspondences (or rimes as he also calls them) that represent essential identities or contrasts between there and then and here and now. (p. 59)

There are other implications for the "derivative" nature of Duncan's writing. One of them has to do with what makes his poetry recognizably different from any one else's. Though he wants to pay attention to the poem's (not his *own*) intention, and though he doesn't consider his work personal, it does bear his imprint or "signature," as he calls it. It might seem that an enraptured author, reading the message or poem informing creation, would contribute nothing of his own to a poem and would act simply as a transparent medium bringing it into existence. That's not what happens. Those myths that take hold of Duncan naturally assume the bent of his mind. He has a hand in them. We note his hand in the manuscript, his handling of the material. He inevitably transposes the numinous powers pushing through him into the work at hand as he inscribes the poem on the page. Through his hand, in his hand, instrumental in its sounding.

Duncan necessarily acts like a prism which refracts the light passing through it. The rays take on the artist's colouring because he is neither passive nor empty. . . . Although Duncan cannot make a poem happen, he does not sit idly about waiting for one to arrive. As a matter of fact, he prepares himself, like Blake, through "demanding years of work and constancy in poetic inspiration and craft, demanding arduous study and ardent thought" for the moment when he catches fire. (pp. 60-1)

A poem arrives as a command to the artist; it is presented not invented. Duncan must serve what the poem requires, not what he desires. He must flow with the poem, wherever it takes him, because only then is he faithful to the evanescent, ever-changing appearance of it. To be responsible for the poem he first has to be responsive to it.

Catching the moment as it flies means that Duncan must take what comes, however unwelcome it might be. To do anything else would mean violating the vision. . . . (pp. 61-2)

Most readers believe that a serious writer must carefully and sometimes extensively modify a first draft, the common assumption being that systematic polishing is an essential part of the poet's craft. Never altering a poem, the argument goes, leads to shoddy work. Knowing the risk, Duncan insists that if his poems are to be faithful to their source and fitted to his vision, they should remain essentially as they first appear. (p. 63)

An unsympathetic reader might suppose that Duncan's poems are careless. In fact, they *never* are. They appear only after he has taken great pains in getting ready for them and in attending to them as they assume their almost inevitable but unpredictable configurations. In contrast to the views of more traditional writers, Duncan thinks of craftsmanship as coming into play *before* and *during* the poem's emergence, not after it has formed. To his mind, art is more a matter of preparing for and composing a poem than repairing it.

Still, whatever Duncan might say about not being able to modify the words that first occur to him, he in effect does some editorial work. Though he never takes a blue pencil to a poem, he will often re-do it completely, sometimes making substantial changes in it. His method of re-vision is fairly simple. The first appearance of a poem remains untouched and he reworks the whole thing by writing an entirely new version of it. (pp. 64-5)

Duncan's composition methods clearly are romantic. So are many other features of his work. His open, organic forms, as well as his beliefs in an inspired, expressive, and affective art, stem out of the radical romantic tradition. His preference for a poetry that includes outlawed words, forms, and perspectives also originates in that sensibility. Since art should not be "prophylactic," Duncan thinks it ought to open up to manners and matter normally rejected out of fear or propriety.

Opening the poem, or *The Opening of the Field* as Duncan calls his leading book of poems, means not only incorporating "unpoetic" or "impure" qualities, but letting the line open out as well. (pp. 65-6)

Part of the distinction Duncan is making about the nature of poetic lines originates with Charles Olson's influential essay, "Projective Verse." Arguing that the line is a breath unit, Olson says that a verse will depend on the temperament and immediate disposition of a poet in the midst of composing. (p. 66)

A poet-shaman seized by the energies of eternity will inevitably use a form that carries the power and fullness of that life. A tight, clipped line, like a set stanza or sonnet, cannot convey such explosive release. Extending beyond mental categories means opening up the stiff, constricted forms that accompany and express that containment. The kind of fervour pushing through Duncan's poetry cannot be held in neat, restrained, and regular lines, just as the pressure of Blake's prophecies ruptures his early short lines and neat stanzas. When the spirit breaks through the walls break down.

The romantic poet's activities are sacramental as well as rhetorical. Duncan frequently speaks of his "conversion" to poetry, of the poet's role as priest and witness, and of the reader as communicant in a mass. What is needed in literature, he thinks, is an end to masterpieces and the beginning of testimony . . .—a movement from aesthetics to ecstatics—because "In Art as in Religion it is by faith we move."

Duncan hopes that his inspired vision will infect readers with his dis-ease and that they will "come down with" a case of poetry. He often complains about the stubborn literal-mindedness of an age that distrusts imagination, but he still thinks that a prophet's fictions can change the minds and therefore the behaviour of people. Like the radical Romantic visionaries, Shelley and Blake, he believes that human activity is shaped by the imagined orders in our minds. (pp. 66-7)

Duncan's essential romanticism is clear in the visionary sources, the organic forms, and the vatic ardour of his writing. That romanticism, of course, is entirely consistent with his peculiar strain of post-modernism, which appears in the open, elliptical, and irregular forms that dominate his work. At the same time his work in many ways is modern. It is characterized by allusiveness, complexity, and a deep dislike of the official culture around him. By the same token, his erudite subjects and at times abstruse vocabulary look peculiar alongside the tough, breezy language and the everyday topics found in much recent writing. Although Duncan's words and themes might offend genteel aesthetes, he does not usually possess the graphic immediacy found in many recent poets, including most of the "Black Mountain" poets with whom he is often indiscriminately linked. As Williams once complained of him, his poems are almost never idiomatic and straight-forward. The words he likes tend to be a bit abstract, at times almost academic, while his images are surprisingly infrequent and primarily limited to visual references when they do occur. His subjects, seldom local and ordinary, usually are based on poetry, archetypes, dreams, and occult lore. In fact, Duncan's voice is for the most part literary, mythic and associative. He seeks a special heightened language to convey his awesome regard for that world, knowing that an ordinary or more vernacular way of speaking would not work for him. (pp. 67-8)

Apart from Duncan's abiding interest in spiritualism, the scarcity of tangible passages in his work may derive from his notion, perhaps picked up from the Symbolists, that writing poetry is like composing music. In pursuing what, in the spirit of Pound, he calls the tone leading of vowels and consonants, he from time to time gets so caught up with tracing sounds that he fails to root his poetry deeply in the material world. Duncan's writing keeps moving toward an associational and psychological reality within the poem and within his mind rather than referring to outward physical experience, favouring conception more than perception. It is a tendency that he is aware of and occasionally at some pains to resist.

There are more obvious and important reasons why sensations of the external world are less important to him than the workings of his own inward life and the overpowering presences, charged with energy and in constant fluctuation, that he senses behind and within the physical universe. He is more fascinated with forms and trans-form-ations than solid fixed matter, preferring "not objects but operations," . . . not substances but actions. That kaleidoscopic view reduces the prominence of discrete things in his work to the point that there are surprisingly few concrete nouns and adjectives. In much of Duncan's poetry there is scanty celebration of smells, textures, and sounds (though Duncan does not see the numinous world as distant and transcendent but ineffable and elusive). The problem he must struggle with is how to give colour and body to the immanent presence of God, no easy matter when his apprehension of dynamic presences, met in a fleeting moment, draw him to the verb more than the noun. Given his mythic view of life, Duncan is inclined to see physical things as storming knots of energy or nets of swirling turbulence whose boundaries are constantly dissolving and reforming. No-thing holds in an event-ful world. His preference for a moving, shimmering universe that is surging with power produces the abundance and force of verbs in his writing. Appropriately, many of them are intransitive and in the continuous present. That emphasis is not surprising because Duncan believes in ultimate reality as something that is being and becoming, rather than determined and determining. Events just happen, they are not caused.

Clearly Duncan is aware of what he is doing as a poet. His remarkable vision incorporates, in a complex syncretic way, whatever is pertinent to it. There is nothing unsuitable about his manner of writing, either. Knowing that forms are not neutral, Duncan has found a vehicle that effectively carries and articulates his outlook. "Only the extremely simple, or the extremely sophisticated," the biologist C. H. Waddington writes, "are likely to stray into the realm of [organic] form which is the proper outcome of the blind but complex forces of life." In his remarkable mixture of naivete and erudition Duncan has found that organic form. (p. 69)

Dennis Cooley, "The Poetics of Robert Duncan," in boundary 2, *Vol. VIII, No. 2, Winter, 1980, pp. 45-73.*

GEOFFREY O'BRIEN

When Robert Duncan announced in 1969 that he would not publish another book for 15 years, it seemed a theatrical gesture, as if the exuberant cacophony then reigning on the poetic scene could be topped only by withdrawal into monkish silence. . . .

Now that *Ground Work* has arrived as scheduled, its immediate effect is to point up what a difference those 15 years have made—not in Duncan but in us. When we last heard him at this length, his voice was one element of an ebullient chorale. Now it's a solitary sound, like the speech of an astronaut who has emerged from his capsule to find the home planet irrevocably altered. . . . Duncan's career has always run parallel to wider movements—from Black Mountain and the San Francisco Renaissance to the Aquarian apotheosis—but today he seems without heirs, a rhapsodist intent on ecstasies which those around him would rather deconstruct.

Thus in *Ground Work* we can finally see Duncan as an isolated figure rather than as a front-runner for "projective verse" or "field composition" or "the new American poetry." Whatever his involvement in those old battles, Duncan's writing has always centered to a remarkable degree on himself. With what some might take for supreme hubris, he mythologizes his own life, casting himself as the mystical initiate who transmits the oracles of invisible hierophants; when he says he serves the Muse, he isn't speaking metaphorically. . . .

[The] poetry risks becoming ludicrous at every step, and Duncan's relentless pursuit of the divine afflatus—along with his sometimes Shelleyan vocabulary—can sound hollow to an unsympathetic ear. It's easy to shy from a voice which exclaims: "Everything speaks to me!" But in *Ground Work* he justifies his prophetic stance with poems that are simpler, clearer, more penetrating than anything he has published. The singlemindedness of his life's work shows itself in the confident energy of every line; in an era when poets exercise their "craft" and "control" with defensive restraint, *Ground Work* exhilarates by its utterly uncautious raid on the sublime.

Duncan's poetry is best approached not through hermetic doctrine, or even through imagery—his images, although frequently powerful ("The river of her being is in flood"), sometimes melt into a wavering maze of luminous abstractions. It's best to read him in terms of the music that grounds his ethereal vistas and gives him a place in the real world where he can stand. Duncan's music is syntactical: its rhythm shuttles between the sentence's tendency toward closure and the voice's desire to flow on forever. By a kind of foliation his poetic line stretches itself out, putting forth new shoots, new twists of grammatical structure: "the structures of rime extend into / the fit of the parts at the finger tips." . . .

There are cultures in which an individual receives a single sacred song, to keep his vision alive by constant repetition. Although Duncan's words change, he has been chanting essentially the same melody all his life. The words seem at times only a running commentary on the poem itself, like someone singing a song whose lyrics are: "I am singing a song." The trancelike qualities of Duncan's art have never been more apparent than in **"Circulations of the Song,"** his undulating set of variations on the Sufi poet Rumi, which fittingly closes this splendid book:

> I reflect
> passages of what is moving as I catch it,
> the shadow of the expanding depth,

the glance fugitive and sparkling
　　of but one among a million
promises.

　　　　　Geoffrey O'Brien, in a review of "Ground Work:
Before the War," in VLS, *No. 30, November, 1984,*
p. 5.

H. FOX

In *Ground Work,* Duncan is, as always, a pale echo of Charles
Olson and Ezra Pound, still without either Olson's or Pound's
fire and humanity. The ultimate test of any poet is his "humanity," but Duncan's work from the beginning to now reads
more like the notes of a philologist lost in a classics library
than a poet concerned with the human. And Duncan seems to
be acutely aware of his own limitations. In **"Despair in Being
Tedious,"** he goes into a bar: "Some listened and some tired
of me. / I do not know if I am bound / to run upon this wheel,
wound up, / excited in a manic spiel of wheel in wheel, / or
if I'm free to talk wherever they are free / to listen." There
really are no people in *Ground Work,* even in **"Despair in
Being Tedious."** Ideas, yes, and a lot of Greek, and a whole
"suite" in homage to the 17th century.

　　　　　H. Fox, in a review of "Ground Work: Before the
War," in Choice, *Vol. 22, No. 4, December, 1984,*
p. 554.

MARK RUDMAN

Camus said that Kafka's art consisted in forcing the reader to
reread. The same holds true for Robert Duncan, if for opposite
reasons. His work is difficult right on the surface. His sheer
reach and range of associations and patterning are so complex
that the reader is forced to scan the page as one scans a horizon
and register some sense of a visual whole before proceeding
to the parts. Since *The Opening of the Field* (1960), he has
been engaged in a search for what Alfred North Whitehead
calls "the right chaos, the right vagueness." But for all his
erudition and allusiveness, he is not a poet for scholars only.
If his *oeuvre* can fairly be viewed as a grand collage, the leaps,
gaps and juxtapositions stimulate the reader to uncover, in his
words, "resonances of meaning exceeding what we / understand, words freed from their origins." . . .

Ground Work: Before the War is Mr. Duncan's first major
collection in 15 years. It is also a series of sequences or books
within books, including **"Passages," "Structure of Rime,"**
**"A Seventeenth Century Suite in Homage to the Metaphysical
Genius in English Poetry (1590-1690)"** and **"Dante Etudes."**
Mr. Duncan dwells in other texts; reading for him is an active
process that generates poems. He takes inspiration equally from
the word and the world. . . . (p. 13)

The continued interlinking sequences lead one to think of all
of Mr. Duncan's books as one book. He is the author of 12
books of poetry; a penetrating essay, **"The Truth and Life of
Myth"**; and **"H.D.,"** a book he adds to continually and which
provides a framework for him to harness his central concerns.
And though his gesture goes against the idea of "anthology
pieces," he has written superb poems of all conceivable lengths
that demand to be singled out, from **"An Essay at War,"**
**"Apprehensions," "Night Scenes," "My Mother Would Be
A Falconress,"** to the later sections of **"Passages"** in *Ground
Work* and some fascinating poems like the ongoing **"Structure
of Rime."** . . .

In **"Passages"** Mr. Duncan manages to unite all of his impulses—bard, reader, observer, lyrist, commentator—and he
needs a large framework to give his imagination free rein. He
seems to work best in a series, denying the necessity of ter-
minations and knowing before he begins that the end of the
sequence will not necessitate the end of the poem. . . .

Our categories of description cannot contain Mr. Duncan. His
work is lyric and epic, condensed and expansive, hieratic and
quotidian, avant-garde and traditional. And what holds the
reader through so much diversity is what separates poetry from
verse and resists paraphrase—sound clusters, the subtlety of
rhythmical variation, the emotional drive of the cadence. . . .

"Passages" deepens upon each reading, and its poems are
among the finest written in our time. While it brings together
impulses Mr. Duncan locates in the work of Ezra Pound, Charles
Olson and William Carlos Williams, it points toward new possibilities for the long poem—"this art an aggregate of intentions." (p. 14)

　　　　　Mark Rudman, "The Right Chaos, the Right Vague-
ness," in The New York Times Book Review, *Au-*
gust 4, 1985, pp. 13-14.

GEORGE F. BUTTERICK

There are poems [in *Ground Work: Before the War*] worth a
world. The fact that the volume includes some of the finest
"Passages," those originally published in 1970 as *Tribunals,*
guarantees its significance. I am of an age that I cannot read
"Before the Judgment," for example, and not feel the old
surge of righteousness in my veins, my body alive in an all-
stage alert, morally armed. It is a poem that continues the
themes of **"Multiversity"** and the other **"Passages"** of the
war, the litany of fiends: "Rubin, Hayakawa, Alioto, Reagan,
Nixon / as we go upward the stupidity thickens." These were
poems that gave focus and legitimacy to our feelings, that gave
leadership—when poets could still command audiences of
thousands, by the authority of their words. I cannot tell how
the coming generation might respond. Does the power work
for them too? It is incredible to think otherwise, that the language doesn't quake throughout time, and that Duncan hasn't
successfully done what it is so hard to do, instruct, command,
uplift, and write an effective political poem.

The subject of the poems of *Ground Work* remains knowing
(gnosis), revelation, abiding love, and protest against the violation of the natural order by systematic viciousness. In a
poem like **"An Interlude of Winter Light,"** all the major familiar devices are present: the willingness to announce a theme,
like Whitman (in this case an "oracular" one); contrasts of
light and dark; the dance; the "rapture"; the puns and advan-
tageous "mis-takes"—all the advantages and ingenuities of a
mature artist. One knows that the work of the greatest poets,
if it doesn't decline, always starts over again, is self-regener-
ative, rather than steady progress up an inclined plane. The
poetry here, by the volume's very title, is not offered as "new"
poetry, even thematically. It is anticipatory—a foundation, preliminary—in this case, to the workings of old age and, perhaps,
of a new world.

Duncan composes by books, and this one—which was typeset
under his direct supervision, almost from his own typewrit-
ing—was allowed the announced space of time to assemble
itself, to discover itself, even though we might not readily
perceive a necessary pattern. (It's too large. It's like finding

a constellation. *The Opening of the Field* was a manageable size for book-length composition and comprehension; this is larger than *Bending the Bow,* almost as extensive as *Roots and Branches*.) Nonetheless, there are individual poems so remarkable that one can be content just to accept the fact and catch radiance from them for the time being, until the book can be lived with a while longer. One thing is immediate, however—. . . Duncan's power is undiminished.

It is the subtitle that is most intriguing at present and remains unexplained, formally, by the volume. There is no introduction as in *Bending the Bow,* only preliminary instructions as to how to read or conduct the score of the poems. The subtitle reads, "Before the War." A war that is inevitable, a WW III, the fabled nucleonic End itself? What dire prophecy? Light's war against the Dark? Life against Death? Although begun during an actual war, the undeclared one raging in Southeast Asia at the time, which *Tribunals* and "Santa Cruz Propositions" directly confront, nothing in the volume explicitly indicates what war is promised. . . . One must return to the introduction of *Bending the Bow,* in the first section there titled "The War," to find that these are "the last days of our own history," in which "living productive forms in the evolution of forms fail, weaken, or grow monstrous, destroying the terms of their existence." It is a war, then, for the hope of the species. Duncan continues the tradition of the poet as prophet, a tradition that is as postmodern as it is primitive.

Not all the poems are of equal merit or appeal, of course. The "Seventeenth Century Suite" may have been useful exercises or evenings at home for the poet, but there's not as much there for readers striding along in the traffic of the days. Its outsized "Coda" suffers from the language of "symphonies," of "ghostly paths," "darker reaches," and "trembling lives." And it may be that, finally, Duncan has more kinship with the nineteenth than the seventeenth century. "An Interlude of Winter Light" is a drama easy to lose track of by an impatient reading. . . . It is a poem that hardly reflects the larger questions of the day, those "political issues of our sad history" promised on the book's back cover. On the other hand, there is "The Torn Cloth" some poems earlier. It was probably written amid the dissolution of Duncan's relationship with Denise Levertov, who had shared his correspondence for so long; a strife-torn poem from strife-torn times, it extends beyond the merely personal.

But "Santa Cruz Propositions" is Duncan's great political poem, cosmogonic yet political poem, the central technique of which is the collage, never more skillfully used. From the flaming heart of the revolutionary sixties, he assembles his most dynamic collage, rapid-fire, "crackling," and closely timed section by section. There is a fuse on the poem, reminding us, now, how close to conflagration, how superheated, the society had been. The sections dated down to the hour are like news bulletins. Here Duncan accomplished a mimesis of communications reality—how the reports of events are fed to us. (pp. 273-76)

At least, at the very least, ["Santa Cruz Propositions"] raises the questions of art in life, art as life, and art versus life.

Quite apart from the specific issues the poem goes on to develop, there is no doubt that the opening section (of three) is among the largest and most active Duncan has ever written, indeed one of the great sea poems of all times. It includes a lovely opening metaphor for the poem, the poem as wave—

the line of surf and the poetic line—the "litterd margin" of the beach and, of course, the poem's page. (p. 276)

Thus we have one of the great political poems of the sixties—followed, however, by a strange little bouquet or nosegay of highly personal, sentimental short lyrics, pressed flowers out of the pages of a nineteenth-century album or Godey's almanac. . . . It's clearly a retreat into relief after *Tribunals* and the Santa Cruz upheaval, but this is where it can be difficult to perceive a pattern to the volume. Such small relevancy after poems of such high moment. If there's an hermetic and visionary strain to Duncan, and a highly romantic (High Romantic) strain—and there obviously are those—this is the embroidered strain in Duncan, the Victorian, the lamp with fringes. Sweet opalescence. (p. 277)

Duncan is a poet who has found his themes and continues to play them, more resonantly with each stroke of the bow. We watch and admire, even when it is "thru the frosted panes, thru the inner glass/burnt with aromatics and with gold." There is a sense of an orchestra playing in Duncan's poems, at least since "Apprehensions." No solitary pipings at a mountain pass. Stereo in effect, the peaks ring. The majestic strains are the same, the setting continues to be on the grand scale: maximum magnificence. Yes, Duncan orchestrates his own nobility of gesture, but has he lived among the universals too long? For some, it will be like reading the hymnal during an overlong service, with Poetry in the pulpit. They will cry, "Take poetry out of the pulpit and put it back at the altar where it belongs." Or *on* the altar, where it can be the sacrifice it's meant to be! Duncan will wither them down. His grandiloquence of purpose brooks no such niggling. Duncan will never be for those who prefer reduced, portable images, lamps that can be carried around like flashlights, or who (as I myself often do) welcome epigrams. He writes in skeins not purls of wisdom. He requires more space for development than some readers are prepared to grant. Very broad organ music in a very large cathedral; drafts upon drafts of sound. Choirs, not ballads. No poet is equal in majesty (if majesty is what we need, say those others). Yet, how many poets ennoble the profession? Who else could fit the role, fill the robes with such magisterial splendor? (pp. 279-80)

Duncan's vocabulary is rich, but not startlingly so. There is a suppression of denotative particulars to waves of speech; the lack of hard diction gives a heady evanescence to the lines as we read them ("the forces of Speech give way to the Language beyond Speech"). How he achieves his resonance without such distinct particulars is more of the marvel. His diction is surprisingly consistent in *Ground Work*—aside from a few borrowed words. . . . (p. 280)

In sum, what have we in the meantime? The "Passages" from *Tribunals,* further "Passages" and sections of "Structure of Rime" like "The Missionaries" and "In Memoriam Wallace Stevens," "The Museum," two or three of the "Dante Etudes," and "Santa Cruz Propositions"—added up, at least a dozen major poems in as many years. I mean poems on the scale of the "Dejection Ode" or "Hymn to Proserpine" or "Crossing Brooklyn Ferry." Enough to last any reader's lifetime. (p. 283)

George F. Butterick, "Seraphic Predator: A First Reading of Robert Duncan's 'Ground Work'," in Sagetrieb, *Vol. 4, Nos. 2 & 3, Fall & Winter, 1985, pp. 273-83.*

MICHAEL DAVIDSON

[Much] of *Ground Work* concerns the material form in which poetry appears and the narrative it articulates. For Duncan, poetry is not a matter of individual poems but of Poetry, "Grand Collage" of the individual's creative potential. The immediate event—a slight pause between two words, the distinction between two phonemes—represents entry into what Duncan calls a "felt architectonics . . . of the numinous." This phrase could describe the ways that poetry participates in a structure larger than itself (the origins of one's language, the numinous presence of Deity) but which is "felt" as a structure that one creates. Dante is the genius of this notion for Duncan, and he is, to some extent, the book's patron saint.

Because the book is written from the standpoint of testimony rather than from an assertion of artisanal mastery it will be all the harder for some to read. The language is often vatic and rhetorical, and the diction archaic and abstract:

> Oh Need, beloved Adversary to Love's settlements,
> Invader, the halcyon days are over.

Although the thematic material of the book extends from *Bending the Bow,* the strong precursor to this book is *Roots and Branches* with its high romantic diction and neoplatonic subjects. During the period of *Bending the Bow,* when the nation needed the demotic voice of "Up-Rising" to shake it loose, Duncan's tone could be heard with the full urgency of its occasion, but one wonders if in the discursive 1980's it will be heard as clearly.

The best introduction to *Ground Work* is the poet's 1968 essay, **"Man's Fulfillment in Order and Strife"** (printed in *Caterpillar*) in which Duncan articulates "the great theme of War" that haunts both *Bending the Bow* as well as the current volume. In that essay, he contrasts the productive role of contention in poetry with the authoritarian version of contention embodied in the Vietnam War. For the poet, "the very life of our art is our keeping at work contending forces and convictions." This is the "creative strife" of Heraclitus who sees War as the principle of generation. Modern warfare in southeast Asia, on the other hand, makes war "too terrible for men to wage," as Duncan says in **"Up-Rising."** *Ground Work* begins in the late days of that unhappy adventure, and in many respects the relation between individual volition and political hegemony forms the primary theme of the book's opening poems.

But the thematics of War and conflict are only half of a dialectic that advances the book's Heraclitean subject. In a line from **"Empedoklean Reveries"** Duncan makes this dialectic painfully clear:

> "Because of what we love we are increasingly at War."

The poet's operative spacing nicely illustrates the indissoluble bond between desire and conflict: we are because of what we love and we are, by this desire, increasingly at war. The near rhyme of "are" and "War" adds to the paradox by linking Being and opposition in sound. The interplay between love and war animates all of the poems in the volume. In Duncan's rendering of Southwell's great poem, **"The Burning Babe,"** for example, the sixteenth-century poet's mystical experience of Christ's incarnation becomes, for the contemporary poet, a doubled vision of sacrifice in the ricefields of southeast Asia. . . . It is not that Duncan denies the possibility of incarnation because of the Vietnam holocaust (and how easily a lesser poet would "make use" of Southwell's imagery for an ironizing

intent!) but that the same creative heat that generates belief is, by a perverted zeal, turned into the flames of a secular martyrdom. In this poetry of secular and sacred incarnation, Duncan is most like his metaphysical forebears and really has no peer in the modern period.

The "Great Theme of War" is dramatically evident in the group of **"Passages"** that were printed as *Tribunals* and which appear in the early part of the book. **"Before the Judgment"** is one of Duncan's most powerful declamations against the misuse of power, a poem written in the strident voice of earlier **"Passages"** like **"The Multiversity"** and **"The Fire."** . . . These War passages rival Pound's Hell Cantos in their invocation of a contemporary bolgia of the war makers, but Duncan recognizes his own complicity in the making of war, even as it infects poetry. . . . It is such caution that Duncan urges towards his own peers, particularly Denise Levertov in **"Santa Cruz Propositions,"** that in protesting the historical war we do not become the very warmakers we attack.

Ground Work is dominated by several long series or sequences in addition to the **"Passages"** that appear throughout the volume. **"Santa Cruz Propositions," "Poems from the Margins of Thom Gunn's *Moly*," "A Seventeenth Century Suite . . . ,"** the **"Dante Etudes"** are, in a sense, books within the book. Like many of his earlier poems they are "reading writings," poems that take their impetus from other texts but find their own resonance in the poet's immediate concerns. Newspaper accounts of a grisly murder in the Santa Cruz mountains provide a backdrop for a lengthy meditation on Plato's theory of love; Thom Gunn's book, *Moly* generates a series of poems on homosexual themes; the "metaphysical genius" of Herbert, Southwell, Jonson and others provides a frame for variations on theological and aesthetic subjects; Dante's prose advances propositions of social and poetic order in **"Dante Etudes"**; and in **"Circulations of the Song,"** the work of the Persian poet, Rumi, is the basis for a series of love poems. These are difficult series, written so close to the rhetoric of the source text that they often exclude the reader, yet they are basic to Duncan's practice. They show the poet treating his language as part of a common inheritance in which he is both original and derivative. (pp. 134-37)

The poet's biography becomes a narrative, no less subject to variations than the myths and stories out of which his poetry is composed. Duncan could hardly be considered a "confessional" poet, but when he focuses on specifically personal matters (as he does in many of the book's shorter lyrics) he is painfully honest even while projecting their narrative dimensions. My favorite among the shorter lyrics of this order is **"Despair in Being Tedious"** in which Duncan reflects on his own volubility. . . . (p. 138)

I mentioned at the outset that this book will be hard for some to hear. The proposition that "Everything Speaks to Me" may be read by others as "I exclude all but my hearing," and indeed, Duncan often admits to a one-way conversation with his poem: "My world in speech / answers some ultimate need I know, / / aroused, pours forth upon the sands / again and again / lines written for the audience of the sea." The burden of testimony and belief is that at the moment when language is asked to speak for a realm beyond itself it must relinquish its power to speak at all. Duncan's recent poems approach an almost Mallarmean opacity and spareness, as though sieving out all grit of local association and leaving the sheer performative power of the single word. He wants to name ''It'' without naming any contingent reality to which ''it'' refers. One may prefer those pieces in which Duncan's syntactic and semantic playfulness is most at work (the homages to Jack Spicer, Wallace Stevens and Jess for example), but the point is not which poems one ''prefers'' but one's willingness to see the larger ground of **Ground Work.** And that larger ground, curiously enough, concerns the reader—the degree to which he or she is willing to go along with the sweep and flow of Duncan's unfashionably eclectic intellect. (pp. 138-39)

Michael Davidson, ''A Felt Architectonics of the Numinous: Robert Duncan's 'Ground Work','' in Sulfur 12, *Vol. IV, No. 2, 1985, pp. 133-39.*

Lawrence (George) Durrell

1912-

© 1986 Thomas Victor

(Has also written under pseudonyms of Charles Norden and Gaffer Peeslake) Indian-born English novelist, poet, dramatist, short story writer, travel writer, translator, editor, and critic.

Durrell is known primarily as the author of *The Alexandria Quartet,* a tetralogy of novels widely considered to be among the finest achievements in twentieth-century fiction. Continuing in the tradition of James Joyce and D. H. Lawrence, Durrell experiments with the structure of the novel while also probing the human psyche. His work is infused with observations on the nature of reality and sexuality, based in part on the theories of Albert Einstein and Sigmund Freud. In *The Alexandria Quartet,* for example, Durrell employs the Einsteinian notion of space-time continuum to explore the elusive nature of truth and the potential for an infinite number of ways to approach the same material. His novels often feature a number of characters with varied interests, enabling Durrell to examine and contrast different cultural and philosophical ideas. Durrell's baroque, sensuous prose style and his vivid description of landscape have been highly praised.

Born in India to Anglo-Irish parents, Durrell was sent away from the Himalayan region of his childhood at age eleven for schooling in England. During the 1930s, he initiated correspondence with Henry Miller, whose erotic novels greatly influenced Durrell's work. Following Miller's advice, Durrell published *The Black Book* (1938) in Paris after it had failed to pass British obscenity regulations. Regarded as Durrell's first accomplished work, *The Black Book* protests the sterility of English society, which he termed ''the English Death.'' By this time, Durrell had abandoned England for the Greek island of Corfu and has since lived and worked in several areas near the Mediterranean Sea. These locales figure prominently in Durrell's fiction and poetry and in his admired trilogy of island books: *Prospero's Cell: A Guide to the Landscape and Manners of the Island of Corcyra* (1945), *Reflections on a Marine Venus: A Companion to the Landscape of Rhodes* (1953), and *Bitter Lemons* (1957), whose subject is the island of Cyprus. During World War II, Durrell served in the British Diplomatic Corps as a press attaché; his experiences are related in his satirical *Antrobus* stories, which feature the title character's exploits as a British diplomat. These stories, which were published in several volumes, are collected in *Antrobus Complete* (1985).

Durrell had originally planned to be a poet, but his voluminous output of verse has met with mixed critical reaction. As evidenced in *Collected Poems, 1931-1974* (1980), Durrell's poetry blends the sensuousness of the Mediterranean world with traditional lyric forms of the West in an attempt, in his words, to ''match passion and clarity.'' Durrell's verse plays, *Sappho* (1959), *Acte* (1962), and *An Irish Faustus* (1963), are based on myths and legends and adhere to classical dramatic principles. Written in blank verse, these works explore the ways in which the pursuit of knowledge is hindered by traditional beliefs.

Although Durrell's early novels met with little success, he developed through them the techniques which won him acclaim and recognition with *The Alexandria Quartet.* Composed of *Justine* (1957), *Balthazar* (1958), *Mountolive* (1959), and *Clea* (1960), the tetralogy offers several perspectives on events which involve essentially the same characters. The protagonist, Darley, is a novelist; like the many other artists in Durrell's fiction, Darley attempts through art to rework reality in order to find patterns of significance and meaning in a world devoid of philosophical absolutes. The experimental structure of the novels reveals the subjective nature of reality. While *The Alexandria Quartet* was faulted by some critics for the decadence and violence it portrays, others admired Durrell's evocation of the exoticism of Alexandria, Egypt.

In his next two novels, *Tunc* (1968) and *Nunquam* (1970), known together as *The Revolt of Aphrodite*, Durrell employs science fiction techniques to examine modern cultural values in relation to capitalism and technology. Durrell next created the ambitious *Avignon Quintet,* comprising *Monsieur; or, The Prince of Darkness* (1974), *Livia; or, Buried Alive* (1979), *Constance; or, Solitary Practices* (1982), *Sebastian; or, Ruling Passions* (1984), and *Quinx; or, The Ripper's Tale* (1985). Arranged as a quincunx, these novels echo the successful multivolume strategy of interrelated books of *The Alexandria Quartet.* However, as Graham Hough notes, ''What we have [in the *Avignon Quintet*] is not a story told from different viewpoints, but duplicated themes and situations, the same motifs working themselves out with different characters.'' Through a large cast of characters from different professions and cultural backgrounds, Durrell explores themes related to Eastern and Western religions and philosophies as well as sexuality and the art of writing fiction.

(See also *CLC,* Vols. 1, 4, 6, 8, 13, 27; *Contemporary Authors,* Vols. 9-12, rev. ed.; and *Dictionary of Literary Biography,* Vols. 15, 27.)

CAROL RUMENS

Lawrence Durrell, as the baroque architect among modern novelists, is still adding elaborate extensions to the palace that he began with *Justine,* the first book of the *Alexandria Quartet.* *Sebastian* is the fourth book of the 'quincunx' that is his current project, the term 'quincunx' designating the spatial, rather than chronological, arrangement that he employs, and which is one of his most intriguing innovations.

The new novel shows Durrell's wonderfully mythic imagination still deeply engaged with matters Alexandrian, and not altogether at ease with the modern, or at least post-war, *Zeitgeist* which it is now seeking to absorb. (Psychoanalysis, itself perhaps a myth, is more easily accommodated.) 'Surely the insidious goblins of love had ceased to exist on the thin moral fare offered by the modern world?' worries Sebastian Affad, but it is merely a rhetorical question. Playing a dual role as Constance's lover and as disciple of a gnostic sect devoted to the 'primal trauma' (i.e. death), Affad embodies the spirit of old Egypt against which Constance, the would-be rationalist, is powerless in the traditional romantic way. The depth of her involvement with the past is symbolised by the 'new' scent she uses—and whose smell helps bring about the cure of Affad's autistic son—Justine's *Jamais de la Vie.*

There are difficulties for the reader in taking this novel as a self-contained entity. A knowledge of the preceding novels is required to flesh out the minor characters in particular; and for an incomparably vivid evocation of Alexandria itself it is necessary to turn back to *Justine.* As always, there are queasy moments when the high style gets above itself: 'She felt the wild pang of her lover's absence like a knife-thrust in the loins.' But there are also the usual striking set-pieces and individual portraits. Mnemidis, a wily paranoid schizophrenic, is particularly memorable in his disguise as a nun 'with a face full of unhealthy confessional secrets,' listening ecstatically to Strauss and Delibes while 'his fingers caressed the forms of the knives which lay so quietly obedient upon his thighs.' Such passages concentrate the essence of Durrell's imagination; its romanticism and its fascination with violence, its tactile precision and freakish wit. When Eros or Thanatos rule the narrative the results are usually impressive; it is the more philosophical flights that seem strained.

> Carol Rumens, "Eros and Thanatos in Alex," in The Observer, *October 23, 1983, p. 32.*

VALENTINE CUNNINGHAM

[*Sebastian or Ruling Passions,* the] fourth volume in Lawrence Durrell's fine Avignon or Provençal quintet is still a fiction of the middle of things; but only just. It begins at an end-point, at the end of the Second World War, with the smooth assembly of key units of a now familiar cast, the Prince, Affad, Constance, Felix Chatto, the writers Blanford and Sutcliffe. In the company of other survivors from previous volumes they're despatched to Geneva for sorting out, almost like the mails (and, indeed, one key strand of this novel concerns what happens to a letter sent to Affad in Geneva), before being posted on at the end to Avignon, there to await the Durrellian Last Things, in his and their final tome. The narrative's pace and inventiveness are flagging not at all. No signs of wear and tear are visible. In fact, verve and dash seem to be increasing as Durrell sniffs the final straight. But still, this is the penultimate volume, and tidying and tying up have evidently begun.

Not that you should expect things that were previously a bit murky to be made specially clearer hereabouts. The Prince and Affad are still heavily into a set of gnostic practices and Manichaean beliefs whose doctrinal outlines never got rescued from obscurity in earlier volumes, and don't get clarified much here. The novelists Blanford and Sutcliffe are still occasionally made the occasion of some Chinese-boxing in the cause of fictional self-reflectiveness. But *Sebastian* is simpler than its predecessors. For a start the cast has thinned and continues in *Sebastian* to thin out, which makes the visibility somewhat clearer. What's more, Durrell has by and large stopped trying to fill us in on the details of the Egyptian hermetic arcana. And he has also largely abandoned modish narratology-within-narrative and goes in here for what he's still astonishingly good at—an older-fashioned brand of storytelling. And all this simplifying isn't at all disagreeble in its effects.

Doctrinal subjects haven't, of course, gone away altogether. The debate, for instance, between Affad's Eastern, Greekish cultism and Constance's Western psychiatric medicine is still being vigorously mounted. But the ideas and the mongers of ideas are being continually forced to give place to the enactments, the practical results of ideas. Jewish idealists, Christian theologians, all sorts of mystical bags of tricks, come in for a good deal of scathing, especially from Constance's colleague Dr Schwarz. He can't stand Jewish talkers, or jargonizers or Left Bank intellectuals and all their ilk. (He singles out for dispraise Lacan as well as Sartre—which makes him in 1945 a pretty well-read shrink.) And what beliefs do to people is now the central issue. The chickens are coming home to roost. The murderous Mnemidis stokes up the novel's distresses on reading from Constance's copy of the Bible. Affad's cultic death-wishes end in something no reader has trouble understanding: his death. The autistic son of Affad and poor demented Lily (we see her as an aphasic hermit shut away in a Coptic monastery, and eventually hear tell of her as a skeletal survivor of a death-camp), a boy whose mental state has made a grim emblem of the earlier novels' labyrinthine complexities, is brought back to tears, smiles and speech through Constance's ministrations. And not because of any bookish wisdoms or acquired psychiatric skills, but because she chances to start wearing Lily's brand of perfume (*Jamais de la Vie* it's called, with some pointfulness).

Deaths accumulate in this novel against a background of wider wartime horrors. Criminal violence is all about. But Durrell's tone remains astonishingly unoppressed and unoppressive. It's as if this central resurrection of Affad's son into fuller humanness, and the light and love of Constance's surrogate mothering, prove pervasively redemptive. Death-camps, murder, suicide, become much more bearable in its vicinity. Suddenly, and without the previous ponderous accumulations of theological luggage, what Affad's and his cronies' wish to confront death might be all about, seems to come clear. After grief and death, resurrection and life. The quincunx turns into a kind of divine comedy. Or just a comedy. At any rate a comedy of Durrell's own kind, unsentimental, blasphemous possibly, marvellously loud-mouthed in its sustained scurrility.

Sebastian has at least five great narrative set-pieces. Again and again one is made think that Durrell really can tell a story, and command his narrative tone. . . .

[What] incites admiration is his variety of touch, his refusal to settle oppressively into a single register, mode or mood, which have never been better demonstrated than here. And it's a demonstration, in effect, of the necessity, survival and continuing power of language and fictions—his own and his characters'. Words and texts are, of course, shown to have their problems in this novel as elsewhere in the quincunx. Intellectuals are just contriving a Babel, we're told. Several times the complaint is made of philosophy that it is destroying itself in a vain semanticity. Constance meditates at the end on the feebleness of language to "circumscribe the inexpressible bitterness of death and separation. And love, if you wish." But "Mr Schwarz he dead", a black stretcher-bearer reports, still clinging in that awful moment to words. And to texts, for his line is sunk into somebody's reading of Conrad even at so grievous, so silencing a moment. It's an instructive as well as a greatly moving effect.

> Valentine Cunningham, "After Grief and Death," in The Times Literary Supplement, No. 4204, October 28, 1983, p. 1184.

HARRIETT GILBERT

One suicide, two knifings and one mock crucifixion, in a brothel, occur in the course of Lawrence Durrell's new novel. Whatever their relevance to plot, character or theme, they do at least jolt the reader awake from the tired old springs and loose, frayed webbing of everything else in *Sebastian.*

Durrell's prose can batter the senses with its beauty. In this fourth part of his 'quincunx', it sags with clichés and repetitions and meaningless, verbal space-fillers. Exclamation marks stagger to the rescue, but fail to add excitement to the desultory doings and half-baked thinkings of Constance—whose psychiatric methods have developed a B-movie ludicrousness; of Affad (Sebastian), her Gnostic lover, whose pursuit of death one would like to encourage; of Schwarz; of the Prince; of Lord Galen; or of any of the rest of that curiously drifting, expatriate, dilettante gang—whose lives we take up where the last volume ended, in Geneva, at the end of World War II.

The 'quincunx' attempts to synthesise the dualisms of West/East, Ego/Id, Male/Female, Creator/Created, etc. This thematic ambition has always exceeded its author's intellectual concentration—in *Sebastian,* it has also exhausted his sensual imagination. One passage only, in which Lord Galen rampages, on behalf of the governments of Europe, in search of a post-war 'culture'—'It's all very well to suggest, as someone did, that we might get a book like this *Ulysses* rewritten in a more acceptable and forward-looking manner by someone like Beverley Nicholls . . .'—is alive with Durrell's precocious-adolescent flair. The rest is an unconvincing and unconvinced bluff.

> Harriett Gilbert, "Uses of Literacy," in New Statesman, Vol. 106, No. 2747, November 11, 1983, p. 30.

GRAHAM HOUGH

It is not the easiest thing to discuss a novel that is the fourth of a series of five. *Sebastian* is not properly intelligible without an acquaintance with its predecessors, *Monsieur* (1974), *Livia* (1978), *Constance* (1982); and the ultimate destination, if there is to be one, is not yet visible. As it happened, I read them in the wrong order, but such is the vitality and attack of Durrell's writing that it hardly mattered. Enter them anywhere and one is sucked into the stream.

The series is called a 'quincunx', which suggests a fifth central element tying the whole pattern together. For that we must wait and see. The structure at first recalls that of the *Alexandria Quartet*, but this is a mistake. What we have here is not the same story retold from different viewpoints, but duplicated themes and situations, the same motifs working themselves out with different characters. Two siblings deeply involved with each other and a third person who loves them both; homosexuality, especially among women; mental breakdown, especially among women; suicide, or (which is not the same thing) voluntarily accepted death—these all recur with an ominous regularity that is not that of realistic narrative. Yet if you require a novel to be one entire and perfect chrysolite in the Henry James manner, Durrell is a non-starter. His fiction is made up of wildly different elements which there is no attempt to harmonise. He has ebullient moods and phases, and he wants to get them all in. There are the great descriptive set-pieces, often motivated by the spirit of place—here Egypt and Provence: Christmas in a crumbling chateau near Avignon, a ride across the desert, a boat journey up the Nile. Such passages in the Alexandria series were sometimes frowned on as over-luscious, but they are not so here. They remind us that Durrell began his career as a poet, and they bring in an element of poetry that the dusty shop-window of the English novel has not seen for a long time. There are the surrealist-erotic episodes, Durrell the farcical pornographer in the Henry Miller manner. Opinions may vary, but for myself a little of this goes a long way. There are reflective and speculative interludes, on the nature of art and the conduct of life. Recurrently through the series the doctrines of a certain Gnostic sect are discussed and partly expounded—to what effect is not yet wholly apparent. Their central tenet is that the good God has been dethroned and the government of the world usurped by a malign impostor—a doctrine not difficult to sustain, but as with most Gnostic sects, it is not clear what we are expected to do about it. Then, like a train coming out of a tunnel, we find stretches of straight historical-social narrative: a picture of the French Midi during the German occupation, for example.

Freud is a considerable presence throughout—not swallowed whole, but acknowledged as an essential interpreter of our state. Happily it is the square old Freud we learnt at our mother's knee—infantile sexuality and the family imbroglio—not the deranged semiotician lately invented by the French. And since *Constance,* the protagonist of the last two volumes, is a clinical psychiatrist, the Freudian reflections are firmly built into the narrative. Elsewhere it must be admitted there are lapses. The Henry-Millerish episodes can sink into bar-room smut, the speculative musings into yoga for beginners. There is some by-play of a rather Nouveau Roman variety by which the personages of the story are represented as each other's imaginary creations. Two of the characters are novelists, and one of them starts life simply as a 'character' in one of the other's books. But he later takes his place on equal terms with the rest of the cast, and is no less substantial. This bit of bafflement is little more than a decoy to lure the unwary into Pseuds' Corner; but at least it touches with an engagingly light hand on some recent critical worries; and it leads to a brilliantly witty dialogue between the author and his creature in the first fifty pages of *Livia*. Or, as you might prefer to put it, the occultation of the proairetic code foregrounds by its intertextual reference the multi-level fictionality of the metanarrative text.

There is a tendency in the austerer literary circles to regard Durrell as a slightly obsolete, over-theatrical decorative painter, a sort of Frank Brangwyn of the novel. Every reader may well find something to make him bristle in these pages, but where we don't like it we had better lump it. Otherwise we shall be missing a great deal: missing a last lingering regard, from a very odd angle, on some odd but representative corners of the old world, Europe and the Near East, with its inherited squalors and grandeurs, its richness of feeling, and its decay—before the last war delivered it over finally to the hypermarkets, the word-processors and the terrorists. For all their complex interconnections, each volume has its own centre, and sufficient integrity to function independently. *Sebastian* is largely a pendant to *Constance,* and carries a huge load of retrospect, hard to hold together in the mind and impossible to summarise, but it has two new themes of its own, one touching, the other tingling with suspense. The scene is principally Geneva, and the central thread is the relation of Constance with her enigmatic lover Affad, which now seems threatened. The new themes are the healing by Constance of Affad's autistic child, and her simultaneous treatment of a dangerous criminal psychopath. Neither of these has any roots in the previous complex of episodes, yet they seem to arise out of it, surprising but inevitable, like most of Durrell's prolific inventions. These novels forego the support of portraying a settled society. The characters are mostly transients and immigrants in the places where they find themselves. Their loyalties and affections are directed to a few kinsfolk or a small group: but for all the betrayals and violent disorders of feeling, they have loyalties and affections. There is a range and freedom that we do not find among the pinched ironies of much contemporary fiction.

> *Graham Hough, "Auld Lang Syne," in* London Review of Books, *Vol. 5, Nos. 22 & 23, December 1 to December 21, 1983, p. 14.*

WILLIAM BOYD

Without doubt *Sebastian* is the least successful of the four novels in the [*Avignon*] sequence so far published, and there are, it seems to me, a number of contributing factors that explain this deficiency. First, the balance of moods is singularly uneasy. The novel skips maladroitly from vein-throbbing romantic lyricism through turgid pontificating to a kind of high-camp grand-guignol. And when these ungainly tones of voice are combined with the hermetic obscurities of the quincunx form, the uninitiated reader is left very much in the dark. Reading the preceding volumes does admittedly make things somewhat clearer, but behind the (as it were) *ad hoc* difficulties lurks the more general metafictional tricksiness.... Apart from the various levels of fiction (is this Durrell's, Blandford's, or Sutcliffe's novel? Is this Durrell writing a book about a man writing a book about a man writing a book?), the original cast we encountered in *Monsieur* is transmogrified into other char-

acters about and around whom other stories revolve. To take one example: at the end of *Sebastian* Constance meets Sylvie again. Sylvie is mad and is also the eponymous Livia of novel two. Moreover, she believes that Constance has been away in India and when they meet she utters words that echo a paragraph from the opening pages of *Monsieur,* words which she wrote in a letter to her brother Piers. What possible significance can this have? Or is it nothing more than an indication of the "organic" relationship between the novels?

Perhaps it is premature and a little obtuse to seek to understand and make demands of a work still missing its final part, but the interconnections between the novels of the quintet seem of an entirely different order than that of its sibling, *The Alexandria Quartet.* There the multilayers and time sequences served a valid narrative role, the relativity of viewpoints nicely revealing psychological truths and ambiguities. But in the quincunx, the suspicion emerges that in the web the spider spins here complexity is being indulged in purely for its own sake—clever, glittering, intricate, but without any real strength.

Durrell, doubtless, would see this sort of reaction as typical—given the nationality of this reviewer, typically British. And to some degree his published assessments of his own critical reception in England are just. Durrell's books—raffish, vaguely decadent novels of ideas—don't sit particularly happily within any broad English tradition. His dandiness, his ornate verbal facility, his paraded symbols, and his dallying with esoteric philosophies—all ally him more with the French, with writers like Huysmans, say, or Baudelaire. (p. 34)

I have never shared the condescending put-downs of *The Alexandria Quartet* and have always admired Durrell's pointed rejection of Little-Englishness and his exuberant internationalism. For all that, however, *Sebastian* takes only a few pages to become bogged down in its own pretentiousness.... There are pages and pages ... of unreadable leaden dialogue as Durrell remorselessly compels his characters to thrash out their theories on Gnosticism, entropy, the Primal Trauma of Death, and so on. Grand ideas, admittedly, but hardly the stuff of engaging or compelling fiction, especially when presented in such unadulterated style. (pp. 34-5)

I suspect that when we are finally presented with the full set we will applaud Durrell's tireless invention and energy and particularly admire the Blandford/Sutcliffe relationship. Whenever these two are the focus of attention the books come alive, and *Sebastian* suffers from their being too little present. Without them, its tone is either toilingly verbose, romantic-insipid, or simply ludicrous.... [The] flaws of *Sebastian* might not be so apparent, but, set out on the floor on its own, it appears a distinctly rickety piece of work. (p. 35)

> *William Boyd, "Strung Quintet," in* The New Republic, *Vol. 190, No. 16, April 23, 1984, pp. 33-5.*

PETER KEMP

The fifth volume of Lawrence Durrell's *Avignon Quintet,* **Quinx** is intended as the one in which everything at last adds up. What in the earlier books—*Monsieur, Livia, Constance, Sebastian*—seemed disparate units are now to be made to tally. Things in the narrative may still look at sixes and sevens, but Durrell divulges that the solution to all problems is the number five.

The mystic significance of this digit is resoundingly stressed. 'The power of five,' we're told, 'is the riddle of the Quinx.'

In keeping with this, attention is emphatically drawn to 'the five senses, the five arts', 'the five-sided truth about human personality'. It's in the fifth chapel of a church that a crucial meeting occurs which leads to the long-deferred discovery of the Templars' treasure, that glittering goal sought throughout this five-novel sequence: the charismatic cache, it emerges, is hidden under the Pont du Gard in quincunx-shaped caves, for 'in architecture the quincunxial shape is considered a sort of housing for the divine power.'

This numinous numerology, along with a kind of esoteric eroticism, is revealed as the most valuable haul the Templars brought back from their sojourn in the East: their 'real treasure was the Grail, the lotus of insight'. Though the book ends with millionaire Lord Galen leading his troop of treasure-trackers into the warren of caves below the Pont du Gard (where, characteristically, the trove is guarded by a network of bombs and booby-traps governed by 'five master-keys or detonators'), we never learn what is unearthed. For Durrell's point is that none of the possible material rewards have any real substance; it is the spiritual largesse which his more enlightened seekers have found during their quest that matters.

It is doubtful, though, whether any particularly rich gains have been garnered by those readers who have patiently followed the mazy convolutions of these five books. Even the supposedly epitomising aphorisms and keys to magic mathematics with which this last volume is littered seem—though flashy—profitless. . . . (p. 31)

In *Quinx,* by dint of the therapeutic massage and yogic discipline she learnt from an Egyptian lover in an earlier volume, [the character Constance] eventually kneads Blanford—the book's novelist-figure—back to supple vitality. Durrell's treatment of this and of the couple's ensuing ecstasies is, however, curiously unwieldy and heavy-handed—like so much of this novel. Loitering through dissertations on its gnostic nostrums, *Quinx* then lurches awkwardly across its narrative stretches. Even a climactic scene such as that where Blanford saves the symbolically cramped Constance from drowning is recounted with almost comic lameness.

Peopling these technicolour tableaux are Durrell's usual band of gaudy two-dimensionals: a fabulously priapic amputee, gorgeous blonde bisexuals, saturnine dark geniuses, a Cambridge graduate turned Romany seer, a magnate of Croesus-like wealth. Inserted into the story at intervals, too, are sadistic little scenarios of a type his fiction has always favoured—such as the hunting down and tearing apart by hounds of a young gipsy and her baby. Conducting this atrocity gives one man an orgasm; hearing about it leaves another 'quite pale with lust'.

This combination of sex and savagery strikes a *fin-de-siècle* note—as do other aspects of *Quinx*. The language is sometimes tinged with preciosity—'tintinnabulous belfries', 'Lips uncials of sweet compliance'. There is a relish—like that of the Decadents—for recherché words and cabbalistic creeds. Durrell's palette is thickly encrusted with period tints—'mauve sands', 'skies of old rose and madder'. And he has a turn-of-the-century enthusiasm for Gothic frisson, doppelgängers, artifice and the perverse. (p. 32)

> Peter Kemp, "*Five Sides and Two Dimensions,*" in *The Listener, Vol. 113, No. 2911, May 30, 1985, pp. 31-2.*

KEITH BROWN

Quinx completes Lawrence Durrell's Avignon "quincunx" (five interrelated novels, not forming a continuous sequence) and is also the last of the dozen novels by which he has said that he would wish to be remembered: *The Black Book,* the *Alexandria Quartet, Tunc* and *Nunquam,* and the Avignon books. Durrell's career has brought him international celebrity, but also the persistent scepticism of the London literary world: and thereby hangs our tale, for neither the quincunx nor the proud epigraph to its concluding volume ("must itself create the taste by which it is to be judged") will be rightly appraised if the grounds for Durrell's resigned impatience with that scepticism are not grasped.

The quincunx novels (*Quinx* itself is effectively an appendix to the series, and cannot well be independently discussed) are set mainly in the late 1930s and the following decade, and present a rather classy set of young professional people—doctor, diplomat, don, novelist, psychoanalyst, etc, all sexually entangled—and their shadow-doubles. The full supporting cast includes Catholic Nazi General, Egyptian Prince, Jewish Plutocrat Peer, and (in *Quinx*) hundreds of gypsies. *Constance,* the numerically central volume, makes a rather worrying effort to fit the moral and psychological facts of the Nazi horror into our picture of the era, but also depicts a triumphant *affaire* between the psychoanalyst Constance and Affad, an Egyptian gnostic. Affad's fusion of sexual gifts with mystical insight, fertilizing Constance's own Freudian training, carries her far beyond Freud to a deeper, if still half-intuitive vision of what genuinely healthy human relationships—whether overtly sexual or not—should really mean. This vision, essentially identical with the sex-mysticism associated with more than one Asian faith, is the only therapy that Durrell can prescribe for that sickness-of-the-soul in our civilization of which atom bombs and Nazi atrocities are merely the most dramatic symptoms. At one level his aim in these volumes, in short, is no less than that which Chesterton credited to Dickens: to change the world by changing the expression on the face of mankind. Yet his fable is no *folie de grandeur:* he knows the difficulty, obscurity and remoteness of the hope he offers, just as he knows that the East, for all its mystical wisdoms, can be as spiritually ugly as the West. . . .

[A] conventional résumé of the quincunx would . . . be absurd: the work is a reviewer's minefield, deliberately sown. . . . Normal novel-reading expectations are aroused repeatedly, only to be led gently into a bog: thus the cod climax of *Quinx* does not actually bring us to the Templar treasure, which now seems to represent True Reality. Not that this will prevent the reader enjoying yet another assemblage of Durrell's enamelled descriptions, exalted sex-mysticism, glimpses of ancient wisdom and running psycho-chatter: so who need worry that the connective tissue this time seems so oddly weak? Yet why that spiky epigraph?

Doubtless most writers feel that critics never do them justice, but in some respects Durrell has undeniably been the victim of an irony in the history of modern literary criticism. Now that historical irony has been repaid by a sort of serious practical joke. There has always been in him a vein of unremitting philosophical curiosity about the way literature works, concealed by the fun that wells from his belief in the novelist as *homo ludens*. Thus much scornful ink was once poured on his cheerful analogy between the *Quartet* and the Einsteinian space-time continuum; that the *Quartet* is virtually a literary laboratory, trying out one good question after another, was less frequently remarked. (What happens to the autonomy of the text, for example, when *Balthazar* shows the narrator of *Justine* to have been as aware of its *Rebecca*-like limitations as we are?) *Tunc* and *Nunquam*, behind much else, are a sort of field-test of Renaissance literary theory. Whether or not this vein of literary reflectiveness makes Durrell a better novelist than already supposed, it does make him a rather different one. Ironically, too, his career has coincided with a period in English criticism when we (leaving aside social comedies) have steadily required of new English novels—though not of American, nor of the great names of our own past—that tightly "organic" or crystalline quality that the New Criticism loved. This critical primness has been unjust to any gifted writer like Durrell (again, in this respect at least, comparable to Dickens) who needs to be allowed room to write badly if he is also to write well.

But now, after decades of being addressed by the censors as if he were someone else, Durrell has simply blown up the Examination Halls. In recent years he has found his way into a growing involvement with Tibetan Buddhism, whose metaphysic genuinely rejects that hard-edged, materialist, ego-centred Western world view of which the novel is perhaps our clearest literary reflection. Is it, then, possible to write a "Tibetan" novel—that is to say, a new, more fluid, open-ended kind of fiction, still recognizable to novel-readers though largely shedding the usual assumptions of the genre? The quincunx is Durrell's attempt to find out, or at least, by breaking down, gently, our normal novel-reading expectations, to open our minds to the possibility of a fiction based on a radically different metaphysic. I am not sure the attempt succeeds, nor how far what is envisaged could ever in practice differ from, say, a mistier version of the usual anti-novel, or attempts to bring fiction closer to the condition of music. Yet the reader will have missed something who fails to follow Durrell, if at times over patches of slightly stony ground, up to that Pisgah-sight. Some of the non-philosophical jokes are very nice too.

Keith Brown, "Up to the Pisgah-Sight," in The Times Literary Supplement, *No. 4287, May 31, 1985, p. 597.*

PATRICK PARRINDER

Quinx or The Ripper's Tale concludes a sequence consisting of *Monsieur or The Prince of Darkness, Livia or Buried Alive, Constance or Solitary Practices* and *Sebastian or Ruling Passions*. This series of novels-with-two-titles, containing characters with variable names and fluctuating identities, is (as we should expect) suffused with radical ambiguity. The *Avignon Quintet* which Durrell has now completed is an enigmatic and secretive work, a cluster of dark passages and gaudy treasure-filled caves beside the thrusting baroque edifice of his earlier *Alexandria Quartet*. The very titles of the 'quincunx of novels' terminated by *Quinx* confirm this sense of Durrell having gone underground. At the same time, his art is undiminished in scale, in inventive gusto and fictive extravagance. Durrell remains unrepentantly committed to the view that a classical fiction for our age can only emerge out of formal experimentation—in this case, the pursuit of 'soft focus palimpsest' in place of the 'linear' novel of the 19th century. Where the *Alexandria Quartet* referred back to Einstein and Proust, the comic anarchy of the *Avignon* novels is post-Joyce, post-Pynchon and post-Flann O'Brien.

In terms of subject-matter, Durrell has a shrewd eye for the sensational. Readers of the *Avignon Quintet* can steep themselves in the secrets of the Templars, gypsy forklore, Nazi atrocities, the mysteries of the sperm, sexual yoga, and the rituals of an Egyptian Gnostics' suicide club, without any of the vulgarity of solutions, explanations or no-holds-barred investigations to be found in pseudo-historical best-sellers and popular journalism. Durrell's ideal of the novel is one of *haute cuisine* with great quantities of pepper and garlic, and the brew that results is more highly-flavoured than that of any other contemporary English novelist—a feature that sometimes reminds us of Dickens. The difference lies not in the ingredients of the brew but in the fact that the spirits do not always come when Durrell calls them.

At bottom, the *Avignon Quintet* is a deliberate romance, with a Holy Grail, a magic circle or Round Table of characters equipped for the quest, and a threat of apocalyptic destruction regardless of whether the quest succeeds or fails. There are several allusions to the Arthurian story, and a major concern is the history of the Templars, whose legendary Grand Masters were to Languedoc and Provence what Arthur is to Wessex. One aspect of Durrell's ambiguous Grail consists—as befits a banned author of the Thirties and a former associate of Henry Miller—of 'love-lore' or the secrets of sex. These, which have something to do with 'dual control' in the love-act and simultaneous orgasm, are passed down from master or mistress to hand-picked pupil in certain rare and long-delayed bouts of sexual intercourse. The characters of Durrell's charmed circle work through many of the possible erotic combinations with one another, but only the favoured few join the inner ranks of the sexual magi. Those who do, convinced of 'the existence of lovers as philosophers', tend to wax eloquent about it. Sometimes, we are told in *Quinx,* this makes them a bit of a bore. It is nice to think that their author has noticed.

Another aspect of Durrell's Grail is that it embodies the secrets of novel-writing, of producing a work of art which (again, as we are told in *Quinx*) 'should show high contrivance as well as utter a plea for bliss'. This quest is pursued by means of facetious dialogues between two would-be novelists, Sutcliffe and Blanford, one of them supposedly the other's creation, and both a curious blend of Oscar Wilde, Peter Pan and *l'homme moyen sensuel*. The mist of uncertain identity which shrouds Sutcliffe and Blanford radiates out to the other members of the charmed circle. *Monsieur,* like *Justine* at the commencement of the *Alexandria Quartet,* must now be regarded as a hoax-novel offering a compellingly melodramatic but wholly misleading introduction to the characters and themes of the series as a whole. Akkad, the Gnostic seer in *Monsieur,* later appears as Affad or Sebastian, an Egyptian banker whose story implies a Manichaean struggle between eros and thanatos, or procreation and suicide. *Constance,* the mid-point of the *Quintet,* is named after Durrell's principal female character, a sober and capable psychoanalyst: but Constance is unable to impart sanity or constancy to the others. Her place at the centre of the quincunx is that of a beleaguered queen whose companions and courtiers, including such carnival creations as the millionaire Lord Galen and the gypsy sibyl Sabine, are for the most part dedicated to maximising anarchy.

The charmed circle or square of the *Avignon Quintet* may be said to include all Durrell's characters—those to whom he has given names. That is, the bond of naming proves stronger than merely human hatred or enmity. The novels span the years of the Second World War and the Nazi occupation of France, with *Quinx* supposedly set immediately after the war's end. Extremes of murder, torture and insanity in the earlier novels have not sufficed to alienate Durrell's characters permanently from one another. In *Quinx* there is a series of unlikely reconciliations of old enemies, including Nazi officers and supporters of the Resistance. Hatred, for these characters, is simply the inevitable obverse of love, so that to be beyond the reach of reconciliation and blood-fellowship is to remain anonymous.

Quinx takes in a grand celebration of blood-fellowship in the form of the first post-war gypsy festival at Les Saintes Maries de la Mer in the Camargue. Durrell gives no hint that those who gather there must be the lucky survivors of persecution and the death-camps: this would tend to undermine the general atmosphere of bonhomie. Constance and her companions go down to the Camargue in a hired bus crammed with 'hampers of elaborate food and wine', which give the trip 'the allure of a scouts' picnic'. This is not the only occasion when Durrell seems to be reducing life to the level of schoolboy japes. . . .

Orgy and feasting, the revelry that turns sour, and the intimate connection of *petite* and *grande mort* are, here as elsewhere, Durrell's specialities. *Quinx* (like *Livia*) ends with a banqueting scene beneath the Pont du Gard, prior to the opening-up of the Templar treasure—an ending indicative of the author's Pied Piper's view of the narrative art and his sense of the novel itself as a treasure-chest. . . . [As] G. S. Fraser once put it, Durrell combines a 'delicate mastery of his craft' with effects sometimes 'insolently and boldly shoddy'. Such a paradox is already implied in the double title (not, I think, a title and subtitle) *Quinx or The Ripper's Tale*. The Ripper may be the Bulgarian count, he may be Sutcliffe (referred to on one occasion as 'the old Ripper'), Blanford who is supposedly Sutcliffe's creator, or possibly others among Durrell's cast of characters, who all belong to the fellowship of the rippers, the ripping and the ripped. (Or, of course, he may be Durrell himself.) The title "The Ripper's Tale" is, in fact, a floating signifier which short-circuits the cognitive function of naming. It is one of the built-in redundancies of a profuse and intricate text which, like a Pynchon novel, abounds in systemicity holding out the—constantly deferred, and perpetually subverted—promise of an overarching system. Sutcliffe in *Quinx* has some unkind and contemptuous remarks about the American novel, which Pynchon presumably exemplifies: but that is all part of the magician's patter and bluster. (pp. 22-3)

Patrick Parrinder, "Naming of Parts," in London Review of Books, *Vol. 7, No. 10, June 6, 1985, pp. 22-3.*

JOSEPH CARUSO

Readers of the four previous novels of *The Avignon Quintet* will be compelled to go on to *Quinx,* which completes what Lawrence Durrell calls his quincunx: an arrangement of five objects so placed that four occupy the corners and the fifth the center. Durrell's admirers should prepare—after the fairly straightforward narratives of *Monsieur, Livia, Constance,* and *Sebastian*—for an exuberant potpourri of conflicting themes and vignettes, dozens of characters, and a plot that builds to what is, finally, an inconclusive end. Those who have not read the four previous novels probably need to do so.

Like his 25-year-old *Alexandria Quartet, The Avignon Quintet* displays Durrell's masterly, and masterful, artistry—as well as his preoccupation with the sexual act and its relation to unattainable love, a preoccupation that goes back 50 years to *The Black Book.* But even with the other four novels framing it, *Quinx* is frustrating. Most annoyingly, the quintet's plot has

been usurped almost entirely by abstract musings about how to make The Novel.

These speculations seem no more integrated with the narrative for having been shoved into the mouths of the characters Aubrey Blanford and Robin Sutcliffe, two novelists who create each other, each the other's doppelganger. (Who created whom becomes intentionally unclear.) Here is Blanford, repeating "to his own mind, 'I dream of writing of an unbearable felicity. I want to saturate my text with my teleological distress yet guard its slapstick holiness as something precious. To pierce the lethargy, indolence and distress of my soul.'" One wishes Durrell actually had done in *Quinx* some of the provocative things his characters keep suggesting a novelist can, and should, do.

In *Quinx* the plot of the quintet jerks to an anticlimactic finish. Lord Galen leads a long search for the Templar treasure, a cache—buried in Avignon during the 14th century by the heretical Knights Templar—that just might include the Holy Grail. A host of love-crossed characters joins him in his obsessive quest, which runs from just before until just after World War II, primarily in southern France. The characters' search for the treasure becomes as labyrinthine as their attempts to find love. (p. 9)

Certainly, Durrell uses the Templar treasure plot mainly to fuel the complicated relationships which he delights in unfolding. And he employs the scheme of multiple narrators as writers of novels within (and of) his own novel throughout the quintet. But in *Quinx,* the pretext of the plot's importance fades. And the once subtle narrative techniques grow obtrusive and silly. Durrell makes a joke out of the very things he took seriously for 1,400 pages. At last, just when the Templar treasure becomes as fascinating as it is near, Blanford transforms any discovery into the abstract "thought that if ever he wrote the scene he would say: 'It was at this precise moment that reality prime rushed to the aid of fiction and the totally unpredictable began to take place!'"

In *Quinx,* Durrell seems most of all to be exploring the Idea of the Novel. But he fails to do so by means of his characters. As Constance, much less individuated than previously in the quintet, is made to explain: "'We exist in five-skanda form, aggregates, parcels, lots, congeries. They cohere to form a human being when you come together and create the old force-field quinx, the five-sided being . . .'" She has been made a mouthpiece, as have the other characters, for Durrell's abstract expressions. Anyone in *Quinx* could have said Constance's, or nearly anyone else's, lines because all the characters' voices are similar; when they are not similar, they are the same. Durrell's names are interchangeable.

The Writer is a despot in *Quinx.* Narrative technique, plotted through characters who seek hidden love and treasure, has been reduced to a private jest. Durrell did not have to stop developing his plot and his characters to make the point that both love and treasure may be unattainable. *Quinx* possesses more of Durrell's flat assertions than it does of his elegant art.

Of course, the subtitle is "The Ripper's Tale." Durrell slashes his characters into shreds of frivolous dialogue about what a grand writer can or should do, instead of doing it himself. He has his laughs, and loses his story.

In the end, though, *Quinx*'s faults hardly matter. Lawrence Durrell may have failed to bring off the final volume of *The*

Avignon Quintet, but he remains a writer whose novels will be read as long as people care for books. (pp. 9, 13)

Joseph Caruso, *"Unravelling the Riddle of the Quinx,"* in Book World—The Washington Post, *September 1, 1985, pp. 9, 13.*

BARBARA FISHER WILLIAMSON

[In **Quinx,** the final volume of the *Avignon Quintet,*] all the characters who have not been killed and who have not lost their reason during [World War II] reunite in Avignon when it is over. They are a remarkable lot—two novelists, a psychoanalyst, a German double agent, a Cambridge-educated gypsy, a Jewish lord, a schizophrenic young woman and an Egyptian prince.

When the plot emerges from the interminable opening religio-literary-sexual-psycho babble of the two novelists, it centers on Constance, the psychoanalyst. In the course of the novel, she uncovers a nasty incest story about her brother and sister, finishes mourning a dead lover, gives up an infatuation with a former patient and finds at last her proper union. Bits of other plots straggle toward completion, and all join in what promises to be an illuminating and redemptive final act—the search for the oft-mentioned treasure of the Templars, a medieval Gnostic order of knights. The treasure is entombed in caves that are sacred to the gypsies and that were mined with baffling ingenuity by the Germans during the war. The caves have the shape of a quincunx, the four points of a square plus a single point at the center, which is considered a "sort of housing for the divine power," and which is also the shape formed by two conjoined human bodies. The shape, like the treasure, is teasingly referred to throughout the novels, but it never reveals its secrets.

Over and over again, patterns dissolve and systems fail. The psychoanalyst betrays professional ethics, a man whose death has been elegantly planned by the members of a death cult he belongs to is senselessly killed, the lovers who achieve mystical union never reproduce, and the novelists create this long joke of a book. The final sentence of the last volume of the quintet makes the whole 1,300-page cycle a shaggy dog story. As the narrator says toward the end, "There is no meaning and we falsify the truth about reality in adding one. *The universe is playing, the universe is only improvising!*" Another, more hilarious work of teleological distress, Rabelais's *Gargantua and Pantagruel,* ends with a similar anticlimax, when the long-sought-after oracle of the holy bottle speaks the single nonsense syllable "trinc." Although the truth never appears, the search is nonetheless worth the effort.

The sensual beauties of Mr. Durrell's text suggest a further similarity with Rabelais. Here, as in his famous *Alexandria Quartet*, Mr. Durrell writes descriptions that can take one's breath away. Avignon, ancient city of kings and popes, comes gloriously alive. The physical pleasures are the only ones that can be counted on in this world of teleological frustration.

The reliance on the physical is apparent in each volume, but the shaggy dog structure of the whole is impossible to detect if one reads only part. What makes the single volumes most perplexing is that the systems the different characters propose to give life meaning—Gnostic religion, Freudian analysis and mystical union through simultaneous orgasm—are described with such conviction and passion that they seem sufficient rather than provisional and flawed. Reading the theories in any one volume alone, one is tempted to think Mr. Durrell is silly. Reading them all, one is convinced he is wise.

Barbara Fisher Williamson, *"Links and Winks,"* in The New York Times Book Review, *September 15, 1985, p. 16.*

PUBLISHERS WEEKLY

How the diplomatic corps of the British Foreign Service—as portrayed in the loosely connected sketches collected in [*Antrobus Complete*]—managed to survive until now is one of those mysteries before which the mind boggles. Featuring amiable, deadpan loopy Antrobus as narrator and prototype ("we dips," he says in all innocence of himself and his colleagues), these tales of comic woe, small disasters, goofs, gaffes and misadventures from the ridiculous to the absurd depict the vaudeville of a government bureaucracy. How, for example, the dips could bring themselves to accept an invitation from the Kurdish Embassy to a circumcision (smelling salts, stiff upper lip, stiff drink and sheer courage) is still not fully clear. Durrell's aim is to amuse while he instructs, and he succeeds with unfailing good humor.

A review of *"Antrobus Complete,"* in Publishers Weekly, *Vol. 228, No. 15, October 11, 1985, p. 58.*

E. S. TURNER

Literary quiz question: which well-known novelist sends a susceptible American novelist to Egypt on leave with Lawrence Durrell's *The Alexandria Quartet* under his arm, and brings him back, thoroughly Muslimized, with a string of little black wives, saying "Durrell's right. Down there everything goes"? The answer, of course, is Lawrence Durrell, and the incident occurs in one of his rightly esteemed [stories contained in **Antrobus Complete**]. His cheek is to be admired as much as his resolve not to be awed by his own reputation. In these very funny "sketches from diplomatic life" he is like an air traffic controller who relaxes from juggling with jumbos by tossing round the light stuff, which can be even dodgier to handle.

The Antrobus tales first came out in enneads, to use a word airily thrown up by a Faber blurb-writer; that is, in sets of nine. In 1974 the three slender volumes *Esprit de Corps, Stiff Upper Lip* and *Sauve Qui Peut* were ransacked to produce the still-slender *The Best of Antrobus;* and now we have *Antrobus Complete,* by no means a damned thick book, though one ennead ahead of *The Best.* The first volume was dedicated to "the members of the Chancery, H.M. Embassy, Belgrade, 1951". Many of the adventures vouched for by the deprecatory Antrobus have a Balkan setting, suggestive of Evelyn Waugh's *Scott-King's Modern Europe.* Here are calamitous *vins d'honneur* and *trains d'honneur,* along with wanton manifestations of culture which, as Antrobus warns, can spread like mumps ("All culture corrupts, but French culture corrupts absolutely"). Yet it is a world of curious innocence; the Ambassador, Polk-Mowbray, is never called on to apologize for British soccer fans and nobody worries about defections and leaks. To be sure, there is a character called Ponting, but he is only a drunken press officer, permanently *en poste.*

Durrell's style in these sketches has been likened to that of Sir Harold Nicolson teamed with Wodehouse, but some may nominate Peter Fleming (with all those capital letters) rather than Nicolson. If the plots are wild, the manner is disciplined and the wit elegant. There are some captivating conceits: ''[The Ambassador] groaned and moved from side to side, as if he were representing Colic in a charade''; ''[the saluting gun] would give a hoarse boom at sunset while a pair of blue underpants, which had been used from time immemorial as wadding for the blank charge, would stiffen themselves out on the sky''; ''[The embassy cat] was at the top of the elm tree, quietly, effortlessly, brilliantly fielding sparrows as they passed''. Perhaps Durrell is really the cat up the tree?

E. S. Turner, ''From the Embassy,'' in The Times Literary Supplement, *No. 4316, December 20, 1985, p. 1453.*

T(homas) S(tearns) Eliot

1888-1965

American-born English poet, critic, essayist, and dramatist.

Eliot is one of the most important literary figures of the twentieth century. While both his poetry and his prose are frequently cited as having helped inaugurate the modern period in English and American letters, Eliot is best known for his distinctively erudite and innovative verse. His poems often combine classical forms and concerns with elements drawn from contemporary culture in a format which sometimes juxtaposes fragmentary, disjointed surfaces with underlying philosophical significance. Throughout his career, Eliot strongly advocated the development of a "historical sense" which he claimed, in his essay "Tradition and the Individual Talent," is "nearly indispensable to anyone who would continue to be a poet beyond his twenty-fifth year." Consequently, an awareness of his literary and cultural heritage is one of the most prominent features of Eliot's criticism and poetry. In his dual roles as groundbreaking poet and eminent critic, in addition to his less prominent position as a playwright, Eliot has maintained an influence in literature that some critics claim is unequaled by any other contemporary writer. In 1948 Eliot was awarded the Nobel Prize in literature. In an essay summarizing Eliot's poetic achievements, Hyatt H. Waggoner noted that what "Eliot has left us with is a distinguished volume of poems, long and short, . . . poems that give us still today the words to express, and thus be better able to understand and cope with, our own experience, our distress, our fears, and our occasionally possible hopes."

Eliot was born in St. Louis, Missouri. He moved to England after graduating from Harvard University and lived there for the rest of his life. Although Eliot's first volume of poetry, *Prufrock and Other Observations,* was not published until 1917, he wrote several of the poems while he was a student. This volume established Eliot as an important new voice in English and American poetry. "The Love Song of J. Alfred Prufrock," in particular, encapsulates the distinctive techniques that Eliot employed throughout his career. James F. Knapp described the poem as "one which helped to change our conception of what kind of shape a poem might take." "The Love Song of J. Alfred Prufrock" is a lyrical, dramatic monologue spoken in the voice of a middle-class male persona who inhabits a physically and spiritually bleak environment. Although aware of the possibility of personal fulfillment, the speaker is afraid to act, unable to claim for himself a more meaningful existence. Many critics noted in the poems in *Prufrock and Other Observations*—including "Preludes," "Rhapsody on a Windy Night," and "Portrait of a Lady"—the influence of the French symbolists, especially Jules Laforgue and Charles Baudelaire. These poets had impressed Eliot with their realistic portrayals of urban landscapes and their bold use of irony and symbolism. Eliot's early poems feature similar qualities: they are characterized by their often sardonic tone, strong rhythms achieved by blending formal and informal verse forms and speech, and vivid, startling metaphors. *Prufrock and Other Observations* was immediately lauded by, among others, Ezra Pound, who became Eliot's friend, literary advisor, and editor during this period.

In 1915 Eliot married Vivien Haigh-Wood, an Englishwoman from an aristocratic family. The failure of their marriage is often seen as having contributed to the despair in the poetry Eliot wrote at this time. *Ara Vos Prec* (1922) contains several of Eliot's best-known poems, including "Gerontion," a dramatic monologue featuring a disillusioned protagonist who may represent Prufrock as an old man, and "The Hippopotamus" and "Mr. Eliot's Sunday Morning Service," which satirize the Anglican church. The poems in this volume anticipate *The Waste Land* in their evocation of the barrenness of modern life.

The Waste Land has generated voluminous critical commentary since its publication in 1922. When the book-length poem first appeared, response was divided—some considered it immensely significant, while others found it obscure. However, most critics agree that *The Waste Land* holds an important and influential position in the development of English and American poetry. Its five sections—"The Burial of the Dead," "A Game of Chess," "The Fire Sermon," "Death by Water," and "What the Thunder Said"—are composed of apparently random, disconnected images and scenes and are spoken by several different voices which blend together at various points throughout the poem. Eliot evidenced his belief in historical precedence by incorporating into *The Waste Land* a complex network of allusions to literature, anthropology, pre-Christian and Christian myth, and other sources, as well as lines written in such foreign languages as Latin and German. He also included a section of notes at the end of the poem to identify the sources of many of his references. Although Eliot has been faulted for his learned approach, which some critics claim makes *The Waste Land* inaccessible, he is more often praised for the scholarship, philosophical depth, and original poetic techniques exhibited in the poem. The meaning of *The Waste Land* is a subject of much debate, but scholars generally agree that it presents a metaphorical portrait of the modern world as dry and desolate and of humanity as emotionally, intellectually, and spiritually empty. Among the many themes in the poem are death and rebirth, time, sterility, and the failures of sexuality. The traditional interpretation of *The Waste Land* as the quintessential expression of the post-World War I generation's disillusionment and alienation is now considered limited and inaccurate, particularly in view of Eliot's later declarations of personal and political conservatism. Although Eliot described the poem as "a heap of broken images" in "The Burial of the Dead," it retains great power to affect its readers and, as Donald Hall observed, "resolves . . . an extraordinary manyness and diversity, deeply historical and deeply psychic."

Eliot's next major piece, *The Hollow Men* (1925), with its tone of overwhelming desperation, echoes the concerns of *The Waste Land*. But in the volumes which followed, Eliot's work underwent a significant change. In 1927 Eliot was baptized into the Anglican church, and several months later he became a British citizen. *The Journey of the Magi* (1927) and *A Song for Simeon* (1928) retain the basic elements of Eliot's style while introducing a religious dimension to his thematic concerns. The poems in these collections combine realistic detail with visionary imagery and biblical references, portraying the doubts and pain of the religious convert. Similarly, *Ash-Wednesday* (1930) has been interpreted as a direct declaration of Eliot's Christian orientation. It too describes the difficulties and indecision of his new commitment while emphasizing the value of spirituality in a highly secular age.

In the years immediately following the publication of *Ash-Wednesday,* Eliot wrote several plays in verse but produced little poetry, concentrating primarily on criticism, lectures, and his position as an editor at the London publishing house of Faber and Faber. This relatively unproductive period ended with the publication of *Four Quartets* (1943), comprising four previously issued volumes: *East Coker* (1940), *Burnt Norton* (1941), *The Dry Salvages* (1941), and *Little Gidding* (1942). The title of each section refers to a geographical landscape of significance to Eliot; these include his family's ancestral village in England and the Massachusetts coast where he spent his childhood summers. A long meditation on a variety of themes—most notably time and history—*Four Quartets* is marked by its attention to sound and music, its generally optimistic tone, and its skillful blending of philosophical complexity and lyricism. Although some critics claim that *Four Quartets* is weakly executed and pretentious, most consider it a fitting and powerful culmination of Eliot's poetic career, and Eliot himself felt that it was his best work.

Eliot's work for the theater consists of six plays, each written in verse rather than standard dialogue. His high regard for Elizabethan and Restoration drama led him to attempt a synthesis of modern theatrical techniques, classical poetic form, and mythical references and devices. Eliot's first effort, *The Rock: A Pageant Play* (1934), was commissioned by his church and is explicitly religious. Written in collaboration with E. Martin Browne, the play features Greek choruses whose speeches

were Eliot's contribution. *Murder in the Cathedral* (1935), widely recognized as Eliot's most successful play, was also commissioned by the church and again employs choral verse. This play recounts the martyrdom of Thomas à Becket, Archbishop of Canterbury, who was killed in 1170 by knights of King Henry II. Eliot's later plays are generally considered less effective than *Murder in the Cathedral*. In *The Family Reunion* (1939), *The Cocktail Party* (1950), *The Confidential Clerk* (1953), and *The Elder Statesman* (1958), Eliot hoped to achieve philosophical depth in a context that would be appreciated by a wide audience by fusing contemporary settings, situations, and dialogue with classical forms and allusions. Although several of his plays were well attended, their popularity is usually attributed to the fame of the author, who by this time was an established cultural figure.

Eliot has also exerted considerable influence on twentieth-century literary criticism. A. Alvarez claimed that "[our] interests and standards in literature are Eliot's creation. . . . His critical pronouncements were made valid by his poetry. So he did more than change the standards of critical judgment; he altered the whole mode of expression in order to make room for his originality." Eliot's work is considered a major force behind the rise of New Criticism in England and the United States during the 1930s and 1940s. This movement advocated a move away from Romanticism toward a more intellectual and methodological evaluation of art. Two of Eliot's concepts are considered important contributions to critical analysis: "objective correlative" and "dissociation of sensibility." In the essay "Hamlet" in *The Sacred Wood: Essays on Poetry and Criticism* (1920), Eliot defined the objective correlative as "a set of objects, a situation, a chain of events which shall be the formula of [a] particular emotion" and which have the ability to evoke that emotion in the reader. This idea, in its insistence on expression that is balanced and objective, runs contrary to Romantic tenets. "Dissociation of sensibility," as described by Eric Thompson, "is the dislocation of thought from feeling and feeling from thought that occurs when language orbits too far out from a metaphysical center." For Eliot, the dislocation of sensibility began in English literature in the early seventeenth century. He cites Dante, John Donne, and John Dryden as poets whose work encompasses metaphysical conflicts. In essays collected in such works as *The Use of Poetry and the Use of Criticism* (1933), *After Strange Gods: A Primer of Modern Heresy* (1933), and *Poetry and Drama* (1951), Eliot stresses the importance of tradition, religion, and morality in literature and society.

Beginning in the 1950s, new experimental techniques in poetry, the revival of the Romantic belief in the primacy of the individual, and the emergence of personal or "confessional" poetry led to a decline in Eliot's authority and popularity. In his 1928 essay "For Lancelot Andrewes," Eliot had declared himself "an Anglo-Catholic in religion, a classicist in literature, and a royalist in politics," and this conservatism also contributed to his fall from favor. Most recent critics, however, while expressing occasional reservations about Eliot's personal ideology, agree that his profoundly innovative, erudite approach to poetry and criticism has had a permanent impact on literature. The divergence of critical opinion on the ultimate worth of Eliot's accomplishments continues, but, as Northrop Frye observed, "A thorough knowledge of Eliot is compulsory for anyone interested in contemporary literature. Whether he is liked or disliked is of no importance, but he must be read."

(See also *CLC*, Vols. 1, 2, 3, 6, 9, 10, 13, 15, 24, 34; *Contemporary Authors*, Vols. 5-8, rev. ed., Vols. 25-28, rev. ed.

[obituary]; and *Dictionary of Literary Biography,* Vols. 7, 10, 45.)

A. D. MOODY

With the completion of *Four Quartets* Eliot ceased to be a poet, and became in his art simply a dramatist. His pre-war drama had worked on both levels, the human and the transcendental; but in the three plays produced in the last twenty years of his life the metaphysical poet disappears in the writer of well-made drawing-room comedies. Regrettable as this may be, it was not simply a consequence of failing powers. For one thing, the poet could only have repeated himself, having said all that he had to say in the perfected Quartets. For another, it is just by their not being poetry that the late plays add something to his *oeuvre.* It is not a new vision that they offer, but a progressive revision of that of the poet who would be a saint. *The Cocktail Party* transposes *The Family Reunion* and *Four Quartets* into the audience's own terms, and in doing so significantly alters the emphasis towards the occupations of 'most of us'. In *The Confidential Clerk* the dramatist develops a point of view distinct from that of the poet, and for the first time in Eliot's work the poet is observed in a light other than his own. Then *The Elder Statesman,* which is in certain respects a summing up of the whole of the poet's life-work, brings us at the end to a radical revaluation of it.

This last play gives us something genuinely new and shocking to reckon with. In it the poet, that ideal, elected self, fashioned throughout a lifetime's death in love, who had already turned back to be the dramatist of his world, assumes an ordinary personality and declares himself a human lover like any other. By way of the dedicatory verses with their obvious connection with certain passages in the play, Eliot as good as made a personal appearance on the stage, affirming his need to be loved by a woman and his joy in the liberating experience of sexual love. This was to come back out of the refining fire and through the looking-glass into the secret rose-garden—to go back on the poetry, and to give the last word to the human being whom the poet had all his life been struggling to transform and to transcend. It can't cancel or invalidate the poetry, which remains what it is. But it does establish a new frame of reference, to thus celebrate the union

> Of lovers whose bodies smell of each other
> Who think the same thoughts without need of speech
> And babble the same speech without need of meaning.

That subordination of 'meaning' to the natural communion of lovers affords a new point of view; one which may detach us finally from the poet's, and enable us to understand the void at the heart of his work. . . . (pp. 267-68)

The happy ending to his life and work must have taken Eliot himself by surprise. But the confining of his drama to the prosaic sphere of human action had been a matter of deliberate effort. Questioned about his intentions in *The Cocktail Party,* he gave the dry understatement: 'I intended to produce characters whose drawing-room behaviour was generally correct.' That was probably the literal truth and not a snub, but it cut deeper than would appear. It needs to be set alongside his altered view of *The Family Reunion:* 'my sympathies now have come to be all with the mother, who seems to me, except

perhaps for the chauffeur, the only complete human being in the play; and my hero now strikes me as an insufferable prig.' In 1938 he had regarded Amy as 'merely a person of tremendous personality *on one plane*'; but it was that plane which now interested him most. He was therefore being quite consistent with the theory and practice of his pre-war drama in laying down for himself, when he wanted to represent 'our own sordid, dreary daily world', 'the ascetic rule to avoid poetry which could not stand the test of strict dramatic utility: with such success, indeed, that it is perhaps an open question whether there is any poetry in the play at all.' To adapt his writing to 'the needs of the stage' meant keeping it down to the level of ordinary awareness.

At the same time it does seem perverse to choose to represent ordinary reality according to the artificial conventions of drawing-room comedy. . . . I suspect that . . . it was precisely the vapidity of conventional realism which made it good for his purposes. If it offered only a world of outward appearance and illusion, so too, in his view, did the ordinary world. Its unreality would be the perfect expression of the audience's failure to exist on the moral plane. Moreover, it was the appropriate way to make them aware of that. . . . In a sense they already knew what he had to say to them there, that what they agreed to take as real was mere pretence. To make them fully conscious of this he had only to reveal that this theatrical world was a true expression of their mode of existence.

To bring home the unreality of what we ordinarily call reality—to effect a positive dis-illusionment—had always been an element in Eliot's work, notably in *The Waste Land* and in the satiric treatment of the visionless world in the dramatic writing of the 1930s. But hitherto the aim had always been to dismiss and to transcend it. Now, in the post-war plays, the ordinary human plane, 'unreal' as it is, is accepted as one on which the spiritual action may take place. The development follows on from that of the wartime Quartets, which discovered how consciousness of the 'meaning' could transform the life of the world from a hell into a purgatory. Their dominant concern was the occupation of the saint, whereas the later plays are concerned with more ordinary lives, but the moral is still the same. Whatever one's fate, whether it is to be a martyr or an ordinary person, that is what one must accept in order to be free. 'Resign yourself to be the fool you are', as Sir Henry Harcourt-Reilly advises Edward Chamberlayne, and in that way 'work out your salvation'. That was the odd beginning of the dramatist's finding his peace in human love.

The first thing to be said of *The Cocktail Party* (1949) is that it repeats the essential action of *The Family Reunion.* Celia, a simplified version of Harry, follows out the same 'process by which the human is / Transhumanised . . . on the way of illumination'. By the stages of disillusionment, discovery of solitude, and recognition of sinfulness, she comes to a knowledge of 'the void at the heart of all human relations', and so to the necessity of atonement. She achieves that, we are assured, in accepting her destiny: 'a happy death' in the desert, 'crucified / Very near an ant-hill'. Hers is in every way the strongest part of the play, and it is exactly what we should expect of Eliot. There is one other important respect in which the later play corresponds to the earlier. As Harry was helped on his way by the Eumenides and Agatha, so Celia is directed on hers by the trio of 'Guardians'. Julia and Alex, the intrusive 'kindly ones,' save her from error; and Reilly's office, like Agatha's, is to make her understand her fate so that she may assent to it. These three act and advise with the assurance of those who know the law of things—the Logos; and so may be regarded (if we can take them so seriously) as God's messengers and ministers, spreading the conviction of Original Sin and of peace in His will. Thus far the design of the two plays is identical.

But then the Guardians differ from the Eumenides, and even from Agatha, in being thoroughly adjusted to the modern comedy. They are not in the least supernatural, nor are they saints or visionaries. . . . If they are distinguished from the merely commonplace characters, the Chamberlaynes and Peter Quilpe, then it is by their confident enlightenment or knowingness; and also by their playing the silly social game with the light-headedness of those who don't mind being ridiculous. In a world of fools and saints they belong with the fools, only they would be wise fools. (pp. 268-70)

The dramatic effect of Harry's leaving Wishwood to follow the bright angels was to kill Amy and show up the incomprehension of the comic aunts and uncles—that is, it should detach us from the plane of ordinary consciousness. In *Murder in the Cathedral* the effect of the martyr's death, as mediated through the Chorus, was similarly to bring to the common man an apprehension of the ways of God. But the shock of Celia's death in the desert is used for an opposite effect: to confirm the commonplace couple in their mediocrity. 'The dull, the implacable, / The indomitable spirit of mediocrity' is the essential quality of their characters and of their relationship—meaning that they have never been borne out of themselves by the passion of love. Such a marriage without ecstasy was the pollution which made Harry's hell, and from which he had to purge himself. But the Chamberlaynes, once the Guardians have brought them through the breakdown of their illusions and self-deceptions, are simply reconciled to their condition. It would be hell, as Edward finds and as Reilly tells Celia, to remain oneself alone 'in the phantasmal world / Of imagination, shuffling memories and desires'; but honestly to face the fact that one is not capable of real love, and not really lovable, makes it a purgatory and one way of salvation. Eliot explained in a letter that when Reilly says these things his 'universe of discourse' is governed by 'two primary propositions: (1) nobody understands you but God; (2) all real love is ultimately the love of God.' Because she has really loved, Celia is set upon the way of illumination. The Chamberlaynes' enlightenment is to know that they cannot really love each other—and that this is why they are bound to each other. Theirs is 'the human condition' as Reilly describes it:

> tolerant of themselves and
> others,
> Giving and taking, in the usual actions
> What there is to give and take. They do not repine;
> Are contented with the morning that separates
> And with the evening that brings together
> For casual talk before the fire
> Two people who know they do not understand each
> other,
> Breeding children whom they do not understand
> And who will never understand them.

'Is that the best life?' Celia asks. 'It is a good life,' Reilly insists; and he adds later, 'Neither way is better. / Both ways are necessary.' That affirmation has to make all the difference from the putting down of the common man's 'living, and partly living', in *Murder in the Cathedral;* and from the feeling in *The Family Reunion* that to be out of love was to be cursed and polluted. The Chamberlaynes are not to be plucked from

their burning, but must go on with the cocktail party as their form—the banal, commonplace form—of the *via negativa.* (pp. 270-71)

That there should be any degree of reconciliation with 'the human condition' is a notable advance upon Eliot's pre-war work. But we should not exaggerate the matter, or take it for something other than it is. . . . The change that has taken place in Eliot's work is simply this: that from fear and terror of the ordinary human lot, he has come to accept it as inescapable, and therefore as necessary for ordinary mortals. This is the very reverse of an escape from or transcendence of mediocrity. It is a coming to terms with it, by comprehending it within the pattern of fate. 'The waste sad time' becomes in the simplest way 'ridiculous', to be laughed at; and the importunate negative is discovered to be the absurd side of Providence.

This should make the play a comedy in a deeper sense than is intended by the term 'drawing-room comedy'. Yet what sort of comedy is it? Celia's death, from the Christian viewpoint, is certainly a sort of happy ending. Possibly, still from that point of view, the fate of the nun who escaped but 'Will never be fit for normal life again' should evoke 'a tremor of joy'. But this is the comic sense of the saint. The comic sense which would reconcile us to the human condition differs from it as it has a different object. Its basis appears to be the conviction that in this world we are all of us fools, and that the wisest are those who laugh at themselves for being 'only human'. To them is granted the assurance that in the end 'all shall be well, and all manner of thing shall be well', and this makes them glad to be ridiculous. But this means that, ultimately, both fool and saint are seen in one and the same Christian vision. A natural association of ideas might lead one to speak of this comedy as introducing a new humanity into Eliot's work; but to look at it from a humane point of view is to discover its limits. Erasmus' *Praise of Folly* would be a useful guide to the play's discriminations of the different kinds of fool there may be in the world; and at the same time, fully understood and taken with his *Dialogues* and other writings, it gives a measure of how far short the play falls of a complete Humanism. Erasmus, without being any the less Christian, was genuinely in touch with the Greek sense of man—which Eliot repudiated even while drawing upon Greek sources for his plays. He was, moreover, a genuine precursor of the Shakespearian comic vision, in which Puck's 'Lord, what fools these mortals be!' is only one note in the gamut, and one fully resolved in the final harmony of nature, when 'all the story of the night . . . grows to something of great constancy'. The truly humane sense of comedy does not leave out of its sense of life all that makes for life, for its power and substance and intensity. In its light, the human wisdom of *The Cocktail Party* is only that of the void heart, conscious only of failure and defeat and alienation; a wisdom valid for lightening the burden of *Angst* by giving it a meaning and a purpose; but hardly one which ministers to the sane and joyful fulfilment of mankind in its own nature. From the point of view of a comedy which celebrates the possibilities of our world, the Guardians look like a bunch of creeps, dangerous because they think they know all, and because their cure is to confirm the disease. The spreading of their 'enlightenment' to the Chamberlaynes, and from them to Peter Quilpe—and from the play to its audience—calls for Blake's penetrating critique, in *Songs of Innocence and of Experience,* of the passing on of the oppressive evangel of sin and sorrow like death itself from generation to generation. Even from a point of view near to Eliot's own the humanity of the play must appear very restricted: Dante's *Divine Comedy* does not make fools of us.

The Confidential Clerk (1953), though it is generally regarded as the lesser play on account of having even less 'poetry' in it, is both more of a comedy, and a more humane one. This is because it doesn't merely reconcile the mediocre to their lot; but does this on the basis of their having something worthwhile to be reconciled to—a positive human potential which the play works to release and fulfil. Moreover, from that there follows a surprising further reconciliation within the deep and tangled complex of emotions which had dominated Eliot's poetry up to *The Family Reunion,* and which had seemed to be finally, if rather violently, resolved there. Most surprising of all, there is a distinct suggestion, which becomes a fairly definite conviction by the end, that his typical hero is not being taken so seriously as hitherto, and that he is being exposed in a not wholly flattering light.

The most obvious advance upon *The Cocktail Party* is that here Eliot committed himself, for the first time, to making a play that would work in purely worldly terms. Certainly the worldliness is kept on a tight rein, by the artifice of the plot, which owes even more to Plautus and to Oscar Wilde than to its declared 'point of departure', the *Ion* of Euripides; and also to the seeding in of images, puns and allegorical hints to intimate the existence of another world. Nevertheless, it was a great leap for Eliot to do without a saint and martyr. The several characters who are in search of themselves and of their children or parents, have all to find their real identities and relationships in the actual world. Along with this, Eliot brought down his divine agents to the level of the everyday, making the one a tightly rolled confidential clerk, devoted to his duties and his suburban garden; and the other a prim widow in a flowery hat and drab coat who minds other people's children.... [What] directly characterises them, first and last, is their ordinariness, and their possessing no special wisdom or mystery. If they represent the Christian way of life, the one in its positive and the other in its negative phase, they do it in the forms of normal worldly behaviour.

The action of fate as they unravel it appears relatively simple, its complications only those of a romantic tale designed to bring us through confusions to the truth which makes a happy ending. Sir Claude Mulhammer thinks Colby Simpkins is his son; Lady Elizabeth, his wife, persuades herself that he must be *her* long-lost son; in fact he belongs to neither of them. Their real children are, respectively, Lucasta Angel—whom Sir Claude would like to be rid of, and of whom Lady Elizabeth does not approve—and B. Kaghan, whom she doesn't approve of either. When Lucasta and B. decide to marry, Lady Elizabeth has to accept them both together; while Sir Claude fears that he is losing Lucasta just when he has found that she is all the children he has. Colby was Mrs Guzzard's son; but she had given him up to Sir Claude so that he might have a better start in life, and she does not mean to reclaim him now. Instead she sets him free to follow his wanting to be an organist in spite of knowing he will not be first-rate, by telling him that his real father was an undistinguished musician. Thus far we appear to be in the realm of *The Cocktail Party*'s ordinary good life. Colby is happily resigned to being the mediocre musician he is; and the rest of the household are composed into a contented family group, tolerant of themselves and of each other, and reconciled to 'the human condition' in just the way Reilly prescribed.

It makes an immense difference, however, that instead of this condition being reserved for the loveless, all the characters are moved by love in one way or another, while the facts they must adjust to are the real substance of their loves. Sir Claude and Lady Elizabeth in losing their illusory children discover their true ones; and they also discover each other. Lucasta finds the kind of love she needs with B. Kaghan—one which has the security of being without illusions. Eggerson, in looking after Colby, seems to find again his own son who was 'lost in action'.... The larger group of characters are composed in the finale into a family tableau, united in the spirit—if not quite in the same tone—of this speech which was drafted for Monica in *The Elder Statesman:*

> any words are silly between people like
>   ourselves
> Who've no vocabulary for love—but is there one
> For love within a family? That love is most in silence,
> For it's the love on which all else depends, the love
> That stands between us and destruction, love that's
>   lived in
> But not looked at, love within the light of which
> All else is seen, the love within which
> All other human love finds speech ...

That quality of love is not explicitly stated in *The Confidential Clerk,* but it is both the end towards which it progresses, and the ground of its action. This of course is a striking development in Eliot's work, that instead of unfamiliar Love being all, there should be a positive valuation of love as men and women commonly know it in their human relationships.

Colby and Mrs Guzzard are got off stage before the final tableau, and they don't belong in the family group. They rather enact 'the pattern' of the earlier works; but with a difference that arises in part from the way in which they do it, and in part from the way in which the pattern is woven into the 'ground' of the family relationships. As in *The Family Reunion,* the son's life is made to depend upon his mother's love, but Colby is given no cause to kill Mrs Guzzard. The analogies with Orestes and Oedipus, and with Hamlet and Coriolanus, simply don't apply. Thinking back to the earlier play in 1951, Eliot reflected, 'we are left in a divided frame of mind, not knowing whether to consider the play the tragedy of the mother or the salvation of the son. In *The Confidential Clerk,* written about that time, the two things are reconciled. This is done by allowing the mother to be to the son both an Amy and an Agatha, so that her tragedy is his salvation. As his natural mother she showed her love in sacrificing her own claims for the sake of his worldly prospects; when she renounces that hope and reveals the truth of his origins, she brings him to birth in his spiritual existence. So the son seeking his soul's fulfilment, and the mother who wants him to do well, are reunited in a common action. This amounts to a reconciliation of the two realms of flesh and spirit, such as seemed inconceivable in *The Family Reunion.* But there is still the persistent suggestion of a division between the natural and the spiritual, and of the natural life being set right only by an action on a 'higher' plane. Mrs Guzzard, at least, is required to follow the negative way, in consciously sacrificing her own will to her son's destiny.

Colby's destiny is to follow his love of music, and there is something supernatural about this too, although it is brought down to earth. It seems that in order to be sure about it he needs to know who was his real father, and here the connection with the *Ion* becomes illuminating. Young Ion's problem is that he doesn't know whether he is of divine or human origin, and he can find no answer in the evidence offered by both gods and men. But that drives him back upon his own nature, and there he finds his answer: he must follow what Arnold would call his best self. His divine father, Apollo, having absconded, the divine inspiration is to be sought within the human spirit itself. In his own fashion, by having Colby become an organist, though an indifferent one, Eliot also rediscovers the divine principle within the human.

The play makes much of the passion for music, and for art in general—we need to remember that Apollo was the god of music and the arts. Colby's music, and Sir Claude's love of ceramics, enable them to pass from the unreal into the real: the form, the pattern, transports into the realm of immediate experience which is 'life itself'. More than that, the creative impulse is understood as an impulse towards the absolute—that is, towards the unification of all one's being into a single intense and perfect whole. The terms used recall **"Burnt Norton"** 's analogy between the shaping power of human art which is inspired by love, and divine Love which shapes all things. But in this case it is the likeness which is brought out, not the disparity: what is affirmed is simply the creative principle within human nature. Moreover, the quest for integrity no longer requires the annihilation 'of all that's made'. 'Life itself' does not lie through a metaphysical looking-glass, but is realised within the mirror of a natural love raised to the power of art. This means that the aspiration towards the condition of music should not be at odds with the human condition—as it had been in all of Eliot's work since **"Portrait of a Lady"** and **"Prufrock"**. (pp. 271-76)

Now we come to the heart of Colby's problem. He loves his music, which Lucasta calls his secret garden; but being alone there makes even it unreal, as well as everything else. . . . [He] is beginning to hope that Lucasta might walk there with him. But just as they are finding that they could love each other, the natural development of their feelings is prevented—exactly as in *The Family Reunion,* though by nothing so sensational as the Eumenides—by the discovery of the 'fact' that they are brother and sister. The shock serves to make them sublimate their love for each other, even after the supposed fact is disproved; and Colby is confirmed in his solitude. His impulse to love another person thus follows the pattern adhered to from **"La Figlia Che Piange"** right up to *The Cocktail Party*—though with the modifications that he does not have to suffer a terrible disillusionment and conviction of sin, that his separation from Lucasta is not violent and absolute, and that his being impelled towards the divine union is merely hinted at.

This leaves him rather undeveloped in the end, and rather exposed to criticism. The design of the earlier drama and of *Four Quartets,* which I have been tracing out here in a distinctly humanised and more comic form, would lead us to expect that he has been detached from the human object of his love, and born again in the calling of his real father, in order that he might conceive the Word. But we don't see him in that ideal relation: we see him in his human relations, and in a context where human relationships have been given an unprecedentedly positive value. In this perspective it becomes possible to reflect that if his real self can walk only with God, the reason might be that his natural development has been arrested. The quest for integrity of self, which involves separating himself from unreal or falsifying relations, is undeniably a virtue; but it becomes vicious if it leads to being self-enclosed and incapable of entering into real relationships with other persons. Eliot accurately described Colby as having 'a certain deliberate ambivalence: egotist and ascetic'; and while we may choose to regard him as a potential saint, we are shown him as actually something of an egotist. That must make us a bit dubious about his budding sanctity.

The doubt is enforced by the way the play is shaped towards the final family group, from which Colby stands aside; and even more by the treatment of Lucasta, the *jeune fille* as Eliot would once have called her. She is the first of his characters to be a truly *other* person, and not a projection of his hero or of his own feelings and preconceptions about others. . . . Lucasta is the product of sympathetic observation and understanding, and becomes a thoroughly real woman trying to be true to herself in a world that seems to consist mainly of artifice and false relations—Eliot's 'Roaring Girl', as one might say. Now such a recognition of another person could be the first step towards, as it is the necessary basis for, a true union of a man and of a woman. Lucasta's feeling for Colby is primarily in her recognition of what he is in himself; and her relationship with Kaghan is founded upon their mutual recognition of each other. But Colby doesn't seem capable of that. He is really rather afraid of Lucasta; is willing to meet her only upon his own terms—in his own private garden; and is so bound up in himself that he has no real sense of her as a person at all. Looked at in this light, his love appears to be in the immature, narcissistic stage—one of the stages of adolescence. And his sublimation of it would be a way of keeping his ego intact from a woman who was too grown-up for him.

None of this invalidates his quest for integrity, but it does question the form it seems likely to take. So far as he has the character of the metaphysical poet who would be a saint, he is a portrait of that poet as a young man. A first principle in reading Eliot is: the poet is not to be identified with his personae. Now we discover that the dramatist is not to be identified with the poet, but has become the detached critic observing him. He has not disowned the poet, nor the occupation of the saint; but his interest in human characters and human relationships has developed into a new point of view, and so arrived at a new understanding of the impulse towards the ideal. Instead of making that impulse the measure of all else, he has shown it in a way which allows it to be measured by other possibilities. One consequence is that the self-perfecting alien ceases to be the unquestioned hero of the drama, but is seen to be making the best of a bad job after his own fashion. Another is that human beings are found to have rather more to offer than the poet had been willing to credit.

The interest of *The Elder Statesman* (1958) is all in its relation to its author: to the poet he had been, and the man he now showed himself to be. Eliot's remark that its model was Sophocles' *Oedipus at Colonus* recalls what he had said in 1938 about *The Family Reunion:* 'Harry's career needs to be completed by an *Orestes* or an *Oedipus at Colonus*.' That was because Harry had not fully understood what the Furies were telling him, that 'the only way out is the way of purgation and holiness'. The poet had followed that way to its end in the *Quartets*. But when Eliot came to write his *Oedipus at Colonus,* for performance in his seventieth year, he rather abruptly took another way out. His view of life had of course undergone a significant alteration since 1938. But a revolutionary change seems to have followed upon his falling in love with and marrying his secretary, Valerie Fletcher, at the stage when he was writing Acts I and II. The dedication draws attention to the reflection of that event within the play, where the discovery of love does appear to supervene upon an action quite differently conceived. It was to have shown the process of Lord Claverton's purgation and finding the way to die in peace. The celebration of the love which unites his daughter and her fiancé is superimposed on that, and in rather an awkward fashion, since their love for each other is somehow made to fulfil his need to be loved for himself. The awkwardness prompts us to see through the dramatic illusion to the private reality, where there were not two relationships but only one; and where the need which had been turned towards purgation and self-transcendence, was answered by an unhoped for love, and satisfied in a relationship not allowed for in the initial conception. For the play itself this is quite shattering—I don't see how it can be pieced together into a convincing whole. But it becomes all the more eloquent on that account as a human document, and one which suggests a shocking revaluation of Eliot's life-work.

The play remains concerned with the Elder Statesman's purgation except at its beginning and its end. Lord Claverton is an ambitious, successful and honoured public man. Retired because of bad health, he finds himself for the first time since he was plain Dick Ferry with a blank engagement book, 'contemplating nothingness' and terrified of solitude. The self he had been in public life is a thing of the past, yet it is all that he is in the eyes of others: where is his real, his authentic self? For the first two Acts it seems that he must rediscover that through coming to terms with the ghosts of his youth who return to haunt him.

The first of these was a friend whom he helped go to the bad, but who has since changed his name and made good in a Central American republic where corruption is a respectable way of life. This Federico Gomez is clearly Lord Claverton's double; most of all in having so thoroughly changed his identity as to lose himself and become cut off from others. He hopes to be restored to reality by having his old friend accept both the man he used to be and the one he has become—that is, the hollow man he knows himself to be. When Claverton refuses to admit the likeness, Gomez tries to bring it home by recalling the occasion when Dick Ferry ran over a body on the road and didn't stop: thus reviving the shameful, sordid memory of a moment of truth when he had thought only of saving himself. As in **"Little Gidding,"** his double is offering 'the rending pain of re-enactment / Of all that you have done, and been'. By refusing to meet him on their common ground of humiliating egotism and error, he must be confirming his own imprisonment in unreality. For he needs exactly what he is denying Gomez: to be recognised as the small soul he really is, and to be loved as that.

His second visitant cuts nearer to the heart. If Mrs Carghill is a woman with a past, then, in the same sense of the phrase, she is his past. But he had thought to buy her off and bury the affair; whereas she makes no secret of having been Maisie Montjoy the musical comedy star, and of his having been her first lover. . . . He is prepared to remember only 'a brief infatuation' and 'a lucky escape'. But for her their relationship, though brief, was intense and remains a permanent reality:

> It's frightening to think that we're still together
> And more frightening to think that we may *always* be
>   together.
> There's a phrase I seem to remember reading
>   somewhere:
> *Where their fires are not quenched.*

Mrs Carghill is a very near relation to the women of *The Waste Land;* and Claverton seems to have belonged with the loitering heirs of City directors. He has not let 'The awful daring of a moment's surrender' bring him into existence as a moral being; and still, in refusing to acknowledge any relation with her, he is preferring to keep up appearances. Yet Mrs Carghill touches more deeply than Gomez his terror of being irredeemably unreal because hollow at heart—incapable of loving another, and justly unloved. This, his most deeply repressed anxiety, is his worst shame and original sin. That means, according to the example of *The Hollow Men* and the later poems, that it is what he needs to confess and accept as his purgatorial fire. What he is refusing in rejecting Mrs Carghill's ambiguous advances could be his salvation.

Because he will not acknowledge them, these two ghosts can only turn the key upon his imprisonment within an unreal public image—they prove ineffectual Eumenides. A third encounter, with his son Michael—a second self—exposes his present cowardice and hypocrisy. Michael is not impressed by his father's public image, and feels falsified by the expectation that he should live up to it. He wants to be himself and make his own way; which seems to mean taking after Gomez. Shocked and disappointed, Lord Claverton accuses him of being 'a fugitive from reality', of trying to hide from his past failures. What he will not admit is what he most needs to admit—it is the only way to remove the barrier between them—that he has himself been doing the same all his life; and that what really shocks him is Michael's frankly confessing to being no better than he ought to be—like the true son of his shameful, secret self. For the third time he refuses to come clean, and rejects the opportunity to set right his relations with himself and with others.

Nevertheless, at the end of that second Act, he does begin to acknowledge his hypocrisy, in admitting to his daughter Monica that he is himself a coward trying to escape himself and his past, and that he should set himself to be schooled by his humiliations. He must have been moved to this by her declaration, following his scene with Michael, that there must be 'love within a family', and that she would give her life for him. It is a short speech . . . but it is the crucial moment for Claverton and for the play. Up to this point the governing 'reality' has been that there is no love and no truth in his relations with himself and with others. By the established pattern of Eliot's work, the way out of his hell of loneliness and shame should be through suffering it in full consciousness. But everything is altered by the sudden discovery that he is loved after all; and the most profound change is that this enables him to get scot free of his unreal and shameful selves, and to enter directly into 'the illumination/Of knowing what love is'.

The first thing love means to Claverton is confession—showing one's real self to another person, and being really known by that person. But then his confession proves to be essentially a mode of communion, or an approach to communion, in which all sense of self is lost. His shames and failures come to seem unimportant; and what gives release from them is simply the being able to confess to the one person who loves him. Moreover, the meaning of the confession is that he loves that person:

> If a man has one person, just one in his life,
> To whom he is willing to confess everything . . .
> Then he loves that person, and his love will save him.

The manner in which it saves Claverton has little to do with the confession of sins, or with the liberation from humiliation by humiliation called for in the early notes and drafts. While he sees himself 'emerging/From my spectral existence into something like reality', he dismisses Gomez and Mrs Carghill as 'not real'.... [He admits] only that he nourished faults and weaknesses the friend of his youth had been born with; and as for the woman who 'had a peculiar physical attraction/Which no other woman has had', and whose first lover he was,

> Maisie loved me, with whatever capacity
> For loving she had—self-centred and foolish—
> But we should respect love always when we meet it;
> Even when it's vain and selfish, we must not abuse it.
> That is where I failed. And the memory frets me.

What a paltry phrase, and what a patronising 'confession'! He is really setting himself in judgment upon the others whom he fears and wants to be rid of, while taking as little as possible upon himself. In regard to himself, he is mainly appealing for Monica's 'protective affection'—asking for her love to save him from himself and from his past. Her response answers precisely to his need. Aided by her fiancé, Charles, a rising politician, she shows loving devotion towards him, and drives off the 'intruders' with legal menace and chilling snobbery. So far as they are concerned the confession is in effect an exorcism. For the rest it is a confession of love: of his need for love, and the difference it makes to be loved.

The most striking measure of the difference is that in his end he becomes the first of Eliot's personae and protagonists to find his peace in human love, and not by the way of purgation and holiness.... He joins himself ... with his truly loving daughter and his new son—which is rather as if Oedipus were not to pass into the other world, but were to enter into a marriage of Antigone and Theseus. The manner in which he enters into this human communion is perhaps slightly veiled; yet an acquaintance with Eliot's habit of using personae and doubles should make it transparent. The 'daughter', by a reversal of the mode of sublimation practised in **"Marina"** and *Ash-Wednesday,* becomes his beloved; and the man she loves is himself, his 'real self' brought into being at last in love.

In the 'Love duet finale' of *The Elder Statesman*—as also in the discovery of love in its first scene—Eliot was making a transparent confession of his own personal happiness. The characters of Claverton, Monica and Charles all dissolve into Eliot himself, and the words they speak are 'private words addressed to [his wife] in public'. In these passages, as in the 'Dedication', the writing breaks the decorum of impersonal art, and becomes awkwardly intimate:

CHARLES   Oh my
> dear,
> I love you to the limits of speech, and
> beyond.
> It's strange that words are so inadequate.
> Yet, like the asthmatic struggling for breath,
> So the lover must struggle for words.
MONICA   I've loved you from the beginning of the
> world.

The mawkish sincerity of the writing enforces the declaration that it was Eliot himself, the man who suffered among other things from emphysema, who had been 'brushed by the wing of happiness'.

That was 'In spite of everything, in defiance of reason'—and in complete contradiction of his life's work. The basic premise and inspiration of that had been the conviction that the 'barriers between one human being and another' were indestructible;

that there was an 'awful separation between potential passion and any actualisation possible in life'; that 'the void . . . in the middle of all human happiness and all human relations' could be filled by only one thing—Atonement with Christ. The final Act of *The Elder Statesman* breaks that pattern, and affirms the contrary. It finds a new life in the human union, the being at one with each other of a man and a woman in love, 'conscious of a new person / Who is you and me together'.... 'The divine union' is simply not in question . . . , one way or the other. That underlines the wonderful fact that Eliot should end his career as an artist by asserting as actual what his writing over fifty years had maintained to be impossible in life.... The need for self-transcendence in love can now be seen to have been the deepest and most consistent motive in all his work. When it seemed unattainable, frustration and failure grew and were deliberately cultivated into 'the death motive': *Angst,* alienation and the sense of sin; then suffering and death embraced as the way of purgation into the realm—mystical, transcendental, ideal—of perfect Love. Yet all this pursuit of the Absolute through negations is exposed, by the actual experience of love, as necessary only because he was out of love, and only for so long as he remained in that state. When he found himself in love, he found the fullness and harmony of being for which he longed—and his poetry could be seen for what it is, a supreme expression of the negative phase of desire. (pp. 277-85)

A. D. Moody, in his Thomas Stearns Eliot: Poet, *Cambridge University Press, 1979, 365 p.*

RONALD BUSH

[How] did the author of *The Waste Land,* one of the most highly charged, dramatic poems of the twentieth century, come twenty years later to write a masterpiece of deferred immediacy like *Four Quartets?* Eliot's development, it hardly needs saying, points beyond itself and calls up other questions—questions of what modernism was, why it flourished and why it eventually became a lifeless fossil rising over the landscape of contemporary literature. Had new literary currents changed Eliot's course, affecting his verse at the same time that they altered the literary assumptions of his generation? That would be the simplest explanation of the growth and decline of the modernist movement, but it fails to satisfy. In Eliot's case, although it is possible to locate figures who influenced him after his thirty-fifth year (Marianne Moore, St.-John Perse and Stéphane Mallarmé come to mind), the causes of his evolution were there from the beginning.

Recalling the great French poet who said his complete works "datent de quinze ans," the elements of Eliot's later verse can be found in his first mature poems. This is not to say he did not change. He did—radically—but his development worked out potential he had always possessed. Like the modernist movement as a whole, his early work nurtured two conflicting literary forces he had inherited from the romantics. At mid-career these forces were each so strong only the power of a master could join them. Then in Eliot as in his contemporaries the bond between the forces snapped, and the international style of 1922 became a thing of the past.

The inclinations I am referring to are . . . : first, a tendency, inherited from French symbolism, toward a literature stripped both of outside reference and of the voice of the poet who presided at its birth—a poetry, so to speak, of pure music. And opposing that, a disposition, already pronounced by the time of Wordsworth, toward fidelity to the subtlest expressions of the innermost self—a disposition which would lead to the extraordinary internal monologues of the twentieth century. For a brief moment in the late teens and early twenties, these forces reinforced one another, so that in the masterpieces of high modernism we find, as Eliot found in the *Cantos* of Ezra Pound, a "nearly continuous identification . . . of form and feeling." In *The Waste Land* or *Ulysses,* an ornate pattern of myth and music coexists with the most radical kind of emotional sincerity. But by the time of the *Four Quartets* or *Finnegans Wake,* the modernists' understanding of sincerity (and of the self) had been transfigured. No longer driven to seek their buried selves, Eliot and Joyce were free to pursue their symbolist inclinations to an extent unprecedented in English writing. (pp. ix-x)

As his admirers have always known, the power of Eliot's early verse comes from an almost unbearable tension between romantic yearning and intellectual detachment. Significant areas of Eliot's psyche are invested in both, and, forced to choose, we would have to say that the yearning, not the intellect, dominates. Eliot was not the kind of second-order artist who, as Henry James says about George Eliot, "proceeds from the abstract to the concrete" and whose "figures and situations are evolved, as the phrase is, from [the] moral consciousness." Eliot made that clear when he criticized Edgar Lee Masters for writing a poem of ironic autobiography which lacked foundation in the sensuous reality of individual consciousness. Masters, Eliot said, "sometimes fails in a situation . . . because he does not fix before you the contact and cross-contact of souls, the breath and scent of the room. His mind is reflective, not evocative. . . . In descriptive passages . . . we have a vision from the moral emotions, not an immediate application of all the senses."

This is not to say that the moral frames of Eliot's finished poems are to be taken simply as reflex defenses against the discomfort of unexpectedly full experience. Eliot remembered that "I never knew my grandfather: he died a year before my birth. But I was brought up to be very much aware of him: so much so, that as a child I thought of him as still the head of the family—a ruler for whom *in absentia* my grandmother stood as viceregent. The standard of conduct was that which my grandfather had set; our moral judgments, our decisions between duty and self-indulgence, were taken as if, like Moses, he had brought down the tables of the Law, any deviation from which would be sinful. Not least of these laws, which included injunctions still more than prohibitions, was the Law of Public Service." . . . As Eliot hints in what follows these remarks, this need always to choose "between duty and self-indulgence" was an extremely uncomfortable one. But he adds that after much contemplation he had come to the conclusion that "it is a very good beginning for any child, to be brought up to reverence such institutions, and to be taught that personal and selfish aims should be subordinated to the general good which they represent." And we may apply the latter remark to his own life and poetry.

Whatever its psychological roots, Eliot's rage for order, his need to impose clear moral outlines on the world, was the source of real clarity, stability and good, not only in his writing but in his personal relations. . . . As regards his poetry, if he sometimes disfigured an emotional sequence with a rigid and unsuitable frame, his frames (witness **"Prufrock"**) often redeem verse that might have degenerated into mawkish self-pity. In the infrequent instance when the emotional source and the intellectual armature of a poem coincide, it is Eliot's intellectual clarity that raises his work a step above the achievements of his greatest contemporaries. Eliot once said that what flawed the most serious poetry of Ezra Pound was that Pound rarely "has an image of the maximum concentration, an image which combines the precise and concrete with a kind of almost infinite suggestion." It is just this combination, I think, that makes a minor poem like **"A Song for Simeon"** instantly memorable and the emotional force of many of Pound's *Cantos* opaque until the third reading.

Still, **"A Song for Simeon"** *is* a minor poem. In the major poems, obvious in *The Waste Land,* less obvious in *Four Quartets,* Eliot's power is a result not of feeling and intellect working hand-in-glove but of powerful emotion held in powerful check. So constructed, the poems mime the central configuration of their author's psyche. . . . Writing at Easter 1928 to his religious confidant William Force Stead, Eliot told Stead that he needed the most severe kind of discipline. It was, according to Eliot, a question of compensation. Nothing, he said, could be too ascetic, too violent, for his needs.

The discipline that Eliot sought in his life, and felt he achieved only sporadically, permeates his work, where his success was more frequent, though never complete. If we forget this tension between what may be variously seen as impulse and discipline or sympathy and judgment, if we forget what may be generalized as the conflict between the "inside" and "outside" perspectives of Eliot's work, then we lose touch with what makes it most valuable and most characteristic. And if we choose to read Eliot's work primarily in terms of its anti-romantic attitudes, we are guilty of a shallow Puritanism of the kind that Eliot . . . [differentiated] from the vital Puritanism of the American tradition. (pp. x-xii)

If Eliot pursued the modernist dialectic between music and monologue throughout his career, then, it was not simply because he possessed the finest critical intelligence of the age; it was also because the dialectic was grounded in his character. A need to encounter his personal demons and a need to control them, a rebellious self-assertiveness and a compulsive self-censorship, began their quarrel in his psyche before he began to think of them as poles of stylistic choice and long before he was aware of them as issues in contemporary literature. Which is probably why his "rhythmic grumbling" has had such resonance in our time. The circumstances of Eliot's life made his acceptance of acquired conventions of speech repellent. He came instinctively to distrust received forms, and his aversion harmonized with his generation's dislike of rhetoric and later with the deconstructionists' awareness of the rhetoricity of language itself. Other writers incorporated the stylistic fashions of the time into their work or attempted to ignore them. Eliot seems to have had little choice. His genius fulfilled what his character demanded. (p. xii)

Ronald Bush, in a preface to his T. S. Eliot: A Study in Character and Style, *Oxford University Press, 1983, pp. ix-xiii.*

HYATT H. WAGGONER

In 1950, in the *The Heel of Elohim,* I could write, confident of general agreement, of T. S. Eliot as "the greatest poet writing in English today." My subject was American poetry, and the poets whose work I was comparing his with were Pound and Frost, Stevens not yet having been "discovered" by the critics I most respected. (p. 432)

Even by 1950 there had been some early signs of a poetic revolution to come that might have made me frame my judgment more cautiously. Delmore Schwartz in 1938 had already violated the cardinal Eliotic rule of "impersonal" poetry by doing without a persona and writing brilliantly of himself and his life, and Theodore Roethke in 1948 had published his autobiographic *The Lost Son;* but I did not yet realize Schwartz's immense promise, and it would be some years before Roethke's work was widely recognized for what it was and what it meant for the future of poetry.

By the end of the fifties there were unmistakable signs that Eliot's reign in modern poetry would not last much longer. Now the Beats were howling their discovery of Whitman and the open road, rejecting culture and tradition and taking to Zen and meditation. More significantly for poetry Lowell and Berryman were struggling to find their own voices, with Lowell's *Life Studies* (1959) being the first important, and ultimately the most influential, poetic rejection of the early Eliotic standard—a standard that Eliot himself of course had discarded in *The Four Quartets* and was busy now apologizing for in lectures. Meanwhile Randall Jarrell in *Poetry and the Age* (1953) had rescued several poets whose reputations had been hurt by Eliot's influence, especially Whitman, Frost, and Williams; and in 1960 we were urged by James Miller, Bernice Slote, and Karl Shapiro to "start with the sun" and rediscover Whitman and "the poetics of the cosmic poem."

After Eliot's death in 1965 rejection of him as man, poet, and critic quickly became the dominant fashion of the day, first among younger poets, then among younger critics. His Catholicism, at once religious and poetic, was swept aside as just as irrelevant as his announced "royalism" and "classicism" by the poetic reformers, along with all the rest that, rightly or wrongly, he was taken to stand for—cultural conservatism, "poetry of the library," and "impersonal poetry" particularly—in favor of poetry of the heart or of the psychiatrist's couch. The "invisible poet" was discovered to be visible behind his masks. To younger readers now Prufrock's trouble seemed to be not loss of belief but his excessive fastidiousness and his neurosis. . . . The New Critics might still occupy positions of power in English departments, but younger critics would soon make Stevens, not Eliot, the touchstone of the modern. A new romanticism was the order of the day, and any variety of classicism or formalism could be rejected without comment as we moved toward what one anthologist called the new naked poetry. (pp. 433-34)

Downward reassessments, after their deaths, of writers who have achieved great fame and influence during their lifetimes are commonplace; but the reaction against everything Eliotic was unusually strong, widespread, and uncritical. The effort was not to reach a more balanced judgment of his achievement but to reject, if necessary with ridicule and misreading, all that he had done and seemed to stand for. This man who had been, as John Ciardi called him, the literary equivalent of the Vatican's infallible Pope of our literature had become the enemy who must be routed if we were to move beyond modernism. Charles Olson urged his Black Mountain followers to get on with the job of "clearing away the junk of history"—religious, philosophic, and poetic. Eliot seemed to many, as he did to Williams, to be at once the spokesman for and the embodiment of that junk, so that what was called for was not a critical reassessment but a wholesale repudiation. The poetry could be ignored, but the authority of the man, with his values, attitudes, and commitments to the western tradition and particularly to

an Anglo-Catholic version of that tradition, had to be rejected. The parallel with the Protestant Reformation is suggestive on several levels. The fierceness of the rejection was a measure not so much of the achievement of the poet as of the power he had wielded. (p. 434)

Enough time has now elapsed to allow young poets to find themselves as poets without being forced to choose between obedience and open rebellion and to permit the rest of us to read Eliot's poetry as we read Emerson's or Whitman's or Hardy's, not primarily as supporting or challenging our own views and values but as *poetry.* . . .

How good a poet was Eliot? What did he accomplish in his verse? Which poems seem likely to be remembered longest? His achievement as a critic seems to me to have been adequately discussed, but such questions as these seem seldom to have been addressed directly in this post-New Critical era.

What I think we should do is to follow the advice in the last words of Pound's brief contribution to the Eliot *Sewanee* issue, "READ HIM"—the poems, not the library of explications and source studies. (p. 435)

Many of the poems I once enjoyed have been spoiled for me now by too much explication. I have found it very hard, and sometimes impossible, to get a fresh impression of them when the margins of my books are cluttered with explanatory notes. But by using the one edition in my library with clean margins, I have arrived at an impression of which poems now seem to me the most rewarding to reread, volume by volume as they came out. The best of them strike me as very distinguished poetry indeed, fine enough to support the view that Eliot was one of the several greatest poets of the first half of our century, with no need for any help from all the adulatory criticism by those who not only admired the poetry without reservation but shared the poet's values and beliefs.

The poems in *Prufrock and Other Observations* (1917) that strike me as most likely to endure are ["**The Love Song of J. Alfred Prufrock**"], "**Portrait of a Lady**," and "**La Figlia che Piange.**" Many of the others seem, in varying degrees, dated, or derivative, or trivial, or, at best, not clearly superior to similar poems by other poets of about the same time or a little later. (Surely for example one could find more impressive Imagist poems than "**Hysteria**" or satirical portraits not surpassed by "**Aunt Helen.**") But the three I have named, all of which either start from the poet's personal experience—"**Portrait**"—or express feelings we can safely assume he had known, pass the test Eliot would much later, in "**A Note on War Poetry**," when he had ceased demanding "impersonal" poetry, express as "private experience at its greatest intensity / Becoming universal."

A writer need not have been as self-conscious and fastidious as Prufrock to suffer from a loss of direction and meaning in that—or our—time and to connect that loss with the loss of living myths. . . . Then and now Prufrock's problem of knowing too much to be able to believe in anything might be called the problem of the well-educated for the last century or more. His monologue is at once that "confession" of an age that Emerson thought every generation needed from its poets and an expression of the modern conflict between knowledge and commitment, fact and value, that put epistemology at the very center of philosophy in our century.

Of "**Portrait**" and "**La Figlia**" I would say only this: that Eliot's "**Portrait**" is richer in meaning than Pound's or Williams's poems of similar title, and that **"La Figlia"** is a classic statement of the problem of the artist at any time, Hawthorne's for example, as he is not just tempted but in some sense required to *use* life, including other people and himself, as objectified material to be shaped into art. By contrast **"Morning at the Window"** seems to me to express only depression and snobbery, common enough of course but not interesting. It is too obvious that not all housemaids have damp souls.

In *Poems, 1920* there are three poems I can still read with real pleasure, the two Sweeney poems and **"The Hippopotamus"**; one, **"Gerontion,"** that I can admire without enjoying; and one, [**"Burbank with a Baedeker: Bleistein with a Cigar"**], that I find positively distasteful. The others I should be happy never to read again. Despite the Brahmin attitude toward the South Boston Irish in the Sweeney poems, the speaker in them seems to feel more pity than scorn for Sweeney, who is pictured as unaware but is not pushed outside the human race, as Bleistein is. The poems are an early and brilliant expression of that alienation of intellectuals from the popular culture of the masses that was noted by Unamuno and is still a feature of our unhappy century. **"The Hippopotamus"** is still funny and all the better because its satire of the church expresses the disappointment of a would-be convert.

"Gerontion" remains an historically important poem, despite its antisemitic lines and its hints that sex is nasty (there is much more of *this* in the parts of *The Waste Land* that Eliot deleted from his final version), for it gives powerful concrete expression to the alien universe and knowledge-as-destructive-of-value-and-meaning theme, the "nothing but" syndrome, that would soon become so common in the work of many of the greatest writers of the century. Reading it, we can better understand Eliot's later conversion, as well as the whole neoorthodox movement. Gerontion is Prufrock as he will be in a few years, unless he can find something to give more meaning to life than Henry Adams's dynamo. **"Burbank"** I find simply too repulsive for comment, and not only because of its antisemitism. The only possible reason for rereading it would be to remind us of how far Eliot himself had to travel in his effort to remake the man he found himself to be in his youth.

The Waste Land has been far too much explicated and discussed for me to feel that I have anything to add about it, except as the perspective provided by sixty years and the publication of Valerie Eliot's edition alter our response or judgment. The poem both gave a name to a period in literature and helped create that period. Its diagnosis of the period, at least as far as intellectuals and writers sensed it, was amazingly acute: the failure of both love and belief to provide meaning for our lives. Though Eliot would later dismiss it as no more than a "personal gripe," the finished poem does rise to that universality of meaning that Eliot demanded of poetry. The passages in the early drafts that most strongly suggest merely personal gripes were omitted from the finished poem—mostly, it would seem, by Eliot himself, not as a result of Pound's marginalia. The result is both a less personal and a more unified, if perhaps superficially less coherent, poem suggesting that if life is taken as a game, it's a game that can't be won. "Hurry up please, it's time," but time is precisely what we won't have when closing-time comes. The speaker at the end is still fishing in the dull canal and waiting for rain, so perhaps he will have time to profit by the words of the thunder. (pp. 435-37)

The Hollow Men (1925) and *Ash-Wednesday* (1930) both seem to me now to represent some falling-off of power. *The Hollow Men* spells out at tiresome length what had been more eco-

nomically and memorably, if ambiguously, implied in **"Gerontion"** and *The Waste Land,* and *Ash-Wednesday* is too dependent on the Ash Wednesday service in the Book of Common Prayer, rather thin by comparison with *The Waste Land,* and finally expressive only of the new convert's effort to put aside his learning and his pride and *really* believe the words of the service he hears and says. (The last section though I still find moving.)

Far better, it seems to me, are the two earlier postconversion dramatic monologues, **"Journey of the Magi"** and **"A Song for Simeon,"** and the beautiful lyric **"Marina."** Both the monologues seem at once more formally "impersonal" than *The Hollow Men* and *Ash-Wednesday* and yet more meaningfully revealing of what we can suppose were the poet's own thoughts and what he really felt. The biblical characters from Matthew and Luke are fully realized figures, and it is safe to assume that the poet felt a special affinity for them, for the three kings or "wise men" whose long and difficult journey had left them unsure of what the birth meant, and for Simeon, who had to be content with the knowledge that he would never be a saint, a martyr, or a mystic granted the ultimate vision.

"Marina" seems to me the most rewarding short poem to reread that Eliot ever wrote. Though the ambiguity first introduced by the title and the epigraph is maintained throughout, yet this poem is a happy one, even a joyous one. The images seem drawn not from ancient myth but from the poet's early experience of sailing off the coast of Cape Ann, with the mythological Philomel replaced by the common woodthrush. The speaker finds the natural world no longer disgusting, boring, or ultimately threatening, even though the boat he has made for his journey is far from perfect, his exact location uncertain in the fog, and of course the whole feeling of being on the way may be only a dream: he cannot *know,* but seems content not to. Untypical of Eliot's poems though it is—except in the allusiveness of its title and epigraph—**"Marina"** is surely one of his greatest.

The Four Quartets may not be, as Randall Jarrell once called it, "the greatest long poem of the 20th century," but despite its unevenness it remains not only a very distinguished poem but a very moving one. . . . When it speaks to us most strongly, it could be described as a meditation on time and eternity, or life and death. Only in the lyrics that make up section four of each quartet does doctrine seem to be not only influencing but controlling the poem, and these parts may be skipped by readers who are not Anglo-Catholic without great loss to what I take to be the final impression left by the poem, of the limited value of "knowledge derived from experience" and the consequent need of a faith that goes beyond the "evidence."

Despite the explicitly doctrinal passages, the poem expresses feelings and attitudes that link it with the work of Emerson, especially in his journals, and of Whitman, especially in "Lilacs" and other late poems. We find Emerson's dissatisfaction with the quotidian and Whitman's late conviction that though grand is the seen, the unseen is grander still. Of course the dark view of life's possibilities, despite the work of "the wounded surgeon," is here also, to remind us both of how different Eliot's temperament was from Emerson's and Whitman's and of the fact that the poem was written in a less hopeful age, so that such abstract parallels must not be pressed too far. (pp. 437-39)

It was probably Bergson more than any other philosopher who prepared Eliot to write the meditative parts of the poem on time and memory (especially **"Burnt Norton"**) and matter and spirit, or spirit's involvement with nature (**"The Dry Salvages"**), as Bradley had been drawn on earlier for "the thousand sordid images" of which the soul was said to be constituted. In the Quartets we are beyond the Realism/Idealism choice, as Bergson had felt he was. Real time is not measurable in terms of space or in any way quantifiable, so that we cannot move beyond philosophic dualism. "The salt is on the briar rose" and "The river is within us." From Bergson to an Anglo-Catholic understanding of the meaning of the Incarnation is not an impossible leap, as the relation between Bergson's belief that it was necessary to affirm both that "we are, to a certain extent, what we do, and that we are creating ourselves continually" and many passages in the Quartets should illustrate. "Not fare well, / But fare forward, voyagers," choosing freely within strict limits the kind of self we would be.

The voice we hear in *The Four Quartets* is Eliot's own, as there is no need to surmise when we note the pronouns on the first page of **"Burnt Norton"**—*my, I, we*. What this means we discover as we read on: no more "poetry of the library," no more personae, no more "mythological method"—in short a dropping of masks and defenses. The poet who in **"Prufrock"** and **"Gerontion"** had dramatized aspects of himself that he did not like now feels secure enough to speak to us directly from his experience and belief—though still, of course, without becoming "confessional" in Roethke's way.

I suspect that Eliot had found the myths of the Garden and the Fall expressive of his own experience and that his conversion helped him to see that experience as part of the human condition, not uniquely shameful. Earlier, feeling terribly vulnerable, he had adopted various stratagems to make himself invulnerable, both personally and poetically. He had been, as a man, highly mannered as well as fastidious and proud. . . . Aware of his vulnerability now but better able to accept it, as a poet he can stop hiding behind masks, and as a man he can dispense with the more outrageous mannerisms and the courteous arrogance that had once been his way of coping with his shyness.

After more than thirty productive years he could stop writing lyric poetry, except for an occasional poem. Having urged old men to be explorers, the "aged eagle" who had spent his youth anticipating the losses of age, fearing he might become a Gerontion, now explored the possibilities in verse drama, though here too, as in his occasional poems, the quality of his writing seems to me to have declined as the anxiety lessened. I find *Murder in the Cathedral* and *The Family Reunion* far more impressive than *The Elder Statesman,* in which I can applaud only the theme: love can save us. Or, again, a comparison of **"The Journey of the Magi,"** which expresses the disappointment of the convert at not finding himself suddenly "born again," with the late **"The Cultivation of Christmas Trees"** may secure my point: the better man has become the lesser poet. The weariness and disappointment of the Magi, along with the fatigue, boredom, and disgust of **"Preludes"** and **"Morning at the Window,"** are gone, replaced by healthier and more charitable attitudes and by greater wisdom; but the language of the early poems seems much more memorable, however we may deplore the attitudes. (pp. 439-40)

What Eliot has left us with is a volume of distinguished poems, long and short, a volume slender by comparison with Williams's or Stevens's total output but never filled with mere notes for unwritten poems like Williams's or repetitious and predictable like Stevens's: poems that give us still today the words to express, and thus be better able to understand and cope with, our own experience, our distress, our fears, and our occasionally possible hopes.

The "lost generation" was followed by a new generation equally or more desperately lost, as the lives and the work of Jarrell, Berryman, Lowell, and Roethke illustrate; then by several generations of poets unable to take seriously what Eliot, Hemingway, Faulkner, and others thought had been lost but also generally unable to find a satisfactory substitute, until today, when we may expect many of our most honored poets to indulge in word games or to remain locked within purely private experience. Eliot's way of retrieving what had been lost may be impossible for most poets today, but it offered him a way of living in and writing about the world we all briefly inhabit. Like the other modernists Eliot rejected popular culture, but unlike some other artists he did not rely on shock effect to express his radical rejection. His poems no longer shock us, but they still stand up under critical reading. Though reflecting wide learning, they do not require that we read the explications first, as many of the Cantos do, to find out what they are all about. Randall Jarrell was right . . . when he noted in 1962 that the poems were not really "classical," objective, impersonal, etc., but "subjective and daemonic." The best of them, early and late, free us from "the illusion of technique" and help us to know, if not what must be believed, at least what our choices are and in what direction we must travel if we are to find meaning for our lives in a time when all life on earth is threatened by the results of our knowledge and the power over nature it has given us. The great poet writes such poems of lasting "universal" significance whatever his poetic mode.

If we are to do T. S. Eliot's poetry justice in this time when the waste land is no longer a metaphor for cultural decline but is a literal physical possibility, we shall first of all, I think, have to reject Eliot's own early rejection of Emerson's half-truth—that the true poet, not just versifier, must first be a Seer in order to be a Namer and Sayer. What Eliot "saw" and gave us the words for in his poems has already outlasted the New Criticism and will I suspect outlast us, along with the best poems of Yeats, Frost, Stevens, and perhaps Pound. (pp. 440-41)

Hyatt H. Waggoner, "Eliot as Poet," in The Sewanee Review, *Vol. XCII, No. 3, Summer, 1984, pp.432-41.*

DAVID SPURR

In his 1930 essay on Baudelaire, T. S. Eliot suggests that the formal concerns of some nineteenth-century poets support or conceal "an inner disorder" and that in Baudelaire's poems "the content of feeling is constantly bursting the receptacle." Eliot's distinctions between form and content, and between conflicting elements of the Romantic sensibility, may or may not further our understanding of Baudelaire and his contemporaries; they do, however, both suggest and sanction a valuable line of approach to his own poetry. A forty-year tradition of Eliot scholarship has established plausible grounds for narrative coherence in each of Eliot's major poems, and continues to reveal an ever-widening range of literary influences on the poet's work. This same tradition, however, has left largely unexplored the sources of structural tension in Eliot's poems and the problem of relating these tensions to a developing poetic consciousness. Eliot himself says of Baudelaire's poems, "Their excellence of form, their perfection of phrasing, and their superficial coherence, may give them the appearance of presenting a definite and final state of mind.'' But then he goes on to argue a discrepancy between what he calls their external and internal forms. In a similar paradox, Eliot scholarship has created a superficial coherence in his work by assuming a definite state of mind or point of view in each poem. In their tendency to accept Eliot's critical and poetic statements at face value, scholars have overlooked the fundamental conflicts that lie below the surface of Eliot's language.

While the mainstream of this critical tradition continues to take Eliot's pronouncements on poetry as the authoritative guide to his own work, the influence of emerging critical methodologies in recent years has generated a subversive countercurrent to this tradition. This relatively new critical attitude attempts to identify the submerged conflicts of Eliot's language and generally sees his poetry, like his critical writings and even his personality, as divided against itself in various ways. (pp. xi-xii)

The reading of Eliot that I am proposing . . . shares with psychoanalytic approaches to literature the attempt to establish connections between the text and the author's unconscious, while it also follows certain deconstructive procedures in its refusal to take for granted the textual coherence of any poem. This kind of reading not only treats the poem as reflecting the inner forces of the poet's imagination; it also assumes that these forces may run at cross-purposes to one another; the multilayered quality of psychological motivation accounts for a similar quality of the text.

Those who have identified the problem of a divided sensibility in Eliot's poetry all make a basic distinction between forces of order and disorder. My own study leads to a somewhat different formulation, which sees Eliot's poems as enacting a dramatic rivalry between the two kinds of order, one rational and a product of the poet's intellectual power, the other intuitive and a product of the more primitive and spontaneous aspect of the poet's imagination.

Intellectual order, or the poet's attempt to make rational sense out of the world around him, manifests itself typically in Eliot's images of concentration, division, and apportionment. The impulse ''to have squeezed the universe into a ball,'' as well as the image of a ''still point of the turning world,'' reflects a desire to master existence through the phenomenon of spatial concentration. A voice cries out of **The Waste Land,** ''Shall I at least set my lands in order?'' while a later voice can state with confidence in divine dispensation: ''This is the land. We have our inheritance.'' The aspect of the poet's sensibility that seeks a rationally comprehensible world often seeks the intervention of forces from outside this world as external sources of order. The prophet Lazarus, Christ the tiger, the speaking thunder, and the Lady of silences all represent other-worldly forces to which the poet looks, however momentarily or equivocally, for a way of defining his own world. The function of such imagery is continually supported on another level by the language of mental activity—of thought, knowledge, and memory—which reveals the poet's preoccupation with the nature of the conscious mind and its relation to experience. . . . (pp. xii-xiii)

These approaches to the meaning or ''acts of mind'' embodied in Eliot's language and imagery have in common a tendency to *impose* order on a world that, left to itself, would fly apart at the seams or drift forever in aimlessness: ''We cannot think of a time that is oceanless / Or of an ocean not littered with wastage.'' The ordering principle thus appears as external to a world in need of order; Lazarus must come from the dead,

the thunder must speak from above, the mind must deliberately ''construct something / Upon which to rejoice.''

''There is a logic of the imagination as well as a logic of concepts,'' Eliot writes in the preface to his translation of Saint-John Perse's *Anabase*. Lifting this remark out of its original context, we may borrow Eliot's distinction between imagination and conceptual thinking in order to define the polarity of his own poetic consciousness. Over against his ''diurnal'' tendency to master experience through images of division and concentration and through a corresponding vocabulary of conscious mental activity, there lies a ''nocturnal'' aspect of the poet that seeks to describe a set of relations which could not be defined in terms of a purely conceptual framework—Eliot's relatively undeveloped version of Baudelaire's *''ténébreuse et profonde unité.''* By referring casually to this diurnal tendency as ''intellect'' and to the opposing nocturnal tendency as ''imagination,'' we may say that where the intellect seeks control of subject over object, the imagination joins the two: ''You are the music while the music lasts.'' The ordering principle of the material of the imagination arises internally rather than being imposed from without, as in the figure of the Chinese jar, which ''Moves perpetually in its stillness.'' As the imagination conceives of order dynamically rather than statically, so ''the detail of the pattern is movement.''

Ordinarily when we speak of poetic imagination we use this term in a general way to include the various psychological phenomena that enter into the creative act. Certainly in this conventional sense all poetic images—natural or supernatural, architectural or mechanical—are expressive of the imagination. But for purely practical purposes here I wish to limit the meaning of *imagination* by using it exclusively in connection with the isolated aspect of Eliot's consciousness that produces his version of the Romantic or Symbolist vision, often dreamlike in quality, which conforms to organic rather than conceptual principles of order. This ''visionary'' imagination creates in Eliot's poetry a symbolic structure that defines itself primarily in images of flight, expansion, depth, and response. The spatial character of these images combines with their semantic value to create a set of interlocking themes that together constitute Eliot's Romantic-Symbolist vision: purity, the descent to a submerged inner world, the merging of the human and the natural. (pp. xiii-xiv)

The forces of imagination moving through images . . . constantly challenge the intellect for domination of the poet's sensibility in a way that affects the overall structure of each poem. The poet's intellect serves his will; but as [the critic C. K. Stead] remarks, Eliot relies for inspiration on creative moments that occur independently of the will. Both kinds of order are positive, but they remain for the most part unreconciled: the imagination in its subaqueous plunges and its angelic flights tends to evade the task of conquering experience that the intellect sets for itself, while the intellect in turn denies the validity of the imagination's life, of ''The empty forms between the ivory gates.''

Between the ideals of imaginative order and intellectual order in Eliot's poetry lies a disordered middle ground, a ''place of disaffection'' where the poet records mimetically the raw data of seemingly random experience, without according it any particular ontological value: ''empty bottles, sandwich papers, / Silk handkerchiefs, cardboard boxes, cigarette ends.'' This area of the poet's sensibility belongs neither to the intellect nor to the imagination in the limited way we have used these terms as principles of order; disorder is simply disorder. The poetic persona remains for a time passive in the face of his chaotic universe. This is, of course, to treat the disorder of experience as part of the poem's subject matter, the monster of horror and *ennui* the poet-hero must either conquer or evade. Thus in Eliot's work the images of disorder have their own structures of fragmentation, isolation, circular movement, endless repetition, aimless wandering, and random profusion [as in these lines from **"Burnt Norton"**]:

> Tumid apathy with no concentration
> Men and bits of paper, whirled by the cold wind
> That blows before and after time,
> Wind in and out of unwholesome lungs
> Time before and time after.

Time here is the dragon of endless succession, which if the poet cannot slay (''Only through time time is conquered''), he can flee from at privileged moments into the timeless sanctuaries of a visionary world populated by mermaids, hyacinth girls, laughing children, and antic musicians. (pp. xiv-xv)

One could describe [Eliot's] career as a series of confrontations with a visionary imagination that [he] can neither conquer nor reconcile wholly with other aspects of his poetic consciousness. The nature of these confrontations changes with the evolution of Eliot's poetic identity as reflected in the character of the ''speaker'' in each poem. The rivalry between intellectual and imaginative order establishes itself in the two great poems of Eliot's early period, **"The Love Song of J. Alfred Prufrock"** (published 1917) and **"Gerontion"** (published 1920). In each of these poems the failure of a self-conscious mind to master its own situation amid images of random profusion and labyrinthine space leads to escape into images of purity, flight, and intimacy. The form of the dramatic monologue, however, provides an ironic distance that allows Eliot to discredit his visionary imagination. **"Prufrock"** takes a dream-vision worthy of Nerval or Baudelaire and attaches it to a Laforguian character ''Full of high sentence, but a bit obtuse.'' The speaker of **"Gerontion"** dismisses the Mallarméan flight of his imagination (''Gull against the wind'') as ''Thoughts of a dry brain in a dry season.'' In both cases the visionary imagery testifies to a source of inspiration that runs at cross-purposes to the poem's surface rhetoric.

Eliot's poetic persona breaks down in *The Waste Land* (published 1922) to produce a multiplicity of voices scattered throughout the poem. This phenomenon combined with the actual fragmentation of linguistic forms sabotages the visionary imagination by allowing it to surface only in bits and pieces uttered by a profusion of different speakers. One hears at different points in the poem and in apparently unrelated contexts a Wagnerian sailor singing from the mast, Verlaine's children singing in the tower, and a hermit-thrush singing in the pine trees. On one level of reading, the isolated nature of such fragments simply conforms to the poem's general ethos of disorder and random destruction. On another level, however, the images conform to a symbolic structure that joins images of elevation, music, and purity to images of descent and fusion with nature. This symbolic alliance points to a visionary inner world of the poet's consciousness that remains intact despite the poem's more obvious rhetoric of collapse, like oceanic depths undisturbed by storms at the surface.

The disintegration of Eliot's persona in *The Waste Land* signals a crisis of poetic identity, which, after a long period of silence, leaves him with the notion of speaker as mask alone in *The Hollow Men* (published 1925): ''Such deliberate disguises /

Rat's coat, crowskin, crossed staves.'' This denial of identity provides Eliot with a new line of assault on the visionary imagination. If the speaker amounts only to a scarecrow's mask, his Edenic vision can only belong to ''Death's dream kingdom.'' This very abdication of self-identity prepares for the adoption of a Christian persona in *Ash-Wednesday* (published 1930); for in Eliot's version of the ascetic process, the individual must purge himself of his own being in order to be filled by God. In this poem Eliot's Romantic vision surfaces in images of expansion and correspondence with nature that repeatedly frustrate more conscious movements of concentration and *askesis*—the Christian process of self-purgation involving the deliberate ''emptying-out'' of the soul. The speaker's Christian role allows him to attack the natural vision on theological grounds: the attraction to nature distracts the soul from God.

Eliot's role as the aging poet in *Four Quartets* (published 1943) signals a final attempt to reconcile the divergent forces of his sensibility by assimilating the forces of the imagination to a larger conceptual framework involving notions of time. Having evolved beyond an orthodox Christian attitude, Eliot now comes closer than ever to his Romantic and Symbolist predecessors by ascribing mystical significance to his moments of vision. Imagination once more conflicts with intellect, as the poet attempts unsuccessfully to formulate a worldly meaning for his mystical vision. The poet's ''undisciplined squads of emotion'' again defy the intellectual order which the poet attempts to impose on his experience when they move toward a form of order independent of the intellect. The struggle to conquer time cannot succeed when what the poet really values is not to be found in time.

In certain respects the fundamental divisions of Eliot's consciousness can be seen as paradigmatic for the poetic act itself: to some extent all poets are drawn to both rational and visionary unities in giving form to an essentially chaotic experience. But what sets Eliot apart from his great spiritual and artistic models—Dante, Baudelaire, Yeats—is the intensity with which this polar opposition pulls the text apart at various levels and therefore becomes itself a kind of demon to be exorcised. It may be said of the other great poets, I believe, that a rational construct provides, trellislike, the very framework that allows the visionary experience to unfold: Dante's ordered ascent, Baudelaire's controlled sonnet form, Yeats's dialectic between self and image. Eliot's visionary unities, on the other hand, surface around the edges or between the crevices of his rational construct. While other poets have brought about the fusion of intellect and imagination, in Eliot these forces either diverge or come together in recurrent struggles for supremacy.

The terms in which I have described the evolution of Eliot's embattled sensibility make it possible to divide his career into two stages. In the first stage, the ironic persona of the early poems eventually disintegrates under the pressure of the poet's inner conflicts; *The Waste Land* shows us a fragmented persona whose different voices express opposing factions of the poet's consciousness. The process that culminates in *The Waste Land* has its parallels with the process that begins with *The Hollow Men* and culminates in the *Four Quartets*.

In the second stage of Eliot's poetic evolution, he adopts an external set of values rather than an ironic persona, but this new role serves somewhat the same function by providing a structure to combat the forces of a visionary imagination. In this respect Eliot's Gerontion and Eliot's converted Christian unite in a common defense against an imagination that threatens to engulf the poet's mind—hence, in *Ash-Wednesday,* the simultaneous love and fear of "the lost lilac and the lost sea voices" and the speaker's redoubled effort at concentration and prayer: "Teach us to care and not to care / Teach us to sit still." The *Four Quartets* represent a development beyond the limited context of this Christian poem, just as *The Waste Land* signaled a development beyond the dramatic monologue and the quatrain poem. Rather than a final synthesis of psychological values, however, Eliot's last great work enacts an elaborate unfolding of divergent impulses that it can only claim to unite on a rhetorical level. For all their deliberate formal order, the *Four Quartets* reveal as much internal divisiveness as does *The Waste Land* (pp. xvi-xix)

[This] evolution of Eliot's sensibility develops in his critical writings as well as in his poems. The tensions involved here lend strength to poetry, but apparently they can be ruinous to the poet himself. Either from the ascetic demands of spiritual devotion or from weariness with continual raids on the inarticulate, Eliot allows the *Four Quartets* to stand as his farewell to poetry. From this point on, his critical work also loses much of its bite, taking the form of official pronouncements from the elder statesman of letters: "**What Is a Classic?**", "**The Aims of Education,**" "**The Classics and the Man of Letters.**"

An analysis of Eliot's work that divides his sensibility into separate and identifiable components no doubt threatens to become a reductivist portrayal of an extremely complex artistic mind and, in a way, imitates Eliot's own passion for logic and apportionment. The violence of such an approach may perhaps be tolerated, but with the reminder that the notion of "forces" and "movements" in the poet's consciousness are intended simply as metaphors for various levels of the text. Only in the interest of elucidating the text is it useful to speak, again metaphorically, of its sources in "sensibility," "mind," "intellect," or "imagination." Finally, an analysis of a poet's work that discovers unresolved conflicts and ambiguities should not necessarily be regarded as an attack. On the contrary, it seems more likely that the life of an artist's work is sustained by the energy of inner forces in opposition, whether one calls them intellect and imagination, conscious and unconscious, or thought and emotion. Eliot's poetry represents a consciousness whose emotional intensity derives from an awareness of its own inner divisions; its strength lies in its refusal to allow the controlling power of the intellect or the controlling form of the poem to annihilate the dark impulses of horror and ecstasy. (pp. xix-xx)

David Spurr, in an introduction to his Conflicts in Consciousness: T. S. Eliot's Poetry and Criticism, *University of Illinois Press, 1984, pp. xi-xx.*

F. T. PRINCE

What will always matter is the poetry of [Eliot's] *Collected Poems* . . . ; the poetry guarantees a lasting but lesser interest in the prose, the plays, and the biographical record, such as it is. If Eliot had not created unique poetic objects in a new poetic idiom, his criticism would never have had such prestige; at its best it has more than documentary interest, but it flagged, and in later years he himself began to cut it down to size. Even at their best, his plays are comparatively factitious. Like Yeats, he turned to the theatre when his 'lyrical' inspiration seemed to come to an end, and profited from the new experience to return to poetry (*Murder in the Cathedral* led him to "**Burnt Norton**"). He had no natural gift for drama, in this too like Yeats, and his plays of modern life may be regarded as an old

man's amusements, though hardly 'dotages', as Dryden said Jonson's last pieces were.

'Old men should be explorers.' Distinguished as poet, critic, and ideologue, 'the agèd eagle' would stretch his wings in the hope that his experiments might contribute to a new English verse drama. He would let nothing pass that was not very carefully thought out and precisely expressed, both profound and ingenious. But it was a serious handicap that he could only re-use, and use to less effect, the experiences which had given life to his poetry up to and including *The Waste Land.* Harry Monchensey and Celia Coplestone can only spell out, diluting them in the process, the horror and disgust and sense of guilt which are more effectively dramatised in "**Gerontion,**" "**A Game of Chess,**" and "**The Fire Sermon.**"

As for the private life, the recent remarkable biography by Peter Ackroyd [see *CLC,* Vol. 34] gives all that we need to know, and somewhat more. (p. 82)

The enemies of Eliot's work and fame may hope or imagine that they have found more evidence against him, as biographical details are filled in; but only malice or prejudice can regard . . . [the story of his life] as damaging. The story as we have it (and we have it so fully that it is not likely to change much) is one of misfortune and effort, of endurance and achievement. What emerges—and no doubt it will be a stumbling-block to many—is that, in spite of Eliot's 'deliberate disguises' and his capacity for survival, he was a *poète maudit.* The disguises present him successively as a sleek, brilliant, though languid, young Harvard 'patrician', a bowler-hatted City clerk equipped with foreign languages, a London editor and publisher with a European vision, a modernist poet and playwright of international fame, and an Anglo-Catholic sage. . . . If a *maudit* has to spoil his life, Eliot seems not to have done so. Indeed there is no dissipation or disintegration, but the biography records so much suffering, and we can trace so deep a connection between that and the poetry, that the rather un-English tradition of the poet as scapegoat is certainly relevant. Eliot wished us to accept a doctrine of separation between 'the man who suffers and the mind which creates' ("**Tradition and the Individual Talent**"); and his mind was so remarkable that we may want to agree. But in such cases as his, and perhaps in all major literary reputations, there cannot fail to be a personal legend, the other side of the work achieved, which the work will have to carry with it for all time, 'A sort of battered kettle at the heel'.

The irreducible core of Eliot's work, the poetry, offers a clear 'spiritual autobiography' of a kind which is rare in English poetry. But such a record is bound to have a 'political' aspect, and like a purely political equivalent, it must make as many enemies as friends. An art which begins as experimental and subversive and ends as an expression of faith in traditional religion and culture is doubly provocative. It is not surprising that many of Eliot's contemporaries stood back or were alienated, or that scepticism and distaste should survive him. His unfriendly critics will have, and should have, their say, but they have to submit to examination in their turn. We should beware of moving towards such criteria as those of some American editors, who say they will consider only 'positive' poems, to be written presumably by 'positive' people. The distinctive greatness of Eliot's poetry, at least in its first two phases, is that it derives from 'negative' emotions and experiences, the areas of experience which he found had been explored in French by Laforgue and Baudelaire, and in English by the Jacobean dramatists and Donne. He discovered procedures by means of which he could make his own, new kind of poetry out of the 'negative' vision, procedures or methods which continued to serve him when his life and poetry took another direction, and found new ways of dealing with the 'negative' experience.

Can we trace and define these methods? He tells us that Laforgue and the Jacobeans helped him to begin, and in versification the debt is obvious. Verse, the aural component, is indeed consistently one decisive factor for him, and so a part of his method. When he achieves a musicality that satisfies him, the poem has arrived and stands free. Such musical invention springs from a depth below consciousness, and so of course must much else—images, sensations, associations of all kinds. Eliot's method, as far as it can be traced . . . , was to empty his conscious mind, to keep open house for what might come (from the half-glimpsed *donnée*, the scene, verbal accidents, or whatever): but to subject what did come to repeated critical revisions, and always to try to order it within a pattern, a framework of themes or concepts. For example, there is the patterning of **"Rhapsody on a Windy Night,"** the alternation between observation and reflection: the street lamps briskly punctuate the speaker's walk and number off its stages, the things seen in or from the street set off straggling private associations which have their own sinister logic. Or there is the use of the turnings of the stairs in *Ash-Wednesday,* or the threefold Sanskrit injunctions in **"What the Thunder Said."**

Patterning, a habit of schematism, of imposing analytical or categorical blueprints on experience, gives a durable toughness to all of Eliot's constructions, in drama and criticism as well as in poetry. Yet one may feel that the writing loses in intensity, as his 'ideas' grow clearer and harden. The scheme or pattern most relevant to the poetry is stated in *The Use of Poetry and the Use of Criticism* (1934), in the reference to the poet's need to see 'the boredom, the horror, and the glory.' The essay on Dante (1929) had already indicated a triad of moral consciousness based on Dante's three worlds, suggesting that Purgatory and Paradise lie beyond 'the ordinarily very limited human range.' In *The Waste Land* we are undoubtedly in Hell: the typist's 'boredom' is seen as 'horror' by Tiresias. 'Glory' is to be seen, if at all, in glimpses, though one could argue that it is somehow present in the movement towards purgation and the total organised vision of the poem. But as early as the set of four **"Preludes"** Eliot had built on three levels of consciousness: first, anonymous urban life ('Morning comes to consciousness', II; 'The conscience of a blackened street', IV); next, the 'vision of the street' that 'the street hardly understands', in the worn-out waking woman in III, and in the trampled dissenting 'soul' of the city-dweller in IV; and finally the moving glimpse of 'The notion of an infinitely gentle / Infinitely suffering thing' in IV.

Fitting material into patterns or schemes makes possible both a concentration on essentials in small units and a bringing together of diverse materials in larger units. *The Waste Land* drafts show the importance of a framework in these processes of stripping and concentrating, on both the large scale and the small (Pound's comments and advice contributing to both). In the drafts the 'song of the first Thames-daughter begins as seven limping lines of direct statement, unconvincing as a voice for the supposed character and founded uncertainly on Eliot's view from the outside of lower-middle-class London. It ends, after Dante has helped in the use of place-names, as four short rhymed and dancing verses, and both place-names and dancing rhythms and rhymes give the cue for the next two women. And this small piece of concentration and patterning is held in place by the larger framework of **"The Fire Sermon,"** which begins and ends with the river and circles round Augustine's 'cauldron of unholy loves'.

Eliot's modernist revolution set out to make poetry ('of the first intensity') out of the ordinary and the unpoetical. He wrapped himself in the appearances of ordinariness, defining himself at one moment as 'a practitioner of poetry', at another as not a poet, but a man who sometimes wrote poems. In spite of the mask of ordinariness, nothing about him was ordinary— neither his mind nor his personality, nor the circumstances of his early life, nor his life as it took shape when he came to England and married. His poetry was born of and developed through crisis, the crisis first of a prolonged inexperienced adolescence, then of prolonged frustration in marriage; the crises of the First World War and its aftermath, and of the Second War and its preliminaries. . . . The power and fascination of his poetry lie in its use of a subdued rational manner of speaking to deal with the violent irrational forces of human experience, whether of darkness or light—whether opening up abysses of horror and suffering, or pointing to 'the heart of light, the silence'. (pp. 83-6)

> *F. T. Prince, "The Man and the Mind," in* Agenda, *Vol. 23, Nos. 1 & 2, Spring & Summer, 1985, pp. 82-6.*

CLEANTH BROOKS

In the years before Eliot took out British citizenship, his friend Sir Herbert Read was aware, he tells us, of "the struggle going on in Eliot's mind" between the claims of England and his native America. In the essay which Read contributed to *T. S. Eliot: the Man and His Work,* he does not state what he believes was the decisive factor in Eliot's ultimate decision; instead, he simply prints the following excerpt from a letter that Eliot wrote to him on 23 April 1928.

> Some day [Eliot wrote] I want to write an essay about the point of view of an American who wasn't an American, because he was born in the South and went to school in New England as a small boy with a nigger drawl, but wasn't a southerner in the South because his people were northerners in a border state and looked down on all southerners and Virginians, and who so was never anything anywhere and who therefore felt himself to be more a Frenchman than an American and more an Englishman than a Frenchman and yet felt that the U.S.A. up to a hundred years ago was a family extension.

Just how seriously are we to take all this? Is Eliot simply being playful with his friend? Even if the account contains its grain of truth—and I believe it does—it also clearly contains a good measure of exaggeration. Nevertheless, it is Eliot's first and indeed, so far as I know, his only reference to his having a southern connection. (p. 914)

[The] Page-Barbour Lectures, which [Eliot] gave in 1933 at the University of Virginia, can tell us a great deal about what he thought of the South. The lectures were published in 1934 under the title *After Strange Gods.* The first lecture, addressed specifically to the Virginians, is a carefully considered statement of ideas and principles that are integral to Eliot's later work and thought.

In this first lecture, he says that he had never visited the South until he crossed the Potomac in 1933 on his journey to Charlottesville. Though in his 1928 letter to Read he does claim to have been born in the South, we remember that he immediately goes on to qualify this statement by telling Read that his parents were northerners living in a border state; for Missouri, though it can claim one of the stars in the Confederate Stars and Bars, is in fact more accurately described as a border state in which the Union sympathizers were very numerous and soon gained control.

At any rate, Eliot makes it quite clear that he regarded this visit to Virginia as his first to the South whose tradition he meant to discuss as having proved special and important on the North American continent.

The close relation of these Page-Barbour lectures to Eliot's developing ideas is confirmed by his statement that he was taking this first visit to the Old South as an apt occasion for a reformulation of his early essay, **"Tradition and the Individual Talent."** In that essay he had been concerned primarily with the individual writer. Obviously he meant now to discuss tradition in its larger terms as affecting a whole society. Because Eliot saw in the American South an example of what he meant by a tradition still alive and relatively coherent, his lectures in Virginia would offer a proper occasion for such a reformulation and for an extension of such an examination. True, Eliot avoided mere flattery. He described in more guarded terms the cultural situation as it now existed: he told his audience that he expected to find in Virginia "at least some recollection of a 'tradition' such as the influx of foreign populations has almost effaced in some parts of the North, and such as never established itself in the West," though he immediately added that "it is hardly to be expected that a tradition here, any more than anywhere else, should be found in health and flourishing growth." (pp. 915-16)

Just how seriously can we take the compliments that Eliot addressed to his southern hosts? Eliot is known for his civility and his courtesy. Besides, a lecturer is not only tempted but licensed to give a certain amount of praise to his auditors, especially if they comprise people of another nationality or even of another pronounced regional difference. . . . Eliot does show his acute awareness of his cultural difference from his hosts. Thus, at one point he tells his Virginia audience that a complimentary remark that he had just made "should carry more weight for being spoken by a Yankee."

Nevertheless, I believe that what Eliot says in *After Strange Gods* on the subject of southern culture he did mean very seriously; and especially what he had to say about tradition, about the relation of the region to the nation, and about the nature of culture and the character of the good life. But he speaks as a realist. In fact, in his first lecture he fully recognizes the intense pressure on the South to change its ways and the difficulties that it would find in preserving its own identity. It is not too much to say that *After Strange Gods* amounts to a grim warning rather than an invitation to self-congratulation.

How can I be so confident of this estimate? Because of two considerations. The first is that Eliot had evidently read with deep interest and sympathy *I'll Take My Stand* [the manifesto of the group of southern writers who formed the Agrarian Movement advocating a return to the values of a pastoral culture], which had been published three years earlier. So he was well aware of the analysis that a group of southerners had

recently made of the present plight of, and future prospects for, the region.

In short, the Yankee visitor, now a British subject, had not simply succumbed to the charm of Charlottesville and Mr. Jefferson's University of Virginia. Very early in his first lecture he refers to *I'll Take My Stand* by name, and throughout the course of that first lecture he refers to Agrarianism and to what he chose to call the neo-Agrarians.

Yet he could not have been unaware of the fact that many southerners thoroughly disagreed with the Agrarians and that the University of Virginia itself could hardly be considered to be a stronghold of the Agrarian movement. . . . But it should make plain that in his first lecture, Eliot knew that he could not take for granted that he was preaching to the converted and had no reason to assume agreement from his listeners when he praised the virtues of the older southern culture.

There is a second and far more cogent reason for taking seriously Eliot's praise of the South's regional culture. Fifteen years later he would publish his *Notes Toward a Definition of Culture*, a much more elaborate formulation and development of the position he sketches in the first of his Page-Barbour lectures. In spite of the modesty of its title, the *Notes* constitutes a detailed elaboration of Eliot's ideas on the nature of a culture and the mode of its transmission from one generation to another. Its third chapter, entitled "Unity and Diversity: The Region," has a particular relation to what Eliot told his Virginia audience about the relation of southern culture to American culture generally considered. Naturally, in the *Notes,* a book that was calculated to the longitude of Great Britain, the regions with which Eliot is principally concerned are Ireland, Wales and Scotland. But the principles involved apply fully to the relation of America's most self-conscious region, the South, to the United States as a totality.

So it was not the tradition-laden atmosphere of the Old Campus at Charlottesville, Jefferson's beautifully planned arrangement of buildings and grounds, that drew from Eliot as visitor indulgent comments on regionalism and culture of the South's older day. On the contrary, Eliot obviously did see in the American South at least some residue of habits of mind and of a traditional way of life which he regarded as having universal value. (pp. 916-18)

That Eliot regarded as fully relevant to the American South his discussion of the relation of the cultures of Ireland, Wales and Scotland to the dominant culture of England becomes fully clear in the following passage from his first Page-Barbour Lecture:

> No one, surely, can cross the Potomac for the first time without being struck by differences so great that their extinction could only mean the death of both cultures. . . . to come into Virginia is as definite an experience as to cross from England to Wales. . . .

Eliot argues that a national culture would be poorer if it were strictly uniform in its makeup. Variety among its various parts constitutes a stimulating force. A strict uniformity lacks the richness and depth that come from a measure of diversity. Thus, in obeying the natural instinct of human beings to realize themselves, the people of a region are actually nourishing the national culture. If a regional culture is suppressed or obliterated through some facile notion of cultural uniformity, everyone loses.

Eliot provides a concrete illustration by pointing out the ways in which the poets and fiction writers of Scotland, Wales and Ireland have enriched the literature written in the English language. It would be easy to make the same case for our southern writers. Imagine the impoverishment that American literature would suffer if one subtracted from it Katherine Anne Porter, Eudora Welty, William Faulkner and R. P. Warren. (pp. 918-19)

Eliot's *Notes Toward a Definition of Culture* is a closely argued book. I shall make no attempt at a full examination of it here. It will serve my present purpose well enough simply to call attention to some of the issues in which it closely resembles the Agrarians' *I'll Take My Stand*.

First, both books call for resistance against economic determinism. Our reasonable goals and ends ought to determine our means, rather than the most efficient means forcing upon us the ends we are to pursue.

Second, both see a very close relation between a people's religion and its culture. Indeed, in a very meaningful sense the culture is an extension and expression of a people's ultimate values—something that neither Eliot nor the Agrarians hesitate to call by its true name: religion.

Third, both emphasize an actual community in being. No amount of planning or social engineering can create a community. The community is the reality with which one must deal. It cannot be ignored, and if it is destroyed the possibility of developing a genuine culture may well be destroyed with it.

Fourth, the transmission of cultural values is best done through the family, and the family must be preserved. (pp. 919-20)

I must now turn back to *After Strange Gods*. One large question about that book still remains to be answered: Why did Eliot never allow it to be reprinted? It is, I believe, the only one of his books that has never been reissued. I think that I know the answer, and if I am correct, his decision not to reprint it had nothing to do with his approval of regional cultures and regionalism, but with what he had to say in the second and third Page-Barbour lectures.

In writing a book entitled *After Strange Gods,* with its provocative subtitle, *A Primer of Modern Heresy,* Eliot was risking trouble and almost certainly inviting misunderstanding. The phrase *After Strange Gods* is itself provocative. It has a definitely biblical ring, though I have not been able to find this exact phrasing in either the Old Testament or the New. The phrase would seem to be an amalgam of a number of texts found in the Scriptures, texts which reproach various persons or peoples for going "a whoring after" gods other than the true God, and of several other texts which carry a similar reproach for seeking after "strange gods." I expect that the phrasings "after other gods" and seeking "strange gods" simply fused in Eliot's memory. The amalgamation probably sounded so right that he didn't take the trouble to look it up. (p. 920)

Yet the title would probably not have aroused so much hostility had Eliot not added his subtitle. By declaring his book to be *A Primer of Modern Heresy,* Eliot was here surely trailing his coat as if inviting a fight. Our age in particular is sensitive to anything that smacks of heresy-hunting. We associate it with intolerance, some priestly group turning over a victim to the secular arm for dire punishment. In a permissive age, the person who even appears to be himself intolerant can expect to be treated with intolerance.

Worst of all, in his second and third lectures, Eliot illustrated his statements about the heresies of the age with examples from the works of living (or only recently deceased) writers, writers such as Katherine Mansfield, D. H. Lawrence and Thomas Hardy. With these illustrations the fat was indeed in the fire.

It did not avail that Eliot pointed out that he was not in this instance judging their literary art—which he conceded to be great—but was writing as a moralist, concerned with the moral disorder of our world as reflected in their art. Nor did the fact that Eliot made it plain that he regarded Lawrence and Hardy, for example, as distinguished literary artists, even though their fiction revealed the disorder and growing cruelty of the world in which they and he lived. Nor did it apparently help very much that he made a related judgment of the mind and sensibility of his old mentor at Harvard, Irving Babbitt, and of Ezra Pound, his warm friend, whom he tells us in his second lecture is "probably the most important living poet in our language." (pp. 920-21)

[Perhaps Eliot] believed he made his purpose plain when he wrote in his second lecture that he was not concerned here "with the author's *beliefs,* but with orthodoxy of sensibility and with the sense of tradition. . . ." He also mentioned in this second lecture the "alarming cruelty in some modern literature," but the general context indicates that he meant the alarming cruelty of our world as reflected in modern literature. If so, this is very close to Yeats's remark on the "growing murderousness of the world"—certainly not an unwarranted observation.

Most damaging of all, Eliot made a remark in his first lecture that seemed distinctly anti-Jewish: unity of religion, he wrote, made "any large number of free-thinking Jews undesirable." As far as his argument is concerned, *free-thinking* is the key phrase. Thus, even the ultra-conservative Old South got along with its God-fearing Jews very well. There was perhaps less anti-Jewish feeling in the Old South than anywhere else in the United States. "Free-thinkers"—whatever the final merits of Eliot's argument—would have been the accurate term. And if free-thinking was the issue, whether the ancestors of the free-thinkers were of the Jewish, Catholic or Protestant faiths would not matter. Yet Eliot, in the light of his later statements, must have bitterly regretted what he had earlier set down.

As a matter of fact, the anti-Jewish passage aside, the argument advanced in the last two lectures could not be expected to thrive in the intellectual climate of the 1930s or, for that matter, in that of the 1980s. In any case, whatever has merit in Eliot's position is better stated in the *Notes,* with the appropriate reservations and qualifications to be found there. Clearly Eliot later on preferred to write *Notes Toward a Definition of Culture* than to reissue *After Strange Gods*.

There is an . . . epigraph on the title page of *After Strange Gods* which so far seems to have attracted no notice at all. As we know, Eliot liked to employ epigraphs. He frequently uses them to preface individual poems, including even some of his short lyrics. The epigraph I am concerned with here amounts to two and a half lines of verse from Sophocles' *Oedipus Rex*. . . . The Greek seer Tiresias speaks as follows: "Go think this out. And if you find that I am wrong, then say that I have no skill in prophecy."

We have encountered Tiresias before in Eliot's poetry. In *The Waste Land* Tiresias is made to witness the love-making that is not loving or fulfilling or life-giving, but sterile and meaningless. . . . In the notes to *The Waste Land* Eliot tells the reader: "What Tiresias *sees* . . . is the substance of the poem." I propose here that what Mr. Eliot sees in the modern world is indeed the substance of what he has to say about it, not only in *After Strange Gods,* but also in his *Notes Toward a Definition of Culture.*

Are we to conclude then that in *After Strange Gods* Eliot means to assume the mantle of the prophet Tiresias? Well, at least Eliot seems to see a parallel between Tiresias and himself. Both are conscious that their predictions are almost certain to be disregarded. The ears on which the words of each will fall are deaf indeed. If none are so blind as those who will not see, none are so deaf as those who will not hear.

Yet I mustn't make Eliot seem too serious here. He had an excellent sense of humor with which he is not often credited. His reference to Tiresias is so well hidden as to seem sly: only for the observant eye is the admission apparent. Though aware that what he is going to say will not be understood, he will make his statement anyway. In that matter at least Eliot has proved to be a true prophet: he has been regularly misunderstood.

Yet now in the 1980s the content of the prophecy is worth reexamining. Modern Western man, and especially his American version, is predisposed to *hubris*: an overweaning pride in his own powers and achievements. Now he may be threatened by the very success of some of his most brilliant achievements. Eliot was probably aware that even his choice audience of traditional Virginians were also Americans and might stand in need of such a warning. To have solved, as Oedipus did, the riddle of the Sphinx does not mean that one knows the whole nature of man or that he can accurately read his own future.

It would be foolish to claim too much. Eliot was never the unregenerate southern rebel, and long, long ago he had put away his southern drawl in favor of an impeccable British accent spoken after the manner of Oxenford. His visit to Virginia in 1933 was apparently his last—not only to Virginia but to any other state of the old Confederacy (with the exception of a brief visit to the University of Texas in 1958). Nevertheless, his concern for the older southern culture was considered and genuine, and he established a lasting friendship with one of the most thoughtful of the southern Agrarians, Allen Tate. When Eliot's letters are finally published and the remainder of Tate's, that correspondence, though probably not extensive, may tell us a great deal about a warm and enduring relationship and one founded on common sympathies and understandings of our twentieth-century world. (pp. 921-23)

> *Cleanth Brooks, "T. S. Eliot and the American South,"* in The Southern Review, *Vol. 21, No. 4, Autumn, 1985, pp. 914-23.*

STEPHEN BERG

The tone, rhythm and pace of Eliot's poetry rarely seem charged by *personal* passion. He became an echo chamber for the poetry he loved; his work rings with a mixture of others' voices which became his voice. It is hard to believe anyone in particular is speaking in *The Waste Land, The Rock, Four Quartets*. Eliot's primary literary inheritance is the Greek chorus, that mediating anonymity near the beginning of our literature—inclusive, impersonal, fluctuating between talk and song as it expresses the minds of society, of the characters, of the audience. That is the formal source that lets Eliot manage the problem of merging personal urgency with impersonality. It was a vital discovery for Eliot, whose emotional struggles clashed with his need to express them, which was in turn obstructed by his habit of withdrawal. Inspiration was not the movement of one's own private consciousness discovering itself faced with a new combination of experiences demanding to be shared, but the transformation of that consciousness into a voice modified to become everybody's, anybody's, as in prayer. Think of the character of an intelligent rural citizen in Frost's poetry, or of the questing, elegant, urbane thinker informing Stevens' work. In Eliot's poetry there is no particular character at all, only a voice seeking absolutes, laws, some universal hub that will not crumble under the pressure of daily uncertainties and the ego's fragile defenses. Eliot's poetry becomes more and more aloof, renunciatory, general, until it culminates with wonderfully intense diffidence and vulnerability in *Four Quartets*. Yet a special quality permeates his work—perhaps the most touching, permanent and courageous aspect of it—the tentativeness, the broken groping, the thirst for certainty and the abysmal suspicion that there is none. Of all "great" poetry in this century, none that I know displays so honestly and with such necessity a collision of inner conflict with style. By that I mean Eliot's emotional/spiritual condition constantly threatens to destroy semblances of poetic form. Even the *Quartets,* structurally solid and symmetrical as it seems, drifts and slips—often with great power and grace—within the five-part sections. Eliot discovers the perfect tone for his passage through the abiding agony of life. Whatever seasonal, musical, philosophical, religious guides Eliot uses to organize his most important poems, the human awareness within the structure is simultaneously definitive and splintered with doubt. Eliot's great achievement is to have presented the possibility of faith in something beyond and greater than the time-bound physical world, yet something that may be experienced in the present, and is, however potentially consoling, a result of incurable doubt and nameless suffering. *Four Quartets* is the only convincing modern poem in search of faith whose terms are equally secular and religious. Its exact emotional opposite is [Walt Whitman's] "Song of Myself." Eliot's interest as a poet depends on his relentless confrontation with personal suffering and his desire to submit that suffering to metaphysical solutions that others may apply to their lives. The personal struggle, the struggle to heal a deeply wounded self, is always a threat to the formal coherence of the poetry, since it is at least as urgent a force as the need to shape, to find a form for the language that makes true poems possible. It was just that agony, forging the man and his work, that disrupted Eliot's ability to apply his knowledge of the formal achievements of the past with the equanimity of someone born to inherit all that is truly his. His torn psyche kept Eliot innocent, as a poet, of easy access to the tradition he worked so hard to acquire. The poems verge continually on fragmentation and the impossibility of saying what has to be said. They possess none of Williams' casual, blustering precisions and reckless lapses, none of the personality which sticks its nose and fingers and tongue through the speech. In that sense they are innocent, in that sense the speaker and his mastery are being sundered and remade again and again. Eliot cannot plow through or plunge in; he is too self-conscious. His originality and daring are outgrowths not of any strong personal desire to innovate based on what he knows of the past and of himself, but of his temperamental inability to make complete and balanced poetic structures of the kind he admired so much in others' work. . . . [Eliot] turns all to abstraction so that the ordinary world occurs against the backdrop of his inclusive vision. Eliot's desire to dissolve the world in a vision of redemption and unity is familiar. Behind it lurks our own pain and ambivalence. It culminates in the storyless autobiography of the *Quartets,* whose excitement depends on unpredictable shifts of attention, grand and often true definitions of our existence, felt paradox and contradiction, an overall tension that comes, I think, from our inability to grasp what the speaker is really saying much of the time while the solemn, spooky music seduces our interest. Later, we can go back and try to figure out what has been said, how one thing connects to another. But it is odd how Eliot's "mistakes" are so temperamentally honest, so touching in their stubborn idiosyncratic nature. The very end of *Four Quartets* adopts a prosodic strictness and stiffness, a formal corseting which does nothing to embody the ideas, the states Eliot is trying to present—form and content are utterly severed from one another; the moment in the rose garden, the intersection of the timeless with time, Eliot's moment of incarnation and transfiguration and ultimate meaning, is given as pure commentary—a bad translation whose original has been lost—and is utterly buried by his resignation to abstraction, assertion, musical monotony. After so much passion and intelligence, what sadness. But how appropriate. Eliot leaves us with the *wish* for his revelatory condition, and ours, for he has never experienced it, nor have we, and one does not go around inventing such things; one tells the truth: about desire, about impossibility, about the improbability of salvation and all the rest of it. Eliot's heroic attempts to define *our* element—time— and what it means to us is a great reminder of our mortality. He surely knew Baudelaire's "Time eats life," as most of us have known a lover. Impaled on the tines of that sentence, *his* lifetime burning in every moment was perhaps, luckily for us, too much for language to bear. (pp. 1139-42)

Stephen Berg, "Eliot's Pleasure," in The Southern Review, Vol. 21, No. 4, Autumn, 1985, pp. 1139-42.

M. L. ROSENTHAL

I am trying to reach back to what it was in T. S. Eliot's poetry that so attracted me and my little gang of adolescent literati pals in the early 1930's. . . . I speak of a time before **"Burnt Norton"** appeared, when Joyce's *Ulysses* had just been published in the United States—to the shocked fascination of Miss Hughes, my charming, encouraging English teacher in Cleveland, where in 1933-34 my stepfather had a job. The year before, we had lived in Boston, where my previous little gang and I had taken to Eliot over the dead bodies of our teachers. Free verse was still a topic of hot debate, especially the part of people who hadn't a clue one way or another. As for me, at ages 15 and 16, I certainly thought well of the word "free."

It takes a bit of recalling—or rather, perhaps, believing—some things in Eliot that caught our unfledged attention. Not his "obscurity" or "erudition" or religion or thoughts on tradition and the individual talent. I look back (surprised that I still share it) to our glee over **"The Boston Evening Transcript,"** a pre-20's Menckenish squib enlivened by an opening that is still visually hilarious: "The readers of the Boston Evening Transcript / Sway in the wind like a field of ripe corn." . . .

After those two lines a subtler Eliot insinuated himself into our innocent souls with his play on the word "evening" and his deliberate air of intellectual superiority (not in this instance too far out of our ken) that stirred up hidden instincts for random snobbishness. . . .

If I hadn't lived in Boston, this poem might never have caught my attention. After all, the world of Cousin Harriet and The

Transcript—the world of genteel Boston—was light years away from the somewhat bohemian immigrant Jewish circle of my parents, working people who were interested in ideas and art and world politics although they had little formal education. Among them were some Yiddish-speaking poets who in the course of their development had picked up a mixture of influences ranging from German Romanticism and French Symbolism through Russian Futurism to the cadences of Whitman. I listened to them recite their pieces receiving what they had to offer as best I could. . . . Oddly enough, given Eliot's second-rate politics and ignorant cracks about Jews, I was prepared for his sensibility by these men and women despite my inability to appreciate their art thoroughly. If their sense of humanity was larger and more adult than his, their wry mixture of strong feeling with a zest for the ridiculous had obvious affinities with his irony.

Of course, there's a strongly adolescent flavor to a great deal of Eliot's poetry, although at the same time a highly sophisticated mind and vision are at work. The adolescent element in Eliot (like the limbic system in the human brain) is a constant, underlying the complex overlay. It accounts for the dreary sexual and political infantilism in his mentality that made him, despite his infinitely superior genius, a child (sometimes ugly, sometimes dangerous) of American provincial prejudices.

Leaving aside the well-phrased sniggering in pieces like **"Mr. Appollinax"** ("Priapus in the shrubbery / Gaping at the lady in the swing") or the prose poem **"Hysteria"** ("I decided that if the shaking of her breasts could be stopped, some of the fragments of the afternoon might be collected, and I concentrated my attention with careful subtlety to this end"), Eliot's most striking early work is all in the adolescent keys of unresolved self-doubt, endlessly self-directed sensitivity and defensively cruel cool posturing. I hasten to add that I am not calling into question his poetic success, only pointing to an important element in what his poetry was successful in projecting—an actual inner state or quality of reverie, doubtless a reflex too of one type of cultivated American male psyche of Eliot's generation.

"The Love Song of J. Alfred Prufrock" is a perfect instance. Whatever else one may say about this first poem of Eliot's to command strong attention, it positively sweats panic at the challenge of adult sexuality and of living up to one's ideal of what it is to be manly in any sort of heroic model. Those challenges are the special monsters haunting adolescent male imagination, especially of the more introspective and introverted varieties. The furtive restlessness of the start, the fear of women's ridicule, the sensual longings, the forebodings of loneliness and eternal frustration, the painful self-mockery side by side with the persistent romanticism—these are the very stuff of that imagination. The age of the "I" of the poem, who is not in any case a sharply-delineated dramatic character but rather a half-delineated one (the other half being the kind of floating sensibility both Eliot and Pound were to evolve a little further down the line), isn't specified. He may be an unusually self-conscious very young man, or perhaps he is older. It really doesn't matter. Adolescent readers took to him because he expressed their feelings while seeming to be someone other—the stuffily named and brought up "Prufrock" of the title. Fear of impotence, failure and isolation continue into adult life, of course, but they are the particular unwanted burden of the young.

"Prufrock" holds all this burden of vulnerability, and also the accompanying need to mask desire ("Is it perfume from a dress / That makes me so digress'') and not give the game away to "the women" as they move about and chatter and seem so politely, unshakably self-contained. How old was Eliot, actually, when he wrote the poem—about 21 or 22? It is a poem whose essence is distilled from teen-age memories, felt as deeply private yet almost universally shared—"I have heard the mermaids singing, each to each. / I do not think that they will sing to me."

Exactly! And that is why we could recite the poem at the drop of a hint, and could absorb its music unthinkingly, so that it mingled with equally rueful tones and rhythms out of Edwin Arlington Robinson and Robert Frost in the great American symphony of unrealized grace and heroism. (p. 3)

But the great lyrical triumph of the *Prufrock* volume was **"Rhapsody on a Windy Night,"** in which many of the motifs of **"Prufrock"** reappear in altered context. **"Rhapsody"** offers the same murkily squalid context of seedy late-night streets, the same horror of sex (here focused in the figure of the prostitute who "hesitates toward you in the light of the door / Which opens on her like a grin" and again in the image of the moon as a crackbrained old whore), and, at the end of the poem, the same fear of waking into ordinary life. If **"Prufrock"** merged in my mind with poems like Robinson's "Eros Turannos" and Frost's "Reluctance," the music of **"Rhapsody on a Windy Night"** very largely displaced the others.

Eliot's narrow psychological base remained intact (the adolescent limbic system); yet it became identified with the harsh metropolitan awareness of Europe, specifically of the darker side of Paris, and beyond that with the sense of brute impersonality as the key to what memory means and to a pervasive gross atmosphere of madness. Adolescent terror is thus stretched beyond itself and assimilated to the gathering blackness of the West not long before World War I. This sense of dread imminence, not necessarily objectified as the definable pressure of a historical moment, is rhythmically mobilized in the irregularly patterned verse units that mark out a four-hour procession through city streets in a waking nightmare beginning at midnight. The succession of distorted, skeletal, mechanically grasping images, phallic gone sterile, adds up, as the slightly overexplicit ending explains, to a desperate vision of life's macabre essence. It is like the shock of death-realization in puberty.

Now, our own historical moment in the 30's was a reprise, with differences, of Eliot's around 1911. We were a generation that had grown up with the sense that we were doomed to have another such war—only worse, because Mussolini and, especially, Hitler were worse than their imperial predecessors, and because the weapons were bound to be worse.... Our premonitions were basically our internalization of the past; and in its violent images and death-march sense of an irreversible destiny, Eliot's morbid vision of the inner reality of things confirmed what we felt in our bones, no matter how blithe or hopeful our essential personalities might be or how optimistic our surface attitudes concerning the possibility of preventing a new war.

All this happened without our needing to identify it consciously, and was felt independently of what our political views might be. For Eliot transmitted what W. H. Auden, in another, though related, context, was later to call "the unmentionable odor of death" of our century; he also transmitted a raspingly disturbed sense of a world out of kilter and out of control. The European generation of Auden and Bertolt Brecht did not ques-

tion the pervasiveness of that traumatized awareness, although many in Eliot's own generation—and Eliot himself—resisted accepting it. Their religious inheritance and conservative ideas of social and political order (or a mystical neo-primitivism) helped them refuse the evidence of their deepest psychological perception.

Nevertheless, Eliot's most telling poetry before **"Burnt Norton"**—that is, his most telling poetry as it came to me in mid-adolescence—conveyed that perception incisively and beautifully and also insidiously. We have had no other poet, I believe, whose phrasing infects the reader's nervous system as Eliot's infected that of embryonic poets of immediately succeeding generations. William Butler Yeats remains our greatest modern poet, Ezra Pound our great embroiler and William Carlos Williams our great humanizer; but Eliot, while he was still enmeshed in unresolved youthful struggles of spirit, showed us a decisive image of ourselves in the mirror of a terrified age being quick-marched nowhere though still capable of making wonderful jokes about it all. The major work that made up this psychic mirror consisted of **"Rhapsody on a Windy Night,"** *The Waste Land, The Hollow Men,* the Ariel poems, *Sweeney Agonistes* and **"Coriolan."** (pp. 3, 37)

> *M. L. Rosenthal, "Adolescents Singing, Each to Each—When We and Eliot Were Young," in* The New York Times Book Review, *October 20, 1985, pp. 3, 37.*

HAROLD BLOOM

Thomas Stearns Eliot is a central figure in the Western literary culture of this century. His undoubted achievement as a lyric and elegiac poet in itself would suffice to establish him in the main Romantic tradition of British and American poetry that moves from Wordsworth and Whitman on to Geoffrey Hill and John Ashbery, poets of our moment. There is an obvious irony in such a judgment. Eliot's professed sense of *the* tradition, *his* tradition, was rather different, tracing as it did the true line of poetry in English from its origins in medieval Provence and Italy through its later developments in France. I borrow that remark from Northrop Frye [in his essay "Antique Drum"]. Eliot's polemical stance as a literary critic can be distinguished from his rhetorical stance as a poet, and both postures of the spirit are fortunately quite distinct from his cultural position, self-proclaimed as Anglo-Catholic, Royalist and Classical.

An obsessive reader of poetry growing up in the nineteen thirties and forties entered a critical world dominated by the opinions and example of Eliot. To speak out of even narrower personal experience, anyone adopting the profession of teaching literature in the early nineteen fifties entered a discipline virtually enslaved not only by Eliot's insights but by the entire span of his preferences and prejudices. If one's cultural position was Jewish, Liberal and Romantic, one was likely to start out with a certain lack of affection for Eliot's predominance, however much (against the will) the subtle force of the poetry was felt. If a young critic particularly loved Shelley, Milton, Emerson, Pater, and if that same critic did not believe that Blake was a naive and eccentric genius, then regard for Eliot seemed unnecessary. Whatever he actually represented, a neochristian and neoclassic Academy had exalted him, by merit raised, to what was pragmatically rather a bad eminence. In *that* critical climate, Hopkins was considered the only valid Victorian poet, greatly superior to Browning and Tennyson, while Whitman seemed an American nightmare and Wallace Stevens, if he passed at all, had to be salvaged as a Late Augustan. Thirty years on, these views have a kind of antique charm, but in 1954 they were at least annoying, and if one cared enough, they had some capacity for infuriating.

I resume these matters not to stir up waning rancors, but to explain why, for some critics of my own generation, Eliot only recently has ceased to represent the spiritual enemy. His disdain for Freud, his flair for demonstrating the authenticity of his Christianity by exhibiting a judicious anti-Semitism, his refined contempt for human sexuality—somehow these did not seem to be the inevitable foundations for contemporary culture. . . . [An] Academy that found its ideology in Eliot was not a place where one could teach comfortably, or where one could have remained, had the Age of Eliot not begun to wane. The ascendency of Eliot, as a fact of cultural politics, is something many among us could not wish to see return.

Eliot asserted for his poetry a seventeenth century ancestry, out of Jacobean dramatists and Metaphysical lyricists. Its actual forerunners are Whitman and Tennyson, and Eliot's strength is felt now when we read "When Lilacs Last in the Dooryard Bloom'd" and "Maud: A Monodrama," and find ourselves believing that they are influenced by *The Waste Land*. It is a neglected truth of American poetic history that Eliot and Stevens are more Whitmanian than Hart Crane, whose allegiance to Whitman was overt. Though Eliot and Stevens consciously did not feel or know it, their poetry is obsessed with Whitman's poetry. By this I mean Whitman's tropes and Whitman's curious transitions between topics, and not at all the example of Whitman, far more crucial for Crane and many others.

It is the pattern of Eliot's figurations that is most High Romantic, a pattern that I suspect he learned from Tennyson and Whitman, who derived it from Keats and Shelley, who in turn had been instructed by Wordsworth's crisis lyrics and odes, which go back yet further to Spenserian and Miltonic models. Consider Eliot's *Ash-Wednesday*, his conversion-sequence of 1930. The poem's six movements are not a Dantesque *Vita Nuova*, despite Eliot's desires, but a rather strict re-enactment of the Wordsworthian drama of experiential loss and compensatory imaginative gain. (pp. 1-2)

Eliot is hardly unique among the poets in having misrepresented either his actual tradition or his involuntary place in that tradition. His cultural influence, rather than his polemic, was closer to being an unique phenomenon. To have been born in 1888, and to have died in 1965, is to have flourished in the Age of Freud, hardly a time when Anglo-Catholic theology, social thought, and morality were central to the main movement of mind. . . . Frank Kermode, a distinguished authority on Eliot, writing in 1975, insisted "that Eliot profoundly changed our thinking about poetry and criticism without trying to impose as a condition of his gift the acceptance of consequences which, for him, followed as a matter of reason, as well as of belief and personal vocation." It may well be that the largest difference between Kermode's critical generation, in England, and the next generation, in America, is that we changed our thinking about poetry and criticism in reaction against Eliot's thinking, precisely because Eliot's followers had imposed upon us consequences peculiar to his belief and his personal vocation. Whether Eliot's discriminations were so fine as Kermode asserts is yet another matter. Shelley's skeptical yet passionate beliefs, according to Eliot, were not coherent, not mature, not

founded upon the facts of experience. Eliot once gave thanks that Walter Pater never wrote about *Hamlet;* would that Eliot never had done so. We would have been spared the influential but unfortunate judgment "that here Shakespeare tackled a problem which proved too much for him." Eliot doubtless is in the line of poet-critics: Ben Jonson, Dryden, Dr. Samuel Johnson, Coleridge, Poe and Arnold are among those who precede him. As a critic, he does not approach the first four, but surely equals Poe and Arnold, equivocal praise, though he certainly surpassed Poe and Arnold as poets. It is difficult to prophesy that Eliot's criticism will prove to be of permanent value, but perhaps we need to await the arrival of a generation neither formed by him nor rebelling against him, before we justly can place him.

That Eliot, in retrospect, will seem the Matthew Arnold rather than the Abraham Cowley of his age, is the sympathetic judgment of A. Walton Litz. For motives admitted already, one might prefer to see Eliot as the Cowley, and some celebrated passages in *Four Quartets* are worthy of comparison with long-ago-admired Pindarics of that forgotten wit, but Arnold's burden as involuntary belated Romantic is indeed close to Eliot's. A direct comparison of Eliot's elegiac achievement to Whitman's or Tennyson's seems to me both more problematical and more inevitable. . . . The phantasmagoric intensity of [Eliot's] best poems and passages can be matched only in the greatest visionaries and poets of Western literature. It is another paradox that the Anglo-Catholic, Royalist, Classical spokesperson should excel in the mode of fictive hallucination and lyric derangement, in the fashioning of nightmare images perfectly expressive of his age.

Eliot's influence as a poet is by no means spent, yet it seems likely that Robert Penn Warren's later poetry, the most distinguished now being written among us, will be the final stand of Eliot's extraordinary effort to establish an anti-Romantic counter-Sublime sense of *the* tradition to replace the continuity of Romantic tradition. That the continuity now has absorbed him is hardly a defeat; absorption is not rejection, and Eliot's poetry is securely in the canon. Eliot's strength, manifested in the many poets indebted to him, is probably most authentically commemorated by the poetry of Hart Crane, which engages Eliot's poetry in an agon without which Crane could not have achieved his difficult greatness. One can prefer Crane to Eliot, as I do, and yet be forced to concede that Eliot, more than Whitman, made Crane possible. (pp. 4-6)

Eliot, writing in 1948, ended his *Notes Toward the Definition of Culture* by affirming that the culture of Europe could not survive the disappearance of the Christian faith, because: "It is in Christianity that our arts have developed . . . It is against a background of Christianity that all our thought has significance." That seems to be the center of Eliot's polemic, and each reader must make of it what she or he can or will. The Age of Freud, Kafka and Proust, of Yeats, Wallace Stevens, Beckett: somehow these thoughts and visions suggest a very different definition of culture than the Eliotic one. Perhaps it was fortunate for Eliot that he was a Late Romantic poet long before he became, for a time, the cultural oracle of the academies. (p. 7)

Harold Bloom, in an introduction to Modern Critical Views: T. S. Eliot, *edited by Harold Bloom, Chelsea House Publishers, 1985, pp. 1-7.*

Carlos Fuentes

1928-

Mexican novelist, dramatist, short story writer, scriptwriter, essayist, and critic.

Fuentes is regarded by many as Mexico's foremost contemporary novelist. His overriding literary concern is with establishing a viable Mexican identity, both as an autonomous entity and in relation to the outside world. Myth, legend, and history often intertwine in Fuentes's work, as he examines his country's roots in order to discover the essence of modern Mexican society. Fuentes commented: "Our political life is fragmented, our history shot through with failure, but our cultural tradition is rich, and I think the time is coming when we will have to look at our faces, our own past." This tradition includes the Aztec culture, the Christian faith imparted by the Spanish conquistadors, and the failed hopes of the Mexican Revolution. Fuentes uses the past thematically and symbolically to comment on contemporary concerns and to project his own vision of Mexico's future.

Fuentes first gained international attention as an important writer associated with the "boom" in Latin American literature. During the late 1950s and 1960s, Fuentes, along with such authors as Gabriel García Márquez and Julio Cortázar, published works that received widespread acclaim and drew international attention to the important contributions of Latin American authors to contemporary literature. Fuentes's work, like that of several writers associated with the "boom," is technically experimental. Through such methods as disjointed chronological development, varying narrative perspectives, and rapid crosscuts between scenes, Fuentes creates a surreal atmosphere. For example, in his first novel, *La región más transparente* (1958; *Where the Air Is Clear*), Fuentes uses a series of montage-like sequences to investigate the vast range of personal histories and lifestyles in modern-day Mexico City. This novel provoked controversy due to its candid portrayal of social inequity and its socialist overtones. In addition, the work expresses Fuentes's perception of how the Mexican Revolution failed to realize its ideals, a recurring theme in his work and the basis for one of his most respected novels, *La muerte de Artemio Cruz* (1962; *The Death of Artemio Cruz*). The title character of this work is a millionaire who earned his fortune by ruthless means. Using flashbacks, the novel shifts between Cruz on his deathbed, his participation in the Revolution, and his eventual rise in business. Through this device, Fuentes contrasts the high ideals that fostered the Revolution with present-day corruption. *The Death of Artemio Cruz* is a complex work that demands active participation by the reader.

In the novella *Aura* (1962), Fuentes displays less concern with social criticism than in previous works and makes greater use of bizarre images and fantastic developments. The plot of this novel involves a man whose lover mysteriously begins to resemble her aged aunt. In *Cambio de piel* (1967; *A Change of Skin*), Fuentes uses disordered chronological development to present a group of people who relive significant moments from their past as they travel together through Mexico. Fuentes's concern with the role of the past in determining the present is further demonstrated in *Terra nostra* (1975), one of his most ambitious and successful works. This novel exceeds the scope

of his earlier fiction, extending the idea of history as a circular force by incorporating scenes from the future into the text. The work is divided into three sections: "The Old World," which concerns Spain during the reign of Philip II; "The New World," about the Spanish conquest of Mexico; and "The Next World," which ends as the twenty-first century begins. By tracing the evolution of Mexico beginning with the Spanish conquest, Fuentes depicts the violence and cruelty that began in the Mediterranean area and was perpetuated in Mexico through Spanish colonialism.

In *La cabeza de hidra* (1978; *Hydra Head*), Fuentes explored a new genre—the spy novel. Set in Mexico City, this work revolves around the oil industry and includes speculations on the future of Mexico as an oil-rich nation. Fuentes's recent fiction investigates Mexico's relationship with the rest of the world. In *Una familia lejana* (1982; *Distant Relations*), for example, the plot involves a Mexican archaeologist and his son who meet relatives in France; on another level, however, the work is about the interaction between Mexican and European cultures. Fuentes employs shifting narrative perspectives in this work, as an old man relates the tale to a man called Carlos Fuentes, who in turn relates the tale to the reader. Through the inclusion of ghosts and mysterious characters, *Distant Relations* also illustrates how Fuentes introduces fantastic events into otherwise realistic settings. This technique, found in many Latin American novels, is often called magic realism. In *The Old Gringo* (1985), a study of Mexican-American relations, Fuentes creates an imaginative scenario of the fate that befell American journalist Ambrose Bierce after his disappearance in Mexico in 1913. Michiko Kakutani stated: "[Fuentes] has succeeded in welding history and fiction, the personal and the collective, into a dazzling novel that possesses the weight and resonance of myth."

In addition to his novels, Fuentes has written several plays, including *Orquídeas a la luz de la luna* (1982; *Orchids in the Moonlight*), and has published the short story collections *Los días enmascarados* (1954), *Cantar de ciegos* (1964), and *Chac Mool y otros cuentos* (1973). Many of his short stories appear in English translation in *Burnt Water* (1980). Fuentes is also respected for his essays, the topics of which range from social and political criticism to discussions of Mexican art. In 1956 Fuentes founded the prestigious journal *Revista Mexicana de Literatura*.

(See also *CLC*, Vols. 3, 8, 10, 13, 22; *Contemporary Authors*, Vols. 69-72; and *Contemporary Authors New Revision Series*, Vol. 10.)

WILLIAM KENNEDY

Distant Relations is a ghostly poem, a vexing puzzle, an amazingly constructed argument on the relatedness of human spirits, past and present. It is a work which reads better the second time than the first. Two readings are required merely to grasp the meaning of the story that rides along the surface.

Since it is a ghost story, it immediately rends all realism. Fuentes dedicates the novel to his friend, Luis Buñuel, the great surrealist filmmaker, and as one reads it one yearns for Buñuel to transform it into a film. Even if Buñuel did make it, the film would only begin to evoke the mystery, the convolutions, the infinity of meaning the book presents.

It is not difficult to read. It begins in a Jamesian way in The Automobile Club in Paris, overlooking the Place de la Concorde, where two men sit, one talking, the other listening. Talking is the Comte de Branly, an 83-year-old French aristocrat. Listening (and transforming Branly's words into the pages we are reading) is an unnamed younger man who turns out to be a fictional character named Carlos Fuentes. (p. 1)

The book is a game of matching names involving many members of the Heredia family of Mexico, of France, of Haiti, of Spain. There are, for instance, two Victor Heredias in the book, one a boy who becomes both an angel and half of a drowned fetus, the other a man who might be 160 years old but who is really a white-maned and ageless phantom. Branly meets the young Victor's father, Hugo Heredia, in Mexico, where Hugo is an archeologist, more enamored of Toltec stones than he is of men.

Branly becomes a figure wrapped in a mysterious conspiracy by the Heredias, past and present—their name in Spanish suggests heredity, inheritance—which injures him and makes him a bedridden quasi-prisoner in a strange old Parisian mansion. In his illness Branly meets many specters and phantoms of the Heredia family—from both its French and its Spanish lines—and he also encounters his own lifelong specter, who turns out to be a phantom member of the Heredia family, a woman who is also the personification of his own forgotten love.

I don't expect anyone to really understand the preceding paragraph. You barely understand the book as you read it, for Fuentes withholds a great deal of information as he goes, to enhance his suspense. But you read on, held by the strangeness of it all. Yet even if he so chose, Fuentes could not have explained each mystery as it occurs, for the mystery requires the entire book in order to be fully unraveled as a mystery; solving the mystery will take much longer. (pp. 1, 17)

There is a natural inclination to grow impatient with Fuentes at points along the way, where he seems to be excessively abstract, or unnecessarily dense with historical detail. But that is the nature of his game—he always succumbs to the temptation to elaborate. Eventually he returns us to new action, which always deepens the complexity and density of the tale.

The book is a labyrinth of symbol and allegory and metaphysical conjuring. Fuentes gives his own shape and definitions to demons and angels, specters and phantoms, and they do not always intersect with the definitions in common use. He slips into the surreal with regularity, explaining his method (as he likes to do) by invoking Buñuel's film, *Un Chien Andalou*, "in which the heroine opens her door on the sixth floor of a Parisian apartment house and steps directly onto the beach: Cabourg, sea, sand."

Branly, the Heredias, the assorted specters, and finally Fuentes, all live in this non-sequential world, and when Fuentes is not busy expatiating, that world becomes excitingly bizarre. Also his settings are sensually visual, like great paintings (as usual he invokes the names and work of many painters and writers: Delacroix, Ingres, Balzac, Dumas, others) and his language is appropriately lush, elegant and baroque. . . .

[*Distant Relations* is] a story of the war between cultures—the European and the mestizo; between Branly and his aristocratic progenitors on the one hand and the Heredias and their Indian and Franco-Hispanic ancestors, their Creole heritage, on the other.

Branly says Hugo Heredia "had that quality so characteristic of cultured Latin Americans: the passion to know everything, to read everything, to give no quarter, no pretext, to the European, but . . . above all, to demonstrate to the European that there is no excuse not to know other cultures."

Fuentes certainly has demonstrated just that to Europeans, and everyone else as well, in his cosmopolitan novels. In this new book he affirms in a most mystical way his identity with Hugo as well as his difference from him. He asserts that the various cultures are not separate but unified in dream and fantasy through history, populated by ghosts and specters who refuse to die, and who live their afterlives through endless time in ways that reshape the present.

Fuentes' mystical beings, and his speculations about them, are not unlike the speculations about the angels who used to dance on the head of the medieval pin. His meaning is not only deliberately incomplete at novel's end—leading perhaps into a novel yet to be written, with Carlos Fuentes as the central figure—but is always, throughout the story, an effort to fix boundaries on the ineffable, to fence in a cloud. Yet out of his effort comes a new feeling for the mystery of tradition, of continuity, of Heredia.

Fuentes the listener hears Branly say something and it sounds as if Heredia is saying it: "Everything depends on your understanding the words. You had a past, but you do not remember it. Try to recapture it in the little time you have left, or you will lose your future."

This is what Branly does. This is what the listener Fuentes begins to do. And this is also what Fuentes the author seems to be doing himself in writing it. (p. 17)

> *William Kennedy, "Carlos Fuentes Dreaming of History," in* Book World—The Washington Post, *March 14, 1982, pp. 1, 17.*

GUY DAVENPORT

Halfway through this metaphysical ghost story [*Distant Relations*] we become deliciously confused. Are we in the imagination of a Henry James, where ghosts are psychological projections of inner states? Are we exploring, as in Balzac, the elder Dumas, and Poe, edges of reality where reason frays into myth and fantasy? Or has reality been distorted into strangeness just enough, as in Luis Buñuel, to whom this novel is dedicated, to sharpen our attention?

Carlos Fuentes in all his books draws tight a tense conjunction of opposites: the sensuously beautiful and the horrifyingly ugly, innocence and evil, past and present, the familiar and the strange, nature and culture. In *Distant Relations*, a novel in which two boys fuse into one and a man disintegrates in a shower of dead leaves, these tensions operate in a cat's cradle of a plot, crisscrossing each other to make a puzzle worthy of Poe or Borges. (p. 3)

The plot changes shape according to angle of vision. The narrator, Branly, is at first a passive observer, then a bit player when the story still seems to be nothing but an idle game; but as the novel pitches into its momentum, he becomes the protagonist. Along one line of development, the plot goes this way: A Mexican archeologist, Hugo Heredia, has lost his wife and one of his two sons in an airplane crash. He and his remaining young son are very close. In a life full of movement, from digging sites in Mexico to cities all over the world where Heredia lectures and attends scientific congresses, father and son play a game. They consult the telephone book in places they visit to see if either's name appears. The son finds his name, Victor Heredia, in the Paris phone book, and the aged Branly, their host in France, goes along with the game and drives the boy to the address of his namesake, who lives in a chateau in the suburb of Enghien.

The Parisian Victor Heredia is middle-aged and has a son the same age as the Mexican Victor Heredia. Here, in the style of the most shameless of the old Gothic romances (but as modernized by a Surrealist), the plot begins to display dimensions of myth, fantasy and dream, but always refocusing back into a logical world. Fuentes plays a game of his own with his readers: How many times can he disarrange reality just enough to make us wonder if he will explain all the mysteries, or end in a mystery that has moved beyond the logical world? He does both.

The elder Victor Heredia . . . , it turns out, was years ago a lonely child who longed to play with Branly and his friends in the Parc Monceau. He once threw a ball into the park, which Branly might have thrown back, thus making friends with him. Branly didn't, and since then he has lived with the guilt of flubbing the opportunity. Now Heredia holds him and the young Mexican Victor Heredia captive in the chateau, appropriating the young Heredia to be the playmate for his son that Branly refused to be to him.

Probably none of this happened. It is Branly's explanation, based on his guilt.

Another explanation grows out of another set of events from the past, events having to do with a woman Branly loved during the First World War, but having also to do with the poet Rimbaud, with class struggles and with the European exploitation of the New World. (pp. 3, 26)

In one sense this novel is a meditation on Latin Americans who, like Fuentes, chose French culture as the context in which they could create best. A poem, "The Adjacent Room," by Jules Supervielle (who was born in Uruguay) serves as an epigraph to the novel and as a text that Branly and Fuentes quote to each other to interpret Branly's strange story. Jules Laforgue, Paul Lafargue, Isidore Ducasse (Lautréamont), Reynaldo Hahn—the list is a long and distinguished one of South Americans (Alexandre Dumas not the least of them) whose presence in French literature has a special aura. This influx, as Fuentes shapes it in his imagination, is of an exotic, primitive, chthonic nature long ago civilized out of European culture.

Is this dispersed and returned heritage a welcome return, or is it a kind of revenge? In the two endings of this novel we have both meanings. Insofar as the Old World and the New World can fuse, the crossbreeding (exemplified by the French setting of a novel by a Mexican writer which we are reading) is something wholly new, an invention. The fusion is of the intuitive and the logical . . . , of nature and culture . . . , of the primal and the derivative. . . .

But the fusion can breed a monster, or something that we think is a monster because of its strangeness. Fuentes gives us many examples of this cultural fusion, some of them wonderfully disturbing. The French Victor Heredia's son is "not well made." When we see him out of his sailor suit, making love to the Mexican Victor Heredia in the back seat of an automobile, he is as hairy and goatish from the waist down as the god Pan. Do these two boys really join bodies and become the handsome young waiter with panther tread and animal gaze who comes and goes in the Automobile Club de France while Branly is telling his strange story?

Why does the French Victor Heredia live in a house that once belonged to Alexandre Dumas? Why does his past as he tells it belong to a generation before he was born? These questions have answers. Fuentes is a novelist who builds structures in one's imagination. We feel that even at his most fantastic there is nothing trivial in his work, or merely sensational, or merely decorative. On the contrary, he writes with the authority of a great poet who, like his master Buñuel, needs a realism accurately perceived and sensuously felt as a medium for getting at the dark interior of the past, without which, as a character in this book remarks, we cannot have a future at all. (p. 26)

> *Guy Davenport, "The Novel: A Conjunction of Opposites," in* The New York Times Book Review, *March 21, 1982, pp. 3, 26.*

ADAM MARS-JONES

In his new novel Carlos Fuentes sets out to combine the virtues of Proust and Borges, and ends up with those of H. P. Lovecraft; *Distant Relations* is a B-movie masquerading as an art film.

The story straddles the Old World and the New, just as the style seeks to accommodate both realism and prose-poetry. . . .

[The] story is a preposterous mess, claiming to explore the high themes of heredity, identity and memory while allowing its author to overdose on mannerism and flabby Gothic.

While the author basks, the reader flounders. Fuentes loads his text with allusions and fireworks, without ever producing a memorable phrase or a vivid image. Branly's Spanish servants are introduced with a comparison apiece: ashen José looks "like a figure in a Zurbarán painting", while florid Florencio resembles "an exhausted jai-alai player". This is as much character-drawing as Fuentes provides in this case; the two phrases, which insist on their own precision but convey no information, are repeated word for word a hundred pages later, when the servants reappear. . . .

Stilted, snobbish, charmless and elephantine, *Distant Relations* is unlikely to make any converts for Carlos Fuentes. In spite of its dedication to Buñuel and its insistent references to Supervielle, to Lautréamont, to Holbein the Younger, to Quevedo, to Laforgue, to Lafargue, to Musset, to Nerval, to Vallejo, to Neruda and to Paz, its closest links are to pulp fiction in the Lovecraft mould. . . .

In the closing pages of *Distant Relations* the narrator is named by the Comte de Branly as "Fuentes", but the reason for this personal appearance by the author is never made clear. Having his name on the spine and the title page should have been embarrassment enough.

> Adam Mars-Jones, "Discreet Charms and Eternal Squiddities," in The Times Literary Supplement, No. 4136, July 9, 1982, p. 739.

LUIS LEAL

Carlos Fuentes has stated that fiction can be useful in looking at history from new perspectives, and this is precisely what he has done in most of his novels, wherein he has presented a vision of history that cannot be gathered from the reading of history books. And, even more, he has reinterpreted history to present a new version of its development, a version reflected by a mind keenly conscious of the significance of past events in the shaping of the contemporary course of human events. In most of his novels he has gone one step further, to the recreation of history by the combination of realistic and mythical structures. The purpose of this essay is to trace the intrusion of history and myth upon Fuentes' narrative, and to observe how he has solved the technical problems involved and yet has managed to produce novels that are aesthetically satisfying. (p. 3)

One of the characteristics of the writers of the new Spanish American novel . . . is the tendency to create pure fiction. One of the leaders of this trend has been Carlos Fuentes. He, like other new novelists (García Márquez, Cortázar, Rulfo, etc.), has moved in this direction by combining two narrative modes, the realistic (historical) and the mythical. Northrop Frye has discussed these two modes at length, and he differentiates between them by saying that realism is the art of verisimilitude, the art of implied similarity, and myth the art of implied metaphorical identity. However, he says that the presence of a mythical structure in realistic fiction "poses certain technical

problems for making it plausible, and the devices used in solving these problems may be given the general name of *displacement*." (pp. 3-4)

[In the story **"Chac Mool"** from his first book, *Los días enmascarados*], Fuentes solves the problems of displacement by the use of realistic motifs: the action takes place in Mexico City and Acapulco; the two characters are clerks in a government office; and Filiberto, the protagonist, purchases a statue in a well-known market. To introduce historical fact, the technique of the diary, in which conversations are recorded, is used. The fictitious Filiberto writes about historical events in his diary, such as the introduction of Christianity after the Conquest and the effect it had on the conquered people. In the other aspect of the story Fuentes recreates the myth of the eternal return by the illusory transformation of the statue of the god which Filiberto had placed in the basement of his home. Chac Mool comes back to life with the coming of the rains and takes control of Filiberto's life, finally driving him to suicide. Thus Fuentes skillfully blends the historical and the mythical into a continuous narrative form which derives its structure from the tension created by the interaction between two different cultures, that of ancient Mexico, represented by Chac Mool, and the contemporary, represented by Filiberto.

The technique used in this early story was soon perfected and expanded in the novel, and it has become the distinguishing mark of Fuentes' fiction. The models that he followed for this mode of fiction he found principally in William Faulkner, Malcolm Lowry, and Miguel Angel Asturias. From them he learned the art of utilizing myth, either as form or theme in the context of the realistic novel. (pp. 5-6)

The novels of Fuentes, with some exceptions, can be considered as mythical approaches to history, or creative history. The success of his novels is due in great part to this use of myth to interpret history; for history, as Ernst Cassirer has observed, is determined by the mythology of a people. . . . In his first major work, **Where the Air Is Clear,** Fuentes presents a mythical history of Mexico City and its four million (1958) inhabitants. The characters who represent the historical aspects of the novel are products of the Mexican Revolution and, at the same time, representative of Mexican society during the 1950s: Robles, the revolutionary turned into a conservative banker; his wife Norma, the social climber who marries for money; Zamacona, the brooding intellectual who becomes one of the sacrificial victims; the decadent Bobó, from the new upper middle class; Gabriel and Beto, the displaced *braceros* back from California; and the Ovando family, the impoverished representatives of the dethroned porfiristas.

In the novel, the representatives of its mythological counterpart are found in the old lady Teódula Moctezuma and Ixca Cienfuegos. They symbolize Mexico's past, a mythical Mexico that still survives and believes in ritual, in sacrifice as the only way for man to redeem himself. The Mexican people have been chosen by the gods to feed the sun and keep it moving so that mankind can survive. Without sacrifices this would be impossible. Displacement in the novel takes the form of parallel action in the fictional world representing history. Both Norma and Zamacona are sacrificed to modern gods. This revelation of the mythical nature of Mexican history is accomplished by the use of image and metaphor. The characters, the description of the city, the action, and the plot are all expressed by uniting two worlds, that of the remote past and that of the present. The interaction between the characters representing both cultures becomes the central technique of displacement. Mythical episodes are used by Fuentes to give his work a pure, literary quality. History and myth balance each other to give the novel equilibrium. (pp. 6-7)

The Death of Artemio Cruz and *Aura* were published the same year, 1962. While in the latter work the mythical predominates, the historical elements surface in *The Death of Artemio Cruz,* but even here mythical aspects are evident in the structure of the subject matter and the characterization of the hero. After writing the social history of Mexico City in *Where the Air Is Clear,* Fuentes continued and recreated the history of modern Mexico in *La muerte de Artemio Cruz,* approximately from the era of Santa Anna to the 1950s, with the period of the Revolution receiving the most attention. Historical personages are freely mentioned, as are historical facts and events. . . . It is also a history, as seen through the eyes of Artemio Cruz, an unreliable character. The mythical structure is found in the use of the myth of the descent into hell to depict the career of the hero who recreates in his mind, just before he dies in the hospital, the twelve most important moments of his life. These twelve days represent the twelve circles of Dante's Inferno, as well as the twelve months of the year. This mythical motif is repeated in the temporal structure of the novel, in which the narrative time covers the last twelve days in the life of Artemio. (p. 8)

In the novels published after *The Death of Artemio Cruz*—*Aura* (1962), *Zona sagrada* (1967), *Cambio de piel* (1967), *Cumpleaños* (1969), *Terra Nostra* (1975), *La cabeza de la hidra* (1978), and *Una familia lejana* (1980), Fuentes has given more emphasis to the mythical than to the historical, but never forgets history or the social condition, which underlies all his fiction.

In *Aura* he gives expression to the historical and the mythical by creating characters symbolic of both forms of thought. Two male characters—Llorente, a general of the period of Maximilian's Empire, and Felipe Montero, a young contemporary historian who later turns out to be the general's double—represent the historical component in the novelette. For balance, there are two additional archetypes, both female—Consuelo (Llorente's wife and a sorceress), who conquers time by recovering her youth, and Aura, her counterpart as a young girl. (pp. 8-9)

[Some of the mythical elements in *Zona sagrada* occur] in the thematic content, the relation between Claudia Nervo, the mother, and Guillermo (Guillermito, Mito), the son. The first chapter, entitled "Happily Ever After," narrates the myth of the sirens in the story of Ulysses, but in a present-day context—a football game which is played in a sacred zone, the staked field. In the last chapter, "Zona sagrada," Mito is transformed into a dog. While in *Where the Air Is Clear,* the beginning and the ending of the novel are in opposition (mythical introduction, historical epilogue), in *Zona sagrada* they are parallel. The novel ends with the episode of Circe, the sorceress who changes men into animals. Since Claudia Nervo is associated with Circe, the transformation of Mito into a dog becomes a part of the myth. As a theme, the myth of Ulysses has also been recreated, for the characters represent Penelope and her son Telemachus. Even Telegonus, the son of Ulysses and Circe, is there, under the name of Giancarlo. The historical part of the novel is based on the life story of a famous Mexican movie star.

Cambio de piel (A Change of Skin) signals a change of attitude in Fuentes as a novelist. Here for the first time he builds a purely fictional construct. . . . Displacement is achieved by introducing numerous realistic motifs, starting with the date when the events in the novel begin—Palm Sunday, April 11, 1965. On that precise, historical day two couples leave Mexico City in a Volkswagen on their way to Veracruz, taking the old road and stopping at Cholula, where the rest of the action takes place, at a second-rate hotel and inside the great pyramid. This, however, is preceded by a prologue with a displacement function and in which the destruction of Cholula by Cortés and his men is recreated. (p. 10)

[The theme of *A Change of Skin*] is the mythification of history. In history there is no progress, time has been abolished, as in myth. This explains why the violent acts occurring at the end of the novel—the death of Franz and Elizabeth in the center of the pyramid, the killing of Isabel by Javier in the hotel—are structured in parallel trajectories with some of the most violent events in history: the destruction of Cholula by Cortés, the massacre of the Jewish people. (p. 11)

Cumpleaños (1969) is the first novel by Carlos Fuentes in which the action takes place outside of Mexico. It is also the first that transcends his preoccupation with Mexican history and myth, being based, instead, on European history and myth. However, there are, as in his first novels, both historical and fictitious personages. Also, in *Cumpleaños,* as in previous novels, there is a sacred place, where the theologian, accused of heresy, takes refuge to escape his enemies. This place becomes a bedroom in a contemporary London house where the old man, Nuncia, and [a] boy live. Both places merge into one labyrinthian residence symbolic of the universe. In the bedroom the old man remembers his past life which extends back to the thirteenth century, since he is the reincarnation of Siger de Brabant, a theologian from the University of Paris persecuted for his ideas by Etienne Tempier and Thomas Aquinas. In the present he is George, an architect in London, husband of Emily and father of Georgie, whose tenth birthday they are celebrating that day. This novel is the least realistic of those written by Carlos Fuentes; yet, even here, there are historical elements in the plot, in the artistic motifs, and in the description of the milieu: books read by the boy (*Treasure Island, Black Beauty,* etc.); realistic descriptions of London. . . . (pp. 11-12)

In *Cumpleaños* all traces of Mexican history have disappeared, but the same is not true of *Terra Nostra, The Hydra Head,* and *Una familia lejana. Terra Nostra* deals with the history of Spain during the Renaissance period, but in the second of its three parts, "The New World," the subject is pre-Hispanic Mexican myth and the conquest of the land. By the use of history and myth Fuentes attempts to apprehend the meaning of the age of Philip II and, therefore, the destiny of the Hispanic people, both in the Old World and in the New World, and even in "The Other World," the title of the last part of the novel. As a technique he superimposes several historical periods, going back to the age of Tiberius and pre-Hispanic Mexico, and forward to the end of the century. By this means he creates a new historical reality which, although it is purely fictional, is based on empirical fact and real historical personages. The figure of Philip II, however, becomes an archetype, since it is a composite of several Spanish rulers who have exercised absolute power, and it is this obsession with power on the part of Philip II that gives universality to the novel.

Terra Nostra opens with a scene in Paris on a precise day, July 14, 1999, and ends there on the last day of the same year, the end of the millennium. Thus, the entire narrative partakes of the apocalyptic myth. In the second part, Fuentes creates a space in the New World where historical, fictional, and mythical characters act their roles in a purely mythical time. But even here are found the everpresent historical references, presented with the techniques of fiction. (p. 13)

[In] *The Hydra Head* and *Una familia lejana,* history plays a secondary role to fiction. A current event, the struggle for the control of Mexican oil deposits, is the subject of the first, a detective novel. The protagonist, Félix Maldonado, is patterned after a present-day mythical archetype, James Bond. In *Una familia lejana* Fuentes tries to establish, in a minor way, the cultural relations between Mexico and France, as he had done with Spain in *Terra Nostra,* but in a more personal way. The protagonist, Mexican archeologist Hugo Heredia, husband of a French girl, Lucie, and father of two sons, Víctor and Antonio, delivers a long, historical essay in the first part of chapter 20. At the same time, the author identifies himself with the protagonist, thus becoming the hero of his own novel. . . .

Mythical elements in [*Una familia lejana*], which predominate, are given expression by means of several devices: the association of the characters with the mythical past of Mexico (Lucie as La Llorona); the use of the double (Heredia and "Heredia"); the use of motifs related to the "Día de Muertos" (November 2); and, especially, the use of fiction itself as myth. (p. 14)

In general, then, it can be said that the narrative of Carlos Fuentes swerved strongly at the beginning toward the historical, and strongly after 1969 toward the mythical, but never in a pure form. His idea of history, however, is not that of the empirical historian, but goes beyond fact to a reality that includes myth and legend, so important in the shaping of the Mexican mind. Quite often he fills the lacuna of the historical record with oral history, legend, or myth. His fiction reveals that history itself often becomes myth; and although it is based on a collection of facts, the mythical consciousness of the author is ever present before the facts are verbalized. . . . By fusing history and myth in his novels (and the same can be said of his play, *Todos los gatos son pardos*), Fuentes has been able not only to reveal important aspects of the mind and character of the Mexican people, but also to project his own hopes and aspirations, one of which is not to kill the past. (pp. 15-16)

> Luis Leal, "History and Myth in the Narrative of Carlos Fuentes," in Carlos Fuentes: A Critical View, edited by Robert Brody and Charles Rossman, University of Texas Press, 1982, pp. 3-17.

GLORIA DURÁN

Fuentes has been less than successful as a playwright possibly because the form of dramatic art that has influenced his fiction is not the stage play but the movie. Up to now he has written plays that create imposing technological problems in a stage presentation, problems that can be solved only by the magic of the screen.

But perhaps there is magic in the number three. His third play, *Orchids in the Moonlight,* seems clearly to be written for the stage, yet it is inspired by his overwhelming love for the movies. If we judge by conventional standards, it is his most successful play to date: it has enjoyed a six-week presentation by the American Repertory Theatre in Cambridge, Massachusetts. . . .

However, judging by both the production and the manuscript, I would not say that this is Fuentes's best play. . . .

How then, can we account for the play's relative success? A factor of some significance may be that the play was written by Fuentes directly in English. In view of his growing reputation in the United States, and especially in academic circles, we may suspect that the potential audience for his dramatic works is also growing. But another factor of some importance may be the interview with Fuentes by Arthur Holmberg, published in section 2 of the Sunday *New York Times* of 6 June 1982, three days before the play's premiere. In this prominent, illustrated interview, Fuentes describes his play and emphasizes its feminist content. Talking about his two protagonists, Dolores Del Río and María Félix, film stars of the thirties and forties, Fuentes says: "I loved these two actresses because they were strong and independent. They shattered all the macho myths. They were not what Latin American women were supposed to be. They were not little dolls men could cuddle. María Félix was a Pancho Villa in skirts." (p. 595)

Orchids is a play about the relationship between two women. But although this is a feminist play, at least on its most conspicuous level, *Orchids* is not readily understood by a public who may not be conversant with Fuentes's constant recourse to archetypal characters. . . . As in his earlier works, he is fascinated by all the physical attractions that turn women into symbols rather than people. He also makes feminists wonder how these women can be both sexy and anti-sexist symbols, archetypes of the glamorous female and also role models for average Latin American women. Yet in all fairness to Fuentes, in the Holmberg interview he warns us that this play will not be easily understandable: "My play is about the myth of culture and the culture of myths," he says as he describes movies as "bearers of the collective unconscious, the warehouse of modern myths."

The initiate, therefore, is forewarned that *Orchids in the Moonlight* will be feminism passed through the sieve of Jungian psychology. The feminist element will be supplied by the fact that now, for the first time, female archetypes are to be examined from their own viewpoints rather than from the perspective of a male protagonist. They will become the "we," not the "they." Fuentes accomplishes this transformation by intruding upon the sacred area inhabited by his archetypes. Possibly he is describing this process when he says in the playbill: "That is the thing about archetypes: they fascinate you but you dare not touch them. They nurture you but who nurtures them? Who is the archetype of the archetype, the star of the star, the model of the model? Who is Mother?"

In the above passage Fuentes shows that he is no longer using these archetypes in the classical Jungian sense of projections by our collective unconscious, projections which we incarnate in other people. Rather, his new archetypes will now generate their own archetypes, much as Borges's dream characters give birth to new dream characters and in so doing attempt to convince themselves of their own reality. In fact, the only female character in the play who remains a true archetype is the one who never appears—"Mummy." Mummy is the Great Mother, the unseen psychic presence against whom the protagonists must struggle in order to assert themselves as human beings rather than popular fantasies. Although Mummy may have nurtured them, as Fuentes indicates, she has nurtured only their public images, their *personas.* She stands in the way of human fulfillment. To a certain extent the dialogue of the two actresses can be seen as a psychoanalytical attempt to integrate the Great Mother archetype through a dialectical process. (pp. 595-96)

María is the more liberated of the two women. She is portrayed as an earthy Chicana with few illusions about her past. In realistic details she closely resembles Fuentes's earlier characterizations of María Félix in *Zona sagrada (Holy Place)*. María is relatively free of the escapism of the older Dolores, who lives only for her memories. Dolores's memories, like Elizabeth's in *Cambio de piel (Change of Skin)*, are apocryphal, a collage of movie make-believe. Dolores seems to be a Mexican version of Gloria Swanson in *Sunset Boulevard*. Enmeshed in her own narcissism, she is relatively passive to the professed love of María. María reiterates that she loves Dolores only for herself, and that she is the only person—not excluding Dolores—who loves her for what she is rather than for what she appears to be or to have been. Although in the archetypal image that she represents to others María is a femme fatale, in her love for Dolores she is all too vulnerable. When she imagines that she has lost Dolores, she commits suicide, like a modern Juliet. And yet ironically, Dolores, by her departure, finally shows that she has come to grips with María's love and is capable of reciprocating it. A brief reference to the plot as it unfolds in the second act should explain this cruel paradox in the play's conclusion.

The private world of the two actresses (a windowless apartment with huge mirrors, racks of clothes and oversize bed) is breached when Dolores, still playing the great actress, makes a telephone call. Stopped by María, Dolores does not manage to identify herself over the telephone, but nevertheless the call mysteriously summons forth a fan, an ardent admirer who has seen every one of Dolores's films. María, now torn by suspicion and jealousy, identifies the male intruder as a prying newspaperman whose real motive in seeking out Dolores is to do research for an obituary column. Reacting to María's accusations, the jovial intruder becomes menacing. He threatens to publicize a pornographic film once made by María and which she believed was destroyed. It is at this point that Dolores appears to forsake María by going off to marry the fan. But when she returns after María's dramatic suicide (accomplished by an overdose of sleeping pills as she attempts to reenter a film that is being projected on the boudoir walls), Dolores reveals that she had accompanied the fan only to kill him and thus save María's reputation. Her apparent betrayal of María was in fact her greatest proof of love.

Clearly, the only real similarity between *Orchids in the Moonlight* and *Zona sagrada* is that both deal with the life of María Félix. But in the play María loses her archetypal, magical properties. She is far more than a sex goddess. In fact, if we compare elements of plot, *Orchids* is far closer to an earlier work of Fuentes, the novelette *Aura* of 1962. In both this work and the play Fuentes deals with two exotic women of indeterminate age (the manuscript for *Orchids* suggests that they should appear to fluctuate between thirty and sixty years of age) who inhabit a mysterious, private world. The women's goals in both cases are love, youth and immortality. In both cases the moonlit world is breached by a young, male writer. In *Aura* the writer pays for his folly by a relinquishing of personality. In *Orchids* the penalty is greater; his very person is sacrificed on the altar of love.

Thus, in schematic terms, the basic elements of plot in both *Aura* and *Orchids* are similar. Yet in psychological terms, the two tales are poles apart. In *Aura* we see the world through the perspective of the male protagonist. He is mesmerized and immobilized by the archetypal female figure, incarnation of the Great Mother, and so succumbs to the power of the collective unconscious. Instead of achieving an integration of personality as a result of his struggle with his archetype, he accepts its total disintegration. In *Orchids,* on the other hand, a decisive difference is effected through change in point of view. Although the male character is still a victim, his fate becomes inconsequential. Instead it is the women who are the real protagonists; it is they who must struggle with their own archetypes, the foremost being Mummy. . . . María defies and fears Mummy. Dolores is constantly apprehensive about the possible reactions of this omnipresent figure who lives on "the upper floor." It is only at the play's end that she can call Mummy "the atrocious old lady, believing she can take life because she gave us our life, the hypocritical whore older than all the dead." . . . Her liberation from Mummy has been accomplished by the intervention of "the Fan."

Who is this character whom Fuentes identifies only as "the Fan"? We are told almost nothing about him. His motivations are uncertain. It is never made clear whether he imagines himself in love with Dolores or merely wishes to blackmail María. . . . [Fuentes] identifies him as a punster. The Fan enters the scene almost as a court jester, paying Dolores the lavish compliment of remembering every detail of each of her films. He is jovial and boisterous like a gust of fresh air that ripples across an ill-ventilated room. But when María accuses him of pretense, his ribald personality turns menacing. Eventually both women regard him as demonic. If we seek the Fan's identity in the archetypal world described by Jung, the Fan can be easily assimilated to the figure known as the Trickster.

Writing on the psychology of the Trickster figure, Jung describes him as a "shape-shifter" with a "dual nature, half animal, half divine," and traces him back beyond Hermes. (pp. 596-97)

[For Fuentes] movies are often both the seed and the fruit of literature. Instinctively he seems to know that the medieval fables about the sly fox who is eventually outfoxed have their modern cinematic counterpart in the "private eye" figure, the ethically ambiguous detective who often reveals truths that those who summon him would rather not accept and whose services, therefore, are not always fully appreciated. Some of Humphrey Bogart's famous roles have a true Trickster dimension; he is the tough guy who evokes both laughter and tears. (p. 597)

[The] appearance of the Trickster in the second act transforms *Orchids* from a play about memory, which is static and interesting mainly to those who share Fuentes's nostalgia for the two actresses, to one of dynamic action. The fantastically rapid pace of events in this act is probably welcomed by the average member of the audience, who sees the Fan as a dynamic third character. Yet for those familiar with Fuentes's work, third characters are suspect insofar as they often turn out to be new versions of existent characters. . . . Thus Fuentes cognoscenti may share my suspicions that the Fan is an incarnation of the unconscious of Dolores, the dreamer, or, as already suggested, a collective mirage for both actresses. If the latter is the case, the action may be regarded as taking place on two levels, as reality and as imagination.

This dual interpretation of the action enhances not only the metaphysical significance of the work but also its unity and esthetic value. If we do not give an oneiric interpretation to the second act, it becomes inexplicably different from the first one, where there is a Tennessee Williams atmosphere of escapism struggling against harsh reality. The second act, by way of contrast, seems to be a hybrid of film and dreams. The film is out of Del Río's early period, where action appears accelerated. The dream is also an actress's dream, where "real" life and film are intertwined. At the moment that the actresses sing their tango about dreams, the Fan knocks at their door, almost as if conjured out of their collective longing. Curiously, they both fear at first that the impossible apparition will turn out to be Mummy.

The first act of the play, therefore, broadly hints at the unconscious world dominated by archetypal characters. The second act immerses us in this world, where one such character, the Trickster, materializes and combats the other, the Great Mother. In keeping with the myth of the Trickster, the Fan becomes too clever for his own good and is himself tricked and sacrificed. Fuentes's female protagonists thus emerge as far more able to combat the emanations of the collective unconscious than his male protagonists. In this respect, if in no other way, we may say that *Orchids in the Moonlight* is a truly feminist play.

Yet *Orchids* is not only a feminist play. In his stage directions Fuentes even (jokingly?) suggests that the protagonists could be played by two men. Fuentes emphasizes that *Orchids* is a play about authenticity versus the role-playing which society forces upon us and which we come to accept as definitions of our personalities. He portrays a Del Río so identified with her public image as a movie star that loss of public recognition undermines her belief that she is still herself, necessitating constant confirmation by María for her to continue to exist. Thus the play continues to explore the theme of continuity of personality which has been a preoccupation of Fuentes in most of his fictional writings.

For critics attuned to social commentary in Fuentes's works, the character of Dolores may also be seen as a vehicle for the author's condemnation of Mexico's middle class, its self-deception, sentimentality and escapism. Against Dolores's genteel world of make-believe he contrasts the coarse realism of María, a lowly Chicana, who is innately generous in her capacity to love.

Beyond feminism and social commentary, *Orchids* is a drama about psychic growth, about maturing and facing death. Since the loss of youth and beauty is more painful to bear for those who have become identified with them, the two Mexican actresses make excellent protagonists. Dolores, moreover, with her suggestive name (*dolor* = pain), becomes a symbol of the human condition. *Orchids,* therefore, is a metaphysical play which Fuentes has packaged in the attractive allure of Hollywood, in part perhaps to draw an audience, but also because, as he has said, "movies are bearers of the collective unconscious." (pp. 597-98)

> *Gloria Durán, "'Orchids in the Moonlight': Fuentes as Feminist and Jungian Playwright," in* World Literature Today, *Vol. 57, No. 4, Autumn, 1983, pp. 595-98.*

LANIN A. GYURKO

Orquídeas a la luz de la luna provides a fascinating evocation of two of Mexico's greatest cinematic actresses, Dolores Del Río and María Félix. This complex drama constitutes a play-within-a-play. It presents two aging *chicanas*, Dolores and María, living in seclusion in an apartment in Venice, California, who identify so strongly with the screen personalities of Dolores Del Río and María Félix that they—paralleling the self-deluded Don Quijote, who, intoxicated by his readings of the *novelas de caballerías,* sallies forth as a *caballero andante*—believe, in their self-delusions, that they actually have become these two cinematic stars. Thus they seek desperately to convince one another, the very audience watching *Orquídeas a la luz de la luna,* and the mysterious and sinister Fan who one day arrives at their apartment, that they are these two legendary actresses.

Having failed at their cinematic careers in their native land, Mexico, the two central characters of Fuentes' drama emigrate to the United States, where they attempt to pursue the glamorous illusion of a Hollywood film career. Denied entrance to their El Dorado, they are forced instead to dwell in a limbo realm, a shoddy apartment that is more like a penitentiary cell, symbolizing how much they remain entrapped in their fantasies. Here the two *chicanas* engage in a bizarre cult of their cinematic idols, even constructing altars to them, thus from the very start transforming María Félix and Dolores Del Río into household gods. The impoverished and desolate lives of the *chicanas* are, paradoxically, both fulfilled and destroyed through this fanatic cult of the cinematic Other, which both provides the means of communicating with one another, of transcending their solitude and alienation, and yet finally devours their original personalities and prevents them from responding to each other except as cinematic roles, as celluloid illusions. Their days are spent either in the obsessive viewing of the many films of Del Río and Félix, films like *Flying Down to Rio,* in which Del Río played the role of a glamorous and sophisticated socialite, Belinha de Rezende, dancing with Fred Astaire, and whose lilting tango, "Orchids in the Moonlight," gives its title to Fuentes' drama, as well as films from the later, Mexican period of Del Río's remarkable career, like *Las abandonadas* and *La selva de fuego.* Fuentes' María, brash and impetuous, constantly identifies with the María Félix of *Doña Bárbara,* the powerful *devoradora de hombres,* and even attempts to play this role in real life.

The art of Fuentes is one of constant role reversals, of *cambios de piel,* in which the *conquistador* becomes the *conquistado,* and vice versa. In *Orquídeas a la luz de la luna,* the standard roles—so very different—with which each of these two actresses is identified, are suddenly and brutally exchanged. Throughout her career, in both the films she made in Hollywood, such as *Ramona* and *Resurrection* and *Revenge,* as well as in many of her Mexican films, such as *María Candelaria,* Dolores was cast in the role of the downtrodden *campesina,* or, as in King Vidor's *Bird of Paradise,* the exotic Polynesian maiden who sacrifices herself to placate her angry gods, whereas in film after film, María Félix has played just the opposite role—the fierce and dominating and castrating woman, the "Doña Diabla." Yet in Fuentes' drama, it is María who succumbs, taking her own life, unable to live in complete isolation after she mistakenly believes that Dolores, her soulmate, has abandoned her for the Fan. And the timid and subservient Dolores, in a stunning departure from the majority of roles played by her screen idol, becomes transformed into the vengeful *tigresa,* suddenly killing the Fan who has come, ostensibly to render homage to them, but in reality to blackmail María with a pornographic film that she had made in her youth, in the silent era of film, and that he now projects—demonstrating the power of the image not to redeem but to destroy. Through this sudden role reversal, Fuentes underscores the theme reiterated throughout his drama, that Del Río and Félix are components of the same haunting and mesmerizing self. (pp. 3-4)

In *Orquídeas a la luz de la luna,* Fuentes continues his masterful exploration of a theme that has preoccupied him since his very first collection of short stories, *Los días enmascarados* (1954)— that of the relationship between individual and national identity. Throughout his work, Fuentes creates characters who function convincingly as both individuals and symbols of *la mexican-idad*—Artemio Cruz, whose complex personality, a fusion of opposites, of idealism and corruptness, of cowardice and bravery, of social responsibility and ruthlessness, is developed as a continual paradox in order to grant him the weight and intricacy to symbolize an entire nation; Federico Robles and Rodrigo Pola in *La región más transparente,* who symbolize various phases of the Mexican Revolution and post-Revolutionary society; the commanding Claudia Nervo in *Zona sagrada* who in her immense wealth and power and international fame attains the status of a national symbol, and the despised La Malinche, whom Fuentes in his drama *Todos los gatos son pardos* vindicates, elevating into an eloquent and fiery advocate of the new Mexican nation, the fusion of both Indian and Spanish, that will emerge from the conflict and devastation of the Conquest. Instead of adhering to the traditional portrait of La Malinche as the Mexican Eve, as the betrayer of her people to the *conquistadores,* Fuentes portrays La Malinche as both conscience of Cortés, urging him to become the Quetzalcóatl, the god of life and love, that the Indians see him as, and as a bold resister of foreign domination. In *Orquídeas a la luz de la luna,* Dolores Del Río and María Félix emerge as positive national symbols, as exemplars of the cosmopolitanism and sophistication of modern Mexico, as well as its rich and variegated culture. Thus in *Orquídeas,* Del Río and Félix are evoked on myriad levels, as radiant and constantly changing cinematic images, as vibrant and authoritative exponents of the emancipation of women in Mexico, and as national institutions.

On the one hand, *Orquídeas* is one of the most cosmopolitan of Fuentes' works, with its inclusion of both Mexican and North American characters, its evocation of both Orson Welles and H. G. Wells, its use of intertextuality—the inclusion of a seventeenth-century poem by the baroque author Luis Sandoval y Zapata, and intervisuality—allusions to Verdi's *Aida* and to Michelangelo's *Pietá.* Yet, like all of Fuentes' works, *Orquídeas* is at the same time international in scope and, in its essence, uniquely Mexican. The two deracinated *chicanas,* and in particular María, feel the constant pull of the origins. At the end, right before her death, María engages in an elaborate ceremony of both evocation and exaltation of her Mexican past, acknowledging her identity not as the domineering María Félix but as the humble Maclovia, reaching out to the Mexican *pueblo* for spiritual support. . . . The Mexican cult of death—death as not divorced from life but life's constant, inseparable companion—is portrayed throughout the drama. María evokes Venice not as a joyous realm of imaginative liberation but as a death city; the malevolent Fan, who writes the obituary column for a leading newspaper, seems to be an incarnation of death itself, suddenly appearing to fulfill the deepest desire of María. The weird and powerful Mother, like so many of Fuentes' mothers, Teódula Moctezuma in *La región más transparente,* Carlota/Consuelo in *Aura,* Isabel in *Terra nostra,* Claudia Nervo in *Zona sagrada,* and Ruth in *La cabeza de la hidra,* emerges as a mother of physical and spiritual death, of death-in-life. The two *chicanas* attempt to hide the newspaper from this *mater terribilis,* who daily pores over the obituary columns, gloating whenever she encounters an item describing the death of someone younger than herself. Like the fierce Aztec goddess Coatlicue whom she seems to represent, the goddess whose immense statue is in the National Museum of Anthropology in Mexico City, with her skirt of serpents and gruesome necklace of severed human hands and skulls, the goddess who demands human sacrifice in order to nourish herself, the ominous and unnamed mother of Fuentes' drama derives new life from death. A Mexican Bernarda Alba, the Mother perhaps keeps her two daughters imprisoned in a state of living death, compelling them, as the only means of escaping from her despotism, to identify with the two titanic women presences, Del Río and Félix, who defeat the Coatlicue myth, who have been able to defy and escape from oppressive, tradition-bound familial structures, to transcend their pasts and to become symbols of the power of women to create and assert their own identities, freeing themselves from role-incarceration, oftentimes so severely imposed on women in Latin America—roles as dutiful and obedient wives, long-suffering mothers, and respectable society matrons.

In this drama as in so many of his works, Fuentes approaches his homeland as an outsider, through the perspective of the *chicanas,* who defend both their filmic idols and their native country, but from within the United States. The fact that Dolores Del Río herself transcended affiliation with a single country to become a universal symbol provides the bilingual/bicultural model on which this drama is based. In a major sense, *Orquídeas a la luz de la luna* is a continuation of Fuentes' novel that immediately preceded it, *Una familia lejana* (1980), in which for the first time in Fuentes' work, the Other is not the North American or European mask over the autochthonous identity assumed by Mexicans in order to bolster the weak, insecure, or unsophisticated self, as it is so feverishly done in *La región más transparente, La muerte de Artemio Cruz,* and *Cambio de piel,* but rather the Other, outside identity is the Mexican identity itself. In *Una familia lejana,* the only work in which Fuentes himself appears explicitly identified as a character in his own novel, the Francophilic "Carlos Fuentes" openly rejects his Latin American origins. . . . Instead, Fuentes strongly identifies with the elegant and cultured Count Branly, and seeks to construct a new French identity, on the model of other illustrious Latin American writers like José María de Heredia and Jules Supervielle who became completely integrated into French culture, wrote in French, and are now considered as French authors—despite the pronounced Latin American tone and even thematic influence on their art. But in both *Una familia lejana* and *Orquídeas a la luz de la luna,* the origins cannot be negated. In both works the origins appear as a supernatural force, linked with death—in the form of the monstrous Mother in *Orquídeas* from whom Dolores at the end vows to hide the body of María so that she cannot claim a triumph, and in the figure of the diabolic master of time, André Heredia in *Una familia lejana.* In *Una familia lejana,* the eloquent attempts by "Fuentes" to negate his origins are futile; the Latin American past rises up as a demonic power at the end, pursuing him to what he has all along self-deludedly believed is his sanctuary in Paris, in the sophisticated and genteel French Automobile Club, rapidly undermining his newfound and much-prized French identity, founded on Cartesian rationalism. Instead, the helpless Fuentes, like the victimized Felipe Montero in *Aura* who is also caught up and destroyed by the origins, by the ancient Mexican past that imposes itself as a present reality, is swept back into a phantasmagorical jungle. At the end, an internal, metaphysical vision assaults Fuentes' mind—images of a monstrous, even hellish jungle world reminiscent of the "green inferno" so terrifyingly evoked by the Latin American novelist José Eustasio Rivera in his epic novel *La vorágine.* In *Orquídeas a la luz de la luna,* as in *Una familia lejana,* the Latin American identity is always evoked from the outside. For the self-exiled María, Mexico is but a nostalgic memory that she evokes poignantly and fervently at the very end. Yet despite this brief, symbolic return to the origins by María, who orders an elaborate meal of Mexican delicacies, the predominant image of Latin America in *Orquídeas a la luz de la luna,* present in the very title of the drama and continued throughout, is the Hollywood image of Latin America as exuberantly represented in *Flying Down to Rio*—tropical island paradises, dark beauties on moonlit beaches, orchids blooming like weeds, sensuous Latin rhythms of the tango and the samba, endless gaiety of dance and song. Fuentes deliberately and ironically evokes Latin America not as a Latin American writer normally would, but from the perspective of a Hollywood film producer. Thus the Mexico that is finally conjured up by María is a combination of Aztec ceremony and mariachi bands, of Aztec and Hollywood rituals, of Nubian slave girls who might have stepped out of a Cecil B. DeMille epic motion picture of Cleopatra. Even truth itself is cinematic—the Fan makes a polar contrast between the verbal and the visual; the language that is used to deceive and the image—a veiled reference to the film that he has brought with him—that reveals the truth. . . . (pp. 5-8)

From the beginning to the end of Fuentes' drama, which expertly combines various levels of fantasy—dreams and reveries and nightmares, psychological and supernatural fantasies; artistic fantasies, murals and songs and poems, and the play-within-a-play, as dramatic actresses play the roles of *chicanas* who play the parts of cinematic actresses—it is the cinematic image, the cinematic presence, and not the degrading and brutalizing marginality of the real-life existence of the two *chicanas,* that is the most important. At the very end, the sound of the shovelsful of earth that are burying María is drowned out by the music, "Orchids in the Moonlight." So strong is the grip of illusion on the fragile mind of Dolores that, instead of confessing the truth to the Fan that they, like he, are impostors, Dolores kills him in order to defend the reputation of María, and in order to protect her precious cinematic illusions, which she exalts as part of the funeral ceremony for María. . . . Through their total identification with the screen, in life and even after death, as Dolores props up the body of María and projects on the screen in front of them the images from the films of their idols, the two *chicanas* ironically gain what so many of Fuentes' characters obsessively search for—immortality. They preserve themselves as eternally young and eternally beautiful—the obsession of the wizened sorceress Consuelo in *Aura* and of Claudia in *Zona sagrada,* who like Dolores fanatically courts the camera, insisting that she be photographed again and again, as a means of defying her Nemesis, Time. (p. 23)

Lanin A. Gyurko, "Cinematic Image and National Identity in Fuentes' 'Orquídeas a la luz de la luna'," in Latin American Theatre Review, *Vol. 17, No. 2, Spring, 1984, pp. 3-24.*

MICHIKO KAKUTANI

[The title character of *The Old Gringo*] happens to be Ambrose Bierce, the American journalist and short-story writer who left for Mexico in 1913—presumably to join Pancho Villa's revolutionary army—and who mysteriously disappeared. What Mr. Fuentes has done is to imagine Bierce's subsequent life—and death—there in the desolate desert reaches of northern Mexico, and in doing so, he has succeeded in welding history and fiction, the personal and the collective, into a dazzling novel that possesses the weight and resonance of myth.

Mr. Fuentes, of course, has long been interested in the history of his homeland, and in such novels as *Where the Air Is Clear* and *The Death of Artemio Cruz,* he has already examined the effects of Mexico's 1910-20 revolution, and that country's tangled relationship with America, the sprawling, imperialist giant to the north. None of his earlier works, however, illuminate those issues with the assurance evinced by *The Old Gringo* or use his gifts for magical realism with this book's passion and precision. In *The Old Gringo,* Mr. Fuentes has found a form and a subject that enable him to exploit his favorite techniques and explore some of his favorite themes (from cultural and Freudian determinism to the nature of reality and art) and give them their fullest expression.

Cutting back and forth in time, *The Old Gringo* is, on one level, the story of Bierce, as recollected by Harriet Winslow, an American spinster whose encounter with the journalist will have tragic consequences for both of them—as well as for their friend and adversary, a Mexican general named Tomás Arroyo. Yet if Harriet's attempts to come to terms with this experience through memory and imagination underline Mr. Fuentes's own concern with the uses of fiction, hers is hardly the only voice that compels our attention in *The Old Gringo.* Within her account, we also hear the voices of Bierce and Arroyo, and we listen to the voices, too, of assorted Mexicans—other officers in Villa's army, their women and their hangers-on, who together form a Faulkner-like chorus, articulating Mexico's past and present. . . .

Certainly the hard-bitten author of "The Devil's Dictionary" does not share the bright illusions of Harriet Winslow—this spirited Jamesian heroine, who has left behind her safe little home in Washington to teach young Mexican children, and who naively clings to her missionary faith, even in the midst of a chaotic revolution. And yet taken together, these two norteamericanos form a sort of composite portrait of America, an America that will come to stand in shadowy contrast to the Mexico of Tomás Arroyo and his people. America, a land of changing seasons, a country built upon the ideals of order and democracy and individual will, and so devoted to the notion of progress as to obliterate the past; and Mexico, a land of eternal summer and "memorious dust," a country unable to forget its history of conquest and unrequited blood—these two nations, so representative of our inability to comprehend the differentness, the plain otherness, of the foreign, will become the poles from which the tragic action in *The Old Gringo* springs.

Such a summary tends to make this book sound a good deal more schematic than it is, for while Mr. Fuentes is concerned with cultural and racial myths, he is even more interested in how those forces intersect with the private lives of individuals. Indeed, he makes it clear that the triangle among Bierce, Arroyo and Winslow is the product both of their idiosyncratic psychic and familial histories and larger, social movements beyond their control. By grounding the more symbolic actions of his story in a welter of biographical details and minutely imagined facts, Mr. Fuentes persuades us that the love Harriet Winslow inspires in both men—the old gringo, who believed that his cynicism protected his heart, and the young revolutionary, who believed that no woman could come between him and his cause—is as inevitable as it is real.

Although Mr. Fuentes's lyric tendencies occasionally result in rather clotted passages—there are a few too many vague, incantatory musings about the meaning of life and death—his gift for metaphor lofts *The Old Gringo* out of the realm of naturalism and invests its more didactic social impulses with the fierce magic of a remembered dream.

Michiko Kakutani, in a review of "The Old Gringo," in The New York Times, *October 23, 1985, p. C21.*

PAUL WEST

[*The Old Gringo* is] a cleverly conceived and crisply rendered book about Ambrose Bierce's mysterious last days, as an old man, in the Mexico of 1914.

The book's premise is that Bierce went to Mexico to die, in the army of Pancho Villa, because death is what Mexico is good at. It would be easier to explore this premise if Fuentes had come closer to Bierce's most hidden motives, but he backs off, only occasionally allowing Bierce to speak out, or dream forth, in his own words, in an idiom different from that of the novel's narrator: "This handiwork of man and beast, this humble, unheroic Prometheus, comes praying, yes, imploring everything for the boon of oblivion." The reader has to guess, wondering if indeed the old gringo saw a Mexican death as a fitting punctuation mark because death in Mexico, as distinct from death anywhere else, is more imposing, satisfying, incongruous or whatever.

After all, the author of "An Occurrence at Owl Creek Bridge" had a vested interest in death, its protocols and mannerisms. Shot, Fuentes imagines, in the back by a capricious junior general of Villa's, after making a solo horseback charge of indelible, reckless bravery, and after encountering too late for anything to come of it the exquisite and chaste Harriet Winslow of Washington, D.C., Bierce suffers a death every bit as enigmatic as his initial decision to go south of the border. Did Arroyo the general shoot him for being too brave, in other words for setting too high a standard; or for burning Arroyo's box of private papers? Take your choice. Or, better, shelve the question as if the novel were a movie (which it is going to be). Eye the events and decipher them as best you can in the absence of narrative help. I am not sure we aren't dealing here with an *acte gratuit* much as we find it in André Gide. At any rate, Bierce wanted his death, and got it, so for him the causation could hardly have mattered.

To some extent, then, this general Arroyo is a contraption, but contraptions fit well into Fuentes' highly schematic book, fraught with echoes, parallels, and doubles, almost like an enfolded rose. To both Harriet and Arroyo, the old gringo is a father figure. She has lost her father, at first thought killed in the war, but revealed to have run out on his family. Arroyo is the unacknowledged son of a grandee. In the end, Villa, himself a father figure to Arroyo, has Arroyo shot for shooting Bierce, but not before he has him dig up the old gringo's corpse for "execution" from in front by firing squad, to keep up appearances. There are other such patterns and their interaction, like something underwater as you sail through the clear prose element above, imperils and thickens the action, turning everything that looks straightforward into something indisputably richer and stranger. Fuentes understands how the mind, especially in his myth-rich native land, modifies whatever it attends to, and in this case he allows room for the accomplice-reader to become part of the sea-change itself.

What looks, at first, like an almost allegorical tale becomes something much less obvious, less fathomable. Old gringo, young gringa, young general, older general, begin to overlap more than they don't, and in a weird way their roles drop away from them until each—Bierce, Winslow, Arroyo, Villa—begins to get lost in the others, not on the level of character, but in a hortatory ballet, staged with phantoms in the neutral desert.

Looking back on it all, Harriet Winslow can hardly credit what she lived through, remembering best her mental affair with the old gringo, her intense physical one with Arroyo. She has discovered contingency, what Henry James called "the insolence of accident." She cannot separate the inevitable from a whole series, a concatenation, of flukes, which has nonetheless defined her forever. A traumatized survivor, she inherits the theme *"I cannot take it all in such a short time,"* and you wonder if, without realizing it, it is history she's talking about. Mantegna's Christ invades her mind, obsesses it, not least because she cannot link the old gringo as she knew him to the Ambrose Bierce who wrote the books. (pp. 1, 15)

It's a haunting novel, easier to focus on with the second reading, and—although a blaze of fierce action—a book of interacting levels, one of which is contemplative: where the reader begins and ends, pondering the enigma of Ambrose Bierce, who became as baffling as Mexico in order to die at its visionaries' hands. (p. 15)

Paul West, "Ambrose Bierce's Last Days in Mexico," in Book World—The Washington Post, *October 27, 1985, pp. 1, 15.*

EARL SHORRIS

Ten years ago, Octavio Paz told an interviewer there was not one Carlos Fuentes, but two, the European voice and the Mexican voice. Since then, more have emerged. Carlos Fuentes has been the palimpsest of Mexican history and culture separated into its discrete layers: Indian, Spanish, French, revolutionary, aristocratic, leftist, centrist, expatriate. In this analyzed presentation of the person, this soul shown after the centrifuge, Mr. Fuentes demonstrates the complexity of the Mexican character and the artistic difficulties peculiar to the novelist born in the Naval of the Universe, which is where the Aztecs placed Mexico.

For the North American reader to appreciate the levels and enjoy the discoveries of the sensual and mind-pleasing new novel by Mr. Fuentes [*The Old Gringo*], it may be helpful to provide the context to a tale that is, on casual reading, an imagined conclusion to the life of Ambrose Bierce.... (p. 1)

The pattern of the Mexican character was set early in the 16th century: When the Spaniards came to Mexico, they put the conquest of the population in the hands of the priests, and those wily psychologists chose to overlay Christianity on pagan religions like paper on a wall.... On the very hill where the Temple of Tonántzin had been, the Church of Our Lady of Guadalupe, patron saint of Mexico, was erected; the soul of a nation in the form of a palimpsest was carved in stone, and the problems of the Mexican in life and art were forever complicated.

The intellectual and social life of France was then piled on the converted Indian during the brief reign of Maximilian, who arrived in 1864 and was executed in 1867. Yet the positivism of Auguste Comte was the main philosophical influence in the oppressive government of Porfirio Díaz, which was overthrown in the revolution of 1910. The Socialist constitution of 1917 added another layer. Then came the betrayal of the revolution by a class of robber barons like Artemio Cruz, the dying monster of Carlos Fuentes's best known novel [*The Death of Artemio Cruz*]. But in all these changes nothing disappeared; there were only additions: Every Mexican knows that we live in the fifth and final age, *quinto sol,* and that the world will end in earthquake and fire; every Mexican has a *nahual,* an alter ego, a magical twin, a mirror image; no Mexican can help but be awed by the figure of Coatlícue, she who exists between life and death, reaching into both, mother of the moon and the stars, the goddess who swallowed a white feather and gave birth to Huitzilopochtli, the warrior sun, Coatlícue the earth and Our Mother; and every Mexican knows what lies to the north and how behemoth America affects every moment of his days and nights for as long as it suffers him to live.

It is in this Mexican mind that Carlos Fuentes sets his most ambitious novel, the first in which he attempts to integrate all that he knows and can call up of history, myth and thought. He uses the opposition between nations, the tension of unequals that share a common border, to drive the plot of the novel and to motivate the revelations of history and analogue. He calls North America "the land without memory" and says there is a "memorious dust" in Mexico that blows across the river, all the way to Washington, where the heroine of the novel, Harriet Winslow, now sits and remembers. So begins the story of *The Old Gringo,* looking down through the topmost layer to the exhumation of the body of the old writer who had said, "To be a gringo in Mexico, that is euthanasia."

The exhumation and manner of death of the old gringo echo the killing of William Benton by one of Pancho Villa's generals during the revolution that began in 1910. Benton, a British citizen with connections to the great landowners of northern Mexico, was bludgeoned to death, causing an international scandal. Pancho Villa ordered the body dug up, properly executed, and sent home. It is a grisly incident even in a revolution, but Mr. Fuentes uses it as a turn of plot and a layer of imagination. Before half a dozen pages have gone by, the mind of the reader has been awakened to the author's dissatisfaction with history. The Miranda ranch in the novel will resemble the famed Terrazas ranch, which before the revolution was so large the owners replied to an order for 10,000 head of cattle by asking, "What color?" The generals of the novel will resemble the generals of history, but nothing will be exact, everything will be imagined from the shards of history and made to serve the fiction. Even Ambrose Bierce's famous story of patricide, "A Horseman in the Sky," will appear in the novel as past and present, imagination and history, part of the distinction between Mexicans and North Americans. Quotations from his stories will be revised to fit the Ambrose Bierce invented by Mr. Fuentes.

In a novel of layers and connections such as this, the surface action must move quickly, there must be a good story to keep the reader from drowning in the depths. The genius of *The Old Gringo* is the choice of a character as rich as Ambrose Bierce, who is at the center of a famous mystery. At the age of 71, tossed between memory and death, Bierce crossed the border into Mexico in search of Pancho Villa, perhaps to find the stuff of stories again, perhaps to soldier as he had during the Civil War, perhaps to die. (pp. 1, 46)

The novel has the magical form invented by the Mexican novelist Juan Rulfo and carried on by Gabriel García Márquez, Mario Vargas Llosa, Mr. Fuentes and others. In this form, roles change, characters exist and speak in more than one frame of time on the same page, dream and reality are interchange-

able, inconsistencies abound and lead to revelations. The intellectual excitement of these novels is often greater than their poetic achievement.

Distance is not a problem in this book, however. Carlos Fuentes is not a cold writer.... (p. 46)

The oppositions in *The Old Gringo* are like armies across a border, waiting for the starburst that signals the commencement of war. Bierce and Winslow, Arroyo and La Luna; and after these surfaces the nation of the mother and the nation of the father, Coatlícue and Zeus, Freud and the poet/kings of the Valley of Mexico. "Half of the world is transparent; the other half, opaque," according to Mr. Fuentes. On one side, the people do not move from the place in which they were born; on the other side, their restlessness knows no limit. On one side there is no memory and on the other even the dust carries a history. War is engagement, however, and revolution is always parenticide; it is the same in both camps.

The truth of the conflict, however, may be revealed by the dominant symbol in *The Old Gringo,* the mirror. In the mirror we see ourselves or the opposite of ourselves; the reflection proves the reality of the viewer or the existence of the *nahual.* If the father of the schoolteacher from Washington died in Cuba, who is the old gringo who has come to die in Mexico, and how is he related to the teacher and to Arroyo except as a symbol? How is the moon-faced woman who sleeps with the young general connected to the sun? In the intertwining of the schoolteacher and the general, the child of the father and the child of the mother, who will dominate? And what have these symbolic children to do with the death and exhumation of the old gringo?

There are devilish bargains, the destruction of a precious patrimony, murder, betrayal and a great deceit, all growing out of the reconstructed, comprehensible history imagined by Carlos Fuentes. It is the kind of work one hoped would follow the brilliant excoriation of a perverted revolution in *The Death of Artemio Cruz,* which was published more than 20 years ago; it is the work of an integrated personality, the artist who contains and illuminates all the layers of all the times and cultures of a nation.

If there are moments in the novel when the artist is overwhelmed by the analyst, or the political fervor of the author leads him to write an unseemly rhetoric into the mouths of his characters, the reader does best to move on, keeping to the pace of the plot, ignoring the fleas. The only serious flaw for me is that the book may be too concise; I wished for details to more fully realize the characters, to limit them less by their symbolic roles. Perhaps that would have obscured the depth of the novel; I don't know; the book is a siege of echoes, it goes by in a moment, and that is enough. (p. 47)

> *Earl Shorris, "To Write, to Fight, to Die," in* The New York Times Book Review, *October 27, 1985, pp. 1, 46-7.*

JOHN UPDIKE

[*The Old Gringo*] is a very stilted effort, static and wordy, a series of tableaux costumed in fustian and tinted a kind of sepia I had not thought commercially available since the passing of Stephen Vincent Benét....

We are asked to believe that Ambrose Bierce—perhaps the least appealing figure of enduring worth in American literature—joined up with Pancho Villa in 1914; this has been often rumored, but the verifiable facts show only that he disappeared into Mexico in 1913. (p. 102)

The Greek chorus of talk about the central figure (''The old gringo came to Mexico to die;'' ''Yes sir, you could see 'farewell' in his eyes'') doesn't bring Ambrose Bierce to life; nor does the occasional paraphrase of one of his stories. He doesn't even have a sense of humor, this writer of a thousand sardonic jokes. He remains a fist clenched upon nothing, upon the announced intention to die, as Harriet Winslow and Tomás Arroyo remain clenched around a few stylized, heavily insistent memories. The most vivid and least programmatic pages of *The Old Gringo* portray a middle-class Mexican woman's reaction to a sudden onslaught of rebel forces; these kindle an unforced interest and power, as if taking by surprise Fuentes's stiff army of symbols. But generally the only thing moving in this sere landscape is the author's mind as it spiders among his checkpoints, thickening the web of mirrors and keys and Oedipal fixations.

On the back of the book jacket the author states, ''I have lived with this story for a long time.'' He conceived it forty years ago, wrote the first ten pages in 1964, and took it up again for a month in 1970. He held the inspiration and its emblematic figures too long in his head, perhaps; they became petrified. Although the novel goes through the motions of establishing geographical and historical authenticity, we learn little about Mexico we didn't know after seeing *The Treasure of Sierra Madre* and *Viva Zapata!* The glimpses of Washington, and Harriet's life there, seem more animated, more exciting to the writer, than the horde of rebel Mexicans, with their slit eyes and terse mutterings. Revolution . . . has become in *The Old Gringo* a stock phantasmagoria the writer has sought to enrich with portentous Freudianism. Apropos of international as well as personal relations, Fuentes makes a point—''Did you know we are all the object of another's imagination?'' . . . Fuentes is certainly intelligent, but his novel lacks intelligence in the sense of a speaking mind responsively interacting with recognizable particulars. Its dreamlike and betranced glaze, its brittle grotesquerie do not feel intrinsic or natural; its surrealism has not been earned by any concentration on the real. Latin-American surrealism has enchanted the globe, but its freedoms cannot be claimed as a matter of course. Mere mannerism results. (pp. 103-04)

John Updike, ''Latin Strategies,'' in The New Yorker, *Vol. LXII, No. 1, February 24, 1986, pp. 98, 101-04*

Alasdair Gray

1934-

Scottish novelist, short story writer, and illustrator.

An innovative contemporary Scottish writer, Gray achieved recognition for his first novel, *Lanark: A Life in Four Books* (1981). Through his combination of realism and fantasy and his structural experimentation, Gray has created an idiosyncratic style noted for its complexity, wit, and energy. His fiction is multidimensional, enhanced by illustrations and typographical experiments, and the breadth of its scope has led to comparisons with Dante and James Joyce. Much of Gray's fiction satirically or allegorically explores the oppression of the working class and presents a dark vision of modern Scottish and British society. Echoing the opinions of many reviewers, David Lodge stated that Gray "is that rather rare bird among contemporary British writers—a genuine experimentalist transgressing the rules of formal English prose . . . boldly and imaginatively."

Like the majority of Gray's fiction, *Lanark* is characterized by a disjointed narrative that emphasizes the book's surreal and dreamlike qualities. In this work, Gray creates a stark and prophetic vision of a dystopian society where the governing elite depend upon and perpetuate the gradual dehumanization and decay of its citizenry. Merging a realistic depiction of contemporary Glasgow with a nightmarish account of its decadent future, *Lanark* is at once an Orwellian portrait of the individual in the context of society; a social, political, and economic critique of Glasgow; and, in a larger sense, an allegory, according to Douglas Gifford, "of the decline of the bigger West, the barren city failures of Europe and the world beyond."

Gray's second novel, *1982, Janine* (1984), is similarly disjointed and surrealistic. Revolving around the thoughts, memories, and sadomasochistic fantasies of protagonist Jock McLeish, the novel takes place during one night and portrays a despondent, apathetic man attempting to cope with the mediocrity of his life and the emotional burden of his past. The violent nature of McLeish's sexual fantasies has generated controversy. Some critics, while acknowledging Gray's intent to discredit pornography, found his use of sexually explicit language and imagery unnecessarily offensive and unsuccessful in achieving his aim. David Lodge, however, contended that Gray "is continually deconstructing the discourse of pornography, by parody, metafictional commentary . . . and the interpellation of another, more authentic discourse—the discourse of confession—which eventually dominates the book."

Gray's recent novel, *The Fall of Kelvin Walker: A Fable of the Sixties* (1985), chronicles the adventures of a man raised in a strict religious environment who embarks on an odyssey in search of fame and fortune in London. Although similar to Gray's earlier novels in its social commentary, this work was not as well received. Gray has also written a collection of short stories, *Unlikely Stories, Mostly* (1983), which, like his novels, blends realism, myth, and humor in a structurally inventive and imaginative exploration of religious, social, political, and sexual themes.

Photograph by Eric Thorburn, Glasgow

ERIC KORN

For Alasdair Gray, Glasgow is twinned with the sunless phantasmagoric city of Unthank, and the hero of this huge, exacting and intermittently inspired novel [*Lanark*] is a citizen of both. The persevering reader is richly rewarded with a fine traditional biography, a hyper-real fantasy, a variety of good jokes and bad tricks, and any amount of argumentation "about morality, society or art." . . .

Without the "anti-novel" mayonnaise, *Lanark* has two ingredients, "cemented by typographical contrivances rather than formal necessity" says Gray, but he isn't serious. There is a straightforward and gripping portrait of the artist as young schizoid, a bildungs-and-demolitions-roman; and there is the surreal tale in which it is embedded, a world either posthumous, or allegorical or imaginary. Duncan Thaw, eczematic, asthmatic muralist and moralist, is incapable of closeness to family (there's a fine portrait of his well-meaning father), friends, teachers, or distant and wounding girls.

Gray is admirable in his evocation of the drear society of Unthank, where time is unreliable, and the citizens are consumed by strange diseases, the outward manifestations of inward disorders, "mouths, softs, twittering rigor, dragonhide," and the still more phantasmagoric Institute, which purports to cure but feeds on Unthank's ills. Cannibalism is for Gray the pattern of all human relations: "Man is the pie that bakes and eats itself and the recipe is separation." Lanark escapes through the Intercalendrical Zone, in quest of sunlight, and is charged with defending Unthank against the machinations of the Council, the Institute, the Creature: respectively, let us say, authority, reductionist science and multinational capitalism.

He does not wholly succeed; nor does Gray, though he is not entirely defeated; on the way to a rather smudged finale there are many excellent jokes. I had sworn not to use the word "dour," but Gray insists so much on Glaswegiosity it sets me wondering if fantasies of cosmic conspiracy are an especial part of the provincial sensibility. Gray's fantasy may be more Clyde and less Bonny than most, but it's a bracing air if you don't inhale.

> Eric Korn, "The Cannibal Culture," in The Sunday Times, *London, March 8, 1981, p. 42.*

DOUGLAS GIFFORD

Lanark undoubtedly will stand as one of the greatest of Scottish novels. . . . But this—though true—denies the novel its other singular achievement and significance; which is, that it singularly and effortlessly manages to find equal footing and fruitful comparison with the best of great surrealist and dystopian fiction throughout the world. *Lanark* is not beggared, but enriched by comparison with *Gulliver's Travels, Don Quixote, The Green Isle of the Great Deep, 1984,* Kafka—and yet it's undeniably Scottish in character. How has Gray achieved this? He has made his picture of Glasgow and the West of Scotland in decline his *Waste Land*—with its exaggerated images of sterility and decay thus becoming the images of the decline of the bigger West, the barren city failures of Europe and the world beyond. Using Glasgow as his undeniable starting point, Gray makes virtue out of necessity and transforms local and hitherto restricting images, which limited novelists of real ability, like Gordon Williams or Archie Hind or George Blake, into symbols of universal prophetic relevance. (pp. 229-30)

To begin with—*Lanark* is not about Lanark. . . . No, Lanark is a person, and the name chosen arbitrarily (if one can accept that "choices" like this are ever artistically "arbitrary"). He is a displaced, memory-less, impoverished traveller whom we first meet in a Glasgow once-plush cinema cafe, amongst the seedy intellectuals and their ladies. But before the atmosphere becomes too reminiscent of Sauchiehall Street and the environs of the Art College, weird glimpses that this city is *not* Glasgow disturb, increasingly, till shortly it bursts upon us that we are living in a Kafka nightmare. This city has little or no sunlight, and its inhabitants have lost memory of or need for the sun. Its inhabitants tend to disappear suddenly, at nights, when alone—without much note being taken. Its industry has either disappeared, rotting away, or is focused in the curious cylinders of sinister but undefined function which rust on the muddy banks of a shrunken Clyde. Gray's evocation of a sterile and Wasteland Glasgow is without parallel—harsh, bleak, yet horrifyingly and naggingly relevant and prophetic. His exaggerated description of the loss of population, the emptying inner city, the gloom and mood of sallow misery has the power of Thomson's *City of Dreadful Night* or Smith's "Glasgow"—yet what makes it worse is that all the time the reader is enabled to make the modern connection, seeing that the reason for the

disappearance of people is indeed the Glasgow disease, that unemployment is in reality too little commented on, that the mood—say, of Glasgow after yet another industrial closure is announced—is increasingly of apathetic despair.

This is vision of a very high order indeed. Yet before we are overwhelmed by this mood, Gray moves us along in Lanark's bewildered mind, trying to grasp where he is, who he is, and where he's come from. All he knows is that he's come to the city (later named as Unthank) by railway, with some few tokens of a past life—a map, some stones, a compass—and an odd haunting sense of former identity. Thus Lanark's is a nightmare quest, an Everyman journey, which introduces him to some strange but all too convincing types, from bureaucratic social workers who don't seem greatly concerned or perplexed by him, to corrupt city politicians making a killing on the misery. . . . [Lanark eventually discovers] the way through the baffling surface appearance of this "civilisation" to the organizing Power behind it and other "civilisations"; the Institute, Academy, or University, or Civil Service or Hospital Board, it is a huge, amorphous, familiar body of professional people, their meetings, theories, places of work, which in essence is the privileged heart of our society.

Gray's portrayal of Lanark's discovery of the Institute, and the horrific impression he succeeds in giving of its vast but rather demented rights and power, is amongst the astonishing achievements of the book—made all the more effective for being realized in down-to-earth harsh concrete detail, where reality and fantastic nightmare merge.

The Institute helps those it finds to be worth helping—but Lanark looks (literally) over its dark edge to the pit beyond, where the sighs, moans, and darkness of the mass of humanity are heard and seen. He discovers, to his horror, that the Institute actually feeds on this sub-strata of humanity. He himself has come close to being such fuel-fodder; for throughout his Unthank days reference is made in a most unpleasant and itchy way, to his "dragon-hide," his scaly patches of skin—which are the novel's way of expressing the hardening, the alienation, the sealing-off behind selfish carapace, of the lost individual. Such "dead" individuals—fermenting inside themselves—are about to explode (suicide? outrageous social gestures?)—and as they go "supernova" the Institute actually *uses* their combustion as energy-fodder. Thus we feed off our weakest, says Gray. His scaly new limbs take over a volition and power of their own—Gray's way of expressing something of the dehumanization of unemployment and despair in the lost soul. . . . Lanark is haunted by a recurrent vision, sometimes glimpsed through high windows of the Glasgow-Infirmary-like windows of the Institute, of hills, and greenness, and most of all, sunlight. This lyric and immensely refreshing counter-theme relieves the darkness of city and underground vault. Lanark becomes last home of the human urge for freedom and light, and Gray makes us feel the need to find the open spaces of mountain and sea. And besides, Lanark is haunted also by a memory of *déjà vu,* of having seen all this through other eyes, of having been before—and *part one,* which is described as *Book Three,* ends with Lanark finding, through the oracle, his real past life as Duncan Thaw, Glasgow child and art student. Now *Book One* succeeds *Book Three*—and, with Tristram Shandy logic, there *is* poetic sense in having the novel open at its third movement so that we have to go back two moves to discover the beginning.

In effect one could start to read the novel at page 121, since it's cyclic, or seamless. Thus the opening part, the surrealistic or fantastic dream part, prefaces the naturalistic account, in *Book One* and *Book Two,* the next two parts; while the sandwich is completed by the return of *part four* to Institute and Unthank.

If this sounds over complex or pretentiously obscure, it is not so in reading. As we follow the traditionally told events of Duncan's life, the pattern and meaning of the telling become eminently clear. Duncan *is* Lanark, in an earlier life, yet still they are the same; Duncan not with dragonhide, but a skin disease which makes him horribly shy, affecting all his relationships. Here, in "reality" is the origin of Lanark's nightmare loneliness, dragonhide. This inner novel, so close to *Portrait of the Artist as a Young Man,* is the moving description of the agonizingly sensitive and yet absurdly humour-filled life of Duncan Thaw. It's far from self-indulgent reminiscence. It's cruel about self, embarrassing in its revelation of private detail, hurtful in its familiarity—and very funny. But the overall movement is to an agonized realization of our loneliness, as friends fail to be enough, as his mother "disappears," as love doesn't work and sexual satisfaction is unattainable. (pp. 230-32)

It's the very normality, humanity, and sometimes physical beauty of Duncan's surroundings that highlight his tragic dilemma—that he is not born to know sexual love, that he cannot translate these hopeless feelings into an Art he finds acceptable as substitute.

Therefore he commits his "suicide," if it be that—and his "murder" too, if hints are taken. And thus we return, after "death," to the Limbo-land of Unthank, where Duncan has become Lanark, where he has to work out his salvation, if there be salvation. Here, after bizarre journeys and rejection of what the Institute stands for, Lanark has his family—but finds, in [his lover] Rima's rejection and his separation from his son Alexander, yet again alienation and frustration.... [Slowly], Gray's conflicting human struggles resolve themselves. There is a moment of communion between Alexander and Lanark, on a hill, in the sunlight, when Lanark thanks life for sunlight, and that moment, if for nothing else. There is, amidst the nightmare political struggles between Unthank and the Institute at the end, acceptance by Lanark, amidst the wreckage of the Cathedral and Glasgow/Unthank, of his place in what is finally seen as an upward human movement—slow, incredibly encumbered and frequently farcical—but *upward.*

Having said this, there is another way of reading **Lanark** which has disturbing implications for the idea of the book's unity. One of the most striking features about it is its painful honesty; and one cannot go far into this novel without becoming aware of just how personal and autobiographical it is.... Thaw's life is remarkably close to Gray's, so that one eventually speculates that the opening nightmare scenes are actually Gray's way of looking at Glasgow when utterly depressed or even from the viewpoint of nervous breakdown.... Gray and his personal life seeth under the phantasmagoric surface of this novel, so that despite all advice to oneself *not* to fall into that trap James Joyce warned us about in *Portrait of the Artist as a Young Man,* wherein we confuse author and hero, one feels that Gray wants desperately for both escape in the Kafka-esque sense and self-dramatization to go on at the same time. Thus on one hand disguises everywhere, so that Gray is Nastler is Thaw is Lanark, and models of other imagined universes from Gulliver's to Don Quixote's and Kafka's are cited as examples of what Gray is doing here for Glasgow; while on the other hand the story can be read as changing visions of Glasgow from

within one head only, Alasdair Gray's, with everything else changing disguise for events in real life.

This way of looking at the novel would be quite acceptable but for the fourth book, which both widens out to look at world politics of the future and to trace the speeded-up movements of the rest of Lanark's life. That is to say, it departs from the kind of satire with which the Institute was presented wherein recognizable stereotypes such as university teachers, social workers, politicians were found amidst settings which were amalgams of Glasgow establishments, and breaks the novel's by-and-large autobiographical mould. In the end Lanark is a kind of extrapolation of Gray/Thaw into the future, thus lacking the marvellous echoes and resonances which brought phrases from Thaw's life into the Institution ("Man is the pie that bakes and eats itself," "you need certificates," phrases from conversations Thaw had throughout his life). *Book Four* has none or little of this double register and is the thinner without it. But the work is nevertheless majestic in conception.... (pp. 233-34)

Douglas Gifford, "Scottish Fiction 1980-81: The Importance of Alasdair Gray's 'Lanark'," in Studies in Scottish Literature, *Vol. XVIII, 1983, pp. 210-52.*

DANIEL EILON

Unlikely Stories, Mostly is copiously illustrated in a style which sometimes descends to coy greeting-card formalism—inanely grinning dogs, twinkling stars, nymphs with perfectly rounded breasts and perfectly circular nipples, muscular workers, a conquistador complete with Spanish moustache, an eastern scene composed of pointy pagodas. Prospective readers should not be daunted; Gray's prose is seldom crass. Some of Gray's experiments are daring gambles: in one story he choreographs four parallel texts on the page (edited from the lucubrations of the great and good Sir Thomas Urquhart, a fellow Scottish patriot and eccentric genius), prints the vowels and consonants of a passage on separate pages, and interrupts the text with blank sections (where the manuscript was supposedly nibbled by mice). Not all of Gray's literary adventures are as successful as these; indeed, the editorial rodents should not have released this book from their clutches until it was seventy pages shorter. The first seven stories are pleasant and amusing enough, and are doubtless included to indicate the range of Gray's imaginative talent. However, compared to the five central interlinked stories which take up the bulk and constitute the real achievement of this work, these minor excursions are negligible. The last two texts in particular, labelled as 'likely stories' and each five lines long, posit a tawdry domestic realism (within symmetrical pre and post-marital situations) as a bathetic contrast to the 'unlikely' fictions of the rest of the book. The gnomic closure of these scraps is pretentious, and their cynicism is trivial.

When Gray is not under the impression that he is the reincarnation of Blake, and eschews prophetic sententiousness, his work is masterly. The cadences of prophecy and its inebriating correspondences are temptations for him because of the sublime coherence of purpose in his central work. Temperamental radicalism, militant humanism and a number of recurring sexual, linguistic and aesthetic themes are woven together into a prose full of recondite allusions and brilliant innovations. *Unlikely Stories, Mostly* is a gothic structure of myths, ancient and bespoke. In the "Axletree" stories (inspired by Kafka's elaboration of the Babel myth), the primeval imperial instinct and its most recent avatar, multinational capitalist enterprise, are portrayed in a tale that is at once timeless and timely. One of the specifically contemporary details in this representation of an Empire devoted to the idolatry of exponential growth, is that a sizable proportion of the imperial revenue is spent on unemployment benefit to prevent mass revolt. Although the syndrome of a cyclic succession of civilisations that degenerate into barbarism and extinguish themselves is fast becoming commonplace—see, for example, Keith Roberts's so-called 'SF classic', *Pavane* . . .—Gray's exploitation of the theme is not merely conventional. His intelligent, idiosyncratic and formally sophisticated analysis of the powers of language to bind and blind likens the cultivation of linguistic differences to the human habit of proliferating weapons of destruction. Semantic disarmament is the common aim of Urquhart's universal language (elaborated in **"Logopandocy"**, an extraordinary feat of imaginative insight) and Pollard's dictionary of definitions (in **"Prometheus"**): Gray suggests that it is impossible to deceive or suppress fellow-men with these ideal linguistic systems. The strictly hierarchical society in **"Five Letters from an Eastern Empire"** develops the logic of mass-suppression to political perfection: whole sections of the population are declared to be 'unnecessary people' as the labour market that sustained them is withdrawn. A government decision to suspend the livelihood and usefulness of certain men and women resembles a sentence from the Empire's draconian Court of Irrevocable Justice, where people have things removed that cannot be returned, like eardrums, eyes, limbs and heads. Gray's parable seethes with righteous indignation. . . .

1982, Janine is as tricksy, eclectic and scintillating as its two distinguished predecessors, *Lanark* and *Unlikely Stories, Mostly*. Like Gray's other books, this novel politely says goodbye at the end; like them, too, it tries to pre-empt ingenious critical comparisons to Dostoevsky, Kafka, Nabokov, Flann O'Brien, Joyce, Cummings and others by supplying a systematic schedule of allusions and literary credentials (in *Lanark* this took the form of an Index of Plagiarisms). This novel also experiments with alternatives to the serial ordering of prose on the page, most dramatically in a traumatic central chapter where Shandean print patterns explode and converge. Less spectacular but highly effective is his use of a synoptic 'Table of Contents' and marginal half-titles for time-keeping and ironic commentary. . . .

The novel is set, on a dark insomniac night, inside the head of a divorced, alcoholic supervisor of security installations, who is quietly pickling his conscience in malt in a small hotel somewhere in Scotland. For some years now his nocturnal life has been of a solitary nature, so he passes the hours by creating fetishistic stories of bondage, rape and prostitution. Being a stolid corporate man, his onanistic fantasies have a sound business footing; he is the managing director of the largest international white-slavery syndicate ever imagined. One or two other unusual features punctuate his otherwise bland and mild-mannered conventionalism: he has never cried since he was 12, never slept since his wife left him, he carries an emergency bottle of Scotch in case his memories get out of control, and a bottle of barbiturates in case the bomb goes off before he reaches a shelter.

Jock McLeish is a failed cynic. For obscure reasons (which are buried in sub-plot, but gradually emerge) he has plunged himself into selfishness and mediocrity ('not a bad marriage', 'quite a good job') consciously and with a vengeance, as if miserable alienation supplied him with some kind of desperate

integrity. He finds ironic detachment from his own degradation marginally preferable to self-pity. . . . Clearly, his emotional economy is such that he cannot afford to ignore the small profit margins that contempt offers, and equally clearly, he has long since given up trying to persuade himself that he isn't a shit. . . . In a Falstaffian Britain where the ancient pageant of feudalism has been revived (its colour and brio produced by the lively contrast of winners and losers), McLeish sniggers meanly at corruption and cowardice. He has attempted to destroy those faculties that refuse to be anaesthetised, to sublimate suffering into rage, but in the process has lost all self-respect. In fact, his failure to simulate carelessness seems like a tribute to his moral resilience. . . .

Gray's thoroughly democratic sensibility recounts the 'very ordinary and very terrible' private tragedy of McLeish's emotional history. The novel's disruption of temporal ordering is partly a realistic device, imitating the non-serial structure of recollected experience. But in McLeish's case, the pathological reticulation of narrative is symptomatic of a dangerously fissile involuntary memory. His reflexes are in a state of trauma. . . . McLeish resorts to his emergency bottle, bangs his head against the wall, falsifies his own perversions, and indulges in strange moral and stylistic excesses in order to suppress his recalcitrant past. In contrast to the filmic myths of his youth and his profane nightly imaginings, his own personal narrative does not conclude with consummation. . . . McLeish's petulant repetitions, threats, jokes and diversions, and his addiction to the 'what I should have said' school of retrospect, all contribute to a portrait of a mind that is not in control of its experience.

The novel does not merely display the dark creatures of McLeish's imagination, but follows his progress in taming them. A significant stage in his self-diagnosis occurs when McLeish realises the implications of the cruel and insane 'educative' system of a belt-wielding teacher he had encountered at school. Mad Hislop's attempts to make a man of Jock so far succeeded that subsequently he has been locked into a machismo notion of maleness (in fact, a worthless defiance of pain) which corrupts women who admire bullies and killers as much as it brutalises men themselves. A second anagnorisis, that finally allows McLeish to resist evasive digression and recount his story in straightforward fashion, is the realisation that all his sado-masochistic fantasies of bondage and entrapment have insisted upon the *femaleness* of the central victim in order to resist the truth that he has been telling the story of his own enmeshed life.

In spite of one's first impressions (cultivated in the unregenerate early sections where McLeish's pornographic imagination is given its head) the sexual politics of this novel are mature and progressive. Jock McLeish is a fallen man, but it is clear that his youthful idealism, suspended and betrayed in the course of twenty-five years of moral inertia, had included a proper contempt for masculine delusions of mastery. Though profoundly ignorant of women in his childhood, and for many years a mental hoarder of volumes of sexist crap (identified as such near the end of the novel), his true attitudes towards women are marked by respect, need, and a sexual honesty which stops short only of recognition of the feminine in himself. . . .

A few minor shortcomings of this novel are that McLeish's straw Conservatism is never convincing, that the bondage and prostitution metaphors, initiated in the early sections of the book, are sometimes clumsily mobilised, and that pietism and schematic simplifications (either you're part of the problem or part of the solution) occasionally obtrude. The breadth of this work is most impressive, one indication being the sheer range of radical concerns that are raised, including the post-Holocaust conscience, exploitation of the Third World, the ill-defined goals of technology, the manifold tyrannies of capitalism, the garrotting grip of conventions (and the fear of scandal), and even the iniquity of the social security cohabitation rule ('the assumption that a woman living with a man is a self-employed whore is good practical Conservative economics'). The existential ethic of the novel demands of sentient characters that they take responsibility for their own lives instead of allowing themselves to luxuriate in the inevitability of Nature, Politics and Economics: McLeish eventually rises to the challenge.

In a glorious vision of his youth, Gray's hero looks towards the Great Future of Mankind with boundless hope, declaring in radiant capitals that 'it is technically possible to CREATE A WORLD WHERE EVERYONE IS A PARTNER IN THE HUMAN ENTERPRISE AND NOBODY A MERE TOOL OF IT', insisting as a prerequisite that we must 'EMPLOY EVERY LIVING SOUL TO FERTILISE OUR OWN DESERTS, RE-STOCK OUR OWN SEAS, USE UP OUR OWN WASTE, IMPROVE ALL GROUND, NOURISH EDUCATE DE-LIGHT ALL CHILDREN ...' (p. 19)

> Daniel Eilon, "Unnecessary People," in London Review of Books, Vol. 6, No. 8, May 3-May 16, 1984, pp. 19-20.

LEWIS JONES

Alasdair Gray's first novel, *Lanark,* occasioned comparison with Dante, Joyce and many more. This was partly because Mr Gray had plagiarised Dante & Co. (engagingly, he provided an 'Index of Plagiarisms') and partly, it must be said, because he comes from Scotland. Still, it is a wonderful novel....

1982 Janine, Mr Gray's second novel, resembles *Lanark* in its structure, theme and hero: it differs in the nature of its preponderant fantasy.... This is described exactly in a discussion between Lanark and a dragon, once a woman, whom he falls in love with when in Hell. In the hope of undoing her metamorphosis, he reads books to her, of which her favourite is *No Orchids for Miss Blandish:*

> 'Oh, yes I like this book! Crazy hopes of a glamorous, rich, colourful life and then abduction, rape, slavery. This book, at least, is true.'

> 'It is not true. It is a male sex fantasy.'

1982 Janine is about a night in the life of Jock, a middle-aged security technician, spent in a Scottish hotel room. For the first 150 pages or so, Jock masturbates, fantasising about Janine—a figure he has devised over the years, who has crazy hopes and the rest of it. The fantasy is repeated with variations—figures such as Superbitch and Big Momma are brought into play—and constantly interrupted.... After much fantasy, whisky and soul-searching, Jock becomes nauseated by himself and, in a chapter that is a monument to the craft of the typographer, tries suicide; he is saved, though, by God. Repentant, he decides to give a true account of the life we have so far only glimpsed at. Over the next 100 pages, Jock tells of a fairly harsh childhood, a very nice family and an adolescence of high artistic promise. Again, it is wonderful—funny, true and imbued with noble sentiment; and again the life is ruined by a failure to connect sex and love.

Pornography is problematic. Mr Gray seeks to disarm criticism, both by anticipation ... and by intimidation....

My only objection to pornography is that it is dead: it can excite a part of the imagination, but comes to bore and then sicken it—it cannot engage the whole imagination. This novel certainly is pornographic, but the purpose is apparently to demonstrate the nature of the stuff—that it is exciting, boring and sickening.... As in *Lanark,* Mr Gray intends the fantasy part to be an allegory of the realistic part; he tries to incorporate the pornography in an imaginative whole.... After his suicide attempt, Jock decides that his Janine fantasy is really the story of his life. He has never noticed it before, because of 'the *femaleness* of the main character ... My fancies keep reliving that moment of torture for Janine because I have never fully faced it in my own life ...' At the end of his story, having come to face it, he returns to his fantasy and finds it changed: 'O Janine, my silly soul, come to me now. I will be gentle. I will be kind.'

1982 Janine, then, tries to be an onanist's Song of Solomon.... I think the attempt is brave and clever; I don't think it succeeds, though. It is perhaps better that it should be inspired by gentleness than by rage, but a wank's a wank for a' that. Mr Gray shows pornography to be dead and then attempts to bring it to life. One cannot expect miracles.

> Lewis Jones, "The Self and Its Abuse," in The Spectator, Vol. 252, No. 8130, May 5, 1984, p. 27.

JONATHAN BAUMBACH

1982 Janine has a verbal energy, an intensity of vision, that has been mostly missing from the English novel since D. H. Lawrence. Mr. Gray is not a great original, though there are various postmodern devices in [his] books (for instance, typographical play, metanovelistic self-consciousness), but his torrential energy spills over into risk. He is a didactic wild man, willfully subversive of his own puritanical penchant. The impulse to outrage is the transforming element of his work.

Janine, who gives her name to this serious comic novel, is only one of several stock figures in the sadomasochistic fantasies of Jock McLeish, the guilt-ridden protagonist who tells his own story....

The novel moves between fantasy and memory, editorializing from time to time on the state of the real world. The various intrusions keep the reader from getting caught up in the pornographic fantasies, which are never really erotic in any event, but only deformed versions of Jock's life. That his characters enact cautionary tales and are punished for presumption and desire is indicative of Jock's ingrained puritanism. Misbehavior earns punishment, grandiosity engenders abasement. The punishment his characters receive for transgression is a way of justifying for Jock his own timid behavior in events past. It is the punishment, not the transgression, that fills Jock with desire.

Gradually, the interludes of memory break through—the interruptions become the text—and Jock's real story is given voice. At first the story reveals itself through association but later, in the second half of the novel, through straightforward narrative. Ultimately, everything we want to know is made explicit, all mystery clarified....

Mr. Gray is almost always more interesting as a realist than as a visionary or innovator, more alive when dealing with human issues directly than through abstraction or allegory. The idiosyncratic formal play enlivens the book though it is tangential to its main achievement. Mr. Gray is a natural storyteller and it is the wit and energy of his language that keep the rendering of Jock's lonely, wasted life from being unbearably depressing. The richness of this novel and the pleasures of its language and form are sufficient affirmation, a real message of hope.

Unlikely Stories, Mostly—an unfortunate title—confirms Mr. Gray's considerable gifts, though it contains more uneven work than the novel. Sometimes it is hard to separate Mr. Gray's best aspirations from pretension or indulgence. The stories, which are if anything more idiosyncratic than the novel, are not enhanced by Mr. Gray's clever (and fussily self-insistent) illustrations. At its worst *Unlikely Stories, Mostly* is an advertisement for its author, a showcase exemplifying the impressive range of his skills. What the stories share with the novel is a dazzling command of rhetoric, a willingness to take large risks and a handful of obsessive themes. Mr. Gray has a predilection for creating mythologies, though in his best work the narrative takes charge and creates its own sense of purpose. In almost every one of these stories, in one way or another presumption is its own undoing.

"The Comedy of the White Dog," my favorite of the collection, just misses being a masterpiece. Its mode is dreamlike. A naïve young man named Gordon goes to dinner at the house of Nan, a woman he loves (though he barely knows her). At the house, there is a white, piglike dog with an insinuating manner. The dog seems to have some mysterious power, particularly over women, which Gordon contrives to ignore. "Gordon prided himself on being thoroughly rational, and thought it irrational to feel curious about mysteries." At some point, the dog drags a woman named Clare into the bushes while the men watch shamefacedly, afraid to interfere. Nan runs off with Gordon and moves into his apartment with him. The night before their wedding, she asks Gordon to leave under the guise of honoring convention. We suspect what's going to happen but Mr. Gray insists—his worst fault—on clarifying the mystery of the white dog for us. The brilliance of the ending comes close to redeeming the story from its own overexplicitness.

Each of the stories tends to construct worlds that reflect allegorically on our own. **"The End of the Axletree"** is a highly inventive, somewhat laborious parable touching on the insanity of the nuclear arms race. **"The Great Bear Cult,"** in the form of a television documentary, is the mock history of a movement in which people identified their secret natures by dressing up as bears. In **"Prometheus,"** a Parisian dwarf named Pollard, apparently a literary giant, exposes his unfinished epic poem, "Prometheus Unbound" to an ideologically rigid feminist poet with whom he has fallen in love. The dwarf is himself a version of Prometheus and the poem he conceives is a grandiose vision of liberation from the tyranny of ambition (and from his own deformity) and from the ordinary failings that flesh is heir to, from mortality itself.

Alasdair Gray takes matters one step further in **"Prometheus"** and breaks the illusion the narrative has hitherto sustained. "I am not a highly literate French dwarf," his narrator confesses, "my lost woman is not a revolutionary writer manqué, my details are fictions, only my meaning is true and I must make my meaning clear by playing the word game to the bitter end." This statement articulates the esthetic that informs most, if not all, of Mr. Gray's fictions. Mr. Gray is a desperate rebel against an internalized tyranny. Both *1982 Janine* and *Unlikely Stories, Mostly,* are violent gestures toward esthetic and moral freedom, a melancholy and sometimes ecstatic rattling of chains, an insistence—through the example of their humor, power and beauty—on the transcendence of the imagination.

Jonathan Baumbach, "The Impulse to Outrage," in The New York Times Book Review, *October 28, 1984, p. 9.*

DAVID LODGE

1982 Janine is a confession, a venerable form of narrative that goes back to Augustine. Though it is described in the author's self-mocking blurb as "mainly a sado-masochistic fetishistic fantasy," and indeed incorporates large dollops of undiluted pornography, it is essentially a story of conversion, the awakening of conscience and spiritual rebirth. It is a very modern example of the genre, not only in giving rather more attention to sin than to the state of grace, but also in narrative technique. Alasdair Gray is that rather rare bird among contemporary British writers—a genuine experimentalist, transgressing the rules of formal English prose, and its typographical representation, boldly and imaginatively. The influence of James Joyce, and that eighteenth-century avant-gardist Laurence Sterne, is very evident, but Gray does not seem merely derivative from these matters. He is very much his own man. (p. 43)

1982 Janine was highly praised on its publication in Britain last spring, but some readers queried Gray's extensive use of the discourse of pornography. For Anthony Burgess, who greatly admired Gray's first novel, *Lanark,* the new one "raised problems because I found it pornographic . . . it does excite the glands." Another reviewer, while acknowledging that the book as a whole was a critique of sexism, observed, with a witty allusion to Robert Burns, that "a wank's a wank for 'a that" [see excerpt above by Lewis Jones].

In this respect *1982 Janine* merely exemplifies in a particularly obvious way a general trend in the contemporary novel. The increasing exploitation of pornographic images, motifs, situations, and rhetoric in "serious" literary fiction is manifest to anyone who reads it regularly (and often a shock to anyone who encounters it accidentally). The novel has always given a disproportionate amount of attention to the sexual dimension of our lives, partly because it is concerned, much more than other narrative forms, with the private, inner life of persons, which psychoanalysis has taught us is dominated by desire. In the permissive society there are no taboos on the explicit representation of sexuality in art, while commercial pornography thrusts itself upon our attention from every newsstand or video shop. It may be regrettable, but it is hardly surprising, that the imagery of pornography has impressed itself upon the literary treatment of sex. Experimental, avant-garde fiction is often more deeply implicated than mainstream work, and it has been irreverently suggested (by Susan Suleiman, for instance, an academic critic of the *nouveau roman*) that without such a lure few readers would persevere with its repetitions, permutations, and dislocations.

It would not be fair to say that of *1982 Janine,* which is thoroughly readable throughout. And although the novel, like any sexually explicit text, may be erotically stimulating or disturbing to individual readers, anyone who resorted to it for that purpose would probably be frustrated by the *coitus interruptus* of Gray's narrative technique. He is continually deconstructing the discourse of pornography, by parody, metafictional commentary ("is that anatomically possible in that position?" Jock asks himself anxiously at some crucial moment of his fantasy) and the interpellation of another, more authentic discourse— the discourse of confession—which eventually dominates the book.

If the novel is vulnerable to criticism, it is that the "real history" of Jock's relationships—with his working-class parents, his women, and his charismatic friend Alan—when unscrambled and narrated in a relatively straightforward fashion, seem a mite sentimental and/or implausible. Also, that the socio-political *pensées* of which Jock delivers himself in the course of his journey to the end of a long night, though shrewd and thought-provoking, seem less and less like the opinions of a Tory-voting supervisor of security systems and more and more like the views of a romantic utopian Socialist who aspires to be the modern Scottish equivalent of William Blake.

Like Blake, Alasdair Gray is a visual as well as a verbal artist. . . . [*Unlikely Stories, Mostly* is] a collection of Borgesian fables elaborately illustrated by the author in an exuberantly eclectic style. The contents include a story about a man who splits in half, a short revisionist history of the Industrial Revolution in which Hargreave's spinning jenny is displaced by McMenamy's knitting Granny, and several letters home by a poet at the court of China in the days of Marco Polo. It's a beautifully designed book, but I found it more fun to look at than to read. Here fantasy, unchallenged by the reality principle so tangibly evoked in *1982 Janine,* quickly degenerates into whimsy. And it isn't even very sexy. (pp. 44-5)

> David Lodge, "Sex and Loathing in Scotland," in
> The New Republic, Vol. 191, No. 3643, November
> 12, 1984, pp. 43-5.

SCOTT L. MALCOMSON

Gray said that he had worked out the essential line of [his first novel, *Lanark* (1981),] by the time he was 18. Parts of it do read like that, but the novel's overall vision is clearly that of a mature man trying to reconstruct his past and the past of his country. . . .

In Gray's portrayal of postwar Glasgow, there are two linked political themes: the problem of marginality, and the choice between grudging cooperation and rebellion. Marginality in *Lanark* goes from being a specifically Scottish problem to being a universal state of being. There are those in power, and there is everyone else. Though the book is long and detailed, the arrangement of power is ultimately fairly simple. The world is run by a small group of petty administrators with high opinions of themselves. Lanark/Thaw's choice is whether or not to join them, that is, the choice of the aspiring middle class in a time of ever-increasing polarization. In the sci-fi world of *Lanark* the choice is especially stark after Lanark/Thaw discovers that the main source of fuel for the global administration is the otherwise "useless" bodies of the unemployed.

The same choice animates Gray's second novel, *1982 Janine* (1984). It was greeted rapturously by the British critics and, together with his story collection *Unlikely Stories, Mostly* (1983), cemented Gray's adoption by the Scottish press as the greatest literary Scot since Hugh MacDiarmid (if you haven't heard of *him,* blame your English department). Partaking of a particularly Celtic form—the drunken long look backward—Gray's narrator Jock McLeish sustains a harrowing monologue through a restless night in a Greenock hotel. The resultant portrayal of

a middle-aged life is about the price of security: a story of compromises and small insults, sexual fantasies and real-life failures, and political polemics from a man who sees in Scotland's predicament a mirror of his own. (p. 15)

The choice between being in the trap and helping to make it is the freedom of the middle class. Jock's decision repeats Scotland's perennial choice of getting a little English security in exchange for giving up any chance of self-determination. But the profits of Scotland's traps remain, for the most part, far away, in Surrey homes with security systems. In a bleak moment McLeish describes the Scots as "these arselickers of instruments, these stoic and hysterical losers." This vision becomes more than slightly paranoid when he dwells on the British government's tendency to keep its nukes in Scotland— part of a plan, he reasons, to make the Clydeside region a national sacrifice area as a master stroke against unemployment. When he reaches this point in his history of Scotland, McLeish realizes that even the freedom to be an instrument may be disappearing. The political context of his 30 years' compromise has changed. McLeish finally resolves that now is the time to fight, and the dark night ends (though the new day is a bit gray, this being Scotland). . . .

The resolutely working-class outlook Gray and some of his fellow Glaswegian literati have brought to Scottish letters may not set the heather on fire. But at least it moves the locus of Scottish literary discourse firmly away from tear-stained memories of Culloden and into the crucial conflicts of the present. (p. 17)

> Scott L. Malcomson, "Alasdair Gray Paints Himself
> Out of a Corner," in VLS, No. 31, December, 1984,
> pp. 15, 17.

TOBY OLSON

In notes at the backs of *Unlikely Stories, Mostly* and *1982 Janine,* Alasdair Gray acknowledges sources not only for brief moments and lines but for major themes and characters in both. . . .

The straightforward crediting in these notes is as purely exuberant as the books themselves, and it is this unqualified openness and warmth that American readers should find refreshing, for while Gray marks the traditions from which he comes, he is in no way bound by them. There is a complete lack of the tentative in his writing, a sureness that seems almost naive. It may be that Scotland stands to England as Canada does to the United States, free of those matters of literary propriety that can urge writers to be careful, properly pessimistic, tasteful. Gray, at least, stands free of them; he is none of these things, and these two books, though full of invention, read as if the prose were completely transparent. It is hard to describe them as beautifully written; they seem to sustain their power purely on the unmistakable energy of their author.

1982 Janine is the first-person narrative of Jock McLeish, an insomniac and alcoholic who gets through the one night of the novel in a hotel outside of Glasgow by drinking and constructing elaborate pornographic fantasies. . . . They are mostly sadistic, bondage fantasies, complex and constantly frustrated. . . . What frustrates them is both McLeish's desire to prolong their climaxes and the constant intrusion of memories from his life—memories of parents, lovers, his ex-wife and friends. As the fantasies grow and change, the issue of frustration intensifies, and McLeish begins to recall elements of frustration in his own life and in the political and social life of Scotland and of the world at large, both in history and in the present. (p. 10)

Finally, the thing that holds *1982 Janine* together is its political intent, one that would argue quite optimistically for drastic and wholesale social change.

Political concern, though it is present in a veiled way, is less important to the success of *Unlikely Stories, Mostly,* a gathering of 14 fictions published by Gray between 1951 and the present. The book is a wonder of ingenuity, a varied and rich collection in which Gray's abilities as a visual artist and illustrator are placed not only beside but within the products of his fertile imagination as a writer. In **"The Crank That Made the Revolution,"** a nutty piece of revisionist history dealing with the *real* cause of the Industrial Revolution, for example, careful drawings of ''McMenamy's Improved Duck Tandem'' propulsion device are an integral part of the story.

There are children's stories here, brief fables, stories that are guides to the reading of visual matter, a piece called **"The Great Bear Cult"** that could be a script for Monty Python, strange science fiction/fantasy pieces, stories like **"The Comedy of the White Dog,"** which contains a unique mix of humor, myth, and painful anxiety, and three longer pieces, **"The Star of the Axletree," "The End of the Axletree,"** and **"Five Letters From an Eastern Empire,"** that are gorgeous in their fabulous detail and elaboration. They read like a world created by Escher or Bosch, and though they tend to swallow the reader in their magic, like the thrust of *1982 Janine,* their lesson is social and political, their ironic and witty worlds cautionary.

In the middle of *1982 Janine* there are pages in which Jock McLeish is fighting with drugs and alcohol, attempting to either die or come through and get free of his fantasies. In his delirium, he hears the voice of God, which enters in small print, pushing against the larger type of his ravings. Something God says is repeated on the first and last pages of *Unlikely Stories, Mostly,* complete with illustration and the words ''Scotland 1984'' beside it. God's statement is ''Work as if you were in the early days of a better nation.'' It is the inherent optimism in that statement that perhaps best captures the strength of Alasdair Gray's fiction, its straightforwardness and exuberance. (pp. 10, 14)

> Toby Olson, *"Eros in Glasgow,"* in Book World— The Washington Post, *December 16, 1984, pp. 10, 14.*

HERMIONE LEE

Alasdair Gray's robust, sardonic little fable, *The Fall of Kelvin Walker,* was first drafted as a drama, and it still has the air of a morality play, rather stiff and two-dimensional, with a frieze of caricatures taking up positions behind its anti-hero. Gray's ''Fable of the Sixties'' is prefaced by a quote from James Barris—'There are few more impressive sights in the world than a Scotsman on the make'—and at the start of this Puritan's Progress we find Kelvin, fresh in London from Glaik, armed with his Nietzsche in a furious revolt against the 'headmaster of the universe' and his representative, Kelvin's father, Session Clerk of the John Knox Street Free Seceders Presbyterian Church of Scotland.

Kelvin attaches himself to a bohemian, quarrelsome couple— a painter, Jake (rather like the tormented Duncan in Gray's *Lanark*) and his put-upon girlfriend Jill—and sets out to take London by storm. Pluck, gall, and self-esteem make him into an overnight telly star—he's the answer to the BBC's quest for 'interviewers with firm regional dialects.' But the Nietzschean opportunist in swinging London is only the other side of the Presbyterian minister. As artist Jake gets more frantic and unhappy, his alter-ego Kelvin becomes increasingly dour and disciplinarian, and ends up 'as the official spokesman for all that's most restrictive in Scottish religious and social opinion.' . . .

Gray is a funny, garrulous, erudite visionary, passionately political, very odd, and always worth attending to. But this satire on the Calvinist drive for power, though a jolly *jeu d'ésprit,* doesn't allow him the big scope he thrives on.

> Hermione Lee, *"Partners in Fantasy,"* in The Observer, *March 31, 1985, p. 26.*

STUART EVANS

[The protagonist of *The Fall of Kelvin Walker*] is a staid, humourless, hilariously formal young Scot who arrives in the London of the sixties to make his fortune. More naive than Candide, he has discovered a more dangerous mentor than Pangloss in Nietzsche. . . . Befriended by an insouciant girl and her turbulent lover, he cons his way into various high places before being thrown out. Eventually he finds a niche in television, where they need ''a simpleton who asks out of sheer naiveté, all the most pointed and devastating questions.'' But Kelvin, in attracting the girl away from the lover, discovers that God is alive and well and on his side. . . .

The satire is deadpan and ferocious. Kelvin's absurdity underlines the ridiculous values which doom him to success. The resolution is acid enough, but the so-called ''anticlimax'' is vitriolic. It is hardly necessary to comment on the high quality of the writing.

> Stuart Evans, *"The Maze as a State of Mind,"* in The Times, London, *April 4, 1985, p. 13.*

HUGH BARNES

The Fall of Kelvin Walker skirmishes around Gray's favourite themes—politics, sexual politics and religion—without engaging any of them for very long. Perhaps this comes with the territory. The novel embarks on an odyssey of tricks, and the most daring of all of them Gray plays on the reader. Guidelines are few and far between, and the rest of the novel is aphoristic warnings: 'certainty isn't easy in a world as big and as strange as this one.' The world may be large and difficult, but Gray's treatment of it in this novel is uncharacteristically minute. On his first evening south, Kelvin meets Jill, a vapid bohemian; perhaps he even chooses her for her imagined Nietzschean flavour. Jill introduces the homeless saviour to her boyfriend Jake, brutal but artistic (a saving grace as far as Kelvin is concerned), and offers him sleazy shelter. What Gray has contrived is clearly not so much a fable as a morality drawn up on strict Presbyterian lines. Kelvin's upbringing in the shadow of his merciless father, a latter-day John Knox, has taught him spartan conduct and rigid self-discipline. The result can be absurd, since Kelvin suffers his various slings and arrows with persistent Panglossian good humour. (pp. 22-3)

The Fall of Kelvin Walker seems a perplexing departure from Gray's earlier work, disarmingly simple in construction and typographically unadventurous. (p. 23)

Hugh Barnes, "Fraynwaves," in London Review of Books, Vol. 7, No. 8, May 2, 1985, pp. 22-3.

JOHN CROWLEY

After reading Alasdair Gray's *Lanark,* a first novel published in England in 1981, Anthony Burgess declared Mr. Gray the most important Scottish novelist since Walter Scott. This reviewer is not qualified to dispute that judgment, though Robert Louis Stevenson does come to mind. It is probably safe to say that *Lanark* is not very much like any other Scottish novel, but it does have antecedents in literature—in Bunyan, in Blake, in Dante. . . .

Lanark, subtitled "A Life in 4 Books," begins with Book Three which is followed by Books One, Two and Four. In a rainy, gray, depopulated city called Unthank, something has gone wrong with the sun; it comes up, but never very far, never shining strongly. An amnesiac young man, who does not remember who he is or how he comes to be in this city, has chosen the name Lanark—which he saw printed under a photograph of a landscape—because he does not remember his own. He spends time in a cinema cafe among aimless young people without jobs or families. Around him, people disappear, sucked into the sky or the ground without warning. Others suffer from strange diseases with names like twitters, mouths and softs. Lanark has contracted dragonhide—a patch of hard, insensate skin on his arm is spreading. A woman he meets has a worse problem: she opens her palm and shows him the speaking mouth that has appeared there. . . .

At length, Lanark too disappears from Unthank, climbing into an enormous summoning mouth that appears before him, and the story takes the first of several very sharp turns.

Lanark awakens in "the institute," a huge mental institution or hospital that seems to exist outside time and space. His dragonhide is cured, and he is expected to join a staff of bustling and self-important doctors and cure others. It begins to appear that the various diseases of Unthank are equivalents of psychic and moral ailments—dragonhide is an inability to love—and the reader also apprehends, with something of a sinking heart, that he himself has arrived in what is almost certainly an allegory.

No help for it—but the novel staves off the tedium so common in allegorical stories partly because Mr. Gray's characters and incidents multiply so rapidly. Yet what looks like a proliferation of new faces is actually the same people reappearing. In novels like this, characters often seem to double and triple their parts, like actors in a touring company. (p. 14)

From Book Three, the reader enters Books One and Two, which tell of the birth and growth of Duncan Thaw—Lanark's name in his previous life—in the recognizable and more or less naturalistic Glasgow of the 1940's and 50's. . . . These central sections of *Lanark* are a *Bildungsroman* of almost unrelieved sadness and bleakness, a *Portrait of the Artist as a Young Man,* had it not been saved by Joyce's extravagance. Thaw's story

is made only just bearable by our knowledge that Lanark—post-Thaw—comes to learn of love and the possibility of completion and adventure.

In Book Four he quits the institute with his beloved to find a city where the sun still shines. But he must first return to an Unthank surrounded by motorways, covered with advertisements, crowded with uprooted people—Glasgow today apparently, as the Unthank at the beginning was the Glasgow of Mr. Gray's youth.

But at this point Mr. Gray's enterprise gets out of hand. His allegory has the structure of a Möbius strip: the naturalistic Glasgow of Books One and Two is as much an allegory of Unthank as Unthank is an allegory of Glasgow. As the novel reaches for larger and larger moral and political pronouncements, the allegory and the allegorized become virtually identical. This unfortunate tendency seems to be inherent in the form. Made-up names are substituted for real ones and realism is lost with no corresponding gains in descriptive power. The longer the book goes on, the more rapidly its magic leaks away.

An epilogue placed well before the end takes the form of a dispute between Lanark and a character—not named Alasdair Gray—who says he is the author of the novel. The two argue about how the story should end and we are given an elaborate lecture on the novel's plagiarisms and antecedents, complete with footnotes. (This sort of self-reflexive set piece will one day seem as corny and as redolent of this period as deathbed scenes of Victorian novels seem now.) *Lanark* is not the sophisticated modernist work of art this epilogue seems to suggest, not John Barth's *Giles Goat-Boy* or Flann O'Brien's *At Swim-Two-Birds.* It is more like the great homemade books, the all-encompassing works that have always been constructed not of mainstream materials but of the author's own peculiar mud and straw: *Pilgrim's Progress,* say, or Branch Cabell's *Jurgen.* Like Swedenborg's *Divine Love and Wisdom, Lanark* is built on the conceit that the universe has the shape of the human body.

Such homemade structures can be accessible and popular, like the Watts Towers in Los Angeles, or private and obsessive, like a yacht built in a basement. Which is *Lanark*? It is a question to which a purely literary judgment is not a sufficient answer. The book often seems provincial, both in the narrow angle of its vision and the great size of its ambitions. It is a quirky, crypto-Calvinist *Divine Comedy,* often harsh but never mean, always honest but not always wise. Certainly it should be widely read; it should be given every chance to reach those readers—for there will surely be some, and not all of them Scots—to whom it will be, for a short time or a lifetime, the one book they would not do without. (p. 15)

John Crowley, "From Unthank to Glasgow and Back," in The New York Times Book Review, May 5, 1985, pp. 14-15.

KATE FULLBROOK

If any evidence is still needed to secure Alasdair Gray's reputation as one of the two or three most powerful new forces in British fiction [*The Fall of Kelvin Walker*] provides it. Gray's previous novels *Lanark* . . . and *1982, Janine* . . . are both large sprawling affairs that exempt no one and nothing from the author's sardonic vision. In *The Fall of Kelvin Walker* the same satirical genius is displayed in miniature in a perfect parable for the latter half of this century that is at once wonderfully funny and superbly acute. The tale recounts the progress of the battle campaign of the hero, young Kelvin Walker from Glaik in Scotland, who has picked up a few Nietzschean clichés in the local library, and who arrives at Victoria Coach Station to secure his place as one of the supermen in the London citadels of power. . . . Walker is, of course, undone, but not before Gray brilliantly raises questions about most of the bases of personal and political power on which the culture rests. The book is a complete success—hilarious, ferocious, satire at its best.

> *Kate Fullbrook, in a review of "The Fall of Kelvin*
> *Walker: A Fable of the Sixties," in* British Book
> News, *June, 1985, p. 361.*

Vasily (Semёnovich) Grossman

1905-1964

(Also transliterated as Vassili Grossman) Russian novelist, journalist, dramatist, and poet.

Long recognized as an important writer in Eastern Europe, Grossman has recently received significant attention in the West. He began his career in the 1930s and won widespread national acclaim for his novels and his journalistic coverage of World War II. After the war, however, Grossman became a victim of the anti-Semitic climate and official restrictions on artistic freedom in the Soviet Union. As his work became increasingly critical of the Soviet state, he was viewed as subversive, and a number of his works were suppressed. After Grossman's death, two of his works which had been confiscated by government officials, *Vse techet (Forever Flowing)* and *Zhizn' i sud'ba (Life and Fate),* were smuggled out of Russia and have since been published in the West.

The first of Grossman's suppressed works, *Forever Flowing* (1972), concerns a man who has been freed after spending thirty years in a Siberian work camp for making a speech that differed from official Communist doctrine. The novel details the man's journey through Russia, during which he meets former friends and relatives who express guilt and embarrassment over the disparity between their comfortable lifestyles and the suffering the man endured in prison. Grossman interweaves the protagonist's ruminations on his fate with historical passages and philosophical digressions, questioning why his country's revolutionary ideals were never realized. Despite Grossman's pessimistic view of Soviet society, an underlying belief in human kindness and in the eventual triumph of liberty emerges from the novel.

Grossman's second book to be smuggled abroad, *Life and Fate* (1985), is a sequel to his novel *Za pravoe delo* (1955). *Life and Fate* centers on an extended family during the German seige of Stalingrad in World War II. The novel's historical setting and vast range of characters have elicited comparisons to Leo Tolstoy's *War and Peace*. In addition, Grossman, like Tolstoy, employs long, philosophical asides to reflect upon the human condition. In *Life and Fate,* Grossman contends that tyranny is the greatest cause of suffering, and he presents a harsh commentary on the totalitarianism of both the Nazi government and Joseph Stalin's regime, essentially equating the two. He denounces those who forsake their humanity by mindlessly adhering to a political ideology. As in *Forever Flowing,* however, Grossman offers hope in the small, selfless acts of the individual. Fernanda Eberstadt commented: "[*Life and Fate*'s] great subject is human freedom, as exercised in those minute acts of 'senseless kindness' by which ordinary men and women wage war against the forces of enslavement. . . . Grossman's excoriation of these evils is the more effective and the more ennobling for being clothed in a gently majestic humanism which renders this work not only an evocation of an era but a novel for all time.''

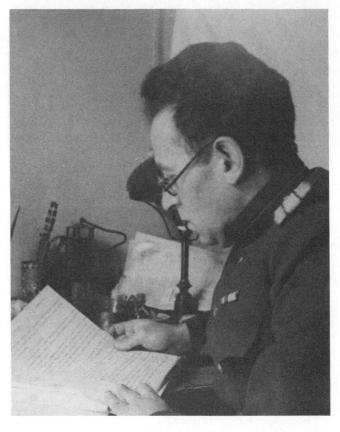

Savfoto

IRVING HOWE

For two centuries now, under czars and commissars, Russia has given us the most brutal autocracy and brilliant literature. During the last 20 years its best writing has come from poets, novelists and essayists who cannot publish in their own country but whose work, in defiance of the bureaucratic fist, finds its way into the West.

Some of these writings, like Alexander Solzhenitsyn's novel, *The First Circle,* Andrei Sinyavsky's essay, "On Socialist Realism," and Nadezhda Mandelstam's memoir, *Hope Against Hope,* are masterpieces. Their strength comes not merely from a high order of individual talent, but from the unconditional attachment to freedom that is the animating idea of Russian underground literature (*samizdat*). Indeed, at a time when some Western intellectuals have again yielded themselves to authoritarian dogmas and charismatic dictators, it is these brave writers of the East—not only Russians but also Poles like Leszek Kolakowski and Yugoslavs like Milovan Djilas—who best uphold the values of independence, freedom, dissent.

Vasily Grossman's *Forever Flowing,* written shortly before his death in 1964, is another of these remarkable books, known only to a few friends (and no doubt the secret police). It is a novel portraying the experiences and reflections of a man who returns to Moscow after 30 years in the Siberian labor camps;

it contains pungent discussions of political ideas; and it trembles with the vision of freedom. At least in this book, Grossman is not so good a novelist as Solzhenitsyn or smooth an essayist as Sinyavsky. Yet in one major respect his book seems the boldest to emerge from the suppressed literature of Russia: It is the first, to my knowledge, that comes to grips with the myth of Lenin.

Grossman's career holds remarkable interest, precisely because for so long a time it was quite ordinary. He began to publish in the 30's, when a novella of his attracted the favor of Maxim Gorky. Other writings established him as a gifted novelist who was especially admired by Russian literary people for his style. Apparently a decent man, he tried to maintain his integrity and nurture his talent during the Stalin years without paying too great a price in shame. Neither heroic nor slavish, he remained silent when he had to, but meanwhile kept his mind alive, storing up explosive ideas and impressions.

In 1946 he published a play, *If You Believe the Pythagoreans*, that was denounced by the party-line critics, and then, during the anti-Semitic campaign against "homeless cosmopolites," he was attacked again. (p. 1)

What seems most striking about his career is that, in ways not entirely clear from a distance, a man like Grossman could experience a major intellectual and moral transformation over a period of time—by himself? together with friends?—in which the received ideology of the Communist state was discarded and the scorned, "obsolete" values of liberalism or social democracy became a cherished possession. Reading the pages of *Forever Flowing* with their glow of humane reflectiveness, one wonders: How did people like Grossman hack their way out of the ideological jungle in which circumstances had trapped them? How, in their enforced isolation, did they find a path, and by no means uncritically, to the best of Western thought? Whatever the answers, one is almost tempted after reading this book to accept Grossman's view—a view not exactly encouraged by recent history—that there is a "natural, indestructible striving toward freedom inherent in human nature."

Forever Flowing begins in a familiar manner: a worn old man is on a westward-moving train to Moscow. Mocked by the louts and officials who share his compartment, he keeps his silence. Ivan Grigoryevich is returning from the camps to which, half a life earlier, he had been sent because of an impulsive student speech deviating from Communist orthodoxy. The figure of the returned prisoner is a central one in recent Russian writing: the victim, the survivor, the man who remembers.

Ivan visits his cousin and boyhood chum, Nikolai, a small-talented scientist who has toadied a little over the years and now lives in "a world of parquet floors, glass-enclosed bookcases, paintings and chandeliers." One man well-fed, smug, and uneasy; the other gaunt, tormented and irritable. Ivan makes no accusations. It is his very silence that provokes Nikolai into self-defense: "I went through trials and tribulations," though "of course I did not ring out like Herzen's bell." It is hopeless, a dialogue of the deaf. What can a man from the camps say to a man with an apartment?

Beyond these acrid, sharply-contoured opening chapters, *Forever Flowing* has little plot. (pp. 1, 16)

Ivan moves to a town in southern Russia, works as a laborer, meets a woman also worn out by suffering. She lived through Stalin's campaign against the kulaks and the forced collectivization. They have a few moments together, not exactly of

happiness, but of the peace that comes when people can at last speak with honesty. The woman dies. Ivan is again alone, with his thoughts and questions, "gray, bent, and changeless."

Woven through this simple story are linked segments of incident and passages of reflection. Two scenes are especially strong. One is an imaginary trial, perhaps running through Ivan's mind, in which the informers who had sent millions to the camps are now arraigned. Each speaks freely, from his own motives, for his own skin. (pp. 16, 18)

The other scene, rich with Dostoevskian echoes, consists of Ivan's recollections of a critical moment in prison. . . . [A] fellow-prisoner believed "in the law of the conservation of violence." The history of life, he insisted, "is the history of violence triumphant. It is eternal and indestructible." To Ivan the pain of these words seemed greater than the pain of the interrogator's blows a few hours earlier. . . .

The chapters of intellectual reflection are meant, no doubt, to be taken as the thoughts of Ivan. But perhaps because Vasily Grossman could not properly finish his book or perhaps because he wrote out of so urgent a passion that he brushed aside the formal niceties of composition, these chapters have to be taken as set-pieces not well integrated with the plot. No matter; they are striking in their own right.

Grossman is fascinated by the paradox that runs through the whole Russian revolutionary movement. How can it be that in the same people there exists a "meekness and readiness to endure suffering . . ." together with "contempt for and disregard of human suffering . . ."? Grossman finds his answer in the tradition of Russian messianism, a "sectarian determinism, the readiness to suppress today's living freedom for the sake of an imaginary freedom tomorrow."

In a powerful sketch of Lenin, he connects the revolutionary leader with this two-sided tradition: the gentle selfless man who loved music and showed tenderness toward friends, and the harsh politician who, in rage against heresies, laid the basis for the party-state dictatorship. This kind of revolutionary Grossman sees as a man who fancies himself a surgeon of history: "His soul is really in his knife." Grossman's Stalin reduced Leninism to its political essentials.

But Grossman does not stop there. Through a confrontation with those notions of a unique Russian destiny that course through the work of Tolstoy and Dostoevsky as well as, less assertively, Solzhenitsyn, he performs a first-rate intellectual service. The great Russian writers, both the reactionaries and some revolutionaries, professed to find unique qualities in the Russian soul, which they regarded as the last unsullied vessel of Christian purity; they sneered, too often and with disastrous results, at the liberalism of the West. All these prophets "failed to see that the particular qualities of the Russian soul did not derive from freedom, and that the Russian soul had been a slave for a thousand years." . . .

This is the voice of a "Westerner," the kind of Russian intellectual who, alas, never has had enough influence in his own country. But now, after the ordeal of the past half-century, what Grossman wrote in the privacy of his study, perhaps without expecting that it would ever be published, takes on the strength of a central truth. It is, I think, the one supremely revolutionary idea: that without democratic freedoms no society, whether it calls itself capitalist or socialist, whether it has an industrialized or backward economy, can be tolerable.

It is also the one permanently revolutionary idea, for no one can say with assurance that it will survive our century and every thoughtful man knows that it will always have a precarious life, its triumph never assured. (p. 18)

Irving Howe, "A Bold Underground Novel of the Split Russian Soul," in The New York Times Book Review, *March 26, 1972, pp. 1, 16, 18.*

THOMAS LASK

[*Forever Flowing*] is as eloquent a memorial to the anonymous little man in the Stalinist state as *Dr. Zhivago* is to the artistic spirit in post-Czarist Russia and *The First Circle* to the scientific intelligentsia.

Forever Flowing is a look at the Soviet state from the very bottom, not from the bottom of society or the political spectrum, but from the place where all the lofty decisions from on high, all abstractly conceived theories, all high sounding resolves are translated into human endeavor and measured by human results. It is the place where all theories are made flesh. Grossman judges all theories by a simple rule: What happens to the people to whom they apply?

As he follows the results from the time of Lenin to that of the post-World War II leadership, he concludes that the state is a rapacious, relentless, soul-crushing adversary—an enemy of the people. Yet so powerful is the embracing magnetism of the state that the citizenry contrive at their own downfall. At the worst it allows the scum, the Yagodas and Berias to come to the top; at best it corrupts even the well-meaning and men of principle. The real saints are few and far between.

Ivan Grigoryevich has been given his freedom after 30 years in the Russian slave labor camps, and he returns to Moscow, to Leningrad, to once familiar places an old, gaunt, bent man. As he visits a cousin, encounters a comrade who had denounced him to the prosecutor, finds lodgings and a job for himself, Russia's history, his own past and that of so many he knew boil and bubble in his mind. His reappearance disconcerts those he meets; they find their dormant consciences flickering to life, unpleasant memories floating to the top of their minds. Some had given in to base demands a little at a time only to find themselves so far in, it was as distasteful to turn back as to go on. Some had believed that they were working for the good of the state. Some were greedy, some were seduced by ambition or high office. The motives and the reasoning were always complicated, intertwined, rationalized. And as the author points out the thinking inside the camp was exactly the same as that of the world outside. The ideologies of the prisoners were as varied and ingenious as the men who had put them there. They were after all the same Russians. . . .

[*Forever Flowing*] has not been published in Russia for reasons that will be clear to every reader.

One of them is that [Grossman] goes beyond Stalin to Lenin when he comes to place the blame for the excesses of the Soviet state. He dismisses the human side of Lenin, his personal modesty, his courtesy, his love of music, his patience with a citizen, not because they are not true, but because they did not really count in guiding the revolution and in establishing the new state. These took intellectual arrogance, ruthlessness, insulting impatience with opposition and contempt for western notions of individual freedom. Those who shared Lenin's gentler side, Bukharin, Rykov, Kamenev and Zinoviev, were crushed as mercilessly by Stalin as these qualities were eliminated from the body politic. Stalin, says the author, was Lenin's true heir. The force that fashioned the revolution later guided the purges.

But an idea of even greater abhorrence to the Russian hierarchy as well, perhaps, to the Russian people, is the one that sees the Soviet state as a natural result of Russian history. The serf-like mentality of the Russian people has been a weight on the liberating spirit of the country for a thousand years. In a passage that shoots a sharp light into the discussion, Grossman argues that Lenin was chosen by the Russian people. He was their kind of leader.

In spite of all his pessimistic assessments, he contends that the spirit of freedom lives on in the Russian heart and that it will ultimately flower even in his native land. How this will come about in the light of all he has said is never made clear. Very likely it was Grossman's last wan hope. By the time he died, perhaps there was nothing left.

Thomas Lask, "When Theories Are Made Flesh," in The New York Times, *April 1, 1972, p. 21.*

PATRICIA MEYER SPACKS

[The protagonist of *Forever Flowing*] has suffered the archetypal fate of his generation: thirty years in an Arctic labor camp, during Stalin's regime and after. Returning to civilization, he finds himself alienated; his one viable relationship, with his landlady, ends soon with her death. Most of the second half of the novel consists of his reflections on the meaning of his fate.

The human situation of this man has almost automatic power over the imagination. The bare words, "thirty years in an Arctic labor camp," evoke so much history, so much suffering, involve the reader in his own political guilts and make him guiltily conscious of his good fortune in avoiding such a fate: part of the novelist's work is done already. The rest, unfortunately, never quite gets done at all; the alternate journalistic flatness and rhetorical insistence of Grossman's prose (at least in translation) may suggest why. . . . (p. 507)

[It] is not the prose of fiction, but of argument. One may point to analogues in, for instance, George Eliot; but George Eliot's arguments, justifying the operations of her imagination, do not take its place. The purpose of *Forever Flowing* is to persuade: it is, in short, rhetoric. That rhetoric is often compelling, as in the accounts of permitted starvation, the exploration of possible judgments on a stool pigeon. But it is not compelling as a novel is compelling, it does not absorb the reader into a new form of life, it judges experience instead of rendering it. (p. 508)

Patricia Meyer Spacks, in a review of "Forever Flowing," in The Hudson Review, *Vol. XXV, No. 3, Autumn, 1972, pp. 507-08.*

THE TIMES LITERARY SUPPLEMENT

Grossman was an important Russian writer, little known in the West, who . . . established himself as a novelist before he was thirty, and became famous during the Second World War for some impressive works of reportage and for a novel, *The People is Immortal,* which rose above the prevailing level of social patriotism. Despite his considerable contributions to Soviet literature, however, he got into trouble towards the end of Stalin's life, when his old play *If One Believes the Pythagoreans* and his new novel *For the Just Cause* were suppressed. After

Stalin's death he spent several years writing a bitterly subversive book called *Everything Flows*. . . .

[The title of the new translation of *Everything Flows*], *Forever Flowing,* is rather misleading. Grossman was of course quoting one of the old Heraclitan tags, which is repeated in the book, together with a grim parody of another—instead of "You cannot step into the same river twice", he says, "You cannot get into the same prison train twice." The whole book, in fact, is permeated with the metaphysical ideas attributed to Heraclitus more than 2,000 years ago; and, while this destroys its literary quality, it gives it a special historical and philosophical interest.

Everything Flows is not really a novel—or rather, it begins as a novel, describing one of the "Returners" (*vozvrashchentsy*), a man who has come back from the labour camps after thirty years and finds that everyone has flowed, everything has changed, and the revolutionary enthusiasm of the old days has turned into sour disillusion and narrow careerism; but it soon breaks down into a series of semi-fictional stories about various aspects of the Stalinist dictatorship which are never properly drawn together but are linked and eventually overshadowed by a long meditation on the meaning and purpose of the phenomenon of Stalinism.

Grossman is remarkable among Soviet writers for seeing this not as some kind of error in development or interruption of progress but as an essential culmination of the whole course of Russian history. . . .

Some of the stories [within the novel] have considerable power, especially those about Masha, the wife of an arrested man who is arrested in turn and suffers and dies in the camps, and about Anna, the Party activist who witnesses the Ukrainian famine at the beginning of the 1930s during the compulsory collectivization of the land. But the main story, about Ivan, the hero whose life has been ruined by the regime, is weak, and the whole book leaves an impression of artistic confusion mixed with intellectual conviction of a disturbing kind.

Everything flows, and yet remains the same; tyrannies rise and fall, but tyranny lasts forever. Grossman hints that liberty will come in the end, but it is hard to see how this fits into his scheme, and the terrible vision of Russia enduring perpetual slavery is the most striking feature of the book. It is a pity that, in spite of the time he spent on it, Grossman didn't manage to make it as good as it deserved to be.

> *"Synthesis with Slaves," in* The Times Literary Supplement, *No. 3703, February 23, 1973, p. 197.*

ROSETTE C. LAMONT

[*Zhizn' i sud'ba*] is a great epic work in the Tolstoyan tradition. Its other presiding spirit is Anton Chekhov, whom [Grossman] considered the great master of humanist realism. Grossman's novel is also an astonishingly bold piece of socialist realism in the best sense of that much-abused term. It differs from the typical examples of the genre in that it is entirely free of inflated rhetoric, pathos and bathos, blatant propagandist ideology, and clichéd posturing. It presents Soviet society during the siege with unflinching directness. The reader is taken into the Russian trenches as well as behind enemy lines. Grossman shows us German prisoner-of-war camps, concentration camps, and the recesses of KGB jails ultimately opening, for the interrogated victims—most of them loyal party members—onto the Siberian wasteland dotted with Gulags.

Although his novel appeared long after the publication of *The Gulag Archipelago* . . . , Grossman preceded Solzhenitsyn in his depiction of what the French call "l'univers concentrationnaire." He even shows in detail the German engineers' planning of the crematoria. In one of the most horrifying and magnificently realistic scenes in this courageous novel, the writer depicts the small private feast served Adolf Eichmann within one of the future gas chambers he has finished inspecting. A table has been set up in the center of the room, laden with hors d'oeuvres and graced by a bottle of fine wine. Reichsführer Liss, who is accompanying Eichmann on his inspection tour of the death camp, raises a glass to the organizer of the Final Solution. Eichmann accepts the toast with modest pride: "Imagine two years hence, when we'll sit down again at this cozy table, we'll be able to say: In the space of twenty months we solved a problem humanity struggled with for twenty centuries." . . .

The subtitle I would give Grossman's book is "The Courage to Tell and Show All." Like André Schwarz-Bart in *The Last of the Just* (1959), Grossman introduces us into the gas chamber after having allowed us to follow the victims' via dolorosa until the very end. Whereas the French writer sentimentalizes the ultimate moments of his characters, however, Grossman remains resolutely sober and truthful. I know of no such scene in all of Holocaust literature.

The same lucidity is brought to bear on the description of Krymov's tortures and interrogation by the KGB. This authentic, formerly ruthless commissar has at last fallen victim to the kind of denunciation he has practiced throughout his life. He cannot comprehend how this could have happened to "Comrade Krymov, a Bolshevik, a Leninist," a loyal party member and citizen of the state. Under torture he comes to realize that "the new age needed nothing but the revolution's skin; they now skinned men alive and those who did not salute the coming era were cast upon the dung heap." . . . Still, a principle of freedom exists within the depths of the commissar's being: his love for the wife who left him because he was too inhuman. He has never forgotten her, and although she loves and is loved by a brilliant young general in command of a tank division, she gives up the possibility of fulfillment in marriage when she hears that her former husband is in jail. She travels to Moscow to be closer to him and sends him a note to let him know of her presence. It is this message that will help Krymov endure his suffering and his dreadful isolation. Although Grossman does not sympathize with the Krymovs of this world, he recognizes in him a fellow idealist, a utopian dreamer unable to see his perfect world turning into a nightmare. In prison he is simply unaccommodated man, naked, stripped of all the trappings of former glory. To him the writer gives grudging respect.

The breath of spiritual freedom courses through the entire novel, even at moments of dire danger and repression. It unites the small, heroic unit of resistance fighters of the house 6 Bis on the Stalingrad front. Their leader, Grekov, feels that the spirit of liberty that arose under fire will have to shape the Russia of the future. Commissar Krymov writes a report against him, but since the whole house is destroyed by enemy fire, no arrest will be made. Had Grekov survived, he would have been sent to a labor camp or executed.

The leading character of *Zhizn' i sud'ba* is the research scientist Victor Strum. It is at a moment when his mind indulges in the free play of creative imagination that he solves a particularly difficult problem and creates a revolutionary theory in physics, a real breakthrough. Although he is a theoretical physicist, his findings will obviously be of practical application to the war effort. For a while Strum is the victim of envy and anti-Semitism in his laboratory, but after Stalin telephones him to inquire about his project, he becomes a much-revered colleague. Grossman shows the baseness of human nature, even in the privileged milieu of the intellectual elite.

We owe the publication of *Zhizn' i sud'ba* to an admirable rescue operation. Once the microfilm of the novel reached the West, two dissident scholars, Efim Etkind and Simon Markish, reconstituted its original structure to the best of their ability. Some gaps remain because in the process of photographing the manuscript some pages were lost. Perhaps they were also missing from the archives. The novel would undoubtedly have benefited from the author's final revisions and some reorganization, had he had access to his manuscript. However, even as it stands, the book is one of the most luminous masterpieces of our time. It is the result of a kind of "conversion." The story of its own "life and fate" makes one wonder how many wonderful books were killed by censorship and self-censorship. At least we have this one. (p. 48)

> *Rosette C. Lamont, "Vassili Grossman's 'Zhizn' i sud'ba': The 'Life and Fate' of the First Soviet Dissident Novel," in* World Literature Today, *Vol. 59, No. 1, Winter, 1985, pp. 46-8.*

JOHN BAYLEY

Robert Chandler writes: '*Life and Fate* is the true *War and Peace* of this century, the most complete portrait of Stalinist Russia that we have or are ever likely to have.' Chandler, who has had the herculean task of making a good translation of this long, moving and very remarkable novel, puts forward that claim in his Introduction. When a long honest novel comes out of Russia today comparisons with Tolstoy are routine—I have made them myself—but in this case it seems worth asking rather more rigorously than usual what they really mean.

In the first place, no novel that merely resembled *War and Peace* could be anything like it, or indeed any good. Tolstoy himself said that *War and Peace* was not a novel, nor a piece of history, but something unique which he felt he could make, and which the situation called for. But apart from that, all long socialist realist novels coming from Russia since the Revolution, including those of Alexei Tolstoy, have in fact taken *War and Peace*, consciously or unconsciously, as a native model. That is one reason why most of them are so bad. What works for a genius will not do so for those who try to avail themselves of what seems his formula. *War and Peace* depends as heavily on the social and fictional conventions of its time, and on the way of life of the Russian nobility, as it does on Tolstoy's genius. You cannot transpose its method into a wholly different social ethos and scene.

Technically speaking, the panoramic method of *War and Peace*, which made Henry James refer to it as a 'loose baggy monster', is far more cunningly ordered than it looks. No one is dropped or forgotten; scene dovetails neatly into scene; above all, the central event—the attempted seduction of Natasha by Anatoly Kuragin—works by placing a girl, whose 'reality' has been totally established, in a totally conventional fictional situation. Tolstoy's timeless truths depend on their liaison with stock events in the novels of his time, just as his characters get their living three-dimensional selves from a participation in such events.

The instinctive confidence his characters feel in themselves comes from the fact that Tolstoy always starts on the inside of life, always with what it feels like to be oneself. . . :

Grossman's method is indeed socialist realism, used with a wholly Tolstoyan truth and honesty. This itself makes a disturbing, an explosive mixture. But where creating individuals is concerned, Grossman uses Tolstoy's art just as ineffectively as the merest party hack. It is not his fault. Though individuals remain basically the same, their true innerness has no chance to be revealed in a work devoted to the miseries and splendours of Russian wartime society. External pressures are too great. Grossman simply cannot afford the sense of leisure and repose which is the ground of Tolstoy's art, even though Tolstoy's *deux cent familles* offer some kind of correspondence with the Soviet Nomenklatura, the list of in-people suitable for high office which is kept by the Party. These persons have neither the time nor the inclination to be conscious of themselves, and they offer decidedly meagre fare to the novelist who wishes to establish his characters in a solid perspective of familiarity. So a gap yawns in the centre of *Life and Fate*. The Shaposhnikov family not only do not have the great unifying function exercised by the Rostovs in *War and Peace*, but are the only characters in Grossman's novel who are positively null, even boring.

War and Peace is much more a large-scale domestic novel than in any sense an 'epic' (how much Jane Austen would have enjoyed Vera Rostova, and the incomprehensible, but absolutely authentic difference between herself and the rest of the family), and it may be that art can no longer handle that basic material of the individual and the family. It is no longer thought of as 'serious' and 'important'. (And yet was it ever seen as being so? Probably not.) Grossman replaces it with a pattern of arbitrary fates—who was killed where, who starved, drowned, was shot, gassed, or relapsed into anonymous existence. We follow to Auschwitz Sophia Levinton, a Jewish doctor, a major in the Medical Corps, captured at Stalingrad, because she happens to be a friend of Yevgenia Shaposhnikova. The latter's brother-in-law Viktor, an atomic physicist, the most important but least realised character in the novel, is there to make the painful points about the scientist's role and responsibility under Soviet Communism.

By the same paradox that operates in *Dr Zhivago*, the author, in the process of operating the random arbitrariness of coincidence and destiny, puts himself too much to the fore and becomes an all-powerful instrument of fate rather than an artist. Tolstoy is all-powerful too, but, as he himself emphasised, the novelist must by some mysterious divination of art know what is, as it were, the true fate of each character, instead of merely allotting them a part. No doubt that is simply not possible these days, and the artist who aspires to paint on the widest canvas the travails of a revolutionary society in war and peace can only imitate the honest eye-witness who is doing it 'for the record'. Grossman in fact bows to this technique, using it in a way that is quite exceptionally powerful and moving. His novel is a series of scenes and records, which Tolstoy's is not, although it may seem to be. In some ways Grossman is much more like Isaac Babel, on a huge scale.

So much for the stock claim in terms of construction, technique, effect. But what about the message of *War and Peace*, its celebration of Russian life, the drive of its propaganda? This is a different and more complex matter, and it must be said at once that Grossman really has managed to breathe into his novel something of the inner spirit of Tolstoy's. Tolstoy never pretended that he was writing about the whole people of Russia. What interested him was his own class, and the part it had played during the French invasion and the glorious year of 1812. Yet with his massive and almost invisible diplomacy Tolstoy manages to associate all that was best and simplest in Russia with that class—which was under strong attack at the time he was writing *War and Peace*—and with its achievement. He suggests that 'good' Russia is, and always has been, classless. Such a claim is never uncommon among those at the top of the tree in any country, but Tolstoy makes it with great certainty and subtlety. So although the literary method is quite different, inevitably different, there is an almost exact subterranean correspondence between what Grossman wishes to say and what Tolstoy wished to say.

Both see with penetrating clarity that everything bad comes from the state 'machine', from the people who create it and devote themselves to it, and the mass of people who submit themselves—often willingly—to its disciplines. With the French occupation of Moscow in 1812 this 'machine' (his own term) is seen by Tolstoy as working with its own particular sort of mad efficiency. The 'human' French soldiers consent and defer to it utterly when they are required to shoot civilians or march out the prisoners. And by one of his characteristic sleights Tolstoy suggests that the 'machine' is a peculiarly French organisation, pitted now against good-hearted Russia and the simple human instincts of Russians. So compelling is the machine that it not only dehumanises the naturally good and makes them do evil acts, but paralyses those who have created it and are a part of it. Under its influence Napoleon has no choice but to march on Russia, and further into Russia.

This business about the machine, and the human goodness it corrupts and nullifies, is of course sufficiently old hat, and it takes a creative writer of the first power, like Tolstoy, to bring home to us what it means, and to move us deeply with the spectacle. It says much for Grossman that he can do this too, using the same basic ideas, and conveying them with the same transforming passion of art. But though his position is essentially Tolstoyan, it is more complex than that of Tolstoy in *War and Peace*. Without straining the probabilities too far Tolstoy was able to oppose Russian 'humanity' to French 'machine'. For Grossman, naturally enough, the picture has to be different: his 'machine' achieves a virtually identical perfection in two places, Stalinist Russia and Hitlerite Germany. Germans have the same *entrée* to *Life and Fate* as the French had in Tolstoy's novel, and their language is frequently used in a Russian context. This tacit but significant interchangeability—of the one country and the other—would itself be abhorrent to the orthodox Soviet line, even if there were no other offences in the novel. Its time sequence is that of the siege and relief of Stalingrad, though there are frequent references back and forth, particularly to 1937, the year of the purges. A number of scenes take place on the German side, in German camps, on the trains to Auschwitz and Dachau, and in the dug-outs and headquarters of the German Sixth Army at Stalingrad: and there is no great difference in tone between the reflections and conversations on both sides. Real persons are introduced in speaking parts, as in *War and Peace* and in Solzhenitsyn's *August 1914;* there are identical attitudes, ambitions and ideologies among Soviet and German *fonctionnaires*.

The genius of both novelists appears in the compelling and spontaneous way they juxtapose the human and the non-human in scenes of swift unspoken analysis. Towards the end of *War and Peace* Colonel Denisov, now a partisan commander, dis-

cusses the fate of the French prisoners with the sinister roué Dolokhov. He is furious with Dolokhov for expressing total cynicism on the point, even though he admits the prisoners will probably die anyway, of cold and hunger. An almost exactly similar scene occurs after Stalingrad between two Russian officers, one of whom has just casually kicked a wounded German by the roadside. The fury of the other, and their quarrel, illustrates with silent irony the difference between spontaneous human goodness and the equally spontaneous need to maintain appearances. The two things depend on each other, and validate the conviction that Russians, or Germans, or English, just don't behave like that. 'Are we Germans or something?' cries Natasha, when it is a question of the wounded using the carts in which the Rostovs are evacuating their belongings. How *we* behave fuses nationality with humanity in a way essentially absurd, but also saving. The machine, whether Soviet, German or English, has no time for such incongruities.

In the face of the machine, even certain kinds of smallness and selfishness become allies of human dignity. When Field-Marshal Paulus surrenders at Stalingrad his captors wait curiously for him to utter some appropriate sentiment—appropriate, that is, to one machine that has been put out of action by another. What went wrong? Where was the decisive error? Instead he says shyly: *Sagen sie mir, bitte, was ist Makhorka?* A heavy smoker, he is enquiring about Russian tobacco. All he can think of is will he be able to get something to smoke and eat, be given some warm place to sleep. He has been reduced to just the same small preoccupations and anxieties as the ordinary soldier. (p. 3)

Faithful to the spirit of his model, Grossman celebrates the defence of the homeland against the Germans, as Tolstoy did against the French: but both deprecate the un-Russian spirit of mean efficiency, and ruthless indifference to the human cost, which seeks to carry the war into the enemy country and liquidate him like the kulaks or the party dissidents. When her sons have saved Russia the Party steps in and takes the credit, giving the cold shoulder to uncommitted loyalty and decency. Stalin in the Kremlin reflects that success has now condemned his victims to limbo: 'Nobody quarrels with a victor.' The commander of the tank corps which successfully completed the encirclement of Stalingrad is reported on unfavourably by the corps commissar for holding up his attack for a few minutes in order to ensure his men won't be decimated for lack of artillery support; and at the end of the novel he seems headed for demotion and possible disgrace. As at the end of *War and Peace,* victory seems only to have confirmed tyranny and made it both more confident and more suspicious.

Of course everybody knows this now. Grossman's fervour is years out of date, and even at the time must have seemed a voice crying in the wilderness. The old paradox obtains. What for Suslov must not be published for two hundred years, lest it amaze and confound the faithful, is in the West merely a repetition of what we have been told many times, or what we can work out for ourselves. We can also raise our own objections, for Grossman's propaganda is no more absolutely true than Tolstoy's. Patriotism and decency are all very well, but what won the war was the sheer brutal discipline and drive of the Red Army and the Party—their ability, by whatever means, to keep up the ammunition supply, to get the guns and the conscripts into action. (p. 4)

Rather engagingly, Grossman has a weakness for the old thriller technique in which villains love to make long speeches to helpless heroes in defence of their policies, speeches of great elegance and philosophical subtlety. O'Brien does it in *1984*, and the interrogator Gletkin in *Darkness at Noon*. In *Life and Fate* a cultured SS officer of high rank, a friend of Eichmann, enjoys long discussions with his old Bolshevik prisoner from Stalingrad, remarking that it doesn't really matter which side wins, since both stand for the same thing, and thus victory for their joint policy is assured. Towards the end of the novel the same kind of talk takes place in a cell in the Lubianka, where Krymov, one of the party faithful arrested at Stalingrad for not taking a more vigorous line about House 6/I, finds himself incarcerated with another unexpected victim, a veteran Chekist whose aesthetic love for the whole system is so great that he imagines a time when there will be no difference between being in a camp and outside one.

Naturally, the old Bolsheviks are appalled and agonised by the cynicism of the SS man and the old Chekist, who treat them as no different from themselves. To the reader, however, the tableau is both commonplace and unconvincing. Russians love to talk, and the way they talk (lying under an idea as if under a stone, as Chadayev said) is more intense and dramatic than anything that usually takes place in a free society. But conversations designed solely to emphasise a point to the reader are unconvincing in any fictional context. SS and KGB men are far cruder and more naive types than this, and their conversation would most likely be meaninglessly depressing, or as banal as the chat of businessmen in a bar. Equally unconvincing are the sentiments of the heroic 'housekeeper', Grekov, to the lads in House 6/I. . . .

Unexceptional sentiments, but they are fatally compromised by being set in the socialist realist mould. They might fascinate and appal the Russian reader (though would they really today?), but us they excite as little as would their mirror image in the same style of a young soldier proclaiming Lenin's beneficent divinity. The medium, in a sense, nullifies the message. We can also understand why, in a piece entitled 'Le Cas Grossman' in a French periodical (*L'Age d'Homme*, 1983), Simon Markish quoted a Russian friend's comment on *Life and Fate:* 'Yes, all this is noble, elevated, morally irreproachable, but I don't need a follower of Leo Tolstoy's.'

That reaction is natural, almost unavoidable, and yet the novel survives it triumphantly. I strongly agree with Chandler, who in his excellent introduction is aware of all such criticisms ('the novel is indeed a remarkably old-fashioned one') and yet remains convinced of its inherent freshness and importance. The defects and drawbacks are obvious: ideology, propaganda, 'the clash between freedom and totalitarianism'—all these things take on an academic quality from the fact that they are painted as the old academicians used to paint. And yet the novel can still present a disturbing, an explosive mixture.

Structurally, it is dead: spiritually, it could not be more alive. There is even a certain justice about the fact that Grossman, who detests all forms of political and moral organisation, should himself be unable as a writer to organise his book on such lines. Although the scale is so impressive, the detail so varied and compelling, the true life of the book seems obstinately to exist independently, between and among all these forces that have been marshalled to make it. This is its truest, most secret relation to *War and Peace*. . . .

What fill the mind at the end of *Life and Fate* are the innumerable glimpses the book contains of 'senseless kindness'. This is the phrase used by a dotty old creature who has ended up in Dachau, and who has managed to preserve a kind of

essay, a very Tolstoyan document, on what men really live by. This gets into the hands of the SS officer Liss, who maliciously conveys it to the old Bolshevik prisoner Mostovskoy, whom he loves to talk with and ideologically torment. Both regard the document, whose insertion has a parallel in the Grand Inquisitor passage in *The Brothers Karamazov*, as a piece of crazy nonsense, beneath contempt: and yet the old Bolshevik, who will soon be liquidated anyway, is secretly tormented by it as much as he is by the SS man's affable intimacies.

Senseless, unwitnessed, such kindness is 'outside any system of social or religious good'. It is 'as simple as life itself', and yet 'even the teachings of Jesus deprived it of its strength.' Christianity in its time killed it as effectively as modern totalitarianism. The sentiments of the holy fool are not particularly original—indeed it could be said that acts of 'senseless kindness' are usually no more than gestures of human self-satisfaction, the universal sentiment Tolstoy understood so well—and yet in some extraordinary way Grossman's entire novel endorses the old madman's point with all the secret force of which the language of art is capable. 'Art' is the operative word, for Grossman's old-fashioned simplicities, and his extensive use of second-hand techniques, might lead the reader to suppose that he is not an original artist. The proof that he is is shown more than anything by the fact that we are not 'moved' or 'horrified', in the obvious sense, by the most memorable scenes and sequences in the novel—like the one in which a trainload from Eastern Europe arrives at Auschwitz, to be followed through the 'bath-house' into the gas chamber. Art here shows itself to be deeply, and as it were naturally, in league with 'senseless kindness', as at the moment when a woman in the queue for the gas chamber painstakingly brushes the mud off the back of another's dress, or when a small boy sees the movement as a fan starts in the ceiling to suck in the cyanide, and thinks that some bird or animal has been trapped up there. One of the most memorable scenes in the novel, quite near the beginning, simply describes how a mother goes to the cemetery of a military hospital to visit the grave of her son, a lieutenant who has just died of wounds. She hugs his grave, as if she could still warm him and comfort him inside it.

Art in the novel is no good without a personality to go with it. Not only is Grossman's extremely appealing, but it is part of the nature of the appeal that it escapes from 'the machine'— the full gruesomeness of whose impact upon the lives of Soviet citizens it continually but almost incidentally reveals—without rejecting it. It sets up no counter-philosophy, like Solzhenitsyn's, to fight the system: and partly for this reason, Grossman's personality, and awareness of things, are much more congenial than Solzhenitsyn's. Only a man indifferent to the real voice of art, a man who insists that the novel must above all things be *novel*—aligned with whatever kind of Modernism is currently valid—could dismiss *Life and Fate* as merely 'noble, elevated, morally irreproachable'. It is a work whose greatest recommendation is that it has no need to be in tune with the times. And yet, as Suslov inadvertently pointed out, in his act of refusal and denial to its author, the times are all too likely never to be out of tune with what Grossman has written, and how he has written it. (p. 5)

John Bayley, "Off the Record," in London Review of Books, *Vol. 7, No. 16, September 19, 1985, pp. 3-5.*

APRIL FITZLYON

Everything about [*Life and Fate*] is exceptional: the history of its gestation and publication; its length—over 800 pages; its scope; the quality of the writing; and the author's deep compassion and moral indignation. It is a chronicle of life in Stalinist Russia, a kind of tapestry in which the personalities, lives and fates of a vast number of very disparate people are interwoven. (p. 94)

[Almost] every long novel in Russian—*Quiet Flows the Don, Dr Zhivago,* and even more unlikely candidates—has been marketed as a new *War and Peace*. However, in the case of *Life and Fate* it is legitimate to make that comparison. It is legitimate not only because Grossman does deal with war and 'peace'—the twentieth-century variety; not only because the scope of the novel is comparable (although Grossman deals with more different facets of society than Tolstoy does); but principally because the two writers' style and technique are so similar. Like Tolstoy, Grossman is the authorial god; he knows what goes on in the deepest recesses of his characters' minds, and he describes their thoughts with extraordinary subtlety. Like Tolstoy, he is the master of the interior monologue. Like Tolstoy, Grossman is an adept at describing how people do one thing, while thinking or experiencing something quite different. Like Tolstoy, he is able to get under the skin of the most disparate characters: generals and ordinary soldiers; intellectuals and workmen; dyed-in-the-wool Bolsheviks and dissidents; women, teenagers, and children; the staff of concentration camps—Germans and Russians—and their victims. His description of a mother's grief when her son is killed is profoundly moving; and his analyses of the minds of party hacks, top scientists and old peasants ring equally true. Like Tolstoy, Grossman is able to make all the members of this vast cast come alive; they are rarely wholly good or bad, just human—with all that implies. And like Tolstoy, and despite the appallingly tragic scene he is depicting, Grossman has a sense of humour.

Paradoxically, war—Stalingrad—in *Life and Fate* is much less horrific than civilian life. At the front the worst that can befall a man is to be killed by the Germans; he knows who his enemy is; and there is a spirit of camaraderie amongst soldiers united in a common aim. Civilian life is much more dangerous and terrifying: denunciations, interrogations, concentration camps; a chance word to a close friend may cost you your job, your freedom, and even your life. No one knows who his enemy is. No one can guess of what he may be accused. No one—even the highest official—is safe.

Like Tolstoy, Grossman is prone to philosophizing. Briefly, his philosophy is that all ideologies—religious, political, social—are evil; in the name of Good—but whose Good?—followers of these ideologies have committed terrible crimes. The only defence the individual has against this collective Good is the small, individual good, often senseless and useless, but 'evil is impotent before it'. Throughout this long novel Grossman gives countless examples both of the evil, collective Good, and the true, individual good.

In his introduction Chandler is, I think, too apologetic about Grossman's old-fashioned style. It is true that he writes in the style of nineteenth-century realism, and is untouched by Modernism; but it is not true to say, as Chandler does, that Grossman writes 'according to the doctrine of Socialist Realism'. Socialist Realism demands that art should reflect man's struggle towards Communism, and must breathe a spirit of hope and optimism; heroes must be positive. No one could accuse *Life and Fate* of any of that; and Grossman's passionate championship of the individual and of individualism is directly contrary to Socialist Realism. Old-fashioned *Life and Fate* may

be; but it is one of the most important novels to come out of Russia since 1917, a worthy memorial to the millions of people on whom Hitler and Stalin inflicted such terrible sufferings. (pp. 95-6)

April Fitzlyon, "Unacceptable," in London Magazine, *n.s. Vol. 25, No. 7, October, 1985, pp. 94-6.*

RONALD HINGLEY

[In *Life and Fate*] Grossman's faults are the usual faults of Socialist Realists as exemplified in hundreds of run-of-the-mill Soviet works of fiction published over the last half century. The extraordinary thing is to find this puddingy and conformist technique employed by an author who has so triumphantly rejected the political conformism that is supposed to go with the technique. And the novel indeed does triumph in the end, defects and all, stodge or no stodge. It triumphs through the high seriousness of Grossman's grand theme and through his compelling historical, moral and political preoccupations.

Notable among these is his faith in erratic, spontaneous, unscripted human kindness, as preached from inside a German death camp by a certain Ikonnikov, one of those saintly, philosophizing half-wits so beloved of Russian fiction writers. Such (as it were) extracurricular kindness is seen as an ineradicable human characteristic. It is presented as the sole guarantee that victory need not go in the end to the world's great cruel ideologies, among which Ikonnikov does not hesitate to include Christianity alongside Marxism and Nazism. The thesis may sound trite, but Grossman illustrates it poignantly.

The prehistory of the book goes back to 1943, when Grossman began work on an earlier, widely forgotten novel entitled *For a Just Cause*. That book hinges on the opening phase of the Battle of Stalingrad.... (pp. 1, 38)

What of the relations between these two linked novels? Subplots and major characters straddle them, though not to the extent of making the sequel impenetrably obscure to those ignorant of the predecessor. Closely linked in this way, the two works yet offer a sharp contrast in political attitude. It is a contrast between the conformism of the earlier volume and the militant nonconformism of the later.

For a Just Cause was only another sample of Socialist Realist (that is, caponized) fiction, and it was even described as a potential Stalin Prize winner. True, the first published version came under attack and had to be rewritten. But that happened even to the most orthodox of Stalinist authors....

Thus, the news that he was working on a sequel to *For a Just Cause* in the late 1950's would have been unlikely to create a stir in the Soviet Union or anywhere else. All that could be expected was another gelded fictional brontosaurus like its predecessor, the umpteenth such carcass to litter the landscape of officially approved Soviet literature. Who was to suspect that there was another, a secret, Grossman, a Grossman painfully aware that his own Government was responsible for a large share of the appalling sufferings that assailed Europe during his middle life? Here, it turns out, was a loather of totalitarianism in both its guises, the Stalinist no less than the Hitlerite. *Life and Fate* is a passionate onslaught against state-sponsored political terror....

In portraying Hitlerite and Stalinist totalitarianism as closely resembling each other, the novel is not unique among Soviet-banned works. Aleksandr Solzhenitsyn has made a similar point, just as he has also tended to agree with Grossman in suggesting that Lenin rather than Stalin was the true founder of Soviet-style totalitarianism. But Grossman deploys these important arguments with a force and slant all his own.

His book is also remarkable for the attention given, by an author himself Jewish, to the Jewish situation. The hero is a Soviet Jewish nuclear physicist. Soviet persecution of Jews is a major theme—a shade anachronistically, for attitudes more characteristic of the Soviet Union in the late 40's are here attributed to the war period. But all that is nothing, of course, compared with the pages on the sufferings of Jews caught up in Hitler's "final solution." For example, the reader of *Life and Fate* enters a gas chamber and breathes in an asphyxiant, the notorious gas Zyklon B. You need a steady nerve to read parts of this novel.

Grossman also pictures the horrors of the Soviet death camps and takes the reader inside the unspeakable Lubyanka Prison in Moscow. His account of Soviet life—penal, military and civilian—is encyclopedic and unblinkered. On the military side it embraces adventures in an encircled strongpoint in Stalingrad—artillery bombardments, air raids, hand-to-hand fighting, the relations between commanders and military commissars and life in the army on the move and in the rear areas. Then there are the experiences of civilians—in the provinces, in evacuation to the temporary wartime capital, Kuibyshev, and in Moscow itself. Love affairs, divorces, the problems of acquiring a ration card or a residence permit—they are all here, the tragic and the trivial side by side.

It is all enormously impressive too, but the level is decidedly uneven. And there is so very, very much of everything. One wonders, not for the first time, why Russian authors are so relentlessly committed to fictional gigantism. One cynical explanation is that they are perverted for life because they are paid by the page and not on the basis of sales. A less cynical explanation puts it all down to their wish to emulate Tolstoy's *War and Peace*. But when Robert Chandler . . . calls it, in his preface, "the true *War and Peace* of this century," I incline to cavil, though I can see why he thinks so. For example, Grossman does vie with Tolstoy in embracing so many events and personages of historical importance: Stalin, Hitler, Eichmann and not a few real-life Soviet generals are among his minor characters. But his chronological range is far more restricted than Tolstoy's. Then again, Tolstoy's great novel has itself been criticized as loosely shaped. But it does at least *have* a shape of sorts—more so, anyway, than Grossman's sprawling work. This book has little in the way of compelling plot line, while samples of narrative skill are all too sparse. A little suspense here, the occasional surprise there, the odd humorous or sarcastic touch: it doesn't add up to much in the way of vibrancy.

Above all Grossman lacks Tolstoy's flair for characterization, as do so many other modern Russian fiction writers. Whether we think of the endless minor figures in the novel, introduced so lavishly as to put even *War and Peace* in the shade, or of the handful of major male heroes, or of the comparably featureless Lyudmilas, Yevgenias and Alexandra Vladimirovnas—everywhere we find the inability to breathe full conviction into the printed word. The man can make residence permits, army rations, booze-ups in dugouts, gas chambers and mass graves credible. What a pity, then, that he can't do the same for human beings. Yes, yes, he does hand out various physical characteristics, a ginger-colored mustache here, a twitching

right eye there. But his brain children largely tend to be stillborn.

This is true even of the novel's main character, the nuclear physicist Viktor Shtrum. Here is a politically ambivalent figure given to dropping indiscreet remarks. His star seems ascendant when he makes a crucial discovery in theoretical physics, but he soon becomes the target for an anti-Semitic witch hunt at his institute. Only at the last moment, when he seems firmly marked as concentration camp fodder, is he unexpectedly rescued by one of Stalin's famous *deus ex machina* telephone calls. This redeems Shtrum's position. But it also—more significantly—effects his ideological seduction from the status of political waverer to that of enthusiastic pillar of the scientific establishment. Perhaps Grossman is here apologizing, through his hero, for his own many accommodations with the literary establishment which so richly rewarded him. In the light of such speculations Shtrum's dilemmas become considerably more fascinating than Shtrum himself. . . .

[*Life and Fate*] is, at very least, a significant addition to the great library of smuggled Russian works by Pasternak and his many successors, works written in the Soviet Union but destined almost exclusively for the un-Kremlinized reader. (p. 38)

> Ronald Hingley, *"Stalingrad and Stalin's Terror,"* in The New York Times Book Review, *March 9, 1986, pp. 1, 38.*

FERNANDA EBERSTADT

Since the early '60s, when Nikita Khrushchev's "thaw" unloosed an avalanche of dissident novels and plays, we have come to expect certain traits from Soviet writing, at least of the kind that finds its way to the West: innovative techniques, surrealism, the fancy footwork of multiple puns and ironies. Thus we have the black humor of a Sinyavsky, the picaresque satire of a Vladimir Voinovich, the modernist pointillism of the late Yuri Trifonov. What, then, is the American reader accustomed to the experimentalism that has characterized much of dissident Soviet fiction to make of *Life and Fate*—a 900-page epic about the siege of Stalingrad, written in the solemn, lucid and philosophical manner of a 19th-century master? Read it, and rejoice that the 20th century has produced so thoughtful and so profound a literary humanist.

Vasily Grossman's life and the bizarre fortunes of his masterpiece, *Life and Fate,* are a macabre emblem of the history of the modern Soviet state. . . .

Among the novel's chief protagonists are Mostrovskoy, an Old Bolshevik imprisoned behind enemy lines; Viktor Shtrum (clearly a self-portrait of the author), a Jewish physicist evacuated to Kazan, and his sister-in-law Yevgenia, an enigmatic siren torn between her love for a tank commander at Stalingrad and her loyalty to her ex-husband who has been arrested on charges of espionage.

The sufferings and self-revelations of these characters provide us with some of the most troubling and occasionally uplifting examinations of the human heart to be found in contemporary literature. Under this category comes the letter Shtrum's mother writes on the eve of certain death in a Nazi-run ghetto, and the confrontation between the fanatical Marxist Mostrovskoy and a German interrogator who tries his faith by revealing the undeniable congruence between communism and fascism. Under this category, too, comes the epiphany of an elderly spinster, Sonya Leviton, who discovers in the Nazi gas chamber a sudden and boundless love for the Jewish people akin to a mother's love for her children.

Grossman's view of human nature is at once tenderly forgiving and quite merciless. We are exposed, for instance, to the all-too-realistic succession of emotions—from exultant resistance to depression and submission to gloating smugness and final resolve—that accompanies Viktor Shtrum's buffetings by the state: first lionized for an important scientific discovery, he is then denounced by the party as an enemy of the people and finally saved at the 11th hour by Stalin's intervention and persuaded by sheer relief to sign a letter vilifying other prominent Jewish intellectuals.

Life and Fate is not without its failings. Grossman was deprived of any chance to revise his manuscript as he intended. It is blunt and sometimes hasty in style . . . ; the dialogue occasionally clanks with the rather mechanical effusions characteristic of socialist realism. In addition to these drawbacks, only a handful of the novel's cast of hundreds (including such historical figures as Hitler, Stalin and Eichmann) achieve a distinctive individuality. At the same time, however, so compelling are Grossman's dramatic powers that the reader feels himself by turns to be suffocating in a Nazi gas chamber, undergoing torture at the hands of the Soviet secret police, and gaining victory on the battlefield.

Life and Fate is above all a novel of ideas, in the 19th-century sense. Its great subject is human freedom, as exercised in those minute acts of "senseless kindness" by which ordinary men and women wage war against the forces of enslavement, forces which are embodied in our own time by communism, fascism, and their common scourge, anti-Semitism. Grossman's excoriation of these evils is the more effective and the more ennobling for being clothed in a gently majestic humanism which renders this work not only an evocation of an era, but a novel for all time.

Fernanda Eberstadt, "Suppressed Epic of Stalingrad," in Book World—The Washington Post, *April 6, 1986, p. 5.*

Ernest (Miller) Hemingway

1899-1961

American short story writer, novelist, nonfiction writer, journalist, poet, and dramatist.

Hemingway is regarded by many as one of the greatest writers of the twentieth century. Considered a master of the understated prose style which became his trademark, Hemingway was awarded the 1954 Nobel Prize in literature. Although his literary stature is secure, Hemingway remains a highly controversial writer, and his novels and short stories have stimulated an enormous amount of critical commentary. His narrow range of characters and his thematic focus on violence and machismo, as well as his terse, objective prose style, have led some critics to regard his fiction as shallow and insensitive. Others claim that beneath the deceptively limited surface lies a complex and fully realized fictional world. His supporters note the extreme importance of the things left unsaid. As Hemingway commented in *Death in the Afternoon* (1932), the "dignity of movement of an iceberg is due to only one-eighth of it being above water." Despite the fact that his style is variously applauded and denounced, Hemingway is one of the most widely imitated writers in modern literature.

Critical assessment of Hemingway's writing frequently focuses on the connections between his life and his work. Born and raised in affluent, suburban Oak Park, Illinois, Hemingway spent the greater part of his life trying to escape the repressive code of behavior set by his strict, disciplinarian parents and their society. His first break from home came in 1918, when he volunteered for service in World War I. Hemingway was stationed in Italy for only a few weeks before he was wounded and forced to return to Oak Park. Scarred physically and emotionally from the war and stifled by his home environment, Hemingway, according to some critics, began a quest for psychological and artistic freedom that was to lead him first to the secluded woods of northern Michigan, where he had spent his most pleasant childhood moments, and then to Europe, where his literary talents began to take shape.

The similarity between Hemingway and his characters is most clearly evident in the stories revolving around Nick Adams, a character who spent much of his youth in the northern Michigan woods, went overseas to fight in the war, was wounded, and returned home. The first in the line of Hemingway's "fictional selves," Nick Adams is often discussed as the quintessential Hemingway "code hero." While this hero appears tough and insensitive on the surface, many critics contend that his toughness stems not from insensitivity but from a strong moral code that functions as the character's sole defense against the overwhelming chaos of the world. In an influential study, Cleanth Brooks, Jr. and Robert Penn Warren noted that while this hero seems to lack spontaneous emotion, he "sheathes his [sensibility] in the code of toughness" because "he has learned that the only way to hold on to 'honor,' to individuality, to, even, the human order . . . is to live by his code."

The code hero is also found in Hemingway's most celebrated novels. Jake Barnes in *The Sun Also Rises* (1926) is both disillusioned and emasculated as a result of the war, and he establishes his own code of behavior because he no longer

believes in the dictates of society. Frederic Henry in *A Farewell to Arms* (1929) finds order in his life through his love for a woman, maintaining his dignity even when she dies and the structure of his world collapses. Robert Jordan in *For Whom the Bell Tolls* (1940) is an American who dedicates himself to the Loyalist cause during the Spanish Civil War and ultimately dies for his convictions. These men demonstrate courage and perseverance in the face of adversity, thus exemplifying Hemingway's concern with fortitude and personal commitment.

With the novella *The Old Man and the Sea* (1952), for which he received the Pulitzer Prize in fiction, Hemingway turned from themes of love and war to focus on a lone fisherman's struggle to capture a large marlin. The protagonist, Santiago, heroically fights the elements, only to lose all but the fish's carcass to sharks. As is characteristic of Hemingway's fiction, the terse, almost journalistic prose, the compressed action, and the subdued yet suggestive symbolism point to a deeper meaning than appears on the surface. Hemingway stresses Santiago's heroism through subtle allusions to Christ, and the simplicity of action serves to underscore the hero's nobility. Although Santiago is hindered by age and misfortune, he persists with dignity, thereby gaining a moral victory and demonstrating Hemingway's lifelong interest in maintaining "grace under pressure."

Hemingway's nonfiction often explores themes similar to those in his novels and short stories. *Death in the Afternoon* comments on the stylized ritual of bullfighting and reveals Hemingway's great admiration for the toreador's bravery in the face of death. Hemingway himself faced danger hunting big game in Africa, and *Green Hills of Africa* (1935) records one such experience. The work is noted for its introduction of his novelistic techniques into nonfiction.

Although Hemingway committed suicide in 1961, continued critical attention and the posthumous publication of several works testify to his enduring importance. Among the books published after his death are *The Garden of Eden* (1986), a novel which Hemingway began in 1946 and was edited from his uncompleted manuscript; *A Moveable Feast* (1964), an acclaimed collection of autobiographical essays which recount Hemingway's life in Paris during the 1920s; and *The Dangerous Summer* (1985), a re-edited version of an essay about the rivalry of two toreadors which was originally published in *Life* magazine in 1959.

(See also *CLC*, Vols. 1, 3, 6, 8, 10, 13, 19, 30, 34, 39; *Contemporary Authors*, Vols. 77-80; *Dictionary of Literary Biography*, Vols. 4, 9; *Dictionary of Literary Biography Yearbook: 1981;* and *Dictionary of Literary Biography Documentary Series*, Vol. 1.)

HERBIE BUTTERFIELD

[In the story that concludes *In Our Time*, "**Big Two-Hearted River**", Nick Adams puts the] stuff of nightmares behind him, 'everything behind, the need for thinking, the need to write, other needs', . . . [and] heads away from the road for the woods and the river. Far from other human sound, he fishes, pitches his tent, builds a fire, cooks a buckwheat flapjack, brews coffee. 'He was there, in the good place. He was in his home where he had made it.'

It is a familiar American literary moment, this sealing of the solitary compact with nature, marked most famously amongst Hemingway's predecessors by Thoreau, in *Walden* and his other journals and natural histories. Thoreau was a writer who on the face of it would appear to have been unimportant to Hemingway. . . . However, that he sensed a kinship between himself and Thoreau can be gauged from the fact that in the first draft of "**The Snows of Kilimanjaro**" the names he gave to the dying writer, who, simply because he is a writer, is the closest representative in the fiction of Hemingway himself, were the determinedly significant ones of Henry Walden. He soon suppressed the association, but an underlying connection had briefly surfaced.

There were of course immense differences between the times and the lives and personalities of Thoreau and Hemingway. For Thoreau, self-encouragingly, 'the truest account of heaven is the fairest', where Hemingway had early on seen things that permanently disturbed his sleep, so that the dark was full of terrors and empty of God. Conversely, there were compensatory pleasures of the body, of board and bed, that Hemingway joyously rendered, but that Thoreau for whatever reason denied himself; just as, gregarious, amatory, and self-damagingly restless, Hemingway envied Thoreau's capacity for solitude. But at the core, at the still centre, as Hemingway recognized, there

was affinity of spirit. In different accents each spoke the language of a radical, isolate individualism that separated them from others, the mass of men leading lives of quiet, or hectic, desperation, and beckoned them towards an unpopulated nature. Each in fundamentally Protestant manner knew that what a man does with his solitariness is the true subject of philosophy. And each to be renewed, to be made whole, went home to nature, to earth and water, to Walden Pond and Big Two-Hearted River.

To be sure, where Thoreau levels a long, steady gaze at nature, Hemingway, as here with Nick, offers only brief homecomings; where Thoreau evolved into a herbivore, Hemingway remained a predator; and where Thoreau in his narratives has his solitude interrupted by only occasional or chance meetings, Hemingway's fictional world is often densely populated. But the important point is this, that whether the world be as uninhabited as Nick's in "**Big Two-Hearted River**", or as crowded as the expatriate caravan of *The Sun Also Rises*, the essential condition of life for Hemingway is solitary, and the interesting, the properly serious business, is the management of that solitude.

Thus, in *The Sun Also Rises*, which was published exactly a year after *In Our Time*, Jake Barnes managerially 'did not care what it was all about. All I wanted to know was how to live in it', the primary characteristic of 'it' being a loneliness that is in fact in the general nature of things, though for Jake it has been given particular immediacy by the war-wound that has deprived him of the possibility of sexual love and comfort. To the problem of how to live in the days there are simple solutions; they can be filled with activity, people, laughter, and one more drink to fend off the night. 'It is awfully easy to be hard-boiled about everything in the daytime, but at night it is another thing.' There, alone, the dark is a place less of pointless yearning than of terror. . . . The fear is not of hidden presences, but of emptiness, universal absence, oblivion. It is of course a legacy of the war. . . . The war as a cause, though, is scarcely important; what matters is the reality of its effect, the knowledge of the fearful loneliness, the 'it' that must be lived in. There are the daytime distractions, which give to the novel such colour and movement; there are the natural world's healing balms (fishing at Burguete, bathing at San Sebastian, reestablishing footholds upon the earth that abideth forever); and for the nominally Catholic Jake there are some very flimsy 'consolations of religion'. But the continuing impression and the final picture (Jake sardonically puncturing Brett's wishful daydream of togetherness) is of a solitariness, that must be borne, coped with, lived in. And this is not just because of Jake's exceptional status, imposed upon him by the misfortunes of war. Other figures, central and peripheral, for whom we feel sympathy, are similarly marked, whether Brett in her loneliness of spirit careless and abandoned, or the Englishman Harris and fat Count Mippipopolous in theirs composed and dignified. Indeed, it is almost a precondition of our sympathy. Only the despised, those outside the circle, those who try too hard or not hard enough, seem not to know of such loneliness. (pp. 186-89)

[Hemingway's novels *Across the River and Into the Trees, To Have and Have Not,* and *For Whom the Bell Tolls*] all bear witness to . . . his obsession with death. All end or reach their climaxes with the death or impending death of the principal characters, figures as various as a small-time smuggler, an idealistic young guerrilla fighter, and a cynical middle-aged professional soldier. *Across the River and Into the Trees* (1950) closes with Colonel Cantwell, after a night of love and a day of duck-shooting, dying from the heart condition that has tracked and threatened him throughout. Cantwell is a representative Hemingway leading character, even if a rather coarse and unpleasant version, and as such he need not detain us here. The two earlier novels, however, offer the interesting difference of being consciously political in a way that his previous books had not been. *To Have and Have Not* (1937) is an emphatic protest against corruption, exploitation, political hypocrisy, and the immorality of gross inequality; while *For Whom the Bell Tolls* (1941) commemorates three days of a guerrilla action in the Spanish Civil War, on which Hemingway had reported as a passionate adherent of the Loyalist cause. Hemingway's basic politics were consistent with his individualism, which is to say that they were anarchic, libertarian, and humanist. . . . On such grounds, entirely to his credit and in contrast to a notorious number of his literary contemporaries, he had early on laid his unambiguous opposition to Italian Fascism and his immediate hatred of Hitler. But if it was 'natural' for a libertarian individualist to detest totalitarianism, it was not 'natural' for one such to take up left-wing collectivist politics. And it is from the resultant uncertainty as to political identities that the relative failure of *To Have and Have Not* stems. Harry Morgan, named after the pirate Henry Morgan, is precisely piratical, a swashbuckling individualist, given to private criminal enterprise. He dies an appropriate violent, heroic death. What does not convince, though, what is not in character, is the swansong he utters while dying, the halting knell of that individualism: 'One man alone ain't got. No man alone now. No matter how a man alone ain't got no bloody chance.' The words may fumble towards a historical truth, but they have been learned in a politics lesson, rather than derived from Harry Morgan. The character and his incipiently political message have been separately conceived; and that absence of conceptual integrity accounts also for the clumsy obtrusiveness of the methods whereby elsewhere in the novel injustice is exposed. Hemingway's sentiments in this context are generous and admirable; but it did not come easily to him to give those sentiments a political cast. In fact, in the film made several years later, Faulkner in his script, Hawks in his direction, and Bogart in his starring role were between them, in being unfaithful to *To Have and Have Not,* being more faithful than Hemingway to himself.

For Whom the Bell Tolls is a greater work altogether, albeit an extraordinary combination of the exhilaratingly good and the embarrassingly bad. Neither for the first time nor for the last it is in the recreation of love that Hemingway goes astray. In the depiction of the loss of love that leaves a man bereft he excels; but in the description of lovers together he is ever liable to an excessive, distorting sentimentality that infantilizes, demeans, or renders ridiculous man and woman alike; never more so than here, with Jordan's and Maria's brief affair. Conversely, as in *A Farewell to Arms,* nearly all that has to do with war is excellently done: the characterization of the members of the guerrilla group; the comradeship, the hatred of enemies, the respect for enemies, the bravery, the brutality, the self-transcendence, the self-debasement. There are at least three permanently memorable narrative scenes: Pilar's tale of the murder of the Fascist civic leaders, El Sordo's last stand on the hill-top, and the mining and blowing up of the bridge. *For Whom the Bell Tolls* is a story of men and women in action together, dependent upon one another, fighting for a common cause; yet here again in its final picture the light falls not upon that cause, upon history and politics, but upon two lone individuals, both about to face their deaths; upon Lieutenant Berrendo, the decent Fascist, 'his thin face serious and grave',

riding into Robert Jordan's range, and upon Jordan, dying for the cause, yes, but also dying for himself, alone, with courage and honour. Beneath the new political clothes, it is the same man.

We are each of us alone, then, at home in nature when we can find our way there, but amongst others solitary individuals rather than members of a community; alive, we suffer, in body and mind; and, knowing that we will die, we dwell upon death. That is the human condition as it appeared to Hemingway, or as it appeared important to him. The ways he proposed of meeting or managing this fate were various and distinct, so that in different aspects his values may seem, loosely, stoic, heroic, Protestant, or hedonistic. Pleasure, sensuous pleasure— food, drink, and all kinds of physical activity—he conveys with a rare, discriminating vividness, especially in the early writings and in the retrospective *A Moveable Feast* where, aided by his recently rediscovered notes, he shows a quite remarkable ability to recapture poignantly the look, smell and taste of things thirty and more years ago. If it is a world of pain, it is also one of pleasure, of visual beauties and tactile delights that ease our passage. (pp. 192-94)

The principal element, though, in Hemingway's imaginative world, the quality with which in some form or other virtually all his best writing is concerned is courage: simply, courage. If life is intrinsically painful, and the prospect of death omnipresent, the act of living becomes by definition a test of courage. The courage required may be moral, or mental, or physical; it may be passive or active; it may be as ostensibly minimal as bearing it, with or without grinning, or it may be the stuff of awards for gallantry. The active exemplars include the bullfighters, boxers, hunters, soldiers, and guerrilla fighters, men and women: Pedro Romero; Manuel Garcia; Jack Brennan; Wilson, the white hunter; Agustin; Pilar. The passive models cover a moral range from those who merely refuse self-deception . . . to those who exhibit varying degrees of what Hemingway famously termed 'grace under pressure'. Some are with faith, like the priest in *A Farewell to Arms* or Anselmo who was 'a Christian. Something very rare in Catholic countries'; some without faith, like Count Greffi who 'had always expected to become devout . . . but somehow it does not come', and the waiter of **"A Clean, Well-Lighted Place"**; but all are seen to bear with grace—it is a matter of courage and a quality of the spirit—the pressures that fate exerts upon them.

The last and longest test of courage, beyond which there was really no need of further testing, was that undergone by the fisherman Santiago in *The Old Man and the Sea,* who after months of failing to catch anything wrestles day-long and night-long with the great marlin, only to have his magnificent fish devoured by sharks. Published in 1952, the long story proves a splendid exception to the otherwise poor or drastically uneven writing that Hemingway was doing at this time; and with its knowledge of mystery and its natural reverence . . . it represents also a marvellous renewal after the morally and imaginatively dull record of competitive killing into which his previous saga of man and beast, *Green Hills of Africa,* had degenerated. *The Old Man and the Sea* is a story of skill, of all kinds of courage, of defeat in the flesh, of victory in the spirit, of pride humbled and self-respect earned, of suffering, and of final great peace of mind. It was the last fiction that he published.

The Old Man and the Sea is not a novel, but a long story, in its texture self-consciously and I think effectively poetic. The point has often been made, in one form or another, that Hemingway was essentially a poet rather than a novelist. . . . Certainly in his attitude to language and the tools of his craft Hemingway was far closer to many poets, especially amongst his contemporaries, than he was to at least the more utilitarian of novelists. What is the famous diatribe against the rhetoric of war in *A Farewell to Arms* but an emotionally charged, morally urgent elaboration upon Pound's Imagist dictate to 'go in fear of abstractions'? What is the lament in *Death in the Afternoon* that 'all our words from loose using have lost their edge' but a sparse precursor of the passage in Eliot's "Burnt Norton", where words 'slip, slide, perish, / Decay with imprecision, will not stay in place, / Will not stay still'? . . . Concentration, understatement, significant omission, antiphonal repetition and variation, austerity, verbal propriety: these are some of the technical devices or aesthetic values that he came to cherish, learned from others (Turgenev, Twain, Crane, and Conrad; Anderson, Stein, Ford, and Pound), but mastered for himself. With such literary priorities and with the priceless gift of his extraordinarily fine senses, especially of sight and taste, he developed an art capable of rendering outer and inner worlds alike, not with miniscule detail or complexity, but with startling, lucid simplicity. His achievements with language are on a par and of a kind with the great modernist poets of his generation. (pp. 195-97)

> Herbie Butterfield, *"Ernest Hemingway," in* American Fiction: New Readings, *edited by Richard Gray, Barnes & Noble, 1983, pp. 184-99.*

FRANK McCONNELL

In 1944 the Second World War was virtually over, the Axis will and neck all but terminally broken, Paris retaken, and Ernest Hemingway a picturesque but faintly absurd epiphenomenon of the tidal wave rolling toward Berlin. The most important American novelist of his time (but that time was passing), a sometime war correspondent (but his war correspondence was muddled), and a self-styled soldier on behalf of the civilized world altogether (though the civilized world, at that crucial moment, had very much larger things to worry about), he was lurching between bravery and silliness in a way that boded ill, indeed, for the remainder of his career. (p. 193)

For, just as the First World War virtually made Hemingway a serious writer—second only to T. S. Eliot as the chronicler and anthem-writer of a whole generation's despair—so the Second World War effectively marked the end of Hemingway's moment: or, at least, appeared to do so. 1944, the year of Allied victory and Hemingway foolishness was also the year of a new and startling talent in American letters. For while Hemingway was hoping to get into Paris without getting shot, Saul Bellow was publishing his first novel, *Dangling Man*. It is the fictionalized journal of 'Joseph', a Chicago-based intellectual and agonized draft-resister, a sensitive man who cannot even decide if he should enter the war to which Hemingway gave himself so enthusiastically. And it begins with what is essentially a refutation of the entire Hemingway mystique. . . . (p. 194)

In retrospect, there is something a little *too* cruelly parodic about . . . [the opening] sendup of the 'tough boy'. Much of our contemporary sense of Hemingway, after all, is precisely the sense of how far from 'tough' he really was, all along. Philip Young was probably the first critic to demonstrate compellingly what an ocean of self-doubt and vulnerability underlay that charade of gusto. But we do not, now, even need Young: we have the suicide. And in the glare of the suicide we can

see that Nick Adams, Jake Barnes, Frederick Henry, Robert Jordan and the whole Hemingway crew were always, in one way or another, weak men overcompensating desperately for their weakness. Bellow goes on . . . to observe that the hard-boiled writers tend to be deficient in the finer senses of despair and possibility. They are unpractised in introspection, he writes, 'and therefore badly equipped to deal with opponents whom they cannot shoot like big game or outdo in daring'.

Badly equipped, yes: but one wonders about that word, unpractised. Is anyone *well* equipped to deal with the monsters inside, as opposed to outside the head? And isn't the man who quests obsessively for beasts in view, for clear and evident monsters to kill, perhaps also the man who understands best how unkillable are the monsters within?

To ask such questions is, of course, to re-romanticize Hemingway, to return him—man and style—to the arena of melodrama he himself felt most comfortable in. But that itself might not be a bad thing to do. In the twenty-odd years since his death, Hemingway has been subjected to much more blatant, and much less understanding, kinds of parody than Bellow's treatment in *Dangling Man*. And most of the worst of it has come from the literary critics.

He was a sad man. His bluster, his bullying, his loud adventurism were a mask for a deep-seated insecurity. He was . . . a *miles gloriosus*, a braggart soldier who could be taken as a mere, absurd figure of fun. So much is true, and is eminently acceptable as an attitude to strike toward Hemingway in the American academy. For so much is, to put it bluntly, reassuring. One needn't fear the braggart soldier, just because he *is* only a braggart: we know that by the last act he will be revealed to be a coward, like us.

But, I want to suggest, Hemingway managed to be all those absurd, laughable things, and also to be something else, something permanently valuable for American letters. He managed to be a hero of consciousness, a writer and a stylist who made his cowardice, and his knowledge of his cowardice, the very stuff of his heroism and his endurance. This is, again, a cliché of a certain strain of romanticism: the Byronic. And yet the evidence of American fiction after Hemingway is that he, like Lord Byron, was the kind of truly great clown whose special talent is for making that kind of cliché vital and serviceable. (pp. 194-95)

Both Byron and Hemingway were dandies: ostentatious, elegantly vulgar men who made their insecure egotism the subject of their art. Hemingway's most lasting importance, indeed, may be that he was the first great American dandy of this century (only Whitman and Twain come to mind from the nineteenth century); and that, like all the truly valuable members of the sect (e.g. Byron, Baudelaire, Wilde, T. E. Lawrence), he shows us something of the cost, as well as the value, of the dandy's pose.

Francis Jeffrey wrote what is probably the definitive analysis of the literary dandy, in his review of Byron's *The Corsair;* and his analysis applies with striking appropriateness to the Hemingway persona, also. Why all this fascination, in a civilized country, with violence, adventure, and deep melancholia, he asks. Because the very civilization with which we have surrounded ourselves puts us out of touch with certain primal instincts, rages, and passions that are necessary to our souls. So that Byron's 'primitivism' is not primitivism at all, but the very sophisticated nostalgia of an over-complex victim of the modern age. (p. 196)

The dandy values style above substance . . . because he finds the world of substances empty, void, a sham. This is the Byronic abyss of cynicism, this is Lawrence's profound despair at politics, and this is Hemingway's celebrated *nada*. The dandy confuses the life and the work: to the degree that his heirs or his successors must laboriously separate the life from the work, in order to see the work afresh. The dandy loves to show off; loves to be sketched or photographed in the various poses and costumes of his dandyism: see the portrait of Byron in Albanian garb, or the photos of Hemingway, smiling over dead buffalo, in his white-hunter slouch hat and khaki.

And the dandy loves war. He loves war for the same reason he loves stylized brutality, because war *is* stylized brutality, the absolute triumph of technique over value and therefore the permanent, the true condition of humankind. Patton and Montgomery are two dandies *manqués*—neither wrote well—in that they both seemed to understand war as theatre, as a riotous backdrop for their own performing selves.

But the dandy loves war as he loves everything else: ironically. 'Abstract words such as glory, honour, courage, or hallow were obscene beside the concrete names of villages, the numbers of roads, the names of rivers, the numbers of regiments and the dates.' That, of course, is Frederick Henry in *A Farewell to Arms:* one of the most often-quoted, and one of the most crucial of Hemingway passages. Byronic romantic that he was, Hemingway believed in this wounded emptiness before he ever saw it manifested in the War (think about his jejune parody of Anderson's sentimentality in *The Torrents of Spring*). But he welcomed the War—and became its chief elegiac voice—just because it was the manifestation of the *nada* he carried inside himself.

And that gift of irony, that sublime hollowness, is his bequest to later American writers. (pp. 196-97)

Hemingway—as writer and as presence—broods with a particular urgency over the writers who come after him. I have said that the literary dandy confuses his life and his art. In Hemingway's case that confusion has been unusually productive, and unusually indicative of shifts in the national self-consciousness. We can take Hemingway as the first successful American romantic after Walt Whitman, the first man to identify a style of writing with a style of being in the world, and to make the indentification popular. He *was,* largely, the Byron of his age: so much so that 'Byronic' and 'Hemingwayesque' are the only two terms we normally apply as adjectives to the word, 'hero'. (p. 201)

If Hemingway is the American Byron, we might expect that his influence and his presence would be, like Byron's, both blatant and subtle. And so it has been. Indeed, like Byron, Hemingway has had at least as important an influence on so-called 'popular' culture as he has had on so-called 'serious' writing. His very short story, **"The Killers"**, from *In Our Time,* has provided a title and at least the bare bones of a script for two excellent gangster films (one directed by Robert Siodmak, 1946; one directed by Don Siegel, 1963). But beyond this explicit influence, it is also evident that Hemingway and the Hemingway style have exercised a strong, probably determinative, effect on the whole course of the American detective story in both film and literature.

Dashiell Hammett and Raymond Chandler are usually credited with being the originators of the American or 'hardboiled' style of detective writing. But, as the phrase itself, 'hardboiled' may indicate, both Hammett and Chandler—and their contemporary

heirs, Ross Macdonald, John D. MacDonald, Lawrence Sanders, and Stuart Kaminsky—would not really be possible without Hemingway. Indeed, the Hemingway hero is, by and large, the classic American hardboiled private eye; and the prose style that goes along with that peculiar figure is, by and large, the prose style Hemingway developed for a very different kind of character: i.e. the wounded, disillusioned veteran of the First World War.

'Doctors did things to you and then it was not your body any more', thinks Frederick Henry in *A Farewell to Arms,* returning to the Front. 'The head was mine, and the inside of the belly. It was very hungry in there. I could feel it turn over on itself. The head was mine, but not to use, not to think with, only to remember and not too much remember.'

'Only to remember and not too much remember': that may be the distinctive definition of the Hemingway style. For at its best it is a style that places a screen of words, a screen of short, ritualistically declarative sentences between the narrator/perceiver of the action and the horrendous, tragic quality of the action itself. Jake Barnes *is* impotent; Frederick Henry *does* fail to make a 'separate peace'; Robert Jordan *does* die needlessly; Santiago *does* fail to catch and bring back the great fish. It is a universe of defeat and disillusionment, and yet that telegraphic style . . . almost reconciles us to the horror, since it all but masks the horror within an ironic, primitive, unremembering articulation.

This is to say that the Hemingway style is a direct equivalent of the celebrated 'code' of the Hemingway hero; for both are deliberate reductions of the flux of life to the dimensions of an elaborate game—the one in the world of behaviour, the other in the world of utterance. And that, of course, is precisely the tone of the classic American detective story, whether in film or in literature. It is a deliberate unremembering: a recapitulation of the violent past that filters the horror of the past—the horror of betrayal, of failure, of psychic impotence—through the obsessive detail of its descriptive style. In American film this is the tradition of the *film noir,* from classics of the '40s like *The Maltese Falcon* and *Double Indemnity* to recent attempts at recapturing that special tone like *Chinatown, The Godfather,* and *Body Heat.* What all these disparate films have in common is their celebration of a certain tender cynicism, a certain conviction that, rotten at the core and inevitably entropic as human history may be, there is a kind of existential toughness, a bullet-biting disengagement that can survive the ravages of time with something like dignity.

That is the Hemingway tradition at its most popular—and perhaps also at its most dangerous. The self-advertising 'toughness' . . . can also be adopted at its most vulgar and arrogant pitch of *machismo*. No one, for example, could seriously argue that the popularity of the Hemingway hero is directly responsible for the obscene bullyism of America's venture into Vietnam. But, on the other hand, one could argue that the Hemingway vision is symptomatic of a certain strain of irresponsiblity, of cruelty, of dangerously arrested adolescence that is a permanent flaw in human character and a fatal flaw of empires. (pp. 202-04)

If indeed there are two Hemingways, the self-aggrandizing man and the writer who was a hero of consciousness, it may be fair to say that his heirs have learned an important lesson that he never learned: how to keep the two separate. And they have learned it, of course, from his example. His presence grows increasingly analogous to Byron's presence in the nineteenth century: a sensibility and a style impossible to ignore, and a personality impossible to emulate.

The work of Thomas Pynchon is the best and richest place to track Hemingway's ghost. Pynchon's two massive novels, *V* and *Gravity's Rainbow,* and his novella, *The Crying of Lot 49,* may be the most important fictions produced in America after the Second World War; they are certainly the most apocalyptic. Pynchon's vision is of an absolutely paranoid universe, presided over by giant cartels and international war machines whose grand design is to turn human beings into mere mechanisms. It is a vision of plastic entropy very like Joseph Heller's vision of the War in *Catch-22,* except that its grimness is more unrelenting and its comedy even blacker. And it is, of course, a vision directly inherited from Hemingway. In the same paragraph where Jake Barnes reflects on not too much remembering, he meditates on the surgery that has been performed on his knee:

> Valentini had done a fine job. . . . It was his knee all right. The other knee was mine. Doctors did things to you and then it was not your body any more. The head was mine, and the inside of the belly. It was very hungry in there.

This very famous passage might almost be the epigraph for all of Pynchon's fiction. . . . Life is increasingly encroached upon by the technologies of war and healing, both of which have the effect of robbing life of its vitality, and the only escape from that warfare is into the Switzerland of 'the head and the inside of the belly'. Pynchon's heroes . . . are the contemporary reincarnations of this mode. Benny Profane in *V,* Oedipa Maas in *Lot 49,* Tyrone Slothrop in *Gravity's Rainbow*—they are all weaklings, wounded and put-upon losers who are shocked into rebellion and a separate peace by the discovery that they are being turned into *someone else's* creation.

Their retreat is into style, into canniness . . . and into the kind of bitter, end-of-the-world charity that also characterizes the best of Hemingway throughout his career. In *V* the jazz musician McClintic Sphere articulates, in a brief scene, what may be the summary statement of the dandy's ironic humanism: 'Keep cool, but care.' And in the toughness and tenderness of that short line one hears echoes of all the sensibilities we have been examining, but with Papa at the centre.

No final assessment of the Hemingway presence can really be made, of course. This has been a century of triumph of partial visions, all of which have left their mark on what comes after. But Hemingway more than any American novelist of the age represented and lived the vocation of art as *risk,* as a deliberate gamble with one's chances for sanity in a mad world. And in that he became a paradigm—something much larger and subtler than an 'influence'—for the most serious American writers of the post-War years. His ghost, the ghost of his finest perceptions and strongest acts of literary courage, is a very unquiet ghost indeed. And its rumblings are an inescapable part of the splendid dissonance that is contemporary American fiction. (pp. 210-11)

> *Frank McConnell, ''Stalking Papa's Ghost: Hemingway's Presence in Contemporary American Writing,'' in* Ernest Hemingway: New Critical Essays, *edited by A. Robert Lee, Barnes & Noble, 1983, pp. 193-211.*

JAMES A. MICHENER

[*The Dangerous Summer*] is a book about death written by a lusty sixty-year-old man who had reason to fear that his own death was imminent. It is also a loving account of his return to those heroic days when he was young and learning about life in the bull rings of Spain. (p. 3)

In 1930 [Hemingway] had published in *Fortune* a longish, knowing article on bullfighting as a sport and an industry and this led, two years later, to the remarkable illustrated essay **Death in the Afternoon.** A disaster with the critics, who could not understand why a writer of his talent should waste himself on such arcane material, it quickly became a cult book. (p. 12)

In 1959 Hemingway went back to Spain and during that long, lovely summer when he was already beginning to suffer the ravages which would in the end destroy him—monomania about being spied upon, suspicion of his most trusted friends, doubt about his capacity to survive—this powerful man, so much a legend of his own creation, returned to the vibrant scenes of his young manhood. With great good luck he arrived in Spain just as two wonderfully handsome and charismatic young matadors, brothers-in-law, were about to engage in a protracted mano a mano, hand-to-hand duel, which would carry them and their partisans to most of the famous bull rings in Spain.

The matadors were Luis Miguel Dominguín, thirty-three years old and usually the more artistic, and Antonio Ordóñez, twenty-seven, the brilliant son of Cayetano Ordóñez (who fought under the name Niño de la Palma), whom Hemingway had praised in **Death in the Afternoon.** Fairly matched in skill and bravery, they were sure to put on a stupendous show. It proved to be a glorious summer, a most dangerous one, and Hemingway adopted that concept for the title of his three-part series, **The Dangerous Summer.**

Certain facts about the manuscript he produced are significant. *Life* had commissioned him to write a crisp, 10,000-word article about what it was like to go back, but he became so obsessed by the drama of the summer—much of which he superimposed upon a solid base—that he was powerless to halt the flood of words. The first draft ran to 120,000 words. The polished manuscript, from which the *Life* excerpts and the present book were edited, ran to about 70,000. (pp. 12-13)

My own judgment, then and now, was that Hemingway was unwise to have attempted this return to his youth; that he tried to hang far too much on the slender, esoteric thread of one series of bullfights; but that he produced a manuscript that revealed a great deal about a major figure of American literature. It is a record worth having.

To the lover of taurine literature, Hemingway's description of the historic Málaga corrida of 14 August 1959 in Chapter 11 is one of the most evocative and exact summaries of a corrida ever penned. It is a masterpiece. That afternoon the brothers-in-law fought an exceptional set of Domecq bulls, and the fame of the corrida still reverberates, because the two men cut ten ears, four tails, and two hooves. There had never before been such a performance in an arena of category.

Hemingway could have ended his manuscript on that high note, but because he was an artist who loved both the drama and the twists and turns of the arena, he ended his series with a corrida of much different quality, and on its tragiheroic note he ended what he had to say about the two men whose footsteps he had dogged like a star-struck little boy.

To those, and they are legion and of good sense, who will protest that Hemingway should have wasted so much attention on a brutal affair like bullfighting, or that a major publisher should resuscitate his essay, or that I am defending the work,

I can only say that many Americans, Englishmen, and Europeans generally have found in the bullfight something worthy of attention. That one of our premier artists chose to elucidate it both in his youth and in his older age is worthy of note, and I have never been ashamed to follow in his steps. (pp. 16-17)

Of course, bullfighting has elements of brutality, but so does surgery, hunting, and the income tax. *The Dangerous Summer* is an account of the brutal, wonderful, challenging things that happened during one temporada [bullfighting season] in Spain. (p. 18)

Hemingway's essay in its present book form will be treasured by two special groups of people. Devotees of American literature who revere Hemingway, of whom I am one, will find in these pages a confused farewell from a great and legendary figure. We witness his curious behavior toward his wife when he adopts various attractive young women during the feria at Pamplona. We see the longing with which he returns to those singing woods near Roncesvalles. We come suddenly upon his own assessment of *The Sun Also Rises:* "I've written Pamplona once and for keeps."

Certain passages reverberate with the authentic Hemingway touch. . . . (p. 36)

We get many insights into Hemingway's character, his bravado, his preoccupation with death, his intolerance toward inferiors, his wonderful generosity when he identified with someone he deemed worthy of respect. In these years he met two young American friends of mine, John Fulton, a Philadelphia boy who aspired to be a bullfighter, and Robert Vavra, a California lad who wanted to be an animal photographer. Listening to their stories, he impulsively drew from his wallet a check which he signed for one hundred dollars. When they tried to thank him, all he could say was: "Buena suerte."

But he could also be miserably aggressive. When he met another friend of mine, Matt Carney, who knew more about bulls than Hemingway, he goaded the young man into agreeing to a fist fight and then withdrew before any blows were exchanged. (pp. 36-7)

I cherish the throwaway paragraphs in which Hemingway reminds us of the sparse way he worked and of his refusal to use commas. . . . (p. 37)

[Most] treasurable bits have been retained, and they provide affectionate glimpses of the man and the writer. On the other hand, the purely bullfight passages have been sharply cut, so that the devout aficionado will miss details which he would have savored. Both the *Life* editors and those responsible for the present volume decided—properly so, I judge—to eliminate from most of the corridas the names and work of the matadors other than Dominguín and Ordóñez. But someone like me, knowing the matadors thus eliminated and their histories, regrets the loss of revealing paragraphs. . . . (pp. 37-8)

[Yet] whereas aficionados like me have lost something through the cutting, the typical reader has not. Indeed, a plethora of such material—and there are long pages of it left on the cutting floor—would so alienate the general public that the manuscript would probably never be finished by most readers if it were published intact. (p. 39)

> *James A. Michener, in an introduction to* The Dangerous Summer *by Ernest Hemingway, Charles Scribner's Sons, 1985, pp. 1-40.*

MICHIKO KAKUTANI

It's immediately clear why bullfighting exerted such a visceral hold on Ernest Hemingway's imagination. Bloody yet magisterial, the sport dramatized his own obsessions with violence and death, and it also struck him as one of the ultimate tests of a man's ability to sustain "grace under pressure." Like big game hunting, boxing and combat, bullfighting seemed to personify the aggressively masculine values that he'd championed in his fiction and his life, and he came to regard it as an art— the art of "killing cleanly," with courage and with style. . . .

[In his introduction to *The Dangerous Summer,* (see excerpt above), Mr. Michener] admits to feeling that Hemingway "tried to hang far too much on the slender, esoteric thread of one series of bullfights," and he strains to find reasons to justify this book: He quotes a punctuation-less passage that, he says, "reminds us of the sparse way [Hemingway] worked and of his refusal to use commas." . . . Certainly this discursive, flaccid volume offers the reader little else—except an unnecessary and unflattering portrait of Hemingway in decline, his masculine esthetic hardening into macho posturing; his fine, spare use of language dwindling into empty mannerism.

What Hemingway did in the 1920's was to invent a new style of writing, a style whose austerity and precision implied a moral outlook, a way of looking at the postwar world, as much as a narrative strategy. Unfortunately, however, as the author's own confidences were shaken, as he became increasingly trapped within the armor of his public image—"Papa Hemingway," great white hunter, confidant of generals and darling of the gossip columns—only an attitude and the outward remnants of a technique remained. As a result, the writing began to sound synthetic—*Across the River and Into the Trees* reads like a parody of the early Hemingway; and *The Old Man and the Sea,* while deftly controlled, has a reductive, vestigial feel to it, as though the author were just going through the motions of writing something remembered dimly from long ago.

Although a few of the action sequences in *The Dangerous Summer*—particularly those describing the fierce, balletic contest that took place in Málaga—demonstrate Hemingway's old gift for narrative, vast stretches of this book are laid down in painful pastiches of the writer's famous style. . . .

[One] must question the decision, on the part of his estate and his publishers, to issue a volume that does little but underline, again, the degree to which Hemingway's talent and psyche had come unraveled.

In the end, though, it's unlikely to have the slightest effect on the author's reputation. Hemingway believed that a writer is judged on the sum total of his work; and even such a flimsy book as this cannot detract from the achievement of *The Sun Also Rises* and his glorious, early stories.

> *Michiko Kakutani, "Hemingway at Sunset," in* The New York Times, *June 1, 1985, p. 34.*

JAMES F. VESELY

[*The Dangerous Summer*] is a book for men to read alone at night when it is possible to look back to the way it was in the summer of 1959 when Ernest Hemingway was still alive.

Hemingway spent that summer watching bulls die in the arenas of Spain and noting with detail the flourishes of two men who were dueling for some unspoken title as Papa's favorite killer of bulls.

This is also a book about traveling through Spain, a journey that for Hemingway could only have seemed a return to his greatness. For those who have been to Spain only through his eyes, it is another chance to see the country in his hard-polished way of describing the people, the dust and the *corridas* where men and bulls meet. . . .

Perhaps Hemingway scholars will dance away from *The Dangerous Summer* because it is an old man's last ramble, filled with too much detail for such a spare writer. In his last *corrida* with a typewriter, Hemingway could no longer discipline his wandering mind to write in his accustomed style, lean as grass.

The duel of the summer of 1959 was between Luis Miguel Dominguín and Antonio Ordóñez. Hemingway favored Ordóñez from the beginning the way a writer of boxing will sometimes see more skill in a fighter from the home gym. So not only is this a book about Spain and Hemingway's last paw into its earth, but it is also a book by a sportswriter who notices the movements of athletes. . . .

Papa was 60, and having trouble. He was not so right in the head any more. But later, while in Cuba working on the manuscript, he was able to pull together enough sinew to get some things right on paper. Chapter 11 of *The Dangerous Summer,* for instance, describing the way Dominguín and Ordóñez fought their bulls, gives us the twitch of the killing sword, the softness of the sand and the rush of the bull as it tries to hook into a matador's groin. It is quite powerful. . . .

[The] solidity of Hemingway's writing lingers on each page of *The Dangerous Summer.* The final chapters in particular are packed like a snowball; despite his age and declining powers, the man had enough strength left to pitch his story right into your gut.

> *James F. Vesely, "The Summer of Hemingway's Last*
> *'Olé'," in* The Detroit News, *June 9, 1985, p. 2K.*

WILLIAM KENNEDY

[In *The Dangerous Summer*] we have a great writer who set out to write an epilogue that turned into a book-length manuscript that died of unwieldness but was years later edited to its literary essence and became a book, truly, and is here with us now, and is good.

The epilogue was conceived by Ernest Hemingway in 1959 to conclude a new edition of his 1932 treatise on bullfighting as life and art, *Death in the Afternoon.* . . .

Hemingway's subject for the epilogue was the *mano a mano* (or hand-to-hand, a duel) between Spain's two leading matadors, Luis Miguel Dominguín and his brother-in-law, Antonio Ordóñez. (p. 1)

[Hemingway] turned both the *mano a mano* and the epilogue into a quest for, and a statement about, his own youth, his own heroism, his own art, his own immortality; for he was dying, psychically and artistically, and he seems to have intuited that.

Hemingway had begun his writing career in journalism and though he denigrated it in later life . . . , he never really left it. The last two books on which he worked so diligently before his death in 1961 were this one and his superb nonfiction sketches of Paris in the 1920's, *A Moveable Feast.*

He lived all his life with his own *mano a mano* between nonfiction and fiction, primarily believing that fiction was supreme. (pp. 1, 32)

His use of the novelist's tools—dialogue, scene construction, interior monologues—in *The Green Hills* was the style that such New Journalists as Gay Talese and Tom Wolfe would popularize so abundantly well in the 1960's. Hemingway's Ego Journalism, wherein the writer's point of view is more important to the reader than the subject matter, would be carried to splendid new heights in a later generation by writers like Hunter Thompson and Norman Mailer.

The Green Hills of Hemingway, however, was only a valiant failure. The book perished in the bush from overkill: too much hunting detail, too much bang-bang banality, insufficient story. By contrast, his two fictional stories of Africa, **"The Snows of Kilimanjaro"** and **"The Short Happy Life of Francis Macomber,"** were both masterworks.

By 1959, when Hemingway was 60 years old, his plan to write the bullfight epilogue trapped him anew in journalism, and he went to Spain. He followed the *corridas* (afternoons of bullfighting) in which Dominguín and Ordóñez fought the bulls. He worked manically at recording the small and large details of it all, wrote voluminously for five months and in September 1960 published three articles in Life.

I remember the articles. I looked forward to them but could not read them. I don't think I finished even one of the three. The great Hemingway had resuscitated all the boredom I'd felt in reading *The Green Hills.* This was also the response of Life's other readers. The articles were a disaster. Nevertheless, plans continued at Hemingway's publishing house, Charles Scribner's Sons, to publish a book from the material. For many reasons, chief among them Hemingway's suicide in 1961, the book remained a manuscript with elephantiasis until now, 26 years after the writing.

The Dangerous Summer is a singular document, as studded with ironies as it is with taurine terminology. What it is also, because of the long hiatus between inception and publication, is the centerpiece of a much larger composite work that readers may put together for themselves. The basic books required for this composite are Hemingway's *Selected Letters;* the autobiography of his widow, Mary, *How It Was;* A. E. Hotchner's peculiar but valuable 1966 memoir, *Papa Hemingway;* Carlos Baker's biography, *Hemingway: A Life Story;* James A. Michener's nonfiction book on Spain, *Iberia;* and a long and sensitive memoir by a Spanish journalist, José Luis Castillo-Puche, called *Hemingway in Spain.*

When they confront the subject of the aged Hemingway, from 1959 until his death and its aftermath, these books together offer a prismatic vision of the dying artist, a complex and profoundly dramatic story of a man's extraordinary effort to stay alive; so that when we come to Mr. Baker's succinct and powerful final sentence in the biography, we have a new comprehension not only of a writer's despair but of suicide as a not unreasonable conclusion to a blasted life. (p. 32)

> *William Kennedy, "The Last Olé," in* The New York
> Times Book Review, *June 9, 1985, pp. 1, 32-3, 35.*

REID BUCKLEY

I read *The Dangerous Summer* with a keen and very particular ache in my heart. Hemingway's fascination with bullfighting is easily explained, creativity being intimately of the stuff of death, sex, and religion. About religion he was callow and formally ignorant. And hubristic. Death therefore rode him like an obsession, and at the end, though he fought and defied Death, which stood for the extinction of his literary powers, it claimed him. Turning sixty at the time, Ernest Hemingway was desperately attempting to recover his youth and failing art. (p. 44)

[Hemingway] could be superb, and there are very good things in this book, good Hemingway, descriptions and narrations especially of action that only Hemingway could have written. Like Dominguín, he was great, a disciplined stylist, a *domador* of prose, at his best wonderful, but . . . he was making the mistake of coming back, of pitting himself in the arena again, and it did not work out; he must have recognized in his own overblown, overlong, overdramatic manuscript that he was through. The summer was dangerous for Ordóñez and Dominguín, but it proved to be mortal for Ernest Hemingway.

It makes me unspeakably sad adversely to criticize this book. Hemingway boasts in it that he had "written Pamplona once and for keeps." Well, maybe so. But I had freshly re-read *The Sun Also Rises* that summer, the novel that made him famous, and I was shocked by my disappointment. I thought that if the characters took one more drink *I* would throw up. How tedious the drinking is. The novel is ultimately juvenile, its perceptions banal. Hemingway's short stories, his *Old Man and the Sea,* and maybe *A Farewell to Arms* are "for keeps." . . . As he grew older he had become arrogant, and intolerant, and there was a spiteful nastiness in the man that transpires in such as his scathing remarks about a young fellow-American (not I; he didn't know I existed) who had the temerity to write about bullfighting too. Hemingway was nasty about F. Scott Fitzgerald, he was nasty about Dos Passos, he disparaged Faulkner. He could not bear to share the limelight. There is his absurd machismo, which translates too often into affected working-class solecisms (thats for whos, whos for whoms) and awful, tough guy prose that falls into bombast and groans with the hinges of empty significance, as in, "We tried to count the number of mountain ranges we had crossed and figure the mileage we had made and then we gave it up. It did not matter. It was made," end paragraph. (p. 46)

When the toughguyness isn't plain awful, it is awful and embarrassingly punk, as when he boasts of getting into a cage with a wolf, which we are given to understand does not harm him because the wolf comprehends that the great Hemingway is an admirer of wolves; or when he boasts of knocking the ashes off cigarettes Ordóñez held in his mouth with a .22 rifle "seven times" at a portable shooting gallery his wife Mary had hired for his 60th birthday party, with Ordóñez "puffing the cigarettes down to see how short he could make them." There is everything wrong with this. The trick isn't that impressive, the distance being under two yards, so there is nothing to boast about, other than Hemingway's steady hands after a heap of drinking and his and Ordóñez's stupidity.

The reader winces. There are times in *The Dangerous Summer* when the reader cringes, as when Hemingway's adulation of Ordóñez reduces a great writer to a fawning hanger-on. But we, who have received so many gifts of the imagination from Ernest Hemingway, must sympathize with him in his agony. And what about this exquisite *veronica* from a master of English prose? "Any man can face death," he says at one point, "but to be committed [as Antonio Ordóñez was that summer] to bring it as close as possible while performing certain classic

movements and do this again and again and again and then deal it out yourself with a sword to an animal weighing half a ton which you love is more complicated than just facing death. It is your performance as a creative artist each day and your necessity to function as a skillful killer." What *The Dangerous Summer* is about is the act of writing. (p. 47)

Reid Buckley, in a review of "The Dangerous Summer," in The American Spectator, *Vol. 18, No. 10, October, 1985, pp. 44-7.*

E. L. DOCTOROW

Since Hemingway's death in 1961, his estate and his publishers, Charles Scribner's Sons, have been catching up to him, issuing the work which, for one reason or another, he did not publish during his lifetime. He held back *A Moveable Feast* out of concern for the feelings of the people in it who might still be alive. But for the novel *Islands in the Stream* he seems to have had editorial misgivings. Even more deeply in this category is *The Garden of Eden,* which he began in 1946 and worked on intermittently in the last 15 years of his life and left unfinished. (p. 44)

The hero of this radically weeded *Garden of Eden* is David Bourne, a young novelist and veteran of World War I, who is traveling with his wife, Catherine, through Spain and France in the 1920's. The couple are on their honeymoon. In their small black Bugatti, they drive from the seaport village of Le Grau-du-Roi, where their stay has been idyllic, to Madrid, where the first shadows appear on their relationship. Catherine evinces jealousy of his writing. At the same time she demands experimentation in their lovemaking—she wants them to pretend that she is the boy and he is the girl. At Aigues-Mortes, in France, she has her hair cut short, and later she insists that he have his cut by the same hairdresser in a match to hers, so that he will look like her. David complies in this too, though not without some resistance and a foreboding of the ultimate corruption of the marriage.

Going on to La Napoule, near Cannes, they engage rooms in a very small hotel, where it is quiet because it is summer, the off-season in the south of France. One of the rooms is for David to write in. He has just published his war novel in America and received in the forwarded mail the press clippings and publisher's letter telling him he is a success. This news disturbs Catherine. The differences between them sharpen as she presumes to tell him the only subject worth writing is their life together on their honeymoon.

One day drinking at the cafe terrace of their hotel, they attract the attention of a beautiful young woman named Marita, who is very impressed by this darkly tanned couple with their newly dyed, almost white hair, and French fisherman shirts and linen trousers and espadrilles. She moves to their hotel. Catherine fulfills David's forebodings by commencing an affair with Marita. In further sign of her instability, she encourages David to embark on his own erotic relationship with the woman, who makes it easy by privately confessing to him that she has fallen in love with both of them. He succumbs. The ménage swims from the deserted beach coves of the area and sunbathes nude. David sleeps with one or the other as they designate in their time-sharing with him. Every day consists of a good deal of drinking, of martinis, which David himself mixes and garnishes with garlic olives at the small hotel bar, or absinthe, or Haig pinchbottle and Perrier, or Tavel, or carefully prepared Tom Collinses. The mixing and consuming of drinks is the means they seem to have chosen to adjust to the impact of their acts and conversation on one another.

It is Catherine who begins spectacularly to come apart under the strain. Becoming, in turn, bitter or remorseful, she either excoriates David for his relationship with Marita, or condemns herself for making a mess of everything. As a defense against the situation, and what he perceives as his wife's clearly accelerating mental illness, he begins to write the story he has been resisting for years, the "hard" story, he calls it, based on his life as a boy in East Africa with his white-hunter father. This story gradually intrudes on the main narrative as the boy David sights the bull elephant with enormous tusks that his father and an African assistant are looking for; he reports his sighting and lives to regret it, as the father tracks down the great beast and destroys it. The climax of the novel has to do with Catherine's reaction to this story, which David has written by hand in the simple cahiers used by French schoolchildren. A disaster then occurs which is the worst that can befall a writer as a writer, and the ménage breaks up forever, two to stay together and one to leave.

At first reading this is a surprising story to receive from the great outdoor athlete of American literature. He has not previously presented himself as a clinician of bedroom practices. Even more interesting is the passivity of his writer hero who, on the evidence, hates big-game hunting, and who is portrayed as totally subject to the powers of women, hapless before temptation and unable to take action in the face of adversity. The story is told from David Bourne's masculine point of view, in the intimate or pseudo-third person Hemingway preferred, but its major achievement is Catherine Bourne. There has not before been a female character who so dominates a Hemingway narrative. Catherine in fact may be the most impressive of any woman character in Hemingway's work, more substantive and dimensional than Pilar in *For Whom the Bell Tolls,* or Brett Ashley in *The Sun Also Rises.* Even though she is launched from the naïve premise that sexual fantasizing is a form of madness, she takes on the stature of the self-tortured Faustian, and is portrayed as a brilliant woman trapped into a vicarious participation in someone else's creativity. She represents the most informed and delicate reading Hemingway has given to any woman.

For Catherine Bourne alone this book will be read avidly. But there are additional things to make a reader happy. For considerable portions of the narrative, the dialogue is in tension, which cannot be said of *Across the River and Into the Trees,* his late novel of the same period, and for which he looted some of the motifs of this work. And there are passages that show the old man writing to the same strength of his early work— a description of David Bourne catching a bass in the canal at Le Grau-du-Roi, for example, or swimming off the beach at La Napoule. In these cases the strategy of using landscape to portray moral states produces victory.

But to be able to list the discrete excellences of a book is to say also it falls short of realization. The other woman, the third main character, Marita, has not the weight to account for her willingness to move in on a marriage and lend herself to its disruption. She is colorless and largely unarticulated. David Bourne's passivity goes unexamined by the author, except as it may be a function of his profession. But the sad truth is that his writing, which we see in the elephant story, does not exonerate him: it is bad Hemingway, a threadbare working of the theme of a boy's initiation rites that suggests to its own

great disadvantage Faulkner's story on the same theme, "The Bear."

In David's character resides the ultimate deadness of the piece. His incapability in dealing with the crisis of his relationship does not mesh with his consummate self-assurance in handling the waiters, maids and hoteliers of Europe who, in this book as in Hemingway's others, come forward to supply the food and drink, the corkscrews and ice cubes and beds and fishing rods his young American colonists require. In fact so often does David Bourne perform his cultivated eating and drinking that a reader is depressed enough to wonder if Hemingway's real achievement in the early great novels was that of a travel writer who taught a provincial American audience what dishes to order, what drinks to prefer and how to deal with the European servant class. There are moments here when we feel we are not in France or Spain but in the provisional state of Yuppiedom. A reader is given to conclude that this shrewdest of writers made an uncharacteristic mistake in not finding a war to destroy his lovers, or some action beside their own lovemaking to threaten their survival. The tone of solemn self-attention in this work rises to a portentousness that the 70,000 words of text cannot justify.

But here we are led back to the issue of editing a great writer's work after his death. As far as it is possible to tell from biography, and from the inventory of Hemingway manuscripts by Philip Young and Charles W. Mann, Hemingway intended *The Garden of Eden* as a major work. At one point he conceived of it as one of a trilogy of books in which the sea figured. Certainly its title suggests a governing theme of his creative life, the loss of paradise, the expulsion from the garden, which controls *The Sun Also Rises* and *A Farewell to Arms,* among other books and stories. Apparently there is extant more than one manuscript version for scholars to choose from. Carlos Baker mentions the presence of another married couple in one of the versions, a painter named Nick, and his wife, Barbara. Of the same generation as David and Catherine Bourne, Nick (is Adams his last name?) and Barbara live in Paris. And there may be additional characters. Presumably the material involving them is in a less finished state and easily stripped away to find the spare, if skimpy, novel we have now in print. But the truth about editing the work of a dead writer in such circumstances is that you can only cut to affirm his strengths, to reiterate the strategies of style for which he is known; whereas he himself may have been writing to transcend them. This cannot have been the book Hemingway envisioned at the most ambitious moments of his struggle to realize it, a struggle that occupied him intermittently for perhaps 15 years. And it should have been published for what it is, a piece of something, part of a design.

For there are clear signs here of something exciting going on, the enlargement of a writer's mind toward compassion, toward a less defensive construal of reality. The key is the character of Catherine Bourne. She is in behavior a direct descendant of Mrs. Macomber, of **"The Short Happy Life,"** or of Frances Clyne, Robert Cohn's emasculating lover in *The Sun Also Rises,* the kind of woman the author has before only detested and condemned. But here she has grown to suggest in Hemingway the rudiments of feminist perspective. And as for David Bourne, he is unmistakably the younger literary brother of Jake Barnes, the newspaperman wounded to impotence in that first expatriate novel. But David's passivity is not physical and therefore more difficult to put across. He reminds us a bit, actually, of Robert Cohn, whom Jake Barnes despised for suffering quietly the belittling remarks of women in public. Perhaps Hemingway is learning to dispense his judgments more thoughtfully. Or perhaps David Bourne was not designed as the hero of the piece at all.

With a large cast and perhaps multiple points of view, something else might have been intended than what we have, a revised view of the lost generation perhaps, some additional reading of a kind of American life *ex patria* with the larger context that would earn the tone of the book. There are enough clues here to suggest the unmistakable signs of a recycling of Hemingway's first materials toward less romance and less literary bigotry and greater truth. That is exciting because it gives evidence, despite his celebrity, despite his Nobel, despite the torments of his own physical self-punishment, of a writer still developing. Those same writing strategies Hemingway formulated to such triumph in his early work came to entrap him in the later. You can see this beginning to happen in his 1940 novel, *For Whom the Bell Tolls,* where implanting the conception of the book in geography, and fixing all its action in time and relentlessly understating the sentences, were finally dramatic strategies not formally sufficient to the subject. I would like to think that as he began *The Garden of Eden,* his very next novel after that war work, he realized this and wanted to retool, to remake himself. That he would fail is almost not the point—but that he would have tried, which is the true bravery of a writer, requiring more courage than facing down an elephant charge with a .303 Mannlicher. (pp. 44-5)

> E. L. Doctorow, "Braver Than We Thought," in
> The New York Times Book Review, *May 18, 1986,*
> *pp. 1, 44-5.*

JAMES SALTER

Hemingway believed deeply and demonstrated that there is a way to put words together that is invincible, but he is not a profound writer or one who had a great maturity. What he does offer and abundantly is an almost physical excitement and pleasure. His lines, unspoiled by ornament, are beautiful to see and hear, and the Europe and Africa that he discovered and brought to us are still remarkably fresh. Europe in particular remains his Europe, the Paris and Spain, the towns of northern Italy, the rivers, forests, waiters, and hotels. He and his work have remained so much alive that there have been 10 books published posthumously although only one of them was a novel, *Islands in the Stream.*

Among the manuscripts he left after his death was one he began working on in 1946, just after the war, and on which he continued to labor for 15 years. It finally reached a length of more than 200,000 words which is even more impressive considering how carefully he wrote, keeping track of his daily output like a bank clerk. This long, unperfected novel was called *The Garden of Eden.* It appeared to be unpublishable.... Then along came a young editor ..., not a Hemingway scholar, who undaunted by previous failures sat down and, working for nearly a year, unearthed what we may accept as the book that was always buried in the rubble. In his lifetime Hemingway submitted to almost no editing. Even Maxwell Perkins had to be diplomatic and cautious about seeking any changes he thought necessary. Tom Jenks, who was a boy of 10 when Hemingway died, has had unprecedented freedom but has worked in a very respectful way. No words that were not Hemingway's have been added. Certain things have been rearranged. The unnecessary has been discarded. The result is a sleek, taunting novel that possesses both Hemingway's considerable strengths and also his weaknesses.

The book is about a newly married writer, his beautiful, destructive wife, and another young woman, also beautiful, who joins them. In short, a *menage à trois* in the south of France. It is also about getting dark from the sun, hair cut very short, lesbianism, clothes, drinking, writing in the morning, and abnormal sex that involves what is called role change, generously hinted at but fortunately never fully described. Also embedded in the book, nearly complete, is a story the young writer, David Bourne, writes about Africa, his adored white hunter father, Juma the guide, and a great bull elephant they are tracking to kill. Here is the best of Hemingway, his great love and feeling for Africa and the wild, his knowledge of beasts and the hunt, and his ability to make these things win one forever. No one else writes like this and when they do they are imitating him.

The reader will also learn those things that once informed the unsophisticated: the feel of life in the south of France, how to eat gazpacho, the effect of drinking real absinthe, and how to look at paintings. What is marvelous about the book is the dialogue and pace—the hard, oblique, unreal lines that Hemingway's people often speak. What is less brilliant is the depth.

David Bourne is unmistakably the young, enthralled Hemingway, even to the khaki shorts, the love of drinking, and the cheap, lined *cahiers* in which he writes. As in **"The Snows of Kilimanjaro"** there is the writer writing about the writer, what he thinks, writes about and doesn't write about. Much is recognizable as what Hemingway thought and many times spoke of, and there are very few people who make you feel like writing or make you envy the writer as much as he does. (pp. 1-2)

As long as you can work, David Bourne says during the course of the long idyll and eventual crisis, nothing can touch you.

Catherine Bourne, on the other hand, stunning in both speech and appearance, barely 21 years old, is the sort of woman any sensible man would throw out in five minutes and in a large measure the book reveals the consequences of not doing so. Selfish, possessive, perhaps insane, she has money and takes more than one bite of the apple that means expulsion from paradise. "I'm your lazy naked wife," she says, and there are times one adores her. In the end there is a denouement, the loss of something irreplaceable, that is similar to a shocking episode in Hemingway's own life. Lady Ashley and Mrs. Macomber, to name two preceding goddesses, were achieved with briefer, more Picasso-like lines—Catherine tends to be on stage too long but like Lady Ashley she is the kind of woman who can destroy a weekend or a marriage and then without embarrassment reappear and with one fearless gesture or the gift of a dazzling line be irresistible.

Marita, the mysterious companion and rival, is like her in many respects, at least in her compliance, her way of talking, and her aplomb. She is also, we sense, just as possessive. One knows nothing of her past. She appears in a cafe, she is not entirely real. Neither of these women is, that's part of their power. They are Hemingway's women—he has created them and given them lines, we try not to believe them....

Hemingway was and remains an intensely masculine writer. It is surprising and a tribute to what he was able to achieve that the feminist revision of literature hasn't taken it as goal to whittle him down. This final novel had as its theme, in his own words, "the happiness of the Garden that a man must lose.'' Perhaps. Compared with things that matter, *The Garden of Eden* may be somewhat slight, but compared with things that don't it is solid and sure. It has the additional poignance of being probably the last novel that will reach us from the master's hand, his farewell, mannered, thrilling, spoiled, pure, loyal to its monumental maker and itself and with no knowledge of coming darkness. (p. 2)

James Salter, ''Ernest Hemingway's Last Farewell,'' in Book World—The Washington Post, *June 1, 1986, pp. 1-2.*

WILFRID SHEED

Up to now, it has been generally assumed that [*The Garden of Eden*] wasn't published in the Fifties because it was so bad. This is possible—although the book isn't so much plain bad as what the kids would call ''weird.'' But there are at least a couple of other perfectly good reasons for Hemingway's reticence in the matter.

The first might be simple decency, or caution. The story is, superficially at least, a heavily mythologized version of the breakup of his first marriage, and both women involved, Hadley and Pauline, were not only still alive, but attempting to mother his children. In *A Moveable Feast,* Ernest inadvertently summarizes the plot thus: ''An unmarried woman becomes the temporary best friend of another young woman who is married, goes to live with the husband and wife and then unknowingly, innocently and unrelentingly sets out to marry the husband.'' And there, if you throw in Martha Gellhorn, Lady Brett, Jane Mason, and the rest of the menagerie, you have it.

In *The Garden of Eden,* the husband's seduction is entirely artificial, and way beyond libel: it is turned into a sort of erotic charade, until nothing remains but a bitter taste, the essence of the affair. Even by the late Forties, Hemingway was long past doing this as well as he wanted to, and at times the dialogue is so remorselessly kittenish that one imagines a person at the next table sorely tempted to empty a pitcher of ice water over all three (fortunately there is no person at the next table—this being the Garden of Eden), but the book does do something, and becomes more intense and disquieting than anything in the novels Hemingway *didn't* consider too bad to publish after the war.

In fact, *Eden* has haunting links with his prewar work, links which he snapped smartly, and perhaps intentionally, with his decision not to publish. He had just finished liberating the Ritz and all that, and the feel of prewar Europe still comes fresh off the page, as it never would again (the watery graveyard of Venice in *Across the River and into the Trees* marks the end of all that). The principals are all young again, and what is even better, Papa, the bore's bore of the Fifties, seems to be nowhere in sight, or even any dauntless old men in fishing boats. The hero, David Bourne, is actually closer to Jake Barnes: to wit, he is passive, rueful, flawed, and much more dominated than dominating.

Or so it seems at first. In fact, Papa is absent only in the sense in which Adam tries to make himself scarce from the original Garden of Eden legend. ''The woman tempted me and I did eat.'' All his life, Hemingway had a diabolical trick of coercing his women to act out his dreams for him (or imagining they had if they hadn't) and then treating the result as acts of the eternal feminine. Nobody ever really talked like that, the reader thinks—but Pauline Pfeiffer did, almost on contact with him;

Martha Gellhorn wrote stories just like his; and poor Mary Welsh saw him through his last days babbling the lingua *finca,* or Indian baby talk, that he'd spun around them. *Tout ensemble* his wives must have sounded like Buffalo Bill's roadshow featuring Sitting Bull.

Meanwhile, the author having thus created these women truly and well in his own image, could safely withdraw and leave them to it or, as in this case, simply go passive all over, and let it look as if *they* were corrupting *him.*

The Garden of Eden opens upon a young couple, David and Catherine Bourne, who are living a life of carnal innocence (nice work if you can get it) on and around the French and Spanish Rivieras. Hemingway could still make the sensual life mesmerically appealing for a few pages, but ultimately nerve-racking. (The Garden of Eden is a bore. It needs a good snake.) His paradise here seems to consist of a lot of eating and drinking—as a novelist, Hemingway could never pass a bar without doing something about it—along with swimming for distance (the booze does no harm if you get enough exercise, explains David) and what sounds like highly calisthenic lovemaking. And then sleep, really good sleep. The latter may seem like an odd item in a honeymoon couple's agenda, but it may also be one clue among several that our hero is not quite as young as advertised.

The drinking may be another. Not only David but both his women put away enough hooch each day to make writing one's signature a problem, let alone a great novel. But fictionally speaking, it is only stage booze, warm tea, and has no significant effect on the novel, except to fill up space. What it does for the author is another story. One imagines old Hem hunched over his famous writing board in the bone-dry dawn of Cuba, unable to imagine a Garden of Eden without a fully stocked bar.

Anyway, as noted Hemingway tended to transfer his own wishes onto his women, and both his slender wife and his petite, snake-in-the-grass mistress are as thirsty as dockwallopers throughout; no one ever has to force a drink on *these* girls, not even Papa, whom they have by now absorbed entire.

They do have to force some things on David, though. Catherine, whom he calls Devil from the outset—perhaps to establish that Woman will be both Satan *and* the snake—decides without preamble to get her hair cut like a boy's, and just like that asks David to be *her* girl for just one night. Smitten with love, and riddled with manly confusion, he complies to the fullest extent imaginable—which suggests another, possibly conclusive reason for not publishing. Hemingway might have had a hard time calling himself Papa after this fling at being the Little Woman—whose run incidentally is extended over several days and nights *passim.*

David having bitten into the apple decides to go on chewing helplessly, and the next thing we know Catherine has wheedled him over to the hairdresser to have his head cropped close to match hers, and dyed silver so that the two of them will even *look* interchangeable. Reading this can give one a strange start, because everyone knows—he scarcely bothered to hide it—that it was Hemingway himself and his fictive representatives who were forever cajoling their women to crop their hair, or grow it out, so that they can alternately be boys and girls as the spirit moves. So this goes a little beyond the usual crass displacement of responsibility, and into territory where at last the author can no longer hide. Like some medieval saint, David naturally feels that any temptation so vile must come from outside; but he has no doubt either that he has conspired fully in his own corruption, and he blames no one. It's hard to tell what will set a man off, but David feels irredeemably damned with this second cut and dye. And as if to show how far an author will go to get his material, Mr. Meyers in his [*Hemingway: A Biography*] reports that Hemingway himself "accidentally" dyed his own hair blond in the course of writing the book.

In the midst of all this, washing and rinsing enters the new girl, who significantly will not go along with the tonsorial games, although she goes along with just about everything else. After one chance meeting in a cafe, Catherine greedily foists "the girl" (as she is mostly called) on their happy home. In a spirit of pure inquiry she herself has a lesbian trial run with "the girl," with a view it seems to a *ménage à trois* with herself in the middle. This is more than all right with the girl, who instantly points her cap at David, promising to be his girl and Catherine's girl and anything else that's doing. But David, in a burst of primness, draws the line at this.

One feels a mild shock to find David drawing the line at anything, but this apparently is it, like the word "upstart" that sets Groucho off in *Duck Soup:* the spirit of Papa finally rises from the woolly depths to condemn all this foulness, and out of the Garden the three scamper. David falls in love with the girl, who has after all been practically flung at his head (what's a man to do?) but he feels rotten about it. His only consolation now is his Work ("From the sweat of thy brow wilt thou toil").

Well, the Garden was never much of a place for work anyway. Catherine hates the stuff because it tends to break the spell. Both she and the girl break Catherine Barkley's old indoor record for repeating how happy they are, as if the state at its fullest requires constant awareness of itself. Perhaps it does. But exhausting. In this light, David's scribbling becomes not only damnably distracting but a sort of treachery, and a terrible risk.

Bernard Shaw's hobbyhorse about women vs. artists gets a thorough workout every time David sneaks off to his study and it's not always to the artist's advantage. Early on, Catherine flies into a sarcastic rage when she sees David poring over his press clippings. "Who are you now, you or your press clippings?" she asks later in bed, and we feel she has got Hemingway dead to rights. At another point, the author allows her to make rather startling fun of him. David has just said, "The sea was very good," and Catherine purrs back, "You use such interesting adjectives. They make everything so vivid." David gets even with her a few pages on when she refers to the girl as his "paramour." He goes into a fine little cadenza on the word, to wit, "I had absolutely no hope of ever hearing it in this life . . . to have the sheer naked courage to use it in conversation," etc. Brittle stuff, and some distance from Sloppy Joe's in Havana. The picture of Hemingway beating his women by outbitching them, by outwomaning them, takes us back for the last time to the world of *The Sun Also Rises,* the last book in which the author felt free to be himself.

Un-Papa-like exchanges like the above (and they are not infrequent) are enough to break the heart of a Hemingway admirer. It seems as if the boy wonder was making a last stand in this book against the old rumpot, winning a page here and losing three there. The result is wildly, almost zanily, uneven, and as such may serve as the last missing link between Nick Adams and Colonel Cantwell.

Ominously, the girl is mad about David's work, and can't get enough of it. This is how his girls will be from now on. Catherine, contrariwise, in a last truly flamboyant gesture, burns every scrap of his writing that she can get her hands on, declaring that it is no good anyway and that he should start all over. This, for Hemingway, is like finally coughing up a fish bone. Many years before, his first wife had left a suitcase full of his early work, plus copies, on a train for a few minutes, and had returned to find them all gone, and Hemingway had been brewing up theories about it ever since, none of which included accident. Sexual jealousy, artistic jealousy (all the *copies,* for Christsake!)—he juggled every dark possibility before arriving at the combination in this book, presumably his last word. After the fire, David feels at first as his creator must have felt (it rings terribly true), that it is all over, that he can never get it back now. Then in despair he returns to the story he has been working on, an African hunting yarn that has been running through the book as a kind of counterpoint, and he finds that *it* is still there, it will always be there when he wants it. Alas, poor David, poor Hemingway.

Obviously, a great deal depends on the quality of this African story. If it is going to save his life and career, it had better be pretty good—had better, in fact, have been written by the young Hemingway, just to be on the safe side. Fortunately, it is not bad at all. Who knows from what mysterious notebook the old master dug it out (there tends to be a mystery about his notebooks), but it contains all the sights, smells, and textures of Hemingway at his best. And it has enough left over to serve a double purpose, that of offsetting the childish corruption of the Riviera with the deeper and more interesting kinds of corruption available to men on the hunt.

Warts (if that is word enough for certain cancerous blemishes) and all, *The Garden of Eden* is surely the novel Hemingway *should* have published after the war—supposing, that is, that he still knew how to edit as sharply as Tom Jenks at Scribner's, which seems possible. The parlor Freudians, who had been baying after Hemingway for some time anyway, would have had a field day of course, but it would only have been a day. In the longer run, this complex journey into a fetish would have served Ernest far better than the crude analyses that nowadays are slapped on him routinely and randomly by his inferiors. Whether it speaks to you or not, Hemingway's recurrent theme of communion under pressure between bully and victim, hunter and hunted, man and woman, so that each becomes the other, deserves better than being labeled the theme of a "closet queen." No doubt he asked for it, with his playground fag-baiting, but what's the point of giving it to him now? If a major, but very dead (as he would say), writer is slighted, the loss isn't his.

Before *The Garden of Eden* can be recommended less reservedly than that, I suppose the usual warnings should be read out about the later Hemingway prose. All the primary adjectives are here in force. "Dark," "cool," "cold," "hard," and "very" all of the above. Such words are obviously meant to make you see more clearly, and perhaps they do, except that you keep seeing the same thing or types of thing. It's like being trapped in an endless exhibit of primitive paintings. Why, one wonders again and again, did so gifted a man chain himself to so narrow a method? (pp. 5-6)

Wilfrid Sheed, "A Farewell to Hemingstein," in The New York Review of Books, *Vol. XXXIII, No. 10, June 12, 1986, pp. 5-6, 8, 10, 12.*

Stefan Heym

1913-

(Born Hellmuth Flieg) German novelist, short story writer, translator, editor, and poet.

Heym is regarded as one of East Germany's leading contemporary authors. His war novels, written during the 1940s and early 1950s while he lived in the United States, have an anti-Nazi focus, while his later novels, written in East Germany, utilize parable and satire to comment on modern political circumstances in Soviet bloc countries. Although Heym received the German Democratic Republic's National Prize in 1959, his recent works are considered too controversial for East German publication and have been issued only in the West.

Heym fled Germany when Adolf Hitler took power in 1933. He immigrated to the United States in 1935, became a citizen, and served in a psychological warfare unit of the United States army during World War II. His first novel, *Hostages* (1942; republished as *The Glasenapp Case*), is a suspenseful narrative about a group of Czech civilians who are falsely accused of murdering a Gestapo officer. Although some reviewers considered the book overly moralistic and simplistic, Heym was generally praised for his insight into the psychological states of his characters and his sincere, passionate style. Orville Prescott called *Hostages* "vastly superior, tense, tautly constructed, swift and terrible." In *Of Smiling Peace* (1944), a similarly didactic and moralistic work, Heym celebrates American idealism and the Allied intervention of World War II. This novel, set in North Africa and presented from the viewpoint of a propaganda officer, is an examination of war and its effect on men of differing attitudes and backgrounds. *The Crusaders* (1948), Heym's most ambitious and complex war narrative, centers on the efforts of American soldiers to overcome Nazi forces despite greed, moral cowardice, and divisiveness within their own troops. *The Eyes of Reason* (1951) is a historical novel involving three Czech brothers with conflicting political views just prior to the Communist occupation of their homeland.

Heym left the United States and settled in East Berlin when McCarthyism and the Korean War escalated in the 1950s. In the majority of his later works, Heym addresses the problem of remaining true to one's beliefs and honestly expressing one's opinions in a country which prohibits even mild dissension. Most of these novels, which were written in English and later translated by Heym into German, are allegorical satires in the manner of Voltaire, Jonathan Swift, and Bertolt Brecht. *The King David Report* (1972) is set in biblical times and reflects Heym's position as an East German writer. The plot of this work involves an ancient historian who is asked to produce an "accurate" but agreeable report on King David for David's successor, King Solomon, who wishes his own views established as incontestable truth. The novel, which Heym called a historical and biblical work "charged with political meaning," is indirectly concerned with Stalinism and the corruption of ideals. Similar themes are evident in the short story collection *The Queen against Defoe and Other Stories* (1974), in which Heym explores such topics as historical persecution and East German party politics. In *Five Days in June* (1977), Heym analyzes the brief period in 1953 when East German workers

ignored government edicts and went on strike for the first time in twenty years. Heym again examines the Communist writer's conflict with authority in *Collin* (1979), the story of a dying East German novelist whose final act is to expose the concealed crimes of his government's elder members.

Heym's first East German novel to attract widespread attention in the United States was *The Wandering Jew* (1984), a complex work of theological satire set concurrently in the sixteenth century, the present, and an eternal, timeless region. The novel concerns the efforts of the title character to persuade a latter-day Christ to take responsibility for the world into his own hands and avert human misery rather than directing the wrath of God against innocent people. This work, which alternates several story lines, was praised by D. J. Enright as a "brilliant theological fantasy, simultaneously profound and comic, spiritual and fleshly." Heym's next novel, *Schwarzenberg* (1985), concerns a group of German anti-fascists who make a futile attempt to establish an independent republic in a small, unoccupied border region of Czechoslovakia.

(See also *Contemporary Authors*, Vols. 9-12, rev. ed. and *Contemporary Authors New Revision Series*, Vol. 4.)

ORVILLE PRESCOTT

[*Hostages* is] a book that unquestionably will be ranked with the finest novels of 1942, if not of a much longer period. . . .

It is the best novel I have seen about life under the Nazis, the undying revolt of the supposedly conquered peoples and the methods by which the Nazis strive to rule. Compared with it, most other novels about similar material seem like mere romantic thrillers or overly optimistic examples of wishful thinking. . . .

Hostages is the story of the events immediately following the disappearance of a drunken German lieutenant from a Prague bar. It looked at first like murder, but even after the Gestapo sleuths discovered it was suicide they preferred, for devious reasons of their own, to insist on calling it a murder. They arrested all the patrons of the bar, among them five of the eight principal characters of this novel. The hostages were a curious group who shared one cell and soon learned to know each other all too well in their few remaining hours of life. One was a psychiatrist, one a boastful actor haunted by a sense of inferiority, one a young newspaper man, one a powerful industrialist and former Cabinet member who had traitorously "collaborated," and one a tough, superficially naïve but actually wily lavatory attendant and former tramp who was an active member of the underground.

What happened to them, the methods chosen by the Gestapo to break their spirit and learn their secrets, how they met the terror of death and death itself, is the major theme of Mr. Heym's tragic, pitiful story. A minor and complementary one is the story of two Czech patriots who remain outside the prison walls. . . . The remaining important character is the Gestapo chieftain, a brilliantly done characterization showing all his pride and weakness, his bestial shrewdness and complete viciousness.

Hostages is violent, harsh, excruciatingly painful. It is revolting, sickening and hard to bear. It is as frightful and true and heroic as is so much of life in so much of the world today. As a novel it is unusually distinguished on at least three counts. One is its thrilling suspense, its terrific excitement, its great dramatic power. Another is its brilliance and fascination as a psychological study of diverse characters under the fear and certainty of imminent death. The last is a more general and moral significance, for like all writers of stature and significance Mr. Heym is acutely aware of moral values. So *Hostages,* which tells of seven Czechs and one Nazi, never forgets that they are only a minute fragment of a greater tragedy, and that all over Europe, from Narvik to Suda Bay, from Cherbourg to the bloody rubble of Stalingrad, innocent men and women by scores and hundreds are imprisoned, tortured and murdered every day in retaliation for acts of war which they did not commit.

> *Orville Prescott, in a review of "Hostages," in* The New York Times, *October 16, 1942, p. 17.*

ROBERT PICK

In a Prague riverfront café, a German officer vanishes. There are five Czech people on the spot: the psychoanalyst Dr. Wallerstein, the actor Prokosch, a young journalist, the big Quisling industrialist Preissinger, and Janoshik, the toilet keeper. They all are seized as suspects by the Gestapo. . . .

The situation [of *Hostages*] is grandiose, and no-one can blame Mr. Heym for not living up to it. It would indeed require the power of a Dostoievsky to give an adequate presentation of these five people, who not only know they have to die shortly but also come to realize gradually that there wasn't any crime committed at all, and that they are nothing but tools in a ruthless and cynical campaign.

The characters of the unfortunate captives are not too happily chosen by the author: three of them are intellectuals, one is a realistic politician, and none of them has been living the uneventful life of plain Czech folk. Only by confronting—as reality does—the hideous hostage system of the German conquerors with average men and simple family life could the monstrosity of the German method have been fully exposed. But these five are very peculiar persons. The actor and the newspaperman are mutually entangled in a rather unfortunate affair, and Mr. Heym goes to some lengths in portraying their unique troubles. He is, quite obviously, fond not only of the romantic—which makes him frequently run into melodramatic and rhetorical *scènes à faire*—but also of sex and brothel scenes which he depicts with a naturalism which can hardly be surpassed.

By intertwining the original plot with an "underground" yarn, the author, apparently, wanted to give his story both a wider background and a deeper political meaning. But, unfortunately, he seems to have been carried away by his sense of the theatrical. . . .

The most inspiring figure of the novel is Janoshik, the toilet keeper. True, he owes most of his outward traits, especially the quixotic habit of telling seemingly pointless anecdotes, to Jaroslav Hašek's immortal "Good Soldier Schweik." But, in the end, he grows and gains the originality and the real stature of a hero—not only in the theatrical sense of the word. Here, the author has not failed. He has succeeded in making credible the fact that a simple Czech handy-man uses, in his last breath, the very words which Jan Hus spoke centuries ago at the stake.

Mr. Heym has remarkable skill. In spite of the shortcomings and the patent unevenness of this first novel, both his power of imagination and his psychological insight are notable. Nor is there any doubt as to the sincerity of his wrath. His trouble is that his own ardent desire for retribution gets the better of him as a narrator.

> *Robert Pick, "Hostages to the Dark Ages," in* The Saturday Review of Literature, *Vol. XXV, No. 43, October 24, 1942, p. 20.*

HAROLD STRAUSS

There is good melodrama which need not blush in the company of the season's best fiction. The author accepts his characters for what they are, personifications of good or evil, and gets on with the business of history. But there is also moralistic melodrama such as *Hostages,* in which the author's first concern is to insist, and insist again, that his heroes are good and his villains evil, as if their qualities were still open to question.

Actually, his characters have made their decisions long before the opening scene. They do not grow or change. In other times another author might ask how Janoshik, the sturdy Slav peasant, grew into his role of leadership, or how Lev Preissinger, the capitalist, managed to worm his way into a position of power in which he could toady to the Nazis. Even Reinhardt, the chief of the Gestapo in Prague, who had charge of the twenty hostages seized for the murder of Lieutenant Glasenapp in a waterside café, might afford interesting material. But Mr. Heym makes him so much the weakling and fool, the coward and pervert, that he is a perilous opponent only because of his ability to torture his prisoners brutally.

The situation revolves around the fact that Glasenapp was not really murdered, but committed suicide out of loneliness. Because the Nazis look greedily on the coal mines of Preissinger, and also because of their quaint notions of disciplining the Czechs, they wish to conceal this fact and go ahead with the announced execution of the hostages. On the part of the Czech patriots, the objective is to expose the utter irresponsibility and viciousness of the Nazi measures by broadcasting the truth to the people. And Janoshik has a further objective of finishing a job to be done by the underground—of blowing up certain munitions barges in the Danube on their way to the Russian front.

The story is particularly concerned with five of the hostages and two patriots outside. In his cell the utterly craven Preissinger cannot believe until the very end that his position and money will not save him. He twists and squirms like a worm on a pin, and as a last desperate act accuses Janoshik of the non-existent murder, simply on a class basis. With him is Prokosch, the actor, who disintegrates in a different way, and, because of his egoism, tries to confess to the murder. Then there is Lobkowitz, a newspaper man and the lover of Prokosch's wife, who is the only one who understands Janoshik's heroism. And finally, there is the curious psychiatrist, Dr. Wallerstein, who prepares a learned article on the behavior of his fellow-prisoners which he tries to persuade Reinhardt to have published after the execution. Of the two outside, one is a lovely Czech girl, Milada, who possesses the clue to the death of Glasenapp, and thus becomes Reinhardt's victim; and Breda, who engineers the dramatic broadcasting of the truth about the suicide. . . .

In the last few pages the story rises above itself and comes to a sufficiently moving conclusion.

Harold Strauss, "A Czech Patriot," in The New York Times Book Review, *October 25, 1942, p. 28.*

JAMES GRAY

Of Smiling Peace is the testimonial of a recently adopted American to the youth, the strength and the idealism of his new country. War is the laboratory in which this alert and explorative young novelist undertakes to analyze the essential traits of Germans, Frenchmen and Americans. The scene is Algiers. To it come the innocently exuberant men from Wisconsin and Illinois and no chemical dissympathy could be greater than theirs for the Vichy collaborationists and the Nazi spies with whom they come in contact.

In the central figure of his novel, Stefan Heym has created a counterpart of himself. Bert Wolff, European born, has survived mistreatment by the Nazis, has fought in Spain and finally has reached America, there to become a citizen and an officer of Intelligence in the Army. This parallels the author's own odyssey which has led him by a circuitous route back to Europe in active combat duty as a sergeant of a psychological warfare unit.

Lieutenant Wolff has his first personal triumph against his ancient enemy when he presides single-handed over the surrender of the whole Nazi Armistice Commission. . . . [Dutiful

to what they believe to be their Fuehrer's orders], they allow themselves to be herded into a truck and led away to safe-keeping.

But there are others who are less bound by military decorum and more adept in a kind of slimy improvisation. . . . There are spies like Jerez, who lives by selling the shabby tatters of his intellect to any buyer. Most particularly there is Major Lizst, the Nazi, who despite the fact that he is intellectually a rubber-stamp and morally a coward, still manages to fancy himself as the perfect model of the superman.

The narrative resolves itself into a struggle to determine which of these implacable opponents shall survive. The American officers and men of whom Heym has created a large and likable company flounder at first in the muddy waters of international diplomacy. This is as much because of distaste for the noisome environment as from ineptitude. But in the end their rugged gift for survival makes them outlast even the most cunning and contemptuously treacherous of their rivals for domination.

Lieutenant Wolff's own final fulfillment comes about, as Stefan Heym seems to suggest, because America has refreshed his European mind. Despite their blunders, the novelist says in effect, Americans are the pure in heart and society must look to them to create an innocent new world.

Of Smiling Peace is perhaps less moving than Stefan Heym's first book, *Hostages*. That is because its mood is less tense and tragic. But the new novel is likely to give more satisfaction to a greater number of people. Our contentious world has offered writers a quite legitimate opportunity to try to blend the best features of *War and Peace* with those of a novel by E. Phillips Oppenheim. Stefan Heym is deeply, soberly and intelligently concerned with the great issues of life and death, of honor and human dignity. But he can also tell a racy story of intrigue and flight. As Major Lizst makes his hairbreadth escapes and wriggles with a verminous agility out of every trap Stefan Heym achieves many scenes of tension and excitement, tossing in a few that are pure Hollywood as well.

Of Smiling Peace is an immensely likable and intelligent study of spies, slaves and men of honor. It makes the best of the two worlds of ideas and of adventure.

James Gray, in a review of "Of Smiling Peace," in New York Herald Tribune Weekly Book Review, *October 22, 1944, p. 8.*

NONA BALAKIAN

It has been said—and perhaps there is some truth in it—that after five years few of us really know the total meaning of war. . . . Stefan Heym, famed author of *Hostages,* makes this startlingly clear in [*Of Smiling Peace*], a tumultuous novel that some will find hard to digest except in small doses.

A soldier and a European, now serving as a technical sergeant in a "psychological warfare company," Mr. Heym approaches the mechanics and politics of war in no uncertain terms. In his "experienced" hands, the familiar sordidness becomes more sordid: war seems no longer—as we are used to thinking of it—a temporary interruption of peace but inherent in the natural order of things, with no beginning and no end. His setting is itself suggestive. It is French North Africa in the days of Darlan and our first invasion force. Thieves and traitors walk the streets of a frightened Algiers; behind guarded portals, panic-stricken officers of the Nazi Armistice Commission brutally lambaste each other one moment before the final hour....

Now and then, we catch a glimpse of something wholesome— a word, a thought from an American soldier; from "Shadow," who ingenuously sums up the war as "grown-up men playing the games of wild children"; from Lieut. Bert Wolff, who has fought in Spain and knows that "victory must consist in the proof that the enemy was weaker than he, morally, spiritually and ideologically."

But it is the Nazis and their collaborators who set the tone of the book. The tide of the war has turned.... Maj. Ludwig von Liszt, who embodies all the diabolical traits of all Nazis ever created, is "suddenly hypnotized by the discovery that there existed tanks which could move against him." His immediate impulse is to flee. But first he must carry out the one scheme left to save the German army in Africa....

It would be possible to dismiss *Of Smiling Peace* as melodrama a shade higher than Hollywood level, were it not that Mr. Heym gives more than an occasional hint of his interest in the psychological and moral problems involved. His conclusion that the anti-human system of the Nazis must eventually be its own destruction is, of course, plausible. But to truly understand and convey the inner weakness of the enemy, one must set it up against the greatness of the force opposing it—and this is where Mr. Heym, to this reader, seems to fail. Perhaps because positive qualities of character are harder to objectify, the American soldiers never really come to life. They speak eloquently now and then, but when the time comes to act, their heroism appears unreasonable or inadequate. This could suggest that the real strength of the American soldiers lies not so much in their physical courage—which is all Mr. Heym really attempts to show—but, as John Hersey so clearly made evident, in their basic faith in Man, and, in the end, in their natural resistance to war itself.

Nona Balakian, "The Days of Darlan," in The New York Times Book Review, *October 29, 1944, p. 22.*

JEROME D. ROSS

[In *The Crusaders*] Mr. Heym has set out to do a panoramic picture of the war, his canvas stretching from Normandy to the final victory and aftermath in Germany. This is a thickish book, for the author has grappled with almost every conceivable phase of the struggle.... [Many] dissimilar events and situations are fastened together by a shaky framework of plot and by a handful of soldiers and civilians who work overtime dashing about in tanks and jeeps to turn up, breathless but on schedule, in episode after episode.... Mr. Heym has sought to depict the war by means of the cumulative method, and the result is a long drawn-out, ponderous serial. For all the wealth of incident and for all his characters' rapid movements in this most mobile of wars, *The Crusaders* remains curiously static.

Chiefly, the fault lies in Mr. Heym's failure to develop his main characters. They are mostly American officers and G.I.s assigned to psychological warfare work, plus a few combat troops, a familiar egomaniac general (this time equipped with a whip instead of pearl-handled revolvers), and a smattering of women, including a ubiquitous gal-correspondent. Stereotypes to begin with, each one reacts with distressing uniformity throughout.

The book's premise is founded on the thesis that among the American liberators you found crusaders and you found scoun-

drels, good people and bad people, and somehow the war was fought and won while the two groups were at loggerheads. There are the idealists like Lieutenant Yates and Sergeant Bing who believe in the Four Freedoms and kindred texts which they read to the Germans over front-line loud speakers.... On the other hand, men like Colonel Willoughby, Captain Loomis and Sergeant Dondolo aren't merely bad; they are very very bad. Sergeant Dondolo, to escape a black market rap, railroads a buddy to the mental ward. Loomis' crooked deals in Germany are foreshadowed in his treatment of a nice girl in Paris. As for Colonel Willoughby, he amply proves his pragmatism—he promotes a vast international steel cartel with pro-Nazis; he chisels into Loomis' petty thievery and, as if this were not enough, he carries on shamelessly with a hussy....

From Normandy to the banks of the Elbe, these types go on repeating their behavior patterns, laudably or culpably as the case may be. It is the endless repetition of them that makes the book so boring. One can find no fault with a number of the background situations. Mr. Heym has a keen reporter's eye. His descriptions of a concentration camp, of German townspeople trapped in a mine of tanks and armored vehicles on the move, are all strikingly vivid. But these situations lose their force the minute the main characters appear.

Jerome D. Ross, "Panoramic Picture of the War," in New York Herald Tribune Weekly Book Review, *September 12, 1948, p. 8.*

RICHARD PLANT

At first glance it seems as though Mr. Heym's title [*The Crusaders*] must be ironical. American soldiers, so we read in the leaflets of Propaganda Intelligence, are the crusaders, smashing the Nazi machine, bringing freedom to the oppressed of Europe. Yet while the war is still being fought, Major Willoughby ... starts his promising business deals with those Nazi collaborators and partisans, the Rintelen trust and Prince Yasha Bereskin....

[The question posed is: Is America] justified in crusading for a moral cause or in telling anyone in Europe anything?

Lieut. David Yates and Sergeant Bing of Propaganda Intelligence, the protagonists of this large-scale, complex and splendidly brought-off novel, believe we are. Although during four years of fighting they have learned what war does to victors and conquered alike, they do not believe it was fought for a caprice. It is to Mr. Heym's credit that neither Yates, a former instructor of German, nor Bing, the German-born broadcaster, are given to editorializing. During a broadcast at the front, Sergeant Bing is killed by one of our own planes—one of the many perverse and tragic ironies to be found in Mr. Heym's story.

However, Lieutenant Yates and his superior, old Colonel DeWitt, survive to see the SS leader with his schemes of a revenge war blown to bits. They catch up with the racketeers in their own ranks, witness the removal of the Nazi Mayor and, finally, watch a group of emaciated, pitiful DP's settle in the luxurious mansion of the Rintelen estate. Perhaps, Mr. Heym seems to say, there existed a few honest crusaders among us, knowing they could never achieve their goal, but trying, nevertheless. At the close of the book, the title doesn't sound so painfully derisive. (p. 4)

During its first two-thirds, the events are centered on Sergeant Bing, an expertly rounded character. Slowly we are made to understand the core of his anxiety; does he, the German-born, possess some of those traits he abhors in the Nazis? Isn't he efficient at his job precisely because subconsciously he understands part of what he hates? There is no answer to this; but as long as Bing is alive, the novel has a sun around which to revolve, with all its larger and smaller planets neatly in place. When Bing is killed, it appeared to me as though a central power had vanished, and people and plots overwhelm the author.

This is not to imply that Mr. Heym's writing loses its power in these latter chapters. Throughout, he keeps his fervor, his anger, his compassion under control; his restraint makes the grim episodes the more effective. . . . (pp. 4, 37)

General Farrish is only one of the many acidly drawn characters of *The Crusaders,* but he is the one most likely to be remembered because of his resemblance to [General Patton]. . . . Mr. Heym, a former soldier, pulls no punches, and his gallery of brass and rank is as vivid as it is sardonic. The note of bitter resignation, so prevalent in books on this war, can be found, too: the men who really do the job never get the credit.

Undoubtedly, the book is too long. Perhaps the author could have left out the parts dealing with the occupation. Furthermore, although Mr. Heym was born in Europe, the weakest figures are the Nazis, such as *Obersturmbannfuehrer* Pettinger. They never come to life. While Mr. Heym has caught splendidly all sorts of GI's, in speech and mannerism, he is ill at ease with most of his European characters.

At times I couldn't help noticing how very much the book resembled a novel of World War I. It has become fashionable to say that our younger generation of soldiers fought the last war without illusions. This, I believe, is itself a delusion. The good novels that have come out of the last war have dealt with one sort or another of disenchantment.

When the soldiers of *The Crusaders* take Paula camp, even the most inarticulate GI feels he is eradicating a poisonous sore, something that should never have happened in our civilization. Those same GI's knew later on, that somewhere, on the way, we muffed our victory. The good novels of World War I and World War II are similar as far as this basic issue is concerned. Mr. Heym's novel, not only a good book but a brilliant one, proves it again. (p. 37)

Richard Plant, "A Study of GI Good and Evil," in The New York Times Book Review, September 12, 1948, pp. 4, 37.

MALCOLM COWLEY

[*The Crusaders*] is the story of a Propaganda Intelligence Unit that landed in Normandy just after D-Day and followed the foremost American troops across France into Luxembourg, where it took over a powerful radio station, and then through Germany to the first meeting with the Russians. . . . [Much of the book] is invented, and if the inventions are not always fresh, they are at least varied and abundant. The novel has everything, in the Hollywood sense of the phrase. It has combat, pursuit, cruelty, sex, a host of characters including General Patton and a story that plunges ahead like an armored division to the final pages. . . . It also has a thesis and a sound one, namely, that the war was fought against evils some of which exist in our own army and nation.

There is only one thing the novel lacks: the respect for his characters and for truth as opposed to bombast that one has a right to expect from a writer of Heym's talent. I spent a whole day reading *The Crusaders* . . . and finished it with a feeling of resentment at having wasted my time. The end of the book is so unmistakably contrived, the characters are so hastily maneuvered into one place and then the evil ones are so miraculously confronted with evidence of their evil-doing that the whole story dissolves into Technicolor. Even the honest and powerful passages, of which there are many, become falsified as one looks back at them; and the sound thesis is weakened by being presented with something less than literary integrity. *Gone with the Wind* was bigger and better and truer to its author's purpose. (pp. 33-4)

Malcolm Cowley, "In Love with Germany," in The New Republic, Vol. 119, No. 13, September 27, 1948, pp. 33-4.

FREDERIC MORTON

[The setting of *The Eyes of Reason*] is Czechoslovakia, dangling between East and West. The time, 1945 to 1948, a queasy period after the liberation yet before the Communist coup. The protagonists are three brothers, bedeviled heroes, who represent the clashing values of the mid-century. . . .

[It is strange] that *The Eyes of Reason,* so far Mr. Heym's most profound novel, should impress one also as his most static. It lacks the suspense of *Hostages,* nor does it possess much of the sharp-etched effectiveness of *The Crusaders.* The characters seem too carefully planted into their positions; frequently one wishes that their postures were less stiff, their dialogue more fluid. But as the story unfolds and the threads of plot and subplot converge, such flaws recede. The movement of the whole fuses life into less vividly projected parts. In the second half of the book the full measure of the author's social understanding becomes apparent. One begins to savor the resolute impartiality he applies to issues that explode daily into angrier headlines. It takes considerable courage to dissect dynamite with Mr. Heym's thoroughness. And if the characters in *The Eyes of Reason* never attain the depth of fully realized individuals, they do emerge in the end as important and representative social types, masterfully analyzed.

One objection may be raised: in his pursuit of non-partisanship Mr. Heym occasionally overshoots the mark. His version, for instance, of the Communist coup in Prague will be accepted by few Americans. But the significance of the novel is not wholly dependent on the accuracy of its historic framework; nor need the reader agree with all of the author's conclusions to appreciate the impact of a message well worth remembering.

Frederic Morton, "A Novel of Czechoslovakia in Crisis," in New York Herald Tribune Book Review, February 4, 1951, p. 4.

MARCIA DAVENPORT

If it could be presumed that Czech people are deficient in sentiment, in personal or atavistic or national emotion, in warmth, in humor, in historical pride, in gaiety, in color, in common-garden humanness, then to some readers [*The Eyes of Reason*] might be believeable. But the book will not be believable to any person who knows its scene, its chronology, and the prototypes of many of its characters. That may be a special objection; the more general fact is that this is a novel without a heart, contrived by a cold, dialectically disciplined brain.

Mr. Heym has spent substantial amounts of time in Czechoslovakia, both in Prague and in a provincial town upon which he models the place he calls Rodnik. The most recent of his sojourns has been since the Communist seizure of the country in 1948. . . . No foreign writer can live and work in this or any other Communist state without . . . official blessing or be free of the minutest secret-police surveillance. These facts are the key to *The Eyes of Reason*.

The early chapters are somewhat disarming, seemingly drawn with tolerance and a broad philosophical point of view. Mr. Heym pursues the problems and the fates of three brothers who, each having fought the Nazis in his own way, return to their birthplace in Czechoslovakia in 1945 to begin their lives anew and to take part in the construction, reconstruction, or destruction—according to one's own politics—of the Republic. Joseph, from the Czech Squadron of the RAF, is Mr. Heym's capitalist and reactionary. Karel, from the Nazi concentration camps, is his Communist—strong, simple, unconfused. Thomas, from refuge and war work in the United States, is the intellectual, the confused liberal, the anachronisitic man of frustrated good will whose torments all too clearly are destined from the first to end in suicide.

The scene moves between the industrial town of Rodnik, where the brothers are the inheritors of a family glass factory, and Prague, which Mr. Heym rather against his own design, one suspects, contrives to make as dreary and dour as its present masters have done. Nowhere does Prague's magic, its beauty, its tragic tenderness, its wealth of historical atmosphere touch this icily materialistic book. The three years of struggle, confusion, treachery, and tragedy culminating in the debacle of 1948 are the span of the novel; but to the author and his key characters 1948 was no debacle.

A considerable mass of facts, mostly of such political detail as to be uninteresting to the ordinary reader, fills this long and not very readable book—facts used or abused with the utmost cynicism. In the later chapters the veil not immediately perceived dissolves from the face of these facts, and Communist jargon rolls forth with increasing momentum. (p. 12)

Czechoslovakia as the three Benda brothers and their subsidiary characters live in it and deal with it post-1945 is a horrifying mess of disorganization, dishonesty, and disruption, but that is not the work of the Nazis; that is capitalist reaction endeavoring once more to enslave the people. The final chapters of the book, which cover the 1948 crisis in Prague, are with certain clumsily artificial incidentals a straight pro-Communist version of what to the Reds is victory, to Western civilization catastrophe.

Further, the non-Communist politicians—whose shocking failures of statecraft, vision, and courage are bitter truth enough—are caricatured in a snarl of preposterous conspiracy. The Communists emerge shining white, their Gottwald strong and simple, a man of no oratory, no grandiose gestures. Mr. Heym appears not to realize that some of us are witness in the flesh and to the facts.

Even more cynical is his curious dragging in of the tragic march of the university students, trying vainly to see President Benes. To Mr. Heym they were a disorderly, bragging mob duly subdued by earnest, patient police and by a platoon of workers, hard-faced and armed with carbines. To us who stood in that

street and watched a drilled rabble of ruffians with red flags round their arms—armed civilians—roughing up thousands of young men and women, Gottwald's "new country of the working people, a happy country" is a place of terror, slavery, and death, no hint of which peeps through *The Eyes of Reason*. If the book were written with any sign of real passion or with real art it might be terrible even if preposterous. As it is it does not manage even to be insidious. (p. 13)

Marcia Davenport, "Prague without Magic," in The Saturday Review of Literature, *Vol. XXXIV, No. 6, February 10, 1951, pp. 12-13.*

ELIZABETH JANEWAY

Stefan Heym has taken as the scene of his new novel, *The Eyes of Reason,* Czechoslovakia in the months between its liberation from Nazi rule and the Communist coup of February, 1948.

His publishers have chosen the word "controversial" to describe Mr. Heym's book, and it is easy to see why—for Mr. Heym's sympathies are clearly with the Communists. "Controversial," nonetheless, is the wrong word. . . . Falsification is not "controversial." Mr. Heym's retelling of the tragedy of Czechoslovakia is one long exercise in distortion, in omission, and in begging the question.

Mr. Heym consistently ignores the fundamental fact of Soviet imperialism. In the face of this omission, even his absurd misrepresentation of the American point-of-view dwindles to mere caricature—shocking, but relatively insignificant. No Soviet pressure was put upon the Czech Government, Mr. Heym would have us believe; and this being the case, he reduces the struggle of Czech patriots to retain their independence to the effort of a group of corrupt and greedy men to keep themselves in power for their own ends.

But what, the novel-reader may ask, about the book? Granted that Mr. Heym's grasp upon political reality may be weak (to say the least), may he not have written an interesting and exciting story? We need not accept Tolstoi's view of history to enjoy *War and Peace*, or Dostoievski's morality to be moved by *The Brothers Karamazov*. Cannot a book which is morally bad be aesthetically good? Alas, Mr. Heym spares us the interest of this argument. His book is bad clear through. It is so bad, indeed, that it exerts a kind of horrid fascination. One comes to read it, after a while as one reads a case history, discovering as chapter follows chapter, the all-too-familiar symptoms of the patient's obsession. . . .

[The story is] overlaid with much incident with many vignettes of the wholesome working class and the sly and grasping bourgeoisie. Interestingly enough, however, Mr. Heym never allows a confrontation between the democratic and the Communist point-of-view. Whenever we think that we are at last to have an argument, the scene shifts and opponents walk past each other talking to themselves. . . .

Perhaps Mr. Heym believes that democracy has no arguments. Or perhaps, one is tempted to think, he is aware that even his American readers (whom he surely conceives as being the stupidest people in the world) would notice what was going on if he allowed communism to argue down democracy. So he begs the question. It is one of the most irritating features of this exasperating book.

Two observations remain to be made. First, *The Eyes of Reason* is a valuable book in the sense that its denials, distortions and omissions can teach us a good deal about the kind of mentality we are up against in our struggle with communism. And secondly, though Mr. Heym uses his American to make a mock of American freedom of speech, how deeply vital in spite of all his protestation his own calculation upon it must be—to have led him to write for American publication a book which insults democratic beliefs on every page.

> Elizabeth Janeway, "The Case of a Novelist," in The Christian Science Monitor, *March 1, 1951, p. 15.*

RUSSELL DAVIES

What a curious tale the career of Stefan Heym has made. Quitting Hitler's Germany and joining the US forces, he served through some nasty times in wartime Europe, consoled perhaps by the prospect of extracting some good literary mileage from his baleful experiences; but hardly had he begun to reel off his best-sellers back in the US when the Korean War and Mc-Carthyism got going. The disgusted Heym not only sent back his medals to that admittedly unlikely champion of the literary conscience, Dwight D. Eisenhower, but thumbed his nose at the Western world in general by taking up residence in East Berlin.

The delight of the Ulbricht boys in welcoming him to the Democratic Republic was tempered a little when he began to write again, in English, translating himself laboriously into his native tongue. Nowadays he is ostracised, his work appearing only in the West—all of which adds up to a life of ceaseless outrage and indignation that has left Heym feeling understandably peeved.

It is to his credit, then, that Heym has managed to work up such a temperate, even agreeable satire as *The King David Report* in illustration of his own predicament. Not until the last pages, when the historian Ethan ben Hoshaiah receives the judgment of King Solomon on his efforts, does the book's message take on the tone of the Party Spokesman. . . .

Heym concentrates pretty strictly on the course of Ethan's researches, his attempt to produce, at Solomon's behest, *The One and Only True and Authoritative, Historically Correct and Officially Approved Report on the Amazing Rise, God-fearing Life, Heroic Deeds and Wonderful Achievements of David, son of Jesse,* a work referred to in the text, as often as not, as 'The Report on the Amazing Rise and so forth.' This little throwaway mannerism is strongly reminiscent of Heinrich Böll's style in his recent *Group Portrait with Lady,* and it is interesting to note that the cover of this work of Heym's is conspicuously plastered with enthusiastic comments by Böll; and no wonder, for Heym's investigative-narrative style here . . . is remarkably similar to [Böll's]. . . .

It may be that a new, classifiable form is beginning to organise itself here, the multi-faceted Novel of Uncertainty, or Doubt-Ridden Documentary, wherein the author impersonates a bemused researcher doomed to discover only a dismally garbled version of the hoped-for objective truth, plus a daunting realisation of the limits of his own capacity for certainty. This is all Ethan ben Hoshaiah gets, to be sure, for the nearer he gets to the full conviction that the late King David was an intolerable opportunist and despot, not unlike J. Stalin to modern eyes, the less likely it is that he will be assisted, much less encour-

aged. Cynics will doubtless argue that the difference between Ethan and Heym is that the former was 'commissioned,' or ordered, to fulfil his task by a similar tyrant, Solomon; whereas Heym seems to have chosen, in a fit of disillusionment, a foreseeable doom. But however oddly willed the irony of his situation, he has certainly produced a literary oddity to match it.

> Russell Davies, "Uncertainties," in The Observer, *July 29, 1973, p. 31.*

THE TIMES LITERARY SUPPLEMENT

The King David whose history is recounted in I Samuel 6 to I Kings 2, is a figure romantically sprung from obscurity who becomes a mighty ruler capable of great mercies; a sinner greatly repentant; an ancestor of Christ, and later, in the writings of the Fathers, actually a type of Christ. . . .

[Research] commissioned by King Solomon from Ethan the historian [in *The King David Report*] uncovers another David altogether. Annals, army records, letters, songs, legends and testimony of eye-witnesses contribute to a picture of a ferocious killer who was also a poet, an unscrupulous overlord who shaped a nation from a handful of restless tribes. Ethan's investigations fasten on the several anomalies in David's story, the most obvious being the tradition by which David came first to Saul's court with healing music, compared with the one which has him first appearing as the shepherd boy with the sling. Zadok the priest and the other members of the *Report* commission smoothly enjoin that such contradictions shall be played down, and a blend of plausibility and acceptability be the great aim. . . .

Stefan Heym has said elsewhere that he sees David as a revolutionary, succeeded by the despot Solomon. In a postscript to the *Report* he calls it both a biblical and an historical novel, and "a story of today charged with political meaning". In West Germany it has been greeted as a satire on the writer who seeks truth among all the perils of a dictatorship. In fact it is stylistic tricks that make the points and carry the book along, rather than any intensity of political parallel. Cutting from Ethan's own account of his inquiries, to the depositions of witnesses, to the minutes of committee meetings . . . , with a great many other devices the composite picture takes shape. But the modern applications are resting shallowly in these devices; they do not spring naturally from the sum of the book's implications. The sub-biblical cadences are trying, and one or two outbreaks of rather inferior stream-of-consciousness are jarringly inappropriate to the half-flippant, half-elegiac tone of the whole.

> "David Re-done," in The Times Literary Supplement, *No. 3726, August 3, 1973, p. 893.*

ALVAH BESSIE

Born in 1913 in Chemnitz (now Karl-Marx-Stadt), Stefan Heym immediately attracted Nazi attention as an anti-Nazi poet when Hitler came to power. He went into exile—first in Czechoslovakia and then in the United States. In New York he met and married Gertrude Gelbin, who helped him perfect his English and who was his editor until she died in East Berlin in January 1969. His first novel [*Hostages*]—written in English—was a modest success [and] was sold to the movies. . . .

[*The Crusaders* is] indisputably one of the best novels about World War II on the Western front, written by any participant in any language. For Heym served in the Army of the United States, was decorated and became an American citizen. But when he received "Greetings" from President Truman at the outbreak of the Korean "police-action" and was ordered to report to his reserve unit, he said to hell with it and, with his American wife, left for Europe.

He returned to Czechoslovakia, and then, in 1951, to the German Democratic Republic . . . , and Heym himself had every reason to expect to be an ornament of the new Socialist regime, together with Arnold Zweig, Heinrich Mann, Ludwig Renn and Anna Seghers.

He did become such an ornament, winning the National Prize in 1959, but he is said to have considered the award a bribe for discreet silence about his unpublished novel [describing events of the 1953 East German uprising, *A Day Marked X*]. Heym had not been silent under Hitler, nor under reactionary pressure in the United States of the McCarthy days when his novel *The Eyes of Reason* was attacked as Communist propaganda because it was a startlingly acute (and sympathetic) portrayal of the transition from capitalism to socialism in Czechoslovakia. (p. 88)

Never a member of any Socialist party, [Heym] is a dedicated Socialist and at the same time an articulate, cogent and unabashed critic of socialism in action. His criticism was beginning to get him in trouble even before 1956 when a column he was writing for the *Berliner Zeitung* was closed down. In 1965 Heym was denounced—together with other [German Democratic Republic] writers, poets and editors—at the eleventh plenum of the Socialist Unity Party, and he became a nonperson: no longer permitted to publish books or articles, nor even to speak in public. He has lived since then on his savings, his domestic royalties, which were small, and his royalties from both the capitalist and Socialist worlds, which have been considerable at times. And he has kept right on writing.

But times change and regimes change with them. The withering away of the cold war; the thaw between West Germany and the GDR following the Willy Brandt *démarche*, which finally recognized that the Socialist third of Germany was there to stay; the necessity for trade and improved relations on all levels between West and East—all these shifts in international relationships brought about changes in what Marxists call the superstructure of the GDR: a relaxation of controls, however small. . . . (pp. 88, 90)

Today, [Heym's] last three novels—*Uncertain Friend,* about Ferdinand LaSalle, one of the founders of German social democracy who broke with Karl Marx; *Queen Against Defoe,* which deals with the persecution of the great satirist for fighting censorship; and his latest, *The King David Report,* are all certain of publication in the GDR.

Anyone reading these books will find that the man who fled Nazism at 20, then fought it in uniform, who abandoned his adopted land, where he had been successful, when it embarked upon imperialist adventures in Korea—returning his citizenship papers, his commission, his medal and citation to President Truman—is still the same cantankerous character whose self-assurance has annoyed many people; whose charm has endeared him to many more; whose resistance to criticism has disturbed not only his critics but his friends, and whose insistence on writing in English, then translating himself into Ger-

man has infuriated nationalistic German publishers, not least because he charges them for the translation.

Certainly the cultural leaders of the GDR would know what Heym was up to in all these works, as well as in *The King David Report,* even if he had not told them in the postscript to the novel. For this is a story that operates simultaneously on three levels. It is a short Biblical epic and is fascinating on that level alone; it is an often hilarious satire on the Old Testament and its people (derived from the Saul-David-Solomon legends of Samuel and Kings); and it is an audacious modern political parable concerned with Stalinism, the uses of demagoguery to attain power, the corruption of good ideals in that struggle, purges and show trials to enforce conformity of opinion, the sort of nepotism that flourishes under all governments, the rewriting of history to suit those who hold the reins of power, the role of an honest man in a crooked society, the role of an honest *writer* in a rigid regime determined to tell him how to think, the making of an un-person and his rehabilitation.

All these facets of life today in our capitalist and Heym's Socialist world are examined in the story of a Biblical personage, Ethan ben Hosiah, a poet and historian who is called in by King Solomon to write (under the aegis of a royal commission, of course), [The King David Report]. . . .

Like all honest writers, Ethan is consumed with the need to write the truth—and the parallel need to keep his head on his shoulders, feed his family and live as long as possible. The danger he faces becomes apparent immediately, for he discovers that David was not only a great soldier who unified the tribes of Israel and forged a nation in the midst of revolution, but he was also a thorough-going bastard, thief and killer; a man capable of being a whore to both men and women; a hypocrite who talked directly to God and did not hesitate to murder his own son to consolidate his rule.

In the telling of this tale Stefan Heym demonstrates not only his diabolical ingenuity as a satirist—he is of the order of Defoe and Swift—but also as a stylist in English who is a match for those other foreigners, Joseph Conrad the Pole and Vladimir Nabokov the Russian, who abandoned their native tongues to write in ours.

He is more than that. He has been a nonperson in two countries, who has been rehabilitated in his own lifetime without going through the obligatory ritual of "self-criticism" or confession by the Establishments of this world—Socialist, capitalist or in transition. (p. 90)

> Alvah Bessie, *"The Captains and the King's Remains,"* in The Nation, *Vol. 218, No. 3, January 19, 1974, pp. 88, 90.*

JOHN WILLETT

[*The Queen Against Defoe*] is more a testimonial to the deserved success of [Heym's] last novel, *The King David Report,* than a book which can stand on its own feet. Certainly it displays many of the talents that so sparkled in that work, and as a result most of it is well worth reading. But it is a very slight book and seems to have been thrown haphazardly together.

The four stories occupy in all about a hundred pages. Half this space is occupied by the title novella, which has enjoyed a certain reputation since its rejection in East Germany on the ground that it "might be misunderstood". It proves to be a lively and all too convincing pastiche account of the measures taken by the Earl of Nottingham, through a nasty group of creeps and hirelings, to punish Defoe for his *Shortest Way with the Dissenters* and discredit him in any way possible. . . . [It] gives a perfectly credible picture of the motives and actions involved in the control of writings embarrassing to political leaders, whether past or present, and ends very satisfactorily with the sacking of the unsuccessful provocateur.

Minions come and go; the system carries on. This is the depressing moral of the second and third stories, which are perhaps essays in the sort of thing Defoe might be writing today. In the simpler of the two the theme is the changing reactions of a Czech scientist's wife to her new neighbour, a powerful and sinister public figure who seems to have been one of the prosecutors in the Slánsky case; the sting lies in the fact that his fortunes are changing too. **"A Very Good Second Man"** is more ambiguous, describing not merely the hogging of all credit for a major engineering project by an officially favoured incompetent but also the "very good second man's" strange acceptance of this. Why? "Because I'm a responsible citizen of a Socialist Republic", he tells the narrator; and again at the (seemingly "positive") conclusion: "because I happen to be a Communist!" The lesson seems to be that party discipline leads intelligent men to accept phonies; but it remains unclear just who in turn accepts this. Does the author? Do the East German Communists? The neatness of the story is deceptive.

The book is rounded (or squared) off by a mildly amusing fantasy about sex change . . . and an "encounter with Stefan Heym", under the ludicrous title **"The Creator and the Commissars"**, in which the author speaks like a man of genuine independence:

> QUESTION: Is creativity flourishing in the German Democratic Republic today?
>
> HEYM: Yes, and I think the very restrictions we have contribute to that. People are thinking much more. . . .

John Willett, "Hired Hands," in The Times Literary Supplement, *No. 3825, July 4, 1975, p. 732.*

JULIA O'FAOLAIN

Stefan Heym is driven to deviousness for political reasons. The title novella in **The Queen Against Defoe** is an exhilarating and persuasive account of Defoe's treatment at the hands of undercover agents working for the Earl of Nottingham, who had been enraged by the publication of *The Shortest Way With The Dissenters* and thought he scented a conspiracy. . . .

Heym's other stories here are direct and less effective. One feels an essay struggling to break out of the short-story form and it is a relief to find the author frankly speaking with his own voice in the final piece [**"The Creator and the Commissars"**]: an interview where he discusses censorship in Germany and America. . . . Here he is stimulating, acute and obviously no conformist. This sent me back to the shorter stories wondering about their sententiousness. I think the fault is with the form. The brief short story would seem to be a perfect medium for reflecting the fragmented consciousness of our bourgeois world. Like a bit of broken mirror, it can catch shifts and doubts, render one or more of Tennessee Williams's humorous or horrid perceptions, but is too frail to carry the ideological coherence striven for by writers like Heym.

Julia O'Faolain, "Cats on a Hot Tin Roof," in The Observer, *August 3, 1975, p. 21.*

LORNA SAGE

[**Five Days in June**] is a fictional analysis of those days in June 1953 when workers in East Berlin went on strike for the first time in 20 years—and when (so the blurb suggests) Stefan Heym first realised his own 'equivocal' position in East Germany. Certainly it's a novel shaped by political self-searching. Heym is focusing on those particular events because then (for once is the ironic implication) ordinary individuals felt close to the centres of power, and therefore it's an episode that must yield some relevance to the present, not least in justifying Heym's vocation as a critic from the inside.

He sees the brief struggle staged in factories and bombed-out streets less as a confrontation between State and workers than as a self-division in all the participants. East Berlin, in the background, sets the tone—a mixture of 1984-style squalor (foul food, irrational shortages, slum housing) and sudden space, a sort of historical interval. The characters likewise are caught between old habits of repression and new roles they can't believe in. They're all somehow maimed by the past: Witte, long-time party faithful, now secretary of the Union Committee of his factory, drags a gammy leg from the prison camp; Dreesen has caught the Russian bureaucrat's bad heart; Banggartz develops psychosomatic colic every time he has to act without orders.

What's special about the five days, when the Government reveals its uncertainties by first imposing new work norms, then rescinding them, is that people have to act inventively, in ways that show up their real character. . . . At the same time, though, the plot stresses the dead ends and the accidents, the confusion that is going to justify a resumption of rigidity once the crisis is over. A clause about 'self-criticism' finds its way into the constitution at the next party congress, but Witte is eased out of his job into 'a year of theoretical studies.'

The novel tries to live up to the ideal of self-criticism, with deliberate variations of viewpoint and narrative strategy, but it has something of the old-fashioned 'socialist realism' stiffness still. The excitement of the events is lacking; instead you get conscientious map-making, meant to bring out the typical significance of what's happening. The characters, too, seem over-carefully constructed for their tasks. And the result is that, from here, Stefan Heym's controversial independence is less visible than his basic conformity to the role of socialist intellectual.

Lorna Sage, "Crisis in Berlin," in The Observer, *January 2, 1977, p. 25.*

JULIAN BARNES

Five Days in June, which deals comprehensibly with the causes of the 1953 strike by East Berlin workers against norm raises, is 'no political tract'. It's true that various questions of emotional loyalty are thrown up by the strike, but the central personal drama is that of a trade unionist's political conscience; while the helpings of sex appear particularly contrived beside, say, a canteen argument over the posting of an illegal notice. Unquestionably, the novel's driving force is dialectical passion; and Heym's account of a historic protest, and his practical comments on it, are our main reasons for curiosity.

Five Days in June purports to be as documentary as possible, with quotes from newspapers, ministerial statements, and American zone radio; yet often, oddly, one is left grasping for more detail. This seems less a matter of being an insufficiently politicised reader, more of the fact that Socialist Realism, compared to, for instance, Zola's realism, is often inadequate. . . . Workers grumble about the government's previous mistakes; but we are given no hint of what these mistakes are until a speech of Ulbricht's is quoted two-thirds of the way through. Not that this vagueness extends to the novel's robust and serious centre, where the political questions are sharply crystallised. What does it mean when workers strike against a workers' government? How far do you order people to do what you know is good for them? When does criticism become counter-productive? Heym's sane but probably unacceptable answers emerge in a unionist's closing speech to a girl secretary; though if these two pages are not tractish, then neither are the last movements of Socialist symphonies. (p. 95)

> *Julian Barnes, "Pressgang," in* New Statesman, *Vol. 93, No. 2392, January 21, 1977, pp. 94-5.*

WES BLOMSTER

The value of [*Collin*] lies . . . in Heym's discussion of the dilemma of the writer who desires to serve a state with integrity and without debasing himself as a puppet of a political system. To this story all too often heard from writers in the Eastern nations Heym brings a new perspective through the question of whether the relativization of the categorical imperative through the new ethic of the proletarian revolution is not in fact illusory and whether in reality the old moral laws do not retain their validity.

Despite the universal excitement conditioned by this mammoth question, the narrative energy present at the outset of the novel flags before the end thereof. It is as if the fatigue of the central figure, seeking escape from his dilemma through illness, infects the book itself with a leaden ennui which causes the reader to put it aside more with a feeling of relief than of profit. *Collin* is undoubtedly an honest chapter in the story of Heym's self-confrontation; the great expectation remains, however, that a complete account of the inner life of this near-septuagenarian . . . will someday appear.

> *Wes Blomster, in a review of "Collin," in* World Literature Today, *Vol. 54, No. 1, Winter, 1980, p. 96.*

NICHOLAS SHRIMPTON

Stefan Heym is a writer whose career bears more than a passing resemblance to that of Brecht. . . . Since [his return to East Germany] he has shown a very Brechtian ambiguity in his relations with the state. His fierce criticism of Stalinist repression and his fervent support of the artist's right to free speech have led to his expulsion from the Writers' Union. His last five books have all been first published in the West, *Five Days in June* and *Collin* still being banned in his own country. Yet he remains a Marxist and continues to live in East Berlin. . . .

[*Collin*] reflects this ambivalence. Though some of its most sympathetic characters retain their faith in the theory of surplus value, it contains a savage attack on the geriatric oligarchy which rules the GDR. Hans Collin, an elderly novelist in a cardiac ward, is determined before he dies to record the secret crimes of the 'old comrades network'. But the theme is not

Solzhenitsyn's heroic sense of the writer's duty, owed to mankind, to preserve historical truth from revision and suppression. Instead, Heym is concerned with the writer's duty to himself. Only accurate confession and honest statement, he suggests, will keep the creative arteries open. Heym's own literary heart and lung system is clearly in good order and, within its carefully drawn limits, this is a skilful and courageous book. (p. 18)

> *Nicholas Shrimpton, "Bucolic Bones," in* New Statesman, *Vol. 100, No. 2578, August 15, 1980, pp. 17-18.*

EVA HOFFMAN

The Wandering Jew, for all too understandable reasons, has been a durable symbol; he has been seen in legend and in literature, in folklore and high art, as a personification of exile, uprootedness and a specifically Jewish fate. . . .

[In *The Wandering Jew,* Heym] uses this suggestive figure in yet another way—as a kind of subversive prophet, an oblique vantage point from which to reinterpret the entire story of creation, of Christ and of much latter-day history. It is a grandly, almost quixotically ambitious project—and in struggling to fill its dimensions, Mr. Heym achieves moments of poetry and moral passion. If he doesn't entirely succeed, it's because, in his many-layered design, myth is too much separated from the fictional consciousness, and ideas are insufficiently fused with embodied characters or action.

In Mr. Heym's time-leaping parable, the Wandering Jew, or Ahasverus, is introduced as a kind of third term in the perennial opposition between good and evil, between God and Satan, and later between Lucifer and Jesus. He is first seen as one of Lucifer's companions in his banishment and fall, but unlike Lucifer's, his is not the rebellion of pure rejection and denial. He is a revolutionary of a distinctly modernist cast, an angry idealist who wants to defy authority to improve the world. Later, when Reb Joshua (the Hebrew name for Jesus) makes His appearance, the already age-old Ahasverus sees in Him a possibility of redemption—although his hope is hardly of the traditional Christian sort.

In some of the novel's most lyrical and provocative passages, Ahasverus follows the very human and conflict-torn Reb Joshua into the wilderness and tries to persuade Him that martyrdom will accomplish nothing, that the way to change the course of history is not by submissiveness, but by taking fate into His own hands.

It is when the action of *The Wandering Jew* falls into that real history that it becomes, for all its picaresque twists and its jauntily colloquial language, oddly predictable and stilted. The central narrative is set in Luther's Germany, and it concerns the temptation of Paul von Eitzen, Luther's protégé and follower, by Hans Leuchtentrager, Lucifer's hump-backed and cloven-footed current incarnation, and Ahasverus, his intermittently vanishing and reappearing Jewish friend.

Von Eitzen is a kind of lumpen Faust—fascinated by the dark forces he intuits in Leuchtentrager and yearning after a luscious Margriet, but mostly just too timid, smug and unquestioning to engage with the challenges to his faith, or his own irrational impulses and desires. He is also a theological opportunist, who, succumbing to Luther's attacks on the Jews and the time's rising anti-Semitism, in effect condemns Ahasverus to death.

The episode is central to the novel, for it stands for the visible fulfillment of Ahasverus' prophecy and the failure of Jesus' sacrifice. And perhaps in making an unprepossessing and dim-witted apparatchik the instrument of this great injustice, Mr. Heym is trying to suggest something about the banal and undignified origins of evil.

But the novel's main protagonists are simply too indistinct and insignificant to carry the burden of such weighty historical drama. Ahasverus becomes, in these sections, a marginal character, too remote to command our sorrow, or betoken a whole people's suffering. As for Leuchtentrager, he is a rather tame tempter; his magic tends to the trickster's variety, and his suggestions that man is a creature of lust more than reason, or that evil is an intrinsic part of the world's scheme, are unlikely to unsettle readers well accustomed to literature that gives the Devil his full due.

These are not supposed to be realistic characters, but even within the rules of fable, they serve too much as allegorical straw-men for the novel's manifold arguments, tracts and disquisitions. . . . [Mostly], the ideas reverberate as if in a fictional echo chamber—resonating with allusions to Milton and Blake, Nietzsche and Goethe—but too familiar, even in their putative heresies, to startle us into moral or intellectual surprise.

And yet, moral provocation—and inciting righteous astonishment at the wrongness, the corruption of human arrangements—is clearly one of Mr. Heym's aims. But he is, paradoxically, most effective in this when he gets away from the generalities of "great issues," and grapples with those primordial, concrete stories of human origin and suffering that are still potent detonators for imaginative and emotional energies. The novel's philosophical strands receive a kind of resolution in a weird, nuclear-style Armageddon in which Ahasverus is again reunited with Reb Joshua and God.

But in the end, the scene that imprints itself most forcefully on the mind is the anguished wrestling of Reb Joshua, before His fate was yet decided, with the possibility that He might simply be choosing the wrong path. It is revealing of the biblical story's deep-rootedness in our culture that such a radical re-writing of it can still produce a genuine philosophic amazement—the amazement that Mr. Heym struggles hard and sometimes daringly to achieve—proceeding from the thought that the world does not necessarily have to be what it is, that the progress of our history has been only one possibly misguided and quite arbitrary course.

> Eva Hoffman, in a review of "The Wandering Jew," in The New York Times, February 23, 1984, p. C19.

ERNST PAWEL

[**The Wandering Jew**] is an often brilliant, always imaginative journey through milleniums of bigotry and greed. Along the way, Mr. Heym skewers many a worthy target and offends a broad range of constituencies, from devout Christians and Jews to no less devout Marxists. He has the courage of his convictions—an overrated virtue in the age of kamikaze terrorists, but in this instance it makes for some highly effective satire. The correspondence between Prof. Siegfried Beifuss, head of the "Institute for Scientific Atheism, Berlin, Capital of the G.D.R." and his superior in the East German Ministry of Education, about the purportedly 2,000-year-old Israeli citizen Ahasverus, a shoemaker in Jerusalem's Old City, is the sort of parody that bureaucrats of the German Democratic Republic

are unlikely to forgive, if they are bright enough to recognize it as such.

But at the heart of any true satire lies a sense of despair, and this is what comes through most clearly here in the end. Our world may have started with a "big bang," but only faith can make one believe that it can survive the next one, and his former faith is precisely what Mr. Heym seems at last to have lost.

The conclusion drifts into allegorical pomposity with the Second Coming of Reb Joshua, descended this time to judge rather than be judged. What he finds is humanity unredeemed, riven by hate, on a planet bristling with weapons of mass destruction. Armageddon takes merely the touch of a button. But in the cosmic silence that follows, Ahasverus at length is forgiven, and thus an impressive tour de force ends on a note of banality.

> Ernst Pawel, "Fantasy of a Loyal Dissident," in The New York Times Book Review, February 26, 1984, p. 14.

D. J. ENRIGHT

Beer and onions, bums and breasts, metaphysics and damnation, slapstick and horror. . . . This is the matter in which the German genius is most at home. Stefan Heym has surpassed himself [in **The Wandering Jew**], sustaining his imagination and maintaining our engagement with it; and by force of wit holding in check what might be thought—or are we merely jealous of the love that exists between angels?—a drift toward sentimentality. Heym, who lives in East Berlin, spent some twenty years in the United States and writes English with brio and apparent ease; he has a weakness for the progressive form— "I am still seeing the Rabbi's face growing pale"—though such minor eccentricities may be supposed appropriate to the story's time and indeed its timelessness.

A writer-character in Heym's previous novel, **Collin,** gave as his reason for staying in East Germany the opportunities provided for observing so much that is contradictory. And Heym has remarked *in propria persona* that East Berlin is a fascinating place for a writer to live in because "there are a lot of contradictions." It is perhaps no contradiction that **The Wandering Jew** is unpublishable in the author's country. Its meaning, or part at least of the fable's meaning, present in Ahasverus's conviction that man is free to make changes and redemption requires revolution, may appeal to the authorities. But, even if the story's Manichaean implications are glossed over, Heym's metaphors are likely to appall them. He arrives at what might just be considered sound doctrine via distinctly unscientific means. And, what is worse, while his narrative is full of vigorous *disputatio,* its use of dialectics smacks of the sterile formalistic device known as parody. It occurs to us that the Devil cited scripture when, in tempting Leverkühn, he dismissed parody as a form of aristocratic nihilism generating little profit. (p. 46)

> D. J. Enright, "Beer, Onions and Damnation," in The New York Review of Books, Vol. XXXI, No. 7, April 26, 1984, pp. 45-6.

TIMOTHY GARTON ASH

[In **Schwarzenberg**], Heym imagines that in 1945, through an oversight, a small corner of Germany on the Czech border is left unoccupied by both the Western allies and the Russians. His "novel" recounts how independent, upright, democratic German antifascists strive to build their dream of a "free German republic." In the end they fail—Schwarzenberg falls into the Soviet zone—but to most of his readers Heym's "realistic" ending will be less important than the "dream" he paints with such manifest sympathy: a "political utopia" which, as the blurb quite unhistorically asserts, "might almost have become reality." *Schwarzenberg* speaks powerfully to a notion abroad in Germany today—not a popular notion, but a quietly influential one— ... that, left to themselves, the survivors of the German antifascist resistance in 1945 could have found their own way forward to an authentic socialist democracy in a demilitarized united Germany. (p. 38)

> *Timothy Garton Ash, "Which Way Will Germany Go?" in* The New York Review of Books, *Vol. XXXII, No. 1, January 31, 1985, pp. 33-40.*

WES BLOMSTER

"Political fairy tale" would be a fitting designation for Heym's new work [*Schwarzenberg*], were it not so painfully rooted in the political reality of postwar Germany. In his new novel (published, like all his recent books, only in the West) the senior GDR author gives a fictive account of the short-lived "Republic of Schwarzenberg," a small region on the Czech border. ... The dream enshrined lovingly by Heym in the book is that it would be a better world today had the Germans been left to design their own future upon the end of the war, and therewith to digest the past that continues to plague them even now.

Heym's dream is an attractive one—in part because of the humane idealism that informs it, in part because the author constructs it with that easy narrative passion that is the trademark of his work. However, is the dream of convincing validity before the critical eye of modern history? The answer to this question is necessarily negative, if hesitantly so. Even to those sympathetic to Heym's thought, the adolescent naïveté of the seventy-two-year-old writer, who has rejected—and been rejected by—most political systems of the modern world, is as astonishing as it is enviable.

> *Wes Blomster, in a review of "Schwarzenberg," in* World Literature Today, *Vol. 59, No. 4, Autumn, 1985, p. 585.*

Eugène Ionesco

1912-

Rumanian-born French dramatist, essayist, scriptwriter, novelist, and short story writer.

A major figure in contemporary drama, Ionesco is linked by the thematic content and techniques of his plays to the Theater of the Absurd. He creates darkly comic portraits of the human condition by exploring such themes as alienation, the impossibility of true communication, and the destructive forces of modern societal pressures. As is characteristic of the Theater of the Absurd, Ionesco's drama is experimental. He replaces the traditional structure of plot, action, and denouement with an oneiric drama composed of contradiction, nonsensical dialogue, and bizarre images and situations. Central to his approach is the projection of dreams onto the stage. Ionesco, who often draws upon his own dreams for dramatic material, stated: "Dreams are reality at its most profound, and what you invent is truth, because invention, by its nature, can't be a lie."

The absurdity of language and communication is a dominant theme in Ionesco's early works, including his first two plays, *La cantatrice chauve* (1950; *The Bald Soprano*) and *La leçon* (1951; *The Lesson*). In the first play, which was inspired by the text of an English primer, Mr. and Mrs. Smith engage in a cliché-ridden conversation, while their visitors, Mr. and Mrs. Martin, speak as though they are strangers until realizing that they share the same home and child. The dialogue among the four characters eventually disintegrates into meaningless sounds. In the second play, a professor tutors a female student in several subjects, ranging from the logical constructs of mathematics to the less rigid rules of language. As the language lesson progresses, the professor becomes increasingly agitated, and the play climaxes in an orgiastic frenzy when he stabs the student during a discussion of the word "knife." Both works end as they began, the only difference being that the two couples in *The Bald Soprano* exchange roles. Through the circular nature of these two plays, Ionesco conveys a sense of hopelessness and a pessimistic view of the fate of humankind.

As his career progressed, Ionesco began to use a multiplicity of objects as a metaphor to further examine the absurdity of life. In one of Ionesco's most acclaimed works, *Les chaises* (1952; *The Chairs*), an elderly couple serve as hosts for an audience who assemble to hear an orator deliver a message that will save the world. As the couple arrange seating for their guests, the stage becomes inundated with chairs. Again, a pessimistic viewpoint is expressed as the audience is revealed to be imaginary, the couple commit suicide, and the orator turns out to be a deaf-mute. Other plays demonstrate a similar proliferation of objects: in *Victimes du devoir* (1953; *Victims of Duty*), coffee cups multiply; in *Amédée; ou, Comment s'en débarrasser* (1954; *Amédée; or, How to Get Rid of It*), a corpse grows until it begins to dominate an apartment; and in *Le nouveau locataire* (1955; *The New Tenant*), the protagonist's apartment eventually becomes filled with furniture. By increasing the size and number of objects onstage, Ionesco suggests the alienation and loss of identity experienced by people in modern society.

Beginning in the late 1950s, Ionesco wrote a number of plays that center on Bérenger, a modern-day Everyman. The best

© Jerry Bauer

known of these works is *Rhinocéros* (1960), which is considered one of Ionesco's most accessible plays. As the play opens, Bérenger is conversing with his friend Jean and displays only mild interest when a rhinoceros charges by. Soon, however, everyone except Bérenger has been transformed into a rhinoceros. Bérenger questions whether he should join them, but when he realizes he cannot, he decides to fight them and thus defend humanity. While the inspiration for this work came from Ionesco's reaction to a friend who joined the Nazi party, the play's significance extends beyond the confines of any single ideology to denounce mindless conformity and mob mentality. *Rhinocéros* was adapted for film. Other Bérenger plays include *Tueur sans gages* (1959; *The Killer*), in which Bérenger searches for a nameless killer to whom he falls prey, and *Le roi se meurt* (1963; *Exit the King*), in which Bérenger is a king who is told he will soon die.

The subject of death becomes an overriding concern in many of Ionesco's later plays. For example, in *La soif et la faim* (1966; *Hunger and Thirst*), the protagonist attempts to escape death as represented by his wife and child, and in *Jeux de massacre* (1970; *Killing Game*), an epidemic kills the inhabitants of a village. Charles I. Glicksberg explained: "Death for Ionesco represents the upsurge of the uncanny, the threat of nothingness, the quintessence of the Absurd." The dreamlike images that pervade Ionesco's drama also become more prominent in his later works. In *L'homme aux valises* (1975; *Man with Bags*) and *Voyages chez les morts; ou, Thèmes et variations* (1980; *Journey among the Dead*), the protagonists engage in conversations with the dead. The episodic nature of these plays, coupled with their metaphysical qualities, creates the impression of a dream. Commenting on the influence of dreams on Ionesco's work, Rosette Lamont stated: "Ionesco believes that an interpenetration occurs between the conscious day life and the subconscious night existence, for dreams contain fragments of the day's impressions, and the latter are encrusted with bits and pieces severed from the psyche's intense activity in its nightly revels."

Although best known as a dramatist, Ionesco has also written a novel, *Le Solitaire* (1972; *The Hermit*), and several volumes of essays and criticism. These works, like his drama, are marked by a sense of anguish and a vehement opposition to totalitarianism and oppression. Many of his essays offer incisive comments on his drama. Faulted as obscure by many critics at the beginning of his career, Ionesco's innovative drama has gained international acclaim, and a number of his works are now considered seminal pieces of the Theater of the Absurd. In 1971 Ionesco was elected to the prestigious Académie Française.

(See also *CLC,* Vols. 1, 4, 6, 9, 11, 15; *Contemporary Authors,* Vols. 9-12, rev. ed.; and *Something about the Author,* Vol. 7.)

ALBERT BERMEL

Now that Eugène Ionesco has an assured place in the republic of letters, as well as a *fauteuil* in the French Academy, criticism of his drama, which gushed forth for a few years, has dwindled. The playwright's reputation, trussed and ticketed, sits in a box smelling faintly musty and labeled either the Absurd or the Grotesque, depending on whether researchers read their catalog cards from the west or the east. His plays purportedly deal with "nothingness" or "absence" or "silence," words lifted—in conformity with what used to be called the intentional fallacy—from the author's own collection of prose writings, *Notes and Counter Notes*. Commentators have observed that he propels himself toward the "nothingness" with the aid of distorted language, which demonstrates that words are meaningless, not merely unavailing but a handicap to communication. In addition, he shows us objects and other inert matter taking over from people—that is to say, death triumphing over life—and he draws on anti-logic in the making of his anti-plays.

Looking back over the books and essays devoted to Ionesco in whole or in part I find many that read like metaphysical treatises. Sometimes these solemn documents serve as pulpits from which this or that critic preaches his disaffection from the playwright's "negative philosophy." Little of the criticism addresses itself to the man's positive artistry, liveliness, and humor. (p. 411)

Ionesco is in some ways a thoroughly traditional playwright. His distinction, once we adjust to the novelty of his techniques, lies in his having explored afresh the possibilities of farce and occasionally—as in *The Chairs*—having combined farce with tragedy in a mode I would call the comic agony. *The Chairs,* far from being "about nothingness," happens to be rich with "somethingness"; it consists of a character study blurred by dreamlike, farcical circumstances that have a tragic outcome. The hyperboles of tragedy and farce do not alternate; they cohere and lend each other support; they blend so subtly that it is hard, until the end of the play, to be sure which of them predominates.

The Chairs describes the end of a marriage. It therefore amounts to a sequel (and complement) to the play Ionesco wrote a year earlier, in 1950, *Jacques, or the Submission,* the action of which leads up to the beginning of a marriage. The pair of characters in *The Chairs,* an Old Man aged ninety-five and his wife, an Old Woman of ninety-four, open the play with some verbal sparring that sounds offhanded, if not desultory. Gradually the author transmutes the tone and narrows the direction of the dialogue, working it into and out of some masterly stage business, until the activity climbs to a feverish climax.

The old people speak of the building they are in as their home. From their description it sounds like a tower or lighthouse surrounded by stagnant water: it has the shape of a phallus, the environment of a womb. The set represents about one-half of this tower's interior. Instead of a rear wall it has a semi-circular cyclorama, a construction that supports a row of ten doors and two windows. The scene thus appears to be a modified throwback to the settings for late nineteenth-century domestic farces, such as Feydeau's, in which the actors' entrances and exits (some of them more like eruptions and explosions) provide a heavy proportion of the entertainment. The rest of the stage is sparsely furnished. The playwright calls for stools below the two windows, a blackboard and a dais for an Orator, who will be coming later in the evening to address a crowd of distinguished guests, and a gas lamp that gives out a green light. (p. 412)

The Chairs is a memory play, the memory of a life and a marriage. But whose memory? In the text the Old Woman has almost no independent life, no story, of her own: "Tell me the story.... It's also mine; what is yours is mine." Her recollections do no more than sustain or counteract his. Together they are reliving snatches of *his* life. She reflects and refracts him back to himself. She came into being when he was a year old, an age when infants begin to differentiate themselves from the world around them, to become self-conscious entities. Now, as an "orphan" crying for his mother, he takes her as a mother. When he blames life for its knocks, she substitutes for his conscience and reminds him of his faults.... (p. 415)

This married couple is a single person. It must die whole, united, as the Old Man's rhyming verse suggests when it speaks of their lying, dying, and rotting together. Yet [at the play's end] their bodies plunge separately into the water from the opposing windows. Only beyond that moment of drowning will they become one.

If the Old Woman represents the Old Man's baser self, the other live character, the Orator, stands for his higher self, the source of his message to humanity, somebody to be listened to. But the Orator "must appear unreal." This higher self is a delusion, the Old Man's dream of himself magnified and elevated on a dais. The Old Man "has difficulty expressing" himself, but he can at least speak. The Orator, after his stunning entrance, not only cannot choke out anything but noises; when he attempts to write he deforms one of the commonest French words [adieu].

The three visible characters in *The Chairs* are "one." But the guests, those unseen and unspeaking presences, also belong to the "one." They are people he has known, remnants of the Old Man's past accusing his present, compelling him to confront the big question, What have you made of your life since we occupied it? . . . He has fallen into rationalizing and evading all his life. He wants to be judged—condemned—by these distinguished, imaginary "intellectuals and proprietors" who have made good since he knew them, who do not need to speak or be actualized but will let him damn himself without interrupting.

Then there is the *most* distinguished of the guests, the Emperor. Even more a figment of the Old Man's crumbling mind than the Orator, he is a vision of God. When he first "enters," *"the light reaches its maximum intensity, through the open door and through the windows; but the light is cold, empty."* This empty God provides yet another reason for the Old Man to avoid taking the blame for his wasted life: "I might have been something, if I could have been sure of the support of Your Majesty." Just as the semicircular setting and its chairs breach the boundaries between the stage and the auditorium, so the unification of visible and invisible characters destroys the boundary between what is real and unreal on the stage and helps to expose the play's metaphor.

The Chairs is a theatricalized portrait of a death; its action lengthens out to about an hour the last few seconds before the Old Man's death, which culminates in his suicide. As the invisible presences, the memories, flow into the room in dribs and drabs, and then in overwhelming numbers, the past returns to him in a trickle that turns into a flood. The Old Man not merely calls back his memories while he is dying, he insists on inhabiting again those pockets of his life that cause him pain in retrospect. They show him to himself as a loser when he is on the rim of death and it is too late for him to allay his losses. He summons an audience and a God to listen to his self-justifications—when he says farewell he also asks for God's mercy (*à Dieu:* may God dispose!)—and he summons his higher self to orate to them, but the Orator only confirms his failure as a human being. He has had an abnormally long life—what every person yearns for; longevity is next to immortality—but his ninety-five years have gone misused, squandered. He did not even get to be one hundred. So death does win—but not triumphantly.

The mounting excitement as the guests invade the tower, as the Emperor makes his "cold, empty" entrance, as the Orator strides into view (a surprise, because the play has led us to expect that the Orator will be invisible, too), as the old couple leap from their windows, and as the Orator blunders into his speech-which-is-not-a-speech—this fivefold climax is the spurt of final consciousness: the Old Man's life rallies its weakening forces before it evaporates. The last image of *The Chairs* is of life departed: *"The stage remains empty with only the chairs, the dais, the floor covered with streamers and confetti. The main door is wide open on to darkness."*

The feature of Ionesco's work that has given rise to most critical discussion, and most misunderstanding, is his verbal idiosyncrasy: the bastardized and dissected words, the neologisms, the illogic, the playfulness that is not quite playful. Some of these practices go back at least as far as Shakespeare. We could take a remark of the Old Woman's ("I haven't got thirty-three hands, you know, I'm not a cow") or a line spoken by the father in *Jacques* ("Your descendants will never see the light of day for they'll prefer to let themselves be killed before they

ever come into being") and find it comparable to the nonsense of Dogberry, Holofernes, or Bottom. In Ionesco, however, such lines are liable to be uttered by any of the characters, not necessarily by one who has been established as a clown. Some critics have therefore assumed that Ionesco finds words meaningless. To say this is to deny him his comic gifts. His plays reveal how words *can be* used without regard for meaning, and often are, especially platitudes and misplaced proverbs. He demonstrates the power and powerlessness of words, their might and fragility, their incantatory and somniferent properties. They can defy sense, adapt their meanings to different settings, and even take on startling new identities. When words are repeatedly intoned they can acquire a life of their own which may not match any formal definition. They can be raised to the status of objects, just as objects can be raised to the status of human beings. And like objects, words committed aloud can become enemies, intimate acquaintances which turn against the mouth that gives them life. (pp. 416-18)

In *The Chairs* the Old Man's unspoken intention is to offer a performance that will enable him by reenactment to escape from a clinging childhood, from the time of preliteracy when his fears first took ineffable shape. But childhood and adulthood, dependence and independence have grown confused. They are aspects of his oneness, which he must try to recover and master. His struggle to expose these aspects of himself arises from the opposition of a profoundly troubled psyche to a comic celebration, a social gathering. (pp. 418-19)

The conflict Ionesco detects within one soul between a social man (the adult) and a presocial, preliterate man (represented by the childish talk) gives rise to an antisocial being who is not at home in society, and yet cannot use his instincts properly; they have become defective organs. Such a being will find himself at odds with any setting he is put into by the dramatist. This particular setting, a weird half-tower with *"water under the windows, stretching as far as the horizon,"* does double duty: it belongs to the Old Man's "oneness" because it constitutes his stage; and it also defines his isolation from the rest of the world. In it the character who cannot pull himself together, who is literally and figuratively a nonentity, undergoes agonies of remorse and self-chastisement—which we laugh at. But at the last, as we too are drawn into the "oneness" of the action, the laughter stops up our throats. This is not "nothingness" or absurdity or abscence, but the presence of a keen sorrow sheltering behind a ludicrous mask. (p. 419)

Albert Bermel, "Ionesco: Anything but Absurd," in Twentieth Century Literature, *Vol. 21, No. 4, December, 1975, pp. 411-20.*

ALFRED SCHWARZ

[The] key to Ionesco's and Beckett's almost lyric use of the theater (a histrionic lyricism) [is] to bind actor and audience in a shared consciousness of the essential condition of man. If we take tragedy, in the traditional way, to be the rehearsal of our worst fears in order that we may master them, or at least try to understand and accommodate disorder within a provisional framework of order, the theaters of Ionesco and Beckett demonstrate that such mastery is impossible, such an attempt at understanding is vain, and that therefore we can only create absurd gestures of collapse to indicate what it feels like to exist in the twentieth-century theater of the world. The nightmares of history have resulted in a nightmare of individual and collective consciousness which cannot be accommodated to anything else because there is nothing else. (p. 336)

When Ionesco writes, "To become fully conscious of the atrocious and to laugh at it is to master the atrocious," he means something less than gaining upon the threat of chaos, or mastering the incomprehensible evil by making it comprehensible. In another context, he had written, "The unendurable admits of no solution, and only the unendurable is profoundly tragic, profoundly comic and essentially theatrical." . . . The problem is how to give shape and objective validity to such despair. Ionesco hopes that if he succeeds in "materializing" on stage "the unseen presence of our inner fears" . . . his personal anguish will be expressive of everyone's anguish. . . . In his early plays, Ionesco was above all concerned with inventing a theatrical language that would externalize his personal (and, one might add, not particularly novel) feelings of bewilderment at the contradictory aspects of human existence: that we are social beings and yet utterly alone; that the "joy at existing" is matched by a feeling of emptiness; that material presence is negated by spiritual absence; solidity by evanescence. The paradox of life itself is that man is destroyed by time. . . . The uncertainty of existence leaves him simply perplexed; yet in the short plays of the 1950s he created a series of brilliantly executed confessions of his comic despair.

Ionesco's theater is predominantly comic because it grows directly out of his ambivalent and provocatively subjective view of the world. At first, he professes not to be able to separate comic from tragic in his experience. "Wonder . . . is my basic emotional reaction to the world. Not tragic—all right; then comic perhaps, strangely comic indeed, derisory, this world of ours. And yet if I take a closer look at it, a kind of searing pain takes hold of me." . . . This type of experience is described in several places: what appears to be a strange, implausible, even nonsensical universe when viewed from the outside, in a state of detachment, causes him intense distress when he realizes that it is the sole reality of his existence. But the comic impulse prevails. Looking back upon his work, Ionesco singles out this gift of detaching himself from the world as the reason why he can view even the painful aspects of man's existence as comic in their improbability. . . . He is nothing if not coy in his description of the unexpected effects of his first plays upon the audiences. They laughed at *The Bald Soprano* when he thought he had written the "Tragedy of Language." They found the sadistic business of *The Lesson* highly amusing. Conversely, the "classic vaudeville situation" of *The Chairs* struck them as peculiarly macabre. . . . The fact is, of course, that the audiences respond precisely to Ionesco's manipulation of his ambivalent feelings in any given situation. However, his detached view is not a substitute for an objective universal view of the human predicament (such as Beckett's); therefore, he succeeds in achieving only a detached recognition on our part of his particular version of an imcomprehensible universe. Since he exaggerates, or makes grotesque in other ways, the precarious nature of our existence, the audience laughs. It recognizes its image, but so enlarged or frantically distorted that it fails to share Ionesco's submerged anguish.

If indeed, as Ionesco claims, the writing of *The Bald Soprano* (*La Cantatrice chauve,* 1948; first performed, 1950) was attended by physical anguish, nausea and vertigo, why is so little of that transmitted to the audience in performance? Why does the "Tragedy of Language," or (in Jean Vannier's more precise description) the "destruction of language" which ushers us into the "Kingdom of Terror" . . . make us laugh? Because

his characters are so far stripped of thought, emotion, personality, having lost their identity in the world of the impersonal, that we presume to watch them from a safe distance. Ionesco writes the comedy of dehumanization. By translating the breakdown of communication into the automatic give and take of the English Language Manual, he calls attention to his detached comic view of man totally lost (or to use his own word, "steeped") in his social environment. The only indication of his terror comes in the end when the tone of petit bourgeois complacency rises to a pitch of incoherent madness. . . . But because this typical rhythm or pattern of intensification reflects the eminently subjective response of a sensitive mentality, we feel free to stand back and laugh (perhaps cruelly) both at the comic side of his discomfiture and the grotesque expression of his terror. Ionesco's plays, as he never tires of saying, are about himself struggling to find theatrical equivalents for his own states of mind and feeling. That is really the point of his elaborate self-justifications in the *Notes and Counter Notes,* as well as his speculations about the relation of comedy to tragedy.

Hence he belabors the problem of how to get from his intensely subjective apprehension of the world to a more universal, tragic vision. He declares that Beckett, in contrast to Brecht, is essentially tragic because he brings the whole of the human condition into play, not man in this or that society, because he poses the problem of the ultimate ends of man. Although Ionesco ranges himself on the side of Beckett in his concern with the "authentic reality in which man is integrated" . . . , there is this difference to be observed between them. Ionesco does not possess Beckett's objectivity and therefore not his universality. It does not escape him that he can speak of *Endgame* in the same breath with the lamentations of Job (Job "that contemporary of Beckett") or the tragedies of Sophocles and Shakespeare . . . , whereas his own plays (with the possible exception of *The Killer* and *Exit the King*) hardly grasp the "essentially tragic human reality" . . . in any universal sense. Rather they tend to fluctuate between derisive laughter at his caricatures of human behavior and sudden pain when he discovers that his invented situations accurately render his own desolation. He follows the rhythm of his intuitions and feelings instead of the logic of the invented dramatic situation. (pp. 336-39)

Beckett's comedy, on the other hand, is integral to his tragic vision. It does not compete with it (as is the case in Ionesco's tragic farce), but forms a part of the general rhythm of the play: the stalemate of *Waiting for Godot* or the descent to nothingness in *Endgame* and *Happy Days.* Nor are any of the celebrated enigmas of Beckett's drama—the identity of Godot or Clov's discovery of the small boy—evidence of his personal bewilderment or subjective expressions of his uncertainty in the face of an incomprehensible universe. Though rationally inexplicable, they are in each instance part of the objective tragic reality depicted in the play, relating to the fate of the *protagonists.* In fact, Beckett fulfills Ionesco's theoretical idea of tragedy, the creation of a mythical cosmos and a "pure drama" of universal significance that reproduces "the permanently destructive and self-destructive pattern of existence itself: pure reality, non-logical and non-psychological." . . . But, writing in 1953, he admits ruefully, to make such a world which is peculiarly *one's own* communicable and identifiable to others is perhaps impossible. (p. 340)

For the most part, his talent, contrary to Beckett's, leads him to what Francis Fergusson called the partial perspectives of the modern theater, "highly developed fragments of [the] great mirror.'' He only touches upon the tragic reality underneath the comic surface of life. The conformist, the ideologist, the purely social or ''sociologized'' man negates his humanity and thus becomes an object of derision; but insofar as in organized society man is reduced to his function in that organization, he is alienated from other men. . . . Concealed under the comic picture of a life emptied of meaning lies the horror of solitude. The insight is sharply realized, for example, in the automatic chatter of **The Bald Soprano** and in several other plays; but typically it has the limitations of a theatrical essay upon one of his favorite themes: that it is the human condition which governs the social condition, not the other way around. . . . More ambitiously, as in the masterpiece among his short plays, **The Chairs** (*Les Chaises*, 1951), he tries to deprive us of our sense of the real. The apparently harmless hallucination, begun in the spirit of vaudeville, progressively reveals the ''gaps in reality.'' The proliferation of chairs to accommodate the invisible guests suggests a more than physical absence; and at last he succeeds in expressing the void, ''the unreality of the real. Original chaos.'' . . . But, as he points out in **''La tragédie du langage,''** the tragic character does not change; he is wrecked; he is himself, he is *real*. Comic characters, on the other hand, are people who do not exist. . . . (pp. 341-42)

That the Smiths and the Martins in **The Bald Soprano** are perfectly interchangeable, because of ''the absence of an inner life,'' makes them comical in the way that puppets can be taken as abominable imitations of humanity. Accelerate their mechanical babble to the point of incoherence, and their behavior becomes painful, a kind of threatening disorder. Although Ionesco had in mind at least two explosive endings, involving the audience in a scene of mayhem, extending as it were the ''collapse of reality'' from the stage to the auditorium, circumstances forced upon him the more brilliant idea of returning to the opening scene as the curtain slowly falls. Thus the comic spirit supervenes. The Martins take the place of the Smiths, easily assuming the identity of any member of the ''universal petite bourgeoisie''; they are people who are nothing in themselves, therefore they do not exist. The loss of identity, the absence of real people, in **The Chairs** is a decidedly more serious matter. Now Ionesco looks beneath the surface of actual existence and finds a void. . . . The frantic stage business, the fabricated dialogue with the absent crowd of guests—the whole grotesque effort to conceal the failure of a lifetime (perhaps of a civilization) and to push back the encroaching emptiness, inevitably breaks down. But again, face to face with the terrifying void, Ionesco truncates his statement by arranging a convulsive, farcical ending: the Old Man and the Old Woman attain their false apotheosis by leaping into the abysmal water outside, in a double suicide, and the Orator, who was to deliver the Old Man's message of salvation to the assembled guests, only gurgles and scrawls inarticulately. Ionesco's vision stops short because he is perplexed by what he has discovered; the tragic ''unreality of the real'' is a condition of chaos with which he cannot deal in a meaningful way. (pp. 342-43)

Alfred Schwarz, ''Condemned to Exist,'' in his From Büchner to Beckett: Dramatic Theory and the Modes of Tragic Drama, *Ohio University Press, 1978, pp. 334-56.*

CHRISTOPHER INNES

Ionesco is normally interpreted in terms of the 'philosophy of the absurd' outlined by Camus in *The Myth of Sisyphus*. His theme is said to be a statement of the impossibility of communication and the futility of life in the face of inevitable death, illustrating Sartre's proposition that the consciousness of existence leads to an awareness of 'the nothingness of being'. This is used to explain what is seen as a rejection of the whole concept of personality in the transferable or transforming characters of plays like **The Bald Primadonna** (*La Cantatrice chauve*, 1948, produced 1950) or **Victims of Duty** (*Les Victims du devoir*, 1953), the reduction of social reality to clichés and empty formulas, and an attempt to create an 'abstract' theatre where the primary function of a play is to reveal and express the formal principles of the theatrical art form. Such analyses of Ionesco's work as dramatic statements of a philosophical position, 'pure' theatre, or anti-theatre in the sense of parody drama—and given his assertion of the identity of contraries in an early essay with the title of **''No!,''** it would be perfectly legitimate to interpret his plays as simultaneous expressions of all three—all have a certain validity, and can be clearly derived from some of Ionesco's own theoretical statements or from selected comments about drama put into the mouths of characters in his plays. But there is a mythical, even mystical aspect to his work that is frequently overlooked, as is his relationship to the whole avant garde movement from Jarry to the surrealists. Ionesco's appreciation of *grand guignol* puppet theatre and his position as a 'Grand Satrap' of the Collège de Pataphysique link him to Jarry. His post-graduate thesis on Baudelaire indicates his interest in the symbolists. Surrealists like Phillipe Soupault and André Breton have hailed his work as a natural extension of their own. A play like **Hunger and Thirst** ((*La Soif et la faim*, 1966), originally titled 'Life in the dream', is on one level a reworking of Strindbergian themes, with not only a structure derived from *To Damascus*, and disgust at existence symbolised as in *A Dream Play* by dirt covering the walls of a family home, but also a hero—simultaneously a Christ-figure and a projection of the author—whose pilgrimage in search of an elusive ideal in female form ends in a 'monastery-barracks-prison' where inmates are brainwashed into believing themselves to be poisoned by thoughts of freedom. And even though Ionesco rejects Artaud's theory of cruelty, he acknowledges his work to be following Artaud in his aim of creating a 'metaphysical' theatre, 'to change the metaphysical condition of man, to change life, but from within out and not the reverse, from the personal towards the collective', as well as in his attack on 'petit-bourgeois' attitudes as a 'false culture' that 'separates us from everything and from ourselves'. For Ionesco 'it is precisely the process of this devitalised culture, imprisoning us in an inauthentic reality which Artaud perceived' that defines one pole of his work, and his solution also parallels Artaud in the consequent 'necessity of breaking language in order to reconstitute it, in order to ''touch life'', to put man back in contact with the absolute'.

From this perspective Ionesco's attack on the banality of social behaviour and the meaningless clichés of everyday language in parodies of family life like **The Bald Primadonna** and **Jack, or The Submission** (*Jacques, ou la soumission*, 1950, produced 1955) take on new meaning. The pressures of conformity that have produced carbon-copy characters, whose activities and relationships are therefore arbitrary and nonsensical, are not exaggerated to reveal human existence itself as absurd, but only the forms of social conditioning that destroy individuality. 'Inauthenticity' is only contingent, not necessary. What is being attacked is the contemporary emphasis on rationality, with its accompanying materialism and devaluing of the subconscious or spiritual levels of the mind; a dualism which either produces a zombie-like vacuity, or perverts one half of the psyche into inhuman violence, as in **The Lesson** (*La Leçon*, 1951) where a professor is shown gaining total ascendency over the thirty-ninth in an endless series of pupils, which in each case leads to the rape and murder of an unresisting girl. This clearly relates to the sexual nature of power or the negation of individuality by the educational system, but on a more basic level it is an image for the domination of the intellect (in the rather over-obvious symbol of the professor) over the instinctive and physical side of human nature (the student being finally reduced to an awareness of herself solely as a body). In this symbiotic couple the Professor can only establish his dominance by repressing the Pupil's natural vitality, and the result is insanity. The point is even more explicit in **Rhinocéros** (1959), where the surface reference is political, the metaphor for men turning into rhinoceroses coming from Ionesco's personal journal of 1940 where it is specifically used to describe the dehumanising effect of Nazi propaganda. But for Ionesco politics as such is only a symptom, and he defined the play as 'mainly an attack on collective hysteria and the epidemics that work beneath the surface of reason and ideas but are none the less serious collective diseases passed off as ideologies . . . concealing beneath a mask of cold objectivity the most irrational and violent pressures'.

In this light the proliferation of objects in his early plays, mounting piles of coffee cups, multiplying furniture that entombs one character, or the fungoid growth of a corpse that pushes others off the sides of the stage as it expands are not intended to represent the human condition *per se*, but only the effect of materialistic rationalism. The power of Ionesco's images may have made it appear that they embody an irremediable existential state, but in fact they are supposed to be a challenge to the audience, an exaggeration revealing what we commonly define as existence to be unnatural in order to provoke rejection as well as recognition, to make us aware that we are *more* than the empty figures representing us on stage, that there is a more authentic level of existence available to us. Hence the overt travesty in *The Bald Primadonna,* where the Martins meet as strangers and only discover that they are husband and wife by learning that they live in the same house and sleep in the same bed—yet the genesis of this situation (a game played by Ionesco and his wife on the subway) demonstrates the very capacity to care and share that the play categorically states to be non-existent—or the provocation of the original ending, where the author was to come forward and shake his fist at the audience, crying 'You bastards, I'll skin you alive.'

This challenge is both subtler and more explicit in the final image of *The Chairs* (*Les Chaises,* 1952), where the whole of an invisible fashionable society is ushered in, seated in serried ranks of chairs, sold programmes and refreshments to hear 'a message for all men, for all mankind', so forming an on-stage mirror of the real audience. The Orator, as a man who rhetorically presents another's words, is the actor; and the impossibility of communicating anything meaningful rationally, since he turns out to be a deaf mute, though as an image his 'performance' contains a great deal of meaning, repeats Ionesco's own dramatic approach in microcosm. This non-existent on-stage 'audience', described only in superficial and social terms by profession or dress, reacts in a purely rational manner once the Orator leaves—'snatches of laughter, whisperings, a "Ssh!" or two little sarcastic coughs', sound effects clearly designed to duplicate the probable response of the real audience—and we are left with a vision of ourselves as a void. The intention of this ending was specifically to block rational psychological interpretations of the play that could lead *The Chairs* to be seen as a *folie à deux*. Dramatically, the old couple

and their dialogue, which comprises the 'action' in a conventional sense, is no more than a prologue. The whole weight is on that final stage picture: on the audience as 'an absence of people', on 'the unreality of the world, metaphysical emptiness'. Yet obviously the real audience cannot be actually made to feel that they do not exist. To claim that what we are accustomed to accept as 'reality' (which after all is only a concept—as Ionesco agrees 'the world is a subjective and arbitrary creation of our own minds') is illusory, presupposes that other levels or alternative definitions of reality, represented by the Orator's 'ANGEPAIN . . . ADIEU' (Angelbread . . . God), are at least as valid. And if anything the spectator is being made aware that he does indeed exist, though only in very different terms to the 'nothingness' by which his social and material being is represented on the stage. For Ionesco the conceptual structure of reality is on the point of collapse, and his plays are 'helping to accelerate this process of disintegration', by reproducing in the spectator those states of awareness 'that could set the world ablaze, that could transfigure it' for him. . . . (pp. 202-06)

In his early work the emphasis is on creating the pre-condition for this 'transcendence'. And it is this that explains the breakdown of language and the reduction of those logical concepts, like time, by which we structure our lives, not just to farcical absurdity, but to arbitrariness (as in *The Bald Primadonna,* where a clock strikes the hours out of sequence and irrelevantly). In the same way the menacing magnification and proliferation of objects in a human vacuum, where characters are literally 'dispersed' by reduplication and therefore lack inner being, and even the characteristic rhythm of his plays, with their mad mathematics of 'dizzying' geometrical progression and acceleration that he compares to Feydeau's farce, are designed to drain all social and material existence of meaning, while simultaneously accentuating its external qualities to the point where it becomes unendurable. But the purpose of this apparent negation is to persuade the audience to affirm the (carefully unstated) opposite. . . . (p. 206)

As he noted with reference to Kafka, it is 'when man is cut off from . . . his religious or metaphysical roots' that activity becomes senseless, and this is his real criticism of society. Ionesco's vision is essentially a religious one, even if it stands outside 'official' theologies, and it is here that his apparently 'Absurd' work links up with the preoccupations of Brook or Grotowski. The motive force behind this transcendence, what makes it possible for man to escape from the 'stereotype' to which he has been reduced by society is 'God', defined as 'the universal energy that we partake of and participate in . . . a universal consciousness'; and in a play like *Victims of Duty* both poles of his vision are presented, the 'forgotten archetypes' as well as the stereotypes.

On one level this is the 'pseudo-drama' its sub-title calls it, with the same emphasis on the inauthenticity of socially defined existence. There are the expected transferable identities and confusions between different people with similar names (Madeleine changes from dull housewife to siren, to old woman, to the detective's mistress; the anarchist who murders the detective takes his place; the 'problem' of the play is whether the previous tenant of the Chouberts' apartment spelt his name 'Mallot' with a 'd' or a 't'), and the usual multiplying objects (by the end the whole stage is piled with the coffee cups of social convention), plus the theme of repressive conformity. On this level the play is also a parody of all the traditional dramatic assumptions about intellectually analysable meanings, logical motivation, or cause-and-effect plot, since, according to Choubert, 'All the plays that have ever been written, from Ancient Greece to the present day, have never been anything but thrillers. Drama's always been realistic and there's always been a detective about. Every play's an investigation brought to a successful solution.' . . . [In *Victims of Duty*] the detective's 'investigation' becomes a search into the Chouberts' subconscious and the banality of the Chouberts' bourgeois sitting-room dissolves into the protagonist's psyche. The empty reality of material objects and socialised people becomes dreamlike, while dreams become real.

In Ionesco's own production of *Victims of Duty* in 1968 in Zürich, it was this level of the play that he emphasised. Outlining his motive for writing as 'spontaneous research' into 'the unconscious', he stated that the scenes were transcriptions of his own dreams—in particular the central sequence where the protagonist, entangled in a wood, sinks down into a bottomless pit of mud, reappears as a child and climbs up a ladder to fly in a strong blue light—and noted that these were dreams which Jung had classified, thus linking his subjective experience with archetypes. The social surface was only to be considered as the catalyst for this transcendence. Conventional identity, already empty on that level, dissolved into projections of the psyche, affirming the awareness of 'true' personality on a fundamental, universal plane.

Choubert becomes the ego, 'the inner I', Madeleine the id and the stage a mindscape, with Madeleine and the detective acting as twining creeper and tree in the forest. 'In my original vision . . .' was repeatedly used by Ionesco, prefacing his directives to the actors. Their portrayal of the roles had to correspond to his original dream, and the figures were not to be presented in psychological terms as individuals. Their changes in age, relationship or attitude were sudden switches intended to reproduce the startling transformations, arbitrary contrasts and irrationality of dreams, and the actors were forbidden to search for personal motivations. At the same time the dream sequences were acted with as much physical realism as possible. The descent was illusionistic with Choubert, lit by a green light from beneath, gradually sinking through a trap downstage centre, while for the flight a ladder was lowered from the flies and the actor's climb was real, not mimed. This followed Ionesco's principle that 'authentic realism only exists in concrete images', which is the only way 'essences' can be represented in art.

It is on this surrealistic, Jungian level that Ionesco sees his drama as myth, a point he makes repeatedly in calling for a universal and 'primitive . . . drama of myth' springing 'from the soul of the people' (by extension his own, a subjective problem at its most fundamental expressing 'the problems and fears of literally everyone'), or drawing an explicit parallel: 'truth lies in our dreams . . . there is nothing truer than myth'. Almost all of his later plays are interpretable as dreams; in *Exit the King* (*Le Roi se meurt*, 1962) the stage is literally the consciousness of Bérenger, Ionesco's self-projection, whose castle is the inside of his head which disintegrates in death as he and the figures representing the different elements of his psyche dissolve into the neutral gray light of nothingness; while transcendence in the image of flying recurs in *Amédée* (1954) and *A Stroll in the Air* (*Le Piéton de l'air*, 1963), though in none of his plays can this state of integrated and liberated awareness of being be maintained, reflecting Ionesco's personal experience of its transitoriness. Myth therefore exists more as a potential in his plays than an actuality, though his consistent dramatic aim has been to create a 'drama that is not symbolist, but symbolic; not allegorical, but mythical; that springs from our everlasting anguish'.

It may be largely the association of Ionesco with 'the Theatre of the Absurd' that has given his work its popularity by setting it within a comprehensible intellectual framework, but this has led to a misleading emphasis on such themes as the isolation of the individual, the meaninglessness of human activity and the attack on a mechanical civilisation. In other words the negative preliminary part of his visionary process is taken as the whole, and the mythic and metaphysical dimension of his plays, with its return to 'primitive roots' in the subconscious, tends to be overlooked. . . . (pp. 206-09)

> *Christopher Innes, "Mythic Dimensions and Modern Classics," in his* Holy Theatre: Ritual and the Avant Garde, *Cambridge University Press, 1981, pp. 202-40.*

PHILIP THODY

In *Voyages chez les morts ou thèmes et variations* we again see Ionesco who keeps the promise of his title by exploiting his obsessions. For the play is a dream—or, more accurately, a nightmare—in which a man, known simply as Jean (like the hero of *La Soif et la faim*)—travels among the dead.

Neither the terrors which he undergoes nor the occasional flashes of political satire are likely to surprise anybody familiar with the atmosphere of Ionesco's later work. For when Jean's father describes how he found it quite natural to change from being a defence lawyer to writing novels for the police when the new régime asked him to do so, the anti-totalitarian Ionesco is as visible as it is in the *Journal en miettes* or *Présent passé, Passé présent*. Nor do the cultural references or philosophical jokes require much elucidation, welcome though they are in a text which reads dangerously like self-parody. It may be ingenious to show Jean's disappointment at finding himself still surrounded by "approximations" even when the archetypal chair is there to be seen and touched in the world of essences, but Ionesco's anti-Platonism is a little too obvious. . . .

Voyages chez les morts has not yet been performed on stage. This is not perhaps surprising, since it is hard to see how the printed version could be made into a viable play. It is too long, too episodic and too self-indulgent. A recent reviewer in the *Nouvelle Revue Française* wondered whether it might not be addressed "aux psychanalystes plutôt qu'aux metteurs en scène", and a play in which the Quest for the Mother leads the anxious son into the presence of a ferociously finger-nailed harpie is indeed so open to Freudian explanations as to be positively embarrassing. The October 1981 issue of the *NRF* contains, as it happens, a terrifying account by Ionesco of his first visit to a brothel, at the age of sixteen. Coming as it does after some very pertinent if rather right-wing comments on the Toxteth riots and the Royal Wedding, this extraordinarily honest piece of self-analysis raises the question of whether he is not now ready to move away from the theatre and towards a relatively new status as social commentator and auto-analyst of the Rousseau kind. The oneiric autobiography offered by *Voyages chez les morts* suggests that this is what now really interests Ionesco, and it may well be that the theatre is no longer as suitable a medium as it was for the language-games and surrealist imaginings by which he first added so original a note to French literature.

Philip Thody, "Auto-Analysis," in The Times Literary Supplement, No. 4112, January 22, 1982, p. 86.

ANNA OTTEN

Jean, the protagonist, sleeps. [*Voyages chez les morts: Thèmes et Variations*] is a sequence of dream images more intense and real than reality itself. Verbalizing deep-seated memories and thoughts, the author creates themes and variations structured like a musical composition, about nothing less than life and death. The experience that his play conveys is overpowering. From the opening painful encounter with his father, Jean tears open layer after layer of nightmarish memories of himself, his family and humankind that regain ominous presence and momentum as Jean bares his innermost thoughts.

Ionesco, to be sure, has always been very candid in his plays and prose, particularly in his *Journal en miettes* and *Présent passé, passé présent,* which shed much light on his life and intimate thoughts. Although the theme of death has been prominent in his works, not until this play have final questions about humankind been propounded with such urgency, honesty, clarity and force. Tragedy hand-in-hand with farce (since nothing makes sense in the face of death) mark the journey which takes Jean to the deepest images that dwell in a person's mind and to the questions that thoughtful people have asked since the beginning of time: Why do (or did) I live? Is there another world? Where am I "at home"? Are the writings in "ancient books" still valid? Does nothing belong to anybody, or does everything belong to all of us?

These questions torture Jean. He was happy only as a child and, later in life, in a luminous city that he calls "Aluminia, city of my heart . . . my dream . . . my true reality." The very name of Aluminia, when spoken, blots out shadows and grayness and fills his world with light. But happiness is brief. His father and oppressor, from whom the young man fled at seventeen, confronts the son once more: "You were famous among the living, that is to say, the dying; do the dead remember you?" Only then does Jean realize that fame too is ephemeral; instead of answering he indulges in tragicomic wordplay. He fears that he has confused dream and reality, presence and appearance, skill and vocation. After a long search for his mother and grandmother from whom he hopes to get support, he receives only accusations of neglect. A friend, once dear to him, blames him for having broken their friendship.

The luminous city is far away as he stumbles through dim corridors and pitch-dark rooms to a dingy basement apartment and a hostile environment. His greatest fear is of being engulfed in a black tunnel or bottomless hole into which the dreamer would be hurled to fall vertiginously for eternity. . . .

Throughout the play unanswered questions abound. A lonely man in the middle of an empty stage, surrounded by the unintelligible murmurs of the crowd behind the scenery, a tragicomic modern Everyman who has dared to undertake a voyage to the very end of the world of human experience, pronounces the final sentence: "I do not know."

Anna Otten, in a review of "Voyages chez les morts: Thèmes et variations VIII," in World Literature Today, Vol. 56, No. 4, Autumn, 1982, p. 647.

MARTIN ESSLIN

Ionesco, I know, does not want critics to chase after influences for his work. And nothing could be further from my intention. What I should like to do is to try and draw attention to an area of literature which seems to me to exude an atmosphere, a spirit very closely akin to much of Ionesco's *oeuvre* and to situate him if not within its confines so at least within the penumbra, the outer sphere of radiation of that world: the world of the fairytale.

I dislike the term fairytale. I think it has slightly pejorative connotations in English; there is an element of condescension inherent in the word. Nor do I think that the French equivalent *conte de fées* is a particularly felicitous one. There are not always fairies in fairytales. That is why I much prefer the word *Märchen,* which is merely a diminuitive of a word meaning story, just as the Russian word *skazka,* or the Italian *fiaba* or *storiella,* or the Danish *Eventyr*—which H. C. Andersen used— with its connotation of adventure, the wonderful event. (p. 21)

Where does the genre of the fairytale situate itself among the many types of popular narrative literature? The exact boundary lines between myth and Märchen on the one hand, and Märchen and saga, legend, fable, anecdote, *facetie* (Schwank—joke) on the other, are difficult to trace.

I should say that the fairytale (Märchen) shares with myth the occurrence of miraculous and dreamlike events. But while myth is on a lofty scale and deals with Gods and heroes that are the embodiment of tribal or national ideals and aspirations, while myth concerns itself with events on a cosmic scale, the fairytale or Märchen remains on a domestic, family level. One might say that in the sphere of myth the individual or the tribe or the nation dream of enlarging themselves to a cosmic plane; that the myth transfers individual problems and aspirations to a cosmic level, while the fairytale, although still using such elements as kings, queens, and princesses, brings them *down,* reduces them to a domestic, family scale. We tell our child a story about a king and a queen and a beautiful little princess, but the child knows that we are only talking about father, mother, and herself. Also: myth is on the whole tragic; the narratives of myth often have unhappy endings. The fairytale tends to end on a happier note. Myths are there to accustom us to the harsh ultimate realities of the human condition. Fairytales, on the whole, serve the purpose of reassurance. At the other end of the spectrum the fairytale does merge into the animal fable (there are talking animals in both the saga or legend and even the *facetie,* but these more earthy forms of folk narrative do not rise too high above the ground of everyday, non-miraculous events).

There is, of course, also a significant connection between the fairytale, the Märchen and the dream. . . . [To paraphrase Novalis]: "A fairytale is at bottom like a dream image—without internal logical connection, an ensemble of miraculous things and events, for example a musical improvisation—the harmonic sequence on an aeol's harp—*nature itself.*" Here we are, I feel, very close to what we know of Ionesco's own method of composition, the dreamlike trancelike yielding to the images that come flooding in and which play on the writer (whose skills, linguistic and intellectual, are like the strings of the aeol's harp) as the wind itself plays on that instrument.

But, if Ionesco's method of composition has points of contact with the very nature of the fairytale, is not his vision, unlike that of the fairytale, ultimately a tragic one?

I should, on reflection, dispute that view. Ionesco's vision is, above all, a comic vision, even though a tragicomic one. But are his *endings* really tragic? Does not Amédée float up into the air, freed from his domestic entanglement? *Le piéton de l'air,* admittedly, has seen a terrifying vision of ultimate destruction and the void, which the bystanders do not believe in. But that play also ends on a note of acceptance, however ironic.... (pp. 22-3)

Bérenger *has* seen the abyss and the void, but perhaps what matters even more is that he has accepted that vision. And similarly, the old man in *Les Chaises* dies happily, believing in the transmission of his message to future generations. Does it matter that his optimism has been unfounded? He too has accepted his situation and come to terms with it. What, then, of Bérenger in *Rhinocéros*? I also feel that the ending of that play is ultimately a good ending. Bérenger is refusing to become a pachyderm, we leave him in the hour of his triumph, his victorious, if perhaps futile, defiance. And the Bérenger of *Tueur sans gages*? Does he not submit to the knife? Yes, but does he not do so willingly, having accepted the ultimate absurdity of death and of the *condition humaine?*

There is thus in these plays of Ionesco's—and one could give other examples—a point at which the inherently terrible and tragic ending is, at the last moment, reversed, by the very act of the acceptance of the tragic situation. It is like the point of reversal in those fairytales when the hero or heroine accepts the necessity of doing something deeply repugnant, like that of kissing a horrible beast, or going to bed with a frog, and by that very acceptance reverses the situation into its opposite.... [There] is one play of Ionesco—a highly significant and important one, though also much neglected—namely *Le Tableau,* in which such a transformation actually occurs rather than being merely potentially possible and hinted at.

In that play the fat gentleman transforms his ugly sister Alice into a beautiful princess by shooting her with his pistol, and he does likewise with the ugly old neighbour woman, and finally transforms the painter, also by shooting him, into a Prince Charming. Only the fat gentleman himself remains as ugly as he was before. And so he begs the audience [to shoot him].... (pp. 23-25)

In *Le Tableau* Ionesco probably comes closer to the actual world of the fairytale than in any of his other plays, the world, that is, of the folk fairytale, which is the outcome of the collective subconscious of a whole nation, a whole culture. Many of the stories in the Bible, in Homer's *Odyssey,* and in Ovid's *Metamorphoses* fall into that category, as do many of the stories collected by Perrault, the Brothers Grimm, and other collectors of genuine folk fairytales. But parallel to the folk fairytale there is the Kunstmärchen, the consciously artistic fairytale written by known and often highly admired authors. How far back should we go to the earliest examples of this kind of consciously composed fairytale? Probably as far as Hellenistic times. Lucian's stories are *Kunstmärchen* and so is a work like *The Golden Ass* of Apuleius. I feel also that Rabelais' work is a prime example of a very early highly artistic use of the fairytale form. His Gargantua, and his Pantagruel, are, after all, modelled on the giants of the folk tale, and so is the story of a voyage or quest. Moreover, there is a quality of dreamlike fluidity and improvisation in Rabelais that I, for one, find very closely akin to much in Ionesco. And are there not affinities between the fragments of speech that float through the arctic region, which are frozen particles of language now melting in the sun, and the dead fragments of speech floating around in

La Cantatrice Chauve; are not Rabelais' orgies of language, his long lists and accumulations of synonyms somehow reminiscent of the verbal gymnastics in plays like *Salutations?* (p. 25)

But the practitioner of the *Kunstmärchen* closest perhaps in spirit to Ionesco is Hans Christian Andersen, that truly childlike fantasist from Odense on the isle of Fyn. I feel that a play like *Le Roi se meurt* with its transposition of a bourgeois family situation into the milieu of a bedraggled and decaying royal household is very close indeed in spirit to many of Andersen's tales, which incidentally, have repeatedly been dramatised and have thus played a noticeable part in the literature of fairytale drama. (p. 27)

Well, perhaps all this may seem to have very little direct bearing to our reading and understanding Ionesco. But I for one believe that we can gain a better insight into the nature of all that fairytale literature itself and of Ionesco's *oeuvre* if we set them side by side, without wanting to construct too many direct connections (although I have pointed, tentatively and humbly to one or two) and try to find the common ground from which they spring.

There is first of all, Ionesco's insistence—most eloquently and memorably expressed in *Découvertes*—which I regard as a masterpiece of critical insight into his own creativeness, one of his least-known but most important works—that to him the state of mind of the child, the freshness of his vision even as a child of two is the very basis of his creativeness. *Retrouver l'enfance* is the motto under which, at the end of that great book, he establishes his hope for the future. It is the world of the fairytale, the *Märchen,* which, in all literature is the closest to the spirit of that freshness of vision, that total lack of preconceptions which such a freshness entails.

The fairytale, like Ionesco's oeuvre, above all manifests an immense capacity for wonder. Ionesco has stressed, over and over again, that the essence of his *oeuvre* is that sense of wonder before the world's infinite capacity to surprise us. *L'insolite* is the *primum movens* that informs all of Ionesco's plays and narrative prose. No wonder, then, that it has its affinities with the world of the fairytale. The fairytale is the most *fluid* of all literary genres, the one in which the imagination is at its freest. (p. 30)

But if the fairytale contains a maximum of *l'insolite* it can also accommodate a maximum of another of Ionesco's favourite ingredients, *le cocasse:* in no other literary genre can the poetic and the grotesque live in such happy symbiosis side by side, can the transitions from the avowedly sentimental to the most grotesquely comic, or indeed horrible or obscene, be so easily accommodated and accomplished, without a break in style, atmosphere and consistency. And similarly in this genre there is no breach of any etiquette or convention, if the profoundest and deepest matters of life and death and the last things, the cosmic problems of the universe are mixed and intertwined with social satire, topical comment, or simple nonsensical fooling. Where everything is possible, where the imagination can move without let or hindrance, there are no disharmonies, no inconsistencies or illogicalities, provided, of course, that the tone of the narration, the tone of voice of the playwright, remains within that mysteriously delimited area which marks the boundaries of the fairytale style; that is: a directness and simplicity, a genuine naiveté of vision, without pretention, without affectation, without obvious attempts at cleverness or profundity. For this is the ultimate criterion here: we intuitively *know* whether a narration has that fairytale tone or not. Attempts have been made to define it. The fairytale has been categorised as being the *simple,* as distinct from the complex, forms of literature; it has been said that it is uni- or two-dimensional, flat, linear; and there is a good deal of truth in that too, but it is not a weakness here: The characters in the fairytale *need* no great introduction or exposition. They are simply there and we instinctively know their motivations and their natures. In this, Ionesco's work really harmonises with the fairytale tradition: do we need to know who *le nouveau locataire* is? or Jacques? Or Amédée? or indeed the Bérenger of the plays in which he appears? They are immediately accessible and defined, characterised and intuitively understood, simply because they are *the given,* the basis of a whole world; they are the consciousness of the dreamer and as such immediately identified with by the audience who is taken into the dream, in exactly the same way in which the child does not need to be told what kind of psychology the youngest son of three has, who is going out into the world to seek his fortune, because he or she immediately knows that the youngest and most vulnerable child is him- or herself. And the other characters then, being seen through the eyes of the self, have the simplicity and clarity of "the others" that are seen from the outside and thus appear simple and well defined.

Ionesco has achieved the immensely difficult feat of retaining the freshness and clarity of his childlike vision; hence his direct appeal to the child—which is to say our basic being, or archetypal self, before it has become encrusted and polluted with all the accidentals of the outside world. That is why we can intuitively and immediately identify with Ionesco's archetypal dreamer, his basic character, whether it is Choubert, the victim of duty; or the Professor of *The Lesson,* who, also basically, is only a naughty boy, or indeed, the girl pupil in *The Lesson* who is the archetypal schoolgirl; or Jean or *L'homme aux valises* or any of the other leading characters in Ionesco's plays and stories. In the sense that these characters are all ourselves, that they are Everyman—or rather the Everychild that hides in every man or woman—Ionesco's *oeuvre* is very close to the world of the fairytale.

And that, at least in my scale of literary values, is very high praise indeed. (pp. 30-1)

> *Martin Esslin, "Ionesco and the Fairytale Tradition," in* The Dream and the Play: Ionesco's Theatrical Quest, *edited by Moshe Lazar, Undena Publications, 1982, pp. 21-31.*

DAVID BRADBY

Like Beckett's theatre, Ionesco's is self-conscious and self-critical. Indeed, Ionesco was far more explicit about this aspect of his work, and produced quite a body of dramatic theory, whereas Beckett wrote none at all. Like Beckett's, too, his theatre was a theatre of shock tactics and here again he was rather more explicit than Beckett. . . . [In *La Cantatrice chauve,* our] common perceptions of reality are systematically undermined and language, our principal means of apprehending and controlling reality, is pushed out of control. By the end of the play a kind of linguistic terrorism has broken out and the projected endings were intended to drive home, in terms of concrete action, the aggressive power of language that has gone mad. (p. 74)

[*La Cantatrice chauve*] seemed totally destructive, but he continued to write, discovering that by rejecting all established conventions he had created a new one. The new convention relied on a number of confusing paradoxes. Most obvious of these was their combination of hilarity and despair, summed up by Ionesco in the phrase 'tragic farce'. Equally paradoxical was the fact that while their action was literal, often very physical, their principal subject was language. Ionesco returned again and again to the treachery of language, its apparently straightforward guarantee of meaningful communication, together with its disturbing ability to mean whatever we choose to make it mean. His most memorable image of the incapacity of language to bear the weight we place on it is the orator who appears at the end of *Les Chaises.* His is the appearance for which everything in the play has been a preparation; he is the one who will deliver to the world the message composed for the occasion by Le Vieux and his wife. This is to be the moment when a life-time's wisdom and experience is distilled into language. But when the orator gets up to speak it becomes apparent that he is deaf and dumb and can only make mysterious signs on a blackboard.

This attack on language led to such plays being labelled 'theatre of non-communication', which Ionesco objected to, claiming that he believed that people communicate only too well. What he wished to suggest was that the rational, discursive use of language was not the only, nor even the most powerful means by which people communicate. *Rhinocéros* contains a passage in which Jean, who is admonishing Bérenger for his moral laxity, and the Professor, who is conducting a logical argument on another part of the stage, end up saying exactly the same lines, echoing one another in perfect unison although their intended meanings are entirely different. The effect of this device is to arouse laughter in the audience and to discredit both rational discourse and the uses to which it is frequently put. The inarticulate roars of the rhinoceroses, however, are able to communicate directly with those who are beginning to feel tempted to join them. As they listen to the roarings and trumpetings, they are drawn like metal to a magnet straight out into the street to join the herd. In *La Leçon,* the Professor is able to rape and kill his pupil by means of the simple word *couteau* and in *Jacques* an ecstasy of orgasmic dimensions is achieved by the chanting of the word *chat.*

Rather than proclaiming non-communication, Ionesco displaces our attention from rational uses of language, refusing to treat it as central focus of the dramatic action. Instead of responding intellectually to his plays, Ionesco wants us, first and foremost, to respond with our senses. We witness a dramatic action in which things occur that are by turns shocking, funny, cruel, absurd. Illogicalities are left unexplained, paradoxes unresolved, but as the action progresses the tensions that are set up by this process generate a dramatic image of a nightmare world. (pp. 74-6)

In some ways Ionesco can in fact be best understood as a Surrealist dramatist. He has explained that his work originates, not from ideas, but from two basic states of consciousness, one of evanescence, light, release, the other of weight, opacity, confinement. His plays can all be interpreted as a struggle between these two forces, now one, now the other predominating. The paradoxical image of Amédée, at the end of *Amédée ou comment s'en débarrasser,* floating up into the sky suspended from the body that has formerly oppressed and crushed him is entirely Surrealist. . . .

Ionesco himself has declared that, although interested as a young man in Surrealism, he is not a Surrealist. He accuses the Surrealists of having become fixated on manifestos and systems and he feels that he differs from them in his working methods. . . . But even if his methods do not always coincide, his fundamental aim, to liberate the subconscious levels of the mind from the straitjacket of logic and to achieve this by means of a dream-like style of theatre, is very similar to the programme of the early Surrealists. Although he rejects the name of Surrealist, Ionesco is a member of the Collège de'Pataphysique, a mock-scholarly gathering devoted to the science of 'pataphysics invented by Alfred Jarry, who defined it as 'the science of imaginary solutions'.

In the place of rational argument or neatly constructed plot, Ionesco relies upon dreams. He claims to have been strongly influenced by the Jungian concept that every man suffers from the separation between earth and sky. Only in childhood, during a holiday visit with his mother to the village of La Chapelle Athenaise, did he ever experience unity and harmony. This experience was like being taken right out of himself and finding the world around him totally transformed. For its short duration he experienced a feeling of indescribable bliss and total release so that even gravity seemed to lose its power over him. In many of his works he draws on memories of this experience of bliss and also of the moment when it left him. (p. 77)

In order to maintain the 'sharp' and 'pitiless' quality ('acuïté impitoyable') of [his] dreamed realities, Ionesco chooses to avoid conventional dramaturgical methods. . . . He repeatedly describes his plays as 'abstract theatre', 'pure dramas', in which the rise and fall of dramatic intensity should be compared more to that experienced when listening to music than to a conventional play. (p. 78)

In point of fact the term 'abstract theatre' is rather misleading because the force of his plays relies so much on the very concrete, literal embodiment of his stage images. But it is true that through all their variety of situations, Ionesco's plays rely on exploiting a limited number of dramatic rhythms or progressions. The experience of Bérenger in *Rhinocéros,* which has some claim to being a political play about the rise of fascism in Roumania, is precisely parallel to that of Le Monsieur in a thoroughly apolitical, surrealist piece called *Le Nouveau Locataire.* Le Monsieur moves into a nice new appartment only to be followed by a stack of furniture that grows and grows to the point where he is first walled in and then literally buried beneath the mass of invading objects. Bérenger's revolt against the invasion of pachyderms is the same as the revolt of Amédée against the body that crushes him or the revolt of King Bérenger against the onset of death in *Le Roi se meurt.* In each case we witness an individual crushed by inhuman forces from outside that threaten to invade or annihilate him. The precise nature of these forces is less important than the accelerating rhythms with which they proliferate and finally overwhelm the protagonist. (pp. 78-9)

As the influence of Brecht became more pervasive in the course of the fifties, Ionesco found himself cast as chief opponent of political theatre. It was a role that he accepted with enthusiasm and has kept up ever since. He took every opportunity to satirise the supporters of left-wing political theatre in his plays, but did not stop there, spreading the polemic to other channels of communication wherever possible. In 1958, in *The Observer*, Kenneth Tynan accused him of writing plays that had no contact with reality. An exchange of articles followed, in which Ionesco argued that his plays did indeed have an impact upon reality, but one that was achieved through language and the artistic means of expression, not through political or historical contact. His claim was that he had enlarged the possibilities

of theatre language and that this had a more revolutionary effect than plays about revolution. 'To renew the language is to renew the whole conception or vision of the world. A revolution is a change of mentality. Every new artistic expression enriches us by answering some spiritual need and broadens the frontiers of known reality.' . . . (pp. 79-80)

Ionesco's claim to have renewed language, conception and vision must depend for its justification upon his exploitation of the rich resources of the stage. Every element in his plays becomes a bearer of meaning. Inanimate objects are as important as animate ones. Since they conjure up a dream reality, the plays depend a lot on atmosphere, which is generated by the use of settings, lights, colours, sounds, and on unexpected transformations, as one character dissolves into another, or some basic law of nature is denied, as when Bérenger finds he can fly (in *Le Piéton de l'air*). For their thematic content the plays are much less original, dealing with the themes that have traditionally preoccupied European dramatists, such as freedom, guilt, love, death. The most important of these themes and the one that recurs most frequently is that of death, a subject that has always obsessed Ionesco. . . . *Le Roi se meurt* provides the most sustained example of a play on the theme of death in Ionesco's theatre. The dramatic rhythm of this long play is provided solely by King Bérenger's attempt to fight off the inevitable approach of death. The conflict in the play arises from his repeated attempts to restore his regal dignity which is repeatedly undercut by Marguerite and the Doctor. In King Bérenger is summed up the most consistent tragicomic tension in Ionesco's work: the attempts of men to assert their dignity in situations where they are merely laughable. He never appears to be more than a grotesque mockery of a king. . . . He stands as a figure for Everyman and the play follows a similar pattern to the medieval morality play of *Everyman*. As in that play, Bérenger finds himself gradually stripped of all things that he relied on for support: his wealth, his power, even his love for the young Queen Marie, and, ultimately, his sense of selfhood. But unlike the medieval play, it does not end on a note of certainty. Rather than the soul ascending to be with Christ, we see nothing but a greyish light invading everything as Bérenger finally dies, the walls of his palace disappear and we are left with an immense, blank question mark.

This play shows Ionesco attempting to supply a rite of passage for a culture in which the power and efficacity of the traditional rites is no longer axiomatic. The public nature of the theatre and its traditional preoccupation with death make this a naturally tempting project. It has always been one of the functions of theatre to reconcile its audience to even the most unacceptable aspects of the human condition. Ionesco, in his own way, tries to do this. He offers a ritual for people who no longer believe in rituals; a passage from life to death that we can never take quite seriously, that seems to be mocking itself just when it is at its most serious, a ceremony that fully deserves the epithet grotesque: both comic and repulsive.

In the last analysis Ionesco's work must be seen as that of a mystic. A mystic for whom faith seems impossible, but for whom the traditional questions still nag with an undiminished urgency. . . . Rather than present his audiences with stories, debates or information he tries to administer a shock to their sensibilities that will remind them of what it feels like to live and to face death. In doing this, he succeeds in creating literal, concrete images of guilt, fear, isolation and so contributes to the forging of a more direct and more effective language of communication in the theatre. But this achievement is limited by Ionesco's inability to pass beyond the expression of individual joy or depression to the social dimension. When his characters experience lightness, joy, evanescence, it is always a solitary emotion. They cannot derive joy from togetherness with others. In fact it is almost always the pressure and intrusiveness of social existence that destroys their inner sense of bliss. In other words, Ionesco is incapable of seeing the world of personal relationships as anything other than smothering and stultifying and this in turn makes it impossible for him to deal with society in terms other than caricature. Although Beckett's plays could be said to be open to the same objection, they do not invite it in the same way because of their strict adherence to the treatment of isolated, marginal characters. Most of Ionesco's plays are set recognisably in the context of society at large. Yet Ionesco the mystic cannot see society as anything other than detrimental to the soul. As he said of his first creations in *La Cantatrice chauve,* they are 'hollow, purely social characters—for there is no such thing as a social soul'. . . . (pp. 80-2)

David Bradby, "The Parisian Theatre II: The New Theatre," in his Modern French Drama: 1940-1980, *Cambridge University Press, 1984, pp. 53-86.*

Franz Xaver Kroetz

1946-

German dramatist, scriptwriter, and nonfiction writer.

Among the foremost contemporary dramatists to emerge in West Germany during the 1960s, Kroetz favors linear structure, absolute realism, and minimal use of dialogue, a style of drama that Robert Brustein termed "modernist realism." Kroetz's plays depict in explicit fashion the sexual, cultural, and socio-economic conflicts of West Germany's rural and urban working classes, reflecting the influence of the *Volksstück,* or "folk play," a form originally characterized by the use of colloquial language and lower middle-class settings. Kroetz's dialogue, which consists of a rigid, barely articulate Lower Bavarian dialect punctuated by aphorisms and clichés, is often less meaningful than his characters' gestures and silences. According to Kroetz, "the most important action of my characters is their silence. . . . Their problems lie so far back and are so advanced that they are no longer able to express them in words."

Kroetz studied acting in Munich and Vienna before turning to playwriting in the late 1960s. His earliest plays eschew conventional moral standards and often graphically depict shocking acts of sex and violence. However, these scenes are presented in the same flat, banal manner as his dialogue to evoke an authentic sense of fatalistic tragedy. When a young girl's parents oppose her affair with a young man in *Wildwechsel* (1968), she resorts to patricide. A mentally retarded peasant girl is impregnated by an old farmhand in *Stallerhof* (1971; *Farmyard*), and in a sequel, *Geisterbahn* (1975), the same girl murders her child rather than submit to city officials who wish to place it in a foster home.

Kroetz became an active member of the German Communist Party in 1972, and many of his subsequent dramas reflect his belief in Marxism. These realistic works expand on his early depictions of working-class conflicts by focusing on the effects of consumerism, capitalist society, and popular culture upon lonely, lower middle-class individuals. *Wunschkonzert* (1972; *Request Concert*), an unusual play lacking dialogue and conflict, depicts an evening in the life of a lonely woman, who maintains a precarious sense of order and purpose through her performance of such everyday activities as watching television, eating, and cleaning. Her suicide, within this context, is equally mundane, attributable only to the sterility of her existence. Many of Kroetz's subsequent plays reveal a less relentless fatalism. In *Through the Leaves,* a revised version of Kroetz's early drama *Männer Sache* (1971; *Men's Business*), a middle-aged woman tolerates the abuse of her occasional lover because he fills a void in her life, but she retains her dignity when he leaves her. A similar optimism prevails over economic pressures in *Oberösterreich* (1972; *Upper Austria*), in which an expectant married couple contemplate abortion for financial reasons but decide to have the child despite their problems. In a related play, *Das Nest* (1975; *The Nest*), the family is almost destroyed by the husband's participation in a corporate scheme involving illegal disposal of toxic chemicals. With the aid of a union, however, he decides to oppose the corporation's wish to keep him silent. *Mensch Meier* (1978), according to Kroetz, completes the trilogy begun with *Upper Austria* and *The Nest.*

In this play, a working-class family is undermined by a number of problems which Kroetz relates to capitalism.

In addition to his dramas, Kroetz has written numerous scripts for film and television. Many of these works are collected, together with journalistic articles relating to political topics, in *Weitere Aussichten* (1974).

DRAGAN KLAIĆ

Who is Kroetz? An unexpected discovery: a German playwright who emerged after Weiss and Handke to create a substantially different style and dramaturgy in German drama. Kroetz is both a newcomer and an outsider. He has a fondness for life, not in general, but for what he experienced in his earliest surroundings, among the peasants and workers of Bavaria. Therefore, his plays have a clear and easily recognizable geographical and social framework. The dialect Kroetz uses makes his work particularly distinctive. His heroes are small peasants with their wives, children, and servants; industrial workers in the first period of urbanization; small shop-owners. They work in their courtyards or workshops, they cook and eat meals, sit in the gardens of small inns while drinking beer and talking in their rigid, condensed idiom. These are the people who never appeared in the plays of Brecht, Weiss, or Handke.

Kroetz knows that an idyll can be banal while banal life can be tragic. The banality of quiet domestic life, as led in *The Stallers' Yard* (*Stallerhof*) and in *Dear Fritz* (*Lieber Fritz*), is almost intolerable. The peasant Staller family, which appears in the first play, and the florist Otto and his family in the second, have their daily order, their fixed world, their small duties, their security and peace in the same way that in *Men's Cause* (*Männer Sache*) Marta, who sells bones and giblets for pet food, has her independence, her prosperous business, her fantasies. Miss Rasch in *Music on Request* (*Wunschkonzert*) has her everyday ritual of returning home and of housekeeping.

Behind this order and illusory self-satisfaction with a modest but constant prosperity, lies the loneliness of characters, their struggle to win a happiness which they always miss. A hint of disorder and even a pinch of perversion emerge behind these conventional existences, ready to create, at the right moment, the atmosphere of tragedy. Beppi, the retarded daughter of the Stallers, is unable to resist the old servant Sepp. In *Ghost Train* (*Geisterbahn*), a continuation of *The Stallers' Yard,* she is Sepp's common law wife who overcomes her idiocy by motherhood. The idyll is disturbed by Beppi's unexpected pregnancy, and then renewed by her relationship with Sepp and the birth of their child. Sepp's sickness and death destroy the achieved balance and turn the young mother into a child murderer. Banality and tragedy continue to co-exist: Beppi remains in jail while her parents continue their petty life.... Lonely Miss Rasch (in *Music on Request*), after cleaning, washing, cooking, and dining, finishes her daily ritual by commiting suicide. Since she lives alone, there is no one to witness this act, and the radio set monotonously broadcasts music requested by listeners.

Idiocy, sexual crimes, perverse passions, pathological and suicidal obsessions cannot imperil the conformity of modest Bavarian life, but at the same time, cannot remain hidden and repressed forever. When they come out, these deviations from the accepted standard of Kroetz's world must disturb the flux of trivia. The social and familial environment defends itself, pushing strongly toward the previous state of decency, e.g. banality. When this condition is re-established, the deviant character is left hopeless, lonely, victimized. His or her intimate suffering or personal debacle cannot affect anyone else. The character is speechless; perhaps some semi-articulated words can be muttered at the end, such as Beppi's ''Papamama.'' Miss Rasch dies at the end of *Music on Request* without having said a word during the entire play. She has no one to speak to.... Kroetz's works remain truthful to life, even though they lack the careful selection of elements chosen solely because they are ''representative,'' ''typical,'' or ''significant''—a characteristic of naturalist creation. An absolute ideal of truthfulness leads to a kind of realism which, because of its sincerity, completeness, and clarity, becomes magical and fascinating. This is achieved mainly through Kroetz's attitude towards the selection of his dramatic material and its timing within the play. In our time, we have developed a certain aversion to realism, considering it dull, straight, without deviation, without fantasy. It is easy to object to realism on the grounds that it is more concerned with the detailed process of reconstruction than with the material under examination. The ultimate goal of realism can be seen as an imitation of life which tries to be perfect, so that the illusion cannot be distin-

guished from the reality. An impulse towards imitation causes the playwright to neglect the demands of theatre, misusing the time and the patience of the spectators. When it lacks dramatic effects, tension, and originality, this self-concerned realism is selfish and boring. In the process of playwriting, the author cannot avoid condensing, choosing, speeding up, and intervening in his initial material.

Kroetz, however, refuses to condense an event, to make an action out of it, to bridge gaps of low dramatic density, to pick up exciting moments and drop the uninteresting ones. He is open-minded and patient, ready to accept in his plays the long intervals of passivity and immobility, the everyday, simple and conventional operations, the meaningless dialogues, the acts usually considered inappropriate in public. Life has its own natural rhythms, with periods of tension and relaxation; the spectator feels pleasure in experiencing the amplitude. And even immobility can be viscerally exciting for the audience. Simple actions, when performed carefully and without theatrical exhibitionism, strike us by their complexity, logic, and order. Empty words and sentences . . . , [platitudes and proverbs, and ready-made expressions] are a large part of everyday conversation. In Kroetz's plays they become self-sufficient and do not conceal anything. They do not stand for something that cannot be said, they do not disguise some passionate feeling (as in the case of Chekhov's plays where trivia covers the internal turmoil of a character.) In Kroetz's open concept of theatre, banality—banality for itself and not as a symbol for anything—has its place because it dominates the life of the characters.

Banal dialogues and actions become attractive and dramatic because Kroetz is never in a hurry. He always gives enough time to his characters, leaving the normal rhythms of life undisturbed by the demands of theatricality. The analytical character of this realism is what makes it so fascinating.... The performers do not distract or confuse the spectator since they give him enough time to absorb sensations from the stage. Indeed, the usual becomes unusual, the simple becomes complicated, and everything opens to the spectator's examination and reflexion.

Of course, a certain selection has been made, not within a given scene, but only in choosing which action will create the scene. Kroetz takes an action in its entirety, and, in placing it on the stage, changes nothing.... In deciding what will form a scene, Kroetz rejects any moralistic considerations, scruples, or general standards of decency. In this way, he imposes some demands generally thought impractical from the theatrical point of view (the presence of the animals on the stage, the active role of children in a play, etc.) Kroetz introduces some actions which are ''tasteless,'' ''shocking,'' and ''not for the stage'' (and which really might be tasteless, shocking, and not for the stage in the opinion of some spectators): onanism, intercourse between an old man and a retarded girl, an unsuccessful abortion, the strangling of a baby, the torture of a dog, etc. Such actions, performed with the ease of drinking a glass of beer, and with a precision and openness hardly ever seen on the stage when such matters are involved, counteract the apparent banality of previous and subsequent acts, reinforcing the extraordinary character of everything that happens on the stage and demonstrating the force of Kroetz's realist instinct. (pp. 94-7)

These acts, (obscene, private, cruel ones) which are reserved only for life penetrate the theatre, but in their execution a mobile border line between the life-event and the stage-event, between reality and illusion, is drawn. The magic force of the theatrical act lies precisely in the vacillation between two realms, in the constant and delicate movement of the borderline. Where Kroetz succeeds is in presenting these exciting vibrations while dealing with material whose untheatricality comes so deeply from within the realm of life. He turns this into theatre, combining it with other elements (cruel, private scenes) which are even more from life and even less appropriate for the stage. Absolute realism in the execution of the first kind of scene and a compromise in the execution of the second balance each other. The first brings the stage very close to life; the second, as a warning, points out the distinctive nature of the theatrical action. Realism, even that which tends to express itself as absolute, still remains but one among many possible theatre styles. (p. 97)

Dragan Klaić, "The Theatre of Franz Xaver Kroetz," in yale/theatre, *Vol. 6, No. 1, Fall, 1974, pp. 94-7.*

MARTIN ESSLIN

Five years after his breakthrough into success Kroetz has an *oeuvre* of some twenty plays and screenplays to his credit. He has also, as an active member of the West German Communist party, taken a vigorous stand in a number of polemics. *Weitere Aussichten* is a massive collection of his journalistic output together with a number of older and newer plays, screenplays, radio and television scripts. The principle of selection is none too clear: Kroetz's best-known and most successful plays are not included, probably because they have already been published under other imprints. So the older and less successful scripts and the newest plays which are to be found in this *Kroetz-Primer* . . . seem to be an almost random assembly of leftovers and not-yet-placed material. But perhaps even this explanation does not hold water: for, curiously enough, the book . . . is in fact an East German publication. . . . So perhaps the selection merely reflects those aspects of Kroetz's work which have found favour in the East and can be offered without risk to East German readers.

That Kroetz is a playwright of exceptional talent is beyond doubt: the precision and originality with which he handles Bavarian dialect is masterly and so is his ability to let the unspoken thoughts of his primitives shine through the grunts and groans, the hums and haws of their speechlessness. The question which this particular selection of his writings poses, however, is the age-old problem of whether party political commitment might not be detrimental to an artist's development and achievement.

The juxtaposition, in this volume, of the author's dramatic writings with his political journalism and polemical outbursts sheds a peculiarly useful light on this problem. Those of Kroetz's plays in the book which are free from an over-obvious propagandist bias seem far more effective—even as political polemics—than his heavy-handed attempts to inject party-political object-lessons. . . .

[A] somewhat simpleminded inability to see the reality of the West German scene beyond the smokescreen of pseudo-Marxist dogma pervades [*Weitere Aussichten*]. In a number of articles Kroetz bitterly complains about the repressiveness of the German theatres and television channels, who prevent playwrights of his political persuasion from reaching the masses, while the blurb on the jacket and the eulogistic preface stress the fact that Kroetz is among the most frequently performed playwrights in West Germany and has reached millions through his television and radio scripts. Contemporary West Germany

may have its ugly, cigar-smoking capitalists and nouveaux-riches, but nothing could be further from the truth than the idea that left-wing ideas are suppressed; on the contrary, a "Marxist" stance is almost compulsory if one wants to get access to the most reputable publishers or theatres. . . .

Kroetz never tires of stressing that his motivation in turning communist is his *Mitleid*, his compassion for suffering humanity. Yet in one of his political writings in the book, a reportage on cooperative agriculture in the GDR . . . , he shows a less compassionate side. In talking about the process by which agriculture was collectivized—the land was first *given* to agricultural labourers and ten years later they were forced into collectives—Kroetz discusses those farmers who did not want to join the cooperatives—in theory a wholly voluntary decision:

> The struggle for the total collectivisation of agriculture lasted till 1960. Many could be persuaded, some also fled to the West; and there were also those who, when they realised that you could not escape the agricultural collectives, took a rope and hanged themselves. . . .

Compassion indeed! Reading this kind of writing one is forcefully reminded of that famous Nazi publication about prominent Jews, which after each biography of people like Einstein or Stefan Zweig added in brackets *Ungehängt*—"Not yet hanged".

Kroetz is very talented. But for real greatness as a writer more is needed than mere talent—a truly important writer must also have intelligence, insight and critical self-awareness. And that means knowing that compassion with suffering humanity also includes farmers who do not want to be forced to join a "voluntary" cooperative.

Martin Esslin, "In the Mouths of the Speechless," in The Times Literary Supplement, *No. 3941, October 7, 1977, p. 1163.*

PAUL ALLEN

[*The Nest*] deals with the attempts to create a totally self-contained, controlled world for their coming baby by a working class couple.

Their attempts fail because the overtime being worked by the lorry-driver father . . . eventually involves dumping poisonous waste at a beauty spot, where in due course it badly burns the new baby. The message is ambiguous: one closing line suggests it will be all right if he joins the union, but a more persuasive conclusion is the decision to let the baby play unhindered among the manicured flowers; you can't tie up the world in neat parcels.

But it wasn't the message that seemed the important thing. Kroetz is an extreme naturalist, and his instructions, that we be shown, for example, the labour of emptying all eight containers of the poison, were carried out to the letter in one of two wordless scenes lasting twenty minutes each. A point is made, but it's a laborious one, and it doesn't bear repeating. I was glad to have seen it, once.

Paul Allen, in a review of "The Nest," in Drama, *No. 139, 1st Quarter, 1981, p. 45.*

ROWENA GOLDMAN

[*The Nest*] is an example of the most powerful type of political theatre. It presents an apparently simple family drama of love and disruption after an inevitable chain of events, and then hits home hard with the realisation that economic motivation lies behind it all.

A hard-working lorry driver, John, and his pregnant wife Martha, plan diligently for the arrival of their baby. . . . [But the father] has unwittingly disposed of highly toxic industrial waste [for his boss], resulting in the near death of the baby and the temporary breakdown of the marriage during which John attempts suicide.

The play has a united-we-stand, divided-we-fall philosophy. John promises to expose the boss who in his turn threatens to hand John his cards, leading the hero to his ultimate belief that he must join the union—for two reasons. First, to prove to Martha that he is not just an "organ-grinder's monkey", but a brother in solidarity, and second, for protection, because "in the union you're not alone".

Through subtle suggestions Kroetz implies that whether capitalist employer or downtrodden employee, the need to survive is the force behind every action. One feels that even if John had known the real content of the barrels he would have gone ahead with his task, because the promise of a £50 reward, and the knowledge of what that money will bring, induces a more powerful feeling than the fear of the maybe. . . .

The Nest bears all the marks of a mature work with a political point to make. . . .

> Rowena Goldman, in a review of "The Nest," in Drama, No. 141, 3rd Quarter, 1981, p. 31.

RUSTOM BHARUCHA

Franz Xaver Kroetz's *Request Concert* is a rarity in the contemporary theater: it has the daring to confront the banality of its subject matter. (p. 66)

The action of the play is without incident even though it is packed with details—the non sequiturs and minutiae of everyday life. There is no plot; in fact, it would be more appropriate to speak of a scenario of gestures. There is only one character—a nondescript middle-aged woman—who does not speak a word in the course of the play. . . . *Request Concert* exposes the life of this woman on one particular evening when she returns to her apartment alone. For more than an hour, the audience surveys her most private and inconsequential actions, gestures, and movements. Voyeurs in the dark, they watch the woman undress, cook, watch television, listen to the radio, eat, defecate, wash dishes, embroider, sleep, get up from bed, and then commit suicide.

What is so terrifying about these actions is not just their triviality and absence of nuance, but the fact that they lead to preparations for a suicide that are no less prosaic than the actions which preceded it. One would expect the suicide to be charged with a significance that would contradict the banality of the play. One would expect it to stand outside the framework of the play by virtue of its extremity and suddenness. But the suicide in *Request Concert* remains unquestionably within the confines of the play. It is the very apotheosis of banality. (pp. 66-7)

[The] woman radiates an antiseptic aura one associates with models in television commercials for deodorants and antiperspirants. Her movements are brisk, her actions defined. The only casual business that interrupts her metronomic routine is invariably inspired by her obsession to keep the apartment *clean.* . . . The efficiency of her gestures is quite formidable.

This obsession to order an environment which is already ordered stimulates the woman to create additional jobs for herself. For instance, while cleaning the sink, she just cannot resist rubbing the kitchen cabinets on top of the sink. They are spotless like all the fixtures in the room. And yet, even though the apartment is scrupulously clean, it is somewhat sterile. One can almost smell the slightly acrid odor of the various sprays used by the woman in the course of the play. . . . [The woman's activities] seem to reassure her that her life is busy. (p. 67)

Another more suggestive and lingering revelation of the woman's inner life occurs when she rubs her hands with cream while waiting for the soup to boil. For a few moments, [she] ceases to bustle around and stands still. She rubs her hands slowly, even sensuously, and stares almost directly at the audience even though she seems to be lost in her own world. Her face gradually reveals a range of infinitesimal emotions, a combination of pain and longing and intense sexual frustration. She seems to be isolated from any possibility of a relationship with another person; she seems quite estranged from the world.

It is not easy for an audience to determine whether she had an earlier relationship or whether she was once married. In a somewhat arbitrary note to *Request Concert,* Kroetz mentions that his character, whom he names Miss Rasch, had once experienced a painful love affair that was followed by years of sexual abstinence. . . . Kroetz is, perhaps, more eager to *explain* his character in the note to *Request Concert* than he is in the text of his play which consists of two pages of stage directions.

Apart from emphasizing the early romantic experience in the life of Miss Rasch, Kroetz asserts that "she became susceptible to advertising and consumerism during the years of sexual abstinence." Though this connection seems somewhat contrived, it tells us something important about how Kroetz wants his character to be viewed by the audience. Clearly, he is not merely interested in exploring the psychology of an unmarried woman, who lives all by herself in an apartment, lonely and emotionally desolate. He is not interested in her predicament alone. He is more concerned with that quality of urban life in a technological society that produces predicaments such as the one dramatized in *Request Concert.* For Kroetz, the psychology of an individual is directly related to the social circumstances that shape it. (p. 68)

What is so pitiful about the woman's gestures is their inauthenticity. Most of her gestures are not her own: they have been borrowed from images in fiction and catalogues. Even her use of toilet paper seems to be inspired by advertising techniques. To watch [her] dexterously fold toilet paper around her fingers, then turn to the audience with her eyebrows arched and her mouth gaping wide, then clean her rear end with a rhythmic rotation of her hand, is to confront the juxtaposition of a very intimate act with a very contrived set of gestures. Even when sitting on the toilet, the woman in *Request Concert* cannot resist posing and playing out a fantasy inspired by postures of models in magazines. So, even her process of defecation has, in a sense, been influenced by her submission to consumerist lures.

For those readers who may be shocked by this seemingly risqué interpretation of a very basic human act, it is necessary to point out that, for Kroetz, no human act is too embarrassing or too intimate to be enacted on stage. In *Farmyard,* a retarded girl has diarrhea on stage, and in the same play, a character casually masturbates. These actions are brutally unsettling compared to the act of defecation in *Request Concert* . . . which is less shocking than illuminating: it tells us something about the woman. It is not simply there to elicit a visceral response from the audience, unlike the actions in *Farmyard*. It is ironically viewed and enacted, and consequently, it demands some kind of "intellectual" response from the audience. The longer one views the act of defecation in *Request Concert,* one becomes increasingly convinced that it is not significantly different from the other actions performed by the woman such as her cooking and cleaning and tittivating in front of the mirror. Her defecation is as banal and contrived as any of these actions. (pp. 69-70)

On the surface, the preparations for the woman's suicide are as meticulous as the preparations for her dinner. She places a napkin on the table and empties some sleeping-pills from a box on the napkin where she spaces them at regular intervals in two neat rows. . . . One by one, the pills are swallowed, but then, there is a hitch. There is no water left in the glass. The woman rises and fetches a decanter of wine and a solitary wineglass that she seems to have kept aside for "special occasions." She returns to the table and celebrates by pouring herself a glass of wine. Quite inadvertently, she spills some wine on the table. It is her only *untidy* action in the entire production, and the effect is startling. One gasps at her clumsiness. She, too, seems to be taken completely by surprise and utters an ingenuous and heartbreakingly spontaneous exclamation. She then makes a gesture that is even more startling than her pouring of wine on the table: she actually *wipes* the wine-stains on the table with the sleeve of her precious polyester nightgown. There is an unconscious finality to this gesture, more chilling, to my mind, than the utterance of any suicide note. Finally, there is just one submission to pathos when the woman timidly lifts the wine glass for a second and toasts a silent "cheers" to no one in particular. It is a deeply sentimental and moving moment. After drinking the wine, the woman continues to sit at the table, very still, without seeming to think of her action. Insofar as her silence "expresses" anything, it is a sign of what remains inarticulate within her. It is an acknowledgement of what she cannot express. (p. 70)

Kroetz's rationales for survival seem pedantic when one confronts the desolation of the woman's life in *Request Concert.* In the New York production, the choice of suicide seemed inevitable, even brave. One did not question its validity. One accepted its swiftness, its silence, its absence of motivations. It is possible, of course to agree with Dragan Klaic (the author of the only comprehensive study of Kroetz's plays in English,) that the woman commits suicide because she wants to remove herself from the order she has regimented for herself. But it is less easy to accept his interpretation of this action as a "rebellion against order."

"Rebellion" is, perhaps, too strong a word to convey the passivity of the woman's suicide. It also implies a level of consciousness about her action and its implications that she does not seem to possess. . . . In her final moments, the woman reveals no resentment, no suggestion of anger, no sign that she is committing suicide because she is *against* anything. She simply goes through her actions without trying to justify herself or prove anything. When she finally drinks the wine and sits at the table, she astonishes us with her grace. (p. 71)

Rustom Bharucha, "*Kroetz's Act without Words,*" in Theater, *Vol. 13, No. 1, Fall-Winter, 1981, pp. 66-71.*

COLETTE BROOKS

[*Request Concert* exemplifies] various aspects of Realism. To begin with, we are forced to exercise our powers of observation: over the course of seventy minutes (real time) we simply watch as a woman . . . moves about her apartment—eating, watching television, working on a rug, reading. There is no dialogue, there being no one to speak to; the play is simply a series of discrete actions strung for our inspection.

More than most "realistic" drama, *Request Concert* seems to *be* what Baudelaire termed "a fragment torn from our planet"— a piece (or slice) of life as contained and as *present* as is possible in art. This has less to do with our "being there" than with the manner in which the evening unfolds. Each action is absolutely itself, each moment accorded the single-minded, unthinking attention that is best described as autonomic. Until the very last moment of the play, when she takes an overdose, Ms. Rasch has done nothing *remarkable*—nothing "conspicuous, unusual, or worthy of notice"—and her final action (the sort that impels normally eventful dramas) cannot be considered apart from the number of smaller moments that have preceded it. During the play, one doesn't think to wonder *why* the character changes clothes, or *why* she eats, or *why* she washes the dishes; at play's end, this cumulative lack of consequence takes its effect, and questions as to why she kills herself seem oddly out of place, or beside the point, as well.

Because the woman doesn't reveal herself through "significant" action, or muse aloud as one might in a monologue, the curious spectator is forced back upon inference; for the "inner life" of this character isn't to be seen on the surface. (pp. 49-50)

What may be most "realistic" about *Request Concert* is its rendering of a human being's electronic relationship to the external world—a modern circumstance that has altered our conception of what constitutes experience and has, in the process, made us as much "prisoners" of our homes as the soul was once said to be of the body. Ms. Rasch's radio and television are sensors, tracking and pulling in signs of life from elsewhere, serving to affirm the existence of a world that is truly *without* her. . . . In this age, the media have become the "eyes" and the "feet" of man, and *knowledge* has become *information;* a diminutive comprised only of raw data, existing quite independently of a mind that need know or digest it. This modern form of "knowing" is not, however, without resemblance to its ancestral archetypes: when Ms. Rasch periodically adjusts her set to get "the sharpest signal she can," she is doggedly pursuing the Cartesian ideal of the "clear and distinct" perception.

In *Request Concert,* in fact, Realism has come full circle: we are back in Plato's cave, that "prison dwelling" representing the "region revealed to us through the sense of sight," lit now by a flickering television tube. Without leaving her apartment, Ms. Rasch is able to see and hear more than past ages thought possible; yet the world so faithfully rendered is arguably more remote than ever. . . . The absolute luminosity once granted only to "God" is now licensed out to others, and this illusory omniscience promises to make us newly blind. To see everything is to see nothing, finally, to value the sensation of light rather than the world that it illuminates. (pp. 50-1)

Colette Brooks, "*Remarks on Realism,*" in Performing Arts Journal, *Vol. VI, No. 2, 1982, pp. 46-51.*

FRANK RICH

The radio is almost always on in *Through the Leaves,* the latest Franz Xaver Kroetz play to appear in New York. The dial is tuned to an easy listening station that broadcasts lulling songs like "Moon River" and "Chances Are". Yet there are few other soothing sounds in this acidic account of a woman butcher and her abusive lover. When the heroine's yelping dog isn't drowning out the radio, we're likely to be assaulted by the cacophonous grunts of crude sex—or the grinding of a butcher's saw cutting through a thick bone.

Through the Leaves is not pleasant, but it sticks like a splinter in the mind. Mr Kroetz is a young West German dramatist who chronicles the alienated working class, and he practices kitchen sink realism of the grimmest sort. (Let Mr Kroetz's characters approach a kitchen sink, and they're likely to stick their hands into the disposal.) The playwright's abrasive style is so distinctive that he's fast becoming as cultishly popular in New York as his fellow Bavarian (and one-time collaborator), the late film maker Rainer Werner Fassbinder. . . .

In Mr. Kroetz's view the butcher's plight begins with her job. Annette's butcher shop is a specialty operation that sells only the inferior "utility" cuts of meat—the entrails used primarily as animal feed. Annette herself might as well be a discarded animal organ. Though she delights in her status as an "independent" business woman, we see that she is chained to dehumanizing drudgery by day and to her adding machine at night.

[Victor], the man who suddenly invades Annette's constricted existence, is also a prisoner of economic circumstance. He's a brutish, beery laborer who regards "freedom" as the right to disappear on weeklong drunken binges. A slave at work, he likes to be "the boss about everything" with women during off hours. When he has sex with Annette, he mocks her frumpy middle-aged appearance and tells her not to waste his time by disrobing completely. "Just get rid of the underpants," he commands.

Annette obeys the oppressive Victor—not because she's a fool, but because she's desperate for any human contact. Throughout the play, we hear the butcher's diary entries, and while they often end with phrases like "everything is fine," it's clear that Annette knows better. Unlike her lover, she's introspective— she dreams of finer things like "imagination" and at one point composes a homely poem. What Annette doesn't know is the cause of her distress, or its cure. She believes that "being diplomatic" will arrest Victor's endless badgering, and she rationalizes her subjugation with tortured logic: "Maybe he'll kick me so far down that he'll pick me up again."

The action unfolds in stark fragments that are set both in the gleaming butcher shop and its squalid back room parlor. . . . After a while, the two characters begin to resemble the calf's head that's displayed behind plate glass in the butcher shop's refrigerated display case. But there's some gallows humor to lighten the chill. When Victor and Annette decide to partake of the leisure and fun that is their reward for hard work, they dress up in incongruous costumes from *My Fair Lady* to go to a "Night in the Tropics" ball. . . .

[A great] distraction is the director's decision to take . . . [the] pungent English translation, which retained the play's German setting, and relocate it in Queens. [Another director] similarly transposed *Request Concert,* but the switch didn't seem too far fetched in a piece that contained no dialogue. In *Through the Leaves,* the social texture remains Germanic (as typified by the specialty butcher shop)—and both lovers seem too unworldly to be inhabitants, however downtrodden, of an America in which everyone is exposed to "The Phil Donahue Show."

Frank Rich, "Kroetz Play Is His Third This Season," in The New York Times, *April 6, 1984, p. 3.*

ROBERT BRUSTEIN

A surprising development of one recent form of modernism has been the revival of a meticulous painstaking realism. This, after all, was how the modern dramatic movement began—in the naturalistic novels of Zola and the domestic plays of Ibsen— but for over a half century now realism has been primarily identified with mainstream theater. . . . [In] Germany, largely because of Franz Xaver Kroetz, such realism has recently been identified with the most advanced form of playwriting. (pp. 25-6)

[*Through the Leaves*] represents a good introduction to modernist realism. . . . As in most of his work, Kroetz is here concerned with moments of crisis in the lives of desperate depressed people living barely at the level of consciousness; and, again as in most of his work, his treatment of this victim class is pitiless, harsh, remorseless, cruel, redeemed only by fitful flashes of compassion. Annette is a middle-aged spinster who makes her living by cutting up "utility meats" for dog food; Victor is a coarse unemployed roustabout who occasionally services her crudely in a room behind the shop. . . . But Victor is not only frequently unfaithful, he also deserts her frequently for long periods of time. . . . Each time Victor returns, however, he is more abusive, insensitive, and violent. Witnessing the lovemaking of this unappealing, overweight couple is sometimes indistinguishable from watching two sides of beef having their loins rubbed in her butcher shop; at one point he tries to take her while she is chopping up a mess of calves' liver.

Annette's generous if bovine love for Victor, however, is not entirely free of resentment, and there are occasional hints that she would like to carve him up with her cleaver. Still, in exchange for his intermittent company and occasional spurts of pleasure, she passively accepts her role in what amounts to her complete abasement and humiliation, never totally losing her cheerfulness even when he deserts her for good at the end ("All alone—longing—period").

Kroetz, a Marxist, makes little effort to dramatize the dignity of working-class people, whom he shows to be leading lives of noisy desperation. Relatively tender toward women, he displays no feeling whatever for his males, who are almost invariably depicted as human brutes living at the lowest scale of existence. As a result, his plays usually emerge as laborious documentaries of man's inhumanity to man (and, more often, to women), making no concessions either to theatricality or to the pleasure principle—grim and squalid vignettes of humanity in extreme circumstances, a poetry of aesthetic abstinence. (p. 26)

Robert Brustein, "The Premature Death of Modernism," in The New Republic, *Vol. 190, No. 21, May 28, 1984, pp. 25-7.*

ROGER DOWNEY

To appreciate Kroetz's achievement fully, he must be seen in context, because in many ways Kroetz began his career as, and remains even today, something of an outsider: a cuckoo in the nest of German *Kultur*. (p. 6)

A man who loves independence, Kroetz was fortunate in his birthplace. Munich is one of the very few cities in West Germany where a lively "free-theater" scene exists and thrives. Like his compatriot and exact contemporary Rainer Werner Fassbinder, Kroetz was free to develop his craft in his own wayward fashion, free to act, direct, write as he pleased, paying little regard to "the Culture Industry" as embodied in the vast production machines of the state-subsidized companies.

By the time Kroetz arrived at maturity in the late 60s, those machines were beginning to creak dangerously. The postwar German theater had been explicitly designed as a sanctuary, a place devoted to the classics. . . . If critical attitudes to contemporary society were expressed at all, it was allegorically, through the neo-Expressionism of writers like the Swiss authors Frisch and Dürrenmatt. But by the mid-60s, a post-war generation full of nothing but contempt for *Kultur* and its smug consumers was ready to take on contemporary reality again. In Franz Xaver Kroetz they found a dramatist eager not only to portray reality, but rub his audience's nose in it.

All the most striking characteristics of Kroetzian dramaturgy appear already fully-formed in the earliest play in the published canon: *Game Crossing,* which dates from 1968. The play's 27 short scenes occur in more than a dozen locations centering on a crowded working-class family apartment. Scenes begin and end sharply, abruptly—once Kroetz employs the theatrical equivalent of a film jump-cut with particularly telling effect— but within each scene the timing and texture are those of the most miniscule kitchen sink realism: people take showers, use the toilet, eat meals, wash dishes, shop, picnic, make love, work, tell dirty jokes. The dialogue is couched in the most ordinary of ordinary language, broken by half-completed sentences and desultory silences.

The author's notes on performing style in *Game Crossing* are exemplary for virtually all his later work. "The baldness (*Kargheit*) of the language should be matched by an economy in the stage picture. Projections could be used to sketch in the various realistic settings quickly and simply. Alternatively I recommend a bare stage with only the most essential set pieces." The cast of *Game Crossing* is equally exemplary: a truckdriver, his wife and teen-aged daughter, and the daughter's boy friend. (Six other figures appear briefly: in later Kroetz pieces the number of characters is pared down as ruthlessly as the language and settings, to the bare minimum necessary to the action.)

In plays set in Austrian hill-towns, on remote Bavarian farms, in urban high-rise apartments, the same figures recur again and again: truck-drivers, *Hausfrauen,* half-grown children, common laborers, facing again and again the same situations: lack of money, lack of a job, family frictions, unwanted babies, trouble with the cops, the boss, the neighbors. (pp. 6-8)

The reality depicted in all Kroetz's earlier work is penetrated through and through with violence and the threat of violence. Some German critics found the plays melodramatic, even sensationalistic, and certainly there is hardly a piece before 1974 without its rape, abortion, baby-murder or suicide, its half-wit, cripple, or fumbling petty criminal. To an American familiar with the popular dramatic literature of the 1930s, the Kroetzian milieu may recall that of John Steinbeck—or, even less flatteringly, Erskine Caldwell.

But even Kroetz's earliest plays are devoid of the sentimentality, the romantic idealization of poverty and ignorance, that make *Of Mice and Men* or *God's Little Acre* such queasy reading today. In early Kroetz, a flat, hard light beats down on everything, for characters and audience alike: there are no shadows to creep into, no corner to hide in. The characters are so rigidly confined by circumstance, by character, by the very language they speak, that violence seems only the natural outcome of unbearable pressure.

Kroetz is, through and through, a political playwright: given the seething political and social currents of West Germany and West German theater between 1965 and 1975, he could hardly have been otherwise. But in the early plays, political or social criticism is entirely implicit: a society capable of producing the stunted, half-timid half-ferocious figures that populate them must *ipso facto* be rotten, root and branch.

In 1973, Kroetz was the most-performed living playwright in the German language, but found himself at something of a dead end in his work. He began striking out in new and controversial directions. Always the maverick, he joined the fearfully unfashionable Deutsche Kommunistische Partei—the most conventional and doctrinaire of left-wing West German parties. . . . Most of his time over the next year and a half was devoted to reportage and adversary journalism: his "creative writing" was limited mostly to adaptations of other writers' work and to "agitprop" pieces, stylistically quite uncharacteristic of his earlier work.

When after more than a year Kroetz wrote his next straight play for the stage, he returned to the form and milieu of the earlier plays, but with a different attitude toward his materials. *The Nest,* written in 1974, premiered in 1975, is a free-standing work, but also a kind of commentary on an earlier play: the two-character *Upper Austria,* written in 1972. To make sure no one misses the connection, Kroetz takes extreme measures. Not only are the characters of *The Nest,* sociologically speaking, identical with those of the earlier piece: the two plays begin with an identical situation—a couple sitting in their living room at the end of an evening of tv.

But *The Nest* begins with a warm, impersonal voice on the tv announcing "you have been watching *Upper Austria,* a play by the Bavarian dramatist Franz Xaver Kroetz"! What's more, Kurt and Martha casually discuss the play they've seen before going to bed, even making some elementary connections between its story and their own situation. Such self-consciousness, such awareness of the possibility that things can be different than they are, would have been far beyond the capacities of the dreamy, feckless Heinz and Anni of the earlier play.

Upper Austria is, among the early plays, strikingly placid in event. Truckdriver Heinz does *not* murder his pregnant wife; Anni does *not* get a backstairs abortion. But the play provides little reason to expect the couple's future to be brighter than their past: the play ends as it began, with dreams of a trip to Vienna, accompanied by a Strauss waltz wheezed out on a concertina.

Martha and Kurt in *The Nest* are not dreamers but, however fumblingly, doers, and the sphere of their activity is meticulously defined. In the third scene of the first act Kurt and Martha spend a long Saturday afternoon calculating the cost of having a baby. The text of the scene is little more than a catalog of nursery items, brand-names, and prices; but before it is over we know not only the precise economic situation of the little family but also its members' attitudes to the outside world and their perceptions of self: Martha's fiscal naivete and tv-commercial-cultivated "consumerism," Kurt's paternal attitude to his wife and his dependence on the boss's continued favor, the couple's unquestioning submission to the rule of "keeping up with the neighbors."

The Nest is also novel in the intimate linkage established between the private lives of the characters and a specific external condition that concerns society at large. Partly through ignorance, partly through a stubborn refusal to face inconvenient facts, Kurt makes himself responsible for (literally) poisoning his private Paradise, a little Alpine lake, and thereby for the illness of his baby son. In accepting that responsibility, Kurt implicitly accepts responsibility for his own life. The individual does not make the world he lives in; but any change in that world begins with an individual choice. The play ends with Kurt's decision to be no longer, in his own words, "a trained ape" in someone else's circus.

The Nest is a transitional work in Kroetz's *oeuvre*. The private and public worlds of the play make contact but do not, so to speak, interpenetrate, and the manner in which contact is brought about seems a little mechanical, if only in comparison to the seamless dramaturgy of the "private" scenes in the play. In Kroetz's later pieces, the great world outside continues to shape and color private experience, but never again does it obtrude into the action in such a direct, "plotty" way.

Three years later, *Mensch Meier,* described by the author as the completion of a trilogy with *Upper Austria* and *The Nest,* had its simultaneous premiere at four West German theaters. It is difficult not to regard the play as Kroetz's masterpiece. In this tale of a jittery, imaginative Munich assembly-line worker, his vague, housebound wife, and their silently observant teenage son, he has achieved an almost perfect blending of family microcosm and societal macrocosm, finding ways to deploy the action on the largest emotional and thematic scale without violating his own strict canons of verisimilitude.

The development of Kroetz's worldview and dramaturgy during the 1970s is easy to discern through a comparative reading of the successive versions of the dramatic material first published as *Men's Business* in 1970. This first portrayal of the relationship between a female butcher and her laborer lover ends with a scene of expressionistic violence. The final version, *Through the Leaves,* first performed in 1981, begins with identical characters and an identical situation; but the development of the action reflects an enormous maturation both in social understanding and in subtlety of dramatic technique.

Since 1978 only three new Kroetz plays have appeared on German stages: comparatively few for an author of such eruptive productivity. This slowing-down reflects in part Kroetz's determination not to repeat himself, the difficult self-imposed task of extending the range of his dramatic technique without sacrificing any of the terrain he has already conquered. But it also reflects vagaries of taste—professional, not public. West German theater over the last 10 years has increasingly become director's theater, stage designer's theater, dramaturg's theater, critic's theater—anything but playwright's theater. Indeed, the living playwright is often perceived as an impediment to dramatic process, annoyingly insistent on the integrity of the text and objecting to its reduction to a mulch in which the director's and designer's interpretive fancy can grow luxuriantly.

On the whole, the most-produced living German authors tend to be those, like Botho Strauss and Heiner Müller, whose scripts more closely resemble a set of intriguing raw materials

to tickle a director's imagination than they do free-standing works of art. An author like Kroetz, only too clear about what his plays are and mean and determined to see his ideas reflected in the final product, offers little scope to the superstars of *Regietheater*. (pp. 8-10)

Kroetz's most recent play, *Fear and Hope of the Federal Republic of Germany* premiered in late January 1984. Formally, the new work represents a great departure from Kroetz's customary technique. The play's 15 scenes do not form a continuous narrative but a panorama of scenes from ordinary West German life in a year troubled by political reaction, unemployment, and renewed fear of nuclear war.

The title indicates affinities to the exiled Bertolt Brecht's 1938 propaganda play *Fear and Misery of the Third Reich . . . ;* an attempt to alert the world to the realities of life and society in Nazi Germany. Kroetz's dramatic technique is similar, but its target is different. *Fear and Hope* aims to alert the cultivated German public—at least that portion of it which still attends the theater—to the corrosive currents circulating through the German body politic; to give these currents a visceral reality and generality of application which the most vivid newspaper or television report cannot attain. (p. 10)

But the mix-and-match structure of *Fear and Hope* also indicates a desire on the part of Kroetz to create a new kind of theater which might be called *Gebrauchstheater*, theater for use: a hybrid of straight play and propaganda piece, performable in its entirety in the palaces of culture but also constituting a kind of library of dramatic materials to be drawn upon for educational, inspirational, agitational purposes, and performable in non-traditional venues as various as living room and union hall.

It may seem optimistic of Kroetz to compose in this fashion, but he has every reason to believe in the technique's efficacy. In the United States, Kroetz's plays are considered even by their admirers to be difficult, downbeat, painfully serious. Hard as it may be to believe, this is not their impact in their native land. There Kroetz is a popular playwright—not in the sense of one aiming at commercial success, but one who has achieved both commercial success and access to a broad audience without compromising his principles. I will always remember the evening I spent in the little Frankfurt suburb of Neu-Isenburg at a performance of Kroetz's *Neither Fish nor Fowl*. The hall was flat-floored, the seating folding-chairs; the production was a tackily-mounted quasi-commercial tour, and the size of the audience due no doubt in part to the presence of the author (something of a TV star, thanks to his appearance there as the star of his own *Mensch Meier*) in the cast. But for whatever reason they were there, the audience—as ordinary-middle-class an audience as I have ever seen outside a high-school auditorium at school-play time—was wholly absorbed with what they were seeing: an examination of life as they live it, shot through with gentle but persistent encouragements to consider why it is lived that way. It would be difficult anywhere in North America to find an audience of the kind I saw in Neu-Isenburg at a "serious" theatrical performance. And the reason may well be in part because there is no playwright in North America so wholly dedicated to finding that audience and communicating directly with it. (pp. 10-11)

Roger Downey, "Kroetz Before 'The Nest' and After," in Theater, *Vol. 15, No. 3, Summer-Fall, 1984, pp. 6-10.*

LANGDON BROWN

Mensch Meier demonstrates the difficulty of creating an articulate dramatic work using inarticulate characters. West German author Franz Xaver Kroetz's play depicts familiar victims of capitalism: three members of a working class family. Father Otto Meier is an assembly line worker whose limited view of the world is summed up in his description of laid-off fellow workers "from down the line"—he can't identify what they do, and seems resigned to never finding out. Otto rails against a system that "plugs him in" to work and unplugs him for the weekend. He vents some of his rage on his wife Martha, who bravely struggles to maintain the semblance of family life in the face of her husband's alternating impositions and inattentiveness, and in the face of the family's primary problem, son Ludwig. Ludwig is a sullen teenager whose ambition to become a bricklayer's apprentice clashes with his father's desire that he go into banking. Otto extracts revenge by asserting a petty economic tyranny over Ludwig, mirroring that exercised over Otto by his boss. Although Otto can act out on his family the same excesses which are destroying his own peace of mind, he is incapable of identifying or engaging his enemy. The audience quickly accepts the improbability of any member of the Meier family summoning the ambition or intelligence to reverse his or her fortune.

Having abandoned traditional dramatic interest in plot development, Mr. Kroetz attempts to stimulate his audience with a rapid and antagonizing sequence of scenes graphically depicting dehumanization. (p. 426)

As is typical in this sort of exposition of the evils of capitalism, the goaded characters, unable to think their way out of their difficulties, resort to attacking each other. Although this play is not as violent as some of Kroetz's other works, there is a notable explosion when Ludwig is denied the 50 marks he needs to attend a rock festival and steals the required amount from his mother's purse. Otto and Martha discover their loss at the supermarket, and are humiliatingly forced to return items to the shelves when they are refused credit. Otto reacts by destroying the family living room and driving Ludwig out of the house. Otto's outburst sparks a mini-revolution on the part of Martha, who leaves him and takes a room in a boarding house only slightly drearier than the apartment she has escaped from.

At this point the play surrenders its logic. As Act II progresses, Martha finds a job in a department store, Ludwig begins training as a bricklayer, and both refuse to come home to Otto, who pleads for the restoration of their former life. Martha and Ludwig seem to have achieved some sort of apotheosis, although Mr. Kroetz does not make clear why Martha's job selling bedroom slippers or Ludwig's laying bricks fails to inspire the same anguish as Otto's assembly line job. A modest form of happiness for these people seems to reside in accepting the awful fate that capitalism has in store for them, leavened by the kind of hope Martha wanly expresses in looking forward to the day when she is allowed to operate the cash register. . . .

[The production is most successful when the characters are depicted] in moments of escape from their deadening routines. Otto's moving escape into a fantasy world where he flies a model airplane in the European championships sets up the disconcerting moment when he erupts and destroys his plane. After the family goes for an outing, the pleasant memory is displaced by Otto's mistaken recollection of an error a waiter made on their bill, reinforcing the intrusion of economics into the fabric of their lives. Even Otto's attempt at making love is a failure because he can't forget that his boss has failed to return his ball point pen.

At such moments, we have a Chekhovian sense of the characters' immediate dispossession of any sensation of pleasure. But on the whole, the power and vision of the play are undercut by a directorial concept antithetical to the text, and are also diminished by the author's odd journey from emotional grand guignol to a sentimental ending. (p. 428)

> *Langdon Brown, in a review of "Mensch Meier,"* in Theatre Journal, *Vol. 36, No. 3, October, 1984, pp. 426-28.*

VARIETY

It's too bad such good theater as **Help Wanted** is also so completely depressing. That's the case with German playwright Franz Xaver Kroetz's 10 vignettes about the homeless, the unemployed, the suicidal and the lonely.

The ensemble performances, which in nine out of 10 cases is a pairing of a man and a woman, depict scenes where at least one of the characters is on the brink of desperation—the most poignant being that of an unemployed bookkeeper . . . who asks his wife if she wants to commit suicide by burning to death under the tree on Christmas Eve. The scene is aptly titled "Christmas Death."

In another, a desperate and drunk single woman pleads with a man to marry her knowing full well he doesn't speak a word of English. . . . [The woman] is perfectly balanced by her mystified Haitian guest . . . who utters not a word but whose expressions reveal his growing revulsion. . . .

Although **Help Wanted** is the work of a German, it has been translated and adapted to give it a distinctively American feel, including references to Social Security, unemployment compensation and President Reagan.

What is retained throughout is the Marxist undertone fostered in all of Kroetz' plays, most of which are about the exploitation of the proletariat.

> *Brit., in a review of "Help Wanted," in* Variety, *February 5, 1986, p. 152.*

Peter (Chad Tigar) Levi

1931-

English poet, novelist, translator, and travel writer.

A former Jesuit priest, Levi writes classically influenced poetry characterized by graceful rhythms, casual rhyme schemes, and a subdued tone. His verse reflects his concerns with nature, death, human relationships, and humanity's proper role in the world. These themes are affected by Levi's awareness of and concern for the spiritual nature of all things. Levi often relies upon emotional responses to deeply personal experiences; as a result, his poetry has been described as elusive and cryptic. However, Martin Booth stated that Levi's poetry "has, in recent years, become far more accessible and exacting, gathering in force, excitement and power while at the same time not losing its calm and authority."

In his first book, *The Gravel Ponds* (1960), Levi celebrates with simple language and gentle rhythms the beauty of life and nature. Many critics consider *Pancakes for the Queen of Babylon: Ten Poems for Nikos Gatsos* (1968) to be Levi's finest early work due to its sharp images and broad thematic scope. Consisting of a cycle of poems dedicated to the Greek poet Nikos Gatsos, the book evokes surrealist effects through visionary pastoral imagery. In his well-received volume *Private Ground* (1981), Levi's concern with landscape and nature centers on death and rebirth in the natural world and in human life. Levi's use of the elegy form emphasizes his tone of integrity and sadness as he explores friendship and love in the context of death and grief. *The Echoing Green: Three Elegies* (1983) furthers Levi's work with the elegy form.

Levi has also written two complex and erudite thriller novels, *The Head in the Soup* (1979) and *Grave Witness* (1985). These works relate the adventures of private detective Ben Jonson against the exotic backgrounds of archaeological explorations and art museums. In addition, Levi is the author of several popular travel books, including *Atlas of the Greek World* (1980) and *The Light Garden of the Angel King* (1983).

(See also *Contemporary Authors*, Vols. 5-8, rev. ed. and *Dictionary of Literary Biography*, Vol. 40.)

Oxford and County Newspapers

Levi is good, as in ["**The Gravel Ponds**"], when his *cri* seems correctly adjusted to his *coeur*. And there are other poems and parts of poems which are exact in their feeling and memorable in their expression. I dwell on the failures because they could so easily be mortal. In the rhetorical 'the terrible rain'; in the falsely simplistic 'He was a small, delightful, active man, / I was glad it was on Good Friday he died'; in the hollow "**For Robert Frost**" and the specious "**When Poisoned Socrates**", there is a streak of the kind of phoneyness which can become wildly popular. It will be a good thing for poetry, as well as for the author, if Peter Levi acquires that self-torturing concentration which must expel the fraudulent.

> Donald Hall, "*True and False Feeling,*" in New Statesman, *Vol. LIX, No. 1517, April 9, 1960, p. 530.*

NORMAN MacCAIG

Peter Levi's book [*The Gravel Ponds*] puzzles me. His lines move with an easy and graceful gait. His language is simple and natural. The atmosphere of his poems has nothing in it of the murky, the prophetic, the apocalyptic. And yet, quite often, I boggle at such imprecisions and implausibilities as:

> Saturday
> Was the colour of his socks.

DONALD HALL

Peter Levi has written in *The Gravel Ponds* a mixture of seriously good and seriously bad poems. The good ones depend on exactness of feeling; and the bad ones are bad because the feeling does not ring true. Poets who are mainly emotional, who depend not on the graces of form nor the compulsions of argument, rely on an *instinctive* verification of their own feelings. When their instinct fails—or when they fail their instinct—they fake. 'Sincerity' is a technical term; when a man uses clichés, hollow literary rhetoric, and confused metaphor, we doubt the authenticity of his feelings: a verbal chicanery evades the reality of his emotions. One of the few benefits of a training in technique is that it gives the poet another weapon against self-deceit.

Or:

> the dead with suddenly sweating wrists
> cry out for birth.

Why wrists?

Does this seem niggling? If there is a note of petulance here, it comes from observing an obviously sensitive, unpretentious and honest mind just failing to create the poems of its intention because of a fault that is exactly the one you wouldn't expect it to have. There is something wrong when one is continually questioning the words as one reads them.

> Angels and pit-ponies are blind.

One assumption and one error in one wee line. There are complete poems which come off, quite a number of them. But I fancy Mr. Levi's next book will be a better one than this. (p. 583)

Norman MacCaig, "Noise and Solemnity," in The Spectator, Vol. 204, No. 6878, April 22, 1960, pp. 582-83.

ROSEMARY F. DEEN

The poems in *The Gravel Ponds* have a grave and quiet air partly because of their technical qualities: the simple diction, the easy control of the line, and the shapely stanzas. In addition there is something pastoral about Peter Levi's themes. The pastoral traditionally springs out of a nostalgia for a place of peace and a state of innocence. Many of Mr. Levi's poems celebrate intellectual order. The poem **"Over the Roof . . . ,"** a kind of small-scale "Il Penseroso," describes a remote, hexagonal room, a retreat for "a mind at peace." Some poems mourn for the peace that life allows only within sharp limitations, as in a poem about slum lovers for whom loving "made nothing better":

> So they loved,
> like the aimless air
> or like walking
> past shut doors
> in a never quiet street and talking.

Mr. Levi knows how to use images from pastoral nature as symbols for powerful ideas. The poem **"My Mind Reads . . ."** grieves for Adam's punishment and loss in an image of "his deer, moving without cover."

But the pastoral tradition is not simple or "escapist," as it is popularly supposed. It is *about* innocence and not itself naive. Milton's thoughtful man ends by aspiring not to seclusion but to "something like prophetic strain," and this strain of passionate thought is a supreme theme of Mr. Levi's. ["**The Gravel Ponds**"] laments the loss of "wilderness"—the innocent animal vitality and freedom killed in "the long distraction / of the heart's inaction." . . .

It may be startling to hear in the measured tone of voice of these poems evocations of an elemental vitality: sea monsters in whose "water-muted ear" the clamor of the docks is only half-heard; a sibyl prophesying under a tree "bloody with fruit"; or a seasonal sacrifice, "some rite of the blood's heat" like a "slaughter of ships and cocks." But one of the great themes of modern poetry, expressed in Eliot's "Christ the tiger" and in Yeats's swan, "brute blood of the air," is a need to refresh the idea of the unity of life and the deeps from which it springs. Mr. Levi joins this tradition in a poem such as the beautiful

"An Angel Sat on a Tomb-Stone Top . . ." The setting seems pleasantly archaic: wind in the pines, shepherd's flute, and shepherds telling the story of the death of Daphnis. But the story is only "half-remembered," and the angel warns them:

> Sing when thin cicadas chir in the heat, and the thickets
>   have their leaves.
> Autumn is coming and that will pick them clean.
> Winter is coming with his claws of ice to break the
>   flute and bend the pleasant pine.
> At the year's end stands Christ in a pillar of fire.

> (p. 405)

Rosemary F. Deen, "One of Poetry's Great Themes," in Commonweal, Vol. LXXII, No. 16, August 5, 1960, pp. 404-05.

R. I. HAMILTON

Peter Levi is a fluently obscure writer—[in *Water, Rock and Sand*] he deals obsessively in a narrow and unvaried range of bleak landscape imagery that never quite reveals a coherent or identifiable shape. R. P. Blackmur, talking of E. E. Cummings's 48 uses in one book of the word 'flower', concluded that Cummings used the word very much as 'the incomplete mystic repeats the name of god to every occasion of his soul.' There is something of this inscrutability in Levi's use of his very personal idiom—the question is always whether or not the reader can possibly have shared his special experience of it. There are few distinct visual or dramatic situations here— landscape offers figures but not experiences, it is submitted to a private system of rhetorical selection but is rarely felt to be the invigorator of the arguments it serves. Levi establishes a relationship between concrete and abstract in which both are diffused and generalized. The result is a thinly textured and elusive poetry. (p. 839)

R. I. Hamilton, "Plain-Dealing," in New Statesman, Vol. LXIV, No. 1656, December 7, 1962, pp. 839-40.

THE TIMES LITERARY SUPPLEMENT

Father Levi undoubtedly has an ear for original and acceptable variations on the familiar stanza-forms and on the more soporific harmonies of word-sounds. His poems [in *Water, Rock and Sand*] are like the motions of a stylish conductor's baton— they startle attentiveness in the reader, draw his attention quickly on, hold him poised or distract him, then lead him swiftly on again; and they can keep this up.

But generally there seem to be no instruments being led by the baton. Each of the poems has indeed some pretence to a theme— schoolboy memories, images of departure, Prospero, Death the Huntsman. But allusion to a theme seems only a negligible part of the duty of the words in each poem. The important reason for their presence there is to construct, out of their play of sounds, the baton and its fascinating movements. However the baton does successfully bemuse—and it is just as well that it does. For anything like normal attention to the meaning and tone of the words makes one realize, with a start, that Father Levi has pressed into his service abstractions and images and clichés, rhetorical and colloquial and plain-ugly expressions, without regard to any kind of wholeness in the poems apart from their new formal patterns. . . .

The few poems in **Water, Rock and Sand** with anything like a coherent meaning to make its mark are those where the word-material includes plenty of landscape items and colours:

> The faceless sun
> rising in a sky of sharp grey
> infuses hanging vapour with a clear
> lemon wrack of light.

Here the prevailing wintry imagery seems in loose momentary accord with the spectral abstract music. But all in all there is a long step for Father Levi to take from his present command over initially seductive form to the writing of poetry that may sustain its command over the reader; and it seems a pity that this volume is so wholly devoted to the first.

> *"Form and Feeling,"* in The Times Literary Supplement, *No. 3186, March 22, 1963, p. 202.*

THE TIMES LITERARY SUPPLEMENT

Peter Levi is an altogether gentle poet, yet in [**Fresh Water, Sea Water** he] has some hot tussles with the physical world: "I fume coarsely along in the fine air", and so on. But . . . Father Levi uses old-fashioned watercolours, and even his most vigorous and would-be muscular exercises have a wan elegance, a pallor of the study. There seems to be an oddly adolescent infatuation with "being a poet" in these poems, and many of them are no more than vaguely affirmative noises about the mystery of creating. In **"Poem in March"**, for example, he looks at

> Builders at work high up printing on air
> one economic movement, climbing in
> the leafless forest of the scaffolding,

which is neatly if unadventurously observed, but then goes on to relate the seen thing to "human life":

> For things so bare so rhythmic and so tough
> I cannot find a word simple enough.

But this is too artfully empty an abnegation, so he ends

> and the religion of my poetry
> is this, what life is or what it could be.

Such abstract trailings away into mere musing make one wonder whether such a poem has any more impetus than the desire to make a poem. The ingratiating tone of **"Science Fiction"** seems to underline an inability to come to terms with anything but whimsy:

> I belong to the Monster Society,
> they are my only ramshackle heroes,
> I really love them, and whenever I see
> monster films I cheer them from the back rows.

This is embarrassing. "I have lived ten years in a kind of dream", writes Father Levi, and it is not mere coarseness that makes one mutter, "Well, snap out of it".

> *"Poetic Postures,"* in The Times Literary Supplement, *No. 3391, February 23, 1967, p. 139.*

HOWARD SERGEANT

Father Levi, a delicate landscape artist of the first order, seems to be far more at ease with the landscape than with people and there are times, when reading [**Fresh Water, Sea Water**], that one could wish to find a little of [Peter] Redgrove's earthiness

and vigour, [Thom] Gunn's penetrating vision, Stevie Smith's sly humour, or failing these, at least some sense of compulsion about Peter Levi's work. In the opening poem he describes a scene in terms which might justifiably be applied to his poetry:

> Humanity deserts the public beach.
> Humanity should have died out in us,
> we should be as the stones are, should retire,
> retire, retire. . . .

for if he writes occasionally about human beings he keeps them strictly at a distance, and retires as soon as he can to his **"Landscape with a Wish,"** **"The Tractor in Spring,"** **"Landscape with Poet"** or his reflections upon **"Thirty Ways of Drowning in the Sea."** Technically, Peter Levi is competent indeed, and he describes what he sees with the sensuous eye of a painter, with great feeling for language, if only as a complement to his pastoral moods and impressions. (p. 50)

> *Howard Sergeant, "Individual Talent,"* in Poetry Review, *Vol. LVIII, No. 1, Spring, 1967, pp. 48-50.*

MARTIN DODSWORTH

Fresh Water, Sea Water is a difficult book. . . . The tone is extraordinary, an aloof declaration of belief in human qualities, so cryptic as to belie the human altogether. I do not fully understand the book, nor do I find what I understand of it at all sympathetic. It is very much a book of Christian verse, meditating on the way in which human imperfection makes redemption possible. The long poem **"Thirty ways of drowning in the sea"** is not yet another variation on Wallace Stevens. It takes up the reference in David Jones's inscription to 'Him who freed the waters et qui maxima quaeque sacramenta in aquarum substantia condidisti'. This is done in a very oblique fashion; the obliquity, whilst making it *new,* for no one has written in English in this way before, also gives the poetry a chilly feeling. The poems want to work at a level that is not rational, and yet there is little sense of the spontaneous and unwilled. The result is memorable, ponderable, but inhibiting. . . .

> *Martin Dodsworth, in a review of "Fresh Water, Sea Water,"* in London Magazine, *n.s. Vol. 7, No. 1, April, 1967, p. 114.*

TULLY POTTER

I wandered lonely through Peter Levi's new collection [**Pancakes for the Queen of Babylon**]—feeling I might as well be a cloud for all the contact with reality his "Ten Poems for Nikos Gatsos" provided. At last I decided reluctantly I must leave the poems to Mr Gatsos—reluctantly, because Peter Levi is a poet of brooding integrity and these latest poems are shot through with insights. The images are there, too. Key images flick in and out like leitmotifs throughout the book, and they are images which seem to be worth tracing.

So I did not feel I was being conned; I felt more as if Mr Levi had shuffled his images, his ideas—his very lines—and had dealt them without turning up a single straight flush. The music was sparse and sporadic as in a Boulez composition, without the mathematical compensations of Boulez.

Mr Levi has taken off out of this world, but he has failed to convey this reader into the next. I have failed, too. I appreciate the working of an intense talent, but I fail to receive his communication. I hope Mr Levi's new departure will lead him through chaos to the harnessing of chaos. I am sure he is poet enough to do it. I respect his having made the initial leap. (pp. 296-97)

Tully Potter, "Casting Off," in Poetry Review, *Vol. LIX, No. 4, Winter, 1968, pp. 296-97.*

THE TIMES LITERARY SUPPLEMENT

The ten poems in *Pancakes for the Queen of Babylon* are dedicated to the Greek poet Nikos Gatsos; and bearing in mind recent political events in Greece, it seems likely that the poems express Father Levi's concern over the widening gulf between the laws of men and the Law of God. But this unfortunately is more guess-work than confident interpretation. The poems are dense, sometimes unapproachable, and after several readings they are still reluctant to yield up much meaning.

> The universe has once been magical
>
> a grain of sugar for the kettle
>
> one who came back
> naked under his bronze and linen
> his face scarred by planets
>
> this freedom is my theme

Law and freedom are certainly the keywords, but any understanding of the poems on a textual basis is impeded by what appears as an almost wilful arbitrariness in which image is piled on confusing image and nouns are linked with adjectives that seem no more useful to them than many others might have been.

A review of "Pancakes for the Queen of Babylon," in The Times Literary Supplement, *No. 3479, October 31, 1968, p. 1220.*

ROBIN MAGOWAN

We may know of Levi as the author of three books of awkwardly rhymed, neo-Georgian verse, all having sea or bay or something like that in their title. In [*Pancakes for the Queen of Babylon*] all that discipline, Horatian stoicism, has been converted into an exciting and I think probably very important book. The excitement is that of reading a poet who doesn't know where he is going, but who doesn't care—knowing that he is a poet, that if he will follow his words long and hard enough they will take him somewhere. To truth. The poet is naked. All he wants is to see the world enormously. "In the deserts of my imagination poetry is the naked exercise of the entire man." . . . In this pamphlet we have the joy of a well-trained man discovering in quasi-journal form how very much of the world he can embrace—and embracing it. (p. 202)

Robin Magowan, "Pancakes for You and Me," in Poetry, *Vol. CXVI, No. 3, June, 1970, pp. 193-202.*

ANNE CLUYSENAAR

The poems in *Life is a Platform* defy repeated readings because the language is (despite a first-glance polish, even shimmer) amorphous. Take for example the opening two verses of **"Kapetan Michalis."**

> He has gone, leaving written papers.
> To many houses, all stone and sky,
> Some green growth in summer, some deep snow in spring.

Thousands of words of dream scribbled on a bedsheet.
This man tore down the fruit of solitude unripe.

> In these woods, in the first leaf of the elm
> when the stone becomes shadow
> the most tormented mind is motionable
> it will be stony,
> can settle among trees like an enormous butterfly
> and shadow becomes stone.

The patina of repetition and balance, of the cunningly contrasted romantic and everyday wording, is immediately evident. This looks like poetry of some kind. But there are problems. Are we to read from line one into lines two-three, so that *gone . . . to* is the grammatical interpretation? Or does the sentence-break indicate that the construction is, rather, comparable with *To John, much love?* Why are houses stone and *sky?* Windows? Or a religious reference? Linking up, perhaps, with *words of dream?* There is some uncertainty, too, about *unripe:* should we understand 'tore the fruit down unripe' or 'tore down the unripe fruit'? Not that it seems to matter much, except for the hesitation this confusion causes: why not a comma after *solitude* or, alternately, a change of sequence between the last two words (since rhyme is no object and rhythm could be altered)? But verse two raises worse difficulties. Why does the first leaf of the elm (= spring?) coincide with stone becoming shadow? Because sun shines only in warm weather? But even this unlikely notion won't work, since stone doesn't become shadow in sun, but *has* a shadow, which it must, indeed, be *sunlit* to have. It becomes less not more shadowy in spring. Then, what is a motionable mind? Flexible, emotional? Why the invention, which introduces a note of preciousness which seems to have no role to play. If the mind is motionable in spring, when will it be stony? And why do we whip from present to future—*is/will be*—and then apparently back to the present with *can?* Or is *can* to be taken as a possibility in the future, when the mind will be stony? If so, though, why the butterfly simile? And how are we to link up the last line—to line two, so that stone and shadow become each other? Or to line four, so that we have states following each other in time? But what of *becomes?* (Not *become*). Finally supposing that the whole verse relates to the present (with line three as it were in brackets, as a general statement, and *it* referring back to *mind* despite the grammatical oddity), one still has to make sense of the stone becoming shadow, mind stony, shadow stone: the equivalences seem to cancel out, so that mind might equally well be shadow *or* stone, since stone becomes shadow. In all this, I have tried to summarise some of the thoughts I had while trying to discover what was being said. As will be seen, I did not succeed. Details like the vague reference of *these* in *these woods* only add to the confusion.

Levi's public poems are difficult in a different way. What does the **"Christmas Sermon"** add up to? It seems to be a traditional Jesuit meditation without the ancient virtues of structure and sense-intellect involvement and control. There are, also, minor oddities.

> I am colder than Christ was

for example raises doubts as to how hard Levi is thinking—why the geographical oddity of assuming that Christ was born in cold? Or, if this is irony, it seems irreverent. The rhyming couplets, triplets, quads *et cetera* of these pieces do not work, to my ear. Full-rhyme so often occurs that when off-rhyme does, one is tempted to misread, sometimes with comical results:

> In the moisture and mist a bird or two
> bubble in watersprings, they come and go.
>
> (pp. 77-8)

Anne Cluysenaar, in a review of "Life Is a Platform" and "Death Is a Pulpit," in Stand Magazine, *Vol. 13, No. 2 (1972), pp. 77-8.*

ALAN BROWNJOHN

[Levi's *Collected Poems 1955-1975*] gathers up the work of 20 years scattered among out-of-print hardbacks and pamphlets (including his promising debut with *The Gravel Ponds*) as well as available volumes. By current standards, Father Levi has been prolific. But he hasn't greatly varied the content and the texture of his work: it's substantially about the life of the seasons and the validity of his faith, all done in a fairly muted, somewhat repetitive diction, and slack verse forms which employ an irksomely recurrent habit of casual and obfuscating rhyming. All this means that it's, frankly, a labour to read outright, and more rewarding to read selectively. Occasionally he has abandoned his all-too-gentle and meandering cadences, re-ordered and sharpened his diction, and produced poems like **"Pancakes for the Queen of Babylon"** and **"Pigs."** . . . But mostly he seems to feel that his poems need not or should not venture out to grip the reader by his lapels. There is enough here (just) to suggest that this has been a mistakenly modest strategy. (p. 654)

Alan Brownjohn, "Metre Maid," in New Statesman, *Vol. 91, No. 2358, May 14, 1976, pp. 653-54.*

COLIN FALCK

Peter Levi's earlier poems tended to founder in their own rather mannered obscurities ('Triumphal corrupted stone / hangs down from the mind's bone') but he could occasionally come up with a clean image that seemed to open the way for some real dealings with the world. . . . None of the poems came very near to expressing a personal vision of life but there was something personal in their rhythms which made one go on reading even when one's mind had given up hope of finding much to get hold of. Lines came over as unmistakable poetry which might have come over as a good deal less if they had been differently worked out on the page. . . . The explanation of this state of affairs that might suggest itself to the hindsighted reader of Levi's *Collected Poems 1955-1975* is that the poet's official beliefs—he is a Jesuit—must have been constantly on hand to impose their own organising demands above a certain level of concrete particularity; that nothing but an uncontainable imaginative force would have been likely to break through such a censorship; and that since Levi's imagination was not that kind of force (his few full-blown early images seem like products of a part of his mind—the poetic part—which the more dogmatic part hadn't got round to tidying up yet) his genuine self-expression found itself repressed to a sub-articulate rhythmic level where the censorship couldn't operate. For a poet—rather than a musician, say—this means very little self-expression indeed. Levi goes readily enough to detail and can even be handy with general ideas (non-heretical ones, presumably) or—on the occasions when he comes any distance away from nature—with an easy-going Audenish shorthand for gesturing towards the modern world ('Now to the groaning of murdered

Europe close / your ears . . . / . . . not in hotels . . .' etc.). Where he misses out is on the crucial middle level where the mind does its real imaginative work and where genuine self-supporting poems get created.

The obscurities are mostly ironed away in the second half of *Collected Poems 1955-1975* but the clarity that replaces them isn't a poetic one. Any sense one had of a distinct person with distinct emotions at least partly at work in the poems has by now given way; and the world itself, whether natural or human, has been made to sacrifice its wonder or magic in favour of a doctrinaire conception of what that wonder or magic ought to be like. . . . The general glazing-over of content goes with a smoothing-over of the once-alive rhythms, and the resulting combination of greater-than-ever fluency with blander-than-ever response is a reliable formula for arousing the reader's boredom. A sense remains of some kind of remote initiating self behind the poems but it seems rootless, ageless and generally sublimated into everyman-ish abstraction. There are hints of worldly interests, including an interest in politics—even some mutterings about revolution: . . .

> *Vox populi ira Dei,*
> voice of the people wrath of God, say I

—but it all comes over as pretty cryptic and evasive (as well as reminding us rather disturbingly of the *ira-Dei*-type justifications that were adduced for, say, the Nationalist atrocities in the Spanish Civil War). **"Poem 177"**, subtitled "The Law School Riots, Athens, 1973", is so riddlingly indirect in its approach to its subject as not perceptibly to approach it at all, and the relevance of the title of a poem called **"A Few Words About Fascism"** is so far from being obvious as to make one reflect that almost any poem could as well be called by that name; future inquisitions might find it hard to know which side this poet had really been whetting his knife on. One might wonder why most of Levi's later poems are in fact left untitled—until one realised that he must have known what he was doing since hardly any of them are really about anything in particular. What they all lack is the sense of an authenticating actual life that finds its way into the poems and provides them with a reliable starting point; even where there is imagination at work in them it usually fails to arrive anywhere because it rarely has anywhere to set out from. Around the middle of the book one picks up murmurs of religious doubts and anxieties, but they get smoothed over again without being built up into a poetic structure (as they would have been by Donne or Herbert or Hopkins with their persisting sense of their own human actuality). One's sympathies get ready to extend themselves, but one is given nothing personal enough to sympathise with; in the end all one can do is to register sympathetically what seem to be the desperation-signals of someone who has founded his life on untruths and—having once been a poet—must be more than intermittently aware of it. (p. 55)

Colin Falck, "Catholicities," in The New Review, *Vol. III, No. 28, July, 1976, pp. 55-6.*

BLAKE MORRISON

Peter Levi's debut as a thriller writer [*The Head in the Soup*] has many of the elements we'd expect from a poet and don—impressive descriptions of landscape, a good poetic name for his archaeologist hero (Ben—you've guessed it—Jonson), and some donnish epigrams: 'Lunch in an old-fashioned college is like a family Christmas where all the guests have stayed too long, and the hosts have retired to bed and left them to it.' For a time it looks as if Levi is going to focus on Oxford much as Edmund Crispin did in his novels featuring Gervase Fen, but contemporary thrillers usually prefer to cast a wider net, and Jonson is soon sent darting about the globe (Paris, Geneva, Rome, Crete) in search of lost treasure. There's a rather implausible dragging-in of just about every political group going (the CIA makes its compulsory appearance, and in there too are the Israelis and Arabs, Fascists and Communists, and various secret police bodies); but this is the Greece of the Colonels in 1972 and political wheeling-and-dealing is certainly afoot. It's no great shakes as a thriller but Levi knows at least some of the tricks of the trade (his handling of Jonson, Grimble and the photographs is particularly well done) and keeps the pace up to the end.

Blake Morrison, "Making Tracks," in New Statesman, *Vol. 98, No. 2523, July 27, 1979, p. 137.*

SHAUN McCARTHY

In Peter Levi's poems there is a recurrent concern with landscape, but never any names or specific locations. The title of this collection, *Private Ground,* is well chosen. Perhaps it is the poet's rendering of a particular, known landscape, or it may consist of elements that coalesce only in his head—which in those poems where this perspective is most evocative, accord in some way with the solipsistic world within our own. . . .

In the sectional poem **"Village Snow"** Levi creates a patchwork of a world where snow has fallen. It is crowded with well-observed detail: pensioners complaining, news of snowfall on other parts of the globe, snippets of nature described (snow-laden trees, fields, deer in the woods). We see a complete, but unspecifiable landscape. Levi often begins by locating the reader in such a place, then moves him into deeper, more unknown areas. In the thirty short sections that comprise **"Village Snow,"** this transition towards conclusions can be imagistic in its focus and terse precision. . . . (p. 8)

In **"248"** a similar course is followed. A metaphysical train of thinking is begun with a view of a winter garden bounded by a churchyard wall. The frost-gripped masonry, temporarily devoid of its summer vegetation, becomes a motif for the cycle of natural and human decline and resurgence:

> now they die back, then they branch again green,
> they are revived by what we might have been,
> the swallows and sunsets
> and dawns that this house sees,
> the light souls of poets,
> the dark heart of roses.

This is the final poem in a group of six (243-8), which although not titled overall like many of the rest of the poems in the book, nonetheless form a thematically cohesive unit. Their common theme is an awareness of time that has passed and temporal irreversibility; their common tone (excepting the perhaps religious implications of **"248"**) is one of quiet sadness and acceptance. This very human theme is dealt with through constant reference to the more obvious register of decline in the natural world. Levi uses this imagery to evoke some powerful insights. . . . (p. 9)

But of these six poems, **"247"** is the exception and the most powerful, for here the poet tackles the overall theme in directly human terms. Many of the other poems rather overwork the same concerns, diluting the effectiveness of the subject/theme association. But, in **"247"** (quoted in full below) Levi is op-

erating without the intermediate landscape, revealing the strong emotional drive of this group of poems:

> I have consumed forty-seven years
> building an aeroplane of paper-clips,
> it will not fly, only the shadow flies
> and on the clear sand under the clear sea
> shadow and light will tumble together.
>
> I would not want to relive my life,
> but a few minutes over and over,
> in love, in love among the paper clips,
> and to live and relive the sandy sea.

While the other poems contain some fine lines, it is a pity that **"247"** has to stand among so much work on the same theme. It is also a pity that in *Private Ground* Levi does not more often deal so directly with his themes. (pp. 9-10)

Levi, it would seem, is concerned, perhaps more than some other poets, to communicate to a public and to be seen to be communicating. Thus his vivid landscapes serve to lead you into his thinking; unreal and fluid, yet studded with details that are designed to evoke exactly the parallel vision that Levi requires in the reader's imagination. Thus, too, the grouping of poems within this collection into expositions of common themes. When reading these poems one is made aware very quickly of at least some of the beliefs, moral and philosophical, which Levi is at pains to expound. In places one feels that he is overworking themes in his desire for clarity. There are points where poems seem unnecessarily to overlap thematically their numerical neighbours, and places where an idea, or means of expressing that idea, is over-used. This does not necessarily lead to dull or weak poetry, but to too many often good poems expressing similar notions.

Technically, Levi is a fine craftsman; all the poems in this collection are well shaped; as a poet he has a keen eye for subject and an ear for the exact words to express it. His language is straightforward, often authoritative, occasionally repetitive. *Private Ground* is an essential volume for anyone who has Levi's *Five Ages* for the concerns, like the numbers, continue without interruption from that previous volume. Indeed, *Private Ground* breaks little new ground; Levi does not seem concerned to develop new styles or interests, but to refine those he has already explored in some degree.

It is however of interest to anyone who wishes to enjoy a poet who, whatever his faults, is seriously and passionately concerned with making his verse a forceful means of communication. (p. 11)

Shaun McCarthy, "Peter Levi," in Agenda, *Vol. 19, No. 4 & Vol. 20, No. 1, Winter & Spring, 1982, pp. 8-11.*

GAVIN EWART

Peter Levi's *Collected Poems 1955-1975* (1976) were followed by *Five Ages* (1978). [*Private Ground*] is his second book since the main collection. His verse is formal, classical, impersonal and (apart from **"The Shearwaters,"** written in 1965 and one of the very best long poems of our time) almost completely hermetic, the very opposite of 'confessional' poetry, the 'I' scarcely seeming to exist. The reader knows that the writer is living in the country when landscapes are described, but not what he had for breakfast. History does not intrude, and there are almost no cultural references (God, Christ, Shakespeare,

Hardy, Edward Lear, Victor Hugo are the only proper names; place names are not common either). Instead, there are key words: wind, snow, stars, sun, blue, green, white. The poems are all numbered, from the *Collected Poems* onwards, and this volume contains poems 243-75. Since Levi married and left the Roman Catholic priesthood, there has been a slight relaxation: 'I am free to speak of money these days. / The expense of my life horrifies me'. The simplicity (which is often not comprehensible) pays dividends: 'How we pass time, and how it used to pass: / a poem as anonymous as the grass'. . . . There is a very original rhetoric of plants and flowers: 'the cabbages are dignified in death', 'and motionless carnation in his rage'. This verges on wit, as in the fine **"Village Snow"** sequence: 'Do nations get the snow that they deserve?' The sonnets are among the best poems, and there is something very Elizabethan about Levi's verse so that the rare quotations from Shakespeare and Marlowe do not seem out of place. There are beautiful lines ('Age is vigil, an ache worse than a stone', 'The vault of heaven sweetens with a sigh'). One gnomic lyric (**"269"**) has a Ninetyish beauty but still remains impenetrable. These poems are remarkable, entirely unlike anyone else's, and their virtue is their uniqueness.

Gavin Ewart, in a review of "Private Ground," in
British Book News, *March, 1982, p. 181.*

TIM DOOLEY

The poems in Peter Levi's latest collection [*Private Ground*] are, for the most part, untitled, and continue the system of numbering used in *Five Ages* (1978) and *Collected Poems 1955-1975*. The effect of this is to underline the suggestion that Levi's work is all of a piece, and to encourage the reader to see in the new volume an extension of the concerns of his previous poetry. Levi clarified those concerns in the introduction to his collected poems, where he said that what he wanted was "to be believed, not applauded". . . .

What Levi has attempted to be truthful about is summed up in a comparatively early poem, **"The Tractor in Spring"**:

> praising heaven I ever took for theme
> this planet, its unnatural wishes,
> common reason and human justice,
> and growth of life, the last increase of time

In exploring these themes, Levi is scrupulously faithful not only in his descriptions of physical nature (writing of horse-chestnuts in **"No 113"** that "the fruit was coffined, asleep") but in the care he takes to give the abstractions he deals with a recognizable physical and emotional setting. As he acknowledged in *Pancakes for the Queen of Babylon* (1968), he finds it difficult to "keep proverbs out of (his) voice" and his writing is shot through with resonant, if sometimes resistant, epigrams ("God is a kind of unenlightenment", from **"Christmas Sermon"** is a typical example). These resounding phrases can be deceptive. Their function is not to encapsulate and define, but to provoke feeling and thought. They serve a dramatic function in poems that tend to veer away from conclusion and certainty—poems less concerned with interpretations of experience than with the difficulty of making such interpretations. In Levi's exploration of his "planet" one rarely feels that an observation is being made to serve a preordained argument. Rather, like the central figure in his **"Five Ages of a Poet"**, "He is a scholar reading from a tree / some innermost of dignity in trees."

The search for order in the flux of time has been a recurring obsession in Levi's work, and regret for the passage of time sounds an elegiac note through many of the poems in *Private Ground*. . . .

In the past Levi's poems have sought escape from this sense of flux in the incarnation of an idea from outside time: a revelation or a revolution. **"No 148"** allows for both options: ". . . God will make them come true in the street one day. . . . And God shall fulfil this with his Amen." A change of gear can be felt in *Private Ground*, in the sense that time itself may be capable of producing solutions for the problems it sets. After reading this collection, it is difficult not to feel intimately acquainted with Levi's village garden: its pear and plum trees, its wild cherries. Here the change of seasons demonstrates an order that needs no intellectual theory to support it, only "the motions of weather and of love". The **"Five Short Moral Poems"** which make up **"No 266"** concentrate on immediate, animal reactions to the natural world. Where once, Stevens-like, Levi might have hoped for a supreme fiction which would hold decay in stasis, now:

> Fiction withers away on the branch,
> novels of wanderings in pure places
> with watersprings under towering trees,
> gods at midday, adventurous dreams;
> that is all ashes. Life, unexpected,
> has offered the simplest solution,
> life is an old unlikely servant.
> There is no other place like this place.

"Comfort at Fifty", the most impressive of the longer sequences in *Private Ground*, underlines the commitment Levi now feels to the accidental beauties of nature, rather than the essential beauty of an ideal. These "antiplatonic sonnets" contrast the pure but evasive quality of the world of spirit with the plural, and graspable, here and now. While "these problems about what the mind knows / are too ragged to be penetrated", Levi finds the natural world's moralities clear and readable. . . .

An unaffected attachment to the seasonal rhythms is matched here with an unabashed sensuousness and a calm treatment of traditional lyric forms. Levi has not compromised his high-principled view of the poet's calling, but his own vision has softened and become more tender in these recent poems, with the result that *Private Ground*, while still carrying the sense of authority that was recognized in his earlier work, will seem to many a warmer and more fully humane volume than any he has previously published.

Tim Dooley, "The Fruits of Time," in The Times
Literary Supplement, *No. 4122, April 2, 1982, p.
393.*

PATRIC DICKINSON

[*The Flutes of Autumn*] is a rather odd piece of semi-autobiography. It may be outrageous to say of the work of an ex-Jesuit priest that his book is a bit of a curate's egg but so it seems and since, manifestly, Peter Levi has little sense of humour, perhaps one can get away with it. His parents were both Catholics, his father also a mercantile Jew. Levi was born in Ruislip in 1931. The family, though reasonably prosperous, felt rather 'apart'. He describes his boyhood in the second world war freshly and entertainingly; then his schooling at Prior Park (near Bath) and Beaumont: Catholic, of course, and 'Irish', out of which he seems to have come with a passion for archaeology, a sentimental regard for the indomitable Irishry, and the conviction that he had a vocation.

The training of a Jesuit takes quite a time, and in that time Levi became a happy and egregious scholar. . . . Levi makes his training sound too like living on a generous kind of Catholic dole. Finally, he had to get out and do something—teach: in London, at Stonyhurst, which he regarded as a prison (he might have been sent to school there himself), and as a priest visiting Brixton prison where naturally he got matey with IRA thugs. There are many moments when he breaks off from narrative to give one the benefit of his considerable knowledge, but debatable views, on the past England he would like to have been different. These disquisitions, like bits of lectures, are often fascinating, often pedantic, not seldom boring. And then, as laconically as one might write 'I became disillusioned with the British Council', he writes, 'By 1974 as a priest I was falling to pieces . . . so the next spring I left the Jesuits and got married having been more or less in love for 13 years'. As an agnostic one finds this bland account of Levi's life dispiriting; even his Requiem Sermon for David Jones is both mannered and rhetorical. Can one give up these vows and beliefs so easily? Refusal to sign the 39 articles drove Clough from Oxford and horribly damaged his life. As an archaeologist Levi says he has never discovered anything in England 'except one badly-made flint arrowhead'. One might be forgiven for thinking he meant his own heart. (pp. 118-19)

> *Patric Dickinson, in a review of "The Flutes of Autumn," in* London Magazine, *n.s. Vol. 23, No. 8, November, 1983, pp. 118-19.*

MARTIN BOOTH

[Levi's] poetry, originally somewhat academic, has, in recent years, become far more accessible and exacting, gathering in force, excitement and power while at the same time not losing its calm and authority. He is a poet who increases in stature with every new book; [*The Echoing Green: Three Elegies*] goes a long way towards building up a solid reputation, for the contents are exceptional.

The book contains three poems about the deaths of three close friends, one of whom was Vasko Popa's translator, Anne Pennington. Though elegies of a sort, the poems are also reassessments of life and friendship, a reordering of the bases upon which relationships are founded and a realization of what love between people can amount to. Levi insists that the poems be read as a sequence and, obeying his instructions, one sees the development through the poems of elegiac thoughts, religious conviction and aspiration and, finally, rage at death's robbery. This last emotion is especially keen as the subject of the final poem, Colin Macleod, committed suicide.

It is not easy to draw quotations from the poems to illustrate their efficacy for they are so tightly controlled; however, the following gives a sense of the directness of imagery, the integrity of the poetry, that makes it so successful and accessible to both the grief and the triumph of friendship:

> The shadows shifted, he played on and on;
> his game of patience came out in the end,
> and straggling shadows drowned in the deep dark,
> the windows flamed and died for our one friend:

as if she walked outside under the trees
to hear a nightbird then lie down alone,
then talking to herself just one moment
she smiled as she was drowsing into stone.

> *Martin Booth, in a review of "The Echoing Green: Three Elegies," in* British Book News, *March, 1984, p. 180.*

LACHLAN MACKINNON

Peter Levi's *The Echoing Green* begins with a damaging preface which explains that his elegies for friends who died early "must be taken together", elucidates some allusions and tells us that "Anne Pennington's is the Christian centre-piece, and Denis Bethell's is a pure elegy . . . but Colin Macleod's is the climax, it expresses unconsoled grief and unreconciled anger." This unwillingness to trust the reader is misguided, because its account of the poems bears little relation to their real effect.

The opening of the elegy for Anne Pennington gives a better picture of the poems' strength:

> Early awake, a sunrise in treetops,
> a million green feathers at tree height:
> then on the garden floor the sun let fall
> vast playing-cards of shadow and of light.
>
> The shadows shifted, he played on and on;
> his game of patience came out in the end,
> and straggling shadows drowned in the deep dark,
> the windows flamed and died for our one friend.

Each poem opens with rhymed quatrains appropriate to the month of its subject's death and proceeds through the same number of sections in blank and rhymed verse. This traditional formality suits Levi's tone, which is pitched high and rises at one point to a verse sermon, but disguises the poems' true structure, which is essentially symbolist. Recurrences of green and white bind the poems into a "musical" rather than argumentative unity: the model is *Four Quartets,* and like Eliot, Levi is by turns lyrical and sententious ("Courage to live at all is our one pride"). There are more allusions than the preface states: the patience-playing sun here should probably remind us of the chess-playing nights in Pasternak's "Marburg", and the image of Anne Pennington's having spent her time "as though / a life lived is an hour in a meadow" tactfully adjusts the proverbial wisdom of the earlier poet's "Hamlet". These echoes are fitting to the subject.

But the writing is self-consciously beautiful. In the passage above, the image is over-extended: where Pasternak surprises us, Levi moves just too slowly, and the metre requires the repetition of "of" in the fourth line, which feels pedantic rather than necessary. The end of the elegy for Colin Macleod ("I say your likeness is to an old stone: / upright, raineaten, mooneaten, alone"), which classes the sequence, has too knowing a dying fall. Though often impressive and moving, the poems are glazed over by old-masterly deliberation.

> *Lachlan Mackinnon, "Preening and Glazing," in* The Times Literary Supplement, *No. 4243, July 27, 1984, p. 838.*

REGINALD HILL

Classicist and archaeologist as well as poet, Peter Levi displays his reverence for the past in the manner as well as the matter of *Grave Witness*. It belongs firmly in that tradition of exuberantly witty and erudite crime-writing whose roots run back to the 1920s and which flowers most abundantly in the hothouse atmosphere of Oxbridge. Between the soufflé Grand Marnier and the port of the High Table dinner with which the novel opens, we encounter Campbell's *Gertrude of Wyoming,* Hobbes's translation of Thucydides, Wood's *Palmyra in the Desert,* Sir Philip Sidney and the later writings of Henry James before we get a sniff of the plot.

This, when it appears, is centred on the provenance both ancient and modern of a collection of Grecian potsherds allegedly discovered in a sixth century BC grave in Oxfordshire, an event apparently calculated to set the archaeological mind racing with speculation and suspicion. The mind in question belongs to first-person narrator, Ben Jonson, whose heart is simultaneously set pounding by the appearance of a young girl of heavenly beauty called Joy. Together in Oxfordshire, London and the Isle of Wight, they overcome dangers, track down killers, unravel mysteries, and also pick a few flowers along the way.

Typically in books of this genre, the supporting cast tend to have suggestive names and engage by their oddity rather than their humanity: Saintly, Stoup, Frowser, Iggleby fit the bill nicely on both counts, though there are hints enough throughout his characterization to show that Levi will be able to plumb greater depths when he chooses. At present his main problem seems to be his poet's way with narrative, hopping around in a manner which lovers of a good tale well told may find a little irritating. Effective set pieces of rapid action and high excitement occur from time to time, atmospheres are powerfully evoked, no precious stone is left unturned, and there is always something rich and strange to catch the ear or the eye, but on the whole the extremely complex plot is unfolded a little awkwardly.

> *Reginald Hill, "Out of the Hothouse," in* The Times Literary Supplement, *No. 4279, April 5, 1985, p. 394.*

MICHAEL DIRDA

Much admired in England, Peter Levi's *Grave Witness* ... depicts the adventures of a classical archeologist who becomes involved with Greek pottery, shady art dealers, an eccentric English antiquarian, his beautiful niece (the love interest), and a variety of crimes including murder, theft, kidnapping, and an elaborate con game. Certainly, there is enough here to make a thrilling novel à la John Buchan or a witty and learned one in the style of Edmund Crispin and Michael Innes. The only trouble is that Levi tries to blend the two, and doesn't quite pull it off.

For instance, the hero Ben Jonson (a peculiar ostentation) opens his story with a portrait of his academic archenemy, one Frowser: "The reference books credit Frowser with a critical volume called *Sentiment and Metaphor.* I have heard it said that his chapter on Gertrude of Wyoming opened the eyes of the learned world to new delicacies in the shorter longer poems of the earlier middle century." Funny yes, but a rather familiar kind of academic humor.

A similar wanness characterizes the tidy love affair and rather unthreatening adventures. Jonson is knocked on the head at the shop of a dealer in artifacts, he is kidnapped twice (once would have been enough), his involvement with Joy proceeds far too smoothly, and there is an obtrusive use of foreshadowing, even of the old-fashioned "Had I but known" convention for which Mary Roberts Rinehart was notorious.

Still, *Grave Witness* partially redeems itself with eccentric characters. . . . The writing is certainly fluid and competent, as one would expect from Oxford's current professor of poetry, himself a well known classical scholar. In short, this struck me as a mildly diverting mystery, but not half so clever or thrilling as it would like to be.

> *Michael Dirda, "The Greeks in Oxfordshire," in* Book World—The Washington Post, *September 15, 1985, p. 6.*

Janet Lewis (Winters)

1899-

American novelist, poet, short story writer, editor, and author of children's books.

Respected primarily as a novelist and a poet, Lewis is praised as a master stylist whose careful attention to detail and language has resulted in literature of subtle yet powerful impact. Much of her work revolves around the tenets propounded by the *Gyroscope* group, a circle of scholars who founded a short-lived but influential literary journal in 1929. These writers, including Howard Baker and Lewis's husband, Yvor Winters, staunchly favored classicism over contemporary trends in modernism and romanticism. Lewis's fiction, adhering to the precepts of the *Gyroscope* group, is distinguished by spare, lyrical prose, tragic plots, and an emphasis on moral rectitude. Lewis's early poetry, while generally observing traditional forms of rhyme and meter, is more optimistic in tone. Her later poetry, often written in free verse, displays the influence of the Imagists and Japanese haiku.

Lewis's best-known novel, *The Wife of Martin Guerre* (1941), is the first of a series of novels based upon actual incidents described in Samuel M. Phillips's *Famous Cases of Circumstantial Evidence*. *The Wife of Martin Guerre* concerns a sixteenth-century French woman who, eight years after her husband has disappeared, suspects that the man claiming to be her husband is an imposter. In spite of the prosperity and happiness that this man brings to the family estate, the wife's traditional morality, coupled with her suspicions, causes her to bring him to trial. *The Trial of Sören Qvist* (1947), based upon a famous case in Danish legal history, recounts the story of a pastor who is prompted by his religious and philosophical beliefs, as well as by the strength of the evidence against him, to confess to a murder he did not commit. *The Ghost of Monsieur Scarron* (1959), another novel based on historical fact, relates the story of a seventeenth-century bookbinder who is both cuckolded and framed by his wife and assistant for publishing seditious pamphlets. These novels were praised for Lewis's accurate detailing of historical settings and for her meticulous development of austere themes. Fred Inglis commented: "[The] moral standards contained in the books are lucid and definable, and human behaviour may be checked against them, consciously and rationally. The tales embody a moral judgement, rigorous and severe: it becomes diffuse, fluid, uncertain when we absorb it into the muddy medium of our own undefined values."

Lewis has also published fiction based on her personal experiences. Her first novel, *The Invasion: A Narrative of Events concerning the Johnston Family of St. Mary's* (1932), chronicles three generations of a family of Irish and Ojibway descent in Northern Michigan. This book was influenced by the Indians and landscape Lewis became familiar with during her travels to Michigan's Upper Peninsula. *Against a Darkening Sky* (1943) is set in California prior to World War II. In this novel, Lewis explores the encroachment upon traditional ethics and institutions by modern values and technology. Lewis's volume of short fiction, *Good-bye, Son, and Other Stories* (1946), consists of thematically linked tales dealing with death and nature.

Photograph by Alva Henderson

In her poetry, Lewis focuses on many of the same moral and aesthetic concerns of her fiction. She underscores the theme of rational thought versus passionate action by experimenting with various lyric forms and attending to precision of detail and language. Her first volume of poetry, *The Indians in the Woods* (1922), like *The Invasion,* is concerned with the experiences of the Ojibway Indians. Another volume, *The Ancient Ones* (1979), recounts Lewis's visits to the Hopi and Navajo villages of the American Southwest. Among Lewis's other important collections are *Poems, 1924-1944* (1950) and *Poems, Old and New, 1918-1978* (1981). Of her poetry Robert Pinsky stated: "Musicality, clarity, directness of address, boldness of conception: Janet Lewis has used these gifts of talent superbly. . . . Her poetry is at once lucid and subtle, cosmopolitan and deeply American, formally serene and full of the moral passion that makes her directness possible."

(See also *Contemporary Authors,* Vols. 9-10 and *Contemporary Authors Permanent Series,* Vol. 1.)

JOHN CHAMBERLAIN

The Invasion is a historical novel of several generations that is a curious combination of a genealogical compendium and descriptive writing of a cool, translucent beauty. Unfortunately, the sense of beauty that is Janet Lewis's is the sense of beauty of a poet of the external world; it is not made germane to the problem of the novelist, historical or otherwise. What lives in this story of the Johnstons of Michigan's Northern Peninsula is not so much the people, Indian and English and French, as it is the country itself—the country which, even as late as the middle of the nineteenth century, remained the primitive wilderness of the early voyageurs. Lake Superior in squall, in mist, in placid Summer, the woods, in Winter, when the snow breaks under the sharp hoofs of the deer and the Indians spear sturgeon through the ice; the Northern Spring, when the dogtooth violets are appearing—these are Miss Lewis's own material. But the people—even John Johnston, the founder of the family, who comes to the "Soo" country from the North of Ireland at the end of the eighteenth century—remain wraiths, names, unfilled outlines, wandering, living and dying in a setting that lives all around them but is never reflected in them.

Miss Lewis's prose is hushed, unaccented; pages of it are a pure pleasure to read with a slowness requisite to the savor. It is questionable, however, that it is the proper instrument for a chronicle, where movement is literally the *sine qua non* of success, and where the dramatic must be accorded at least a trifle more space per item than the facts on pages that are essentially information-giving. Miss Lewis takes almost everything—a birth, a cold Winter, the removal of an Indian tribe to the further West, the War of 1812, and the fact that "Atala" was published in Europe by Chateaubriand—in the same stride. Girls meet a bear in the woods—and Miss Lewis dismisses it in a line. This method has about as much relation to the novelist's art as the chronicling on a gravestone has to the art of biography. It is a method that moves so rapidly that often an effect of absolute stillness is achieved.

Nevertheless, there are compensations. It is enough that the region glows. It is enough that we live with a country and its legends; it is enough that we see the Ojibway and the Ottawa pass from the domination of the French, through the American agency stage, and into the tripping falsifications of Longfellow's "Hiawatha," the genesis of which forms the gist of some of Miss Lewis's most interesting pages. It is enough that we see the Indians driven out by vicious treaties removing them to the West, when copper and iron give the white man cause to move in.

And there are parts of the novel that are humanly interesting. . . . But the human interest of the Johnstons is largely the human interest that absorbs the antiquarian. *The Invasion* will be treasured by the hunter of Americana who is particularly interested in the Great Lakes region, its early history and its development from the days of the fur traders to the era of the whaleback and great shipments of ore. It will also be treasured by those with a taste for imagist poetry.

John Chamberlain, "A Chronicle of the Old Northwest," in The New York Times Book Review, October 2, 1932, p.7.

J. V. CUNNINGHAM

The publication of *The Invasion* by Janet Lewis . . . turns public attention on the [*Gyroscope*] group, for this novel is the most extended piece of work by any one of them as well as one of the more important novels of the season. *The Invasion* is a chronicle of the Johnston family of the Sault Ste. Marie; its theme is the dispersal of the Indian culture, and, in the gradual decline of the family fortune, the failure of the assimilation of the two cultures which it represented. John Johnston, an Irish gentleman, entered the fur trade at the Sault in 1791, and, in a few years, married the Woman of the Glade, daughter of the hereditary chieftain of the Ojibway nation, a splendid woman who is the central character of the book. The children were thus, as Johnston proudly said, of the royalty of two continents. Mrs. Winters knows both the region and Indian life thoroughly. She brings the tale—crowded with historic characters and incidents, the rivalry of the great fur companies, the War of 1812, the industrialization of the Great Lakes area—down to the present day. One of the firmest descriptive passages of modern literature, toward the close of the book, pictures the freighters passing through the locks, engaged in the iron trade. An exciting novel, it is also history, ably summarized, dramatically presented, and thoroughly documented.

The Invasion is perhaps the best example we have of the regional chronicle, and should serve as a model to the many in America who are reconstructing the history of their locality, for to accomplish this is to do more than arrange and enliven documents. Historical workers are seldom rhetoricians. Yet dispassionate history is not the result of a disinterested scientific approach—disinterest is boring—but of an adequate rhetoric which, although it may give false information, never gives false values. Livy is thus superior to those who refute his facts; and Mrs. Winters excels even Livy in this one respect, that her facts are documented and sound. Her most valuable quality, however, is a sustained and capable comment, a rhetoric more able than that of any other woman in America with the exception of Miss Katherine Anne Porter and a few others.

Each chapter of *The Invasion* presents a key incident, or series of incidents, in novel form. The interval between chapters, with other antecedent information, is adroitly worked into each opening; an extraordinary amount of fact and historical summary is slipped over with only occasional confusion, and without requiring any effort from the reader towards mastering the material. This method, however, effective as it is, becomes the only serious limitation to the book, and it could not honestly have been avoided. Continuous narration requires a simple scheme which events can be seen to justify, so that pointing the moral will occupy the transitions. That is the common historical method, but, in this case, the available schemes are suspect. The story of the Ojibway could have illustrated either the supremacy of the white and the degeneracy of the Indian, or the converse, which is the more popular theme today. With an admirable hesitancy, and a method appropriate to it, Mrs. Winters has gathered what is known of the case for both races. Hers is the only book I know which treats the Indian as casually as the white.

Mrs. Winters's poems, though few, are even more distinguished than her prose. They are quiet and calm, untroubled by the modern nervous disorders, and they have a personal charm which arises from her settled background and from the sense of assurance afforded her by the consciousness . . . of being part of a continuing literary and family tradition. Technically, the poems are remarkable for swift and successful metrical variations within common forms. Two early pamphlets of verse have been published, *The Indians in the Woods* (1922) and *The Wheel in Midsummer* (1927); a general collection should be eagerly received. (pp. 703-04)

J. V. Cunningham, "The 'Gyroscope' Group," in The Bookman, New York, Vol. LXXV, No. 7, November, 1932, pp. 703-08.

MAY LAMBERTON BECKER

If we could be as sensitive to beauty this year as we were in 1927, [*The Wife Of Martin Guerre*] would have the reception then accorded to *The Bridge of San Luis Rey*. It has the same pellucid—and deceptive—simplicity. No doubt there was an actual *cause célèbre* of the middle sixteenth century in Gascony, from which it arises. But its relation to fact is that of a flower to seed. No doubt a young husband, heir to a rich farmer, did leave home to carry out a project of which the father did not approve, and stay away so long that when some one appeared, in possession of the name, the person and the past of Martin Guerre, he was taken, even by the wife at first, for Martin returned. There have been other trials to establish identity, at which waves of witnesses swore in good faith to contradictory statements. But all this is . . . a starting point for exploration of a soul. The soul is that of Bertrande, married at ten to a lad no older, whose first matrimonial gesture was to scratch her face because he disliked being married. So did she, but though they were not royal, their land-owning families amounted to dynasties, and their property must be united; they sympathized with each other, grew up together and were deeply in love when Martin went away. When the bearded traveler returned and Bertrande was bearing his child, the reason she began to doubt was that Martin would never have made her so happy. Why she brings her child's father to trial, what forces evoke the witnesses to confute or to confirm him, why, at last, Martin himself comes back and acts as he does—these are mysteries of human character, not tricks of plot.

> *May Lamberton Becker, in a review of "The Wife of Martin Guerre," in* New York Herald Tribune Books, *February 22, 1942, p. 10.*

ROSEMARY BENET

It is a relief to find a normal, reasonably happy, well adjusted mother in *Against a Darkening Sky*. Mary Knox Perrault, whose domestic life makes this book, was originally Scottish. She came from Campbeltown in Scotland to California, where she married a Swiss-French gardener and settled in a little community near San Francisco. The marriage was a happy one; they were poor financially, perhaps, but rich in experience. When the book opens she has four children. Her eldest, a daughter, Melanie, is about sixteen, and there are three sons, Andrew, Duncan and young Jamie. Life in the Perrault household is hard-working, pleasant and not uneventful. . . .

The details of a full domestic life are well set down. There is a good deal, for instance, about subjects as diverse as rabbit breeding, which is one of Mr. Perrault's hobbies, and the mother-daughter relationship which is one of Mrs. Perrault's preoccupations. . . . Particularly well done are Mary Perrault's memories of her own girlhood, and her working out of this mother-daughter relationship. There is a true picture of the pull and yet the tie between Mary and Melanie, the worry, the things left unsaid on both sides, the inevitable reticence that exists between generations, however sympathetic the understanding.

There is a curious realism about it all, a "like-life" lack of pattern to the book. The automobile accident, which looms so large in the beginning, fades into the background, for example, as it might fade from memory and we go on to other concerns. The end does not tie up any loose strands, or lead up to any given dramatic point. It is rather like a full, quiet stream that flows along, taking its own course and its own time as it goes.

There is no shadow of the war yet on the Perrault lives. That "darkening sky" is yet to come. That and the warm, fulfilled emotional quality make it seem, in spite of the various problems, almost a peaceful picture. This is a well written account of a woman who accepts what life brings.

> *Rosemary Benet, "Quiet Flowing Stream," in* New York Herald Tribune Books, *January 24, 1943, p. 4.*

ROSE FELD

Goodness in a character, that is, strength and kindness and understanding, is something that most novelists shy away from and with good reason. For the description of these qualities is a difficult thing to achieve. Unless the work is leavened with sound good sense and hard reality, the character dissolves into a weak-spined personality or one treacly with sentimentality.

In her portrait of a mother which is the essential core of Janet Lewis's new novel, *Against a Darkening Sky,* goodness assumes the dignity and strength of a rock battered by angry seas. Mary Perrault, poor in worldly goods but rich in native intelligence and a sympathetic heart, emerges as a convincing person blessed with a salty serenity of character.

Scotch by birth, Mary Perrault had come to the United States in her youth and married a man of French descent, a simple, kindly person, who earned his living as gardener, as general handy man, as collector of water rates in the small community of Encina in California. In her portrayal of both these two Miss Lewis succeeds admirably in bringing out the differences and the likenesses of their background; the woman, quiet and reserved in her words and acts; the man, charming and sensitive, with a touch of Gallic color that expresses itself in his activities and his relationships with the members of his family. The marriage is a good one, deeply rooted in mutual respect and affection. If Perrault's rabbit breeding is not always successful financially, it is no matter of grief to his wife. She knows he finds happiness in this work, and it means no outrage to her dignity to bolster up the family's funds by going out to do a day's cleaning occasionally. Friends and neighbors in Encina recognize her as a fine woman. . . .

Against a Darkening Sky has the quality of a moving tone poem, with the conflict expressed through the exploration of a woman's heart and mind. The writing has the same high quality of serenity as the splendid woman it portrays.

> *Rose Feld, "Strength and Goodness," in* The New York Times Book Review, *January 24, 1943, p. 32.*

WILLIAM E. WILSON

Any consideration of the writing of Janet Lewis becomes inevitably a consideration of style. In *Good-bye, Son,* she exhibits a classical purity that is rare in an age of writing that is often either mannered or without craftsmanship. Each sentence is labored over, each paragraph put together with painstaking precision.

Yet, as a story-teller, Miss Lewis succeeds best where she labors least. Many of the stories in this collection composed of the most carefully-set gems of sentences have almost no point and very little emotional or esthetic impact as stories. One is often not quite sure what Miss Lewis is trying to say, as in the story **"Proserpina"**; one is even more often in doubt as to the actual identity of her characters. It is as if the author, in her concentration upon the perfection of parts, had forgotten the intention of the whole.

Two of the longer stories—**"People Don't Want Us"** and **"Good-bye, Son"**—are the best in the volume, because they are the most spontaneous and seem to arise from a total concept. In them, Miss Lewis maintains her stylistic perfection, but in the genuine emotion that she feels and conveys, in her absorption in the whole story she is telling, she lapses into a more human idiom. **"People Don't Want Us"** is a simple analysis of the affectionate relationship between an American and a Japanese woman in California soon after the outbreak of the war. **"Good-bye, Son"** is a ghost story, perhaps in the Jamesian school, yet wholly original and convincing. These two stories alone lift the volume above the rather dull category of just good writing.

> *William E. Wilson, "Craftsman vs. Story-Teller," in* The New York Times Book Review, *March 24, 1946, p. 32.*

THEODORE ROETHKE

[There] is a temptation, when given a book by a neglected writer, to correct the balance by an uncritical "appreciation." In the case of Janet Lewis, this is not difficult, since she is a poet who always maintains her own tone, even in less successful pieces; whose work is marked by an absolute integrity of spirit and often by the finality in phrasing that can accompany such integrity; whose best poems recall the tenderness, the pure intense feeling, the simplicity and subtlety of early English religious poetry.

Some of her poems [in *The Earth-Bound, 1924-1944*] re-create a moment in time; in a sense the poem is the means whereby the author escapes from time, as in **"Remembered Morning"**:

> The axe rings in the wood,
> And the children come,
> Laughing and wet from the river;
> And all goes on as it should.
> I hear the murmur and hum
> Of their morning forever.
>
>   (p. 221)

For me, the line "And all goes on as it should" has the peculiar power of summation, of drawing together experience in condensed statement that sometimes occurs in the Elizabethans. The "forever" at the end of this stanza and the last line of stanza two ["Of my heart parcel and part"] are a descent from this level; but the whole poem remains in the mind, fresh and immediate. (p. 222)

Other work that can be ranked among her best includes **"The April Hill,"** one of several elegiac pieces; the slight but charming **"Lost Garden"**; and some of the poems to children. **"In the Egyptian Museum"** has a surface excitement that for me disappears in subsequent readings: the rhythm seems wrenched; the diction over-decorative, even for the subject; the whole poem "written." **"Country Burial"** relies too heavily on abstractions in the opening; later after the veritable detail of the daisies that

>   bend and straighten
>   Under the trailing skirts

it lapses into the clichés of prose:

>   and serious faces
>   Look with faint relief and briefly smile.

and the ending falters, it seems to me, in its effort to express too much. Possibly the theme of the poem could have been conveyed more obliquely by understatement, by detail that deepens into symbol.

But it is unfair, particularly in the work of Janet Lewis, to quote lines out of context because her poems are the sort that, in their total effect, rise above inadequate phrasing or archaic language. It is not always true that a poem is just as good as its weakest word. In these poems, sometimes the diction seems to consist of mere poetic counters, but the poem as a whole will be deeply moving, warm and luminous.

It is perhaps enough that lyric poetry be intense and passionate, however narrow in range. Nevertheless, while one is grateful for the candor, the deep tenderness and simplicity of the best of these poems, one keeps wishing that Miss Lewis would break into other areas of experience. The nursery, the quiet study, the garden, the graveyard do not provide enough material for a talent of such high order. (pp. 222-23)

> *Theodore Roethke, "Integrity of Spirit," in* Poetry, *Vol. LXIX, No. IV, January, 1947, pp. 220-23.*

EUGENE GAY-TIFFT

Exquisite craftsmanship, a cool perfection of utterance have long been the enviable property of Janet Lewis.

The Trial of Sören Qvist, a novel, and the latest work to leave her hand, represents her talent at its best. She has taken a deeply moving seventeenth-century tale, has transmuted it into winey prose. The poise and restraint which have always stamped her verse have now involved her scholarship, with the result that the latter is at last in proportion. Too, she has somewhere discovered along the way the art of narration and in the present book has almost succeeded in offering that necessary degree of suspense which the mind craves along with other virtues of story-telling.

It is a grim drama, played in an atmosphere of clinging fog and drafty candle-light, which crowds the heart from first to last with inexorable and almost grotesque tragedy. It relates how an innocent man—a minister of God during the early reign of Christian IV, and the soul of virtue in his rural community—could be ensnared in a net of circumstantial evidence manufactured by a diabolically crafty enemy, and how that evidence in its cumulative effect could be so imposing that in the end even the accused was convinced of his own guilt and testified against himself. . . .

The main part of the book is devoted to the events out of which the cynical plot against the pastor was woven. It is a story of weird, medieval conflict; of spurned suitorship and revenge, of virtue at grips with vice, of superstition darkening the mind's enlightenment, of love and loyalty wrestling in the dark with hatred and contrivance.

There is, during the later unfoldment, little in the way of suspense. The plot has already been given away, and we follow the sweaty struggle through to its inevitable conclusion not as sleuths but as students of human nature. Of love in this tale there is little, of physical passion none at all; but there is much in the way of emotional struggle and of loyalty. Of action there is less than of brooding talk, and of warmth there is only that upon which the Jutland fog is constantly creeping; but there is atmosphere as rich and authentic as that of life itself. There is excellent characterization. And last of all, there is throughout the book a charm which is born of Miss Lewis' peculiar eloquence and which rides down every other consideration.

> *Eugene Gay-Tifft, "Justice, Perverted," in* The New York Times Book Review, *March 23, 1947, p. 12.*

VIRGILIA PETERSON

[The] old tale of the Danish pastor whose head was chopped off by sword for a murder of which he was guiltless has taken root in the folklore of Denmark as a symbol of uncompromising integrity. More than a century ago the Danish writer Steen Steensen Blicher, a collection of whose stories was published in America last year, told it with characteristically bony simplicity under the title of "The Parson of Vejlbye." Now, in *The Trial of Soren Qvist*, Janet Lewis, a young writer of no mean talent, has infused the same historic legend with fresh color and sound and feeling. While Blicher kept the quality of the spoken tale and the stark outlines of northern reticence, Miss Lewis, though faithful to its spirit, has added some interpretation of character and dappled the harsh facts with the sun and rains of a more yielding moral climate. Thus the old tragedy of the soul's conflict with itself comes closer, more movingly alive, to the modern temper. . . .

Here is the same armature as Blicher's, the noble, God-fearing pastor who refuses the hand of his bright-haired daughter Anna to the local devil Morten Bruus, and, giving in to his only weakness—a hasty temper—boots Morten Bruus from the door, thus provoking a vengeance which slowly but inevitably brings ruin upon himself and his daughter and ashes to the mouth of the young judge who was to have become his son-in-law but was compelled, instead, to pronounce his death.

But only the armature of Miss Lewis's tale is the same as Blicher's. Over it, she has fashioned a far more complex account of human motives. While never allowing herself to depart from the basic facts, she has managed to give the parson the stature of some tragic Greek; she has invested Anna Sörensdaughter, the pure and obedient virgin of the folk-tale, with the tender vulnerability of a young doe; she has enriched the character of Vibeke with that untutored but sound intuition which is to be found in simple women of all eras and all lands; and she has made of the judge, whose rigid honesty was tinged with an all too human ambition for his calling, a far more understandable figure than the stern arbiter of law as depicted by Blicher. These characters—not only the parson, the judge and the girl, but also the devil Morten Bruus and his younger brother, Neils, who served him unwittingly as half-baked disciple and chief weapon of revenge—are imprisoned, like all mankind, in eternal conflict. But to this plot, which is somewhat stereotyped in its horror and so clearly related to the old morality plays, Miss Lewis brings the green fingers of her imagination to give it a lyric quality all its own.

> *Virgilia Peterson, "A 'Greek Tragedy' in Denmark," in* New York Herald Tribune Weekly Book Review, *March 30, 1947, p. 21.*

MAURICE H. IRVINE

Miss Lewis' short lyrics [in *Poems 1924-1944*] deal mostly with children, gardens, music and the transitory nature of human experience.

Miss Lewis' taste for Landor is evident in some of the shorter pieces. Two that are addressed to the poet himself have something of his reflective and concise grace. Herbert and Herrick are probably other favorites. Though some of the poems leave no particular impression on the reader, only **"White Oak,"** a soliloquy by the tree itself, is a real failure. Miss Lewis is at her best on the wonder and promise of childhood and in **"April Hill," "Candle Flame," "No-Winter Country"** and **"Lost Garden." "Helen Grown Old"** (after the fall of Troy) strikes just the right note of detached interest on a familiar theme. These last are poems to remember.

> *Maurice H. Irvine, "Gardens and Music," in* The New York Times Book Review, *April 8, 1951, p. 17.*

JOAN BRACE

Janet Lewis, the author of such memorable novels as *The Wife of Martin Guerre* and *The Trial of Soren Qvist,* has once again proved the excellence and purity of her style and her rare ability to translate the mustier aspects of historical research into clear and shining prose [in *The Ghost of Monsieur Scarron*]. . . .

As in *The Trial of Soren Qvist,* Miss Lewis has taken the facts of an actual incident, the publication of a scurrilous pamphlet directed against Louis XIV and Madame de Maintenon (the former Mme. Scarron) and the king's punishment of a bookbinder in whose possession it was found, as the scaffolding of her story, which is as simple and inevitable as a Greek tragedy.

The tragedy is particularly moving because it follows inexorably the one weak act of passion in the life of a thoroughly good mother and wife. It is "a novel of innocence and betrayal," of the implacable forces of good and evil in a kind of Jansenist world where free will is inoperative. It also is a novel of vengeance.

Miss Lewis . . . is a good scholar as well as a good novelist. She reports soberly, gravely, exactly, the excesses of the latter part of Louis XIV's reign—the artificial and organized excesses of the court and the spontaneous excesses of a goaded populace.

Her descriptions of the daily life of a family, Larcher, bookbinders, give quiet evidence of an understanding of 17th century life. . . .

Miss Lewis has placed years of historical learning at the service of a style as clean and neat as can be found today. To that she has added what cannot be learned—an intuitive knowledge of man's long struggle between passion and reason.

> *Joan Brace, "Musty Facts Transmuted into Shining Prose," in* Chicago Sunday Tribune Magazine of Books, *February 22, 1959, p. 3.*

FRED INGLIS

[Janet Lewis' prose contains] the confidence and sure judgement of a moral historian; it contains also a remarkable leanness, an exact purity in the selection and disposition of its syntax which comes, I should say, from close, and repeated scrutiny of poets like Jonson and perhaps Horace, Valery and Landor—though without any of the latter's petrified self-indulgence. It is steady, meditative and pure; in a remarkable way Miss Lewis retrieves the original, *essential* qualities of a simple vocabulary. . . . Miss Lewis in her conscious and scrupulous art recreates an ethos of her own in which her prose seems similarly to contain the resonance of a homogeneous culture and a secure grasp on moral standards. It is a courageous act of recreation, a dogged reforging of traditional instruments, and an achievement, I should guess won only at considerable cost. . . . [This] prose is mature but not—as I understand the word—subtle. It is not able to record the minute discriminations of Henry James, but then its author wouldn't regard this as her object; nor is it able to explore the flux of subconscious feeling, like a Lawrence or a Dostoyevsky. Again, I take it that Miss Lewis would not want to attempt such an exploration—but her specialized prose would fail in such an attempt because the moral standards contained in the books are lucid and definable, and human behaviour may be checked against them, consciously and rationally. The tales embody a moral judgement, rigorous and severe: it becomes diffuse, fluid, uncertain when we absorb it into the muddy medium of our own undefined values. I do not mean that Miss Lewis sternly but naively holds certain moral views incompatible with the twentieth century (although I am certain that she *does* hold moral views, and I honour her for it), but rather that the recorded morality of say, Gascony in *The Wife Of Martin Guerre* collides with our own vague humanitarianism and challenges us to a salutory clarification. The moral intention is collision. Thus the prose, in its poised wisdom is not intense, as we may find the nervous and marvelously perceptive intensity of Lawrence, nor is it subtle, as the evaluation of the complicated society of Middlemarch is; it has at its best however a third quality no less valuable, an inclusive, compassionate generality.

Inevitably, then, the task suggests itself to Janet Lewis as in some degree involving the historical sense, a sense of the past and its *pastness*. A useful quotation from Professor J. V. Cunningham may illuminate what I mean: "Our purpose in the study of literature . . . is to erect a larger context of experience within which we may define and understand our own by attending to the disparity between it and the experience of others." . . . Her task then is to make this attention as complete as possible by presenting the past as entirely as possible, and one of the conditions of such an intention will be historical truth. *Waverley,* which I take (after reservations) to be a very distinguished historical novel, is weakened by the fiction; in spite of the thoroughness with which the Waverley traditions are described, the reader is uneasy when Waverley meets the great historical characters—Charles Stuart, for example. The issues at stake are enormous, but such encounters reduce the stature of the book momentarily to daydream. This shortcoming applies neither to *The Wife of Martin Guerre* nor *The Trial of Soren Qvist,* but in both cases very little is sacrificed to historical significance. The third historical novel, *The Ghost of Monsieur Scarron* seems to me altogether less successful. (pp. 52-4)

[In *The Wife of Martin Guerre*] Miss Lewis has so refined and pared down her theme and her material, that the characters, for all their physical solidity, are only significant socially and morally. They are invested with such social importance, woven so deeply into the dense, rich texture of the moral and social order that, as with the heroes of Racine and Ben Johnson, our central preoccupation is with their abstract moral importance. The details of individual personality which are so important to the theme of the twentieth century novelists are here reduced to a minimum. The conflict is between "natural" passion and a moral duty which amounts to passion. The judgement Janet Lewis asks us to consider is not easy but it is, I think, decisive. . . . [We] are not invited to pardon everybody as victims of an unfortunate misunderstanding or a recalcitrant Provi-

dence; rather, we should arrive at an accurate evaluation of two acts of wrongdoing and even more importantly correctly evaluate the resolution compelled by Bertrande's moral scheme. Such an evaluation depends on a living morality of our own: Miss Lewis, as I have said, drives us to define it.

The Trial of Soren Qvist is the second of the three historical novels which make up, as far as method, tone and pattern go, a sort of trilogy. Probably it is the most perfect of Janet Lewis' novels, and among the most perfect of any novels. And here it is worth mentioning that we consider the books in terms of "perfection" of moral form, much as we would consider a short poem. . . . The affinities of these novels are . . . towards the formalism of the great poets of the Renaissance lyric, and we should read them with such related expectations.

I do not need to recapitulate the story of *Soren Qvist* by way of illuminating the method. It is enough to say that here too we have the recording of historical fact, the social importance of the main figures, the apparent violation of received morality and the anguish, in the pastor, of an involuntary responsibility. (pp. 57-8)

[It] may well be objected that Janet Lewis' view of experience is sour and pessimistic, and that what she presents us with in this book is a brutal, savage and meaningless world in which the Pastor is the voluntary victim of an absurd and empty code of morality. I suppose that is how M. Sartre would read it, and find it, as such, satisfactory. But I think this would be to damage beyond repair the whole meaning of the book as it presents itself in narrative, tone, imagery and positive statement, and we have no right to neglect the cumulative effect of the components as we read and re-read. The statement, finally, it seems to me is of a piece with *Martin Guerre* and *Against a Darkening Sky;* Miss Lewis finds the meaningful and enduring patterns of morality to be strengthened and affirmed by the acts of individual human beings. The determination of Soren Qvist to face Punishment for what he was sure was a sinful act, finally conquers the evil which has seemed to triumph over him. No doubt this seems mere sentimentality to the believers in the absurd, but the quality of Soren Qvist's character is too solid, strong and admirable to be interpreted any other way. (pp. 59-60)

I have done something to suggest the kind of reading this fine novel requires. In a real sense we have a tragic novel—more genuinely tragic than *Tess of the D'Urbervilles,* because there is no sense of contrivance and there is, at the end, an act of choice which is in fact triumphant. What we have witnessed is the destruction of the good by the evil, and yet in so doing we have experienced the tragic effect which isn't medicinal but a sense of challenge and "enhanced vitality". The values held by Soren Qvist are felt as ultimately more significant than the individual valuer, and his recognition of this represents the positive affirmation of tragedy, and this novel. (p. 61)

After these two very considerable works, *The Ghost of Monsieur Scarron* is a severe disappointment. It suffers from having no historical substance for the main characters, although the story itself has some basis. But as in *Waverley* the detailed reconstruction of the life of Louis XIV and his minions is unsatisfactory and over-thorough. The insistence on the presence of assorted literary names—Fenelon, Racine and so on—makes the novel read too much like a well-sugared history textbook for reluctant pupils. The book describes the publication of a scurrilous pamphlet by the 'ghost' of the sharp-tongued courtier M. Scarron and its savage suppression by

Louis and his police, especially because it hurt the feelings of Mme. de Maintenon. The public theme is conscientiously related to a private one in which a bookseller is first cuckolded and then framed by his assistant who leaves copies of the pamphlet in the bookseller's house. The bookseller is executed and after some hiatus, the wife and the assistant live together until they are denounced and murdered by the bookseller's son returning after a long exile in England. There appears to be some intention to consider the conflict of justice and political dictatorship as they appear in a fair-minded but wrong-headed king, yet if this is the intention it is cursorily done and less exactly and subtly than in *Darkness at Noon*. At the same time although there appears in the private theme to be some similarity of intention to *Anna Karenina*, that is to show the moral degeneration of an individual dominated by a joyless passion, I do not think Miss Lewis' perception nor, therefore, her prose adequate to the carrying out of such an object. The last pages of the book have a certain brute power, but we expect more from a novelist than coercive power, and I think that when we look elsewhere in this novel for that something, we are disappointed, and probably bored. The book is longish, but it gives none of the evidence the other two contain of being consistently re-worked and refined. The two themes never coalesce, their links remain arbitrary so that the repetition of historical dates becomes irritating, and the characters are tasteless and rather stale.

I have left *Against a Darkening Sky* to the end, although it was written in 1943, four years before *Soren Qvist,* because it is a contemporary novel and therefore raises special problems of its own. Certain hints are implied in the title, which is clearly more allusive, more "symbolic" than the direct unambiguous *The Trial of Soren Qvist*. Much of the approach is, as we would expect, recognisably the same: there is the same careful construction of a way of life with strong healthy roots in a natural landscape, and hence a careful, sensitive and (in an undenominated way) religious response to that landscape. . . . The book describes two or three years in the life of a family living somewhere outside San Francisco in the early thirties. . . . It is entirely fictive, and of its nature cannot contain a circumscribed tale like the other novels, and Miss Lewis is too intelligent and too intent on the incompleteness inferred by her title to provide the novel with a spurious climax on which to lower the curtain. Yet the book describes the attempt of Mary Perrault, the mother and principal character, to impose a moral pattern on the intractable amorphous material of twentieth century life, to do this against a sky darkening with economic disasters, moral incoherence and, ultimately, war. Her struggle to order without extinguishing the deep vitality of the family's sprawling lives gives the form of the novel a profound symbolic force. If its success is only partial, as I think, this is because the presentation of Mrs. Perrault, utterly admirable as it is, is finally inadequate to unify the novel and to sustain the passages in which she is only an unseen presence. But the successes of the novel are far from being merely local ones, and the greatest one is no doubt the presence of the Californian landscape and the subtle alliance created with Mary Perrault's Scottish landscape, and her husband's Swiss one. (pp. 61-3)

[Janet Lewis] built a literary tradition for herself by "intelligent saturation" in certain traditional modes. The process enabled her to ignore the merely technical innovators of the century, and she created by sheer hard work a prose and a novel which would support her intention. . . . Janet Lewis has also found for herself a way to state a moral position without elaborate qualification and defensiveness, self-mockery or naivety. The voice is quiet in which she does it, but it seems to me in every way preferable to Hemingway's adolescent nihilism or the fashionable quietism of novelists as different as Henry Miller and Evelyn Waugh. It is a small body of work and it may be unspectacular and unsensual, so it is never likely to be fashionable. But in three novels it is sane, honest and courageous and, as I think, more enduring than most of the novels of the last thirty-five years. (p. 64)

Fred Inglis, "The Novels of Janet Lewis," in Critique: Studies in Modern Fiction, *Vol. VII, No. 2, Winter, 1964-65, pp. 47-64.*

DONALD DAVIE

The entire genre of "the historical novel" needs to be vindicated anew. It has been vindicated in the Communist world, preeminently by George Lukacs, to the extent that the social-realist novel about the present day is, in Marxist thinking, virtually a historical novel set in the twentieth century; but in our noncommunist world "the historical novel" is in common acceptance a necessarily unserious form, a charade or costume pageant.

Fortunately it is not necessary to exhume and vindicate the historical novel as a genre, in order to take the measure of Janet Lewis' distinction. . . . *The Wife of Martin Guerre* (1941), *The Trial of Sören Qvist* (1947), and *The Ghost of Monsieur Scarron* (1958) all recreate plausibly the form and body of life in society in a vanished era; all of them, in a way which Lukacs would admire, present in action the dynamics of historical change from one form of society to another. But in no case does this seem to have been the prime intention. Grateful as one may and must be for such fruits of the historical imagination, in each case they are provided as a sort of incidental bonus. The storyteller's imagination is focused elsewhere. Each of the three books is a fable about authority. They are books about politics, only incidentally about history. To call them "fables" does violence to the density and concreteness of these narratives; the political lesson is not to be read out of them at all so unequivocally as I shall pretend. But I believe that they are distorted less from this point of view than from any other. (pp. 42-3)

[Like] Shakespeare in his cycle of History Plays, Janet Lewis investigates [in *The Wife of Martin Guerre*] the nature of political authority by taking the crucial case of the usurper. And, again like Shakespeare, she presents the question at its sharpest in that she makes the usurper in some ways more able, as well as more agreeable, than the rightful ruler whom he displaces. This is where she traces the dynamics of historical change more subtly, as well as more profoundly, than a Marxist is usually prepared to recognize. For she sees the historical change (for instance, the change in ideas of authority and sovereignty) as the emergence of a new psychological type on the stage of history. The pretender, Arnaud du Tilh, who masquerades as the lost Martin Guerre, is as vigorous and dignified as the true husband was, but he is also courteous, gracious, considerate, flexible and tactful, capable of tenderness. When Bertrande has taken him to her bed, having as yet only faint suspicions that he is not what he seems, her passion for him makes the sensuous world about her more vivid and immediate than before. . . . The dangerous complexity of these feelings, in which dread lends an edge to pleasure, characterizes possibilities of experience outside the range of the Homeric King and the Gascon patriarch. These possibilities are opened up to Bertrande, a woman of the old style herself, by the man who, when she brings herself to arraign him in a court of law, regards her "with a look at once patient, tender and ironic." Nonplussed by the look, she asks herself: "Who was this Arnaud du Tilh. What manner of man was he that he did not return her hatred with hatred. . . .?" And though Bertrande cannot answer her question, we surely can: Arnaud, the usurper and imposter and true lover, is a *modern* man, a man to whom the Renaissance has happened, an individualist. As an individualist, his world is not structured and governed by those hierarchies which govern Bertrande's world. Since human relations are no longer for this modern man controlled by the traditional hierarchies, he has learned to be infinitely more skillful, perceptive and resourceful in such relations. Most of Bertrande's associates, including (a fine touch) the parish priest, are won over by the stranger and by the modern behavior he stands for. Bertrande, though he charms her, resists him, and when she arraigns him she holds by the standards of the old and vanishing world she was born to. I am reminded of Walter Pater's unfinished novel, *Gaston de Latour,* where Ronsard is seen by a representative of Old France in the same double-edged way: the new ways of feeling are an enrichment or a corruption, a rebirth or a decadence, according as one sees them from one set of assumptions or another. "Ironic" is one of the attitudes Arnaud du Tilh is capable of, which marks him off from both the Martin Guerres and from Bertrande. (pp. 45-7)

[Arnaud du Tilh, the] adventurer and self-made man, is condemned, but he is a portent: within a century the self-made Oliver Cromwell will overthrow the kingdom of England and institute a Republic; and in another century after that, "He has a good heart, that is all" will have quite a different ring—Fielding will assert, in the figure of Tom Jones, that to have a good heart is all that matters. On the other hand, in this modern world, where the authority vested in the offices of king, father, and husband will seem no longer inviolable but dependent on the good conduct of the office-holder, there will still be those to claim that the authority of the father in his family is the model for all political authority whatever. And the theme of *The Wife of Martin Guerre* is thus a living issue, and can never cease to be so, since the questions surrounding the concept of authority will always be questions of life and death in any political establishment whatever. The perplexity which we feel as the fable gradually unfolds these perennial issues before us is a measure of how scrupulously the storyteller's imagination has refused to simplify them. (pp. 47-8)

By 1625, at Vejlby in Jutland, the problem of authority is already more perplexing still, not just by reason of the lapse of time, but because in some areas (and Denmark is one of them) the intervening years have seen the triumph of the Reformation, bringing with it revolutionary changes in the theory and practice of politics. In the case of the Danish pastor Sören Qvist, the image of serene and naturally-sanctioned authority which corresponds to the image of old Martin Guerre as a Homeric King is already a much more complicated image. . . . In a Protestant polity the image of natural authority is no longer the father as husbandman, but the father as farmer *as priest.* In this case, as in the case of Martin Guerre, this authority both underwrites and is underwritten by the authority of the monarch. . . . [In] striking contrast to the direct chronological line of the story of Martin Guerre's wife, the story of Sören Qvist plays tricks with time, and much of it is told in flashback. . . . But as we should expect from our experience of *The Wife of Martin Guerre* . . . , [an early flashback in *The Trial of Sören Qvist*] serves many more functions than simply to pin

us down in recorded history. For one thing, coming so early as it does, it serves to advise us that the Protestantism we are to be concerned with is not Puritanism, in the sense of a more or less hysterical fear and hatred of the flesh: on the contrary it is this Protestantism, rather than the Catholicism of Bertrande de Rols, that has, for what it is worth, the sanction of atavistic connections with the carnal and the earthy—a connection to be dwelt on later, with a rather different inflection, when the Pastor's hands which baptize the human child are also the stockbreeder's hands which had helped a cow to calve. Moreover, if we turn back to these earliest pages after we have read through the story, we perceive that in Denmark the Gascon situation is reversed: in Denmark the royal authority in the kingdom, though menaced, holds fast while the pastoral authority in the parish crashes in ruin; whereas in France the authority of the Gascon head of the household holds fast, even as the authority of the king is challenged and overborne. . . . (pp. 48-50)

The authority of Parson Qvist is undermined, and at last destroyed, because the authority of the priest, which might have seemed to buttress Qvist's authority as head of his household, in fact works against that authority and saps it. He is liable to fits of violent anger: as the farmer that he is, he could have removed temptation from his path by dismissing the idle and churlish servant who continually tempts him to give way to this human infirmity; but as the pastor and priest, the man of God, he feels that the provocation offered by the servant is sent by God to try him, and so he mortifies himself by keeping the hired man in his employ. By doing so he permits his enemy to "frame" him for a murder he did not commit: his office as priest betrays him into dangers which his office as farming patriarch would have saved him from. (p. 51)

The Wife of Martin Guerre is, I suppose, a *nouvelle;* at any rate one feels of it that it is just as long as it needs to be. This is not what I feel about *The Trial of Sören Qvist:* though the issues raised by the later story, as they are more complicated, require more expansive treatment than the *nouvelle* allows for, the fable and the cast of characters are still too spare to sustain such treatment. Accordingly the second story has its longueurs; the narrative is sometimes slowed down beyond what seems called for. Related to this is some uncertainty about the point of view from which the story is told: the story of Sören Qvist is not told from the standpoint of Anna Sörensdaughter at all so consistently as the story of Martin Guerre is told from the standpoint of Bertrande de Rols. And finally the narrative style is not always held to a consistent level. One character calls another "a clever varmint" and explodes on the next page into, "Damn it all," but also into, "Oh, the devil take it"; whereas another character exclaims, "he will not, the poltroon." Elsewhere I detect traces of self-consciously "fine" writing, embellishment without function: "The name drifted to the old man, through the darkness, through the chill air, like some petal loosened from a flowering bough remote in spring." I would not insist on these blemishes, if that is what they are, were it not that in the last pages the political focus seems forgotten and Sören Qvist's dilemma is presented as a purely ethical one, as if the author had herself succumbed to the individualistic heresy, and were considering the ethical dilemma of an individual as if it could be divorced from the social milieu and matrix which conditioned him and the situation in which he finds himself.

On the other hand, whereas Mr. Inglis finds *The Ghost of Monsieur Scarron* "a severe disappointment" [see excerpt above]

I believe that it is a consummate performance. It is the one among the historical narratives which has the scope and shape of a full novel. This is not to say that it is an "advance" on *The Wife of Martin Guerre;* for the *nouvelle* does one sort of thing, the *roman* another—and the difference between the two kinds of fiction is not one of arbitrary word count. In *The Wife of Martin Guerre* the clean run of the narrative line produces an effect of tragically inexorable logic such as *The Ghost of Monsieur Scarron* aims at but does not achieve at all so certainly. On the other hand the world of Jean Larcher is more densely peopled and densely furnished, so that we seem to live in that world smelling its smells and hearing its sounds, more absorbedly than in the world of Bertrande de Rols. And yet this is not to say that the novel makes more concessions to "local colour." There is in *The Wife of Martin Guerre* a marvelously rendered and memorable description of Bertrande's housekeeper sitting near the doorway killing doves; and this, beautiful as it is and easily justifiable even in the tight economy of a *nouvelle,* is much nearer to "local colour," has a much less clearly symbolical or allegorical relation to the main plot, than has a comparable episode from *The Ghost of Monsieur Scarron,* a chapter in which Madame Larcher and her lover watch an uncle, a beekeeper in the country, smoking bees from the hive to take their honey.

The greater "fullness" of *The Ghost of Monsieur Scarron* has everything to do with the intensive researches of its author. For one note that Miss Lewis struck in the first of her narratives, *The Invasion,* has been constant with her throughout: she is a realist in the straightforward and now rather rare sense that she uses her art to embellish history and to clarify it (the embellishment is in the clarifying), but not at all to supplant the historian's truth by the allegedly superior truth of art. For her the art supplements and sharpens, makes poignant, the truths that are available in other forms, for instance in historical records; the art does not in her understanding give her access to a realm of truth of which it has the monopoly. Thus each of her narratives rests upon a solid basis of scholarly research; and it is obviously of great moment to her that she does not *create* her plots, but *finds* them, or at least the vestiges of them, in recorded history. (pp. 53-4)

It is these trivia, and our trusting our author to have got them right, which make the world of Jean Larcher so *solid*. And solidity matters more in the world of Larcher than in the worlds of Martin Guerre and Sören Qvist. For Larcher is a bourgeois, a man to whom property matters. And this in fact is the new challenge which Miss Lewis takes up with this book: what happens to the allegedly natural authority of the father as head of the household, when the economy of that household is no longer agrarian but *commercial?* We ask the same question, only lifting it to another plane, when we ask: can monarchical authority be maintained, has it still "natural" sanctions to appeal to, when the kingdom has become largely mercantile? These are the questions posed by *The Ghost of Monsieur Scarron* as a whole. For the moment what needs to be noticed is that with this story, when Miss Lewis focuses her attention on a bourgeois household, a household where property matters greatly, she has suddenly a strong card to play. She is at an advantage simply by being a woman, or, more precisely, by having known what it is to be a housewife. (p. 56)

[Walter] Scott found a way of analyzing in fiction the dynamics of historical change by poising between political and social orders in conflict the figure of a wavering and youthful unheroic hero, uncommitted to either side but attracted to both. Janet

Lewis in each of her narratives casts a woman for this central role; and this enables the central figure to become once again heroical, as Bertrande de Rols certainly is. For the woman is poised undecided between the conflicting orders, not because she cannot make up her mind, but because she is committed to both sides at once. Bertrande is torn between her ties to her legal husband on the one hand, and the pretender-husband on the other; Anna Sörensdaughter is tied on the one hand to her father, on the other to her fiancé, the judge who on the evidence has to find her father guilty; and Madame Larcher is torn between her husband and her son. It is her love for her son which first makes her sap a little her husband's authority; and when the son has disappeared, his friend whom she takes as her lover is much of the time only a sort of shadowy surrogate for the son who is offstage.

It may be objected that, by my own account, these stories are academic in conception, and that the interest which they excite, sustain, and satisfy, is an academic interest. Indeed, they are "of academic interest," if (as I suppose) it is the responsibility of the academy to analyze and clarify rather than vehemently to protest and exclaim. The tool which this analyst employs is however the imagination, preeminently that species of imagination which consists in sympathetic identification with the painful plights of other persons. The narratives of Janet Lewis exemplify an art of literature which happily, though not humbly, collaborates with, and yet transcends, the disciplines of responsible scholarship. (pp. 59-60)

> Donald Davie, "The Historical Narratives of Janet Lewis," in The Southern Review, *n.s. Vol. II, No. 1, Winter, 1966, pp. 40-60.*

EVAN S. CONNELL, JR.

Recently I reread [*The Wife of Martin Guerre*] for the first time, although I have been mentioning it and handing out copies for quite a while. I had no interest in reading it again, because some books, like certain scenes, print themselves permanently on the mind. However, it is not tedious to read a second time, and it remains for me one of the most significant short novels in English. (p. 152)

That a factual case is always a precarious base for fiction is demonstrated by the general mediocrity of historical fiction, and the usual novelist would have written a melodramatic, implausible book from such melodramatic, implausible history. Janet Lewis wrote something else.

If there is one characteristic of the book that distinguishes it, I would call it dignity. This quality cannot be manufactured, as certain qualities can; it emanates from the author. And it is here as plentifully and as unmistakably as grain in the fields of Languedoc. Out of a few documents Miss Lewis created a man named Martin Guerre who returned from the wars, arrogant and unforgiving, without one of his legs, to demand his rightful place; Arnaud du Tilh, obliged by his respect for Bertrande to become a finer man than he ever had been, or expected to be; and Bertrande, who could not live with suspicion. All of them are aware of themselves, which is the true definition and the prerogative of dignity. I think it is because of this uncommon self-knowledge that they continue to live.

I do not much like extravagant praise, either to hear it or to employ it, and I am reluctant to use the term "masterpiece," which is used indiscriminately. I am not sure if *The Wife of Martin Guerre* qualifies; but I approach it with respect. (p. 156)

Evan S. Connell, Jr., "Genius Unobserved," in The Atlantic Monthly, *Vol. 224, No. 6, December, 1969, pp. 152-54, 156.*

SUZANNE J. DOYLE

Returning to the subject matter of her first book of published verse, *The Indians in the Woods, 1918-1928,* Janet Lewis's most recent volume of poems, *The Ancient Ones,* concerns itself again with the experience of the American Indian. This new sequence of poems, based upon the poet's experience during a visit to the Southwest in 1976, deals with the Indians of that territory, specifically the Navajo and Hopi. While *The Indians in the Woods,* concerning the Ojibway tribe, was a volume of poems chiefly employing free verse and Imagist techniques, *The Ancient Ones* is a collection of poems which experiments with the possibilities of the longer free verse line.

The earlier Indian poems owe much to the Imagists, whose intention was to capture the isolated perception with such precision, clarity, and harmony that it would suggest a considerable depth of conceptual content. . . . The concentrated line of the Imagist poem intentionally offered no opportunity for reflection or commentary upon the experience described. In the years 1918-1928, Janet Lewis used these limiting, Imagist techniques in such a way as to unify the inner and outer realms of experience captured in the poems, a possibility which is implicit in the form. These poems reveal the intimate relationship between the natural world and a people whose bond with it was of life and death importance—a simple but intense experience itself, like the best of the Imagist poems. The spiritual consciousness of the Indians arises out of this vital relationship with the natural world, and in the poems concrete detail, or the Image, is the embodiment of the spiritual disposition. In this respect, the early poems clearly resemble the Japanese Haiku, a form which the Imagists greatly admired and sought to imitate. (pp. 531-32)

Unlike those of the earlier poems, the principles of organization in the poems of *The Ancient Ones* are not primarily Imagist. The exceptions are **"Deer Dancers at Santo Domingo"** and **"Kayenta, Arizona."** (pp. 532-33)

In the more thematically ambitious poems, such as **"The Anasazi Woman," "The Ancient Ones: Betátakin,"** and **"Awatobi,"** the Imagist method is abandoned in favor of a longer free verse line which allows the poet the freedom necessary for generalizing upon the experience. **"The Anasazi Woman"** is a poem in which the speaker reflects upon having viewed a "sun-dried mummy in the museum / In Tucson." This is not a persona poem at all; the voice is the voice of the poet, Janet Lewis. Here the lines are organized basically in terms of syntactical units with runovers gracefully turned to sustain a quiet rhythmical continuity. Stanza length varies and is determined by completed units of thought. The train of thought is associative; the vision of the mummy gives rise to the question of how old she was when she died, and this to an imaginative reconstruction of her consciousness by the poet, who views the Indian's simpler, elemental world with nostalgia: "I . . . / Think of the peace and splendor of her days." The poem concludes with an explicit recognition of the woman as a spiritual sister. (pp. 533-34)

["The Anasazi Woman"] is very similar in style and intention to poems written in the Romantic tradition of Wordsworth and Coleridge, albeit the rhythm and tone seem to me far more elegantly sustained and emotionally restrained than nearly any-

thing in *The Prelude* or "Frost at Midnight." The diction and syntax are those of everyday speech, occasionally elevated for effect with the rhetorical "Oh" and minor syntactical inversions, which lend an archaic quality to the tone. The voice, as mentioned above, is personal, the experience is private and "recollected in tranquillity," but its subject is not spiritual revelation. This is a poem about spiritual discovery, the discovery of spiritual identity. It is an anti-Romantic poem in that there is no surrender of the individual consciousness to the overwhelming elemental forces of nature. Instead, the individual is brought into relationship with those forces, as a sister, as a friend to another human being who also understood the proper relationship, one of reverence and respect, to the natural forces which shaped her life. The traditional Romantic identification with Nature would, to such a consciousness, be an offensive act, a blatant *hubris*.

I find it interesting to note that what is discovered by the poet in **"The Anasazi Woman"** seems to have been a tacit assumption in all of the poems in *The Indians in the Woods:* a temperamental affinity of the poet for the Indian consciousness. The difference lies in the fact that here it is the poet's personal voice and consciousness which gives form to the idea in explicit commentary in the poems. Some explanation of the return to the old concerns and attitudes by a different road seems to be offered in **"The Ancient Ones: Betátakin."** The concluding lines of this poem explicitly discuss the problem of artistic form and by implication the form of one's life, which is discovered in Time as it leads the individual toward death:

> Time stays, the canyon stays;
> Their houses stay, split rock
> Mortared with clay, and small.
> And the shards, gray, plain or painted,
> In the pale roseate dust reveal, conceal,
> The patterns of their days,
> Speak of the pure form of the shattered pot.
> We do not recreate, we rediscover
> The immortal form, that, once created,
> Stands, unchanged,
> In Time's unchanging room.

The Platonic Form here is not only that of Art but includes the universal, eternal Forms of human experience and relationship. This conclusion is arrived at through meditation on a landscape, the ruins of the civilization at Betátakin. The delicate depiction of the natural details, animal, vegetable, and elemental, which were experienced by the Indians in the same Form provide the link between the present and the past, allowing the poet to recognize that she, too, although subject to continual mortal change in Time, is a carrier of that eternal pattern of human experience. This same paradoxical, divine discovery is symbolically realized in a single line, perhaps the most beautiful image in the entire volume, in the poem **"Paho at Walpi":**

> The sunlight pours unbroken through the wind.

It is difficult to sustain rhythmical tension in a free verse line in which general statement is being attempted, especially if the poem is of considerable length. The language tends to fall into prose rhythms when a metrical norm has not been established to define the line. The natural rhythm of the language, its underlying iambic measure, then threatens to take precedence, unless grammatical inversions, among other devices, are repeatedly employed and the stress value of the "charged" words remains sufficiently emphatic. The repeated coincidence of line break with syntactical unit also presents the danger of the emergence of a kind of pattern, which undermines the integrity of the free verse form, a form which has as its single definition "perpetual variation" according to Yvor Winters in his book *In Defense of Reason* (1947). Syntactical disruptions through precipitous line breaks, necessitating rapid runovers, and variable line length soon become ineffectual mannerisms. The Imagist poets discovered these problems in their longer poems and for these reasons it seems to me that it is much more difficult to write a poem in free verse which successfully balances the general and particular statement, if the general statement is at all ambitious and particularly if a historical narrative is attempted. But Janet Lewis manages in **"The Anasazi Woman"** and **"The Ancient Ones: Betátakin"** to work these devices unobtrusively and effectively, sustaining an appropriately dignified tone, striking a balance between the concrete and the general in which each informs the content of the other. I do not find this to be true, however, in the poem entitled **"Awatobi,"** which begins:

> "This is holy ground," he said, our Hopi guide,
> And he was right to say so; but I think
> It was not sanctified for him
> Because here died
> Of Christian martyrs a great number.

This seems to me to be very fine prose, but the quality of the language and the rhythm of the free verse are leveled to the point of falling flat. There are an insufficient number of strongly stressed syllables or "charged," suggestive Images to maintain the integrity of language existing in lines. Always the danger of the longer free verse line, this falling off is repeated throughout the poem.

"Awatobi" is an attempt at a historical narrative of the destruction of the village of Awatobi during an internecine war waged with a neighboring tribe of the Three Mesas. Awatobi was attacked because of the cultural assimilation of the Catholic religion into the traditional worship there. The poet's vision is broad and sweeping; it is a poem about holy wars in general and the art which miraculously survives them. To illustrate this an eleven line stanza is devoted to drawing parallels between the events at Awatobi and the corresponding situation in France during the same historical period, where the art of Racine and Purcell survives despite the persecution of the Huguenots. Janet Lewis has dealt with such grand themes very successfully in *The Invasion*, her first novel; in fact, *The Invasion* reads like a prose poem, it is so richly and gracefully written. There she has the time and space, the formal structure, necessary to handle the epic scope of the subject, the transformation and gradual obliteration of the Ojibway culture. But here, in **"Awatobi,"** the form is insufficient to the subject. (pp. 534-37)

In general, *The Ancient Ones* demonstrates a return to what were for Janet Lewis her concerns as a young poet and fiction writer. Thematically, she seems to have come full circle in an impressively productive literary career. While the virtuoso rhythmical touch evident in the earlier free verse and traditional forms manifests itself in such poems as **"Deer Dancers at Santo Domingo,"** **"The Anasazi Woman,"** and **"The Ancient Ones: Betátakin,"** the longer free verse line attempted here is less successful than the handling of the rapid movement of the early Imagist poems or the refined, stately measure of the poems in traditional forms which she has done. It also seems to me admirable and worth mentioning that at the age of eighty Janet Lewis continues to experiment with new forms and reflects in these very poems the struggle of most contemporary free verse

poets to discover a form that will allow for more general statement and narration, while sustaining rhythmical variety and freedom apart from traditional meters. (p. 537)

> *Suzanne J. Doyle, "Janet Lewis's 'The Ancient Ones'," in* The Southern Review, *Vol. 16, No. 2, Spring, 1980, pp. 531-37.*

HELEN P. TRIMPI

The poetry of Janet Lewis that is collected in *Poems Old and New: 1918-1978* ranges over a period of sixty-two years, for it may be noted that despite the dates of the title there are poems included which were written since 1978. From the earliest poem included, **"The Freighters"** (which won her entrance into the Poetry Club at the University of Chicago in 1918) to the latest, **"Words for a Song,"** richness of intelligence and centrality of human concerns have characterized her poetry.

The earliest poems, written from 1918 to 1927, include a sequence on Ojibway Indian themes that is reprinted from her first book, *The Indians in the Woods*. . . . It is no coincidence that the American Indian consciousness reemerges as a theme of her later verse, in the seven poems beginning with **"Kayenta, Arizona, May, 1977,"** for one might almost say that she is haunted by that consciousness, except that, perhaps, it is we who haunt the landscapes in which they more integrally lived. The Indian habit of mind, with its intimate relationship to the natural world, its dependence upon the changing seasons, and with its ordered understanding of the basic experiences of human life, has an affinity with her intelligence.

The general human significance of the themes on which she writes is, perhaps, her greatest source of strength. Her preoccupation is not with the odd vision, the oblique angle, the distorted lens, or the procedure that becomes of more interest than the subject itself. Her method does not become her matter. The perennial matters of human experience, approached directly, are her subjects: birth, the perception of good and evil, the battle against passion, choice, love, loss and death. By way of comparison, it may be noted that while none of her poems has the sharp, powerful intensity of the specialized vision of Louise Bogan's "Exhortation," she has in its place a breadth of experience and experiential understanding that is beyond Bogan's. The reader should weigh against the strong and acute, but narrow, vision of Bogan's poem the equally strong, but broader, power of Lewis's poem **"For the Father of Sandro Gulotta."** There are not many good poems about the death of a child; they are harder to write than poems about human depravity because sentimentality is difficult to avoid.

In a poem on the human consciousness, **"Time and Music,"** Lewis states a concern with time as the element in which we live, as a necessary condition of our being—a concern that appears frequently in her poetry as well as in her novels and stories: ". . . Time for us / Both snare and breath and motion is." In this she looks back to the pre-Kantian and pre-Cartesian concept of the consciousness in which the human person was thought to exist as a real independent entity in time and space—as does every other real thing—and was not thought to be able to "create" the conditions for his or her own existence. Such a consciousness is not "primitive" but perennial. It is not something "to go back to" but something to rediscover in the present and to find the contemporary language by which to explore and express it. To the extent that she finds a contemporary language for perennial experience Janet Lewis's work is original and enduring. (pp. 251-52)

For this reader, Janet Lewis's two best poems are two poems on death—the early lament, **"In the Egyptian Museum,"** written during the 1940s, and the comparatively recent elegy, **"For the Father of Sandro Gulotta,"** written in 1971. . . . **"In the Egyptian Museum"** is a meditation on death considered generally, without reference to a particular death. It avoids overgenerality, however, through the use of particular visual detail, consisting in the sharp description in stanzas 1 and 2 of objects seen in glass cases in a museum of Egyptian burial artifacts. . . . All the objects represent the attempt of the living mourner to overcome his or her pain through the orderly beautification of the dead. Then, in qualification of her description of the objects seen, Lewis introduces quietly the "anguished mind" of the imagined Egyptian mourner, which becomes the fulcrum upon which the poem turns, for the anguished mind—the one that may be supposed to have made or had made the objects surrounding its beloved dead—becomes in the last stanza a living voice speaking from the vacancy of the electrically lighted exhibition cases. Ironically, she says, objects intended to allay sorrow have become the means for the long-lasting expression of sorrow. . . . The rhetorical movement is masterly. Yet, unlike **"For the Father of Sandro Gulotta,"** . . . this poem does not convey a powerfully rational ordering impulse. The subject, by the close, seems to be grief rather than the right ordering of grief. To the extent that the expression of grief dominates the poem, it is marred. But it does not entirely dominate emotionally, because most of the poem . . . concerns the artistic (ordered) objects that represent the command of grief by the imagined Egyptian mourner. They form the background—firm and concrete—for the ghostly, half-subjectively created cry of the mourner who made them. Hence, the preponderance of feeling, despite the strength of the conclusion, remains with the ordered expression of grief, not the disordered cry of grief. The cry seems framed by the earlier part of the poem.

"For the Father of Sandro Gulotta," composed by Janet Lewis upon request for the father of a seven-year-old boy dying of leukemia, neither of whom she had met, draws, in its profundity of feeling and mastery of technique, upon sources of emotion far beyond the immediate occasion. . . . Lewis accomplishes here something that she approaches doing in several earlier poems but never quite so successfully as here: she captures the apparent simplicity of the child's life (which is really only a formal simplicity) through the figure of the day lily. The day lily functions as a metaphor for all the formal organizations of time—hours, days, years, etc.—that structure individual existence and that in structuring it grant lastingness. The child is perceived only as alive, both in the day lily, to which he is likened, and in the "children" called from their play. He is not seen as called beyond time to an eternal life nor to a blank nothingness that human thought cannot grasp. Time as a form, as measure, is itself timeless and unchanging; it can take various embodiments, giving structure to them. (pp. 255-56)

Helen P. Trimpi, "The Poetry of Janet Lewis," in The Southern Review, *Vol. 18, No. 2, Spring, 1982, pp. 251-58.*

J. D. McCLATCHY

A Collected Poems by any artist who works, like Janet Lewis, with slow precision within a very narrow range is in danger of being either neglected or overestimated. With her late husband Yvor Winters, she shares an abiding interest in American Indian culture; a sequence on Ojibway themes leads off [*Poems Old and New 1918-1978*], and it concludes with an even better set on the Anasazi and pueblo life. In both groups, a screen of sentimentality is in place, along with the expected details: the Edenic forest, river bank and hawk, the ceremonials. Though there are successes ("**Awátobi**" is one, a fine one), Lewis is more convincing with lyric abstractions. Time—"the substance and the breath"—is her theme, and Yvor Winters's dry aesthetic is, again, her guide. Her material has been refined to the point she wants to make about it; her imagination is demure, and thoroughly traditional; her rhythms are exact; her tone nostalgic, often stiffly so. Many poems are occasional—several elegies and memorials, or the likes of **"Lines with a Gift of Herbs"**—and none is ambitious. . . . Lewis is best known as a novelist. Whether or not poetry has been merely a sideline, her gift for it is slight—I mean, both delicate and minor.

J. D. McClatchy, in a review of "Poems, Old and New, 1918-1978," in Poetry, *Vol. CXL, No. 6, September, 1982, p. 349.*

TIMOTHY STEELE

The excellence of [Janet Lewis'] work results partly from the simple fact that she writes very well, hers being a style that combines clear speech with distinctive and personal inflection and perception. Lewis' achievement, however, involves not merely stylistic properties, but sympathies that issue from a life richly and thoughtfully experienced. To read her is to read someone who has been a child, sibling, friend, spouse and parent, and who has clearly cared as deeply about these aspects of her life as she has about those aspects connected with her art. . . .

Because her writing is so restrained and clear-sighted, one might almost overlook the fact that much of Lewis' work is about sex. The subject commonly receives gaudy treatment, and a jaded reader may not recognize it in Lewis' plainer settings. Marianne Larcher, of Lewis' *The Ghost of Monsieur Scarron,* is an individual who, by failing to resist infatuation with the feckless Paul Damas, brings about her moral annihilation, not to mention the physical annihilation of everybody around her. Bertrande de Rols, the young heroine of *The Wife of Martin Guerre,* a beautiful short novel based on a legendary case in French law that also served as the basis for a recent film, is both betrayed and ennobled by her love for a clever and affectionate adventurer who poses as her long-lost husband. (Lewis' novel, which anticipates by several decades many of the motifs of the feminist movement, presents the story in a way considerably different from that of the movie.) Bertrande's initial acceptance of the imposter is a triumph of understandable but misguided desire over instinct and reason alike. Her ultimate rejection of him is a triumph of courage over deception and self-deception, though the cost of the triumph is heavy, for Bertrande must see her lover condemned to execution and herself to public shame and dishonor.

A second, equally central concern in Lewis' work is with the past. This is reflected generally in the historical materials on which four of her five novels draw. More particularly, the concern is reflected in the characters in the novels, a number of whom are people trying to establish, often under more difficult conditions, a sense of community and tradition. This is especially true of John Johnston and Neengay of *The Invasion.* In the wake of the ruin of his family's fortunes, the young Johnston comes from his native Ireland to the New World, where he finds himself totally isolated from his heritage. Neengay is by no means isolated from hers, but she sees it being eroded by the encroachments of the fur trade and the military power of the Europeans. Johnston and Neengay's marriage is in one respect an assertion of the hope that they will be able to found a new ancestry to replace the lost or dying lineages.

A similar theme is sounded in *Against a Darkening Sky,* which is set in a semi-rural community on the San Francisco Peninsula during the Depression. The novel's plot involves Mary Perrault's attempt to communicate stable values to her four children, whom she sees growing up in the rootless and anxious society of modern California. An immigrant from Scotland, Mary Perrault has herself great strength of character; but she realizes that this strength is owed to her having been reared in a world more ordered than that which her children occupy. As she observes, in words that will be readily appreciated by many current residents of this state, "The fault lay in the lack of faith, the lonely and independent lives—every man for himself and the devil take the hindmost—the shifting communities whose constant change made it impossible for anyone to live as she had lived as a girl, in a community as in the center of a family."

Lewis' concern with history appears as well in certain poems dealing broadly with the human condition—with the fact that our species, though subject to biological process, has somehow stepped from merely material existence into self-awareness and a recognition of time. One of the most interesting of these poems is **"Fossil, 1975,"** the opening lines of which describe a fossilized fern and affirm that durable patterns of existence can and do survive the ceaseless flux of things. . . .

Faith is another central motif in Lewis' work. Her belief that lacking spiritual support human beings are vulnerable to moral corruption or despair, is explored in detail in *The Trial of Soren Qvist,* a study of a decent but flawed parson whose faith is tested by a terrible personal catastrophe. And the theme is examined again in **"The Candle Flame,"** a poem in which

Lewis suggests that only a kind of divine grace can counter the instability of human passions and behavior. . . .

It remains to say that Lewis' work, as somber as it sometimes is, maintains a joyful appreciation of the world in all its transitory loveliness. Nowhere is this appreciation more evident than in **"Country Burial,"** a poem distinguished by finely rendered physical details, such as that of the women following the casket out through the meadow: "The daisies bend and straighten / Under the trailing skirts."

The poem concludes with the observation that the mourners can relate the mystery of death only to the wonder of life, the vital sum and limit of their experience.

> Into this earth the flesh and wood shall melt
> And under these familiar common flowers
> Flow through the earth they both have understood
> By sight and touch and daily sustenance.
> And this is comforting;
> For heaven is a blinding radiance where
> Leaves are no longer green, nor water wet,
> Milk white, soot black, nor winter weather cold,
> And the eyeless vision of the Almighty Face
> Brings numbness to the untranslatable heart.

For more than half a century, Janet Lewis has been writing verse and prose about "the untranslatable heart." She has devoted readers and has been widely praised by her peers, among them Louise Bogan, Theodore Roethke and Tillie Olsen. Evan S. Connell has written of her: "I cannot think of another writer whose stature so far exceeds her public recognition." Because of this situation, this year's Robert Kirsch Award to Janet Lewis may rightly serve two functions: to honor a wonderful writer and to bring her to the attention of new readers.

Timothy Steele, "Janet Lewis and the Untranslatable Heart," in Los Angeles Times Book Review, *November 3, 1985, p. 2.*

Ross Macdonald

1915-1983

(Born Kenneth Millar; also wrote under pseudonyms of John Macdonald and John Ross Macdonald) American novelist, short story writer, critic, editor, and nonfiction writer.

Together with Dashiell Hammett and Raymond Chandler, Macdonald is considered one of the most prominent authors of "hard-boiled" American detective fiction. Best known for his popular series of novels featuring detective Lew Archer, Macdonald is credited with enlarging the moral and psychological scope of contemporary crime fiction while downplaying the genre's characteristic emphasis on sex and violence. Set in southern California, the Archer mysteries display Macdonald's ability to objectively but sympathetically probe the effects of time and change on rootless people drawn from all phases of society. Dick Adler echoed the opinion of many critics when he deemed Macdonald "not only the best in his field but an important novelist on any level. I know of no other writer who catches the spectrum of California life so succinctly."

Macdonald's earliest books, written under his real name, Kenneth Millar, are spy and crime novels influenced by the fiction of Hammett and Chandler. These works include *The Dark Tunnel* (1944), *Trouble Follows Me* (1946), *Blue City* (1947), and *The Three Roads* (1948). Millar adopted the pseudonym John Macdonald and introduced Archer in *The Moving Target* (1949). Although he acknowledged his debt to Hammett by naming his hero after Miles Archer, the partner of Hammett's detective, Sam Spade, Macdonald based his hero's personality on actual detectives. Reserved but sensitive, Archer functions in Macdonald's early novels as a man removed from his past, a resigned but sensitive observer of the exterior world. Novels written under the pseudonym John Ross Macdonald include *The Drowning Pool* (1950), *The Way Some People Die* (1951), *The Ivory Grin* (1952; republished as *Marked for Murder*), and *Find a Victim* (1954). In these novels and in his first work to appear under the pseudonym Ross Macdonald, *The Barbarous Coast* (1956), Archer compassionately examines the process by which victims become victimizers.

In 1956 Macdonald began psychotherapy to help him confront memories of his traumatic childhood and his abandonment by his father. Macdonald's subsequent novels deal with such topics as broken homes, child custody battles, and neglected or abused children. Macdonald stated that *The Doomsters* (1958) signaled "a fairly clean break with the Chandler tradition . . . and freed me to make my own approach to the crimes and sorrows of life." This work established the major themes which distinguish his later fiction: the complexity of human motivations and interactions and the traditionless, alienated nature of urban life. In this novel and in *The Galton Case* (1959), Macdonald's focus begins to shift from Archer to the characters he observes. Archer becomes, as Macdonald noted, "less a doer than a questioner, a consciousness in which the meanings of other lives emerge."

Macdonald's fiction of the 1960s is considered to be among his most complex and mature work. He continued to explore variations on familial and psychological themes in such novels as *The Zebra-Striped Hearse* (1962), *The Chill* (1964), *The*

Far Side of the Dollar (1965), *Black Money* (1966), *The Instant Enemy* (1968), and *The Goodbye Look* (1969). Ecological themes dominate many of Macdonald's novels of the 1970s. *The Underground Man* (1971), for example, is a highly-praised account of an arson-related forest fire, and *Sleeping Beauty* (1973) concerns the effects of offshore drilling upon ocean ecology. Of *Sleeping Beauty* Jean White commented: "All of Macdonald's trademarks are there—the crisp, crackling dialogue, a beautifully constructed story skein that unwinds inexorably, the search into past and psyche, the frantic southern California life."

Although occasionally faulted for overly complex plots and a self-conscious literary style, Macdonald has been praised for mastering the techniques of detective fiction and for broadening the concerns of the genre. Macdonald's hero Archer is also featured in the short story collection *The Name Is Archer* (1955), and several of Macdonald's Archer mysteries are collected in the volumes *Archer in Hollywood* (1967), *Archer at Large* (1970), and *Archer in Jeopardy* (1979). Macdonald also wrote a nonfiction work, *On Crime Writing* (1973). *Self Portrait: Ceaselessly into the Past* (1981) is a collection featuring Macdonald's introductions to his novels and journalistic essays on ecological topics.

(See also *CLC*, Vols. 1, 2, 3, 14, 34; *Contemporary Authors*, Vols. 9-12, rev. ed., Vol. 110 [obituary]; *Contemporary Au-*

thors New Revision Series, Vol. 16; Dictionary of Literary Biography, Vol. 2; and Dictionary of Literary Biography Yearbook: 1983.)

ANTHONY BOUCHER

Just at the time that the tough genre in fiction needs revitalizing John Macdonald turns up. There is nothing startlingly new about Mr. Macdonald's plot [in *The Moving Target*] (though there is great technical dexterity in his interweaving of three levels of criminal endeavor); kidnapping, contraband, decadence and brutality are familiar elements of the hard-boiled school. The outstanding freshness of this novel comes, instead, from the fact that Macdonald as a writer, as a weaver of words and an observer of people, stands head and shoulders above most of his competitors. He can evoke pity and terror for his "foreshortened figures with blood and money on their minds," and probe the social and psychological implications behind crime and detection—and do this without sacrificing for a minute the impact of a tautly paced, tightly constructed story.

> Anthony Boucher, in a review of "The Moving Target," in The New York Times Book Review, April 3, 1949, p. 28.

ANTHONY BOUCHER

Dashiell Hammett and his many admirable pulp colleagues gave a vitally needed blood transfusion to the detective story with a more nearly realistic approach to crime and punishment, a faster tempo and added narrative vigor, and a prose at once simpler and more colorful than that prevalent in the trade at the time. Yet, just as the overardent admirers of Charles Fort have turned the conjectures of that valiant antidogmatist into a dogma of their own, so the imitators of the hard-boiled school have turned a fresh approach into the tiredest of formulas. . . .

The entrance upon this jaded scene two years ago of John Ross Macdonald was [highly welcomed]. . . . [*The Way Some People Die*] is probably his best [novel] to date—and thereby automatically the top hard-boiled novel of the year. Macdonald has the makings of a novelist of serious caliber—in his vivid realization of locale; in his striking prose style, reminiscent of Chandler and yet suggesting the poetic evocation of Kenneth Fearing; in his moving three-dimensional characterization; and above all in his strangely just attitude toward human beings, which seems incredibly to fuse the biting contempt of a Swift with the embracing love of a Saroyan.

The plot of the latest Macdonald (starring, as usual, the private detective Lew Archer) is a complex study of the heroin racket and its impingement on an assortment of characters of all social and cultural levels; but for all its complexity, it's a tighter and better organized plot than that of either of his previous stories. Which makes this (to stick my neck out) the best novel in the tough tradition that I've read since *Farewell, My Lovely*. . . . and possibly since *The Maltese Falcon*.

> Anthony Boucher, in a review of "The Way Some People Die," in The New York Times Book Review, August 5, 1951, p. 16.

JAMES SANDOE

John Ross Macdonald began (*The Moving Target*, 1949) as an adept writer of pastiche in Chandleresque vein and [in *The Ivory Grin* (1952), as in his second novel, *The Drowning Pool* (1950), he] demonstrates his imitative capacities with a good deal of skill.

With *The Way Some People Die* (1951) Macdonald reached beyond clever imitation to a position of his own at once sardonic and compassionate as it was steadily hard-driving. Now *The Ivory Grin* consolidates this position in a tale with a contenting simplicity of plot and the same sharply observant set of senses to report what Lew Archer saw and felt in trying to discover what happened to spoiled, harassed young Charles Singleton.

Macdonald's sense of vivid similitude still overpowers him occasionally and he might now set to work to make his conversation as well heard as his milieu is well observed. But he is even now an admirably corrosive teller of tales and one of the few responsible and gifted practitioners in the hardboiled vein. It is possible to accept his creatures, tormented and twisted as they may be, as credible and worth compassion.

> James Sandoe, in a review of "The Ivory Grin," in New York Herald Tribune Book Review, May 4, 1952, p. 11.

ANTHONY BOUCHER

Macdonald is Kenneth Millar, whose first novel (*The Dark Tunnel*, 1944) I recall as one of the best of all debuts in the espionage-pursuit field. . . .

Find a Victim (titled from a striking and significant quotation from Stephen Crane) is the best yet of the novels about Macdonald-Millar's private detective, Lew Archer—which means that it is about as good as the hardboiled detective story can get. The writing is as incisive and perceptive as ever, and the action as forceful and fast-paced; and the plot is more powerful and personal than earlier Archer stories—a strange and haunting blend of professional crime and private psychological complexities. This is, in fact, so much more satisfactory, whether as a thriller or as a novel, than most other private-eye books that it seems to belong to an entirely different genre of its own.

> Anthony Boucher, in a review of "Find a Victim," in The New York Times Book Review, August 1, 1954, p. 15.

ROGER SALE

[Ross Macdonald's *The Zebra-Striped Hearse* provides] a model to show what care and patience can achieve. . . . It has taken Macdonald ten years and as many novels, all about private eye Lew Archer, to learn finally how not to imitate Raymond Chandler. . . . Macdonald has gradually created his own form, after a number of attempts to rewrite Chandler's, by turning to the lives of quiet bourgeois desperation that are the legacy of California's passionate belief in unreality. Anthony Powell uses coincidence marvelously to show how people who speak the same language are never far apart; Macdonald uses coincidence equally marvelously to show how a life gone out of control, moving as fast as California makes it move, must intersect with countless other lives of which it knows nothing. . . . The plot is extremely complicated, but it is also the perfect instrument for rendering, question by question, the way pointlessness in Malibu leads to colonies in Mexico, Nevada, and other celebrations of the grotesque, and how these, in turn, lead to horror and violence. It is a limited and stylized mode, but it dramatizes, as few others can, genuinely contemporary experience—here violence is not gratuitous, sexual disaster has no overtone of the salacious, and heroism has no more than its just share of muscularity. (p. 148)

Roger Sale, "Gossips and Storytellers," in The Hudson Review, Vol. XVI, No. 1, Spring, 1963, pp. 141-49.

WARNER G. RICE

The hearse which gives occasion for Mr. Macdonald's title [*The Zebra-Striped Hearse*] does not figure prominently in his story, nor do the beach bums who drive it to Malibu or Zuma play more than an incidental part. But the indecorum of the vehicle is significant, and its owners are representative of the society in which the action moves—they are rootless and immature, without firm purpose, without character. Archer, Mr. Macdonald's private eye, responding sensitively to the world to which he is condemned, accepts it with resignation, and is thoroughly at home in the police stations and mortuaries, the seedy back streets and restaurants, the artists' colonies, bars, and motels through which he passes in his resourceful, persistent search for a half-dozen victims and their destroyer....

Mr. Macdonald, always a superb contriver of puzzles, again gives his reader a full measure of excitement and suspense, and of satisfaction with the resolution of his plot. The first problem presented is the identity of Burke Damis, a mysterious painter, talented, but hostile and uncommunicative, who carries off the infatuated Harriet Blackwell very much against the will of her father, a wealthy retired colonel. The discovery of Damis' true name and history proves to be not very difficult; but as the clues are followed up they lead into a perplexing tangle of relationships, ambitions, intrigues, and violent acts, all of which must be unravelled before the fate of Harriet can be known.... [Archer] is tireless, determined, incapable of admitting defeat. Except for Damis, all the people with whom he deals are familiar—he has met them before, under different names, and he reads their natures quickly and accurately. They are not, to be sure, very profound.

Mr. Macdonald writes excellent dialogue, and his descriptions of people and places are masterly in their economy and precision. The fastidious reader is occasionally brought up short by gaudy splashes of figurative language . . . ; but since these passages never occur in the language which Archer reports, but only in the paragraphs in which he tells what he himself observes, they may be attributed to his taste rather than to lapses on the part of his creator, and help to define his *persona* as author.

Warner G. Rice, in a review of "The Zebra-Striped Hearse," in Michigan Quarterly Review, Vol. II, No. 3, Summer, 1963, p. 212.

ANTHONY BOUCHER

Without in the least abating my admiration for Dashiell Hammett and Raymond Chandler, I should like to venture the heretical suggestion that Ross Macdonald is a better novelist than either of them. He owes an immeasurable debt to both in the matter of technique and style; but he has gone beyond their tutelage to develop the "hard-boiled," private-eye novel into a far more supple medium, in which he can study the common and the uncommon man (and woman) as well as the criminal, in which he can write (often brilliantly and even profoundly) not only about violence and retribution but simply about "people with enough feeling to be hurt, and enough complexity to do wrong"—to quote from his latest *The Far Side of the Dollar*....

A 17-year-old boy has run away from a curious sort of psychotherapeutic prep school, and private detective Lew Archer is called in to find him. It is a quest which illumines the war of the generations, odd corners of Hollywood, a 20-year-old sin and even a part of Archer's own past. It involves . . . above all a compassionate understanding of people, old and young, caught up in this moment of time.

Anthony Boucher, in a review of "The Far Side of the Dollar," in The New York Times Book Review, January 24, 1965, p. 42.

HENRY A. WOODFIN

Ross Macdonald writes detective novels, so he is seldom dealt with in serious literary quarters. This is everyone's loss. He is a skillful and intelligent novelist, albeit a minor one, who provides those essential insights into character and milieu which are the major functions of his craft. But, since his protagonist is a California private detective, Macdonald is usually spoken of as a follower of Dashiell Hammett and Raymond Chandler—to the disadvantage of all three. While he is not without some indebtedness to Chandler, the body of his work is very much his own; he has found his particular subject and his personal way of handling it.

His investigator, Lew Archer, is an ex-Los Angeles police detective who has weathered the aftermath of a disastrous marriage and, for undisclosed reasons, gone into private practice. He is a man of realistic compassion and understanding, called upon to look into the details of the private and non-villainous lives of individuals living in more or less quiet desperation in the anomic world of Los Angeles and its environs....

Macdonald depicts the members of the Southern California middle classes, the real subjects of his novels, as rootless, usually without real connections where they have chosen to live. Archer's efforts to make sense of their shattered lives, in this microcosmic climate of physical comfort and moral collapse, can provide no relief other than knowledge, and knowledge uninformed by an organizing principle to make the miniscule tragedies and crimes either bearable or expiable....

Though the violence of the third-rate private detective thriller is conspicuously absent, Macdonald's universe is replete with malevolent activities and psychological violence—more convincingly frightening as the reader realizes the veracity of the account.

Black Money is, I think, his best book yet. The usual Macdonald themes are present, but they are treated with even greater lucidity and sharpness than before. His portrait of life in a state college and the desperate striving for accomplishment is consistently pointed and concise. The interconnections in American life between the Las Vegas casinos, the new underworld of quasi-respectability, and the middle classes are conveyed in human terms, with all parties damaged by the reticulated corruptions.

Macdonald combines the elegiac theme of *The Great Gatsby* with scrupulous observation of the minute details of modern life—all rendered in neatly balanced prose that make his characters both individuals and types. In these days of dreary fiction, Ross Macdonald is a boon.

> *Henry A. Woodfin, "Desperation in the Suburbs," in* The New Leader, *Vol. XLIX, No. 8, April 11, 1966, p. 26.*

ANTHONY BOUCHER

More and more critics, not only of the suspense novel, but of general fiction, are coming to discover that Ross Macdonald is an important novelist of the American scene in the 1950's and 1960's; and they have particularly noted that Macdonald is one of the very few novelists in any genre to write with genuine insight and perception about the peculiar microcosm that is labeled "Hollywood." . . .

[*Archer in Hollywood*] contains *The Moving Target* (1949), *The Way Some People Die* (1951) and *The Barbarous Coast* (1956)—respectively the first, third and sixth of Archer's book-length cases. At the time, I noted of *The Way* that it "manages somehow to fuse Swift's contempt for humanity with Saroyan's love" [see excerpt above]. This combination of two inescapable emotions characterizes most of Macdonald's work. And perhaps as Macdonald comes to be esteemed as a serious writer, I should add the reminder that he also writes beautifully plotted detective stories, with a precise balance of action and character.

> *Anthony Boucher, in a review of "Archer in Hollywood," in* The New York Times Book Review, *February 19, 1967, p. 46.*

ANNETTE GRANT

Macdonald's detective fiction is always as violent and unsentimental as a Los Angeles freeway, where many of his characters travel to and from desperate deeds. . . . [In *The Goodbye Look,* Macdonald] once again probes the effect of big passions on small people. The result is as ominous as a ticking parcel.

A local aristocrat hires hard-boiled private eye Lew Archer to recover a missing Florentine gold box. The case looks open and shut until a corpse appears. All the evidence points to the client's nice but disturbed son who disappears only to turn up at the scene of a second murder. To solve the crimes, Archer must slice through a layer cake of family intrigue three generations deep and expose secrets neither pretty nor face-saving, even for the innocent. This book, an exploration of guilt, greed, exile, revenge and causality, confirms Macdonald's metamorphosis from an imitator of Dashiell Hammett and Raymond Chandler into a novelist who uses the detective tradition to explore the modern American psyche. (p. 82)

> *Annette Grant, "Summer Sleuthing," in* Newsweek, *Vol. LXXIV, No. 4, July 28, 1969, pp. 82, 84.*

DANIEL R. BARNES

[Twentieth-century] writers have with increasing frequency turned to the first-person as a congenial point of view. And, perhaps most important, many have consciously exploited the limitations of their narrators as perceivers. The first-person detective novel would appear to be the single notable exception. [Wayne Booth] has observed, for example, that "In fiction, as soon as we encounter an 'I,' we are conscious of an experiencing mind whose views of the experience will come

between us and the event"; yet we have seldom if ever been conscious of this in detective fiction, because we continue to assume the reliability and objectivity of the narrator. . . . However true of most detective novels, this assumption deserves closer scrutiny.

Generally, I think it is safe to say that detective novels written in the first person nearly always fall into one or another of two fairly obvious categories. The first comprises those which are narrated by someone other than the Great Detective, an observer, usually a close companion or confidante. (p. 178)

The second category includes those novels narrated by the detective himself. This group would seem to present fewer difficulties, for unlike the observer-narrator the detective who tells his own story is more fully a participant—even if only intellectually—than anyone in the first category. Because his accounts are "inside narratives" his reliability and judgments are seldom questioned. . . . Despite our inclination [to assume the narrator's objectivity], however, it is also true that as we come closer to a fully realized narrative voice in any fiction—as revealed through style, diction, imagery—the generalization of the narrator's objectivity breaks down. And with the collapse of that single assumption comes our realization, perhaps for the first time, that the detective-narrator, because he combines *in a single personality* the dual functions of observer and "experiencing mind," is a far more complex figure than we might otherwise have imagined.

The Lew Archer novels of Ross Macdonald offer a significant case in point. Archer is on occasion a less than objective reporter of factual data; indeed, he is, in this respect, a particular kind of "fallible narrator." Consequently, he is also a good deal more than the reporter of the traditional detective novel, whose objectivity we have continued to assume central to the form. Archer's observations, and the style through which he presents them, reveal an added dimension to his character. . . . (p. 179)

Most of his readers are well aware that Macdonald's fiction is heavily imagistic and metaphorical. Eudora Welty, for example, in her review of *The Underground Man,* remarks that "A great deal of what [Macdonald] has to tell us comes by way of beautiful and audacious similes" [see *CLC*, Vol. 2]. Miss Welty is quick to add, however, that "Descriptions so interpretive are of course here as part and parcel of the character of Archer who says them to us." Miss Welty's perceptiveness appears, however, not to have been shared by Raymond Chandler. In a 14 April 1959 letter to James Sandoe, Chandler faults the similes in Macdonald's *The Moving Target.* He finds particularly offensive Macdonald's description of a car as "'acned with rust,'" and sees it as typical of "The simile that does not quite come off because it doesn't understand what the purpose of the simile is." . . . [However, in] accusing Macdonald of "stylistic misuse of the language," Chandler fails to take into account the presence of the narrator; if the reader's attention is "jerked away from the thing described," it is jerked towards—not the "pose of the writer"—but Archer, the teller of the tale.

To ignore this distinction is to ignore as well a basic epistemological distinction. . . . The traditional reader of the detective novel is interested primarily in acquiring knowledge about the real weather of the fictive world in which he finds himself. What is he to do, then, when confronted with the experiencing mind of Lew Archer who, like Prufrock, is not above poeticizing the evening sky into something quite different? Is he, in short, to accept Archer as an "unequivocal spokesman" for Ross Macdonald or as "a fallible character in the story"?

The problem may best be approached, I think, by concentrating upon a singular "poetic" feature of Archer's narration: his perennial fascination with eyes. As with his recurrent interest in moonlight and birds, Archer's concern with eyes is to some extent inevitable; it is an obvious and necessary constituent of scene. And sight and vision are, of course, particularly essential to first-person fiction, which must present its world literally through the eyes of one who, like all of us, "knows" his world primarily through those eyes. Thus, Archer depends upon his eyes to know, following the predictable conventions of all fiction; what makes him remarkable, however, is the extent to which he relies as a detective upon his ability to read the eyes of others and to make and revise his judgments of them largely, if not solely, on that basis. In no way do his subjects reveal to him their duplicity or their innocence, their fears and anxieties, more than by their eyes. . . . Conversely, the only real and immediate limitation of Archer's power to ferret out the truth lies in his occasional inability to penetrate the eyes of others, to strike through the mask. This is especially true in the case of those stock figures from the hard-boiled tradition and before—the exotic Orientals, Mexicans, Indians, and Blacks, as well as that old standby, the curt receptionist with "cold green eyes." But in the Archer series it is no less true of virtually anyone who wears glasses (note Archer's frequent descriptions of reflected glare, of fogged and dark lenses). . . . (pp. 179-81)

Archer's ocular fascination extends, however, far beyond his interest in subjects or in arriving at truth. For one thing, it contributes a whole battery of images to his vocabulary. Among the most common of these are his repeated references to lights, windows, and guns in ocular images. . . . Such imagery emphasizes Archer's conscious or unconscious belief that he is the object of scrutiny, the *observed* rather than the observer. (pp. 181, 183)

These metaphors of fear clearly signal that Archer's preoccupation with eyes amounts to nothing less than an obsession. Perhaps it may be explained as being related to Archer's sense of guilt at earning his living as a "private eye at the keyhole of illicit bedrooms". . . . But the fear goes much deeper than this—and farther back into Macdonald's canon. . . .

> The things you see, the eyes, and the people
> that follow you, are almost certainly imaginary.
> The fears themselves are real. We are all pur-
> sued by fears from birth to death, from the fear
> of being born to the fear of dying. There is no
> one who has not seen those eyes in the night.
>
> (*The Three Roads*)
> (p. 183)

Because of [Archer's] own obsessive fear, . . . [some observations] seem less valid as empirical descriptions, less a function of the "real world" than a consequence of Archer's projections of that fear onto the landscape. If the pictures are grotesque, they are so because Lew Archer has painted them that way. Describing the sun metonymically as an "insane red eye" tells us little about the real weather of this novel but a good deal about the inner weather of Archer's mind. His is the experiencing mind, his the perceiving eye, and what he sees may often be . . . an optical illusion.

What makes this all the more intriguing, however, is the ample evidence in the novels to indicate that Archer's eye fixation is directly related to yet another of his anxieties, a pathological fear of blindness. (p. 185)

I have said nothing of the high incidence of eye injuries in these novels, nothing of the dozens of characters whom Archer describes as astigmatic, myopic, shortsighted, or cross-eyed, nothing of the abundance of asymmetric eyes which contribute to the grotesqueness of so many characters, nothing of Archer's fondness for Cyclopean imagery and statues of "Blind Justice." Nor is there space here to indicate how, in novels like *The Moving Target, The Galton Case, The Chill,* and *Find A Victim,* Archer's eye imagery and blindness motifs thematically support the larger patterns of light/dark or, more significantly, the Oedipal pattern which consciously informs so much of Macdonald's fiction. But integral as Archer's eye fixation may be, it is but one function of his role as narrator.

The limitations imposed upon a novel by the author's choice of a first-person narrator are many; the most important of these affects what I have termed the novel's epistemology. Though we may legitimately discuss a novel like *The Galton Case* in terms of its theme, its formal unity, its sense of moral and aesthetic order, we should always remember that these elements are—given that point of view—created and sustained, indeed imposed, by the narrator. And if, as I have suggested earlier, that narrator's attempt at *telling* us about the real weather *shows* us in the process something of his own inner weather and its capacity to color the empirical phenomena of his world, the question of his limitations becomes a real one. The degree of reliability, even within a single narrative voice, will vary as that voice functions as a mouthpiece for its creator, as a teller of the tale, or as an unconscious betrayer of itself. And surely Lew Archer functions for the most part as a reliable teller of tales; indeed, this is his single most important function. But like so many of his counterparts, in first-person fiction, he occasionally makes the reader aware of his distance from the norms of both reader and author; like them, in telling his tale, he sometimes calls attention to the mystery of his own personality; and like them, finally, he unwittingly provides clues towards cracking it.

In short, Archer's penchant for ocular images affects significantly his characerization both as a detective and as a narrator. Far from indicating a paucity of inventiveness or "the stylistic misuse of language" on Macdonald's part, the pattern of eye imagery in the novels actually draws our attention to the experiential side of the observer's character; it reminds us that, like *The Great Gatsby,* these novels too are woven of a "seamless web of observation and experience," sustained solely by the presence of Archer's narrative voice. (pp. 187-88)

> *Daniel R. Barnes, " 'I'm the Eye': Archer as Narrator in the Novels of Ross Macdonald," in* The Mystery & Detection Annual, *1972, pp. 178-90.*

L. MOODY SIMMS, JR.

Kenneth Millar, who publishes under the pen name of Ross Macdonald, is frequently asked why he chooses to write detective fiction instead of straight fiction. Millar's most interesting response to this question involves his reading and understanding of Frank Norris's essay, "The Responsibilities of the Novelist." In this essay, Norris makes it plain that he is a true believer in democracy. Art must be understood by the people; art that the people do not understand dies. . . . Norris's creed as a writer holds that the novel is a social instrument, charged with a popular significance, democratic in its ingredients, realistically and faithfully American, regional but never provincial. (p. 89)

In his Lew Archer novels, [Millar] has dealt with the rush of change which started during World War II and which accelerated afterwards, especially in the empty spaces of southern California. "It seemed," observes Millar, "that a brave new world was being born here, on the last frontier, and people migrated to it as we had from all over the continent." Millar's style—which tries to catch the words and rhythms of everyday language—lends itself to the depiction of the open society which California was struggling to become in the years just after the war. And as for crime, it is seen as a complex product of society and not simply as an intellectual puzzle.

Over the years, Millar's Lew Archer, the tough guy hero, has become a modern Everyman. He represents modern man in a technological world. Though homeless and virtually friendless, he behaves "as if there is some hope in society, which there is. He's a transitional figure between a world that is breaking up and one coming into being in which relationships and people will be important." (pp. 89-90)

> *L. Moody Simms, Jr., "Kenneth Millar/Ross Macdonald, Frank Norris and Popular Literature," in* North Dakota Quarterly, *Vol. 49, No. 1, Winter, 1981, pp. 89-90.*

GARY GIDDINS

Consisting of 21 brief essays (including the two valuable studies previously published as **On Crime Writing**) rather than a fluid autobiographical narrative, [**Self-Portrait: Ceaselessly into the Past**] is a vague, prissy rummage through the writer's soul. Macdonald has many interesting things to say about detective fiction, his peers, the relationship between his past and the particular wrinkle he brought to the genre with **The Galton Case,** but he's hardly a lively anecdotalist—he doesn't even explain why he switched to Macdonald from his real name, Kenneth Millar. Like Ray Bradbury, Macdonald drowns vivid memory in lachrymose nostalgia, exacerbated by the deja vu that follows when he repeats the same phrase from essay to essay. Not that he's entirely consistent: on page 100, he writes that Hammett's prose "could say almost anything but often chose not to." Ten pages later, he demonstrates, "Hammett's prose is not quite a prose that can say anything, as Chandler over-enthusiastically claimed it could." None of the tough-guy writers delivered themselves of an autobiography, and it looks as though Macdonald won't either. I wonder if he writes good letters. (p. 45)

> *Gary Giddins, "Pulp and Circumstance," in* The Village Voice, *Vol. XXVI, No. 48, November 25-December 1, 1981, pp. 42, 45.*

JULIAN SYMONS

[*Self Portrait: Ceaselessly into the Past*] is a collection of pieces written over nearly twenty years. Some are related to Macdonald's interest in ecology, and concern such matters as the Santa Barbara oil spill of 1969 and a projected new road that would have affected local condors, but most are introductions to collections of crime stories. . . . [As] Eudora Welty says in a foreword, they contain a strong autobiographical element. They are, indeed, the nearest thing to an autobiography we are likely to get. The illness that affects Macdonald has, at least for the visible future, brought his writing life to an end. This short book is extremely informative about the pressures that have produced his novels.

Most of them since **The Galton Case** (1959) have concerned a broken family and a lost father, and to this aspect of his early life the articles return again and again. One might expect that Kenneth would feel bitterly about the father whose departure left the family in penury, but that is not the case. . . . Young Kenneth Millar felt much more tenderness for the father who left him than for the mother who stayed, and the significance of **The Galton Case** for the author was that it represented the emergence in his fiction of "the epic theme of a lost father". . . . If one reads the later books, roughly half Macdonald's output, with this theme in mind, the repetitions of it become obvious. For several years, as he has said himself, he has been playing variations on the same basic tale. Most writers, he says, work out of their obsessions, and certainly that is true in his own case. To produce a work of fiction is "to struggle with demons, to get them under control. . . . I mean problems, memories, or whatever else makes up one's psychic life".

With the appearance of **The Goodbye Look** in 1969, Macdonald was hailed in his own country as a major novelist, a writer whose "worth and quality surpass the limitations of the form", to quote one review typical of many. Yet he has always respected the crime story's form, as Eudora Welty says. A mystery must be created, and interest maintained in readers who mostly ask for no more than an undemanding tale of crime and retribution. These are problems for any writer trying to extend the boundaries of the crime story—Chandler, Highsmith, Nicolas Freeling, even Sayers in *Gaudy Night*—and each finds a different answer. In Macdonald's case "I sacrifice, if sacrifice is the word, everything to those two requirements" of holding the reader's attention by surprising turns of plot, and concealing what has actually happened.

In England Macdonald has received little serious critical regard, being viewed as a rather faint carbon-copy of Hammett and Chandler. Yet the differences are greater than the similarities, how much greater may be seen by comparing Philip Marlowe with Lew Archer. Marlowe "is the hero, he is everything", in Chandler's words. Archer, as Macdonald says here more than once, is not the central character, nor the main object of interest, in the books where he appears. He is simply the man to whom people talk, the surveyor discovering the crack in the family's apparently irreproachably sound building. This was not always true. If one looks at early and late Archer it is plain that Macdonald has consciously tried to reduce the detective's importance and eliminate him as a personality, so that he shall not stand between the reader and the books' real subject, the rediscovery of the past.

It would be foolish not to admit that there have been losses, as well as gains, in Macdonald's singleminded pursuit of the past. . . . The early books do show debts to Hammett and Chandler, but they have a verve and an audacity in the use of simile and metaphor that is restricted, almost placed in cold storage, in the later ones. **The Way Some People Die** and **The Ivory Grin** are particularly exciting and enjoyable. But as Macdonald has said himself, the blaze of youth does not last, "one writes . . . on the backs of torn-off calendar sheets", and the later stories are immensely more subtle and serious. At times the symbolism is too insistent, like the forest fire in **The Underground Man,** "much like the Coyote Canyon fire that threatened Santa Barbara", Mr Sipper tells us, that is reflected in the purgative fire burning out the secrets of the Broadhurst family. Yet the opening of *The Blue Hammer,* which casually mentions "the towers of the mission and the courthouse half submerged in smog", most delicately suggests the mists and confusions through which Archer will look for the truth about Richard Chantry's missing painting.

This last, or most recent, novel is in some ways the peak of Macdonald's achievement, bringing to the unravelling of past guilts much of the sparkle in the early work. A choice of books that suggest his range as crime writer and novelist might include the early ones already mentioned, together with *The Zebra-Striped Hearse* and *Black Money,* two of his own favourites, plus *The Far Side of the Dollar* and *The Blue Hammer.* When one sees the increasing skill, subtlety and sense of purpose shown in the course of Macdonald's writing, it is obvious that he has had in England much less than his due of praise. He stated his intentions with clarity in an interview given several years ago: "I've been trying to put into my books the same sorts of things that a reader finds in a general novel, a whole version of life in our society and in our time. . . ."

> *Julian Symons, "In Pursuit of the Past," in* The Times Literary Supplement, *No. 4122, April 2, 1982, p. 369.*

PETER WOLFE

Anything by Ross Macdonald can be read with pleasure and profit. **"The Writer as Detective Hero"** (1965) and **"Writing The Galton Case"** (1969), arguably the two main essays in *Self-Portrait: Ceaselessly into the Past,* may be indispensable to serious readers of the American murder mystery. No comparable works demonstrate as well how hardboiled literary detection has served as a model for life and action. Many of the other pieces in the book, like **"Homage to Dashiell Hammett"** (1964), contain insights that sound as fresh and accurate today as they did when first framed. In some of them lie the seeds of Ross Macdonald's peerless art. **"A Death Road for the Condor"** (1964) and **"Life with the Blob"** (1969), for instance, aren't just worth reading for themselves; the moral commitment to wildlife and the environment informing them returned in the Lew Archer novels, *The Underground Man* (1971) and *Sleeping Beauty* (1973).

As valuable as *Self-Portrait* is, though, it can't be called autobiography. Eighteen of the twenty-two selections included in the book have appeared before; none extends more than twelve pages; none has come out since 1979. The reader deserves to have this information before he/she thinks seriously of buying the book. The appearance of the Acknowledgments page, where this information is reflected, one page from the end, rather than in the front-matter section, might rankle the unwary buyer. But not every buyer: Ross Macdonald wrote twice as many novels as Hammett and Chandler combined; he took American literary detection away from the mob and dropped it into the middle-class family; his turning the fictional private eye from a tough guy into a man of compassion brought the genre a moral and historical depth it had never enjoyed before. In his last book, this master novelist set forth the main impulses, both literary and personal, behind his work. One selection in the book reads:

> I think a murderer is someone who has been very severely injured, morally and emotion-ally. . . . The average murderer in the United States is a man or a woman who kills somebody he knows. Often, it is his wife or husband, or

some member of the family, or someone close to the family. It is very often done on the spur of the moment under the influence of severe stress. I try to write about the domestic cir-cumstances that might produce this kind of sit-uation.

Where have we come to when a book by someone who can write with such tragic insight into motives needs to be reviewed with a warning? (pp. 426-27)

> *Peter Wolfe, "The Critics Did It: An Essay-Review," in* Modern Fiction Studies, *Vol. 29, No. 3, Autumn, 1983, pp. 389-433.*

MATTHEW J. BRUCCOLI

At thirty-two, Millar wrote his first breakthrough novel, but didn't know it at the time. He was trying to write a novel that he hoped would sell: "I was in trouble, and Lew Archer got me out of it." (p. 27)

In *The Moving Target* [1949], Lew Archer is a Los Angeles private detective who operates a one-man agency. He is thirty-five years old and separated from his wife, who dislikes his work. Formerly a member of the Long Beach Police Force, he had been fired for his opposition to municipal corruption. Archer is intelligent, courageous, and good with his fists. He absorbs beatings and administers them; Archer vows to get one of his assailants and drowns him. If Millar had a model for Archer, it was Chandler's Philip Marlowe rather than Hammett's Sam Spade (who appears in one novel, *The Maltese Falcon*). Like Marlowe, Archer is a knight-errant, a free lance with a highly developed system of morality; but he is less romantic than Marlowe and, at the same time, more intro-spective in this first appearance. (p. 30)

Lew Archer provides what Millar has described as a welder's mask or a protective shield between author and material that is too hot to handle. Archer not only tells the story; his in-vestigations cause things to happen and extend the web of causality. But he is not the hero; the novels are not about Archer. "He is less a doer than a questioner, a consciousness in which the meanings of other lives emerge. This gradually developed conception of the detective hero as the mind of the novel is not wholly new, but it is probably my main contribution to this special branch of fiction." Millar had been impressed by "the talking voice" in Cain's *The Postman Always Rings Twice* (1934): "You can say almost anything about almost anything with a tone like that, I realized." (p. 31)

In *The Moving Target* Archer is hired to find a missing oilman. (Oilmen reappear as figures of corruption in the Archer novels.) The intricately plotted case takes Archer through the Southern California underworld of new money, easy money, dirty money. Santa Teresa, one hundred miles north of Los Angeles, is the principal locale and is loosely based on Santa Barbara. Al-though sense of place is strong in Millar's fiction, he does not work close to his sources; he avoids the Gibbsville-Altamont approach to fiction. Santa Teresa has the social ambience and moral climate of Santa Barbara, but it is not a factual recon-struction of the city.

Millar . . . [remarked] that "the basic evil" of Santa Barbara "is the book's real subject." He probably meant that it was about what money does to people. Archer's cases come down to sex and money, and Millar observed that all crimes are ultimately sexual. F. Scott Fitzgerald told Harold Ober: "I have never been able to forgive the rich for being rich. . . .'' Neither could the grown-up charity boy.

Millar regularly reread *The Great Gatsby,* which he has described as ''the closest thing we have to a tragedy illustrating our secret history.'' There are no admirable wealthy people in Archer's world, and the ways they have acquired their money are frequently corrupt and corrupting. Money is a main subject of the Archer novels. (p. 32)

The Moving Target is what the book trade calls a ''page-turner''; and Millar has described it as ''a story clearly aspiring to be a movie.'' . . . Millar has said that his books have more story than the reader expects, and he has described his plotting as ''a moral and imaginative tontine.'' That is, ''I always start with an idea, and the idea usually contains in it the possibility of a strong reversal. . . . The reversal is actually an illumination of what has gone before.''

The writing in *The Moving Target* is a refinement of the hard-boiled style of [Millar's early novel] *Blue City* [1947] to a style appropriate to Archer's sensibilities. . . . Millar has defined style as structure in miniature. However, some critics have cited him for an overdependence on the simile, a rhetorical figure that calls attention to itself. (pp. 32, 34)

''In order to have a democratic society, you have to have a classless language.'' When this statement was queried by a friend who insisted that speech always stratifies the class of the speaker, Millar replied, ''What I would wish is that the various strata should be available to the speakers of the language.'' This issue identifies a problem in his technique. Whether the result of his Canadian exile or the result of his theories about the democracy of literature, Millar did not possess a sharp ear for American speech. Yet he was convinced that his printed prose retained the force of the spoken language. (p. 38)

Lew Archer would be the narrator in seventeen subsequent novels. . . . There are obvious benefits and liabilities for a writer in maintaining a series character, and there is ample precedent in the mystery field from Poe through Doyle to Christie, Gardner, and Stout. (Archer—unlike many series detectives—is not an eccentric.) Readers like the reappearance of a familiar figure; and audience was a crucial consideration for Millar. He never aspired to be a mandarin author—despite his academic background. From the inception of his career he sought to write popular fiction: not for commercial reasons, but because his boyhood reading—reinforced by Frank Norris's ''The Responsibilities of the Novelist''—persuaded him to seek a general readership.

The chief disadvantage of using a series character is that it takes pressure off the author. Instead of inventing new protagonists, he puts the same one through the same paces; and the reader's sense of familiarity may yield to boredom. This problem is largely obviated in the case of Lew Archer because he is the observing participant—not the hero. Millar does very little to fill in Archer's personal history in the subsequent novels. It is almost as though Archer has no life between cases. (pp. 38-9)

The Moving Target was followed by three Archer novels in three years—*The Drowning Pool, The Way Some People Die,* and *The Ivory Grin.* With *The Drowning Pool* Millar altered his pseudonym to John Ross Macdonald after John D. MacDonald protested. (p. 41)

The Drowning Pool (1950) . . . introduces the themes of concealed parenthood and distressed children. Since the daughter

does not learn the truth of her paternity until the end of the novel, it avoids the child's quest for identity—which would become the dominant theme of Millar's fiction with *The Galton Case* in 1959. (pp. 41, 43)

In *The Way Some People Die* (1951) Archer encounters his first homicidal female as a missing-daughter case involves him in the drug racket. This novel marks the emergence of what some critics have discerned as Millar's misogyny. Most of his killers are women; they kill not for love, but for security. He has explained that women are frequently victims of society, and victims tend to victimize. The locale is Pacific Point, south of Los Angeles; Pacific Point resembles Santa Barbara in terms of social stratification, but is ''a little more touched by the Orange County feeling.'' Millar tried to alternate Santa Teresa and Pacific Point settings to avoid getting stale. (p. 43)

The Drowning Pool and *The Way Some People Die* reveal a sentimental streak in Archer that would be suppressed for a time. In *The Drowning Pool* he gives $10,000 to a hooker, along with the lie that it was left to her by a criminal who loved her. And in *The Way Some People Die* Archer allows the murderess to keep $30,000, for which she killed three men, to use for her legal fees.

The cast of characters in *The Ivory Grin* (1952) includes a syphilitic gangster, a corrupt beauty, and a deranged, puritanical doctor. Millar, who regarded it as his best novel so far, explained to an editor . . . :

> In my opinion, the distinctive qualities of *The Ivory Grin,* and the valuable elements in the convention from which it derives, are vividness and honesty of characterization, the close technical interaction of ''narrative'' or ''drama,'' and plot. . . . The physical violence which has become the hallmark of the ''hardboiled school'' has tended to kill it off with literate readers, and *Grin* was written in rather explicit reaction to this excess, the idea being to increase the psychological, social, moral range of the form while retaining the virtues noted above.
>
> (p. 44)

[Millar's] novels were carefully planned; and he spent almost as much time on his notes for novels as on writing them, tracing the ''relationships between people and events'' that provide the plot lines. . . . It has frequently been claimed that mystery fiction is plotted backward—that the writer devises the ending first and then works toward it. This generalization—which applies to some straight fiction as well as mysteries—has many exceptions, and its application to Millar is doubtful. Although his books end with one or more reversals, it is by no means evident that his narratives are constructed for the sake of a surprise climax. His plots are not Procrustean; the reader has the sense that the plots find their meanings in the process of composition. There is a strong likelihood that Millar began writing his novels with several possible conclusions in mind, discarding alternatives as he progressed. His mind was fertile with plots, and by 1953 he had accumulated some twenty plot notebooks. (pp. 46-7)

Howard Cross, the narrator of *Meet Me at the Morgue* [1953; a novel not included in the Archer series], is a probation officer who becomes involved in a case when one of his clients is suspected of having kidnapped a child. There is no compelling reason in the plot for dropping Archer; perhaps Millar wanted to demonstrate that he wasn't dependent on a series private eye. The substitution of Cross permitted the introduction of a love interest for the narrator. At the end he marries the child's mother, who has been widowed during the novel. (p. 50)

With *Meet Me at the Morgue*, Millar's plotting tentatively began to seek more depth. A disgraced father trying to establish contact with the grown son he had abducted in childhood is introduced as a parallel to the kidnapping case.

Millar returned to Archer in *Find a Victim* (1954), a novel in which the killer is a deranged woman trying to preserve her marriage. Millar's victims are often self-victims, a thesis enforced by the epigraph from Stephen Crane: "A man feared that he might find an assassin; / Another that he might find a victim. / One was more wise than the other." Although his plots are catalyzed by sex, the sexual encounters occur off the page—usually in the past. Archer is himself remarkably chaste for a fifties private eye. He does not bed a woman until *The Galton Case* (1959), and his couplings are not graphic. In the entire Archer series he sleeps with four women. (p. 51)

With *The Barbarous Coast* (1956) Millar settled on the pseudonym Ross Macdonald. Arguably his best novel to date, it explored the ramifications of power and corruption at a California beach club. In this novel he touched on his Canadian roots for the first time by introducing a Toronto reporter seeking his wife, but Millar was not yet ready to reopen that wound. Like several of his female victims/victimizers, the runaway is from a family that has lost its money. . . . Another woman, the neurotic daughter of a movie mogul, is reacting against the death of her father and her husband's infidelities. Lost security—especially when combined with the loss of a father—is a powerful trauma in Archer's world. What critics would label Archer's almost Christ-like goodness emerges in this novel. . . . The plot of *The Barbarous Coast* involves assumed identity, which became a favorite Millar reversal device. (p. 52)

Millar has described [another Archer book, *The Doomsters* (1958)] as "a work of tolerance trying to reach beyond tragedy." It probes the past crimes that cause present crimes in a moneyed family. Again, the killer is a victimized woman. Carl Hallman, an escapee from the state mental hospital, seeks Archer's help. Hallman carries a heavy load of guilt. He holds himself responsible for the death of his father, Senator Hallman, because he argued with the old man, who had a heart condition; he also blames himself for his mother's suicide. His wife, Mildred—one of Millar's women from a declassed family—had pressured him into marriage because he represented security and restitution. "Money. That was what set him off from everyone—the thing that made him so handsome to me, so—shining." . . . Mildred, the least likely suspect, killed Carl's mother after a forced abortion and then committed three more murders—including that of the Senator—to protect her stake in the Hallman fortune.

The Doomsters, Millar wrote, "marked a fairly clean break with the Chandler tradition, which it had taken me some years to digest, and freed me to make my own approach to the crimes and sorrows of life." Chandler wrote connected scenes; but Millar treated "plot as a vehicle of meaning." Marlowe's voice is stylized and "limited by his role as the hard-boiled hero." Archer has a wider range of expression because he is less encumbered by the requirements of his character and because a certain distance developed between Millar and Archer. Millar observed in a 1976 interview: "It took him [Archer] a while to develop into anything substantial. The real change in him, I think, occurred in *The Doomsters;* he became a man who was not so much trying to find the criminal as understand him. He became more of a representative of man rather than just a detective who finds things out." The clearest way in which *The Doomsters* departs from Millar's previous novels is that Archer is personally involved in the events and might have prevented three of the murders. . . . Yet it is out of character for Archer to provide autobiography because his own life is suppressed. Millar told an English interviewer: "He lives through other people. He's the shadow of the novelist." Thereafter Archer resumed his role as outsider. (pp. 55-6)

Matthew J. Bruccoli, in his Ross Macdonald, *Harcourt Brace Jovanovich, 1984, 147 p.*

André Pieyre de Mandiargues

1909-

French novelist, poet, short story writer, critic, essayist, travel writer, dramatist, translator, and biographer.

Among France's most respected contemporary prose stylists, Mandiargues is an author of allegorical fantasy whose works often reflect the influence of surrealism. Beneath the strange, lyrical surface of his prose lies a mixture of the appealing and the terrifying, the erotic and the grotesque. In his mystical narratives, Mandiargues unites metaphor with ornate detail to evoke a bizarre, dreamlike world in which characters seek the correlations between flesh and spirit, sexuality and death. Thomas Bishop noted that Mandiargues's universe ''is marked by a fusion of the extraordinary and the erotic; it is a sensual sphere placed beyond the realm of reason, halfway between wakefulness and dream.''

Mandiargues's earliest writings anticipate his later concern with such subjects as birth and death, violence, and sexuality. *Dans les anneés sordides* (1943), his first collection of prose poems and fables, also reflects his interest in the visual arts in its depiction of caverns and landscapes inhabited by anthropomorphic insects similar to those in the paintings of Hieronymus Bosch. Mandiargues's works after 1947 reflect the influence of the French surrealists, particularly André Breton and Guillaume Apollinaire, with whom he associated following World War II. Mark J. Temmer stated that these early works ''tend to be somewhat unsubstantial and uncohesive like many texts written under the sign of Surrealism, [while] his later stories are grounded in a lyrical awareness of the senses, tempered by a delicate rigor and irony, and shaped by an allegorical and fabulistic conception of life.'' Many of Mandiargues's later works reflect the influence of Carl Jung in their concern with the individual's need to attain psychic and spiritual wholeness. In the novel *Murbre* (1953), for example, a man comes to recognize both the male and female sides of his nature and strives to unite the two to become a more complete individual.

Supernatural and mystical elements, including the Tarot, alchemy, astrology, and, in particular, sacrificial and initiatory rites, recur in Mandiargues's later novels. In *Le lis de mer* (1956; *The Girl beneath the Lion*), a virginal noblewoman instructs her lover in her sexual initiation. In *La motocyclette* (1963; *The Motorcycle*), an allegorical novel which recalls the myth of the Black Knight and blends classical and mechanical imagery, a young woman meets her death while speeding on her steed-like motorcycle toward an adulterous meeting with a mythic lover. *La marge* (1967; *The Margin*), Mandiargues's first work to achieve significant international attention, concerns the fate of a man on a business trip who receives a telegram alluding to his wife's suicide. Refusing to acknowledge the telegram and its contents, he lives temporarily in the seedy districts of Barcelona. Some critics suggested that the novel, for which Mandiargues received the Prix Goncourt, functions both as a work of inner perception and as an examination of Spain under the rule of Generalissimo Francisco Franco.

Mandiargues is also praised for his work as an art critic, translator, and essayist. His essays and lectures collected in *Le*

belvédère (1954) and *Le cadran lunaire* (1958) feature, in addition to several travelogues, studies of such European artists as Max Ernst and Paul Klee. *Arcimboldo le merveilleux* (1977; *Arcimboldo the Marvelous*) is a critical biography of Giusseppe Arcimboldo, a sixteenth-century artist renowned for his bizarre portraits of fish, fruit, and birds. Mandiargues has also written several plays, including *L'école des pères, comédie en cinq actes* (1957), *Isabella Morra: pièce en deux actes* (1973), and *La nuit seculaire* (1979).

(See also *Contemporary Authors,* Vol. 103.)

VERNON HALL, JR.

Habituated as we are to the clinical details of the modern sex novel, we may tend to forget that, like everything else in our own emotive life, sex may be made into poetry. André Pieyre de Mandiargues has reminded us of this in a charming novel [*The Girl Beneath the Lion*]. . . .

His plot, and it has no more complications than that of a short story, is as follows: An eighteen-year-old Italian countess by the name of Vanina goes to Sardinia for a vacation. . . . All is perfume, sun, salt water, sea lilies, and bronzed young people. The asexual god of the Christians has no place here. The great Pan, himself, is alone worthy of worship.

Seeing a beautiful young man who reminds her of a painting by Giorgione, Vanina promises herself to him if he will follow certain instructions. First, he must come to her window at night and gaze upon her virginal and candlelit nudity without uttering a word or attempting to enter her room. Second, the following night he must meet her on the beach, tie her hands behind her back, and ravish her as if she were a sacrificial lamb upon the altar. He agrees and follows her elaborate rites in every detail.

The next morning Vanina leaves the world of love for the workaday life of the mainland. But she is no longer the searching semi-adolescent who arrived in Sardinia. She is a woman. . . .

[In *The Girl Beneath the Lion*], André Pieyre de Mandiargues has successfully created and sustained a poetic mood. Slight as is his plot, his ability to evoke the sights, sounds and tastes of Sardinia as well as the emotions of his heroine makes this little book a lovely and memorable thing.

> *Vernon Hall, Jr., "Novel of Sensuous Beauty," in* New York Herald Tribune Book Review, *November 23, 1958, p. 4.*

MARK J. TEMMER

A former disciple of Breton, Mandiargues circumvents the traditional domains of Surrealism in order to enter the confines of an innocent universe that is revealed by pure sensation. . . .

[Mandiargues has stated]: "It is one of my favorite ideas that a book, essay, poem, or narration is, all in all, a rêverie, a meditation, more or less directed, prolonged (at times during an entire life), sustained by a verbal rhythm." . . . Indeed, one notes throughout his works prose cadences worthy of Bossuet or Bourdaloue, rhythmic forms into which are poured, like gold and silver, the verbal counterparts of his sensations. Lastly, intellect imposes a syntactical order in harmony with the inner logic of the dream, or, as in his later stories, with the general thread of the narrative. Just as sensations follow one another with inexorable necessity—does one ever cease to feel?—Mandiargues' prose consists of uninterrupted sequences of phantasmagoric visions whose plenitude is reminiscent of Descartes' continued creation. Odor, touch, and sight are the vortices of this extravagant and frivolous universe that is curiously devoid of sound and time. It is a world that knows no calm, has no fixed shape, but which is composed of mirages that dissolve as does sugar on the tongue. (p. 99)

[A representative example of Mandiargues' early writing] evokes a sumptuous vision of love that suggests influences ranging from E.T.A. Hoffmann to the Flaubert of *Salammbô*, or Huysmans and André Breton: "That night was for Camille de Hur a magic estrangement, for Damien, a crucible with a russet sheen in which melted like coarse wax all the forms that had haunted his memory only to reappear in keener moulds and shapes." . . . The rhythm of these periods, classical in its measure, contrasts with the romantic deployment of luminous motives among which are interwoven designs of fabulous creatures that seem to have escaped from the *Apocalypse* illustrated by Picasso, Buffet, and Dali. (p. 100)

Unlike traditional characters with a specific biography, the inhabitants of Mandiargues' kingdom appear and vanish in the form of states of consciousness against the fantastic backdrop

continually recreated by the author. Moved like flotsam by invisible currents, these beings suffer the pressures of a universe that abhors a void, and disintegrate under its cosmic weight. Then their minds break, and their psychic energies fuse with the sensation or element that caused the fatal crack. For example, an archeologist, gazing at the Adriatic, suddenly finds himself within its glaucous mass, confronted by Venus sculptured in green marble; or a young woman, enraptured by the fire of a perfect diamond, discovers herself prisoner within the crystal. Thus, personal identity always threatened by sensory explorations and explosions, self-knowledge becomes at best a cruel adventure. . . . [By] the very nature of his viewpoint, Mandiargues dispenses with first and final causes. This is not surprising, for it is his imagination that shapes the destinies of his characters. Submitting themselves fatalistically to playing either the rôle of executioners or sacrificial lambs, they contemplate their victims or their tormentors with a monstrous detachment and accuse or confess with theatrical nonchalance. . . . (p. 101)

No less passive in their demonstration of love than in suffering, Mandiargues' characters disregard all tenderness in their reciprocal relationships. These are, at best, a pretext for poetry . . . and, at worst, an alignment of two bodies in space where the opposite number resembles a quantity infinitely approaching zero. Such indifference points to Sade and his apostles whose homilies preach a union of sex and intellect that excludes moral and esthetic sensibilities. Indeed, Mandiargues assures us in an essay on Balinese dancers that one may allow oneself the greatest deviations or *égarements* of the body without losing one's lucidity . . . and reassures us, furthermore, that "Eros is probably the only guide capable of leading us wide-awake on the roads of the subconscious and of granting us a little of that absurd happiness which, at times, we have known in dreams." . . . (p. 102)

But Eros also leads to death, for—in principle at least—eroticism destroys both mind and flesh. One of Mandiargues' finest stories, **"Le nu parmi les cercueils,"** offers a splendid illustration of his seductive thesis. This curious parable exemplifies the drier, more ironically objective style of his later works. Its hero, Daniel Point, about to take a siesta in his Mexico City apartment, suddenly sees in the mirror above his divan a young lady standing in a hall filled with coffins arranged in four parallel lines. . . . Mariana Guajaco, for that is the name of the apparition, relates her story. A Mexican midinette, abandoned by her lover, a night watchman in a motel *de passage*, Mariana has become the captive of a mad undertaker who, nightly, forces her to perform a strip-tease with metaphysical implications, reducing her to a *thing* situated in an intermediary position between life and death, flesh and dust, instant and eternity. The allegory ends with an apostrophe from which wit and irony have been banished: "And you, sprawling amidst your cushions, who watch me tell my adventure, . . . are you sure that it will be different for you—that each and every one of your adventures or entire lives, dreamer, reader, author, is anything but an infinitesimal moment in the dream of an enormous drunkard sprawling on his clouds, or a nervous contradiction in the depth of the infinite matrix whence perhaps sprang forth the universe? Outside of the coffin-shop and beyond the room in which you rest is the great night. Do you hear the sirens of the ambulances, coming and going, in search of victims?" . . . (pp. 102-03)

Here fantasy leads to reality, wantonness to sobriety. The hero's realities shatter under the impact of the vision, and our tragedy begins when we know his dream to be true. Reminded that all is precarious, we then seek reassurance by dismissing, although *à contre-coeur*, Mandiargues' *carnaval fantastique* whose brilliant life is predicated on our willingness to believe. Like any superior writer, our author is his severest critic: "My mirages exist only insofar as one grants them reality, and dissolve most often into stumps and bushes when one tries to examine them closely.".... It would be erroneous to mistake this confession for a general flaw, for, while it is true that his earlier *Fantasiestücke* tend to be somewhat unsubstantial and uncohesive like many texts written under the sign of Surrealism, his later stories are grounded in a lyrical awareness of the senses, tempered by delicate rigor and irony, and shaped by an allegorical and fabulistic conception of life.

Further proof of the author's vitality and critical powers are his essays, which have been published in two volumes. The first one, *Le Belvédère* (1954) contains a series of studies on Ponge, Klee, Max Ernst and Germaine Richier, as well as some travel essays, notably on the monsters of Bomarzo, an ensemble of ferociously baroque statues in the Italian province of Viterbo. Mandiargues is a superb Baedecker. A witness with a *parti pris* for matters fantastic, his style is both light and precise, sustaining a *ton* that blends lascivious, tender, and humorous notes.... The second volume, *Le cadran lunaire* (1958) maintains his high standards of artistic and personal integrity. And there emerges from all these texts, as well as from his prose poems (*Dans les années sordides*, 1948; *Astyanax*, 1957) and volumes of poetry, a portrait of one of the most original literary figures of recent years, an aristocratic writer, free of prejudice, deeply committed to hierarchical principles in art and thought.... Artistically influenced by the Italian baroque tradition, Agrippa d'Aubigné, the Elizabethans, the German Romantics, Coleridge, Rimbaud, Lautréamont, and, of course, the first generation of the French Surrealists, André Pieyre de Mandiargues ranks, with Julien Gracq and Noël Devaulx, among those writers who continue the renaissance initiated by Surrealism and who exploit, each in his own manner, the riches of fantasy and allegory. (pp. 103-04)

> *Mark J. Temmer, "André Pieyre de Mandiargues," in* Yale French Studies, *No. 31, May, 1964, pp. 99-104.*

WILFRID SHEED

[*The Motorcycle* is] a tender story of a young girl's love for a motorbike. Rebecca Nul is a traffic-stopping nymph with clumps of hair on her back, bird-legs, and a modified crewcut. Her inventor, André Pieyre de Mandiargues, is a veteran male author in the mid-fifties, and Rebecca's viewpoints keep slipping into those of a veteran male author too, with a special, somewhat severe interest in the minutiae of mechanics and botany. However, M. de Mandiargues is not trying to create a real person, but a legend. He has taken one of the mythic figures of our time—the black knight on the motorcycle—and has created a special sensibility for it, a motorcycle-sensibility. Rebecca Nul is a classical figure, a boy-girl-animal, mounted on a flying iron horse, her soul fusing with the pistons.

The whole book is taken up with one long journey, which sends Rebecca zooming and bounding from her husband in Alsace to her lover in Germany.... The lover is himself a mythic character, a sort of human motorcycle, and Rebecca has extended reveries about him en route. It seems that they have had a sequence of pagan ritual encounters, in the snow, in the woods, etc., and these run counterpoint in her mind to her affair with the *real* motorcycle.

This blend of classical and mechanical mythology produces some strange and interesting effects in the course of this lengthy prose-poem. For the unmechanical reader, these tend to get buried in sprockets and spark-plugs and gear changes.... But the central image remains powerful: the black-leather suit, as cryptic as black armor, and the rider herself, half master and half slave of her machine.

The novel teems with more symbols than you can shake a wrench at. Its rich, metallic language is well suited to the more erotic aspects of machinery.

> *Wilfrid Sheed, "Love a la Mode," in* The New York Times Book Review, *May 16, 1965, p. 26.*

THE TIMES LITERARY SUPPLEMENT

In this immaculate novel [*La Marge*] André Pieyre de Mandiargues has again used his surrealist shotgun to marry off the poetic to the perverse; the flagellation is done with flowers. But as well as the thoughtful and inventive eroticism which one would expect, *La Marge* also contains a very clever device for lending to an everyday reality the emotional intensity of a dream. The hero, Sigismond Pons, is in Barcelona when he receives a letter containing the news of a domestic tragedy, but he refuses to capitulate there and then to such an abrupt fatality.... For the next three days he is able to exist in the "margin" of the title, doomed but not destroyed, doing little else but walk the narrow streets of the *barrio chino* amidst the prostitutes.

Sigismond's one-man saturnalia is a restrained but intense experience, because it is one he has often dreamed of when lying in bed with his wife.... [His movements] are controlled mysteriously from within, where the archetypes are hard at it in the battle for his soul.

But the implications of this struggle are more than merely private, because Sigismond is able to extend the radii of his dark sun to shine on the Catalonian people as a whole. The "bubble" which protects him from a direct contact with the world comes to be equated with the present regime in Spain, and his own father with the *caudillo*, Franco. When the bubble is finally burst its personal and political significances diverge violently, since the suicide of Sigismond must also be read as a sign of hope for an oppressed people. It is hard to be sure whether *La Marge* sets out to work from Sigismond to Spain or from Spain to Sigismond, but in either case the book, for all the stylization of its vision and its syntax, is far from being remote or heartless.

> *"Spanish Tragedy," in* The Times Literary Supplement, *No. 3407, June 15, 1967, p. 543.*

THOMAS LASK

[Both J. M. G. Le Clezio's *Terra Amata* and Pieyre de Mandiargues' *The Margin*] are written from the point of view of the hero, not only from his point of view but also from a point within his skull. The outside world beats on the mind of the observer and the contact between event and brain brings on those reflections and those states of feeling that are the novel. The speakers are in a constant condition of rumination, of constant awareness, and they respond to every shift in the psychological and environmental weather as a vane to the wind.

The novels are intense but also hothouse, the parts glinting by silvered or artificial light; even the outdoors are interiors. The effects are often quite brilliant, but just as often quite literary. This is a lot less true of Andre Pieyre de Mandiargues than of Mr. Le Clezio. It is only when you begin to ask what makes the people think the way they do that the novels begin to look and sound less than convincing. Both books require that you go along with them rather than push against them. This attitude works well with *The Margin*. . . .

The Margin, winner of France's Prix Goncourt, is a novel split into two simultaneous parts: they exist side by side. One part is a travelogue through Barcelona. . . . With an expert hand the author has summoned up both the physical characteristics of [its] places and their pervading mood: poor, cheap, coarse, grotesque at times, but also vital, basic, living. Mr. Mandiargues is expert in describing the foods and special sauces . . . , the beverages and the services that go with them.

We also meet a long train of street walkers including the one our hero, Sigismond Pons, a Frenchman on a business trip to Spain, encounters. For a change we encounter a lady of the night who is seen as she is. She is sympathetically drawn, but with more objectivity than sympathy. . . .

The reason a respected businessman is indulging himself in this way—not the usual reason—makes up the second part of the book. Traveling as a wine merchant, Pons receives a letter from a servant. He reads only a few lines, enough to convince him that his wife has taken her life. This knowledge puts him into a stupor and he wanders through the city sampling the low life and contrasting mentally the promises and the fictions of Franco's regime with the actualities before him.

It is hard to believe that Pons would act as he does; his mind is too powerful, his awareness too socially anchored. There is a strength of character in the man that doesn't fit in with this aimless wandering. The whole affair is too idyllic for a man overcome with grief. But if you can forgive the reasons for his actions, you will find the trip with him one not easy to forget.

> Thomas Lask, "Man and His Woes," in The New York Times, *April 3, 1969, p. 41.*

THOMAS BISHOP

When *The Motorcycle* was published in France in 1963, André Pieyre de Mandiargues, after more than twenty books, gained a sizable reading public for the first time. *The Margin* . . . enlarged his French audience and finally earned Mandiargues, at the age of fifty-eight, the acclaim he so richly deserves. Not only has he long been one of France's finest modern prose stylists; he is also one of those rare writers capable of creating a unique fictional universe, into which the reader is lured, then trapped and enthralled by a strange yet compulsively appealing hot-house atmosphere.

The world of André Pieyre de Mandiargues is marked by a fusion of the extraordinary and the erotic; it is a sensual sphere placed beyond the realm of reason, halfway between wakefulness and dream. Although at least tangentially in the lineage of surrealism, his baroque distortions of reality are constantly held in check, as it were, by his classic mode of expression, direct and devoid of romanticism. In his predilection for the fantastic, Mandiargues delves neither into science-fiction nor even quite into the supernatural, but rather into the nebulous inner world of the imagination. His eroticism is coolly evoc-

ative and intimately linked to the characters' interior landscapes; it is never gratuitous nor excessively descriptive.

Like most of Mandiargues's works, *The Margin* demands of the reader a certain willingness to follow the author's initial premise—a tacit agreement not to say, "People wouldn't do that." Because some do, or at least one might. Sigismond Pons, a fortyish Frenchman, leaves his young wife and their son for a few days to go to Barcelona on a business trip as deputy for his cousin. . . . After checking in at a hotel, Sigismond goes to the Post Office hoping to find a letter waiting in General Delivery from his wife, Sergine. . . . [After reading a passage that reveals his wife's suicide, he decides] not to read on, not to know the beginning and end of this dreadful message—at least, not yet—as if the notion of his wife's death were too overwhelming to be confronted directly. And so, while the fateful letter waits ominously for him in his hotel room, Sigismond Pons sets off on a two-and-a-half-day odyssey through the most notorious section of Barcelona.

This "margin" of life that he has granted himself, as if he had not yet received the letter, takes the form of a hallucinatory sixty hours spent among prostitutes, perverts, and pimps, dwarfs and sailors—a symbolic descent into hell, whose circles consist of Barcelona's narrow backstreets. What this modern-day Dante . . . seems to be seeking without knowing it is some *raison d'être*, some inner strength on which to draw now that he is going to be left alone. But as the mental images of Sergine multiply and grow more obsessive the reader becomes aware of Sigismond's love for and reliance on this apparently captivating woman. Moreover, his wanderings throughout the grotesque labyrinth of the Catalonian city lead to no fruitful answers. Even several touching encounters with an attractive and very young prostitute leave him unfulfilled; throughout he remains a spectator and not a participant.

Thus, when finally the insistent presence of the letter makes it impossible for him *not* to read it, Sigismond finds out that the truth he deciphers is even more tragic than he had assumed. Overwhelmed by his own spiritual emptiness, he realizes that he has lived his life "in the margin" (thereby giving the work's title a double significance).

This beautiful novel contains more riches than can be analyzed here: the ferocious satire of Franco; the almost compulsive descriptions of objects, streets, faces, and meals, which combine to create a delirious sur-reality: the vivid portrayal of medieval religious paintings in all their sadistic violence; the subtle, mysterious symbolism on almost every page. The narrative, related strictly through Sigismond's subjectivity . . . , helps us fathom the thrusts and gropings of a man's mind.

In *The Girl Beneath the Lion,* Mandiargues reached a denser consistency of poetry; in *The Margin,* a sumptuous meditation on love and death, he displays greater complexity and maturity, which fashion a richer fabric of fiction. (pp. 27, 30)

> Thomas Bishop, in a review of "The Margin," in Saturday Review, *Vol. LII, No. 22, May 31, 1969, pp. 27, 30.*

DAVID J. BOND

It is presumptuous of any critic to attempt to "situate" a living writer who is at the height of his powers and still producing works of art. In this case, it is doubly presumptuous, for Mandiargues eschews categories and "schools," and has the kind of genius which it is very difficult to limit to a recognizable mold. (p. 95)

The critic's task in describing Mandiargues's place in French literature is made more difficult by the breadth of this writer's interests, his undoubted erudition, his fascination with all that is curious, beautiful, attractive, marvelous, or that, in some way, holds his attention. He has a particularly keen interest in modern art and literature, and he attempts to keep abreast of all that is valid in contemporary art, so his interests are constantly developing and expanding. At the same time, he is aware of the contribution that writers and artists of the past have made to modern art, and he shows a particular interest in the baroque, the Elizabethans, and in any work of the past that displays fantasy and imagination. His artistic and literary criticism extends from Bernini to Max Ernst, from Zurburan to Tapies, from Sade to *Le Con d'Irène;* his boundless curiosity for the unusual spectacle embraces the Mayan ruins of Palenque and the Paris Métro, the monstrous statues at Bomarzo and the dancers of Bali. His erudition touches on alchemy, mythology, astrology, archaeology, and literature in all its ramifications and obscure byways. For his wide interests (especially in the obscure and the occult), for his appreciation of modern art, and for his own production of creative works one can compare him only to the poet-critic Baudelaire, whom he calls "our perpetual hero" in *Troisième Belvédère.*

But Mandiargues is also a man of his times and has necessarily been influenced by them. Since we are concerned here with his fiction, it is as well to begin by examining how it fits into the main trends in modern fiction. Perhaps the most influential movement in this field in France since the Second World War has been the *nouveau roman.* Mandiargues, aware as always of the directions being taken by literature, has shown a keen interest in this type of novel and its practitioners. . . . [Michel] Butor's novel *La Modification* is one of his favorites, for he calls it "a book that I like immensely" and adds: "But for it, perhaps I would not have written *La Motocyclette.*"

This comment on *La Modification* is not surprising, for both it and *La Motocyclette* use the framework of a journey to convey one person's experience of time, memories, and external reality. They put us inside an individual's consciousness and we move freely with that individual's thoughts between past, present, and future, liberated for the duration of the novel from "real time." *La Marge* too uses a rather similar technique, and all three novels present a wealth of objects and detailed descriptions of things observed in the course of a journey. We are taken on a guided tour of Barcelona, swept along the highway to Heidelberg, just as in *La Modification* we are taken by train to Rome and shown the countryside passing by, every railway station, and every physical detail of the compartment where the narrator sits. We notice and organize these things into meaningful patterns through the consciousness of the characters who experience them. Each detail, each incident is liable to provoke memories, anticipations, and reveries which we share with the characters.

This does not mean, of course, that *La Motocyclette* and *La Marge* are *nouveaux romans,* simply that Mandiargues has adapted some techniques of this genre to his own use. Although we experience time as the characters do, for example, it is made clear when we are experiencing memories or anticipation of the future. Another important difference is that the world of Robbe-Grillet, Butor, and the other writers of the *nouveau roman* remains relentlessly opaque; it assumes only the meaning that the characters impose on it. There is no pre-existing

pattern in the world as they depict it. Mandiargues's world, on the other hand, is closer to Baudelaire's: it speaks to those who listen, it provides clues to the course of future events, and addresses signs to those who know how to recognize them. Nowhere in the *nouveau roman* does one have the feeling that the screen of appearances is about to be rent asunder and that the extraordinary, the impossible, and the unreal are about to spill onto the scene. Never does one feel that sense of anticipation, of things about to happen that one senses in such tales as **"L'Homme du parc Monceau"** or **"Le passage Pommeraye."** The world of the *nouveau roman* is organized according to a human consciousness, and has no power of its own. (pp. 95-7)

The style of Mandiargues's novels is also very different from that of the *nouveau roman,* which avoids metaphor and concentrates on concrete detail. Although he picks out the details of the material world, he expresses them in a highly poetic and sometimes baroque style. Only Montherlant among modern writers shows the same sense of style, and he also shares Mandiargues's taste for the Mediterranean world. (p. 97)

Mandiargues's use of fantasy links him to such modern writers as André Dhôtel, Marcel Bélau, and Boris Vian, although there are obvious differences of style. His depiction of a dreamlike reality in which death and desire combine, his love of German romanticism, and his fascination with magic worlds, castles, and enchanted forests all remind the reader of Julien Gracq. The combination of fantasy and the erotic suggests comparisons to Michel Bernard, while the cruel sado-erotic vein in many of his stories puts him in a stream of underground erotic literature which is well represented in France, and passes from Sade through Guillaume Apollinaire, Louis Aragon, Georges Bataille, and Pauline Réage.

Although the comparison may seem fanciful, there is also some similarity between Mandiargues's view of life and that of another important group of modern French writers: the "absurdist" philosophers. Mandiargues too sees man as separated from the world in which he lives. Rebecca, Vanina, Ferréol, and several other characters long to achieve contact with nature precisely because they are different from the rest of the created world, and they are aware of that difference. They also realize that the world is potentially hostile. Indeed, some of them are destroyed by the powers hidden in creation, and their destruction makes one think of Camus's remark: "The primitive hostility of the world throughout the millennia rises up towards us." The difference, however, lies in the fact that for Camus the world is nearly always hostile, and, at best, indifferent to man. In Mandiargues's fiction, it is only hostile when men interfere with or offend the "panic" forces. Nor are his characters totally alienated in the world. Unlike the "absurdist" writers, Mandiargues believes that contact with the world is possible, that there are forces both inside us and within the world which may be united. This goes far beyond Camus's lyrical appreciation of natural beauty, for Camus believes that this beauty is totally impervious to human feelings and that nature has an existence radically different from man's.

Where Mandiargues differs most strikingly from the "absurdists," and from many other modern writers, is in his attitude to death. For Camus, Malraux, and Sartre, death is the final proof of the absurdity of existence. It dominates their novels and fills their characters with anguish. Many other writers share their attitude to death: Louis-Ferdinand Céline, Samuel Beckett, Eugène Ionesco, and Jacques Chessex to mention only a few. For Mandiargues, death is as natural a part of existence as the life forces themselves. Indeed, he sees death as one of the marvels of life, an experience to be savored as much as anything else that life offers.

Mandiargues's ability to see the marvelous everywhere, his belief that the world has hidden depths that may reveal themselves at any moment, his search for experiences that deny logic and everyday rationalistic ideals all link him firmly to surrealism. It is the surrealists whom he praises most consistently and warmly in his essays. . . . (pp. 97-8)

The bond of feeling between Mandiargues and the surrealists is due in some measure to a shared taste for certain writers and artists. Baudelaire, whom Mandiargues frequently praises, Jarry, Rimbaud, Mallarmé and Lautréamont, whom he calls in *Le Cadran lunaire* the "four great poets who appeared in France after Baudelaire," and the Marquis de Sade, whom he claims in *Le Désordre de la mémoire* to "love and admire," are all seen by the surrealists as predecessors who anticipated their own views. . . . The Gothic novel, which exercised a considerable influence over the surrealists, is another shared taste and Mandiargues speaks warmly of Maturin, Horace Walpole, Lewis, Anne Radcliffe, and Beckford in *Le Troisième Belvédère*. They also have in common their love of romanticism. (p. 98)

In their artistic theory and practice, and in their general attitudes, Mandiargues and the surrealists are often indistinguishable. They both praise and use fantasy in their art, seeing it as a means of liberating man's imagination from the shackles of cold logic. In Mandiargues's fiction, unsuspected possibilities open before the reader's eyes, fantasy liberates the mind from logical thought, and the imagination is set free. . . . Mandiargues attacks the stable, fixed nature of the world by changing the conditions under which it normally operates. He makes characters change shape and size, transports them to other domains, alters the flow of time, and makes dream project into reality. (p. 99)

For the surrealists, another way of liberating the imagination was by use of the marvelous, and they attempted, in their writing and their paintings, to show it hidden in the world around us. As [C.W.E. Bigsby] puts it, they believed that: "The true purpose of art and indeed of life itself was to expand our definition of reality until it included the marvelous." Mandiargues more than once expresses similar ideas, pointing out that the unexpected may be found in the tiny details of life, the objects that surround us, the events that we take for granted. In his fiction, Vanina finds the marvelous in a flower, Rebecca discovers it in a motorcycle, Pascal Bénin in a stone.

The marvelous and the hidden face of the world were often revealed to the surrealists by what they called "objective chance." They believed that chance events could suddenly plunge them into the world of the surreal, as when Breton, quite by chance, met Nadja, or when he discovered, in a Paris flea-market, an object which seemed to speak to him in some mysterious way. . . . In his fiction, it is this "objective chance" that leads Pascal Bénin to pick up the stone that causes his death, that impels the narrator of "**Le passage Pommeraye**" to enter the sidestreet, and that brings together Ferréol Buq and the old man who guides him to the death ceremony. Often, as in the case of Breton and Nadja, it is a woman who is sent by fate. She is the instrument of the marvelous for Mandiargues, since she reveals the essence of life and death (the dying woman in *Marbre*), lures the hero to undertake mysterious journeys ("**Le passage Pommeraye**" from *Le Musée noir*

and "**L'Opéra des falaises**" from *Soleil des loups*), acts as the vehicle of dreams and revelations (the prostitutes in "**La Grotte**" from *Porte dévergondée* and "**L'Enfantillage**" from *Feu de braise*), and is the receptacle of the life forces (Vanina, Rebecca, and Sarah). Mandiargues, when he depicts woman as the vehicle of the marvelous and says in *Le Désordre de la mémoire* that she is, for him, "together with poetry, my most powerful mobilizer of emotion," is in a surrealist tradition. The surrealists too saw woman as the projection of marvel and beauty into life. (pp. 99-100)

Woman is often seen by the surrealists as an instrument of the marvelous because she inspires love. The same is true of Mandiargues, whose words in *Le Désordre de la mémoire* that love is "the great reason for living" echo Breton's: "There is no solution except love." Although love plays a lesser role in Mandiargues's work than eroticism, there is no doubt that, in his life, it has played a critical part. His love for Bona, described in *Bona l'amour et la peinture,* is depicted as a *coup de foudre*, a poetic and idealized love that changed his life as does *l'amour fou* in surrealist mythology. This love is the inspiration of much of his poetry, as it is of Breton's, Eluard's and Aragon's.

In addition to love of this kind, both Mandiargues and the surrealists recognize the importance of desire. . . . The sexual variety is evident in the vein of sado-eroticism in nearly all his fiction which culminates in the scenes of sexual excess in *L'Anglais décrit dans le château fermé*. The desire to escape the limits of self, either in erotic abandon or in "panic" experience has also been described in some detail. It is sufficient at this point to remind the reader of the furious desire for the world experienced by many of his characters, the longing to merge with nature that culminates in "panic" communion.

The same will to shock lies behind much of the uncontrolled eroticism of the surrealists and of Mandiargues's writings. They attempt to scandalize, to flout bourgeois morals, and to shake people out of rigidly set attitudes. The anti-conformism that surrealism inherited from Dada is precisely one of the things that endears both movements to Mandiargues, and he has said in *Le Désordre de la mémoire* that, "like any surrealist worthy of that name, I am naturally disrespectful." He and the surrealists believe that the tension created by unconventional attitudes, and especially by sexual excess, adds excitement and power to a work of art. (pp. 100-01)

Mandiargues insists on accurate detail in his description of the world around him, and, as he himself points out, this is also true of the surrealists. This similarity of technique is due to a shared vision of the objects of reality. Surrealism takes objects, observed in all their detail, and removes them from their utilitarian context. When they are placed in a new context, in proximity with things not normally associated with them, new potential is released in them. Mandiargues recommends the same method, and he speaks, in a passage from *Le Belvédère* . . . , of the resonances set up when an object such as Bernini's statue of Louis XIV is placed in unusual surroundings. The statue that Férreol Buq finds on the deserted island, the ruins in the midst of the Mexican jungle described in *Deuxième Belvédère,* the insect scuttling across his desk at the beginning of *Marbre* are just a few examples of how Mandiargues, in his own work, shows us objects which interact in unusual ways with their surroundings.

He is also fascinated, like the surrealists, by objects found by chance which capture the finder's imagination and which meet some kind of unconscious need. The wooden spoon and the mask found by Breton and Giacometti in a Paris flea-market are the best known examples of this phenomenon. They served as a catalyst to free the artists' imagination, just as the insect, the paperweight, and the list of names inspired *Marbre.* (p. 101)

Mandiargues has also talked of the artist as a medium, and has, on occasions, practiced a kind of automatic writing. He believes too that it is necessary to be in a particular state of mind in order to create. His interest in dreams is at least as keen as that of the surrealists, and is based partly on the belief that they reveal the inner recesses of the self. Like Breton, Mandiargues would like dreams and reverie to affect reality, to change the course of events, and in such tales as **"Le Marronnier"** and **"Le Triangle ambigu"** (both from *Mascarets*) this is what happens. He also sees dreams as a means of enriching his writing and of making it appeal on a kind of subliminal level at which dream images and symbols operate.

The surrealist attempt to project dreams into life, to liberate the inner self, to reconcile what lies inside us with life outside all show a desire to bring together the forces within us and the ones that direct our waking life. This is also the goal of many of Mandiargues's characters, and it is achieved by Vanina, Rebecca, and others when they experience "panic" communion with the universe. Dream, reverie, the mysterious forces of life within and without us all mingle in Mandiargues's fiction to achieve that surreality which is the goal of surrealist art.

In addition to these similarities of aims, attitudes and techniques, there are, naturally enough, certain motifs and recurring situations in Mandiargues's work that may be considered typically surrealist. The surrealists are, for example, fascinated by castles (and this may possibly reflect the influence of the Gothic novel on their sensibility). . . . Mandiargues sets *L'Anglais décrit dans le château fermé* in an isolated castle, as well as the culminating scene of **"La Vision capitale."** Damien visits Camille de Hur in her castle, and Frederick II's Castel del Monte is the subject of **"L'Espion des Pouilles"** in *Le Cadran lunaire.* The delight that surrealists show in museums and collections of unusual objects finds its echo in the museum that Sigismond visits in *La Marge,* the one where Conrad Mur sees the wax statue, and the strange collection made by Father Athanase in *Marbre.* The markets that exercised such fascination for Breton, because of the possibility of finding an interesting object there, can also be found in Mandiargues's work, for example the market that Sigismond visits in Barcelona, and the one described in **"Les Marchés du Temple"** in *Le Cadran lunaire.* One story, **"Le passage Pommeraye,"** depicts a street that is very reminiscent of the passage de L'Opéra, the setting of Aragon's *Le Paysan de Paris.* Indeed, the idea of "passage" conveyed by both these stories is a common surrealist concept. The surrealist motif of a passage or link between this world and the one of surreality is reflected in the bridges, corridors, and streets of many of Mandiargues's stories.

We are obviously dealing here, not so much with an "influence" exercised by surrealism, as with a shared sensibility. Of all the trends in modern French literature, this is the one with which Mandiargues has the most affinity. Yet he did break with the group, was associated with it for only a few years, and was just peripherally involved in its activity. He *is* a surrealist in many ways, but not entirely so. He is too independent, too determined to be bound by no imperatives, too much an individual to belong completely in any one group. His genius cannot be limited to one set of theories and practices, however

much sympathy he has with them. . . . Paradoxically, Mandiargues is never more a surrealist than when he affirms the spirit of freedom and revolt, and takes his leave of surrealism.

One major point on which he parts company with them is their attitude toward the artist. Although he has used techniques similar to automatism, and although he sees the artist as a medium and a *voyant,* he does not have the surrealists' disregard for the artist's creativity. The logical consequence of belief in the passivity of the artist is the idea that little creative activity is involved in producing works of art. . . . Mandiargues's comment in ***Troisième Belvédère*** that the novelist is a dreamer "sustained by the gift or the acquisition of a style" shows that he believes the writer is not *just* a medium: he must also fashion his dreams and inspiration into something stylish. The artist's will has a part in the creation of works of art in his opinion. . . . The tight control that Mandiargues exercises over his medium, the careful, calm, and deliberate balance of his prose show that he does not simply let inspiration pour through him. His evocation of dream, passion, ecstasy, and the black demons of the self is cunningly and consciously done.

Another point on which Mandiargues takes issue with the surrealists is their hermeticism. They often seem, in his opinion, to scorn the public at large and to see any attempt to appeal to a wider group of readers as being sordidly commercial. . . . He himself thinks that more and more people have open and inquiring minds, and are interested in the avant-garde. It is the artist's duty to appeal to as many of these potential readers as possible.

One thing that makes Mandiargues's work more accessible than many surrealist writings is that much of it is fiction. Although some of the surrealists wrote novels, they generally affected great scorn for fiction. They saw the novel in particular as subservient to logic, to rational development of character and of plot. It pandered, they believed, to bourgeois tastes for rational categories. When they do turn their hands to novel writing, the result tends to be works with little concern for the logical development and plot of traditional novels. Mandiargues's fiction, although it often has a rather thin plot, nevertheless has one, and a recognizable story line is developed. (pp. 102-04)

Perhaps Mandiargues's relationship to the surrealists may best be seen as a sharing of certain attitudes that have always existed. Surrealism is a complex of beliefs and ways of looking at the world which are timeless, and which existed before the term "surrealism" was coined. . . . Mandiargues holds many of the same attitudes, and saw in the surrealists *frères d'élection* with whom he could sympathize. The movement was never viewed by him as a series of beliefs to which he must rigidly adhere. In fact, although he may share some of the surrealists' attitudes, there are certain others, just as old, which form an integral part of his work. These are his mythical beliefs.

The language of myth is an ancient one that still finds expression in Mandiargues's fiction. As Jung has pointed out, the symbols and language of myth are also those that the unconscious uses to express itself in dreams. (p. 105)

[Mandiargues] naturally uses the language of myth because his view of the forces at work in the world, and of man's relationship to them, is identical with that of ancient myth. Although his fiction appears, at first glance, to be only lighthearted fantasy, there is more to it than that. His fantasy is deliberately worked into certain recurring patterns, the strange events in his works are repeated, the ritualistic situations reappear, the same metamorphoses overtake his characters, time follows similar unusual paths because Mandiargues is expressing a particular view of life in all his fiction. He molds his fantasy to the same mythical patterns because these are the patterns that best express his view of human existence. Fantasy in Mandiargues's work is not the equivalent of frivolity; it is used to tell us something about the nature of life.

Myth conveys in symbolic language truths that are not comprehensible by logic alone, and Mandiargues tries to convey the same incomprehensible truths as myth. His heroes discover these inexplicable realities because they are willing, like the heroes of myth, to leave the security of everyday life and face trials and ordeals. There is a movement from a limited, inhibiting (though often comfortable) social setting towards a wider world of secrets that encompass the whole of humanity. This represents a rupture, not just with a particular social setting, but with a whole complex of inhibiting attitudes. As Campbell puts it, "the rupture is rather with the comparatively trivial attitude toward both the human spirit and the world that appears to satisfy the great majority."

Mandiargues's fiction cannot be defined entirely by its relationship to other contemporary artists, trends, and movements. Because of its striking similarity to the archetypal myth, it appeals to part of the human mind which is timeless and which still thinks in certain "primitive" patterns. By appealing to this part of us, Mandiargues invites us to reject the "trivial attitude" to which Campbell refers; he invites us to abandon the superficial view of life that looks no further than appearances and to travel, as the mythical hero does, to another realm of perception. Here we will discover truths that are best conveyed in mythical terms; we will see those forces that, according to myth, surround and inhabit us all the time; we will become aware of the beauty and mystery of life; we will know a world that opens and speaks to us. This is the "message" hidden in his work. The function of the recurring motifs and themes in Mandiargues's fiction is to provide us with a way of looking at the world with new eyes. (pp. 107-08)

David J. Bond, in his The Fiction of André Pieyre de Mandiargues, *Syracuse University Press, 1982, 133 p.*

Patrick McGinley

1937-

Irish novelist.

McGinley writes darkly comic novels about the Irish which typically evoke the rich landscape of Donegal county, where he was born and raised. His intimate knowledge of rural life lends authenticity to his work as he explores the philanderings, homespun philosophies, and petty jealousies that arise amid the insular communities of western Ireland. Critics commend McGinley for the accuracy of his dialogue, noting especially his ability to capture the ribald wit that characterizes pub conversations.

Murder is integral to the plots of McGinley's first three novels. In *Bogmail* (1979), a pub owner kills the man who seduced his daughter; *Goosefoot* (1982) concerns an innocent young heroine whose neighbor is stabbed to death; and in *Fox Prints* (1983), an unknown psychopath murders several women. While mystery and murder add intrigue to the plots, McGinley's primary concern is with his characters and the bizarre circumstances of their lives. *Bogmail,* for example, focuses more on the odd assortment of customers who congregate at the local pub than on the murder. These novels also demonstrate McGinley's linguistic virtuosity. In *Goosefoot,* he contrasts the erudite conversations of Dubliners with the earthy language of Irish rural residents, and in *Fox Prints,* the action, humor, and names of characters and places are all in some way related to the word ''fox.''

With *Foggage* (1983), McGinley turned from the subject of murder to focus on the lives of farm dwellers in rural Ireland. At the center of the work is an incestuous relationship between Kevin Hurley and his sister, Maureen, that becomes complicated by Maureen's pregnancy and Kevin's marriage to their neighbor. A change in tone occurs in the novel when the focus shifts from Kevin to his wife; the lewd humor of the first half gives way to the more refined language of the second. McGinley returned to death as a catalyst for action in *The Trick of the Ga Bolga* (1985), in which an unknown corpse floats ashore outside of Garaross, a Donegal town. The novel's protagonist, an Englishman who fled to Ireland to avoid involvement in World War II, becomes inextricably involved with the townspeople and the strange events in their lives. Sheila MacLeod commented: ''To an outsider, eccentricity is the hallmark of Garaross. But it is an eccentricity which has a logic of its own, being rooted in Ireland's everpresent past and a peculiar mix of Celtic myth and Catholicism, where nothing is ever quite what it seems.'' This work, like McGinley's other novels, has been especially commended for its recreation of the manners and beliefs of Irish country folk.

PETER KEMP

Bogmail is a powerfully surprising book that pushes your expectations pleasingly askew. Opening as a murder story, it retains elements of detective writing to the end, but grows into

something else: the rather eerie presentation of a remote Donegal community. In a damp cranny of that region, strange-named locals—Roarty, Rory Rua, Cor Magaill, Gimp Gillespie—fester ominously. Contact with them leaves one outsider dead, another smarting with betrayal. The book ends with the community closed in upon itself and left to its ingrown devices. One of these is the acquiring of recherché knowledge. Erudition here, it seems, is a valuable weapon in one-upmanship—not to mention knocking people down: the murdered man is smartly felled by Volume 25 of the *Encyclopaedia Britannica* (1911 edition). (p. 735)

Peter Kemp, ''What's in a Name?'' in The Listener, Vol. 100, No. 2588, November 30, 1978, pp. 734-35.

ROBIN W. WINKS

[*Bogmail*] is perversely brilliant. I had read it when it was published in Ireland two years ago and hoped that someone would extend some hands across the sea. The rather intelligent publican in a village in the west of Ireland kills his assistant with an encyclopedia, having failed to poison him with toadstools in his omelette. In disposing of the body in a nearby bog, our pub keeper is observed, and his punning moral pursuer submits him to bogmail, demanding £30 a week for silence. The cast of likely characters, all frequenters of the pub, includes a seedy and well-read Englishman sinking ever deeper into the spiritual bogs of Ireland, the local policeman, and several poetic types who can describe a sunset, a lough, or a rather grimy sexual experience with drunken music. In many ways the book is unpleasant, for all speak as they think, and their thoughts are explicit and crude; yet the writing is so skilled, the power to evoke a sense of lush, green landscape so great, that one is fascinated with the perversities of the human character, perversities that seem all the more morbidly fascinating for being expressed in a lilting Irish voice.

> *Robin W. Winks, in a review of "Bogmail," in* The New Republic, *Vol. 184, No. 18, May 2, 1981, p. 38.*

NEWGATE CALLENDAR

The dust jacket describes [*Bogmail*] as "a novel with murder." Which indeed it is. It starts with a lovely paragraph. Roarty, the owner of a pub in a seaside Irish village, is busy making an omelet, mixing in poisoned mushrooms with the sort of manic energy that Mime demonstrates while preparing the potion for Siegfried. Roarty wants to murder his bartender, who has corrupted his daughter. . . .

In a crazy kind of way all of this is completely incidental to the book, a wonderfully charming, amusing look at the Irish—who are, as we know, great talkers. And there is mighty fine talk here about religion, about life, about murder, about philosophy. Mr. McGinley (who has woven a vein of black humor through his book) has avoided stock characters. At the end, justice definitely does not triumph. Somehow, one does not care. A murderer who loves Schumann and who has all but memorized the 11th edition of the Britannica cannot be all bad.

> *Newgate Callendar, in a review of "Bogmail," in* The New York Times Book Review, *August 2, 1981, p. 27.*

MARY CANTWELL

Patricia Teeling [protagonist of *Goosefoot*] is a country girl. She has just received a first in agricultural science from University College, Cork. Her bachelor uncle, Lar, wants her to run his farm for him. Eventually she will inherit it; and in Ireland having land is tantamount to having money. But Patricia wants to see the world for a year or so, or at least that part of the world which is Dublin. . . .

Patricia Teeling is what F. Tennyson Jesse, the author of the classic *Murder and its Motives* calls a murderee. "Perhaps, at some future date," Miss Jesse wrote many years ago, "when the laws of attraction and repulsion are more fully understood than they are at present, it will be discovered that murderers and murderees send out waves that correspond to the waves of wireless between certain stations."

It is Dublin that sends out waves to Patricia Teeling, a tall, big-boned, slope-bottomed innocent. She gets a job teaching science in a school whose headmaster, a man whose mustache is always dripping, sits under her classroom windows "like a red-brown stag with upturned nose" checking her performance. She discos with strangers and takes coffee with her neighbor, Gladys Baggotty, whose writer-husband, it is rumored, beats her. The husband, Bernard, turns out to be the "Austrian osteopath" who was once Patricia's dancing partner. His wife, he says, enjoys obscene phone calls.

Patricia's flatmate, Monica, is fond of talking about, though not experiencing, what they choose to call the membrum virile until they realize that it might be "unscholarly" to assume that all membra are virile. . . . The landlord, Mr. Mullally, is deaf as a post and buried in racing forms. Dublin is "a cold desert on a dark night." The reader, who likes Patricia, begs "Go home, go home, go home."

Patricia does go home at Christmas. Uncle Lar is drinking, led into liquor by his young cousin, Hugh, who's emerged from Australia with his eye on Lar's farm. . . .

Back [Patricia] goes to Dublin, to find Gladys Baggotty stabbed to death, possibly by Bernard. He declares himself innocent and, not incidentally, in love with Patricia. An inspector comes to call, a Detective McMyler. . . . There is something strange about Detective Inspector McMyler. Patricia is drawn to him; Bernard is afraid of him. Bernard calls him Goosefoot.

If mystery fiction is literature about a world in which no crime goes unsolved and unpunished, then Patrick McGinley is an accredited practitioner of the genre. True, who murdered whom was no secret in his first book, *Bogmail,* but who is blackmailing the murderer was. Everyone, however, gets a comeuppance: Mr. McGinley observes the rules of the game. But within the perimeters of mystery fiction, he has created a place in which lust and guilt are inseparable, and everybody talks as if an angel's got his tongue.

That place is recreated in *Goosefoot.* Patricia's and Monica's virginity hang over their lives like a shadow over a landscape. Still, there is no joy in sex, only the fascination of the abomination. Phone calls are obscene in their elegance, not in their matter. In the country Uncle Lar is drinking himself into the grave; in the city Bernard is scaring himself into his. There's a murderer about, but how can you spot him when everyone is moon-tetched? (Or maybe it is simply that everyone, except for Bernard and Gladys Baggotty, is Irish, which, Mr. McGinley implies, is the same as being moon-tetched.) And Patricia, who doesn't know "the nature of the experience she craved" finishes each day "inchoate and incomplete." It will take disaster to order her chaos.

There are crimes in *Goosefoot* and solutions, but there is also Ireland and coruscating conversation, wit that scalds and sins that are no less sinful for being uncommitted. Mr. McGinley may never have a large audience, but he is certain to attract a fervent cult.

> *Mary Cantwell, in a review of "Goosefoot," in* The New York Times, *September 27, 1982, p. C16.*

RICHARD FREEDMAN

In his superb first novel, *Bogmail,* Patrick McGinley wove a complex Irish plaid with strands of murder and blackmail, and as garrulous a crew of pub philosophers as you'll find outside the works of the late Brendan Behan. The pattern works nearly as well again in *Goosefoot,* which suffers slightly from second-novel letdown; but not so you'd notice if you hadn't read *Bogmail.*

Where that thriller remained deeply implanted in the Donegal bogs, this time Mr. McGinley moves the action to Dublin. Where *Bogmail* had a charming murderer for hero, *Goosefoot* has a charming victim as heroine.

She's Patricia Teeling, a tall, strapping country lass who leaves her loving Uncle Lar and the promise of eventually inheriting his farm for a job teaching science in a ghastly Dublin secondary school. . . . One of Patricia's fellow teachers is friendly enough and buys an occasional drink, but has a disturbing fetish for balloons. And a neighbor, Bernard Baggotty, poses as an Austrian osteopath and makes occasional crank calls to his own wife. Like the character of Potter in *Bogmail,* he's an Englishman ill at ease with Celtic modes of thought. . . .

Bernard Baggotty seeks Patricia's counsel and company. Nothing can come of it. Not only is he married—until his wife is mysteriously murdered—but Patricia has her heart set on Mr. Right. For although she has many suitors, including her hulking cousin Hugh back home, Patricia is perhaps the most resolute virgin since Richardson's Pamela, a delightful anomaly in today's fiction.

As a thriller, however, *Goosefoot* disappoints somewhat. The mystery of Mrs. Baggotty's murder comes too late in the story to seem more than an afterthought. And before then, Patricia's teaching adventures in Dublin too closely resemble Jenny Bunn's career in London in Kingsley Amis's 1960 *Take A Girl Like You* to live up to the high expectations of originality aroused by *Bogmail.*

Still, the lyrical wit of Mr. McGinley's writing makes one await avidly his Opus 3.

> *Richard Freedman, in a review of "Goosefoot," in The New York Times Book Review, October 24, 1982, p. 42.*

GEOFFREY STOKES

[*Goosefoot*] overflows with rich language and the stink of repressed sex.

For McGinley, the two seem intimately connected, almost as though sudden effusions of poetry in the most prosaic circumstances were not a sublimation of the Celtic carelessness crushed under centuries of Jansenism, but a joyous bursting of the bonds—an ecstatic entry of a whole priest-ridden people into a realm foreclosed them by the long denial of their flesh. As a novelist, McGinley finds the swap nearly irresistible, inventing a piece of pub talk that might have been lifted whole from *Passing the Time in Ballymenone.* . . . (pp. 3-4)

[Pub talk] is Patricia Teeling's home language, and hearing it, she feels "in collusion with the farmers, a party to the secret life of the country. . . . It was a gift from heaven that no amount of negative living could now take away from her." The talk of the city, of negative living, is by comparison mad. In study—a fellow teacher's compulsive pseudo-Joycean word-play, her English neighbor's university wit, the relentless fancifying of self-proclaimed poets—is corruption. Plucked from the ground and set in a vase to serve as decoration, the language of the land grows overblown and sick.

In McGinley's Ireland, experiments with freedom, linguistic or sexual, are doomed. Whether Patricia is to die at the hands of a maniac or to suffer the slow suffocation of "negative living" matters little in the long run; poisoned sex has poisoned the nation. Yet despite the grimness of the vision (in *Bogmail,* conventional sex leads to murder, but a child-molester is a village joke), McGinley makes Patricia a hugely appealing character. Big-boned and muscular, she brings a young baccalaureate's still-damp enthusiasms to the farm and a farmer's common sense to Dublin's excesses. Perhaps the most determined virgin in recent literary history (for reasons the men she meets make thoroughly sensible), her bedtime conversations with Monica, her flat-mate, reveal a restless curiosity about sex more suitable to a schoolgirl than a schoolmistress.

Except, of course, in Ireland, where the primary mode of sexual expression seems to be the snigger. The only other choices are a sad celibacy, or an adolescent Don Juanism that shades through ever deeper degrees of misogyny to a battered corpse in a roadside ditch or a bog.

This, finally, is McGinley's great theme. Darker, despite the many moments of charm, in *Goosefoot* than in *Bogmail,* it is also a trifle less convincing. Because the earlier book played itself out within the confines of the mystery genre, McGinley's inventiveness kept itself in check. But *Goosefoot* is too laden with coincidence to satisfy as a mystery, too conscious of its obligations as a thriller to stand as the novel McGinley is obviously on the way to writing. In its flirtation with "serious" literature, it is, in fact, his Dublin, and only its sequel will tell if he has survived his adventure. (p. 4)

> *Geoffrey Stokes, in a review of "Goosefoot," in VLS, No. 13, December, 1982, pp. 3-4.*

PATRICIA CRAIG

[*Goosefoot*] is nothing if not eclectic. Clearly it was conceived as parody, but parody not confined to one genre only: among its targets are the self-discovery novel, the Dublin pub novel, the idiosyncratic-Irish novel, the realistic rural novel, the comic-erotic novel, the whimsical novel, the aphoristic novel, the detective novel and the romantic thriller. There are moments, too, when parody gives way to something more straightforward; any of these categories is liable to surface briefly in an authentic form. The author suffers from a slight uncertainty of tone; humour suits him best, but he doesn't always try to be funny, and he isn't consistently successful when he does. His addiction to the cryptic quip and the outlandish foible sometimes gets the better of his literary judgment. Setpieces, to a certain extent, take the place of plot. You could say the novel is all but immobilized by its desire to take off in a number of different directions at once. For the author, you feel, the ingredients are of more consequence than the end product.

What do we have? An Irish virgin, an agricultural maid, albeit a modern one equipped with a science degree and endowed with the capacity to drink four pints of stout at a sitting, turns her back on the chance of a farm of her own and heads for Dublin. . . . In a novel in which the sex-rôles of characters are often reversed, Uncle Lar is the fairy godmother, Cousin Hugh an ugly sister whose ploys pay off, Patricia the younger son whose path is beset with symbolic difficulties. Among these is the problem of distinguishing between those who wish to help her progress, and those who mean to hinder it; in this area, the world of the folktale and that of the picturesque thriller converge, with the heroine ultimately endangered by her inability to tell a joker from a killer.

There's an ordinary story, or at least the bare bones of one, superimposed on all this. Patricia Teeling moves into a furnished flat with a girl called Monica, secures a post as science mistress in a boys' school, and wards off the advances of Bernard Baggotty, a married man and an English journalist to boot, who lives in the flat downstairs. But ordinariness, and the odd forms it sometimes takes, do not have too secure a hold on the author's imagination. He has a much surer instinct for full-blown bizarrerie. Knicker omelettes, balloon enthusiasts, those who like dowsing for coins in women's underclothes, inept poets who dream of ostrich farms, goose-steppers and pussy-footers are dotted obtrusively about his narrative; he isn't at all averse to gaudy decoration. He goes in, in about equal measures, for inconsequentiality and aplomb; and he offers, in his more inspired passages, a celebration of Irish verbosity and virtuosity.

Patricia Craig, "Virgin in Danger," in The Times Literary Supplement, *No. 4167, February 11, 1983, p. 130.*

PATRICIA CRAIG

Geese and foxes, their symbolic function and the puns they generate, preoccupy Patrick McGinley. . . . Hard on the heels of *Goosefoot* . . . comes *Fox Prints*. This is a story about an Irishman, an Englishman, a Scotsman and a Welshman. The Irishman goes under the name of Keating, and the other three are Quilter, Garlick and MacGeoch. McGinley assembles his comic quartet in a London suburb called Wistwood East, where the architecture is mock-Tudor, and where the illusions or delusions of the inhabitants are a fit subject for mockery.

"Foxgloves" is the detached residence where Keating, newly arrived from Ireland, goes to earth for a time before searching around for a journalistic post. In the meantime, he cooks for his keep, as well as contributing to the Celtic ballast which is supposed to contain the Anglo-Saxon buoyancy of Quilter. The latter, a *Telegraph* employee and self-styled major, has imposed a pseudo-military character on his domestic arrangements. . . .

In the tame woodlands of Wistwood East a predator is on the loose: three young women are done to death in circumstances which lead a Fleet Street newspaper to dub the killer "the Wistwood Fox." Keating, from whom a succession of right answers is required by the major, broods about the murders, throws himself into the play-acting at home and conducts his amorous engagements elsewhere, ingratiating himself with a voracious widow by passing himself off as a salesman complete with the "F" volume of an encyclopedia filched from MacGeoch ("Foxgloves" contains the light-fingered as well as the red-handed). . . .

The Scotsman, MacGeoch, we may infer, is not a suitable candidate for the part of the fox, since his name lets us know he's the son of a goose—unless, of course, this detail is thrown in to fox us. What's plain is that a prodigious amount of leg-pulling goes on at "Foxgloves," where someone's goose is about to be cooked, and throughout the narrative as well, where the author's distinctive humour inclines him towards riddling, ribaldry and a kind of frivolous abstruseness which enlivens the bulk of his dialogues. As an exercise in diversion, *Fox Prints* is thoroughly commendable; Patrick McGinley has manufactured a satisfactory literary manner from the impulse to lay a false trail for his readers.

Patricia Craig, "False Trails," in The Times Literary Supplement, *No. 4198, September 16, 1983, p. 1001.*

TOM PAULIN

Visiting Ireland in the early 1890s, Henry James complained of "the sinister shabbiness of this tragic country." James wrote as a tourist in a country whose enduring impoverishment had forced his paternal grandfather to flee a century earlier. Although James viewed Ireland as an exasperated outsider, his vision has been endorsed by many Irish writers. In *Dubliners*, for example, Joyce aimed to design a city with a "special odor of corruption" and Samuel Beckett has also developed this theme of corruption and despair. Writers who take rural Ireland as their subject—Patrick Kavanagh and John McGahern, for example—have similarly insisted on the pitiless drabness and frustrations of Irish life. In Kavanagh's classic poem, "The Great Hunger," there is a lacerating presentation of spiritual and physical squalor as a frustrated rural bachelor watches his life slip past him. . . . Kavanagh describes the monotonous awfulness of his protagonist's life and he rigorously excludes any idea of redemption from the banal hell of the poem. Like Swift, Kavanagh shows a world of grinding poverty and folly which is incapable of giving even the most minimal of satisfaction.

It is essential that the reader of Patrick McGinley's new novel, *Foggage,* understands that it belongs to this richly pessimistic tradition of vehement anti-pastoral. Like Kavanagh, McGinley is concerned to describe a society which is almost medieval in its stagnation and fixity. His central character, Kevin Hurley, is a bachelor farmer who is oppressed by a profound sense of sin and a disquieting disgust for his bedridden father. . . .

This is Eamonn De Valera's Ireland, a neutral isolated island which has been transformed into a permanent state of mind. With an almost savage relish, McGinley offers images of a country frozen "into a mould," a place which is both static and festering like the gossip in Kevin's village.

Unfortunately, McKinley is unable to extend the vision which he has inherited from the tradition of Irish anti-pastoral I have just outlined. He is torn between a disgusted attitude of repudiation and a Lawrentian ambition to describe Kevin's incestuous relationship with his sister, Maureen, as something which is essentially noble and life-enhancing. Thus Maureen is described, with gauche and tacky irony, as "assiduous in bed and equally assiduous in the farmyard. She would shuffle about in wide unlaced shoes with splashes of slurry on her unstockinged calves, and when she stooped over a tub to mix the hens' feed she would place her flat feet apart, and her unkempt hair would hang down like thrums about her face." That unexpected and accurate word "thrums" redeems this queasy description only slightly, and it's clear from the gloating repetition of "assiduous" that the prose contains more than [an] element of interested prurience.

At times, McGinley appears to be stewing together ideas and images drawn from *Wuthering Heights* and Lawrence's *The Fox.* He then tries to deny his literary debts by suggesting that he is really writing an ironic and subversive fable of rural passion and guilt. His dialogue is curiously clumsy and the long monologues of the local vet, Festus O'Flaherty, have a thickly self-conscious, stage-Irish quality. At one point O'Flaherty gets drunk and exclaims "Ah, Kevin, me darling, me onlie begetter of foggage and its myriad applications!" This blethery tradition has been in existence since Shakespeare's time and it deserves to be repudiated by everyone who tries to write about Ireland.

Even so, *Foggage* has something which is compelling and exact—a disgusted cosmic despair which, just at times, is given a precise and almost-theological structure. . . .

[McGinley] ties Kevin's introverted peasant agony to a landscape which at times seems derelict and metaphysical, like

Beckett's. If McGinley's narrative manner is often tedious and secondhand, there is a talent in *Foggage* which may yet find its proper style and form.

Tom Paulin, "The Importance of Being Irish," in Book World—The Washington Post, *December 18, 1983, p. 11.*

MORDECAI RICHLER

Forty-year-old Kevin and Maureen are twin brother and sister. And incest, Kevin's conscience tells him, is wrong. On the other hand, if the story of Adam and Eve were true, he speculates, it follows that we are all the children of incest. Yet incest was forbidden in every country of the world, even in countries where cannibalism was still practiced.

We are only 15 pages into Patrick McGinley's new novel *Foggage* when Kevin's problem is compounded. "I'm pregnant," Maureen tells him.

Together, brother and sister contrive to tempt a hired man onto the farm. The bovine but calculating Maureen will seduce him, Kevin will surprise them in the act and expel the outsider, whom the neighbors will then accept as the father. The hired man, the frog-faced Billy Snoddy, a mere cottager's son, turns out to be a sneak, and Kevin is soon upset that Billy is having Maureen as well.

Enter the refined, troubled Elizabeth Quane, a schoolteacher, the spinster from the adjoining farm whom Kevin marries. As a student in Dublin, Elizabeth had known only weedy little men from life's infantry until she lost her virginity to a callous English technical journalist. Actually, he raped her. . . .

A saddened Kevin allows that, in that case, Elizabeth is foggage. "You know! Grass after the first cutting. Autumn foggage isn't as rich in nutrients as spring grass, but I'm not complaining. You'll have to do."

Up to this point, *Foggage* struck me as an imaginative, expertly turned dark comedy, informed by some splendid dialogue and a sensual feel for the claims of the soil. Then, suddenly, Mr. McGinley . . . switches gears. Elizabeth is so fully realized and sensitively drawn a character that she literally appropriates the story, tipping the comic balance. It is as if, having begun to read a novel by Erskine Caldwell at his best, we end up with something by Carson McCullers.

The novel is still dark, certainly, but now more tragic than anything else. Mr. McGinley is so talented a writer that he could easily have either sustained the comedy or written a tragic tale. In *Foggage,* however, the two approaches seem contradictory, they fail to mesh. The ending, with its gentle hint of redemption, smacks of manipulation. Even so, everything is redeemed by the high quality of the prose. Patrick McGinley is a very gifted man. He knows his Irish bog as well as Isaac Bashevis Singer does the *shtetl,* and he can sing about it with something like the same magic.

Mordecai Richler, "Siblings in Love," in The New York Times Book Review, *December 25, 1983, p. 6.*

RHODA KOENIG

Foggage is the grass left on the ground in winter. [In *Foggage*] Kevin Hurley, a Tipperary farmer, is consumed by the Foggage Principle, his idea for extending the grazing season later into the year. If this sounds like a sexual metaphor—think of the expression "getting one's greens" or the three-letter word Norman Mailer made up to get *The Naked and the Dead* past the censors—there's a good reason. Kevin is frugally making use of the only sex partner available to him, his twin sister, Maureen. Forty years old, the twins have been mating, more like farm animals than lovers, since they buried their mother three years before. Unaware of the depravities enacted on the floor below, their ninety-six-year-old bedridden father clings spitefully to life, determined to outlive his enemy, the neighbor.

Kevin is not plagued by guilt, or so he says. . . . But while neurosis and superstition leave Kevin unmoved, his scientific knowledge has given him cause for worry. Lately he has felt a pain in the scrotum after sex with Maureen. Could he have cancer? (Religion is old-fashioned, therefore contemptible, but cancer is modern.) His worries increase when Maureen tells him she is pregnant.

Kevin's attempts to drag home a victim for Maureen to seduce and then charge with paternity provide the novel's coarsest and most grotesque humor. Here we enter a world of lewd music-hall jokes, of shaggy pub stories that go on longer than they should and get funnier as they do. Without giving away the punch lines, I'll just say that these chapters treat death, even at its most undeserved and undignified, as part of the ludicrous comedy of life, and make it no less pathetic for that. Throughout Kevin's futile and increasingly desperate efforts to procure a fall guy, Maureen won't let him alone. "I'm dying for a rub of the relic," she insists, pinning him to the bed between funerals. Kevin begins to think the whole business may have been a bad idea.

Maureen's problem is eventually solved, but in the process Kevin sickens of their earthy, slovenly life. Even his leisure moments provide no variety—boozy confabs in the pub with Festus O'Flaherty, the philandering veterinarian, who tells him: "Most men would prefer to be seen out with a filly in the evening, but they'd prefer to spend the night with a heifer." To mortify and cleanse himself, Kevin decides, he will marry Elizabeth Quane, the spinster schoolteacher who just happens to own a nice bit of land. After a courtship conducted largely in silence, Elizabeth accepts him in a manner that encourages his hope of further trials. . . .

At this point, about halfway through the book, McGinley does something very daring—he breaks his story in two, and bends it back on itself. Elizabeth's point of view takes over the novel. Soon twigging to the fact that it will take a lot more than a bidet to civilize Kevin and Maureen, she goes to work on the marriage in her own way. She is hampered, however, by her ignorance of all the clauses in the contract. The language turns sparer and more delicate as the sensitive, reflective school-mistress ponders her lack of success. In one sense, this is a loss, as it's hard not to feel a falling off and thinning out from the more robust earlier section of the book. But as Elizabeth's intelligence circles in on Kevin and Maureen's secret, the tightening gyre of fear alters our perception of *Foggage.* We are forced to consider Kevin not as a natural animal but a civilized member of the outside world—marriage has a way of doing that—and to regard his new life as he comes to see it himself. From a penance, Elizabeth evolves into a blessing; he is touched by her efforts to understand as well as domesticate him, although Elizabeth understands both too much and not enough. Her faith in education, in words, is a frail weapon for dealing with the semisavage Maureen, but the course that *Foggage* takes toward its close demonstrates how powerful words can be. . . . In one terrible scene of McGinley's novel, the educated person's dream of power and the superstitious peasant's fear of a curse converge. Looks may not kill, but words can. (p. 76)

Rhoda Koenig, "The Blind Side of the Heart," in Harper's, Vol. 268, No. 1604, January, 1984, pp. 74-6.

PATRICIA CRAIG

[In *Foggage,* the] gloom of Patrick McGinley's opening paragraph recalls the gloom of "The Great Hunger", though the hunger Patrick Kavanagh had in mind is appeased in the hero of *Foggage* by means of an aberrant liaison: this . . . is a story of incest in the Irish midlands and its comic-opera effects, deviously orchestrated. The ill-luck attaching to such violations of nature is deflected away from the principals—an awful pair of middle-aged twins by the names of Maureen and Kevin Hurley—but not too far; retribution keeps lighting on those innocently entangled with the siblings.

Kavanagh's "His sister grunted in bed. / The sound of a sow taking up a new position" finds an echo in McGinley, who makes no bones about rendering to the fullest extent the charmlessness of Irish country ways. Women, though on the whole less attractive than heifers, thrive, as cattle do, on reasonable treatment. So muses Kevin Hurley, dullard, beef-eater, schemer and hypochondriac. . . .

It's impossible not to see in *Foggage* a falling away from the splendid antics and involutions of *Fox Prints* (1983) and even from the playfulness of *Goosefoot* (1982), a kind of muted coprophilia having taken the place of the cleverness we'd come to expect from Patrick McGinley. *Foggage* reeks not so much of the earth as of the earth closet. This naturally witty author doesn't rise here to anything wittier than "you can't have your grass and eat it"—apropos of *foggage,* a farmers' conservation principle extended here to include the conserving of semen. The book is also a bit uneven in tone. Kevin comes to understand that what's most natural to him is also most unnatural; but the author hasn't quite decided whether to treat the impasse as paradox or farce.

Patricia Craig, "Unnatural Hungers," in The Times Literary Supplement, No. 4249, September 7, 1984, p. 988.

ALAN RYAN

On the road between Malin More and Glencolumbkille, on the westernmost peninsula of Donegal in northern Ireland, a handsome hotel stands quite by itself on a hillside. You can have a fine meal there—a good thing, too, because you can't have any sort of meal anywhere else for miles and miles—and enjoy good service and study the sheep on the opposite hill while you dine and watch the sun set slowly across the waters on Malin Bay. But afterward—if you're staying in a Glencolumbkille farmhouse, as I was a couple of years ago—you must take your life in your hands and brave the fog and the treacherous, narrow road that twists across a landscape so barren, so alien, that it might be the mountains of the moon dressed up with purple heather, muddy sheep, and the ever-present mist.

Irish novelist Patrick McGinley has made this Donegal setting, and the sturdy people who survive it for the length of their lives, indisputably his own. . . .

[In *The Trick of the Ga Bolga*] Coote, an Englishman in his thirties and "a man of many part-selves," goes off to remote Donegal to "find unity of experience" while chaotic war breaks out in Europe in the 1940s. He settles into a rundown farmhouse and slowly, living like the local people, is absorbed into the rhythm of the land and the seasons, into the life of the tiny village and its characters. And there is plenty here for him to absorb in turn. There is the lifelong feud between two cantankerous farmers, Salmo and the Proker. There are two very different women, the earthy Imelda and the aptly-named Consolata. . . .

There's also the dead Englishman who floats ashore one night on the tide with £300 in his pocket, which the priest at once appropriates to build a bridge across the inlet. Then there's the tragicomic race between a donkey and a dying horse. And there's a brutal murder . . . or what appears to be a murder. And the mystery of the split potatoes. And a suicide. And an angry wronged husband. And, most telling of all, there is Coote's wondering whether he is the catalyst that set all of the trouble in motion.

That question, in fact, is at the heart of this book. Can this life, with its ancient rhythms and patterns, be changed? Can a stranger become part of it, or is it a closed circle? Symbolically, although McGinley is never heavy-handed about this, Coote is engaged to design the local bridge. Despite blessings by the priest and the strength of primitive rituals, Coote has a hard time of it. The world he has touched resists him. . . .

The particular locale of the story lies in the shadow of a mountain, "Screig Beefan, mute but not long-suffering, in a tunic of ferns that concealed a heart of stone." That is the key to understanding. "In a place like this, sanity and salvation were to be found in ritual and magic—in establishing a precise order of actions that in time would become the prescribed order with its own value and significance." It is not so much that man seems small, but that man persists in a context that is larger than himself, and long-lasting. The survivors are the ones who see this.

McGinley's story is by turns funny and ferocious. His characters live. His dialogue rings true. His world is as real as the book in your hand. His writing combines the unrelieved darkness of John McGahern, the grim solemnity of Bernard MacLaverty, and the dry, controlled elegance of William Trevor, and then adds a generous touch of ribald Irish earthiness. In the end, this intensely Irish novel is really about people who "live in one another's pockets." And you don't have to be Irish for that.

Alan Ryan, "Ritual and Magic in a World Elsewhere," in Book World—The Washington Post, May 5, 1985, p. 10.

SHEILA MacLEOD

If Patrick McGinley had set out to write an anti-tourist tract, hoping to keep us Brits out of Ireland forever, he could hardly have succeeded better than with *The Trick of the Ga Bolga.* The small, isolated Donegal community of Garaross is not one that any outsider would lightly decide to settle in. But in 1943 or so the Englishman George Coote, a gritty loner disinclined to fight in the war, comes more or less innocently to such a decision. And with fatal results.

Coote finds himself in an emotionally claustrophobic environment where everyone knows everyone else's business and is keen to bring him up to date with their own version of native events and characters. The priest and the Protestant schoolmaster vie for his religious allegiance. His two closest neighbours, Salmo and the Proker ('Everyone has at least one nickname') exist in a state of potentially lethal enmity. And as far as women are concerned, his favours must be divided between the handsome, sexy Imelda, a war grass-widow, and the schoolmaster's virginal daughter, Consolata. The more Coote tries to remain distanced and uninvolved, the more he becomes enmeshed with all his neighbours.

To an outsider, eccentricity is the hallmark of Garaross. But it is an eccentricity which has a logic of its own, being rooted in Ireland's ever-present past and a peculiar mix of Celtic myth and Catholicism, where nothing is ever quite what it seems. Coote assumes the trick of the Ga Bolga to be some esoteric sexual manoeuvre but discovers too late that it is in fact a combative sleight-of-hand. Amid the general boozing and hilarity, other illusions are similarly shattered.

Patrick McGinley seems to be telling us that it is impossible to remain uninvolved, whether with national struggles or with our fellow-creatures. Not only the forces of history but the all-too-human existence of other people obviate the sort of lone neutrality which poses as amoral but is in fact a form of immorality. This is a strange, elusive novel which sometimes verges on the blarney, but is never less than excellently written and, once read, remains a powerfully haunting presence.

> *Sheila MacLeod, "Foreign Ways," in* New Statesman, *Vol. 110, No. 2841, August 30, 1985, p. 26.*

DAVID PROFUMO

"The universe is suffering from a deep and lasting mayonnaise," observes Salmo, the massive inhabitant of Garaross in Donegal, where George Coote takes refuge during the height of the Second World War. And so it would seem, for the world of [*The Trick of the Ga Bolga*] is one where the centre cannot hold—the rural community and its dramatic environment of moorland and seascape come to reflect an unnerving malaise that has driven the enigmatic Coote from the city, "from silly buggers and solemn suburban apes." *The Trick of the Ga Bolga* describes the chain of catastrophe that gradually unwinds during this foreigner's residence, and in many ways it makes enthralling reading.

Garaross is a place where anyone of note has at least two nicknames. No sooner has he moved into his smallholding than Coote finds colourful neighbours pressing their attentions on him; the otherwise gentle Salmo wages a vigorous feud against a spindly rival called the Proker, while Timideen (the cocky ex-schoolmaster) lectures Coote on the desirability of taking a wife, to wit, his virginal daughter Consolata. All of this leads to difficulties, as the Englishman is drawn into local affairs and against the odds becomes the folk-hero they desire, winning a horse race and supervising the building of a much-needed bridge. But there is something mighty wrong with his state of mind. Coote seems poisoned by self-analysis, and the strange new surroundings begin to work on him, further blurring his perception of what may be real. Occasional letters from his estranged friend Philip Woodwind—"a journalist and a vulgar man"—emphasize that he is in danger of losing his grip on things. . . .

The novel includes many dark touches, and achieves an often beautiful evocation of this particular type of Irish community.

McGinley's prose glints with visual precision, and the dialogue is remarkably crisp; but the book's flaw is the central character, whose neurosis never comes convincingly into focus, his behaviour remaining unaccountable. Coote's own confusion simply confuses the reader, and the ironic motif of the Ga Bolga—actually Cuchulainn's treacherous weapon—becomes a heavy symbol of larger elemental forces that are not sufficiently well evoked. Still, though it doesn't quite come off, the book is everywhere free from clichés of plot and expression, and is full of haunting peculiarities which accumulate to leave the impression of something mysterious and durable.

> *David Profumo, "The Ultimate Manoeuvre," in* The Times Literary Supplement, *No. 4302, September 13, 1985, p. 1000.*

CLANCY SIGAL

"The joke has gone far enough," says Charles Keating, the sex-obsessed fugitive hero of [*Foxprints*]. . . . A puzzled reader sympathizes with Keating's complaint. Mr. McGinley, the talented Donegal novelist whose . . . [other] works, like *The Trick of the Ga Bolga,* have shown a wonderful eye for Irish landscape, seems less at ease in the Home Counties England he has invented for his shaggy-dog, or rather shaggy-fox, tale.

Keating's real name is Martin Reddin; he has run away from an intolerable wife in Ireland to London's forgiving anonymity. Having shaved off his beard to change identity (he left behind circumstances suggesting suicide), he wants to become "one unremarked and unremarkable man among several million." But *Foxprints* is not a thriller in the ordinary sense. Keating is befriended by "Col." Peter Quilter, who hires him as a cook and major domo in Foxgloves, his mock-Tudor home in the London suburb of Wistwood East. The house is shared with a kilted, portly Scotsman, MacGeoch, and a disputatious Welshman, Garlick. All of them are overeducated and divorced or separated . . . and have vague journalistic connections.

So there's an Englishman, a Scotsman, a Welshman and now, with Keating, an Irishman—but what's the joke? I suspect that in the author's eyes, the situation itself, so suggestive of non-sensical pub ribaldry, is by definition hilarious, or at least funny in a double-take way. . . .

Mr. McGinley is at great pains to establish that Keating is a "cook-general in a madhouse that was probably saner than any other house around." I wonder. Suburbia knocking is no longer quite my measure either of humor or mental stability; it's an old joke, a clichéd target, unless the writer does something fresh with it. Mr. McGinley tries, perhaps too hard. Some local women are murdered, always with a fox connection. . . .

Keating falls in love with the married woman across the way, a theological hardcase who wants to save his soul. (Only toward the end do we understand that Keating's soul may in fact be lost and why.) And there is endless talk about foxes—as food, varmints and I suppose symbols. If foxes, their droppings and puns about their symbolism are your thing, Mr. McGinley is your man.

The line between bloodlessness and artful self-consciousness can be paper-thin in a novel so obsessed with words as this. Mr. McGinley's descriptions of sex are absurdly fussy, even if they are meant satirically. His observations on suburbia are correct, if overintellectualized—the London suburbs *are* the heartland of English fantasy, but saying it isn't the same as showing it. In Mr. McGinley's novel, suburbia is where misogyny and misanthropy meet, mate and spawn a kind of depressed verbosity.

Somewhere in his schema, Mr. McGinley was on to something original with Colonel Quilter, whose rage, intellectual aggression and culinary fastidiousness reflect the awful claustrophobia that afflicts the Englishman who is self-condemned to live in his imagination "because England is no longer wide enough to accommodate the sweep of his dreams." The Colonel really is no joke, or if he is, he has lost his own point and therefore loses me as a reader.

Clancy Sigal, "Murder in Suburbia," in The New York Times Book Review, *October 20, 1985, p. 24.*

Terrence McNally

1939-

American dramatist and scriptwriter.

According to Harold Clurman, McNally is "one of the most adept practitioners of the comedy of insult." His plays, whether classified as satire, farce, or melodrama, generally attack complacency, outmoded norms, institutions, and human folly by means of black humor and witty, acerbic dialogue. McNally's early plays, in which he examines the effects of current events upon individuals, are often angry, violent, and bitingly satirical. His later works, while remaining true to their author's savage wit, are lighter and more lyrical in tone, relying increasingly on references to New York and its theater community.

McNally's first play, *And Things That Go Bump in the Night* (1964), is the story of a bizarre family who live in self-imposed isolation in their cellar. Beneath its manic violence and hilarious surface, the play contains serious undertones, as is the case with much of McNally's drama. McNally's reputation increased with his series of one-act plays written for Broadway in the late 1960s. These works explore such topics as adolescent rebellion, politics, popular culture, and personal and social values. Many of these plays feature young protagonists who are angered and confused by the social upheaval of their era. Anarchy in the form of political assassination is the subject of *Witness* (1968), while in *Sweet Eros* (1968), a personable but egocentric young man wrestles with his inability to give or receive love. In *Noon* (1968), an unusually compassionate farce for McNally, an unseen character arranges a sexual rendezvous between five people whose preferences and experiences turn out to be vastly different, resulting in chaos and miscommunication. Like many of McNally's plays from this period, the one-acts *Cuba si!* (1968) and *Next* (1969) focus on political protest. In the latter play, one of McNally's more popular and acclaimed works, an overweight middle-aged man who wishes to fail a physical examination in order to escape the Vietnam draft feels humiliated when rejected by the pompous, authoritarian officer on duty. Several of McNally's one-act plays have been adapted for television.

McNally's full-length comedy *Where Has Tommy Flowers Gone?* (1971) is considered to be one of his best plays. The exuberant, amoral protagonist, a sensitive young man both liberated and traumatized by the events of the 1960s, engages in violent destruction as a means of rebellion. McNally received an Obie Award for *Bad Habits* (1971), a production of two one-act plays, both set in sanitoriums, which feature unusual methods of treating mental illness and human misery. While the patients of *Ravenswood* are allowed anything they desire, no matter how harmful or debilitating, the staff of *Dunelawn* maintain strict control by keeping patients strait-jacketed and drugged. *The Ritz* (1975), first produced as *The Tubs* (1974), is a fast-paced farce in which a naive heterosexual, pursued by his murderous brother-in-law, unwittingly hides in a homosexual bathhouse. Although reviews of the play were mixed, McNally was praised for his creative variations on such burlesque techniques as chase sequences and close confrontations. McNally wrote adaptations of the play for both television and film.

© Nancy Crampton

McNally has become more closely associated with Broadway tradition in recent years, enlarging on earlier concerns through the use of established conventions and references to New York and its theater circles. In *It's Only a Play* (1982), a revised version of McNally's off-Broadway production *Broadway, Broadway* (1978), a producer and the cast of her production throw a party in anticipation of their opening-night reviews, referring to and poking fun at actual New York personalities in the process. McNally provided the book for the musical *The Rink* (1984), a comic melodrama in which a mother and her estranged daughter confront their bitter past and possible futures. McNally's recent comedy, *The Lisbon Traviata* (1986), concerns the efforts of a failing playwright to persuade his lover not to leave him for a younger man. The play is, according to one reviewer, "an attempt to dramatize progressive stages in the disintegration of the hero's personality, with . . . [the] desperate and self-defeating effort to salvage a love relationship presented as an alternative to creative fulfillment."

(See also *CLC*, Vols. 4, 7; *Contemporary Authors*, Vols. 45-48; *Contemporary Authors New Revision Series*, Vol. 2; and *Dictionary of Literary Biography*, Vol. 7.)

CLIVE BARNES

[*The Rink*] is not quite as good as it should have been, but certainly not as bad as it could have been.

The Rink is ambitious, and seems to promise the expectation of grandeur. I think I was even expecting it to be on ice. It is a roller rink—a very seedy roller rink, in an even more seedy amusement park somewhere on the Atlantic seaboard, where casinos haven't reached and the boardwalk has lapsed into tiny decay. It is a bitter playground for muggers.

[Anna] is the rink's owner—or at least co-owner with her long-absent daughter—and she has sold it for demolition, and even now a six-pack wrecker's crew is moving in to start work.

But the daughter Angel . . . has suddenly decided to return from California. She misses the colored lights of the fairground, and the magic of a world that, unbeknown to her, has vanished.

The musical is not about the rink—the rink, its possessions and its future, are simply the arena where a mother and daughter examine their past, and perhaps learn to talk to one another after these years of hurt and dangerous silence.

As the daughter says: "We scream, we yell, we shout, we hate—we don't talk." What can they talk about? The past and its lies, and deceptions. The dead father who wasn't dead, the infidelities, the little girl who felt unlovely and unloved, the mother who felt abandoned, and the church that did little to nurture or comfort either of them.

A serious musical then. Terrence McNally's book is lean and hard even in its sentimentality. It is a musical where dreams twist into nightmares, where sex, not love, is omnipresent, and a joking song about the good old days can disconcertingly erupt into a gang rape.

An innovative musical, then. Yes—McNally uses a very fluid time warp for his story, and all the characters, apart from the mother, daughter and the daughter as a child, are played, irrespective of gender, by the wrecker's crew. The sextet even get to do a roller-skating ballet. (pp. 376-77)

You see everything is there. Or, almost.

The multi-purpose chorus is a cute dramatic idea—but does it actually work on stage? Perhaps not. Certainly it makes the show seem intimate while the sweep of the music is surely show-biz expansive.

Similarly the crisply sophisticated lyrics, bristling with wit, are out of kilter with the more savage, perhaps deeper humors of the book, seeming inadvertently to provide a flippant commentary to real, if funny, pain.

Even the decrepit grandeur of the setting seems wraithlike in the musical's bounce, and yet also, with all that bounce, the very musical itself misses that authentic belting surge it seeks . . . to evoke. It even lacks that final clinching clutch around the heartstrings, what Broadway fondly calls "the 11 o'clock number."

So the sum of the parts does not add up to the sum of the whole, and some of the whole adds up to less than that. What to do—put it all on ice, bring out new skates, and go back to the workshop with, say, an Alpine village?

No. *The Rink* disappoints at the high level it aims at, yet provides much pleasure, as well as real emotion, on the lower slopes. The show has not been either well envisaged or, in final concept well produced—but within those limitations there is much to enjoy. . . . (p. 377)

Clive Barnes, "Chita and Liza Set the Wheels in Motion in 'Rink'," in New York Post, *February 10, 1984. Reprinted in* New York Theatre Critics' Reviews, *Vol. XLV, No. 2, Week of January 16, 1984, pp. 376-77.*

FRANK RICH

The turgid, sour new musical [*The Rink*] . . . is a curious affair. . . . [Much] of it is as polished as [the leading actress's] skills. . . . But no glossy Broadway professionalism can mask the work's phony, at times mean-spirited content—or give credence to its empty pretensions. . . .

The idea behind the show—which often seems a forced hybrid of *Follies,* John Guare's screenplay for *Atlantic City* and a previous [John Kander-Fred Ebb] musical, *The Happy Time*—was to create a Proustian-flavored reunion between a long-estranged mother and her grown-up daughter. The acutely symbolic setting . . . is a decaying roller rink along the boardwalk of a tattered Eastern seaboard resort. Anna . . . , the rink's proprietor, has sold the old joint. But just as the wreckers arrive, her daughter, Angel . . . , returns from a seven-year California exile to search for roots and settle old scores.

What ensues in Terrence McNally's book is a series of repetitious present-day squabbles, punctuated by flashbacks. Mr. McNally is a smart and witty playwright, but you'd never know it from this synthetic effort. His dialogue is banal, and his characters are ciphers. Anna is merely a spunky widow; Angel is a caricatured 1960's dropout defined by scruffy clothes. *The Rink* is static because nothing specific or compelling is at stake for the two women. Their only real conflict is a generalized, all-purpose log-jam: they've never learned how to say "I love you."

To inflate the show, Mr. McNally pays lip service to sociological themes (such as urban decay) and loads the memory segments with lurid, melodramatic revelations that might well constitute a parody of William Inge. We learn that Anna's late husband was an alcoholic womanizer; we also hear of an illegitimate birth, Anna's postmarital promiscuity and a fatal car crash. Though none of these soap-operatic incidents adds depth to Angel and Anna, they . . . do reinforce the evening's distasteful tone. Almost every male character is a crude sexual adventurer, and both women are presented as reformed "tramps."

Mr. McNally paints himself into so many corners that he must resolve the mother-daughter relationship by fiat. Angel and Anna end up on terms of endearment thanks to another plot trick and several lines of "I'm O.K. You're O.K." psychobabble. Mr. McNally also attempts to pander to the audience in a climactic flashback: to free the daughter from her past, he presents antiwar protesters of Angel's generation as bubbleheads who didn't even know where Southeast Asia was. That cynical judgment is then embroidered in [Angel's] final song—in which Mr. Ebb's lyrics characterize the idealists of an entire decade as ineffectual Frisbee throwers and draft-card burners. Somehow this holier-than-thou indictment of the Vietnam War era lacks authority when couched in trivial terms befitting Mr. Ebb's last show, *Woman of the Year.*

Frank Rich, in a review of "The Rink," in The New York Times, *February 10, 1984, p. C3.*

EDWIN WILSON

[*The Rink*] is a mother-daughter saga. Anna's husband, Dino . . . mistreats her and, after returning from the Korean War, leaves her and her daughter. Anna begins to have affairs with other men, which alienates her daughter, Angel . . . , who heads West to become a hippie.

These events are presented as flashbacks: The play opens when Angel, after a long absence, has decided to come back to the rink—to her roots. That happens to be at the very moment when Anna has sold the property to a developer. During the course of the play, the mother and daughter attempt to come to terms with the past and with each other.

The creators of *The Rink* may feel that it has not fared better at the hands of the critics because the critics are not receptive to a serious musical, but they should not deceive themselves. *The Rink* fails not because of its subject matter, but because neither the book nor the musical score of John Kander and Fred Ebb treats the material with bite or originality.

Mr. McNally's book suffers from two problems, the first being that the story is told mostly in cliches. . . . When Anna attempts to justify her affairs, she tells everyone—God, her priest, her daughter—"You don't know what the nights are like." And Angel, in explaining why she left home for so long and was so mixed up, tells her mother that it all goes back to her childhood: "You never told me I was pretty."

A second problem with the book is that it is caught in a time warp of the 1960s, with frequent references to such things as flower children, dropouts and Cambodia. Both the predictable story and its dated quality hit bottom when Anna and Angel, who have been shouting profane epithets at each other all evening, suddenly are reconciled over a joint of marijuana.

A great deal of this might have been rectified, however, by an inspired musical score. Many ordinary stories have been raised to exceptional levels by music—think of any number of operas or American musicals of 30 years ago. . . . But the tawdry or unpleasant incidents that could have been made poignant or painful by a first-rate score are not raised above the ordinary by the only score this show has got.

The Rink does, nevertheless, have a certain number of redeeming features. . . . [But they happen] around the edges—at the center stands the empty rink.

> Edwin Wilson, "*A Turkey on Skates*," in The Wall Street Journal, *February 14, 1984, p. 30.*

JOHN SIMON

Circumstances beyond my control compelled me to see *The Rink* at its antepenultimate preview, though nothing much could have changed between Monday and Wednesday, when most of the critics went. Advance rumors, which one cannot help hearing in this business, were abuzz with references to *The Rank,* and I even heard that certain people couldn't wait to read me on *this* one. I was as prepared for anything as the most dedicated Boy Scout, but—I'm sorry if this comes as a disappointment to "certain people"—*The Rink* is not really rank, only long, intermittently tedious, fairly cliché-ridden, and lacking in any sort of urgency, even the musical-comedy kind. But it has its points, [and] is never unbearable. . . .

The Rink is another pseudosignificant, comi-tragi-sentimental tale of a long and supposedly complex mother-daughter relationship in the manner of *Terms of Endearment.* Here Anna, the mother, is selling the Antonelli roller rink . . . , just as Angel, her 30-year-old hippie daughter (29, according to Anna: "I'm your mother—there's no way I have a 30-year-old daughter!"), makes one of her rare return visits from her roamings, this one meant to be permanent. . . . Will Angel be able to stop [the rink's destruction]? Will Anna finally shake the years of unhappiness with [ex-husband] Dino and after Dino, and go off with "good old Lenny," a devoted but unglamorous suitor of many years, to Rome, freedom, and not quite marriage, because "at our age, people don't get married; they just set up light housekeeping and wait for the Social Security checks to start coming in."

The book is by Terrence McNally, who has written plays with plots, but don't go to *The Rink* expecting a working story. As the time frame keeps fluctuating between past and present, and often fuses the two, there is no coherent, credible action, only clichés and crises, one after another after another. But McNally can create amusing situations and write funny lines, and there are some of the former and quite a few of the latter floating around. There are also some unintentionally funny lines, such as [Angel's] repeated complaint to [Anna], "You never once told me I'm pretty!" (p. 89)

[The rest of the cast] comprises six men—a kind of barbershop, or hair-salon, sextet—who play all the other parts, starting with the wreckers and including various girls and women of diverse ages and conditions. And *The Rink* makes *La Cage aux Folles* look like *Oklahoma!* There is, of course, nothing wrong with a show on a homosexual subject looking and sounding homosexual (*La Cage,* incidentally, seems nowhere near forthright enough). But we have here an ostensibly heterosexual show being, in halfway-in, halfway-out-of-the-closet fashion, homosexualized in sundry ways. Not only could the men in drag have been more suitably replaced by women, but even the two leading roles seem at times to be played by men. Here the direction errs, but much of it has to do with acting styles and writing. For instance, would a mother trying to encourage her shy teenaged daughter to be bolder with the boy she fancies say, "I could go for him myself. See the arse on that kid?" In fact, the entire Anna-Angel relationship comes across more like an endless lovers' quarrel than a mother-daughter imbroglio, which may resemble the former but not that closely. Especially when you consider how pallid and amorphous the Anna-Dino and other heterosexual relations are, not to mention that campy mixture of exaggeration and winking at the audience with which much of the show is played.

And the sell-out audience picked up on the innuendos and kept falling into hysterical ecstasies. The theater was awash with subtexts that had nothing to do with the avowed text. (pp. 89-90)

> John Simon, "*Skating on Thin Wood*," in New York Magazine, *Vol. 17, No. 8, February 20, 1984, pp. 89-90.*

VARIETY

Imagine a revival of the first act of *The Boys In The Band* and the last act of *Who's Afraid Of Virginia Woolf?* and you'll have a sense of the dual artistic personality of *The Lisbon Traviata.* Terrence McNally's new play is a sort of chiaroscuro study of gay obsessions and relationships. The funny first half is very funny indeed, but the somber second act doesn't work.

The hero and presumed authorial surrogate is a once-acclaimed playwright with a bad case of writer's block who has let his obsessive devotion to opera dominate his life. He and another opera zealot, a campy buddy, spend an evening trading inside gags about opera divas and vying in their devotion to Maria Callas. . . .

The bitchy jokes and opera arcana are written from obvious expertise and will be irresistible to opera buffs. Most of the best zingers are given to the playwright's silly, but likable comrade-in-arias. . . .

The tone shifts abruptly in the second act as the writer returns to the apartment he shares with a lover to find him and a new, younger romantic interest arising from bed. The rest of the play is an increasingly tense confrontation as the hero tries to persuade his lover of nine years not to leave him. There's a violent climax.

The play's contrasting sections are an attempt to dramatize progressive stages in the disintegration of the hero's personality, with the first half's vicarious opera devotion seen as a neurotic substitute for life, and the second's desperate and self-defeating effort to salvage a love relationship presented as an alternative to creative fulfillment.

It's not a bad theme, and McNally is a real writer with a flair for crackling dialog. The bloody climax possibly aside, it has the ring of truth. But the hero is already *in extremis* when the play begins, and the audience has to take his human decency on faith. As given, the character's a rather nasty, self-pitying, selfish nuisance. Maybe another scene of character exposition, prior to the opera chat, would provide the stature and dimension now missing. . . .

Lisbon is too indigenously gay and sexually explicit for mainstream popular appeal, but it might well repay an investment as an open-end off-Broadway production in a small theater. It wouldn't hurt to lose 10 minutes of the second act.

Humm., in a review of "The Lisbon Traviata," in
Variety, *July 3, 1985, p. 76.*

JOHN SIMON

Terrence McNally's plays have usually been maliciously funny, and generally more out of the closet than those of his contemporaries. This was most overtly true of *And Things That Go Bump in the Night* and *Noon,* somewhat less obviously so of several others. With *The Lisbon Traviata,* McNally brings into the uptown venue some of the most floridly flagrant excesses of a group of homosexuals whom Julius Novick, in his *Voice* review, correctly termed "opera queens." In the first act, Stephen, in whom we are to recognize a stylized self-portrait, and Mendy . . . are two opera fanatics and old friends relentlessly oneupmanshipping each other with operatic trivia. Stephen, whose roommate and ex-lover Mike is using their apartment to consummate a new relationship, has forgotten to bring along to Mendy's the newly available recording of Maria Callas's Lisbon *Traviata,* which Mendy slavers for with the kind of craving for instant gratification it takes a baby over half a century to perfect. His most outrageous maneuvers to obtain it fail, however, as he and Stephen have at each other verbally.

This first act is extremely funny if you know anything about opera. It is all bitchiness, which, however, like jazz, can range

from hot to cool, from the scatological and obscene to the epigrammatic. But the second act, in which Mendy dwindles to a voice on the phone or answering machine, changes gears completely. Some wit remains; the rest is pure acid and venom. Stephen, next morning, discovers Mike, whom he still loves (or merely craves) with a "trick"—actually, a nice young man—and proceeds to torture them both. Homosexual sex is graphically evoked, shocking at least two of my colleagues audibly. The conclusion may seem tragic to the author but, with its unearned violence, strikes me as only melodramatic and extraordinarily sadistic.

The Lisbon Traviata, unbalanced as it is in more ways than one, offers insight into a type of homosexual psyche in its ripest confusion, at the level where both characters and author lose control, and we get a glimpse into an abyss that is deadly but uncathartic. Consider some key lines, most of them uttered by the author's alter ego. "People who don't like opera, don't like life." This is meant as irony, most opera being a kind of hyperbole antithetical to everyday reality, and *worshiped* by some (as opposed to *loved*) precisely for its unlifelikeness. "What's wrong with quiet [without an opera record playing]?" "You have to listen to yourself think." No comment required. . . . Finally—and in the context of murder, irony fades—this about the Humming Chorus from *Butterfly:* "Sometimes I think this is the most beautiful music ever written. Christ knows it's the most banal." The supreme beauty of banality? This is camp sensibility carried to its horrifying pinnacle. True, the protagonist is half mad by now, yet his murderous act is being justified in strange ways. If the banal can be beautiful, the unworthy can be sublime, the operatic perfectly normal, and murder just a part of life. So what was initially treated as a joke has become at least half accepted as the truth—as Cio-Cio-San's seppuku becomes equated with the stabbing of Mike. (pp. 68-9)

The first act, because it knows what it's about, is cannily funny; the second, because it doesn't, is uncannily revealing. (p. 69)

John Simon, "All Wet," in New York Magazine,
Vol. 18, No. 27, July 15, 1985, pp. 67-9.

JOHN SIMON

If ever a talented playwright suffered from second-act trouble, Terrence McNally is it. By far his most satisfying plays are *Next* and *Noon,* both one-acters, followed closely by *Bad Habits,* a seemingly full-length play made up of short ones. Only last summer, we had from him *The Lisbon Traviata,* consisting of an uproarious first act and an upchuckable second. Still, I for one refuse to give up on him—even as he, albeit differently, won't give up on me, usually sticking a verbal pin into my name in the course of his witty dialogue, thereby making sure of at least one laugh at one performance—mine.

Laughs, however, are not McNally's problem: He gets plenty in the current version of what, under a different title [*Broadway, Broadway*], was seen at least twice before. Now, as *It's Only a Play,* it's on view again, and if you are satisfied with an extremely funny first act and an inoffensive but rather aimlessly dawdling second, do catch this version; it may be months before the fourth one comes along. In a way, it's not McNally's fault if this second act doesn't work, for he has latched on to one of those funny situations that simply cannot be stretched far enough, as Moss Hart also discovered with his similar *Light Up the Sky.*

We have here a *pièce à clef* about a producer, Julia Budder, giving a party in her townhouse after the opening of *The Golden Egg,* written by the promising but frantic young Peter Austin; directed by the new whiz-kid director, Frank Finger, a fellow cursed with success and kleptomania; and having in the female lead Virginia Noyes, a pill-pushing actress who just flunked out of the movies. . . .

I'll tell you that Julia is based on Adela Holzer, the playwright on McNally himself, and *The Golden Egg* on **The Ritz;** for the rest, you're on your own. Among the unseen downstairs guests are numerous show-biz celebrities, named and joked about, and the casts of various current shows. On the phone, periodically, are sundry playwrights, producers, agents. In the dialogue are further references to theatrical figures and plays. *It's Only a Play,* you see, is a sort of grand McNally atlas of the theater, jaundiced as all get-out, and, for one act, just as funny. What it all works up to, besides tiny tizzies for all the players, is the coming of the reviews, notably the decisive *Times* one, and their effect on all concerned. But once the Frank Rich notice is in (and rather less funny than if Rich had written it), the play is played out; there is no more plot waiting in the wings, and, in any case, what further plot could fit into this format?

There are other problems. Some of the in-jokes are bound to elude all but the most ardent theatergoers; and some of the gags have a hard time being timely. When the play was done last, *Annie* was still around, and considerable mileage could be got out of the kiddable kiddies in it. Now, by a merely semantic nexus, McNally has substituted *Orphans,* whose grown-up cast does not fit his jokes. Also, the satire plays it too safe. . . . (p. 56)

> *John Simon, "The Plot Thins," in* New York Magazine, *Vol. 19, No. 3, January 20, 1986, pp. 56-7.*

BRENDAN GILL

[*It's Only a Play*] successfully breaks one of the strictest rules laid down by the founder of this magazine, Harold Ross; to wit, that writers should never write about writers writing. From his choice of a title to the final curtain, Mr. McNally is concerned with nothing but the anguish of being a playwright and the hilarity that this anguish can be made to yield for the rest of us, who are lucky enough not to be playwrights. Ross suspected that writers were too lazy to invent characters who were not writers, but plainly it isn't laziness that has caused McNally to violate the Rossian dictum; his comedy is charged with an energy that leaps and zigzags from the merely frantic to the hysterical. Obedient to the playwright's intentions, I found that the closer the many characters came to total mental and physical collapse the funnier I found them.

To call the plot wafer-thin is probably to insult wafermakers from coast to coast. An excitable young man . . . has written a play called *The Golden Egg,* and a wealthy woman . . . who happens to be wholly ignorant of the theatre has produced the play and is giving the obligatory opening-night party at her mansion on the upper East Side. . . . The tiny hinge upon which the plot turns is Frank Rich's review of the play in the *Times*—will it prove favorable or unfavorable? Such is the agreeable irony of the perpetual interplay between life and art that in the McNally play Mr. Rich dislikes *The Golden Egg* intensely, while in real life Mr. Rich likes *It's Only a Play* intensely. If Rich is the name most often dropped, we hear as well a hundred or so other names that resonate—or give off at least a slight hum—on Broadway, and to each of these names one or more jokes is effectively attached. Every one-liner I laugh at makes me a softer touch for the next; late in the evening, I laughed almost uncontrollably when a character inquired pensively, "How many 'p's are there in 'Papp'?" (pp. 90-1)

> *Brendan Gill, "Nil Nisi Bonum," in* The New Yorker, *Vol. LXI, No. 49, January 27, 1986, pp. 90-1.*

Paul Morand

1888-1976

French short story writer, novelist, nonfiction writer, travel writer, and poet.

Morand was one of the best-known French writers during the era between the two World Wars. In his work, Morand evoked the cosmopolitan atmosphere and energetic social life of this period while creating psychological portraits of hedonistic, often disillusioned characters. His witty, fast-paced, descriptive prose is rich in imagery and has led some critics to categorize him as a French modernist. Like several modernist writers, Morand dispensed with transitions between poignant events and images in order to sustain intense narratives. His work was praised by such literary figures as Marcel Proust, who wrote a preface for Morand's first collection of short stories, *Tendres stocks* (1921; *Green Shoots,* later published as *Fancy Goods*), and by Ezra Pound, an enthusiastic critic and translator of Morand's early work. While Morand was a popular and prolific writer during the 1920s and 1930s, he wrote sparingly after the onset of World War II. He was elected to the Académie Française in 1968.

After publishing two volumes of short, impressionistic poems, *Lampes à arc* (1919) and *Feuilles de température* (1920), which are valued primarily for his application of Dadaist techniques to verse form, Morand gained significant attention for *Tendres stocks.* Each of the three stories in this collection centers on the experiences of a female protagonist in London. Critics noted Morand's unusual use of imagery, which, as Marcel Proust commented, "joins things by new relationships." Morand's next book, *Ouvert la nuit* (1922; *Open All Night*), contains six stories, each set in a different European city, and each featuring a different female protagonist. He was praised for his impressionistic recreation of the atmosphere and idioms of these cities and for depicting characters whose moral confusion represented the feelings of many people during the post-World War I era. Morand's next collection of stories, *Fermé la nuit* (1923; *Closed All Night*), similarly portrays the chaotic lives of characters in various settings. His other short fiction collections include *L'Europe galante* (1926; *Europe at Love*), in which the common themes are love and sexuality; *East India and Company* (1927), twelve stories written in English and set in the orient; and *Magie noire* (1928; *Black Magic*), a series of stories in which black characters living in Western societies feel compelled to return to their African heritage. Morand's novels include *Lewis et Irène* (1925; *Lewis and Irene*), which dispassionately explores the ill-fated marriage of a French businessman and a Greek businesswoman, and *Bouddha vivant* (1927; *The Living Buddha*), which examines conflicts between East and West by depicting a twentieth-century Buddhist priest whose life parallels that of the legendary founder of Buddhism.

While a young man, Morand served as a cultural attaché to England, and he later became a diplomat and ambassador for the French government. In 1925, he began a series of travels to different continents. The speed at which he was able to travel and the wide variety of cultures he observed provided themes and settings for both his fiction and nonfiction. Among Morand's most acclaimed nonfiction works are his *Portraits de villes—New York* (1929), *Londres* (1931; *London*), and *Bu-*

carest (1935; *Bucharest*). Georges Lemaitre described these works as offering "a most original combination of geography, historical survey, picturesque description—and psychology. The blending of these various elements is so harmoniously achieved that at the end of each book the 'personality' of the city with which it deals stands revealed—as real, intense, and complex as that of a living human being."

Morand's sporadic literary output after the 1930s contributed to the gradual decline of his reputation as a popular and critically respected writer. His importance in French literature is debated; critics acknowledge his command of style and technique and his descriptive powers, yet several contend that his themes are often superficial and his observations on cultural characteristics are overly generalized. In addition, when he was first nominated to the Académie Française in the late 1950s, Morand was forced to withdraw his candidacy because he had served as ambassador to Switzerland for the Vichy government of Occupied France during World War II. Nevertheless, Morand's early stories continue to be regarded as representative of international literary and cultural tastes of the 1920s. In a review of *Fancy Goods; Open All Night: Stories,* the 1984 publication of Ezra Pound's translation of *Tendres stocks,* Richard Sieburth stated: "The Morand of these short stories is still news. . . . [He is] one of the great nomads of 20th-century

French literature, racing through the apocalypse with the haste and glamor of an Orient Express.''

(See also *Contemporary Authors,* Vols. 69-72 [obituary].)

MARCEL PROUST

[*The preface from which this excerpt is taken was originally published in* Tendres Stocks *(1921).*]

The Athenians are slow in execution. As yet only three young damsels, or dames, have been given up to Morand our Minotaur [**"Clarissa," "Delphine,"** and **"Aurora"**—the title characters of the three stories collected in *Tendres Stocks*]; seven are specified in the treaty. But the year is not yet over. And many unavowed postulants still seek the glorious destiny of Clarissa and Aurora. I should like to have undertaken the useless labor of doing a real preface for these charming brief romances, which bear the names of these beauties. But a sudden intervention forbade me. A stranger has taken her abode in my mind. She goes, comes, and soon despite her mobility her habits are become familiar to me. And moreover, she has tried like a too long-sighted boarder to establish a personal relation with me. I was surprised at her lack of beauty. I had always thought Death beautiful. How otherwise should she get the better of us? However . . . she seems to be absent for the day, this day. Doubtless a brief absence, if one can judge by what she has left me. There are more prudent ways of profiting by the respite accorded me than to spend it writing a preface for an author already known and who has no need of my prefaces.

Another reason also should have deterred me. My dear master Anatole France, whom I have not, alas, seen for twenty years, has just written in *La Revue de Paris* that all "singularity of style should be rejected." Now it is certain that Morand's style is *singulier,* personal. If I were to have the pleasure of seeing M. France, whose past kindness is still present and living to my vision, I would ask him how he can believe in a unity (or uniformity) of style when men's sensibilities are *singulier* (personal, particular, individual, different one from another). The very beauty of style is the infallible sign that the thought has risen, that it has discovered and knotted the necessary relations of things which their contingence had left separate (inapparent). (pp. 3-4)

The truth (M. France knows it better than anyone, for he knows everything better than anyone else) is that from time to time a new and original writer arrives (call him if you like Jean Giraudoux or Paul Morand, since for some reason unknown to me, people are always bringing Morand and Giraudoux together like Natoire and Falconet in the marvelous *Nuit à Châteauroux,* without their having any resemblance). This new writer is usually fatiguing to read and difficult to understand because he joins things by new relationships. One follows the first half of the phrase very well, and then one falls. One feels it is only because the new writer is more agile than we are. New writers arrive like new painters. When Renoir began to paint people did not recognize the objects he presented. Today it is easy enough to say that he is an eighteenth-century painter. But in saying it one omits the time factor, and it needed a great deal of time, even in the nineteenth century, to have Renoir recognized as a great artist. To succeed, the original painter, the original writer, proceeds like an oculist. The treatment—

by their painting, their literature—is not always agreeable. When they have finished they say: "Now look!" And there it is, the world which has not only been created once, is created as often as a new artist arrives, appears to us—so different from the old one—perfectly clearly. We adore the women of Renoir, Morand, or Giraudoux, whom before the artist's treatment we refused to consider as women. And we want to walk in the forest, which on the first day had looked to us like anything you like, except a forest—for example a tapestry with a thousand nuances, and lacking exactly the nuances of forest.

Such is the perishable, new universe which the artist creates and which will last till a new artist appears. To all which many things might be added. But the reader who has already suspected them will define them better than I could in reading **"Clarissa," "Aurora,"** and **"Delphine."**

The only reproach I might be tempted to offer Morand is that he uses images other than the inevitable images. No, all the "almost" images among images don't count. Water, in given conditions, boils at 100° centigrade. At 98° or 99° the phenomenon does not occur. In which cases he would do better to do without images. (pp. 11-12)

It seems as if our minotaur Morand had up to the present searched the detours of his "vast retreat," as Phèdre calls it . . .—in French and foreign palaces, built by architects inferior to Daedalus. From whence he watches the young ladies in dressing gowns, with sleeves fluttering like wings, young ladies who have had the imprudence to descend into the labyrinth. I know these palaces no better than he does, and would be of no use to him in solving their shrouded and fractious mystery. But if, before becoming an ambassador, or rivaling Consul Beyle, he will visit the Hôtel de Balbec, I might endeavor to lend him the fatal thread:

"Tis, I, my prince, tis I whose useful aid
Hath taught you the wrong turnings of the labyrinth."

(p. 12)

> Marcel Proust, "Preface to 'Fancy Goods'," in Fancy Goods; Open All Night: Stories by Paul Morand, edited by Breon Mitchell, translated by Ezra Pound, New Directions, 1984, pp. 3-12.

THE TIMES LITERARY SUPPLEMENT

After one has read (and thoroughly disliked in as far as an almost complete incoherence made dislike possible) the works of a group of young writers; after one has expressed this dislike quite frankly, it is a great pleasure to find a book by a quasi-member of the group which can be praised almost unreservedly. It is not that the impressive name and discursive reflections of M. Marcel Proust are attached to [*Tendres Stocks*], like a frontispiece of a slightly different style to a piece of architecture; even without M. Proust's guarantee we should have pierced through the prejudices created by M. Morand's former Dadaisme. If any of the other Dadaistes suddenly arrives with a work of prose or prose poetry or *vers libre* or verse as lucid and as brilliant as *Tendres Stocks,* we shall be happy to present him or them with a tribute similar to the barren parsley crown here woven for M. Paul Morand. . . .

To find an author writing with intelligence of a foreign country is remarkable, but to find one of the sedentary race of Parisians writing of England without falling into the absurdities popularized by M. Gabriel de la Rochefoucauld is indeed almost unique. M. Valéry Larbaud has done it and M. Paul Morand has done it, but how many other French pictures of England have been fabricated by the recipe invented by des Esseintes? There is something more than impressive in the thought of how much M. Morand has expressed in these three short studies of women. He gives us three admirable psychological portraits, which by themselves make his book worth reading; but he does very much more than that: he reveals to us a new, subtle, and most interesting personality (his own), an artistic method which is distinctly original; and finally he writes about England far better than most Englishmen. His gift of observation is immense, and if, as M. Proust declares, his images tend sometimes towards the "à-peu-près" the tendency is slight and the compensations manifold. He abounds in pleasing and malicious traits. . . .

M. Proust notes in his preface that a new writer of originality "is generally rather tiring to read and hard to understand, because he unites things by new affinities." This may be true in general, but certainly not of M. Morand in particular, whose prose on the whole is easy to read and to understand.

> *"M. Paul Morand," in* The Times Literary Supplement, *No. 998, March 3, 1921, p. 142.*

EZRA POUND

Proust in his preface to Morand's **Tendres Stocks** [see excerpt above] has greeted Morand and Giraudoux as the standard bearers, or something of that sort, of the new prose. They are different enough, Giraudoux piling up objective detail in a welter of words, trying to construct, and succeeding, along lines which Laforgue had used in satirizing the overloading of Salammbo; Giraudoux writing almost obviously for his own pleasure and out of his own subjectivity; Morand with buddhic eye contemplating the somewhat hysterical war and post-war world and rendering it with somewhat hasty justness. His somewhat unusual title may perhaps be translated Fancy Goods; one has met his ladies *"de par le monde,"* and technically Aurora must be exceedingly good, for one can hear the English woman's voice and speech throughout the story, and it cannot be easy to convey these tones of voice and idiom in a foreign speech. Aurora is English, just as Delphine is not English, and in the later stories I think he has sustained his differentiation of nationalities exceedingly well. And he has surely the first clear eye that has been able to wander about both ends of Europe looking at wreckage, and his present news value need not fail ultimately of historic validity. His people are as definitely real, of the exterior world, as Giraudoux' are subjective mechanisms. (pp. 461-62)

> *Ezra Pound, "Paris Letter," in* The Dial, *Vol. LXXI, No. 4, October, 1921, pp. 456-63.*

AFFABLE HAWK

Morand is the first writer I have come across who has treated like a man of letters those post-war phenomena which in the young generation alarm our moralists, depress our aesthetes and sadly gravel our elderly observers. M. Morand must excuse me if [in reviewing *Open All Night*] I appear more interested in his subject than in his skill. To his skill I take off my hat; but after that salutation I would not stop upon my way if, in my quality of baffled old buffer, I could not button-hole him in the certain hope of enlightenment. It is as a guide to the spiritual and social "devastated areas" I chiefly value his company. Yes, in spite of his tickling my imagination by the fine

precision of his unexpected metaphors, by the sensitive curiosity of his sensuality and his companionable gift of finding the exact and often witty word, I would not otherwise choose him as a companion with whom to explore experience. He has wit, sensibility, and an eye; he knows the meaning of the word "vanity"—great qualifications, but I seem to detect behind the brilliant play of observation and fancy an emotional lassitude. Eureka! I have placed him. Paul Morand is one of those authors who cannot afford, for a moment, to cease amusing and surprising us. If he did, we should hear only a brief little sigh.

It is therefore a sound instinct on his part which makes him decorate the surface of his page with clevernesses: "I loved her plebeian hands, her eyelids the colour of a fifty-franc note." . . . Yet, I must repeat for the sake of emphasis, that his instinct never to cease amusing and engaging our admiration is, in his case, an artistically sound one. As an *amuseur* he can, while thus socially employed, suggest that he is giving us, and indeed often in fact gives us, something more to think and feel about; but were he to approach his subjects directly, that emotional lassitude would betray him. He has no faith in the permanence or profundity of his emotional response to life; but he is artist enough to manipulate that indigence into an irony which flutters, very prettily, to and fro between the scenes and persons he describes and himself.

M. Morand is a post-war Loti. It is instructive to compare and contrast them. The aim of both writers is to capture "the spirit of place"—atmosphere. Both employ the same method; the approach in either case is through a woman. Japan, Samoa, Constantinople—Loti's impressions of these places which he transmits so vividly to us are, in each case, saturated in a particular love episode. It is through Madame Chrysanthème or Azäida that he has come to understand, and ultimately his readers also, Japan and Constantinople. Loti, himself, is always upon the scene, drawing our attention by his own wistfulness, sensuality and sorrowful romanticism at once from and to the places and people he describes. M. Morand is also always upon the scene, and in each case he, too, has his heroine; only as befits a post-war Loti, his affairs make no pretension to stir depths. Loti paraded a heart which was a jar to hold the tears of the world; M. Morand parades rather the gossamer flimsiness of his brief partialities. Indeed, without the spice of detachment, they would hardly be preserved one hour from "quickening into lower forms." Tenderness? Yes, he has it; and pity, too. But it is the tenderness and pity of an exquisitely cultivated sensorium upon which one flibbertigibbet after another impinges. . . .

Loti was a traveller; he visited many foreign lands and places. Although in *Open All Night* we visit Barcelona, Constantinople, Rome, Paris, Vienna, Buda and a Baltic town, and although the atmosphere of these places is wonderfully reflected, M. Morand is not so much a traveller on the face of the world as an explorer of a period in the world's history—the five years which have passed since the war ended. It is as a guide to the devastated spiritual areas that this book is—even waiving its fine literary quality—significant. Considered merely as a document, **"The Turkish Night"** has recorded for ever the mood of the Russian refugees in Constantinople. Nor have I read anything which brought so close to my apprehension the rush of subterranean savagery beneath a shabby yet superficially recovering civilisation, a torrent war has let loose, as the story of **"The Hungarian Night."** Jazz, cocktails, indifference on the top; a sparrow-minded courage that lives from moment to moment; death or sick poverty, an *oubliette* beneath. Let us forget, let us forget; there lies the source of fun and courage. It is at some such diagnosis as this of Europe 1918-1923 that the reader of *Open All Night* arrives when he lays down the book. And the whirling confusion is moreover highly diverting, at least to one who remembers, but without pained loyalty, standards and civilized discriminations. . . .

I have spoken of his emotional lassitude as a deficiency; I must not forget to admit that it is also a bridge between him and what he studies, enabling him to meet craziness half-way and understand it sympathetically. It is an asset to him as an interpreter.

> *Affable Hawk, in a review of "Open All Night," in*
> New Statesman, *Vol. XXI, No. 539, August 11, 1923,*
> *p. 523.*

GERALD GOULD

[*Open All Night*] in its pristine shape as *Ouvert la Nuit,* awakened in many critical breasts an enthusiasm which the English version certainly does not awaken in mine. To those who have read it, or propose to read it, in French, nothing that one can have to say about its English can be of much consequence. But the book is held important enough to be offered us by an English publisher for the English-reading public: and I cannot tell why. For my own part, I have not enjoyed it sufficiently to be tempted towards the original. Critics of weight, critics whose judgment I respect, have admired it extremely. I do not admire it—in English—at all. Mr. Middleton Murry has said: "A great many young Frenchmen have tried to do this kind of thing, and some Englishmen, but none of them have brought it off like this before." What is the kind of thing? The supposed teller of the six tales here collected is experienced, and at home everywhere, and the possessor of a light touch, and not at all afraid of implying, as any Englishman would be afraid of implying, that he is what in certain circles is called "a bit of a one with the girls." He talks about his "lustful, lying and inquisitive French soul." He gives details. **"The Catalonian Night"—"The Turkish Night"—"The Roman Night"—"The Six-Day Night"—"The Hungarian Night"—"The Baltic Night"**—those are the titles: and really it is all rather dreadfully like what those titles imply. There is wit there, and wisdom; but they seem of too narrow a sophistication. The wisest story—because the most human—is about a nobly ridiculous six-day cycle race. For the rest, there is a good deal that is cynical and "daring" on the subject of various types of women. It is a subject I have heard of before.

> *Gerald Gould, in a review of "Open All Night," in*
> The Saturday Review, *London, Vol. 136, No. 3546,*
> *October 13, 1923, p. 408.*

THE NEW YORK TIMES BOOK REVIEW

It is rather surprising that Morand's American publishers did not happen upon *Hothouse Plants* as their title for [*Green Shoots*]. It is certainly the idea that lay in the author's head in giving us his triple study of feminine Byzantism. [The title characters of **"Clarissa," "Delphine,"** and **"Aurora"**] are plants of the orchid family, brave in hue, fantastic, not to say misshapen, in form. They spring from soil enriched by uncanny fertilizers, the sort of soil where hybrids flourish but where a cut or scratch may mean tetanus. . . .

Morand's three studies are fantastic, unreal affairs, brilliantly written and full of what the wise Brontë children, when discussing literature in the nursery at Haworth parsonage, used to term "cleverality." Their author knows something about so many things. His mind is furnished to the point of incumbrance. We are always bumping against furniture or knocking over bibelots and hardly have time to notice the observations that hang framed upon the walls, often of an arresting wisdom and insight. The figures in his triptych are perverse creatures to whom impulse is law and whose characters are a compact of eccentricities. As no one can be held to account for the unaccountable, Morand evades the obligations of psychology which weigh heavily on more sober writers, and can indulge to the full his very real talent for surprising juxtapositions and the syncopation of ellipses. But the composition that results, vividly colored though it may be, is something as artificial and sterile as Clarissa's beadwork garden.

> *A review of "Green Shoots," in* The New York Times
> Book Review, *May 4, 1924, p. 22.*

ISABEL PATERSON

The titular figures of Paul Morand's *Lewis and Irene* are symbols rather than types. They resemble the angularized conventions of modern painting, which returns to the archaic in search of novelty. Lewis and Irene occupy the whole picture, . . . with hardly any background or perspective; yet they are distinctively of the present—contemporary myths, with a basis of fact like all myths.

Lewis is a composite portrait of the speculative promoter, nominally a Frenchman, but adventuring in the field of international finance. In taking up an option on a Sicilian sulphur mining property he found himself outmatched by a Greek firm, the Apostolatos Bank, represented by Irene Apostolatos, a young and classically beautiful Greek widow. Irene was a practical business woman, not a gambler like Lewis, but the daughter of generations of shrewd Greek traders and money changers. Drawn together by their unlikeness, Irene and Lewis fell in love, married, endeavored to give up their work in hope of attaining domestic happiness. Boredom ensued. (p. 83)

Yet though they could make an end of their marriage, they could not sever their business relations. When they ceased to be lovers they became partners. Whether this is meant as irony is not clear. Morand strives for detachment, carefully avoids any hint of a moral or a thesis. The sensualist Lewis is just a bundle of appetites and aptitudes without passion or real intelligence; he has the sleek sufficiency of a beast of prey. Irene is merely his opposite. Their behavior has no ethical meaning; it is like a series of chemical reactions. The book is clever, thin, and dry. (p. 84)

> *Isabel Paterson, "Men, Women and Manikins," in*
> The Bookman, *New York, Vol. LXII, No. 1, September, 1925, pp. 82-6.*

ROBERT LITTELL

Morand hangs somewhere between literature and journalism, in that limbo where notebook observation and creative synthesis work side by side, not fused together. He is a magnificent journalist, with an insatiable eye plundering Europe for acid incident and curious detail, of which he has accumulated such prodigious quantities that he has more than he can use, though he uses all of it. His chief vantage point is express trains, by long practice through the windows of which he has trained himself to catch places and characters on the wing. The stories in *Fermé la Nuit,* while not so well turned or human as those in *Ouvert la Nuit,* exhibit the full extent of his talent for the unusual, whether in people, incident or language. He cannot live without the unusual—upon normal ground he never recovers his sea legs, and seems a rather tired journalist, a little sentimental and strangely lacking in imagination. But in [*Fermé la Nuit*] his hard, restless, unpleasant but enviable talent is at its best.

> Robert Littell, in a review of "Closed All Night," in The New Republic, Vol. XLIV, No. 571, November 11, 1925, p. 312.

SIDNEY SHULTZ

Vulgar-minded folk of Paris or the provinces, whose taste for life's crudities is a stage above that which revels in peep-shows, should find satisfactory entertainment in Paul Morand's *Fermé la Nuit,* and the English translation of the book should bring pleasure to their American brothers. For through it a sensational panorama of exciting times in various cities during post-war days is unfolded, together with flashy records of the "fast women and sloe gin" in each. Gaudy adjectives hop through paragraphs in the volume like insects, and Monsieur Morand, disclosed himself as a kind of noisy ringmaster suffering under Don Juan delusions and a Casanova complex, makes them go through even queerer antics than he did in that earlier performance, *Open All Night.* His scenes, however, are as unconvincing as they are animated. Altho they contain rather clever touches in places, they are, as a whole, quite as unsound descriptions of the hectic period they are sketched from as were those days in actuality.

There is a fascination about these stories, but this is not the result of "strangeness mixed with beauty." Each makes the reader gape by its grotesqueness. One of the stories, concerning an Irish poet, a mysterious siren of a woman and the author, has its scenes laid, among other places, in a New York more fantastic by far than New Yorkers have ever known. (pp. 54-5)

A record of changing political offices in Paris is shown us, with the love for a charmer engrossing the central figure's mind during a political fray. Of this it may be noted that it contains keen impressions on amatory matters, yet these, like those on most other subjects handled by the author, are too burdened with fireworks to be truly effective. (p. 55)

> Sidney Shultz, "Closed All Night," in The Literary Digest and International Book Review, Vol. IV, No. 1, December, 1925, pp. 54-5.

EDWARD DAVISON

If one may be allowed the mixed metaphor, the champagne-like quality of Paul Morand's wit and humor is likely to be caviare to the general. Those who noticed its brilliance and sparkle, its aciduous tang in *Green Shoots* and *Open All Night* will hasten to enjoy [*Closed All Night*]. Morand invites comparison with Oscar Wilde and "Saki" (in his own rare realm of letters one of the inheritors of unfulfilled renown). Unlike his predecessors, however, Morand is not always merely witty for the sake of wit. His world, when we strip it of its high, fantastic colors is considerably less artificial than theirs. Beneath the bright, hard surface of his mind we may discover something of a tender and generous understanding of humanity,

its foibles and aims, such an understanding as Wilde and "Saki" did not know. In short, Morand's satire is not of the same superficial quality as theirs. It is something more than naked wit; it has a philosophic quality outstripping mere paradoxical badinage and persiflage. And yet Morand, though he has direction, appears to lack purpose. He is a philosopher without a philosophy. Most of the fine common sense which flows like an undercurrent against the hurrying stream of his satirical gaiety serves no constructive purpose. Wit rather than meaning is still the most outstanding element of his work. The old Voltairean chill still creeps into its atmosphere, but there is no compensating moment when Morand feels it necessary for man to cultivate his garden. Possibly the comparison takes our author too seriously. But in *Closed All Night* there are hints of a mind capable of deeper purposes than it has yet expressed, suggestions of an equipment which might be used to fine purpose beyond the bounds of mere amusement and gaiety.

Morand conjures with ideas, not for love of the ideas so much as love for the conjuring. He is indirect, preferring implication to his plain statement. He pins down his thoughts in crooked juxtaposition and leaves it to his subtlest readers to straighten things out. . . .

As before there is little that can be called a "story" in any of the four "nights" of the new book. We are carried through Cosmopolis on the same magic carpet that visited the world's capitals in *Open All Night.* There are the same kind of fantastic people and odd places, the same lights and shades of life as before, whether he takes us to Charlottenburg or Venice, New York or Putney. Morand is unquestionably a citizen of the world and he needs a sophisticated reader to appreciate his swift changes of mood and place. Even his casual descriptive sentences are loaded with keen wit of thought or phrasing. . . . And his aphorisms nearly always come home to our business and bosoms. "Women, especially very young women, have such a curious habit of attaching themselves to what is successful, never to what will be successful." Not a page of his book but has something as good as this.

> Edward Davison, "Morand's Nights," in The Saturday Review of Literature, Vol. II, No. 25, January 16, 1926, p. 491.

THE INDEPENDENT

[In the stories collected in *East India and Company*] Morand embroiders strange and exotic situations with patterns of brilliant if inconsequential characters, giving them all a peculiar charm which holds the reader unfailingly—but only until the story is done. It is all very well to say that the author is merely clever in an indolent and epigrammatic fashion. But there is in his writings the barb of indirect satire, the prod of a keen imagination and sometimes a feverish set of sensibilities which become immensely stimulating to the reader who is not bewildered by a sense of humor that beckons to rather than shouts at him or by literary skill that insinuates rather than bludgeons its way along. By their essential triviality are these tales made the more delightful.

> A review of "East India and Company," in The Independent, Vol. CXVIII, No. 4015, May 14, 1927, p. 520.

THE LIVING AGE

[In *East India and Company*] we see the Orient through the eyes of one of our most civilized European writers. All that is bizarre and interesting in the East is grist for the Morand mill, for in this book we find stories of Chinese phantoms, Siamese animal training, Hindu seraglios, international intrigue, and many other similarly diverting subjects.

East and West have been cleverly brought together here, as may be illustrated from the narrative woven around the skull of the horse of Genghis Khan, which, after being found in the heart of the Gobi Desert, must be taken to Paris before the author deems it advisable to conclude its remarkable succession of adventures. . . . Although some chapters smack strongly of being potboilers, [Morand] raises them above the level of hack writing.

Paul Morand, with the probable exception of Marcel Proust, is perhaps more widely known outside his own country than any other modern French writer. In this volume we do not get him at his best, but the delectable Oriental feast to which he invites us is well flavored with European spice and sophistication. It should not be ignored if one has the time and taste for such exotic dishes.

> *A review of "East India and Company," in* The Living Age, *Vol. CCCXXXII, No. 4307, June 1, 1927, p. 1031.*

LEWIS GALANTIERE

[In *East India and Company* we see] Morand's Big Show, playing under twelve tents. Lions, tigers, princesses, coolies, American beauties, harem ladies, ghosts, bolshevists—Paul Morand, Chinese Magician, pulls them all casually out of his silk hat, shows how they work, hands them over for your inspection—and in your hands, somehow, they vanish.

This conjuror never cheats. He makes a little speech before each trick, explains what he is about to do and how he will do it. But the hand is quicker than the eye. Before your believing incredulity has vanished the trick has been performed, and you are moved along to the next tent.

Morand has all the gifts. He knows everything that will please you and he does only the pleasant things, sells none but the most pleasing merchandise. If you ask me, as a shopper among summer books, where you can get more for your money than at *East India and Company,* I confess that I do not know. Swift grace, a light touch, an ingratiating smile, the genuine article as advertised—what reader would ask for more?

> *Lewis Galantiere, "Chinoiseries," in* New York Herald Tribune Books, *June 19, 1927, p. 2.*

CYRIL CONNOLLY

The conflict between East and West . . . is illustrated topically by M. Morand [in *The Living Buddha*]. This writer is always rather under a cloud in England, as he seems to epitomise the fashionable and superficial "valise" literature of France. His work is always an "article de Paris" swayed by clique-life and the export trade. As a matter of fact, he has improved steadily in seriousness and style, and is probably the most competent French epigrammatist now writing in the classical tradition, with depth of observation compared to his glib wagon-lit period. The story is of an Indian prince who goes to Europe led by a French adventurer, and tries to impose Buddhism on France, England and America. He fails and returns to govern his extremely Oriental kingdom. It is a result of M. Morand's Eastern journey and his desire to be in the know on the question of the day; the defeatist leaning of the Continent to the passive indifference of Oriental philosophy. The book is inclined to be too smart, English undergraduates do not make puns on "Universe" and "University." The hero changes too quickly into an ascetic; but the book is lively and illuminating, with a remarkable grasp of English institutions, and that mocking tenderness for France which is M. Morand's most serious emotion. The style is bold, with some perfect sentences, and shows the trend of French impressionist Bars-and-big-business style to leave slick fantasy for the lucid aqueous clarity of Voltaire and the seventeenth century. No amount of smartness unfortunately conceals its sentimentality. M. Morand is too genial and topical to be much more than a highly sensitive barometer, but there is true firsthandedness in his analysis of places, and he makes the apparent world as real as appearances are. The general result is to make one feel socially adventurous and desire to learn more about Buddha and the Orients of London and Paris. It is that competent kind of novel which the French are able to turn out, never tedious, never profound, in which nothing could have happened differently. (p. 358)

> *Cyril Connolly, in a review of "The Living Buddha," in* New Statesman, *Vol. XXX, No. 765, December 24, 1927, pp. 358-59.*

ROY TEMPLE HOUSE

Some European critics do not think so, but it seems to one Anglo-Saxon reader that Paul Morand is growing. *The Living Buddha* has humor, pathos, suspense, vigor, all the qualities of a good story, and withal a light, aristocratically personal touch which gives it a character all its own; and it maintains nearly always a certain thoughtfulness, seriousness, almost tenderness, and teaches a lesson—oh, a very tactful Gallic preachifying, I assure you, messieurs, dames; no indigestible Anglo-Saxon lesson, but a deft patting and tucking in of the covers at the end so that you feel as if something is proved and settled, even though it may have been settled by Buddha's ceasing to be Buddha. It is a book which it is a privilege to read. . . .

The theme is an ingenious inspiration. Paul Morand secured his plot, or a large part of it, by the simple expedient of going back over the recorded life of Gautama Sakya-muni, the Rajah's son of Kapilavastu, who became the Buddha, the Perfect One, and by repeating certain features of that life in a different setting—Kapilavastu, south of Nepal, India, in the sixth century, B.C., becomes Karastra, a backward independent state of Indo-China, in 1925 A.D. Again we have a young prince who despises tradition and longs for the attainment of truth, planning to throw off the fetters of royalty-to-be and seek wisdom honestly and freely. Hampered by a royal father, tempted by a woman, traveling, suffering, begging, loving, forgiving, learning, conquering the universe by conquering himself. (Some young student of contemporary French literature should make at least a Master's thesis out of a comparison of the two Buddhas.) Prince Jàli of Karastra, become King Indra the Third, is discovered at his coronation to have become the living image of the great copper Buddha above the temple.

The story has been told before, probably many times. Hawthorne told it in "The Great Stone Face," but Morand has done a thing which is much finer and more powerful. Hawthorne's edifying Ernest grew very quietly and rather easily to be something which he was clearly intended to be, as the worm becomes a butterfly or the pumpkin seed becomes a large, wholesome and comfortable pumpkin. Morand's Prince Jàli meets a million difficulties. He is misunderstood and discredited, he sees his well meant efforts to do good result in confusion and hurt, like Dorgelès' Saint Magloire. Worse than this, he is bitterly driven to the conclusion that his whole apostleship has been wrong and mistaken, and he finally attains to the Buddha by denying the Buddha, by a compromise, by the acceptance of slavery, by a return to lifeless conventions. . . .

As a story it is absorbing. The disillusioned young Frenchman who drifts into the perplexed East Indian's world as driver of his automobile and turns his thoughts to the mysteriously different mental constitution of the West, and who dies sordidly without having accomplished anything in life—anything except releasing the twentieth century Buddha and through him perhaps millions—touches the button for one of the dizzy world tours which are Paul Morand's specialty.

> Roy Temple House, *"Buddha and the Ku Klux," in* New York Herald Tribune Books, *March 18, 1928, p. 2.*

W. B. SEABROOK

This collection of fiction fantasies [*Black Magic*], shot through with passages of intense realism, is co-ordinated like the movements of a symphony around a central theme which is the stavistic reversion of the individual civilized Negro or Negress to ancestral savagery.

The key motif, however, as treated by M. Morand is far from simple. It develops almost like a wheel within a wheel, the two wheels always turning in opposite directions. In the outer wheel atavism plays the part of the villain; racial inheritance is a sinister, malignant force, almost diabolical, to which the Negro "succumbs," by which he is dragged down. Paradoxically, in the wheel at the core atavism becomes the hero of the dramas, and the Negro, instead of succumbing, as he seems superficially to have done, sloughs off a cheap veneer which is no good to him and harmoniously returns to the heart of life; Morand turns Manichean; the Devil becomes God.

The most extreme example of this wheel within a wheel occurs in a brilliant fantasy called **"Syracuse, or the Panther Man."** Dr. Lincoln Vamp, American Negro, rich, frock-coated, civilized, sound Republican and leader of his race, founder of banks, newspapers and fraternal insurance societies, goes to the Pan-African Congress at Brussels. He wanders into the Belgian Congo Museum and, left alone by chance with the ancient masks and fetiches, reverts completely to savagery and rushes out naked, bellowing. Here, then, is a theme to delight the Georgia colonels and prove their thesis that the Negro, no matter how seemingly civilized, remains always at heart a beast. But now hear the disturbing variations in counterpoint introduced by M. Morand as he develops that theme, with Dr. Vamp standing entranced in the museum:

> Face to face with the ancient masks and the tremendous drums, he saw how silly, how comical by comparison was his Syracuse uniform of Great Steward of the Knights of Samson. And in the faculty of piercing the soul of things those flint spear heads were richer than the science or prayer of the whites; swifter in reaching the core of the great living principle which was called God. Flee, they told him, leave America. Her fertility is but a show, and ruin broods over

her; her progress is an illusion; come back to the land where stones and trees speak in the name of the spirit.

> (p. 5)

Wyndham Lewis suggests, in his *Time and Western Man,* that the white intellectual "is suffering from an inferiority complex in his prostration before the Negro and the primitive in art, music and feeling." If I have suggested, by implication, that Paul Morand upholds any thesis of abstract Negro superiority, I have done him an injustice. He has, I think, an immense admiration for certain phases of the Negro character, and, to quote his own words, "the ultimate wisdom of a race contented with little, like all those who are beloved of God." But wherever the question of comparative superiority of one race or one civilization with another is involved, Morand pins the issue down, in the method of Epictetus, to "superior in what?"—the white, for instance, superior in intellect and industry, the Negro superior in emotional richness and capacity for joy.

The range of this book, geographical as well as psychological, is amazing. Morand knows Negro life in Harlem, Charleston, New Orleans, Hayti, Montmartre, the Ivory Coast, Timbuctoo, the Sudan, Equatorial Africa, Liberia. Before writing it he travelled 30,000 miles and visited twenty-eight Negro countries.

Eight tales emerge, distilled, brilliant, profound, fantastic, and often beautiful, for Paul Morand, now citizen of the world, diplomat, traveller, and many other things besides, began his career as a poet, and remains always above all other things a great artist. (pp. 5-6)

> W. B. Seabrook, *"The Ultimate Wisdom of a Race," in* New York Herald Tribune Books, *April 21, 1929, pp. 5-6.*

THE NEW YORK TIMES BOOK REVIEW

There has never been any particular depth to the work of Paul Morand. Like his Renaud in *The Living Buddha,* he "takes the world of the senses for what it is worth" and murmurs, "What's the use? One is beaten in advance." In *Black Magic* he takes the black races, whether they live in the United States, in Haiti, in Africa, for what they are worth as material for esthetic effects, as the decorative stuff of a smooth, high-geared prose that is modern in its surface aspects and not particularly searching. He uses his "thirty thousand miles" in "twenty-eight negro countries" as so much colored glass to stain the white dullness of this eternity of life, and in so doing he proves a very amusing person. But the words "amusing," "companionable," "witty" about cover this diplomat and littérateur who means to live well, "c'est-à-dire, le plus vite possible."

Black Magic hardly tries to humanize the negro. Its characters, "Congo" Taylor, Octavius Bloom, Dr. Lincoln Vamp, the Dictator Occide, Pam Freedman, King Mongku, are more in the line of silhouettes. Morand puts these silhouettes through many amusing paces, but it is surroundings that interest him to the exclusion of the heart. The Morand mind is like a very swift firefly. It darts, for example, at Octavius Bloom, a gentleman of such little color that he can "pass" for white, illumines for a moment the problem of the negro in Georgia, casts a swift glow on the tribulations of the black man who passes successfully at first in a Delaware seaside resort, only to come to discovery and grief, and then twists the story ironically. You perceive many implications, but Morand doesn't give you time enough to relate them to the individual Octavius Bloom. Thus, where he succeeds as an entertainer and a decorator, he fails as a writer of fiction—whose most profound duty is to create character.

And yet, in spite of his ultimate failure, there is one very fine thing about Morand. He is keenly alive to the details of the modern world; his stories are of our times. For example, he speaks of "two blacks beneath the red lamp . . . like negatives just showing their shape in the developer"—and the simile is distinctly modern. A dance floor shakes "like Brooklyn Bridge when the trolleys pass." . . . Of all the stories in **Black Magic,** **"The Black Tsar"** is the most effective. It combines fantasy and satire. There is fervor in it. In writing it Paul Morand seems to have been touched with some concern for what values are going to govern the world. He doesn't betray himself, but one feels certain that for once Paul Morand has removed his tongue from his cheek.

> *"Tales of the Negro in Paul Morand's 'Black Magic',"* *in* The New York Times Book Review, *April 28, 1929, p. 5.*

WALTER WHITE

Morand, despite his boast of having traveled thirty thousand miles in visiting twenty-eight Negro countries (countries in which Negroes live), might far more profitably have spent all this time and energy observing one Negro and finding out what that Negro's thoughts and reactions really were before he began to write [**Black Magic**]. Morand has most superficially though entertainingly looked at the outermost layers of Negro mentality; the result is an amusing and, at times, well written series of sketches of how Paul Morand thinks *he* would react were he a Negro. The low state of literary criticism in these United States is distressingly revealed by the reviews which have acclaimed Morand's "admirable detachment" and "cool objective realism" and by declarations that Morand's is "the first real picture of the Negro we have had."

Of what does this picture consist? Eight short stories laid variously in the United States, the West Indies, Europe, and Africa. . . . The thesis of them all is that Negroes, no matter of what training, environment, economic circumstance, mental development, character or admixture of white blood, revert to primitive savagery the instant their surface culture is scratched. Consider, for example, Morand's most silly example of hobby-riding in the tale, **"Syracuse."** A Negro, born in America, knowing little or nothing of Africa, a gifted business man and organizer, happens to wander into the Terhueren Museum at Brussels. There he sees a Congo mask—and promptly goes native. . . . **"Good-bye, New York"** tries ludicrously to tell how a colored woman, wealthy, educated, and so fair none could distinguish the presence of Negro blood, also "goes native" when white prejudice causes her to be abandoned on a world cruise in Africa. In only one story, **"Charleston,"** does Morand tread on sure ground when he tells of the results of the attraction a black man has for a Southern white woman in southern France.

Despite its meretricious character, born of mere cleverness with little intellect or intelligent observation back of it, there are in **Black Magic** numerous pages of brilliant descriptive writing. The stories are amusing and interesting. (pp. 770-71)

> *Walter White, "The Road to Africa," in* The Nation, *Vol. CXXVIII, No. 3338, June 26, 1929, pp. 770-71.*

THEODORE PURDY, JR.

Besides being an accomplished traveler, M. Paul Morand has always been a great enthusiast for things American,—even to the extent of comparing unfavorably such charming institutions as the Paris telephone service with the more impersonal American one. It is perhaps not surprising, therefore, that he devotes his new book [**New York**] to a lengthy paean in honor of our largest city, which he has visited and explored much as he visited and explored Timbuctu a few years earlier. His verdict is in the main extremely favorable, and his picture of the city, though in some ways it will be scarcely recognizable to Americans, is likely to be remembered and imitated by other travelers in the future. He has, in effect, provided a guide-book of New York, without the devastating completeness of Baedeker or the annoying lapses and omissions of the purely literary descriptions of the city by foreigners.

His book is addressed largely to the tourist in search of amusement, who expects to be astonished by New York, perhaps horrified, but always amused. There is a good deal in it that is inaccurate, and the spellings of American names are confused as only a French proofreader can confuse them, yet on the whole M. Morand has seen New York well and truly, as well as in the impeccable perspective of modernity which is so characteristic of all his work. . . .

The most striking thing about M. Morand's painless guide-book, however, is that it is already out of date. The interval between the author's last visit to New York and the publication of his book has seen a total shift, for instance, of interest and accent in the skyline of the city. . . . Yet the talent for assimilation, which has always been M. Morand's chief charm, as well as the great obstacle to his chance of writing anything lasting, is in this book ideally employed. Both the native and the passenger on an incoming liner may find things in his book which will bring the life of the city nearer and render it more understandable. In any case, M. Morand's interest in America is liable to repay both himself and the casual reader of his deceptively facile but extremely clever book.

> *Theodore Purdy, Jr. "Mr. Morand's Manhattan," in* The Saturday Review of Literature, *Vol. VI, No. 36, March 29, 1930, p. 876.*

FORD MADOX FORD

I hope a great many Americans all over the North American Republic will read M. Morand's book [**New York**]—and a number of New Yorkers. His New York is not yours nor yet mine, but it is none the less an admirable and legitimate corrective for the wrong ideas of a great many of us. M. Morand is in ecstasies over the Battery and the Aquarium on the Battery and the City Hall and the Fraunces Tavern and the other old "bits" of late eighteenth and early nineteenth century architecture of which there are so many, astonishingly prominent and unnoticed, down town in New York. And these and the history of the city he puts in the forefront of his volume—where none of us would think of putting them. And indeed to these admirable relics he devotes far more care of writing and attention than to the Great White Way, with which most of us would begin *our* accounts. The effect is a little startling, but I do not know that it is any the less salutary. For I do not know that it would do any one anything but good to remember that in New York America has a city that is actually older than St. Petersburg. If that were remembered and held in the forefront of the New Yorker's consciousness Gotham might have bestowed on it not merely the uneasy boastfulness of a population that is half uncertain whether the city's activities are not in the end manifestations of barbarism, but the deep affection that is given by its populations to a city that has ancient traditions and glories gracious in their decay. . . .

So we may well welcome M. Morand's book. It is, as I have said, astonishing in the order in which it approaches the features of the city, for in the case of most cities it is usual enough to begin with history and end with modernities, but the modernities and noises of New York so bang and blare across the oceans and the acres of a startled world that that world is apt to believe that she enshrines no other characteristics such as distinguish the lesser marts and fortalices of this globe. . . .

And the book is doubly astonishing in that it is the work of Paul Morand the brilliant impressionist, who with a few strokes of the pen has made us see half the cosmopolitan cities and barrooms that encircle the earth from China to Peru and then round back again by the other way. Not that there are not brilliant paragraphs devoted to the Paramount and the Roxy, or to the all-star teams of international ice-hockey matches, or to night courts, or to newspaper offices; or to skyscrapers, beauty parlors, Park Avenue, the Metropolitan Museum, Harlem by night or Bill Robinson, Texas Guinan or the downtown Jewish theaters. But these brilliances bulk very little in the book; and that, no doubt, of necessity, since you cannot be both brilliant about and dwell long on such things as the shafts of light over the Broadway after-theater crowd. On the other hand, you can write for long about the place occupied by Washington Square in the development of the early social life of New York, and you can write for long and lyrically about Brooklyn Bridge by night or the Jewish or any other quarter. . . .

So that M. Morand's New York is astonishingly welcome in that it is not a series of coruscations. To read it is to have a justly balanced impression of the city as a workaday place, with its historic evidences and its earnestnesses. The fires of its "night-life" blaze—but only after dark—as if from an immense pyre, the beacon on top of a vast skyscraper; but they remain at the top of the pyre and do not threaten the destruction of the civilization below. Equally Wall Street has its place in M. Morand's record, but not more than its place; indeed it is with singular equanimity that he treads the rough roadway of the usually all too glamorous ravine. Yet in most impressions of New York the loom of the night life and of Wall Street is so all-overwhelming that you might well think that Gotham did not possess anything so sublunary as a municipal government, a laboring population, factories, docks, studios, orchestras and garrets in which starve the poets of tomorrow. And the most numerous and the most harmful impressions of New York are formed by those who have never been there. For them Wall Street and night life stand up as a pillar of smoke by day and of fire all the rest of the time. You gain fifty million dollars in ten minutes and spend the rest of your life among nudities in blazing cellars. . . .

It is that image of corruption—for there is no image so corrupting as that of too easily gained fortune squandered in too ignoble indulgences—that, in vulgar minds, New York presents of herself to the world. And it is because M. Morand's book is admirably corrective of those impressions—because of that, if for nothing else, we should be grateful to him. That you or I or any one else should see eye to eye with him in every particular of his close-packed work it would be unreasonable to expect. You will object to a paragraph on page 131;

your charming cousin will still more dislike the whole of pages 171 and 172. But that is only to be expected. (p. 2)

Ford Madox Ford, "To Gotham in the Fall," in *New York Herald Tribune Books, November 9, 1930*, pp. 1-2.

MILTON H. STANSBURY

As a diplomat and bohemian, Morand was in an excellent position to take the pulse of a shattered and delirious Europe. A part of the routine of his life was to hear the din of cabarets, and to be the guest of many establishments, whether "open" or "closed" at night. Here he heard many a strange tale and confession from the human wrecks who frequented them. The commonplace had no attraction for him, and wishing to make a methodical investigation of strange derelicts whom the War had cast adrift, he scoured the haunts of dissipation and vice in quest of his subjects. He sought the wandering, unprotected girl, the drug addict, the degenerate, the social outcast; in short, any human embodiment of moral and intellectual degradation. Dragged as it was through all the dives of Europe, it is small wonder if his bag became soiled and scarred. Although the pulse he counted was undoubtedly authentic, it was never the healthy or normal one, but always the irregular rhythm of debauch and anarchy. "When Morand learns that a revolution is brewing," jeers one French critic, "he rushes to the place to observe it." From these plague spots he brought back many a fantastic tale to convince the humdrum stay-at-homes of his rare and penetrating psychology. Rareness it possessed, but hardly depth, for in confining his choice to extreme and unusual types viewed from violent angles, Morand was merely reporting what only too glaringly struck the eye.

With his curiosity about life, his genius for taking brilliant flashlights, his ability to capture in a few vigorous strokes the picturesque and essential elements of every scene, and his flair for the eccentric, he extracted from his experiences vivid material for excellent short stories. A superficial thinker, uninterested in the analysis of character, he was not well qualified to be a novelist. Completely indifferent to all moral problems, he certainly had no interest in the soul. He is not even a highly lettered man, and by his own account has reduced his reading to a minimum. Not intellectual, but exceedingly intelligent, he drew his vast information from the spectacle of the world about him, for his special gift is that of the reporter who observes and visualizes. Instead of utilizing his cosmopolitanism to sift out all the qualities of his era, he carefully skimmed it of everything but its deformities and vices, and seems to have explored the globe with the express purpose of discovering only the worst.

Obviously mesmerized by the corruption of post-war Europe, he accepted its demoralization as irreparable. "We are inclined to believe," reads the citation from a treatise on hydrogen oxide which prefaces his *Europe galante,* "that the voluptuous sensations which many people seem recently to have experienced are due to an incipient asphyxia." This would be an appropriate introduction for most of Morand's early work. Attributing the prevailing mental and moral aberration to the purely chemical reaction from these poisonous gases, he applied himself to a cool examination of the more colorful manifestations of the disease. If we are to take him at his word, most of his stories are personal experiences, and reveal the author now at Moscow, now at Constantinople, now at Budapest, as a roving, if usually frustrated Don Juan. Untroubled by conscience, never indulging in introspection, he writes a diary of facts and abstains from personal reflections. In addition, he possesses that rare faculty of being able to judge dispassionately a life of which he has been himself a part. (pp. 84-5)

Where Giraudoux's universe is like a still landscape bathed in sunshine, Morand's much more vigorous art presents a realistic world with sharp architectural lines and intense shadows. Far from ignoring ugliness, Morand welcomes and emphasizes it, for he believes that by coarsening and depoetizing he avoids the commonplace. When his picture needs a cat, he may be depended on to select one that limps. If a theatre is full of people, he focuses the spotlight on those feminine backs with "ossicles and knotty bands, itching and flat like paving stones." Granted that Barcelona lacks beauty, Morand presses the point by comparing its porters' lodges to tumors, its chimneys to varicose veins.

However, it might be a mistake to suggest the removal of these ugly realities, for when in his later books he resorts less frequently to imagery, freaks of style, and brutal fancies, how dull and tame he becomes! Grown used to these verbal cocktails, we find insipid a less highly flavored drink. Expanding his vision in the *Chroniques* and the *Voyages*, Morand devotes less attention to his style, and his literary distinction proceeds in inverse ratio to this expansion. He states somewhere that, weary of his former pyrotechnics, which everyone was imitating, he strove to sober and simplify his phrase. Whether or not Morand has ceased to value sophisticated recognition, he has been content for a number of years to produce a series of none too carefully written best-sellers. He evidently prefers to be read once by the profitable multitude than to be reread by the discriminating few. . . . If formerly he wrote because he traveled, he now travels because he wants to write. Where, in *Tendres Stocks,* you could imagine yourself turning the fanciful if artificial pages of Giraudoux, in *Magie noire* or *Champions du monde* you might be perusing a *Harper's Bazaar,* while much of his travel literature is hardly more than glorified Baedeker. Stepping into immediate fame with *Tendres Stocks,* creating a literary furor with *Ouvert la nuit,* adding to his triumphs with *Fermé la nuit,* Morand never surpassed nor equaled his early efforts. Indeed, it would have been difficult to improve upon his first masterpieces. There were many gifts he lacked; those he did possess were preëminent. A mature and skilful artist from the first, he dazzled the world by the audacity of his imagery, the keenness of his observation, his glitter, originality, and verve. His very vitality proved a pitfall, for in addition to his diplomatic duties and his travels to the four corners of the globe, he likes to keep his name before the public with one book, sometimes two, a year, and it is not to be expected that five novels, six collections of short stories, seven volumes of travels, one pseudo-historical study, countless magazine articles, and, to omit nothing, the inevitable volumes of adolescent verse—all of these appearing within the short span of some thirteen years—could maintain an equal standard of excellence. It is more surprising that his talent was born as it were full grown, than that with time its original brilliance tarnished. (pp. 97-99)

Milton H. Stansbury, "Paul Morand," in his French Novelists of Today, *1935. Reprint by Kennikat Press, Inc., 1966, pp. 83-99.*

GEORGES LEMAITRE

[Morand's] first publications—*Lampes à Arc* (1919) and *Feuilles de Température* (1920)—were collections of short poems, most of them referring to circumstances or impressions of the war and the armistice period, many being obviously inspired by Morand's own experiences in England, Italy, and Spain. They all bore the stamp of a fundamental pessimism and of a restless imagination; with their jerky, syncopated style they sounded an unmistakable note of challenge to *bourgeois* common sense and the rational conception of things. Morand was then in the vanguard of the young artists who thought that the old civilization was dying and that a hard, cold, shoddy, industrial, banal new system was about to take its place. Between the two worlds, one already moribund and the other yet to be born, these young artists were striving to create a strange new language of their own to express their agony and their forebodings.

Tendres Stocks (1921) was conceived somewhat in the same spirit. The three short stories about three young women, drifting in war-time London, were but a pretext for an indictment of the precarious state of contemporary morals; yet the style was less frantic and dislocated than in Morand's previous writings, and his evolution in the direction of the ideals of 'La Nouvelle Revue Française' was clearly marked.

Ouvert la Nuit (1922) and *Fermé la Nuit* (1923) brought Paul Morand instantaneous and lasting fame. In these two collections of short stories, he conjures up with haunting intensity the very atmosphere of some typical social groups in turbid, post-war Europe. *Lewis et Irène* (1924), a full-length novel in similar vein, was not an unqualified success. *L'Europe Galante,* though not published until 1925, belongs to the same group of works; in it the themes previously presented in the *Nuits* were repeated in a more daring key, fully justifying the translation of the title used in the English version, *Europe at Love.*

At this stage of his moral and literary evolution, Morand appeared as the most typical representative of the fascinating though unbalanced post-war period and also as its most genuine and adequate interpreter.

In 1925 Morand's life took a new turn; the Ministry of Foreign Affairs sent him to Siam to assume charge of the French Legation in Bangkok. To reach his new post, Morand crossed the Atlantic, raced over the American continent from New York to Vancouver, traversed the Pacific to Yokohama, skimmed along Japan, saw Peking, Shanghai, Hong Kong, Macao, touched Singapore and finally arrived at his destination—Bangkok. (pp. 319-20)

This trip round the world was for Morand the starting point of a new life and the beginning of an almost entirely different outlook on people and things. Up to 1925, he had travelled to and fro all over Europe, but in most cases these journeys had been made as rapidly as possible from one capital to another, and the main experience gathered from these various trips was a thorough knowledge of the ways and uses of international trains and of the comparatively small steamers which threaded the narrow European seas. The girdling of the earth afforded him entirely fresh revelations—the powerful poetry of distance, the lure of the great open spaces, and the spell of the colourful pageant of a world full of rich contrasts. He discovered new problems, broader, more compelling, than the questions of morals or of maladjustment amongst Europeans which had, until then, claimed the greatest part of his attention. (pp. 320-21)

The way in which he had had to travel seems to have determined definitely the trend of his new ideas about 'the earth.' Receiving orders to proceed at short notice to his legation at Bangkok, he could not roam leisurely about but was obliged to rush headlong to his destination, meanwhile snatching impressions as best he could. The speed with which oceans and continents flashed across his vision forced on him the impression that the earth was very small indeed. Again, his contact with coloured peoples, especially during his sojourn in Siam, caused him to realize the supreme importance of racial even more than national problems at the present day. Henceforward the two questions—the influence of speed of transportation upon contemporary life, and the puzzling considerations of ethnical psychology were to be the main preoccupations of his mind. (p. 321)

His writings during this period were of two kinds. Some were direct accounts of his travels up and down the earth; *Rien que la Terre* (1926), *Le Voyage* (1927), *Paris—Tombouctou* (1928), *Hiver Caraïbe* (1929). Others were more elaborate studies of the moral characteristics of the large human groups, with which Morand had come into contact in the course of his travels outside Europe, and which seem to hold within themselves the future of mankind: the yellow races in *Bouddha vivant* (1927), the black in *Magie Noire* (1928), the American people in *Champions du Monde* (1930). In these ethnical studies which are presented in the form of novels, Morand did not try so much to expound theories or to make predictions as to offer an objective picture of the most typical aspects of the modern world. Appropriately he gave to this series of studies, recording the outstanding features of contemporary civilization, the collective title of *Chronique du XXᵉ Siècle*. The book *L'Europe Galante* is included in the series, though in truth this selection of short stories concerning the ways and byways of love in postwar Europe, belongs to an anterior and different stage of Morand's outlook on life, and seems to have been linked rather artificially to the three other volumes of the *Chronique du XXᵉ Siècle,* perhaps merely for the sake of symmetry, in order to include Europe along with Asia, Africa, and America. (pp. 322-23)

In the mass of miscellaneous writings produced by Morand since [the onset of] the depression, it is possible to distinguish four separate, different trends. First, his most original contribution to literature during this period is perhaps his *Portraits de Villes,* striking and penetrating studies of *New York* (1929), *London* (1931), and *Bucharest* (1935). . . . He had become thoroughly well acquainted with London in his early twenties and he was personally linked to Bucharest by his marriage. In each case, thanks to his own very special *flair,* he achieved, though in different ways, original, and colourful masterpieces.—Secondly, Morand became for a while an aviation enthusiast. His air-travel impressions of South America, described in *Air Indien* (1933), and of Central Europe in *Flèche d'Orient* (1931), struck a shrill, modern note new to his work, though completely in harmony with his general conception of life.—Thirdly, the growing political and social unrest in France about this same time caused him to turn an anxious eye upon the internal troubles perplexing his own country. A retrospective view of *1900* (published in 1931) helped him to take a measure of the rate at which France had been changing since the days of his youth. In the ironical *France-la-Doulce* (1934) and in *Rond-Point des Champs Elysées* (1935) he examined more directly some of the disturbing problems and difficulties which beset contemporary French civilization.—Finally, in the reflective mood of a man in his forties, he began to turn reminiscent and to look back wistfully at his own past life in *Papiers d'Identité* (1931) and in *Mes Débuts* (1933).

These many different and sometimes quite divergent directions which Paul Morand's writings have taken in recent years have

been a puzzle to the reading public and have made it difficult to determine the real import of his work. Yet his work does carry a meaning and possesses an original value of its own. Its unity does not lie in the formal similarity of the various subjects treated but in the identity of spirit which inspires all his books—the spirit of our modern time. Beyond any doubt Morand is the most typical representative and interpreter in French literature of the world of today, with its manifold and rapidly changing phenomena, with its over-intellectual culture, its crude and callous display of efficiency and power, its sharp and violent racial and national antagonisms, its fundamental restlessness, its moral frailty, and its fervent longing for a recovery of order and balance. All these complex and sometimes contradictory feelings and aspirations Morand has experienced within himself, because the circumstances of his life have moulded his personality in such a way as to make him particularly apt to understand and to express the idiosyncrasies of his time. (pp. 324-26)

It is perhaps in his accounts of rapid, hasty journeys that Morand's original qualities are displayed to best advantage. Whereas usually travellers prove most interesting when they have been able to proceed in leisurely fashion, taking time to observe, Morand strikes the deepest, most personal notes when he has been compelled for some reason or other to proceed with all possible speed. He is unrivalled then in his vivid rendering of the fleeting or acute impressions that the traveller experiences on a fast train, a great liner or an aeroplane. (p. 338)

The very speed with which Morand accomplished most of his travels made him acutely conscious of the contrasts between different countries, as well as of the most general and striking features of the regions through which he passed. . . . Moreover, the modern ways of living and thinking, as a result especially of the rapidity in transportation, make it imperative that the whole earth be conceived as a unit and that the relations between its different parts with their prevailing characteristics be understood simultaneously.

Morand's insight is exceptionally keen. When he has to pass through a country rapidly, his vision is thoroughly individual, reaching spontaneously the most typical features, presenting new and unexpected images of reality, and yet conveying the irresistible impression of truth. However, if his pace is slower, his view becomes normal, average, almost banal. His book *Rien que la Terre* is the most typical example of this. The chapters in which he describes his hurried trip round the world have a vivid and fascinating quality; those in which he deals with the customs of Siam—where he stayed for a few months—are reminiscent of the picturesque descriptions in a Baedeker guide-book. Morand is himself, his inimitable self, when he evokes in a few illuminating sentences the fundamental aspects, the irreducible antagonisms, the unsuspected affinities of nations, races, and continents—as seen by a man who really possesses a sense of the earth as one harmonious whole. (pp. 339-41)

Portraits de Villes (*New York, Londres, Bucarest*) offers a most original combination of geography, historical survey, picturesque description—and psychology. The blending of these various elements is so harmoniously achieved that at the end of each book the 'personality' of the city with which it deals stands revealed—as real, intense, and complex as that of a living human being. Though Morand does not rigidly follow the same method in each case, he begins normally with a study of the primary physical conditions, the cradle of the infant city, as it were; then he follows step by step the growth of the developing organism, and finally presents in rich and varied display its present, multiple aspects. At each stage of the exposition, Morand is not content with merely stating the facts—which he does with commendable precision; he is above all anxious to explain their meaning and full significance. His penetrating and intelligent interpretation excels in establishing the constant, interlocking relationship between the material elements and the human factors, in emphasizing the spiritual value of each feature, and also in indicating the relation of the urban development to its national and moral surroundings. New York is shown as a representative and yet abnormal element of American life, London as a faithful expression of English ideals and culture, Bucharest as a mirror of Roumania's unhappy history and everlasting charm. So the very spirit of a city gradually emerges from a multitude of seemingly insignificant details and is vigorously summed up at the end in telling and pungent phrase.

There is nothing theoretical or abstract in these studies of urban phenomena. On almost every page Morand sets forth an original impression, strikes a personal note. Each city is considered from a thoroughly individual angle. (pp. 349-50)

Morand's style to a large extent reflects [his] conception of existence. His sentences are not at all regular, organized, or well composed. They sparkle with intelligence; but the grammatical construction is constantly dislocated for no obvious reason. He pays little attention to the rhythmic cadence of his phrases; he never cares to round off a nice period with well chosen and sonorous words. From time to time, however, there surges up unexpectedly some intense, rich, pungent expression in which all the evocative and suggestive power of the passage is concentrated, giving the reader the shock or the thrill of a direct and entirely unconventional vision of reality.

To achieve these effects, Morand uses the following method: he first writes in a connected manner a full and fluent account of what he has to relate. Then, in the very middle of his text, he deliberately cuts out all the transitions and connexions,— all the spontaneous but superfluous literary padding that has grown round his original, simple, clear thought. He goes even further and strikes out a number of those words that find their way into a clause in order to satisfy the exigencies of the syntax but which do not in themselves carry any particularly interesting signification. For instance, the verb *est* and the expression *il y a* are very often omitted, and many a formal sentence is cut down to a noun followed by several grammatically unconnected attributes. Approximately one third of a first version is eliminated by this method; the rest is given to the public untouched and unpolished, in a sketchy but extremely arresting form.

This manner of composition conveys to the reader an impression of great rapidity. The mind has to leap quickly from one idea to another; all the intermediary stages of thinking have been suppressed; in many a clause only the indispensable element has been retained; throughout the whole the reader is rushed along at full speed as though by a telegraphic impulsion. Yet speed must not be taken here as a synonym for conciseness. Morand does not possess the art of expressing a great deal in a few well chosen and highly significant words. His technique is one of suppression rather than of compression—though the result for the casual reader amounts to practically the same thing. (pp. 387-88)

But the most striking feature of Morand's style is his abundant, queer, and aggressive imagery. The most surprising, far-fetched yet often illuminating comparisons give his prose an entirely personal accent. Many critics have protested against his extraordinary metaphors. . . . The literary images presented by Morand are certainly not inevitable ones; they cannot even be called natural; they rest upon artificiality. For instance, he will quite systematically assimilate some physical feature of a human being, or some normal aspect of natural scenery, to a manufactured object,—and invariably to one, not only of the most trivial use, but also of the most emphatically modern application. Yet after the first shock of surprise one is bound to recognize that these seemingly irrelevant suggestions often indeed disclose subtle, realistic affinities between persons and things apparently very far remote from each other. Thus Morand compares the discoloured eyelids of a *femme galante* to the yellowish-grey French fifty-franc notes. (p. 389)

Fatigue and strain too often result from prolonged contact with Paul Morand's works. A multiplicity of vivid splashes of colour, brilliant touches, and startling contrasts, more or less disconnected, without any toning down whatever of their lurid intensity, flash past our eyes at almost cinematographic speed. The spectacle is exciting, fascinating, intoxicating; but even if new aspects of beauty are revealed now and then, the hard, pitiless light falls more often than not on dismal and distressing objects. The quickness of the pace seems to multiply their occurrence. Contrasts are too sharp, clashes too frequent, changes too rapid—the procession dissolves itself into a dizzy, fluttering show. But who among us would not recognize in these features the very characteristics of our modern times? Morand offers a typical case of perfect adaptation of an author to his chosen topic. His defects and his merits, are they not the defects and merits of the world today? That is why he has been able to express so well its anxieties and its forebodings. That is why his recording of our ordeals and woes will remain permanently one of the most invaluable and illuminating testimonies of the spirit of our age. (pp. 391-92)

> *Georges Lemaitre, "Paul Morand," in his* Four French Novelists: Marcel Proust, André Gide, Jean Giraudoux, Paul Morand, *1938. Reprint by Kennikat Press, Inc., 1966, pp. 303-92.*

PATRICK McCARTHY

Paul Morand's writing is a part now of the early 1920s. His name evokes Bugatti cars, Paris jazz-clubs, Victorian gentlemen ageing graciously in London clubs, American flappers, bankrupt German businessmen and, for a final dose of exoticism, the first snows of revolutionary Russia. The heroines of his early stories flit from capital to capital and make passionless love in luxury hotels. They seem to have turned out badly but that does not matter because, as one of them says, Europe itself has turned out badly.

Morand did not invent the theme that modern sensibility is mobile and fragmented, he inherited it from a writer whom he admired—Valéry Larbaud. . . .

Although he was only seven years younger than Larbaud, Morand looked back at the enchanted world which had been destroyed in 1914. What remained for him, he felt, was the anguish of modernity without the joy. *Chronique du XXe siècle* reprints four of his earlier books, one of which, *L'Europe Galante* (1925), is a series of sketches about modern love. Three women describe the men they love; these men seem to have nothing in common yet they turn out in the end to be the same man. Again, a man who is in love with a woman seduces another woman who resembles her. Morand's characters invent love-objects quite different from the people whom they supposedly love. Experience crumbles, his characters start looking for fresh loves which invariably turn out to be mirages and the heady passions of [Larbaud's] *Les Enfantines* are replaced by emptiness.

The fading of a dream is also the subject of his *Champions du monde* (1930). In 1909 four young Americans are leaving university. Since they are athletic, handsome and talented, the world promises them much. Twenty years later one has been driven to suicide, another is a bored dilettante, the third is an exhausted, puritanical diplomat and the fourth has fled to the Soviet Union where he is, we are to hope, living happily ever after. All of them have been ruined by American women, before whom Morand feels a trembling awe. The dilettante, Van Norden, lives out a silent expatriate's life dominated by his mother. . . .

Morand's work is drearily repetitious. Innumerable cosmopolitan love stories, where only the décor varies, all prove that human beings cannot make contact. The characters are shallow because Morand is not sufficiently interested in them to take them seriously, while the plots move predictably to their gloomy conclusions. Larbaud had understood that the glittering fragment of experience should be allowed to hang in its void, and that a writer who kept lamenting the emptiness of the modern world risked becoming a bore. Although the stories of Morand's *Magie noire* (1928) juxtapose Southern plantations, Haiti and the Congo, the characters all behave in the same way. Blacks, Morand tells us, inevitably revert to the jungle! A black American doctor goes to a museum of African art and regresses into an animal. A black American woman who travels to Africa ends up as the wife of a native.

Larbaud had stressed that cultures resemble one another, but Morand is convinced that cultures are fundamentally different and that "the twentieth-century's only crime of passion will be racial wars". In *Bouddha vivant* (1927) he depicts a Frenchman, Renaud, who visits the East, learns nothing from it and ends up as a chauffeur driving a Bugatti in an Asian princedom. The prince who employs him is inspired by Renaud to visit the West, where he too learns nothing, tries to convert the French to Buddhism and almost dies of starvation.

Morand's cosmopolitanism led him back to a crude nationalism. He believed that France was already losing the racial war. Jazz was the weapon which the mongrel hordes were using to penetrate Europe; American saxophonists were the enemy's cavalry, and behind them came the army of foreign immigrants: Asians spreading Buddhism, refugees from Eastern Europe who were Bolshevik spies, and so on. Meanwhile the French were embracing their conquerors as if in a suicidal frenzy. . . .

Naturally, Morand was antisemitic. In the books he wrote in the 1920s the Jew appears in his usual roles of foreigner, betrayer and insidious immigrant who was able to disguise himself as English banker, Russian revolutionary or even progressive Catholic. The Jew is both victim and executioner. One of the stories in *Ouvert la nuit* (1922) describes a pogrom in Hungary, while in *Les Champions du monde* the Jew, Nadine, first destroys her husband and then rises to become a duchess, her husband having proclaimed that he could not be a part of American society because he was Jewish, that he had "a sick mind in a sick body" and that he carried poison with him at all times because he was fascinated by suicide.

In the preface to *Ouvert la nuit* Morand compares himself with the Jew, his fellow-cosmopolitan, a well-documented trait among antisemites, who feed their own fears. Terrified by his vision of a bankrupt Europe, Morand blames it on the Jew rather than take any responsibility for it himself. Another theme common to so much French antisemitism is the fear of women, especially blonde, Aryan women. In *Bouddha vivant* the prince suffers his final defeat at the hands of a New Yorker, Rosemary, a "tall beautiful Aryan angel" who is initially tempted by the East but later feels for the prince "a terror which rises up from the depths of her race". In general, Morand's heroes, who seem like triumphant Don Juans, are weak when confronted by women and their resentment of this weakness is transmuted into hatred of the Jew, which allows them to assert their equality with the Aryan goddesses who despise them.

In the 1930s Morand grew even more antisemitic. In 1934 he published *France la Doulce*, a banal racist novel about Jewish refugees from Germany who take over the French film industry which displays more than a merely superficial, social antisemitism. His nostalgia for Barnabooth's Europe misled him and prevented him from understanding his own age. . . .

Morand will be remembered for two things: for early books like *Tendres Stocks* (1921), and *Ouvert la nuit* and *Fermé la nuit* (1923) and such travel books as *New York* (1929) and *Londres* (1933).

New York is inspired by the panic-stricken exhilaration which the city inspires in Morand; it is a book about a dream and a nightmare. He admires the aristocratic families who created the city—the Stuyvesants and the Van Cortlandts, the Vanderbilts and the Goulds. He relishes the elegant houses on Washington Square but cannot forget that the men who built them were robber barons, Protestants and captains of industry in comparison with whom a French writer feels unsure of himself. Modern New York overwhelms Morand: the skyscrapers are too high, the *NY Times* is too heavy, the Broadway lights are "epileptic" and thousands of animals have been butchered to make the fur coats which are draped around the elegant, inaccessible women of Fifth Avenue. Morand the cosmopolitan is delighted by New York but Morand the traditionalist is appalled. Sometimes his discomfort is comical: he spends hours looking for an "authentic" black jazz-club in Harlem and gulps down huge, unwanted steaks in bleak self-service restaurants.

London also frightens Morand. In 1933 the streets are full of hunger-marchers and tramps, while the newspapers issue gloomy prophecies of economic disaster. Morand looks back to late-Victorian and Edwardian London, which he half-remembers and half-invents. When he first came here in 1903, English puritanism so impressed him that he did not dare take photographs on a Sunday because he thought it was forbidden. Yet he enjoyed the ceremony of the city. He talks of Victoria's coronation as empress of India and of her funeral, when the Smithfield butchers draped their meat in black crêpe.

Morand inherited the theme of London from Larbaud; both writers declared that their favourite spot here was Chelsea—around Old Church Street, where Larbaud sets his novel *Beauté mon beau souci*. But where Larbaud was unimpressed by English men, to whom he preferred very young English girls, Morand is fascinated by public-schools, cricket-fields and the London clubs where gentlemen read *The Times* in dignified silence.

Morand was frequently overawed and it is this shyness rather than the kitsch of the early 1920s which explains why his first books are his best. *Tendres Stocks* is a portrait of three women seen by a young man who cannot understand much less possess them. . . .

In *Ouvert la nuit* the young heroes spend most of their nights alone because their lady-friends have deserted them: one has been arrested for spreading revolution, while others have run off with cyclists or black clarinetists. The disconcerted narrators are left to piece together their half-finished stories. By the time he wrote *Bouddha vivant* Morand was starting to talk about this fragmentation instead of continuing to allow it to shape his fiction, but his earliest books end on a question which continues to intrigue us sixty years after they were written.

> Patrick McCarthy, "The Anguish of Modernity," in The Times Literary Supplement, No. 4068, March 20, 1981, p. 307.

BREON MITCHELL

In the spring of 1976, an elusive and mysterious trunk once owned by Ezra Pound was reported to have reappeared at last in Fairfax, Virginia. Rumored to contain a treasure trove of literary letters and manuscripts from his Paris years, the puzzling location of the long-lost trunk was of secondary interest. The exact nature of its contents and the question of ownership were of more immediate concern. If speculations were correct, it held several early drafts of the *Cantos*, as well as other material of central importance to Pound scholarship.

The rumors were true—although the trunk itself no longer existed. The newly discovered [Pound] translations of Paul Morand's short stories published [in *Fancy Goods; Open All Night: Stories*] for the first time are but part of the riches which came to light as the story of Pound's trunk unfolded. (p. vii)

[Morand] was already a force to be reckoned with in Parisian literary circles when Pound arrived in the French capital in 1920. Always ready to champion new and distinct voices, Pound praised a "very divergent group of writers under or about forty years of age, writing without humbug, without jealousy, and without an eye on any market whatsoever." Among them Morand, who offered "the first clear eye that has been able to wander about both ends of Europe looking at wreckage," particularly attracted Pound. Having begun translating Morand as early as 1920, he had signed a contract by the spring of 1922 to translate two volumes of his short stories, *Ouvert la nuit* and *Tendres stocks.*

To his dismay, however, the translations were rejected as "unsuitable for English readers," partly on the grounds of sexual frankness, and in spite of all protestations, the contract was canceled. The typescripts of the stories were returned to Pound, he received a single payment of £25 from the English publishers, and the translations disappeared within the trunk.

Morand, who was elected to the Académie Française in 1968, has remained largely unknown to English-speaking readers, in spite of his immense popularity in the 1920s. To what extent his fortunes might have been improved had Pound's translations appeared, as intended, in the early years of that decade must remain a matter of speculation. English translations which did subsequently appear, "nacherly inferior to mine," as Pound was to report with satisfaction in 1935, seemed unable to maintain the reader's interest, perhaps in part because they were bowdlerized by timid publishers.

Morand's place in literary history rests squarely on his short stories from the '20s. Credited with having introduced a fresh and exuberant style into postwar French letters, he created a series of portraits of young women whom, as Proust pointed out, "we refused to consider as women" before such artists as Renoir, Giraudoux, or Morand brought them to our attention. But what was new in Morand was not simply the whirl of exotic places and sensibilities; it was a singularity of style which joined images in a manner striking and original enough to awaken the admiration of Pound. (pp. ix-x)

Like Pound, Morand was frequenting Dada and other avant-garde circles in Paris in 1920, while publishing his first poems, most of which dealt with the war and his own experiences abroad in a manner calculated to send at least minor shock waves through the middle class. His short stories, on the other hand, although saturated with a sensitivity which was thoroughly modern and postwar, were still accessible to the public at large. (pp. x-xi)

By the time Pound first contacted him in August of 1920, Morand was serving in the Ministry of Foreign Affairs in Paris and entering into the period generally considered as the most significant and fruitful of his life.

At age thirty-two, and with his major works still ahead of him, Morand must have been flattered to receive Pound's first letters of praise and encouragement. He responded with a copy of his poems *Lampes à Arc* (1919) and a promise to send him even more recent work. *The Dial* was soon to publish one short story by Morand, translated by another hand, and Pound, as their Paris correspondent, was ready to provide them with more. (p. xi)

[Morand] found himself agreeing with Pound about "the necessity of making an impression on the reader and, if possible, of taking the chance of a knock out. . . . I am sure final version will be quite perfect and it may go to New York at once without my seeing it." "**Turkish Night**" appeared in the September 1921 issue of *The Dial*, a year in which Morand's literary star was at its zenith. *Tendres stocks* appeared to general praise, and in February of 1922 *Ouvert la nuit* proved an instantaneous success. Proust's introduction to *Tendres stocks* had in Pound's words, "shoveled what one hopes is a final funeral clod upon the corpse of Sainte-Beuve," while at the same time setting the official seal of approval upon Morand and the new generation.

Pound's October "Paris Letter" in *The Dial* [see excerpt above] brought Morand to the attention of English-language readers again, as one of the standard-bearers of the new prose. . . . Behind Pound's praise the translator's mind is already at work. (pp. xi-xii)

The Chapman and Dodd contract was signed on May 22, 1922, with Pound agreeing to provide the manuscript of *Ouvert la nuit* by June 30 of that year and the translation of *Tendres stocks* six months later. For this Pound would receive "world rights" to the translation in the English language and a sum of £120, payable in installments as the two manuscripts were delivered and published. Pound at first took exception to the phrase "suitable for publication in the English language" and noted in the margin: "This to mean that publishers may delete what they think likely to upset Smith & Son and similar pests—for which deletions the translator assumes no aesthetic responsibility." (p. xiii)

Pound was understandably furious that Chapman . . . wished to back out of the contract, citing in part the "unsuitability" of the texts for English readers.

Morand himself was obviously embarrassed by the whole affair, particularly in light of the fact that he had indeed reviewed the English versions and approved them and felt a sincere debt of gratitude to Pound. . . . Morand's first interest remained that of securing an English language edition of his works, and he arranged for a meeting with Chapman later that year in London to discuss other possible translators. It may be safely assumed that this defection put an end to further relations between Pound and Morand, while the latter's willingness to authorize new translations sounded the death knell for any attempt at publishing Pound's for years to come.

Thus ended a literary relationship that might well have remained of continuing importance to both men. There was much in Morand that was attractive to Pound, and it is largely an accident of history that so little attention has been paid to the effect of this period of intense interest in the French writer upon Pound's own work. The rediscovery of Pound's translation now opens the door at last for a closer look. (pp. xv-xvi)

> *Breon Mitchell, in an introduction to* Fancy Goods; Open All Night: Stories *by Paul Morand, edited by Breon Mitchell, translated by Ezra Pound, New Directions, 1984, pp. vii-xxiv.*

RICHARD SIEBURTH

Among the most widely published authors of *l'entre-deux-guerres,* Morand remains relatively unknown to English-speaking readers today. In France, despite his induction into the French Academy in 1968, Morand's reputation has never entirely recovered from his participation in the Vichy regime as French Ambassador to Rumania and Switzerland. Stripped of his diplomatic rank during the Liberation, placed on the index by the leftist intelligentsia, Morand was relegated to the same limbo of literary history inhabited by fellow collaborators Robert Brasillach, Céline, and Drieu la Rochelle. Now that the dust has somewhat settled, Morand's 40-volume *oeuvre* is beginning to reacquire some of the readership it lost after the war. The publication of the first unexpurgated English version of Morand's early work [*Fancy Goods; Open All Night: Stories*] is thus all the more timely, since it provides an additional incentive to reconsider an author admired both by Pound and by Proust as a pioneer craftsman of Modernist French prose.

Proust registers the unsettling effect of Morand's experimental prose in his preface to *Fancy Goods.* . . . The "new relationships" that Morand elicits . . . have none of the aleatory feel of Surrealist juxtaposition. Instead, they more resemble the Vorticist esthetic espoused by Pound and Wyndham Lewis—a hard, honed geometry of "planes in relation," words angled against each other in a plastic pattern of precise image and sound. . . .

The short stories gathered in *Fancy Goods* and *Open All Night* tend to take the form of linked vignettes of women etched against a shifting series of backdrops—the night life of wartime London, politics in Catalonia, Russian émigré cafés in Constantinople, a gritty Parisian velodrome, a nudist society in Norway. Their narrative thread is often tenuous; instead they rely on montage techniques that borrow from the vocabulary of film. As Pound observed in a 1921 review, "the visual impressions succeed each other, overlap, overcross, they are

'cinematographic' but they are not a simple linear sequence. They are often a flood of nouns without verbal relations." Morand's prose, in short, provided the perfect vehicle for an inventory of the moral and spiritual devastation left by the First World War. Pound noted, "He has surely the first clear eye that has been able to wander about both ends of Europe looking at wreckage, and his present news value need not fail ultimately of historic validity."

The Morand of these short stories is still news. Much of his later writing (primarily travel reportage) lacks the tautness and the satirical incision of his early work. Morand's forte is the esthetic of aftermath and, more particularly, the portraiture of the desperations of modern desire. The sheer shapeliness of his prose recalls Hemingway; the urbanity of his self-destructiveness compares with Fitzgerald's; and his camera eye is as lucidly stroboscopic as that of Dos Passos. He is, like Victor Ségalen, Blaise Cendrars, Valery Larbaud, and Saint-John Perse, one of the great nomads of 20th-century French literature, racing through the apocalypse with the haste and glamor of an Orient Express. It is a pity we should have had to wait this long to catch up with him via Pound.

> *Richard Sieburth, "A New Voice from the 1920's,"* in The New York Times Book Review, *June 17, 1984, p. 10.*

JOHN UPDIKE

[*Fancy Goods; Open All Night: Stories* by Paul Morand] fairly drips with old-fashioned modernist credentials: the jacket lists New Directions as the publisher, Ezra Pound as the translator from the French, and Marcel Proust as the author of a preface.

What dark sun is this, who held such planets as Pound and Proust in his orbit? M. Morand had a long life, from 1888 to 1976, but his artistic celebrity rests upon the short stories he published in the first half of that classic modernist decade the twenties. (p. 136)

Fancy Goods contains three stories—"**Clarissa,**" "**Delphine,**" and "**Aurora**"—and *Open All Night* six: "**Catalan Night,**" "**Turkish Night,**" "**The Roman Night,**" "**The Six-Day Night,**" "**Hungarian Night,**" and "**Borealis.**" Each story has a woman at its center and indeed seems designed to display her, by means of a glittering succession of scenes and anecdotes that yet leave ambiguous, often, her relationship with the narrator. He, though unnamed and passive, is a continuous presence, and by virtue of his ardent voice an emphatic one. In *Fancy Goods*, whose episodes take place primarily in London, during the First World War, the narrator is younger than in the stories of *Open All Night,* where he has become a man-about-Europe, if not a roué. The women flit through his life like large, gorgeous, inscrutable butterflies. Some achieve unhappy ends: Remedios, a Spanish revolutionary, sets off an explosion and is arrested; Isabel, a French coquette in Rome, is found strangled; Anna, a Russian aristocrat reduced to being a waitress in Constantinople, announces her intention of spending two weeks in Paris and then committing suicide; and Zaël, a Jewish dancer in Vienna, demands to be taken back to Hungary and is kidnapped and presumably murdered there. Others simply vanish from view, like Aurora in London: "She makes a sign. Number 19 bus comes docilely to curb at her feet. She ascends the stair like a frieze unrolling itself." The writing is the thing. Whether the prose's confident oddity derives from Morand's original or from Pound's translation scarcely matters. The effect is luxurious, sharp, compressed, startling:

The caged sun went down between tree trunks,
like a red slice of beetroot. The ferryboat came
into dock. Two anchors fell from its nostrils.

(p. 137)

Her eye cast forth its scrutative beam to-me-
ward, and it sank in like a grappling iron.

Her face, smooth as a porcelain bowl, sloped
away in an even curve, holding level in its
surface her two flat liquid eyes, but my memory
hesitated before the softened mouth, weary at
its corners and showing no pleasure in possessing its even teeth. . . .

Such richness of imagery, so quickly folded and superimposed,
feels Cubist. The issues are circled rather than faced. Not so
much the people as the spaces between them are exactly drawn.
The spurts of dialogue, where they occur, are elliptical and
Firbankish. A certain deliberate Gallic wit presides; the humorous rhetorical device of syllepsis occurs perhaps too often:
"freshly caulked keels flaming with red lead and the sunset,"
"a small woman, excessively preserved by milk of cucumbers
and egoism," "I . . . arose with satisfaction and with bleeding
hands." The Zeitgeist is diagnosed in a kindred cadence: "It's
the sacrificed generation, ma'am. The men have gone off to
be soldiers, and the women have all gone crazy." The shattered, frenetic postwar Europe is described in language both
jazzy and coldly detached. (pp. 137, 140)

*John Updike, "Modernist, Postmodernist, What Will
They Think of Next?" in* The New Yorker, *Vol. LX,
No. 30, September 10, 1984, pp. 136-37, 140, 142.*

Richard Murphy

1927-

Irish poet and essayist.

Murphy has often been called a "poet of two traditions" because his work documents both sides of Irish culture—the primarily rural life of the Catholic majority and the former landowning and commercial Anglo-Irish Protestant sector. Murphy employs clear, direct language and frequently uses traditional poetic forms, particularly the long narrative style in which several of his most successful poems are written. While several critics claim that his detached, slightly ironic stance ultimately limits his sensitivity, others laud Murphy's nonjudgmental yet compassionate approach to his central concerns. Maurice Harmon observed that the key to Murphy's work "comes from [a] need to bridge the gap between the two cultures and the two traditions, to achieve a balance between planted demesne and peasant holding, between what he sees as the isolation and rectitude of the one and the sense of community and freedom of the other."

Murphy gained critical recognition with the publication of *The Last Galway Hooker* (1961). The title poem of this volume relates Murphy's purchase and refurbishing of an old "hooker"— an Irish sailing vessel—which he used to conduct fishing trips for tourists. Both *The Last Galway Hooker* and Murphy's next book, *Sailing to an Island* (1963), are steeped in the lore of the western Irish seacoast and populated by the fishermen and itinerant workers who live there. The latter volume contains three of Murphy's best-known poems. "Sailing to an Island" tells of his unsuccessful attempt to sail from Cleggan, the village where he lived, to Clare Island. In "The Cleggan Disaster," Murphy employs vivid descriptions of the sea and recounts a severe storm which destroyed most of Cleggan's fishing fleet in 1927. Critics claim that this poem displays Murphy's ability to convey great drama and pathos in direct language. "The Woman of the House" elegizes Murphy's wealthy, Protestant grandmother, Lucy Mary Ormsby, and blends the history of Murphy's family with that of his country.

The long title poem of *The Battle of Aughrim* (1968), originally a narrative for presentation on radio, relates the 1691 conflict which established Protestant dominance over the Catholic majority in Ireland. Murphy, who claims that his ancestors fought on both sides of the battle, attempts to maintain an objective stance, sympathizing with the viewpoints and sufferings of both Catholics and Protestants, and to demonstrate, as he states in a line of the poem, that "the past is happening today." Another poem in *The Battle of Aughrim,* "The God Who Eats Corn," is set in Rhodesia in the 1950s, and it too relates a painful, complex situation in which one culture, though a minority, holds power over another. This poem centers on Murphy's father, who retired to a farm in Rhodesia after a career in the British Foreign Service.

In 1969, Murphy purchased High Island, located off the Connemara coast, and built a house there. Many of the poems in *High Island: New and Selected Poems* (1974) are dominated by the environment of this area, focusing particularly, as in previous volumes, on the lives of fishermen and tinkers. This volume also includes poems based on the several years that

Murphy lived in Ceylon during his childhood. The trend toward richer, more directly personal verse which critics noted in the recent poems in *High Island* is also evident in *The Price of Stone and Earlier Poems* (1985). The title sequence of this volume comprises fifty sonnets, most of which are metaphorically centered on the building of Murphy's house and other structures; the final sonnet is a tender, lyrical description of his son's birth. Other significant poems include meditations on the deaths of fellow writers Tony White and Mary Ure. Although John Mole characterized parts of *The Price of Stone* as "weighed down by artifice," other reviewers considered the volume to be a positive development in Murphy's poetic evolution. Peter Denman noted that the book retains "the quizzical and detached qualities of his earlier poems, but now set in a new lucidity."

(See also *Contemporary Authors,* Vols. 29-32, rev. ed. and *Dictionary of Literary Biography,* Vol. 40.)

DONALD DAVIE

Richard Murphy has always worked from and in and among his images. In some of his earlier work he stayed so enmeshed among images that no idea emerged from them even by implication. But this is a poet who improves steadily and . . . *The Last Galway Hooker* moves with impressive gravity among limestone quay-walls and larchwood planks, trammels and spillets and Italian hemp, whiskey-bottles and marline, to the muted and modest resonance of

> Old men my instructors, and with all new gear
> May I handle her well down tomorrow's sea-road.

The reined-back rhythms of this verse are especially pleasing. (pp. 91-2)

> *Donald Davie, "Poems and Orations," in* New Statesman, *Vol. LXII, No. 1584, July 21, 1961, pp. 91-2.*

NORMAN MacCAIG

[In *Sailing to an Island*, Murphy shows that he] stands in his own weather, safely to the west of the shadow of Yeats. He has a rhetorical voice but straight things to say, and since his attention doesn't wander from these things, the rhetoric is kept in control; it gives his verse a fine, ringing solidity, and only occasionally flies off on an image that baffles me. He seems best when he looks out from himself at actual events (**"The Cleggan Disaster"**) or actual people (**"The Woman of the House"**). Since that is what he tends to do, there are only one or two poems here that don't, for me, come off. The effect of the ones that do is at once rich and spare—they are sensuous but not clotted; their speech is 'heightened' but the words all work—no idlers allowed. The sensuousness includes an unusual feeling for movement; and of course he has what seems to come naturally to Irish writers, a dramatic sense which establishes the people he describes in a context of others, to their mutual enrichment. (pp. 387-88)

> *Norman MacCaig, "Soaking Acorns," in* New Statesman, *Vol. LXV, No. 1670, March 15, 1963, pp. 387-88.*

GEORGE MacBETH

After a long eclipse there are signs that the narrative poem is on the way back in. The recent taste for verse autobiography . . . has helped to restore faith in the old-fashioned virtues of honesty, concrete detail and story-line. . . . Richard Murphy's *Sailing To An Island* develops this rebellion further, expanding the autobiographical formula to include the history of a family and a landscape as well as a person. His book depends on a clear narrative outline and a severe purity of style which has deceived reviewers into underrating its originality and its excellence.

Richard Murphy's poetry depends on the classical art which Hemingway described in (I think) *Death In The Afternoon* as 'turning the gas as low as possible without letting the flame go out'. In a period when obtrusiveness of phrasing has become widely accepted as a criterion of quality it's easy to underestimate the packed reticence of a line like:

> Her house, but not her kindness, has found heirs.

This line comes from **"The Woman of The House"**, a twenty-six stanza elegy describing the life and death of the poet's grandmother, Lucy Mary Ormsby. This poem has the rare merit of combining an almost Betjeman-like thinginess . . . with the sort of laconic brevity a Greek poet like Simonides used to

aim at in his inscriptions for tombstones. . . . In fact, the Spartan quality of this poetry is everywhere apparent both in its plainness of diction and its coolness of tone. The weakness of this kind of writing, of course, is often in its use of metaphor. Mr Murphy can employ a metaphor with fine economy, as in the line:

> And sometimes the shovels met with a knelling clang

where 'knelling' aptly suggests the sound of the death-bell in the gravediggers' work. This line is from his longest (and perhaps best) poem **"The Cleggan Disaster"** which combines muscular drive with an elegant simplicity of line. Occasionally, however, as in **"The Poet On The Island"** he seems to have been frightened that he was perhaps being *too* plain, and the result is lines of an over-papered vagueness:

> His forehead, a Prussian helmet, moody, domed,
> Relaxed in the sun: a lyric was his lance.

Years of conditioning by the imagists have persuaded one to accept the notion of a helmet relaxing in the sun as a viable, if graceless, anthropomorphism: the helmet is presumed to relax as a man might. What distresses one here is that the precise and concrete image of a forehead relaxing (by the easing of the wrinkles in a frown) has become submerged and blurred. Worst of all, the intrusive helmet has bred a fearful monster in Mr Murphy's comparison of a lyric (and a lyric by that least military of poets, Mr Theodore Roethke) with a lance. There's a special temptation in the steady thump of four-stress lines deriving from Old English which has here led Mr Murphy into the vice of linking by alliteration. (Usually, I hasten to add, he employs his difficult chosen rhythm with a syncopated ease which only R. S. Thomas among living writers has bettered.) In a romantic writer it would be unfair to concentrate on such a minor blemish; but the classical aims of Mr Murphy's poetry depend on the most even level of finish, and the few failures still remaining after the extensive revisions some of the earlier poems have undergone stick out rather jaggedly. If he can eradicate his tendency to indulge in badly visualized imagery . . . and increase his control of pathetic litotes . . . , Richard Murphy will develop into an important force in the poetry of the sixties. Already his Spartan style (and, let's face it, rather Spartan view of the world) mark him out as an individual voice in an age of moral conformism. I should be tempted (were he not an Irishman) to rank him with Gunn, Hughes, Middleton and Porter as one of the half dozen most distinctive English poets under forty. (pp. 87-9)

> *George MacBeth, in a review, of "Sailing to an Island," in* London Magazine, *n.s. Vol. 3, No. 4, July, 1963, pp. 87-9.*

M. L. ROSENTHAL

[The poems in *Sailing to an Island*] are highly local, sentimentally so when they are not rescued by [Murphy's] talent for larding description and narrative with objective detail. Fundamentally, he is an old-fashioned, rather conventional poet.

Reading his **"The Cleggan Disaster"** and **"Sailing to an Island,"** both poems about stormy, precarious sailing off the Galway coast, one wants to check back for comparison to a forerunner like Masefield's "Dauber" or even to the relevant passages in Hopkins's "The Wreck of the Deutschland." Mr. Murphy knows sailing—it is now his trade—and these poetic accounts are brilliantly concrete and exciting, serving a timeless artistic purpose in the way they repossess a particular type of experience and way of life. Nostalgia for a lost and nobler (sayeth the poet) past is heavy in these pieces. It is even heavier in **"The Last Galway Hooker,"** the biography of Mr. Murphy's own ship the Ave Maria, and in **"The Woman of the House,"** a poem about his grandmother and at the same time about his whole family's and country's past, and in a few other poems as well.

Yet for the most part he carries his purpose off through sheer good workmanship and strong but never overstated feeling. A lovely, sad, brief poem, **"Girl at the Seaside"**—in its way the rarest thing in the collection—and a gently understanding portrait of the American poet Theodore Roethke on a not too happy visit to the Irish poet's village round out a book of considerable achievement. It is a crucial question, however, whether Mr. Murphy can continue in his present vein without bogging down in provincialism and repetition. (p. 5)

> *M. L. Rosenthal, "Surrender to Despair," in The New York Times Book Review, December 22, 1963, pp. 4-5, 10.*

ALAN BROWNJOHN

After the variety and sureness of *Sailing to an Island,* Richard Murphy's *The Battle of Aughrim,* originally written for radio, is a disappointment. These evocations of the last battle fought on Irish soil are never less than competent, but rarely very energetic: some good vignettes and anecdotes, but too much merely routine re-creation of historical moments. (p. 363)

> *Alan Brownjohn, "Repetitions," in New Statesman, Vol. 76, No. 1968, September 20, 1968, pp. 362-63.*

GAVIN EWART

One feels that it may not even be very fair to criticize *The Battle of Aughrim* as it were 'from the page', since it was written for sound radio (and I'm sure it sounded fine). Aughrim was the last decisive battle in Ireland, a 'credal slaughter' and part of a 'credal war', and is still celebrated by Orangemen as a Protestant victory. The intermingling of past and present (an Eliot technique) gives it some depth:

> And a rook tied by the leg to scare flocks of birds
> Croaks as I dismount at the death-cairn of St Ruth:
> *Le jour est a nous, mes enfants,* his last words:
> A cannonball beheaded him, and sowed a myth. . . .

This is poor stuff, I'm afraid (though it's not all as crude as this), but as a blow-by-blow account of a not uninteresting battle it could have been all right on the night, on the air. Loosely and often randomly rhymed, most sections are lyrical or ballad-like. . . . Brutality, treachery, heroism, muddle ('the wrong kegs of ball / were consigned to the castle / Irish bullets too large / for French firelocks'), pathos ('A wolfhound sits under a wild ash / Licking the wound in a dead ensign's neck.') This is certainly war; but very little of it is magnificent poetry. **"The God Who Eats Corn"**, a mild, more evenly written poem in honour of his father, shows Murphy in a rather better light. (pp. 93-4)

> *Gavin Ewart, "Old Scores," in London Magazine, n.s. Vol. 8, No. 9, December, 1968, pp. 92-5.*

DANIEL HOFFMAN

The Battle of Aughrim contains but two poems, of which the 47-page title poem is the longer. . . . [The] Battle of Aughrim, fought in 1691, was "the last decisive battle in Irish history". A prose note provides the references that have to be sorted out in order to understand the poem: we must be able to identify St. Ruth, the French general commanding Catholic forces loyal to James II; Patrick Sarsfield (apparently a forebear of Mr. Murphy's), the Irish general to whom St. Ruth failed to confide his battle plan; Colonel Lutrell, the traitor who withdrew his troops after St. Ruth's death in battle ("He'd sold his country to preserve his class"). Some may hold that a poem should contain its own clarifications, but Mr. Murphy, speaking in the present (in his opening section) can justly say, "The past is happening today." The Matter of Aughrim is remote only in its particulars. . . . [The] painful divisions of English vs. Irish, Catholic vs. Protestant interests survive, the unhealed wounds of a country tragically divided.

Mr. Murphy is a proven adept of the long narrative poem, but he has eschewed the straightforward telling of **"The Cleggan Disaster"** in *Sailing to an Island* (1963). A modern poet writing of history cannot help but have in mind the example of *The Cantos,* and an Irish poet must, besides, come out of the long shadow cast by Yeats. Mr. Murphy sounds a different note, his own, by adopting strategies consonant with his rather Augustan sensibility. An inheritor of traditions of the Ascendancy, he takes an objective view of history. His crucial event is chosen from a period not preempted by Yeats—neither the mythopoesis of Bronze Age demigods, nor the Easter Rising. (pp. 342-43)

The first of [**"The Battle of Aughrim"**'s] four sections is **"Now"**, a series of lyrics, some personal, which clarify the legacy of the battle—the despair and hatreds it bequeathed—before we participate in the ironical design of the event. The three succeeding sections are set **"Before"**, **"During"**, and **"After"** the battle. Each contains from five to ten brief poems, some lyric, some dramatic, some narrative, in various forms and meters. One—St. Ruth's sanctimonious address to his troops—is in prose; another, a versified quotation from a contemporaneous English history. Thus the texture is continually varied, juxtaposing effectively to the foreign commander's hauteur, his distrust of the lowly people he was commissioned to defend; juxtaposing to the righteous rhetoric of apologists for either side, the barbarity of both armies toward civilians and to each other; juxtaposing, too, the self-serving treachery of Luttrell and lesser turncoats to the butchery of their defeated countrymen. As Murphy says of Sarsfield, "Nothing he will do, or has done / Can stop this happening."

The directness of diction reinforces the dramatic objectivity of vision, isolating significant action with the economy of an ancient ballad. Though the texture of the lines is simple, the movement of history in the poem is complex. **"The Battle of Aughrim"** is surely one of the most deeply felt and successfully rendered interpretations of history in modern Irish verse, and in poetry in English in our generation. (pp. 343-44)

Mr. Murphy's concluding poem, **"The God Who Eats Corn,"** meditates on that other relevant history, the colonialization of Africa. The poet's late father, a former governor of the Bahamas, retired to a plantation in Rhodesia where he was among the last, perhaps *the* last, of the benevolent British colonists. . . . The sterility of their exploitative society is presented with restraint, in the implied contrasts between the realities of Rhodesia and both the humane ideals of Sir William Murphy and the nearly forgotten ways of the natives before their degradation. When this poem appeared in *The Reporter* (7 May 1964) it detailed brutalities since excised; the poem is the better for relying upon implication. (p. 344)

Daniel Hoffman, *"Constraints and Self-Determinations,"* in Poetry, *Vol. CXIV, No. 5, August, 1969, pp. 335-44.*

COLIN FALCK

'The calamity of seals begins with jaws.' With this mildly preposterous line Richard Murphy begins **"Seals at High Island"**, the first poem in his new book *High Island*. High Island is an island off the Connemara coast and the seals are observed copulating:

> She opens her fierce mouth like a scarlet flower
> Full of white seeds; she holds it open long
> At the sunburst in the music of their loving;
> And cries a little. But I must remember
> How far their feelings are from mine marooned.
> If there are tears at this holy ceremony
> Theirs are caused by brine and mine by breeze. . . .

Lawrence (say), with some self-knowledge and a living rhythm or two, might have carried this off. Ted Hughes would at any rate have had the sense to keep himself out of the poem altogether. Murphy flounders, because he doesn't really know whether he wants to be part of the poem or not and his speculations—though not without a certain verbal distinction—come over as idle and literary. What is the vague and feeble 'marooned' doing here (surely the seals are perfectly in their element?), we might wonder, except meeting the rather lax requirements of blank verse? Who, in fact, *is* this poet, who responds so blandly and yet evasively to such elemental experience? Are seals really *calamitous* (the poem doesn't explain why)? Murphy is a classical, or classicising, poet who mostly settles for a literary and elevated tone and for a stylised, almost token poetic ego rather than for any kind of recognisable self who might appear with actual empirical flesh on in his verse. If he appears in the poems he appears self-effacingly, and the poems make way rather bardically to accommodate him. What we get is Irish scenes, remnants of myth and superstition, anecdotes, bits of nature; what we don't get is encounters with the self or with other selves or anything distinctively about the modern world. *High Island* includes one or two poems about Murphy's Ceylon childhood which momentarily arouse one's subjective interests (after all this time the subject-matter must presumably mean *something* other than just having chanced to be there when the poet walked past it) but which just as quickly disappoint them. Murphy is obviously happier with the kind of poetry where these difficult personal demands don't have to be met. (pp. 69-70)

Colin Falck, *"Leaving Something Behind,"* in The New Review, *Vol. I, No. 11, February, 1975, pp. 69-71.*

DONALD DAVIE

I remember twenty years ago walking across a Wicklow hillside with Richard Murphy, and his Old English sheepdog bounding to meet us. It would be a cruel quip, and yet near the mark, to say that this has been Murphy's trouble all along—an English dog (or an English manner, certainly an English accent) in an Irish setting: There was never anything he could have done

about it; this was his fate and his inheritance. For he is the only accomplished verse writer we have whose poems spell out the agonized impasse at the present day of that brilliant stock which we call the Anglo-Irish. Outside of Ireland, if we have any grasp of this at all, it is thanks to Yeats. And Murphy is not quite Yeats's sort of Anglo-Irishman, but rather of the sort that Yeats celebrated and venerated in the persons of Augusta Gregory and her son Robert; the landed gentry, English by race, usually by religion and often enough by education, who left Ireland characteristically to serve as proconsuls of the British Empire, who nevertheless thought of themselves in most situations as Irish first and British second.

The poet's father, the subject of a long and touching poem, **"The God Who Eats Corn,"** represents the pattern in its purity, except that on retiring from a distinguished career in the British Colonial Service, instead of returning to his native Ireland, he settled in 1950 on virgin land in what was then Southern Rhodesia. It was left to his son to return to what we must call, in justice and yet with bitter irony, "his roots"; and to try to make historical sense out of being, in 1960, the highly specialized sort of Irishman that the history of several centuries had made him. (p. 10)

Among the cards dealt into Richard Murphy's hand, which *High Island* fans out before us (consisting as it does of twenty-five new poems supplementing earlier collections reprinted), we find: a childhood in the tropics, the privileged but also disoriented scion of the colonial overlords, left mostly in the charge of servants from among the colonized; memories, through long-lived grandparents, of the Anglo-Irish Ascendancy in its last traditionally secure though mostly unglamorous years before 1920; and a doubtless sincere attempt to become just another loyal citizen of the Irish Republic, indistinguishable from his mostly peasant or fisherman neighbors in the West of Ireland where he lives.

One has to have lived in Ireland to recognize how impossible that last endeavor is, and so how the hand was ultimately unplayable. The evidence is all there in the poems: in a country where the historical memories are (for reasons we all know about) as long, as tenacious, and as embittered as among the Irish, in a landscape moreover where neither industrialization nor population growth has been such as to erase the sheerly physical and material vestiges of earlier centuries (Murphy has a good poem about a slate that he took from a hedge bottom to pave his garden path, and the uses it could have been put to ever since St. Colman used it)—it is impossible for his neighbors, whatever the good will on both sides, to accept him as one of themselves. By and large, Murphy's poems are good when he acknowledges this impossibility; less good, though all the more touching as human documents, when he tries to deny it.

His most ambitious attempt to deny it is a sort of fragmented and acrid epic, **"The Battle of Aughrim,"** about the Irish Jacobite war which in 1691 finally riveted the Protestant Ascendancy on the whole island. Heroically he here tries to celebrate the losing side, particularly in the famous person of Patrick Sarsfield, Earl of Lucan; but if I read the case aright, all Murphy's forebears would have been on the other, the winning side, and the way of life which they then built up for themselves, a way of life which conditioned Murphy himself, was made possible only by that victory. It was that historical contradiction in the very subject matter which, I suspect, made too much of this poem (it has its good moments) prosy, strained, and wooden. To the American reader, it is just this prosiness and flatness, what Tom Kinsella has called "verse of the lowest possible intensity," that will seem to be the English sheep dog in this Irish garden. The Englishman Larkin, they may feel, handles these muted instruments with more finesse.

Murphy however began as a much more colorful poet, and has adopted this subdued and chastened language as the only means for fulfilling the task that history has landed him with. And at least once, in the long poem **"The Last Galway Hooker"** ("hooker" meaning, it should be said, a kind of seagoing boat), it served him admirably. Only the bare style of the later Murphy could have risen to the splendid and marmoreal lines which give to this poem a conclusion among the most memorable, for dignity and poignancy combined, of any in modern English:

> Old men my instructors, and with all new gear
> May I handle her well down tomorrow's sea-road.
>
> (pp. 10-11)

Murphy's poems, alike the good and the less good, are in any case irreplaceable, as a human witness to a historical predicament more excruciating than most English-speakers will ever have to face. (p. 11)

Donald Davie, "Cards of Identity," in The New York Review of Books, *Vol. XXII, No. 3, March 6, 1975, pp. 10-11.*

ROGER GARFITT

In Richard Murphy's first two collections [*Sailing to an Island* and *The Battle of Aughrim*], direct narrative statement was framed and given perspective by the inflections of a quite different, more intellectually-based style. A slight distance was kept from the reported fact, which enabled statement to be smoothly articulated into image. . . . One remained very aware that this was a narrative conducted in verse: the success of the style lay in its making full use of the rhetoric of verse. . . . (p. 86)

In his new collection [*High Island*] Richard Murphy is concerned to let facts impinge directly, without a controlling inflection in the style. The boy's interview with his father in **"The Fall"**, for instance, says a great deal about a particular culture and class without needing to break the illusion of total recall:

> That night he walks to the chair with long wooden
>   arms;
> Whisky glass, tobacco pouch, crossword puzzle, pen;
> To own up like a gentleman.
> Scent of cartridges ejected from a shotgun,
> Glint of pince-nez, mosaic frown.
> The hand with a gold signet ring bends him down,
> A lion rampant on a little hairy finger.

The series of poems on his childhood in Ceylon is particularly successful in catching the child's ambivalent attitude to his environment: beneath his acceptance of its stranger elements lies the recurrent fear of their foreignness. Incident cannot always provide a sufficient logic, though. Poetry is rooted in metaphor: the imagination combines to create significance. . . . [Metaphoric] life is rare in this collection. What makes some of the Ceylon poems and most of the Irish poems appear inconsequential is that they present isolated incidents which are given no metaphoric value. Where Richard Murphy's earlier work was historical, these poems are merely documentary. The decreased intensity is equally marked in the nature poems, in

the whimsy of **"Stormpetrel"** or the romantic embroidery of **"Seals at High Island"**. Accuracy itself seems to suffer once the imaginative perspective contracts. (pp. 86-7)

Roger Garfitt, "Ceylon & Elsewhere," in London Magazine, *n.s. Vol. 15, No. 1, April-May, 1975, pp. 86-90.*

MAURICE HARMON

From the beginning of his poetic career Richard Murphy worked hard to achieve clarity; the struggle may be traced in the early uncollected pieces with their apocalyptic touches from Dylan Thomas, their austere notes from Milton and their Wordsworthian passion for nature, but it is central to his growth as a writer. He always seeks the exact word and the precise meaning, making it clear being more important than making it new. At the same time he is a formalist who favours traditional verse forms and standard metres.

One of his basic beliefs is the truth of place; he is drawn by the drama of what happened in a specific place—Wittgenstein at Rosroe, Roethke at Inishbofin. His accounts of journeys by sea are based on an actual voyage and an actual disaster. He sets poems in specific places, Brittany, Crete, Creragh, Cleggan, Aughrim, and because of its topographical density, his work has a strong regional dimension.

Another prominent characteristic, arising from his interest in place and event, is the attraction for narrative. He believes that there is truth in accurate historical narrative; he therefore takes great care to establish the reality of particular events, that certain things happened and exactly how. This fundamental need determines both his preparation for the writing of a particular poem and for the method of organisation. His narratives, **"Sailing to an Island"**, **"The Cleggan Disaster"**, and **"The Last Galway Hooker"**, are constructed in such a way that their effectiveness is the result of the careful presentation of their narrative components, their accurate record of things done and said.

The value of these descriptive narratives is relative to their meaning for one mind. "The poet's mind", as Murphy once noted, "has become the stage on which the action takes place, and the myth is treated as an indication or reflection of that mind." That observation, made about the general decline in narrative poetry, is particularly relevant to *The Battle of Aughrim* which, for all its diversity, is a drama of a single consciousness. Murphy's aim is to strip away the myths that time, tradition and conflicting attitudes have imposed on the event, so that its truth can shine through the faithful, almost documentary, narrative. (pp. 7-8)

The key to much of Murphy's work comes from [a] need to bridge the gap between . . . two cultures and the two traditions, to achieve a balance between planted demesne and peasant holding, between what he sees as the isolation and rectitude of the one and the sense of community and freedom of the other. In some respects he seems to be a classic example of a sensibility divided between the two major traditions of Irish life, but the dichotomies that are visible in his work, indeed clarified there for our consideration, should not encourage us to see it merely as a sterotype of the Ascendancy-peasant relationship or to categorise it within a conventional view of that relationship based on a particular period, a particular region, or even its imaginative reconstruction by other poets. Murphy's definitions of ancestry and of self, and his sense of relationships between places and cultures, are peculiar to his own experience. There are many dimensions to his understanding of faded ancestry, poor gentry, plantation and rectory; there are, too, many facets to his vision of people of the other culture, those in between the two and those outside both. Aughrim itself he saw as the "navel", Ireland's geographical centre, and that physical fact confirmed his sense of it as a familial, religious, social, historical and cultural centre as well, from which virtually everything of importance radiates, including his own destiny. *The Battle of Aughrim* itself is a complex act of understanding, as though by working out the problem on the page he could then write Q.E.D. after it and move on to 'more personal poetry'.

The transition to *High Island,* with its three separate but complementary worlds, indicates the discovery of another centre, the preparation of another drama in which a variety of separate actions can be realised. The notes of love and imaginative possession, the liberation of language and feeling, the Hardyesque purity of diction suggest how fruitful this mating of self and landscape has been.

The integrity of Richard Murphy's poetic career is apparent in the successive acts of definition and scrutiny that make up the bulk of his work. As a young man he set sail for an island of vision, but found instead the inner harbour at Inishbofin and men in the real world. Ever since, he has trusted reality and meets it on its own terms. Today his chosen landscape is full of potential for myth or magical incantation, but his manner is still low-keyed and objective. The stormpetrel is his pulse of the rock, her nest a hermit's skull; it is the thrift and sea-campion that flower, the pink granite of St Fechin's church that rises from the dead, aided by the skill of the archaeologists, the cross-slab at Brian Boru's well that retains its power for a thousand years. The corncrake drafts an epic, the petrels compose a nocturne. To these he bears witness in his poetry, to these creatures, these harmonies, these movements and events in the natural and the real world. (pp. 8-9)

> Maurice Harmon, "Introduction: The Poet and His Background," in Irish University Review: A Journal of Irish Studies, *Vol. 7, No. 1, Spring, 1977, pp. 7-9.*

SEAMUS HEANEY

As a poet, Richard Murphy has something in common with the Orcadian poet George Mackay Brown. Both write about islands redolent of old faiths and old customs, about fishermen and tinkers, about landscapes and seascapes. Both manage a language that is objective and concrete, shaped and sided, closer to the staccato and stress of Anglo-Saxon poetry than to the melody and syntactical complexity of the Spenserean tradition. Both tend to keep themselves out of the poem, to be present as observers, anonymous voices, bearers of tales; they strike us as shapers of material rather than explorers of the self. Yet in spite of the facility with which the case for similarity can be made, it is the differences between them that are most significant.

Mackay Brown's style holds the actual world in thrall; his artistic world constitutes a frieze, an illuminated book of cold northern hours; the beauty of the art stands against the mess of the actual, its timeless images and archetypes, its corn and wine and waves and furrows are sacramental, cyclic alternatives to the profanity, vulgarity and decay he sees in contemporary life. The poetry is held like a cross in the face of the

devilish onset of a deracinated materialism, an impious rationalism. It is a sign made in the name of an older, almost medieval consciousness, and its stiffness is the stiffness of ritual gesture.

Murphy's stiffness, on the other hand, is that of a man moving in a constricted space. The elemental characters and incidents in his work are not frozen in a heraldic procession but are in motion behind the pane of the style, where they are observed not with votive attachment but with precise detachment. They represent neither an exemplary nor an alternative world but are rendered as aspects of the world we inhabit and, if the epic note is occasionally sounded above them, they maintain a documentary presence that almost shrugs off heroism. Whereas Mackay Brown offers his world as the emblem of a desirable culture to which he would be affiliated, Murphy conducts us into a bleak and beautiful environment toward which he is sympathetic but finally ambivalent. Murphy's fidelity to the world of boatmen and tinkers and natural beauties and disasters does not altogether constitute a faith in it because that world is inadequate to his social and cultural recognitions. It is valid in so far as the poet participates in it as boatman, as neighbour, as eavesdropper, as annalist, but it is unsatisfactory because this participation can never be total. Murphy will not surrender his sense of caste, his manners, his educated consciousness, his willed individuality to this essentially communal fatalistic and half-literate culture, however attractively that culture presents itself to his imagination. The constricted space he moves in and writes out of is a march between his Anglo-Irish Protestant background and his Irish Catholic surroundings, a space at once as neutral and torn as the battlefield at Aughrim, as problematic and personal as the house he builds for himself from ruined famine cottages, sometimes invaded by nostalgia for the imperial, patrician past, sometimes hospitable to deprivations and disasters which somehow rebuke that heritage.

The title poem of his first collection, *Sailing to an Island,* discovers that space in the shape of a narrow bed, a point of rest attained after some bruising of the social self. The poem is at once a direct narrative about a boat trip, full of the swing and threat of the sea, confident in its relish of sailing lingo, rich in evocation of atmospheres; and at the same time it is a parable of another journey between cultures, from the sure ground of a shared but disappearing Ascendancy world to the suspecting community of the native islanders. Although the boat runs into and negotiates a storm (and there is something Conradian about this test of seamanship), the real test is to survive the scrutiny of these secretive, knowing spectators. . . . (pp. 18-19)

That bed is a point of rest but by no means a point of relapse or repose. There is a strong sense that tomorrow will renew the exposure, the search for balance, the need for skilled navigation. But the poem itself is secure in its art, a beautifully modulated movement from delight to wisdom; it achieves a momentary stay against confusion and by its honest plotting of a rite of passage earns its right to pass. Of course, the felicities of image and expression enrich our response ("the shelved Atlantic groundswell / Plumbed by the sun's kingfisher rod"), although a too literary straining sometimes disturbs it ("the ribald face of a mad mistress"); but the poem's strength resides in the mythic and psychological truths exhaled off its plot. The narrative element is the adequate symbol.

In his suggestive essay, **"The Pleasure Ground"**, (printed in . . . *Writers on Themselves*) Murphy makes an imaginative connection between his childhood entrancement in the overgrown thickets of a pleasure ground and his later discovery of the sea as the first element in which his poetry came to life. The pleasure ground was a walled Ascendancy garden attached to his grandfather's house in the west of Ireland. It had run wild, but under the untutored profusion of yews, laurels and briars there lingered the ordered lines of ancestral care. When he arrived there as a boy with his mother, brother and sister, they made an effort to restore its decorous features, and the delight that came from this adventure of entering and ordering such natural abundance, he tells us, pervaded the disciplines of his education: his study of mathematics, music, painting and poetry was enlivened by the spirit of the garden. The essay ends with this tantalising sentence:

> As I grew older the garden grew wilder, losing
> its form as trees were felled, and its spirit as
> old people died and the young left the country;
> so I searched more and more into the origins
> of that garden till I found them finally in the
> sea.

What does he mean? How does he find the origins of that garden in the sea? The answer to the question must be fundamental to the groundplan of Murphy's poetic imagination. (pp. 20-1)

It seems to me that Murphy exchanged the stewardship of his inherited pleasure ground for the stewardship of his chosen art; his "masculine energy" was directed to the mastery of a way of life among boats that would make him an initiate among the "truly Irish", and directed also to the mastery of the craft of poetry that would enable the rebirth of the self as an artist. As artist, he is impersonal and in control. The contents of his mind, the drift of his feelings, the conflict of his loyalties and recognitions are all materials to be worked, and the poem will have to be a vessel sturdy enough to take the strain of conflicting Irish winds. As Irish artist, both the pleasure ground of the elemental landscape, with its indigenous inhabitants, and the pleasure ground of the ancestral estate, with its colonial ethos, are to be his theme. He will fulfil the paternalistic role of his Governor father and the life-enhancing role of his grandmother by celebrating the noblest aspects of both cultures and perpetuating their purest strengths and values in his work. We might say that the sense of a rest well deserved, which informs the conclusion of **"Sailing to an Island"**, is born from a realisation that perfection of the life has at least guaranteed perfection of that work.

"The Pleasure Ground" was published a year after the appearance of *Sailing to an Island* and stands as a coda to that book, as well as a prologue to *The Battle of Aughrim*. Indeed, although I have forced the essay to stand as a gloss on the title poem of the first collection, it is much more explicitly relevant to the other three long poems in the book, **"The Last Galway Hooker"**, **"The Cleggan Disaster"** and **"The Woman of the House"**. Each of these is severely formal. The first thing we respond to is the finish of the verse, the eccentric stress of the metric, the conscious wording. This is clinker-built poetry and, unless it is buoyant upon deep feeling or strong sensation, it feels cumbersome. For this reason, while I can take pleasure in the poet's pleasure in his last Galway hooker, I feel that that poem's prose sense and mass sink its poetic lift. It is as if we have been provided with a barge where a currach might have been more appropriate. Nevertheless, its theme of inheritance and renewal is central to the volume; more explicit than **"Sailing to an Island"**, though not, I think, as artistically successful, it celebrates the furbishing of a boat and a betrothal

to its mysteries as analogous to the poet's artistic commitment to making, continuing and conserving.

"The Woman of the House" is a grave and tender elegy to that "mistress of a beautiful disorder" whose memory "warms my mind". Beneficent, munificent, she is made to walk again behind the dry-stone walls of the quatrains, each of which forms a kind of invocation.... (pp. 22-3)

She is almost a muse, and [the] echo of a medieval carol to the Virgin Mary is entirely appropriate to our sense of her as a nurturing presence, as a mother of perpetual succour, an intermediary between the extra-mural world of labourers' cottages and patrician evenings with biscuits on a tray and ginger wine. *Gravitas, pietas*—elevating classical notions present themselves when we look for the quick of the poem's feelings. Yet there is a resolute matter-of-factness that does not balk at her certified dotage and gives a hard force to the last snatch of her talk....

The intonations of **"The Woman of the House"** are drawn from the world of phaetons and sermons.... (p. 23)

The opening of **"The Cleggan Disaster"**, on the other hand, bows to the labour of rowing, and is loaded with a different "ancestral bias":

> Five boats were shooting their nets in the bay
> After dark. It was cold and late October.
> The hulls hissed and rolled on the sea's black hearth
> In the shadow of stacks close to the island.
> Rain drenched the rowers, with no drying wind.

The feeling for the sea in this work is very different from Synge's in *Riders to the Sea*. There is no real merging into the fisherman's point of view, no unbending of the authorial voice, no tinge of the *keen*, no surrender to the intimate vocabulary of the fishermen. Instead, there is that strong "masculine energy", a robust framing of the scene, a narrative pace that takes things almost with a tradesman's calm and thoroughness. The result is a beautifully solid, slow and stoic presentation of the disaster. If it misses the *duende* that Synge achieves, it registers authoritatively the *sensation* of the sea's relentless and awesome power.... What we are given is a *via dolorosa* of the waves, and the achievement of its objective bulk must have encouraged the poet to face the larger disaster that happened at Aughrim in 1691.

The Battle of Aughrim is as meditative as it is narrative, in so far as the juxtaposition of the historical elements induces a detached consideration of the meaning of the action (or is it actions?) now, before, during and after the battle. The storytelling voice shifts its perspectives and varies its intonations to enliven different parts of the tale, but its function is finally choric, setting things in an ironic and tragic pattern. (pp. 23-4)

[The] poem is fundamentally connected with Murphy's shaping of his inheritance into a poetic theme: his quarrel with himself is implicit in the lines of the battle, and the violence within modern Ireland "Has a beginning in my blood." He can trace affiliations with both sides. Patrick Sarsfield, Earl of Lucan, darling of the defeated Irish side, is plangently celebrated as "great-uncle in the portrait's grime" and the buoyancy and melody of this section of the poem touch racial stops that the Reverend George Story, author of *An Impartial History of the Wars in Ireland*, would surely find regrettable....

On the other hand, feelings not unexpected from the author of **"The Pleasure Ground"** are raised in a lyric that celebrates the colonist's vision and forges incidentally a thematic link between the title poem and **"The God Who Eats Corn"**, also included in this volume. . . . (p. 25)

And in the **"Now"** section, the poet is affronted by a "kinsman"—and how tactfully his use of that proud noun places him at a distance from the man himself and from the less dynastic consciousness of the "truly Irish"—who violates both the indigenous and the colonial heritages:

> Left a Cromwellian demesne
> My kinsman has bulldozed three bronze age raths. . . .
> He's auctioned grandfather's Gallipoli sword
> And bought a milking machine.

It is by such means that Murphy seeks to pattern conflicting facts and facets of history and Irishry. The whole poem is a tessellation of deliberately shaped lyrics, just in their long views, solid in their crafted shapes, occasionally rich in their violent content—as in the account of the death of the traitor Luttrell—or entranced by the satisfactions of their language, as in the evocation of rapparees who materialise before the battle "Out of the earth, out of the air, out of the water". Yet in this lovely section there is a symptomatic unease between the manner and the matter of the poetry:

> . . . At the whirr of a snipe each can disappear

> Terrified as a bird in a gorse-bush fire,
> To delve like a mole or mingle like a nightjar
> Into the earth, into the air, into the water.

Moles are not to be found in Ireland and nightjars have to my ear an indelibly English literary ring to them, so that at a moment when the tutelar presences of the Irish ground are being summoned, they are subtly debilitated by the idiom in which they surface. It is not that Murphy wishes to rob them of their proper force: it is more that his language retains *its* ancestral bias in spite of his intention to exorcise ancestry as a determining limit of vision.

Mention of the poet's intention brings us to the critical crux. I agree with Edna Longley that "something programmatic in its design and designs . . . stands in the way of total subjection of the offered experience." . . . (pp. 26-7)

It is as if in his first two volumes Murphy is intent on discovering navigational aids to locate the self, to plot its longitude and latitude. These books are the log of an expedition before they are the diary of a soul. In *High Island,* however, we enter more subjective territory and the intimacy of exploration, which Murphy showed himself capable of in his earlier poems about Theodore Roethke and Ludwig Wittgenstein (**"The Poet on the Island"** and **"The Philosopher and the Birds"**), is exercised upon the poet's own life. Solitude and ambivalence, love and loss, become explicitly personal themes. A freeing of the voice occurs and a number of poems combine a lightness of touch and an intensity of feeling that come from a quick surgery of these more intimate veins. (p. 27)

In *High Island* the old preoccupations are more internalised. Small incidents take large strains. We are aware of a sureness of direction in the art and a poised and appeased self-knowledge in the poet. **"Walking on Sunday"**, for example, has the poise of self-possession about it, and a fluency and delight in its own music—a not unhappy music of time and change. . . . Walking or driving or watching or listening, the poet in this volume is typically alone and in the best poems his encounters are translated into states of feeling. The most resonant of these is **"Seals at High Island"**, evocative of place, analytical of feelings, replete with a music of sea and sex and sorrow, moving like a long swell, finding at last a syntax that carries over from line to line so that the effort of making is subsumed into the pleasures of saying. . . . (pp. 28-9)

When read alongside the poems I have mentioned, the uptight bitter anecdotes about clifftop murder, caravan incest and quayside gossip and craft are too cold. On the other hand, the autobiographical childhood pieces about Ceylon are almost overvoluptuous: a wealth of tropical detail luxuriates around the line of the narrative and an unexpected exotic quality enters the poetry. A new pleasure ground, a new myth for what the poetry means, swims into his ken. Sound and self, not social and historical circumstances, are apprehended as the essentials. **"Coppersmith"** finds Murphy in the act of remaking his poetic myth, coming in close to the heart of the feeling, relaxing out happily in the run of the sense and the syntax. It begins in a narrow space but opens generously to concern itself not with the English colonial past but with the poetic resources of the English language, that medium where all of us, "truly Irish" or "Anglo-Irish", must discover ourselves and our directions, the bounds of our outer and our inner space. . . . (p. 29)

Seamus Heaney, "The Poetry of Richard Murphy," in Irish University Review: A Journal of Irish Studies, *Vol. 7, No. 1, Spring, 1977, pp. 18-30.*

JAMES D. BROPHY

The question [of whether Murphy is a poet of nostalgia or 'pietas'] derives most recently from Seamus Heaney's essay . . . [see excerpt above]. It also has a provenance in Donald Davie's 1975 review of Murphy's *High Island* [see excerpt above]. The question, which might be stated more familiarly and polemically as "Can an Anglo-Irishman possess a genuine Irish commitment?," is important to consider because its skeptical prejudgement (more obviously implied in the latter formulation) seriously depreciates Richard Murphy's poetry. In my estimate the position that Murphy adopts a superficial posture toward the Irish sources and material of his poetry is unsupportable. . . . Murphy is not a poet of "nostalgia" with its overtones of insincerity, but is indeed a poet who reveals a genuine commitment to his country—a commitment that might usefully be defined by the Latin term, *pietas.* (p. 49)

Given this background of Murphy's extending back to the "dark poverty of rural" and Catholic Ireland, it is difficult to account for Donald Davie's remark about Murphy's **"The Battle of Aughrim"** that "if I read the case aright, all of Murphy's forebears would have been on the other, the winning side, and the way of life which they then built up for themselves, a way of life which conditioned Murphy himself, was made possible only by that victory." The answer, obviously, is that Davie has not "read the case aright," that a considerable part of the poet's heritage was on the losing side, and, indeed, Murphy has never lost sight of that. (pp. 50-1)

Like Davie's, Seamus Heaney's evaluation of Murphy's poetry is largely depreciative, but, based on the poet's language and style rather than Davie's procrustean sociology, it is more acceptable as literary criticism, although, ultimately, it too has a sociological bias. . . . [Heaney's] sophisticated analysis [of a section of **"The Battle of Aughrim"**] is, unfortunately, ultimately unconvincing as literary criticism. I say "unfortunately," because Heaney, apart from being a first-rate poet, is usually a perceptive and resourceful critic. His error here is falling into the organic fallacy that the form must mirror the content in every way. The logical conclusion of this thesis is that one must write about Ireland in Irish, which, of course, is not what Heaney himself does. . . . To disallow "delve like a mole" as an illustrative simile for a readership that (being in English) would surely extend beyond Ireland is carping of the severest kind. And to make this judgment after the remarks about his own poetic mixture is to compound the issue with hypocrisy. If moles are not to be found in Ireland, the phrase indicts Murphy at most of not being a naturalist. If "nightjar" sounds "English" to Heaney, I submit that to a reader of modern poetry it also suggests Dylan Thomas ("Fern Hill") who is Welsh or Celtic rather than English. Or should we disallow Thomas's evocation of a farm in Wales because he uses a word putatively of English allusion? Heaney's acute perception has the considerable merit of dealing with the language of the poem, but surely his demands for something like linguistic purity are unreasonable. (pp. 51-2)

The basis of Heaney's rejection of Murphy's poetry, however, is that Heaney does not believe that Murphy possesses a genuine sympathy for his Irish subject matter: there is in **"Aughrim,"** for example, according to Heaney, "a lack of sympathetic imagining." And once the critic is armed with this bias the analysis of the language can indeed create supporting evidence. (p. 52)

Heaney, in a passage characteristic of the depreciative tone of his essay, states that "The constricted space Murphy moves in and writes out of is a march between his Anglo-Irish Protestant background and his Irish Catholic surroundings, a space at once as neutral and torn as the battlefield at Aughrim, as problematic and personal as the house he builds for himself from ruined famine cottages, sometimes invaded by nostalgia for the imperial, patrician past, sometimes hospitable to deprivations and disasters which somehow rebuke that heritage." Reading here the deliberate distinction which he makes between Protestant "background" and Irish Catholic "surroundings," one might wonder if Heaney knows (as Davie did not) about Murphy's Irish Catholic background as distinct from more accidental and superficial "surroundings." Since he notes later in his essay concerning the opposing forces at Aughrim that Murphy can "trace affiliations with both sides," one is indeed curious as to why affiliations that go back to 1691 do not qualify as "background" rather than "surroundings." It would seem that a valid case can be made for considering Richard Murphy a poet of *pietas* rather than nostalgia.

The basic, interrelated themes of Richard Murphy's poetry from the poems of his first collection, *Sailing to an Island* (1963), to his most recent edition, *High Island* (1974), are the need for a homeland or home and the requisite search for it. (Since one implies the other, this may be a single theme.) In **"Sailing to an Island,"** the stark, compelling opening poem of his first book, the presence of a relentless drive is acknowledged. . . . The boat labors "all day for our chosen island," and typically for Murphy the choice is an Irish one, "Clare, with its crags purpled by legend," where the poet hopes to "locate in sea, earth and stone / The myth of a shrewd and brutal swordswoman / Who piously endowed an abbey." In a very real sense his third and latest book, *High Island,* demonstrates the completion of that earlier unsuccessful voyage which ended in turning back to Inishbofin for refuge. The poem **"High Island"** does indeed describe the location of "An older calm" amid "the kiss of rock and grass." (pp. 53-4)

Aside from his purchase and care of High Island, one of Murphy's most interesting Irish concerns has been his generous and symbolic rehabilitation of a family of tinkers. In 1972 he learned of an itinerant family in which the parents were estranged and the seven children put into an industrial school and an orphanage. Working to get the family back together, Murphy accepted responsibility for them, and obtained a house for them in Cleggan. (p. 61)

Murphy's poem **"The Reading Lesson"** conveys some of the problems of this rehabilitation of the tinkers, and most importantly, the reason for his work on their behalf. The problems include the tinker's own unregenerate attitude, resisting the difficult business of learning to read:

> He looks at a page as a mule balks at a gap
> From which a goat may hobble out and bleat.
> His eyes jink from a sentence like flushed snipe
> Escaping shot. A sharp word, and he'll mooch
> Back to his piebald mare and bantam cock.
> Our purpose is as tricky to retrieve
> As mercury from a smashed thermometer.

The boy complains, "I'll be the same man whatever I do," and protests, "I'll not read anymore." The poet asks "Should I give up?" and in this is confronted by another problem for the tinkers, the attitude of other Irish toward them: "A neighbor chuckles, 'You can never tame / The wild duck: when his wings grow, he'll fly off.'" But the poet perseveres, because he sees the tinker boy with "hands, longfingered as a Celtic scribe's," and he believes that the tinkers of modern Ireland are the descendants of the Celtic bards who were turned out of their positions by the British invaders to find their lives in the lanes and hedges. Thus, the tinkers are highly and importantly symbolic to Murphy; in helping them he is restoring a rightful Irish patrimony. Regardless of whether Murphy's hypothesis about the tinkers' origin is correct or not, what matters is his commitment to the Irish past and the sense of duty it generates. (pp. 61-2)

It is this commitment to justice that shapes **"The Battle of Aughrim"** as it begins with "Who owns the land . . .?" One notes that only a few stanzas later we read that "a tinker woman hired to stoop / Is thinning turnips by hand." Irony is Murphy's central technique in **"Aughrim,"** and its operation here in this passage is clear. Those who are closest to the earth do not indeed own it, and with the case of the tinkers that fact is even more ironic or distressing. But the role of tinkers in **"Aughrim"** is incidental to the larger, overriding theme of the betrayal of Ireland and the Irish by foreign powers. The force of Murphy's irony is mostly directed at the British planter hegemony, but he demonstrates other ways in which alien powers work against Ireland's ultimate good: the battle itself was directed not by Irishmen but by Germans (on the British side) and French (on the Irish side). Murphy has said that **"Aughrim"** is his attempt to reconcile the division of Ireland in poetry. And his chief method is to dramatize the injustice of the Irish not controlling their own destiny and lives. Mainly the Irish are the victims of the colonial ethos. . . . But they also show some evidence of self-betrayal as alluded to by the woman who brings as a souvenir from Knock shrine "John Kennedy's head on a china dish." Kennedy's presence suggests the Irish dispersion, the "wild geese" who, for whatever good reasons, nonetheless depart and disconnect. The conclusion of **"Aughrim"** makes very clear the irony of Irish rejection of Ireland. And that is an important connection between **"Aughrim"** and **"The God Who Eats Corn"** which documents the father's distance from "the rectory lawn" of Connemara. Murphy depicts the descendants of the Irish who died at Aughrim returning to view the battlefield. They are "strangers." "They know by instinct," he writes, "this cool creek of traitors."

This is sharp indictment indeed, and may be especially rankling to some readers coming from one who can be "Strictly defined as Anglo-Irish." The final line of this powerful poem describes the visitors of Irish heritage as they "turn in time to catch a plane for France." Conquest, abandonment, betrayal—all are shown by Murphy in **"Aughrim"** to be Ireland's burden and trouble, past and present. And what informs the eloquent ironies of their manifestation in **"The Battle of Aughrim"** is the poet's own devotion to Ireland. "Who owns the land?" Ironically, it has not been those of similar devotion, and this has been dire for Ireland and the Irish. For as Murphy consistently shows in his poetry from first to last, from *Sailing to an Island* to *High Island,* an individual's fulfillment is to be found within his own heritage, in the realization of homeland and home. The theme as well as the source of this poetry is *pietas.* (pp. 62-3)

> James D. Brophy, *"Richard Murphy: Poet of Nostalgia or 'Pietas'?"* in Contemporary Irish Writing, *edited by James D. Brophy and Raymond J. Porter, Iona College Press, 1983, pp. 49-64.*

PETER DENMAN

Since *Sailing to an Island* in 1963, Richard Murphy's collections have appeared in a roughly lustral rhythm, although this was maintained in 1979 only by his *Selected Poems,* which did contain some new work as well as revised versions of earlier pieces. *The Price of Stone,* therefore, is the first substantial body of new poetry from him since *High Island* (1974), an important book in which Murphy moved into a new idiom and broadened his range of material. Nevertheless, that book's style of reticent allusiveness, while engaging, constantly gave the impression of something being left unsaid. Such, of course, is the price of reticence, but a search for unspoken communication has been a feature of Richard Murphy's work from the outset.

The Price of Stone is more forthcoming than *High Island.* The title sequence consists of fifty sonnets (cast in the "Shakespearean" form) in which the very stones speak. In each poem Murphy gives a voice to some particular structure (monument, dwelling-place, his old school, etc.) which has impinged on his experience. They speak to him, questioningly, accusingly, or reflectively, about passages of his life. This device of giving mouths to others, and putting words into those mouths, suits Murphy; he can appear to speak frankly to and about himself, and yet remain silent.

The sequence begins with some sonnets which approach the problem of finding an appropriate mode of expression ("a laconic style?" "a chiselled voice?") but it rapidly moves on to the main business: how to obtain a purchase on the events and experience of the poet's past, made numinous by memory and by their projection onto the surfaces of buildings where he has lived. What we have is an autobiography in the form of a verbal *son et lumière.*

In the course of this evocation of his life, Murphy quarries some challengingly unusual words. Try these without a dictionary: rupestral, penetralian, obelize, spall, and (all in one sonnet) cineritious, ithyphallic, and succursal. He also has a trick of shifting a word or phrase between its figurative and literal senses: "A spirited father walked barefoot to Rome," or the surface of an ice rink renewed at night has its "Old scores ironed out." This gentle wordplay not only helps to avoid any monotony in the formally repetitive sonnets, but also serves as a reminder that Murphy inhabits a language-shaped world. The poet works with words, but words play with the poet. . . .

"The Price of Stone" (the title sequence) begins with erections; these are either follies or monuments to the dead. It ends with the birth of the poet's son, with life. It is in this last sonnet that Murphy finally speaks as himself, addressing his son not through any surrogate or interlocutory structure. And the final word of the sonnet, and of the sequence and book, escapes language to affirm an alternative form of communication: "touch." There really is nothing more to be said.

One cannot label all of this as simply being yet more poetry about language. It is more substantial than that, for Murphy's poetry faces up squarely to moral and emotional questions, and to the workings of experience and its ramifications. Furthermore, it avoids the spiritual dimension and rests with the material. This marks Murphy's poetry as essentially different from that of Geoffrey Hill, although it would be to Hill rather than to any Irish poet that one would turn in seeking a writer with whom Murphy's work has affinities of tone and scope.

Of the 21 poems which make up Part I of *The Price of Stone,* the central ones are those dealing with Murphy's friendship with Tony White and White's death in 1976. Death dominates in these introductory poems: the death of friends (**"Mary Ure"**), the death of love (**"Displaced Person"**), and death-in-life (**"Elixir"**). There are also some trial pieces for the later sonnets, and the graceful elegiacs of **"Stone Mania"** serve as a rueful link between *High Island* and *The Price of Stone.* But it is for Part II, the sonnets, that this book will be cherished. As a sequence, they not only embody an intrinsic worth but they also give a retrospective shape to Murphy's work as a whole so far. Those readers who, like myself, have been fascinated by the turns of Murphy's poetry, at once allusive and aloof, will recognize here the quizzical and detached qualities of his earlier poems, but now set in a new lucidity. The book provides not a story, but a history, and adds new lustre to all his earlier volumes.

> Peter Denman, *"Allusive and Aloof, Quizzical and Detached,"* in Irish Literary Supplement, *Vol. 4, No. 2, Fall, 1985, p. 15.*

DENIS DONOGHUE

[In *The Price of Stone* Richard Murphy] leaves a good deal unsaid. The price of stone is high, apparently, but he hasn't computed it in detail; we are meant to leap from one assessment to the next. To begin with, it is the price of trying to build a house in granite, and then of trying to make a life from correspondingly difficult and durable material. The phrase, 'stone by stone / Personified', in **"Cottage for Sale"** marks his poetry and something of his life. He is an Irish poet whose inherited life is compounded of particles Irish, English and South African. The life he has made for himself involves a house in Cleggan, sailing to Inishbofin and other islands, the poetry circuit in the USA, marriage, lovers, children, and sundry affiliations. Many poems in this new collection are tokens of affection, offerings to friends—Tony White, Mary Ure, a dying poet. A few are more public, like the rather unquestioning poem about the Long Kesh hunger-strikers. There is a weirdly memorable poem about a poisoned goat. Fifty sonnets are about buildings, and the price of them: Nelson's Pillar, Kylemore Abbey, a school in Carlow, the Red Bank Restaurant in Dublin. . . .

Murphy's relation to these themes and symbols is unfailingly humane. The poems are personal, but not in any sense that Byron would call vicious. Murphy doesn't force the unspoken claim that these perceptions have issued from him and could not have come from any other source. He implies that he happened to be in the right place at the right time, and that the form of the sonnet was available to note the conjunction. He doesn't come closer to the reader than decorum requires, and he uses a rather curial diction to mark a due distance. (pp. 21-2)

These are good poems, but unvaryingly phrased. Murphy's style has every merit, starting with dignity, but I wish it would allow itself to change, indulge itself in moods, be fractious on occasion. A meditative propriety governs the entire book: excellent if such a degree of government is required, but oppressive on days when we long for Mardi Gras. (p. 22)

> Denis Donoghue, "Ten Poets," in London Review of Books, *Vol. 7, No. 19, November 7, 1985, pp. 20-2.*

BERNARD O'DONOGHUE

[*The Price of Stone*] is in two sections: the first contains twenty-one separate poems and the second is a sequence of fifty sonnets which gives the book its title. Each of the sonnets is spoken in the "voice" of a building with which Murphy has been associated, in most cases addressing him in the second person. The first section is ancillary but important. Some of its poems are in the poet's own voice, balancing his position as addressee in the main sequence, and some allude to the sequence, most crucially **"Stone Mania"** which acts as a keystone to the whole work by contemplating gloomily the time that has been lost in planning and building his house, New Forge, in terms which apply equally to the building poems (evoking, maybe, the same underlying metaphor as in Donne's punning "we'll build in sonnets pretty rooms"). . . .

Superficially, the primary emphasis falls on the relationship between Murphy and the places where he has lived, something which might seem to be a further movement inward from the exteriority of his earlier poetry, beyond the self-reflective *High Island*. The details of the poet's life are so central that one almost wishes Maurice Harmon's excellent biographical note . . . [see excerpt above] had been appended. That, however, might have misrepresented the book in two ways: first, it is by no means only a private document, and many of the poems have familiar public speakers (from Nelson's Pillar to Canterbury Cathedral to a tinker's tent), expressing political awareness; second, it would distract from one of the book's greatest strengths, on the face of it a paradoxical one. Just as Yeats's tower has more importance as a concept than as a dwelling (and it is one of the many themes of Yeats that have crucially affected Murphy), these sonnet houses give detached, objective forms to the poet's concerns. There is an irony here: Murphy's earlier poetry was sometimes criticized for its preoccupation with the nature of Anglo-Irishness. Now, when cultural pluralism in Ireland is debated endlessly, Murphy has moved on to a subtler medium to depict it. Like J. G. Farrell in *Troubles,* perhaps, Murphy's poetry (most memorably in **"The Woman of the House"**) has always looked quizzically, as well as af-

fectionately, at the virtues and unrealities of his grandmother's class in its twilight. The poetry takes its historical responsibilities seriously; Kylemore Castle has a view "improved by famine's hand / That cleared away people", and **"Family Seat"**, one of the finest sonnets, introduces its "grim, grey face / Of limestone cut by famine workmen" before proceeding to a delicate parody of Yeats:

> But love I took from a ruling family,
> And gave them back a wealth of lovely things:
> As a trout river talking with propriety
> Through cockshoot woods, bailiffed by underlings.

The weighted last word is typical of the way in which Murphy achieves balance by letting judgment emerge in the face of the partial personae. . . .

This original method is founded on a familiar sociological fact: buildings express the societies which constructed them; Murphy is giving verbal form to that expression, so the view of each building is partial. But environment also determines the limits of imaginative experience, so the objective imperative in these poems demands an honesty which Murphy produces unflinchingly. Some of the poems are painful in their unsentimental self-accusation; **"Roof Tree"** estimates most expensively the price of the obsession with stone: "To renovate my structure, which survives, / You flawed the tenderest movement of three lives." Perhaps the strongest poem of all is **"Convenience"**, which laceratingly conveys the embarrassment, ludicrousness and seriousness of sexual self-consciousness.

The Price of Stone, even if it hasn't the unflagging expressiveness of *High Island,* is Murphy's most formidable achievement to date. Some of the poems in the early section show him still capable of a rich eloquence. . . . But the characteristic distinction of this volume is not lyricism but exacting honesty. It should restore Murphy to the eminence he held in 1974 when, younger readers may need reminding, only Larkin and Hughes could command as eager a reception.

> Bernard O'Donoghue, "Structurally Speaking," in The Times Literary Supplement, *No. 4314, December 6, 1985, p. 1405.*

JOHN MOLE

Richard Murphy's work is an interesting blend of the sensuous and the austere. *The Price of Stone* is an elegant, highly crafted collection, full of contrivance and patches of very fine writing. It doesn't leave a poem unturned, but too great a sacrifice of material to the demands of construction tends to make a stone of the art. Although the first half of this book contains some fine lyrics, Murphy keeps getting weighed down by artifice. In **"Stone Mania"** he writes of "the house whose construction has kept us entirely apart." This is addressed to a loved one who has had to pay the price of the poet's "passion for building in granite"—a passion which throughout the collection he insists on exploring as a metaphor for the craft of verse—but it also draws attention to a procedure which keeps him apart from his reader. One keeps watching for the next appearance of "a wise old mason", "the stonework of my heart", "each random stone made integral", etc., and rather distantly admires the rhetorical expertise.

The entire second section is a sequence of fifty sonnets in which Murphy traces his lineage and growth as a poet by means of giving a voice to buildings which have had significance in his life (birthplace, school, a friend's cottage and so on). There's a lot of indomitable Anglo-Irishry in this. It's an extremely enterprising project, packed with cunning effects which keep drawing attention to their own literary ingenuity—"to renovate my structure", "plucking lost tunes from my structure", "made me sound in my ruins", "he restored my site." "Much as you need a sonnet house to save / Your muse . . ." begins **"Carlow Village Schoolhouse."**

That sounds rather desperate. It's as if the schoolhouse may have Murphy's number. At times, along the way, as yet one more building bent the ear, I felt that I needed another sonnet like a hole in the wall. It's all so literary, consciously poetic, and rather *vieux château*. Yet what a powerful descriptive gift Murphy displays when he's not labouring on the construction site. . . . (pp. 59-60)

John Mole, "Conceit & Concern," in Encounter, *Vol. LXVI, No. 1, January, 1986, pp. 55-61.*

Diana O'Hehir

1922-

American poet and novelist.

O'Hehir's two volumes of poetry, *Summoned* (1976) and *The Power to Change Geography* (1979), deal with strong emotions and dramatic situations. Many of her poems explore the inward and outward changes that influence personal growth. Although some critics found O'Hehir's range narrow and her verse somewhat humorless, others praised her ability to transform mundane observations into profound truths.

Personal growth is also the central concern in O'Hehir's novel, *I Wish This War Were Over* (1984). The protagonist of this work, nineteen-year-old Helen Reynolds, travels by train from California to Washington, D.C., to try to save her alcoholic mother from self-destruction. Although Helen ultimately fails in her attempt, she comes to terms with her feelings of guilt and resentment and begins to see herself as a unique individual, separate from her mother. O'Hehir was generally praised for the well-rounded portrayal of her heroine and for precisely capturing the essence of America in 1944.

(See also *Contemporary Authors,* Vols. 93-96.)

JAMES GUIMOND

On the dust jacket of *Summoned,* O Hehir says that she considers her poetry as being—among other things—"surreal." Since the 1960's, this kind of statement has become about as helpful as saying that a poet has brown hair or reads Spanish. Nowadays, the Sacred Groves have plenty of mystical, surreal, and "deep image poets." The hard problem is telling the good ones and their poems from the bad.

The surreal should be sur-real, a reality which is above and beyond our regular, rational reality—the geography of another world, the history of dreams. So whatever else it may be, good surreal poetry should have words and images combined in strange, unlikely ways. In one of O Hehir's poems, a mother cleaned offices for years to send her children to college.

> The mother is tall, her hair tied behind her ears in a
> kerchief.
> The worst part of her day is midnight:
> The tiredness of soup, sullen radio,
> Sleeping children, the angel who follows after, wings
> akimbo,
> Edges of feather dipped in paint. It has a neon line
> around it.
> > It says,
> I'll wrestle with you, lady.

Not some Giant Despair, but a jaunty angel ("wings akimbo") for an antagonist—what better creature to tempt a cleaning woman to give up hope? And equally appropriate, the angel has adapted itself to the mundane with a brisk, colloquial familiarity: "I'll wrestle with you, lady."

The poem is a good example of the way O Hehir's poems move surely and quickly from the regular to the surreal to discover extraordinary truths about both realms. In a single stanza she can step from vivid but relatively conventional statements to very unconventional ones. (pp. 56-7)

Poor surreal poetry is predictable in its strangeness, turns the irrational into a routine, demonstrates that the weird can be as trite as the reasonable ever was. O Hehir knows this, avoids it in her poems, and warns against it in **"Some of Us Are Exiles from No Land,"** an excellent satire on the predictable surrealism which flourishes in

> > > . . . a lost country
> Painted by Dali.
> > > > > > (p. 57)

Poor surreal poetry is painless, bland, and sentimental. The most wonderful transformations are achieved by pushing buttons, just like Oz or perhaps Shangrila. Traveling through the other world is not so much different from—but easier than—moving through regular reality. On the other hand, O Hehir's poems are painful and sometimes disturbing. When she goes "underground" it is not a technicolored, magical mystery tour, but a risky journey. . . . And the inhabitants of the other world in her poems are not animals out of *Bambi* but **"People in Dreams"** who are "Dangerous, their palms are puddles of radium. Their lips shine, bones are hollow.'' Or Lady Macbeth saying, "I did it for my children, did it for . . . a solitary walk down a moon-dry road, / My shadow yelling ahead of me, / Boredom trotting my side like an anxious dog."

O Hehir's poems have force and vitality. She knows that you cannot create another reality by simply gawking at it. . . . Instead she tries to be the kind of artist, whom Klee described, that can place herself "at a remote starting point of creation" where she can "state *a priori* formulas for men, beasts, plants, stone and the elements, and for all the whirling forms." And frequently she succeeds. . . . (pp. 57-8)

James Guimond, "Sur-real and Surreal," in Kayak, No. 48, June, 1978, pp. 56-8.

CHARLES MOLESWORTH

The Power to Change Geography, Diana Ó Hehir's second book, lacks the invention and energy of its title; the writing is superficially competent, but hardly polished. The Princeton series has published at least two very good poets (Pinsky and Pevear), and at least one very poor one (discretion draws its silvered veil), but this new title adds little luster to the list. . . . [One] can assume only that her editor found her poetry in some way touching. I doubt he found it profound or richly musical. Here is a typical passage, where the subject is a rather commonplace nostalgia:

Water grinds down the mill of the cliff in surges, picks
    up
All the relics of our past: tokens, rings,

Artifacts painted blue,
They float, frantically, buoyantly, downhill.

(**"Waterfall"**)

The poem ends: "My ears are filled with roaring." Now are the blue artifacts in this passage there for variation? Is the frantic floating there to denote energy? Of course this poem is limited in every way, and one could object that such limits can be freely chosen, self-imposed, but when Ó Hehir aims for the unfettered, she doesn't fare much better:

Around us the weave of an indestructible listening,
Love, a dark heavy sister waits over us,
Her watching so strong it melts the backbone, brings
Our word out of its grave, its hair thick in dust, its dark
    eyes wild.

The occasion here seems a non-specific meditation on her lover, but the poem doesn't have a clear narrative framework. The listening here is no more indestructible than the floating is frantic in **"Waterfall,"** nor is the melting backbone any more vivid or evocative than those blue-painted artifacts. The music of the verse has only stale adjectives to keep it from flattening into prose.

One often feels the strain in this book, to generate feeling, but that strain eventually exposes a weak imagination (as the "so strong" leads into that melting backbone). Ó Hehir's similes are characteristically trite: "leathery as a bat"; "vague as rumor"; a brooding "heavy as low clouds"; "shinny as onyx"; "limp as cotton." One wishes (how one wishes!) there had been an editor who might have blue-pencilled these phrases. But perhaps that's to raise the wrong kind of strictures, the false kind of hope. Ó Hehir's poetry, with its confessional drive for emotional honesty, isn't bad, it's only made to look futile when decked out in book form with a Princeton label. (pp. 241-42)

Charles Molesworth, "Bright Lights and Blind Choices," in Parnassus: Poetry in Review, Vol. 7, No. 2, Spring-Summer, 1979, pp. 239-48.

CHOICE

[The poems in *The Power to Change Geography*] are poems of power, sureness, originality; their imagery is alive and exciting. Ó Hehir writes on a variety of subjects, the unifying theme, in her own words, "perceptions which have pushed me toward change or renewal." **"House"** tells of her visit to her childhood home, where "In the upstairs room is the memory of another solitude . . . [which] filled up the whole house." The poems cannot be classified, but their metaphors show new ways of perceiving. . . .

A review of "The Power to Change Geography," in Choice, Vol. 16, No. 8, October, 1979, p. 1023.

PETER STITT

Diana Ó Hehir's *The Power to Change Geography* is a relentlessly single-minded volume. Every poem is written in a single style—using nearly identical rhythms, figures of speech, rhetorical devices, patterns of imagery—and follows a single form. It is remarkable how similar the poems look as objects upon the page—rarely is there more than a five-line variation in total length. . . . Her favorite figure of speech is the simile. . . . After simile in popularity comes metaphor, that other chief device of comparison or analogy; most things are doubled by Ó Hehir—this is like that, that is this.

The book's unity extends beyond technique into theme, mood, and tone. Rarely have I encountered a book as consistently lacking in humor as this one. Of course, everyone can't be funny all the time. . . . But humor encompasses many things, none of them present in Ó Hehir's poems—no playfulness, no wit, no light-heartedness. Likewise, the book is pervaded by fear, fear of the self's being invaded from without—by visitors from outer space, by fire from underground, by emptiness/fire/water (one poem) from underground, by a criminal intruder, by earthquake, by an executioner. Two other poems are entitled **"Threatened"** and **"Victim."**

This is unsettling in human terms, of course; in literary terms it produces a deadly tone of portentousness that drags the book and the reader deeper and deeper into an emotional swamp. Consider this apparently harmless stanza:

We dip into books as if they were
Wells of pity, cups of
Futures, lendings of light from the genuine owners of
    light,
Shining for miles into the awful garden
Where, deep enclosed, is the Rajah's frightening jewel.

This series of three extended similes is an unvarying cry for help—the speaker seeks pity within apparent lovelessness, light within darkness, a future within hopelessness. Even the light turns horrific at the end, becomes "awful" and "frightening." And yet the lines considered solely as poetry, as language tipped over into song, are unusually good. But however skillful she is at creating single poems, Diana Ó Hehir does not show well in this book. Because of the narrowness of her range—

emotional, artistic, thematic—she ends up writing the same poem almost every time. (pp. 233-34)

Peter Stitt, "Summer Birds and Haunch of Winter," in Poetry, *Vol. CXXXV, No. 4, January, 1980, pp. 229-37.*

DEL MARIE ROGERS

In Diana O Hehir's first book, *Summoned,* there is a wild struggling against the facts of external reality—old age, crippling disease, death, separation—that expresses itself over and over as a willed transformation of that reality. The persona of many of these poems is insatiable, she wants superhuman powers.... She wants to be able to *make* a peace in her life, a peace that probably doesn't exist on earth, and the strength of her wish is immense. Superhuman figures abound—martyr, saint, zealot, Lady Macbeth, the woman who fought for fifteen years with an angel, a woman struck by lightning. Here is no sad-eyed giving in to death or loss, this poet's a fighter.... The reader of these energetic poems begins to sense a religious dimension; this is a constant struggle in which the self is more fully realized, a struggle for individuation. [O Hehir's] poems make me think of a Jungian interpretation of Christianity in which the imitation of Christ is the living out of one's own reality as fully, as intensely, as Christ lived out *his*. In this sort of view, there is a continuing incarnation of God—the more we make ourselves real, the more real God becomes.

There is a great deal of imagery of electricity, lightning, earthquake, and so on, to suggest human force and its sudden changes. While there is no easy optimism in these poems, there is human endurance and power....

One of the most interesting figures in *Summoned* is "the old lady under the freeway." The "old lady" represents a return to psychic depth allied with nature and quietness, as opposed to the technology and confusion that roar nearby. The old lady survives like something subliminal, on the borders of things, but in a world of human longing that is still green, growing. The nature/technology contrasts are by no means simple: there is a danger in opening yourself up to nature and the unconscious, which is clearly presented. The words of the ferns are "unsafe," "harsh and green," and still the old lady carves a tunnel inward.

The final poem of *Summoned* carries the book's problems, but ends with some interesting lines that carry a feeling of the elation and peace that come with accepting the world as it is....

Although a wishing for dramatic change, for a controlling power, is evident in the title of ... *The Power to Change Geography,* this is a very different book. O Hehir goes from an outward wrestling with circumstance and a violent recurring wish for outward transformations that would bring inward peace in *Summoned* to a greater exploration of inward states in *The Power to Change Geography.* The title poem of this second, more inward book is not about outward change, as one might expect, but inward change. In this book I find Ms. O Hehir much more often following an inward thread to the place where it leads, sometimes with surprising results.... In ["Watching"] she is in tune with changes that are happening, natural changes, instead of forcing change from the outside. The same is true of the poem "Waterfall," "All the relics of our past: tokens, rings, / Artifacts painted blue, / They float, frantically, buoyantly, downhill."

A wish for outward, rather than inward, change is still present in such poems as "The Retarded Children Find a World Built Just for Them" and "They Arrive This Morning." In the latter, visitors from outer space hold the key to our lives that we can't possess—"They have mirrors to lighten our waiting." A lover leaves the poet "like a searchlight ray" in "Cars Go by Outside, One After Another." The pattern of looking outside herself for answers exists in the book's title poem.... But it is inward change the poet also wants, and in these poems she is in the process of bringing herself up against the idea that she alone possesses the key to her life. Knowing that her light is of use "to me only," she's on the right track. In "Vision: Fire Underground" there is an inward space, potential.... There is an exploration of *frozen* inwardness in the poet's examination of a dead human being in "Survivor." Somehow the poet has shared this man's condition; she says that his mind holds "What any of us who've been frozen solid can tell you" and this claim seems natural in the context of the poem. A further exploration of frozen inwardness lies in the poem "Recluse," in which O Hehir's protagonist is locked away at incredible distances from other humans: "You can't reach me. Light would wilt my face like a leaf." The poems "House" and "Home" manage to speak of internal and external realities in a steady, calm way—in "Home" "The beautiful roofline folds up into the sky / Closing us out."

In "The Sea Creature" the voice of a primitive animal is one of her inward voices, and it is exciting to hear it.... I don't fully understand this extraordinary poem; it has a mysterious residue; but the animal abandoning the speaker in this poem seems to be her sexual/emotional self abandoning her.

Looking back over both of these books, I find a touch too much apotheosis, a tendency for transformation to the grand, instead of the capacity to follow reality's configurations faithfully that becomes more prominent in *Geography*. Ms. O Hehir besieges us with her titles. Many of the poems are anthology-pieces taken individually, but her violent changes and dramatic titles ("Besieged," "Called," "Vision: Fire Underground," "Survivor," "Threatened," "Victim" in the second book alone) come to seem over-dramatic as a steady picture of the world, a kind of sensationalism, like a newspaper making more and more outrageous claims on our minds instead of the real urgency of a farewell letter from a lover. But particularly in the second book the migration to deeper water, to psychic depth, is so striking that I'm ready to forgive her all her faults, grateful that we have a new artist of this stature.

Del Marie Rogers, in a review of "Summoned" and "The Power to Change Geography," in The American Book Review, *Vol. 3, No. 2, January-February, 1981, p. 6.*

ANNE TYLER

Diana O'Hehir—previously known for her poetry—has managed in her first novel [*I Wish This War Were Over*] to produce a group of characters so complex and particular, so appealing and so heartbreaking, that what happens to them matters far less than who they are. Like real-life people, they draw us into the layers of their personalities, and these form the book's real plot.

The "I" of the book is a 19-year-old Californian named Helen. The year is 1944, a time so vividly re-created that it's practically one of the characters. Trains are full of sprawling soldiers. Banners hang in railroad stations reading "U.S.O.—We

Care, We Share, We're There.'' *Time* magazine shows a weeping Frenchwoman whose dress has been ripped open because she fraternized with the Nazis. . . . Women are sporting a style in which a snarl of bobby pins fastens part of their hair to the front of their heads and part of it to the back. (''I started to say to myself,'' Helen tells us, ''that they looked like the wrath of God and then I had to retract it, because it was not true at all, really. They looked pretty and sweet and charming.'')

In fact, it is probably Helen's distance from the era that allows her to speak so kindly of those women in bobby pins. We don't know her present vantage point; we have no idea what became of her after 1944. But there is a certain tender note in her voice that suggests she is looking backward over a great sweep of time, and that is what makes the book so poignant.

She is tender even toward her 19-year-old self, and rightly so, for Helen at 19 is an admirable young woman—sensible, self-reliant, and gifted with the ability to breeze her way through events that would undo most others. We meet her first as she's setting out on her cross-country journey, hoping to rescue her alcoholic mother from where she's landed on the skids in Washington, D.C. (pp. 36-7)

[Helen is] hardly seated on her train when she encounters one of her mother's old boyfriends. O'Connell (as she calls him throughout the book) is a married man more than twice her age, a union activist who addresses her as ''Butchie'' and ends up inviting her to stop off with him in a Reno hotel. Not the kind of situation we'd like for any 19-year-old of *our* acquaintance, thank you; but that's where Diana O'Hehir's wonderful particularity of characterization comes in. She shows O'Connell and Helen playing poker on the train together:

> After a bit he decided to enliven the game by pretending that additional people were playing and assigning names and personalities to them. Mr. and Mrs. Jones were a meek couple in their forties; Lady Sadie was a stripper; there was also Donald Nelson, the head of the War Production Board; and a fat man named Eustace, who was my son.

By the time O'Connell has peeked at a card, meanwhile explaining that ''he wasn't doing it in his own person, but in that of Lady Sadie,'' we're smitten. Oh, all right, let her stop off in Reno with him. In fact, she'd be crazy if she didn't.

Carry this quality throughout the book—make each person so specific, so lovingly detailed that he might be sitting in the room with us—and you have a novel that sticks in the mind. . . .

Wartime Washington, a Virginia mill town, the bizarre, bleak waiting room of an Army doctor, the crumbling little apartment in which, after Helen's mother goes on a doughnut-frying spree, droplets of grease hang from all the shade pulls—each scene is palpable, meticulously described. And all are deepened by a faultless sense of time. The year 1944 lies over them like a translucent wash of color.

Only rarely are we reminded that this is a first novel. There is a creaky flashback mechanism near the beginning, when Helen is riding the train and rather too determinedly reviewing her life history. And the ending seems hastily conceived; the author's light touch suddenly gives way to overstatement, and her resolution of the plot is not entirely plausible. Until that point, though, *I Wish This War Were Over* seems effortless—a book like a trip, with a sure sense of pacing and a clear destination, and an enthralling view out the window. (p. 37)

Anne Tyler, ''1944 and All That,'' in The New Republic, *Vol. 190, No. 11, March 19, 1984, pp. 36-7.*

LAURIE STONE

I Wish This War Were Over is an economical, wise coming-of-age story—a first novel for Diana O'Hehir, author of two books of poetry. The characters are vivid and worth caring about. They take shape, to a large extent, through dialogue, and the talk is crisp and funny, showing people puzzling out each other's eccentricities. Best of all is narrator Helen's ironic, humane, intelligent voice. It has a '40s tough-girl-masking-vulnerability edge—like Carole Lombard's. It's the sound of the clamorous, anxious country about to jettison innocence—the open-faced rawness Henry James love-hated. Beneath the period style, however, is a familiar, appealing figure who creates herself in every generation: the woman who knows life shrivels if she steers toward protection.

O'Hehir is deft and assured in her feminist skin; there isn't a polemical stutter or sentimental passing of wind in the narrative. Helen doesn't embody ideas; she's a porous consciousness, keen to the dust balls under her mother's bed and the taste of fear in her kisses. Helen's aware, as well, that her emotions color everything. . . .

The considerable tension in the novel derives less from what the characters do than from the way Helen registers her reactions, most interestingly to the combined brutality and rightness of events. Helen sees this in all her relationships, but O'Hehir is especially good at showing it in the O'Connell parts. Intimacy ignites between Helen and O'Connell when a dog dies. They're in a car, arguing about whether she should sleep with him (he's married, he makes her insides melt, he probably made her mother's insides melt). A dog runs onto the road, and it's too late to brake. Watching the animal die, Helen decides to have sex as a way of justifying the carnage. The thought makes sense until O'Connell, fresh and creamy from his shower, scoops her in his arms. She's been doing her nails, and as he kisses her, she plunges a scissor into his shoulder. The stabbing has a logic too, but Helen doesn't spell it out. She's evening the score: shifting the burden of sacrificial lamb to O'Connell and signaling her violence as well. It's a test, which O'Connell passes simply by recognizing it. These two are a good match, O'Hehir shows, because they have the same sense of justice and equal portions of curiosity. The sexiness in their exchanges is a wonderfully real mixture of shared knowledge and private fantasy. . . .

Helen's scenes with [her mother] Selma—who comes alive as the splendidly manipulative wreckage her daughter describes—don't work as well as the O'Connell sections. They're as spare and ironic, but that's the problem. The deeper feelings of watching a mother go down the drain are sometimes muffled by Helen's obliqueness. O'Hehir seems reluctant to dive into them, and the ending is more of a stop than a conclusion. But these omissions are few beside the novel's abundant delights.

Laurie Stone, in a review of ''I Wish This War Were Over,'' in VLS, *No. 25, April, 1984, p. 4.*

BARBARA FISHER WILLIAMSON

Diana O'Hehir's *I Wish This War Were Over* is a finely crafted first novel told through the perfectly pitched voice of 19-year-old Helen Reynolds. Full of wondering incredulity, Helen is alternately unsure or overconfident, always self-surprised and self-amused, full of delight that the world is as weird as she has secretly suspected.

The story Helen tells is about a trip she took in 1944, from her home in California to Washington, where she has encouraged her irresponsible and alcoholic mother to go. Worried about her mother's decline into drunkenness and defeat, guilty over sending her away, Helen sets off to see her. . . .

Although Helen fails to save her mother from suicide, she does succeed in understanding herself. And the line where Helen ends and her mother begins comes into sharp focus. But my one complaint with the novel is that the focus sharpens too fast. At the end, Helen realizes that her mother "wasn't an aching version of me anymore. She wasn't someone whose mistakes I was responsible for, whose mistakes I had to search out and redo. She wasn't me without my father's genes to make me stand up straight. She was somebody different from me." Helen deserves to know this, and we believe that she will some day learn it, but not yet and not so suddenly. Separation and self-definition take years to complete, and I suspect the author knows this.

In its central concern, *I Wish This War Were Over* resembles two other splendid, recent first novels—Marilynne Robinson's *Housekeeping* and Susanna Moore's *My Old Sweetheart*. In all three, young women struggle to define themselves as different from the inadequate and crazy mothers or mother substitutes with whom they live. Who are you if you are not like your mother and, because you have such a mother, not like other normal young women? The deep, demonic pull to be like one's mother, even when she is a lunatic or suicidal, rends the heart, as the dogged, daily push to be something different, and yet something that feels authentic, taxes the strength. Caught between this heart-wrenching pull and this energy-sapping push, the heroines of these novels toil valiantly to become whole people.

In *I Wish This War Were Over,* the struggle more resembles a caper because Helen protects herself from tragedy by her sense of wonder and her inclination for hope. We share her wonder and hope and appreciate her courage because the author tells her story with such rare grace and skill.

Barbara Fisher Williamson, "Puzzled by Men," in The New York Times Book Review, May 6, 1984, p. 24.

ISA KAPP

With its several strands of disorderly life percolating at the same time, and its World War II background of crowded trains, V-Day banners and plans held in suspension, *I Wish This War Were Over* adroitly escapes the confined quarters of fictional innocence and sensibility. The plot is full of motion: strangers meet, families part, and people's views of one another undergo sudden change.

Even in the throes of still another mother-daughter story (and a rather treacly one at that), O'Hehir's touch of levity turns

our expectations around. The formidably self-possessed 19-year-old heroine sets forth from California to bail her childlike drunkard mother out of the disheveled existence she is leading in Washington, D.C. Her first-person narrative style, dry and laconic (with hidden reserves of lyricism) is a direct steal from Humphrey Bogart's Sam Spade, and may well have been devised to counterbalance the tearful denouement. On the train, she runs into an affable middle-aged union organizer, an old boyfriend of her mother's who peppers his conversation with zestful tales of bygone auto strikes. We are distracted from future gloom by their bantering cross-country love affair, convincing in its cautious momentum and unembarrassed physicality. O'Connell is an unusual hero, uneducated but quick-spoken, soft with women, and magnetic at union meetings. . . .

Despite the plot's resorting, as does so much of modern fiction, to a pathological condition as catalyst, there are a number of winning tableaux: the mother decorously serving home-baked cake with burnt berries to her visiting daughter; the daughter putting the debris of underclothes in order, or solicitously reminding her fey parent to button her bathrobe. *I Wish This War Were Over* is corny yet beguiling; its main shortcoming is the impatient and pallid images it scatters of a city as animated and comely as Washington. (p. 7)

Isa Kapp, "The First Time Around," in The New Leader, Vol. LXVII, No. 22, December 10, 1984, pp. 5-8.

ROBERT DAHLIN

I Wish This War Were Over is concerned with 19-year-old Helen Reynolds, whose picaresque adventures take unexpected twists and turns as she travels the United States from west to east on what starts out as a journey of mercy but becomes one of self-discovery. . . .

Helen's epiphany is a familiar one in the long tradition of novels about young people awakening to adulthood, but in O'Hehir's hands the route to the realization is one that's marked with convincing insights into characters who come alive and a companionable understanding of sorrows and satisfactions that are sometimes inexpressible.

It is Helen's compassion masked by a stony exterior that makes her experiences rewarding as they push her along. Her jagged edges of immature resentment and mock hardness wear away, leaving her at book's end not much older, but significantly wiser.

O'Hehir's prose is a joy, unobtrusively poetic when imagistic playfulness is appropriate, tough when conveying deep emotion, and thoroughly in control throughout. It is her accomplishment that the novel speeds by like an adventure story, and yet repeatedly touches the reader with a poignant resonance that is uncannily like real life.

Robert Dahlin, "When a Young Girl Awakens to Adulthood: A Poet's First Novel," in The Christian Science Monitor, March 1, 1985, p. B2.

V(ictor) S(awdon) Pritchett

1900-

English short story writer, critic, essayist, travel writer, autobiographer, and novelist.

An important English "man of letters" whose career has spanned more than fifty years, Pritchett has won enthusiastic acclaim for his versatility and the consistency of his work. Along with his short stories, for which he is most highly praised, Pritchett's canon includes critical essays, travel writing, and autobiography. Pritchett's grasp of character, delineated with a Dickensian eye for detail, a sense of humor, and a deep interest in and understanding of human behavior, is frequently cited as a key element in all of his work. In evaluating the success of Pritchett's short fiction, William Trevor observed that "[the] more parochial and domestic these stories appear to be on the surface the deeper the depths they acquire when considered in retrospect. Pritchett writes of the universal by way of a narrow particular, allowing humor and the variations in human relationships to create his patterns of truth."

Pritchett has written five novels, all of which were published early in his career. Although it is generally agreed that Pritchett's novels are less important than his short stories, they display some of the same concerns and techniques as his other work. Pritchett's interest in Spain is evident in *Shirley Sanz* (1932; published in the United States as *Elopement into Exile*), in which a young English woman elopes to Spain with a man of English and Spanish ancestry. Cultural differences and disillusionment in marriage are among the themes developed in this book. In *Dead Man Leading* (1937), Pritchett departs from his conventional style to employ such experimental devices as flashbacks and stream-of-consciousness prose. Although reviewers did not consider this novel to be entirely successful, they praised its symbolism and vivid portrayal of the Brazilian jungle setting. The central character of *Mr. Beluncle* (1951) is loosely based on Pritchett's father, whose adamant, eccentric religious beliefs, like Mr. Beluncle's, disrupted his family. Pritchett's other novels are *Clare Drummer* (1929) and *Nothing like Leather* (1935).

Pritchett's nonfiction works cover a variety of interests and formats. Prose volumes culled from his extensive travels include *Marching Spain* (1928), *Foreign Faces* (1964; published in the United States as *The Offensive Traveler*), *New York Proclaimed* (1964), and *Dublin: A Portrait* (1967). These books are characterized by their sensitive, detailed observations of people and places. *A Cab at the Door: Childhood and Youth, 1900-1920* (1968) and *Midnight Oil* (1971) are volumes of reminiscences which were praised for their honesty and insight; the latter work chronicles Pritchett's development as a writer. Theodore Solotaroff described *A Cab at the Door* as "a splendid montage of persons and places fixed in their individual being, casting their representative light, and suggesting the evolving personality of the author through his relations with them."

Pritchett's critical essays form another important part of his career. They are written in clear, direct language, and while they contain intelligent appraisals of American and European literature, they usually focus more on the personal lives of the

authors than on textual analysis. Critics compare Pritchett's technique to that practiced by such renowned literary commentators as William Hazlitt and Edmund Wilson, claiming that Pritchett's essays are both intellectually stimulating and entertaining. His best-known critical works include *The Living Novel* (1946), *Books in General* (1953), and *The Working Novelist* (1965). He has also published several volumes on individual authors, including *Balzac* (1974) and *The Gentle Barbarian: The Life and Work of Turgenev* (1977). *The Myth Makers* (1979), a collection of essays on European, Russian, and South American authors, evidences Pritchett's interest in a diverse group of literary figures. In *The Tale Bearers* (1980), Pritchett shares his views on such writers as Jonathan Swift, Joseph Conrad, Rudyard Kipling, and Saul Bellow. *A Man of Letters* (1985) contains a selection of essays drawn from Pritchett's extensive critical writings.

Pritchett is most highly respected for his work in the short story genre. His stories describe the lives of predominantly middle-class, ordinary people through a flood of mundane details and frequently humorous but essentially kindhearted observations. His early collections, including *The Spanish Virgin and Other Stories* (1930), *You Make Your Own Life* (1938), and *It May Never Happen and Other Stories* (1945), contain many of Pritchett's most famous stories, including "The Saint," "Sense of Humour," and "Pocock Passes." Pritchett considers the title piece of *When My Girl Comes Home* (1961) to be his best story. This work centers on the return of a young girl to her hometown of London. Her friends and neighbors, who are under the impression that she had spent the previous years languishing in a World War II prison camp in Japan, are mystified by her evident wealth and well-being and by her tales of exotic travel and marriage. Frequently cited as an example of Pritchett's skillful evocation of character, through which he reveals the complex, poignant inner lives of commonplace people, "When My Girl Comes Home" was lauded for its realistic portrayal of the social intricacies and class tensions of English working-class life. In a review of *Selected Stories* (1978), Eudora Welty summarized Pritchett's achievement: "The characters that fill [his stories]—erratic, unsure, unsafe, devious, stubborn, restless and desirous, absurd and passionate, all peculiar unto themselves—hold a claim on us that is not to be denied. They demand and get our attention, for in the revelation of their lives, the secrets of our own lives come into view."

(See also *CLC*, Vols. 5, 13, 15; *Contemporary Authors*, Vols. 61-64; and *Dictionary of Literary Biography*, Vol. 15.)

RICHARD LOCKE

Literary criticism these days tends to decline into academic drudgery or sacerdotal solipsism; book reviewing frequently becomes an exercise in cultural politics or a clamorous yawp of exhibitionistic ego. In this cultural context, V. S. Pritchett, born in 1900, remains a man of letters in the best unsentimental sense, the last great English literary journalist, a surviving link with the great tradition of English and European literature.

Neither a scholar nor an intellectual in the New York or Continental sense, Pritchett is the supreme contemporary virtuoso of the short literary essay in which, as he puts it, "the writer has to get at an essence, show his wit and his hand, and make his decisive effect with alacrity in fewer than 2,000 scrupulous words." Unlike so many English literary journalists who dash off smooth and slovenly "notices" in a trice and rely on social gestures and what he calls "mellifluous English nonsense," Pritchett is informal but never clubby, witty but never snide or snobbish, precise and always full of gusto—a true descendant of William Hazlitt.

He is impatient with explication, symbolic games and patterns, psychoanalytic clichés and the massive "fact-fetishism" of recent literary biographies. . . . He abhors "the present academic habit of turning literary criticism into technology. . . . Literary criticism does not add to its status by opening an intellectual hardware store." (p. 3)

Pritchett has no great curiosity for "ideas in themselves" or for the structure or philosophy of literature. He stands apart from the two most influential critical movements of the century, the New Criticism of Brooks, Warren & Company and the French formalism (structuralism, post-structuralism, now deconstruction) that has swept American graduate schools during the past decade. At the same time, he is not a literary antiquarian or esthete offering lush impressionistic "appreciations," and he never uses literature as the occasion for a political speech or moral sermon or visionary flight.

Pritchett's essays are sketches of an author's life, times and works. Always the short-story writer, he is fascinated by people,

by characters. He has the lower-middle-class Londoner's quick eye and sharp tongue and appetite for comedy. He's quick to spot pride, the cover-up, flummery, snobbery, cant. From his work he appears to be an emotional, intensely curious man—plucky, blunt, generous. A shrewd and adroit psychologist, he's not interested in digging into psychoanalytic turf: he feels it tends to "standardize [the] subject as a psychological case." He'd rather follow a writer around, seeing him live his life with all his conflicts acted out (or suppressed) and transformed into art. . . . (pp. 3, 22)

Pritchett relies on short sentences, concrete details and brilliant metaphors: nearly all the scholarship and commentary on Joseph Conrad, for example, is dwarfed by Pritchett's short essay in *The Living Novel* with its extraordinary remark that *Nostromo* is a "grim brocade." His essay on George Eliot in that volume is even better: it contains a wonderful narrative description of her pastoral novel *Adam Bede*. . . .

[Almost all of Pritchett's] recent work exhibits a fresh, compulsive curiosity and a vigorous prose style. In this he seems an English cousin of Edmund Wilson in his old age—without the crotchets or the granitic egotism. . . .

To convey Pritchett's distinctive tone and method, his description of E. M. Forster [from *The Tale Bearers: Literary Essays*] serves well:

> He was at once comically drab and alarmingly alive, and so fresh in the offhand private voice speaking in the public place where it disconcerted because it dodged conventional utterance. The voice was the most important thing about him and his prose; it was unofficial, conversational, free of jargon, and dropped a dissident but carefully timed word or two of Edwardian slang into the solemn moments of argument. . . . 'Arguments,' he once said, showing that he was a novelist by nature, 'are only fascinating when they are of the nature of gestures and illustrate the people who produce them.'

Of course, much of this could apply to Pritchett himself.

Yet there's a lot more to Pritchett's greatness than his voice. . . . (p. 22)

[Consider] the beginning of his rapid survey of turn-of-the-century English literature, occasioned by the reissue of the *Lucia* novels, minor entertainments by the once-popular E. F. Benson:

> The Edwardian period in English literature which runs, I suppose, from the 1880's until 1914 was prolific in light, satirical Society novelists of remarkable urbanity and invention. The exclusive [George] Meredith was one of the gods; the moment for high comedy had come. One can see why: an age of surfeit had arrived. The lives of the upper classes were both enlivened and desiccated by what seems to have been a continuous diet of lobster and champagne—a diet well suited in its after-effects to the stimulation of malice. The class system gave the ironies of snobbery their double edge. Society lived out its fairy-tale life, spent its time changing its extravagant clothes several times a day, and was entertained by the antics of social

climbers. And, whether they are writing about manners, high, middling, or low, the light novelists have a common quality: they are accomplished, they are even elegant. . . . I have often thought that professors of English Lit. should take time off from the central glooms of genius and consider these lesser entertainers who are deeply suggestive; but perhaps it is as well that the Academy winces at the idea, for we would hate to see our fun damped down by explication.

Of course, Pritchett is himself a master of the central glooms of genius, but he is also incontestably one of the happy few, a man seemingly blessed in life and work. He still regards literature as a personal communication, a social act, a performance and a mark of character. This is certainly not the only way to read and write, but it carries the cultural momentum and authority of a great tradition with it; and Pritchett deserves our warmest homage and thanks, particularly in an age of rising literary technocrats and declining literary culture and continuity. (p. 23)

Richard Locke, "In Praise of V. S. Pritchett," in
The New York Times Book Review, *June 29, 1980,*
pp. 3, 22-3.

JAMES CAMPBELL

The conspicuous virtue of Pritchett's criticism is that it is itself creative. He uses the occasion provided by [**The Tale Bearers**] to do some writing of his own. Managed by Sir Victor, this method is never impertinent: he is sensitive, informative, critical when need be, and deeply and consistently intelligent.

The essays in his new book are mostly on novelists and were occasioned either by the publication of a new novel or of a biography. As a writer of fiction, Pritchett approaches his subjects with the sympathy of the fellow sufferer. He knows how to convey a narrative synopsis and a sense of character without either giving too much away or letting any of the essential feeling spill from his description. Of the Countess in Angus Wilson's *No Laughing Matter*, for example: 'an Edwardian snob with a false accent—she says "beauteh" for "beauty", "meh" for "me". She lives in dreams of second-rate grandeur, is capricious, petulant, very randy and rather unclean. Her taste in lovers is coarse.' This snapshot—the last two details making the awful 'Cuntess' sound so unappealing yet strangely enticing—is typical of the descriptions not only of characters in novels but also of the subjects of biographies. . . . This encapsulating skill is equally evident when Pritchett is defining the psychological motivations of novelists: Evelyn Waugh's early books 'spring from the liberating notion that human beings are mad; the war trilogy, a work of maturity, draws on the meatier notion that the horrible thing about human beings is that they are sane'. Flannery O'Connor's characters are at the mercy of forces they do not understand—but give them time: 'Satan, they will discover, is not just a word. He has legs—and those legs are their own.'

In writing of biography he is never content simply to retell the facts of an author's life, even when—as, say, in the case of T. E. Lawrence—those facts are interesting enough to command attention in their own right. Always, he is on the lookout for the detail which will cause the fan to spread out and reveal a picture worth a thousand words. Of particular use in this respect is sex, since it is one of the chief driving forces in all

lives. Sir Victor appears to understand its operations quite well. He never generalizes, and chides the easy Freudian trick when it is played: as there are as many manifestations of the sexual spectre as there are human beings, it follows that each will be uniquely haunted. (pp. 88-9)

[Among the authors] whose sexual and literary mentalities are related: Rider Haggard's creation 'comes flawlessly out of the agonies of sexual anxiety'. Discussing *She,* Pritchett is inclined to call Haggard's Ayesha '*He* but—as James Thurber once said about a grand piano—with breasts'. Conrad, who drifted away from sex once he married, created *femmes fatales* which are 'the standard fantasies of the Romantic Decadents'. Kipling, whose love affairs were 'painfully platonic' and who was 'mother's dutiful boy' for more years than he should have been, eventually married a formidable woman who managed his money, opened his letters and dictated their replies, and, perhaps damagingly, 'cut her husband off from intellectual company'. Pritchett sardonically quips that she 'enjoyed hearing that the female of the species was more deadly than the male'. (p. 89)

Some of the other subjects in this collection of 23 essays are Beerbohm, Greene, James, Bellow, Pepys, Swift and Richard Burton. He imitates the nit-picking critic in only one place, and there helpfully to enlighten: one of Mary McCarthy's characters insists that swans do not bite, they strike; not true, says Sir Victor, 'I was bitten by one when I was eight.' This book demonstrates at every turn of the page that criticism can be as pleasurable to read as any other literary form: often more so, since it is pleasurable in the manner of the best conversation. I can think of only one other critic who is so consistently engrossing and entertaining and that is Gore Vidal. But while Vidal has one crafty eye on the author, both of Pritchett's are planted firmly on the page. (p. 90)

James Campbell, "Both Eyes on the Page," in London Magazine, *n.s. Vol. 20, No. 4, July, 1980, pp. 87-90.*

VALENTINE CUNNINGHAM

Matured long ago past the stage of having to strain for a young reviewer's smartness, V. S. Pritchett's criticism practises wisdom. Wisdom comes so naturally to his reviewing pen, in fact, that we end up taking his crisply sage reflections, his most assentable asides, the continual evidencing of hard-schooled and well-tried gumption, almost for granted. . . . Pritchett has clearly been around, as they say, and around a long time. We and the editors of the *New Statesman,* the *New Yorker* and the *New York Review of Books* from which **The Tale Bearers**' pieces have been culled and (in some cases I would guess) stitched together, are lucky still to have him about.

He's probably of necessity still hard at it, of course, for there are no occupational pensions for that breed of writer and critic of which he is one of our last survivors—the old-fashioned Man of Letters. Only men of letters in the new style, the professoriate, get pensions that let them potter and pick after the age of sixty-five or so. The others have to keep treadling. No wonder Pritchett evinces a kind of wry pride in what the journalistic "mill" puts the reviewer through. . . .

No wonder either, then, that the less necessitous academic author is rarely let off without a scathing. Toiling through Felstiner's study of Beerbohm, Pritchett "understood what Max meant when he said that exhaustive accounts of the period 'would need far less brilliant pens than mine'". Conrad's biographer Professor Karl makes too many "solemn and obsequious gestures to the academy". Dr Mack, biographer of T. E. Lawrence, "is no wit". Richard Burton, "a pestiferous pursuer of whatever can be turned into a footnote", had the echt academic appetite "that turns the romantic into a pedant" (and, Pritchett mutters darkly, "One has often seen this happen").

Naturally enough, Edmund Wilson is the kind of critic to whom he warms most.... [Pritchett] is England's nearest living equivalent of Edmund Wilson. And Pritchett's criticism is always warming, like that, to aspects of authors that he himself turns out to share....

Pritchett's power as critic derives from his capacity for giving himself up to "the minds and feelings and interests" of the authors he discusses. It is a process of what he calls "unselfing himself". Unselfing was, he suggests, the strength of Henry Green's fiction. We are not surprised to find him detecting it as the method, too, of Edmund Wilson—inspirited in his turn by his master, the master of historiography, Michelet:

> I mean that he is an artist ... in the sense that
> he is a man possessed. Give him the subject
> and it fuses with his whole person as if something like Mesmer's famous magnetic fluid had
> flowed into him.

It is a consequence of such a saturation in the author and book at hand that no other living critic I know can initiate one so surely, so swiftly, as Pritchett does, in the space of a mere paragraph or two, into the heart of an author's life and matter....

[Pritchett] is exercised by a continually strong moral attentiveness. The English, he suggests, "live on moral tension". He is up on sin ("There is more magic in sin", he declares of Kipling, "if it is not committed"). He wants to repossess the concepts of good and evil from Greene's Catholic clutches ("May not a rationalist be fully conscious of mental degradation or good and evil?").

It is a set of moral concerns which—like the alertness with which he can be depended on to pick up an author's or character's puritanical connection: T. E. Lawrence's or Kipling's mothers, Burton's wife, the theological inheritance of Pepys and Boswell, Rolfe and Gissing—has been bred into him by generations (on his father's side) of Yorkshire Non-conformity. And, conscious as he is of his own family inheritance, he frequently opens his dealings with an author by accounting for the impact of parents. Naturally, Edmund Wilson's *The Wound and the Bow* is acknowledged as a key text ("Lawrence's private story is the story of the wound and the bow"). In its wake, Pritchett has become a connoisseur of the shaping childhood trauma. He is particularly good, as well, on the childishnesses that persist into adulthood....

Pritchett's criticism keeps making deftly impressive connexions between an author's art and his life—keeps refreshing our sense of him as one of our best literary biographers.... Granting full weight to an author's life may in some quarters be thought critically *passé*, but Pritchett's practice keeps justifying its fruitfulness, keeps proving it part of the necessary fullness of attention authors and text deserve.

Axiomatically, for Pritchett, authors live in a real world; so do their books; so must their critics: and he will make us inhabit it with them and him.... You can't quarrel with a critic who's been there. And Sir Victor perpetually convinces you he has been there; so personally, so livingly, so perceptively, in, with,

and about his authors, keeping an always loving but ever diligently sharp eye on their life, works and claims.

Valentine Cunningham, "The Reader on the Scent," in The Times Literary Supplement, *No. 4043, September 26, 1980, p. 1070.*

GEORGE CORE

To read Pritchett's criticism is to understand the relation of the author's world to the life of his writing—or the writer's life to the world of his characters. Pritchett enters so thoroughly into the mind and work of the writer he criticizes that he all but vanishes; the same applies when he writes fiction: the author, although present, does not intrude, and we forget him as we delight in the figures of his fictive universe. His figures are not only animate but inanimate and are bound by unprepossessing metaphors which gradually accumulate effect, echoing and amplifying action and theme. "My stories almost always begin with an image which settles in the mind. In that way it's like writing poetry," he has said.

This image almost invariably sits astride the spine of the narrative. The images are obvious, concrete, active, and inevitable in the making of the fable and the unraveling of the plot....

Image becomes action in **"Tea with Mrs. Bittell," "The Worshippers," "Blind Love,"** and nearly every other story in *On the Edge of the Cliff* and *Selected Stories* (1978). In **"Tea with Mrs. Bittell"** Pritchett mixes the droll and the serious in equal parts, never allowing the humor to become slapstick (as Waugh often did) and never permitting the grim, melancholy, frightening, and pathetic to get the upper hand (as Greene often does). The controlling image is a painting of Psyche that has been in Mrs. Bittell's family forever. A lonely widow, she mistakenly befriends two young men at church, and after several visits one of them returns to pinch Psyche and other things in Mrs. Bittell's flat. She unexpectedly returns, and the ensuing scene—which possesses the terrifying and comic quality of nightmare in slow motion—gathers up the many motifs of the story—imperialism, frustrated heterosexual and homosexual love, fetishism, acquisitiveness. At the end Psyche and her owner have been violated, but they are victorious, if badly shaken. The author leaves the action not quite resolved: this is an earmark of his fictive strategy.

The economy of Pritchett's short fiction is remarkable. Another author might use the material in a Pritchett story for a novel. **"The Wedding,"** a fiction of 7,500 words that is the best story in the new collection, is a good instance. In it we get the biographies of three complex characters, glimpses of various minor characters, two weddings (the one onstage provides the major scene), a symbolic rape followed by a seduction, a compact history of the farming community in which the action occurs, the interiors of three houses, and many other things to boot. (pp. xxxviii-xl)

Love, usually thwarted, always complicated, is the master theme of Pritchett's fiction. Theme as such, action in the abstract, does not hold him as a critic: he looks at the unfolding life of a fiction and lets us see it fully by watching him take its pulse and trace its anatomy. But he is fascinated with the ideological frame of mind—how a particular set of values or a way of looking at the world can harden into orthodoxy, twisting life and wringing the juices and flavour from it. Pritchett is compulsively attracted to puritanism, as Walter Allen has pointed out. (pp. xl-xlii)

One of Pritchett's latest reports on puritanism appears in **"Satan Comes to Georgia,"** the best short essay ever written on Flannery O'Connor.... This piece is collected in *The Tale Bearers,* which presents essays on British and American writers from Pepys to Angus Wilson. Some of the best essays concern Englishmen that Pritchett had previously considered, just as some of the best in *The Myth Makers* concern Russians like Dostoevsky and Goncharov. These books, together with *The Living Novel and Later Appreciations* (1964), are among the best criticism of our time. One reads Pritchett in the *New York Review of Books* or the *New Yorker* to get the report from the front that remains news. When it hits the newsstand, one gets a succinct but comprehensive review not only of the work at hand but of the author who wrote it and of his world; when the piece reappears in a collection, the reader finds it as fresh and acute as it was on first being published. (p. xlii)

The life of art is conveyed by the vitality of V. S. Pritchett's prose and by his unflagging curiosity. The critical prose is less metaphorical, less involved with the idiom of the times and its walks. We get the dazzling generalization ... but not the darting idiosyncrasy that Allen has remarked in the stories.... In the stories Pritchett time and again catches conversation fumbling: people usually talk at each other, pursuing their own obsessions; but in the criticism Pritchett speaks directly to the reader in a unique voice—quiet, measured, compelling. (pp. xlii-xliii)

George Core, "V. S. Pritchett and the Life of Art," in The Sewanee Review, Vol. LXXXIX, No. 2, Spring, 1981, pp. xxxviii, xl, xlii-xliii.

ANATOLE BROYARD

I keep reading and re-reading V. S. Pritchett in the hope of admiring his stories as much as everyone else does. He is so universally admired that I feel deprived of him, tricked by fate out of a pleasure available to my friends and colleagues. I don't have the nerve to suggest that I may be right and everyone else wrong.

Now here's his *Collected Stories,* his own selection from seven volumes and 50 years of writing, and all I can say is that his stories are good, fine, even splendid—but only when he allows them to be. Quite a few of them are spoiled, in my opinion, by what I would call a sentimental humanist assumption.

Mr. Pritchett seems to believe that wholly ordinary people, behaving in a wholly ordinary fashion, can be made to yield literature by good writing and technique. It's as if he thinks it's enough for them to be human beings, or God's children, as if he were saying that in a democracy everyone is interesting and you must love your neighbor as yourself.

I don't know: perhaps from the vantage point of his great age, Mr. Pritchett can see what I can't. Perhaps in his eyes and mind people cast long shadows. He's past 80 years old and it may be that, as one of his characters says, a man of that age thinks of death and the thought of death makes all life beautiful.

There are younger writers like Mary Robison or Raymond Carver, who push the ordinary toward the grotesque and make a kind of literature of it, providing you can suspend your disbelief—but in a man of Mr. Pritchett's wisdom and experience I tend to look for something more. Yet it may be wrong of me to want him to father fiction. If he wants to kick up his heels among feckless characters, I suppose he has his reasons. It

may be more cheerful for him than writing profound stories. . . .

Having said all this, I want to call your attention to some wonderful moments in these *Collected Stories.* There is one story about a woman whose life has been spoiled by a physical blemish and who, when she finds a man who doesn't care about it, cries: "I love you. I feel gaudy!''. . .

A lonely, rigid woman goes to the house of a lonely, rigid man, and Mr. Pritchett writes, "His windows seem to him—and to her—to sob." A man who's having an affair with a romantic young woman has told her that his wife is beautiful. When she meets his wife, who is almost grotesque, she feels that she is the more deceived of the two.

"The secret of happiness is to find a congenial monotony." "The suffering of others is incredible. When it is obscure it seems like a lie; when it is garish and raw, it is like boasting." There are many sentences as good as these, and some of the stories are brilliant. . . .

"The Diver" is a perfect story about a young Englishman in France. It's filled with ingenious centrifugal impulses that all come together in the end, like people coming from different directions to a party. Mr. Pritchett knows how blind men feel with people who can see. He knows how old men feel with young women they desire. He knows what it feels like to be attractive or unattractive. He understands the fascination that insanity can have for the sane. He can make you feel hopelessness as you feel bad weather.

So there it is. After all these stories, I'm no nearer to the secret of Mr. Pritchett. Sometimes he's great and sometimes he isn't. I suppose that's not such a bad way for a writer to be, all things considered.

Anatole Broyard, "The Ordinary People," in The New York Times, April 24, 1982, p. 17.

ROBERTSON DAVIES

[If V. S. Pritchett's] short stories must be nailed down to some particular department of narrative art, they may be called French in quality. Their concision, coolness of tone, controlled irony and economy in describing emotion that is itself far from economical remind us that this writer studied French writing closely as a youth, and lived for some time in France during the years when he was not only forming his style but acquiring his characteristic way of looking at life. The life he looks at most closely and describes most persuasively is not French but English.

English, moreover, of a special aspect that only an Englishman who had experienced it at first-hand could hope to capture and make convincing. A Henry James may perfectly understand the English upper classes, but Pritchett's England is the England of H. G. Wells' *Kipps*; he writes of it better than Wells, because Wells despised it and his mockery and derision cannot be controlled. Pritchett writes of it coolly, but not coldly; his feeling for it is affectionate and understanding, but not nostalgic or approving. As a result, his view of this lower middle-class world is more revealing and more devastating but in no way as cruel as is that of Wells, who was convinced that he was a genius; it is unlikely that such a notion about himself has ever entered Pritchett's head.

How wonderfully he writes about this world of precariously maintained respectability, of shopkeepers who must "refinance'' or ''sink back'' (meaning get their hands on more capital or fail), of all the fine slicing of theology that divides Calvinistic Methodist from Wesleyan, and Congregational from Baptist, to say nothing of that vast world of ''New Thought'' and faiths ''in harmony with modern business.'' How compassionately, but not emotionally, he deals with all the complicated domestic politics of the respectable poor, the martyred or termagant wives, the feckless or drunken husbands, and that terror that walketh by noonday, the mother-in-law. His novel **Mr. Beluncle** is an unjustly neglected comic masterpiece, perhaps because the comedy is too shrewd and not broad enough for those who merely want a funny book. Its comedy is Chekhovian, rather than Dickensian. But then, Dickens believed in Evil, and Sir Victor is too cool a customer for that, and the most piercing comedy demands a moral commitment he does not choose to make. (pp. 1-2)

Sir Victor admits his preference among his short stories; he thinks **"When My Girl Comes Home"** is the best thing he has done, and all critical reason supports his opinion. But I have a special fondness for **"The Camberwell Beauty,"** a story of the antique trade.... In this splendid story Pritchett produces that mingling of the wondrous and the commonplace that marks the finest work of E.T.A. Hoffmann, and which has a power that can only be described as fantastic in the real sense of that battered word. The reader will not soon rid himself of the image of the beautiful girl, prisoner and mistress of one of those rookeries of antiques, blowing on her bugle and rattling on her drum to keep at bay the young man to whom she is the treasure of treasures.

Part of the pleasure of reading [Pritchett's **Collected Stories**] is that he writes about people who are very much in the palpable world, people who go to work because they must, and whose financial ambitions are modest. People to whom the bank manager is a towering and perhaps a minatory presence. People whose adulteries are as compelling as those of Antony and Cleopatra, but who live out their drama against the fusty dullness of ordinary lives and ordinary bedrooms. People who are working-class politicians, driving themselves toward petty goals which may benefit their followers but are principally beneficial to themselves. People in whose lives truth is a conditional, rather than an absolute value. People whose lonely old age is eerily illuminated by cunning, and acute feeling, and loony passion. People who live in that world of unlikelihood which is the very stuff of truth, rather than of careful fiction. If they sound dull or repellent thus catalogued, they are by no means so as he writes about them, because they are all illuminated by understanding, and have the ring of truth. Every word and situation, every queer turn of events, carries conviction.

This is literary achievement on a very high level, and what a relief it is from the tedious stream of stories about privileged people who have time and inclination for foolish mischief, usually of a sexual kind, and who are so frequently authors, or artists, or simply rich idlers, but who are invariably self-indulgent dullards. (pp. 2, 15)

[In his essay **"As Old as the Century"** in **The Turn of the Years,** Pritchett] says that the writer has to work much harder than the mass of employed people, which is what all writers say, but which in his case carries immediate conviction. To see life as steadily as V. S. Pritchett does, and to find the best way to tell us what he sees and to convince us of its reality without ever falsifying detail or tone, is very hard work indeed.... This is the harvest of a life of observation, experience and intuition, a harvest gathered by a man of integrity and

artistic gift. It is this rich harvest that we enjoy with him, and for which we offer him our thanks as he comes rejoicing, bringing in the sheaves. (p. 15)

> *Robertson Davies, ''V. S. Pritchett: Storyteller Supreme,'' in* Book World—The Washington Post, *April 25, 1982, pp. 1-2, 15.*

VALENTINE CUNNINGHAM

If anywhere there lurks any doubt that V. S. Pritchett should carry off the palm as the best living English short story writer, [**Collected Stories**] will surely rout the worriers.... [Here], rewardingly for old and new readers alike, is an enticing trove of around fifty years' worth of the master's mature work, a volume for reading and re-reading, one to dip into and return to, and to be warmly recommended. It comprises a rare set of fictional delights.

And one really is talking about fifty years of mature work. In his preface, Pritchett is not only being perceptive when he describes the stories in his 1920s volume **The Spanish Virgin** as prentice work (and none of them are collected here), he's also right to feel that he had already ''found a distinctive voice'', ''discovered my voice'', by the 1930s. Take the third story in this collection, **"Many Are Disappointed"**, about a quartet of thirsty cyclists on holiday from the office who are looking out for luscious women as well as for the pub and the Roman road marked on their map, and who have to settle instead for the mere cups of tea, dull tomato sandwiches and poorly, faded proprietress of the so-called ''tavern'' they've come across. This story stood out sharply in 1937 from the rest of the ''Seven English Stories'' among which it first appeared in the fourth number of John Lehmann's distinguished magazine *New Writing*. It proved to be as good a story as Lehmann ever published. It sticks in the mind, in fact, as one of the finest short stories to have appeared in the 1930s. And it's as memorable in its way as anything Pritchett was to produce later. By his own and his century's thirties—he and it are the same age—Pritchett was well into his stride: a pace that, astonishingly, he's been able to maintain ever since....

From the start his trademark has been making human moments into epiphanies through memorable phrases, vivid tags and scraps of ideolect captured by roaming and plundering the language registers of an extraordinary breadth of classes and sects, odd social crannies, dark and curious corners of behaviour.

''Many are disappointed'': it's in that phrase of the careful, washed-out tea-lady that she and her story really live. It was in discovering her voice and the voices of her kind that Pritchett discovered his own voice, and how to make his stories speak. And again and again he hits off this impressive trick. ''Do you a nice spotted dick?''; ''Say, we let some Error in that time''; ''This is the job''; ''Ai love it when you are severe''; ''She's played everyone up'': thus the landlocked sailor turned handyman, the podgy transcendentalist, the lustful lay-preacher, the dried-up, masochistic private-schoolmaster, the irked local councillor, reveal themselves to their circle and to us. And when whole conversations are made out of such stuff—as in **"Things As They Are"** ('''Not with a belt', said Mrs Foster, 'I will not be hit with a belt' ''), or **"When My Girl Comes Home"** ('''It was proved in court that he didn't', said Constance briskly''), Pritchett can sound magically anticipatory of Pinter's best.

What he's celebrating is the heroicism of banal life.... Ordinary people, made marginal and socially insignificant by provinciality or lack of intelligence, or by the chosen exiles of enthusiastic religiosity (and Pritchett enters more knowledgeably than anyone else now save perhaps Stanley Middleton the shadowy worlds of the Gospel Hall, the Mission Tent, the faith-healer's parlour): people like this are shown striving to cope, especially by their little sayings, their blunted verbal stratagems, their ritually smoothed out counters of exchange, with the pressing universe of wider experience and bigger words. ''I mean'', slate-miner's son Sidney, who works in a posh grocer's, will ask of everything and everyone, hanging on grimly to the liferaft of a saving concept, are you, is his friend, was the Duke of Wellington ''sincere''? . . .

Pritchett sympathizes most with people who have problems knowing their way round and managing the lingo. About those who manoeuvre more adroitly through the tripwires of words he allows most doubts to settle. He admires their skilled survival, but also distinctly feels that to become too strong, to become at worst all voice, less person than megaphone—like the unfrocked cleric in **''The Voice''** who sings indestructibly from below the bomb rubble of his old church, or the lifelong radical lady speechifier in **''The Speech''** whose words sent boys to their death in Spain—is to have allowed the verbal means of personal salvation to get hellishly out of hand.

The Pauline language—salvation, damnation—comes naturally because it is Pritchett's own. His narratives are full of Bible-punchers, high on Biblical phraseology and the analogies they draw between bombing or bonfires of family heirlooms and Hell. The very first narrator in this collection declares himself a puritan. Lots of the characters are teetotallers. They live within, and are annoyed by, religious constraints.... In Pritchett's fiction religious faith is usually bad faith. And one of Pritchett's virtues is that he refuses to get too heated about that: both he and his people accept a sense of sin, a seared conscience, as normal. Pritchett is superb at presenting the moral lapse.... It's noticeable, however, that Pritchett's tolerance wears thinnest, and his usual worries about the slick language-manipulators are most clamant, in the presence of the powerfully puritanical: people like the awful Charles Thwaite in **''A Debt of Honour''**, the canting Catholic husband who returns after years of absence to squeeze his wife for more cash, and who walks off with her last treasure, her fur coat, after terrorizing her once more with his masterful gibes about sin and divorce and her ''indecent'' pictures.

These twisted puritans—and they include the self-righteous lady sermonizer of the Left, and the Leftist editor whose self-love is quickly uncovered by his third-world female fan—make such powerful fictional presences because it seems that in looking into their deterring depths Pritchett is illuminating something deeply felt in his own. His lustfully corrupt religious men itch to lay bare, to get their hands on the skin beneath women's clothes—a desire oddly akin not just to the story-teller's keenness to expose but also to the fascination repeatedly shown by these stories for the flesh beneath women's dresses. And, not unlike their puritans, Pritchett's stories are often as worried by the business of exposure as they are animated by it. Uncannily, bits of bodies come disconcertingly alive as Pritchett uncovers them for our attention. Teeth have a way of throwing the reader as well as characters when they're bared, as they often are. So, for that matter, do eyebrows, exposed frequently in Pritchett's fiction (as well as in his criticism).... And what about tongues, ultimate instrument of Pritchett's strength and chief

means of such strengths-in-weakness as his people acquire? Mrs Johnson of **''Blind Love''** is all tongue, her mouth hot with Cockney toughness, her body embraced beneath her blouse by a huge birthmark, ''this ugly blob—dark as blood, like a ragged liver on a butcher's window, or some obscene island with ragged edges'': ''like a red tongue''. Living with a tongue like that is evidently difficult. Exposed on her wedding night it shocks her husband into instant separation. A crooked faith-healer prowls about her swimming-pool and craves a sight of it, but only the love of her blind lover helps her to come to terms with her stained self, gaudy tongue and all. **''Blind Love''** her story is titled: and though blind love may not be much, it's better, Pritchett implies, than no love at all when you go about, as his fiction does, in the excitingly worrisome places where people live so vividly by their tongues.

Valentine Cunningham, ''Coping with the Bigger Words,'' in The Times Literary Supplement, *No. 4134, June 25, 1982, p. 687.*

CLANCY SIGAL

Like a great surgeon, V. S. Pritchett wields his literary scalpel to uncover layer upon layer of the insulted flesh of his obsessional, love-hungry, love-frightened characters. His men tend to be crafty, brutal and ungenerous; his women, great quivering monuments to masochistic self-sacrifice and stoicism. He is our Chekhov, dissecting the respectably cadaverous hearts of the sober, puritanical English middle class—especially, the lower middle class—with tender cruelty, and withholding the mercies of sexual fulfilment or a happy death in old age.

Pritchett is not a visionary; indeed, his stories **''The Speech''** and **''The Lady From Guatemala''** . . . make clear that, in the author's view, a political life guarantees both flagrant hypocrisy and contempt for believers. His strength is an enormous faith in, and ironical suspicion of, the guile-encrusted lifemanship of the sort of people slowly passing from the English scene: small-town shopkeepers, rural taxi-drivers, unprotesting widows, and all those Bessie Braddocks of the hearth of whom we see only vicious impersonations by Thora Hird or in *Coronation Street*. As well as being a deceptively 'quiet', and brilliant, storyteller Pritchett is a meticulous historian of the agony of diminished passions of a post-imperial generation, whose largely unheard snuffles and laments most of us still carry unconsciously in our hearts. (pp. 22-3)

Every good story writer invites you into a self-contained world that only inexactly parallels and overlaps the 'real' world. Pritchett's cosmos is dark, lively and full of super-ordinary people who either don't have the sense or don't have the stupidity to be altogether crushed. For better and worse, he is class-specific; his working-class characters are too predictably brutish and limited, but are splendid triggers for Pritchett's cool pathos....

In one of the typical stories [included in *Collected Stories*], **''Handsome Is As Handsome Does''**, the frustrated wife of Coram, an industrial chemist who has thrust vulgarly and blindly up from the working class, falls humiliatingly in love with a 22-year-old boy while on holiday in France. There is a near-drowning; the husband is cowardly, the boy heroic. The middle-aged wife, who had thrown away her class status to marry Coram and so demonstrate her defiance of petit-bourgeois conventions ('I could be a general's wife by now if I'd worn gloves') horrifies herself by trying to seduce the boy in his hotel room. His rejection gives her a small, permanent thrill.

The story is about not sexual frustration but the wife's need 'to abase herself to the depths of her husband's abasement'—his class-rooted, resentful stupidity. People dragging their loved ones down to a sort of 'congenial monotony'—Pritchett's secret of happiness—is what many of the stories dwell on. They are almost horror tales.

Pritchett's gift is for neatly wrapping up people and their relationships in a few words without sounding glib. The Corams 'had no children and, because of the guilt she felt about this and because of the difficulties he saw everywhere, they had become completely dependent on each other'. Mr Fulmino, in **"When My Girl Comes Home"**, 'loved whatever had not happened yet'.

My niggle of doubt stems from the finely sculpted shape and firm tone of the stories. Some, like **"The Wheelbarrow"**, about a nervously bossy widow and her evangelical Welsh handyman, are magnificently elusive. Similarly, in **"The Wedding"**, about the wily courtship of the town scandal by a ferociously land-grasping farmer, there is a welcome unpredictability, a flourish of what-the-hell pursued to whatever surprises a story may suggest. But in several stories, it's as if he has been magically held fast to his original image and, like his characters, cannot or will not break free. His people suffer their author's cheerfully grim determination that they shall not escape.

Pritchett is sadly superb on old age. My choice is **"On The Edge of the Cliff"**, about a surprisingly lighthearted love-affair between a bad-tempered 70-year-old man and a young girl who, despite the odds, have a whale of a time together. But there is not a single story in which Pritchett fails to breathe life through his characters to us—and give us back our lives enhanced. (p. 23)

Clancy Sigal, "Low Lifemanship," in The Listener, *Vol. 108, No. 2772, August 5, 1982, pp. 22-3.*

LYNNE SHARON SCHWARTZ

[*More Collected Stories*] draws on seven collections originally published between 1938 and 1980 in his native England, and show Pritchett to be interested in everything and everyone. He appears, remarkably, to have the inside scoop on doctors and dentists, interior decorators and window washers; boats and the rag trade and the movie industry and mineralogy; marriage and divorce and the isolation of children; the very fat and the very thin; the busy rich and the even busier poor.

His special interest, though, is con artists of every social class, desperate failures whose survival depends on deceiving themselves as effectively as others. In **"The Worshippers,"** for example, Lavender's cherished ancestral portrait turns out to have been bought for 50 pence at an auction; near-bankrupt but gallant, Lavender sleeps in his London office but pretends to walk to work each morning, so that his single employe can maintain his idolatry as well as a sense of reflected glory. The bedridden old lady of **"The Liars"** and the bartender who used to wheel her in a bath chair meet weekly to exchange ever more elaborate epics of their past exploits, mutually—and tenderly—buoying up shakey identities in a vacuous reality. And the inscrutably cunning Nell of **"The Necklace"** baffles her boyish, doting husband when she defends her lies with more passion than most people expend on the truth, and at a ruinous price. . . .

Like a photographer, he loves the interesting situation, the strange, now comic and now alarming patterns human beings arrange themselves in. Each design is new, each demands an original stance. Some even demand slipping past the borders of realism into a quasi-twilight zone, or into pure fantasy. **"The Landlord"** is a highly comic yet chilling story of a self-important wife and self-effacing husband who aggressively insist on buying a house only to find that the landlord goes along with it, as a kind of revenge for their presumption. As the landlord takes over bath, board, and eventually bed, the husband watches with the impotence of a nightmare victim. . . .

The collection is uneven. In the less successful stories—**"The Last Throw"** or **"The Vice-Consul"**—the author's own exuberance sweeps him off on far-flung chases, leaving the disengaged reader behind. The best ones move more slowly and meditatively to unearth psychological secrets at their roots: **"Pocock Passes,"** a brilliant evocation of the bond formed between two immensely fat and fatuous men . . . ; **"The Ladder,"** in which a young girl bereft of her mother cleverly—and wisely, as it happens—helps wreck her father's second marriage; and **"The Satisfactory,"** a wry wartime-London story with a decorator starved for food and his female assistant starved for sex exploiting each other's cravings in a droll complicity.

The dates on these stories, ranging over 40-odd years, are mystifying to anyone looking for gradual development of sophistication, wisdom, or craft. Pritchett seems to have been a virtuoso all his working life. One of the finest and most wrenching, **"The Two Brothers,"** a somber account of the human wreckage caused by the Irish "troubles," reads as if written only yesterday. Its date is 1932. Right there is a luminous example of what it means to be timeless.

Lynne Sharon Schwartz, "V. S. Pritchett's Stories of Craft and Cunning," in Book World—The Washington Post, *October 9, 1983, p. 5.*

HERMIONE LEE

A fat, lazy, fifty-year-old estate agent called Rogers, living in a country town in an alcoholic "stupor of inertia and incompetence", makes friends with another fat drunk called Pocock, who says he is a well-known painter. Pocock dies, no one seems to have heard of him, and Rogers takes home one of Pocock's paintings, an embarrassing nude. "He took the picture because, without knowing it, he felt it symbolized the incomprehensibility of the existence of other people."

The sentence, and the story (**"Pocock Passes"**, 1938), are characteristic. V. S. Pritchett's stories [in *More Collected Stories*] penetrate "the incomprehensibility of the existence of other people" by making the most unpromising characters reveal themselves in absurd and painful ways. Very often the penetration of such lives will centre on a comical object—a set of false teeth, a ladder—which the reader, though not the characters, recognizes as "symbolic". **"Pocock Passes"** is typical, too, for its dingy semi-rural setting and for the rather shamefaced relationship between the two men, each of whom "has passed the crest of his life".

It is reasonable to compare such characters with Dickens's shabby-genteel optimists or Wells's anxious suburban heroes, but Pritchett's England is more peculiar and less predictable than those parallels suggest. The *curriculum vitae* of any of his characters will be found to have odd quirks or gaps. . . . Pritchett's favourite type is anxious, earnest, well-meaning, easily bothered:

Lavender returned, and seeing her near the picture, straightened it and then put his blotter straight on his desk, saw that the telephone books were in the right order on Eeles's table. Then he got his coat from the coat stand, remarking that Eeles had only one bad habit: he often used Lavender's peg by mistake. "Small things," he said, "irritate".

But the attempts to keep order are doomed by the "incomprehensible" strangeness of things. The only way to keep a brave face is to make yourself up. Most of Pritchett's characters are boasters, liars, story-tellers, or, at the least, self-deceivers. When a daughter says of the father whose second marriage is a bad mistake, "It was his chief vanity that he understood his own behaviour", she speaks for them all. . . .

The uncomfortably intimate pairings (banal versions of Conrad's "secret sharers") that recur in the stories—Rogers and Pocock, Lavender and Eeles, two Irish brothers, a film producer and researcher, a bankrupt father and the son he despises—suggest the question: How close can you be to someone without finding them out? Pritchett sees that people can give themselves away with every word they speak, and still go undetected. So, while the characters are often innocently unperceiving, the narrative is wickedly observant. He is rightly famous for his ear; his people, as people do, wear their verbal mannerisms like suits, at once protecting and revealing themselves. . . .

[A] delight in detail is the outstanding quality of Pritchett's work. The narrative is marvellously ironic and precise even when the stories (as with one or two in this collection) are slight. The man "whose slow mind lay down like a dog in the domestic basket", the woman who keeps "breaking helplessly into autobiography", the conversationalist who ends the night "sodden in his own anecdotes, like a fruit in rum", the ship's officer "with an unreasonable chin and emotional knees", the lady "whose upper part suggested a box at the opera in which she was somehow living and sitting": this relish for humane caricature is everywhere sustained, in a collection which ranges from the 1930s to the late 1970s. One of Pritchett's characters is a mineralogist who believes that "no fact, however small, is unimportant. Put all the facts together and one gets the whole." If people were crystals, Pritchett would be their mineralogist.

Hermione Lee, "Boasters on Their Dangerous Journeys," in The Times Literary Supplement, *No. 4205, November 4, 1983, p. 1214.*

WHITNEY BALLIETT

V. S. Pritchett published his third novel, **Dead Man Leading,** in 1937, and it has now been reissued. . . . Pritchett tells us in his second volume of autobiography, **Midnight Oil,** that the book "came out not long before the war started and that killed it." Set in the Brazilian jungle, **Dead Man Leading** deals with the disastrous search by two explorers and a journalist for an English missionary who disappeared seventeen years earlier. (He was the father of one of the explorers.) . . . Pritchett says in **Midnight Oil** that **Dead Man Leading** was an attempt at a "psychology of exploration" and that "the novel was more imaginative than my earlier ones." Indeed, it was an act of imagination that only a young, unstoppable writer has the extra fuel for. Pritchett had never been to Brazil, so he "constructed a small model of my bit of the river in the garden of a cottage we had rented in Hampshire—my explorers were ants struggling through the long grass." Then he imagined the way the Amazon looks in the morning, at midday, and at night. He imagined the garish sounds and deep silences of the jungle, its alarming smells, its leaden noons and chill dawns, its splintering storms. His style—precise, limber, and rich in metaphor—had pretty much formed. . . . The action in the book, slow to mobilize but eventually taut, and even exciting, is secondary to the way Pritchett furnishes it. So are the rather murky motives of his main characters: Gilbert Phillips, the journalist, who is governed largely by fear, and Harry Johnson, the lost missionary's son, who is governed by a kind of Wilfred Thesiger masochism—that is, he gets pleasure from depriving himself of pleasure. Johnson is happiest when, almost dead of thirst, he sets off through the jungle alone and unarmed to find water. Pritchett tells us in the preface to his **Collected Stories** that "by the 1930's I had . . . discovered my voice and that my native bent was to the designs of comedy and its ironies." But there is little comedy in this liquid, green Pritchett jungle, and how strange it seems, for we always hear in his fiction what we hear in Dickens—that constant laughter in the throat. (pp. 127-28)

Whitney Balliett, "Listen," in The New Yorker, *Vol. LXI, No. 7, April 8, 1985, pp. 126-28.*

PAUL CHIPCHASE

V. S. Pritchett has been writing literary journalism for almost 50 years. The earliest piece reprinted in [**A Man of Letters**] dates from 1939; the latest was written last year. The dates given after each essay do not wholly explain themselves; a 1949 piece on Evelyn Waugh also includes reviews of books which appeared in 1961 and 1964. Many of the essays seem to have been composed in this way, by sandwiching together a number of reviews from different periods. The practice leads to a certain amount of repetition—in the essays on Ford and Conrad, for example. The miraculous thing about them is that they show no waning enthusiasm, no decline in their author's nimbleness of manner and catholicity of taste. In fact, I enjoyed the later stuff more than the youthful *New Statesman* pieces, which, for all their compact epigrammatic cleverness, have rather a lot of period intonations on the importance of psychology to the human condition.

I think my favourite piece of writing by V. S. Pritchett is his description of the thieves' kitchen in Madrid in **The Spanish Temper.** I could read with pleasure more or less anything he writes about Spain, but that account of the *cante hondo* singers singing as it were privately, to console themselves, in a wretched cellar full of other intense, ill-looking connoisseurs of the art is remarkable. Considering the opportunities here for pathos and false exoticism, it is also very funny—particularly about the formal manners of the thieves, who rise to their feet as one man, shouting '*Eso no!*'—'None of that!'—when a show-off gypsy dancer starts to remove his jacket. This picture is a cross between Goya and a Bateman cartoon. In the dignified old-fashioned Spain of Pritchett's descriptions, a man and his jacket are not parted.

There are many similar passages of precise and witty writing in V. S. Pritchett's two volumes of autobiography—all crisp similes and sharp observation. It is for this neatness of finish that one reads his short stories, and his literary criticism, too. Book reviews are not such tractable material as Spanish cellars, French landladies, Christian Scientists and life in general. They can't be treated in so cavalier and amusing a fashion. They have no natural vigour. There have to be plot summaries and long quotations and dutiful comparisons and sage judgements and remarks on the nature of Romanticism—all the grim impediments which are liable to crush literary essays into the least tolerable kind of writing in the world. Well, V. S. Pritchett includes all these things, and some of them are boring enough, but he contrives all the same to force strong currents of life and energy into the airless world of literary criticism—partly by the use of bright quick generalisation (which may or may not be true) and partly by his comic and inventive use of words. . . .

As a keen student of graceful cadence he is affronted by the 'painful reiterating English' of George Eliot—a Victorian idol who not only proved to have feet of clay but who appeared to write with them. Connoisseurs of this kind of verbal cartooning will enjoy the sketch of Cyril Connolly as a greedy baby in a pram, and that of Arnold Bennett as a valuer going from room to room in the house of the deceased, glumly ticking off the items in the inventory.

But V. S. Pritchett is not particularly a mocker; all these essays are records of generous enjoyment—but it is his power of caricature to which I look forward. That is the quality nearest to his ordinary attitude to life and farthest from the droning pieties of literary criticism. The George Eliot essay, far from being the destructive piece which my quotations may suggest, praises her in fact for cogency of construction and other worthwhile things. It is typical of V. S. Pritchett to have found in *Middlemarch* a minute touch of irrational comedy which he claims is one of the funniest in the history of the English novel. . . .

Sir Victor Pritchett wrote in his memoirs that 'one or two good stories are worth all the criticism of the world'. I can't disagree. Sir Victor has written a lot of those stories himself, and if I prefer the freedom and elegance of his writing about Spain and about the characters of his youth to his extraordinarily hardworking and enjoyable literary criticism he will not blame me. Who would care to read about the novels of George Sand and E. M. Forster when they could be on the train to Seville with V. S. Pritchett?

Paul Chipchase, "A Catholic Taste," in Books and Bookmen, *No. 361, November, 1985, p. 20.*

ANTHONY BURGESS

'Give all thou canst,' says Wordsworth. . . . I was going to begin by saying that Sir Victor Pritchett is not only our best short story writer but also our best literary critic, but I have no desire to give Sunday morning heartburn to such writers as may read me who think they have as good or better a claim or claims to that/those title(s). Let me then say that we have had no better man in either field, nay, not since the genres of fabulation and literary journalism began.

No one, I think, will dispute a title accorded to him which the literary world is beginning to think *démodé*. This title is also the title which he, with just pride and a little defiance, gives to [*A Man of Letters*]. . . . We have academics and we have media men. Sir Victor does not belong to either category. He is what he says he is.

His preface clarifies the nature of his calling: 'I come . . . at the tail-end of a long and once esteemed tradition in English and American writing. . . . We earn our bread and butter by writing for the periodicals that have survived. If we have one foot in Grub Street we write to be readable and to engage the interest of what Virginia Woolf called "the common reader."' He goes on to say that the tradition, in the days of its greatest esteem, could take for granted a condition for its practice which no longer exists—namely, the unlimited space of the old monthlies and quarterlies. Men like Walter Bagehot and Henry James, to say nothing of predecessors like Macaulay and Scott, could make love or hate to their subjects in a Great Bed of Ware. Nowadays, in the *New Statesman,* the *New Yorker,* and even the *New York Review of Books,* the bedspace is austerely limited. It is an army cot or a palliasse on the floor. . . .

The range of his examination of classical fiction—which includes Ford Madox Ford's *Parade's End* and Evelyn Waugh's *Sword of Honour*—is wide but unsystematic. . . . The brief study of Surtees sums up his essence so well—'he has all the dash, all the partiality and all the prospect of an amateur'— that he equips us to discuss Jorrocks without having to go to the trouble of meeting him. . . .

The section on the European writers . . . avoids sounding scholarly, though real scholars may learn much from Pritchett, through the unfailing awareness on the part of its author that there is a common reader to attend to, and that literary journalism must be entertainment as well as a kind of aesthetic instruction.

The final wonder is that Sir Victor has read so much, and enjoyed so much of what he has read. His kind of literary aficionado is nowadays a very uncommon reader. . . . Some of his best essays belong to his eighty-fourth year. At 85 . . . he remains a shaming example to the academics and pococurantists alike. Books, he says, are life; books are also pleasure. Get all thou canst.

Anthony Burgess, "Pleasures of Literature," in The Observer, *December 15, 1985, p. 20.*

Julian Rathbone

1935-

English novelist.

An author of both suspense and mainstream fiction, Rathbone examines contemporary moral and political concerns in his novels. He has been praised for creating convincing characters and intricate plots and for his descriptive prose, which evokes his exotic settings. Rathbone's experiences as a teacher in Ankara, Turkey, and the culture and landscape of Eastern Europe inform much of his early fiction. *Diamonds Bid* (1966), *Hand Out* (1968), and *Trip Trap* (1972) concern Turkish detective Nur Bey's investigations into assassination plots, Russian spy rings, and drug-smuggling operations. *With My Knives I Know I'm Good* (1969) and *Kill Cure* (1975) feature other Eastern European locales in addition to Turkey. Rathbone has also written several novels set in Spain, including *Bloody Marvellous* (1976), *Carnival!* (1976), and *A Raving Monarchist* (1978). In each of these works, British civilians visiting Spain become embroiled in local intrigue. *Lying in State* (1985) is likewise set in Spain and concerns an Argentinian antifascist exiled in Madrid.

Rathbone's other series of novels, comprising *The Euro-Killers* (1979), *Base Case* (1981), and *Watching the Detectives* (1983), features Jan Argand, a conservative police commissioner of a fictitious European nation who faces such issues as ecology, antinuclear protests, drugs, and civil unrest. Harriet Waugh observed: "The intellectual effort [Rathbone] has to make to encompass the mind of an incorruptible right-wing bureaucrat, despite his own socialist feelings, brings a control and rigour to the novels [of this series]."

Rathbone's mainstream fiction has earned critical praise for his examination of modern moral issues. The protagonist of *King Fisher Lives* (1976) is a college lecturer whose lack of values and fascination with primitive lifestyles lead him to bizarre acts of antisocial behavior. *A Last Resort . . . For These Times* (1980) is a social satire on the double standards and hypocrisy of the established order of a small English seaside town. *A Spy of the Old School* (1982) draws upon an actual spy incident at Cambridge University to comment on immorality and corruption in Great Britain's industry and government. *Nasty, Very: A Mock Epic in Six Parts* (1984) documents the rise of an unscrupulous fortune hunter.

Rathbone is also the author of a historical novel, *Joseph* (1979), which relates the adventures of a young man who becomes a spy for the British army during the Peninsular War in Spain. Rathbone's contemporary version of the eighteenth-century picaresque novel and his grasp of philosophical concepts caused Michael Ratcliffe to praise *Joseph*: "[Behind] all its technical pezazz and glittering entertainment stands an organizing mind uncompromisingly intellectual in its grip."

(See also *Contemporary Authors*, Vol. 101.)

Photograph by Alayne Pullen. Courtesy of Julian Rathbone

NORMAN HORROCKS

For three years, Julian Rathbone, an Englishman, taught in Turkey. Drawing on this experience, he has written [*Diamonds Bid*]; a mystery story with violence and politics thrown in. An English schoolteacher stumbles accidentally on a plot to assassinate the President and Prime Minister during a ceremonial drive through Istanbul. Despite some romantic interludes our hero foils the would-be murderers and is able to take his reward in the international currency, diamonds. Mr. Rathbone is clearly fond of Turkey and the Turks and conveys well their appeal and charm. His writing is a little uneven and might have benefitted from tighter editing. Yet this is a promising beginning.

Norman Horrocks, in a review of "Diamonds Bid," in Library Journal, Vol. 92, No. 14, August, 1967, p. 2811.

THE TIMES LITERARY SUPPLEMENT

As with his last book, almost all Mr. Rathbone's characters are so unpleasant it is hard to care what happens to them; which is a pity, for here [in ***Hand Out***], as before, he makes good use of Turkey, his locale, and the foreign expatriate society of Ankara. (He is, incidentally, very Durrell-conscious, and there is a minor character called Tunc.) The honest Turkish policeman carries over from the earlier book, but we see too little of him. The anti-hero is a British professional spy whose behaviour is so nasty, and who is regarded by himself and his author as so nasty, that it is intolerable he should survive. Cleverness must, however, be granted.

> "Kills and Spills," *in* The Times Literary Supplement, *No. 3466, August 1, 1968, p. 833.*

CLARA CLAIBORNE PARK

[In *With My Knives I Know I'm Good,* a] knife-thrower defects from a troupe of Azerbaijani folk dancers and finds himself the center of an international intrigue involving the Americans, the Russians and a third secret service which you'll probably guess before you get to the end of this exciting spy novel. With sophistication and taste, yet with not too much to detract from the action, Julian Rathbone sketches an attractive hero, cultivated and intelligent, modern on the surface, yet motivated by the ancient Homeric drives to avenge friends and kindred, and to return to a land he can call his own.

Though a Soviet citizen, the knife-thrower is also a Turk, and, for a Westerner, one of the side benefits of this thriller is the realization that there is a whole population for whom Turkey, of all places, has the emotional pull of Greece or Palestine. The book is full of such benefits; the author conveys an insider's feeling for the Near East. Each time the hero eats we are given another exotic dish, and when agent rubs out agent by knife or gun the blood flows over an enthralling background.... The travel writing is excellent, but before we can tire of it we are rushed away, briefly glimpsing the Taurus mountains in a snowstorm, dodging bullets in the frescoed tufa-caves of Göreme. At the end the bad guys, Russian and American, get theirs, and the hero settles down on his hard-won Turkish acres. Which is exactly as it should be.

> Clara Claiborne Park, "Insider's Near East," *in* Book World—The Washington Post, *May 17, 1970, p. 8.*

ALLEN J. HUBIN

With My Knives I Know I'm Good ... by Julian Rathbone is, for want of a better classification, a spy story, but it is also a very descriptive tale—of character, of pride, of racial heritage and tradition—and the thrust is more telling for it. Aziz Milyutin is a Russian-Turk, touring Western countries with a Soviet carnival troupe. He is induced to defect to Beirut, where murder throws him into a multination chase across the mountains to Ankara, and to a Jewish geologist and his crucial discovery. It's a tangled, bloody web. Aziz's progress through it is more at the leading of his heart—for revenge—than his head.

> Allen J. Hubin, *in a review of* "With My Knives I Know I'm Good," *in* The New York Times Book Review, *May 31, 1970, p. 13.*

NEWGATE CALLENDAR

Trip Trap is a novel of relationships as well as a cops-and-robbers story. Rathbone has worked up some credible characters and put them into a realistic background. Everything flows naturally, and there are some interesting insights into Turkish family relationships. But above all this is a story of crime and criminals, of a hard-working cop who manages to

work things out in an ingenious manner. Rathbone is a superior writer, and this book goes to the top.

> Newgate Callendar, *in a review of* "Trip Trap," *in* The New York Times Book Review, *December 31, 1972, p. 18.*

NEWGATE CALLENDAR

[Julian Rathbone's *Kill Cure*] concerns the possibility of a super-destructive force getting into the wrong hands. One of society's present worries is the unpleasant prospect of political activists getting hold of an atom bomb. Rathbone makes it even easier for the activists. Suppose the force is not a bomb but rather a virulent botulin, a few drops of which can spread plague in any city. With that in his possession a fanatical revolutionary can all but blackmail the world.

Rathbone's narrator is a British girl. She thinks she is part of a convoy of trucks taking medical supplies to Bangladesh. She is quickly disabused of that notion. Deftly, almost surgically, Rathbone builds the plot to as exciting a finish as you are going to come across this year.

> Newgate Callendar, *in a review of* "Kill Cure," *in* The New York Times Book Review, *August 17, 1975, p. 26.*

PUBLISHERS WEEKLY

[In *Bloody Marvellous,* smuggling] a vanload of hashish from Morocco to England via Spain is no easy matter, especially if you've decided to betray the man you're working for, and you run into the leader of a rival dope ring, and your traveling companions are a friend and two girls whose loyalty toward you is suspect. The principal setting is scenic southern Spain; the central character is an English schoolmaster understandably fed up with his salary; and the moderately suspenseful shenanigans that make up the action include a bullfight, a shoot-out and plenty of car (and van) chases along winding roads. The star surprise in a story that contains a number of surprises is provided by an Australian "tourist."

> A review of "Bloody Marvellous," *in* Publishers Weekly, *Vol. 208, No. 14, October 6, 1975, p. 80.*

VIRGINIA L. FETSCHER

[*King Fisher Lives*] is a remarkable but flawed novel, more concerned with subjective reality and the relationship between literature and life than with Lewis Fisher, the nominal protagonist. Several layers of narrative of varying degrees of reliability are laid one upon the other, showing less about counterculture intellectual Lewis who frees himself from academe in order to dedicate himself to survival than about his lover's brother Mark, whose journal entries explicate much of the action. Rathbone draws freely on *Timon of Athens* and *Lord of the Flies* for inspiration, but with a touch of Hemingway ethic, Forster description, and a sprinkling of Christian symbolism thrown in. The somewhat rocky beginning may put off some readers, but those who persist may find this a British intellectual gem.

> Virginia L. Fetscher, *in a review of* "King Fisher Lives," *in* Library Journal, *Vol. 101, No. 16, September 15, 1976, p. 1883.*

TOM KEMME

The protagonist of [*King Fisher Lives*], Lewis Myton Fisher, American poet, artist, and writer, is a moral slob. While lecturing as a Visitor of Arts at Hume College in England, Fisher produces Shakespeare's *Timon of Athens*. After the successful production, a party follows which evolves into a sex orgy and a tragic accident.

Fisher illustrates a problem which sometimes occurs in academia. Some faculty members who have the appearance and the credentials of culture, and what would appear to be the fruits of culture, lack values most basic to a civilizing process. Fisher's study of "the New Biology" and paleontology, combined with his misunderstanding of Shakespeare, motivates him to experiment with a primitive "life style" which evolves into cannibalism.

Fisher's personality and "life style" are presented to the reader through a series of documents: three excerpts from a journal kept by Mark Southam, a Lecturer at Christbourne College of Education and the Timon of Fisher's *Timon of Athens;* a B.B.C. television interview containing Fisher's "perceptions" of Shakespeare and the corrupting nature of society; a "perceptive" Fisher lecture on *The Lord of the Flies;* Fisher's notes revealing his passionate attachment to British football; a narrative by Southam containing that portion of his life spent living primitively in Spain with his half-sister Nadia and Fisher; and a narrative by Dr. Garcia, a friend of the Southams, explaining that Fisher was killed by Spanish police who had discovered his cannibalistic habits. . . .

Although Rathbone's novel contains episodes which will test stomachs long exposed to vulgarity, lewdness and violence, it is not without some "redeeming social value." Remember: before donating to the college of your choice, check the eating habits of the faculty. The sole you save may be your own.

Tom Kemme, in a review of "King Fisher Lives," in Best Sellers, *Vol. 36, No. 9, December, 1976, p. 282.*

DAVID CRAIG

The trouble for Colin Shedfield in Julian Rathbone's *Carnival* . . . is that he only has to settle down to a slice of glossy outdoor adultery in Spain and very rough things indeed start happening close at hand. It is just after a fine mountainside session with Purita ('Again? So soon', she wonderingly mutters) that they see a party of dangerous looking lads digging a secret grave, though no corpse is in view so far. And this is merely a start. Later in the book he and Purita—wife of a rich and Rightist bull breeder—are urgently consummating a visit to a dam ('Make love to me now. Quickly.') when a huge track-mounted earth-mover picks up their borrowed jeep in its metal claws and throws it into the lake. A sexual jinx? Although Colin is a gifted performer ('balls like a bull', says Purita, talking shop), regular accompaniments of this sort to love-making could set up a block or two eventually.

It is sad that the sex in *Carnival* should be so thunderous (we're back with the orgasmic 'gasped out oaths and obscenities' and the 'long shuddering moan') because for the most part Rathbone writes a very tidy, alert prose and puts together a believable story. In his previous book, *King Fisher Lives,* the sex as I recall was treated mistily—poetically—and worked pretty well; well enough to help get him short-listed for the Booker. Whatever has happened since, it is not an advance. To his credit,

what he has tried to do in *Carnival* is make the love-affair a real part of the plot, not an extra for the paperback cover. When the jeep goes into the water it is a crucial part of the story. But crucial in a fashion that ignores credibility. Without giving too much away, I can say that we are asked to swallow that a woman would lead her lover into a spot where his enemies can do their dirty worst and, whenever he shows signs of suspicion, grab him by the trousers and cry 'Give it to me now, Col', or likewise, to distract him. This is a pulp situation in what purports—and generally purports very well—to be serious writing. Rathbone knows, of course, that he is pushing his reader's tolerance pretty hard and ends the episode in deliberate comedy, with Colin rounding on Purita and throwing her naked into their picnic. This is a bit late, though. As Bob Woodward said, you can't ask retrospectively to go off the record.

Carnival gives a vivid picture of political conspiracy on the Spanish-Portuguese border, with evil stemming mainly from a big land-owning syndicate. Festival bulls run the streets seeking whom they may trample, but we have come some way from the Hemingway simplicities of courage and glory. Rathbone picks out the complicated tensions in these two countries of recent swift change with what strikes me—an innocent in Iberian affairs of all kinds—as great subtlety and some passion. Shedfield, a historian, is out there making a television film on Wellington's campaigns and is drawn into these newer, small-scale but vicious battles. We have two first-class profiles of policemen, one Spanish, one Portuguese, and a fairly successful avoidance of caricature in the television party. Shedfield himself is that noble creature of thrillerdom, the good little guy accidentally implicated, and his personality has to be the established mix of confusion, hesitancy and misjudgment. That is when he has his trousers on, of course. (p. 62)

David Craig, "Criminal Activities," in The New Review, *Vol. III, No. 33, December, 1976, pp. 61-2.*

JOHN BUTT

This thriller set in post-Franco Spain [*Carnival*] must be the first of its kind. Modern Spain sets a number of alluring traps for the novelist, and Julian Rathbone walks cheerfully into all of them—bullfights, revolutionaries, fiestas, honour and hot-blooded ladies. Nevertheless, he manages to mix the standard ingredients into an oddly touching brew. "Shed", a green ex-academic, a drunken Irish journalist, a don't-mind-if-I-do retired English major, and a Texan who keeps forgetting not to talk Etonian, are making a documentary on Wellington. While filming near the Portuguese border they witness the murder of a well-known Spanish socialist. Their knowledge lands them in difficulties with Civil Guards, landowners and a shady counter-revolutionary conspiracy. A bad business, made much worse by the hero's involvement with the local bull-breeder's wife.

After a shaky start, the story moves towards an exciting climax. Mr Rathbone's knowledge of Spanish life and language is accurate, his enthusiasm for them unbounded. But times have changed in the country which gave us Don Juan, *Blood and Sand* and the novels of Hemingway. The Peninsula was once a field for grim, lean, passionate idealists who slept under the stars. This lot are adventurers of our own times: your two-star demi-pension sort, all open-neck shirts and sandals, here for the *vino* and the local colour. "Shed" is not a poet of the revolution, but a respectable young Englishman interested in rare birds, the Peninsular War and his host's wife, very much in that order. The events of the novel seem incongruous in this context, the sort of nightmare imbroglio every package tourer would like to insure against, but the blend of the romantic and the pedestrian is probably a fair reflection of the realities of the country, no land of heroes as it used to be, and "Shed" perfectly expresses this truth.

John Butt, "For the Birds," in The Times Literary Supplement, *No. 3903, December 31, 1976, p. 1643.*

SUSANNAH CLAPP

A Raving Monarchist bases the capable excitements of its plot on Spanish political scheming, but extracts as many minor frissons from the personal palpitations of its two central figures—a pair of English homosexuals on holiday. Maurice is clever and charming and deeply disturbed, fully equipped with vertigo, bitten nails, a dismal childhood and a murky adolescence. He pouts, giggles and taunts his companion (on the lines of not being 'a clammy knickers' or an 'awful pig'), while Archie, though sometimes 'shrewish', adopts in the main a poetically paternal role, noting when Maurice's hair needs trimming, but attentive also to literature, churches and the sky (variously 'glaucous' and apocalyptic). Slabs of architectural and topographical description are given rather more generous coverage than the political dilemma informing the plot; but since niceness is for the most part cosily co-extensive with right-mindedness (the villain likes Baroque churches with lots of gilt and cupids), this turns out to matter less than it should.

Susannah Clapp, "Suburbanity," in New Statesman, *Vol. 94, No. 2429, October 7, 1977, p. 483.*

PAUL PRESTON

The idea of applying the story of *The Day of the Jackal* to the Spanish political scene [as in *A Raving Monarchist*] could have been expected to produce gripping results. After all, in December 1973 a Basque commando out-jackalled the jackal in assassinating Admiral Carrero Blanco, and terrorists of right and left are still active along the Spanish road out of dictatorship. What then went wrong for Julian Rathbone? His novel concerns a highly implausible New York hitman, Paco Blas, son of an Irish mother and a Puerto Rican father, who has been paid by extreme rightists to kill King Juan Carlos in such a way as to make the blame fall on Basque revolutionaries. His efforts are eventually thwarted by the raving monarchist of the title, Maurice, an English homosexual student who is apolitical but rather taken by monarchical pomp and circumstance. The story is recounted by Maurice's would-be lover, Archie Connaught, whose narration is the main reason for the book's failure. Archie has no idea of what is really happening and Julian Rathbone uses him too readily as a device to keep the reader in the dark about the real reasons behind any number of absurd coincidences. In so doing, he relinquishes the main strength of *Jackal*-style thrillers—the sheer fascination of the mechanics of mercenary killing.

Paul Preston, "The Spanish Cockpit," in The Times Literary Supplement, *No. 3952, December 23, 1977, p. 1513.*

MOLLIE HARDWICK

To describe *Joseph* as a good read would be to under-estimate it. Immensely long, it has the feel of a Victorian penny-a-liner, and couched in period English with plenty of capital letters, it might be an undiscovered work by Thackeray or Lever. Might be, that is, if those authors had allowed themselves a freedom of language and subject which would have been emphatically impermissible in their day, but is rich gamey stuff in ours.

Joseph Bosham is an innocent: at least, he starts out that way. Child of an English pastor who lives by the Light of Reason, he is brought up in Salamanca after his father's flight from Florence in the Republican riots of 1796. He tells us in his opening chapter (in fact an address to the Duke of Wellington, petitioning His Grace for employment on the strength of old acquaintance) that 'beside the bloody strand of War . . . the yarn of my life is flecked with the green thread of Love and the black one of private enmity or vendetta': and so indeed it proves, from the childhood moment when he realises that his Father's decision to have him circumcised, for rational hygienic reasons, may lead to complications.

It does, indeed, among them a terrifying experience of witchcraft and seduction by a very knowing young woman, the first of a memorable gallery of ladies whose bright eyes rain influence on the educable Joseph. But the bloody strand of War tangles up the green one, for the French are on the march and Joseph becomes a courier or secret agent—a fact which his Grace the Duke of Wellington later has difficulty in believing. Fate leads the Boshams, father and son, into the presence of the Tyrant himself, Napoleon Bonaparte, and they spend together what the Emperor describes as 'just a quiet evening among friends'. The description of this unlikely party is quite brilliant; perhaps the most telling fictional portrait of Bonaparte I have ever read. Just as one would have expected, he emerges in this alleged piece of reportage as an early apostle of communism, with Johnny-Head-in-Air dreams of the Cause of Civilisation, Social Unity, Order, the Will of the People (these capitals get tiresome but are inescapable), Metrification, and the Reformation of the Catechism with Bonaparte substituted for God. And so on, unbelievably clever and convincing, until this boring, lonely, ridiculous megalomaniac reaches the coffee stage.

This is the best part of a novel in which the hero's picaresque adventures surpass those of Tom Jones, Roderick Random, or Peregrine Pickle, far too many to recount; a survey of the intriguing jacket will convey the essence of them, but a particularly amusing brothel, some blood-chilling glimpses of the Peninsular War as it really must have been, and a delightful lady called Mistress Flora Tweedy whose hilarious accouchement brings the story almost to its close, stand out.

I read the book not quite at one sitting, but at no more than three, which provoked slight mental indigestion and served me right for greed. It is best read slowly, then set aside and re-read. A previous novel by Julian Rathbone was short-listed for the Booker Prize. I'm not sure which prize I would put this one up for, but there must be one somewhere which it would win at a canter. (pp. 51-2)

Mollie Hardwick, in a review of "Joseph," in Books and Bookmen, *Vol. 24, No. 9, June, 1979, pp. 51-2.*

JOHN MELLORS

Joseph takes us back and forth between the British and French armies and the Spanish *guerilleros* in the Peninsular Wars from 1808 to 1813. . . .

[*Joseph*] brings pain and privation vividly to life when it is dealing with armies on the move and men killing and maiming one another. It is less successful when Julian Rathbone sends his colourful narrator into boudoirs and brothels, gypsy encampments and witches' covens, and introduces him to a bawd who turns out to be his mother, to a wet-nurse who bares 'the most mountainous breast in the World, a monstrous rolling lolloping blubbery lardy thing'—and even to Napoleon.

The book conforms closely to the pattern of the picaresque novel as described by Joseph's supposed father. The *picaro* or rogue has all sorts of adventures, and the skill of the author lies in presenting his character's development from lively lad to adult scoundrel, keeping the *picaro* himself unaware of his descent into rascality.

John Mellors, "Booker Wars," in The Listener, *Vol. 102, No. 2635, November 1, 1979, p. 611.*

MICHAEL RATCLIFFE

[The] work of a novelist whose intelligent thrillers and adventures receive regular, approving attention (one of them, **King Fisher Lives,** was even shortlisted for Booker in 1976) *Joseph* was totally ignored by the national Press. The pathetically 'saucy' dust-jacket in which the publishers sent forth this breathtaking novel of the Peninsular War into the world suggested that perhaps they hadn't read it either—or, more likely, that they had, and nervously divined the truth, that behind all its technical pezazz and glittering entertainment stands an organizing mind uncompromisingly intellectual in its grip.

It is this quality that takes *Joseph* well beyond the mimicry and pastiche implied in its 'period' prose and picaresque form and gives it a firm, late 20th-century character of its own. The philosophical heart of the book is an informal field supper with Napoleon, in which the Emperor expounds with great charm the Imperial plans for creative social revolution in Europe—one of the most plausible reconstructions of its kind that I have ever read, and double-edged with sardonic premonitions of the totalitarian state. ('I have been told there is no new literature in my Empire. Well, that is the fault of the Minister of the Interior. I shall look into it').

Mr Rathbone is, in fact, an historian *manqué,* yet with his uncommon gift for presenting characters round historic moral abstractions—personal fidelity, the faith in pure Reason, the coward's instinct for survival—then swiftly fleshing them out in sensuality and affection, he is the true novelist, too, transcending the detached narrative convention he has chosen to revive. The emotional heart of the book is the love of a venial son for an honourable father, told with fine sentiment and destroyed in a chaos without meaning. The visions of Goya, from the enchanted picnics and parasols of the Prado cartoons to the black bones and white bandages of *The Disasters of War,* are never far off. Indeed, Mr. Rathbone stands on the ground of 1800 so convincingly that his mind remains half in the Enlightenment, with the father and the wisdom of Voltaire, and half in Romanticism with the son and the pantheistic egoism of, say, Jean-Paul. (The passionate exactitude of his response to the wild flowers and bird life of Castile, on the other hand, suggests the gentleman-traveller of Victorian England.)

Joseph begins as it means to go on, with dazzling landscapes and piercingly sharp boyhood memories of an evil feud and the first French army's arrival in Spain, and it is actually a fault that, nearly 500 pages later, after countless set-pieces and scenes of comparable beauty, there seems no earthly reason why it should ever end—one characteristic, I suppose, of the virtuoso performance. Certainly Mr Rathbone can't think of one and, chopping the manuscript off in mid-sentence, he simply pretends there is no more.

Since *Joseph* purports to be the discovered memoirs of Joseph Bosham, a gentleman-rogue from Naples and Salamanca whose tenuous connection with Wellington's army permits him to tell the story of his life to the Duke in pursuit of a British pension, the novelist gets away with it—just. But what count and remain unforgettable are the tireless inventions of Joseph's adventures within the parentheses of a terrible war and the book's unforced response to the indestructible joys of everyday life, all recorded in prose as strong, clear and unclouded as the light of Castilian day. If ever a novel were compulsively *writeable,* this is it. (pp. 682-683)

Michael Ratcliffe, "Booker Dark Horse," in New Statesman, *Vol. 98, No. 2537, November 2, 1979, pp. 682-83.*

PUBLISHERS WEEKLY

[In *The Euro-Killers*] Commissioner Jan Argand is a police officer of the old school, who disapproves of the turmoil the 1970s are bringing to Brabt, a fictional Benelux city on the North Sea. As the most honest and dependable civil servant in the province, he is assigned to the politically delicate EUREAC case. The vice-president of that conglomerate is missing, possibly kidnapped. An environmentalist group has been strenuously objecting to the expansion of a EUREAC chemical plant that will destroy the wetlands; the fanatics in the Red Spectre organization have threatened the corporation. Both these groups send ransom notes, but Argand has a feeling they're hoaxes and that the vice-president disappeared for reasons of his own. He patiently interviews all the quirky folks connected with the case, and after the suicide/murder of one of them, finds himself getting deep into a sticky maze. Though Commissioner Argand is sometimes reminiscent of Maigret, everything else about this story is refreshingly new and pleasing: the solid plotting, the unique characters, and the intelligent commentary on the economic and social unrest in a prosperous Europe.

A review of "The Euro-Killers," in Publishers Weekly, *Vol. 217, No. 2, January 18, 1980, p. 136.*

NEWGATE CALLENDAR

The Euro-Killers is a well-written book that attempts a look into the mind of a high-ranking police officer. The locale is the province of Brabt in an unnamed country that could just as well be called Belgium. The officer is getting on; he is a conservative man near retirement, a bit puzzled by the new kind of world surrounding him, unsure of how to handle a case with international ramifications. One thing he does trust, and that is his own integrity.

An important industrialist disappears. His company had been about to construct a huge chemical factory on the ocean shore. Ecologists swing into action. So do religious fanatics. So do two different terrorist groups, each of which claims to have kidnapped the industrialist. Murder follows. Tremendous pressure is applied, and the cop is taken off the case. Is there a conspiracy of some kind, in which the terrorists are as much the victims of an outside force as the inspector is?

The ending is sharp and bitter. Mr. Rathbone seems to have few illusions. His story takes place in Belgium, but it could just as well have been put in France, Germany or the United States.

Newgate Callendar, in a review of "The Euro-Killers," in The New York Times Book Review, *May 18, 1980, p. 16.*

NICHOLAS SHRIMPTON

A Last Resort, the preface tells us, was written when Julian Rathbone was the recipient of a Southern Arts Bursary and he has done his best to represent his patrons' territory. The setting, as the punning title suggests, is a Sussex seaside town. And the fictitious name of Brinshore is not there merely to protect the guilty. With his usual, lively sense of literary precedent, Rathbone has developed a detail from an earlier South Coast novel. In Jane Austen's fragmentary *Sanditon* Brinshore was the insalubrious rival to the village somewhere 'between Hastings & E. Bourne' which Mr Parker was attempting to develop.

The rate-payers of Southern England may feel that he has done them justice in rather the sense in which Judge Jeffreys understood the term. Twentieth-century Brinshore is a piece of maritime suburbia, blasted by a fatal combination of unimaginative developers and venal bureaucrats. The prevalent ethic, captured in a series of wickedly accurate saloon-bar conversations, is a philistine materialism. Saturday's joyless wife-swapping gives way to the meaningless rituals of an irreligious Sunday. The working week, whether spent in boardroom or workshop, is a sequence of cynical fiddles. As an image of contemporary Britain the novel communicates something not much short of despair.

Against this bilious picture of our life and times are set two very different strands of protest. One is a shadowy Marxism. The other, oddly, is a highly conservative Leavisite aestheticism. Dickens's *Little Dorrit* is repeatedly celebrated as a touchstone of spiritual values, to such an extent indeed that even the Barnacles of the Circumlocution Office become retrospectively admirable. Julian Rathbone's sense of place is marvellously sharp. But on this occasion he has allowed it to overwhelm both his characteristic grasp of plot and a necessary clarity of argument. (p. 936)

Nicholas Shrimpton, "Seaside Judge," in New Statesman, *Vol. 99, No. 2570, June 20, 1980, pp. 936-37.*

JENNIFER UGLOW

Julian Rathbone is a versatile writer with a gift for parody. His last work, *Joseph,* was an imitation of an eighteenth-century novel but in *A Last Resort* he dons the guise of a twentieth-century satirical realist, producing the familiar shabby, academic anti-hero—in this case an art teacher at a local comprehensive—who stumbles to self-knowledge through a series of confrontations with the prejudices and pretensions of the society surrounding him. . . .

The novel progresses through a series of events which are dated very precisely (a week in June 1978) by references to radio and television programmes, newspaper articles, political events, and songs—if the book has a theme tune it is Ian Dury's "What a Waste". With equal precision the large cast of characters are trapped like specimens, their particular place in a subtle class structure defined by minute descriptions of their habitat and way of life—make of car, dress, interior decoration, food, drink, sexual fantasies. Sometimes this smacks of self-conscious cleverness, patronizing to characters and readers alike, and gives a sense not of period but of datedness. But there is much that is fierce and funny and the effect of the careful detail is to create a general picture rather than individual histories. . . .

The week's happenings include the death of an elderly worker, an epic struggle to extract a rebate for dental treatment from the Department of Social Interference (updated Circumlocution Office), the pranks of two well-heeled adolescent arsonists, and a school disco. All illustrate the gross stupidity, inhumanity and pretentiousness of the contemporary establishment, as revealed by church, council, educational theorists and civil servants, and the even more dangerous tendencies of a rising managerial class, whose creed of self-interest blots out the past and threatens the future. The families in Merriedale estate are shown to live in an atmosphere of uneasy hedonism which drives the men to fascism, the women to tranquillizers and the children either to court or to the psychiatrist.

We are allowed three lucid commentators on this self-deluded society. All three are artists: Frank Dangerfield, teacher and painter of realist pictures which do not sell; Ern Copeman, council surveyor with a private crusade to reverse vandalistic bureaucratic decisions and amateur painter of romantic sunsets which do sell; and Miriam Trivet, a working-class student. While the two men tend to avoid confrontation, Miriam is depicted as a fighting spirit, clinging to the image of Dickens's physician in *Little Dorrit,* whose *"half grain of reality . . . will favour an enormous quantity of diluent"*.

A Last Resort is full of splendid set pieces—parodies of a sermon, a headmaster's speech, an essay, and a scathing account of "Will Shakespeare" on television. But the mixture is bitter rather than blandly comic. In a central incident an iconoclastic sixth-former hands in a sententious essay on the choice of a career, which meets with such official approval that it is read out at assembly, but later turns out to be by Karl Marx. The perpetrator of this hoax is black, from a single parent home—he is suspended from school with consequent risk to A levels and future career. Meanwhile a white middle class child responsible for £50,000 of fire damage escapes a court appearance as a result of "contacts" between headmaster, police superintendent and the father's managing director.

Despite the attack on late capitalist hypocrisies and the very sympathetic presentation of a Marxist analysis, this is conservative rather than revolutionary satire. It is full of nostalgia for tradition and historical continuity and it ends appropriately in a stone age ring on a ridge of the Downs. The full title reads *A Last Resort . . . for these times* and the pun refers not only to the town itself but to the place of art in a world full of Brinshores. Ern and Frank both turn to art as a refuge whereas Miriam urges that it should be a "beginning". The novel itself is stronger in attack than in positive theorizing and, as one suspects that Rathbone is admitting, may deserve Miriam's comment on Frank's painting of the vandalized shelter and Leisure Centre: "sort of arrogant. And yet 'so-what-y', passive. Ironic, which I liked, but impotent".

Jennifer Uglow, "Scandal by the Sea," in The Times Literary Supplement, *No. 4030, June 20, 1980, p. 718.*

NEWGATE CALLENDAR

Jan Argand, that complicated man who is the Commissioner of the Brabt police, returns in *Base Case* by Julian Rathbone.... Previously, in *The Euro-Killers,* Argand had a case that rested on ecology. Now, recovering from a mental shake-up, he has been sent to the Virtue Islands off the coast of Spain. Argand's job in the Canary—excuse me, Virtue—Islands is to work with security people at a nuclear base that is being built by Americans and that has a great many people up in arms.

The skillful Mr. Rathbone weaves many strands into *Base Case.* The island hosts a literary convention, and scholars from all over the world are in attendance. Mr. Rathbone, a former English teacher, is conversant with the murderous seriousness of scholars defending their arcane specialties. And he finds some deep-running humor in the literary experts' habit of jumping at each other's throats.

Argand is as much a specialist in his field as the literary scholars are in theirs. But he is also not in the best of health, and prone to nearly hysterical fits and periods of black dejection. He is not your average kind of cop, nor is *Base Case* an average kind of thriller, though it has a murder and some dealers in drugs and stolen gems, as well as political idealists who want to fight the nuclear station. In fact, suspicious operators are all over the place, not the least paranoid of whom is Argand himself.

Base Case is unusually literate and a joy to read. Its characters and their milieu come vividly to life—even though Mr. Rathbone is utterly dispassionate in his clinical dissection of people and their motives.

> *Newgate Callendar, in a review of "Base Case," in* The New York Times Book Review, *May 17, 1981, p. 37.*

DAVID WILSON

Base Case features drug smuggling, a bomb at an airport, an attempted separatist coup and some shady manoeuvring by agents versed in dirty tricks. Not to mention the Foreign Legion and a literary congress.

Julian Rathbone's detective, Commissioner Jan Argand, belongs to the old school of hunch and instinct, but knows his way round the acronyms of multinational newspeak. Argand is seconded from his home base of Brabt (on the coast between Holland and Belgium) to act as security adviser to ISOBRAS, a EUROSTRUCT subsidiary contracted to build an American nuclear base on the Spanish Virtue Islands....

Occupying a middle ground between detective story and political thriller, the novel needs time to reflect on the broader implications of Argand's investigation. The case against the base, for instance, is put during a chance conversation which Argand has with a local on a bus. Most of these passages, weighing the political and economic issues of nuclear sites on foreign soil, are plausibly dovetailed into the narrative, but some of them stretch coincidence too far. Even less persuasive is the part played by the academics assembled on the island to do honour to its one literary light (along with guavas its only exportable commodity). Julian Rathbone has some fun "quoting" from the texts delivered at this congress and even involves Argand in a debate on Marxism and literature: but, although the parody is accurate, it is hard to see why the book needs these peripheral allusions. In this context a reference to "the essential instability of texts" seems more double-edged than was perhaps intended.

A similar rather forced irony may be the point of Argand's remark that he never allows the possibility of a coincidence:

in fact the plot hangs on coincidence. That this is less troublesome than it might have been is a tribute to Julian Rathbone's dryly engaging style. He is an excellent mimic, and can etch a character in a few lines of dialogue. Argand himself is an interesting creation, by no means entirely sympathetic. A man of moral certainties, he can beat up a suspect in the course (and cause) of duty but is genuinely shocked when he finds the same man tortured and garotted. It's a nice point that the final ramifications of the plot (a triumph of tragi-comic description as the island's bid for independence is launched in the middle of a garden party) depend on his sense of what ought to happen, even if he is not wholly certain why it is happening. The book ends, happily, with the promise of another case.

> *David Wilson, "Hunch and Instinct," in* The Times Literary Supplement, *No. 4081, June 19, 1981, p. 710.*

REGINALD HILL

It is a truth occidentally acknowledged that Cambridge in the Thirties was positively incarnadine with trainee traitors. Chroniclers of espionage, in both fact and fiction, have found it hard to keep up with the flood in recent years. Many are still fumbling with Philby, but Julian Rathbone in *A Spy of the Old School* ... has gone bounding beyond Blunt. Such nimbleness, little surprising to those acquainted with the great range and high skills of his writing, is a family characteristic if we are to believe the information (given in an aside too gratuitous to be untrue) that the Rathbones got out of slaves and into cotton two decades before Wilberforce's abolition bill. This Hitchcockian flash of self is not out of place in a narrative often cinematic in its use of dissolves and close visual detail as the tension mounts in the hunt for Sir Richard Austen, war-time cryptologist, eminent archaeologist, and unrepentant spy. Since Blunt, of course, the rules of the game have changed. In fiction, mole-hunting is old hat. Now the game is a competition between those who want to punish the traitor by long imprisonment and those who want to slap his wrist and extort a promise that henceforward he will be seen but never heard....

Mr Rathbone is not original in any flashy way. The tracing of Austen's past from childhood to manhood showing how he has become what he is—the privileged upbringing, the almost obligatory prep-school scenes, the top university—all this is a familiar path to students of the genre. But Mr Rathbone's handling of it is exquisitely done, giving us a double view, first through extracts from Austen's published autobiography and then by flashbacks to the events themselves. His characters live, he writes with elegance, with wit, and with conviction. What more to say?

> *Reginald Hill, "Espionage and Kidnapping," in* Books and Bookmen, *No. 326, November, 1982, p. 24.*

HARRIET WAUGH

Julian Rathbone's *A Spy of the Old School* is a rather uncomfortable novel. The central character is based on a Blunt stereotype. Sir Richard Austen is a highly respected archaeologist and director of the Gold Museum. He has recently published his memoirs, which are written in a silly, chatty style. In them he writes about his left-wing sympathies as though he were being daring and original. The memoirs and Sir Richard's authentic memories are juxtaposed with an M15 investigation by one of its operatives into Austen's wartime intelligence work at Bletchley Park. There were known to have been leaks to Russia but this had been put down to a man who went missing during an air-raid. Now 40 years later there is reason to think that those leaks had gone on long after the disappearance of that suspect. The finger points to Sir Richard and soon all sorts of machinations start among the powers-that-be to obliterate the truth.

The story, with its twists and unexpected happenings, is excellent, but it has been written in a hysterically bitter style so that there is no differentiation between the paranoia and crippled personality of its central character, which is perfectly well explained and acceptable to the reader, the dubious morality of the intelligence service, the corrupt self-interest of industry and government as against the comparative innocence of society at large. It adds up to an unacceptably paranoid view of life.

> *Harriet Waugh, in a review of "A Spy of the Old School," in* The Spectator, *Vol. 249, Nos. 8058 & 8059, December 18 & December 25, 1982, p. 43.*

HARRIET WAUGH

Julian Rathbone's new political thriller, *Watching the Detectives,* returns to his imaginary European setting starring his right-wing hero, Commissioner Jan Argand. . . . In this case Argand is appointed to head a bureau investigating police brutality. Rathbone's Europe is only democratic in so far as ignorant people like myself see it as so. In fact it is as politically circumscribed in a right wing way as the Soviet Union is to Western eyes in a socialist manner. Inside this Europe, Jan Argand is a natural bureaucrat of the state. He has little liking for democratic practices, and in his personal life is paranoiac and obsessively set in routines with a strong dislike of civil disorder, homosexuals, hippies and other manifestations of modern laxity. However he does believe in the rule of law. So when he is appointed to head the Bureau he investigates the complaints with an impartiality that goes against his natural inclinations.

As the investigation gets under way tension is increased by lack of cooperation from the different sections of the police force who seem unusually aggressive. Their aggression culminates in a horrifying massacre of citizens at an anti-nuclear rally when a policeman is knifed. Gradually a sinister picture emerges, one that Argand, suspicious of his own capacity for paranoia, slowly accepts.

This series of novels is among Mr Rathbone's best. The intellectual effort he has to make to encompass the mind of an incorruptible right-wing bureaucrat, despite his own socialist feelings, brings a control and rigour to the novels missing in some of the others.

> *Harriet Waugh, in a review of "Watching the Detectives," in* The Spectator, *Vol. 250, No. 8091, August 6, 1983, p. 25.*

AMY PERSHING

Julian Rathbone's *Watching the Detectives* is his third thriller to feature the good Commissioner Jan Argand of Brabt (a fictitious country located somewhere between Holland and Belgium). This time, the all-powerful Secretary Prinz has named Argand to head a fledgling bureau to investigate complaints of

police harassment. A decent, conservative, middle-aged policeman, Argand does not relish his new job, the sorts of people he finds himself defending (nude Marxists, union activists, homosexuals) or the fact that the group he seems to be coming up against the most (the Movement for Moral Regeneration) is one whose aims he would normally applaud. Nonetheless, he is finally, reluctantly convinced that the movement has definite National Socialist tendencies. Appalled, he pursues the wrong-doers, his view sometimes narrow, his conclusions often dead wrong, but his sense of justice unwavering.

Argand is a wonderful, solid character, and Brabt, with its complicated parliamentary maneuverings and its politically polarized citizens, is uncomfortably real. But *Watching the Detectives* has one big problem: for a "novel of suspense," there is a conspicuous lack of just that. The book is to a large extent a study of manipulation: industry uses Christian rhetoric to hoodwink the middle class; the left capitalizes on the antinuclear movement; the head of the military police recruits soldiers for fascism; an aging academic seduces his young admirers in the name of Marx. Manipulating them all, however, is the smooth and coldly amoral Secretary Prinz, who has decided— for unstated reasons of his own—against a right-wing takeover. And what Prinz wants, Prinz will get. He knows it, Argand knows it, we know it. And this otherwise fine book suffers for it.

> *Amy Pershing, in a review of "Watching the Detectives," in* The Nation, *Vol. 238, No. 9, March 10, 1984, p. 299.*

JONATHAN KEATES

Nasty, Very is as good as its word. Charlie Bosham's climb to the top has none of your picaresque graces about it: a more laboriously devoted and energetic Sod's Progress it would be hard to imagine, as he lies, blusters, creeps and wangles his way across the landscape of contemporary Britain from Suez to the Falklands.

Julian Rathbone subtitles this unimproving chronicle 'A Mock Epic,' inviting us, in the manner of an Augustan satirist, to see his reptilian grotesque as a creature whose 'heads-I-win-tails-you-lose' crudities have largely been moulded by our nonchalance. Such implicit reproof would be more convincing were Charlie's foulness and that of the rebarbatively southern English atmosphere it pervades not so tiresomely insisted on. Bags of period detail here to enjoy, incidentally, shown best of all in the label-conscious bravura of Charlie's final apotheosis as a Thatcherite diehard election winner.

> *Jonathan Keates, "Autumn in Prague," in* The Observer, *September 2, 1984, p. 21.*

BRYN CALESS

Julian Rathbone chooses to portray a Britain of decline, decay and selfishness in [*Nasty, Very: A Mock Epic in Six Parts*], and carefully selects images of neglect to point up his message. His hero, Charlie Bosham, rampages through each decade since the Second World War, serving simultaneously as the continuing link and as the embodiment of each period. Are we to believe that every Briton who wants to make something of a life must follow the Bosham path? Or is it that people like Bosham have brought us to this pass?

Bosham desires money and power. From humble beginnings, he climbs the slippery slope to fortune by the simple expedient of treading on anyone in his way, or by ruthlessly exploiting them to his own ends. . . . The fact that both Bosham and the novel are stultifyingly boring does not seem to have occurred to Rathbone, for him the message should be the medium as well. Insult is added to injury by the many uncorrected errors that abound in this dismal fiction.

Bryn Caless, in a review of ''Nasty, Very: A Mock Epic in Six Parts,'' in British Book News, *February, 1985, p. 111.*

JOHN CLUTE

In Julian Rathbone's *Lying in State,* yet another old man tries to make sense of his life. But this novel is a thriller, and the route to redemption is suitably melodramatic. Long exiled from his native Argentina, Roberto Fairrie in 1975 is living in Madrid, haunted by memories of Juan Peron and by Franco's interminable final illness. An anti-fascist, Fairrie has spent all his money financing small socialist bookshops. He is now destitute. He seems a figure of pathos. As the novel begins, he is on the run from potential killers, perhaps because an English journalist has involved him in the authentication of some tapes apparently dictated in exile by Peron. Various factions clearly have plans for these tapes.

All this in the first pages. Fairrie starts taping his own reminiscences and through them we enter flashback country, where things get no simpler. It is soon clear that Fairrie is not the innocent he first seemed. The plot thickens several times. Franco dies. Fairrie is nearly killed a couple of times, in the process discovering a long-lost daughter. But Rathbone fails to handle their reunion with any conviction. He is best on Spain and on the muted tussling of the various agents and entrepreneurs as they vie for control. Unfortunately, the plot peters out at the point it might seem we are going to be told something. (pp. 33-4)

John Clute, ''Past Imperfect,'' in New Statesman, *Vol. 110, No. 2846, October 11, 1985, pp. 33-4.*

Peter (William) Redgrove

1932-

English poet, novelist, dramatist, scriptwriter, nonfiction writer, and editor.

Redgrove's poetry is marked by its distinctive exuberance expressed through an expansive vocabulary and a wealth of images. Redgrove attended Cambridge University as a student of natural science, and this background is reflected in his work. Infused with the beauty and diversity of nature, his poems also examine the grotesqueries and brutality that may be found there. Redgrove has referred to himself as a "scientist of the strange," and this quality has led critics to compare his work with that of Sylvia Plath and Ted Hughes, who also frequently employ violent natural imagery. Redgrove's novels, like his poetry, display his penchant for surrealism and his interest in psychology, mysticism, and the occult. Although some reviewers claim that Redgrove's effusive language sometimes obscures his meaning, he is praised for the originality and intensity of his vision.

Redgrove's first two books, *The Collector and Other Poems* (1960) and *The Nature of Cold Weather and Other Poems* (1961), were well received, but it was with *The Force and Other Poems* (1966) that he began to attract more widespread critical attention. Alan Brownjohn claimed that this book, along with Redgrove's preceding volume, *At the White Monument and Other Poems* (1963), shows Redgrove "wandering off exuberantly into ambitious, energetic, baffling poems which work by combining obscure and alarming plots with vast, bizarre assemblages of incisive detail." In such subsequent collections as *Peter Redgrove's Work in Progress* (1968) and *Dr. Faust's Sea-Spiral Spirit and Other Poems* (1972), Redgrove continues to employ his minutely detailed observations of the natural world in an exacting yet exuberant voice. Several critics found this tone problematic; Roger Garfitt claimed that "the quality of thought rarely breaks through the scrum of boisterous verbiage which comes milling into every poem." Generally, however, reviewers praised Redgrove's ability to fuse description and perception. *Sons of My Skin: Selected Poems, 1954-1974* (1975) provides an overview of the first twenty years of Redgrove's career and, along with such later volumes as *Aesculapian Notes* (1975), *From Every Chink of the Ark and Other Poems* (1977), and *The Apple Broadcast and Other Poems* (1981), reinforces his position as a meticulous, energetic chronicler of both the psychic and physical realms. Jed Rasula found in Redgrove's later work, represented in *The Weddings at Nether Powers and Other New Poems* (1979) and *The Man Named East* (1985), an "ever greater refinement, exactitude, and energy."

Redgrove is best known as a poet, but his novels have also won praise. *In the Country of the Skin* (1972), according to several critics, might better be described as a long, surrealistic prose poem in which Redgrove delves into a variety of psychological and sexual themes. Redgrove wrote *The Terrors of Dr. Treviles* (1974) and *The Glass Cottage: A Nautical Romance* (1976) in collaboration with Penelope Shuttle, with whom he had previously produced a volume of poetry, *The Hermaphrodite Album* (1973), and whom he later married. The former novel is composed of a series of short sections dealing both

with scientific theory and the occult. *The Glass Cottage* centers on the murder of a woman by her lover on a transatlantic ocean liner. Anne Stevenson noted that Redgrove's next novel, *The God of Glass* (1979), "begins with murder and exorcism and ends in a celebration of shamanistic birth, trance and salvation through knowledge of evil." In *The Sleep of the Great Hypnotist* (1979), an eccentric scientist invents an instrument for the projection of unconscious images and orders his daughter to use it to rejuvenate him after his death. Both *The Beekeepers* (1980) and *The Facilitators* (1982) are concerned with a mysterious bee cult which originates in an "institute" run by an enigmatic female scientist. These novels feature bizarre rituals and explorations of spiritualism, eroticism, and magic. Although most critics consider Redgrove's poetry to be more successful than his novels, his fiction has gained recognition as an interesting extension of his strikingly original vision.

Redgrove has also written a number of plays and scripts for radio, most of which are adaptations of his own work. *The Wise Wound: Eve's Curse and Everywoman* (1978), another collaboration with Penelope Shuttle, is a nonfiction work which explores the effect of menstruation on the psychology of women.

(See also *CLC*, Vol. 6; *Contemporary Authors*, Vols. 1-4, rev. ed.; *Contemporary Authors New Revision Series*, Vol. 3; and *Dictionary of Literary Biography*, Vol. 40.)

DONALD HALL

There are few poor poems in *The Collector*. Most of the poems are new in their plotting and fresh in metaphor and diction. The rhythms nicely reinforce the sense, and since the sense is repetitive so are the rhythms. Redgrove is particularly successful when he clots his lines with sequent stresses at moments of strain.... The problem of language is beaten (to a pulp) and the poems survive as individual victories. Of course there is little further that a poet can go, if he is restricted to a vocabulary of the intense and painful. But meantime one has some good new poems. (p. 302)

> Donald Hall, "Habits of Language," in New States-man, *Vol. LIX, No. 1511, February 27, 1960, pp. 302-03.*

P. N. FURBANK

Peter Redgrove is half of a very good poet. As a sensibility he is all highly-tuned responsiveness, a bundle of nerve-ends stung and pricked and excited by an active and anthropomorphic Nature. It is a Nature very personal to him. In one of his prose poems (modelled on Rimbaud's *Les Illuminations*) his garden pond gets out of its bed and, wearing mackintosh and galoshes, makes its way into the house, where it starts making love to his wife. This, though not always so whimsically, is the role Nature generally takes in his work. It is the active partner, always nudging, intruding and challenging. Redgrove's verse-handling fits this kind of active intercourse with Nature; it is fluid and nervous, full of energetic verbs and consonantal clashes, weighted with physical reference and alive with extravagant metaphor. There are some splendid things in the poems [collected in *The Nature of Cold Weather*], for instance the stinging actuality and metrical poise in this rendering of a burning match:

> That pet of a matchflame
> Serves me clouds of calm
> At my cigarette,
> Flips shadows about, whispers
> With its tiny sting, wrings
> The wood elderly, pricks at my thumb
> Before my breath splits and garottes it.

The trouble with him is that he is *only* a sensibility. With all their brilliance his poems don't seem to add up to much in the way of meaning. Their inexorable concreteness is not a formula for exact, though untranslatable, emotions; it is an end in itself. The thought holding the poems together, being arbitrary and fanciful, does not put enough control on the metaphors, which at times burgeon as rampantly as some decadent metaphysical's.... There is some doctrinaire abuse of the 'image' in these poems, which makes them exhausting to read in any quantity. All the same, a real talent, I think.

> P. N. Furbank, in a review of "The Nature of Cold Weather," in The Listener, *Vol. LXVII, No. 1715, February 8, 1962, p. 265.*

ROBIN SKELTON

[*The Nature of Cold Weather & Other Poems*] is difficult to evaluate. It has immense vitality, and contains many intense and shrewd perceptions, but is not infrequently shrill rather than passionate, pretentious rather than authoritative. Visual observation runs riot in many poems, and often the raison d'etre of a poem seems simply to be the author's desire to be ingeniously exuberant. I am not sure whether it wouldn't be fair to call the book sensationalist.... [The] poems, as a whole, give an impression of being fragments of experience given strenuous expression, rather than true poems, each having its own inevitable disciplined structure. Even as I say this, however, I remember other poems in which the formal, even incantatory, structure, is heavily emphasised, and in which a witty intelligence has been brought to bear upon the rawness and violence of those experiences in which Mr. Redgrove appears to be most interested.

There is considerable force and vitality in the book, certainly, but there is also a lack of tact. The poems bully the reader. They hector and shout, gesticulate and stamp.... It seems as if Mr. Redgrove is, on occasion, unable to select from the wealth of epithets at his disposal; it also appears as if he must, on almost all occasions, make every word a surprising or emphatic gesture. It is good to meet a young poet so wholeheartedly opposed to the reticent and well-mannered sterilities that pass for poems in so many current collections, but sympathy with the vigour and passion of these poems must not lead us to accept mere violence of diction and manner as the equivalent of passion; nor would it be wise to accept the remarkably skilful prose poems at the end of the book as tokens of supreme originality, reminiscent as they are of much work of the thirties and forties in the surrealist vein. They are, however, again, lively and often funny. The Rimbaudian attitudes are well handled.

I end up, as I read the book for the third or fourth time, feeling less satisfied than curious. There is grand stuff here, and there is stuff that is quite unbearable. Mr. Redgrove's next book is one I am looking forward to with impatience. Is it going to prove windy, violent, over-theatrical, pretentious, sensationalist, and hollow? Or is it going to be original, vital, passionate, authoritative, disturbing, and meaningful? I don't know. (pp. 91-2)

> Robin Skelton, in a review of "The Nature of Cold Weather & Other Poems," in Critical Quarterly, *Vol. 4, No. 1, Spring, 1962, pp. 91-2.*

CHRISTOPHER RICKS

People seem to be going off Peter Redgrove, but it is hard to see that his verse has in any real way changed. Agreed, that too may be a bit disappointing, but he still has his original virtue: a wide-ranging and effectively fertile vocabulary, pressing and evocative in detail. He is still rather prone 'to sate on writhing passages of scenery', but *At the White Monument* confirms, not lessens, the sense that he is gifted. But he is still loath to write whole poems; almost throughout, the basic notion on which a poem turns is simply no match for the tugging, distracting, and in a true sense diverting, effects of the detail. At present the best poems set out to burlesque their own hurly-burly.... Yet often the violence of the diction blunts itself into dull thuds. Donald Davie has deplored much of Hopkins as 'muscle-bound'; it will be a pity if so talented a poet as Mr Redgrove stiffens into the empty flexing of Charles Atlas. (p. 844)

> Christopher Ricks, "Sick Supper," in New States-man, *Vol. LXVI, No. 1708, December 6, 1963, pp. 844-45.*

THE TIMES LITERARY SUPPLEMENT

[In *The Force*] Peter Redgrove is at it again, sweating, guzzling, peering, prodding, holding an enormous magnifying glass up to nature.... There is a sense in which Mr. Redgrove is continually on the edge of parodying himself, and sometimes in his new book he actually does so. His poems boil with an energy that often seems factitious; he is the poetic equivalent of what the Charles Atlas advertisements used to call "dynamic tension", attempting to build up huge muscles simply by flexing them while the body remains inert. Reading him is a physically tiring process because the expansive gestures become abortive and constricted, so that the reader is in the end frustrated by unresolved displays of fierce mimetic description: **"Nothing but Poking"**, to use one of Mr. Redgrove's own titles.

Only when some narrative lies behind the work does Mr. Redgrove show a firmer shaping power: **"The House in the Acorn"**, a strange dream-encounter, displays this briefly. But it is in his longer prose-poem monologues that he best succeeds in exercising and controlling his real talents; one remembers **"Mr. Waterman"** from his earlier work, and in *The Force* Mr. Redgrove almost equals that achievement with **"The Sermon"**.... One feels that if Mr. Redgrove could only stop indiscriminately lashing about with his big insulting stick and would search more calmly for his themes he might be a much more impressive writer.

"Poetic Postures," in The Times Literary Supplement, *No. 3391, February 23, 1967, p. 139.*

D. M. THOMAS

There is a passage in Hermann Hesse's *Steppenwolf,* used by Redgrove as a poem-heading in his last collection, that I think gives us a hint of the Redgrove world: 'Man . . . is an experiment and a transition. He is nothing else than the narrow and perilous bridge between nature and spirit. His innermost destiny drives him on to the spirit and to God. His innermost longing draws him back to nature, the mother. Between the two forces his life hangs tremulous and irresolute.' One is reminded of the 'new swinging bridge' in **"The Old White Man"** by which the men cross and destroy the ruler of the primitive mountain paradise. 'But the beasts were all scared and the men could build bridges, / And this must be the will of heaven.'

Man, in Redgrove's poetry, is the point of tremulous marriage between matter and spirit. The sexual union which the poems in this volume celebrate—man and woman, wizard and witch— is felt as a microcosm of this sacred marriage....

Yet, man, wake up the hidden woman in yourself,
Woman, wake up the man who is the deepest part of
    you.
Find them, they are conversable; you do not know
What could yet flow and change, embrace and speak.
                                    "Signs"

Perhaps we ritualise in our uniquely tormenting sexual obsession the cosmic forces of matter and spirit which have chosen us as the site of their armistice conference; mythology and psychology, summated in Hesse's words, seem to confirm this; language too: matter and mother are cognate. The witch-figure of the poems [in *Peter Redgrove's Work in Progress*] is unmistakably a real woman, having a real love-affair—glimpses of her with 'mud on her jersey', or on a train speeding to meet her man, smoking a cigarette and glad about having men-

struated, are solid and actual—but she has attributes of magic, more frequently shimmers in a mystical atmosphere. In several poems (**"Young Women"** *with the hair of witches and no modesty;* **"Small Dirge"**; **"The Idea of Entropy at Maenporth Beach"**), she is, like Ophelia, vanishing into water or mud. In a sense she is the poet's own body, own youth, slipping away ('It is the body, it is the body, it is the body is the loved thing, It is from my mother, it is my mother's . . . '). She is woman but also that seemingly doomed cosmic force to which our innermost longings draw us back. It is impossible—such is their ambivalent atmosphere—to say whether these are 'love' poems or 'nature' poems. Which means that they are religious poems. **"The Haunted Armchair"** has the scarifying *memento mori* obsessiveness of a Donne sermon . . . 'One humour of our dead body produces worms, and those worms suck and exhaust all other humour, and then all dies, and all dries, and moulders into dust, and that dust is blown into the River, and that puddled water tumbled into the sea . . .' but the differences are more significant; whereas Donne finds this endless destruction a loathsome prospect, relieved only by his faith in personal resurrection, Redgrove fights towards an ecstatic acceptance of it. 'Suddenly everything grants me withering'. 'Grants' is an unexpected and important word. (pp. v-vi)

The flux of opposites, and the refusal of Redgrove's images to exercise polite good sense, *are* relevant and central, whether one finds them irritating or exhilarating. The best of Redgrove's images seem to me to have a concentrated force, as though formed at depth under great pressure....

Stars lie in pools black as pupils
That return their stare, ice-irised...

Each word, each sound, generates fresh energy by its reaction against the others; is like the torrent in one of his finest images, the distaff of itself (**"Young Women"** . . .). Every effort is made to create a mimesis of helter-skelter life. Words spill themselves in repetitive ever-varied seminal abundance. Rhythms are strong, shifting, tidal. . . .

The mountainous sand-dunes with their gulls
Are all the same wind's moveables...

The sound of the second line is directly related to that of the first, is a kind of rearrangement of it, like the sand-dunes of Perranporth that are being described. It is the rhythm of erosion and perpetual new creation. (p. vii)

D. M. Thomas, in an introduction to Peter Redgrove's Work in Progress, *Poet & Printer, 1968, pp. v-vii.*

ALAN BROWNJOHN

[Given] a title which appears to disclaim finality, [*Peter Redgrove's Work in Progress*] might easily be mistaken for a set of drafts, or an interim volume. It is not either of these, but a substantial volume in its own right; a book which no one interested in the work of this enormously talented and perennially frustrating poet should miss.

Redgrove, along with poets such as Ted Hughes and Philip Hobsbaum, came of a Cambridge generation just after that which supplied the local members of the 1950s Movement. His early work was appearing in the magazines in the late Fifties and his first volume, *The Collector,* came out in 1960. His search for range and vigour (in reaction against the limited academicism of the Movement poets) was for a time diverted into the domestic preoccupations of some of the writers associated with the Group. But there was always a kind of feverishly wide-ranging quality about his perceptions, and already in *The Nature of Cold Weather* (1961) all the signs of his later development are apparent. *At the White Monument* (1963) and *The Force* (1966) show him wandering off exuberantly into ambitious, energetic, baffling poems which work by combining obscure and alarming plots with vast, bizarre assemblages of incisive detail. Rhetoric and length go with scientific precision. The very fine title poem of *The Force* provides a kind of key to Redgrove's philosophy in its celebration of the energies of the physical world for their own sake. But both in that book and the new one, discernible plotting and rational argument are becoming harder to trace: Redgrove's ecstatic absorption in the physical forces has taken almost complete command. . . .

D. M. Thomas's introduction to [*Peter Redgrove's Work in Progress,* (see excerpt above)] speaks of personal themes turning into religious themes through their links with 'cosmic forces', while 'each word, each sound generates fresh energy by its reaction against the others'. It seems an ideal recipe for turning this poet's brilliant, seething inventiveness into pure mystical bombast.

Alan Brownjohn, "Physical Jerks," *in* New Statesman, *Vol. 78, No. 2014, October 17, 1969, p. 540.*

CLIVE WILMER

Peter Redgrove has been praised for using a scientific education as the basis for his "imaginative exploration of matter". . . . Precisely what we need at the moment, in my view, is a writer for whom poems are not autonomous and wholly self-justifying, but what Yvor Winters called "forms of discovery", penetrative and exploratory. But Redgrove uses scientific material purely as illustration. Indeed the whole method of *Dr Faust's Sea-Spiral Spirit* is mere amplification. In the title poem, for example, he begins rather well but, after ten lines or so, he starts amplifying and carries on with detail after gratuitous detail to a point where any sense of form or precise articulation just evaporates. It is the method of a whole school of contemporary poets who find formless catalogues an easy substitute for properly structured argument. The villain of the piece, alas, is the Ted Hughes of *Crow*. Redgrove's **"A Taliessin Answer"** reads like a parody of *Crow*, and Hughes's style, somewhat emasculated, ghosts every page of the book:

I am the issue of this divine intrusion,
My heart beats deep and fast, my teeth
Glisten over the swiftness of my breath,
My thoughts hurry like lightning, my voice
Is a squeak buried among the rending of mountains.

This is just pretentious bombast. And what are we to make of the quieter diction? How about the phrase, "Mute parcels of impending forests", describing—God help us—a pile of acorns! This is the worst kind of decadent periphrasis.

As the passage I have quoted should demonstrate, the versification is as blurred as the content. Generally he uses an end-stopped long line that can only be read as prose (and rather primitive prose at that, as the syntax is so crude) unless the reader allows the strong line-end to tense the rhythm. One imagines the latter was intended, but the effect is a kind of monotonous incantation where variety of stress and, hence, all subtlety of meaning are simply annihilated. (p. 545)

Clive Wilmer, "Forms of Discovery," *in* The Spectator, *Vol. 229, No. 7528, October 7, 1972, pp. 545-46.*

DOUGLAS DUNN

Considerable application is necessary before realising that whatever else Peter Redgrove's poems are, they are far from vague. An imagination as odd and bulky as Redgrove's demands a galvanising verbal unexpectedness to spark his universal mysteries and obsessions into poetic form. There were times when poetry of such strangeness used to recommend itself as the only true way, implying that earthen and hydrological mysteries were the prime attention of poets, and that real worlds of commonplace passions were uninteresting, because temporal. Poets dedicated to a single overview—mythological, scientific, Christian, surrealist, or anything else of that sort—have had their day. Redgrove is not, however, a poet of single faith, although his contribution to *the Review*'s symposium on "the state of poetry" must have convinced many people, and perhaps himself, that he is. "Interior sensitivity" was the phrase he used in *the Review*, recommending whatever was meant by that as the most fruitful line of growth in new poetry. Can there be *any* poetry without "interior sensitivity"? And yet, reading **Dr Faust's Sea-Spiral Spirit,** one realises that what Redgrove is recommending—in the book by example, in *the Review* by precept—is that imagination is the essential quality of poetry.

Redgrove's imagery is hard, experienced, seen, felt, smelt, and real. He possesses an extraordinary verbalising gift that associates him with Plath, Hughes, and Roethke. His free verse is—well, is free verse, but interesting free verse. He has taken to heart Eliot's remark that "No *vers* is ever *libre* for the man who wants to do a good job." He can be rhythmical in sudden bursts of energy, and is capable of as many ways of saying as the Prime Minister has suits. . . . His poems are ambitious in the best sense—he doesn't seem to be trying. They have a beautiful and almost haphazard natural exactitude that could be said to be apt in relation to a nervous, bustling imagination, not a preconceived model of how poems should be shaped. Most contemporary poetry moves forward in short, organised narrative steps, dying falls, sinkings, isolated glamorous lines, moral endings. Not so Redgrove's; he jumps in shouting. (pp. 67-8)

Douglas Dunn, "Moral Dandies," *in* Encounter, *Vol. XL, No. 3, March, 1973, pp. 66-71.*

SHIRLEY TOULSON

Within all our heads live many people of all ages and sexes. Peter Redgrove's novel [*In the Country of the Skin*] concerns the ones in his skull; for the dominion of the skin, he reminds us, extends to the grey matter: 'Ectoderm is unfolded to become brain in the foetus.' The characters are the types that psychology has taught us to expect: Silas/Jonas the twin but conflicting protagonists; Teresa, the eternal female; Sarah the old earth woman; Tomas, the wise man; the parents, Mary and Albert. If they lack substance it is because they never interact with the outside world. The country within this skin is isolationist. . . .

It is not easy reading. Admirers of Mr. Redgrove's poetry point to his intrepid originality and say little else: I suspect they find him difficult too. This novel, which contains several passages of verse, presents the same problems as the poetry. His originality comes from what one might call the stream of unconsciousness. 'The stream of consciousness' is a literary form we're all at home with. Its weakness is that by jumping from association to association it tends to reduce people, places and events to a trivial level. The unconscious, that which mostly becomes known through dreams, makes heavily-charged rituals of everything that comes within its grasp. In Mr. Redgrove's case these celebrate and explore the desires and movements of the flesh and the yearnings of the spirit. Perhaps this is inevitable. Flesh and spirit are what remain when logical thought is discarded and there are no external relationships to exercise the feelings. For me it does not do: as a reader I am dependent on Coleridge's 'shaping power of the imagination'. Too much fancy induces vertigo. Reading this novel was like listening to scrambled tapes being played backwards: an essential sorting process but tantalising if one tries to find meaning in the fascination of stray words and phrases. . . .

Despite all I have said I would not be without Mr. Redgrove's visions: they remind me of nothing so much as those late medieval painters who produced canvases crowded with the damned and only slightly lightened by the blessed. Yet I also hope that some day he will write an account of the world beyond his skin.

> *Shirley Toulson, "The Inward Eye," in* New Statesman, *Vol. 85, No. 2198, May 4, 1973, p. 665.*

MARIE PEEL

Most writers of strong originality see and feel ahead of their time. They usually dig deep also in ways that show our constant loss in wholeness and energy through conforming compromise. Most readers shrink from the glare and heat of such vision. They shut their ears to its whispering undermining explosiveness. They prefer interpretations that confirm and protect their own view of things, often seeking to impose this on the writer. But important writers are uncompromising and cannot be manipulated in this way.

I think Peter Redgrove is a writer of this stature and that the time has come for this to be more fully recognized. . . . Reading one or two poems, one is almost certainly struck by his strange memorable quality. Reading further within one volume, one may feel some resistance to the restless fantasy, the constant changes of identity, the startling difficulties or seeming incoherence that shoots out and swirls around one.

This is why I think it adds immensely to his impact to read him more consecutively in a chronological selection such as is offered [in *Sons of My Skin: Redgrove's Selected Poems 1954-1974*]. Then one finds a growing understanding in response, with each poem important in and for itself, but also connecting within and across the books as part of a developing whole. . . . For here is a writer deeply engaged with life and poetry in an interlocking, many-layered way. At times this takes him deep into the physical universe and man's collective unconscious. At others he flares forth, touching with probing power the infinite surface of life, the stretched skin, as it were, of the natural world or of himself as an individual human being. (pp. xi-xii)

[Peter Redgrove shares with Blake] a knowledge of poetry as articulate energy, and of energy as the source of all creative power. "Eternal delight", Blake called it. He also said that all man's ideas of God or gods "reside in the human breast".

Peter Redgrove would agree with this, as he would I think with another of Blake's central convictions: "Everything that lives is holy". But he goes behind Blake with an animistic vision of science that precedes Newton and flares ahead of Darwin. Materialism does not have to be single-visioned and dead. Only those with a strong vested interest in propping up the Christian God call it this. For Peter Redgrove the power and pattern of existence are essentially inherent in the natural world, they are embedded and flowing there. In this sense he is a materialist, but one for whom—to use his own phrase and emphasis—"matter *sings*".

There are other unusual combinations in his vision. For at present he is both evolutionary and individualist; not revolutionary and for the generality of men, as Blake was and as I think Keats would have become, the Keats who knew the greatest poets to be those for whom, as he put it in "The Fall of Hyperion": "the miseries of the world / Are misery and will not let them rest." Peter Redgrove is appalled by these miseries—they were an instinctive part of his rejection of his own privilege—but he did not know them instinctively and for their own sake, as part of the pattern of most people's lives over generations. Everything in his English middle-class background, his education at a minor public school and major ancient university, his education, moreover, as a scientist, prevented his knowing this. It also prevented his knowing that most people need some fuller consciousness of an outward social kind, before they can begin to become fully themselves. His rebellion was essentially *against* consciousness, against what it had done to him through its confident supposed control by his own class. The move for him was irresistibly out, down, away from this form of consciousness towards the unconscious. (pp. xii-xiii)

The evolutionary drive of his rejection seems to have been compulsion—perhaps one could better say *impulsion*—towards non-human nature, the life of the earth and stars and flowing spirit of water. It was essentially away from houses and mansions, symbols of man's need to domesticate himself within the universe. (p. xiii)

Getting out from all this involved unknowing, a *decreation*, a toppling down the storeys of the traditional hierarchy of creation, so that the poet sees and feels with small ground creatures, inhabits trees and woods and stones as well as knowing power in the strata deep below. Once gone there is no holding him, though they drag the lake of the house for evidence of a corpse. He has a sense of glee and freedom in his power to elude his searchers. He delights in coming back, "the colour of ghosts", but with new substantiality, to lick "every corner where I was / To know as I was known." One has no sense of his being pursued or possessed in this process, but rather of swirling manifold being moving out from fixed positions to those of "no conclusions". But the gleeful freedom is often crossed by pain and sense of loss and above all by bewilderment that the nature of his experience should be so utterly not understood by those closest to him.

An essential element of this experience was the descent deep beneath domesticated surface morality to the heat and power at the core of existence. Here the poet knows an *Ur*-morality where conventional distinctions between good and evil disappear in the fusion of creation, burning up traditional moral and emotional layers accumulated over centuries of Christianity. In the magma at the centre, where power puts its finger, "the lines show thick roots of hot blood" that force new creation. Though infinitely minor compared with the actuality of geology, in his own workings, when there is this hot thick-rooted pressure, the poet knows access of power directly corresponding to it.

The quotations I have given come from poems central to this central experience: from ["**The Son of My Skin**" in *Sons of My Skin*], "**The Nature of Cold Weather**", and from "**Power**", "**Decreator**", and "**The Absolute Ghost**", all in the important fourth book, *The Force and Other Poems*. I could have chosen other poems, especially "**Lazarus and the Sea**" from the poet's first book, *The Collector*. But in a sense it does not matter which one chooses for all are aspects of the process at the heart of Peter Redgrove's poetry, that also forms its living skin. Once this is known, one can freely inhabit the varied strata of his poems, stretched deep or lying close beneath the surface like layers of the same skin.

One enters autobiographical strata at different levels, knowing the poet as a boy, relationships within his family, the death of a brother, experience in advertising, a visit to Spain. Most deeply embedded and also most intensively recurrent on the surface is a marriage and all that that then meant. Other allegorical figures join the Decreator and the Absolute Ghost to bear witness from different angles to the poet's drowning-into-life. For instance Mr Waterman (in "**The Nature of Cold Weather**"), who tells a psychiatrist about it; and the Minister in "**The Sermon**" (in *The Force and Other Poems*), who is tempted by his congregation to reveal the secret of godhead and when he preaches immanence, a shard of power in each of us, is assaulted for his truthfulness.

Significant symbols emerge from the allegory. More than once a white-haired old man appears, a blind gardening God the Father, endlessly tending a tamed Mother Earth. He is for ever hedging and clipping and hypothesizing, dividing body and mind, black earth of matter and white light of spirit, and so is drained of living power, which springs only from some fusion of the two. Black and white often recur symbolically as night and day or as symbolic colours in a sexual context, while there is often a similar rich interconnection between sun and moon.

As I have suggested, there are deep geological strata, particularly in the poem, "**The Nature of Cold Weather**", with its manifestation of heat shut up and pressed down within the frozen universe. We see the beauty of the surface under ice moved back to an extinct ice age. Then there is fresh snow, the swirling movement of it, followed by intense painful pricking of the thaw felt across the poet's whole being as he inhabits the landscape. In "**Minerals of Cornwall, Stones of Cornwall**", in the poet's most recent volume, *Dr Faust's Sea-Spiral Spirit*, the image of a white kaolin-station steams deep within the moor, empowering future ages in the gleaming fixed "inclusions" of the rocks; moving also with infinite slowness towards "good conclusions" up above, in the free seeding of the millennia. Other poems are alight with the chemistry and physics of the universe, the beaming power of the sun, the power in water and electricity and in man's human beam, the life-force of his sexual energy.

All these poems spring from the self of the poet, who has utterly lived his own remark "he is dead who cannot change utterly". Before, he was the interested naturalist of "**The Collector**", with his "reasonable curiosity", and "observations in default of love". Now he becomes the man in "**I See**" (in the *Force* volume), loving the natural world in a new way that knows it utterly for itself and for his own relatedness to its processes. (pp. xiv–xvi)

But no one can live wholly and powerfully through the non-human natural world alone. One must have natural human living as well and in this sphere the reborn poet is driven by less fruitful contraries. The Widower, for instance, in ["**The Widower**"] knows what he has done to his wife, a woman who was "daytime to the mind", to whom he brought: "Twelve-hour lyings down for fear of this world". The poem is full of the contraries of day and night, the night full of self-induced, self-justifying fears. Its vision of life grows morbid, "the too-great majority" walking like "a shivering laundry of shifted humanity / And who stink. . . ." The poet quickly repudiates this false emphasis, spawned by the inbreeding of night thoughts, and turns towards the evolutionary truth of day. (pp. xvi–xvii)

But evolutionary vision must be aware of change and of progression through change. All life needs night as well as day for growth. They are true contraries in Blake's sense when he wrote: "Without Contraries is no Progression". But if the psyche is severely disturbed some contraries easily become fixed opposites that entrap and shut one in instead of resolving and setting free. By the end of the poem one may feel the Widower is entrapped in his new freedom. He himself was dead, is now alive, which by too tight a logic turns an unchanged wife into a dead one, himself into a kind of murderer. Looked at more dialectically, the wife must have changed also because of him, as he has done in part because of her.

The poet's rebirth expresses itself in a new range of poetic *personae*, going beneath and beyond Christianity: Taliessin, the Welsh poet, disciple of Merlin, who sought different voices and congenial forms to express the manifold knowing of his imagination; Frankenstein, the modern Prometheus, who created not static perfection, but the suffering complexity of human life; above all Faust, whose Sea-Spiral in the title poem of the last book, *Dr Faust's Sea-Spiral Spirit*, comes sweeping in from the sea, drawing up power and releasing it in everything it touches. The driving force of Goethe is very strong here, a great poet and original scientist for whom our culture has no equivalent because of its static division between arts and sciences, though I think Peter Redgrove will help to change this.

In Goethean science imagination is essential, the scientist must enter the trees and rocks and plants he studies, must know deeply in himself something of the forces working in the universe. For Goethe colours were not made by refraction of white light solely, but by interpenetration of darkness with light, they are equal though different forces. Newton's interpretation, which our culture chose, stresses what the poet calls "exclusive masculinity", the thrust of abstract intellect divorced from deeper knowing. The powerful Earth-Spirit of Part I of Goethe's *Faust* goes far towards accepting the contrary energies of life in all its forms. In Part II there is no one all-powerful Sea-Spirit to equal this, but two elusive spirits both of whom, one senses, would make a strong appeal to Peter Redgrove: Thales, the earliest known Greek philosopher, who taught that the world was made of water; and Proteus, "the Carpathian wizard", as Milton called him, capable of infinite transformation.

Peter Redgrove's Sea-Spiral Spirit infuses and is infused through all the elements. Spiralling across the world, it lifts up and is lifted up by a fifth, the whirling doughnut of energy the physicists call plasma, that creates force at the core of everything. . . . This spiralling spirit does not find the Earth-Spirit too ugly, it knows the spell-bound containment of its power within the earth and Faust's own power of spells to call it up.

A parallel poem, "**The Haunted Armchair**", finally lays the spirit of the jobbing gardener who was God the Father. A voice comes from the chair, itself evocative of gentlemen's libraries, leather-bound volumes, abstract power of mind. Still dividing body and mind, it wants to go on doing so until the end of time. Until, suddenly, a strong new sense of time comes in, which is also immeasurably old, and undermines the man-made separation. He hears time flowing, "time eroding, the cinder withering in the grate". "How much time," he asks, "have I seen withering?" Then suddenly there is release, not into death but into ever-evolving life, as he proclaims: "Suddenly everything *grants* me withering" (my italics).

The personal allegory completing this extraordinary trinity comes through **"The Idea of Entropy at Maenporth Beach"**, which though not specifically written as such is a direct answer to Wallace Stevens's fine romantic poem, "The Idea of Order at Key West". In this sea and sky are given order and meaning for the poet by the beauty of the girl's song. Peter Redgrove endorses the creative power of the artist acknowledged here, but he knows that waves and sky have meaning in themselves, have energy and evolutionary power, however random and boring their incredibly slow process is to restless trapped romantics. His white singer enters the disorderly mud, "From this collision were new colours born" and new power for the poet.

Since his *Faust* book, Peter Redgrove's directions have been many and full of developing contraries, with the prose poems of his novels becoming increasingly important to him. His power has always been a strongly dramatizing one, in the tradition of medieval morality, dramatizing warring elements in the self rather than springing from dramatic absorption in the lives of others. His **"Three Pieces for Voices"** seems to form a dramatic trinity matching the three poems in the *Faust* book, with the first, **"The Son of My Skin"**, recasting God the Father as the Emperor who gives his only begotten self to be flayed alive for humanity's sake and then is radiantly set apart in men's eyes as the Emperor's son. **"The Jesus Apparition"** re-enacts the Ascension as a Descension or Extension of total being, while **"Beyond the Eyelids"**, with its epigraph from E.T.A. Hoffmann's tale, *Rath Krespel*, dramatizes personal experience of the poet knowing himself a protective skin-of-the-eyeball short in intensity of seeing. His novel, *In the Country of the Skin*, extends this hyper-awareness to the skin of the whole body which, when one lives with any conflicting intensity, always records this in its own strange way. The book presents the central experiences of the poet's life I have been referring to, as they happen, in a startlingly direct way and deserves to be read entire for itself. . . .

In Peter Redgrove's more recent poetry there is no longer a sense of marking time in shut-in domesticity, as in a poem like **"Sweat"**, for instance, in *The Force and Other Poems*. Nor of further discoveries of the liberating evolutionary power of time. Instead there is often a joyous offering of the present time, a celebration of unique personal living, an absorption in poetry as spell and ritual. The experience behind this clearly releases powers in the poet, but this does not always make the poetry powerful for others. People need powerful art to energize them for their own living, they don't need that living done for them and in a sense that is what any ritualizing of experience is. The prose poem, **"Really Gone"** (in *The Force and Other Poems*), suggests that Peter Redgrove intuitively knows this and that no art can be a substitute for full and satisfying living. The contraries of his own experience up till that time leap out at one from every page in the *Faust* book, with a poem like **"Tell Me, Doctor"**, for instance, revealing the continuing life

of a relationship supposed dead; **"Half-Scissors"**, the flashing cutting dependence of one very much alive. Some of his poetry since then ignores this contrary, producing its own shut-in ritualistic quality even when enacted out of doors. One misses the cool clear note of the outside world for its own sake, which the poet himself sounds in **"Directive"**, written earlier in answer to **"Sweat"**. Indoors it is at times as if Mr Looking-Glass has succeeded Mr Waterman, with flashing mirrors to look sideways at, rather than doors opening to pass through.

Recent uncollected poems already begin to refute this, showing a new power to enter other people as distinct from divers aspects of himself, or others seen only in relation to himself; and **"From the Questions to Mary"** is a new bringing together of Greek and Christian traditions. . . . **"From the Reflections of Mr Glass"** has a renewal of his original fresh flowing quality, a pursuit of light rather than darkness and so perhaps a movement towards release from any jig-saw puzzle of correspondences for their own sake. (pp. xvii-xxi)

Peter Redgrove has spoken of himself as one for whom "matter *sings*". This is so with the poetry also, the song is very much in the matter, not the manner of it. There is no particular magic in the artistry, no particular outward spell of rhyme or stanza pattern to enact meaning. But there is tremendous store of inner energy, both in rhythm and imagery. Rhythmically one feels this working in a strongly inner, tidal way, with variations in length of lines, speed of movement, degree of poetic pressure. There is also strong entropic power in the compression of what he images, giving back the germ of life, the particle of force, to have its own effect. The tree, for instance, "preening herself with a soft bough-purr"; "the living lips of the worm nibbling air"; "gulls like airships whose furnace draught is screams". These are only a very few grains from the stuffed granary that is there, to say nothing of the radiant outward-flashing power of many other images. (p. xxi)

Marie Peel, in an introduction to Sons of My Skin: Redgrove's Selected Poems, 1954-1974 *by Peter Redgrove, edited by Marie Peel, Routledge & Kegan Paul, 1975, pp. xi-xxi.*

DEREK STANFORD

Some poets, by their form, lead us to think of their creations in non-organic terms. For example, we see Yeats as a mechanical bird 'Of hammered gold and gold enamelling', while Eliot might appear as 'the ancient eagle' on a church lectern. Peter Redgrove, however, is not to be envisaged in terms of inanimate form but rather as some protean shape such as nature assumes with clouds, mist and water. He changes, flows, and transforms himself. He is very like the Old Man of the Sea.

Sons of My Skin, his selected poems, covers the last twenty years of his work, and prints pieces from seven of his books. Marie Peel, who introduces these poems, believes the prolific variability of Mr Redgrove's verse springs from the poet's rejection of what Coleridge calls 'fixities and definites'—the labelling system patented by the consciously disciplined Western mind. In his repudiation of logical, scientific or academic speech (with its carefully stressed contraries: waking/dreaming, right/wrong, life/death, *etc*), she believes he has profited by an immersion into the mental activity of the subconscious. Certainly many of his poems read like purified surrealism, the syntax grammatical while only the thought defies the categories of 'reality'.

Mr Redgrove's poetry may be heard as a voice raised against the all-but-total subjugation of Nature, the organic and the vitalistic by the forces of the man-made and the mechanistic. . . . I can think of no British poet in whom the transforming powers of the imagination are so consistently asserted as in [Redgrove]. If they were accompanied by the workings of the formalising faculty making for unity of composition, Mr Redgrove would be our premier poet. As it is, he remains an astonishing phenomenon of potent individuality.

> *Derek Stanford, in a review of "Sons of My Skin: Selected Poems 1954-74," in* Books and Bookmen, *Vol. 21, No. 5, February, 1976, p. 66.*

JULIAN BARNES

[*The Glass Cottage*] opens with one of those arty killings which (in 'experimental' novels) act as a sort of plot-substitute; thereafter, the scenes shift between an Atlantic liner, a glass cottage in Cornwall and a university in America with such a lack of continuity and such an arch succession of unidentified first-person narrators, that the authors must, one feels, have written it all like a game of Consequences. But then, the book is really an excuse for its prose, which confirms the danger of giving metaphor its head:

> The liner floats on the waves like a large closed volume, its covers tooled in black and white. The sea keeps plucking at its pages but so far has not read it. The sea would like to become acquainted with the ship's contents . . . but so far the liner has displayed only its title—*SS Messenger*—proudly as it speeds like an inter-library loan between Goode Olde England and the Great Universal States.

Can you tell it from Brautigan? Here and there the ceaseless imagising does actually intensify description, and there are a couple of gory bits (a thumb amputation and a self-performed throat operation) which have a repelling precision to them; but too often the book is a wash of self-indulgence. (pp. 420-21)

> *Julian Barnes, "Blood," in* New Statesman, *Vol. 92, No. 2375, September 24, 1976, pp. 420-21.*

NEIL HEPBURN

The Glass Cottage is concerned not so much with the murder of a woman by her lover on board the transatlantic liner *SS Messenger,* which is its formal catalytic event, but with the proposition—and I will not swear to this—that in the sacrificial issue of blood from a woman, whether by menorrhoea or the assassin's wound, lies the key to that Unified Field Theory by reference to which all manifestations of spiritual energy may be understood and evaluated. The obvious corollary to this, the equation of male and female genitalia with weapon and wound, and of copulation with assassination, has been specifically denied by Redgrove-Shuttle. . . .

The Glass Cottage, whatever its true preoccupations, is full of marvellous writing, especially where concrete if esoteric experience is described: some passages, dealing with the vitreously hostile American university at which *Messenger*'s most interesting passengers turn up, or with the real Glass Cottage in Cornwall, are even too good, diminishing the conventional marvels in which the book chiefly subsists and making its metaphysics look distinctly second-hand.

I wish they had tougher editors than themselves: when they have (or, at least, when Mr Redgrove has), the results are powerful.

> *Neil Hepburn, "Strong Meat," in* The Listener, *Vol. 97, No. 2493, January 27, 1977, p. 127.*

VERNON YOUNG

From the early seventies, Peter Redgrove's **"Dr. Faust's Sea-Spiral Spirit"** is a poem he would probably feel represents him better than many I should prefer. . . . The IT in the poem is a kind of underlying, every-where-charging form of energy. . . . [This poem] is not so much the imaging of disorder *by* disorder as it is a desperate attempt to confine ubiquity, contain omnipresence, like stuffing an imp into a vessel too small for it. Sweating to find God or a First Cause without explicit reference to the pre-Socratics or Christianity, the more Redgrove says the more he feels compelled to say; the more he says, of this sort, the less convincing he becomes, either as animist or as poet. Gerard Manley Hopkins once confessed that since "the vice of distinctiveness is to become queer," this vice he had not escaped. Nor has Redgrove. A mixture of the precious and the awkward scatters his calculated effects. The sequence beginning "It electrifies Perranporth sand-dunes" is crude synaesthesia, indeed; how many readings does it take before one understands "blue-slippered prints" as a reference to a slippered lithograph, or the like, on the wall? (*Slippered* is adventitiously employed for the sake of its echo, *slips,* in the next line). Further, "we invaginate, evaginate" and the *ticking* of clocks *welds* to an organ-note? This is associational diction on its worst behavior.

We read with some astonishment the innocent inferences of Marie Peel [in her introduction to *Sons of My Skin: Selected Poems 1954-1974*] when she declares that here is "something we have not had in English poetry before, the scientist's poetic vision of the process." Redgrove is not a scientist: does she mean the *poet's scientific* vision?—in which case, how disingenuous is she being? . . . Redgrove's best is so self-evidently vital in its own right that Marie Peel might well have contented herself with saying that among poets who have been most aware of their community with the elemental in nature, Redgrove has found, very often, a new liberating way of expressing the kinship.

While Redgrove can, and does, concentrate succinctly on one thing for one poem, the total impression he gives is of energy changing its housing from this place, object, or mind to that, with immense agility and nearly always with a view to the transitive, the procreative, the symbiotic nature of the transaction. As close to the center of his Heraclitean source as any poem I'd call his *best* is **"On the Screaming of the Gulls"**. . . . I find this poem more effective than [**"Dr. Faust's Sea-Spiral Spirit"**] because, allowing for some strained metaphors that don't quite rupture, the factual integrity structures the lyric freedom. (Incidentally, there is no science here that would have surprised either Darwin or Wallace!) An even more masterly example of prosody and narrative inseparable, the outside (syntax and vocable) exactly conveying the inside (mental landslide) is **"Decreator,"** one of several poems touching the same subject—"Men beget men, and the angels of chance experiment"—but in this poem the foremost meaning is not necessarily the only one. (pp. 376-80)

I like Redgrove when he's *intent,* bearing down; when observation and metamorphosis (into language) seem to have arrived instantaneously, as he notes "the gnat-worm with smoky feet / Faltering in spirals"; the fly, whose "eyes are cobbled like a road"; the ferns that "dip and spread their fronds / With moisture easy through the stems." A bird "flies worms rot-coated to its children"; " . . . in a downpour cloudy with rush. . . . wet apples [they] sag like a rosy mist" and "Each night from hedgerows / Huge glossy slugs skim out, hour-long transparencies / With mire-cud inset deep that melts. . . ." Noticeably, despite the vast natural forces that sweep through some of Redgrove's poems—the sea, volcanic displacement, wind and rain and transformed energies—his zoology is restricted to the small leafy lives; unlike the England of Ted Walker and Ted Hughes, there are in Redgrove's no predatory creatures much larger than a spider—not a hawk nor a fox nor a shark. Redgrove's bestiary is selected with an eye to ratifying his agreement with Blake (according to Peel): "Everything that lives is holy." There is no sensible foundation for this belief— save as a figure of speech or a premise for Hinduism—once you include piranha, copperhead snakes, and weasels in your catalogue of the living. Another analogy imposes itself. Just as in the poems of Sylvia Plath there is an admirably short distance between word and sensation, between the blood and the lip, so the Redgrove closeup of nature is, like Plath's, odd and Liliputian. She was most at home with snails, cow-parsley, milkweed, moths, and cherries. There resemblance ceases; she felt otherwise threatened by anything that stirred, stung, or writhed. (pp. 380-81)

But there is no parallel in any other poetry, I begin to think, with Redgrove's passionate *weather-consciousness*. He has the most kinetic, virtually disagreeable, ability to make you suffer as you read him—from wet feet, from abrasive wind, from scorching summer, above all from winter: his consummate performance, within my ken, is **"The Nature of Cold Weather,"** a marvelous poem of twenty stanzas he wrote a decade ago. Much of the material in the later selections I can ill judge, for it depends importantly on the context in which these pieces appeared and I have only the *Selected Poems*. Prose poems, prose dialogues, an excerpt from a novel: I am dubious of the scattered directions toward which Redgrove tends and I am not receptive to the messianic touch that increasingly makes itself felt. Whether or not he's the greatest poet now writing in the British Isles I need not decide; certainly his language, exceptions noted, is the most exciting. If he persists too wilfully in his revolt against *consciousness*, if he hunts too strenuously for the quantitative, ransacking the language of botany and physics, he risks arriving at that territory of the inane, inhabited by Hart Crane and Hugh MacDiarmid. (p. 381)

> *Vernon Young, "Romantic Englishmen and Classical Americans," in* Parnassus: Poetry in Review, *Vol. 5, No. 2, Spring-Summer, 1977, pp. 375-89.*

PETER PORTER

Peter Redgrove is the most ambitious poet working in Britain today. That he is not as highly regarded as Ted Hughes, his contemporary at Cambridge, is partly due to poetical reputations being made by teachers and partly to Redgrove's optimism.

From Every Chink of the Ark, at 268 pages, is as long as a novel and three times the length of "Crow," but it is packed with good tidings about living, and, despite the vehemence of much of the writing, offers hope for mankind, at least on an evolutionary scale. The extraordinary changes which make up

Redgrove's world are never Manichean: however violent his metaphors and comparisons, he comes down on the side of humanity and against blackness and the abyss.

Fashion today undoubtedly prefers the certainties of despair, from post-Auschwitzian silence to comic-strip nihilism. However, Redgrove can be quite as full of blood as Hughes, and he is even more wide-ranging in his references. Also he will not suit anyone whose taste is for reticence rather than eloquence.

The most attractive poems in his new book are litanies or antiphons of a restored Church. Thus **"Trashabet"** is an alphabetical listing of the transformations of shards and trash into praise of living, and, by extension, of God. 'C is for cat's fur. If I rub this old plastic haberdasher's hand with cat's fur, it will pick up light buttons by electricity.' Christopher Smart would have liked that haberdasher's hand and also Redgrove's frequent recourse to science, both simple and arcane. For Redgrove, the two cultures have never been at variance with each other: they work together to produce a theology of poetry. There are a number of these Smart-like alphabetical catalogues, and if the method of compilation is simple, the resonance of his language is deep. Naturally, his religious sense is unorthodox, and he can be assertively anti-Christian. Christ is perhaps the most frequent character on his stage, and is most likely to be fitted out with some outrageous form of drag.

But Redgrove's fascination with witches, rituals of magic and the wilder part of anthropology does not make him less serious. Like his concern for minerals and the movement of natural forces such as water and cloud, his examination of psychological factors goes to nourish a sacramental art with room for every aspect of the profane. Everything in Redgrove is News from Somewhere. . . . His optimism does not make him shirk the dark origins of hope. . . .

There is a quality in this book which is relatively new to his work: wit, in its social sense. All his poems to do with university teaching are agreeably mordant, especially **"Dog Prospectus," "Ultimate Professor"** and **"Baby Department."** . . . **"Amazing Perfume Offer"** is a good example of his peculiar ability to humanise the highest of rituals by joking.

There are two reasons why I think Redgrove is an encouraging poet to read, as well as an important one. Firstly, he has an unquenchable love of language at its most exuberant. Secondly, his work is both deeply English and yet completely *sui generis*. He stands outside all the controversies about modernism and Traditionalism.

> *Peter Porter, "News from Somewhere," in* The Observer, *September 4, 1977, p. 24.*

ANNE STEVENSON

There is no poet writing in Britain with a more ebullient imagination than Peter Redgrove. Everything he sees is transformed by that imagination. Everything he thinks or feels emerges in his writing richly embossed with images. The effect can be overwhelming, and readers who prefer to take their reality in sober doses have been known to balk at the demands Redgrove makes on their credulity.

Surely, though, there are enough tidy suburban dwellings in the English literary landscape to make us welcome the daring gothic of Redgrove's cumulative extravaganza. His latest book of poems, *From Every Chink of the Ark,* adds to the impressiveness of the Redgrove edifice, and yet provides rooms for humanity and life that are positively cheering. . . . Readers, of course, must let themselves go with Redgrove's poems. There is no point in sitting on the sidelines griping because some seem long and unwinnowed and others are so gnarled with images as to be obscure. All Redgrove's poems are poured forth with immense force out of the same fecund and original imagination. You either respond to that imagination and are excited by it, or you reject it altogether. There is little middle ground on which to hold rational critical arguments. Indeed, without exception, the poems in *From Every Chink of the Ark* celebrate what is primitive and mystical in existence (the animal instincts that remain when the ark is blown away) at the expense of what is rational.

Redgrove is a great poet of the transforming eye. What he sees things *as* is more immediately accessible to him as poetry than what he actually sees or thinks. Or, to put it another way, whatever he sees and feels is captured immediately by the exaggerating mirror of his mind. Images of mirrors and glass abound in this collection, though artificial fabrications—glass, steel, lenses—characteristically oppose the natural elements— water and ice. . . . In some poems—to me, the best poems— Redgrove uses his eye simply as a magnifying glass; imagination adds subtle but unportentous interpretations to what is observed. In a sequence entitled **"Pictures from a Japanese Printmaker"**, for instance, "Women being carried across a river / On the backs of husky watermen" themselves look like rivers:

> The ladies are particularly heavy, as they are dressed
> In their own rivers of colour
> Heavy with rain, heavy with river;
> Each of the watermen shoulders his individual river.

In this light mood Redgrove is at his most beguiling. There seems to be no moral to his magic; it is presented simply for our delight.

In other poems, however, a fervent idea lies thickly under ornate surfaces. A poem which Redgrove evidently took pains to make allegorical is called **"Aesculapian Notes"**; it is worth looking at carefully to see how Redgrove sometimes builds images out of ideas. The poem as a whole, I think, is a meditation in images on man's peculiar relationship with his own elements on one hand (words, thoughts, the creative mind) and natural elements on the other (clouds, water, air, wind, etc). In the first section Redgrove sees these two kinds of elements as being antithetical. The plane "on its domestic flight", full of its "mineral" passengers, resembles nature's "death-cloud"—meaning not a nuclear cloud, but one of ice crystals. When the plane enters the cloud, the cloud smashes, and in the imagery at least, both plane and cloud destroy each other, "building one large Four-armed flake that howls to the ground / Exploding on impact to smudged immense hieroglyphs / Uttered for miles across the even snow." . . . The rest of the poem is devoted to showing how the "passengers" in their plane (their civilization) may learn to be reconciled to the "deathcloud", or the life-and-deathcloud, by a kind of mythological metamorphosis. To keep alive is to keep in flux, to be the subject and object of change. Moreover, natural elements are the patterns of human elements: wind becomes language, and language, spoken from within the oak tree, becomes the serpent who originally taught us how to create. Only by subjecting themselves to metamorphosis can the passengers on the plane become "passengers on each other", where "the cloud /

Enters the Plane, the plane the cloud / And the changes happen".

In this poem Redgrove is obviously not only the magician but the medicine man, the healer of souls (hence the title, **"Aesculapian Notes"**). At the end he speaks from inside—not a plane or an oak tree, but a warm house in wintry upstate New York. Here he watches flies "woken by their hormone orchestra / . . . Stagger out like old men on black ski-sticks" indoors, while ice-crystals form on the outside of his windows. So the reconciliation is finally made between indoors and outdoors and the poet is imaginatively able to participate in the winter. . . .

I have chosen to look at **"Aesculapian Notes"** in detail because it is central to the theme of Redgrove's book, and also because it illustrates some of the difficulties inherent in his longer poems. There is always a danger in Redgrove that the images will flood the poem. A reader is likely to get lost or impatient without following the twists and turns of his imagination through to the end. Moreover, Redgrove never blanches at ugly turns of phrase. . . .

Redgrove's work is more powerful, more awkward and much greater in range than that of more fastidious surrealists, such as Elizabeth Bishop. There is much humour in Redgrove, but little wit—or taste. His feeling for the deepest, most mystical levels of existence is unparalleled in modern poetry, but his expression can be difficult and clumsy as well as marvellous. However, reservations about his stature have to be niggling, minor reservations—gnats, as Redgrove might put it, biting at the sanguine, healthy flesh. For Peter Redgrove is one of the few writers in Britain to whom the risk of poetry is as natural as the risk of life. That he has chosen in this book to celebrate life rather than denigrate it makes *From Every Chink of the Ark* one of the richest, most valuable collections of poems to appear for some time.

> *Anne Stevenson, "The Voice of the Green Man," in* The Times Literary Supplement, *No. 3947, November 18, 1977, p. 1355.*

ANNE STEVENSON

Peter Redgrove actually calls his novel-poem *The God of Glass* . . . "A Morality." Unlike Ted Hughes, who seems to feel his way into myth by intuition, Redgrove wants us to understand rationally what he intuits. His purposes are evangelical, joyful; he is like a man who has experienced a revelation and wants us to see it too. His partnership with Penelope Shuttle has produced remarkable poems and novels, but the message inherent in *In The Country of the Skin* and *Dr. Treviles* was obscure until the writing of *The Wise Wound*. . . . (pp. 323-24)

The ostensible subject of this fascinating, carefully researched study is menstruation—a topic the authors felt (rightly) has been tabooed by our so-called liberated society, but which has been disregarded at immense emotional cost to both women and men. The deeper subject of *The Wise Wound* is, however, the real subject of all Redgrove's work: that is, intuition or imagination as alternative modes of perception. Redgrove has always been committed to freeing the human mind from the bondages of rationality and sense perceptions. He does *not* mean, I think, that what we consciously see or think or feel is unreal, but that there are important realities which we do not perceive consciously. Redgrove's fictions are always concerned to present unconscious realities by means of images to the conscious mind. The themes of *The God of Glass* are those of *The Wise Wound,* but they were received by Redgrove *first* as images or dreams, and only later treated factually by his conscious mind—and pen.

The plot which holds *The God of Glass* together is . . . improbable and deliberately shocking—though Redgrove's stories are always edged with a certain grotesque humor. Little girls in an English village are possessed by demons, and one of them, offered water in a glass by a priest, breaks the glass and slits the priest's throat. No Christian vicar can exorcise the spirit which finally causes the girl to saw through her own neck, but the village doctor consults an African called Geoffrey Glass who successfully undertakes the exorcism of a second demon-infested girl by freeing and embracing her. Mr. Glass, it turns out, is a shaman and hypnotist who, having murdered and flayed a man shortly after his arrival in Britain, was confined in a solitary cell where, for fifteen years, he "reflected" on the meaning of what he had done. The consequences of this reflection are miraculous. After the exorcisms have made him famous, Glass becomes the leader—or container—of a world-religion based on meditation. Through Glass, the rhythms of his healing message radiate to all civilized peoples. In a last and terrifying scene, Glass, televised, visible to all, "a tiny black figure on the immense platform draped in white by the management of the Albert Hall," describes his crime: "I killed a man very horribly, and was given life." Such is the power of this life that it enables men to share the experience of women; the priest who witnessed the murder of his colleague in the first chapter of this book is delivered of a baby in the last.

Such a plot would be appalling—or simply impossible—in an ordinary story, but Redgrove has used the trappings of the horror tale as Geoffrey Glass has used the flayed man's skin, to deliver his moral. "The apparent violence of certain of the scenes," Redgrove writes in an epilogue, "is the natural accompaniment to the emergence of deeply repressed but healing material. *The God of Glass* is subtitled 'A Morality' because it seeks, by adopting the mode and idiom of a horror story of exorcism, to redirect attention to the serious themes of adult rebirth, and the dire consequences of masculine non-participation in feminine blood-mysteries . . ." (pp. 324-25)

Anne Stevenson, "The Recognition of the Savage God: Poetry in Britain Today," in New England Review, *Vol. II, No. 2, Winter, 1979, pp. 315-26.*

ANTHONY THWAITE

The prolific Peter Redgrove launches another of his unclassifiable fictions in *The Sleep of the Great Hypnotist:* elements of fairy-tale, or myth, of science fiction, combined with jovial exuberance and with a strongly didactic or evangelistic undercurrent, lightened with farce. In Part One, George Frederick Pfoundes has invented an Oscilloscope—'a device for magnifying our unconscious reactions, and playing them back for us to see, so we could co-operate with them.' In Part Two, after Pfoundes's death his daughter manages to exercise this magical and oppressive spirit.

Increasingly, the mark of Redgrove's poetry and prose alike is a dottily sardonic matter-of-factness about (literally) extraordinary physical and spiritual states, so that dreams, trances, and religious ecstasy are presented with plain assurance and total conviction, keeping the whiffs of mumbo-jumbo buoyant

with sheer gusto. It might be nonsense, but it was true nonsense.

Anthony Thwaite, "Switching On the Oscilloscope," in The Observer, *November 25, 1979, p. 39.*

DICK DAVIS

Understatement is not Peter Redgrove's forte. The exuberance of his subject-matter—he seems to have an insistent vision of everything in the universe turning into everything else—is matched by the exuberance of his style. . . . [The sheer bulk of *The Weddings at Nether Powers* gives one] the impression that the author would consider pruning or revision some kind of affront to his fecund muse. Nevertheless, it would be a service to his readers: the riot of images reminds us occasionally of Craig Raine. . . . But where Raine keeps a dandyish distance from his poems, Redgrove plunges into the vortex with a delighted whoop. Unfortunately the reader is left floundering in the headlong spate, gasping for a foothold of definition or precision. The vision is undeniably powerful, but the language seems hurried down pell-mell and is, for this reader at least, confused and confusing. (p. 158)

Dick Davis, "King Image," in The Listener, *Vol. 103, No. 2647, January 31, 1980, pp. 157-58.*

ANNE STEVENSON

Since writing *The Wise Wound* with Penelope Shuttle, Peter Redgrove has drawn three novels out of his researches into the occult. *The God of Glass* grew from his study of blood taboos: subtitled "A Morality", the story begins with murder and exorcism and ends in a celebration of shamanistic birth, trance and salvation through knowledge of evil. *The Sleep of the Great Hypnotist* took up the theme of hypnotism from *The God of Glass,* but in this novel the hypnotist exerts power posthumously by giving his daughter an hypnotic command to raise him from the dead.

Both these novels could be called Moralities and together they give us a good idea of Redgrove's attitude towards magic. Magic, of course, is for Redgrove the stuff of poetry. Good magic is the magic of primitive religion and, indeed, of the Old Testament, with earth, nature and man in a close and fruitful relationship. Bad magic, or black magic, means the manipulation by man of the powers of life and death. A good sorcerer / witch / poet reads the book of the earth and works according to, and with respect for, its laws. A bad magician defies nature and writes his own laws, destroying the balance of existence for his own ends.

In his new book, *The Beekeepers,* Redgrove approaches this obsession with the balance of life and death through the imagery of bees and the plot of a spy story. While the novel explores the uses and misuses of magic, its setting is social, modern and certainly relevant to today. Perhaps because *The Beekeepers* is a novel about people and relationships, rather than an exploration of pure psyche, its structure is tighter and more accessible than that, say, of *In the Country of the Skin.* To experienced Redgrovians it will seem like settled waters after the storm. Previously Redgrove has dealt in multiple identities, ritual violence and the quest for truth through sex, murder and death. *The Beekeepers* is no less violent, but it has a magnetism and even a charm that the other novels lack.

Two poets, Guy, a heavy drinker in his forties, and Matthew, an older man and an alcoholic, decide to give up drink in order to explore the subconscious causes of their addiction. Spiritualism and automatic writing, which they take up for amusement as they might take up chess or golf, reveal the existence of a common, highly destructive *anima,* a terrorist who, according to their independently written but dovetailing automatic scripts, is on the point of destroying herself and hundreds of others in a crowded London pub.

Guy, who lives with his sexy, observant, psychologist mistress, Millie, introduces Matthew to water-divining with the result that Guy becomes transfigured by the spirit of water; Matthew, however, blows his mind. A corporeal manifestation of Matthew's destructive *anima*—Meave—carries Matthew off to a sinister Institute on the edge of London where David, a psychiatrist who has prolonged his life through sex-magic, experiments on the spirits of the dead. The implication is that he can remake "souls" by magnetizing their spirits, by gathering dispersed spirit-atoms together like bees. The honey produced at the Institute is sexual, produced by multiple copulations and incest. Matthew, who becomes addicted to David's brand of sex-magic (just as he was addicted to alcohol), is mysteriously destroyed. It is his ghost that delivers the automatic message to Guy, betraying the terrorists at work in the Institute, but at the same time saving his own spirit through his sacrifice, and Guy's and Millie's lives through his warning. Matthew's final message to Guy is embodied in a play, appropriately called *Finding a Ghost,* which is included as a chapter of the novel—a kind of Grand Inquisitor scene, or play within a play, which contains the novel's moral through its indictment of phony escape-mechanisms and black magic.

There is no doubt that as a work of art *The Beekeepers* is a hotch-potch. Ideally Redgrove needs a Russian-sized canvas to do justice to the size of his ideas. But Redgrove is a poet, and his novels should not be read as ordinary fiction or even as dramatized treatises, but as glosses on his poetry. The finest parts of *The Beekeepers* are poems: a splendid and important poem called **"The Dowser"** . . . and another fine poem called **"The Bombs"**. . . . Even Matthew's death-poem at the end of his play is a superb piece that stands apart from its context.

By contrast, the prose of both play and novel seems rushed, makeshift, endearingly amateur. It is as if Redgrove were so anxious to express his vision that he used whatever words came first to hand so as to get the novel out as quickly as possible. . . . Redgrove has never clarified the role of his characters. Are they symbolic, mythical figures, or are they realistic?

At one moment they are undergoing transmutations into snakes or being caught up in blood rituals or orgasms in mud; the next moment they are eating scrambled eggs or having a shower before supper. It is no good saying this is what happens in "real life", for a novel, whatever its aspirations, is never "real life" and it must be consistent with regard to the aspects of life it represents. Surrealism, possibly, can get away with dripping realistic watches from realistic trees, but Redgrove is too serious a poet, surely, to be taken in by surrealism.

For what Redgrove is saying—sometimes in humour, sometimes in passion, but never in cynicism or despair—is that there are powers at work in our world that will destroy us unless we recognize them and get them into balance. One of these powers is death, another is love; one is male, another female. It is the old story, perhaps, but no less true for Redgrove and the twentieth century than it was for Dante and for Shakespeare. There is much in Redgrove, indeed, that is Shakespearian; his gusto, his scope, his ability to move from comedy to tragedy with a swift shift of emphasis. Only his timing is foreshortened, and his characters are undeveloped; his prose is adequate but workaday. Why doesn't he let his poetry find speech for *all* he has to say—limpidly, strongly?

Redgrove is nevertheless breaking fertile ground, and his imagination and courage set an example to us. If his novels shock us, if they offend aesthetic and moral sensibilities, if they make us laugh or rage or turn our imaginations towards academically disreputable pastures of the subconscious, so much the better.

Anne Stevenson, *"The Powers of the Earth," in* The Times Literary Supplement, *No. 4035, July 25, 1980, p. 836.*

GREVEL LINDOP

Making conscious the hidden powers and terrors of the psyche is important work. Whether Redgrove has found the means to transmute this material into art is another matter. *The Facilitators* is a psychodrama whose central concern is the pursuit of *anima* by *animus,* a dance of male and female elements within the personality. The novel confronts us with a mysterious "Institute", a therapeutic community whose Director is generally known as "Madame"—the suggestion of the bordello is not altogether irrelevant. The Institute, and the elaborate bee-cult associated with it, are derived fom Redgrove's previous novel, *The Beekeepers,* to which there are several hasty references-back. . . .

Obscurities and adventures proliferate as the characters grope their way through the Institute, guided (and guiding each other) by occasional gestures of "facilitation" or therapeutic approval: a friendly wink, a relaxing massage, a readiness to hear confession or indulge a fantasy. Facilitation? "What an ugly word", as one character remarks. "But", comes the reply, "it's a beautiful concept." The exchange has the ring of genuine psychobabble about it, and is not untypical of those passages where action gives way to reflection or exposition. . . . We are in the land of pop-psychology, and it is not long before a jacuzzi, that trendiest emblem of the Good Life, makes the first of its several appearances.

Repeatedly in *The Facilitators* one is disconcerted to find the narrative's inventive surface underpinned by fashionably simplistic notions, and even by a vulgarization of vitally liberating poetic insights. Its sub-title alludes to Blake's proclamation that "There is a Moment in each Day that Satan cannot find . . . but the Industrious find / This Moment and it multiply. & when it once is found / It renovates every Moment of the Day if rightly placed." One character's gloss on this is, "Yeats kept a hole in the day open by means of Swedish exercises and ritual magic. . . . Madame was disingenuous in not making a complete list, surely. A hole is a hole; intercourse and masturbation should have been included, royal roads." The statement is endorsed by the frequency with which masturbation features in the novel as a means to visionary experience and magical power.

There is a reductionism about this, which indicates why *The Facilitators,* despite its flow of incident and weirdly vivid imagery, generates so little poetic or fictional power. It may be that one of the Institute's doctors is offering an account of the novel's own values when she insists, "We don't use that word 'fantasy'. Call it imagination, enthusiastic imagination." The terms recall Coleridge, but the emphatic repetition will not suffice to destroy the distinction between fantasy, or fancy, and imagination. *The Facilitators* seems a work of the fancy, in Coleridge's sense. Lacking both the constraints of realism and a compelling inner logic, it creates a world where anything can happen, hence where nothing has much significance.

> Grevel Lindop, "The Hidden Powers Going Pop,"
> in The Times Literary Supplement, *No. 4150, Oc-*
> *tober 15, 1982, p. 1141.*

BEN HOWARD

To the grim historicity of post-War British verse, Peter Redgrove brings a keen sense of the numinous. In the work of his contemporary, Geoffrey Hill, we gain access to buried saints and Christian mysteries, and in Ted Hughes we confront invisible psychic forces. But it is Redgrove who reveals the radiant auras, the envelopes of energy surrounding common things. Observing a woman bending in a field, he sees a "queen of the wet dust," who "wraps her body in a coat of dew and straw" and trails "an erotic, ghostly atmosphere." And throughout [*The Apple-Broadcast and Other Poems*] Redgrove surrounds objects, landscapes, and people in similar atmospheres, whether his subject is an infant or a policeman, a bicycle or an icon, his erect penis or the Gwennap Cross. When his strategies fail, they produce little more than a blur, a screen of mist between the reader and the object. But when they succeed, as they often do, we find ourselves in a world akin to that of Turner's paintings or Blake's visions. (p. 124)

Redgrove read natural sciences at Cambridge, and Like A. R. Ammons, whom he sometimes resembles, he devotes many poems to the natural world, dwelling on organic process and kinetic minutiae. But Redgrove is an earthier poet than Ammons, and his poems speak not only of the mind and nature but also of his sexual appetites, his liking for food and drink, his hunger for religion, and his love of domestic life. Yet for all his sensuousness, Redgrove's theme is not the pleasures of the senses, nor are his poems given over to earthly delights. His abiding theme is the metamorphic fluidity of things. And within their irregular stanzas, their intricate syntax, his poems seethe and pulse with the energy of transformation. His tone ranges from breathless to ebullient, comic to manic, as he struggles to praise the changes he has seen.

Redgrove rarely describes his subjects. He clothes them in light or water or companions them with spirits. . . . In Redgrove's poems, images of streams, rivers, fountains, wells, urine, and beer mingle freely with images of bones, angels, ghosts, apparitions, and the nether world generally. And through them all runs an image of energy, whether it takes the form of lightning, magnetism, or the sexual drive.

Redgrove's agitated rhythms reinforce that sense of energy. Long dactylic lines crackle with nervous excitement. . . . Often [as in **"A Shirtsleeve Wedding"**] the dactylic rhythms derive from a profusion of present participles, which cluster and swarm in Redgrove's stanzas, creating new shapes and bonds:

We had

A tieless wedding, a shirt-sleeve nuptials, the groom
And the bride wore loose shirts, and the she-baby
Wore within the bride's skin her folding and unfolding
    linens

Floating as the veils float, as the shirt-tails float,
And she with her finger
Hushing her nose, peeking through the round inside.

Discerning a visual similarity between the fluid movements of the amnion and the flowing veils and shirt-tails, Redgrove mimes those movements in the rhythms of his verse. Father, mother, and unborn child seem enclosed in the amniotic fluid. A conventional wedding snapshot becomes a shimmering vision.

Of course, this technique can be overused. Too much movement can tire the ear as well as the mind. Relentless enjambment can be numbing. Fortunately, Redgrove seems aware of these drawbacks, and in his best work he uses an elaborate syntax to constrain the surge and momentum of his lines. Redgrove likes to stretch a single hypotactical sentence over five or more tercets, letting the tight syntax fence a flock of clucking participles. The result is often a sense of balanced forces, of stillness and movement reconciled. . . . In Redgrove's poems . . . such syntax becomes desirable, if not essential, because it helps contain his tendency to ramble. When the syntax loosens, the lines lapse into prolixity. . . . (pp. 125-26)

Excess of another kind weakens Redgrove's imagery. It tends toward the Gothic, and it is often overdone. We can hold out little hope for a poem that opens with these lines:

A great white ear floating in the sky, listening. I say
That your hair is but the beauty of ashes of blood
Passed out through your skin.

Nor can we be very moved, later in the same poem [**"Lecture Overheard"**], to hear that "a great tree of water flourishes over the sea / And begins walking on its visible roots . . ." When the excess is not of the Gothic variety, it appears most often as a glut of images or verbs or as a surfeit of figures. . . .

Yet at his best Redgrove accomplishes his purpose with skill and daring. Objects are transfigured. A spider in its web, a father's "damp last breath," a Persian feast, "the head of my baby with its rinsed mossy smell," urine, feces, a figure of Christ—all are transformed by the poet's touch. Of course Redgrove's magic, like Midas's, can be either a curse or a blessing. It can gild the lily—or it can transmute a common object into a nexus of energies, a luminous storm. The issue is one of balance and tact, and in his strongest poems Redgrove exhibits both, as he pits his native exuberance against severe restraint. . . . (p. 127)

> Ben Howard, *"Erotic, Ghostly Atmospheres," in*
> The Kenyon Review, *n.s. Vol. VII, No. 1, Winter,*
> *1985, pp. 124-28.*

PETER PORTER

A Peter Redgrove poem is the equivalent of an engineer's wind tunnel: huge forces are at large but words are all we have to show for their buffetings. . . .

He is usually greeted with bafflement, since no one else writes like him. He does not carpenter well-made poems, nor invent tricky ways of seeing things. *The Man Named East* is a sort of learned journal of the spirit, and Redgrove can lay just claim to his self-description, a 'Scientist of the Strange.' Fortunately, though much of his work is difficult, he does not eschew the everyday and the comic. Humour, in fact, is one of his modes of ecstasy, and fixing ecstasy is the main aim of his poetry.

In a Redgrove poem, the ridiculous is frequently the sublime. **"A Proper Halo"** starts with this disarming confession: 'In those glad days when I had hair / I used to smarm it down with Brylcreem.' He remembers that decorum admonished him 'to refrain from pomades at one's confirmation.' The poem proceeds through anecdotes and puns, picking up small instances of the riotous beauty of life on its way. . . .

These poems have to be read as one would the revelations of a mystic, an Eckhart or Boehme who is, nevertheless, companionable, clever and warm. When Redgrove writes 'her collar widening like a torch beam' it is a very different effect from Martianism. He wants to join things up, not isolate them in their silhouettes. Redgrove can handle the traditional when he chooses to. **"The Funeral"** is a memorial to his mother, and a record of his and his father's grief, but it is also an imaginative metaphor for that release of feeling, so elusive in life, which comes from attending obsequies.

> Peter Porter, "*Brylcreem Haloes,*" *in* The Observer, *May 12, 1985, p. 21.*

NEIL ROBERTS

The Man Named East is Peter Redgrove's ninth full collection of poems, and although these books have won him a considerable reputation, the reputation has been more formidable than helpful. He is felt to be difficult and eccentric: unlike his contemporaries Ted Hughes and Thom Gunn, he enjoys no widely shared understanding of the nature of his achievement, or even the grounds for critical debate, and there is no provisional canon of his most important poems. This is especially true of his later and most distinctive work, from the early 1970s on, when the very generosity of his talent has perhaps been a handicap. . . . *The Working of Water* (which has several poems in common with *The Man Named East*) [is] a shorter collection with an obvious, dominant theme.

The element of water has been a valuable clew to the intricate but rational labyrinth of Redgrove's metaphors ever since the popular early prose fantasy **"Mr Waterman"**. It is the most easily grasped paradigm of his way of seeing: he habitually sees phenomena, including people, as products of and subject to a transformational flux, and individual forms as the signatures of a hidden, endlessly recreating movement:

> See shells only as seawater twining back
> To the first touch, of seawater on itself;
>
> The water touching itself in a certain way,
> With a certain recoil and return, and the mollusc
>
> Starts up in the water, as though the conched wave
> Had been struck to stone, yet with the touch
>
> Still enrolled in it, the spot was struck
> And life flooded through it
>
> Recording a thin stone pulse of itself.
> Its spiral photo-album, its family likeness
>
> Caught in nacreous layers. . . .

These lines from **"Shells"** show how closely, at his best, Redgrove's distinctive style is bound up with his vision. All readers must be aware of the overwhelming fluidity of his verse, and one dominant cause of this is his use of long, elaborate sentences, usually with unorthodox syntax. He has insisted that there is always discourse in his poetry but it is a discourse that does not lend itself to orthodox sentence construction. The action in the passage above is distributed among a variety of actives, passives and participles and among several different subjects. The water, the creatures, the shells, even "life" itself cannot be taken as the uniquely privileged agent of the process described: all are manifestations of an underlying flow implicit in the syntax or—in the words of the physicist David Bohm, whose work has influenced Redgrove—"implicate order".

This vision may make us acutely aware of the transience of our own manifest natures but the effect is not alienating for, conversely, Redgrove "humanizes" the whole process that includes us, as in [the title poem of] *The Man Named East,* where water "insists / Into my palm with a slight pressure / Like a baby's hand. . . . / The light clasp which is love". And a sequence of poems about his mother's death movingly negotiates between a vision of implicate order and straightforward human love and grief.

Redgrove's way of looking at the world is remarkably free of the Cartesian dualism. In one poem here a pupa cogitates; in an earlier poem even minerals think. Obviously we must be able to enjoy his poetry without committing ourselves to these propositions (I don't mean, either, that they are obviously to be dismissed), but there is one proposition that he forces us to take very seriously: that women are freer of the dualism than men because their thoughts and feelings are more directly influenced by their bodily processes, especially, as *The Wise Wound,* the book Redgrove co-wrote with Penelope Shuttle, argues at length, by the menstrual cycle. The most urgent task of men is to become more feminine. . . . *The Man Named East* contains one of his most pleasing expressions of this idea in the poem **"The Quiet Woman of Chancery Lane"**. . . .

For a man the feminine mode of experience is most directly accessible in the sexual act itself, and Redgrove's later poetry is pervasively erotic—never more so than in the new collection. Erotic experience of the woman is entry into the "grain-shaped cave" but with one's "light held high". Entry into the cave is not the extinguishing of consciousness in a formless darkness but an experience of clarity in a realm where all forms are potential—a "planetarium" whose "domed roof / Repeats the picture-code of night" (**"The Ships"**).

The "planetarium" could stand for much in Redgrove's poetry. His self-description as "Scientist of the Strange" may be accurate but is rather too awesome. He is a *popular* scientist of the strange, his tone—relaxed, intimate and social—that of a friendly guide rather than a cryptic oracle. Identifying that tone is, I think, half the secret of enjoying his poetry.

> Neil Roberts, "*Implicate Order,*" *in* The Times Literary Supplement, *No. 4291, June 28, 1985, p. 732.*

GEOFFREY O'BRIEN

Redgrove, a former research scientist who lists Taoist yoga among his hobbies, is one of the purest visionary poets alive. Indeed, his work sustains such a steady pitch of ecstasy that it can be exhausting. He builds coiling strings of images, metaphors that hatch further metaphors; each poem enacts a process of restless metamorphosis. His new book [**The Working of Water**] steeps itself in water, endlessly evokes its currents and conduits, revels in it, worships it. . . . Redgrove meditates on water wherever he finds it, in the bathtub, in a urinal, walking on the street after rain. . . . Redgrove's poetry insists that the reader accompany its flow. He offers very deliberately a focal point for active contemplation: "So that the stream may glitter / And play more freely with its sounds / And rise in green vibration, fold on fold / Unfolding, this water with its talent / For talking within itself utters woodland." Redgrove restores an elasticity of conception almost unheard of in modern English poetry.

> *Geoffrey O'Brien, in a review of "The Working of Water," in* VLS, *No. 42, February, 1986, p. 16.*

Anne Rice

1941-

American novelist and critic.

In her fiction Rice depicts horrific events through an ornate prose style and a painstaking attention to detail. She blends accurate historical elements with such themes as alienation and the individual's search for identity. Each of her novels centers on characters from an isolated segment of a real or imagined society: vampires populate *Interview with the Vampire* (1976) and *The Vampire Lestat* (1985), the first two installments of her *Chronicles of the Vampires* series; mulattoes and quadroons in New Orleans during the 1840s are the central figures of *Feast of All Saints* (1980); and the castrati of eighteenth-century Italian opera are featured in *Cry to Heaven* (1982). Rice's exotic subject matter, brooding sensibility, and baroque prose style prompted Michiko Kakutani to note: ''Anne Rice has what might best be described as a Gothic imagination crossed with a campy taste for the decadent and the bizarre.''

(See also *Contemporary Authors*, Vols. 65-68 and *Contemporary Authors New Revision Series*, Vol. 12.)

LEO BRAUDY

[In *Interview With the Vampire*] Anne Rice exploits all the sexual elements in [vampire myths] with a firm self-consciousness of their meaning, even to the extent of having a more than usually obtuse and bug-eyed interlocutor, who is taping the vampire's reminiscences in a rundown apartment off Divisadero Street in San Francisco, dig the reader in the ribs periodically just in case some nuance may have slid by unnoticed. Homosexuality—defined here as the refusal of adult sexuality (read heterosexuality)—is the hardly hidden mainspring of Rice's narrative, and her message seems to be: if you're homosexual, it's better to be unemotional about it. The vampire's progress from 1791, when he is initiated, to sometime in the second half of the 19th century is marked by his gradual acceptance of his separateness, his detachment from human nature, and his ''divorce from human emotions.''

Louis, the hero, is initiated by a vampire named Lestat (a political theme here?) after Louis's younger brother has died in an accident for which Louis blames himself. Lestat and Louis thereafter sleep face to face in the same coffin. Later Louis creates a vampire of his own, a young girl of five, who consequently never grows any older. After about 60 years, Claudia, the girl, tries to kill Lestat so that she and Louis can be free of him. Lestat revives and, with a young musician he has initiated, attacks Louis and Claudia. Louis and Claudia flee to Europe to search for their origins and discover the truths of vampire nature, but they wander the Carpathians finding only ''mindless corpses'' on the rampage. In Paris they discover a Théâtre des Vampires where, in good French style, the whole vampire life style is being merchandised for the jaded boulevardiers of the Second Empire. Here, remarkably enough, there are adult women vampires. Claudia adopts one as a mother

Photograph by Stan Rice. Courtesy of Anne Rice

and possible companion for Louis. But Louis is under the spell of Armand, a Parisian vampire. Lestat reappears. Claudia and the woman are killed. Louis kills the others and runs away from Armand to face his destiny alone, reconciled to his necessary solitude.

Anne Rice seems to view all this very positively, and my tone in the synopsis above may sound a little casual because I think that she has failed to give any kind of resonance to what she writes. Her solitary, homosexual, narcissistic vampire is compensating for his alienation from the community of the faithful. As Louis says about the only woman he ever admires, ''Like all strong people, she suffered always a measure of loneliness; she was a marginal outsider, a secret infidel of a certain sort.'' In this connection it's worth noting that among the changes American Catholicism has undergone in the last decade has been the rise in the number of Catholics writing Gothic tales. Until recently Gothics tended to be the preserve of Enlightenment Protestants glancing with mingled fear and fascination at medieval Catholicism. But now the night-stalker is exiled from a specifically Catholic community, with specifically Catholic rituals, liturgical references and theological arguments.

Anne Rice's publishers mention *The Collector* and *The Other*, but it is really *The Exorcist* to which *Interview With the Vampire* should be compared, and both novelist William Peter Blatty and filmmaker William Friedkin, whatever their faults, did it there much better. The themes I have mentioned are not trivial: The desire to be an individual, different from anyone else, and simultaneously to be part of a loving, nurturing community is a basic theme in American culture. But *Interview With the Vampire* states them more than feels them; it exploits them rather than inhabits them. The publicity tells us Rice is "a dazzling storyteller." But there is no story here, only a series of sometimes effective but always essentially static tableaus out of Roger Corman films, and some self-conscious soliloquizing out of Spiderman comics, all wrapped in a ballooning, pompous language. . . . [The] book is too superficial, too impersonal and too obviously made, to touch the sources of real terror and feeling. (pp. 7, 14)

Leo Braudy, "Queer Monsters," in The New York Times Book Review, *May 2, 1976, pp. 7, 14.*

EDITH MILTON

Unfortunately, the catastrophes which come to Anne Rice's mind in *Interview with the Vampire* are none of them quite as awful as the book itself. A *Bildungsroman* about a vampire? Are the Undead, who spend their days in coffins, capable of *Bildung*? I would have thought the whole point was that they got away from it. But that is a metaphysical speculation, and I suspect that in the name of sanity I should avoid metaphysics for the time. Let me say that I like vampire literature. Not just *Dracula,* but modern versions of the theme, like Richard Matheson's *I am Legend,* which terrifies me. I am fond of lamias and werewolves and cat people, in fiction, film and wherever else I can find them, not mainly because I enjoy a tingling spine but because that whole genre of narrative contains a satisfying metaphor for the beast within, for the loneliness implicit in our animal nature, and for the fear that because we *are* animals the dead will reach out to claim what our guilts tell us is already rightfully theirs.

Anne Rice gets away from all that as though it never existed. Louis the vampire is *good.* He is also hardly lonely; he has an assortment of vampire friends and lovers, and a child-vampire mistress, whose lust for blood and adventure is trapped inside the body of a five-year-old. Louis shares his coffin with her. As the title suggests, the novel is in the form of a nightlong interview, during which Louis explains his way of life; and although he complains a great deal about alienation and feeling isolated, he seems quite *au courant.* Alienated vampires simply do not grant interviews.

What a scope for farce! For satire! For, God help us, whimsey! But although one hopes at first that this may all be a hoax, the realization comes at length, painfully, that we are in a serious novel here. Louis' narrative is in earnest, and even some occasional, astute observations are swamped in its bloody march forward: for instance, the fact that Claudia, the vampire-child, sounds wonderfully sinister echoes of the great Victorian love affair with pre-pubescent little girls, and that she is ditched for a male vampire, Armand, who reverberates rather nicely with equally sinister overtones of the Edwardian love affair with world-weary young men. A touch of wit might have turned this into a brief history of changing sexual modes, from incest to sodomy and on to contemporary apathy. But let it go!

I hoped, too, that Louis' self-torment over his blood-compulsion might be informed by the human conflict between the need to kill and the fear of killing; that Louis as vampire might be

given a *raison d'être.* But he beats his breast, poor vampire, without the slightest dimension of metaphor to explain his behavior, and does his best to keep up with the times, and look at home in the changing world to which he rises nightly from his coffin. (p. 29)

But why does this need to be a vampire book at all? Our Louis is a kindly creature who argues about the existence of God and the Devil, falls in love twice without reference to bourgeois moral standards, appreciates art, travels widely. There needs no ghost come from the grave to tell us this! A 200-year-old man would have done nicely. Deprived both of his conventional metaphor of tragic bestiality and eternal isolation, and of his conventional purpose, to terrify, the vampire has only one function left. He sucks blood.

And there you have it. The hell with literary pretensions and Gothic formulae. *Interview with the Vampire* is an erotic novel, where the sucking of blood has replaced more reproductive activities. So what's wrong with that? Dracula was always a bit of a seducer; if you go by recent movies, the vampire kiss is just an epidermal expression of a *Deep Throat* impulse. Whatever childhood nightmares, whatever delicious guilts lead us to find acceptable such an unlikely connection, they find no clarification in this book, which moves from kill to kill, from rat picking to the great feeding-a-crowd scene in Paris with the energy of Fanny Hill drumming up customers in her *Memoirs.* Louis, like Fanny, finds that his little pleasure leads him to remorse. Unlike Fanny, he isn't very funny about it.

After reading the book, I tend to be remorseful myself. Never mind its stylistic solecisms; its gasping need to rely on present participles wherever possible and sometimes wherever not; its thundering banality ("There you were with another vampire you couldn't stand"); its majestic display of split infinitive; never mind that Louis at 220 lapses into words like "maximize" and does Groucho Marx dialogue: "I'm mystified. You're satisfied?" That he spends a night in the Louvre to look at art which it would take vampire eyes to decipher most of in broad daylight. Pass over all that or blame it on bad editing. But to pretend that it has any purpose beyond suckling eroticism is rank hypocrisy.

It is the multiplication of this hypocrisy which finally makes *Interview with the Vampire* worse than a silly book; makes it in fact a rather pernicious book. To mold erotic material to a structure of killing perhaps only appeals to a dangerous and questionable appetite. But sometimes, when the marriage of the salacious and the sadistic works, it works quite marvelously; as it does for Céline and Burroughs, and even poor A. C. Swinburne. Under no circumstances, however, can it work as a respectable union. What makes *Interview* so bad is not that the erotic content is so explicit, but that the morbid context is so respectable. It would barely bring a blush to the maiden cheek: though it is clearly intended to do much more than that for other parts. Death is made sexual here as blandly as if it were just another preference, more socially acceptable, more speakable than most. The addition of a few historical trimmings for the Bicentennial, the popular sensual girl-child thrown in for luck along with a bit of homosexual interest for more varied tastes, some talk of God and the Devil, a bow of respect toward art and beauty, and directions on the proper use of stakes and garlic, come to a sum which smacks of the computer. The book seems to contain nothing which hasn't sold well before, and almost everything which has. Its publication as serious fiction suggests such stunning cynicism that

I suppose it must be headed for almost certain success. (pp. 29-30)

Edith Milton, in a review of "Interview with the Vampire," in The New Republic, *Vol. 174, No. 19, May 8, 1976, pp. 29-30.*

IRMA PASCAL HELDMAN

[*Interview With the Vampire*] lays to rest a prevailing preconception concerning first novels: Even the most hardened skeptics can assume that the work is not autobiographical. One can also discard any and all previously acquired definitive notions as to what makes vampires suck.

Louis, despite his condition, is endearing—yes, endearing. Not since Barnabas, the vampire on the very successful TV Gothic soap "Dark Shadows," has there been a bloodsucking creature with so much charisma. . . .

Anne Rice pulls off her unique tale with a low-key style that is almost mundane in the presentation of the horrific. She has created a preternatural world that parallels the natural one. True, vampires, for all their cerebral meanderings about the nature of human desire, get their kicks in only one way, bloodsucking. Since that can become tedious, *Interview With the Vampire* could have been somewhat shorter.

But that's a minor quarrel, for this novel achieves more than the satisfaction of mere morbid curiosity. While not for the squeamish, it *is* spellbinding, eerie, original in conception, and deserving of the popular attention it appears destined to receive.

Irma Pascal Heldman, "The Fangs Have It," in The Village Voice, *Vol. XXI, No. 19, May 10, 1976, p. 50.*

EDMUND FULLER

[*Interview with the Vampire* is the] quite stunning debut of a young woman, Anne Rice. . . . It is hard to praise sufficiently the originality Miss Rice has brought to the age-old, ever-popular vampire tradition; it is undoubtedly the best thing in that vein since Bram Stoker, commanding peer status with *Dracula.* She has gone off boldly on a tack altogether her own, with assurance, an incredibly controlled craftsmanship for a first novel, and a Gothic style of lustrous polish.

The story will seize you from the first page, in which the 200-year-old vampire from New Orleans begins to tell his life story, by night, in a grubby room in San Francisco, to a recorder-toting boy who likes to interview people. Many vampire "myths" are destroyed as this tale describes how the narrator was made a vampire by another of that kind, the ruthless Lestat, who also made the child-vampire, Claudia, with whom the narrator's supernatural life is oddly linked.

The absorbing plot carries us to Austria, Transylvania (with a surprise!), and to Paris and the sinister *Theatre des Vampires,* appropriate to this Grand Guignol piece. Her power of invention seems boundless. The end contains a fresh surprise. She has made a masterpiece of the morbid, worthy of Poe's daughter. And like Mary Shelley's Gothic triumph, *Frankenstein,* it has even a philosophical level (though a lesser one), for this sensitive vampire suffers an acute anguish of mind and spirit which he pours out, at times, as in his exposition of how it can come about that a vampire dies (no stakes in the heart). Indeed, without obtruding upon the story, her vampires are a

great metaphor of a certain kind of living that is a death. Miss Rice may be at the start of a productive career, but if she never writes another book, this one seems assured of a long life, possibly to match that of its bizarre narrator.

Edmund Fuller, "Sherlock Holmes Meets Dracula Man," in The Wall Street Journal, *June 17, 1976, p. 14.*

ANNE EDWARDS

Halfway through the opening chapter of this romantic historical second novel [*The Feast of All Saints*] by the author of the much praised *Interview with the Vampire* I felt a great thump in my chest. It is a familiar complaint, easily diagnosed, for it strikes whenever I begin to fear that a book I have been looking forward to reading with enormous anticipation is not going to work. In this instance my expectation had been stimulated by recalling the originality of Rice's earlier novel and by her intriguing selection of the world of the *gens de couleur* (mulattoes, quadroons, octoroons) in antebellum New Orleans as a background. . . . However, by the second chapter the narrative, although desperately in need of an editor's unmerciful blue pencil, has a strange and compelling drive to it. My thump eased, but was never to disappear entirely.

Rice places the *gens de couleur libre* (free people of color) who dominated New Orleans' *vieux carré* before the Civil War, under a high-powered microscope. The story, set in the 1840s, weaves intricately around Cecile, dark-skinned mistress of the rich, white plantation owner, Philippe Ferronaire, and their two children, golden-colored Marcel Ste. Marie and his beautiful ivory-complexioned sister Marie, who could pass for white and yet defies counsel and custom by falling passionately in love with her brother's best friend, a young man darker than herself. . . .

A parallel exists with the white aristocracy of the south at the same time. Thus, Rice has a rich tapestry to embroider and after her pretentious start, she draws her needle in and out of the canvas with an artist's sure touch. The shading of her language is lush and often original, as in a passage describing Marcel's visit to the Théâtre d' Orléans: "Music rose violently and beautifully in the dreary gloom. Diamonds winked like stars. It was too solid, too perfect ever to have been, this music. Its rich and startling rhythms were like pure gold, something mined from the earth, and burnt to send its vapor heavenward." . . .

Rice is extremely clever at texturing her characters and their personal stories. Every crease in every face, every stitch in every dress is vividly, minutely and well described. So tightly are the threads of doom woven that there is no possibility of the reader hoping for a miracle or a happy end. There is drama and melodrama rising and falling in a wild pulse beat on almost every page. Why then did I find the last 400 pages so hard to get through? And why did I feel so curiously unsatisfied when I had finished reading the book, considering how surfeited with literary skill I had been?

It seems to me that Rice has been choked out of her own novel much as a weed in an overgrown, overheated conservatory. The voice of the storyteller has somehow been lost. In such an overcrowded, claustrophobic atmosphere and without a single outside character to act as a catalyst or to form some sort of balance that renders a true perspective, the great tragedy of the *gens de couleur libre* is not clearly exposed. And in the end, *The Feast of All Saints* leaves the reader overstuffed by a rich, gastronomically elegant meal where the chef has meanly and most curiously left out the main course.

Anne Edwards, "Sultry Passions in the French Quarter," in Book World—The Washington Post, *January 27, 1980, p. 6.*

ALEXANDER JOHNSON

After *Interview With the Vampire* (1976), her macabre but affecting first novel, we expect the unexpected from Anne Rice. Our faith has not been misplaced. Featuring many of its predecessor's literary traits—the penchant for gothic narrative, the relentlessly dense story line and, above all, the elegant precision of the style itself—[*The Feast of All Saints*] tackles an equally exotic subject.

Rice's focus is on the doomed world of the *gens-de-couleur,* the "free" quadroons and mulattos who crowded New Orleans during the 1840s. Burgeoning into a strange antebellum aristocracy, these cultural hybrids spoke French, purchased their own slaves and, generally, lived a life of studied gentility. Yet their rights, like everything that sustained their identity, were borrowed. In their socially circumscribed world, "Nothing was anything until someone [white] defined it."

The Feast of All Saints tallies the price of life lived in social ellipsis. In particular, it details the destructive social contract of *placage,* that forceful and fatal misalliance between white men and the black women they kept. With architectural skill, Rice builds her harrowing, if occasionally melodramatic, story around the offspring of such an ill-fated union. . . .

Rice's narrative is drenched in detail. She evokes a fine particularity of period and place with a startling vividness. While a winnowing of material would have helped the novel as a whole, nonetheless Rice has done considerable justice to this compelling if neglected subject.

Alexander Johnson, in a review of "The Feast of All Saints," in Saturday Review, Vol. 7, No. 3, February 2, 1980, p. 37.

RHODA KOENIG

The Feast of All Saints, a sluggish, humid novel about the free mulattoes of antebellum New Orleans by the author of *Interview With the Vampire,* falls somewhere between serious historical fiction and enjoyable trash. It's the sort of thing Frank Yerby might turn out if he decided to clean up his act and write a Bildungsroman. We do get a homosexual flirtation, a gang rape, and several more or less conventional heterosexual acts, but they only briefly interrupt the flow of analysis, reproach and constant repetition. After a while, one begins to suspect that this book was really written by David Halberstam: there is the same fondness for the comma connecting two or three sentences, the same belief that, if you can't say something twice, don't say it at all. . . .

Mrs. Rice also likes a nice, comforting cliché now and then, or even a brace at a time. Philippe Ferronaire, we are told, is a "Creole gentleman to his fingertips, and in debt on the next crop to the hilt." But many of these folk are blessed with elegant digits: "Far from being some sow's ear fashioned into a Creole belle, she was a lady to the tips of her fingers." Although the characters toss off an *"Eh bien"* or *"ma chère"* or *"mais oui"* every so often to remind you they speak French,

they occasionally slip into the patois of the guidance counselor. "Shouldn't he perhaps know a little more of the basic skills?" thinks a fond mother; when his friend behaves irrationally, a boy concludes, "It was clear he could not accept the situation."

As one of Mrs. Rice's characters might say, *tant pis.*

Rhoda Koenig, "Two Novels," in The New York Times Book Review, *February 17, 1980, p. 17.*

MICHIKO KAKUTANI

[*Cry to Heaven* is Anne Rice's] latest novel, a dark, humid melodrama filled with assassinations, attempted suicides and incestuous couplings, and animated by such operatic passions as ambition and revenge. Set in the world of the castrati—those castrated male sopranos whose glorious voices once made them the idols of opera houses across Europe—*Cry to Heaven* provides not only a Baroque portrait of 18th-century Italy, but also a fitting showcase for its author's gothic imagination, as well. . . .

Although Mrs. Rice provides plenty of interesting historical details about castrati and the development of opera, *Cry to Heaven* remains, at heart, a kind of Bildungsroman played out against the pageantry of a declining Venice. It is the story of Tonio Treschi, the young heir apparent of a powerful Venetian family—an heir abducted, castrated and exiled from his home, through the machinations of his brother. Two goals obsess him—to become one of the finest singers in Europe and to exact revenge on his brother.

Certainly these aims help propel the narrative toward its predictable conclusion, but Mrs. Rice is equally concerned with Tonio's emotional development—his movement from self-pity to acceptance, from aristocratic arrogance to compassion, from physical passion to true love. "I am only a man," he can say by the end of the book. "That is all I am. That is what I was born to be and what I've become no matter what was done to prevent it." Indeed, it is a testament to Mrs. Rice's ability to portray Tonio's state of mind that the initial curiosity his anomalous condition elicits in a reader is quickly replaced by genuine concern about his choices and his fate.

Unfortunately, the supporting cast of *Cry to Heaven* possess little of Tonio's depth. For the most part, they are pasteboard figures, taken from drugstore romances and old movies: Tonio's mother remains a shadowy creature, a great beauty, sad and mysterious and haunted; his father, a remote patrician intent on furthering his line at any cost. Carlo, the older brother, never really transcends his role as villain, and Christina, the contessa whom Tonio loves, seems just another one of those wispy innocents, waiting passively for her fate.

The problem is certainly not helped by Mrs. Rice's lush, portentous style. She is forever interrupting the narrative to foreshadow a future event—"and then the meeting took place, which was to change the very color of the sky"—and instead of dialogue, she gives her characters declamatory speeches filled with clichés and almost laughable histrionics.

"I am all too human," whispers Tonio's mother. Or, "Weep, yes, weep, little brother," Carlo says to Tonio. "Weep for her and for me! For our rash love and rash misadventures, and for how we have both of us paid for it."

As much as the reader cares about Tonio, it is not easy to read some 500 pages of such prose.

Michiko Kakutani, in a review of "Cry to Heaven,"
in The New York Times, *September 9, 1982, p. C25.*

JOSEPH McLELLAN

Opera could be even more of an ordeal for some of the singers than for the music-lovers in the audience, as Anne Rice demonstrates in her fascinating and colorful third novel [*Cry to Heaven*]. The audience tended to respond to these performances as they would to an athletic event, and a singer who aspired to something more than total indifference or volleys of rotten fruit had to perform with the kind of vigor and versatility we see today in the Olympic decathlon. Partisanship in the audience was loud, violent and unreasoning, with no significant gradations between the singers who were venerated like gods and those who were utterly despised.

The singers who made the greatest sacrifice for their art (involuntarily, as a rule, or before they were old enough to know what they were losing) were the castrati, who are the chief protagonists of Rice's novel: male singers with the power and tonal richness of a baritone operating in the pitch range of an alto or soprano. An estimated 4,000 boys were castrated in Italy for musical purposes in the 18th century, a practice begun and perpetuated largely because of a ban on the use of women singers for opera or church choruses in the papal territories— "Children mutilated to make a choir of seraphim," Rice calls them, "their song a cry to heaven that heaven did not hear." In some of its best moments, her novel is an attempt to evoke that cry for modern readers. . . .

As for amorous adventures, they supply some of the most colorful pages in Rice's book, as they did in 18th-century anecdote; the voice-preserving operation, when performed properly, left all sexual functions intact except the ability to reproduce, giving castrati a sort of sexual freedom that became available to other mortals only with the arrival of the contraceptive pill. They were greatly in demand for both homosexual and heterosexual clandestine affairs, without which Rice's book would be considerably shorter and perhaps less interesting to some readers. (p. 7)

Cry to Heaven is a tale of dark family secrets, Oedipal hatred and vengeance, complex intrigues and routine violence in which someone in fact does go mad, someone dons a disguise, and the central event is someone's abduction and abuse. The abused someone is Tonio Treschi, designated heir to the glory and burden of a leading patrician family in Venice, and the abuse is the most violent possible short of murder. He is castrated because inability to reproduce will automatically take him out of the family's line of succession but, being the stuff that Venetian noblemen are made of, he turns his liability into an asset. He becomes one of the leading castrati of his generation, bides his time until the situation is right, and wreaks a long-withheld, intricately plotted and executed vengeance on his tormentor.

Some idea of the plot's flavor and complexity (much too baroque for complete summarization) may be gleaned from a confession Tonio makes near the novel's end to a Roman cardinal who is also a former lover: "I don't know what I seek, but I must tell you the one who sent men to kill me is my own father, known to everyone as my own brother."

If that sounds a bit like something in the tradition of Dumas, the impression is not entirely incorrect. But Anne Rice repeatedly raises her novel above the routine costume romances that pour out by the hundred each year, partly through the operatic background with the special thematic overtones related to the castrati and partly through careful research and expert writing. Her research is not impeccable—for example, she has people dancing a quadrille a century before this became a common practice—but it is generally impressive, and her ability to block out a scene with proper background, tension, overtones, dialogue and dramatic structure, often gives abiding satisfaction. Besides being a well-tangled story, *Cry to Heaven* is an absorbing look at a fascinating and little-known world. (p. 9)

Joseph McLellan, "Sacrificed for the Sound of Seraphim," in Book World—The Washington Post, *October 3, 1982, pp. 7, 9.*

ALICE HOFFMAN

Anne Rice summons us into a wondrous 18th-century world of midnights and cathedrals, a place filled with vengeance and passions that seem too strong for ordinary mortals. But *Cry to Heaven* is not about the ordinary; this is the world of the Italian castrati, famed male sopranos who were mutilated as boys so that their voices could remain forever high and unchanging. . . .

Cry to Heaven, like Anne Rice's first novel, *Interview with the Vampire*, is bold and erotic, laced with luxury, sexual tension, music. Here passion is all, desires are overwhelming, gender is blurred. Lovers meet and part, cousins couple with cousins, nephews with aunts, eunuchs become the favorites of cardinals, women disguise themselves in men's clothing, and men seductively wear silk and rouge. Music is everywhere: in the voices of the gondoliers, the hymns of the children, the glorious chords of the opera house. Even the bees sing. . . .

Cry to Heaven is in many ways a ghost story of families that haunt us, fates that are sealed, fairy-tale fathers who are not at all what they appear to be, beautiful and cruel mothers who betray us. Even readers who don't believe in ghosts may be convinced by Anne Rice's lush prose. Still, there are times when the novelist seems not to trust herself—the tension is sometimes heightened in ways that seem false: occasional melodramatic dialogue, odd elongations of words, a confusing switch of narrative focus. But these only serve as distractions from what is a spellbinding story. *Cry to Heaven* is so daring and imaginative that it may frighten off some readers, even offend them by its baroque quality. This is a novel dazzling in its darkness, and there are times when Mrs. Rice seems like nothing less than a magician: It is a pure and uncanny talent that can give a voice to monsters and angels both.

Alice Hoffman, "Luxury, Sex and Music," in The New York Times Book Review, *October 10, 1982, p. 14.*

MICHIKO KAKUTANI

Anne Rice has what might best be described as a Gothic imagination crossed with a campy taste for the decadent and the bizarre. Her last novel, *Cry to Heaven,* was about castrati; and her latest novel, *The Vampire Lestat,* is about—what else, vampires. It's not just the exotic subject matter that makes these books feel so baroque; it's Mrs. Rice's whole sensibility and use of prose. She loves to sling around phrases like "Children of Darkness" and "the Devil's Road"; displays an equal fondness for such words as "chaos," "ecstasy" and "death", and she likes to give her characters romantic names like Armand,

Gabrielle and Marius. Reading *The Vampire Lestat,* in fact, is a lot like spending an entire day in a museum featuring only works by Henry Fuseli—all hung in heavy, gilt frames decorated with curlicues and malicious cherubs. By the end, you're reeling from both the strangeness and the surfeit of ornamentation.

A sequel of sorts to the highly popular *Interview With the Vampire,* this novel purports to give us the full story of Lestat, a character who played a subsidiary role in that earlier book....

Certainly in reading this novel, we learn lots of "facts" about vampires and vampire culture. We learn that they cry tears of blood, that they're capable of reading other people's minds, that they can be destroyed by fire and sunlight. We learn that "no vampire may ever destroy another vampire, except that the coven master has the power of life and death over all of his flock"; and we learn that "no vampire shall ever reveal his true nature to a mortal and allow that mortal to live."

In many respects, this vampire sociology, assembled or invented by Mrs. Rice, is more compelling than the rest of the novel. While Lestat's not an unlikable vampire—he doesn't like to kill innocent people, and he regularly writes home for news of his family—it's hard to take his dilemmas all that seriously. For one thing, his rather heartfelt attempts to come to terms with his anomalous condition ("maybe I was not the exotic outcast that I imagined, but merely the dim magnification of every human soul") are buried under heaps and heaps of wordy philosophizing about good and evil, heaven and hell, and even more wearisome meditations about the nature of Beauty and Truth. And Mrs. Rice further distances the reader from her hero by turning his quest for self-knowledge into a laughable twilight-zone trip through history: We see Lestat investigate the mysteries of Isis and Osiris in Egypt; watch him delve into the secrets of vampire lore in Venice and Sicily, and eventually transform himself into a modern-day rock musician in New Orleans....

Some of the scenes are merely lurid in a standard horror movie sort of way—"in a deep prison cell lay a heap of corpses in all states of decay, the bones and rotted flesh crawling with worms and insects"; others so resemble sequences from a poor Roger Corman picture that we're unsure whether they're supposed to be funny or whether they're just bad. What are we to make, say, of Lestat's declaration that a new age requires a new evil, and that he is "the vampire for these times"; or his remark that "maybe people had to be dead six thousand years" for his mother to love them?

If scenes of Lestat roaring around New Orleans on a Harley-Davidson motorcycle are vaguely amusing, however, our enthusiasm for most of his adventures are considerably dimmed by his—or, one should say, Mrs. Rice's—penchant for recounting them in lugubrious, cliché-ridden sentences that repeat every idea and sentiment a couple or more times. For instance, instead of being able to say that he's attracted to a certain female vampire, Lestat says: "I think for one second the concept of eternity burned in me. I knew then what immortality was. All things were possible with her, or so for that one moment it seemed."

It is recurrent passages like that that make the reader attribute Lestat's terminal sense of loneliness less to his condition as a vampire than to his inability to keep his mouth closed.

Michiko Kakutani, "Vampire for Our Times," in The New York Times, *October 19, 1985, p. 16.*

NINA AUERBACH

The Vampire Lestat is a sequel to *Interview with the Vampire,* but its tone, structure and ambitions are radically different. Louis is a brooding self-tormentor; Lestat—Louis's pitiless mentor in *Interview* and the narrator of the present book—is antic and stagestruck. In the 18th century he sacrifices a promising career with the commedia dell'arte to become a vampire; in 1985, he comes into his own as a rock star who has written a best-selling autobiography, also called *The Vampire Lestat....*

The Vampire Lestat is longer and more ambitious than *Interview*; its theatrical narrator stages spectacular answers to the questions that gnawed at Louis. Its myth of the origin of vampires raises more questions than it resolves, leading Lestat not into stability, but into terror and a cliffhanger ending. This second book in Anne Rice's *Chronicles of the Vampires* series is as brilliant as the first; it is funnier, wilder and more disturbing as well.

Sometimes, unfortunately, it is also sillier. The vampires' continual homoerotic posturing palls—too many beautiful young men moon at each other while debating, in strained dialogue, goodness, beauty and their own monstrous natures. There are jarring smatterings of what Stephen King has taught us to call "grue"; fetid graveyard debris intrudes awkwardly on the finely honed and fearful consciousness Anne Rice knows so well. At times *The Vampire Lestat* chokes on its own excesses.

A bracing woman redeems the book. The same is true in *Interview,* whose most vivid character is Claudia, the vampirized child who is eternally preyed upon by two oppressive undead fathers. Claudia scorns moral probing and philosophic compunctions; she knows only rebellion against her unending childhood.

Her counterpart here is Lestat's put-upon mother, Gabrielle, who has no qualms about losing her humanity. She dresses as a boy, becomes a goddess of empty places and never looks back on suffocating mortality. She lives out the rage for freedom her scrupulous son only half acknowledges. Anne Rice's Hamlet-like males quail before the direct and ferocious vitality of the females who rescue their stories from preciosity.

The Vampire Lestat is ornate and pungently witty. In the classic tradition of Gothic fiction, it teases and tantalizes us into accepting its kaleidoscopic world. Even when they annoy us or tell us more than we want to know, its undead characters are utterly alive. Their adventures and frustrations are funny, frightening and surprising at once. Like her own vampires, Anne Rice seems to be at home everywhere. Like them, she makes us believe everything she sees.

Nina Auerbach, "No. 2 with a Silver Bullet," in The New York Times Book Review, *October 27, 1985, p. 15.*

JACK SULLIVAN

Anne Rice narrates the decadent exploits of her Age of Reason vampire [in *The Vampire Lestat*] with blood-drenched exuberance, chronicling his grisly, rather wacky initiation into the black arts; his passing of the Dark Gift to his dying mother (a singularly perverse and creepily erotic scene); his obsessive tracing and retracing of the ultimate origin of vampires, the true Children of the Millennia, in tales within tales of Rome, Greece, and Egypt spun by ancient tellers; his rediscovery of

Louis, the charming and compelling narrator of *Interview With the Vampire;* and his triumph in the 1980s as a rock star simply playing himself, singing music so shrill that, in his mother's words, it can indeed "wake the dead."

Yet despite his great appetite for the "wonders and puzzles of the world," Lestat also discovers a horrible secret—that eternity can get awfully, awesomely boring. There are no Van Helsings who can touch him, no rival vampires who can destroy him, but a terrible ache and emptiness pursue him through the centuries, causing him to create vampire lovers who eventually despise or leave him. Underneath the glitter of vampire hedonism is the same "sublime loneliness" that haunted Louis in *Interview,* depicted here in Lestat's desperate attempt to be part of a world that ultimately has no use for Death and Evil. "There has never been a just place for evil in the Western world," laments one vampire sage. "There has never been any easy accommodation of death."

One thing Lestat does to fill in this great emptiness is talk, and the novel is consequently full of disquisitions on such cosmic matters as death and eternity, spirituality and carnality, and esoteric questions of vampiric identity such as the tension between being an "exotic outcast" and "some dim magnification of every human soul." Like Louis before him, Lestat talks too much, but enough of what he says is fascinating to make Rice's vampire mythos (a third book in *The Chronicles of the Vampires* is on the way) one of the more memorable horror sagas of recent years.

Here then is a supernatural horror novel that seems to have everything—passion, originality, imagination, narrative power, kinky sexuality, and a superbly drawn otherworldly protagonist. The one thing it doesn't have is genuine terror. The book simply isn't scary. Yet literature is full of vampires as worldly and glamorous as Rice's who also managed to be fearful. Le Fanu's "magnificent and sensuous" Carmilla, Stoker's "big ape of the vampires, the hirsute Slav Count Dracula," and other famous bloodsuckers cleverly alluded to by Lestat were all presented indirectly, with the kind of mystery and narrative distance their creators knew were necessary to give us the shivers. Often the point of view was that of the victim, whose growing unease becomes the reader's. But Rice presents everything directly, immediately, from the point of view of the vampire, with non-stop exposition and explanation. "Why should Death lurk in the shadows?" Lestat demands to know, and the answer is that Death is more frightening that way. Somewhere in these colorful and provocative *Chronicles,* a few shadows would be in order. (p. 7)

Jack Sullivan, "Fangs for the Memories," in Book World—The Washington Post, *December 1, 1985,* pp. 1, 7.

Nayantara (Pandit) Sahgal

1927-

Indian novelist, autobiographer, nonfiction writer, and journalist.

Through her novels, personal narratives, and nonfiction works, Sahgal provides insightful analyses of life in post-colonial India. As the niece of former Prime Minister Jawaharlal Nehru and the daughter of Madame Vijayalaksmi Pandit, who held among other positions the Indian ambassadorship to the United States, Sahgal presents an insider's perspective on India's leaders. Many of the characters in Sahgal's novels are modeled after actual political figures, and her nonfiction works—particularly those focusing on India's movement for independence from Great Britain and on the rise to political power of her cousin, Indira Gandhi—evidence her close relationship with the sources of power and change. Although some critics claim that Sahgal's privileged social standing and her proximity to the subject matter prevent her from maintaining a broad-based, objective approach, most praise her elegant narrative style and unique portrayal of an important and controversial period in India's history.

Sahgal's first book, *Prison and Chocolate Cake* (1954), is an autobiographical work which recounts her lively childhood as a member of the Nehru family and her years in the United States, where she attended college. The book ends with her return to India after graduation. *A Time to Be Happy* (1958), Sahgal's first novel, is set in the years immediately following India's independence and centers on problems faced by the newly liberated country, particularly the tension between Indian cultural heritage and the lingering British influence. While faulted for its stereotypical English characters, the novel is considered a significant chronicle of post-independence India. Another personal narrative, *From Fear Set Free* (1962), describes Sahgal's life after college and her marriage to a young Indian businessman. This work is particularly lauded for its vivid, affectionate depiction of Sahgal's mother. *From Fear Set Free* also recounts Sahgal's struggle to reconcile her family background of idealistic political activism with her husband's more pragmatic, commercial interests.

Like *A Time to Be Happy,* Sahgal's novel *This Time of Morning* (1965) is based on political realities. This book involves a young Indian diplomat who returns to his country from abroad, hoping to make a positive contribution to Indian society. His plans are thwarted by governmental inefficiency and divisiveness. *Storm in Chandigarh* (1969) centers on a conflict between two social groups with differing religious, political, and cultural beliefs. The situation in this novel is similar to that which occurred when the Punjab was divided into two states—one Sikh and one Hindu—in 1966. In *The Day in Shadow* (1972), Sahgal dramatizes some of the problems faced by educated Indian women living in a male-dominated society.

A Situation in New Delhi (1977) is regarded as one of Sahgal's strongest novels. This work concerns the relationship between a passionate, dedicated sister of a recently deceased Indian prime minister, recognized by many critics as identical in ideals and other characteristics to Nehru, and a British journalist who is writing a biography of the prime minister. Shyam M. Asnani

described the book as "a novel of political ideas, [including] within its scope social realism, personal failure and private horror. . . . [Sahgal] demonstrates the skill of a mature craftsman in her use of imagery, symbol, humour, and irony." In *Indira Gandhi's Emergence and Style* (1978), Sahgal turns again to India's political realm, specifically the first period of Gandhi's leadership, from her rise to power in 1964 to her defeat in the elections of 1977. Written from a personal perspective, the book suggests that Gandhi's childhood isolation and her determination as an adult resulted in a tyrannical misuse of power.

Rich Like Us (1985) is set amid the disorder in India following the "Emergency," when civil liberties were suspended by the government. This novel centers on two women: the narrator, Sonali, an Indian civil servant, and Rose, the English wife of a wealthy Indian businessman. Both become involved in economic scandals, and both experience the clash between ancient Indian culture and the encroachment of modernity. *Plans for Departure* (1985) also involves the conflict of the old against the new, this time in a remote Himalayan village in 1914. The protagonist of this novel is a free-thinking Danish woman who arrives from England to work for an Indian professor and soon becomes embroiled in a mystery which develops around a reticent district magistrate and his absent wife. John Mellors considered *Plans for Departure* a victory of Sahgal's storytelling ability over her penchant for political journalism, describing the book as "a subtle, sharply imagined novel, skillfully plotted and elegantly written."

(See also *Contemporary Authors,* Vols. 9-12, rev. ed. and *Contemporary Authors New Revision Series,* Vol. 11.)

MARGUERITE BROWN

At a time when writers on Indo-American relations are likely to be somber and "significant" it is refreshing to read a relaxed account of life in both worlds by a young Indian woman. . . . Such is *Prison and Chocolate Cake,* the graceful and light-hearted story of her childhood and adolescence in India and America by Nayantara Sahgal, daughter of Mme. Pandit and niece of India's Prime Minister Nehru.

Using her stay in America as a Wellesley College student as a point of departure, Mrs. Sahgal weaves back and forth between India and the United States. Inevitably it is a story of politics, since politics was the warp and woof of the Nehru family life; but here politics is merely an exciting backdrop to a quiet and warm description of family relationships. . . .

The Prime Minister emerges as a fond uncle who, despite his burdensome preoccupations, takes time to romp with the three Pandit sisters on the floor. We see Mrs. Pandit not as a world stateswoman but an adored mother. . . . (p. 7)

We meet Mrs. Sahgal's revered and scholarly father; the Mountbattens, whose charm equaled that of the Nehrus, and Mrs. Sarojini Naidu, the sharp-tongued poetess and first woman president of the Indian National Congress, who referred lovingly to Gandhi as "the chocolate-colored Mickey Mouse."

Out of this procession of celebrities, Gandhi comes most alive. The last chapter is a moving account of his death. (pp. 7, 24)

The glimpses of America are fleeting, but often telling: the passer-by who identified India as "that country near Egypt" and the salesgirl who was convinced that Tara and her sister would never want to return home now that they had set foot in God's country.

Amusing as these tidbits of Americana are, this reader begrudged every moment spared from the Nehru family in India. . . . [Seldom] does one get a chance to become acquainted with India's great leaders through a young woman so intimately associated with them.

Unfortunately, the book ends with the author's return to India in 1947. Independence and partition were realities and a new era had begun. One can only hope that Mrs. Sahgal will take time to write a sequel to this first effort, which is, so to speak, an appetizer. There is much of the saga of the brilliant and glamorous Nehru family that remains to be written, and Mrs. Sahgal is in a position to do this as almost no one else can. It could be a chronicle which could take a permanent place in the history of India. (p. 24)

> Marguerite Brown, "Uncle Nehru and Family," in The New York Times Book Review, *June 27, 1954, pp. 7, 24.*

MARY ROSS

[*A Time To Be Happy*] is told in the first person by a man in early middle age who renounced his father's business in an industrial city to follow Gandhi in work for the villages, served a prison term for his peaceful liberalism, and, again free in the new India and without need to earn his living, has become an observer of the scene about him as his well-to-do friends seek to find a footing in the new order. Like himself, most of them were educated abroad. . . .

More at home in Paris or Rome than in any but a narrow family groove in their own country, some of these friends wished to continue to be more British than the British even though they returned to a society where club doors were closed to them. Others were inclined toward their own heritage but found themselves blocked by their ignorance of their own people, perhaps unable even to talk with fellow-countrymen from other parts of India in any language but English. Differences between the generations of any people were multiplied by the antiquity and diversity of India's traditions and, among the upper classes, the British veneer that many had sought or accepted.

A Time To Be Happy pictures the lives of two families and more than a dozen individuals, among them some Britishers of the older and newer traditions. It is particularly the story of Sanad, a man younger than the narrator, who had to make his place in a country he hardly knew in terms of the job he wanted to do, the dress and friends he would choose, the woman he would marry.

Mrs. Sahgal writes with sympathy and wit, in concrete human terms; politics enter only as they bear on the lives of the characters. While the background is exotic on occasion to Western eyes, the men and women are wholly understandable. Good reading for its own sake, this novel offers insight into modern life in an ancient land where people, if not situations, are not unlike our own.

> Mary Ross, "A Novel of New India by Nehru's Niece," in New York Herald Tribune Book Review, *February 23, 1958, p. 6.*

THE TIMES LITERARY SUPPLEMENT

[There are in *A Time to Be Happy*] glimpses of well-taken character in the sketches of high-class Indian women and smart young men Anglicizing themselves for purely commercial reasons. There are mildly sarcastic descriptions of expensive Indian parties imitating the English pattern. So far so good. But there appears a radical flaw in the whole conception of the book that destroys its unity.

It is supposed to be told in the first person by a high society renegade who has become a Congress worker, as a study of upper-crust life in the years immediately before Independence. There are the stereotyped grotesques that one expects to represent the Wicked English. But there is nothing in the whole text, in its implicit attitudes, to suggest that its narrator has so much as peeped into an Indian village. Indeed he seems to acquiesce cosily in those very values of wealth and privilege that Gandhi's followers were at such pains to condemn. The projection of some positive viewpoint would have given to the picture of decadence a bite that is altogether lacking.

> "A Clash of Cultures," in The Times Literary Supplement, *No. 2944, August 1, 1958, p. 433.*

MARGARET PARTON

A generation ago fashionable young Indian women were marching in the streets, defying the British, getting themselves thrown into jail in the cause of freedom. But what are today's young women to do, now that freedom has been won, and nothing more exciting than nation-building is going on? Well, get married. Have babies. And turn out a book or two while the ayah sees to the children.

It's all rather sad, really, and perhaps even more so in the case of Nayantara Sahgal, whose uncle is Jawaharlal Nehru and whose mother is Vijayalakshmi Pundit. *Their* banners still fly, of course, but they are almost at the horizon; the stirring music to which they marched has faded. The young can listen for the echoes, but cannot follow. Nor have they yet new music of their own. Not that Mrs. Sahgal says any of this explicitly. But it is certainly suggested [in *From Fear Set Free*]. . . . In fact, almost everything that might have been of real interest is implied rather than discussed.

After her graduation from Wellesley College in 1947 she returned to India and lived with her uncle, who was mopping up the aftermath of the partition riots. Nehru remains a shadowy figure; but we are given a vivid impression of the Gymkhana Club, where the author met the young Punjabi businessman she chose to marry. It was, she admits, a theoretically unsuitable marriage, and she was worried.

"I should shift from a world where men wore Gandhi caps and Indian clothes made of hand-spun cloth to that of European suits and ties, from orange juice . . . to the cocktail circuit, from an outlook that considered these things natural to one that was baffled by them, from the atmosphere of a political crusade to one of commerce."

So what happened to this tug-of-war and to the marriage? All we know is that there were two children (three, according to the jacket), that they live in Bombay, that thanks to sufficient servants Mrs. Sahgal is often free to visit her mother at her various foreign posts or to interview sherpas in Darjeeling. . . .

She is more forthright on the subject of her mother, but still the relationship between the famous and dynamic older woman and her quiet, home-centered daughter remains elusive. "Hurry, a word that for me splintered serenity into sharp fragments, was the key word of her existence." And: "A porcelain figurine, a fine, embroidered handkerchief, scented soap, or tea served in shell-like, transparently delicate china reminded me of her."

Somehow one feels there is more to say about the powerful, politically active older Nehrus and the domesticated, faintly morose younger generation of the family. But Mrs. Sahgal, in this glamorous variation of the familiar housewife's diary, hasn't even begun to say it.

> Margaret Parton, "A Merchant after an Indian Chief," in Saturday Review, Vol. XLVI, No. 40, October 5, 1963, p. 46.

THE TIMES LITERARY SUPPLEMENT

After six years in foreign capitals, a young Indian diplomat returns excitedly to Delhi, hoping to help in the major role his Government must play on the international stage. Sophisticated but still intensely idealistic, Rakesh ought perhaps to cock an ear to the prolegomenon his friend Saleem provides: "You are back in the Ministry of External Affairs", where appointments are decided as though on the advice of an oracle, where decisions pend and muddle pervades, where the initial enthusiasm of power has become the excitement of personalities and cocktail parties.

It is this Delhi, of much-travelled government employees pursuing their private ends in a setting of comfortable well-heeled social gatherings or momentary, intoxicating crisis, that Mrs. Sahgal displays so intimately and wittily in [*This Time of Morning*]. It is a world she knows better than any Indian likely to write novels, since her uncle was Nehru and her mother Mrs. Pandit. To the outsider she may appear almost as involved, indeed parochial, as the characters who flock on to the pages and who are so disparagingly eyed by both young Rakesh and the new man of power, Kalyan. . . . [Interleaved] with a remarkably enlightening panorama of public life are glimpses of how Delhi seduces and saddens private lives. . . .

In all this, Mrs. Sahgal delicately balances affection and satirical candour, so that her novel never appears intended to shock or placate. She writes fluently, recording the splendidly ironic Anglicisms of Indian society—"Elementary, my dear Watson", says Saleem about a particularly humiliating blunder of protocol—and ranging backwards over the Gandhi era with concise, if somewhat flat, historicity. If her novel is somehow untidy and patchy, this is because she has tried to be a camera of cause and effect rather than a manipulator of the scene. Her involvement is in what she finds familiar, yet is not perhaps enough for her to make us care deeply what becomes of any of her many characters.

> "Pending in Delhi," in The Times Literary Supplement, No. 3311, August 12, 1965, p. 693.

JOHN MASTERS

[Nayantara Sahgal] was born to a ringside seat at her country's political arena. She knows personally all the big wheels and many of the lesser ones. She has not merely observed that world but lived it, and knows both the official story and the backstairs gossip, and the worth of each. She has tried to weave a work of fiction out of this knowledge. The dust jacket [of *This Time of Morning*] tells of the intention: "Kalyan and . . . Kailas [represent] the two totally opposed trends within the ruling Congress Party. The struggle of these two men and their sympathizers and supporters provides a broad framework for this rich, multifaceted novel."

Sadly, it doesn't. Nayantara Sahgal's framework has no more strength or breadth than a gossip column. She has invested some of her characters with the responsibility of embodying various ideas and attitudes; but except for the fact that everyone uses fictional names, the book is not a novel. It is an aimless ramble in Mrs. Sahgal's company.

There are dreadful faults of construction and technique. Action, where there is any, progresses at the pace of a convalescent cripple, with pauses to catch our breath while we listen to lectures on extraneous matters. The public figures are given private lives, but they never inter-relate. The two characters chosen to personify the great political struggle seldom meet and never confront each other.

If there are resolutions, they take place off-stage, or among minor characters in remote places, or both. There is no build-up of tension and hence, naturally, no release of tension. There are too many characters who do nothing but muddle the reader. . . .

Most of these troubles could have been avoided if Mrs. Sahgal had written her own story of her own times, and written it straight. But she has not, and the book's sole merit is as a guessing game. Who do you think is lurking behind those false noses? Krishna Menon? Mme. Pandit? (Isn't she wearing male clothing?) The author herself? That sour old type one met at cocktail parties?

References to "the P.M." [Prime Minister] are not, of course, intended to disguise the late Mr. Nehru. But here again Mrs. Sahgal points up her own failure. Nehru's problems and weaknesses and strengths were those of Nehru, not of "the P.M." Once Jawaharlal Nehru has been invoked, a political story has to revolve around him—in the struggle for his attention, for influence over him—because that is what actually happened and everyone interested in Indian affairs knows it.

I fear that such readers will be disappointed in this book.

> *John Masters, "Who's Who in New Delhi," in* The New York Times Book Review, *February 27, 1966, p. 43.*

STUART HOOD

To read an Indian novelist like Nayantara Sahgal is to wonder at the durability of cultural tradition. This is not an Indian writer who has chosen as a matter of convenience, 20 years after the end of the Raj, to write in English rather than in Hindi: it is an English writer working in a tradition which is hers by birth, education and . . . class. But although *Storm in Chandigarh* is firmly in the main tradition of the English novel, and a confident, skilfully handled example of the genre, its moral framework is alien, non-Christian, non-western, being that of the *Bhagavad Gita*, which assumes a caste system as the natural order of things. More importantly for the theme Mrs Sahgal has chosen, it casts light for her sophisticated, whisky-drinking high-caste civil servants and politicians on the nature of action. From the *Gita* one may learn the value of non-attachment, of the need to accept duty unallied to reward—learn, too, that as the Lord advised Arjun before the great chariot battle, there are times when it is cowardly not to fight.

The relevance of this teaching is that her theme is violence set in Corbusier's modular city, Chandigarh—or rather two related, parallel forms of violence: that which springs from political passion and the other which comes from sexual passion, from the tension between man and woman, husband and wife. Her hero, Dubey, is a young civil servant sent to keep the peace between two chief ministers who are the heads of two states born of fission and local tensions. He has to manoeuvre in a world of political bosses, of contingent judgments, corruption and the threat of mob violence. He averts disaster because he is prepared, like Arjun, to fight. He has meanwhile become involved in a marriage where the husband is dominant and apparently strong, the woman apparently weak. He falls in love with the passive gentle wife, for her sake challenges the husband, whose fury is impotent, and takes her back to Delhi with him. There his superiors, men guided not by principles or conviction but by nauseating hypocrisy, rebuke him for the hazards involved in his tough political stand. He has both lost and won. It is a good cool ending to a novel which handles with equal assurance the workings of politics and the mechanisms of the heart. (pp. 761-62)

> *Stuart Hood, "Guided by Arjun," in* The Listener, *Vol. LXXXI, No. 2096, May 29, 1969, pp. 761-62.*

THE TIMES LITERARY SUPPLEMENT

[*Storm in Chandigarh*] treats of events somewhat similar to those that followed the Punjab's second division, into a Sikh and a Hindu state, in late 1966. At the quality-journalism level, Miss Sahgal has much of interest to say, though to get it said she sometimes has to employ such frankly crude devices as "What, for example, did his Brahmin inheritance have to contribute?", and, worse, she slips us without warning from the point of view of one protagonist to that of another, with the inevitable consequence that all her characters are somewhat shadowy.

But she writes of the personal as well as of the political. For the most part these two strains run side by side, the personal having only a transmuted influence on the political, as it should do. But occasionally we do get tantalizing hints of that rarest of birds, the political novel that is both political and a novel.

> *"Shadows," in* The Times Literary Supplement, *No. 3513, June 26, 1969, p. 676.*

MARTIN LEVIN

[In *The Day in Shadow*] Simrit Raman is a divorcée living in New Delhi "with hordes of children and a tax problem the size of a python." She is also a sophisticated, cerebral, and delighted connoisseur of her native milieu. How, then, does it happen that so enlightened a female has been hoodwinked by her ex-husband as though she were a dimwitted slavey? The answer, relates Nayantara Sahgal in her cool epigrammatic style, lies in an environment that is sympathetic to the exploitation of women and encourages their passivity. . . .

[Sahgal] has written no feminist polemic, but a lively explication of the Indian socio-political scene in terms of character. Simrit is in a slough of depression in the aftermath of her good-bad marriage to a Western-style entrepreneur who was atavistic only in regard to his wife. Waiting in the wings is what looks like Mr. Right—albeit slightly Left—an idealistic politician named Raj, who seeks to integrate Hinduism with social progress. And in suspension between the bitter past and a tentative future is Simrit herself, in search of "permanence" and continuity. . . . Mrs. Sahgal assigns to each of her characters sufficient eloquence and clarity to conduct a highly edifying dialogue.

> *Martin Levin, in a review of "The Day in Shadow," in* The New York Times Book Review, *September 24, 1972, p. 40.*

MARIGOLD JOHNSON

[On the surface, *The Day in Shadow*] is a straightforward, rather slow novel about the liberation of one Brahmin literary lady from the flashy security offered by a business marriage, and her tentative discovery of a different, loving future "in full-blown maturity". But it is clear that the author is far more concerned with the political crossroads India has reached, and with the liberation her country must risk if everything Gandhi strove to create is not to be destroyed by the conflicting ambitions and corruptions of Eastern and Western pressures. . . . For Delhi readers, no doubt, her novel provides the additional interest of recognizing not just parliamentary battle-scenes but real Corridors of Power figures: the corrupt radical young Minister, the wise and tetchy old gadfly whose weekly journal continues to provoke the establishment. But because it is Delhi, not Whitehall, the corridors buzz with philosophical as well as plotting conversation, and ruminations on religious or behavioural patterns are conducted with an idealism far removed from the pragmatism of Lord Snow's world. . . .

Mrs Sahgal's careful, understated elegance is occasionally deadening in a novel which depends more on eliciting the reader's thoughtful concern than on its thin, disjointed narrative. She seems ill at ease with the language of private emotions—the alienated schoolboy son, Simrit's love-making—until they can be recollected and analysed in tranquillity. For, despite her idealistic and articulate characters' anguish about the future of their country, Mrs Sahgal's novel is what Raj would call "Hinduism in a nutshell": intelligent talk and theoretical inspiration, rather than "passion and deeds".

> *Marigold Johnson, "The Corridors of Delhi," in* The Times Literary Supplement, *No. 3812, March 28, 1975, p. 329.*

JOHN MELLORS

A Situation in New Delhi is a powerful and thoughtful 'novel of ideas' raising all sorts of questions about democracy, leadership, continuity, revolution, education and government—in particular about government by remote control and according to a 'book of rules' compared with government informed by understanding and compassion. . . . [The 'situation' of the] title is the aftermath of the premature death of 'Shivraj', a thinly disguised Nehru-figure. Michael Calvert, . . . having lived in India to the age of eight and having worked there as a journalist at the time of Independence, goes back to write a biography of the leader who had been his friend. Calvert . . . is a liberal who fell in love not only with India but also with Devi, Shivraj's sister.

Devi is the Education Minister, increasingly uneasy at the attitude of the current ruling clique, dogmatic pseudo-socialists who have lost touch with the people. . . . Devi, like, presumably, her creator, stands for a policy of *festina lente,* in opposition to the hasty implementation of a carelessly conceived blue-print for 'more power to the masses'. The final message of the novel is surprisingly vague and tentative—that 'perhaps the strongest thing in human life was influence, transmittable through one lifetime or the ages' and that 'we've been in too much of a hurry to say he [Shivraj-Nehru] is dead'. *A Situation in New Delhi* is a provocative book, but I am not sure where the thoughts that it provokes are meant to lead us—except to a regret that the example set by Nehru has not been more faithfully followed. (pp. 111-12)

> *John Mellors, "Old Koi Hais," in* London Magazine, *n.s. Vol. 17, No. 2, June-July, 1977, pp. 109-12.*

CHARLES R. LARSON

[*A Situation in New Delhi*] is almost totally preoccupied with the author's desire to turn political and historical personalities into fictive characters. The author's political theme has been so greatly oversimplified that the story line virtually collapses as Sahgal becomes more and more ensnarled in her roman à clef. . . . When the narrative finally unwinds, the author suggests that the only way the country will be able to check the increasing turmoil (and the general lack of leadership in the country) is by proclaiming a State of Emergency. *A Situation in New Delhi* is weakened, I suspect, by the author's emotional involvement with her characters' real-life counterparts. (p. 245)

> *Charles R. Larson, "Anglophone Writing from Africa and Asia," in* World Literature Today, *Vol. 52, No. 2, Spring, 1978, pp. 245-47.*

THEON WILKINSON

[Nayantara Sahgal's *Indira Gandhi's Emergence and Style*] is an intense and heartfelt attempt to expose the abuses of power in her own country, made more poignant from the closeness of the family relationship between author and subject, and gives vent to her sense of outraged betrayal at the daughter of her uncle, Nehru, undermining his life-work of building a free and democratic India. The dust jacket blurb gives no hint of the personal connection and rather naively comments that '*any* thoughtful observer of the Indian scene from 1969 onwards would have observed Mrs Gandhi's flowering as a quest for personal power'. Nayantara Sahgal is no ordinary observer; the family relationship is significant for although it does not detract from this carefully constructed and objectively researched study, it explains the vehemence with which she expresses some of her views and the touching glimpses behind the veils of history from letters between her mother, Mrs Pandit, the sister of Nehru, and the great man himself. These letters reveal that sister and brother were closer in spirit than father and daughter and that after Nehru's death there developed a bitter estrangement between her mother and Indira. . . . (p. 89)

The contrast between these two leading political figures, the daughter and sister of Nehru, was marked. Mrs Gandhi inherited her father's position of power as Prime Minister without ever having faced the electorate. . . . Mrs Pandit inherited her brother's parliamentary constituency after a long and distinguished political career as State Governor and Ambassador to the USSR, the USA and Britain among other posts, making her the senior and more mature Nehru presence in politics. These antagonisms sharpen the controversy and add an extra dimension to the author's description of Mrs Gandhi's pursuit of personal power, riding roughshod over family, friends and the Congress Party. (pp. 89-90)

The author traces Mrs Gandhi's career to the point of her becoming Prime Minister and then gives an astonishing blow-by-blow account of her assumption of absolute power. The mind reels with MISA (Maintenance of Internal Security Act), mass imprisonments without trial running into tens of thousands, election rigging and press censorship, and there are flashbacks to the personal qualities that emerged in childhood and adolescence to explain her extraordinary singlemindedness of purpose. . . . And there are examples of her fearlessness in flying to the centre of trouble spots during the Bangladesh and Pakistan wars, cultivating an almost Joan of Arc image to encourage a modern-style fealty. (p. 91)

Nayantara Sahgal has given us a fascinating study, interlaced with personal observations, of Mrs Gandhi's rise to power and a lesson on how easy it is to slip into the gear of absolutism if democrats are off their guard. But what of the future? The problems of poverty and over-population are so stark and immense there must always be the possibility of political fragmentation or the imposition of a totalitarian solution. But should there be a return to any form of single party government in the future, I hope we will still have exponents of freedom like Nayantara Sahgal to write so passionately about it. (pp. 92-3)

> *Theon Wilkinson, "Brand Name," in* London Magazine, *n.s. Vol. 18, No. 2, June, 1978, pp. 89-93.*

HENRY C. HART

Indira Gandhi's prime ministership is [interpreted in *Indira Gandhi's Emergence and Style*] from the perspective of her personality, in the context of those who supported and opposed her. The account covers the period from her emergence from her father's shadow in 1964 to her surprising defeat in the election of 1977. In its form and organization the book stands midway between the biographies and the journalistic accounts of the Indian Emergency. Nayantara Sahgal has chosen neither to write a complete life story, nor to give a full account of Mrs. Gandhi's period of authoritarian rule, but rather to explain the one by the inner dynamics of the other. She argues that the Emergency was not required in order to maintain stable government in India, nor was it a sudden departure from Indira Gandhi's previous nine years of rule. The book constitutes a convincing case that "Mrs. Gandhi's recourse to dictatorial power was a need of her own temperament." (p. 569)

[Being of the Nehru] family gives Sahgal the feel of personal relationships; it also leads her to give more than proportionate weight to Mrs. Gandhi's harshness toward Mrs. Pandit in the assessment of those relationships. More to the point, Sahgal belongs to that select company of observers (including Zareer Masani) who before June 1975 correctly predicted Indira Gandhi's drive to monopolize power. Sahgal's warning was printed in the April 1975 issue of the *South Asian Review* (London).

This reviewer's principal disappointment with the book is that we are not taken much beyond that penetrating 1975 article toward an understanding of Mrs. Gandhi's personality. To be sure, Indira Gandhi's own recollection of her childhood as "sombre, tense, aggrieved," is pretty convincingly shown to be more a projection of her own emotional isolation than of her early experiences. (pp. 569-70)

Sahgal tells us that Indira Gandhi grew up with the determination not to become dependent on anyone, lest she be hurt. But whence the insecurity, if it be not from the objective context of her childhood? We are not given a satisfying answer. The inference is of some sort of innate perversity. Though the portrait of Mrs. Gandhi is richly colored here, it is not sufficiently precise to give us insight into two directions of her recent behavior which seem at odds with a consuming drive for control. One is the indulgence of her son, Sanjay. We are told that she called the 1977 election partly to assure his succession to power; earlier, however, there is the suggestion that he blackmailed her through his possession of the secret of her rigging of the 1971 election. These are not logically incompatible explanations, but on the other hand they cannot both be projections of the same fear of dependency. The other is her apparent need to legitimize her dictatorship by truly competitive elections. One suspects, but is given no light upon, some emotional resonance within this indefatigable campaigner of the approbation of the electorate which is not wholly consistent with an autocratic temperament.

At two points the book lapses from the standards of investigative journalism to present rather sensational charges against Mrs. Gandhi upon flimsy evidence. The first is the claim of Balraj Madhok (an unsuccessful Jan Sangh candidate) that in some North Indian constituencies her 1971 election triumph was greatly exaggerated by ballot-tampering through a bizarre use of invisible inks. The other is "the Soviet presence" in Delhi during the Emergency "as an armoured escort to Mrs. Gandhi's leadership." The only evidence for this latter charge is that the government denied it.

As one who appreciates Sahgal's clean prose when she is writing up to her usual standard, this reviewer was a bit put off by occasionally awkward sentence structure. Sometimes clauses are connected so loosely as to permit misinterpretation. (pp. 570-71)

These are surface blemishes. What we have, underneath, is an account that makes us feel we know Mrs. Gandhi more closely, and more in the round, than we did before. What we fail to find is an understanding of her need for dictatorial power. (p. 571)

> *Henry C. Hart, in a review of ''Indira Gandhi's Emergence and Style,'' in* Pacific Affairs, *Vol. 53, No. 3, Fall, 1980, pp. 569-71.*

KATE CRUISE O'BRIEN

In the days when Britain was still an empire, Englishmen were wont to say that the colonies were 'not ready' for independence—which conjured up the unlikely vision of a bristling chap in long knee-shorts swishing his backside with his riding crop as he addressed the bemused natives: 'All right, you chaps, anyone here ready for independence?' It was not exactly in the British interest to prepare her colonies for independence; and independence, when it came, came very often in the form described here in Nayantara Sahgal's *Rich Like Us:* 'The British wouldn't leave until *they* decided the game was up, and it would never be up until they saw doom spelled out in a language they understood. When it was, nothing would induce them to stay. An island race needed no second warning of danger.' As Britain pulled out of the colonies, the newly independent states inherited danger, unpreparedness and a habit of dependence. . . .

Two heroines, Sonali, a successful civil servant in the Ministry for Industry, and Rose, the Cockney, red-haired, white-faced No 2 wife of Ram N. Surya, become victims of the new order. Sonali is demoted because she refuses to grant a blanket import licence to a foreign-based factory making a fizzy brown drink called Happyola. 'Policy,' recalls Sonali, 'did not allow foreign collaboration in industry.' But policy has mysteriously changed, and imported car parts are secretly stored beneath the fizzy brown drink. Sonali, disgusted by her own past indifference to the corruption around her, goes to the aid of Rose, whose husband has been paralysed by a stroke and whose stepson Devi (son of Ram's No 1 wife) is trying to dispossess her—or worse. Devi is involved in the Happyola chicanery and Rose is watchful, truthful and indiscreet. As 'sullenness' builds up 'along New Delhi's heavily policed roads,' Rose is isolated before the raw new power in Devi. Ms Sahgal's description of Devi, a kind of vicious teenage adult, a 'fun-and-games man and companion hijacker to the highest in the land', is masterly and terrifying—though vivid flashbacks to the British Raj and to Partition suggest that Devi's savage and powerful irresponsibility is the luxuriant growth of a colonised seed. *Rich Like Us* is funny, readable and startlingly intelligent.

> *Kate Cruise O'Brien, ''Learning Independence,'' in* The Listener, *Vol. 114, No. 2917, July 11, 1985, p. 32.*

MARIA COUTO

With corrupt politicians, businessmen and bureaucrats at the centre of the narrative and a maimed beggar on the periphery, [Sahgal's *Rich Like Us*] offers a cohesive and intimate portrait of the intrigues of power [inside India], but it is unable to attempt a resolution of the conflict between culture and technology. Sweeping, indiscriminate modernization can inspire disgust: "Happyola" imported to slake the thirst of the urban consumer is no answer for mass unemployment and undernourishment. Sonali, the occasional narrator of her own and other histories, resigns from the Civil Service because she will not countenance the production of "Happyola", and is humiliated. Rose, whose robust matter-of-factness cuts through the cant, hypocrisies and subterfuges of the opinion-makers and the wielders of power, is the cockney memsahib who finds poise and equanimity in an uninhibited acceptance of human relationships irrespective of colour and class.

Through her the narrative suggests that the need for economic solutions is only one dimension. She is largely unaware of the refinements of liberal sensibilities back home in England and has little patience for them in her new home in India as the wife of the worldly and urbane Ram. Her relationship with her shrewd father-in-law, a small trader, is perhaps the truest measure of Indo-British dealings. When business is flagging he learns to appreciate her advice for improvements and change, and in the process gets to know and love her personal qualities; but she first learns his ways and communicates with him on his terms, by sitting cross-legged opposite him on the floor.

The novel's many voices recreate family, social and public relationships with accuracy, occasionally slipping into overkill; but suggest only remotely the reverberations of the Indo-British experience outside the structures of power. A discussion of issues such as Sahgal attempts should extend beyond the history and displacement of élites into a recognition of the forces of the land and its people.

> Maria Couto, "Indo-British Displacements," in The Times Literary Supplement, *No. 4293, July 12, 1985, p. 777.*

WENDY LAW-YONE

Plans for Departure concerns a group of people—mostly Europeans—who meet briefly in remote Himapur. The time is 1914, long after the East India Company's heyday, and the Indian Mutiny had produced a backlash in the colonial administration. Unaware that the war in Europe is imminent, Anna Hansen has left her English lover and her Danish relatives to spend a year in India. Anna is a tall, blond "Valkyrie" of independent means and ways, with interests worthy of an early 20th-century Danish eccentric: health food, yoga, emancipation, Indian nationalism, and Theosophy. She has come to Himapur to act as personal assistant to Sir Nitin Basu, a distinguished and crotchety scientist who prefers to keep out of politics and concentrate instead on studying the emotional range of plants.

The person in Himapur Anna is most drawn to, however, is Henry Brewster, the district magistrate who "suffered from philosophy, and had chronic attacks of ruling-class conscience." Brewster is the sort of "DM" who "would have been delighted to see every existing empire pack up." Instead, it's his wife who's packed up and left. . . .

Anna's involvement with Brewster is averted, however, when she begins to suspect that Brewster's wife hasn't actually left Himapur but has been murdered by Brewster himself. Anna

decides to return home to Nicholas as planned. In London, after a little awkwardness, Nicholas and Anna make their peace even though "the public certainties they had taken for granted could no longer be relied on either. Life ahead would have to consist of whatever they could salvage from public and private ruins."

One of the curiosities of this novel is that although it is set in India and written by an Indian . . . , it is almost quaint in its European sensibility—not only in its overriding concerns about the European war, or the contingency of the Indian characters in relation to the Europeans, or even the many allusions to European myth, culture, and civilization. The very spirit of *Plans for Departure,* the language itself, seems embedded in the amber of that European period, with all its slogans, its jingoistic cliches, its ignorance of irony.

Not only does Sahgal inflict upon her characters some crashingly tedious exchanges about the war's unfolding, she herself lapses into the hackneyed idiom of war propaganda: "Crowned heads exchanged telegrams reminding each other of the tender ties of blood and sentiment that bound them. Governments burned the midnight oil trying to keep the Austro-Serbian crisis from spreading . . . His letter rang with the hoofbeats of imperial cavalries at midnight maneuvers . . . He waited for his beloved Europe to plunge a knife treacherously into her own vitals." And so on. In short, I would have to say *Plans for Departure* is an enlightened but uninspired novel; in a word, dull.

> Wendy Law-Yone, "The Rage for the Raj," in Book World—The Washington Post, *October 13, 1985, p. 13.*

JOHN MELLORS

There are two kinds of writer in the fiction of Nayantara Sahgal. One is the imaginative storyteller, the novelist who creates characters and sets their moods and ordains their destinies. The other is the political journalist, preoccupied with reporting and interpreting the stuff of history, anxious to influence voters and legislatures and governments. Sometimes the two Sahgals are mutually supportive. Sometimes one of them, usually the journalist, seems to get in the other's way, so that the novel loses a degree of its impetus and ceases to grip the reader. In *Plans for Departure* the storyteller in Sahgal has the upper hand, and the result is a subtle, sharply imagined novel, skilfully plotted and elegantly written.

Not that the journalist is elbowed out altogether; there are still a few occasions when the reader is force-fed with facts. However, there are far more times when the storyteller uses the journalist to bring in historical facts and political views in such a tactful and appropriate way that the information contributes to the fiction and makes it more telling. The author has set her fancy free while keeping her *alter ego,* the fact finder and commentator, under stricter discipline than usual. (p. 98)

The plot revolves around Anna Hansen. She is an independent woman, something of a feminist before her time. She is a romantic in her view of history, especially of those early periods in which mythology and history are indistinguishable. In certain cloud formations she sees the Indo-Aryan invaders in their three-wheeled chariots, 'victorious drunken laughter echoing in every gust of wind.' Her questing, speculative mind leads her into trouble when she stumbles across the corpse of the dog that had belonged to Henry and Stella Brewster. Although on her way to being at least half in love with Henry, Anna now begins to suspect that he has killed both the dog and his wife.... One had better not reveal what those suspicions lead to, since there is a strong element of mystery in the plot. Mystery and menace are thickened by the background of events in Europe, the murder at Sarajevo and its repercussions, and the outbreak, at last, of that most avoidable of wars. With her two most recent books, *Rich Like Us,* and now *Plans for Departure,* Nayantara Sahgal is en route to becoming a major novelist. (pp. 99-100)

John Mellors, "Fancy Free," in London Magazine,
n.s. Vol. 25, No. 12, March, 1986, pp. 98-101.

Lawrence Sanders

1920-

American novelist.

A popular author of crime and adventure fiction, Sanders is best known for *The Anderson Tapes* (1970), which won the Edgar Allan Poe Award for best first mystery novel. The story, which centers on an ex-convict's plans to burglarize a Manhattan luxury apartment complex, is told through transcripts, memos, and other documents gathered through electronic surveillance by several law enforcement agencies. Reviewers praised Sanders's inventive narrative structure, his extensive knowledge of police procedures, and his deftness at creating realistic dialogue.

Sanders is also well known for his *Deadly Sin* series of novels, which currently includes four books. These works feature Edward X. Delaney, a respected New York City police detective and devoted family man who solves gruesome murders while struggling to maintain his moral integrity. Delaney's criminal foes are often sexual deviants whose abnormal behavior plays an important role in the violent crimes they commit. Although some critics fault Sanders for relying on sensationalism, many regard his portrayal of Delaney as convincing and realistic. Sanders has also written the detective novels *The Sixth Commandment* (1979) and *The Tenth Commandment* (1980).

In *The Tangent Objective* (1976) and *The Tangent Factor* (1978), Sanders examines the world of international political intrigue. Both novels are set in a fictitious West African nation where the protagonists, one an unscrupulous American businessman and the other an ambitious African leader, manipulate the country's unstable government for their own interests. Sanders has also written several mainstream novels, including *The Marlow Chronicles* (1977), a story of a dying man's attempts to enjoy his final days, and *The Passion of Molly T.* (1984), which dramatizes the transformation of a feminist organization from a social activist group to a band of vengeful terrorists. While reviewers considered these novels less successful than Sanders's detective fiction, they acknowledged his ability to sustain interest through his use of detailed descriptions and colorful language.

(See also *Contemporary Authors,* Vols. 81-84.)

CHRISTOPHER LEHMANN-HAUPT

If you're fashionably paranoiac and willing to believe that the whole world is plugged into a tape recorder, you'll have a zippy time with Lawrence Sanders's first novel, ***The Anderson Tapes.*** For Mr. Sanders has given us a hero with the makings of charisma, an intriguing sex life, and an audacious plan. And to give his story the aura of documentary authenticity, Mr. Sanders has told it all through transcriptions of various tape recordings. Fresh from serving a sentence at Sing Sing for breaking and entering, John (Duke) Anderson has found a woman and a home. . . . Her home is a cooperative apartment in a New York City town house on East 73d Street. Duke

© *Jerry Bauer*

doesn't intend merely to make himself at home at the woman's place; he plans to clean out the entire building, at an estimated profit of a quarter-million dollars or so. . . .

[Since] Mr. Sanders has an ear for tough dialogue and the latest word on eavesdropping devices (he has worked at Mechanix Illustrated and Science and Mechanics magazines), we get to listen in at his artful discretion.

A little too artful, the gimmick backfires somewhat. By trying to make his novel authentic and dramatic, Mr. Sanders has to switch from one tape transcript to another with increasing frequency and trickiness as the story peaks. Since the excuses to do so become steadily flimsier, the net effect is more artificial than the straight narrative Sanders worked so hard to avoid.

And the coincidences! It's too much to have to believe that the New York Police Department and the State Liquor Authority and the Federal Trade Commission and a dozen other investigating agencies all just happened to be electronically eavesdropping on every character in the story at every place they met, and never knew about the planned crime. Mr. Sanders tries to divert us with caustic remarks about bureaucratic ineptitude, and with the theory that if everyone had gotten together the robbery would have been snipped in the bug. But it won't do. Only God and omniscient narrators hear everything.

Christopher Lehmann-Haupt, "Gimmicks," in The New York Times, *February 20, 1970, p. 39.*

A. L. ROSENWEIG

Having worn out art, writers now seem bent on lunging at fact as the new art. Witness the rise of the non-fiction novel or the rambling, sensational disclosures of criminal conversations faithfully taped and published by federal agencies. There's a subcontinent of literature to be explored there; instant books at the turn of a switch. Craft is nowhere evident, only fact, as if by the very communication of events and conversations the writer achieves a novel truth.

But some good use has been made of the device and Lawrence Sanders has raised the wire-tap recording to something like art in his suspense thriller **The Anderson Tapes**. . . .

Purporting to be an actual collection of source material, the bugged conversations, letters and interviews tell of an ex-con's daring plan to take over a small posh apartment house on Manhattan's upper East Side, and systematically loot it of everything of value. . . . The lack of connective narrative may tell on some readers, but Sanders's legerdemain with dialogue and the strength of the plot carry the story through to a bangup finish which courts Armageddon with this envoi from a criminal's diary: "Crime is the truth. Law is the hypocrisy."

A. L. Rosenweig, "Thrillers," Book World—The Washington Post, *March 15, 1970, p. 2.*

PUBLISHERS WEEKLY

The author of **The Anderson Tapes** has come up with something much more routine this time around [in **The Pleasures of Helen**] which adds up to fairly entertaining reading of the lost, lonely-lady school. Helen Miley's pleasures are simple: a man to get up with in the morning, dry Rob Roys to make the day in her p. r. office bearable, the kindness of the gods in keeping her thirtyish figure as great as it is for the next few years. The men in her life, however, although they fit right into her bed and her lonely heart, are all pretty weird. . . . In the end Helen is left high and dry, her best friend married, her men all gone. She goes off to her favorite bar, has a few until the bartender says that that nice-looking gentleman at the end of the bar would like to buy her a drink. And he is nice looking, even though he's missing an arm, so Helen says sure, why the hell not. It's all pretty predictable but there is a feminine market for this sort of thing.

A review of "The Pleasures of Helen," in Publishers Weekly, *Vol. 199, No. 2, January 11, 1971, p. 59.*

TONI MORRISON

[The characters in **Love Songs**] step off the bus and say something nasty to a colored man. Then: "'Snakes in Paradise' she said. 'Vipers in Eden' he said." There we have it: two evilies—corrupting innocence or encouraging wickedness in a lovely New England sea town.

Bobbie Vander, successful pop singer, and her musician companion, return, innocently enough, to her home town for some restful work, but their corrosive nature brings out the worst in people, as well as, apparently, the weather. A sweet young thing is pulled into drugs; a charming boy is pushed into murder; a loving sister is driven to drink. But those verbs are not

right—Mr. Sanders's evilies don't force anybody: they simply have lifestyles which stimulate passion in others. His is a more or less routine view of the nature of evil: a childish acquisitiveness, and a loose-ended curiosity about the extent of one's ability to control another. It is my guess that genuine evil is a bit more sinister. . . .

As the title suggests, the book is about love: the absence of, the distortions of, and, at least in one case, the wholeness of. . . .

It all ends rather neatly. The messy ones die; the weak ones atrophy: the good ones exit with dignity and the wicked pop-singer. Something tender is budding there; an "obscene desire to sacrifice." Love maybe? The storm wanes and Eden shuts itself up tight, free of its serpents and free to return once again to its primeval ennui.

Toni Morrison, "Two Views of Evil-at-Large," in The New York Times Book Review, *October 1, 1972, p. 41.*

J. JUSTIN GUSTAINIS

The first fifty or so pages of [**The First Deadly Sin**], which very nearly turned me off on the whole work, is a standard boy-meets-girl routine spiced up with all the references to sado-masochism, masturbation, and homosexuality that some modern readers seem to demand from their fiction. But then the gears mesh and the book enters into Part II, which centers around the frustrations of a hard-bitten New York City police captain. The interest is piqued as we wonder where these . . . seemingly diverse characters will interact.

Then along comes murder. We realize that the "boy" of the aforementioned boy-meets-girl episode has gone bananas and become a homicidal psychopath, picking at random a citizen walking along a dark street, and bashing his head in with an ice ax. We also watch the veteran officer of NYPD get assigned the case of finding the killer. Complications arise immediately. It seems that the randomly-selected victim was a City Councilman from Brooklyn, and a Deputy Police Commissioner with political ambitions is taking a personal (and noisy) interest. . . . (pp. 330-31)

The chess-game-between-cop-and-killer device is not a new one, but I have never seen it done better than it is here. Sanders has a masterful talent for both plotting and characterization. He undertakes one of the most difficult tasks a writer can face, that of stepping inside a madman's head to show how he rationalizes apparently senseless slaughter. Comparisons with Dostoyevsky are, I suppose, inevitable, and in this respect Sanders is every bit as good. . . .

Sanders has a good story, and he tells it well. His protagonist is flesh and blood, with little of the cliche cop in him. As the story evolves, he becomes a man caught between a rock and a hard place, forced to choose between the ethics of his profession, which he cherishes, and the only way he knows will trap the killer. The psychopath is drawn plausibly enough to make you look over your shoulder more than usual as you walk down a dark street, and to fill your dreams with pictures of ice axes in descent. (p. 331)

J. Justin Gustainis, in a review of "The First Deadly Sin," in Best Sellers, *Vol. 33, No. 13, October 1, 1973, pp. 330-31.*

MARTIN LEVIN

The cop in [*The First Deadly Sin*] has written an unpublished article on "the Dostoevskian relationship between detective and criminal." . . . Published or no, this thesis becomes the *modus operandi* of Capt. Edward X. Delaney's pursuit of a mass murderer at large on the East Side. It adds a few more degrees Fahrenheit to the already superheated climate of Lawrence Sanders's sophisticated *roman policier*.

The object of Delaney's cultivated affinity is a computer specialist named Daniel Blank. . . . Blank has always had the potential for schizoid behavior, but he finally comes out of the closet when he takes up with Celia Montfort, a working diabolist who favors simple black dresses and wrist bandages. With her weird townhouse and her satanic mumbo-jumbo . . . , Celia fills in Blank with a whole new sado-maso life style.

The author (who will be remembered for *The Anderson Tapes*) puts the hunter and the hunted on adjacent courses, every inch of which is meticulously described. When the itineraries begin to conform to the detective's Dostoevskian plan, things really boil up. Sanders lingers over gratuitous details . . . , and his prose sometimes hazes into purple. But nothing seriously impedes the violent course of cruel crime and unusual punishment.

> *Martin Levin, in a review of "The First Deadly Sin,"* in The New York Times Book Review, *October 14, 1973, p. 48.*

ROBERT McGEEHIN

The concern for moral and political values evident in [*The Tomorrow File*] places it outside the realm of pure science fiction. Yet it falls considerably short of the other works that comprise this genre. It lacks the somber element of an Orwell or Zamiatin. In its development of scientific probabilities it can't match the imagination and foresight of a Huxley. Nor can it claim the idealism and terse melodrama of an Ayn Rand.

Sanders's strength, once again, stems from his experience in journalism. There are many obvious if over-wrought parallels to the politics and social history of our own decade. . . . The present carnival atmosphere of the nation's capital is translated into twenty-first century terms when the executive and legislative branches of government are present simply to entertain the masses, who are kept in control by computerized public relations policies.

But if the perspective of a journalist provides Sanders with his strength, it is also the origin of some inherent weaknesses. Characterization is exaggerated. The novel is full of people who are just not believable. Dialogue is rather clumsily handled, and the plot is too predictable. And Sanders' descriptions of love-making, though frequent, are neither sensitive nor erotic. . . .

The Tomorrow File has all the elements for success found in the great works of this genre. And it has the added attraction of a protagonist who openly embraces the society he serves. It also contains the two elements most necessary for bestsellerdom: enough novelty to attract attention and lots of sex.

And yet, with both formulae applied, the novel still fails. Small matter. Someday it'll be made into a movie. Starring James Caan.

> *Robert McGeehin, in a review of "The Tomorrow File," in* Best Sellers, *Vol. 35, No. 7, October, 1975, p. 194.*

AL BAROZZI

The political disassociation of Watergate, the moral disassociation of the FBI, and the intellectual disassociation of the CIA show that beneath any human motive there is a constant: a will to grab or keep power at whatever cost and sin.

Lawrence Sanders proves this in the most nuanced and qualified fashion possible [in *The Tangent Objective*]. On one hand, he recognizes man's need for an ordered society that expects morality from its members. On the other hand, he believes that what moves the world is self-interest. Man is not controlled by law, nor faith, nor virtue, nor love, but by greed, deceit, and corruption. . . .

Thus, Peter Tangent, the executive of an American oil company, is willing to commit any sin to make a fortune for himself; Obiri Anokye, the Little Captain in the emerging African nation of Asante, attempts to substitute ethical and military confrontation for unethical and personal gain; Yvonne Mayer, a Frenchwoman is always on the hunt for titillating sexual sensations, which will ultimately pollute her incentives and reduce her life to shattered pieces; and the whole conflicting and vivid human fauna of spies, soldiers, and whores are bound to each other by common venality, stupidity, and comic hubris. . . .

Sanders's imagination is adventurous, with a feeling for life as mystery and riddle. The narrative is an intriguing mixture of contemporary allusions and gothic mystery.

> *Al Barozzi, in a review of "The Tangent Objective," in* Best Sellers, *Vol. 36, No. 9, December, 1976, p. 283.*

EMILY WEIR, C.H.S.

Toby Marlow [the protagonist of *The Marlow Chronicles*] is an aging actor whose entire life was in the theatre. For him the whole world's a stage. . . . His performance is such that (and this is what he intends) those around him do not pity him when he announces to them that the doctor has told him that he has six months to live.

Nor are Toby's last days spent in feeling sorry for himself. There is too much going on for him to waste his time in self-pity. He and his common law wife of forty years plan their wedding. He carries on his perennial mock feud with their housekeeper. He continues his lively interest in the welfare of his son's companion, Barbara, who is pregnant. But, above all, he engages in a heated, constant debate with David, his son, over the standards of the acting profession. This everlasting sparring gives spice to his life, and a vigor that is astonishing. (p. 137)

Not as engrossing as Sanders' *The First Deadly Sin* or *The Anderson Tapes,* this novel does have its merits. The dramatis personae come through with impact. They are not stereotypes nor puppets; neither are they the average person, yet they are real.

This novel is for the sophisticated reader. Barbara Cartland fans won't like it. (p. 138)

> *Emily Weir, C.H.S., in a review of "The Marlow Chronicles," in* Best Sellers, *Vol. 37, No. 5, August, 1977, pp. 137-38.*

EVAN HUNTER

There are two kinds of cop fiction: the so-called procedural mystery and the more serious novel about human beings who coincidentally happen to be cops. Joseph Wambaugh writes serious novels about cops. Dorothy Uhnak succeeds somewhat less effectively in a similar vein. Jimmy Breslin's portrait of an alcoholic cop in *The Gang That Couldn't Shoot Straight* was painful, true and unforgettable. But Lawrence Sanders has written a police procedural with pretensions. In attempting to expand [*The Second Deadly Sin*] beyond its genre he has given us something that falls far short of a serious novel and has blunted the edge of the knife-hard mystery story he might have told.

The sin of avarice spins the plot, of course, but there are seven deadly mystery-writing sins lurking as well in these pages. The first follows from the basic situation itself, that the supercop is called in *after* all the tedious legwork has been done by lesser mortals; each time an already-confronted suspect is reconfronted by Delaney, we are denied the excitement of an initial encounter. The second is Mr. Sanders' condescending habit of leading us through a suspect interview and then rehashing all the new information in tête-à-têtes between patient instructor Delaney and awed student Boone. The third is the constant use of *post* post-mortems between Delaney and his wife, whom he uses as a sympathetic sounding board throughout. Mr. Sanders' style is the fourth transgression, peculiarly ponderous and flat in light of his subject matter. His dialogue is sprinkled with the salty (and true) language common to cops and thieves; he knows his police-routine cold; but he frequently stops his narrative dead to explain how one or another of his cops learned the tricks of the trade, a method that smacks of diligent research inadequately disguised and poorly assimilated.

In the works of early theologians, gluttony was the fifth deadly sin. Mr. Sanders makes copious use of it here. When we are not being spoon-fed facts, we are being sumptuously feasted, Delaney is a street-wise, brownstone-liberated Nero Wolfe, without his culinary taste. There are enough meals sandwiched between the detection and the speculation to fill a massive cookbook. But in addition to detailed lunches and dinners we are given interior-decorator descriptions of galleries, offices and homes; aimless chitchat about who must be dropped off at camp or picked up at school; and sartorial descriptions that Edith Head might envy—most of them extraneous to plot and poor substitutes for true character development. (pp. 15, 32)

Sixth of the sins is the failure to realize Delaney himself. He is presumably intended to be a lovable old bear who is pained and puzzled by the infinite complexities and cruelties of human beings, but he comes off instead as a humorless, didactic, pedantic and often pontifical workhorse. . . .

But the deadliest sin of all is the disservice Mr. Sanders has done to a well-considered plot based on a plausible tax-fraud gimmick. Somewhere in these many pages there lies buried a taut, slender thriller. It's a pity he wasn't willing to settle for that. (p. 32)

> *Evan Hunter, in a review of "The Second Deadly Sin," in* The New York Times Book Review, *August 21, 1977, pp. 15, 32.*

J. JUSTIN GUSTAINIS

When, five years ago, I reviewed for *Best Sellers* Lawrence Sanders' *The First Deadly Sin,* I called the novel a masterpiece,

and I still hold to that judgment. Sanders' newest book [*The Second Deadly Sin*] is a sequel to that widely praised work. (p. 236)

As it was with the first "sin," the matter here is murder. Brilliant, boozing, brawling artist Victor [Maitland] is stabbed to death in his Manhattan studio. Again the ancient question: whodunit? Again the answer is ultimately provided by Edward X. Delaney, who was a precinct captain in *The First Deadly Sin* and is now a retired Chief of Detectives for New York City. Delaney, although not an intellectual, is a cop who reads, remembers, and thinks. More important, he is a man who learns. . . . When the initial police investigation into Maitland's murder grinds to an inconclusive halt, Delaney is called out of retirement to conduct a special investigation (this mainly as a sop to a politically influential relative of the deceased). For an assistant, Delaney is lent a youngish Detective Sergeant who is waging a not altogether successful battle against alcoholism.

Delaney and Sergeant Boone track the murderer through the New York City art world. This sounds like pretty dull stuff, but it isn't, thanks to Sanders' skill. He makes the point that all the jargon and pretension of the art crowd can be distilled down to one thing: greed (in Biblical terms, covetousness—the second of the deadly sins).

What makes the difference between a "masterpiece" on the one hand, and a "good story" on the other? The distinction lies in Sanders' approaches to murder. In *First* the murderer was a sophisticated madman who used to brain random people for kicks. . . . We knew who the murderer was from the outset, and the fascination of the story was in watching Delaney track him down.

Second follows a more traditional formula. The *corpus delicti* appears in the first chapter, the murderer is caught in the last, and everything in between serves to bring the reader from A to Z. Note, please, that the fact that this formula is a little trite does not mean that it cannot be turned into good fiction. Sanders proves it can, here. But it isn't the stuff of which masterpieces are made. (pp. 236-37)

> *J. Justin Gustainis, in a review of "The Second Deadly Sin," in* Best Sellers, *Vol. 37, No. 8, November, 1977, pp. 236-37.*

DONALD GODDARD

Anyone who takes the trouble to invent a West African state teeming with nationalist politicians, underemployed army officers, white mercenaries, multinational oil-company executives, supine ladies and equally accommodating Central Intelligence Agency agents is unlikely to squander it on just one book. Having previously installed Obiri Anokye in the presidential palace of Mokodi, capital of Asante, in *The Tangent Objective,* Lawrence Sanders now organizes Anokye's conquest of neighboring Benin and Togo in *The Tangent Factor,* thereby setting his black Napoleon on the road to pan-African domination in volumes presumably still to come, and opening up geopolitical prospects to tax the narrative powers of a Tolstoy.

But if Mr. Sanders only occasionally measures up to the epic demands of his theme, he does not always disgrace it either. Behind the fashionable clutter of brand names, brutality, oral sex, pop technology and Flemingway prose conventions, a larger world can still be discerned, as in a Polaroid snapshot of tourists at the Grand Canyon. There *are* forces at work in Asante besides greed and lust.

He also tries valiantly to go against type in portraying his white hero, Peter Tangent, chief of African operations for the Starrett Petroleum Corporation. As far removed from the John Wayne *bwana* figure as from the Brando-style Ugly American, Tangent is a skinny, conniving opportunist who has gone to work for Anokye while still drawing his salary from Starrett. He is also impotent (at least until Amina Dunama, the beautiful Hausa, gets hold of him) and knows how to treat a bottle of Latour '53. But these promising differences are less than skin-deep, unfortunately. Whenever the chips are down, Tangent instantly reverts to the standard American hero who knows in his heart that a man can prove himself only in bed or on the battlefield— a view apparently shared by the entire population of Asante, regardless of sex, race, creed or national origin. . . .

Indeed, Mr. Sanders is practically free of that condescension toward the black man—particularly the black *fighting* man— that colors most African adventure stories up to, and including, Frederick Forsyth's *The Dogs of War*. In *The Tangent Factor*, a better book than Mr. Forsyth's in every way, all the leading characters, black *or* white, are equally obnoxious. Only occasionally does the veil slip, and even then to reveal robust commercial values held in common.

> *Donald Goddard, "Flemingway," in* The New York Times Book Review, *April 2, 1978, p. 15.*

NEWGATE CALLENDAR

A big, detailed private-eye book, *The Sixth Commandment* by Lawrence Sanders . . . is completely different from *The Tangent Objective*. . . . *The Tangent Objective,* a cleverly written book about contemporary Africa, was a combination of adventure and sociology. *The Sixth Commandment* takes place in a decaying New York town on the Hudson River, and the only thing it has in common with its predecessor is a snappy writing style.

Snappy, but in this book not very original. The hero, Samuel Todd, is the field investigator for a foundation interested in science. He goes into the small town to look into the application for a grant made by a Nobel laureate who claims to be on the verge of a breakthrough. His field of research is the aging process. Strange things begin happening; unusual personalities are revealed. As for Sam Todd, he is by far the most conventional character in the book. In Mr. Sanders's subconscious the composite private eye exists. Thus Sam is sloppy. Sam is kind. Sam is honest. Sam is tough. Sam drinks an awful lot. Sam is unmarried, but has girlfriends. Sam is cynical. Sam is the salt of the earth. . . .

There is too much two-bit philosophy and moralizing in *The Sixth Commandment,* and the book could be cut by a third. Otherwise it is a competent job, smoothly written, observing all of the amenities. If only Mr. Sanders did not try so hard with his archetypes.

> *Newgate Callendar, in a review of "The Sixth Commandment," in* The New York Times Book Review, *February 11, 1979, p. 26.*

BRIAN QUINN

[*The Sixth Commandment*] is the kind of book which many people will read—Mr. Sanders has a good sales record—and many forget. Many people will read it just to forget. For many years many people have been reading for just that reason.

Not that it is all that bad a book. Only, it is only what it is: a something meant to be bought, read and consigned to oblivion by as many somebodies as possible.

Everybody can sell somebody something, said Gertrude Stein. When they write, they will tell you about the weather and money. Mr. Sanders tells us about the weather and money. . . .

Indeed, everybody can sell somebody something. That has always been true, as has the need for art. *The Sixth Commandment* is not art.

> *Brian Quinn, in a review of "The Sixth Commandment," in* Best Sellers, *Vol. 38, No. 12, March, 1979, p. 381.*

KIRKUS REVIEWS

Sanders tried out the hard-boiled-detective-narrator genre in *The Sixth Commandment* (1979), with mediocre, heavy-breathing, stickily clichéd results. And [in *The Tenth Commandment*] he's going a similar route . . . but with his very New-Yorky tongue jammed completely in cheek. So, though overextended and often a little silly, this is a much more comfortable entertainment. The sleuth is 5'3" Joshua Bigg, resident investigator for a posh East Side law firm—where he's just gotten two separate hot assignments from two senior partners: partner Tabachnick wants Josh to deal with a man claiming to have key info on the will of the late Sol Kipper, a window-jump-suicide textile king; partner Teitlebaum wants Josh to get the lowdown on Prof. Yale Stonehouse, who has mysteriously vanished. Josh tackles both cases: Kipper was murdered, of course (probably by his sexy second wife and her social-reforming minister-boyfriend), with murder too for a would-be blackmailer; meanwhile, missing Prof. Stonehouse, a nasty type, is revealed to have been suffering from arsenic poisoning before his disappearance. Then, inevitably, after 250 pages of predictable sleuthing, the two cases connect. . . . So-so detection—stretched out unconscionably. But Josh is a breezily likable narrator who takes lots of time-outs for musings on shortness and updates on his hesitant sex life. . . . Plus: platonic support from 6'6" secretary Mrs. Gertrude Kletz, a very sharp and engaging lady. Longwinded but mostly agreeable folderol, then, nearly all in dialogue—with Sanders happily at home in jokey, brassy Manhattan.

> *A review of "The Tenth Commandment," in* Kirkus Reviews, *Vol. XLVIII, No. 14, July 15, 1980, p. 936.*

STANLEY ELLIN

The Tenth Commandment [is] a hefty text of almost 400 pages, every single one of which can be read with pleasure. Set in Manhattan, a territory Mr. Sanders evidently knows and cherishes, the story is outstanding in characterization, straight-faced humor and mastery of style.

If there is anything some readers may cavil at here—and they would have to be thin-lipped and costive to do it—it is that there is very little mystery for our hero to unravel. The title of the book itself gives much of it away, and the villain is identifiable well in advance of the denouement. But more than counterbalancing this is the variety of the characters, each of whom springs to life on delivering his or her entrance line and then remains memorable to the final curtain. Even their names, in the Dickensian fashion, are memorable. Thus, in following investigator Joshua Bigg—all 5 feet 3⅜ inches of him—through his adventures, we encounter the luscious Yetta Apetoff, the late lamented Sol Kipper and his glamorous widow Tippi, the missing Professor Yale Stonehouse and daughter Glynis, the troubled Oriental building manager Clarence Ng, the public-spirited Reverend Godfrey Knurr, and a host of others who delectably flavor Dickens with Doonesbury. (pp. 14-15)

The story opens in a leisurely way with a description of how [Joshua] luckily happened to become chief investigator for a prosperous New York law firm. Almost immediately he is involved in an investigation of why a cherished friend of Mr. Tabachnick, senior partner of the firm, has committed suicide without known cause simultaneously with the mysterious disappearance of an esteemed client of Mr. Teitlebaum, a slightly lesser partner. We are then happily ambling through a web of complications in search of motives and methods.

There is also romance along the way, providing its own inevitable complications—short male, tall female—and a charming and instructive romance it is. All in all, what we have here is the right novel for the reader of any size whatsoever. (p. 15)

> *Stanley Ellin, "Criminal Behavior," in* The New York Times Book Review, *September 28, 1980, pp. 14-15, 40.*

KIRKUS REVIEWS

This third outing for retired NYPD Chief of Detectives Edward X. Delaney [*The Third Deadly Sin*] has Sanders' customary low-level, sensationalistic readability—so it will sell. But even by pulp-thriller standards there's an insulting carelessness this time around: a novel, all about a psychopathic killer, which doesn't bother to make the killer's psycho-motives even half-believable. She is neat, mousy, frigid, pill-popping, 35-ish Zoe Kohler, a hotel secretary who once a month (yes folks, "a psychopathic female whose crimes are triggered by her monthly periods") puts on a sexy disguise, picks up an out-of-town businessman, waits till he's naked, and then goes at him (throat and groin) with a sharpened boy-scout knife. Why? Well, there are some vague references to prudish, overbearing parents and a piggish ex-husband—but nothing even close to psychopath-worthy; nor is the surface characterization convincing or consistent. So readers will have to be content with the predictable, much-padded chills here—as chapters alternate between Zoe (her murders, her sexless romance with a kindred mousy soul, her deteriorating health due to craziness and Addison's disease) and Delaney's deductions. (p. 697)

> *A review of "The Third Deadly Sin," in* Kirkus Reviews, *Vol. XLIX, No. 11, June 1, 1981, pp. 697-98.*

MICHELE M. LEBER

If the pace [in *The Third Deadly Sin*] is a bit ponderous, the sociology sometimes simplistic, and the plot somewhat predictable, Sanders still supplies a final shocker and a full measure of satisfaction. His waiting fans won't be disappointed.

> *Michele M. Leber, in a review of "The Third Deadly Sin," in* Library Journal, *Vol. 106, No. 13, July, 1981, p. 1444.*

EDWARD J. MILLER

For nearly fifteen years, Lawrence Sanders has given his followers a succession of well-written novels commencing with the *Anderson Tapes,* followed by the three *Deadly Sins* books, and his exceptional *Tenth Commandment.* His characters have always been skillfully and artfully sketched, as evidenced by Edward Delaney, the retired detective of the *Deadly Sins* books. While Sanders has not produced great literature, he has given us some of the best relaxation reading of the last two decades, and it was with a sense of anticipation that I commenced reading *The Case of Lucy Bending.*

Sanders's latest sleuth is a child psychiatrist, Dr. Theodore Levin, who practices in Florida. Lucy Bending, a child of eight, is obsessed with older men to the point where she caresses, fondles and attempts to seduce them at every opportunity.... Unfortunately, the reason for Lucy's actions becomes apparent to the average reader very early in the book, and the story then becomes hopelessly bogged down in endless psychiatric sessions.

In an apparent attempt to add some further interest to his suburban Florida Gold Coast setting, [Sanders] has several of the main characters involved in a Mafia financed pornographic film production company. Neither plot ever meets the other sufficiently. I constantly felt Sanders had started two separate books, found each one lacking, and drawing them together by a common thread of sex, decided to patch together a quick-sell follow-up to the success of *Tenth Commandment.*

Too bad! Sanders is a gifted storyteller and I felt cheated by this poorly crafted work.

> *Edward J. Miller, in a review of "The Case of Lucy Bending," in* Best Sellers, *Vol. 42, No. 7, October, 1982, p. 262.*

ARNOLD BERMAN

Folks have been swapping birthrights for pottage since the biblical Esau. With Peter Scuro, antihero of Sanders' latest [*The Seduction of Peter S.*], it's more a case of switching from unsuccessful actor (twelve years without a paying part) to partner in what becomes the most fantastic money-making in-house-and-outcall stud service for women you'll ever encounter. It gets so big that Peter and his partner cut in the mob in order to expand.

The book concerns itself predominantly with the minutest details of how this male call house was organized and operated, and how its staff of happy little helpers was recruited (at first from aspiring or failed actors, later from cooperative members of the armed forces on shore leave). Not slighted are blow-by-blow descriptions (that's tongue in cheek) of sexual deportment that make your wildest fantasies of Hollywood seem like pillow parties. Sanders is so much into this sort of stuff that he stops the forward action of the story for a kinky sex flashback which contributes nothing to an already bursting superfluity.

It's entirely too much like a textbook on how to open such an establishment. The pity is that Sanders is a good writer, and beneath all the commercial b.s. lurks a sensitive and poignant love story between Peter and the truly fine woman he loses. The whole thing becomes an overlong short story, even to an ironic short-storylike last line.

Arnold Berman, in a review of "The Seduction of Peter S.," in West Coast Review of Books, *Vol. 9, No. 5, September-October, 1983, p. 43.*

KIRKUS REVIEWS

Sanders, never the most tasteful of potboiler-makers, continues his descent into sheer dumb vulgarity—following **The Seduction of Peter S.** with [**The Passion of Molly T.**] a neanderthal political/sexual thriller about the feminist threat of the future. It's 1987, and the more militant National Women's Union (NWU) has replaced NOW as the most visible feminist activist group. But activism turns into terrorism at the Canton, W.Va., NWU chapter—after Norma Jane Laughlin, chapter president, is murdered by local bigots: her lesbian lover, Molly Turner, teams up with her cop brother-in-law Rod Harding (the local Alan Alda) to take vigilante vengeance. And soon Molly and Rod are leading the Women's Defense Corps (WDC), the NWU's "paramilitary division"—bombing porno-magazines, lynching rapists, etc. Meanwhile, however, there are nasty Washington, D.C. power-struggles going on amongst the NWU's top brass. . . . Virtually all the women here are lesbians or nymphos. The men are cartoon-slime or flat and faceless. The plot's a melodramatic mess, with totally implausible, naive future-politics at every turn. And the trashola prose features regular dollops of sub-literate laziness (including non-words like "arousement" and "assertation"). But, though limply idiotic as suspense and uncommonly vile as an attempt at misogynistic titillation, this is sure to sell fairly well—like **Peter S.**—thanks to the Sanders byline and the below-the-belt, lowest-common-denominator approach. (pp. 596-97)

A review of "The Passion of Molly T.," in Kirkus Reviews, *Vol. LII, No. 13, July 1, 1984, pp. 596-97.*

PUBLISHERS WEEKLY

It's hard to believe that Sanders, a master of the genre, is offering us [**The Passion of Molly T.**] with real seriousness of purpose. It is cast as much in the form of a report as a novel; its major thrust, the rise of a feminist movement through firebombings and assassinations, is not quite credible; and at least one of the characters is so broadly drawn it slips into caricature. But Sanders's practiced hand (**The Anderson Tapes,** etc.) is enough to drive the story steadily forward. (p. 54)

A review of "The Passion of Molly T.," in Publishers Weekly, *Vol. 226, No. 1, July 6, 1984, pp. 54-5.*

CHUCK MOSS

[In **The Fourth Deadly Sin**] Simon Ellerbee, eminent New York psychiatrist, is found with his head hammered in. Clearly someone out there just doesn't handle his emotions properly. Well, the shrink is dead and it's too late for a priest. What's needed is a cop.

Enter Edward X. Delaney, formerly NYPD chief of detectives, now retired. Last seen in **The Third Deadly Sin,** Delaney hears the firebell and trots out as a "consultant." He's got to solve the murder by year's end, and it's already Thanksgiving.

Lawrence Sanders writes mystery novels, not thrillers. There's a measured pace to his books, far removed from the usual Travis McGee-type page-turner. His characters are rarely in any personal danger and cases are solved by attention to detail and donkeywork, not by leaps in the dark with a knife between one's teeth.

So without thrills 'n' chills, Sanders' books must rely on different strengths to hook the reader: wit, setting, characterization, structure. Unfortunately, **The Fourth Deadly Sin** lacks enough panache to carry it through. Unlike the mannered and hilarious **Tenth Commandment,** this novel is just plain boring.

How come? Perhaps the fault lies with Delaney himself. A major literary sleuth must be believable, if eccentric, for no amount of quirks can substitute for humanity. But a reader also needs something beyond daily police blotter stuff to justify accompanying the sleuth for several hundred pages. Pizzazz helps.

Edward X. Delaney lacks that pizzazz. He's of Irish extraction, but there's no effervescent, Andrew Greeley-ish ethnicity to him. He's honest, painstaking and a good organizer. Big deal. His home life is bourgeois; his only vice is moderate gluttony.

True, the endless snack menu makes this a book to avoid if you're on a diet. But a Dagwood orgy is no substitute for characterization. This sad flaw is even sadder because the secondary characters are well-drawn and memorable. . . .

Too bland, too slow, too prosaic. These are what doom **The Fourth Deadly Sin.** It's not a very bad book, and with its crew of loonies it should have been a contender.

But like most jobs, solving murder is 90 percent tedium. Thus this novel is all too real, and ultimately boring—the deadliest sin of all.

Chuck Moss, "Ding Dong, the Shrink Is Dead," in The Detroit News, *July 21, 1985, p. 8B.*

LINDSEY GRUSON

It is a rare opportunity for Lawrence Sanders to exercise his greatest talent, providing a safe middle-class entry into the dark corners of sexually powered violence. [In **The Fourth Deadly Sin**] however, Mr. Sanders resists the temptation to indulge the reader with vicarious thrills. This time his book is not a literary peep show. The result is a leaner thriller. The plodding of Edward X. Delaney becomes intriguing reportage, mitigating Mr. Sanders' tendency to write as if he were giving directions for installing an automatic garage-door opener. That makes solving his latest crime a tantalizing puzzle. (pp. 18-19)

Lindsey Gruson, in a review of "The Fourth Deadly Sin," in The New York Times Book Review, *July 28, 1985, pp. 18-19.*

DONOVAN FITZPATRICK

The admirers of Lawrence Sanders' *Deadly Sin* novels, featuring that estimable retired chief of detectives Edward X. Delaney, are in for a surprise. This new sex and suspense thriller [**The Loves of Harry Dancer**] comes off as a mystery within an enigma. Harry Dancer, investment counselor, is grieving for his lovely wife, dead a month. For reasons that will not be explained later, he becomes the unwitting target of two groups engaged in a savage, all-out war for his . . . loyalty? The Department, whose logo is a blood-red rowel, assigns its specialist in seduction to turn Harry Dancer around. At the same time the Corporation unleashes its own talented seductress to capture Harry's heart. All of a sudden, Harry finds himself in sexual clover. . . . But hold. After some 200 pages, we learn the Corporation offers its converts ''Life Everlasting'' through suffering, sacrifice. Not happiness, but duty. God is the love object. Opposed to this credo, the Department promises wealth, power, physical delights. Hedonistic pleasures. . . . Are the Department and the Corporation the church and the Devil, locked in mortal combat for the souls of the citizenry? Is this perhaps a parable? Even Harry Dancer never finds out.

Donovan Fitzpatrick, in a review of ''The Loves of Harry Dancer,'' in The New York Times Book Review, *December 29, 1985, p. 18.*

Leonardo Sciascia

1921-

Sicilian novelist, essayist, short story writer, nonfiction writer, and dramatist.

Sciascia is among the most prominent contemporary Italian authors. Born and raised in Sicily, where he continues to live, Sciascia writes primarily of the pride, passion, and corruption that characterize Sicilian society. The workings of Sicilian politics and the influence of the Mafia provide the background for Sciascia's exploration of his predominant theme: the struggle of the individual who seeks justice in the midst of social iniquities and official complicity. Many of Sciascia's novels are characterized as detective or mystery fiction. While they commonly depict a detective attempting to uncover the mystery behind a crime, these works are concerned less with "whodunit" than with the workings of the criminal system and the hypocrisy and corruption that permeate all levels of society. Sciascia is considered to be a gifted stylist writing in the realistic tradition, and his novels can be read both as suspenseful entertainments and as serious investigations of political intrigue and conspiracy.

Sciascia's first significant publication, *Le parrocchie di Regalpetra* (1956; *Salt in the Wound*), is a collection of short pieces set in Regalpetra, a fictional town which recurs in many of Sciascia's works and is patterned after his hometown of Racalmuto. Part fiction and part documentary, these essays address the historical realities that have given rise to the housing, health, and working conditions of contemporary Sicilian peasants. Verina Jones observed: "This historical dimension, which persists in Sciascia's later writings, is a fundamental aspect of his approach to social reality. The ills of present-day Regalpetra are not to be seen merely as something to be observed and denounced, but as problems to be overcome." The narrative technique and social realism of *Salt in the Wound* foreshadow Sciascia's later essays, including those collected in *Pirandello e la Sicilia* (1961) and *La corda pazza* (1970), as well as his novels and short stories. As Jones noted, "in Sciascia's subjective judgement the difference between essay-writing and narrative in his own work is marginal."

Sciascia's suspense novels, for which he is best known outside of Italy, include *Il giorno della civetta* (1961; *Mafia Vendetta;* later published as *The Day of the Owl*), *A ciascuno il suo* (1966; *A Man's Blessing*), *Il contesto* (1971; *Equal Danger*), and *Todo modo* (1974; *One Way or Another*). Central to these novels is the political structure of Sicilian society, and central to this political system is *omertà*, which Frank Kermode described as "a concept for which English has no single word. *Omertà* has to do with a manliness that is expressed by silence, like the schoolboy code that will not allow one to name the thief or bully; but its main support is fear of reprisals." The detectives in Sciascia's novels frequently come up against *omertà* in their investigations; citizens are unwilling to talk, officials and criminals alike are elusive, and, as Kermode remarked, "there are . . . no witnesses to a *mafia* murder." The more the detectives seek reason and justice, the further they get from attaining their goals. Sciascia's crime novels generally end on a note of failure and despair, leaving the network of corruption exposed but uncontested.

© *Jerry Bauer*

Sciascia has also written novels outside the mystery genre. *Il consiglio d'Egitto* (1963; *The Council of Egypt*), *La morte dell'inquisitore* (1964; *Death of the Inquisitor*), and *La scomparsa di Majorana* (1975) are historically-based works that exemplify Sciascia's social concerns and his interest in justice and evil. *The Council of Egypt*, set in the eighteenth century, revolves around an incident of forgery and deception; *Death of the Inquisitor* is an investigation into a seventeenth-century murder committed in connection with the Roman Catholic Inquisition; and in *La scomparsa di Majorana*, Sciascia speculates on the fate of Ettore Majorana, an Italian scientist who vanished at the start of World War II. Sciascia is also the author of *Candido; ovvero, un songo fatto in Sicilia* (1977; *Candido; or, a Dream Dreamed in Sicily*), a contemporary version of Voltaire's *Candide*. This novel chronicles the misadventures of Candido Munafò, a young Italian whose simplistic honesty and benevolence disrupt the corrupt established order. The novel displays Sciascia's ironic approach to social criticism. Victor Carrabino praised *Candido* for the combination of "the lightness and the humor with which [its] pages have been written" and the "seriousness and commitment of Sciascia's thought."

Sciascia's prolific output also includes such short story collections as *Gli zii di Sicilia* (1958; *Sicilian Uncles*) and *Il mare colore del vino* (1973; *The Wine-Red Sea*), as well as numerous nonfiction works and two plays: *L'onorevole, dramma in tre atti* (1965) and *Recitazione della controversia liparitana dedicata ad A.D.* (1969; *Story of the Liparitana Controversy*). In all of Sciascia's works, the history, politics, and interplay of crime and authority in Sicily symbolize the greater evils of the contemporary world, leading Bryan Rostron to assert that although Sciascia "writes about his own difficult, intractable island," he is "the most universal of Italian writers."

(See also *CLC*, Vols. 8, 9 and *Contemporary Authors*, Vols. 85-88.)

VICTOR CARRABINO

Sciascia's *Candido* resembles Voltaire's *Candide* both in the protagonist's penchant for simplifying matters and in the very style of the *contes philosophiques*. Besides these similarities, the sly irony of the Sicilian author is felt in every page.

In the present volume Sciascia recounts the adventures and misfortunes of a young Sicilian man, Candido Munafò. The book opens with Munafò's birth in a Sicilian cavern on the night of 9-10 July 1943—the unforgettable night during which the Anglo-American troops landed in Sicily—and closes in Paris in 1977. With the same lightness of touch and rapidity of Voltaire's conte, Sciascia presents events as they took place between those years. He never attempts, however, to closely examine or speculate on them.

Candido Munafò may be considered an orphan. His mother left him while he was still very young, when she ran away to the United States with an American captain. His father, a lawyer, committed suicide a few years later, feeling that his career had been ruined by Candido. Candido was then put in the custody of his maternal grandfather—an ex-Fascist general and later a Christian Democrat delegate. Candido finally finds his ideal double in don Antonio—an ex-priest who later joins the Communist Party. Another Pangloss in Sicilian clothes, don Antonio examines the myths that hover over modern man, such as politics, religion and psychoanalysis. . . .

Candido's way of simplifying everything draws him to a simple yet profound judgment of life—reminiscent of Montaigne's thought. It is through this simplicity that Candido arrives at the essential element of life, at the heart of things. . . . However, this eagerness to simplify everything does not make life easier to our "little monster." Although Candido had found in the Communist Party "l'istinto della conservazione, la volontà di sopravvivere," he was soon expelled from the Party by his comrade, the Party Secretary, whom Candido had ridiculed publicly—Candido had given him the nickname of Fomà Fomíč (a Dostoevskian character known for being utterly loquacious, pedantic and ridiculous).

Once again Sciascia offers the reader a work of art which is truly entertaining and yet invites him to reflect on the true meaning of life. Besides the lightness and the humor with which these pages have been written, the seriousness and commitment of Sciascia's thought invite the reader to identify himself with Candido. . . . Finally, all is simple and nothing is simple: "Greve è il nostro tempo, assai greve."

> *Victor Carrabino, in a review of "Candido," in* World Literature Today, *Vol. 53, No. 1, Winter, 1979, p. 97.*

PETER S. PRESCOTT

[The protagonist of Leonardo Sciascia's *Candido*] is a young Sicilian so innocent that he is regarded by his family as a monster—as well he might be, for inevitably his simplicity produces havoc among all who are touched by it. Because honesty, lack of self-interest and the will to do good to others are qualities the world cannot abide, Candido is roundly punished for presumptuously possessing them. He inherits an estate; by attempting to farm his land he infuriates his tenants who prefer the evils of an absentee landlord. So much for the joys of cultivating one's own garden. He tries to give part of his land to charity—but charity wants only that which is obtained by bribery and price-gouging. He tries to give his entire estate to the Communists—who reject it because peasants prefer to work on other people's land and won't tolerate living collectively.

Candido must submit to more such pummeling before finding tranquillity with his mistress and the defrocked priest who serves him in the role of Pangloss. Life may be, he suspects, a simple thing, but the telling of fables is not necessarily as simple as Voltaire made it seem. Sciascia, the author of a number of brief, sardonic morality tales, is always oblique, at times obscure—the kind of writer who can finish a murder story without feeling obliged to identify the killer. This story, too, has a quicksilver quality—no one in it ever does or says quite what the occasion requires—but it may please readers who have been put off by the bleakness of Sciascia's earlier work. His wintry pessimism seems warmer here, as if, convinced of human incorrigibility, he now sees no reason not to be charming when he must cope with our condition.

> *Peter S. Prescott, "A 'Candide' for Our Times," in* Newsweek, *Vol. XCIV, No. 13, September 24, 1979, p. 102.*

ANTHONY BURGESS

Leonardo Sciascia's new novella [*Candido; or, a Dream Dreamed in Sicily*] is slight enough in bulk to get itself lost among *Chesapeake's Choice* and the rest of the American giants, but its lightness and brevity belie a gravity of achievement that makes many of those giants seem like Macy's Thanksgiving parade balloons. The short way is still the European way: the craft is one of compression, and Mr. Sciascia's title invokes one of the greatest of the compressors. *Candide* has illegitimately fathered many epigoni, but *Candido* is an offspring of which Voltaire himself would have approved had he understood what has been going on in modern Sicily. . . .

Candido, born in 1943, while the Allies are knocking hell out of Sicily, is abandoned by his mother, who goes off to America with a U.S. Army officer; then he unwittingly provokes the suicide of his father, a hapless lawyer, by revealing—on the basis of an overheard conversation—that one of his clients, a man accused of murder and presumed innocent, is really guilty. Brought up by an archpriest, Candido encourages his mentor to act with unpriestly veracity in another legal scandal involving a lawyer who has shot a priest for defiling his daughter. . . .

Candido, who has inherited land, makes himself unpopular with the peasants by working some of the land himself and trying to improve farming techniques. He is not a gentleman: by soiling his hands, he appears to be parodying or mocking those to whom the soil provides an ungrateful living. Like the former archpriest, now known as Don Antonio, Candido shifts his adherence from the Church to the Communist Party, but he always says the wrong thing at party meetings. He cuts through the doctrinaire verbiage to the truth, believing that everything is fundamentally quite simple. . . .

Candido ends up in Turin—which has become an outpost of Sicily—only to find that the Communists there are, in their own way, just as ineffectual. They all talk of enforced exile—in France, Spain, the United States. Why not Russia? asks Candido. That is the wrong thing to say. And so on.

American readers who find American towns also, in some measure, outposts of Sicily will want to know how the Mafia fits into the story. The Mafia doesn't: the Mafia only appears toward the end, when Don Antonio asks the American who has married Candido's mamma why his compatriots put Sicily in the Mafia's hands when they liberated Italy. . . . There's madness enough in Sicily where rigid Catholicism confronts equally rigid Communism, where the deadliest of the sins is generous, innocent simplicity. In this lucid fable, we don't need the Mafia as well.

Mr. Sciascia, who, we are told, has quarrelled with the party, is revealed here as a true Voltairean liberal, dubious about all modes of reform. Perhaps the only solution to the general Italian mess, and, by extension, the world mess, is the cultivation of one's garden, which, in this novel, means earning a living, making love and drinking a little wine. According to Mr. Sciascia, Paris is the place where the gardens of the spirit and the senses may best be cultivated—Paris being the Mecca of all who are exasperated by Sicilian stupidity. How it must feel to be a Parisian Candido is, of course, another story.

I have read this novel in the original Italian and am able to praise the translation as not merely accurate but elegant. This is, after all, a very European story, and the English is properly European. Through this story, the American reader will gain some notion of the grace and wit of Mr. Sciascia's prose. He is a writer of great importance, one of a holy trinity whose other incarnations are Italo Calvino and Alberto Moravia.

Anthony Burgess, "A Very European Story," in The New York Times Book Review, *October 7, 1979, p. 14.*

GORE VIDAL

[*The essay from which the following excerpt is taken originally appeared in* The New York Review of Books, *October 25, 1979.*]

Sciascia is unique among Sicilian artists in that he never abandoned Sicily for what Sicilians call "the continent." Like the noble Lampedusa, he has preferred to live and to work in his native Sicily. This means that, directly and indirectly, he has had to contend all his life with the mafia and the Church, with fascism and communism, with the family, history. During the last quarter century, Sciascia has made out of his curious Sicilian experience a literature that is not quite like anything else ever done by a European—because Sicily is not part of Europe?—and certainly unlike anything done by a North American.

To understand Sciascia, one must understand when and where he was born and grew up and lived. Although this is true of any writer, it is crucial to the understanding of someone who was born in Sicily in 1921 (the year before Mussolini marched on Rome); who grew up under fascism; who experienced the liberation of Sicily by Lucky Luciano, Vito Genovese, and the

American army; who has lived long enough to see the consumer society take root in Sicily's stony soil. (p. 93)

During Sciascia's youth the Sicilians despised fascism because it was not only an alien form of government (what continental government is not alien to the Sicilians?) but a peculiarly oppressive alien government. The fascists tried to *change* the Sicilians. Make them wear uniforms. Conform them to the Duce's loony pseudo-Roman norm. Although Mussolini himself paid little attention to the island, he did manage to get upstaged in the piazza of Piano dei Greci by the capo of the local mafia, one Don Ciccio Cuccia. Aware that appearance is everything and substance nothing, Mussolini struck back at Don Ciccio (he put him in jail), at the mafia in general (he sent down an efficient Inspector named Mori who did the mafia a good deal of damage post-1924), at Piano dei Greci (Mussolini changed the name Greci to Albanese . . . more Roman).

By the time that Sciascia was fourteen years old, Mussolini was able to announce—almost accurately—that he had broken the back of the mafia. Pre-Mori, ten people were murdered a day in Sicily; post-Mori only three were murdered a week. Meanwhile, Inspector Mori was trying to change the hearts and minds of the Sicilians. In a moment of inspiration, he offered a prize to the best school-boy essay on how to combat the mafia. Although there were, predictably, no entries at the time, Sciascia has been trying ever since to explain to Inspector Mori how best to combat or cope with the mafia, with Sicily, with the family, history, life. (pp. 93-4)

[Like] most writers-to-be, the young Sciascia read whatever he could. He was particularly attracted to the eighteenth-century writers of the Enlightenment. If he has a precursor, it is Voltaire. Predictably, he preferred Diderot to Rousseau. "Sicilian culture ignored or rejected romanticism until it arrived from France under the name of realism." Later, Sciascia was enchanted—and remains enchanted—by Sicily's modern master, Pirandello. As a boy, "I lived inside Pirandello's world, and Pirandellian drama—identity, the relativeness of things—was my daily dream. I almost thought that I was mad." But, ultimately, "I held fast to reason," as taught by Diderot, Courier, Manzoni.

Although Sciascia is a Pirandellian as well as a man of the Enlightenment, he has a hard clarity, reminiscent of Stendhal. At the age of five, he saw the sea: "I didn't like it, and I still don't like it. Sicilians don't like the sea, even those who live on its shores. For that matter, the majority of Sicilian towns have been built with their backs to the sea, ostentatiously. How could islanders like the sea which is capable only of carrying their men away as emigrants or bringing in invaders?" (p. 95)

[After the war, although] everyone agreed that Sicily's only hope was industrialization, the mafia fought industrialization because industry meant labor unions and labor unions (they thought naïvely) are not susceptible to the usual pressures of the honorable society which does and does not exist, rather like the trinity. The first battle between mafia and industrialization occurred when Sciascia was twenty-three. The communists and socialists held a meeting in the piazza of Villalba. Authority challenged, the local capo ordered his thugs to open fire. Legal proceedings dragged on for ten years by which time the capo had died a natural death.

What happened at Villalba made a strong impression on Sciascia. Sometimes, in his work, he deals with it directly and realistically; other times, he is oblique and fantastic. But he has never *not*, in a symbolic sense, dealt with this business.

Even *Todo Modo* (1974) was an attempt to analyze those forces that opposed one another on a September day in 1944, in a dusty piazza, abruptly loud with guns.

Today the mafia thrives in Sicily. Gangs still extort money from citrus growers. . . . Mafia gangs control dockworkers, the sale of contraband, construction permits, etc. Meanwhile, as Sciascia has described more than once, those continentals who come to Sicily as prosecutors and police inspectors soon learn that the true lover of justice must love death, too. Many of Sciascia's tales have, at their heart, thanatophilia. Lately, he has extended the geographical range of his novels. All Italy is now in the process of being Sicilianized. (pp. 95-6)

What is the mafia mentality? What is the mafia? What is Sicily? When it comes to the exploration of this particular hell, Leonardo Sciascia is the perfect Virgil. As we begin our descent, he reminds us that like most Mediterranean societies Sicily is a matriarchy. . . . Effigies of the original Great Goddess of the Mediterranean can still be seen all over Sicily. (p. 96)

The sea at the center of the earth is the sea of the mother, and this blood-dark sea is at the heart of Sciascia's latest novel *Candido:* the story of a Sicilian who, during an American air-raid in 1943, was born to a mother whom he was to lose in childhood to another culture; thus making it possible for him to begin a journey that would remove him from the orbit of the mother goddess. (p. 97)

[The] child is named, "surreally," Candido: neither parent has ever heard of Voltaire. The town is occupied by the American army and Captain John H. (for Hamlet) Dykes becomes, in effect, the mayor. Candido's lawyer-father asks the American to dinner, and Candido's mother falls in love with him. Sourly, surreally, the father comes to believe that Dykes is the blond Candido's father even though the child was conceived nine months before the arrival in Sicily of the Americans. Nevertheless, in the father's mind, Candido is always "the American."

As a result of the April 18, 1948 election . . . , the Christian Democrat party doubled its vote and Candido's Fascist grandfather, the General, was elected to parliament while the General's aide-de-camp, a local nobleman, was also elected but on the Communist ticket. Nicely, the two ex-fascists work in tandem. Meanwhile, Candido's mother has divorced his father and gone to live with her American lover in Helena, Montana. Candido is left behind.

Sciascia's Candido is a serene, not particularly wide-eyed version of Voltaire's Candide. In fact, this Sicilian avatar is a good deal cleverer than the original. As a boy, "His games—we can try to define them only approximately—were like cross-word puzzles which he would play with things. Adults make words cross, but Candido made things cross." One of the things that he makes cross . . . cross the shining river, in fact . . . is his lawyer-father who has assisted in the cover-up of a murder. When Candido overhears a discussion of the murder, he promptly tells his schoolmates the true story. As a result of the boy's candor, the father commits suicide and Candido, now known as "the little monster," goes to live with the General. At no point does Candido feel the slightest guilt. (pp. 97-8)

It is now time for Dr. Pangloss to make his entrance, disguised as the Archpriest Lepanto. Highly civilized priests keep recurring in Sciascia's work, although he confesses that "I have never met one."

The Archpriest and the boy spar with each other. "Up to a point, the Archpriest also was convinced that he was a little monster . . . whereas Candido had discovered that the Archpriest had a kind of fixed idea, rather complicated but reducible, more or less, to these terms: all little boys kill their fathers, and some of them, sometimes, kill even Our Father Who is in Heaven." Patiently, Candido sets out to disabuse the Archpriest: "he had not killed his father, and he knew nothing, nor did he want to know anything, about that other Father."

Sciascia's themes now begin to converge. The mother has abandoned the son, a very good thing in the land of the Great Goddess (who would be Attis, who Pan could be?); the father has killed himself because of Candido's truthfulness or candor when he made cross the thing-truth with the thing-*omerta;* now the Heavenly Father, or Aryan sky-god, is found to be, by Candido, simply irrelevant. Plainly, Candido is a monster. He is also free. He becomes even freer when he inherits money and land. But when he cultivates his own land for the good of his tenant farmers, they know despair. When a parish priest is murdered (with the regularity of a Simenon, Sciascia produces his murders), Candido and the Archpriest decide to assist the inspector of police. When, rather cleverly, they apprehend the murderer, everyone is in a rage. They—not he—have broken the code. A theologian is called in by the local bishop and an inquiry is held into the Archpriest's behavior. It is decided that he must

> step down as archpriest: he could not continue to fulfill that office if all the faithful now disapproved of him, even despised him. "And further," the learned theologian said, "not that truth may not be beautiful, but at times it does so much harm that to withhold it is not a fault but a merit."
>
> In handing the theologian his resignation, the Archpriest, now archpriest no longer, said, in a parodying, almost lilting voice, "'I am the way, the truth, and the life,' but sometimes I am the blind alley, the lie, and death."

With that, the moral education of Candido is complete. On the other hand that of Dr. Pangloss has just begun. (pp. 98-9)

The political education of Candido—as opposed to moral—begins in early manhood. Like so many educated Italians of that time, he regards communism as a replacement for a church that has not only failed but in the land of the Great Goddess never truly taken hold. Candido likes the writings of Gramsci; finds Marx boring; as for Lenin, "he had come to picture Lenin as a carpenter atop a scaffolding who had worn himself out hitting the same nails on the head, but all of his efforts had not prevented some nails from being poorly set or going in crooked." (pp. 99-100)

But Candido becomes a member of the Communist Party even though he is more repelled than not by its sacred texts (excepting, always, Gramsci). Acting on principle, Candido offers his own land for a hospital but because of the usual collusion between the *condottiere* of the left and the right, another piece of land is *bought* by the community and the *condottiere* make their profit. Candido is thrown out of the Communist Party. In due course, after he is done out of his fortune by his own family, he goes off with his cousin Francesca to Turin, "a more and more sullen city. . . . The North and the South of Italy settled there; they sought crazily to avoid each other and, at the same time, to strike out at each other; both were bottled up in making automobiles, a superfluous necessity for all, a necessary superfluity for all.'' Just before the young couple move on to Paris, Candido says to Francesca, ''Do you know what our life is, yours and mine? It's a dream dreamed in Sicily. Perhaps we're still there, and we are dreaming.''

In Paris, at the Brasserie Lipp (August 1977), Candido runs into the long-mislaid mother and her husband Mr. Dykes. Don Antonio is also there: he is now as doctrinaire a Communist as he had been a Roman Catholic. Predictably, the Americans have little to say to the Sicilians. But Don Antonio does ask former Captain Dykes: ''How did you manage, only a few days after you had arrived in our town, to choose our worst citizens for public service?'' Dykes is offhand: he had been given a list. Yes, he had suspected that the people on the list were mafiosi, ''But we were fighting a war. . . .''

When Candido's mother, rather halfheartedly, proposes that Candido visit America, Candido is polite. For a visit perhaps. '''But as for living there, I want to live here. . . . Here you feel that something is about to end and something is about to begin. I'd like to see what should come to an end come to its end.' Embracing him once again, his mother thought, He's a monster.'' Mother and son part, presumably forever.

Rather drunk, Don Antonio has, once again, missed the point to what Candido has been saying. Don Antonio says that ''here,'' meaning France, ''something is about to end, and it's beautiful. . . . At home, nothing ends, nothing ever ends.'' On the way back to his hotel, Don Antonio salutes the statue of Voltaire as ''our true father!'' But Candido demurs; and the book's last line is: '''Let's not begin again with the fathers,' he said. He felt himself a child of fortune, and happy.'' *Magari* as the Italians say.

I am not sure just what it is that makes Sciascia's novels unique. Where ''serious'' American writers tend to let the imagination do the work of the imagination, Sciascia prefers to invent for us a world quite as real as any that Dreiser ever dealt with, rendered in a style that is, line by line, as jolting as an exposed electrical wire. I suppose, as a Pirandellian, Sciascia is letting a very real world imagine *him* describing it. (pp. 100-01)

''Remember,'' Sciascia said to Marcelle Padovani, ''what Malraux said of Faulkner? 'He has managed to intrude Greek tragedy into the detective story.' It might be said of me that I have brought Pirandellian drama to the detective story!'' Often disguised as detective stories, Sciascia's novels are also highly political in a way quite unlike anything that has ever been done in English. While the American writer searches solemnly for his identity, Sciascia is on the trail of a murderer who, invariably, turns out to be not so much a specific character as a social system. That mafia which Americans find so exciting and even admirable is for Sciascia the evil consequence of a long bad history, presided over by The Kindly Ones. Whenever (as in *Il Giorno della Civetta*, 1961) one of Sciascia's believers in justice confronts the mafia (which everyone says—in the best Pirandellian manner—does not exist), he is not only defeated, but, worse, he is never understood. (pp. 104-05)

A decade later, in *Il Contesto,* Sciascia again concerns himself with justice. But now he has moved toward a kind of surrealism. Sometimes the country he writes about is Italy; sometimes not. A man has gone to prison for a crime that he did not commit. When he gets out of prison, he decides to kill off the country's judges. When Inspector Rogas tries to track down the killer, he himself is murdered. In a splendid dialogue with the country's Chief Justice, Inspector Rogas is told that ''the

only possible form of justice, of the administration of justice, could be, and will be, the form that in a military war is called decimation. One man answers for humanity. And humanity answers for the one man.''

Although moral anarchy is at the basis of this ancient society, Sciascia himself has by no means given up. The epigraphs to *Il Contesto* are very much to the point. First, there's a quotation from Montaigne: ''One must do as the animals do, who erase every footprint in front of their lair.'' Then a response from Rousseau: ''O Montaigne! You who pride yourself on your candor and truthfulness, be sincere and truthful, if a philosopher can be so, and tell me whether there exists on earth a country where it is a crime to keep one's given word and to be clement and generous, where the good man is despised and the wicked man honored.'' Sciascia then quotes Anonymous: ''O Rousseau!'' One has a pretty good idea who this particular Anonymous is.

It is Sciascia's self-appointed task to erase the accumulated footprints (history) in front of the animal's lair (Sicily, Italy, the world). The fact that he cannot undo the remembered past has not prevented him from making works of art or from introducing a healthy skepticism into the sterile and abstract political discourse of his country. No other Italian writer has said, quite so bluntly, that the historic compromise would lead to ''a regime in which, finally and enduringly, the two major parties would be joined in a unified management of power to the preclusion of all alternatives and all opposition. Finally, the Italians would be tranquil, irresponsible, no longer forced to think, to evaluate, to choose.''

Rather surprisingly, Sciascia seems not to have figured out what the historic compromise ultimately signifies. When he does, he will realize that Italy's two great unloved political parties are simply the flitting shadows of two larger entities. As any Voltairean knows, the Vatican and the Kremlin have more in common than either has with the idea of a free society. Once each realizes that the other is indeed its logical mate, Sciascia will be able to write his last detective story, in which the murder will be done with mirrors. Meanwhile, he continues to give us all sorts of clues; reminds us that criminals are still at large; demonstrates that life goes on *todo modo*. (pp. 105-06)

Gore Vidal, ''Sciascia's Italy,'' in his The Second American Revolution and Other Essays (1976-1982), *Random House, 1982, pp. 91-106.*

JoANN CANNON

Many of Italy's most prominent modern writers have borrowed from the detective story, an exceedingly conventional genre, to create some of the most original and unconventional fiction of our century. . . . Of all of Italy's contemporary writers, Leonardo Sciascia is, perhaps, the most irresistibly drawn to the detective genre. Four of Sciascia's major novels, *Il giorno della civetta, A ciascuno il suo, Il contesto,* and *Todo modo,* take the form of detective stories. (pp. 523-24)

Sciascia's writing generally falls into three distinct categories: historical essays, historical fiction, and ''detective'' fiction. Sciascia's predilection for detection is intimately related to his historical bias: the process of ratiocination whereby the detective assembles the pieces of the puzzle parallels the process whereby the historian retrospectively reconstructs a series of past events. In *Morte dell'Inquisitore,* the author plays the role of the detective as he assembles and interprets fragments of historical documents in an attempt to reconstruct the legend of Fra Diego La Matina, a seventeenth-century Augustinian monk who, persecuted by the Inquisition, assassinated his inquisitor. Sciascia's interest in historical reconstruction is again apparent in *La scomparsa di Majorana,* where the author attempts to solve the mystery of the disappearance on the eve of World War Two of Italy's most prominent young physicist. Time and again Sciascia assumes the task of solving history's unsolved puzzles.

The modes of discourse Sciascia favors, the detective novel and the historical reconstruction, seem to be grounded in an implicit faith in the power of reason. The detective story has been said to have originated in the eighteenth century as an expression of the conflict between rationality and irrationality. Whether this theory of origins is historically valid, the detective story as a *forma mentis* certainly belongs to the Enlightenment, the period to which Sciascia himself repeatedly turns for his models. The prototype of Sciascia's enlightened hero is Di Blasi, the Jacobin lawyer of *Il consiglio d'Egitto,* whose dreams of a Republican Revolution in Sicily and a "mondo illuminato dalla ragione" led him to the guillotine. Several of Sciascia's fictional detectives, Captain Bellodi of *Il giorno della civetta* and Inspector Rogas of *Il contesto,* derive their ideals from the *siècle des lumières.* Sciascia has often identified himself as an "enlightened" man. . . . Yet, unlike the typical *giallo,* Sciascia's detective novels do not present the detective as the embodiment of the triumph of reason; his fictional heroes are inevitably defeated. Moreover, his detective novels invariably deal with unjust, corrupt societies—the antithesis of the "mondo illuminato dalla ragione" in which the classical *giallo* is set. Like many of his contemporaries, Sciascia adopts the format of the detective novel although thwarting to some degree the expectations awakened by that generic choice. . . . Sciascia's increasing departure from the norms of detective fiction [can be seen] as a reflection of the author's decreasing faith in the power of reason in an irrational world. (pp. 524-25)

> JoAnn Cannon, "The Detective Fiction of Leonardo Sciascia," in Modern Fiction Studies, Vol. 29, No. 3, Autumn, 1983, pp. 523-34.

FRANK KERMODE

The detection of crime is a theme of many great novels, but the present century has seen the development of the highly specialized detective or crime story which, in its purest form, is more of a puzzle than a novel. In books of that sort the interest is almost entirely in the intellectual exercise; you must decide what the clues are, for they are sometimes concealed or deceptive and sometimes ostentatious. The detective with whom you are working may be eccentric, an aristocratic loner or a sharp schoolmistress or an Australian aborigine; but the story will only in passing or by inadvertence say anything serious about the society in which these people work, and in which a particular crime occurred. And although the detective will often be contrasted with the policeman, representing the powers of intuition or the free spirit as against routine and plodding intellect, each has society on his side and will bring its enemies to book. (p. i)

Only very rarely can we say of such works that they look at questions of social justice with the informed eye of the intelligent artist. We can, however, make that claim for the stories of Leonardo Sciascia. He has reinvented the detective story

and made it worthy of himself—that is, of one of the best living writers.

Sciascia is a Sicilian, born in 1921 in Racalmuto, the small town where he still lives part of the year, and which figures (as Regalpetra) in several of his books. . . . He is conscious of his descent in a line of important Sicilian writers—Verga, Pirandello, Quasimodo, Lampedusa—who achieved international fame without losing their native tone and color. Sciascia is now famous in Italy and France; acclaim for his work in the English-speaking world has been slow to come, but it is bound to increase. He is no more to be thought of as the novelist of a limited region than Faulkner or Lampedusa.

His Sicily is not the country of the aristocratic Lampedusa; or, rather, it is Sicily seen in a wholly different perspective. (p. ii)

[In Sciascia's Sicily] it seems to be in the very nature of things that the innocent should be oppressed, and that the forces of justice and order should be at the disposal of evil and unassailable men. And so Sciascia's Sicily, though he loves it as his native place, becomes a figure for privation and corruption, and the *mafia* a kind of human version of the horrors of the sulfur mine and the *chiarchiaro* of *The Day of the Owl,* that "black-holed sponge soaking up the light flooding the landscape," which Bellodi, the detective, associates with "the struggle and defeat of God in the human heart."

The history of Sicily in the twenty years or so since Sciascia published *The Day of the Owl* has only confirmed this view of it. The *mafia* began as an agrarian phenomenon, but increasing industrialization has not killed it off, and it has adapted itself to the modern world—and not only to Sicily and the rest of Italy; its business links with the United States are well known. It has thrived on fear and silence, on *omertà,* a concept for which English has no single word. *Omertà* has to do with a manliness that is expressed by silence, like the schoolboy code that will not allow one to name the thief or bully; but its main support is fear of reprisals. There are, as *The Day of the Owl* tells us in its brilliant opening pages, no witnesses to a *mafia* murder. There has been some change of late. . . . [But] it is certainly no less plausible now than it was then to see in the *mafia* an image of an apparently incurable disease that blights civilization and crushes the few honorable and decent human beings who resist it.

Sciascia once said in an interview, "I've tried to understand why a person is *mafioso.* To this end I've written a book—and I still think it's a good book although I don't like it, in a way I detest it, but I think I've explained why an individual is *mafioso.*" To do that, he needed to show that the entire social structure was permeated by the disease; and that is his great, despairing subject, the sickness of human society, of which the *mafia* is only a repulsive symptom. (pp. iii-iv)

We are obviously dealing with a very unusual crime story writer. And we cannot bracket off these short novels as "entertainments" in the Graham Greene sense; they are not to be thought of as a sort of appendix to a body of more serious and important work. Sciascia is a fairly prolific writer, and his work includes historical novels, plays, diaries, and comments on current affairs; but there is no relaxation in the detective stories, rather a continuous and highly literary attention to his great subject, which is often treated with bitter humor. "Italy," remarks a character in *A Man's Blessing*—a man named Benito, of the same age as Mussolini, who is convinced that the taint of Fascism still lingers—"Italy is a country so blessed that for every weed they destroy, two spring up in its place." In Sciascia irony and humor, like everything else, including those long extraordinary conversations on justice which might seem to have no place in detective stories, are at the service of a project that is never less than serious. (pp. v-vi)

[It is] realism that distinguishes the writings of Sciascia from other works apparently of the same genre but in fact more properly thought of as self-indulgent fantasies. "One corollary of all the detective novels to which a goodly share of mankind repairs for refreshment specifies that a crime present its investigators with a picture, the material and, so to speak, stylistic elements of which, if meticulously assembled and analyzed, permit a sure solution. In actuality, however, the situation is different. The coefficients of impunity and error are high not because, or not only or not always because, the investigators are men of small intelligence but because the clues a crime offers are usually utterly inadequate. A crime, that is to say, which is planned or committed by people who have every interest in working to keep the impunity coefficient high. The factors that lead to the solution of seemingly mysterious or gratuitous crimes are what may be called the professional stool pigeon, the anonymous informer, and chance. And to a degree—but only to a degree—the acuteness of the investigators." So Sciascia, explaining why *A Man's Blessing* will remain within the limits of the probable, and why its investigator, an observant but not a wise or street-wise professor, must fail. So must the detectives of *The Day of the Owl* and *Equal Danger,* though they are, each in his own way, more admirable than the professor. The "impunity coefficient" confronting them is just as high. (pp. vii-viii)

Towards the end of *The Day of the Owl* there is a sardonic scene in which two Sicilians attend a session of the Parliament in Rome. Crude, foreign, they murmur the old insult of cuckoldry at the fascist who asserts (with some superficial justice) that in the fascist times Sicily was better run, the *mafia* better controlled; and they hear, too, the government claim that the so-called *mafia* exists only in the imagination of the Left. Back in Parma, Bellodi decides to go back south and try again, as Sciascia himself will, from a perverse love of Sicily.

But the *mafia* phenomenon, being a product of human evil, spreads everywhere. Five years after *The Day of the Owl* Sciascia published *A Man's Blessing.* Here a death-threat to a pharmacist, and the subsequent murder of this man and a doctor friend, when they are out hunting, turns into a matter of national politics—the sell-out of the Communist Party to the Christian Democrats. The Italian title of the book, *A Ciascuno il suo* ("to each his own") is a translation of the Vatican newspaper's Latin motto, *Osservatore Romano, Unicuique suum;* the anonymous letter containing the death-threat had been made up of words cut from that newspaper. The professor who notices this begins an investigation, not because he desires to convict anybody of the murder, but out of curiosity, because he, too, is the product of "the centuries of contempt that an oppressed people, an eternally vanquished people, had heaped on the law." In fact, timid and mother-dominated as he is, he knows less of what is going on than anybody, and becomes a victim of his own sexual frustration. He is very little different from the hoodlums and voyeurs, for all his education and culture, and he ends up dead in an abandoned sulfur mine, having uncovered some small truths but still ignorant of other, larger ones, such as the complicity of the Church in shady political deals.

The professor is not merely a Sicilian, however; he is like all of us who feel uneasy when confronted with the law and the bureaucracy. On his way to get the certificate of a clean police record needed when applying for a driver's license, he "was masochistically mulling over the apprehensions typical of any Italian about to enter the labyrinth of a public office building, especially one that goes by the name of Justice.". . . . We fear both the power of the law and its possible corruption. Perhaps it was to emphasize this universality that Sciascia set his third detective story, *Equal Danger* (1971), in an imaginary country that is and is not Italy. What was called, in *The Day of the Owl,* the "natural tragic solitude" of the Sicilian may now be seen as a universal condition. And, as the author remarks in his concluding note, the details may be Sicilian or Italian, but the substance of the book "must be that of a fable about power anywhere in the world."

The Italian title of *Equal Danger* is *Il Contesto, The Context,* suggesting the scope of the fable: the investigator Rogas is not dealing with the crimes of individual *mafiosi,* but with the whole system, which of course he cannot beat. When the first lawyer is killed Rogas is told that his inquiries must not prejudice the dead man's reputation. As the killings continue, one judge or prosecutor after another, he is again told to abandon his trail, but "Rogas had principles in a country where almost no one did," and carries on, even when demoted. He refuses to accept the "insurrectional cadre" theory because he will not give up the view that the murderer is avenging a wrongful conviction; he has no great faith in official justice, and no desire to cover up the past by falsifying the present. (pp. ix-xi)

As a story of action [*Equal Danger*] ends with a situation of strange and potent ironies. Rogas dies with the Communist leader Amar when they meet in secret at the National Gallery. Amar dies in front of a portrait of a modern Mexican revolutionary leader by Velásquez (one of Sciascia's many obscure jokes); Rogas is found under a fifteenth-century Florentine painting of the Madonna of the Chain (another little mystery, perhaps an allusion to the part played by the Church in the business of oppression). For the convenience of the State, but also of Amar's successor as party chief, the record will show that Rogas killed Amar. Meanwhile the President [of the Supreme Court] has been murdered. As they did in France in 1968, the Communists decide that they cannot risk a revolution "at this moment." Another stranded intellectual, Rogas's friend Cusan, ends the book by hopelessly echoing these words. In his concluding note Sciascia speaks of the "steadily greater degradation" wrought by the concatenated power that "we can roughly term *mafioso*"; perhaps the *catena* of the Madonna refers also to that power. Professing to have begun with an amusing puzzle, a "concatenation of clues," Sciascia says that by the time he had finished, the task he had set himself was no longer amusing; like his hero he sees that the revolution "is already defeated." The victor is concatenated power; against it a just cause has no chance, and is shown in the record as evil. But Rogas would not, though he knew these things, "go home to bed"; and Bellodi does so only to convalesce before returning to the country of the *chiarchiaro* and the society of the *lupara,* where Sciascia locates the symbolic source of the evils that dominate the entire human community. (pp. xii-xiii)

Frank Kermode, in an afterword to The Day of the Owl [*and*] Equal Danger *by Leonardo Sciascia, translated by Archibald Colquhoun and Arthur Oliver [*and*] Adrienne Foulke, Carcanet, 1984, pp. i-xiii.*

MARGHANITA LASKI

[Both] *The Day of the Owl* and *Equal Danger* would seem, from the copyright dates, to have been published in England before. Now, together, they have come for review among crime fiction, and, as such, rate only very moderate praise, being, as crime fiction, unshapely, untense, and with many such unapt longueurs as the judge's comparison of his dispensation of justice to the priest's of the sacrament. Yet, read as literature, we might well rate them as highly as does Frank Kermode in his afterword [see excerpt above]; there is no difficulty in seeing why this moralistic writer appeals to a critic who has recently turned to hermeneutics. (p. 30)

> *Marghanita Laski, "Literature as Death," in* The Listener, *Vol. 112, No. 2881, October 25, 1984, pp. 29-30.*

PATRICK McCARTHY

It is surprising that Leonardo Sciascia's novels are not better known in the Anglo-Saxon world, both because he is surely, along with Italo Calvino, Italy's finest prose-writer and because his books are superficially, albeit deceptively, simple. Many of them are in the form of detective stories in which the crime is gradually obscured rather than explained, and the detective rather than the criminal is punished.

The Day of the Owl (1961) depicts a policeman from northern Italy, Bellodi, who is endeavouring to solve a Sicilian murder. He makes good progress until he encounters a mafioso protected by high-ranking politicians in Rome; at this point a fog of obscurity descends and the policeman admits defeat. *Equal Danger* (1971) is a more complex novel; the detective, Rogas, pursues a murderer of judges only to discover that the ruling élite is manipulating the killings. Blaming them on New Left terrorists and exploiting the climate of fear, the Rome politicians are preparing either a *coup d'état* or a grand alliance between the Christian Democrats and the Communists or else the two things at once.

In the background of Sciascia's books lurk the men of power who are the real agents of evil, even if they cannot control it and may themselves become victims of violence. They appear to the reader via fragments of conversation, telephone calls and brief allusions. Since they stand both inside and outside history it is tempting to interpret Sciascia's novels in political terms, although this is another false trail down which he sends us. . . .

Most readers will rightly ignore [the political references] . . . , but they will not fail to be drawn with a mixture of fascination and repulsion into Sciascia's Sicily, where violence is an organic part of everyday life. Four characters occupy the stage: the bystander, the informer, the detective and the mafioso. The bystander has the simplest role, for, obeying the code of "omertà", he sees and hears nothing while crimes are committed around him. The informer, whom Sciascia depicts brilliantly, walks a tightrope between the mafioso and the policeman, who incarnate equally menacing forms of power:

> To him the law was utterly irrational, created on the spot by those in command. . . . Between rich and poor, between wise and ignorant, stood the guardians of the law who only used the strong arm on the poor; the rich they protected and defended.

The policeman has a different sense of law and he lives by the creed of reason. He quickly discovers, however, that imagination and intuition are necessary in Sicily. Sciascia's detectives are unashamedly literary men steeped in Pirandello and Borges, and they know that every so-called reality is accompanied by several others. The temptation that awaits them is to be drawn into the mystery they are exploring. Rogas, for example, realizes that the murderer Cres is a mirror image of himself; both of them are convinced that Italian life is a vast conspiracy.

Similarly Bellodi comes to understand that his antagonist, Don Arena, is a *necessary* figure in Sicily. Since the island has known only invaders, brigands and distant, inefficient governments there can be no morality or legality. . . .

This is a disturbing theme; Sciascia leaves it dangling. In general his detectives are alert to the danger and they assert, however unsuccessfully, their belief in law against the mafioso and his remote protectors who are also his vassals.

Outwardly simple, these novels are technically complex. One characteristic device that Sciascia employs is to offer chunks of free indirect speech which are both the testimony of one, unreliable individual and a part of the general narrative. Such pages are not easy to render in English but these translators have done a competent job.

> *Patrick McCarthy, "Brothers in Corruption," in* The Times Literary Supplement, *No. 4256, October 26, 1984, p. 1223.*

BRYAN ROSTRON

[Leonardo Sciascia] has written a series of short, powerful novels or fables about the complicities and accommodations of power. He is the most universal of Italian writers, though he invariably writes about his own difficult, intractable island. For it is in Sicily that one finds the abuse of power—and the affinities of crime, church and politics—not only in its most concentrated form, but also paradoxically at its most subtle too.

In the first of these novellas, *The Day of the Owl,* a man is shot as he gets onto a bus in the middle of the town: but none of the other passengers have seen a thing. Bellodi, the policeman from the north, comes up against *omerta* and all the obstinate obscurity of the south. Bellodi is a typical Sciascia hero: an intelligent, literary, rational man who finds himself faced with "power that, in the impenetrable form of a concentration that we can roughly term *mafioso,* works steadily greater degradation."

As usual when Sciascia adopts the detective form, we never find out who dunnit. But what we discover along the way, as we are led down further dark alleys, is a great deal about everyone and their society. Sciascia is a supreme ironist. He is also a beautiful stylist, and here the translators of *The Day of the Owl* have not done justice to his playful, limpid prose.

He is better served in *Equal Danger*. . . . In this book, which was made into a film called *Illustrious Corpses* by Francesco Rosi, Sciascia makes concrete the Orwellian theme of *Animal Farm* where in the end the pigs in charge look like the men and the men look like the pigs and no one can tell the difference. (pp. 32-3)

Equal Danger, though set in no definable country, is about the Italy of the past decade and of today and perhaps the Europe of tomorrow. In a postscript Sciascia tells us that he kept the 'fable' in a drawer of his desk for more than two years because "I began to write it with amusement, and as I was finishing it I was no longer amused." (p. 33)

Bryan Rostron, in a review of "The Day of the Owl" and "Equal Danger," in Books and Bookmen, *No. 350, November, 1984, pp. 32-3.*

VERINA JONES

Most of Sciascia's narrative works begin with an epigraph. Two of these can be taken as statements of the author's views of the status of writing:

> The sulphur-miners from my town call fire-damp *antimonio*. Sulphur-miners believe that this name derives from anti-monk, since in the old days it was used by monks, and, when carelessly handled, it killed them. Also, antimony is used in the making of both gun-powder and type-metal, and was a component of cosmetics in the past. It is for all these reasons that I have given this story the title **"L'antimonio"**.
>
> ("L'antimonio", "Fire-damp", 1961)

> Let it not be supposed that I am detailing any mystery, or penning any romance. Poe, *The Murders in the Rue Morgue.*
>
> (*A ciascuno il suo, To Each His Own,* 1966)

The quotation from Poe warns the reader that the text which follows is not, or not merely, a good yarn to be read as a source of pleasure. The novel, then, is justified by the fact of being something other, or something more, than literature: writing is, or should be, a tool for the understanding of a reality other than itself. The epigraph to **"L'antimonio"** establishes a parallel between the fire-damp which haunts the sulphur-miners, death, gun-powder, the printed word, and the making of cosmetics. Here Sciascia appears to be suggesting that writing is not a neutral, harmless tool: it can be destructive, or it can mask reality, but on the other hand it can be a valid weapon with which to fight. The narrator-protagonist of the story has to be catapulted by the fire-damp explosion in the Sicilian mine 'nel fuoco della Spagna' ('into the burning hell of Spain') before he can 'parlare e parlare' ('talk and talk'), understand himself and reality, and write about it.

Sciascia's view of writing, at least until 1970, is situated consistently between these two poles: writing as mystification of reality, or writing as revelation of reality. This approach would seem to define Sciascia as a perfect example of the 'committed writer' demanded by Neo-realist programmes of literature. His first important book (*Le parrocchie di Regalpetra, The Parishes of Regalpetra*) appeared in fact in 1956, at a time when Neo-realism was entering its crisis. In some important ways this book represents precisely Sciascia's attempt to come to terms with the Neo-realist tradition, to measure his distance from it, and to define his own space within the Italian literary scene.

Le parrocchie di Regalpetra is a collection of nine documentary essays on the life of a poor Sicilian town, Sciascia's own town. The author's investigation encompasses the working conditions of the local salt-miners and sulphur-miners, the sub-standard housing and the under-nourishment to which the poor are subjected, the curse of emigration, the deficiencies of the school system, and also the local folklore, the political intrigues and electoral vicissitudes of the recent past, the role of the clergy, the intellectual and sexual outlook of the middle class who frequent the local *circolo* (gentlemen's club). Although the main emphasis is on the contemporary life of the town, all the essays contain frequent references to the past, and one of them, **"La storia di Regalpetra"** (**"The History (or Story) of Regalpetra"**), is focused specifically on its past history. This historical dimension, which persists in Sciascia's later writings, is a fundamental aspect of his approach to social reality. The ills of present-day Regalpetra are not to be seen merely as something to be observed and denounced, but as problems to be overcome; if they are to be overcome, they must be understood, and an analysis of the past will provide at least an explanation of the present condition. (pp. 235-36)

Although Sciascia's analysis of social reality in *Le parrocchie* is inspired by a broadly left-wing perspective, he rejects the orthodoxies of the left. Both the Socialist Party and the Communist Party are presented in a critical light; the trade unions are shown as incapable, or unwilling, to organize the salt-mine workers; the myth of the *Garibaldini*, dear to the imagination of the left, is pointedly debunked. (p. 237)

While rejecting any specific political involvement, Sciascia bases his writing on a belief in the crucial role of reason. Reason is for him the essential tool for approaching reality. A rational approach to reality will produce positive results, the bringing about of freedom and justice, and writing has the function of enlarging the area of rationality. But the link between writing and reality begins to loosen very soon after *Le parrocchie*. The whole of Sciascia's subsequent career as a writer is marked by a tension between a view of writing as an active intervention in reality and writing as an alternative to reality.

The type of language used in *Le parrocchie* is consistent with Sciascia's view of writing as rational organization of reality. He does not disdain to use the modes of the popular spoken language, with its attendant regionalisms, but does not give them a privileged status. He uses a variety of registers and narrative styles. There is free indirect speech, although not used in a systematic fashion, and not with the function of organizing the narration; it is in fact often manipulated for ironic purposes. There is specialized technical language, as in the description of the salt-mine and the professional diseases of salt-miners, straight reporting language, Sicilian dialect, which is nevertheless consistently presented in italics and therefore distanced from the rest of the text, popular everyday language, highly literary language studded with elaborate lyrical imagery, short isolated one-clause sentences, as well as elaborate sentences with a wealth of subordinate clauses. Sciascia will continue using this type of linguistic *montage,* albeit with the refinements that one would expect from greater experience, in his later works.

Le parrocchie would appear to lay a claim to literal truth. But the real name of Sciascia's home town is Racalmuto; Regalpetra is a fictional name. . . . [The] author might be recognizing implicitly that, apart from the description of salt-mining, his documentary essays do not necessarily relate facts which have really happened, that the Regalpetra of the text is meant to present a synthesis, his synthesis, of Sicilian small-town life, that his essay-writing is beginning to flow into narrative.

Gli zii di Sicilia (*Sicilian Uncles,* 1958) is a work of out-and-out narrative. But it is interesting to note that in Sciascia's subjective judgement the difference between essay-writing and narrative in his own work is marginal; as late as 1970 he declared in an interview with Walter Mauro: 'My subject matter . . . is that of the essayist, which then assumes the "modes" of narrative . . .'. . . . *Le parrocchie* will remain in any case the storehouse for themes, characters, situations, images, turns of phrase which can be traced in his later writings. (pp. 238-39)

In 1961 Sciascia's first full-length novel appeared. This was *Il giorno della civetta* (*The Owl by Day*), and it was a detective story. Sciascia was to write three more detective novels, *A ciascuno il suo* (1966), *Il contesto* (*The Contest* or *The Context*, 1971), and *Todo modo* (*In Every Way,* 1974), with the interlude of the historical novel *Il consiglio d'Egitto* (*The Council of Egypt,* 1963).

Why the detective story? Sciascia's own answer to this question is very simple. He has something important to say and wants to make sure that it is going to be read. . . . Sciascia's detective novels, then, as one would expect, are detective novels with a difference. Once readers have finished reading these compelling stories, they are supposed to have also absorbed a lesson.

Il giorno della civetta tells the story of a mafia murder in an unspecified Sicilian town. Salvatore Colasberna, a local builder who refuses mafia protection, is killed. The *carabinieri* captain in charge of the investigation, Bellodi, doggedly follows the right track, which leads him to arrest the local mafia chief, Don Mariano Arena. But Arena has powerful political connections reaching up to the highest level; so Bellodi eventually fails, and the police investigation is directed along the usual safe lines of the *crime passionnel*. In *A ciascuno il suo* the *crime passionnel* is compounded with an equally powerful political motive. Doctor Roscio is murdered (along with the pharmacist Manno, who receives an anonymous letter warning him of his impending death, the letter having the function of diverting the police investigations onto a false scent) by a killer hired by his wife's cousin and lover, Rosello, a local Christian Democrat notable. Roscio had already discovered the adulterous affair, and also Rosello's murky political and financial intrigues, and had threatened to reveal all if the affair did not stop. While the police soon reach a dead end following up the possible motives for Manno's killing, Paolo Laurana, a schoolteacher, stumbles on a series of right clues, and is silenced with death. (pp. 244-45)

These two novels undoubtedly confront a series of problems, both political and psychological, and attempt to go below the surface, and to offer an explanation for them. The most obvious theme of *Il giorno della civetta* is the mafia, but the book is not simply an attack on the mafia; it attempts to do something more complicated, to reveal what the mafia really is (far worse, far more ominous than it is, or was, generally imagined to be), and also to explain what it is that makes a *mafioso*. Sciascia tries to show that the Sicilian mafia is not merely a more or less colourful protection racket, involved in the acquisition of building contracts and such like; it is also an electoral machine, if not *the* electoral machine, in Sicily, and is in fact an inseparable aspect of the political game at the national level. (pp. 245-46)

In the tension between hope and despair which characterizes Sciascia's writings, *A ciascuno il suo* gravitates towards despair. The detective himself is not particularly far-sighted, nor is his investigation motivated by an ideal of justice: it is mere intellectual curiosity. The whole social fabric of the town is shown as impregnated with hyprocrisy and double-talk. Virtually all the characters, even those who do not stand for evil as such, are imbued with political opportunism. . . . This bleak outlook extends beyond the political dimension: the book also dwells at length on the immature prurient attitude to sex of the

men, and the misguided contamination between sex and concern for property of the women. (pp. 246-47)

A ciascuno il suo also opens the examination of the omnivorous all-encompassing nature of power which dominates Sciascia's later writing. The novel is set at the beginning of the centre-left experiment in Italy, and Rosello is presented very much as the power-seeking politician who will embrace and transform any political ideology to his own ends. But Sciascia also contemptuously begins to dissect the forces of the left, though, curiously, not the Socialist Party who were the Christian Democrats' partners in the centre-left government, but the Communist Party. . . .

In his own preface to the 1967 edition of *Le parrocchie di Regalpetra* Sciascia associated his interest in the detective story with a search for a good narrative technique. Since his aim is 'documenting and narrating with a good technique', he is more interested in following 'the development of the detective story than the evolution of aesthetic theories'. Fourteen years earlier he had published a short article (1953), which shows him to be a keen follower of this aspect of the 'sottobosco letterario' ('literary undergrowth') and related critical writings. At this stage he expressed the conviction that good detective stories have helped the development of main-stream fiction, in that they have conveyed a lesson of taut, stream-lined narration. In particular he admired the lucid, rigorous pursuit of a solution to the puzzle. . . . (p. 247)

When Sciascia comes to trying his hand at using the techniques of the detective story, then, he has at his disposal not only a pretty thorough knowledge of the tricks of the trade, but also certain critical insights into the subterranean workings of the genre. It is interesting to see how his own detective stories make use of these tricks, in a way which amounts to a comment on the whole genre and its common assumptions. What is more, in the light of his insistence on rational understanding, his exploration of a genre which presupposes the essentially rational comprehensibility of apparently inexplicable mysteries becomes a fundamental factor in what he has to say.

Contrary to the expectations of conventional detective stories, where the detective always triumphs at the end, both Bellodi and Laurana fail; Laurana indeed is eliminated. In both cases even their limited successes are made possible by the intervention of elements beyond their control. (p. 248)

[Two] constant features of the conventional detective story are the suspense regarding the correct solution of the puzzle, and the linear summing-up by the detective himself at the end. The conventional story will contain a number of false clues which have the function of sending the reader up blind alleys, with the expectation that everything will be put right at the end by the infallible detective. In both Sciascia's novels the suspense element is shifted very early from the solution of the initial puzzle (the murders) to the question of whether or not the detective will succeed and/or survive. (p. 250)

With *A ciascuno il suo* Sciascia points to the total collapse of reason, and he will return to this theme in *Il contesto* and *Todo modo.* But three years before the publication of *A ciascuno il suo* he had published *Il consiglio d'Egitto,* a historical novel which can be read as an attempt to confront the question of reason in its own historical *locus,* the Enlightenment. *Il consiglio d'Egitto* is set in Palermo in the period 1782-1795. It follows emblematically the descending parable of reason in the *siècle des lumières,* from the enlightened reforms of Viceroy Caracciolo to the turn of the screw against the reformers-turned-

Jacobins after the rumbles from Paris have made the ruling classes close ranks. This novel still has a positive hero, Francesco Paolo Di Blasi: he stands, and speaks, for human equality, freedom, justice, and reason throughout. The book closes with his execution for his part in the Jacobin conspiracy. The council of Egypt of the title refers to a newly found Arabic manuscript which deals a mortal blow to the historical justification for the power of the feudal barons vis-à-vis the crown. However, the council of Egypt is a fake. It is the fabrication of Giuseppe Vella, a poor Maltese priest who hopes to gain glory and wealth as a result. The fortunes of Vella rise and fall with the political vicissitudes of the kingdom. When the struggle against the baron ceases to be the objective of the crown, the mounting suspicions regarding the authenticity of the manuscript gather momentum, and Vella is arrested.

Di Blasi is an aristocrat, and speaks the language of reason; Vella is a man of humble origins who is after personal gain through deceit, or so it would appear at first. But an important theme in the course of the novel is the journey of Vella from selfishness towards enlightenment, a journey in which Di Blasi's personality acts as the catalyst. At the point where Vella reaches enlightenment, the light is about to be extinguished over the brief honeymoon between Sicily and reason, and over Di Blasi's life. Di Blasi speaks the language of reason to the very end. Under torture, his thoughts are of a future world 'illuminato dalla ragione' ('illumined by reason') where torture will be unthinkable. At this point Sciascia intervenes with a direct comment which corrects Di Blasi's historical optimism with a reference to the Nazi genocide and the French authorities' practice of torture in Algeria.... Di Blasi's vision of the world's progress towards a better future is patently wrong, and yet the message of this book is not one of despair. The rational, principled approach of Di Blasi, inadequate at this stage as a tool for sweeping changes, has sown a seed in the mind of Vella, and even affects, at a subliminal level, the brutalized personality of the executioner.

The story of the forged historical manuscripts allows Sciascia to delve further into the relationship between writing and reality. The text of this novel is dotted with references to writing: writing as fraud, writing as truth, even writing as fetish, in the insistent allusions to the tools of writing. What status does Vella's historical fraud have in relation to historical truth? Is it any more fraudulent than the skilful weaving of the feudal legal tradition which Vella's manuscript is now attempting to subvert? Is it not in fact simply the reversed mirror image of the fraud of history? Does history contain any truth at all when it has been the history of 'i re, i vicerè, i papi, i capitani' ('kings, viceroys, popes, generals'), when it has ignored the lives of those who have been unable to write their own history? To these questions, raised sometimes through Vella's own interior monologue, sometimes through direct intervention, Sciascia does not offer clear-cut answers.

Vella exits from the text with the disturbing thought that 'il mondo della verità fosse questo: degli uomini vivi, della storia, dei libri' ('this might be the world of truth: the world of living men, the world of history, the world of books.'), a thought which, significantly, is shared at that very moment by Di Blasi who is about to die. Truth, life, history, writing, form an equation which will no longer be possible without a belief in the rational comprehensibility of reality.

Since *A ciascuno il suo* Sciascia has written two more detective novels, *Il contesto* (1971), and *Todo modo* (1974), and a philosophical fable modelled on Voltaire's *Candide* (*Candido,* 1977).

In *Il contesto* several judges are killed. While the police authorities pursue at first the hypothesis of a mentally deranged killer, and of political murders perpetrated by an extreme left group, inspector Rogas follows up the line of revenge murders by a man who had been unjustly sentenced. But at the point when he has caught up with his quarry, Rogas begins to identify with him, and does nothing to stop him killing another judge. Rogas is found dead, together with the dead body of Amar, the leader of the main opposition party, the Partito Rivoluzionario Internazionale. The revolutionary party does not want the truth about these killings to come out for fear of provoking a revolution.

The novel uses the clichés and devices of the detective story in a paradoxical, parodistical fashion, as Sciascia himself points out in the note appended at the end of the book. The novel ends without a clear explanation of the killings of Rogas and Amar. This open ending postulates a chaotic, elusive reality which reason is no longer able to comprehend, which writing can no longer organize.

Il contesto, unlike Sciascia's previous work, is no longer set in Sicily, nor in Italy. The place is an unspecified country: some features suggest Sicily, some Italy, some a South American environment. This lack of geographic determination would seem to imply, metaphorically, that the total collapse of political opposition, the total collusion of power, is not a peculiarly Sicilian, or Italian, situation, but a universal one.

If *Il contesto* ends without a clear solution to the mystery, *Todo modo* offers no solution at all, it just ends, in the middle of dialogue. *Todo modo* is set in Sicily, but does not carry specifically Sicilian connotations; the bishops, cardinals, industrialists, high-ranking politicians who withdraw to the Sicilian hermitage for a highly suspect session of 'spiritual exercises' come from all over Italy.

The protagonist of *Candido,* Candido Munafo, moves from his native Sicily to Turin in the North, and eventually to Paris. In Sicily Candido suffers a series of disillusionments, personal and political, and his journeys elsewhere only confirm these disappointments but in Paris he escapes into happiness and freedom, away from all authorities, even that of Voltaire. In Candido's experiences Sciascia telescopes his own journey as a writer. Candido is born in July 1943, during the American landings in Sicily, the historical crux of "Breve cronaca del regime" and "La zia d'America". His mother Maria Grazia marries an American officer, and he never sees her again until he bumps into her in Paris, in the last chapter of the book. Maria Grazia has become Grace.... In the Parisian café where he meets Maria Grazia-Grace, Candido is talking with his old mentor don Antonio, newly arrived from Sicily, ...

> of Hemingway and Fitzgerald, ... of the American writers which don Antonio had read during the Fascist regime, and which he had considered great without exception, and which Candido ... had later found uninteresting and even irritating.

The myth of American literature, which the protagonist of "La zia d'America" had to overcome before he could begin to understand, is here reduced to nothing. The book ends with Candido free of Maria Grazia-Grace, who will return to America without him, and free also of the myth of the Enlightenment, which don Antonio is trying to cling to.... Since *Candido* Sciascia has not published any works of narrative. On the other hand, his name has not by any means ceased to appear in print, with essays, newspaper articles, and numerous interviews. Sciascia began writing essays in the early 1950s, and always pursued this activity vigorously, side by side with his narrative works. Sciascia's essays and narrative works are not unconnected: in fact many of his essays can be read as the historical and ideological workshops for his short stories and novels. They fall broadly into two types. The earlier ones consist of analyses and critiques, often extremely well researched, of Sicilian history and literature, such as the collection *Pirandello e la Sicilia* (*Pirandello and Sicily,* 1961), and *Morte dell'inquisitore* (*Death of the Inquisitor,* 1964). Most of the essays published from the 1970s onwards are investigations and reconstructions of real-life mysteries, often based on the examination of historical or judicial documents.... But in recent years Sciascia has acquired increasingly the position of a popular figure whose opinion is much sought, and this reader at least cannot help wondering whether his frequent pronouncements have added anything of value either to Sciascia's writings or to the understanding of the public at large.

Sciascia as a narrator appears to have reached a point beyond which lies uncharted ground. While his earlier works described a series of defeats of reason, they were based on the notion that reality can be understood, even though with difficulty. With the transition to the view of a chaotic reality, where power *per se* is the only certainty, the parameters of reason have ceased to be valid tools for organizing this reality, and the writer is pushed into a position of global critique, often of a nihilist type. This would require the use of completely new narrative tools, which Sciascia appears not to have discovered, or not yet. (pp. 250-55)

Verina Jones, "Leonardo Sciascia," in Writing & Society in Contemporary Italy: A Collection of Essays, *edited by Michael Caesar and Peter Hainsworth, Berg Publishers, 1984, pp. 235-57.*

Wallace Shawn
1943-

American dramatist, actor, and screenwriter.

A well-known actor and off-Broadway dramatist, Shawn writes controversial plays satirizing the follies of human behavior. Regarded by some as a moralist whose plays are exaggerated and lewd comedies of manners, Shawn is concerned with such themes as the dissatisfactions of married life, human cruelty, and the alienating pressures of social propriety. His characters are usually ordinary people involved in such mundane activities as conversing at parties, relaxing in the lobby of a hotel, or eating dinner. Their behavior, however, is unpredictable, and their dialogue is often sexually explicit and vulgar. Shawn's plays consist almost entirely of dialogue, and he deemphasizes traditional forms of structure and plot in order to explore the ability of language to shape reality. While some critics find his plays pointlessly obscene, others contend that Shawn authentically captures the tensions and anxieties of modern life. Lloyd Rose observed that the energy of Shawn's plays "comes not from action but from the seething frustration of the trapped characters."

Shawn's first produced play, *Our Late Night* (1974), earned him an Obie Award. In this comedy, seven guests at a party in New York converse about such topics as sex and food. Discarding the small talk endemic to social gatherings, the characters say the things they are really thinking, with humorous and shocking results. In *Marie and Bruce* (1979), Shawn examines one day in the collapsing marriage of a couple trapped in a love/hate relationship. Focusing on Marie's point of view, the play is filled with her scatological abuse of her husband. *My Dinner with Andre* (1980), originally a play written by Shawn and avant-garde director Andre Gregory, was adapted for film from a screenplay by Shawn. This work consists of a dinner conversation in which Gregory recounts his experiences with experimental art forms and Shawn interjects skeptical responses. *My Dinner with Andre* was praised by Lucinda Franks as reflecting humanity's "search for identity in the contemporary world."

Shawn's recent play, *Aunt Dan and Lemon* (1985), is the story of a young girl's encounters with an eccentric family friend who shapes the girl's social and political thinking. Aunt Dan's defense of Henry Kissinger's Vietnam policies, her apologia for the necessity of government-induced violence, and her admiration for the Nazi party remain unchallenged throughout the play. Shawn presents these ideas in an attempt to stimulate playgoers to reevaluate their own positions on these issues. Paul Berman faulted Shawn for not creating "a legitimate play of ideas" because the arguments of the main characters are easily dismissible on moral grounds. Gerald Weales, however, praised Shawn for devising the play "as an ally of the audience against the characters and their ideas." *Aunt Dan and Lemon* was one of five plays to tie for the 1986 Obie Award.

(See also *Contemporary Authors*, Vol. 112.)

© 1986 Thomas Victor

CLIVE BARNES

Our Late Night is the sickest of sick jokes, but undeniably it is a joke. It is about a party—a horrendous party. It seems to start normally enough, with a host and hostess exchanging connubial unpleasantries before the arrival of the guests. Then the guests arrive, lounging on an enormous sofa and making small talk that rapidly becomes as enormous as the sofa itself.

Guest after guest starts to ramble on in anecdotes that become dirtier and sicker as each freefall garrulity succeeds the next. The most disgraceful and disgusting fantasies come pouring out. Normal conversation becomes abnormal, and even the abnormal conversation becomes more abnormal. A man recites, with desperate relish, an interminable monologue about his sexual experiences in the tropics. People make lewd passes at one another. A man goes offstage to the bathroom to be sick. The host becomes paralyzed with embarrassment. The hostess cowers against him in pain and sickened disbelief. And the guests go on getting weirder and weirder. Until at last they leave—all mock passion spent if not paid for. The couple, left to themselves, show a few darkened monstrosities on their own account. It all ends unhappily in the bile of cities.

Morally there is nothing to commend in this play. But it is funny, especially at the beginning. Eventually the psycho-pathological chatter does begin to pall, and even disgust. But somehow this talk around a sofa—surely the best-informed sofa since Crebillon's—retains most of its totally outrageous charms. If "charms" is really the word. One has rarely seen such pornographic decadence with, guiltily, so much going for it. This is the most obscene show in town, so please don't imagine that you have not been warned. However, the obscenity does have a wit to it, and even some insights on modern society, satirically exaggerated as those insights might be. . . .

No one could call this a pleasant play. Indeed, it is one of the most unpleasant plays I have seen in years. Nevertheless, honesty is to admit that, at least for most of the play's brief passage, its nastiness is given with a kind of defiant stylishness.

> Clive Barnes, " 'Our Late Night', at the Public Theater," in The New York Times, January 10, 1975, p. 20.

BRENDAN GILL

Even for these permissive times, Mr. Shawn [with *Our Late Night*] has written a notably candid play. It is filled to bursting with Lenny Bruce-like scatological bawdry, and it soon becomes evident that bawdry is the means by which the author transforms his high-spirited view of the world into art; the language and deportment of his characters would leave much to be desired in the comfortable, upper-middle-class world that they appear to inhabit, but Mr. Shawn is far from taking a dark view of them. Unwittingly, they strive to follow Forster's admonition "Only connect!," and they always fail, with hilarious, deplorable results. The action of the play is far more mysterious than it promises to be at the start. Its setting is an expensive apartment high above the city; the only furniture is a vast oyster-white sofa, on which the seven actors in the cast sit, slope, slouch, and, in some cases, sleep. It serves as a point of departure for a bout of lovemaking behind its high back and for occasional hurried visits to a bathroom offstage, from which ghastly sounds of regurgitation arise.

A couple occupy the apartment where the party is being given. We do not know if the couple are married, or if they have children, or what their occupations are. We do not know why the guests have been invited, or what, if anything, they have in common. At the start of the play, the host and hostess treat themselves to cocktails so one assumes that the party will include dinner, but after a blackout there are no signs of a dinner having been served. Nor are drinks being served—the astonishing freedom with which the guests speak owes nothing to alcohol. They are clear in their minds and in their utterance, and they are devastatingly uninhibited. Strangers that they are, they speak with the openness of lovers. If a man wishes to kiss the breasts of a woman who happens to be seated next to him, he says so; more elementary desires are spoken of with equal ease and relish. It is hard to give offense in this group, hard not to be all ears. A shaggy-dog tale of a raunchiness Tolstoyan in scale, if not in tone, is related with single-minded, uninterruptible passion by one of the male guests. The hostess cowers. The party draws to an end without civilities; we are not, after all, at Mrs. Dalloway's. There are a number of cinematic blackouts. Host and hostess alone. Awake. Asleep. Awake. Well? Well, what does it *mean*?

And it is true: one resists with difficulty the temptation to make a funny little play like this—it lasts only fifty-four minutes, which isn't a minute too few or too many—stand for something portentous. Surely the author is secretly signalling to us that there is more to his salacious rhetoric than the wish to make

us laugh? Are we not being offered a parable by which to gain salvation? I have to confess that from time to time I was put vaguely in mind of *The Cocktail Party*, but I took care to remain vague. Like most writers with a bent for pornography, Mr. Shawn is on the side of the life-enhancers, while Eliot was on the side of the life-diminishers—the afterlife was what Old Possum smacked his dry lips over. I wish Mr. Shawn's ribald and joyous play to mean no more than it appears to mean; I will be shocked and disappointed if it turns out to contain a message. (pp. 62-3)

> Brendan Gill, "Dead Gull, Live Party," in The New Yorker, Vol. L, No. 48, January 20, 1975, pp. 62-3.

BRENDAN GILL

Marie and Bruce, a new comedy by Wallace Shawn . . . , speaks forthrightly of physical matters Down Here, most of which have to do with the picayune daily miseries of married love. The young couple for whom the comedy is named are first glimpsed in bed—an unlovely-looking couple, in a bed that appears to have gone unmade since the day they purchased it, no doubt from the latest of many previous owners. Bruce, who is small and hairy, is contentedly asleep; Marie, who is much bigger than Bruce, wakes, rises on one elbow, shifts portions of her body from one place to another, and begins to excoriate Bruce in a vocabulary that would buckle steel. It appears that she finds their marriage unendurable and is planning to put an end to it. The precipitating factor in her eyes was Bruce's unmanly distress when, the day before, she threw away his "two-hundred-year-old" typewriter. (Like Albee, Shawn never bothers to tell us what his characters do to earn a living. Since the typewriter meant so much to Bruce, one assumes he is a writer. Marie is obviously unemployable, except as a stevedore.) On waking to a shower of scatological imprecations, Bruce mildly volunteers to make breakfast. They will spend the day apart, meeting in the late afternoon at the house of a friend who is giving a cocktail party.

The heart of the play is the party, and it is very funny indeed. The set is built on a turntable, and as it revolves we encounter again and again, in advancing stages of intoxication, a classic assortment of New York partygoers. Here are the loners who keep silent, and here are the gregarious ones who never stop talking. Here is the pretty Oriental girl, whose seductiveness surely embraces some secret sexual practices out of the mysterious East. Here is the middle-aged businessman bore, who is bumped from group to group and yet never fails to find a fresh group of victims. Marie and Bruce drink a lot at the party. Bruce believes himself to be having a marvelous time and takes advantage of the opportunity to tell Marie that she doesn't make love to him enough. Marie spills drinks—and has drinks spilled—on her sleazy red dress, which she resolutely squeezes dry from time to time, often into a glass and often not.

Marie and Bruce leave the party to have dinner at a Chinese restaurant and talk over their marital problems, and here the play nervily shifts its ground and threatens to become a different play altogether. For Marie is seen to be in earnest in her attempt not merely to leave Bruce but to destroy him. She launches an attack so devastating in its cruelty that we can scarcely believe our eyes when Bruce, in however agitated a state, goes on skillfully manipulating his chopsticks. They finish their meal, get to their feet, and suddenly come to blows; no less suddenly, they are locked in a passionate embrace. To our astonishment, Marie has been transformed into a sort of Manhattan Molly

Bloom, speaking a long and poetic soliloquy, wifelike and motherlike, over her little Bruce. There is a sadness in the innumerable "little"'s that big Marie has uttered; the marriage is terrible and will last forever. It is a daring chance that the playwright has taken, and I find it imperfectly realized, but what an ending it gives us! (pp. 64-5)

Brendan Gill, "Out There and Down Here," in The New Yorker, *Vol. LV, No. 25, February 11, 1980, pp. 63-5.*

JACK KROLL

Marie and Bruce is the best play I've seen this season, a play that sees, hears, smells and tells more about the way we really live now than any American play in years.

Marie and Bruce . . . are your vintage urban couple—the urb could be anywhere from Manhattan to Montevideo to Manila. As with Willy Loman in *Death of a Salesman,* you don't know exactly what Bruce's line is, but he probably has something to do with processing words, because he has a typewriter. Or rather, he had, because as the play opens, Marie tells how she threw out Bruce's beloved typewriter. Husband and wife are lying in bed, although Marie is dressed in a capacious red caftan. It becomes clear that the entire play is being narrated to the audience by Marie and . . . moves beautifully in this double focus, snapping in and out of Marie's storytelling to actual dramatization.

What Marie is telling is the story of the day she tried to break away from Bruce—and maybe or maybe not succeeded. It's not that she has come to despise or hate the man she married—she's literally horrified by him. It's this horror that calls forth her relentless stream of scatological abuse. . . . Strenuously choreographed helplessness *is* funny, as the flailings of Chaplin, Keaton and Woody Allen show us, and Marie's obsessive four-letter rat-a-tat is the verbal equivalent of the slapstick of entrapment. . . .

Bruce, the teensy superschlemiel, . . . meets Marie's bombardment of bad words with a patient counterattack of "Darlings," until that word becomes just as obscene as Marie's gutter-talk. Shawn is showing that the language of hate can really be the language of balked love, while the jargon of love can be the lingo of emotional sterility. No playwright better evokes the anguish and devilish comedy of this moment in which love and hate coexist, locked together in the last tango of the Western spirit. This double bind of love-hate entangles Marie and Bruce with tragic hilarity as they go through their day, visiting a cocktail party which is the ultimate in such urban saturnalias, ending up at a Chinese restaurant where Bruce shows the white feather to a tableful of creeps, and Marie makes one last epic attempt to leave him. And that's the way it is, as Walter Cronkite says; Shawn shows that the big news of such days is in the terrifying spiritual implications of the smallest, most ordinary events.

Shawn's convincing vision of our constantly realienating alienation comes from the startling innocence of his sensibility. . . .

What he is is a true original, one of the most deeply seeing, sharply writing playwrights we have.

Jack Kroll, "I Love You/I Hate You," in Newsweek, *Vol. XCV, No. 7, February 18, 1980, p. 117.*

JOHN SIMON

[Nothing] in the world could save *Marie and Bruce,* which has already wrested the title of worst play within not so recent memory from *The Lady From Dubuque* and another unspeakable item recently exhumed . . . , *The Trouble With Europe.* Written (if that is the word for it) by Wallace Shawn, one of the worst and unsightliest actors in this city, *Marie and Bruce* is the kind of play that, if either our drama critics or our garbage collectors did their work properly, could not have survived one night. . . . It begins with a morning in the life of an unlikely married couple: Marie wants to leave Bruce, but decides to tell him this at a cocktail party later on and contents herself with nonstop insults hurled at him. There *are* witty insults, but what Marie belabors Bruce with for some twenty minutes is every known obscene and scatological term spewed forth over and over again pell-mell, while Bruce endures and utters placating vapidities.

I repeat that this filth is perfectly witless, of the sort that a particularly mindless performer might improvise in some acting or therapeutic exercise (assuming that this distinction still exists). . . . We next go to the cocktail party, which lasts us about 50 minutes, though you and I would have fled such an event in 3 or 4, supposing that anything so stupidly unfunny could have been assembled in life. Here the cast of nine is augmented by strategically posted papier-mâché dummies that you can distinguish from the flesh-and-blood ones by their greater humanity. The chatter is meant to be foolish, but, be it said for Shawn, folly has never before been made so unamusing.

After the party, there is dinner in a Chinese restaurant, where, amid more obscenity and scatology, Marie informs Bruce that she is leaving him. . . . Needless to say, after some twenty minutes and some physical pummeling of Bruce by the basically loving Marie, the two fall into each other's arms. The last scene, of some five minutes (as you may gather, my watch never felt less neglected than during this play), has our couple in bed again, with Marie spewing away once more while Bruce and a not inconsiderable part of the audience are serenely asleep. (pp. 85-6)

The play is performed without intermission or any other mercy, and could have been worse only with Shawn in it. (p. 86)

John Simon, "Harold and Maude and Marie and Bruce," in New York Magazine, *Vol. 13, No. 7, February 18, 1980, pp. 85-7.*

ROBERT BRUSTEIN

[*Marie and Bruce*] is messy and sprawling and ill-formed, but it left me, nevertheless, quite limp and vaguely depressed at its conclusion. I'm not grateful to the author for this reaction, but I have to concede that he achieved it honestly. Though not identified as such, Marie and Bruce . . . are genuinely Jewish characters, and what Shawn has created here . . . is the agony of a really miserable Jewish marriage. I don't mean to say the situation is typical, but it is recognizable as a piece of the truth blown up to monstrous proportions. Performed in a simple, modular, white setting that revolves the scenes from a bedroom to a cocktail party to a Chinese restaurant, *Marie and Bruce* begins and ends with a shriek of marital agony by the female protagonist which does not subside in pitch or volume until the final curtain. "Let me tell you something," she says, sitting up in bed with her husband, her hair decorated with two awful red plastic bows, "I find my husband so goddamn irritating that I'm planning to leave him."

This remark is the signal for a long monologue that her "worthless piece of shit" of a husband who, when he emerges from the bedclothes, seems much too mild a milquetoast to deserve her fury. Yet the odd thing is how Bruce eventually reveals himself as pretty much the monster Marie says he is, not so much from any particular heroic malevolence as from his maddening detachment from his wife's unhappiness. At one of those endless, mindless New York cocktail parties, where leering life-size puppets are indistinguishable from the actual guests, Bruce wanders through the room like a horny Ulysses, attending to his wife's needs primarily by loading her down with six or seven highballs, which she is forced to juggle on her thighs, her dress, in the crooks of her arms. Getting drunker and drunker, Marie suddenly conceives a new sexual passion for her husband while he soliloquizes about the other women he has been attracted to, asking her, when she finally passes out, "Why is it that whenever we have a conversation, you always get sick?"

The final scene, in the restaurant, shows us that the marriage is just about hopeless. As a group of homosexuals discuss their stomach troubles in sickening detail at the adjoining table, Marie launches into her ultimate assault on Bruce, while he keeps his attention fixed on the eggroll and the noodles. "This is very sad," she says, "I mean our dinner is spoiled, but my life was spoiled because I met you." "I don't imagine you'll be wanting any dessert," he replies, as the two sit wanly, desperately, amidst the rubble of their marriage. Bruce has proven Marie's contention that he is not "a living person," and when she proceeds to strike him violently about the head, all he can do is try to hold her hands. It is as if Shawn had taken all the Jewish self-irony previously seen good-naturedly by Woody Allen, Jules Feiffer, Mel Brooks, Marshall Brickman, and numerous others, and shown us its underside in ferocious, sardonic self-loathing. The gold in the streets, anticipated by Jewish immigrants when they first came to this country, has turned into ashes in the bed. *Marie and Bruce* is one of the most savage assaults yet on the failure of the American promise. (pp. 28-9)

Robert Brustein, "Two Couples," in The New Republic, Vol. 182, No. 14, April 5, 1980, pp. 28-9.

JACK KROLL

Hotel Play is not exactly a black comedy but a deeply tanned comedy set at a hotel in the tropics where the guests are having the worst time since man discovered the vacation.

These archetypal neurotics cannot take a vacation from their neuroses. There's a psychiatrist who's infected by the symptoms of his patients, including one who vomits every time he sees an attractive woman. There's a chap in safari drag who settles his nerves by fruitlessly hunting wild boar. There's a young man who's about to score with a girl when three generations of her family break in on their hanky-panky. There's a poor wretch with a vibrating chest, a woman with a nervous parrot, an army of husbands, wives, fathers, mothers and kids who love each other to death. One papa, trying to assemble his family for a happy dip, summons his little boy with a paternal shriek: "You lazy, good-for-nothing, self-pitying weakling!" Shawn himself plays the most ferocious of these citizens, a husband who dissects his gorgeous wife with razor-

edged insults, reducing her to the tearful lament: "I could have been an ordinary woman."

Far from being cynical or contemptuous about "ordinary" lives, Shawn loves them. But his special vision is to see how, in these twisted times, to be healthily ordinary is a positively Utopian goal. Ordinary people who can't be ordinary become monsters both absurd and destructive, and this is the cockeyed, compassionate, painfully hilarious world of Shawn's plays.

Jack Kroll, "Cast of Thousands," in Newsweek, Vol. XCVIII, No. 10, September 7, 1981, p. 81.

FRANK RICH

It's the running gag of Wallace Shawn's comedies—*Our Late Night, Marie and Bruce, The Hotel Play*—that polite literate, seemingly well-mannered people say and do the most outrageous things. The most civilized discourse can, without warning, turn into a beastly description of bodily functions (both sexual and alimentary), frequently punctuated by the word "pig." Mr. Shawn's brave new play . . . *Aunt Dan and Lemon,* is no exception, but this time the people are more refined than ever, their pronouncements the most piggish of all. And the running gag, at long last, reaches its explosive, horrifying punch line— for Mr. Shawn has harnessed it to nothing less than a central moral question of our age.

Simply put, this is a play about how literate, civilized societies can drift en masse into beastliness and commit the most obscene acts of history. The evening opens and closes with monologues in which a creamy-toned young Englishwoman, named Leonora and known as Lemon . . . , very sweetly tells us why she rather admires the Nazis for their "refreshing" lack of hypocrisy. The rest of the play explains, in flashbacks, how Lemon came to hold these pro-Nazi views, and it does so in a most insinuating way. The singleminded Mr. Shawn never supplies a character to challenge Lemon's articulate arguments. Instead, the audience is left to think up its own rebuttal— forcing us to wonder whether we could and would counter the spurious polemics of a clever fascist like Lemon in real life. I can't remember the last time I saw a play make an audience so uncomfortable, and I mean that as high praise.

Along with the discomfort, there is a lot of mordant laughter. Much of it is provided by the character known as Aunt Dan . . . , a friend of Lemon's parents who, during the Vietnam 60s, was the principal influence on the youthful heroine. A brilliant, American-born Oxford don, Dan (for Danielle) is obsessed with defending the honor of Henry Kissinger. . . . Dan's rabid tirades—in which she defends her idol's dates with starlets as strenuously as the bombing of North Vietnam— often backfire hilariously, but she does score some points. Like its companion play . . . , David Hare's *Map of the World* . . . , *Aunt Dan and Lemon* has its own nefarious reasons for giving the right wing its say.

In this play's case, Dan's pro-Kissinger arguments are warped and expanded in her acolyte's subsequent rationalizations of Nazi Germany. But Mr. Shawn goes further still, refusing to settle for blaming Lemon's callous convictions entirely on the political ideology she inherits from Aunt Dan. As we gradually learn, Dan instructed the young Lemon not just in public policy but also in private morality, regaling her with reminiscences of her wild salad days as an Oxford student. Most of these reminiscences center on Mindy—a high-priced prostitute who gleefully murders a client and whom Dan regarded as "the most exciting person" she ever met.

Mindy's amoral escapades—approvingly recounted by Dan and presented voyeuristically on stage in sexually graphic, hallucinatory fragments—are the ultimate dramatizations of what Mr. Shawn regards as the rot eating away at a supposedly civilized world. Throughout *Aunt Dan and Lemon* we are reminded that tabloid headlines like "Mother Eats Infant Baby While Father Laughs" lower our resistance to cruelty, that even an obsessive interest in morbid crime fiction can desensitize us (as it does Lemon) to the crimes of Treblinka. Dan and Lemon stand accused not for the political views they hold but for the compassion they have lost—a point brought home in a climactic scene at the older woman's death bed, when even the friends' compassion for each other goes unexpressed. And it is only compassion that can allow anyone, in prewar Germany or elsewhere, to puncture the smooth but specious analogies with which the shrewdest leaders may argue that the preservation of a privileged "way of life" is worth any moral price.

All of Mr. Shawn's own arguments, including his implicit view of Mr. Kissinger, are open to debate, of course—which, along with his refusal to tell the audience what to think and his omission of any "sympathetic" characters, helps make *Aunt Dan and Lemon* the most stimulating, not to mention demanding, American play to emerge this year. The most artful it is not. One may well want to resist the dramaturgy, which is plotless, all but structureless and almost entirely dependent on lengthy monologues. The crazed language with which the characters plead their obsessions usually, though not unfailingly, carries the speechifying. Only Mr. Shawn could turn even a description of Arnold Schoenberg's music into a memorable riff of Lenny Bruce-ese.

> Frank Rich, "Wallace Shawn's 'Aunt Dan and Lemon'," in The New York Times, October 29, 1985, p. C13.

LLOYD ROSE

Wallace Shawn, whose *Aunt Dan and Lemon* had its American premiere . . . [in 1985], brought the art of conversation and the art of playwriting together when he wrote and starred in *My Dinner with Andre,* in which he turned a series of discussions about art and life which he'd had with the avant-garde theater director Andre Gregory into a play, and himself and Gregory into characters. A film of the play, directed by Louis Malle, was released in 1981, and Shawn, for years a character actor in other people's movies, brought himself to the screen as a homey sensualist, full of common sense and skepticism, Sancho Panza to Gregory's cloud-borne, theorizing Don Quixote. *My Dinner with Andre* is nothing but talk, but it's deliriously good talk, the kind of thing you imagine as an abstraction when reading the phrase, in novel or biography, "brilliant dinner parties." Watching the film is like being an invisible guest at a particularly brilliant dinner party, with the excellent advantage of not being called on to keep up your end of the conversation. (p. 125)

For the audiences who come to see his plays, [Shawn] is always a conversationalist. He isn't interested in the conventional give and take of stage dialogue or, for that matter, in conventional plotting. His plays for the most part lack a beginning, middle, and end, and also scenes in which "something happens." What happens in Shawn's plays is that people talk, often wildly and shockingly—long discourses on obsession, fear, and fantasy, or minute dissections of seemingly everyday events—while others listen with the minimal reaction common to the rigidly well bred and the mad.

Typically, Shawn will place his characters at a party or in a hotel lobby, confronting them with the hopeless task of achieving polite social intercourse. They may make successful small talk for a few minutes, but then, suddenly, foul things will erupt from their mouths: epithets, forbidden desires, threats. "*The Hospital Play* (1971) has a lot of weeping and vomiting," he has written of his own work. "*Our Late Night* (1972) shows perhaps a rather elegant social evening, but weeping and vomiting have their place there too." Eating, as well, always has its place in Shawn's plays—some of his best writing is in his sensual descriptions of food—and the civilized ambience of his dinner with Andre represents a comfortable ideal of the good life, food for the body and for the soul. The rank spewings of his characters' most threatening and shameful thoughts are a metaphor for the impossibility of any true civilization or comfort. His people are always sick, either throwing up or feeling ill, because their souls are diseased, and no amount of raging or confession relieves them.

Scientists have postulated that within every human brain lies a "reptilian brain," in which lurk all the primitive, nonhuman impulses we share with the beasts. It's this brain that suddenly snakes its head up through the consciousness of Shawn's characters and drives them to wildness. It seems appropriate when talking of Shawn's work to use this physical analogy rather than the more philosophical "id" of Freud: his characters' misfortunes arise from being trapped in a body, with its endless demands for gratification and release. Their flesh constantly betrays them with its illnesses, aging, mortality, and amoral urgings. And it forces them to face a reality they would rather avoid: when a young man in *The Hospital Play* tells a woman "I love your hand," she replies, "It's just an animal's hand."

What with all the vomiting and weeping and other unpleasantness, Shawn's plays would be pretty tough going if he weren't such a shrewd, goofy satirist. In spite of the extremities of language and behavior he puts into his work, he's basically writing comedies of manners. His characters' biggest quandary isn't dealing with the moral consequences of their ugly urges, it's how to avoid responsibility for them. Mostly they do this by denial, simply refusing to acknowledge that anything unusual, in themselves or anyone else, is going on. In *Our Late Night* a man at a party recites in lurid detail a horrifying sexual encounter he had in the tropics. The story goes on and on, piling up one painful, crazy incident on top of another, excruciating and embarrassing to listen to. When it's finally over, there is "a long pause." It's as difficult for the audience as for the listeners onstage to think of any sane response. Finally, someone says, "My God—and to think that I planned to go to the tropics on my vacation!"

This remark, with its comically inappropriate egotism and its punch-line placement, is typical of Shawn's writing. He extends the technique to the whole of *Marie and Bruce,* his best-known play after *My Dinner with Andre.* . . . An account of the twenty-four hours that pass between the time Marie decides to leave her husband, Bruce, and then doesn't, it consists mostly of her haranguing him in the sort of language that used to be characterized as unprintable.

She begins on a relatively mild note, shouting at the sleeping Bruce, "Yes! I'm sick of you! Do you get it? You're driving me insane! I can't stand living with you for one more minute! I'm sick of it! I hate it! I hate my life with you! Do you hear me? I hate it!'' To which Bruce replies, ''Oh—hello, darling. Is it time to get up?'' This is the high comedy of the play, the comedy of denial and inappropriate response. And Bruce's passivity turns out to be a weapon of his own—Marie hurls herself against his imperviousness until she's beaten into exhaustion. The play ends not so much in reconciliation as in a draw. In the battle of the sexes Marie and Bruce fight a war of attrition.

Shawn's plays generally end in a draw. The constant confessions to which no one responds, the violent actions to which no one reacts, lead to a sense of stagnation. Nothing quite connects up; no real action seems possible. There are no climaxes (other than the physical kind) in the plays, no release for the characters or the audience. Everything seems caught in some eternal, hellish eddy, whirling nowhere to no purpose, and the energy of the plays comes not from action but from the seething frustration of the trapped characters.

This frustration is Shawn's joke on his characters. It's a good joke—funny and nasty—but it can wear thin. The lack of emotional movement in Shawn's work isn't intrinsically dramatic, and in some ways his writings are more impressive as mordant visions of humanity than as plays. Sometimes, too, the continually blocked action seems more like the writer's limitation than his choice. Shawn's good sense, so evident in his rebuttals of Gregory's more baroque flights of fancy in *My Dinner with Andre,* gets in his way. He can't keep from cocking an ironic eyebrow at his characters' messy fantasies and vile acts—what he has called ''my interior life as a raging beast.'' Irony can keep a writer from sinking into the swamps of sentimentality and excess, but it can also leave him high and dry, too smart and detached for his own good. Shawn may be one of the few writers who don't take themselves seriously enough.

What he does take seriously—what bucks him energetically past his flaws—is language. He isn't poetic, and he doesn't strive for big, mythic effects. His attitude toward his dialogue is familiar and companionable; he loves talk as he loves food. His characters don't talk to avoid action, they behave as if talk *were* action. It's as if they believed that just articulating their hidden thoughts were enough to make something happen, as if language were in itself magic. And Shawn himself has this belief in the power of words.

In the appendix to the published version of *Aunt Dan and Lemon* he writes, ''. . . thinking has its own pathology,'' and he elaborates on influence:

> I speak with you, and then I turn out the light and I go to sleep, but, while I sleep, you talk on the telephone to a man you met last year in Ohio, and you tell him what I said, and he hangs up and talks to a neighbor of his, and what I said keeps travelling, farther and farther. And just as a fly can quite blithely and indifferently land on the nose of a queen, so the thought which you mentioned to the man in Ohio can make its way with unimaginable speed into the mind of a President.

This idea becomes the center of *Aunt Dan and Lemon,* which, though it's told in a fragmented way, is simply the story of how Aunt Dan, corrupted by the stories of murder told by, and the whorish acts committed by, her friend Mindy, in turn cor-

rupts Lemon, the child of close friends of hers. At the play's end Lemon calmly tells us, ''So you have to say finally, well, fine, if there are all these people like my mother who want to go around talking about compassion all day, well, fine, that's their right. But it's sort of refreshing to admit every once in a while that they're talking about something that possibly doesn't exist.''

This conception of the force of words, as if they were a continual stream eroding reality into new shapes, has a certain fabulistic power. And *Aunt Dan and Lemon* is a departure for Shawn, for here, at least, talk really does matter, and one event leads to another. Although Henry Kissinger is used as the symbol of historical wickedness (Aunt Dan's defense of him is proof of her moral vacuity), Hitler, whom Shawn discusses in the appendix, is the evil genius that informs the play. Shawn probably chose to use Kissinger rather than Hitler for the best reasons: to deal with the political crimes of his own country rather than the safer, distant bugaboo of Nazi Germany. This disinclination to let his country and the culture that have shaped him off the hook is courageous and admirable. But honorable choices aren't always the best artistic choices, and as a dramatic symbol Kissinger is hardly a potent substitute for Hitler—not only the most mythical tyrant of this century but also the one who most clearly illustrated the dark magic of words, as he rode the swell of his ranting political speeches to power. Lemon discourses on the crimes of the Nazis at the play's beginning and end, and Hitler haunts *Aunt Dan* like a ghost never allowed to make its entrance.

The conceit of corruption through conversation, when dramatized, is disappointingly thin. You can hardly help wondering why Lemon apparently never talked to anyone else in her life, why her mother, who argues with Dan, has no effect on her. Similarly, Dan appears to have known and been influenced by only Mindy. Their conversions to amorality seem simplistic. They fall too easily; we suspect there was something weak and susceptible in them from childhood, something just waiting to go wrong.

In fact, there *has* been something wrong with Lemon since childhood—she can't really eat. When we meet her at the beginning of the play, about to tell us her story in flashbacks, she is an invalid, able only to drink fruit and vegetable juices and eat a little bread. In spite of Shawn's establishing that she has always been this way, the dramatic power of the image tells us something different. Shawn writes in the appendix that people who give up morality flower and feel free, but in the play the moralist in him becomes a poet: when Lemon announces to us her disbelief in compassion, we feel instinctively, no matter what we've been told, that this is what is wasting her. Shawn may say that he believes in the satisfactions of renouncing morality, but as an artist he cannot imagine them. (pp. 125-27)

Lloyd Rose, ''The Art of Conversation,'' in The Atlantic Monthly, *Vol. 256, No. 5, November, 1985, pp. 125-27.*

JOHN SIMON

Some wicked fairy must have presided over the birth of Wallace Shawn's *Aunt Dan and Lemon.* . . . She must have decreed, ''Thou shalt have neither language nor structure, neither shapeliness nor significance, neither wit nor good sense. Be thou bereft!'' And so there is this poor, unappetizing worm wriggling around the stage and pretending to be an iconoclastic play though it merely offends against taste, intelligence, and basic hygiene as it waits for someone to step on it and put it and its captive audience (no intermission, of course!) out of their misery.

Lemon, to call it by its rightful name, opens with an anemic, anorectic young woman, Leonora, nicknamed Lemon, soliloquizing in her dingy London flat about the uneventfulness, lovelessness, drabness of her idle, reclusive life. Subsisting mostly on a variety of juices although juiceless herself, she thrives on her reading, mostly books about the Nazis, who fascinate her and whose Holocaustal practices she recites with awe and, as we gradually realize, approval. Presently Lemon introduces us to her past. We meet her American father, Jack, a businessman, who promptly gets down to soliloquizing. There is relatively little dialogue in the play, and what there is is usually only thinly disguised monologue: Someone is feeding someone else cues for disquisitions, lengthy reminiscences, elaborate plummetings of fancy in language to make Iowa, by comparison, seem Alpine. . . .

We are, next, given a friend of the parents, Danielle, the youngest American don at Oxford, whom Lemon turns into her beloved Aunt Dan. Dan is an ardent Kissinger fetishist, and explains in interminable, incomparably boring monologues why we need servants and such to do our dirty work, and how Kissinger is just a grave, brave man doing what is distasteful to others but needs doing. Eventually Dan and the liberal Susan, totally incapable of defending her position, part for good; Lemon and Dan continue their discreetly lesbian-tinged friendship until the latter's death. . . .

Even while educating Lemon politically, Dan broadens her sexual horizons. So she introduces her to the friends she voluptuously admires: Mindy, a call girl who, for money, does everything, even kill; and Andy, a cynical roué whose life is all laughs and lechery. The point, I suppose, is that sexual amorality leads to ideological immorality. But Shawn has neither Shaw's wit nor Shaw's intellect with which to interweave plot and subplot dramatically and make antithetical positions come equally alive as they clash and give off sparks. We are tempted to conclude that the supposed intellectual challenge, like the sexual provocation, is only the game-playing of a prurient and presumptuous little boy, egged on by a number of indulgent reviewers. (p. 129)

> *John Simon, "Real Lemon," in* New York Magazine, *Vol. 18, No. 44, November 11, 1985, pp. 129-30, 132.*

ROBERT BRUSTEIN

Constructed almost entirely of provocative monologues, [*Aunt Dan and Lemon*] concludes with a long speech by the sickly young heroine, Lemon, extolling German death camps. . . .

Since Lemon's speech is a monologue, nobody is allowed to suggest that because she is sickly and weak (if not because she talks too much) she herself would have been among the earliest victims of the Nazis. But then I suspect this play has very little to do with credible realities or logical thought. It is really about Wallace Shawn's relationship with his audience. So much of *Aunt Dan and Lemon* is directed out toward the house rather than in toward the other characters that it appears Mr. Shawn is trying to position himself in relation to the sorely besieged pieties of prevailing liberal thought.

For the intellectual heart of this play is a defense of the Vietnam policies of Henry Kissinger. Aunt Dan, an American friend of Lemon's mother and an Oxford don, is infatuated with our former secretary of state not just on account of his mournful countenance but because, Christlike, he took upon himself the sins of an entire nation. "The whole purpose of government," she argues, "is to use force so we don't have to." How dare the "the filthy, slimy worms, the little journalists" attack him for killing peasants? They just "sit in their offices and write their little columns," instead of expressing gratitude to Kissinger for making shattering decisions on America's behalf. Lemon's mother raises a small protest against this reasoning ("Are you saying government or Kissinger can do anything?") but for the most part she, like everyone else in the play, is a mute recipient of totally unchallenged, totally arguable opinions. (p. 26)

Seeing the play doesn't lead one to reargue the virtues of the Vietnam War or even to dispute Aunt Dan's defense of Kissinger. It simply stimulates questions about authorial attitude toward the issues raised, in light of what later prove to be their consequences. For Lemon's defense of the Nazis following Aunt Dan's death seems a direct result of Dan's teachings that governments survive and prosper through the use of violence: "I was on my own," Lemon says. "My education had been completed."

If you think this shows Shawn himself refuting Aunt Dan, by proving that a policy that justifies force leads to a policy that justifies extermination, the play also includes a subplot, otherwise irrelevant, which could be construed as confirming Lemon and Dan's position. This involves some underworld friends of Dan, particularly an attractive blond demimondaine named Mindy who, largely for thrills, poisons and then strangles a foreign drug dealer in the midst of having oral sex with him (echoing raunchier writings by the son of an editor of a chaste periodical popularly known as "Aunt Edna"). Dan and Lemon are both fascinated with Mindy, and Aunt Dan even has an affair with her—an unconvincing mismatch between an elegant middle-aged Oxford scholar and an amoral party girl who have in common only their mutual recognition of the necessity for violence.

I have been discussing *Aunt Dan and Lemon* more as an argument than as a play since it is impossible to evaluate it in dramatic terms. Its failure to create any real engagement between characters, lack of organic development, directionless twists and turns of plot, tortured structure, unending exposition, confusing flashbacks (within flashbacks), and extreme talkiness, all suggest an aesthetic disaster of considerable proportions, if judged by any existing standards of theatrical form. Wallace Shawn, potentially one of our finest dramatists, is perfectly capable of creating strong dramatic action: *Marie and Bruce,* though occasionally disjointed, is a penetrating radiograph of a collapsing marriage. He is also capable of writing a work of genuine intellectual power, as demonstrated in the dialectical *My Dinner with Andre,* where Shawn, playing Sancho Panza to Andre Gregory's Don Quixote, countered his partner's grandiose mysticism with wry mordant realism. But the talk in *Aunt Dan and Lemon* is far from dialectical. It is more like a bleary soliloquy in a college dormitory, interrupted by the merest gesture toward theatrical context ("As we were talking," says Lemon in a typical aside, "night would fall"), causing one to leave the theater as you might stumble into Harvard Yard after having been verbally assaulted by an especially garrulous undergraduate who has proposed particularly provocative premises.

There is, no doubt, a vein of truth in Shawn's presentation. Human beings *are* destructive and violent; governments *do* reflect the aggressive qualities of their constituents. So what else is new? But it is also true that humankind has been struggling since the beginning of civilization to overcome its discontents and control this violence with compassion and understanding, lest we all end up in clumps of corpses or piles of ashes. Liberalism, however discredited, and for all its admitted hypocrisy and frequent silliness, remains committed to the life principle, and to the quest for peace in an aggressive world. And so does conservatism, for all its confrontational "realism" and paranoid style. But this is not true of the ideological extremism expressed in *Aunt Dan and Lemon,* with its effort to elevate a strain in human nature into a general all-embracing dark principle. Which tempts one to say to Wally Shawn, Don't hang back with the brutes.

I'm not really suggesting that Wallace Shawn endorses the reactionary ideas of any of his characters, or seriously entertains their positions. He's more engaged in fashioning acts of provocation. But open season on liberals has been licensed for many years now and the trophy room is getting crowded. I suspect that it might be more daring in the present climate to defend liberalism than to ridicule it, since the hostile audience Shawn is eager to address can be safely assumed now to be conservative. (pp. 26-7)

Aunt Dan and Lemon strikes me as an entirely puzzling performance by a valuable writer trying to create a play of ideas, but too confused by internal contradictions to compose a coherent work. (p. 28)

> Robert Brustein, *"Addressing a Hostile Audience,"* in The New Republic, *Vol. 193, No. 24, December 9, 1985, pp. 26-8.*

GERALD WEALES

The success of *Aunt Dan and Lemon* is something of a surprise since Wallace Shawn does not make things easy for the audience. The play begins and ends with long monologues—very long ones (the closing speech runs almost eight pages in the printed play)—and American audiences are not supposed to be able to listen so attentively. Add that the material of Lemon's speeches—a rumination on human nature that becomes a defense of the Holocaust—is necessarily offensive to many members of the audience. Add, too, that the rest of the play consists of set pieces, most of them by Aunt Dan, or brief scenes, presumably intended as thematic illustrations rather than emotionally absorbing mini-dramas. (p. 179)

Aunt Dan and Lemon is a teaching play of sorts, but the lesson of the play is not the one that the title characters are teaching. As the play opens, Lemon invites the audience ("little children") into her "little flat," into her life. Her explanation of who she is and how she got that way will presumably enlighten us about what human beings are truly like. Lemon is a young woman in her twenties, a recluse living largely on fruit and vegetable juices (a wall of jars full of colored liquids looms behind her, interior decoration as threat) and filling her days with memories—most of them secondhand, having been received from Aunt Dan's stories—and from books about the Nazis. (pp. 179-80)

At first glance, Aunt Dan appears to be a marked contrast to the emotionally desiccated Lemon whose experiences are largely vicarious and whose deliberate speech, . . . underscores the death-in-life quality of the character. The Dan whom we see holding forth to the mesmerized Lemon, at age eleven, is vigorous, raunchy, funny, vituperative. . . . The trick is to step past her surface appeal, actually to listen to her words. The underside of Dan is already detectable in her amusing first speeches, but not as clearly visible and audible as in her long defense of Henry Kissinger, whom she admires as a doer whose ability to make decisions is more important than the moral or immoral implications of his choices. Her long speech, which begins as a reasoned political statement, turns increasingly self-revelatory as her attack on the "filthy, slimy worms" who criticize Kissinger calls up a vocabulary that reveals her own attraction to violence, to blood, to corruption. In the scenes that follow, we see her friend Mindy sell herself for money and then, as a paid killer, murder a man. (Dan's own sexual adventures are depicted as similarly unfeeling if not so venal.)

Lemon is an odd extension of Aunt Dan and her friends. Their playfulness masks a lack of genuine connection (the appeal of Mindy for one of the characters is that "she never asked anyone for anything but money") which becomes in Lemon an almost complete separation from other people. She even turns her back on the dying Dan, whose condition might demand some sacrifice. Dan's refusal to consider compassion as a necessary ingredient in the decision-making process becomes for Lemon an acceptance and finally an embracing of evil. Not only are these people willing to kill to protect their own view of the correct and comfortable life, but the killing itself is pleasing. As Lemon makes her way through her thickets of logical illogic, we can almost see again Aunt Dan, aroused by Mindy's account of murder, reaching out caressingly to touch the lips that tell so enticing a tale.

Lemon's mother is the only character in the play whose feelings and ideas oppose those of Aunt Dan and Lemon. Yet the softness of Lemon's mother is no match for the violence of Lemon's father or the overriding power of Aunt Dan's pseudo-rationality. Drama, the old textbooks tells us, is fueled by conflict, but Wallace Shawn has played an impressive variation on that assumption. The tension in *Aunt Dan and Lemon* is between audience and characters. There is no one on stage to say an effective *no* to Lemon. The audience, unless it is seduced by the plausibility of Aunt Dan and her peculiar pupil, has to do its own rejecting. Some members of the audience, judging by reviews and comments in the theater, reject the play without realizing how carefully Shawn has devised the work as an ally of the audience against the characters and their ideas. (p. 180)

> Gerald Weales, *"Bobbing & Invading: Aunt Dan & Benefactors,"* in Commonweal, *Vol. CXIII, No. 6, March 28, 1986, pp. 179-81.*

Sam Shepard

1943-

(Born Samuel Shepard Rogers, Jr.) American dramatist and scriptwriter.

Shepard is considered the foremost dramatist currently writing for the off-Broadway stage, having won eleven Obie Awards, the New York Drama Critics' Circle Award, and a Pulitzer Prize. His works, including over forty one-act and full-length dramas, convey a surreal vision of contemporary American society in which myth collides with reality. Shepard examines a wide range of topics in his plays, most notably the spiritual dissolution of the family, the corruption of the artist by commercialism, the disintegration of the American dream, and the vanishing Western frontier and its culture. His interest in the legends and myths of the American West dominate his dramas, as do references to jazz, rock and country music lyrics, drugs, Hollywood films, and other components of American popular culture. While some critics label Shepard's work obscure or undisciplined and express difficulty in placing his plays within a specific dramatic tradition, others view his dramas as the most daring and innovative of his generation.

Shepard was born in Fort Sheridan, Illinois, and was raised on his family's avocado ranch in Duarte, California, an area with a diverse population that included farmers, transients, and other people desiring to escape the fast-paced environment of Los Angeles. He describes his family life as less than ideal: "My father was prone to violent bouts with various types of alcohol and his own bitter disappointment with his life. . . . Everything got so hysterical in my family that . . . I fled the scene." Shepard began his theatrical career as an actor in California, but in 1963 he moved to New York City and became involved with several off-off-Broadway theater groups. His first one-act dramas, *Cowboys* and *The Rock Garden,* were produced by Theatre Genesis in 1964. Although virtually dismissed by critics, the plays attracted a sizable cult following, and Shepard soon became off-off-Broadway's most productive dramatist. His subsequent one-act plays are marked by their disjointed structure, visual imagery, and scatological monologues. Shepard continued to explore various combinations of sight and sound in his early full-length dramas. *La Turista* (1966) is a comedy about a couple who succumb to intestinal illness while vacationing in Mexico, and *Operation Sidewinder* (1970) is a satire of the social and political upheavals of the 1960s. These plays were described by Carol Rosen as "freewheeling excursions, [taking] flight through dreamlike torrents of language and image."

Shepard moved to London following the production of *Operation Sidewinder*. While there he wrote several plays which constitute a second period of his career. One of these plays, *The Tooth of Crime* (1972), illustrates Shepard's thematic concerns with Western folklore and popular culture. *The Tooth of Crime* is an allegorical story of two rock musicians, Hoss and Crow, whose battle for prominence in the music industry resembles the actions of gunfighters in the old West. Language plays a crucial part in the play, for Shepard employs urban slang, rock lyrics, and other pop idioms in place of the conventional weapons of gunfighters. At the conclusion, Hoss, realizing that the language he uses for "dueling" is dated,

commits suicide, leaving Crow in command until the next challenger comes along. Praising the drama's cohesive structure and theme, many critics regard *The Tooth of Crime* as Shepard's best play. In the mid-1970s, Shepard resettled in California, becoming playwright-in-residence at the Magic Theatre in San Francisco. His plays produced during this period focus on the artist's pursuit of identity and creative freedom as well as the struggles that result from this search. *Suicide in B-Flat* (1976), for example, suggests the stifling of creativity in the life of a jazz musician, while *Angel City* (1976) satirizes the film industry and the corruption of young writers.

Shepard's major plays of the late 1970s and 1980s are domestic dramas in which working-class families are victims of self-perpetuated violence, guilt, and abnormal fantasy. The dissolution of a southern California family in *Curse of the Starving Class* (1976) symbolizes the demise of the Western frontier and American society in general. *Buried Child* (1978), for which Shepard won a Pulitzer Prize, features a family whose history of incest and infanticide is accidentally discovered years later. *True West* (1980) is about two brothers—one a successful scriptwriter, the other a petty thief—and their different attitudes toward fantasy and reality. The thematic concerns of Shepard's later plays culminate in the Obie Award-winning drama, *Fool for Love* (1983). Obsession, betrayal, myth, and truth are addressed in this play about an incestuous love affair between a half-brother and half-sister. In his recent play, *A Lie of the Mind* (1985), which won the New York Drama Critics' Circle Award, Shepard further explores American families in emotional distress. This work centers on a married couple whose violent relationship both destroys and redeems their families. While some critics voiced concern over the redundancy of character and theme in the play, Jack Kroll contended that Shepard's characters are "battered travesties of the American pioneer energy. . . . Shepard is their William Faulkner; like Faulkner, he writes about them with a powerful blend of wild humor and tragic force."

Shepard is also well regarded for his work in other genres. He wrote the screenplay for the film *Paris, Texas* and adapted *Fool for Love* for the screen. He is also the author of a volume of short stories, *Hawk Moon* (1973), and has published *Rolling Thunder Logbook* (1977), a journal based on his experiences traveling with Bob Dylan's Rolling Thunder Revue tour. *Motel Chronicles* (1983) is a collection of autobiographical sketches and poems. In a review of this book, R. E. Nowicki summarized Shepard's achievements: "[What] is best about Shepard is the way in which he captures the heart and soul of the contemporary American West. . . . Sam Shepard presents a picture of the West that goes against the grain of the glamorous movement to Sunbelt cities."

(See also *CLC*, Vols. 4, 6, 17, 34; *Contemporary Authors*, Vols. 69-72; and *Dictionary of Literary Biography*, Vol. 7.)

RICHARD GILMAN

Not many critics would dispute the proposition that Sam Shepard is our most interesting and exciting American playwright.

Fewer, however, can articulate just where the interest and excitement lie. There is an extraordinarily limited and homogeneous vocabulary of critical writing about Shepard, a thin lexicon of both praise and detraction. Over and over one sees his work described as "powerful"—"brutally" or "grimly" or "oddly" powerful, but muscular beyond question. Again and again one hears him called "surrealist" or "gothic" or, a bit more infrequently, a "mythic realist." . . . To his detractors he is always "obscure," usually "willfully" so, and always "undisciplined." But even some of his enemies acknowledge his "theatrical magic," always with that phrase, and admirers and some enemies alike point to his plays' "richness of texture," always in those words.

The same sort of ready-made language can be found in discussions of Shepard's themes or motifs. Nearly everyone is agreed that the great majority of his plays deal with one or more of these matters: the death (or betrayal) of the American dream; the decay of our national myths; the growing mechanization of our lives; the search for roots; the travail of the family. (The trouble is, this cluster of related notions would apply to a good many other American writers as well.)

Most critics find it hard clearly to extract even these ideas from Shepard's plays, many of which are in fact extraordinarily resistant to thematic exegesis. Shepard's most ardent enthusiasts have got round the problem by arguing that he isn't . . . talking *about* anything but rather *making* something, a familiar notion in avant-garde circles and, as far as it goes, a correct one. They point out that his genius lies not in ideas or thought

but in the making of images; he speaks more to the eye, or to the ear (in terms of expressive sound, though not necessarily in terms of immediate sense), than to the mind.

I don't fully accept this argument, though I see its virtues, and I do share in some of the prevailing uncertainties. I don't mean that I'm uncertain about the value of Shepard's work, but I find the question of "themes" troubling, primarily because I detect a confusion in *him* about them. But the real difficulty I share with many critics isn't so much deciding what the work is as knowing how to write about what it is. How to wield a critical vocabulary that won't be composed of clichés and stock phrases, how devise a strategy of discourse to deal usefully with this dramatist who slips out of all the categories? (pp. ix-x)

If there's a more nearly perfect exemplar of a cultural education gained ("absorbed" is a better word) in the 'fifties than Sam Shepard, I can't imagine who it might be. I first saw him at the Open Theater in 1965, a James Dean-like youth with an un-Dean-like intellectual glint in his eyes. Even after I'd overcome my initial dismay at such easy and untutored confidence, it took me awhile to see that there wasn't any reason he couldn't be a playwright or anything else. For the fifties, out of which he came, or sidled, was the era in which two things started to happen of great importance to our subsequent culture. One was that the distance between "high" and "low" in art began to be obliterated, and the other was that the itch for "expression," for hurling the self's words against anonymity and silence, began to beat down the belief in the necessity for formal training, apprenticeship and growth, that had always been held in regard to drama or any art. (pp. x-xi)

Shepard seems to have come out of no literary or theatrical tradition at all but precisely from the breakdown or absence—on the level of art if not of commerce—of all such traditions in America. Such a thing is never a clean, absolute stride away from the ruins; fragments of tradition, bits of history, cling to every razed site and to one's shoes. But in his case one does see a movement with very little cultural time at its back, or only the thinnest slice of the immediate past, a *willed* movement, it might be said, for one sometimes suspects Shepard of wanting to be thought *sui generis,* a self-creation. That he must, for example, have been influenced by Jack Gelber's 1959 play *The Connection,* by some of Ronald Tavel's work, by certain aspects of Pinter and, more recently, by Edward Bond, as well as by elements of what we call theatrical "absurdity," are things he has never mentioned.

What we do know is that in a sense he's a writer in spite of himself. . . . Shepard's plays sometimes do give off a whiff of reluctance to being plays, a hint of dissatisfaction with the form. And his recent incarnation as a film actor increases our sense that he's had something else, or something additional, in mind all along.

For what was true for him when he started (as it was true for the general culture in its youthful sectors), was that a mode of expression existed more compelling, more seductive and more in affinity with the outburst of the personal than writing in the old high formal sense. In light of Shepard's rock ambitions, listen to him on the genre. It made, he said (without punctuation) "movies theater books painting and art go out the window none of it stands a chance against the Who the Stones and Old Yardbirds Creedence Traffic the Velvet Underground Janis and Jimi." . . .

Nevertheless Shepard did pluck drama from outside the window and became a writer. But the influence of rock is major and pervasive, if most direct in his early plays. It can be seen in the plays' songs, of course, but also, more subtly, in a new kind of stage language, contemporary in a harsh, jumpy way, edging, as both rock lyrics and rock talk do, between pseudo-professional argot and a personal tone of cocksure assertion. It is almost hermetic at times, but one can always detect a type of savage complaint and a belligerent longing. Thematically, rock, or rather the legendary status of its star performers, provided the direct subject of *Suicide in bFlat* and *The Tooth of Crime.*

But rock isn't the only musical style Shepard employs. A whole range of other genres can be found: modern jazz, blues, country and western and folk music of several kinds. Shepard has always claimed, or others have on his behalf, that these musical elements are as important to many of his plays as their speech, and that the same thing is true for his decors. Indeed it's difficult to imagine much of his work without its music, by which I mean that it's not an embellishment or a strategic device, in the manner of Brecht, to interrupt the flow of a sequential narrative, but an integral part of the plays' devising of new consciousness.

Shepard's physical materials and perspectives come largely from developments in the graphic arts and dance during his adolescence and early career. He has said that Jackson Pollack was important to him, but what seems more active in his sensibility are emanations from the "happenings" phase of painting and sculpture, collage in the manner of Johns and Rauschenberg, and the mixed-media experiments of the latter artist with John Cage and others. His sets reveal all these influences at two extremes: their occasional starkness, a bare space in which lighting is the chief or only emotive or "placing" factor, and their frequent stress on dirt, *dreck.* . . . (pp. xi-xii)

More generally, in regard to subject and reference, to iconography, we can observe a far-flung network of influences, interests and obsessions that have gone into the making of Shepard's work. The most substantial of these are the car or "road" culture of his youth, science-fiction, Hollywood Westerns and the myth of the West in general, and television in its pop or junk aspects. Besides these Shepard himself has mentioned "vaudeville, circuses . . . trance dances, faith healing ceremonials . . . medicine shows," to which we might add telepathic states, hallucinatory experiences (drug-induced or not), magic and witchcraft.

Eclectic as all this seems, something binds it together, and this is that nearly everything I've mentioned is to one degree or another an interest or engagement of the pop and counter cultures that had their beginnings in the fifties. When we reflect on what these movements or climates have left us—their presence is still felt in the form of a corpse not quite grown cold—a set of major impulses immediately emerges: a stance against authority and tradition, anti-elitism, the assertion of the untaught self in impatience and sometimes mockery.

But one sees in it all too—something most pertinent to a rumination on Shepard's plays—another and more subtle configuration: a world of discards and throwaways, of a *nostalgie de boue* appeared by landscapes filled with detritus and interiors strewn with debris, of floating images, unfinished acts, discontinuity and dissonance, abruptnesses and illogicalities; an impatience with time for proceeding instead of existing all at

once, like space; and with space for having limits, fixed contours and finality.

This in large part is Shepard's theatrical world. I said that his plays emerged far more from new movements outside the theater than from within it, but what really happened can't be that clear. If he's never acknowledged any debt to the so-called Absurdists, or to any other playwrights for that matter, whether or not he learned directly from them scarcely matters. He learned alongside them, so to speak, or in their wake, in the same atmosphere of rejection of linear construction, cause and effect sequences, logical procedures, coherent or consistent characters, and the tying of language to explicit meanings that distinguished the new drama from its predecessors. (p. xiii)

Most of his plays seem like fragments, chunks of various sizes thrown out from some mother lode of urgent and heterogeneous imagination in which he has scrabbled with pick, shovel, gunbutt and hands. The reason so many of them seem incomplete is that they lack the clear boundaries as artifact, the internal order, the progress toward a denouement (of some kind: a crystallization, a summarizing image, a poise in the mind) and the consistency of tone and procedure that ordinarily characterize good drama, even most avant-garde drama of the postwar time.

Many of his plays seem partial, capricious, arbitrarily brought to an end and highly unstable. They spill over, they leak. They change, chameleon-like, in self-protection as we look at them. This is a source of the difficulty one has in writing about them, as it's also a source of their originality. Another difficulty is that we tend to look at all plays for their single "meanings" or ruling ideas but find this elusive in Shepard and find, moreover, his plays coalescing, merging into one another in our minds. Rather than always trying to keep them separate, trying by direct plunges into their respective depths to find clear meanings tucked away like kernels within gorgeous ragged husks, I think we ought to accept, at least provisionally, their volatility and interdependence; they constitute a series of facets of a single continuing act of imagination.

Beyond this, and as an aspect of it, we have to see Shepard's work as existing in an especially intricate and disorderly relationship with life outside the theater. Such a relationship obviously is true of any drama, but in Shepard's case it shows itself as a rambunctious reciprocity in which the theatrical, as a mode of behavior, takes a special wayward urgency from life, while the living—spontaneous, unorganized and unpredictable—keeps breaking into the artificial, composed world of the stage. (pp. xv-xvi)

The very "rootlessness" of Shepard's theater, its springing so largely from a condition outside the continuity of the stage, is a source of the difficulty we have with it, as it is also a source of its dazzling disturbances. But inside his theater, within its own continuousness, a tragi-comic drama of names and selves unfolds. I think of the frantic efforts of so many of his characters to make themselves felt, often by violence (or cartoon violence—blows without injuries, bullets without deaths: dream or make-believe, something filmed), of the great strand in his work of the ego run wild, of the craving for altered states of being and the power to transcend physical or moral or psychic limitations—and the very alterations and transcendences of this kind carried out in the plays: the transformations, the splitting of characters, the masks, the roles within roles, the mingling of legendary figures with invented ones. And I think of the "turns," the numbers, the oratorios and arias, and especially the monologues or soliloquies that aren't simply contributions to the plot but outcries of characters craving to be known.

The monologues take many forms. One is a kind of technical disquisition, such as Jeez's on deer-skinning in *Shaved Splits* or Howard's on flying in *Icarus's Mother*. They may be prosaic or bizarre but they have the effect of claiming for the speaker an individuality based on some sort of detailed knowledge. More often the monologue is simply a "story," matter-of-fact or exotic, which may or may not contribute to the plot, but which always serves to distinguish the speaker as a voice, as someone with *something* to tell. (p. xx)

The monologues are most often tight, staccato, gathering a strange cumulative eloquence. In their varied voices they reveal as nothing else does Shepard's marvelous ear, not for actual speech but for the imagined possibilities of utterance as invention, as victory over silence. (p. xxi)

In his last three plays Shepard has withdrawn noticeably from the extravagant situations, the complex wild voices and general unruliness of the earlier work. His themes, so elusive before, seem clearer now, if not pellucidly so, his vision dwells more on actual society. Physical or economic circumstances play more of a part than before. (p. xxiii)

In its straightforwardness and sparseness of action *True West,* Shepard's newest play, is surely the least typical of all his works. Its protagonists, two brothers who somewhat resemble Lenny and Teddy in Pinter's *Homecoming* (as the play itself also resembles Pinter in its portentous pauses and mysterious references) clash over their respective roles. Lee, the drifter and man of the desert, envies Austin, the successful screenwriter and takes over his position by selling a producer on an "authentic" Western, one, that's to say, drawn entirely from his own matter of fact and therefore non-artistic, uninvented experience.

Austin, not an artist but a contriver of entertainment, nevertheless represents the imagination against Lee's literalness. Their battle shifts its ground until Austin, in the face of Lee's claim that his story reveals the "true" West, retorts that "there's no such thing as the West anymore. It's a dead issue!" The myths are used up. Still, his own identity has been found within his work of manipulating popular myths and he finds himself draining away under the pressure of Lee's ruthless "realism." The play ends with Austin's murderous attack on his brother, a last desperate attempt to preserve a self.

A last word on *Tongues* and *Savage/Love*. . . . Both are more theater pieces than plays. They're the outcome of Shepard's and Chaikin's experiments with a dramatic form stripped of accessories, of plot elements and physical action, reduced to essentials of sound and utterance. When they rise, as they sometimes do, to a point of mysterious and resilient lyricism, they reach us as reminders at least of Shepard's wide and far from exhausted gifts.

I suspect he'll astonish us again. (p. xxv)

> *Richard Gilman, in an introduction to* Seven Plays *by Sam Shepard, Bantam Books, 1981, pp. ix-xxv.*

JACK KROLL

Joseph Papp's production of Sam Shepard's *True West* . . . is emblematic of the uncertainty of American theater as it enters the '80s. Here's Shepard . . . , who in some twist of cultural prestidigitation has gone from being the darling of the "experimental" theater to winning the Pulitzer Prize, complete with the albatross of being called "America's leading playwright." And here's Papp, who's still a "controversial" figure after a generation of bringing every conceivable kind of theatrical experience to audiences ranging from workshop eavesdroppers to Broadway herds. . . . Now the author has disowned Papp's production of his newest play after a squabble over casting and the resignation of director Robert Woodruff. . . . [And] Papp has sworn never to do another Shepard play with the writer. . . . Both men are innocent and the result is an unfortunate mess.

True West is another of Shepard's attempts to deal with American myths as they curdle into pop fantasies. He is both appalled and fascinated by this process, and this ambivalence is what gives his plays their ambiguous power. *True West* is a kind of pop Cain and Abel; the brothers here are Austin . . . , a screenwriter, and Lee . . . , a truculent weirdo who lives by petty burglary and is envious of his brother's success. The brothers are ensconced in their mother's house somewhere in suburban southern California while she is off vacationing in Alaska. Austin is trying to work on a new movie "project" and Lee is bugging him, swilling beer and relieving his anxiety by swiping TV sets from the neighbors. The mythic switch comes when a chain-wearing Hollywood producer . . . likes Lee's dopey idea for a Western better than Austin's project, and suddenly the Neanderthal Lee is the success and Austin is the envious outsider stealing toasters.

There's a promising idea here. Shepard is dealing with all sorts of themes: the Jekyll-Hyde interchangeability of highbrow and lowbrow; the devastation, spiritual as well as physical, of the West as territory and dream; the civil war in the American spirit between conformity and anarchy. What you see is an effective staking out of these themes, an irresolute development and a botched-up climax. Shepard has protested that some of his text has been changed, but it seems clear that both play and production are at fault. The play falls on both of its faces as myth and reality: Why is Austin an Ivy League smoothie and Lee a desert rat? Why is their mother . . . in Alaska (ah yes, another American frontier), and why is she so damned dissociated when she returns? And why is the final, lights-out combat between the brothers so indecisive? Does one survive? Both? Neither?

Like almost all of Shepard's plays, *True West* is a hybrid: half barbaric yawp, half sophisticated artifact. Papp's version underscores this split. It symbolizes an American theater that, whatever its successes and failures, has yet to produce serious and popular drama that truly reflects the troubled American consciousness.

> *Jack Kroll, "California Dreaming," in* Newsweek, *Vol. XCVII, No. 1, January 5, 1981, p. 63.*

STEPHEN HARVEY

It was, of course, pure coincidence that . . . [a revival of Ibsen's *John Gabriel Borkman* and Sam Shepard's *True West* premiered] almost simultaneously. Yet seeing them within a few days of each other produced an odd and unexpected set of cross-resonances. Both are basically naturalistic pieces that focus largely on the battle for dominance between a pair of adult siblings who have always loathed each other; each veers suddenly into a metaphorically moonlit coda, as its respective set of sisters and brothers merges into one being at the final blackout. In their own way, Ibsen and Shepard alike forged their characters with such rude skeletal symmetry as to demand the most confident, sympathetic direction to give their creations flesh and momentum. Neither play received anything like the production it deserves.

Shepard's play in particular needs a good deal of help lest its endless string of carefully matched dualities be reduced onstage to a willful theatrical tic. The title alludes to two of the conflicts that fuel the play, one general and one highly specific. There is the California of antiseptic tract homes (like the one in which *True West* takes place) at the edge of the feral desert they're gradually destroying. Then there's the romantic Western scenario that professional screenwriter Austin . . . is busy concocting vs. the hokey yarnspinning of his brother, Lee . . . , a lifelong con artist. Austin is a cultivated smoothie, favored since childhood by his bland, bourgeois mother; Lee is the hair-trigger anarchist, his reprobate father's pet, who camps out amid the sagebrush and pinches TV sets for a living. At the play's beginning, Austin is hunched intently over his typewriter at stage left, while Lee the intruder stands in the kitchen on the right, guzzling beer and exuding peeved desperation. For much of the second act, their positions—physical and otherwise—are precisely reversed. Now it's Lee whose saga is destined Soon to Be a Minor Motion Picture, while Austin swills booze, vents his temper, lifts other people's appliances and mumbles of his urge to grasp reality by retreating to the solitude of the desert.

Naturally, both alternatives are revealed as futile. As Austin puts it all too bluntly late in act two, "There is no such thing as the real West anymore"; but we all know what an empty shuck lies in store at the hands of the forces of Mammon. The latter are represented here by a walking symbol of venal old Hollywood, a producer who descends on each of the brothers in succession to weigh their competing movie treatments. . . . [This] unctuous vulgarian is no less transparent a device than the cheap celluloid artifices Shepard so vocally despises. Austin pours contempt on the shoot-'em-up chase scenes Lee has injected into his script (and which the mogul, predictably, loves), but isn't this ostentatious identity switcheroo of Shepard's just another show-biz gimmick of a somewhat flossier order? Local color notwithstanding, *True West* is no more than an uprooted transplant of the Ingmar Bergman *Persona* game, unless we can be persuaded that Austin and Lee recognize enough of themselves in each other to be tempted to trade psyches—or indeed that they exist dramatically in the first place. (p. 123)

> *Stephen Harvey, in a review of "True West," in* The Nation, *Vol. 232, No. 4, January 31, 1981, pp. 123-24.*

ROBERT BRUSTEIN

[I went to Sam Shepard's *True West*] expecting a significant event. The evening was significant, but not quite in the way I had anticipated. What it revealed was an important theater in a state of momentary disarray. (p. 21)

Like *Seduced,* Shepard's recent play about Howard Hughes, *True West* has the feeling of a first draft. Shepard rarely revises any of his work extensively, but at his best (in *Buried Child,* for example), the initial rush can carry him through. In *True West,* his impulse is not sustained; the play looks thin, even emaciated, like a healthy organism turning anorexic before your eyes.

True West is fascinating as long as its design is hidden . . . ; its very symmetry undermines its mystery. I suspect the work will ultimately be of interest mainly to Shepard's biographers, for it is possible to detect in the tension between the two brothers a personal meaning for the playwright. I have a feeling that Lee and Austin represent two aspects of Shepard's career— the increasingly renowned playwright and movie actor on the one hand, the freewheeling coffeehouse writer and carefree musician on the other. It may be that Shepard is working something out in this play, a kind of nostalgia for his past life, which he associates with the real or true West, as opposed to "shopping in the Safeway, riding on the Freeway," the suburban traps in which "There's nothing real down here anymore—least of all me."

The real Shepard is certainly not on display . . . , and that, too, may be the price he is paying for his fame. (p. 22)

[The] evening generally seems to be an exercise in sloppiness, without even the excuse of being a work in progress.

And that, ultimately, is the really pathetic thing about this exercise—that one of the few genuine dramatic writers of our time should have been so shamefully mishandled. (pp. 22-3)

> *Robert Brustein, "Crossed Purposes," in* The New Republic, *Vol. 184, No. 5, January 31, 1981, pp. 21-3.*

MICHAEL EARLEY

For close to two decades Sam Shepard has been an anomaly on the American dramatic landscape. Part of the problem in approaching his plays has been the question of just where to place him within a perceivable tradition—be it theatrical or literary. What, after all, does he owe to American drama? Very little, in fact. Rather he seems to have forged a whole new kind of American play that has yet to receive adequate reckoning. But when you step back for a moment and measure Shepard against the deeper wellspring of American literature, particularly the transcendental and romantic traditions, a whole new way of looking at this complex and curious writer is revealed. He is, after all, an intuitive playwright of exhilarating vision who, to paraphrase Ralph Waldo Emerson in "The Poet," sees America as a drama whose ample geography dazzles the imagination. In placing Shepard within this kind of spectrum, you begin to see possibilities for him and his plays that you never thought existed.

If you take the position, as I do, that Shepard is a true American primitive, a literary naif coursing the stage of American drama as if for the first time, asserting a stylistic independence that has become a central dramatic situation for American writers, then what you begin to see in his plays are innocent gestures and fresh associations that resemble the themes, language, and mythic preoccupations of an earlier group of American writers like Hawthorne, Melville, and Whitman. In fact, a substantial case could be made for saying that Whitman is *the* most apparent influence on Shepard's style. For like the poet in "One's Self I Sing," Shepard's plays are full of Whitman's "Of Life immense in passion, pulse, and power." And yet while whole sections of his writing seem to resemble that of Whitman— even play titles and characters appear to come from "Song of Myself"—Shepard's passion for dark, ominous visions, and greater abstraction runs a clear course back to Hawthorne and Melville. For what Shepard lacks of Whitman's optimism and deep faith in democracy surfaces in sympathies for the darker and more corrosive side of early American fiction. (pp. 126-27)

What you begin to see in Shepard, when viewed through the lens of early American literature, is the sort of pattern that the critic Marius Bewley called the "eccentric design" of American fiction. A design that veers away from observable fact and social manners—a European tradition—and comes into closer contact with abstractions and dialectical tensions that became the core of early American writing. In Shepard those abstractions and tensions come alive in a new way while at the same moment repeating a timeless pattern. The symbolic abstraction of, for instance, Hawthorne's forest, Melville's white whale, or Poe's gothic spaces become echoed in Shepard's desert, sidewinder computer, and farmhouse that hides secrets from the past. *The Scarlet Letter* finds its analogue in the mark of *The Unseen Hand* or the green slime of *Angel City*. These images, and the abstractness of the ideas they represent, gives them the "large and glowing generality" that Bewley attends to their presence in American fiction.

The tension between an American wilderness and a new industrial civilization, a resonant note in American literature, strikes a responsive chord in Shepard, too. His sense of this fundamental conflict is as elementary as anything found in the writing of, say, James Fenimore Cooper. His characters also come as though from an earlier age. Everywhere in his dramatic world there are characters who resemble Natty Bumppo, Ahab, and Huckleberry Finn. For a writer as available to the experience of America as Shepard surely is, such resonances run deep even though they are most certainly unintentional. (p. 127)

Shepard brings to the drama a liberating interplay of word, theme, and image that has always been the hallmark of the romantic impulse. His plays don't work like plays in the traditional sense but more like romances, where the imaginary landscape (his version of America) is so remote and open that it allows for the depiction of legend, adventure, and even the supernatural. Shepard's use of popular iconography is one instance of this impulse at work. But what it allows him to do, and what a similar feat allowed earlier American writers to do, is to transcend normal structures of belief and form. Shepard talks of his idea of drama as an "open ended structure where anything could happen as opposed to a carefully planned regurgitated event which, for me, has always been as painful as pissing nickels." Like the classic American writers that Tony Tanner writes about in *The Reign of Wonder,* Shepard "Thirsts after the primitive, absolute, all pervading truth . . . not content with knowledge of barren insulated facts." Rather than contract experience, Shepard expands it. He takes us to places where experience is fresher to the eye. Even though Shepard is one of our most modernist playwrights—his indulgent surrealism being just one example—what he more keenly resembles is a transcendentalist or new romantic whose "innocent eye" wonders at all it surveys and records experience without censure.

A way of linking Shepard to the more imaginatively playful and less philosophical side of transcendentalism is through the innocent and almost adolescent fantasies in such early plays as *Mad Dog Blues, Red Cross,* and *Cowboys #2.* When Shepard says that his plays are extensions of "the sensation of *play* (as in kid)," he is underscoring something akin to what Leslie Fiedler, in *Love and Death in the American Novel,* found operating in our literature at large: "Our novels seem not primitive, perhaps, but innocent, unfallen in a disturbing way, almost juvenile." . . . That Shepard's plays are filled with adolescent-like characters with innocent eyes who approach experience fresh demonstrates the link he has with a specific trait of native literary values.

By retreating from the "carefully planned regurgitated event" and entering forcefully into the world as "play," Shepard cuts himself off from the strict social, economic, and sexual objectification that have always characterized American drama. For him drama is no longer a set of formulaic codes but rather an open field. Like the literature of Cooper, Hawthorne, Melville, Thoreau, Poe, and Whitman, Shepard's plays construct a homemade world where the building of something new is more important than the architecture of the past. In *Fourteen Hundred Thousand* it comes out in the construction of bookshelves and talk about a cabin. In *The Curse of the Starving Class* it is in the construction of an animal pen and a new door frame. The effort is something like Thoreau's retreat to Walden and to the solace of new imaginative space. In order for the world to be new, a new set of boundaries have to be struck. Like so much in early American literature, the effort in so many of Shepard's plays is to create protective environments that will insulate against the wild perils of the frontier. . . . And yet the frontier is something to be embraced because of the environment of freedom it allows. Both interior worlds and exterior worlds are the dimensions through which Shepard's characters roam. (pp. 127-29)

Thematically, Shepard shows all the terror and wonder of being faced with his new continent as earlier American writers did with theirs. The theme of the frontiersman (*Cowboys #2*), the child lost in the wilderness (*Buried Child*), the journey into the unknown (*The Unseen Hand*), the material world as chaos instead of God's order (*Angel City*), possession and dispossession (*The Curse of the Starving Class*), and adventurous travel by sea and land (*Mad Dog Blues*) show that Shepard has never lost intrinsic contact with American literary instincts. As was the case generally for early American writers, his great theme is American expansionism. Only in his mind unlimited possibilities have been reduced to just a few. Verdant growth has been tamed and even virtually annihilated. By locating himself, as the beats did, in "Kerouac country," Shepard tries to stride the expanse and keep the romance alive. And yet there is trouble in paradise. As Capt. Bovine tells the old prospector Bill in *Operation Sidewinder:* "This country's in trouble. Big trouble. Over the past few years there's been a general breakdown of law and order and a complete disrespect for the things we've held sacred since our ancestors founded this country." Despite, and perhaps because of, the gnawing repression that grips most of Shepard's old-style heroes, they retreat into the vast open spaces of consciousness and imagination.

Like so many similar instances in earlier American literature, Shepard's plays examine how specific selves outgrow their environment. Like Huck Finn's escape down the river and disappearance into a newly generated self, Shepard's characters frequently try the same tactic. . . . The great effort and the great tragedy in American writing has always been the attempt to transform the self into something new; to deny the past. It was true in Hawthorne and Melville and it continued to be true in James and Fitzgerald. In Shepard the dilemma is no less contradictory and dangerous. And yet it's a dream that all his characters attempt in some form or another only to be confronted later with the illusion. Just as Henry Hackamore flies high—"Freer than life"—at the end of *Seduced,* he's still a phantom whose voice fades on the contradictory note, "I'm dead to the world but I never been born."

What Shepard shares with someone like Whitman is an unmediated delight in language as a means of imaginative freedom. Richard Poirier, in *A World Elsewhere,* demonstrates at length how American writers used language as a route to imaginative transports; as "an exultation in the exercise of consciousness momentarily set free." Almost everything that Poirier notes as being true of earlier American writers is true of Shepard as well. Expanding the self through what Poirier calls an "environment of language" is something that Shepard may have learned by way of Whitman. And Whitman learned it first from Emerson. . . . [When Shepard] says "the power of words for me isn't so much in the delineation of a character's social circumstances as it is in the capacity to evoke visions in the eyes of the audience," or speaking of "Words as living incantations and not as symbols," Shepard connects himself with Emerson's notion that "Words are also action and actions are a kind of words."

Shepard's *Action* dramatizes this Emersonian dictum. The play is a sustained demonstration of the ways that words can call into being moments of activity and vice versa. . . . *Action* also demonstrates the Emersonian feeling that "All the facts of the animal economy, sex, nutriment, gestation, birth, growth, are symbols of the passage of the world into the soul of man, to suffer there a change, and reappear a new and higher fact." Shepard offers a similar point of view: "Words . . . possess the power to change our chemistry," they "retain the potential of making leaps into the unknown." This essential transcendental belief in the power of language to transform and take us to a higher plane creates the confluence of intentions that link Emerson with Whitman, and Whitman with Shepard.

Beyond the Emersonian impulse to view words as alchemy of a new sort, both Whitman and Shepard share a similar belief in the range and variety of an American idiom: a delight in vernacular, cant, and slang; a strong lyricism that could compose a language of mind, body, and soul; the imagistic and visual values that could be summoned up through the word; and the incredible, almost cinematic, freedom of words leaping from place to place across the page or across the stage. Both poet and playwright express the similar attitude that language can be sly and playful, and that one of its richest resources is its ability to carry a sustained monologue. Whitman's "Song of Myself" is, after all, one continuous monologue from beginning to end. Few American playwrights before or since Shepard have ever attempted, like him, to take the dramatic monologue to similar limits. Almost as if learning from Whitman, Shepard sees in the monologue the large freedoms it could offer his characters. . . . (pp. 129-31)

When you move through the competing registers of the language duel in *The Tooth of Crime,* to take just one example, you can see how Shepard's characters float into focus and then out, how the essential perception of self which makes up the conflict of that play lives and dies on the field of language. When you compare almost any speech from *The Tooth of Crime* with "Song of Myself" the associations of technique come into sharp relief:

> HOSS: Never catch me with beer in my hand. Never catch me with my pecker out. Never got caught. Never did get caught. Never once. Never, never. Fast on the hoof. Fast on the roof. Fast through the still night. Faster than the headlight. Fast to the move.
>
> (*The Tooth of Crime*)

You there, impotent, loose in the knees,
Open your scarf'd chops till I blow grit within you,
Spread your palms and lift the flap of your pockets,

I am not to be denied, I compel, I have stores plenty to
  spare,
And any thing I have I bestow.

("Song of Myself")

The intriguing way in which the Whitman passage, by the merest adjustment, could easily become Crow's retort to Hoss demonstrates what a deep kinship there is between Shepard's play and Whitman's poem. The large, multitudinous ways in which the reading of one informs the reading of the other illustrates the ties that bind Shepard to Whitman. (p. 131)

Going beyond the themes and conventions of Transcendentalism and Romanticism, and the telling verbal associations that link Shepard with Whitman, one final link needs to be made between Sam Shepard and 19th-century American literature. And that is his recourse to mythic impulses. On one level the reading of myth in his plays is quite classical: the agon between characters of huge proportion (*The Tooth of Crime*). On another level the reading takes a different classical bent: the grievance of son with father (shown in embryo in *The Rock Garden* and in more maturity in *The Curse of the Starving Class*). But for a writer like Shepard, imbued with a whole range of mythic preoccupations that take him as far back as folk and Indian lore, the correspondences run deeper. Shepard himself says: "Myths speak to everything at once, especially the emotions. By myths I mean a sense of mystery and not necessarily a traditional formula. A character is for me a composite of different mysteries. He's an unknown quantity." In fact, what Shepard seems to be saying is that his plays spring from the impulse to get inside this unknown quantity in order to *see* what's there. What's there, of course, is the play he is writing at any given moment. But through exercising the visual side of his imagination and sketching a scheme towards its conclusion, which in *The Tooth of Crime* took the form of Crow, a totally "lethal" and "savage" human who needed a victim, Shepard transforms the mystery into something approaching a known quantity. And yet only *just* approaching. For in no sense does Shepard seem to be writing out of some codified mythopoeic tradition but rather a naive American one that takes its savagery to heart and finds literary structures to exorcise it. As Hawthorne and Poe proved, the strategy need not be at all conscious but comes, instead, out of some deep emotional need to show fear in the face of the unknown and the unseen. In Shepard's dramatic romances and tales fear is a wilderness with no path leading out.

Like those American writers with whom I've tried to connect him, Sam Shepard takes it for granted that the mystery is insoluble and will forever leave its imprint strewn throughout the imaginative landscape of both mind and body. It is simply another feature of his complex and eccentric design. (p. 132).

Michael Earley, "Of Life Immense in Passion, Pulse, and Power: Sam Shepard and the American Literary Tradition," in American Dreams: The Imagination of Sam Shepard, *edited by Bonnie Marranca, Performing Arts Journal Publications, 1981, pp. 126-32.*

JOYCE AARON

Sam is a recorder of the authentic American voice. He starts from a certain perception of daily life, and then transforms that into a specific voice—a voice with its own rhythms and shifting consciousness, its unique, particular curve or leap. You can track that leap by following the flow of his language. Each voice is different, and speaks from a different place inside you.

That is part of the theatrical challenge and wonder of speaking Sam's language.

In most conventional plays, however admirable, there is a certain kind of development—a continuity, some external sense or logic, usually a dialogue of give-and-take, which defines the play's architecture and establishes its focus. You can't look for that, or expect it, in Sam's plays. Very often, he provides you with no transitions. As an actor, you have to live the moment as his plays give it to you—and you have to live it as experience, not as history or chronicle. You have to trust that moment and the language which he has captured in sporadic resonances and reverberations. Unless you trust the reality that he sets up, you can't play him as he demands to be played. . . . You can't impose some linear line on the chain of his moments for your own pleasure or satisfaction, because Sam rarely makes his leaps according to any psychological rules or patterns. If you hang on to the moment, you lose the play—because that one moment has already passed and you are at the edge of another one.

You can't approach Sam's plays according to the usual acting terms and conditions—there are no rules, because he has broken them. You might find yourself opening one of his plays as a character who has to deliver a twenty-minute monologue. The character may be in a kind of "tripping-out" state, veering from paranoia to explosion, and the momentum and intensity of the vocal rhythm never lets up, it hounds you. What you have to do is let that rhythm take you instead of you taking it—you have to surrender to the dynamics of that rhythm, let it possess you. That particular originality is one of the things that makes Sam's dramatic voice so different from any I've experienced.

I first met Sam when I was cast as an actress in his play *Up To Thursday,* done at the Cherry Lane Theatre in the mid-1960s. One of the things the role required was that I *not* stop laughing—the character had to go on laughing beyond the limitations of naturalistic convention; the laughter had to hang in the air almost like text. If I had stopped, paused to ask: Why is this character laughing? Why is she laughing so long? Where is it all coming from?—then I would have been at odds with Sam's imaginative process. The conventional logic and rationale an actor asks for was simply not there. The richness lies in the risk-taking. (pp. 171-72)

Sam's work can be very difficult for actors because they don't quite know how to approach it. They may be seduced by it, charmed or even moved by it. But when it comes to putting the play itself up there on the stage, they have difficulty finding the direction. That happens especially when they become too involved with Sam's "meanings." Rather than exploring what the language reveals and where it will take them, they start to act, and before they know it, they've fallen into the current traps of actor training.

When you do Sam's plays, it's important to remember—and actually you will *feel* it—that you are enacting some aspect of a particular person: not in the conventional terms of character, but rather as a witness to a moment or condition in American culture; that you are enacting on the stage one experience of one person at a particular moment, in a particular state. Often you discover that the particular aspect you are enacting exists within a much larger whole—it is only one reality within a kind of super-reality. But you can't start from that super-reality as a point of departure. Your enactment of some condition of being-in-the-world is what's important.

Your conscious obligation to Sam's plays should be their aliveness, to making them come alive on the stage; otherwise, you'll end up acting the metaphor or the poetry. Your job is not to enact feeling or to embody emotion. What you're enacting is the pulse or heartbeat of feeling, the essence of emotion. If you try to play Sam's language "cold," it won't work either. What you can't do is let yourself be enveloped by the feeling, speak through the tears, say, as you might with Chekhov. Because that way, you're sure to lose the rhythm and the music. There's a tremendous freedom in working this way, because you're not locked into any psychological system that calls for exploring or demonstrating "feeling." It's a mistake, for example, to think of Sam's monologues as an evasion of feeling, when what they really are is an explosion of feeling. It's hard to put this concretely, but when you do Sam's plays, you have to be prepared to bear a kind of witness to yourself—you have to be detached enough to enact yourself. Which is another reason why the tremendous humor in Sam's work is so important—it's a survival technique for his characters, but a survival technique for his actors, too.

There's Sam's imagery, also, which an actor has to accept as part of the whole. You can't compete with it—you have to co-exist with it. The actor must simply accept it being there and work with it. In *Red Cross,* for example, everything on the stage was white: I was dressed in white, I wore white-rimmed glasses, even my shopping-bags were white. When Jim turned around at the end of the play, blood was running down his face. That blood was the only color on the stage. The audience was left with that image. (pp. 173-74)

I had great faith and trust in Sam and his work, in his responses and in the authenticity of what he was doing. I still do. I might say I like one play more than another, but I never doubt what he's trying to make happen on the stage.

I wish he'd write a play for women! (p. 174)

Joyce Aaron, "Clues in a Memory," in American Dreams: The Imagination of Sam Shepard, *edited by Bonnie Marranca, Performing Arts Journal Publications, 1981, pp. 171-74.*

EDITH OLIVER

The [1982] production of Sam Shepard's *True West* . . . is not so much a revival as a transformation, after its unsatisfactory presentation . . . last year—which, as you may remember, the dramatist indignantly disavowed. . . .

Much of Mr. Shepard's writing here is absolutely splendid. There is a monologue spoken by Austin, about the brothers' destitute father losing his teeth one by one, first on his mattress and then on a blacktop road to Mexico, and eventually misplacing his false teeth in some takeout chop suey, which is vintage Shepard, whether it sounds funny or not, and there are other memorable passages as well. What is lost is Shepard's subtle shifts from the comic to the poetic to the sinister (as the howling of coyotes is heard outside), or maybe they are just drowned in laughter; at any rate, I didn't miss them.

True West does not compare in quality with *Curse of the Starving Class* or *Buried Child,* but it is good all the same—much better than most other plays by most other playwrights. There is little passion in *True West,* but Mr. Shepard's dramatic imagination and humor still run riot.

Edith Oliver, in a review of "True West," in The New Yorker, *Vol. LVIII, No. 41, November 29, 1982, p. 160.*

ROBERT MAZZOCCO

When the plays of Sam Shepard began appearing in the Sixties at underground theaters like La Mama or the Caffe Cino he was often thought to be a surrealist dramatist. That's true enough of much of his atmospheric detail, early or late: *Angel City* and its phantasmal green slime, *Operation Sidewinder* and its serpentine computer. At the start of *Suicide in bFlat* we discover, to quote from Shepard, that "the outline of a man's body sprawled out in an awkward position of death is painted in white" on the center of a darkened stage. And it's true that a dreamlike *mise en scène* inhabits most of his forty or so plays.

More likely, though, the boisterously prolific Shepard should be seen as an embattled realist, or an elusive one, with a highly picaresque view of the world, and a roguish sense of himself and of his characters in relation to that world. A number of these characters, whether buried in the "middle of nowhere" or ravaging among the graffiti of the metropolis, dote on the tall tale, are fascinated by the foxiness of old pretenders. Others are a kind of holy fool, drifters who are also questers, outlaws who are also poets. Even the most matter-of-fact are prey to orneriness.... Eventually in the unraveling of the tall tale calamity lurks, the horizon is electric with disaster, while for the holy fools paranoia is always possible, suitably guyed with touches of Shepard's humorous hyperbole: A funny thing happened to me on the way to Armageddon, as one of his characters might say.

Shepard's world, however idiosyncratic, is of course America.... For Shepard's is largely the America of Buffalo Bill and Andrew Jackson, but surely not that of Henry Adams or Henry James; the America of medicine shows and covered wagons, revivalist meetings and rodeos, but hardly of Debs or Sacco and Vanzetti or even of the robber barons of Wall Street. In short, a thoroughly demotic, folkloric America, the American past more or less as a Hollywood cliché—but an America, nonetheless, continually illuminated through the purview of the artist, the artist as tramp or seer.

If one is content to follow this hard-nosed, drug-induced, pop-flavored style, this perpetual retuning of old genres and old myths, one encounters, finally, a profuse and unique panorama of where we are now and where we have been. Because Shepard has written so much, because frequently his plays seem provisional reports whose vitality springs perhaps from a certain disgust with writing plays at all ... it's extraordinarily difficult to write categorically about what goes on in his theater. But surely at the center of Shepard's America must stand his antipodean band of errant sons and ghostly fathers—his assortment of gangsters and gamblers, cowboys and farmers—variants either on the "child of nature" and "noble savage" or on the authority figure of the "old man," an abiding presence, home from the hills and now gone a bit daft. Shepard's women, themselves variants on mothers and whores, sisters or sweethearts, are, not surprisingly, dim in comparison to his macho pantheon, but they too have their moments. (p. 21)

Yet these characters are rarely separable or memorable; they have none of the distinctiveness, the embroidery of portraiture of Blanche DuBois or Willy Loman. Not only do Stu and Chet frequently mimic each other or exchange identities with each other [in *Cowboys #2*] but so also do Kosmo and Yahoodi in

Mad Dog Blues, and Lee and Austin in *True West;* even in the incestuous coupling of *Fool for Love* ..., May and Eddie, half-sister and half-brother, are virtually opposite sides of the same coin. These characters, as Elizabeth Hardwick has observed, are not so much characters as *actors,* members of some sort of revolving repertory company where the impresario is of course Shepard himself, Shepard exuberantly amplifying the possibilities of his own picaresque imagination or poetic roguery, Shepard delighting in the fact that the playwright is, as he says, "the only actor who gets to play all the roles."

In so celebrating the histrionic dexterity of the actor, Shepard is also insisting that we watch as well as listen, use our eyes no less than our ears. In his theater we encounter precipitate alterations of personality, or chimerical shifts in diction or mood or dress (disrobing or a bedraggled sumptuousness are common), and frequently accompanying the long monologues or interwoven among them, another character, on another part of the stage, might suddenly begin shadow boxing, or howl like a coyote, or slowly dance to a blues ballad, or sit in a heavy red armchair and maneuver it till it comes to resemble a "giant tortoise."

Admittedly, at times all this activity can be little more than an avant-garde burlesque of the "stage business" of yesteryear. At other times overall movement clearly falters: Shepard either runs out of gas (the second half of *Angel City* is surely a letdown after the first) or has trouble getting started. But generally such choreography engages us as swiftly or effortlessly as possible; and even when the characters are seemingly doing nothing at all, lying about as if "dead," these moments are purely deceptive—at key points in the concluding sequences of *Melodrama Play* ... each of the "dead" will rise from the floor and exit, and the effect is startling. (p. 22)

The Tooth of Crime, undoubtedly the quintessential Shepard play, is a dazzlingly corrosive work and one of the most original achievements in contemporary theater. It is also the play that best illustrates the various facets—at once highly eclectic and highly singular—of his genius. Though ostensibly a futuristic exposé, with sci-fi trimmings, of the sleaze of the recording industry—it was written in London after Shepard's meetings with members of the Who and the Stones—it is basically a rock fantasia on the new gun in town. Shepard's most bravura touches are here—woozy epithets, internal rhyme, musical syncopation, cockalorum and caricature, a knife thrower's dummy that spills real blood, as well as Shepard's prevailing belief that "language is a veil holding demons and angels which the other characters are always out of touch with." All these, despite some exasperating lapses, rise to a level of perfection that Shepard, I believe, has not matched since. (pp. 22-3)

The intricacy of the play—its multiple "codes" and "rules," approaching at times incoherence—can only be hinted at. In structure, however, *The Tooth of Crime* mirrors the strict pattern of crisis and catastrophe found in Shepard's earlier (and equally incantatory) *La Turista.* ... The first act focuses on Hoss, caught up among his minions in all the cliché paraphernalia of being a "star," a "king," a "fucking industry." Hoss randomly meditates on his fame and his past, on his high school days or on his fear of "losin' direction." The act concludes fittingly in a soliloquy of "shifting voices," through which Hoss speaks both in his own voice and in that of his dead father, "old fishin' buddy," who advises, as always: "The road's what counts. Just look at the road. Don't worry about where it's goin'."

In the second and final act we arrive at the prolonged confrontation scene, Hoss and [his rival] Crow in their virtuoso jousting match, a truly daring example of the interpolative velocity of Shepard's art. Against a suitably mercantile background of rock-and-roll and country-western . . . Hoss and Crow will attempt to outperform or overcome each other, to symbolically attain or retain legendary frontier status. Yet however extravagantly drawn, neither is autonomous. And that is Shepard's point. Each is merely a combinative "pawn" in a "game," and the only way for either to win at the game is to keep reinventing the self, which means to keep proliferating one's "image." . . . (p. 23)

At the end of the play, Hoss, bowing to the implacable style out of which he's sprung, will fire a bullet into his mouth and disappear in "one clean shot." Crow will indolently remark: "I gotta hand it to ya'. It took ya' long enough but you slid right home." The wheel of fashion will spin another turn, and Crow will have to await his own Crow, for the next shoot-out, the next "image" to supersede his own.

For Shepard, this is what the trail (or the "crime") has become: constant flux, which of course is its only permanence, a continual "rollin' down." . . . Here not even Hemingway's idea that "man is not made for defeat," that "a man can be destroyed but not defeated" is applicable. For inverting the Hemingway formula, Hoss is both defeated (by Crow) and destroyed (by himself). (pp. 23-4)

If we look back over the expanse of Shepard's work—the trash of human loneliness or human aggression, a feeling for "images that shine," as he says, "in the middle of junk" (the billboard culture of America serving him here) or for things that time and again are "blown away"—we can see in the jocose desolation or stoical amiability, in the interplay of ego and environment the unstinting vigor and originality of his vision. But also its limitations. Americans—that is, Americans en masse—have always celebrated their own ignorance. . . . And there's no doubt that Shepard, with his tall tales and holy fools, celebrates that national trait.

Superficially his general indictment of American materialism is similar to James's "interrogation of the past" as he gazes upon the industrial gloom of the New Jersey shore in *The American Scene*. But what a difference between Shepard and his lust for the old primordial thrill and the expatriate James and his manifold displacements, his "international theme" of "dispossessed princes and wandering heirs." Though one can find in Shepard any number of spiritual or ceremonial transformations (the mantic strain, the use of paradox and parable, being, I think, as present as the manic), one would be hard put to discover much in the way of cultural or intellectual emancipation. "Myth," as he puts it, "is a powerful medium," precisely "because it talks to the emotions and not the head."

Thus, again and again, what unites his heroes is the division of the spoils, the affirmation through negation. . . . Hoss says of himself, "I couldn't take my life in my hands while I was alive but now I can take it in death." May tells Eddie that "anybody who doesn't half kill themselves falling off horses or jumping on steers" isn't a real "male" in his eyes. It's all vital and genuine, and wonderfully moving and sinister in an aboriginal way, and yet for all that a kind of shuck, a "game."

Of course, as we have seen, Shepard knows very well that it's a game. . . . Shepard enlarges and elaborates upon what he knows, and damns, repeatedly, the computerized and deper-

sonalized world that has arisen from the old partriarchy, the old macho assurances. Still, deep down, his heart goes out to them, he remains in fealty to them, unwilling as he is to demystify or to confront these old myths and their dubious hold upon us or upon himself. Thus the splendor of his tapestries. Thus, too, the laceration of consciousness—"split," one of his favorite words—as we move from a raw and evergreen youthfulness traveling the "territory," constantly upping the ante, to the abrupt disgruntlement or dilapidation of age, and with very little else in between. Then comes the final severance, the final recoil, till one is left a ruminating shadow. . . . (p. 26)

Shepard arrived on the scene at two crucial, if ephemeral, moments in recent American history, each of them bearing heavily upon his own development: during the late Fifties and early Sixties, the salutary aspects of mass culture drawn from such sources as rhythm and blues unexpectedly irradiated high culture, saving it from the academic solemnity or bourgeois conformity that had been stifling it; and the equally radical metamorphosis of the family (or the escape from the family) into a "generation of youth," what one used to call the "new sensibility" of the Sixties. These upheavals, of course, did not last, precisely because they had no real intellectual underpinnings to nourish or guide them; with the result that mass culture, with its assemblage of technocrats, taste makers, and "target audiences," is today far more of a corporate monolith than it's ever been.

From the Seventies to the present, we have been witnessing, with only the rarest of exceptions, and with much lap-dog palaver suggesting the contrary, an unprecedented acceleration of the banal or the bogusly sophisticated in American life and in popular culture—in the megabucks infantilism of the astral sagas of Lucas and Spielberg, in the cornball uplift of *On Golden Pond,* in Yahoo types like Indiana Jones, in the showbiz promotion of American fundamentalism and American politics (the evangelical President Reagan, when not chopping wood or pumping iron, deals in tall tales as if they were facts and figures; he calls his tall tales "anecdotes"), and, finally, in the emergence of a new generation of youth, dumber or shallower, perhaps, than any other generation of youth within memory. Adversary culture, traditionally the air hole of mainstream culture, is no longer a force; the heterogeneity of mass culture, such as it is, is dependent on what's left of the old liberation movements of the Sixties, on feminists, blacks, gays, or on the legacy of rock, as in the current "phenomena" of Harvey Fierstein, Eddie Murphy, or Prince.

Sam Shepard, only a few years out of his thirties, seems at a difficult point of an extraordinary career. Clearly he has been the dominant American playwright of his generation. And he has been more than that, for without him it is by no means certain that the contemporary American theater would have much of importance to speak of, the best of his colleagues, Lanford Wilson, David Mamet, or David Rabe, being in no sense his equals. He has already created a body of work distinctive enough for a lifetime. One may hope that he will not, like Travis at the end of *Paris, Texas,* disappear into more of the folklore of the "far distances," a folklore that has now become as emotionally threadbare as it is ideologically synthetic. (pp. 26-7)

Robert Mazzocco, "Heading for the Last Roundup," in The New York Review of Books, *Vol. XXXII, No. 8, May 9, 1985, pp. 21-7.*

EDITH OLIVER

[The revival] of *Curse of the Starving Class,* Sam Shepard's passionate, funny, and ultimately tragic play about a family shattered by poverty, is better than good enough, although it does not dim in memory its glorious original production . . . in 1978. The action, to remind you as briefly as possible, is set in the kitchen of a ranch house in California. . . . The family acres are yielding little, the animals are dying off, and the efforts, especially of the son, to hold at bay the sleazy lawyer and other disreputable characters who are out to grab the land for purposes of their own ultimately come to nothing. In one brilliant, imaginative soliloquy, the son describes these "zombies," with their bulldozers and wrecking balls, whose aim, he asserts, is to cover the whole country with concrete. This theme, in play after play, has become an obsession of Shepard's, and nowhere is it realized in more masterly fashion than in *Curse of the Starving Class.* If my synopsis has made it sound grim, I have totally misled you; it is so filled with witty lines and quirky comic business that, laughing throughout, we realize only at the horrifying end that we have been watching a tragedy the whole time. Much of the wit (and seriousness) is set forth in soliloquies—verbal riffs so dazzling that they disarm even one as resistant to monologues as I am.

> *Edith Oliver, in a review of "The Curse of the Starving Class," in* The New Yorker, *Vol. LXI, No. 28, September 2, 1985, p. 71.*

ANDREW KOPKIND

A wide expanse of Western desert in the windless afternoon. The camera's lens, like a lone eagle's eye, sweeps over the stones and chaparral and settles on a tumbledown assemblage of shacks and junk at the edge of a lonely land. An old-timer walks among the ruins like a forgotten archaeologist left at a fruitless dig. . . . Wait—I've seen this movie before. Why are they rereleasing *Paris, Texas,* more than a year after its disappointing premiere? (p. 25)

As it turns out, this isn't Wim Wenders's Teutonic attempt to translate Sam Shepard into great cinema; it's Robert Altman's Hollywood version of same. *Fool for Love* is not exactly a foal of the earlier existential horse opera, but it certainly looks like a spiritual stablemate. Shepard merely wrote the screenplay for *Paris, Texas.* This time he adapted the script from his own play and acts the part of the leading man, which gives him ample opportunity to mire the proceedings in more creative muck. Shepard is nothing if not an overachiever. His plays, stories, poems and miscellaneous jottings fill the shelves, his prizes . . . load the mantelpiece. . . . And this is his best year so far, with a new play and a revival in New York, a cover story in *Newsweek,* . . . and *Fool for Love* making its mark on midcult America. Who could ask for anything more?

Zip! Will Sam Shepard ever write a great play? Lorenz Hart gave Gypsy Rose Lee that line about William Saroyan in *Pal Joey,* but it applies as well to the current purveyor of regional Americana in the form of timeless drama. Much of Shepard's stage work has a raucous energy compounded of physical violence and sublimated sins against nature and close relatives. The stuff about the West is mostly boilerplate, a convenient symbol on which to hang his family plots. At his most abstract, Shepard is our Pinter. He taunts us with half-baked hints about the lives of characters before they come on stage (or screen), about the hidden history of their relationships and about their futures. The plays have no beginnings or ends, just middles. It has been said, and it sounds right, that no one can write a Pinter play except Pinter; it may be true, too, that no one can write a Shepard play, not even Shepard. His efforts seem in-

complete, not because they are too short but because they so resolutely resist resolution and abjure antecedents. The danger with modernist abstraction is that its material is so self-referential that it has no meaning outside the mind of its creator. You never know whether the images are classic archetypes, important metaphors or merely patternless pieces summoned at random. (pp. 25-26)

Director Altman must have convinced Shepard to open up *Fool for Love* on the theory that a movie audience would not sit still for 105 minutes as two characters slapped each around on a single set. Altman should have trusted his directorial skills more. . . . The horrible secrets of Eddie and May's past are explicated in a series of monologues and depicted in flashbacks which grow more frequent as the film progresses. We still aren't told everything. The flashbacks are partisan renderings of reality, filled with the lies, half-truths and subjective judgments we loved so much in *Rashomon.* . . .

Let's see, have I forgotten anything? Ah yes, the plot. Eddie and May . . . have been at it for years, whatever "it" is, and the action of the movie involves a few hours of it in Motel Hell. Their obsessive relationship is too hot to handle, but as much as they cannot live together, they cannot stay apart. What binds them is also what repels them: the memory of innocence and the experience of sin, like Adam and Eve, like the West, like America. So they slap and scream, bite and kiss, stalk and pout and try to explain themselves to each other and the world. Often they look at each other with longing, lying eyes, while the minutes fly by like hours. The scene literally explodes at the end, but unfortunately both Eddie and May survive, which suggests that a sequel, though not wise, is always possible. (p. 26)

> *Andrew Kopkind, "Fool for Love," in* The Nation, *Vol. 242, No. 1, January 11, 1986, pp. 25-6.*

LAWRENCE O'TOOLE

In the film adaptation of Shepard's often viciously funny play [*Fool for Love*] humor is the only relief from the fierce intimacy that its two main characters share.

With his inquiring camera, director Robert Altman . . . captures the unrelenting strain of Eddie and May's relationship. After she makes up with him momentarily she kisses him, then instantly changes her mind and kicks him in the groin. They drive each other away out of emotional revulsion and then experience separate outbursts of jealousy. . . .

In *Fool for Love,* passion is heightened into absurd horror. What makes their dilemma especially unusual is that Eddie and May are half-brother and sister. . . . In the play, Shepard diffused the power of his theme of impossible love by introducing the subject of incest. In the movie, Altman tries to avoid that artifice by moving the action . . . into the lonely outdoors near the motel. There, he keeps the camera dancing around like a fighter in a ring, and finds visual tensions to supplement the verbal ones. It is an extraordinary feat of film-making. Unfortunately, the performances . . . are often mannered and too emotionally confined for all the noisy fighting that takes place.

Despite those flaws, *Fool for Love* is sizzlingly effective. What emerges is a portrait of two lives that are painfully, inexorably, even tragically united. The viewer is left with the sensation of watching two lives played out on an eternally unmade bed.

Lawrence O'Toole, "The Knots of Passion," in Maclean's Magazine, Vol. 99, No. 2, January 13, 1986, p. 46.

PAULINE KAEL

On the face of it, Altman and Shepard seem an ideal matchup. The herky-jerky instability of Shepard's plays wouldn't faze Altman—it would delight him.... His collaboration with Shepard [in *Fool for Love*] represents one of the rare opportunities that moviemakers and playwrights have had to work together freely, and its failure can't be blamed on any commercial calculations, or on anyone's not doing his damnedest. You can see an immense amount of effort in the film—perhaps too much. The material seems to congeal on the screen, and congealed rambunctiousness is not a pretty sight.

In the theatre, *Fool for Love* works somewhat like a Pinter play. From start to finish, everything is unresolved but suggestive. Actors delivering fragments of dialogue hold the stage space by creating tensions out of inexplicable transformations and quick changes of mood—aggressions, murder threats, temper tantrums, sudden laughter, pangs of guilt and fear. But Shepard, always manic, loves flamboyant, dreamlike stage images, and he whips up more of a free-for-all ruckus than Pinter does. The high that audiences can get from his plays comes out of his fermented mixture of junk culture, hard-nosed poetic language, and counterculture macho (circa *Easy Rider*) gone mythic. To keep a play cooking, he'll throw anything into the stew—animal, vegetable, or mineral. In *Fool for Love,* it's an automobile graveyard, horses, spurs and lassos, a mad countess in a Mercedes, gunshots, and fire—a whole conflagration. (p. 84)

The 1983 play is about the no-exit, tormented sex relationship between Eddie, a broken-down rodeo cowboy . . . , and his half sister, May . . . , who lives in a cheap motel "on the edge of the Mojave Desert." . . . These two had the same father . . . , who sits on the stage, looks on, and occasionally speaks, but, as the author puts it, "exists only in the minds of May and Eddie." There's too much fizz for the lovers' torment to be strong drink; it's Pepsi-generation existentialism—it's for young audiences taking a deep swig of the dark side of things. But Altman directs this material almost reverently, as a series of near-static pictures.... The dialogue, set off by the compositions, has the sound of theatuh, and, of course, with that phantom father poking around the junk heap outside May's room and making mournful sounds on his harmonica, the movie has the devices of theatre.

Sitting there, you think this stuff isn't much but maybe it could get by as a slapstick dance-of-death entertainment if it were just faster and more kinetic, if there were less mood and atmosphere, and Eddie and May were ferociously passionate and excitable, and we felt the connection between them—felt that they were dangerously alike. But the twists and turns, and the ominous passage when May's gentleman caller, Martin . . . , arrives to take her to the movies and Eddie taunts him, are all fixed in place. What happens is not unlike what happened in the film versions of Pinter's plays. . . . The stage tensions disappear when the camera rules the space. About the only play I can think of that has walled-in emotional violence like that of *Fool for Love* and was successfully transferred to film is Cocteau's 1949 *Les Parents Terribles.* . . . (pp. 84-5)

Shepard calls his adaptation "an exploded play," but to a viewer it looks just like the usual "opening out the play"— he lets the two lovers out of their cage. (It's a fatal mistake.)

And he includes a sticky lament for lost innocence: a lonely golden-haired little girl at the motel represents May as a child, and this ties in with a scene of May regressing—expressing her vulnerability by lying down in a sandbox. The film also brings on Eddie and May and the Old Man in flashbacks to earlier points in their lives, adds characters who are merely referred to in the play, and expands the setting to the whole motel complex and the highway. (p. 85)

What you're likely to experience at the movie is a numbing discomfort—the result of the conflict between Shepard's flinging-things-together method and the flossy high-art embalming he and Altman give the play. There's all this crazy stuff going on. Eddie and May flip out with no visible provocation— they're shouting at each other and suddenly he's tender, or she's clutching him and, presto, she knees him in the groin— and their tussling is pumped up with dead air and country-song interludes, as if this were an American classic about rootlessness (which I guess some people think it is). (pp. 86-7)

And the impresario director never leaves you alone with the characters; you feel him controlling everything, and it can drive you a little nuts. So can the Greek-tragedy aspect of the material: Eddie and May as the incestuous lovers who can't stay apart—who are fated to love each other and suffer for it. Altman and Shepard push fate over the top when the Old Man goes inside the burning wreckage of the motel and stands amidst the flames playing his harmonica. (p. 87)

Pauline Kael, "Lasso and Peashooter," in The New Yorker, Vol. LXI, No. 49, January 27, 1986, pp. 84-9.

PAUL BERMAN

In Philip Rahv's famous classification, palefaces are the American writers who cultivate sensibility, refinement, education and discipline. Henry James, for instance. Redskins are the half-baked mystics, the primitives, the gross naturalists, the writers whose strength is experience and energy. Whitman, for instance. . . . Rahv published this theory in 1939 and wondered whether someday the paleface-redskin split would heal over, perhaps when the country was more mature. But who in the age of John Updike and Sam Shepard will say that it has?

Shepard is, of course, the reddest redskin who ever lived. He gives the impression that he would rather knock your ears off with an electric guitar than do anything so prissy as to write a play. "I don't want to be a playwright," the playwright said in a program note fifteen years ago. "I want to be a rock and roll star." (p. 215)

There's no point in discussing Shepard without acknowledging at the start that he's a caricature. But . . . [he has certain] authentic qualities—his superphysicality and pop culture spontaneity, his abrasiveness and intentional provocation, early-1970s-style. Those qualities constitute one aspect of his redskin originality, though other qualities can be listed.

He has constructed a bleak picture of American life as a cultural badlands dotted with a few national myths as barren of meaning as cactus is of nutrient. This picture meshes perfectly with his abrasive physicality and spontaneity to make scary scenes of astonishing bitterness. "I thought it was going to be turkey dinners and apple pie and all that kinda stuff," says the young woman in *Buried Child*. Goes the reply: "Well I hate to disappoint you." "I'm not disappointed! I'm fuckin' terrified!" A long evening of this makes you feel you've been sitting too close to a madman banging a drum. But it's not a sensation you'll easily forget.

He commands a voice that is well known in American theater. It is the voice that comes to us, perhaps, from Clifford Odets—the eulogistic catch in the throat, the voice of dazed regret or of a slightly embittered nostalgia. In Shepard you hear this voice at the end of plays like *Buried Child* and *Fool for Love*, only since he's not exactly a realist, the voice seems slightly disembodied, and the mood it produces is odd. You feel moved without understanding why; and the combination of being moved without exactly "getting it" is one of his striking effects....

The playwright has jettisoned conventional theater space and time in favor of space and time that are determined by the emotions of his characters. He has made feelings the basis for action and done away with the ordinary restraints on behavior, so that consciousness and not behavior determines the narrative. He has drawn his characters with a kind of spontaneous line instead of striving for anything coherent. And he does all this with perfect unselfconsciousness. Taken together, his novel techniques produce a kind of crazy fluency, coherent one moment and not the next—which is how people generally are.

The fluency above all is what makes Shepard seem a man of today. By this I mean to distinguish him from what is usually called "modern." The modern style is fragmented and angular, and the audience is intended to piece together a significance. But "todayism" has the quality of an unbroken stream, and the audience is not meant to piece together anything at all. Todayism is the quality that you hear in the music of Steve Reich and his colleagues, where the technique is relentlessly soothing. In theater Shepard is its principal exponent, but of course in his case the technique is hardly soothing. It is relentless, though.

Shepard has cultivated a peculiar comic sense. He is a parodist with a pan as dead as a doornail. There are few punch lines, few opportunities to laugh out loud, few lines that seem funny when read instead of performed. Yet a sense of the ridiculous runs through a large amount of his work. (p. 216)

[Since] Shepard goes in and out of parody with the same fluency with which he goes in and out of conventional time and space, you can never be sure when he's making fun and when he's being straight. His work as a whole takes on a semiparodistic quality, which is another aspect of todayism.

Such are the achievements of Sam Shepard. There is, however, a difficulty in the redskin vocation that can't be ignored, though in the atmosphere of Shepard celebration it often is. The difficulty is what to do when a redskin's genius falls short.... Rahv didn't take up this problem in his essay, but it is a grave one. The redskin is always in danger of plunging into the autodidact's vat of sins—into pretension, pomposity, sentimentality, tastelessness and grandiosity. From brilliant originality to painful amateurism is but a moment's leap.

The gap between the best work of a redskin writer and the worst is therefore almost always immense. For that reason the best had better be spectacular, and the worst had better not come too often.... In Shepard's case, no one has wanted to acknowledge just how bad the worst can be. Partly that's because of his origins in the embattled avant-garde of the 1960s, whose advocates have naturally preferred championing their hero to making critical judgments about him. But mostly it is because of his cleverness at parody. You tend to think that an author as devilishly satirical as Shepard couldn't possibly be sentimental, that Sam the rock-and-roller could never be guilty of artiness, that the American pop culture mythology could never mystify a man like that. Having sat happily through witty speeches . . . , you willingly sit through other speeches. For instance, these lines by the brother of the young woman in [*Curse of the Starving Class*]:

> I was lying there on my back. I could smell the avocado blossoms. I could hear the coyotes. I could hear stock cars squealing down the street. I could feel myself in my bed in my room in this house in this town in this state in this country. I could feel this country close like it was part of my bones. I could feel the presence of all the people outside, at night, in the dark. Even sleeping people I could feel. Even all the sleeping animals. Dogs. Peacocks. Bulls. Even tractors sitting in the wetness, waiting for the sun to come up. I was looking straight up at the ceiling at all my model airplanes hanging by all their thin metal wires. Floating. Swaying very quietly like they were being blown by someone's breath. Cobwebs moving with them.

But these are not funny lines. They are not parody. They are, in fact, the worst sort of purple prose, the most obvious effort to squeeze false emotions—boyhood nostalgia, a fake Western wildness ("I could hear the coyotes")—out of a dramatically dead monologue. They are the lines of a showoff, which is to say, of a redskin gone bad. Surely he's got to be playing some new trick on us, we want to think. We withhold judgment, as so many critics have told us to do. And soon enough Shepard perpetrates yet another ghastly monologue or scene, because lapses in the work of Sam Shepard are anything but infrequent. (pp. 216-17)

It would be pleasant to declare that the American theater has produced a new genius, and that Shepard is the man. But the reality is more modest. Shepard has an instinct for staging certain aspects of the 1960s revulsion for the American mainstream, and this instinct has led him to fashion several theatrical innovations, for which he should be celebrated. But he's not a major playwright....

All the rest in regard to Shepard—his movie-star celebrity, the *New York Times* hyperbole—has nothing to do with the art of theater and everything to do with the workings of an American culture that Shepard himself used to know how to satirize. (p. 218)

Paul Berman, in a review of "A Lie of the Mind" and "Curse of the Starving Class," in The Nation, *Vol. 242, No. 7, February 22, 1986, pp. 215-18.*

Stephen (Harold) Spender

1909-

English poet, critic, autobiographer, dramatist, short story writer, novelist, translator, editor, travel writer, and nonfiction writer.

Spender is most often associated with the young Oxford University poets who informally grouped themselves around W. H. Auden during the 1930s. Called "The Auden Generation" by Samuel Hynes, the group produced literature dominated by a social and political consciousness that reflected such turbulent events of the era as the Depression, the Spanish Civil War, the rise of fascism, and World War II. Most critics agree that Spender's verse, particularly during this period, evidences the tension between his attraction to Romantic lyricism and his desire to comment directly on the times. Much of Spender's later poetry examines the nature of existence and documents his continuing search for a rational system of belief. This poetry is written primarily in free verse, as Spender became progressively liberated from meter and rhyme. Although he uses common language, Spender often creates abstract, surreal images that verge on obscurity. While his poetry has been faulted for an idealism close to naiveté and he is considered by some critics to be a poet of unrealized potential, Spender is admired for the lyrical transcendence and powerful images of his verse. After World War II, Spender produced less poetry and directed his energies toward critical and autobiographical writing, editorial work, and extensive lecturing at various universities in the United States and England.

Spender became acquainted with W. H. Auden, Christopher Isherwood, C. Day Lewis, and Louis MacNeice, leading members of the Auden Generation, while a student at Oxford University. Among the most influential authors of the 1930s, these writers did not adopt common aesthetic criteria; rather, they were joined by their social concerns, their aversion to fascism, and their brief affiliation with communism. Their writings of this period display a Marxist stance and examine the economics, unemployment, and politics of England in the midst of depression and on the brink of World War II. While at Oxford, Spender published *Twenty Poems* (1930), containing several widely anthologized pieces, including "Not Palaces, an Era's Crown," "I Think Continually of Those Who Were Truly Great," "The Express," and "Landscape near an Aerodrome." Much of the poetry in this volume was republished in *Poems* (1933). These collections exemplify Auden Generation social and political concerns but also indicate Spender's more lyrical and personal approach to the subject matter.

Upon leaving Oxford, Spender traveled to Berlin, having been attracted by the sexual freedom and the literary communities that thrived there during the Weimar Republic. While in Germany, Spender witnessed the rise of fascism, which culminated in Hitler's election to the chancellorship in 1933. The following year, Spender produced *Vienna* (1934), a poem in four parts that blends details of the fascist suppression of socialist insurgency in Austria with Spender's personal conflicts. *The Still Centre* (1939) records Spender's growing disillusionment with communism and is based on his experiences in the Spanish Civil War. The poems in this volume resemble the World War I poetry of Wilfred Owen in Spender's rejection of the heroic idea of war and his emphasis on the inhumanity inflicted by

combat upon the individual. Other pieces in *The Still Centre* display the more private reflections that exemplify much of his later verse. Poems from these and subsequent volumes appear in *Collected Poems, 1928-1985* (1985), a collection which led critics to assert that Spender's poetry of the 1930s, his most prodigious period, will be his most enduring.

Spender's prominence as a literary figure is based on a wide range of accomplishments in addition to his verse. Spender founded and, with Cyril Connolly, edited *Horizon*, a leading literary magazine. He later edited *Encounter* with Frank Kermode until they resigned after learning that the magazine was partially funded by the American Central Intelligence Agency. Spender's volumes of criticism, notably *The Destructive Element: A Study of Modern Writers and Beliefs* (1935), *The Struggle of the Modern* (1963), and *Love-Hate Relations: A Study of Anglo-American Sensibilities* (1974), evidence his knowledge of modern literature. His autobiography, *World within World* (1951), is a valuable document of literary and cultural history. In addition, *The Thirties and After* (1978), *Letters to Christopher* (1981), and *Stephen Spender: Journals, 1939-1983* (1985) lend his unique insight into some of the most influential writers, public figures, and events of the twentieth century.

(See also *CLC*, Vols. 1, 2, 5, 10; *Contemporary Authors*, Vols. 9-12, rev. ed.; and *Dictionary of Literary Biography*, Vol. 20.)

GEOFFREY THURLEY

If Spender is not the most unfashionable poet in the world at the present time, it is certainly difficult to think of a *more* unfashionable one. He is known universally as a Poet, and as a Social Poet. Yet there are reputable anthologies of middle twentieth-century verse which exclude him altogether, and in the universities he is likely to be scorned. Contempt rather than oblivion has been Spender's lot—contempt for the lapsed fellow-traveller, for the vegetated poet, for the confessor who never quite came clean. The *Encounter* association and divorce only reinforced the common image of the faded pink whose left hand was so ignorant of the right hand's doings that it could work for ten years against its own real interests.

Yet Spender was, I believe, Auden's superior as poet, and, with David Gascoyne, the most powerful English poet of his time: he became, not entirely through his own fault, the victim of the *maladie Anglaise,* a kind of scapegoat. His poetry assumes greater significance today: if we turn to Spender, to David Gascoyne, and Dylan Thomas, ignoring both the more facile Pylon verse and the more gaseous new Apocalypse writing, a different picture of English poetry emerges from the 'thirties, one that suggests a new future and avoids the poverty of New Lines and The Movement. Such a tradition harks back to D. H. Lawrence rather than to Hardy, to Eliot's poetry rather than to his criticism, and to Wilfred Owen rather than to Edward Thomas; it develops through Ted Hughes rather than Philip Larkin. If such a tradition is a conscious construction rather than an actuality, so is any tradition in so far as that tradition affects the way people aware of it think and write. What inscape in the past we see there depends very largely upon what someone has taught or told us to identify and pick out. In such a re-casting of a poetic and critical tradition, then, a just appraisal of Stephen Spender assumes considerable importance.

Spender himself has largely connived at his own dereliction. He suffered the savage fate of a too early and too complete acceptance, that was based upon a serious misunderstanding—or rather upon an even worse half-understanding. For Spender was accepted as a triumvir, the author of **"The Pylons,"** a sidekick of Auden's. Scorned at Cambridge as the 'new Shelley', Spender sank into a curiously public decline, which he seemed willing to accept as heartily as anyone else. Thus, in his brilliant long story, *Engaged in Writing,* he catches himself beautifully, mirrored in the distorting pebbles of Sartre's glasses (the French philosopher is thinly anagrammed as Sarret):

> They approached him as one attending the funeral of his career. He did not altogether regret their sympathy. . . .

—*Pauvre type!* Spender appears to have endorsed the verdict with dogged glee.

Yet he is much closer than Auden to what, for example, a Polish or a Spanish or a Russian poet or critic would regard as *a Poet*—and this fact seems to some extent to explain his fall from grace. The English do not like a Poet, unless he is Celtic: and Spender has always been 'being a Poet'. He has been both hampered and helped by this consciousness of role. Much of the self-conscious symbol-mongering of his later verse stems directly from it. He becomes, as one works through the *Collected Poems,* more and more 'literary' until he cannot open his mouth but to hold forth like a translation of Rilke or Seferis—

> Again, again, I see this form repeated. . . .

At the same time, the appearance he has of being at all times 'a Poet' is not entirely a matter of mistaking the career of the man of letters for the activity later dubbed poetic, nor of laboriously impersonating the style and rhetoric of the classics. Spender appears 'more a poet' than either Auden or Empson because his verse strives more continuously than theirs for a unifying context both transcending and undercutting the immediate perception. Both in rhythm and body of verse, Spender's best poetry is more powerful, and more deeply organized than Auden's. And this reflects the kind of serious commitment of himself that is inherent in the choice of the life of a poet. What is most important here probably is the awareness that a choice has been or has to be made.

It is the early verse, naturally enough, that demonstrates this best. *Poems* of 1933 seems now an impressive achievement. Less precocious than Auden's *Poems* of 1932, less dazzlingly sure of its indefinable subject-matter than Dylan Thomas's *Eighteen Poems* of 1936, it is still a declaration of promise which the later work was never wholly to fulfil. It is startlingly naïve: *viz.* 'How strangely this sun reminds me of my love', which is a good poem, in fact. But the naïveté *is* Spender, or at least an important part of him: it goes along with a genuine innocence of eye, and a capacity not only for being easily and deeply moved, but for honouring that emotion in strong and direct expression. But there is also a most impressive energy here, arching and bracing the stanzas with a strongly emotional physicality, which reminds one of Ted Hughes's *Hawk in the Rain* manner. (Spender's *Collected Poems* came out in 1953—to be savaged in the Leavisite *Delta*—while Hughes was an undergraduate at Cambridge.) This is best seen in the poems which directly address the important question shelved by Auden and Empson in the interests of a vigilant self-awareness,—the obligations inherent in the possession of poetic talent. Auden and Empson, as it were, pretend not to know they are poets. But the young artist is necessarily a hero-worshipper. Hence, Spender's quite legitimate tendency to think 'continually of those who are truly great'. The resignation and envy in the very title of this poem (it makes it clear the poet knows he isn't one of them) are significant in fact. But the awareness of the sort of spiritual quest involved is equally important: it is a far more mature recognition of the nature of the task confronting him than the sincere but inadequate social conscience the volume also flaunts. A more impressive instance of this *Kulturmythologie* is the frankly adulatory poem on **"Beethoven's Death Mask."** Once again, Spender puts a distance between himself and the 'truly great' man, which is clearly going to incapacitate him for the sustained spiritual flight. But again, also, the acknowledgement of the peculiar role of genius is intelligent and constructive. It is also quite legitimate that Spender should explore the possibilities of the spiritual aspiration through the actual achievement of Beethoven—the transition from Scherzo to Finale of the Fifth Symphony in this case:

> Then the drums move away, the Distance shows;
> Now cloud-hid peaks are bared; the mystic One
> Horizons haze, as the blue incense heaven.
> Peace, peace. . . . Then splitting skull and dream, there
>   comes
> Blotting our lights, the Trumpetter, the sun.

Spender's talent is far better exercised here, in the naive imitation of a master (an Imitation of Christ, *mutatis mutandis*), than in the would-be sophisticated knowingness of 'An "I" can never be a great man', in which received twentieth-century ideas are crossed with Negative Capability in an image-less confusion.

Much more impressive than the latter poem in a related vein is **"What I expected"** (poem XIV in the book), which makes an interesting parallel or contrast with Auden's contemporary allegories of the intellectual life,—"Atlantis," for instance, or "The Quest." Where Auden parabolizes in studious disenchantment, Spender eschews the extended allegorical schema, confident in the capacity of a loosely connected sheaf of activities—climbing, struggling, fighting—to coalesce into a composite image of the spiritual experience:

> What I expected was
> Thunder, fighting,
> Long struggles with men
> And climbing.
> After continual straining
> I should grow strong;
> Then the rocks would shake
> And I should rest long.
>
>   (pp. 79-82)

Structurally and methodologically, it is a beautiful piece of work, the parts related simply and subtly to the whole which they modify as they create it, yet still holding the air of an honest and honestly outraged personal testament. Like all the best poems Spender produced at this time, it embodies the message it enunciates: in pursuing the structural argument, one experiences the poem. And this capacity in Spender has a lot to do with his conception of the poem as an act, rather than as a statement. It is this which most distinguishes him from W. H. Auden, with whom he was fatally associated for so long. The Auden association seems to me to have been a disaster. No poet could have been better chosen to expose Spender's deficiencies and undermine his self-confidence than W. H. Auden. Nor, at the same time, could any poet conceivably be further removed from Auden in mind and ability than Spender. They are in fact polar opposites: as so often happens in the history of thought, two temperaments more or less exclusively contrasted become fixed in a polarization at first stimulating, then destructive. As with Wordsworth and Coleridge, the weaker character went under and suffered in the process more or less crippling damage to his self-esteem and identity. In the present case, the extroverted abreactive brain of Auden, scientific and sharply exact in its annotative habits, decisively demoralized the vacillating religiose vagueness of Spender. The decline of Spender's reputation set in when those who had bracketed him with Auden first realized how far he was from fulfilling the Auden norm, a norm he was hopelessly ill-equipped to attempt. (p. 83)

[Spender's] weakest lines are those which attempt to fix the politico-social facts with what he seems to have felt was an Audenesque precision. Now precision is exactly what Spender characteristically lacks—precision and swiftness: the movement of his verse is laboured, heavily stressed, bound up with its own rhyme echoes. If we compare a poem like the much-anthologized **"Fall of a City"** with any of Auden's political poems, Spender will appear naïve and amateurish:

> All the posters on the walls,
> All the leaflets in the streets
> Are mutilated, destroyed, or run in rain . . .

Spender does little to really fix the impression: there is no distinguished touch to the lines. And yet the heavy-handed emphasis on the three verbs—'mutilated', 'destroyed' and 'run-in-rain'—does something beyond and beneath the actual visual content of the words. In fact, what at first appears its embar-

rassing ineptitude (the fact that the three verbs together tell us little more than any one of them might have alone) emerges as its real strength: the compassionate pathos that rubs off or through onto the inhabitants of the city. More, the suggestion in these lines of tears is something Auden would either not have caught, or would have been embarrassed at: it is the limitation of very clever people that they can often only see suffering as a reason for pity, without being able to feel pity itself. (p. 84)

Spender's clumsiness, in the instance under discussion as in many others, derives probably from the fact that he had to make a conscious effort of will to focus the external facts (the posters and leaflets) from which Auden, bad eyes or no, would have extracted the essence in a trice.

Yet the difference between Auden's mind and Spender, lies deeper than this. I have already noted certain similarities in their use of allegory to express the struggle of the intellectual life. Another type of allegoric poem both poets liked to exploit concerns sexual and emotional situations. Here the allegoric narrative is replaced by a single symbol, as in Rilke's great poem "Exposed on the mountains of the heart," from which both English poets, I fancy, learned something. Spender's **"Your body is stars whose million glitter here"** recaptures much of the ecstasy of Rimbaud's *Illuminations* in its frank hyperbolic celebration of the act:

> Our movements range through miles, and when we kiss
> The moment widens to enclose the years.

The explorers invoked in the second half of the poem are not Auden's jaded delinquents—swillers of rare liqueurs in Graham Greene bars—but acolytes, 'explorers of immense and simple lines'. It is in fact, an immense and simple poem, despite its post-coital deflation, which seems less an intimation of disenchantment than a pain of exclusion welcomed as part of a ritual. . . . (p. 85)

We note, by contrast, the purely 'literary' origination of the mountain symbol in Auden's Sonnet, "The Climbers:" the poem becomes a mere exercise, presenting the labours of love in terms of a climb. Imagery of kitting-out, setting off on a gruelling expedition which is not literal but figurative is, I have noted, a common property of Auden's universe. (pp. 85-6)

One turns with a mixture of weariness and disgust, on the other hand, from the inevitable self-accusations of "The Climbers:" phrases like 'Excuse concocted' and 'Cooling my face in the faults' amount almost to self-parody. Why, we ask ourselves, can Auden only prove his integrity by demonstrating his awareness of his own mendacity and failure? In spite of its confessional nature, Spender's poetry is free of this characteristic vice of ironist verse, and it is the consequent openness and fullness, coupled with the greater volume and rhythmic power of his poetry, that establishes his superiority over Auden. . . .

The strenuousness of Spender's language and rhythm is easily demonstrated. It derives from the poet's slow involvement in his emotionally possessed and surrounded objects and observations. The strength and inner life of his metre explain—as they are explained by—that very naïveté and sluggishness which seemed initially to make him such a hopeless straggler in the 'thirties field. . . . (p. 87)

The Spanish Civil War poems are probably on balance the most satisfying in the Collected Spender. Significantly, the fighting and death afforded Spender a profounder vision into reality than they afforded Auden. Where Auden communicates an exciting sense of disaster and anarchy, Spender sees both sides engaged in a conflict which ultimately transcends their partisan differences; he achieves the classic serenity that marks off the merely good from the momentarily great. . . . (p. 88)

Spender's successes come when he has forgotten the wrangle with symbol and image that bogs down so much of his verse; conversely, his poetry loses its point when the symbol takes over. (pp. 89-90)

The strenuousness (body, rhythmic strength), which I have tried to illustrate in Spender, ties in with his genius for metaphor, or his weakness for it, as it often appears. Metaphor is not only Spender's most natural mode of expression; it is part of his conceptual apparatus—everything is seen in terms of something else. Each image breeds an analogical double. Spender has often been described as 'introspective', usually in a loose way, referring to his awkward self-consciousness. It is not merely his penchant for thinking 'continually of those who were truly great', however, that justifies the label. Spender's mind is introverted in a more precise sense, that relates to his actual manner of perceiving reality. Certainly it is no accident that so many of his successful poems take the form of a commentary on his prolonged rumination (it is this, rather than meditation). (pp. 91-2)

As we move through the *Collected Poems,* the hand of Rilke exercises a more and more inhibiting restraint upon Spender's native metaphorical sense. He displays a greater and greater concern for finding analogical correlates for phenomena which do not especially seem to have struck him, and his own natural metaphorical animism gives way to an increasingly literary symbolism.

Ultimately the effort to compete with Rilke (this is how it registers) broke Spender. The single image in which he most seriously strives after a Rilkean universality—**"The Vase of Tears"**—unequivocally announces the failure of Spender's adoption of Rilkean profundity:

> And one by one these bitter drops collect
> Into my heart, a glass vase which reflects
> The world's grief weeping in its daughter.

A co-translator of the *Duino Elegies* ought to have been more aware of the care with which Rilke ensures a feasible analogical form for his symbols. The cause of Spender's failure in these lines is the absence of any visual or other actual support for the symbol. To call his heart 'a glass vase' was bad enough— the metaphor lacks any real analogical basis. But to go on to picture the vase *reflecting* was disastrous: we are forced to conclude that Spender was leaning entirely upon the reader's stock response to the loaded words—heart and tears.

"The Vase of Tears" was published in the 1937-9 collection, *Love and Separation.* Thereafter the imagery and metaphor show an increasing self-consciousness that borders often on the mechanical. The metaphors and similes succeed more and more in fixing only a limited visual effect. An air raid at Plymouth for example, provokes Spender only to a series of more and less successful parallelisms—the searchlight-beams 'fuse in a cone', or smash the aircraft's image like a cup; they are like fencing swords, or they make geometrical patterns, trying to mark the spot with a cross of doom. The cross they make is of course at once a geometrical intersection, an omen of doom, and then the cross that marks the pilot's grave. This kind of ingenuity betrays the gravity of the events observed. The concern for analogical accuracy destroys or precludes any

serious feeling Spender might have entertained. He might be describing a firework display or a circus instead of a struggle in which somebody—the aircrew or the inhabitants of Plymouth—is likely to get killed. The last stanza's Christian sermonizings do not ease matters: on the contrary, the laboured accuracy now connives at a knowing wit—'the waves / Chuckle between the rocks'! No-one who has read Edith Sitwell's 'Still falls the rain' is going to be impressed, either, by Spender's final crucifix reference:

> Man hammers nails in Man
> High on his crucifix.

This kind of image-hunting is still more shocking when the subject is Belsen or Buchenwald. The pilot was out of sight, and after all he was a Nazi. Confronted by the living skeletons of Belsen, Spender—who has shown himself so enormously compassionate, so profoundly moved by suffering in poem after poem; who is dangerously vulnerable to emotion, and half-Jewish at the same time—retreats into a hunt for the appropriate image that genuinely appalls: their skin 'tars the bones' with a 'thin varnish'; their faces are like 'clenched despair' 'Knocking at the birdsong-fretted air'.

Failure in the face of Belsen and Hiroshima cannot be held against any artist: they are beyond sympathy. The attempt to treat them in artistic form is at best misguidedly immature, at worst presumptuously self-important. It was inevitable that someone of Spender's endowment—tremulously emotional and accessible to suffering—should be forced into a total withdrawal of himself in the face of the Nazi camps. Hence, his poem on the subject (self-mockingly called **"Memento"**) not only reveals no evidence whatever of genuine emotional response, it is positively offensive in its unscrupulous seeking after effects: 'birdsong-fretted' in particular, with its Shakespearean overtones, hits an unpleasantly literary note. We resent this display of technique in the context of such suffering, just as we reject the elegance of Sydney Nolan's Auschwitz drawings, and the pious pomp of Britten's War Requiem. All of these performances seem insulting in the circumstances, their 'sincerity' an impertinence, their articulations heartless. Only silence will do, and silence is a failure. (pp. 95-7)

> *Geoffrey Thurley, "A Kind of Scapegoat: A Retrospect on Stephen Spender," in his* The Ironic Harvest: English Poetry in the Twentieth Century, *Edward Arnold, 1974, pp. 79-97.*

PETER STANSKY

[*The Thirties and After*] from Stephen Spender, an odd and fascinating mix made up for the most part of previously uncollected essays, reviews and reminiscences, along with a connecting commentary, achieves coherence through the force of its author's remarkable personality. It is best read as a kind of pendant to his classic self-portrait *World within World,* published almost 30 years ago. Since then a good deal has happened to Spender in the worlds of poetry and politics, and one might have hoped for another full-scale volume of autobiography. In lieu of that the present work will do, and as one might expect, the best writing here is that which is most immediate, most personal, most autobiographical.

There is an unnecessary but characteristic note of self-deprecation in Spender's Postscript: "I myself am, it is only too clear, an autobiographer. Autobiography provides the line of continuity in my work. I am not someone who can shed or disclaim his past.'' And yet he has an almost irresistible tendency to take off from his personal experience, so often touchingly and perceptively described, to discuss in abstract terms what it may mean—to impersonalize it—to expect it to bear more significance than it deserves, in some senses to make it less interesting in making it more significant. Thus a few lines farther on in the Postscript he offers this almost meaningless generalization, whose purpose would seem to be to blow himself up into a universal principle: ''Politics without ideology and with a strong tendency towards autobiography equals liberalism.'' (p. 27)

The world, whether it be that of poetry, politics, or people, is validated when seen from his own perspective, and illuminated by his response to it. Its main point would seem to be its relation to Stephen Spender, poet, political and social being. This ought to be infuriating, yet there is a candor in the writing, waffly though it may be at times, and an authenticity and intelligence that make this book not only fascinating to read but also a crucial document for the 1930s in certain of their literary and political aspects.

Where, Spender seems to be asking, does he fit in the world of literature and politics of this period? By extension he is asking the same question about the group—W. H. Auden, Cecil Day Lewis, Christopher Isherwood, Louis MacNeice—with whom he has been so closely associated. He writes about them with great freshness, and, in the final section, hauntingly, as one by one the dead are recalled: MacNeice, Cyril Connolly (each in a poem published here for the first time), and then Auden, in the talk Spender gave about him at Christ Church, Oxford, a month after his death. . . .

And yet, taken at their public-face value, the pieces of the book add up to an intriguing argument. Quite a few of its pages are devoted to a consideration of three of the masters of modernism—W. B. Yeats, D. H. Lawrence and, most particularly, T. S. Eliot. Spender acknowledges how deeply he and his friends were influenced by them, and shared with them an unshakable commitment to the importance of art and literature, even though they couldn't have been at a farther remove from their right-wing politics. The antithetical tradition—politics first, then art—he evokes in a younger, activist generation, represented by the poets John Cornford and Julian Bell, the first a Communist and the second a discontented liberal, who lost their lives on the government side during the Spanish civil war. In effect, Spender sees himself partaking—though he doesn't say this so bluntly—of the virtues of both traditions: the commitment to literature of the one, and the political commitment of the other. (p. 28)

The 1930s were a shaping time for Spender, casting a long shadow over all that came after, and in that sense the title of the book has a precise, ironic aptness. It would seem that the rest of his life, more even than he may realize, has been a matter of coming to terms with the 1930s, and the conflicting claims of literature and politics as he knew them in that decade of achievement, fame, and disillusion. ''Spain was a death to us, Munich a mourning,'' Day Lewis wrote in his ''Dedicatory Stanzas to Stephen Spender.'' After the traumas of Spain and Munich, one might have expected that Spender would follow the example of Auden, who abandoned politics (and England) at the end of the decade to devote himself single-mindedly to poetry in America, and in the future would revise or disown those poems of his—no matter how famous—that reflected a politics in which he no longer believed.

But Spender, lacking Auden's single-mindedness, attempted to reconcile the seemingly irreconcilable, and in the exhilarating, stepped-up tempo of the war years he was able to put off a recognition of the difficulties inherent in the attempt. This was a rewarding period for him when he seemed able to be everything he wanted: poet, co-editor of *Horizon*, fire-watcher, husband and father. No longer a rebel, he was at the very heart of the English culture establishment. The latter-day Shelley had been tamed. (pp. 28-9)

The 1950s, as he acknowledges, were not his best decade. It is significant that his most enduring achievement from that time should have been a return to his past in *World within World.*

That masterpiece of autobiography, and the best of the poems, continue to remind us how much we owe to the private Spender. As a public figure he is no doubt the more ''representative,'' but the glimpses of his ''other self'' in *The Thirties and After* make one hope again that he will yet write a sequel to his volume of autobiography. In the meantime, it is useful and gratifying to have this memorable collection. (p. 29)

> *Peter Stansky, in a review of ''The Thirties and After: Poetry, Politics, People (1933-1970),'' in* The New Republic, *Vol. 179, No. 13, September 23, 1978, pp. 27-9.*

DAVID WRIGHT

''The thirties was the decade in which young writers became involved in politics''. Thus Stephen Spender, after Auden the best of the ''Thirties poets'', begins a book which is, alas, rather a barrel-scraping job.

The main body of *The Thirties and After* seems to be a collection of old magazine articles, diaries written for immediate publication, book reviews and accounts of various international writers' congresses, e g, the one at Madrid during the Spanish Civil War, at which ''the endless stream of our oratory continued rather ineffectively'' and André Chamson and the author ''arrived at a truth which few of the congress had even glimpsed . . . that the war is terrible'' (such moments of characteristic honesty, or even more characteristic naïveté, are disarming). These odds and ends are linked by four ''background'' essays, one for each decade: amiable, waffly, made up of generalisations rather than perceptions; studded with vogue-names, but occasionally illuminating.

The moments of illumination occur whenever Mr Spender reverts from journalistic generalizations (usually concocted from his reading of books and newspapers) to the particular (some specific experience or perception of his own). Thus no generalization that he makes about Auden's poetry or politics is as enlightening as his description of the undergraduate Auden seeing (and analysing) his friends one at a time in his room ''with blinds drawn, and wearing a green eye-shade . . . and with a lamp behind his chair which showed him in shadow and shed light upon his visitor'' or reciting poetry ''in a detached clinical voice which seemed to drain it of all meaning except that he emphasized certain words . . . as though they were objects like drowned kittens held out at arms' length''.

Reportage, not theory, is Mr Spender's forte. He is at his best in vignettes like **''Polish Displaced Persons''** or **''The Student Aulach'';** and above all in the long, anecdotal, and affectionate **''Remembering Eliot''.**

David Wright, *"We Wanted a War of Our Own,"* in The Times Educational Supplement, *No. 3303, October 20, 1978, p. 22.*

SAMUEL HYNES

In the 1930's Stephen Spender was called the Shelley of his generation and the Rupert Brooke of the Depression. Neither remark can have pleased him much, but each got the essential genealogy right: Mr. Spender belongs to that line of romantic poets who believed that the times demanded something more than individualism. Shelley wrote revolutionary tracts and Brooke joined the Fabians; and Mr. Spender, through a long creative life, has been a politically engaged writer. Yet in spite of his political commitments, he has remained what he always was— a romantic individualist, valuing personal freedom and artistic creation, and seeking a Good Society in which individuals might flourish. . . .

Now, at nearly 70, Mr. Spender is the last of his generation of poets and the one with the least secure reputation. W. H. Auden was recognized from the first as the generation's major talent, Louis MacNeice has always been admired for his fine, though less expansive gift, and Cecil Day Lewis has settled at a somewhat lower, but stable place among the minor laureates. But Mr. Spender is still an open question. The qualities in his poems that one critic praises as unique—his emotional immediacy, the sense he can give of feelings going directly onto the page—another sees as naïveté, undisciplined formlessness, an embarrassing tendency to self-exposure. (p. 9)

Mr. Spender's copious occasional writings [in *The Thirties and After*] constitute a record of the life and thought of an engaged writer during a career that now covers more than half a century, and, though there may not be much glory in that, there is considerable historic value. It is that value that *The Thirties and After* seems to aim at epitomizing and ordering. Mr. Spender's initial intention, he explains in his introduction, was to make a collection of essays, "some of them concerned with the political involvement of myself, as a member of the Thirties' generation, with public events, others of them critical essays and reviews of purely literary interest. I hoped that this would provide a kind of case history of a Thirties' poet in which the connection between different documents would illustrate themes of literature and politics over a period of nearly half a century." Then he remembered the journals that he had kept from time to time, and he decided to add passages from them. So there are three kinds of writings here: political, literary and personal. These he has organized by decades, and to each section he has written an introductory essay on the "Background" of the decade.

The essential book is these introductory essays: They constitute a kind of autobiography (a long footnote, one might say, to *World within World*) with period illustrations in the form of essays and journal entries of the period being described. The materials from the past are lively and readable—Mr. Spender has always been a skillful prose writer—and especially in the extracts from his journals and his accounts of postwar Germany and of the student revolutions of 1968. The literary criticism may seem a bit dated, but it has its interest as an expression of a poet's opinions in his time. The new material—the decade introductions—is judiciously retrospective, sometimes nostalgic, sometimes self-critical, occasionally self-defensive. Together, past writing and present writing compose a stereoscopic

personal history—Mr. Spender writing *about* the past, *now,* and then Mr. Spender writing *in* the past, *then.*

It is a good idea for a book, and it ought to be a better book. What is wrong with it is mainly a failure to follow the implications of the book conceived as a case history. Mr. Spender has included pieces that might well have been omitted and has excluded material that would be more central to his "case," and here and there, quoting from his journals, he has allowed himself to slip into name-dropping, reporting not very interesting things that Stravinsky said and what Malraux did after dinner. In the end the book seems random, when it ought to seem constructed.

I can imagine another, better book. It would include these introductory essays, but for its evidences it would draw mainly on Mr. Spender's journals: the **"September Journal"** of 1940, the journal-like reporting of *European Witness* and *The Year of the Rebels,* the *Encounter* diaries of the 1950's. Such a book would make the past clearer and more continuous, and would keep the two histories—the topical history of the moment as it was lived, and the retrospective view of it—separate and counterpointed. And it would make clearer what this book leaves blurred—the image of Mr. Spender, the poet, the liberal, the well-meaning man, who lived through these troubled years. (p. 80)

Samuel Hynes, *"An Ambassador of Letters,"* in The New York Times Book Review, *November 26, 1978, pp. 9, 80.*

JOHN BAYLEY

The special flavor of Stephen Spender's writing [in *The Thirties and After*] is, above all, a political flavor; its true originality that of a poet who swims in political and social speculation like a fish in water. Almost alone among authors who reflect upon the times (and they are not in short supply) he has a style of great directness and simplicity which, whether in poetry or in prose, seems to dissolve the hard gritty concepts and abstractions, the self-importance and self-protectiveness which the most sensitive intellectuals clutch about themselves and weave into their syntax and grammar. In a critical essay Spender once made a distinction between opaque and transparent styles. His own is extremely transparent: it seems artless, but without wishing to seem to conceal art.

The question of style is important, because it is by the formation of what may be called a style that most poets, novelists, and intellectuals who are associated with attitudes to events of the Thirties and after responded to those events. The most obvious style would be the jargon of the Party, with its comforting stress on the correct line, the historically inevitable solution. Malraux, Sartre, Koestler, Graham Greene—even, in their almost comically different fashion, Auden and Isherwood—exhibit subtler versions of this protective extrusion of style, a verbal version of the need to escape from the imbecile irrelevance of a society falling apart, to create a world elsewhere. The great strength of Spender, which gives a curious authority to his recollections, his narrative of his own and others' feelings and responses, is that he never seems to have needed such a world or made any attempt to create one. His curiosity, his creative energy seem alike much more literal, more simplistic in a way, and all the more effective for that in presenting a medium in which other worlds may appear like the weeds and stones a fish encounters, in which the Thirties and the Seventies both seem present and alive, unhistorical and all around us.

He regards the phenomena past and present in his life with an imagination of his own, which does not seem to be a literary imagination.

Spender has often been lumped together, as a convenience, with Auden and Isherwood, but that could not be more misleading. As an essayist and creative writer he functions in a manner radically different from either of his two contemporaries. To put it in the simplest terms, they were idealists and he was a realist, notwithstanding he was often assumed to be the most sentimental, indeed naïve, of the three, writing poetry full of aspirations and romantic hopes for himself and society. But whatever the appearances, he and his art were living in the real world in a sense in which they and theirs did not. . . .

Auden insisted on the absolute gap between poetry and life. When he made the ritual pilgrimage to the Spanish civil war as an ambulance driver he returned in six weeks and "never spoke of his experiences"; nor did they become in any sense a part of his life—perhaps his actual experiences never did.

Spender, by contrast, has been reflecting and commenting ever since on the significance of his time in Spain: he did so in his autobiography, *World Within World*—one of the funniest and most penetrating of all contemporary essays in this genre—and he does so, even more illuminatingly, in [*The Thirties and After*]. He is fascinated by the reactions to it of himself and other intellectuals, and the lessons he learned from it. Like his other experiences it has directly influenced his poetry. He wrote poems there, some of his most moving and beautiful poems, which, like some of Whitman's, are actually about impressions of war seen by a sensitive and observant poet, on the spot and without preconceptions. Incongruities are recorded there, as in the section on Spain in this prose collection, in a peculiarly individual and firsthand way—the cossetted machine-gun wrapped up like a granny in a shawl, the look of the dead under olive trees, the bizarre involuntary intimacy of friend and foe in trench warfare, "as if these enemies slept in each other's arms." Auden's "Spain" is a mythological set-piece, like Yeats's "Easter 1916," almost a recital piece, intended to order and sanctify the muddle and dishonesty of the whole business, keep it at arm's length from the poetry, the poet, and ourselves. None the worse for that—it takes a great poet to achieve this time-honored function of the poetic—but it is a very different thing from the lyric and lucid curiosity with which Spender has felt, seen, and recorded his experiences. (p. 33)

Spender might seem to have been the archetypal hero-worshipper, a bit crazy, full of abounding ardors; but underlying this was a shrewd perception and common sense that would not have been possible in the specialized worlds of Auden and Isherwood, who were apparently so much more sure-footed and beady-eyed, patronizing in an amused way the enthusiasms of the one who seemed to them the most unworldly member of their trio.

Spender of course knew, or came to know, Germany very well. In an extract of this book called **"September Journal,"** written just after war broke out in 1939, he reflects on visits there and friends, especially Ernst Robert Curtius. The picture of Curtius, "an egoist of the liberal, Goethe tradition," is done with the kind of sympathy and warmth that only a very good novelist can command—understanding through loving, as Henry James said it should be done—and is as absorbing to read as those of the many other friends we meet in the book, like Cyril Connolly and Louis MacNeice. It is a pity that Spender has

not written novels (we learn that he once wanted to be a novelist as much as to be a poet) because he likes people for their natural egos, instead of using his understanding of these against them, as usually happens in memoirs and recollections. . . .

[Spender's] intuitive feel and sympathy extends to societies—Spain, Germany, and America—and the interrelation within them between personalities and political and social trends. Having myself been in Germany at the end of the war I can testify to thinking that the only account of it that made sense was Spender's in *European Witness,* which appeared in 1946. A selection from it is reissued for the first time in this volume. It is an admirable example of Spender's tentacular and sympathetic curiosity, applied to personalities he met in those ruined and helpless cities, like the student Aulach, who was already exhibiting some of the same symptoms—in particular the invocation of a new charismatic authority to exorcise and replace the old—that appear today among the following of the Baader-Meinhof group. (p. 34)

The empathy and the capacity for poetic identification—that Protean gift valued in poets by Coleridge—is the same whether in prewar Spain, pre- and post-war Germany, or present-day America; though on an American campus today Spender feels no sense of identification with that rather creepy detachment about their own lives and habits which is fashionable among some poets and intellectuals, and which is perhaps not entirely unrelated to the attitude of Aulach. What Spender reacts against here is a certain dehumanizing of ordinary life, and his reaction to it shows a hard reef of humanist morality underlying the ebb and flow of his sympathetic responses. . . .

Merging naturally with these personal impressions are essays on writers of the Thirties and today, reflections on modern poetry, on "late Stravinsky listening to late Beethoven," and accounts of the founding of *Horizon* and *Encounter* and of Spender's resignation when the latter magazine was found to be subsidized by the CIA. Of particular interest are the prewar essays on joining the Communist Party, on Wyndham Lewis as a poet, and on Aragon's collection of poems, *The Red Front,* which the young Spender dismissed with an independence most unusual in that circle at that time as odious and worthy of the Nazis themselves.

One of the best essays is on the verse plays which Auden and Isherwood wrote before the war, *The Ascent of F6, The Dog Beneath the Skin,* and *On the Frontier.* Spender is particularly well qualified to write of these because his own play **Trial of a Judge** is certainly the most effective and most moving of all these prewar poetic dramas; I would put it higher even than *Murder in the Cathedral.* The reasons are connected with what I earlier defined as Spender's realism, in contrast to the fantasy worlds invented by the others, which would not exclude the special type of Anglo-Catholic apologetics canvassed by T. S. Eliot. A surprising thing about the theater is that it requires a more generalized representation of "reality" than need be necessary to either poetry or the novel: the action of *Hamlet* must really seem to take place in the Danish court, and Shakespeare has seen to it that his representation of the Danish court is an entirely convincing one.

This aspect of dramatic verisimilitude, which Spender instinctively understands, was ignored by Auden and Isherwood. As Spender points out, Lord Stagmantle, the newspaper proprietor in *The Dog Beneath the Skin,* and Valerian, the international industrialist of *On the Frontier,* are simply not convincing as portraits of men in their respective callings. Their authors are not interested in making them live, as Brecht or Shaw were careful to make their ideologically oriented characters live—Spender instances the portraits based on Asquith and Lloyd George in *Back to Methuselah.*

He points out that the art of such portraiture concentrates on the gap between the private man and the public one—"the interplay between the littleness of the man and the greatness of his position." In Shakespeare, of course, the contrast between the two is much more subtle than this; but it exists, making such figures as Anthony and Cleopatra far more dramatically alive than they would be if the play concentrated on either their private lives or their public personalities. And Spender's own *Trial of a Judge,* in addition to the beauty of its poetry, is moving and intricate in the ways in which it reveals in depth the dilemma of its characters, a dilemma in which—unlike those in the other poetic dramas of that time—all the private and political consciousness which we share is involved. It is rumored that Spender has been engaged for some time now in writing another verse play. Its production will be an event to look forward to. (p. 35)

> *John Bayley, "A Poet in Politics," in* The New York Review of Books, *Vol. XXV, Nos. 21 & 22, January 25, 1979, pp. 33-5.*

STEPHEN KOCH

The *Letters to Christopher*—written by Stephen Spender to Christopher Isherwood during their hectic youth between 1929 and 1939—are documents from the dawn of a phase in literary history which now is in its evening. Back then, Isherwood was in his famous boarding house, writing *The Berlin Stories,* witnessing the pauperized death of Weimar; Spender was busy on the London literary scene—as he says, "dining with the Woolves." He was also visiting Berlin itself, Spain, and other sites of the emerging international horror. Both were staking out their relation to the dominating intellectual energy emanating from their friend W.H. Auden—a third party, very present in his absence here. But the literary youth of "the Oxford boys" (Edmund Wilson's phrase) is anything but obscure; probably only Bloomsbury has been more copiously documented—and you would have to be very interested in its slighter details to snap up *Letters to Christopher.* Even helped by Lee Bartlett's lucid notes, these letters are pretty scrappy stuff. Certainly nobody will turn to them before the two men's autobiographies: Isherwood's *Christopher and His Kind,* and Spender's gossipy, underrated, *World Within World....*

I am at a loss to explain why Bartlett has relegated to the shadows of an appendix two long sections of Spender's 1930s journals—they are far more interesting than the letters that get top billing. The most interesting is begun on September 3, 1939, two days exactly after the start of World War II, two months exactly after Spender's first wife unceremoniously left him. Hurt, confused, Spender journalizes in search of his emotional and intellectual bearings, (so advised by *both* T.S. Eliot and Virginia Woolf: even de profundis Spender is never *very* far from Fame), and the results are shrewd, twilit memories of Weimar; anecdotes about the great German critic Ernst Robert Curtius; talk about wild escapades; reflections on love and loss—until at last the man's irrepressible curiosity, irrepressible hopefulness, reemerge.

This gives the book all the charm it has. The tall, strapping, smart young man we glimpse through the narrow slats of these letters (and the better view from the journal, along with a good

collection of photographs) is a kind of romping, raucous intellectual Saint Bernard—joyously plunging after every idea, every impression, opinion, poem, dream, person, that passes. He is full of gossip. He is boisterously affectionate. (The sundry dilemmas of Spender's bisexuality are frankly, though inconclusively, revealed.) He is passionately interested in everything—a bit more interested than he is interesting, in fact. He *is* a little shallow, but he is marvelously, boisterously alive. I can see that for all the clumsy charm, he might have been trying as a friend; at one point he and Isherwood had a short but mean drop-dead set-to, in which Isherwood cooly tells him Berlin isn't big enough for both of them. And Spender does look like he could fill more than half the town.

Meanwhile where is the other half? Isherwood's letters do not appear at all. The result is that what at best is a document becomes more like half a document. That may have a certain value, I suppose—and the journals are better. But as they stand, these letters have a bit the sound of one hand that is not clapping.

> *Stephen Koch, "'The Oxford Boys'," in* Book World—The Washington Post, *February 15, 1981, p. 7.*

PHILIP GARDNER

The earliest full-length survey of the poetry of the 1930s was Francis Scarfe's collection of essays *Auden and After,* published in 1941. In it Scarfe predicted that Stephen Spender would become a more considerable poet than Auden. In view of the sensitivity and impressive originality of Spender's *Poems* (1933) and *The Still Centre* (1939), the prophecy was understandable; but History, that Goddess of the 1930s who "may say Alas but cannot help or pardon", has not made the prediction come true, turning Spender from a fine poet to whom critical justice has not yet been fully done into that valuable but lesser being, an entrepreneur of letters. In this capacity, as impresario of his own literary career, Spender has allowed the publication of [*Letters to Christopher*], edited by a young Californian scholar, Lee Bartlett.

It consists of forty-two letters written to Christopher Isherwood between January 1929 and August 1939 . . . , together with two journals, belonging to late 1932 and late 1939. . . . Useful as the editorial apparatus generally is—biographical commentary, annotation, bibliography, and a list of *dramatis personae* which identifies the "Elizabeth" and the "Jimmy Younger" of *World Within World* (1951), though not yet the undergraduate "Marston"—it can hardly avoid stamping the book as a product of the light industry of "1930s studies". Without wishing to be ungrateful to Dr Bartlett, one must say that its real value lies in its primary material, which documents Spender's experiences and feelings during the decade of his best poetry, thus complementing with first-hand immediacy the maturer recollections of his autobiography.

Like Auden's 1930 volume of the same title, Spender's *Poems,* or at least its 1934 reprint, is dedicated to Isherwood: both poets acknowledged the slightly older novelist as their literary mentor. But the letters printed here do not, as the editor claims in his introduction, trace the evolution of an important literary friendship; for that one would need Isherwood's replies, and it is a pity the book does not include them. One reads of Spender's partisan admiration for *The Dog Beneath the Skin,* "which pushes most serious poetry and most novels completely into the background", and for Isherwood's novel *The Lost,* whose retitling as *Mr Norris Changes Trains* seemed to Spender "arty" and mystifyingly gave him "a sense of earrings". One can also infer how valuable Isherwood was to him as a congenial confidant, as well as in his rôle as lonely, dedicated maker. But what is mainly conveyed by this book is the development of Spender himself, a portrait of the artist in a hurry to fulfil the ambitions burning so proteanly in him "to be a real great writer", but also of a man who, at the end of the 1930s, reaches the realization that "no one would want anything except to find his place in life, the centre of his potentiality to love and be loved."

What a peripatetic decade it was for Spender! There are letters from Oxford, London, Vienna, Dubrovnik, Salzburg, Barcelona. Only one short letter relates to Spain at the time of the Civil War, though a description, in the 1939 Journal, of a moon which "takes a farewell look at our civilization everywhere", recalls the lucid staring moon of his poignant poem **"Two Armies"**. . . .

If, since the war, Spender's creative engine has run at less than full power, one remains grateful for his best work, the context of which is fascinatingly provided by these letters and journals.

> *Philip Gardner, "Running the Engine," in* The Times Literary Supplement, *No. 4072, April 17, 1981, p. 446.*

STEPHEN COREY

Letters to Christopher is really two books fated to appear in the card catalogue as one: the first book contains forty-two letters, written between 1929 and 1939, from the young poet Spender to the young novelist Isherwood; the second book consists of two journals Spender kept during that same decade, one in 1932 and the other in 1939. Editor Lee Bartlett's failure to mention the journals in the title is unfortunate, I believe, because ultimately they seem likely to prove more interesting and valuable to most readers than will the bulk of the letters.

A paradox exists concerning our expectations for literary letters—one that makes few of them fully satisfying. We want them to rise above the millions of ordinary letters written every day, and in so rising to speak to *us* with as much (or more) importance as they did to their original recipients; yet if the letters smack of the literary, if they seem written with an ear toward a larger audience, we distrust them—for what kind of person would use private correspondence to further his career? What we seek, then, is offhand wit, casual genius, universality in spite of itself.

Spender's letters to Isherwood, written in the 1930's as both men moved from obscurity to national reputation, would seem likely candidates for success as literary letters. Because he felt Isherwood to be an intimate friend, Spender confided in him seriously and fully. But because Isherwood was a writer as well, Spender often used his letters for theorizing about art, for discussing books he had read and literary figures he had met, and for giving critiques of Isherwood's writing and responding to comments on his own work. The stage would seem to be set, in short, for letters in which the tones and motivations are sincere and the subjects are often of interest to a broad readership. Nonetheless, most of the early letters and many of the later ones may prove unexceptional for all but students of the two principals involved—not because Spender isn't honest and sincere (he always is here), but because, on balance, too much of the letters is taken up by gossip and mundane daily

details. In 1929 Spender was twenty and in some ways still an adolescent, despite the intellectual and literary precocity that would help him to publish six books in four genres before he turned thirty. The first few years' worth of letters although dotted with interesting bits of observation and commentary, are dominated by the very ordinary voice of a boy who wishes his life were better and fears that it won't be: "Damn Oxford. When can one escape from such a place and live in peace?" Still, here and there Spender gives hints of the honest and precise self-analysis to come in his beautiful autobiography, *World Within World* (1951)—the kind of self-analysis a reader feels not as confessionalism but as a revelation about human nature. (p. 431)

The two journals appended to *Letters to Christopher* will make engaging reading for anyone interested in modern art, politics, and culture. In both journals, Spender sets out with the primary intention of recreating a world—Spain in the 1932 entries, Germany in those of 1939. This focus on the public realm counterbalances Spender's leanings toward self-absorption. . . .

Spender's 1939 journal is the most important and fascinating part of *Letters to Christopher.* He began it out of desperation on 3 September, the day England and France declared war on Germany: "I am going to keep a journal because I cannot accept the fact that I feel so shattered that I cannot write at all." But there are few better examples in our literature of a weakness converting to a strength; over the next ten weeks he gives a grim yet lyrical reminiscence of a Europe conditioned to an astonishing degree by the population's general awareness, years in advance, that World War II was inevitable. (p. 432)

After Spender has shown us this tormented Europe so carefully and coherently, despite his initial claim to have been silenced by public events, something is ironically appropriate about the very last entry in the 1939 journal (and of the book itself). Apparently a *non sequitur,* this final sentence could be read as a bizarre coda to life in the 1930's—life in a time whose absurd outlines rendered all details equally significant and pointless: "Two days ago, I went out with my sister to a cocktail party given by a Catholic lady doctor." (p. 433)

> *Stephen Corey, in a review of "Letters to Christopher: Stephen Spender's Letters to Christopher Isherwood, 1929-1939," in* The Georgia Review, *Vol. XXXV, No. 2, Summer, 1981, pp. 431-33.*

IAN HAMILTON

Some would say that Spender has made a career out of seeming to be over-sensitive. Poets warm to the image he projects: they too would like to look like that (it's odd, when you think of it, how few tall *and* good-looking poets there are in the world). Non-poets—university professors and cultural bureaucrats—enjoy his company because he puts them at their ease. He looks like a poet but he doesn't behave like one; his diffidence persuades them that it doesn't matter much if they don't read his work. It also pleases them that the work he is most famous for was written a long time ago.

This unkind view of Spender would continue thus: his looks and charm, it would assert, have splendidly equipped him for a cushy, ambassadorial status in the world of letters, and he has been shrewd enough not to rock the boat by publishing new poems that might dim the lustre of his early fame. After all, it was an accident of history that made him seem important in the first place. He is thought now to have "substance" as a poetry-figure because whenever Poetry of the Thirties is under discussion, he too will be discussed. No anthology of modern poetry would be historically plausible if it did not include half-a-dozen of his early works. Even though he had a good deal less natural talent than, say, Norman Cameron or Bernard Spencer, he was lucky enough to attach himself to a teachable poetic movement, and he has been living off it ever since.

And so on. It is a familiar view, and no one can be more familiar with it than Spender himself. Hence, possibly, [this collection, *Stephen Spender: Journals 1939-1983*]. Spender's image might be one of other-worldliness, but he long ago learned how to keep one step ahead of his opponents. His method is quite simple; he forestalls them. He owns up in advance to whatever feebleness or folly he's about to be accused of. And it is thoroughly consistent with his method that he should choose now, in his seventies, to publish not an autobiography (although this is what many would have wished for from the author of *World Within World*) but a carefully edited selection of the journals he's been keeping for some forty years.

The journal is an ideal form for one who might be nervous of final, summarizing judgments—his own, or other people's. In a journal, everything is present tense, provisional; no one is going to rebuke the author for some bygone frailty when he himself has so willingly exposed it to the public view. The reader is forced into the role of eavesdropper, and any evidence he picks up is either inadmissable or has already been neutralized by means of a confession. Moreover, a journal isn't really a book; it is something that just happens to have dropped between hard covers. Matters of structure and balance are not relevant: you can't really *blame* the author for jotting down too much stuff about dinner parties and not enough about Vietnam. Who knows what noble thoughts he might have had if he had supped at home?

To our unkind observer, then, it will seem that Spender has pulled it off again. He has appeared before his public bruised, self-knowing and making only the most sheepish of bids for critical forgiveness. "I imagine the young reading nothing of me but the bad notices other young critics write." But how could even the youngest of young critics kick a man who keeps on saying, or implying, that—if he'd known better—he would certainly have kicked himself? How can rigour be exercised against a spirit so emptied of vile hubris? . . . It is easy enough to point to moments when humility shades into saintfulness and it is even possible to isolate brief passages of snobbishness and malice. The journal form decrees, though, that such lapses must be placed in fleeting contexts. All in all, the opposition is thoroughly disarmed.

The trouble with the opposition, however, is that it has all along—in Spender's case—been carrying ridiculously heavy weapons. Also, its motivation has been faulty. The assumption has been that Spender has had a career that can be envied, that he has somehow duped the world of letters into giving him a better deal than he deserves, and that his early success has always worked—or been worked—to his advantage. Accusations of guile and main-chance disingenuousness have tended to be based on suppositions of this kind. In fact, an opposite narrative could just as plausibly be framed, a narrative in which the hero spends a lifetime having to be Stephen Spender, famous poet of the 1930s: indeed, famous, young, overrated poet of the 1930s.

Spender was only twenty-three when he thought "continually of those who were truly great", and perceived a resemblance between pylons and "nude, giant girls". Now seventy-five, he is thoroughly aware that of all the lines he has composed since 1932, none is likely to lodge in the public consciousness as these have. And this is not a realization he has painfully arrived at in old age: he has surely known it all along. And he has also known that neither of these lines, nor several others that made him famous as a youth, are really valued as "good lines"—by him, or by anybody else. If anything, they are remembered because they are so strenuously maladroit—and therefore "of the period". . . .

What to do about his early poems and about his early, famed poetic self has been a problem that has dogged Spender for some forty years. His success was unrepeatable; it was the sort of success that is impossible to build on or develop—it was too deeply tied in with the mythic requirements of the day and too anxious, therefore, to gloss over Spender's essential limitations of both language and technique. A fragile lyric promise was trumpeted as "new" because it had wrapped itself around a few lumps of industrial machinery. Spender needed only to rest his fevered gaze on "cripples . . . with limbs shaped like questions / in their odd twist" for him to be hailed as an exemplar of "compassion". No one was prepared to say that there was something hideously literary and callous in the use of words like "shaped" and "odd". Nor would anyone—not even T. S. Eliot—rebuke this young bard for the often ludicrous self-centredness that unbalances so many of his flame-eyed excursions into World Events. The age demanded that bourgeois intellectuals agonize in public about their torn sense of responsibility: to art, or revolution? Spender was elected to act out this inner drama in his verse. Cooler heads were happy to nod in approval, happy that someone else had got the job. (p. 1307)

[By the outbreak of war the] poet's by now well-known attachment to the grand poetic flourish no longer had much power to thrill. "Scalding lead anxiety", "skies stained with blood", "The defeated, filled with lead, on the helpless field", and so on: the adjectives were pumped up as before, but with a stunned, defeated air. Spender's instincts were pacifist, he had had a long love-affair with Germany throughout the late 1920s, and his politics had all along been ruled by a sentimental idealism about personal relationships: "Under wild seas / of chafing despairs / Love's need does not cease". The beautiful young comrades of his 1930s poems had been acceptable to his audience not because they were socialists but because they were standing in for their older brothers, for the beautiful young comrades-in-arms who had been slaughtered a dozen or so years earlier. "Born of the sun, they travelled a short while toward the sun": it is no accident that Spender's well-known line echoes Laurence Binyon's "They shall grow not old, as we that are left grow old". . . .

And this, it might be said, is the fag-end of Spender's public inspiration. From now on, the poems that matter are all personal. To me, this is the period of Spender's career, from the mid-1940s to the early 1950s, in which his voice becomes both distinctive and controlled. He is still compulsively adjectival, and he persistently overstates, goes on too long, or strains for profundities in a way that undermines the poems' concrete force, but even so there are stretches where some tender and particular preoccupation insists on its own rhetoric and, so to speak, removes it from the author's charge: one thinks of **"Elegy for Margaret"** (and especially Section 3) and **"Sirmione**

Peninsula"—a poem which, unaccountably, Spender now seems to have disowned.

It is in this period that Spender's *Journal* actually begins, although he also prints his written-for-publication diary, *September 1939,* and gives us a four-page account of what happened to him in the war (not very much, although there are some nice anecdotes about the founding of *Horizon*—it almost got called *Sirius, Scorpio, Equinox* or *Centaur*). The life that is chronicled here is not the Life of a Poet, but the life rather of someone who now and then writes poems. It is also the rather touching tale of someone who is "in demand" because of the poems he once wrote. Spender never stops feeling that he "should" be writing poetry, but the obligation is often made to seem like an annoying irritant in his otherwise busy and rewarding daily round. . . .

The book's real anecdotal meat is in its literary portraits, and in its portraits of close friends. Cyril Connolly and Christopher Isherwood are affectionately *there* throughout the book, and there are neat (not so affectionate) sketches of Louis MacNeice, Sonia Orwell, Ruthven Todd, Conrad Aiken, Humphrey Jennings and a dozen others. There is also a superb passage on the death of Allen Tate. Altogether, the loose diary genre gives Spender just the scope he needs to demonstrate both his gift for friendship (in addition to the names we've heard of, there are mysterious characters with names like B and D who make regular appearances throughout) and also his oblique, almost clandestine waspishness. More than once the benign mask is allowed to slip, revealing a useful-looking, if rather dainty, pair of fangs.

The book's overshadowing presence, though, is that of Auden: priggish, bossy, selfish, and a bore, if we are to believe Spender's fond account. Auden from time to time turns up at Spender's London home and takes it for granted that the household will instantly revolve around his every whim. And he's not in the least nice about it. Why—or how—Spender put up with him is hard to say, since Auden gives his old friend absolutely nothing in return. When, at one of his American Auden lectures, a student asks Spender if he ever really "liked" Auden, the question seems unanswerable. Auden, after all, is Auden. At another point, Spender benevolently advances the theory that Auden was irritable because he wished that he'd had children. He would have made an excellent father, Spender pleads, although everything he has said about him suggests quite the opposite. It's a strange relationship—strange from the start—and one feels that Spender still cannot quite bring himself to probe it very deeply.

Certainly, no attempt is made to do so in his **"Auden's Funeral"**—the strongest among several poems of reminiscence that appear toward the end of his reissued and revised *Collected Poems.* The revisions are drastic. Spender has once again left intact the well-known anthology pieces—although **"The Funeral"** has gone—but elsewhere the surgery is brutal. Homosexual love poems are either toned down, made more laconic (the "pretty mouths" of boy-whores become the "guilty mouths"; "How strangely this sun reminds me of my love" becomes "How it reminds me of that day") or they are dropped altogether. I can't imagine that many readers will miss pieces like **"Your body is stars whose million glitter here"**, or strain to remember lines like "Even whilst I watch him I am remembering / The quick laugh of the wasp-gold eyes", but even so, it *is* the bold awfulness of works like these that give the young Spender some of his distinctiveness. He was, after all, the bard of wide-eyed affirmation in those days and it does

seem a bit like cheating when he now edits poems of young hopefulness so as to make them seem merely resigned. Take a poem called **"The Little Coat"**, included in a section once called **"Love and Separation"** but now called simply **"A Separation"**. The poem used to end:

> Hold me in that solemn kiss
> Where both our minds have eyes
> Which look beyond this
> Vanishment: and in each other's gaze
> Accept what passes, and believe what stays.

This stanza has now gone, and the poem is made to end with a dismissive shrug towards "the Springs of yesterday".

Throughout, Spender seems to be saying "O, come off it" to his younger self. "I corrupted his confidence and his sun-like happiness", he used to say. No longer. "I am the coward of cowards" now reads "But fear is all I feel". The fifty-line splurge of pretentiousness called **"Exiles from Their Land, History Their Domicile"** is now six lines of off-hand but grown-up wisdom. There is also a political purging—the image of the hot young revolutionaries is severely doused ("Oh comrades, step beautifully from the solid stone" is now "O comrades, step forth from the stone") and a good deal of period stuff is hacked away (the whole "Hitler" stanza of **"The Uncreating Chaos"** has now disappeared). Even a famous poem like **"Landscape Near an Aerodrome"** does not escape the knife: the Church that used to block the sun is now—timorously?—lowercase. Also purged—the unkindest cut of all?—are all grandiloquent references to the poet's own prospects of high immortality.

The urge, Spender says in his introduction, is towards greater clarity, and in many cases the poems *have* been made a little less obscure. On the whole, though, I think most readers will prefer to stick with their *Collected Poems 1955,* and treat this new book as covering the thirty years of Spender's work since then. (p. 1308)

Ian Hamilton, "Owning Up," in The Times Literary Supplement, *No. 4312, November 22, 1985, pp. 1307-08.*

RUPERT CHRISTIANSEN

Some of the material [in *Stephen Spender: Journals 1939-1983*] has appeared before, in *The Thirties and After* and elsewhere, although the starting-point is 1939, where his autobiography, *World Within World,* begins to tail off. The emphasis is on the personal life, rather than public and political events, about which he perhaps feels he has written enough already. A lot of time is spent in America and Provence; the cast of friends is impressive, if somewhat predictable. (p. 29)

This spirit of tact and avoidance of confrontation is pervasive and crippling. The journals are not, in a word, candid. They are confessedly written with one eye on a possible future readership, and there is a lot of tiresomely nudging explication of the sort associated with the first act of a Victorian melodrama, as when the reader is told 'I have a German relative who is the wife of a U-boat commander'—the stuff of an editorial footnote, which no truly personal record would bother with. A journal is, surely, precisely the refusal to respect privacy; but Spender's is full of discreetly shutting doors, the anonymity of initials, and homosexuals, even dead ones, appear in the company of 'friends'.

The dullness often sinks into sheer banality. . . . An evening with Mishima in Tokyo concludes with visits to 'two or three bars, which had very much the atmosphere of Berlin of the 1930s': go on, go on please—but he doesn't. Sometimes the stylistic model seems to have been the deathless diary of Mrs Betty Kenward. At dinner with the Eliots he meets Sylvia Plath, who 'talked more' than her husband and was 'a very pretty, intelligent girl from Boston'. Edmund Wilson, you will be amazed to know, was 'a man of great brain power' and *aficionados* will be thrilled by mention of the 'thistledown movement' of Margot Fonteyn's dancing.

Of course, these are some of the more grotesque lapses, but they are not unrepresentative of the generally sluggish and unarresting prose. Meditations on the larger issues of Art, Christianity, and Time ('the present is a fixed point where one is') fall flat enough, but more excruciating are the efforts at epigrams or metaphorical encapsulations. (pp. 29-30)

Spender accepts with grace that he is only 'a minor poet' and is fond of quoting the line 'All things tempt me from this craft of verse.' The journals are indeed dominated more by the picture of the 60-year-old smiling public man (a third of the book is taken up by the years 1974-83) than of someone possessed by his muse, or her desertion of him. . . .

Spender is right to incriminate himself for allowing a poetic talent to slide on to the periphery. 'I'm struggling at the end' he laments, 'to get out of the valley of hectoring youth, journalistic middle age, imposture, money-making, public relations, bad writing, mental confusion.' The way out, as Spender sees it, is up the steep hill of art, but one doesn't find in these journals much sign of the compulsion to make the climb. (p. 30)

Rupert Christiansen, "Spender the Man," in The Spectator, *Vol. 255, No. 8212, November 30, 1985, pp. 29-30.*

ELIZABETH JENNINGS

Spender has sometimes been a visionary poet, by which I mean neither a gift for prophecy nor an association with a particular creed. I am speaking of a certain cast of mind, a deep awareness of his own inner experiences. This led early on to flights of imagination which resulted in poems like "**The Truly Great**". . . . (p. 30)

Spender has been extremely ruthless while putting [*Collected Poems 1928-1985*] together. He has omitted many early poems and revised a number of others so that only just over a hundred poems remain here. He is a great translator of Rilke and shares with him an inwardness, a sense of spiritual search. The poems here are not placed under the titles from the books in which they first appeared but arranged under such headings as "**Preludes**," "**Exiles**," "**Ambition**," "**War Poems**" and so on.

Spender has rightly retained the splendid "**Beethoven's Death Mask**" and "**Not Palaces**," yet I think the poems which best represent him are the ones concerned deeply with his family and friends. He has retained, fortunately, the affecting "**Elegy for Margaret**," a poem about the death of his brother's wife. . . . There is a remarkable poem reprinted here called "**The Double Shame**" which expressed an experience in love which many of us know but few can articulate. It is notable, too, for the

way in which Spender is prepared to display his own vulnerability. The poem ends,

> At first you did not love enough
> And afterwards you loved too much
> And you lacked the confidence to choose
> And you have only yourself to blame.

Such poems as these are much stronger that those about aerodromes or political ideologies. Spender's warmth and passion really take fire in his love poems and his elegies. Among the new poems which he has added I particularly like the one called "**Auden's Funeral**". Here there are no generalisations but a simple setting of a scene in which the poet pays tribute to a life-long friend. . . . The best poems in this book have a lively force which leaps out and captures our attention. The Thirties is now a dead epoch but Spender is more than a Thirties poet. (pp. 30-1)

Elizabeth Jennings, "Spender the Poet," in The Spectator, *Vol. 255, No. 8212, November 30, 1985, pp. 30-1.*

FRANK KERMODE

[Spender's] juniors have not always thought well of his verses, and in spite of Auden's pronouncement that it was his capacity for humiliation that made him a poet, there were periods when he declined to publish verse out of fear of reviewers. He has evidently got over that worry, and now at 76 produces another *Collected Poems*—an earlier one appeared in 1955. The poems he has chosen to preserve, from almost sixty years of work, are only enough to fill 180 pages.

The severity of this culling he attributes to a change in his way of judging his poetry. Whatever now seems confused or verbose is dropped, and many poems are rewritten to conform more closely with original intentions still remembered. As in the earlier *Collected Poems,* most of the anthology pieces are left untouched; in a sense, as he said thirty years ago, they no longer belong to him, and in any case he thought he needed to own up to such poems as "**The Pylons**" and "**The Funeral**" ('They record simply / How this one excelled all others in making driving belts') which also have a certain historical interest. As it happens, "**The Funeral**" has now disappeared.

The poems that remain are sometimes quite drastically rewritten; some of them, already purged for the 1955 *Collected Poems,* are now purged again. This kind of revision has been done before, with rather mixed results. Yeats did violence to his early poems, sometimes converting them to an inappropriate modern harshness; nobody seems to like John Crowe Ransom's reworkings; and Auden's revisions and exclusions sometimes seem petulant or even perverse, as if he had decided not to understand his own poems. Since the original versions remain accessible this is not a matter of high importance: still, one is bound to try to understand the motives that prompt these renovations. Sometimes they are a mature desire for tidiness and lucidity, sometimes the poet thinks he has caught himself out in a fraud, and one can see why. But I confess I don't know why Spender has turned against what seem to me among his finest poems, the group in *Ruins and Visions* about the end of his first marriage. It is not a compensation for the loss of "**No Orpheus, No Eurydice**" to have revived an early poem about Van der Lubbe. However, a new section labelled "**Ambition**" includes the candid and interesting poem "**The Public Son of**

a Public Man'', and of course there are also poems, many of them about family and friends, written since 1955.

It has often been remarked that Spender's manner has changed far less than might have been expected over so long a career; the potent influences of Auden and Eliot were early assimilated, and the moods and fashions of half a century have left them pretty well untouched. Of course he has changed and now wants to be rid of things that seem palpably false, though in their own day they perhaps had a bold propriety. . . .

There are . . . instances of profitable rethinking. **''The Uncreating Chaos''**, a long poem from *The Still Centre* (1939), was much revised in 1955 and is now revised once again. It is greatly changed, and its final section, already one might have said well-wrought, is not exempt. That these renewed attentions are valuable is evident from a comparison between 1955 and 1985:

> The simple machinery is here
> Clear day, clear room, plain desk,
> The hand, symbol of power,
> Here the veins may pour
> Into the deed, as the field
> Into the standing corn.

> The simple machinery is here
> Clear room clear day clear desk
> And the hand with its power
> To make the heart pour
> Into the word, as the sun
> Moves upward through the corn.

This same poem tells us that lucidity is holy, and these corrections are devoutly intelligent. Now the poem *uses* the hand instead of making it a symbol and dismissing it, and it is more appropriate than 'veins', just as 'word' is more proper than 'deed', to the act of writing poetry. The notion of field pouring into corn is acceptable but hardly lucid; the revision is for the good. And it is as if the nearly homophonic 'power-pour', which by hindsight we see was doing very little in the older version, is now put strongly to work. This is by no means the sole example of successful revision in the new *Collected Poems.*

The allusion to Rilke in **''The Uncreating Chaos''** has gone, and so has the paraphrase of 'Orpheus Eurydice Hermes'. But a general affinity with Rilke is still evident. It arises, perhaps, from a tendency to allow a great gap between idea and image, a sacrifice of simple metaphoricity to a sort of aura or luminescence. Though Spender's later tendency is to cut down on this sort of thing, it is often effective, as in the last stanza of the many-toned poem **''The Public Son of a Public Man''**:

> O father, to a grave of fame I faithfully follow
> Yet I love the glance of failure, tilted up
> Like a gipsy's amber eyes that seem to swallow
> Sunset from the evening like a cup.

This is an elaborate conceit, but very unlike those of the Metaphysical poets Spender admires for knowing so much and putting what they knew to such use. A Donne conceit surprises because in defiance of probability it works out, but here we have a conceit that surprises and makes its effect by not working out: there is no neat fit. You might expect the glance of failure to be downward, not tilted up like the eyes of somebody looking at a sunset. Then, why a gipsy, and why amber eyes, unless by affinity with some sunset tint? And why is the figure of the gipsy developed in another figure, of drinking with the eyes from the cup of the sky? In this way the whole notion of 'the

glance of failure' is enormously elaborated so that it includes the notion of something beautiful as perceived by a person extraordinarily well qualified for such perceptions by his own beauty, his own outsider status, his difference: so that it is only in this variety of failure that success can be found. (p. 6)

Frank Kermode, ''Spender's Purges,'' in London Review of Books, *Vol. 7, No. 21, December 5, 1985, pp. 6-8.*

ROY FULLER

Surely no-one whose intellectual life has substantially overlapped that of Stephen Spender (born 1909) will fail to be absorbed by [*Stephen Spender: Journals 1939-1983*]. Parts of it have previously appeared, in less full or fuller form, but I leave any bibliographical donkey-work to others. It is an immensely long book, giving little sense of *déjà vu*. It begins with a journal kept in the September of the outbreak of war, and continues, in mainly substantial wodges, until 1983. The selection has been made by the editor (who does not contribute any editorial voice, seemingly not even in the footnotes), with the author exercising a controlling power. . . .

The principal theme, I suppose it can be said, is the author's ambition to write an immortal literary work—an ambition frustrated (certainly in the author's view) over the whole period covered by the journal. The work is therefore potentially tragic or, at any rate, pathetic. However, for several reasons the underlying tone is comic—partly unconsciously, but in the main deliberately so. The extraordinary figure who entered the literary scene in Isherwood's *Lions and Shadows* ('He burst in upon us, blushing, sniggering loudly, contriving to trip over the edge of the carpet—an immensely tall, shambling boy of nineteen, with a great scarlet poppyface, wild frizzy hair, and eyes the violent colour of bluebells') time has, of course, toned down, but the journals go on revealing mishaps and tactless frankness, and a reckless zest for social and personal relationships. (p. 136)

The purely physical obstacles to writing an immortal work arise not so much out of the necessity to earn a living (working on the magazines *Horizon* and *Encounter*, a professorship at London University, and many visiting American university posts—soft options, we may suspect, compared with a nine-to-five job), as from a gratuitous compulsion to be (to put it crudely) 'in the swim'. This takes several forms, both public and private: travel, conferences, parties, entertaining (and, as to the last, Lady Spender is the almost silent heroine of the book). A tithe of the material accumulated—music and gossip heard, pictures and physiognomies seen, and so forth—would be sufficient for any number of masterpieces. Spender puts this side of his persona down to his political and journalistic ancestry, but it may be to some degree merely compensatory. And, as in the case of many famous people, one is not always sure why he is famous.

As for the interior obstacles to the creation of masterpieces, it could be argued that Spender being the type of poet whose best work is substantially done in youth, is flogging a dead horse writing poetry through old age in the expectation of amelioration. Remembering the disasters of the revisions revealed by the 1955 *Collected Poems,* he makes our flesh creep when he mentions further revisions, even the re-writing of whole poems. For to me there is no doubt about the genius behind the original texts of the earlier poems, and of their lasting quality. As to the prose, he seems plainly not a natural fictionist, interesting though his work in that area has been; and the same remark, *mutatis mutandis,* could be applied to his criticism.

Is the present book the immortal work unaware, so to speak? I would guess not, though we haven't before us its entire extent (the amatory side of life, for instance, is almost entirely omitted, save for a mention of a late friendship with a scientist simply referred to as 'B'). The thumb-nail portraits are usually brilliant and, in my experience, accurate (that of Ruthven Todd is a good example); the Dickensian character recurrences (Connolly, Auden, Sonia Orwell, *et al*) likewise. The general reflections on art and life are sometimes interesting, sometimes less so, but tremendously worthwhile at their best. Sometimes the entries degenerate into mere lists of names, almost absurd in their fashionableness: it is on such occasions we may feel that the author's sense of the comic has abdicated, leniency taking over. However, the book has surely another great virtue, besides its extreme readability: its hero is likeable—generous and courageous without in the least advertising such qualities. One would hope to be spared to re-read it a few years hence, when its fascinating newness has worn off, to see how it is standing up to the destroyer and preserver of literary works. (p. 137)

Roy Fuller, "Out to Lunch," in London Magazine, *n.s. Vol. 25, Nos. 9 & 10, December, 1985 & January, 1986, pp. 136-37.*

Mark Strand

1934-

American poet, short story writer, editor, translator, and author of children's books.

Strand's verse is characterized by its plain yet compelling language and its imaginative depth achieved through a minimum of detail. Although some reviewers claim that Strand's poetry is weakened by solipsism, most praise its dynamic clarity. Robert Pinsky stated that Strand's "short lines and . . . short, spare sentences provide an elegantly terse vehicle for [his] impetuous, exciting imagination: a busy fountain of mysteries, brooding formulae and images, disciplined by the curt, declarative form."

In his first book, *Sleeping with One Eye Open* (1964), Strand explores the difficulties and contradictions of self-definition through tightly controlled verse, employing surreal imagery and a somewhat foreboding, mysterious aura to present dualities of identity. *Reasons for Moving* (1968) and *Darker* (1970) are similarly infused with an element of anxiety and, like Strand's first book, center on the struggle to recognize and reconcile conflicting selves. *The Story of Our Lives* (1977) marks the beginning of a change in Strand's approach. Critics noted that while his earlier work features a primarily solipsistic focus, the poetry in this volume is more involved with the world outside the poet's mind—particularly the world of his childhood and his present life. Strand also begins to employ a less abbreviated but still concise style to accommodate the rich resources of his personal past. The immediacy of Strand's later work is strongly evident in *The Late Hour* (1978) and *The Monument* (1978), a meditation in prose. In a review of *Selected Poems* (1980), Peter Stitt observed that "most of these new, nostalgic poems are triumphs—true not to the poetic fashions of the day but to the knowledge inherent in the heart."

Like many of Strand's poems, the short stories collected in *Mr. and Mrs. Baby* (1985) are brief exercises in surrealism. For instance, in "Dog Life," a man informs his wife that he was a dog before he met her, and in "The Tiny Baby," a woman gives birth to an infant so small she is able to carry it in her purse. While several critics faulted these stories for unconvincing whimsicality, others found them witty and entertaining. Strand has also edited several anthologies of the work of other poets and has translated the poetry of Rafael Alberti, Carlos Drummond de Andrade, and Jorge Luis Borges.

(See also *CLC*, Vols. 6, 18; *Contemporary Authors*, Vols. 21-24, rev. ed.; *Something about the Author*, Vol. 41; and *Dictionary of Literary Biography*, Vol. 5.)

PETER STITT

Mark Strand has always had a subtle command of language, an innate sense of rhythm, an eye for the telling image. These gifts are apparent on nearly every page of his ***Selected Poems,*** a treasure house of finely-wrought, technically-accomplished verse. . . . I come away from the volume with a strong suspicion

that, for most of his career, Mark Strand has used his considerable gifts on behalf of a false aesthetic—false at least for him, if not for the world.

The kind of poem I am referring to has often, if incorrectly, been called surrealistic; it reads like a parable, is clever, stylized, highly artificial, even arch. Most important, it is a poem divorced from everyday truth—its opening lines are likely to establish a situation we immediately recognize as, in some basic sense, false. A few examples: . . .

> Let us save the babies.
> Let us run downtown.
> The babies are screaming.
>
> ("The Babies")

> It is autumn. People are jumping from jetliners;
> Their relatives leap into the air to join them.
>
> ("The Door"—second stanza)

There is a serious purpose behind such poems, to be sure—Strand creates his parables in order to express large human truths, generally having to do with suffering, insecurity, or guilt. But the method used is so extreme—so clever, so pretentious, so false to the actual, the situational, truth of our suffering, insecurity, and guilt—that the poems now look like just so much self-conscious preening. In its own day, of course, this mode was much more palatable to our taste than it is now, as the dated praise of Harold Bloom and Richard Howard [see *CLC*, Vol. 18] makes clear. Carried to its extreme, this mode results in poems that are downright irritating because of what seems a totally insensitive cleverness. (pp. 874-75)

Strand's most successful earlier poems are generally the ones that sound the simplest—spoken in a quiet first-person voice we can believe, they achieve an elemental personal truth, despite showing the external trappings of parable. An example is **"The Remains,"** which concludes: "My parents rise out of their thrones / into the milky rooms of clouds. How can I sing? / Time tells me what I am. I change and I am the same./ I empty myself of my life and my life remains." Poems like this one are highly successful because they have the solidity of truth about them. And it is poems like this one that point the way to what I believe is Strand's true mode, albeit mostly a mode (for him) of the future. By far the best poems in this selected volume are those most recent ones deeply animated by a feeling of nostalgia, dealing truthfully with the scenes, events, and persons of the poet's early life. In reading Strand's earlier books (before *The Late Hour*) I always wondered about his origins—the childhood spent on Prince Edward Island— wondered because there was almost no trace of this to be found in the poems. It is almost as though he spent years trying to deny his heritage, replacing it with the "sophistication" and cleverness of the city. Well, Mark Strand's best poems deal with those early, authentic times, and we must be grateful that he has finally gotten around to writing them.

There are even signs in the poems themselves that Strand himself knows he has found the true vein; **"The Coming of Light,"** which opens *The Late Hour*, begins: "Even this late it happens: / the coming of love, the coming of light." Since I am talking about something very special, which occurs in only a relatively few poems, I want to give a precise listing of titles before discussing one of these poems in greater detail. I would, then, single out: **"So You say," "Snowfall," "An Old Man Awake in His Own Death," "For Her," "Poor North," "Where Are the Waters of Childhood?," "The Garden," "Night Piece," "Nights in Hackett's Cove," "A Morning," "My Mother on an Evening in Late Summer,"** and **"Leopardi."** The list comprises twelve of the last sixteen poems in this volume, which is why I feel confident that this is the direction Strand foresees himself following in the future. In these poems, Strand shows a newfound sensitivity to the reality outside of himself—a breakdown of the earlier tendency towards solipsism. Typical of this, and of the very high level of writing we also find in these poems, is the remarkable opening stanza of **"My Mother on an Evening in Late Summer"**:

> When the moon appears
> and a few wind-stricken barns stand out
> in the low-domed hills
> and shine with a light
> that is veiled and dust-filled
> and that floats upon the fields,
> my mother, with her hair in a bun,
> her face in shadow, and the smoke
> from her cigarette coiling close
> to the faint yellow sheen of her dress,
> stands near the house
> and watches the seepage of late light
> down through the sedges,
> the last gray islands of cloud
> taken from view, and the wind
> ruffling the moon's ash-colored coat
> on the black bay.

The first thing to notice is how very different this is from even the best of the earlier poems—so much more direct, concrete, so much more true. All traces of cleverness are absent, and yet the overall effect is one of great subtlety; Strand has ever been a master of free verse, the plain style, but rarely has he attained so pure a lyricism as is present in these most recent poems. This stanza is typical, permeated by an interlocking grid pattern of assonance and consonance. There is a danger inherent in poetry of this type, and Strand has not yet learned entirely how to avoid it. **"Shooting Whales"** is an example of how narrative, with its concomitant anxiety to get the details straight, can wash poetic effect away on a flood of literal fact. But most of these new, nostalgic poems are triumphs—true not to the poetic fashions of the day but to the knowledge inherent in the heart—and they bode very well for Mark Strand's future work. (pp. 875-77)

> *Peter Stitt, "Engagements with Reality," in* The Georgia Review, *Vol. XXXV, No. 4, Winter, 1981, pp. 874-82.*

R. W. FLINT

[The] jacket of Mark Strand's *Selected Poems* tells us that the poet's parents were both American and that he was "raised and educated" in the United States and South America. That leaves a reviewer little but poetic license to dwell on the strangely fitting circumstance of his birth on Prince Edward Island, in Canada between the Gulf of St. Lawrence and Northumberland Strait. To anyone who knows that red-earthed, beach-bound, potato-growing, tourist-cosseting tract of unimpassioned tranquillity—incongruously moored in northern seas—its value as a clue, both positive and negative, to Mark Strand's work is irresistible. Gulfs and straits abound in this poetry, not to mention an unflinching martyrdom loosely akin to that of Saint Lawrence himself. And an unearthly mildness at the center, like a sudden Melvillian calm or perhaps the outer lip of Poe's maelstrom where waters relentlessly circle. As a state of mind and soul, the hidden generative presence of Prince Edward Island in Mr. Strand is to the normal Canada about which one jokes and wrings one's hands as Atlantis is to the Atlantic Alliance. With his first breath and—to cite three stanzas of **"My Death"**—very likely his last, Mr. Strand has taken its measure and found it not much less than, certainly no other than, himself:

> Sadness, of course, and confusion.
> The relatives gathered at the graveside,
> talking about the waste, and the weather mounting,
> the rain moving in vague pillars offshore.
>
> This is Prince Edward Island.
> I came back to my birthplace to announce my death.
> I said I would ride full gallop into the sea
> and not look back. People were furious. . . .
>
> Now I lie in the box
> Of my making while the weather
> builds and the mourners shake their heads as if
> to write or to die. I did not have to do either. . . .

Depressiveness this grave and uncompromising, this self-assured, would be remarkable at any time, even if it hadn't more or less coincided with W. S. Merwin's elegantly melancholy sequence of the 1960's, or Richard Hugo's pungent bulletins from the Far West. Were it not for its sturdy clarity, its lurking wit, its homely figuration, its mostly impeccable grooming and tuning, Mr. Strand's poetry might seem on the surface a mere minatory black shadow. It is much more than that, not least because of its strong, mysterious intuitions of presence on which any effective poetry of absence must be grounded.

Indeed, for all the phlegm that weakens the lesser poems and despite the growing overtness, warmth and gusto of his recent work, selected Strand vividly conjures up, from page to page, decade to decade, a forgotten vein in the Romantic synthesis: the cult of ruins and fragments, accompaniments whose melody is missing, echoes of no known sound, Chinese boxes of receding memories, dreams. . . .

The parsimonious acumen with which Mr. Strand put together the five slim volumes that make up most of this book has insured that his selected volume is almost as full, as complete, as a possible collected one. Omissions are few and well chosen; the original order of poems is scrambled, but the poems themselves are almost untouched. Of the five new poems, **"Shooting Whales," "My Mother on an Evening in Late Summer"** and **"Leopardi"** are handsomely written. He is one of the lucky writers whose control of memory increases with age. His affinity with the supreme master of his obsessive themes, Giacomo Leopardi, could hardly have escaped him. His recasting of Leopardi's *"La sera del dì di festa"* (as **"Leopardi"**) is not exactly a translation, nor an "imitation" like one of Robert Lowell's that underlines the translator's distance from the original. Rather, it's a forthright appropriation of the elements in Leopardi that confirm him in his special vocation, an act of comradeship and luminous homage.

> *R. W. Flint, "Strong Intuitions and Lurking Wit,"*
> *in* The New York Times Book Review, *January 18,*
> *1981, p. 13.*

HUGO WILLIAMS

Strand at times reads like a counterfeit wild man, cooked up by a desperate committee, and as such is the recipient of every literary prize on the non-playful side of American letters. He is a career visionary and he shoulders every honour. There is a photograph on the jacket [of *Selected Poems*] which shows that he, too, suffers from a powerful Walt Whitman complex. A bar of sunlight touches his right shoulder, as if to suggest that he is chosen.

But what is it he does? According to Octavio Paz, Strand "explores the terra infirma of our lives. Fascinated by emptiness, he conceives of the poem as a description of absence . . . as absence of meaning: being cancels significance." Quite accurate really. If it sounds promising, in practice the holes eat up the substance and we are often left swallowing on nothing. Strand relies on high poetics for his effect, but these feel counterfeit because they so seldom touch on a verifiable world. What he does is deploy various elemental signs and symbols in an effort to say the unsayable. He has learnt how to do this from Latin-American surrealists like Paz and Vallejo and from Central Europeans like Popa and Holub. . . . Repetition is one of the games: you start every line with "If" or "Not" or "I praise the . . .", filling it in with arbitrary inspiration. There is also the question-and-answer session. . . . What Strand aims for is a visionary purity, like that of James Wright, with lots of snow and silence and unexplained transformations and "leaps". What he achieves is often no more than translationese.

Hugo Williams, "The Jotter by the Ashtray," in The Times Literary Supplement, *No. 4081, June 19, 1981, p. 707.*

IRVIN EHRENPREIS

The theme of Mark Strand's seductive poetry—amply represented in his *Selected Poems*—is the elusiveness of the self. We all assume by instinct that there exists in each of us a quintessential person separate from the physical appearance, separate from the clothes and actions, the thoughts and feelings, separate from one's history and expectations.

But how can we represent or even know this self when language can only render the visible, the tangible, the conceivable? Either we can try to strip away the externals or bring them into consciousness and so get beyond them. But the effort is defeated because the self we are defining changes during the process, and a new person displaces the old even while the old persists. . . .

Besides, the forces that change the self are not in one's control. They act mysteriously and capriciously. Especially is this true of other people. We are one person when alone but somebody else in the company of a friend. . . .

The poet is the man who does not merely submit to these operations. He studies them, and his imagination deliberately employs them to produce aesthetic forms of relationship, symmetrical analogues to the evolution of self from self, choreographies that will endure when the elusive performers are gone. In Strand's work what seem to be people are sometimes characters waiting for a poet to invent them. Or his people may create themselves by writing the story in which they will appear.

A self is the creation of one's memories. But since these cannot be verified, a poet may imagine a past and challenge recollection to oppose it. Indeed, since all memory is partly invention, we are constantly remaking ourselves. Let speculation move a step further, and we may say that to make up a story is to create a memory. Such paradoxes excite Strand's imagination in poems like **"The Story of Our Lives"** and **"The Untelling"** (both too long). He seems drawn to write parables of the act of literary composition.

In Strand's somewhat Proustian view of the human condition we are doomed to cling to evanescence. The world which the self loves decays as the self changes. The person yearns for an intimacy which is unattainable because each lover alters in the presence of the other. To understand and describe another human being, we must not render him as an independent figure but as conceived by a friend or son or wife, and preferably as himself facing the process of decay. (p. 46)

The shape of a poem by [Strand] is almost always pleasing, with his favorite images and epithets (light, shadow, dark, moon, sun, water, rain, mirror, etc.) slipping easily into place, and with subtle rhyme schemes or patterns of assonance supporting the quiet repetitions and variations that lead to a sudden opening as the focus changes from something seen, remembered, or felt, to something still being written—the poem itself.

It is in fact this turning on itself, the movement toward solipsism, that weakens Strand's work. Many of the poems seem written to exemplify designs, to show how felicitously a dream or panic could be given satisfactory form but not to illuminate an experience so that readers might match it with their own.

If I recommend the short lyric of self-definition as the proper modern poem, it is not because the character of a poet is the most important focus of a literary work. It is because through this frame the poet can describe human nature and the world. . . .

For all his mastery of rhythm and music, Strand does not open the lyric to the world but makes it a self-sustaining enterprise. His forms tend toward the infinite regress of a mirror watching a mirror. In his realm you can realize your own self only by imagining another self which in turn is imagining you. That other may be a lover, a wife, a child. It may be your own old self which the new one has destroyed and replaced—after, of course, being imagined in advance. But the movement of all the profound self-awareness is toward decoration rather than abundance. Caught up in the subject-object relation, Strand sees the world as what the perceiver is not, and the perceiver as what the world is not. . . . (p. 47)

> *Irvin Ehrenpreis, "Digging In," in* The New York Review of Books, *Vol. XXVIII, No. 15, October 8, 1981, pp. 45-7.*

ROBERT B. SHAW

Mark Strand's *Selected Poems* comes as a generous reminder of the new tones and perspectives he has brought to American poetry. Together with a few other poets in the Sixties (I think particularly of Bly, Merwin, and Simic) Strand initiated a fruitful commerce between our poetry and that of Europe and Latin America. He did this both through translation of foreign masters, and through taking hints from them in the shaping of his own work. He has assimilated influences to his own unmistakable voice, and has become an influence himself. Strand is surely one of our most imitated poets; but the imitations seem vacuous when set against their original. It must be that the mannerisms of his poems sit still to be copied while the vision that informs them eludes all but the poet himself. By "vision" I mean something beyond a distinctive point of view, although that is part of it; I mean, rather, a freeing and an enlargement of consciousness akin to that which religious mystics seek to attain through spiritual disciplines. Strand has developed an uncanny ability to step beyond the bounds of ego and experience, and to view the self as other, from a vantage point of radical estrangement. The view is that of a spectator and the tone is that of a spectre. It is as though one newly dead were to see himself still going through the motions of a life already ended. The voice issues as if from a trance, untouched by passion. . . . Strand breaches not only the bounds of consciousness but the bounds of time as well: many of the poems are rapt with a sense of the future foredoomed. . . . In his latest work Strand has turned his attention away from imagining the future and toward recapturing the past. He presents childhood memories with the same visionary clarity that distinguishes the rest of his work. **"Where Are the Waters of Childhood?",** **"The House in French Village," "Nights in Hackett's Cove,"** and other recent poems amply confirm his talent as they increase his range. I had feared, in reading some of the longer pieces in *The Story of Our Lives* (1973), that Strand's work was growing mannered and attenuated; but the selections from *The Late Hour* (1978) and the "New Poems" included here present him at a new peak of achievement. This *Selected Poems* seems, as few volumes do nowadays, an entirely necessary book, perhaps a classic. (pp. 175-77)

> *Robert B. Shaw, "Quartet," in* Poetry, *Vol. CXXXIX, No. 3, December, 1981, pp. 171-77.*

LINDA GREGERSON

> . . . it seems to me that we should rather be the flower than the bee. . . .
>
> John Keats to J. H. Reynolds, February 19, 1818

When Mark Strand reinvented the poem, he began by leaving out the world. The self he invented to star in the poems went on with the work of divestment: it jettisoned place, it jettisoned fellows, it jettisoned all distinguishing physical marks, save beauty alone. It was never impeded by personality. Nor was this radical renunciation to be confused with modesty, or asceticism. The self had designs on a readership, and a consummate gift for the musical phrase. . . . (p. 90)

The poet's career has thrived on the honey of absence and, mid-career, Mark Strand has come forth with *Selected Poems*. The overview is both impressive and timely. Beneath a changing prosody, the central poetic strategies exhibit remarkable coherence. On the stage it had cleared, the self divided itself for dialogue: the *I* became an *I* and a *you*, an *I* and a mailman, an *I* and an engineer; the face appeared on both sides of a mirror, both sides of a picture window, both sides of the printed page. In 1978, with the simultaneous publication of *The Late Hour* and *The Monument,* the divided persona became a divided corpus. *The Monument,* a prose collage, is the logical extension of all that went before it: here the poet divests himself of even his poems. In *The Late Hour,* conversely, and surely as a consequence, the banished populations begin to reassemble: place names, personal names, the items of use and the trappings of memory resume some luster of their own. The habitual and strategic renunciation that characterized the earlier poems has been siphoned off into an extra-poetic territory. The new poems, those in the last third of *The Late Hour* and those that complete [*Selected Poems*], have thus been freed for the work of restoration. (p. 91)

In *Selected Poems,* "Exiles" becomes the fulcrum for change, the site on which the work of restoration commences. Its first section follows the plot more or less of Albee's *A Delicate Balance:* a certain "they" find life disappearing around them and run to "us" to be taken in. In the second section, they reverse their course, in what might be a prologue to the poet's later work:

> And on their way back
> they heard the footsteps
> and felt the warmth
> of the clothes they thought
> had been lifted from them.
> They ran by the boats at anchor,
> hulking in the bay,
> by the train waiting
> under the melting frost of stars.

This reunion with the world does not exactly end in a wash of optimism:

> They lay in their beds
> and the shadows of the giant trees
> brushed darkly against the walls.

It is, nonetheless, a reunion of moment, and here are the gifts that accrue: St. Margaret's Bay, the North West Arm, Mosher Island, Wedge Island, Hackett's Cove, Fox Point, Boutelier's wharf, Albert Hubley's shack, a furniture store, a black baby Austin, brants and Canada geese, a mother, a father, an uncle, a grandmother, and Winslow Homer's *Gulf Stream.* The change is enormous, this change that begins with the final third of *The*

Late Hour, and it's not imparted by proper names alone. If the ravellings and auras of personal memory find quarter for once, this is not to suggest that the earlier poems had no sources in biography, or that the current poems never invent or lie. The *appearance* of personal history is what was not encouraged before and is very much encouraged now. When place names appear, as they occasionally do, in the earlier poems, they are poised on the scales of dislocation. . . . Heretofore, the memory Strand was interested in was the memory he could engineer, the memory he could become. In recent poems, he grants some affection to the merely historical, some credence to the merely found, and he diversifies the methods of provoking recognition. No attentive reader will expect biography to "solve" a good poem, or will underestimate Strand's loyalty to the methods and discoveries of fiction. But when the poet begins to grant the past and the reader some license of their own, this loyalty is being reconstrued.

The final sections of **Selected Poems** include work as purely lyrical as any Strand has written; the phrases are more extended, the mimetic strategies far less guarded than any the poet has used before. One poem, based on an ominous survey of the Thames in Bleak House, assembles a central sentence of twenty-eight lines, whose eddyings and sweep reproduce the course of the river itself. As to the elevation of the quotidian, one final example demands our attention. The poem has provoked a fair amount of skepticism, even among Strand's admirers, and may therefore be a useful test of his continuing strength and perspective. The poem is named for the thing itself: **"Pot Roast."** . . . The senses that feed on well-being [in **"Pot Roast"**] are those most resistant to the embrace of language. The taste of a roast, the smell of an onion have the power to translate the speaker to another time precisely because they resist translation. The sensations of taste and smell withstand the dilution and obfuscation that readier equivalents inflict upon the process of sight. . . . The title—**"Pot Roast"**—partakes of that poker-faced hilarity that alerted us to double meaning in earlier poems, but it's not reinforced by obvious gestures in kind. The poem relies on internal transformation, and accomplishes what it does by assuring that it will first be underestimated, even dismissed. In this manner the poem mimes its subject, and confesses to a diminished version of the myth it reenacts. History repeats, with some chagrin. To achieve his final proportion and tone, the poet has only the disposition of literary antecedents, the necessary and sufficient motives for parody, and the manifest subject of celebration.

Having channeled his most distinctive accomplishments into a poet's prose that sidesteps or cagily reroutes generic expectations, Strand is now experimenting with various reconstructions of the lyric voice. He's relaxed his censorship of quotidian detail; he's trying a gentler hand with the past and a lusher version of literary homage; he's practicing a less austere, more personalized and impure fable. Are the poems a dilution of the former enterprise? The poet himself has signalled a shifting of loyalties: "I'm really less interested in writing magazine verse or individual poems than in creating a literary spectacle . . . a little like *Barthes on Barthes*" (*Missouri Review,* Summer 1981). But Strand has always enacted the spectacle he describes. If all writing distributes allegiance between an audience and a subject of regard, if all writing occupies a place on the spectrum that runs from the presentational to the contemplative or exegetical, Strand's characteristic work has steadfastly been of the former kind. The poems were rhetorical, which is to say they were designed to move an audience; the self was a rhetorical construct built in view of that audience; the argument

was all *ad hominem.* Their beauty notwithstanding, the poems written since **The Monument** may prove to be something of a sideline. On the other hand, as a poem like **"Pot Roast"** should alert us, the play of presence and absence continues in all its vitality, even when, on first glance, presence seems to have become less problematic. The new bifurcation of voice, one part spoken by an altered lyric, one part by all that is left of the old, may signal the start of a dialogue we will all do well to attend to: the flower *and* the bee. (pp. 109-14)

Linda Gregerson, "Negative Capability," in Parnassus: Poetry in Review, *Vol. 9, No. 2, Fall-Winter, 1981, pp. 90-114.*

LEONARD S. MARCUS

The poet Mark Strand is an elegist for whom questions of loss—the loss of a parent, the poignant separation one can feel from one's own past, the loss of self experienced as the imagination presses toward visionary limits—have had the peculiar urgency and fascination of a radical obsession. In **The Planet of Lost Things** . . . Strand has attempted to restate this obsession on an imaginative ground accessible to children curious about night, day, lost socks, forgetfulness and other similar mysteries. . . .

Strand's book is ambitious in the very fact of its taking on such a many-layered riddle, but confused and divided about the terms of the story's resolution. A boy dreams he has piloted his rocket to a planet he has never in his far-flung imaginary travels observed before, a Borgesian puzzle-planet on which he finds gathered all the dogs that ever strayed from home, all the letters lost in the mail, all the money fallen from people's pockets, all the hats blown away in the wind: a vast collection of collections not less thorough about such intangible losses as forgotten thoughts and unrecorded sounds as about misplaced keys and umbrellas. Going for a walk around the planet, the boy meets two of its inhabitants, a kindly if bewildered man and woman who introduce themselves as an Unknown Soldier and Missing Person. They point out various sights of their world as the three companions wander aimlessly together; the boy himself meanwhile has forgotten where he left his rocket. "That's par for the course up here," says the Unknown Soldier. "No one is supposed to remember." (But how, then, an inquisitive child might logically ask, do he and his friend even recall they are "missing" and "unknown"? remember how to talk?) "Have a balloon," offers the Missing Person, motioning to the accumulated mass of the world's mislaid helium-filled toys.

The trio passes the region inhabited by extinct animals but do not stop there. "Too bad we can't pay them a visit," says the Unknown Soldier, sounding disconcertingly like a tour guide impatient about schedules. (Here the reader wonders whether the powerful images Strand evokes do not actually call for a much longer, more discursive narrative.) "They are dangerous," the Soldier says concerning the animals, "and, besides, it's out of our way." Anticipating the boy's (and reader's) disappointment at this news, the Missing Person promises a still more interesting adventure to come.

"This," she announces at last, "is where everything goes that magicians make disappear." . . .

[The] boy and his companions do indeed arrive at a colorful stage-flat house of cards, charmingly decked out with magician's tables and turtle doves, top hats, scarves and rabbits.

But no performance is in progress, no adventure at hand; moments later, the three wanderers have already departed and the boy has boarded his spacecraft for the flight home, there to awaken in his familiar bed, his dream all but forgotten.

Strand is a master of a certain type of absurdist wit that arises out of his pressing a world of commonplace wishes, fears, thoughts and occurrences to their extreme logical limits. *The Planet of Lost Things'* beguiling, rarefied atmosphere is the aura of the uncanny. In such an atmosphere, so aptly fitted to the open-ended, unself-conscious questioning of children, the final resort to stage magicians' vanished properties is a diminishment, a sentimental reduction of the story's sense of the magical; the boy's "perfect" takeoff as he heads home seems emblematic of a sleek technical exercise at the end of which *The Planet of Lost Things* remains largely unexplored.

> Leonard S. Marcus, "The Search for Something Missing," in Book World—The Washington Post, November 7, 1982, p. 17.

PETER STITT

Viewed from the perspective of his *Selected Poems*, the career of Mark Strand appears to have two distinct phases. In what we may call the later poems—which begin to appear in *The Story of Our Lives* (1973), become dominant in *The Late Hour* (1978), and completely take over the "New Poems" section of the selected volume (1980)—Strand writes concretely of remembered places and people. In the early poems—all those in *Sleeping with One Eye Open* (1964), *Reasons for Moving* (1968), and *Darker* (1970), and some of those in *The Story of Our Lives* and *The Late Hour*—the real world is held very much at arm's length. In the Winter 1981 issue of *The Georgia Review*, I reviewed the *Selected Poems* [see excerpt above] but concentrated my positive attention entirely upon the later poems. Because Strand's most characteristic work is found not in the later poems but in the early ones, I would like to turn back now and consider those poems. What we see there is a dissociation of sensibility not unlike that which Eliot used to speak about, in which the mind feels alienated from the "body" (meaning the flesh or material substance, as opposed to the spirit). The word *feels* is important in this context—the central issues in Strand's early poetry are psychological and depend far less on reality-states than on the impressions, feelings, and beliefs of a single, perhaps atypical, perceiving mind.

The poems Strand has chosen to reprint from his first book, while not many, are crucial in establishing a solid conceptual basis for the rest of the selected volume. They also introduce us, inevitably, to the characteristic speaking voice of nearly all early Strand poems—the consciousness through which everything seen, thought, felt, is filtered. Undoubtedly, this character is very nearly identical to Mark Strand himself, and yet to equate him with Strand would be to deny the role which the imagination plays in these, as indeed in all poems, however directly "confessional" they may appear to the naïve reader. The character's sense of alienation from the real world is expressed most pointedly in two poems that appear back to back in the *Sleeping with One Eye Open* section here. In **"Taking a Walk with You,"** the speaker notices the countryside which, though "Lacking the wit and depth / That inform our dreams' / Bright landscapes," "Is no less beautiful / For being only what it seems." But the man feels that he can find no home there because it was not "planned / With us in mind." Therefore, we can "stay in a place / Only long enough to find / We don't belong." And in **"Keeping Things Whole"** the speaker announces his conviction that "In a field / I am the absence / of field. / This is / always the case. / Wherever I am / I am what is missing." With respect to the world of physical reality, the speaker feels himself to be a void, a nothingness.

A partial explanation for this intense sense of alienation may be found in how this early speaker characterizes reality. It is perhaps his paranoia that makes him emphasize so strongly the dangers that lurk there. Injury and illness are among these, but most important is the fact of death, the ultimate assault of nature against the self. The poem **"Violent Storm"** expresses much of this feeling by talking about the dangers inherent in bad weather. Superficial people may be able to party as the hurricane bears down upon the coast, it is true,

> But for us, the wide-awake, who tend
> To believe the worst is always waiting
> Around the next corner or hiding in the dry,
> Unsteady branch of a sick tree, debating
> Whether or not to fell the passerby,
> It has a sinister air.

This central consciousness is also fastidious, apparently finding much of the real world ugly—certainly much uglier than the "bright landscapes" he concocts in his own head. The poem **"The Way It Is"** is an attempt to define the general appearance and nature of the world, with its epigraph taken from Stevens ("The world is ugly. / And the people are sad.") and its direct concluding stanza: "Everything dims. / The future is not what it used to be. / The graves are ready. The dead / shall inherit the dead."

So deeply does the speaker feel the ugliness of reality, its power to render death and destruction upon him, that he attempts to retreat farther and farther from it. Through his death-consciousness, he diminishes the world until it virtually disappears into nothingness: "I grow into my death. / My life is small / and getting smaller. The world is green. / Nothing is all." Another poem expresses the same desire paradoxically: "More is less. / I long for more." The closer reality draws to nothingness, the greater looms the power of the mind and the world it creates for itself. This movement gives rise to two of the most important issues in Strand's early poetry—the question of identity and the question of knowledge. How is man to be defined if he is this radically alien to nature? And what can such a man know of a world so foreign to him?

The question of identity has been generally singled out by critics as the central theme of Strand's early poems, and the term most often invoked to explain the fissure that scars the visage of our hero is *doppelgänger*—the self senses the presence of an elusive other self, for which he searches and to whom he wishes to speak. I would prefer to approach the issue through a slightly different concept, one having the additional advantage of correlating with Strand's sense of alienation between mind and body. Ralph Waldo Emerson defined the self in relationship not just to itself (as the *doppelgänger* concept does) but in relationship to its total environment, spiritual as well as physical. Emerson divides the all into two massive components—the "Me," which may be thought of as the mind, the soul, the personality; and the "Not-Me," which comprises all else, significantly including "my own body." The world of poetry is obviously controlled by the Me, which possesses all the ideas and has the intellect necessary to render them into stories, poems, and dreams. The Not-Me is merely a physical entity, sometimes pretty, but certainly dumb as dirt. Moreover, the Not-Me is subject to all the ravages reality has to offer—illness, injury, death. Thus the speaker of the poems, the Me, exists in a very uneasy relationship to his own body, part of the Not-me; he feels an inevitable attraction but also a powerful repulsion. In general we may say that the situation makes him miserable—which is why he mopes around so much in these poems and why Strand has been so often accused of expressing self-pity in his early books.

Strand's most extensive treatment of the Me/Not-Me dichotomy occurs in the long poem **"The Man in the Mirror."** The action begins in the present time, as the Me approaches the mirror wherein he will see the Not-Me. . . . The Me remembers a time when the two would "stand / wishing the glass / would dissolve between us," deep in their narcissistic love. Suddenly the Not-Me bolted, apparently in pursuit of a more physically satisfying life; the Me drifts about the house, heartsick and forlorn. When the Not-Me finally returns, the look of death is upon him—the Me sees "flies / collected in your hair / and dust fell like a screen before your eyes." There is still a sense of recognition between them—"I look at you / and see myself / under the surface"—but the fear which grows from the Me's sense of alienation is profound: "I stand here scared / that you will disappear, / scared that you will stay."

The world of the mind is clearly predominant in the early poems of Mark Strand; reality is capricious, not to be trusted, even unknowable in any certain sense. The question of knowledge for Strand depends upon the question of perception; reality is so inconstant that the observer cannot trust what he seems to see. In his later poems, Strand will write with a good deal of confidence about the world of outward reality; in the early poems his trust is placed instead in the world of the mind. Thus these poems reproduce not images perceived "out there" so much as the images imagined "in here." Strand's major subject, then, becomes the question of human perception and how this can result in poetry. (pp. 201-04)

[The point of such poems] is to strip away the outer world so as to make the subject of poetry the act of perception in the mind, the creation of the poem on the page. At a slightly later stage in the development of this type of poetry (in which the theme is the method, the method the theme) the version of reality created on the page can come back and determine the course of reality in the world. Which is precisely what happens in **"The Story of Our Lives,"** where the action of the poem is defined early: "We are reading the story of our lives / which takes place in a room." Mark Strand is, in many ways, a latter-day symbolist, though his system is neither elaborate nor especially consistent. . . .

Most typical among Strand's early poems are such primitivistic, parable-like narratives as **"The Tunnel,"** **"The Mailman,"** and **"The Accident."** These works use accoutrement drawn from the real world but actually take place within the mental landscape. They are not stories told so as to make the reader feel that meaning has grown organically out of the action; rather, the meaning is clearly known to the poet at the start, and he then creates action to illustrate it. It is somewhat curious that Strand's retreat into a world of the mind should be accompanied by such extreme reductiveness. Somehow the method does not so much liberate the imagination as confine it. Being released from the demands of reality has meant for many writers a lush flowering of creativity within which they could go ahead and make up anything. . . . It is a mark of identification for Strand and his followers that they prefer the safety of nothingness, an imagined world that excludes not just the world of

reality and its actual, human people but even other imagined selves. It is this fact that accounts for the feeling of sterility one has when reading the early Strand and some of the work of his followers. Conversely, this fact also helps to explain why the later poems in this book are so especially satisfying—they please not just intellectually, as the early poems do in abundance, but emotionally, humanly, and warmly as well. (p. 205)

Peter Stitt, "*Stages of Reality: The Mind/Body Problem in Contemporary Poetry,*" *in* The Georgia Review, *Vol. XXXVII, No. 1, Spring, 1983, pp. 201-10.*

PHILIP COOPER

In mid-career, a year or so before the publication of his *Selected Poems* (1980), Mark Strand began publishing humorous stories in the *New Yorker*. They acted as a relief perhaps from the sameness of dark tone that stamped his poems—although his poems were often marked by wit, a certain dry humor that may be a distinctive feature of his voice, and that laces the dreamlike, haunting, impressionistic nostalgia that characterizes a great many of his poems. For example, the poem I like best, **"Keeping Things Whole,"** handles serious paradox with a playful tone—although when I remarked how funny it is, Strand demurred:

> —It's a paradox. I wouldn't put that in the class of humor. It's a paradoxical situation: wherever I am, I am what is missing. I mean, in effect it simply says, I suppose, in the end, that the world can get along very well without me, and in fact that my being there is . . . an interruption. The presence of consciousness is altering, disturbing, isolating. . .
>
> —But then the wonderful throw-away humor of "We all have reasons for moving./ I move to keep things whole.". . .
>
> —It's rather jaunty, you're right.

With that concession, the conversation moved on to the stories, but I wish I had pressed the question of the poem a moment longer. The seriousness of the subject was not in doubt, but it may be that the handling appears more complex—more humorous—to me than it does to its author. (p. 2)

Thinking of the fiction as a clue, a new approach, I asked him about the stories. But first, since the stories entail a more complex texture of writing, and in view of the fact that Strand comes to poetry from painting (he was a student of Joseph Albers at Yale), I asked whether the spare style of the poetry derives in any way from minimalism in art.

> —No, he replied, it derives from insecurity to write more complicated sentences. I mean I think I began with such uncertainty as a writer that I clung to the simplest formulations, verbal formulations, that I could, in order to stay out of trouble. And it took years and years for me to gain confidence enough to write in a more complicated fashion. These stories would've been unthinkable years ago—though my turn of mind hasn't changed or altered so much. It wasn't suddenly that I discovered a funny-bone in my body and began writing this sort of fic-

tion. I could never string together enough sentences that I was sure of before. . .

(p. 3)

The story **"True Loves,"** for example, . . . is reminiscent of *Lolita* in tone and erotic subject, though the humor is broader, closer to slapstick, and the texture of the writing less dense. In the developing picture of his work the stories are comic relief—relief from solemnity, from the lyric oddness that is the defining characteristic, perhaps, of Strand's individual poetic style—relief from the severely minimal diction, the disarming tone but high compression, the startling speed of the typical Mark Strand poem. Consider **"The Marriage,"** for example. . . . The combination of simple diction, surreal time and journalistic concreteness of detail makes this a good example of what Strand has called (in an interview with Wayne Dodd and Stanley Plumly) a "new international style." "I feel very much a part of a new international style that has a lot to do with plainness of diction, a certain reliance on surrealist techniques, a certain reliance on journalistic techniques, a strong narrative element, etc. . . . "

In contrast to the speed and compression of **"The Marriage,"** the story **"True Loves"** is absurdly expansive, romping through a succession of marriages and infatuations, marriages *as* infatuations, all over the globe: Machu Picchu, the New York subway, Hollywood, Australia, Nova Scotia, Belgrade, Venice, Rome. Strand, the quintessential New Yorker, is nothing if not cosmopolitan, a citizen of the globe, debonair, Nabokovian, smart. But also wandering, lonely, lost. Lost, melancholy in many of the poems; jovial, recreational in all of the fiction. (pp. 3-5)

The phase of the fiction may signal a change in the center of gravity of his work. There was, to be sure, always a narrative impulse, but it was curtailed, parabolic, or sometimes a touch too portentous. . . . There was, just as surely, a considerable lightness and humor among the poems, for all their predominant dark. . . . Conversely, among the stories, **"The Tiny Baby,"** for all its comic beginning, ends in an enigma as heavy and dark as many of the poems. The story of the tiny baby, hardly a story at all but a hyperbolic image, a caricature perhaps of something like the "viable fetus" in recent abortion controversy, plays with the sentimentalities of the fatuous mother ("she kept the baby in her purse so she wouldn't lose it") until suddenly the tiny baby has become the smallish woman who is "watching the street for a sight of her favorite hairdo," and who is left, in the end, with the darkly ambiguous thought that "Death will not have me."

Even **"Mr. and Mrs. Baby,"** though in keeping with the title it is a light spoof throughout, has, as good humor must, a serious core. Strand commented on the characters:

> —I just thought of them as Americans, a people who have never grown up. I mean we are a young country, we behave like youngsters . . . we are, well, consumers in the way teenagers are consumers. We are lost.

Lostness, emptiness, uncertainty: the central theme of Strand's work is elusive . . . or is elusiveness itself. Elusiveness as a motif may be the link that unites the two sides, the light and the dark. Among the poems it is present in **"Darker," "The Untelling," "My Mother on an Evening in Late Summer,"** and **"Where Are the Waters of Childhood?"**—examples of the graver mood—as well as in the comic **"Eating Poetry," "Marriage,"** and **"Courtship,"** for example. The surreal hu-

mor of **"The Tiny Baby"**—"She told the sitter, 'The baby's in the living room, but it's real small. If you don't see it, don't worry' "—may be a way of moving beyond ordinary discourse, a way of creating, like "the feel of not to feel," the feel of unknowing, of the elusiveness of meaning, of the uncertainty of human *being* itself. (pp. 5-6)

As he said in connection with **"Keeping Things Whole,"** "the presence of consciousness is altering, disturbing, isolating. . . . " But when we are alone, truly alone, like Meursault at the end of *The Stranger,* the freedom to celebrate being in the world may rise like a tide of light, an illumination both secular and numinous, a dawning:

> I have carried it with me each day: that morning I took
> my uncle's boat from the brown water cove
> and headed for Mosher Island.
> Small waves splashed against the hull
> and the hollow creak of oarlock and oar
> rose into the woods of black pine crusted with lichen.
> I moved like a dark star, drifting over the drowned
> other half of the world until, by a distant prompting,
> I looked over the gunwale and saw beneath the surface
> a luminous room, a light-filled grave, saw for the first
>   time
> the one clear place given to us when we are alone.

> ("A Morning")

The luminous room, the light-filled grave, is the void, is the waiting dark made clear and inviting, once and for all.

If the romantic affirmation of **"A Morning"** seems too easy, seems even with its understatement to claim too much, consider another late poem, **"For Jessica, My Daughter."** Here the central question is posed with disarming, translucent directness.

> Jessica, it is so much easier
> to think of our lives,
> as we move under the brief luster of leaves,
> loving what we have,
> than to think of how it is
> such small beings as we
> travel in the dark
> with no visible way
> or end in sight. . . .

Never was the virtue, the artifice of artlessness more skillfully directed, more touchingly employed. The archaic simplicity of the theme and the plainness of the diction join in perfect song. It is as moving as it is unpretentious. It is a measure of the temper of our time. (pp. 6-7)

Philip Cooper, "The Waiting Dark: Talking to Mark Strand," in The Hollins Critic, *Vol. XXI, No. 4, October, 1984, pp. 2-7.*

WENDY LESSER

There is something about Mark Strand's short stories that suits them to brief rather than extended exposure. One or two at a time can be savored and enjoyed, their separate parts appreciated in detail, but a whole book—even a very short one— gets rather wearing. Mr. Strand himself . . . may even suspect as much, for brevity is one of the guiding forces behind the 14 stories in **Mr. and Mrs. Baby,** his first collection of short fiction.

At their best, the stories in this collection are sharp and idiosyncratic, with unusual twists given to expected realities. In the opening story, **"More Life,"** a young man keeps sensing the presence of his late, estranged father in the creatures around him: "This is hard to account for but I was suddenly convinced that my father had returned. He had come back as a fly." In another story, a man named Glover Bartlett admits to his wife Tracy, in the privacy of their pillow-talk, that before he met her he was a dog. And in a surprisingly apt modern retelling of the myth of Cephalus and Procris, a young woman named Betty gets punished by being turned into an elephant midway in the story. "Even tonight, if you go down the right street," the story concludes, "you may see Betty with her long, delicate legs almost hidden by the great bulk of her upper body, and Cephalus sitting, forever stunned by the gross, magisterially still creature that faces him, proof that the power of the gods to change the shapes of things is boundless."

It is Mr. Strand's own belief in that power—or at least his ability to evoke it convincingly—that makes the human-animal transformations in this collection work so well. We are never sure, in the better Mark Strand stories, whether the evident craziness is attributable to the character alone, to the fictional world he inhabits, or to our larger world that encompasses his own.

Such idiosyncrasy has a very short half-life, however; it decays easily. In longer stories such as **"True Loves"** or **"Mr. and Mrs. Baby,"** Mr. Strand's obvious desire to create surprising effects gets tiring and redundant. By the time the narrator of **"True Loves"** has described one or two of his great passions, we know with irritated certainty that the remaining four or five will be equally evanescent, equally frustrating. The rampant insignificance of Mr. and Mrs. Baby's life—though that is the point of the title story—is similarly tedious. One shies at the subheading "Mrs. Baby Has an Experience," then shudders at the subsequent "Mr. Baby Also Has an Experience," knowing full well that one is about to be dragged through further displays of pointless sarcasm.

This sarcasm reaches its weakest pitch in Mr. Strand's pseudo-political satires, which are characterized by a kind of smart-alecky narcissism that congratulates itself on its own wit. . . .

It's odd that a writer who in his poetry succeeds by making things new should here cling so desperately to the redundant and the predictable.

Most of all, Mr. Strand's stories suffer from the absence of anything beyond tone. When his voice is unusual and captivating—as it is in **"More Life," "Dog Life," "Cephalus"** and briefly at the beginning of **"The Tiny Baby"**—the stories stay afloat. But in the majority of stories in this collection, the heavy, self-consciously surreal, pointedly eccentric tone drags the stories down, with no real plots or characters to buoy them up. It is a great risk to write fiction that depends utterly on tone, and it is a gamble that Mr. Strand more often loses than wins.

> *Wendy Lesser, "Metamorphoses," in* The New York Times Book Review, *March 17, 1985, p. 16.*

ELIOT FREMONT-SMITH

Now here's a thought. If one's theme is the utter futility, emptiness, and boredom of life, one had best be brief about it. Go on too long, and the audience illustrates entropy. Here and there in *Mr. and Mrs. Baby And Other Stories* . . . , Mark Strand goes on too long. It's a problem because repetition and redundancy are, after all, prime exhibits for the prosecution—it's hard to prove ennui without them.

Take the title story, which presents a typical humdrum day in the monotonous existence of Bob and Babe Baby. The presentation covers 10 pages, including the subtitles for its 10 parts, or scenes, or aperçus: "MR. AND MRS. BABY WAKE UP," "HOW MR. AND MRE. BABY LOOKED," "MR. AND MRS. BABY AT BREAKFAST," "MRS. BABY HAS AN EXPERIENCE," "MR. BABY ALSO HAS AN EXPERIENCE," "MR. AND MRS. BABY SKIP LUNCH," "MR. AND MRS. BABY HAVE A GOOD CRY," "MR. AND MRS. BABY HAVE A TALK," "MR. AND MRS. BABY GO TO A PARTY," and "MR. AND MRS. BABY GO TO SLEEP."

Scan these, and who needs a text? Of course, some aperçus are amusing. In "HOW MR. AND MRS. BABY LOOKED," we learn that they looked "familiar"—that is, like bits and pieces of movie stars. Thus, Babe Baby's nose "was not perfectly shaped like Gloria Grahame's, not barren like Betty Hutton's, not swaybacked like Ingrid Bergman's, nor with oversized nostrils like Donna Reed's or Joan Bennett's; it was a nose like the radiant Janet Blair's. It was perky without being prying, it was cute without being cheap, it was noble without being undemocratic."

On the other hand, the Babys are headed not for joy but for sadness, the day's "ordeals of fixity, of ornament, of responsibility: Baby Hades." We know this from "MR. AND MRS. BABY WAKE UP." And we know from "MR. AND MRS. BABY GO TO SLEEP" that it will all be repeated on the morrow. The story is a kind of *Mary Hartman! Mary Hartman!* meets *Dead of Night.* In the middle ("MR. BABY ALSO HAS AN EXPERIENCE"), the point is driven home. Bob Baby, vaguely distraught, writes his first poem; it's about "why he was here and not there, why he had chosen the life he had instead of the life he hadn't, why he felt as he did and, sometimes, as he didn't."

Mark Strand is nothing if not affable. This is necessary; it masks his (and our) sneering at the Babys—or, for that matter, sympathizing with the mother in another story, **"The Tiny Baby,"** whose offspring is so minuscule she must carry it in her purse. In his poetry . . . Strand can express bleakness unalloyed. But his stories are a different matter. Aside from the hurdles of plot, character, and action—formidable for a minimalist, really tough on ennui—a more varied and supple tone is required. In fact, everything turns on tone, its exact manipulation through these 14 sorties or exercises. It cannot be preachy or too morbid; it must seem caring yet, in fidelity to theme, totally uninvolved; it must amuse and be sometimes flip, but not cruel, never judgmental. To judge would convey an interest in consequence, a hint that life offers meaning. The same with sentiment, excitement, bitterness, regret. All of these are out. What's left are affability and sadness (these would be out, too, except nobody would read pure apathy) and the act of control itself.

One witnesses this—conniving is discouraged—with a mixture of admiration for Strand's self-appointed task, bafflement over its innate contradictions, and exhaustion. Nothing is more quickly tiring than the argument that everything is futile, empty, and boring—unless it is the profound self-regard required to put forth the argument.

Strand is aware of this and, controller that he is, aware of our awareness. Thus his description of Bob Baby's poetry parodies a possible description of his own. It is disarming, even briefly charming, and in **"The Killer Poet,"** which ends the book, he repeats the conceit. Only this time it turns on him, and the act of control seems more like an exercise in extrication.

The narrator of **"The Killer Poet"** is a much-honored member of the National Literature Board, which is charged with naming the year's best book. (Strand has received "numerous awards and fellowships," the jacket informs us, "and in 1981 was elected a member of the Institute of Arts and Letters.") The board voices the usual "complaints of spiritual aimlessness" in the submissions for the prize, and one member insists that poets are "advocates of absence, refusal, and negative quantities," arguing that "too many of them believed their power to be directly proportional to what they left out of their work."

But one book of poems, a first collection by the narrator's long-ago friend Stanley, impresses the board with its "eerie solemnity," "mystical consistency," and "honesty." Clearly Stanley deserves the prize. The only trouble is that Stanley has murdered his parents; indeed, his poems are his confession, without remorse.

The board considers the problem to be "both absurd and difficult." As one member puts it, "to reward [Stanley] for sincerity might seem a way of excusing his crimes, just as dealing exclusively with his crimes would be over-looking the accomplishment of his work." Then the narrator suggests that the board withhold a prize—"after all," he demands, "what kind of poet is it who wins official approval during his lifetime!"—and instead ensure Stanley's immortality as "a martyr for poetry, a special saint," by executing him.

The board approves the plan, the narrator calls Stanley, who is willing . . . , and a limousine is dispatched. And so, after a minimum of fuss, is the poet. But then comes the subtitle, "STANLEY'S LAST WORDS."

The attempted extrication is, as usual, from possible misunderstanding. Stanley wants to explain himself, just as (one thinks) Strand wants to explain himself, after all these tales of numbness, refusal, and absence. Stanley (Strand?) wants particularly to explain how offhand the murders were and to thwart psychological interpretation. . . .

"Clearly I am not a bad person," his last words go. "If I seem hidden or guarded, it is because I never understood how candor benefited the imagination. I chose not to shed light but to embody darkness, not to reveal order, but to withhold it. I was alive with the negative certainty of my passion [pun no doubt intended]. Each day I luxuriated in the possession of myself. My sight was always turned inward."

Which is, seriously, Strand's constant theme. In **"Under Water,"** a story told three times with slight variations, the narrator plays solitaire (and wins), recounts incidents of loss and death (his parents'), and embraces a shrinking world: "When I am fourteen my mother encourages me to take out girls. I have nothing to say to them. I close myself up in a room and paint self-portraits. Each is more detailed than the last. I look so hard in the mirror that I see nothing." Identity eats itself, in a room that's not even described as his. . . .

In several stories, desire battles stasis; stasis always wins. One story juxtaposes, in serial form, five failed marriages with six unconsummated **"True Loves,"** all over the world, from Machu Picchu to Australia to the IRT. The romance is with place. In **"Zadar,"** which is set on the Dalmatian coast, the narrator actually gets into bed with a woman, while her silent husband watches. Sex is a possibility, but probably doesn't happen: "My desire seemed borrowed and remote." Even in **"Ce-**phalus,"** the most passionate of the stories, the sex is passive and the passion hinges on the greater thrall of temptation to doubt: no love can be true, and lust exists only to prove it.

In this story, a woman turns partway into an elephant. In the opening story, **"More Life,"** the narrator's frustrated (and failed-writer) father is perhaps reincarnated successively as a fly, a horse, and the narrator's girlfriend. When he cries, "Dad, it's you, it's you," she is suitably disconcerted. A similar idea is funnier in **"Dog Life,"** in which a man confesses to his wife that he used to be a collie and recalls a copulation:

> "Did you love her?" the wife inquires, anent the bitch.
> "No, not really. I admired her more than anything."
> "But there were dogs you did love?"
> "It's hard to say that dogs actually love."
> "You know what I mean."

It's hard to say exactly what Mark Strand means. Understandably, he's been accused of rampant narcissism, but the accusation has a tinny ring. His stories betray no envy; he regards the mirror excessively but without the slightest twinge of arousal. (*Publishers Weekly* calls the book "erotic," which is about as far off the mark as the companion blurb, "satirical.") At most Strand seems sardonic, bemused by his own lethargy—or stance of same.

For, of course, these fables have been worked on hard; there can have been no lack of zeal in getting things just right—the philosophical commitment, the control of tone, the curling redundancies, the enigmatic smile. But if one accepts that—the investment of energy—then what about the futility, etc., the stories are supposed to illustrate? The problem is credibility: presence subverts nihilism, effort shafts ennui.

Or—here's another thought—Strand is dumb to logic, a foolish writer. And I am a fool for logic, a dumb reader. We're as trapped as the Babys, and in our Baby Hades probably just as smug. Put that in your purse.

Eliot Fremont-Smith, "Baby Hades," in The Village Voice, *Vol. XXX, No. 16, April 16, 1985, p. 42.*

ELLEN LESSER

Those who look to fiction for the conventional pieties of plot and character may be disappointed [by *Mr. and Mrs. Baby*]: the pleasures of these tales—by turns surrealistic and wry, whimsical and confessional—lie elsewhere. . . .

[Half of these stories] are fueled by a "magical realism" reminiscent of the Latin Americans. In **"The Tiny Baby,"** a woman gives birth to a child so small it could be a goldfinch or chickadee. The boy in **"Drogo"** may be the narrator's surrogate son, but more likely he is born of the man's imagination. Strand's surrealism is never gratuitous; he uses it in service of the real, to expose the marrow of human relationships. Sometimes this intersection of the fantastic and the mundane yields dry humor, as in **"Dog Life,"** where a man admits to his wife that he used to be a collie. After an elegy to his moonlit barking sessions with the neighborhood canines, he says, "'Darling, there was something about those nights I miss.' 'Are you telling me that something is wrong with our marriage?'"

While critics have seen a dark or lurking wit in some of Strand's lyrics, humor has never been the dominant feature of his poetry. In his stories, he is playful, openly satirical, in a way that readers of his quiet meditations on being and absence might not expect. Strand gives us a president who devotes his entire term to glorifying the weather and trying "to make nothing happen," a general who's rewarded because his losses prove the nation's humanity.... Even poetry is not exempt. The book closes with **"The Killer Poet,"** full of jabs at that most exalted of professions. When the homicidal Stanley R. speaks in rapturous tones of his "anguished humming into the empty corridors of the future," and his "plangent dialogues with absence," one can't help thinking of Strand's own poetic legacy.

Though he's never numbered among the "confessional" poets, Strand achieves something of that intimate tone in his stories about men and women. The hero of **"True Loves"** is a would-be Don Juan in need of assertiveness training. There is a disarming innocence to his obsessive appreciation of the depth or opacity of a woman's eye, the arch of an eyebrow, the "careless grace" of crossed legs; and to "the nervous joy . . . the sweet excitement, the familiar yet unfathomable fear" that comes over him.

By far the greatest pleasures of *Mr. and Mrs. Baby* are not to be found in its mysteries, comic vision, or even its hapless picture of the contemporary male, but rather in the writing. On practically every page, one can be dazzled by Strand's language. When it comes to turning a shimmering phrase, he has the touch of a poet.... At a time when what passes for prose style is often its absence, Strand's intoxication is a welcome indulgence.

Ellen Lesser, "Baby Talk," in The Village Voice,
Vol. XXX, No. 18, April 30, 1985, p. 47.

ALAN CHEUSE

"Then I stopped and looked around, and the world for an instant assumed a deep benevolence that was strangely charged and that lifted me from the possibility of resignation, numbness, or despair.... It was still early and the surrounding silence seemed enormous, as if the world were holding its breath for a momentous occurrence."

Privileged moments such as this occur often throughout the dozen and more stories [in *Mr. and Mrs. Baby*]—well, "stories," you may want to call most of them, since only a few have what we might notice as plots.... Of the few that resemble the classic short story, two of these, **"More Life"** and **"True Loves,"** stay in the mind along with some of the best fiction in recent years. The former is the first-person account of a man who discovers that his late father is returning to haunt him, first as a fly, then as a horse, and then in even more surprising reincarnations. The latter from which I've taken that opening quotation, gives us the story of a man driven always by the possibility of impossible love.

The other selections in the book vary in form and effect. [**"Mr. and Mrs. Baby"**] lays itself out like a miniature novel: "Mr. & Mrs. Baby Wake Up" is the first heading for a "chapter" of about a dozen lines. Then comes "How Mr. & Mrs. Baby Looked," and next, "Mr. & Mrs. Baby at Breakfast" and so on to the end of the 9½-page narrative whose mood is a mixture of irony and affection. The privileges of this story's moments come with the reading rather than anything felt by the figures in the tale.

"Dog Life," another of my favorites, purports to be the testimony of a man who came into this world first as a collie and one night confesses to his wife about the happy times he had while bounding "about in the yellow twilight" of autumn, "excited by the clicking of branches and the parade of odors making each circuit of air an occasion for reverie. . . ." (pp. 1, 11)

Strand, one of the reigning masters of North American plain diction, rescues a number of other speakers and characters from such a limbo . . . , and at the very least, we get included in the enactment of a series of impressive exercises in the creation of image and feeling moment. Like the newspaper pieces of the late Eugenio Montale, one of modern Italy's finest poets, these prose inventions give us the privilege of watching a first-rate artist try out his genius in another mode. (p. 11)

*Alan Cheuse, in a review of "Mr. and Mrs. Baby
and Other Stories," in* Los Angeles Times Book
Review, *June 2, 1985, pp. 1, 11.*

Graham Swift

1949-

Photograph by Mark Gerson

English novelist and short story writer.

Swift writes intricately structured psychological fiction marked by a sophisticated use of symbol, allusion, and metaphor. His central themes include the relationship between the present and the past, the nature of historical inquiry, and the emotional strains of domestic life. These concerns interweave in his fiction, resulting in several levels of meaning. Although some critics fault Swift for a tendency toward verbosity and claim that he is more concerned with ideas than with characters and settings, he is often praised for his subtle yet sophisticated narrative style and his insights into family life.

Swift's first novel, *The Sweet Shop Owner* (1980), details the final day in the life of a British shopkeeper and incorporates, through flashbacks, four decades of his family's dour history. Swift examines the tenuous relationship between family members and the role of the past in shaping the family's present. His second book, *Shuttlecock* (1981), is a psychological thriller in which a law enforcement research investigator attempts to uncover the truth behind his father's activities as a spy during World War II. While a mystery novel on the surface, the book also explores the dynamics of love and cruelty, loyalty and betrayal.

Swift's third novel, *Waterland* (1983), is narrated by Tom Crick, a history teacher on the verge of dismissal. Crick has given up conventional methods of teaching in favor of delivering lengthy discourses on his family history and the history of England's Fen Country, replete with elaborate digressions on a multitude of subjects. While including local detail and an elaborate plot involving sordid family activities, *Waterland* also reflects Swift's concern with the nature of the historical process. Observing Swift's treatment of the role of myth in history, John Brewer and Stella Tillyard stated that "*Waterland*'s narrative not only reflects on the meaning of history but itself exemplifies the difficulty in distinguishing history from fiction."

Swift has also written a collection of short stories, *Learning to Swim and Other Stories* (1982). Blending the domestic and the fantastic, Swift employs a variety of voices in these stories to convey the emotional hardships people endure in moments of crisis. These tales, like Swift's novels, emphasize his concern with the haunting influence of the past on the present.

(See also *Contemporary Authors,* Vol. 117.)

FRANK RUDMAN

Willy Chapman is the sweet shop owner of Graham Swift's impressive first novel [*The Sweet Shop Owner*]. Ostensibly conformist and unassuming, but equally determined to get his own quiet way and prepared to wait a lifetime of snubbing and self-effacement to obtain his ends, Willy marries an insistently assertive shrew, a frigid near-hysteric who retreats into illness and invalidism. Irene, who comes from a family with money, sets up Willy in the High Street sweet shop largely in order to keep him safely and happily engaged away from home and any importunate demands he might make upon her as a husband. Out of misplaced and regretted sense of duty, Irene relents just once and gives Willy a daughter, Dorothy (Dorothea: God's gift) who grows up unable to forgive either of them.

Willy's moment of triumph comes when he suddenly pays off everybody, shuts the shop, all duty done, hoping that the ungrateful Dorothy will return to look after him (*After all, she never said she wouldn't*) as he struggles home with angina tearing away inside his chest. The Chapman family's bitter history is brilliantly chronicled by Graham Swift who captures the essence of the small, modest but obliging variety of family establishments that made up High Street business before the remorseless blight of supermarkets and building society boxes squashed them out of existence.

Frank Rudman, in a review of "The Sweet Shop Owner," in The Spectator, *Vol. 244, No. 7920, April 26, 1980, p. 23.*

JOHN MELLORS

Graham Swift advises readers of **Shuttlecock** 'not to peer too hard beneath the surface of what it says'. First impressions only, please. No second opinions. Accept everything at face value. What is he frightened of when he warns us to beware of the dog beneath the skin? That we might find nothing there, even though, up on the surface, 'the mysteries don't stop'? (p. 88)

Swift *does* have interesting things to say, and it *is* rewarding to peer beneath the plot and consider his views on love, cruelty, conscience, power, responsibility, loyalty and betrayal. 'Love ought to be simple, straightforward, but it isn't,' says Swift's narrator. He had found with his pet hampster, when he was a small boy, that cruelty was involved, if only as 'a way of making remorse possible'. Everybody in *Shuttlecock* seems to be spying on and persecuting somebody near or dear. There is the narrator's 'assault course sex' with Marian, his wife, which he explains as a search for enlightenment. His elder son, Martin, appears to be following him across Clapham Common on his way home from the Underground station in the evenings. His boss at work is either testing his nerve or being gratuitously cruel. And then, of course, there is Dad; is he a victim or a villain?

During the War, Dad had been in the Resistance in France. Later, he had written a book about his experiences, a book called *Shuttlecock*. In it he tells of being caught and tortured by the Gestapo and of his escape from the cellars of the chateau in which he had been imprisoned and stripped naked—'of all the humiliations and cruelties . . . none . . . was more demoralizing, more appalling than this nakedness'. Now, after a breakdown, he is in a mental hospital, unable, unless he is pretending, to recognise even his own son.

But is Dad the hero-victim that he appears to be? The narrator's boss, in the Kafkaesque office near Charing Cross, has access to files which suggest that Dad's first breakdown had been in wartime, that he had betrayed other agents in the network, that his 'escape' had been set up for him by his captors as a *quid pro quo*. Dad is in no position now to defend himself and to say whether his book had been true or false. The doubts remain. The narrator destroys the vital file without himself examining it. The mystery is left unsolved.

Is Swift suggesting that knowledge is dangerous and breeds unhappiness and that only ignorance enables us to enjoy life? Seeing people chatting and laughing as they drink at a table outside a pub, the narrator thinks: 'these people are happy because of what they don't know'.

So, is *Shuttlecock* poppycock? Or is it worth the reader's while to peer beneath the surface? It seems to me to succeed on several levels. It is a novel of ideas and it leaves one with food for thought. It is an entertaining psychological mystery-thriller. The style is clear, smooth, fast-flowing. And, as happens in all the best novels, there are many incidental pleasures in the author's parentheses and digressions. (pp. 88-9)

> *John Mellors, "Beware of the Dog," in* London Magazine, *n.s. Vol. 21, No. 8, November, 1981, pp. 88-90.*

BRYN CALESS

Graham Swift's previous forays into fiction included two novels (*The Sweet Shop Owner* and *Shuttlecock*) and he has regularly published short stories, some of which are collected in this new volume [*Learning to Swim and Other Stories*]. . . .

Swift's general theme is that people—be they the doctor in **"Hypochondriac"**, the small boy in **"Chemistry"** or the adoptive father in **"The Son"**—are 'distrustful of happiness' . . . , and his characters go out of their way to deny happiness to themselves and others. This distrust is partly conditioned by upbringing—the narrator of **"The Watch"** is dominated by a timepiece made to cheat time two centuries ago—or by an internal sterility and denial of enjoyment in others. Now, it all may be true and we may indeed be living on a blighted planet in which any pursuit of life for its own sake is a pathetic illusion. Certainly it may be true that other people, from whatever motive, may deny love to us or spoil happiness when we've got it. What I find difficult to accept is that such blighting is so universal or so unremitting. No life is without pain but, equally, very few lives are *all* pain. Swift's characters would disagree with the last part of that cliché, and so would the author. Judging by the fact that all the stories are narrated in the first person and give a continuous, subjective throttle to the emotions, Swift feels it necessary to create story-teller *personae* to give ideas life. In only one story, **"Gabor"**, does the author give substance to the ideas by creating contrast. All the others are stark statements against which *The Waste Land* seems positively frivolous.

> *Bryn Caless, in a review of "Learning to Swim and Other Stories," in* British Book News, *December, 1982, p. 768.*

HUGH HEBERT

It is not after all a wilderness but an arena. Graham Swift chose to set large parts of his new novel *Waterland* in the low sodden reaches of the Fens because of their potential for metaphor, because they are flat and empty, waiting to be filled. Their most extended metaphorical use is for the ordinariness of the life that is the reality, the reality in which nothing happens, which denies what he calls the sudden hallucination of events.

Yet within this uneventful reality he tells a family saga of incest, madness, murder and suicide that in its raw state would make the average thriller reader's toes curl. He does not offer it in the raw state, of course, but transformed by memory and desire and a sense of history though his attitude, and the attitude of his narrator Tom Crick, to history is deeply ambivalent. History only teaches us, he suggests, the dogged and patient art of making do. . . .

Swift says that Crick, the teacher, offers several views of history, but two in particular. History as instructor, pointing out errors that may be avoided in future (though we all know they never are); and history as drama, as the peg on which we hang our myths and our dreams, what Swift calls "our fabulous requirements." . . .

Yet reality itself remains a puzzle in much of Swift's fiction, a series of possible alternatives shifting as the silt of the Fenland rivers. "Is reality an everyday thing, something we know? or is it something we don't know about until some great crisis occurs?" Is war an interruption of peace, or the other way round?

Waterland is Swift's third novel, and though each is very different from the others, they share several important and powerful themes. *The Sweet-shop Owner* (1980) announced one of them, the relationship between parent and child, past and present. The shopkeeper of this story is on the point of giving it all up. His wife is dead, his daughter will not come to see him even to collect her inheritance, send it by post, she says, and he reviews his past through eyes dimmed with disappointment.

For Swift it was a comprehensive rejection of the traditional first autobiographical novel. Almost nowhere did it touch on his own experience, and the part that did—memories of the sixties—was the most difficult to write. It was a sustained and surprising imaginative flight that brought admiring reviews.

Shuttlecock (1981), his second novel, was subtitled a "psychological thriller," and though the stately pace of Swift's narratives makes the description slightly absurd, it does have Kafkaesque pretentions. The narrator, Prentis, works for a mysterious branch of the police archives dealing with dead cases that come to life again, or are finally dropped altogether.

His relationship with his two sons and his wife is difficult and suspicious, and Prentis himself feels in the shadow of his war hero father, and of his boss Quinn whose job and high-perched office he thinks he will inherit. One of his hesitant investigations leads to discoveries about his father that finally release him from the dead hero's dominance.

At one point Prentis says: "Now let me tell you something. We are all looking for a space where we can be free, where we cannot be reached, where we are masters." The sweet shop is such a space, so is Quinn's office, from which he could look down on his underlings. The theme continues, in *Waterland*, but transformed. The space where Tom Crick wants to be free and master is his classroom but, denied that, he seeks to escape into that abstract concept we call history, his subject.

> Hugh Hebert, "Fens for the Memory," in The Guardian, *October 1, 1983, p. 10.*

SALLY EMERSON

Waterland is a big, ambitious English novel by Graham Swift, one of our best young novelists. His two earlier novels, *The Sweet-Shop Owner* and *Shuttlecock,* received widespread praise but neither has the broad imaginative sweep of his latest.

The narrator, Tom Crick, is a history teacher about to get the sack who neglects traditional lessons to tell his class of his own history and the history of the Fens. From his rich, rambling stories interspersed with dissertations on eels, the Fens and the nature of history, there emerges a picture of old England splashed with Dickensian glory and gore.

The story weaves backwards and forwards beginning in the cottage of Tom's father, a lock-keeper, by a river in the middle of the Fens. Tom is just 10 and his elder retarded brother, "potato-headed" Dick, is 14. At once Graham Swift establishes a strong sense of place, of the brightness of the multiplying stars, the sounds of the frogs croaking in the ditches and the poignant and nostalgic smell, half man and half fish, of the water in the lock. It is into the sluice that the body of Tom's friend, Freddie, floats in July, 1943. Who killed Freddie, how and why, is one of the themes to which the novel constantly returns, helping to give it a strong narrative thread.

In firm, memorable strokes, Graham Swift peoples his book with numerous strong characters, including Tom's 18th-century ancestor Thomas Atkinson who drained 12,000 acres of the Leem river and hit his lovely young wife Sarah in a fit of jealousy so that she lost her senses. He died of grief while she lived, staring out of the window, transformed in the minds of the people into a visionary presence.

The tone of the novel—questioning, teasing, instructing, mischievous, confident—invites comparison with the work of Salman Rushdie. Both writers have a delight in magic and in myth and a zest for the eccentricities of human existences. But towards the end of *Waterland* some of the instructional passages—on eels, for instance—become a little tiresome, as by now all the narrative threads are ready to be tugged into the final pattern and it is irritating to have to wait. Also, at times the narrator's declarations about history do not carry quite the weight they should. Graham Swift lacks the intellectual stamina of Salman Rushdie.

The best passages—of which there are many—describe Tom Crick's childhood, swimming in the lock, playing at sex with his future wife Mary, his fear of his elder brother, 15-year-old Mary's nightmare abortion. All these scenes are presided over, actually or in spirit, by the eerie and powerful presence of potato-headed Dick who is in a way far more the tragic hero of *Waterland* than Tom Crick, bright and full of rhetoric. Dick is part of an older England, the England of Fen and fairy tale.

> Sally Emerson, in a review of "Waterland," in The Illustrated London News, *Vol. 271, No. 7024, November, 1983, p. 92.*

WILLIAM H. PRITCHARD

Graham Swift, who has published two previous novels and a collection of stories within the past four years, is committed among other things to history and to story-telling (the narrator and hero of *Waterland* teaches history in a London secondary school), therefore to making things difficult for readers who want easy and direct access to the facts.

As if to warn such readers, Tom Crick, the narrator, tells us on the novel's first page that when he was young—he is now 53—he, his father, and his retarded elder brother Dick "lived in a fairy-tale place."

"In a lock-keeper's cottage," he continues, "by a river, in the middle of the Fens. Far away from the wide world. And my father, who was a superstitious man, liked to do things in such a way as would make them seem magical and occult. So he would always set his eel traps at night."

Everything in these sentences is thoroughly expanded in the book that follows. A few pages later, one of Tom Crick's students scornfully interrupts his teacher's history lesson on the French Revolution by insisting that history is a fairy tale; while the lock, the river, the watery Fens ("Ours was the marsh country," an epigraph from *Great Expectations* alerts us) are present throughout the book. And the eels not only have a role in the narrator's story ("*Historia.* . . . any kind of narrative: account, tale, story" says the other epigraph) but receive a 12-page excursus on their genesis and (as it were) life style.

Any attempt to steer an orderly course through such a novel is perilous, since *Waterland* is designed to subvert such an operation. Though the book is filled with continuities, its essence is discontinuity; its narrative style varies from catechism and self-laceration (the history teacher at his lesson), to "impersonal" accounts of a family's history over the generations (the Atkinsons, of whom Tom's mother is one) to disquisitions on drainage in the Fens, or the malign effects of the east wind, or the migration habits of eels. But essentially *Waterland* unfolds from two events presented at the outset. First, the discovery, one summer night in 1937, when the narrator was a boy of 10 living in the lock-keeper's cottage on the river Leem, of a dead body—Freddy Parr, rival for the girl Tom is later to marry—washed up against the sluice gate. Second, the grown-up Tom's discovery, 43 years later, that he is to be retired from his school and that his subject, history, is being "phased out." But in fact the phasing out of history is really a phasing out of Crick's history, since his childless wife has scandalized the community by stealing another woman's baby. History is indeed his and her story, and Tom reacts by telling bits of these stories to his class.

Mr. Swift is an extremely self-conscious novelist, and a most resourceful one. Sometimes, one feels, almost too resourceful. . . .

Mr. Swift is so committed to seeing around perspectives, undermining his own assertions, squeezing the narrator between the pincers of past and present, being ironic at the expense of what somebody didn't know but somebody now does, that the effect he creates is rather like that of a three-ring circus. One yearns for a whiff of directness, a change in the narrative weather. "Once upon a time there was a future history teacher and a future history teacher's wife for whom things went wrong, so—since you cannot dispose of the past, since things must be—they had to make do." Assuredly, and in Mr. Swift's novel, as in history, things are *bound* to go wrong. Yet the admission could perhaps be made less theatrically and with less self-congratulation (look how much I know about my own and mankind's ignorance, presumption, folly, inevitable self-deception). In such a book of "reality-obscuring drama" there is also a quotient of hot air. . . .

But these are excesses of what is, throughout the book, a sustained narrative energy. Mr. Swift has some strong writers behind him as precursors. . . . Yet he is his own man insofar as he manages to bring off more than one extended sequence which, though recognizably a tour de force, also comes across, for all the narrative self-consciousness and protective irony, as splendid realistic presentation. There is the chapter entitled "About the East Wind," for instance, which begins by tracing that wind to its source ("It has its birth in the Arctic Ocean, north of Siberia. It steals round the northerly tip of the Urals.") and ends with it dispersing the mists and rustling the river Leem—and also rustling the holly bushes in Hockwell Churchyard where Tom's mother is buried, a victim of the influenza the wind had brought in its wake.

It is finally the past in its pastness which the novel and the novelist most care about. For all the book's ironical awareness directed at the perils of nostalgia, there is a moment late in the story when the narrator speaks parenthetically to his insane wife: "Do you remember, Mary, long ago, long ago? When there were no TV sets or tower blocks, no rockets to the moon, no contraceptive pills, no tranquillisers or pocket calculators, no supermarkets or comprehensive schools, no nuclear missiles . . . when there were steam-trains and fairy-tales . . . when the lighters passing on the Leem still wore on their prows, from olden times, two crossed yellow ears of barley? Do you remember, that windmill? That journey we made to Wash Fen Mere?"

Suddenly the novel's elaborate structure seems less interesting than the core of feelings touched through the juxtaposition of modern conveniences with those yellow ears of barley and that journey to Wash Fen Mere. Yet, as in fact the memory of lost treasures takes on poignancy only through such a contrast, so moments of simple yearning, simple truth as in the above memory, take on their charm through the complicated, even tortured narrative out of which they emerge. "Curiosity begets love. It weds us to the world," says the narrator at one point.

Obviously Graham Swift agrees, and has written a book in rueful praise of these essentially human, and doomed, qualities.

*William H. Pritchard, ''The Body in the River Leem,''
in* The New York Times Book Review, *March 25,
1984, p. 9.*

MICHAEL GORRA

Waterland has the ambition and intelligence, but not the passion or courage, of a masterpiece. The first book by the young English writer Graham Swift to be published in America, it is an absorbing novel of ideas presented as the *apologia pro vita sua* of Tom Crick, an English history teacher in his mid-50s who, as the novel opens, has just been forced to accept early retirement. In response to his students' belief that history is a "fairy-tale" and only the "here and now" matters, Crick has abandoned the formal curriculum to tell stories about his childhood in East England's Fens. (p. 392)

Waterland is a deeply conservative novel, but its conservatism is built not on complacency but on a classical stoicism.

Where *Waterland* fails is in its style. Tom Crick is too much the phlegmatic Fenman, too completely the dispassionate historian of the *Annales* school, to bother much about individuals, and since Swift does not undercut him, his limitations are the novel's. *Waterland* lacks passion, or rather its passion is all for history itself and not for the people who are affected by it. It is so enthralled by the idea of the inescapability of the past that it denies its characters the free will and emotional range that its plot of murder, madness, abortion, incest and suicide requires. The novel is consequently most successful the more nearly it approaches a work of history. Crick's impersonal account of the growth of the Atkinsons' wealth, for example, carries far more conviction than that of his reaction to his wife's madness.

Waterland's weaknesses stem from the fact that Swift is far more interested in the metaphoric qualities of the Fens than in their physical ones. For all the brilliance of his controlling metaphor, Swift's language is not resourceful enough to convey a landscape richly, intensely, passionately seen. No matter how often he mentions their monotony, one never quite feels the power of the Fens as a motive force in the lives of their inhabitants, never feels the psychological effects of landscape as one does in Hardy or Bruce Chatwin's recent *On the Black Hill*.

Small wonder, then, that *Waterland*'s characters come close to being props through which Swift can express his persuasive but programmatic vision of history. He lacks the novelist's final courage, the willingness to be surprised by what his art discloses. *Waterland* is intellectually bold, provocative and challenging in a way that many nearly perfect novels are not. But it is too sure of itself, too convinced a priori that phlegm and silt are all that matters, to earn fully the praise with which one would like to reward its strengths. (pp. 393-94)

Michael Gorra, ''Silt and Sluices,'' in The Nation,
Vol. 238, No. 12, March 31, 1984, pp. 392-94.

JONATHAN PENNER

All but one of the stories [in *Learning to Swim and Other Stories*] are first-person narratives. Many concern men of science—chemistry, medicine, mathematics, zoology. Most stake their plots on the fens of family, on the marshes of marriage.

They seem, in part, repetitive. Swift has a favorite epistemological question—if a thing exists but is not known to exist, is that different from its not existing?—and a favored ending device—the imagined reappearance of someone who had died. And yet, these stories are also rich in unusual situations, fresh writing and original insights.

Often their opening lines are particularly deft, showing how well simple means can draw a reader into a story: ''Mrs. Singleton had three times thought of leaving her husband.'' ''Uncle Walter had his own theory of the value of zoos.'' ''The day they let me out of the hospital I went for a long walk round the streets.''

As may be guessed already, Swift's forte is psychological dissection. He is particularly acute on the war between the sexes, leading us through labyrinths that tunnel to the enemy's heart:

''I blamed my wife because I myself felt to blame for what had happened and if I blamed my wife, unjustly, she could then accuse me, and I would feel guilty, as you should when you are to blame. Also I felt that by wronging my wife, by hurting her when she had been hurt already, I would be driven by my remorse to do exactly what was needed in the circumstances: to love her.''

The best stories are the first two [''**Learning to Swim**'' and ''**Hoffmeier's Antelope**'']. . . .

These first two stories suggest a quirkily strong collection and most of the remaining nine contain passages, at least, that are vividly imagined. Even unforgettable: a frenzied gang of boys using a dead pigeon for a soccer ball.

But several of the stories are peculiarly impersonal. They suggest studies in the economics of emotion: arid Anyman versus angry Anywoman. They are more concerned with feelings than with the characters who feel them.

Other stories fall into contrivance and melodrama. In ''**The Son**,'' for instance, a man devotes his life to concealing from his adopted son the facts of his birth. At the end of the story, in a pat reversal, the son stuns his adoptive father with the news that the latter was himself adopted.

The last and longest story, ''**The Watch**,'' has a frankly supernatural premise. Because they possess a perpetual-motion watch, males of the Krepski family never die of natural causes. The story works itself out with Gothic twists, including death by lightning-bolt, until the watch is finally stopped by the touch of a newborn baby. When such mysterious powers control a story, the human characters hardly matter at all.

These stories are of thoroughly mixed merit. Swift writes grand scenes, magical paragraphs—and finds as many ways to fail as succeed. There is something intrepid in his readiness to follow his nose. His story collection looks like the laboratory of a novelist.

Jonathan Penner, ''In the Laboratory of a Novelist,'' in Book World—The Washington Post, April 14, 1985, p. 8.

MICHAEL GORRA

Taken together, **Learning to Swim and Other Stories** and **The Sweet-Shop Owner** suggest the degree to which the theme of **Waterland**—the inescapability of history—provides a motive for Mr. Swift's work as a whole.

In all his books he suggests that inescapability by concentrating on families whose very structure provides a reminder of the past—families marked by death or divorce or perhaps, as in **Waterland**, by a retarded child. In the story ''**The Son**,'' for example, Mr. Swift adopts the voice of a Greek restaurant owner in London, who has never been able to tell his son, who is now 35, that he was adopted after his natural parents died in World War II. Then the son goes on vacation to Greece, and in their old neighborhood learns—but why spoil it? Yet while Mr. Swift does provide an ending out of Maupassant, both unexpected and convincing, it does not surmount the author's inability to create a voice with the bite and tang of the immigrant's demotic the story requires. Unfortunately, many of the stories in **Learning to Swim** suffer from similar flaws. Mr. Swift often writes in the first person, and yet the voices he adopts in doing so seem awkwardly worn, like a jacket, borrowed for a special occasion, that does not quite fit. While the appeal of **The Sweet-Shop Owner** outweighs its interest as a prelude to **Waterland** and increases my admiration for Mr. Swift's work, most of his stories seem minor—pleasant reading but no more.

Two of them, however, do stand out. In ''**The Watch**'' Mr. Swift makes time itself his subject, in an engagingly gloomy fantasy about a magic watch, ''proof against age and against all those processes by which we are able to say that a man's time runs out.'' (p. 11)

Even better, though, is [''**Learning to Swim**''], a perfect, very English piece about a bad marriage, written with the merciless intelligence of a story by Doris Lessing. . . . By exploring their memories, Mr. Swift manages to collapse their whole hate-filled married life into a brief account of a swimming lesson Mr. Singleton gives their son, Paul, off a beach in Cornwall—an action that takes just the few minutes one needs to read the story itself. Mr. Swift cuts the story loose from chronological time, not to escape it but to suggest how the seemingly random events of the past have conspired to produce this particular moment, in which both story and marriage crystallize around Paul's decision, in swimming for the first time on his own, to strike out to sea alone.

Mr. Swift uses a similar technique in **The Sweet-Shop Owner**, which describes the last day in the life of its title character, Willy Chapman. But in moving through Willy's memory with all the skill of an impressionist master like Ford Madox Ford, Mr. Swift makes that day contain all the others. . . . [The] plot here does not matter as much as Willy's consciousness, and in particular his consciousness of his own life's rhythms: ''Up at five-fifteen. Wash, shave. . . . Breakfast: two eggs, soft-boiled . . . tea and toast, at five-thirty. Time enough not to hurry, to dress neatly, to gather his briefcase . . . to kiss her . . . to drive to Briar Street in time to collect and mark up the papers, to arrange the shelves, to open at seven-thirty. And Sundays the same, only an hour later.''

And so on, through an oddly poetic life, made—like most poetry—of a rhythmic repetition and variation, a rhythm whose power Mr. Swift suggests through the way in which Willy not just varies but violates that rhythm on his last day alive. (pp. 11-12)

Mr. Swift alternates chapters describing Willy's last day with others containing his memory of his life as a whole, a technique that as Willy's memory approaches the novel's present produces a terrifying and painfully sad sense of the way time's passage makes the walls of his life close in. To me that sense far outweighs the novel's main weakness—its defective analysis of the emotional web within Willy's family. . . . ***The Sweet-Shop Owner*** is on the whole a remarkable novel—remarkable for its evocation of the catch in the throat of fatherhood, for the sharp comedy with which Mr. Swift describes the bickering of Willy's shop assistants, above all for the skill behind Mr. Swift's ambitious account of the changes time brings to the street where Willy has his shop, to the greengrocer across the way, the barber, the real-estate agent. There is a touch of Joyce in Graham Swift's revelation of the hidden poetry of small men's lives, and ***The Sweet-Shop Owner*** joins *Waterland* in establishing him as one of the brightest promises the English novel has now to offer. (p. 12)

Michael Gorra, "When Life Closes In," in The New
York Times Book Review, *June 23, 1985, pp. 11-12.*

Guy Vanderhaeghe

1951-

Canadian short story writer and novelist.

Vanderhaeghe is the author of two collections of short stories and a novel. His first book, *Man Descending* (1982), gained popular and critical acclaim and was awarded the Governor General's Literary Award for fiction. Critics praised Vanderhaeghe for his accurate dialogue, precision of detail, and skillful character development. Most of the twelve stories in this collection revolve around characters who are despondent, aimless, and unsuccessful. As David Carpenter noted, however, "it's the small glow in the best of these people—the thing that makes them human—that you remember, that hopeless hope of one leper comforting another."

Vanderhaeghe's second collection, *The Trouble with Heroes and Other Stories* (1983), likewise depicts unheroic men and their uneventful lives. While the stories in *Man Descending* are primarily set in and capture the mood of the Saskatchewan prairie, the stories in *The Trouble with Heroes* include such subjects as early biblical tales and American and Parisian historical events. *My Present Age* (1984), Vanderhaeghe's first novel, revolves around Ed, the protagonist of the title story and of "Sam, Soren, and Ed" from *Man Descending*. The earlier stories depict Ed's failing marriage and his attempts at reconciliation; the novel continues to explore Ed's efforts to piece together his life. While Vanderhaeghe's later work has been less favorably reviewed than *Man Descending*, Louis K. MacKendrick acknowledged the "sometimes arresting imaginative touches" of the stories in *The Trouble with Heroes,* and Douglas Barbour claimed that *My Present Age* "isn't simply the apprentice work of a coming writer but a highly successful work of art in itself."

(See also *Contemporary Authors,* Vol. 113.)

W. P. KINSELLA

In *Man Descending,* Vanderhaeghe demonstrates a great deal of poise and maturity as he explores men at various stages of life, through the eyes of narrators both very young and very old. There is also a wide diversity in tone and voice, while the moods of the stories range from manic to morose.

The best stories in any collection are invariably ones of high energy, of intensity, where no matter the moral or the message, the reader is first entertained. Such a story is **"Drummer,"** not only the best in the collection, but one of the strongest stories I have encountered in recent years. **"Drummer"** can be, and I have used it as, a teaching model for the short story—voice, tone, mood, character development, are all used to perfection. (p. 14)

In **"Drummer"** bewildered teenager Billy Simpson tells the story. He has a star-athlete, hell-raising older brother, who is also a bully and an informer. On a bet, the brother dates a girl Billy cares for because "she seemed like a very nice person

Photograph by Adrian Ewins. Courtesy of Guy Vanderhaeghe

who maybe had what Miss Clark says are principles." The older brother discovers that the girl does indeed have principles, abandons her to Billy, escaping with Billy's more worldly date. Much to Billy's chagrin the girl's "principles" dictate that to the end of the harrowing evening she is still the brother's date. At 16 Billy's life may well be in descent, as he attends the girl's church, against his father's wishes, trying vainly to understand why the girl behaves as she does. What makes this story a bittersweet sensation is Vanderhaeghe's perfect ear for dialogue.

Billy Simpson appears again in **"Cages,"** a brilliant story about choices, a story where man is descending literally, as well as figuratively, for the cages of the title are the elevators used to transport miners to the interior of the earth.

In [**"Man Descending"**], Ed, a self-indulgent loser, finds his marriage breaking up. On one hand he wishes to prevent the break-up, while on the other hand the break-up fits his theory about life. Ed believes that each life and career follows an arc, peaking, then, descending. Ed believes his life is in descent. A self-fulfilling prophecy. The descent continues in the closing story **"Sam, Soren, and Ed,"** where Ed comes at least partially to terms with his inability to will himself to do what must be done.

What these stories have in common is that in each story there is a man descending. (pp. 14-15)

In a number of these stories the descent is toward mental un-
balance and death. . . .

These are technically delightful stories with multi-themes and
layers of meaning. The "death stories" though often moving
and profound, are less successful than, say, **"Drummer,"**
"Cages," and **"The Watcher."** However, at all times Guy
Vanderhaeghe is a writer in command of his subject matter;
he displays a deftness of touch and maturity of vision seldom
seen in first collections. These are stories to be reread and
remembered. (p. 15)

W. P. Kinsella, "Lives of Boys and Men," in Books
in Canada, *Vol. 11, No. 7, August-September, 1982,
pp. 14-15.*

CARY FAGAN

Virtually all of Vanderhaeghe's stories [in *Man Descending*]
concern men losing their hold on their destinies and struggling
feebly to cling to what little dignity is left. Powerlessness is
often due to place as characters writhe in hospitals and asylums
or in the more subtle situations endure unemployment and early
retirement. Or else they're not in control for another reason;
they're children. Even for adults the condition of descent is a
kind of return to childhood's subservience, only without the
promise of growing up. Managing to kill that early promise
are marriage, work, drink and the inevitable disillusionment
of time. Vanderhaeghe is more interested in marking that downward slope than he is in showing how a man got started down
it to begin with.

I suspect that the story **"Reunion"** will be widely anthologized,
as it deserves. About a prairie boy watching his mother and
father feud over a visit to her relatives (the father knows her
family perceives him as a failure) and their weary reconciliation, it is told in a voice as clear as crystal. It's too bad that
Vanderhaeghe pushes the climax just beyond the edge of credibility, but the last lines, a kind of sigh, are near perfect.

"What I Learned From Caesar" and **"Man Descending"** are
both intelligent and heartfelt works, told with precision and
style. The writer's narrative technique is admirably fluent and
he changes perspective easily like the focus on a camera. A
humorous, more earthy tone comes through in stories like
"Drummer" and **"Cages"** but the Holden Caulfield imitation
tires and Vanderhaeghe has trouble grafting in a serious theme.

The first story in the collection, **"The Watcher,"** shows both
Vanderhaeghe's skills and weaknesses. A sensitive boy observes the adult world of morality and sex with puzzlement,
finally discovering a small insight. Neatly done, it still shows
the marks of formula and is hardly fresh. Vanderhaeghe is one
of the few Canadian writers who sounds occasionally too slick,
as if he had his eye on the *New Yorker,* but I admire him even
for that ability.

I won't bother to dwell on the marginally interesting or even
quite bad stories such as **"Dancing Bear,"** **"A Taste For Perfection,"** and **"Sam, Soren, and Ed."** That the author should
have written them is no crime, but they don't belong in this
collection. In **"Going To Russia"** the narrator tells how he
likes Russian novels because only in them does "unhappiness
find a meaning." In a few good stories Vanderhaeghe has
depicted how that unhappiness feels. Now I'd like to see him
tackle, like the Russians, what it means.

Cary Fagan, "Down but Not Out," in The Canadian
Forum, *Vol. LXII, No. 721, September, 1982, p. 34.*

ARITHA van HERK

[The stories in *Man Descending*] are good stories, extraordinary
stories. They have the smell, the look, the accent of fiction
that introduces an archetypal but strange world, a world that
predicates fiction. It is a world born out of Saskatchewan, a
Saskatchewan idiosyncratically and flavorfully itself rather than
a romantic rendition of prairie and sky. For too long we have
measured Saskatchewan by W. O. Mitchell's ruler, *Who Has
Seen the Wind.* That vision of the Canadian prairie was certainly
valid, but how refreshing now to have Vanderhaeghe swivel
the mirror and show us another side of both the landscape and
the young boy growing up within it.

These twelve stories fall into roughly two halves. The first six
deal with childhood and adolescence, the adult world as perceived through the eyes if not the point of view of those who
stand to inherit it. Vanderhaeghe captures the intricate vivi-
sectionings of family politics and the tension between appearance and reality the way these things strike children. Still, his
little boys are more than round-eyed spectators; they participate
in the twistings of fate and the fruits of action. In **"The Watcher,"**
for example, a young voyeur is confronted with the responsibility of seeing and forced to choose between truth and complicity.

The last six stories show how age and maturity do not necessarily dissolve bewilderment or preclude indecision and anxiety. **"Going to Russia"** and **"A Taste for Perfection"** reveal
how mental and physical sickness can exhilarate or numb a
man. Man's furious revolt and puzzlement in the face of growing old dominate **"The Expatriates' Party"** and **"Dancing
Bear."** **"Man Descending"** and **"Sam, Soren, and Ed"** are
about middle age's degeneration and regeneration.

These stories, however, are not filled by inertia. They have a
force and body that is mesmerizing; their author's range is
reflected in their content. Vanderhaeghe has an ear for vernacular that is flawless. His characters would fit in the American Gothic tradition, but with what virile anger, what righteous
persecution. (pp. 267-68)

Without a doubt, **"Drummer"** and **"Cages"** are the best stories
in this collection. They are both devastating depictions of male
adolescence, sibling rivalry, man love/hate. The poignant image of "two people who can't dance dancing to the beat of a
guy who can't drum" evokes the terrible hopefulness of the
young. It is in these stories that the author reveals his best
sense of character; I have never read a more honest portrayal
of young males, their rage and brutality, their tenuous broth-
erhood. It is in this area that Vanderhaeghe excels. He is clearly
a man's writer, who shows us the male world from childhood
to old age without apologizing, without adding the ballasts of
philosophical motivation, a representation of the human condition. (p. 268)

Vanderhaeghe's stories are not without faults. The inevitable
bleakness of his vision is sometimes itself pretentious, and he
needs to overcome a young writer's dependence on overt and
not always appropriate symbols. But this is a fresh voice, one
to be welcomed. I only hope it indicates a new direction in
"men's writing." (p. 269)

*Aritha van Herk, in a review of "Man Descending,"
in* Western American Literature, *Vol. XVIII, No. 3,
November, 1983, pp. 267-69.*

ANTHONY BUKOSKI

I remember W. P. Kinsella two summers ago telling me about Guy Vanderhaeghe's wonderful stories. A little later that summer, in a review of *Man Descending* in *Books in Canada,* he wrote that Vanderhaeghe "displays a deftness of touch and maturity of vision seldom seen in first collections," and called *Man Descending* "stories to be reread and remembered" [see excerpt above]. Unfortunately, I can't say the same of this slim, leather-bound volume, *The Trouble with Heroes and Other Stories,* which apparently was written before *Man Descending* and held until now by Borealis. The one memorable piece here, **"Parker's Dog,"** is marred by sloppy editing. (p. 19)

"Parker's Dog" takes place in what to Vanderhaeghe appears to be a familiar world—greasy spoons, third-rate hotels, guys down on their luck. I appreciate his ability to capture that milieu. Vanderhaeghe is a "bump-and-a-beer" kind of writer, judging from **"Parker's Dog"** and several other stories here. Not for him tea dances and white wine. After Roy, one of the lost in **"Parker's Dog,"** despoils Kilber's car outside the Dream City Motel, he heads for an Al-Anon meeting. "My name is Roy," he says, "and I'm an alcoholic," and so begins his attempt at self-respect. **"Parker's Dog"** is a funny, tough-edged story that succeeds partly because of Vanderhaeghe's ear for dialogue and irreverent, inventive phrasing. (pp. 19-20)

Three other stories exhibit a tough-guy sensibility. Though captivating in its dialogue and black humour, the title piece ends so abruptly it remains a vignette. **"The Trouble with Heroes"** deals with returning Second-World-War veterans, one of whom, a burn victim, wonders whether to wear the rubber nose they've given him in the hospital. The protagonist's dilemma is deliberately ironic: how to make his return to Saskatchewan appear heroic and triumphant when in reality he'd lost his nose falling under a car after a drunken sexual encounter.... More fully developed, this story, like **"Parker's Dog,"** would have been a thoroughly memorable journey into a world without heroes.

All seven stories deal with failed heroes of one sort or another and vary widely in time: **"No Man Could Bind Him"** takes place during the time of Christ; **"Cafe Society"** during the Paris Exposition of 1889; **"The King Is Dead"** during the November of John Kennedy's assassination; and **"Parker's Dog"** the present.

Vanderhaeghe possesses great talent and promise, but in this early work he has fallen a bit short. (p. 20)

Anthony Bukoski, "Waking Up in Dream City," in Books in Canada, Vol. 13, No. 3, March, 1984, pp. 19-20.

MATTHEW CLARK

Guy Vanderhaeghe's earlier collection, *Man Descending* . . . , received a 1982 Governor General's Award and a great deal of well-deserved praise. *The Trouble With Heroes* is perhaps not quite so good, but his gifts are still evident. Vanderhaeghe's control of style is unfailing in a variety of modes: in **"Parker's Dog,"** for example, his capturing of the vernacular is perfect. This collection ranges more widely than *Man Descending* both in setting and points of view. One story is set in Paris in 1889, and two others are Bible stories retold from a minor character's point of view. Not every story in this collection convinces me entirely—the endings of **"The King Is Dead"** and **"Parker's Dog"** seem weak, for instance—but every story has its virtues.

Vanderhaeghe's greatest gift is his ability to make his stories matter to the characters and to the reader.

Matthew Clark, "Travelling Beyond the Boundaries of Small-Town Realism," in Quill and Quire, Vol. 50, No. 6, June, 1984, p. 32.

DAVID CARPENTER

[What *Man Descending*] offers us sounds dubious at the outset, a descent into the squalor and pain of the world's losers: children at play who learn almost nothing about recreation, much about joyless endurance; people losing their jobs, their sanity, their lives; marriages in which genuine affection breeds little more than futility. Our descent into these lives involves a remarkable process of discovery, one made possible by Vanderhaeghe's thorough grasp of his prairie people, radar ears for dialogue, and thorny, elegant prose. One breathes in the squalor, seizes at best a guarded hope which is close to despair and returns, perhaps to the relative comfort of home. One comes to know his people so well that one participates vicariously but powerfully in their agonies. Of course what I'm getting at is empathy; reading a Vanderhaeghe story at its most significant level becomes an act of empathy.

His plucky women, tough kids, cage dwellers, farmers, and invalids never kill themselves. A bit like the characters of Sinclair Ross, they endure until the end of their story. The best of them learn how to accept their limited habitat. This seems to be the biggest step toward perceiving the human possibilities of this bleak terrain. . . .

The worst of them sacrifice others. Big Paul of **"How the Story Ends,"** a monster of insensitivity, suppresses human instincts in anyone he comes near. Gene Simpson's violence smoulders in one story (**"Drummer"**), and breaks out of control in the other (**"Cages"**). Robert Thompson preys upon the weak once too often and is finally broken by the biggest hen in the barnyard (**"The Watcher"**).

It's the squalor of this world that hits you first, but it's the small glow in the best of these people—the thing that makes them human—that you remember, that hopeless hope of one leper comforting another. In **"A Taste for Perfection,"** for example, the dying protagonist Tom Ogle finally looks his mortality in the eye, accepts it, and learns to comfort an old woman who keeps mistaking him for her dead husband. Almost all of these stories, in one way or another, are about love. (p. 116)

The weakest story in the collection, I felt, was **"The Expatriates' Party."** It seemed a bit crowded: too much detail and too many partially realized characters for twenty-two pages. Joe's story is a compelling one but it takes on the dishevelled quality of his mind as he gropes for his identity in his retirement years. I thought it might have been better as a novella.

I'm quibbling. The critic can do little else with a book of stories as deftly plotted and penned as these—except rave, applaud, pray there are more to come. (p. 117)

David Carpenter, "Form & Empathy," in Canadian Literature, No. 101, Summer, 1984, pp. 115-17.

ALBERTO MANGUEL

Every hero is an outcast, and Ed, the hero of Guy Vanderhaeghe's first novel, *My Present Age* . . . , is no exception.

Singled out from the fold, the hero looks at society from a vantage-point, a Darien (as Ed, inspired by Keats, calls it). Ed is fat; Ed is boorish; Ed is a would-be (or rather would-not-be) writer: for a long time he called himself a novelist, then produced a mock-western that he despises, and now lives with the guilt of this *oeuvre manquée*. But above all, Ed is a man with a knightly mission: to rescue a damsel in distress—his wife who, fed up with him, has left.

Everything and everyone conspire against Ed's heroic deed: his downstairs neighbour wants him evicted, accuses him of being a pervert, parks his car in such a way that Ed's mini cannot enter the lot; Ed's college roommate has become Ed's wife's lawyer in their divorce suit; Ed's wife, who once saved him from a band of thugs and who believed in his literary talents, now cannot stand the sight of him and refuses to be rescued. And then there is the Beast: the host of a "public opinion" radio show, upholder of public morality, a dangerously successful bigot. In spite of the world's hostility, like Don Quixote, Ed battles on. . . .

[Guy Vanderhaeghe] has built his novel around (and in the style of) Ed's paranoia: *My Present Age* is the portrait of one man seen by himself in the distorted mirror of his own mind. Too witty for his contemporaries ("Any idea what genius is? The infinite capacity for taking pains?"), too ill-suited for an acceptable place in this world ("I found myself in the unfamiliar position of having no one to disappoint"), Ed is a hero who is also the village idiot.

Unfortunately this concentration of character works to the novel's disadvantage. In the short stories in which Ed appears (in *Man Descending*) the reader bears well Ed's maddening efforts to impose himself and his views. In the novel the reader reading for the plot finds Ed's efforts trying, his quest interminable, his paranoia unpleasantly disturbing, and soon loses interest in the thinly imagined adventures. Vanderhaeghe's talent lies in the crafting of characters, not in devising the characters' actions, and a novel such as *My Present Age* seems to require a story that would justify Ed's heroics.

> *Alberto Manguel, in a review of "My Present Age,"*
> *in* Books in Canada, *Vol. 13, No. 8, October, 1984,*
> *p. 31.*

MICHAEL THORPE

The last two stories of Guy Vanderhaeghe's *Man Descending* centred on one fat Canadian misfit and mocker of self and others named Ed. In one story his marriage to the beautiful Victoria is adrift, in the other they are separated and his attempted reconciliation fails. Ed is a comic study in intelligent incapacity for action. His talent for wry self-analysis is concentrated in the final words of **"Sam, Soren and Ed"**: "Between understanding and willing is where excuses and evasions have their being." The words are from Søren Kierkegaard; Ed places them self-mockingly as the epigraph to his only completed novel, a western stuffed with the clichés of the lone frontiersman.

The stories read like extracts from a longer narrative, and now we have one in *My Present Age* whose title evidently stems (though not overtly) from Kierkegaard's anatomy of his corrupt world, *The Present Age*. Vanderhaeghe does not cite it, but such extracts from Kierkegaard as these seem appropriate: "to be neither moral nor immoral is merely ambiguous"; "the present age is essentially one of understanding lacking in pas-

sion." Ed had already in **"Sam, Soren and Ed"** likened himself to Kierkegaard "who, at least in the flesh, seemed to have much the same effect on people that I have. Like me, the gnarled little Dane didn't mix well at parties, was inclined to goad people into a frenzy, and made too much of a love affair."

Ed introduces himself wallowing in his sleazy apartment, deserted by Victoria, "shovelling home the Cocoa Puffs" while his next-floor neighbour McMurtry vilifies him on "Brick Bats and Bouquets," the call-in show of Tom Rollins, whom Ed dubs the Beast. His ludicrous vendetta with McMurtry and the Beast pads out the central action which, moving somewhat jerkily between past and present, explores Ed's failure in life and love—though, if one recalls the earlier stories, it will seem more embroidery than exploration. The first person, present tense narrative would be virtually static but for periodic excursions into farce and slapstick.

In the second chapter Ed, and perhaps his creator, shows his hand. He recalls his never convincing seduction of the beautiful Victoria—"everything I wasn't, assured, idealistic, ungrubby." Yet it is "Fatso" we must recognize as an idealist within. When Victoria leaves him, instead of "acting like an adult" and "bowing out nobly" according to "the standards of the present age" he goes "in hot pursuit of the woman I love." When he discovers Victoria's dilemma, that she is pregnant by her lover—Ed's *döppelganger,* a fat up-and-coming academic who is a success, or will be if she aborts and gives him time to finish *Fantasies and Fasces: A Study of the Ideology of Popular Fiction in the Modern Age*—he sees an heroic opportunity. His picaresque pursuit of her, the action's main thread, he hopes may achieve reconciliation and anchor his rudderless life. . . .

The end is consistent with Ed's pathetic degeneration, but not intensely engaging; Vanderhaeghe has failed to bounce us beyond the *Man Descending* stories. Ed cannot develop, only expand, in an inflated—if sometimes funny and satirically acute—novel which compels reluctant sympathy with Victoria's rejection of its anti-hero in **"Man Descending"**: "being married to an adolescent is a bore."

> *Michael Thorpe, "Absorbed by His Dream," in* The
> Canadian Forum, *Vol. LXIV, No. 743, November,*
> *1984, p. 35.*

SUSAN GRIMBLY

[Vanderhaeghe's *My Present Age*] is his first novel, and with the longer form, he finds himself in a spot of trouble.

My Present Age takes a closer look at Ed, a cynical slob who figured in two stories from the first book. Ed has cashed in his life-insurance policy and quit his Eaton's job, content to hang around his apartment reading youthful adventures such as *Shane* and *The Adventures of Huckleberry Finn*. Alas, there is an ornery neighbour downstairs who's sure Ed's on the dole, a radio announcer, a female friend, a student writer, and Victoria, the ex-wife, who proceed to clutter up Ed's life, trying to motivate him.

Ed tries to disentangle himself through buffoonery and practical jokes, but things get out of control until eventually he loses his hold on reality. . . .

It's an intelligent novel, questioning contemporary values, but it lacks cohesion and narrative power, and this stems from a central flaw in the author's creation: we are never given any reason why Ed falls to pieces. As nothing motivates Ed, so nothing motivates the story. There would seem to be a parallel with the grown-up Huck Finn character that Ed imagines as a broken-down drunk—the innocent dreamer sullied by society. But the parallel is not strongly drawn, and Ed is too sour to seem to have ever enjoyed such rapt Finn-like innocence.

Nevertheless, within the tragi-comic world Vanderhaeghe describes, he does forge a chain of emotionally potent scenes. Meshed together, they would have proven a more powerful novel.

> Susan Grimbly, in a review of "My Present Age," in Quill and Quire, Vol. 50, No. 11, November, 1984, p. 35.

LOUIS K. MacKENDRICK

[The title story of *The Trouble with Heroes*] and its successors are almost programmatically about consequences and the relativity of heroism. They have a similar perspective on existences that have the ostensible appearance of the antiheroic. **"The King Is Dead"** has the Kennedy assassination as its base measure, in "the limbo of unreality," as opposed to two boys' break-in at an arena and their killing of a scavenger's aged dog. The mean unheroic parallel with the Dallas event is implicit: more important is the narrator's final near-freedom from his more anarchic peer. **"The Prodigal"** is losing his painting, his woman, and his father in a prolonged deathwatch. The story is of failure of seeing: of perception, of insight, of literal sight. The heroism is in a final poignant reconciliation of the underachieving, irresolute son and his father—"I led him, blind man leading blind, both lost now in the strange empire of the senses." **"Parker's Dog,"** with its unhappy rash of typos, is a low-life tale of behaviour modification and oddly symbiotic relationships in the significantly named Dream City Motel. This narrative of dominance, alcoholism, obsession, and mean streets is almost perversely antiheroic in its demotic flavour.

"No Man Could Bind Him" fleshes out the biblical story of the madman of Gadara and Jesus' restoration of his humanity, here proposing a Greek half-brother to the demon-possessed Jew—indeed, many characters in this collection have particular demons. The effete Greek tells the before- and after-life of this man "too uncertain of his demons to be trusted." The "metamorphosis of madman into mystic" opposes the Grecian conception of the heroic life with the mean living and dying of those not living a romantic philosophy, those with a sense of sin. The lesson is absorbed: ". . . finally it was the invisible which allowed my brother to fling himself into freedom and cut the bonds of pain and necessity which bind most." The narrative remains virtually a schematic argument between two contrasting philosophies of life and belief. In another biblical story, **"Lazarus,"** the celebrated protagonist's afterlife is one of solitude; he believes he is condemned to await the Second Coming as Christ's only living witness, immortal but immortally weak in the flesh. (p. 88)

"Cafe Society" suggests another fundamental reduction, in the historical figure of Gabriel Dumont. "Commercially speaking you are a nonentity," he is told, as his sponsor seeks backing for a proposed Wild West Show in Paris of 1889. The Eiffel Tower stands as a metaphor for the superficiality of this society; it epitomizes a frivolous world where the hunter Dumont is lost "in an unfamiliar forest of silk hats." This hero is redeemed only by our recognition of his rank in Canadian history, and of his noble pathos.

The stories of **The Trouble with Heroes** generally lack the maturity, the balance, the fluidity, the thoroughness of character, the virtually seamless craftsmanship, the compelling nature, the dimension of emotion, the naturalness, the sheer narrative interest, and the depth of articulation of the writer's **Man Descending** (1982). One is led to suspect that they are his earlier work—yet to call them "promising" would deny their sometimes arresting imaginative touches and range, their prospects. (p. 89)

> Louis K. MacKendrick, "No Time for Heroes," in The Fiddlehead, No. 143, Spring, 1985, pp. 88-90.

DOUGLAS BARBOUR

Guy Vanderhaeghe has followed his impressive debut as a writer of short stories—**Man Descending** is certainly a worthy winner of the Governor General's Award, with its deadly accurate dialogue, its effective imagery and descriptions, its wit, and its humorously harrowing insight into the feelings of people who have somehow found themselves on the outside looking in, yet in a quaintly twentieth-century bourgeois fashion are so aware of the failings of those who are inside they wouldn't (and couldn't) join them for anything—with an equally impressive debut as a novelist in **My Present Age**.

Some early reviews of **My Present Age,** while acknowledging Vanderhaeghe's continuing power as a writer, suggest an unease with the novel. It is precisely that unease, plus the crafty way he goes about developing it, which convinces me that **My Present Age** isn't simply the apprentice work of a coming writer but a highly successful work of art in itself. For Vanderhaeghe, in choosing to write at even greater length about, and in the narrative voice of, Ed, the feckless protagonist of the final two stories in **Man Descending,** has chosen to attempt one of the most difficult feats in fiction—to make an unsympathetic character sympathetic without ever losing focus on the traits that make him such an unloveable S.O.B. He succeeds; in fact, he succeeds so well he had me laughing out loud one minute and stunned into silent shock the next. Such success is more than reason enough to praise and recommend **My Present Age** to all who care about contemporary fiction. . . .

Those who have read **Man Descending** will recall that in ["**Man Descending**"] and "**Sam, Soren, and Ed,**" Ed and Victoria suffered marital difficulties and breakup, though Ed fought hard to prevent Victoria from getting wholly out of his clutches. Many must have felt, as I did, that Ed's story was far from finished, and wanted to find out what happened next. What is causing unease in some readers is not that **My Present Age** doesn't answer the question but that it pulls no punches, and that although there are still scenes of extreme if also excruciating comedy it is essentially a work of palpable darkness, perhaps even defeat. (p. 151)

Vanderhaeghe masterfully shows everything from [Ed's] point of view yet also reveals his failings as an observer. Nevertheless, for all his faults, Ed has an unerring eye and ear for phoniness, and Vanderhaeghe allows that to emerge again and again. Indeed, it is because Ed is so wittily insightful that we put up with him, for he is even capable of seeing himself clearly upon occasion. But he is also obsessed: with a vision of a perfection that never existed except in his mind and which drives him upon his quest but makes him unable to offer Victoria anything she needs when he finally finds her.

Vanderhaeghe has created a sad-sack loser whose wit and intelligence render him somehow worthy of our complicity in his superb failure to measure up to society's demands. As his tale careens from slapstick comedy to unnerving *angst*, Ed holds our attention and our concern. . . .

Where [Vanderhaeghe] will go next, I don't know, but on the evidence of *My Present Age* as much as *Man Descending* he will go far. I for one look forward to reading the maps he will surely send back from his future forays. Meanwhile, *My Present Age* is black comedy at its intimate and subversive best. (p. 152)

Douglas Barbour, "Black Comedy," in Canadian *Literature, No. 105, Summer, 1985, pp. 151-52.*

ALASDAIR GRAY

In the 12 stories of *Man Descending* we meet a tough farming widow with a waitress daughter and a sick grandson, a miner with a teen-age family, a Belgian immigrant salesman and some professional people, most of whom are retired or dying or unemployed. Guy Vanderhaeghe is a prizewinning young Canadian writer introduced here to American readers for the first time. He convincingly describes more kinds of people than most writers, and uses a variety of voices. When he writes in the authorial third person and lifts his eyes from his characters to the scenery his prose once or twice becomes pulpy and inflated, but usually it is careful and easy to read. And what the stories have in common, besides their mostly Canadian settings, is a special sort of rage and hatred, the chilled social sort called contempt. Few books have shown it working in so many ways.

In **"What I Learned From Caesar,"** a Belgian salesman, married to "a woman of British stock," tries to do better in the world by hiding his origin. He has taken a step along the road to self-contempt, and, as his son observes, it gets him nothing in return: "My father was a lonely man, a stranger who made matters worse by pretending he wasn't." In 1931 the salesman is sacked by a boss whose last words are "Good luck, Dutchie!" This nickname has never before been used to his face. Brooding on it (having nothing else to do), he imagines the whole community has conspired against him, goes mad, assaults a local official and is put away.

"As the air to a bird or the sea to a fish," says William Blake, "so is contempt to the contemptible." But nobody can believe he is thoroughly contemptible and live for long. The salesman is a swimmer who manages to keep his head above a sea of contempt (mainly his own) before dismissal shoves him under it and he drowns. But this story is told by his son. How can the son, without despising himself, accept that his father was killed by a scornful word? In Caesar's *Gallic War* he reads that "of all people the Belgae are the most courageous."

"I read on, sharing Caesar's admiration for a people who would not submit but chose to fight and see glory in their wounds. I misread it all, and bent it until I was satisfied. I reasoned the way I had to, for my sake, for my father's. What was he but a man dishonoured by faceless foes? His instincts could not help but prevail, and like his ancestors, in the end, on that one day, what could he do but make the shadows real, and fight to be free of them?" Notice the lovely irony of this. The boy builds a respect for his father and himself on the one fact that his father tried to hide: the Belgian origin.

In **"What I Learned From Caesar"** the language picks carefully through the sad facts of the past for some grains that can be respected. Most of these stories can be coupled. **"The Watcher"** also has a narrator recollecting some events from his childhood, but here the language works in the opposite direction by cheapening everyone: "I trailed after her as she slopped back into the house in a pair of badly mauled, laceless sneakers." And often using glib insults to do it: "The silly bugger laughed." Or: "But any damn fool could see she was only waving goodbye."

A boy of 11 is watching his grandmother try to rid her home and her daughter of a smug, impudent student who forces his way in, having made the daughter pregnant. Had this story been told by Flannery O' Connor in words that conveyed squalor without underlining it, describing what was said and done without scornful comment, it would have been heroic. In Mr. Vanderhaeghe's story the narrator's contempt pours over everything like a thin, rancid custard, not least on the child who is the watcher. The boy enjoys spying on his sister's lover and lying about what he sees to the police, who finally take the man away. Had he told the truth, his grandmother would have made him suffer, and he is a sickly child afraid of pain, though with a sneaking pleasure in causing it. The contemptuous words that first seem a yellow custard poured over something finer become, on second reading, a deliberately presented jaundiced view, with a jaundiced observer squinting through his disease at events that confirm it. But I hate that shade of yellow.

The hard-boiled reader will prefer **"The Watcher"** to **"What I Learned From Caesar."** The soft-centered will reverse this preference. Mr. Vanderhaeghe's book should satisfy both. . . .

In her guide to Canadian literature Margaret Atwood suggests that Canadian writers are preoccupied by defeat because their country has a tradition of being managed by other people. . . .

"The Expatriates' Party" tackles the national problem . . . positively. It shows Canadians in London in the Royal Jubilee year: "They didn't much like England. But they could leave it at that. Home was what bothered them, seemed to nag at them like a sore tooth." A Québécois among them has an assurance that the rest envy. Someone asks him why he is so "together," so Québécois. "'What is the secret of our success?' said Daniel. 'We're like the Irish, or the Jews, or the South of the Confederacy. We don't forget. Anything. The good or the bad.' He laughed. 'You can see it in our faces.'" . . .

At the end of *A Portrait of the Artist as a Young Man*, James Joyce describes himself leaving a country he can hardly stand in order to forge the conscience of his race by writing books. The grounds of conscience and consciousness are always strengthened when a writer makes an entertaining communal memory out of our local catastrophes. If I made these tales sound dreary I have misled you. Nearly all repay close reading with solid entertainment.

Alasdair Gray, "Varieties of Contempt," in The New *York Times Book Review, October 13, 1985, p. 28.*

Geoffrey (Ansell) Wolff

1937-

American novelist, biographer, autobiographer, and critic.

Wolff is respected for his satirical novels and his nonfiction works in which he explores such themes as familial love, civic decay, freedom of choice, and the role of art in contemporary society. His characters often experience defeat, either through fate or their own personality flaws, yet Wolff tempers their failures with comic scenes and sardonic commentary. Wolff is generally praised for the humorous aspects of his works and for his vivid, exacting use of language.

In his first novel, *Bad Debts* (1969), Wolff depicts his protagonist, Benjamin Freeman, as lacking both emotional and financial resources. Through flashbacks, Wolff relates the disastrous effects Freeman has had on the people closest to him: his wife, who leaves him; his son, who inherits his father's flaws; and his cousin, a lawyer from whom Freeman frequently seeks aid. John Wain praised *Bad Debts* as "the work of a writer who has an excellent ear for the way people talk, an understanding eye for the way comedy intertwines with pathos, and a penetrating curiosity about human beings." Wolff's second novel, *The Sightseer* (1974), has as its protagonist a documentary filmmaker whose acclaimed first picture records the last days of his dying father. His manipulation of reality for the sake of art is contrasted with the humanitarianism of his twin brother. The central character of Wolff's next novel, *Inklings* (1977), is a literary critic who gives only negative notices to the books he reviews because of his own inability to write a novel. He is kidnapped by one of his former students and forced to edit the kidnapper's novel as well as to write a critical appraisal of it. *Providence* (1986) is generally considered to be Wolff's most accomplished work. This novel is set in Providence, Rhode Island, and chronicles the moral and physical decay of the city and its inhabitants. Wolff balances the tragic lives of his characters with witty dialogue to create what James Carroll termed "a novel to be read for pleasure, for pure enjoyment, because it brings a supremely light touch to its heavy subject."

Wolff's nonfiction works include *Black Sun: The Brief Transit and Violent Eclipse of Harry Crosby* (1976) and *The Duke of Deception: Memories of My Father* (1979). *Black Sun* is a biography of Harry Crosby, an avant-garde literary figure of the 1920s who is remembered more for his eccentricities and his bizarre suicide than for his work. *The Duke of Deception* is an affectionate reminiscence of Wolff's relationship with his father, a confidence man who spent several years in prison. Wolff has also contributed literary criticism to such periodicals as *The American Scholar, The New Republic*, and *Saturday Review*.

(See also *Contemporary Authors*, Vols. 29-32, rev. ed.)

SARA BLACKBURN

It's obvious from the first page of this funny, sad book [*Bad Debts*] that its author is a real writer, and it's just as evident

by the last that he is better than his material. Geoffrey Wolff's fifty-five-year-old hero, a pathological spendthrift and con man named Benjamin Freeman, here takes his place in the respectable literary tradition of endearing and memorable punks, and the process by which he does so is always really clever and really inventive.

Freeman is only one of the four stars featured in *Bad Debts:* the others are his colorless estranged wife . . . ; his anxiety-ridden cousin and lawyer, Maurice . . . ; and Freeman's son, Caxton, a veritable marvel of mediocrity who is repulsively at home in the scathingly observed world of middle-level Washington politics which provides part of the novel's setting. Each of these characters is beautifully realized, and there is a remarkable cameo appearance by the wife of a New York waiter, surely one of the most devastating harpies to have appeared in recent fiction.

Freeman's decision that he and Ann should live together again sets off a series of reverberations that form the novel's skeleton, but it is the flashbacks into the separate pasts of its leading characters, with their descriptions of the particular kinds of havoc Freeman has wreaked upon their lives, that give the book its substance. . . .

The trouble with *Bad Debts* (the year's best title) is that Wolff is doing it all with his left hand. His control is always perfect, but he is a writer of such imagination and skill that one feels he is being confined by his material instead of using it and taking risks at broader and (shudder) more important work. The obnoxious-but-lovable-little man who lives out his fantasies in real adventures which are, if not predictable, then predictably outrageous, has become too much of a dead-ended genre in current American fiction. This novel places Wolff at the top of that genre, but he should leave it to less talented writers; he deserves a category of his own, and I hope this flawless first novel is a giant step in that direction.

> *Sara Blackburn, "A New Star in the Tradition of Memorable Punks," in* Book World—Chicago Tribune, *November 23, 1969, p. 16.*

RICHARD P. BRICKNER

Bad Debts has scenes in it that make one wince in delighted discomfort. These scenes are in the same league with the best bitterly comic writing of recent years.... Even though it ends up failing for lack of emotional thrust, *Bad Debts* is a novel with honest-to-God touchstones in it, a novel to be recommended for virtues rare enough that one is grateful for even their qualified appearance.

In narrating the effect of Benjamin Freeman (né Freudemann), a toweringly rotten father and husband, on son Caxton and wife Ann, Geoffrey Wolff draws upon an extraordinarily rich bank of accurate and imaginative behavior, most generously in setting forth Benjamin's pretentiousness, selfishness, *schnorring,* and attendant paranoid bitching. Benjamin refuses to demand of himself everything he demands of those around him. His only job is the full-time acting-out of his versatile grandiosity....

Benjamin Freeman is a given evil. We know nothing about why he pretends and cheats—of what was done *to* him. This must be the chief reason the book is a gleaming car with an engine too small. Lacking an impelling history of his own, thus lacking the excuse that would give him more body and tension, Freeman can't give the novel of which he's prime mover a sufficient momentum. What the author is interested in doing, and succeeds in doing through beautiful, grim, slow-motion farce at the middle of his book, is to reveal that Caxton has been congenitally saddled with a treacherous version of his father's psychological syphilis.

Caxton is a bureaucrat on the make and on the rise in Washington, D.C. Going blind with his success, he commits a bad blunder he doesn't realize he's made until it's just a little bit too late to correct it: half-unwittingly, he flashes a potentially damaging hunch about his superior to a columnist, in the half-conscious hope of usurping his superior's place. Coming to, he tries to prevent the column's publication—frantically. Yet, when he is booted out of his job, he can't quite believe it: he has expected the chance to make it up to his boss "somehow," as Benjamin, more baldly, has lived in the expectation that he would get without having to give.

The entire Washington section of the book is marvelous, humanly letter-perfect.... [Mr. Wolff's] knowledge of the capital's avenues of ambition, and how their traffic writhes and bolts, is so complete the reader feels surrounded by it, invested with it.

We are left, though, after Caxton's climactic loss of footing, with half the novel to go, and it goes only fitfully. Towards the end, the characters and their emotions seem loosely connected, as if the emotions had been plucked down and attached to their owners without sufficient care. But so much of *Bad Debts* hums so firmly, so deeply, with accurate life, we can expect Wolff to pay what he owes us against our aroused expectations.

> *Richard P. Brickner, "A Grim, Gleaming Farce," in* The New York Times Book Review, *February 1, 1970, p. 46.*

JOHN WAIN

Bad Debts is a skillful and amusing book with an aftertaste of reflective sadness; a farce, if you like, containing a message about integrity. Its hero, Benjamin Freeman, is a free man in the sense that he skates perilously on the surface of the glossy, heartless consumer society. The characters who surround him—his estranged wife, his son, an empty-hearted careerist, his cousin, a faceless lawyer—act as effective foils to his large, purposeless vitality. Freeman is a liar and cheat who yet seems more honest than they do: the extravagant stories he makes up about his exploits, the wiles he employs to obtain on credit goods that he cannot afford, are an instinctive protest against the empty, senseless life that goes on around him....

Bad Debts is technically very accomplished; not original, it follows well-marked-out paths of narrative method, and perhaps owes something in tone and pace to the Saul Bellow of *Seize the Day.* But it is the work of a writer who has an excellent ear for the way people talk, an understanding eye for the way comedy intertwines with pathos, and a penetrating curiosity about human beings. (p. 36)

> *John Wain, "The Very Thing," in* The New York Review of Books, *Vol. XIV, No. 4, February 26, 1970, pp. 35-8.*

PAUL EDWARD GRAY

Benjamin Freeman, hopeless spendthrift, congenital liar, failed husband and father, and general all-around rotter, is the central character in Geoffrey Wolff's *Bad Debts,* a bleakly comic first novel. Neither his wife, a dull woman who hides in Connecticut from his entreaties, nor his son, an ineffectual Washington bureaucrat who pays to keep him at arm's length in New York, wants anything to do with Benjamin, and the novel tells of two days during which he tries, by means of threatening telegrams, to reunite this happy clan. (p. 436)

Wolff's understated narrative scours these characters with exasperated contempt, but the Freemans are so unwaveringly insensitive, so implacably selfish and self-deluding, that contempt ultimately seems wasted on them, in much the same way that scorn for the immobility of the rocks in one's garden would seem an example of misapplied energy. Narrative contempt is best reserved for characters who could be, or who could have been, better than they are; since it is never clear how the Freemans came to be so hopeless, we are never convinced that they had any choice but to be the way they apparently were born. *Bad Debts* is a rigorously moral novel without a clear moral focus. It is also, improbable as this may sound, extremely funny, and its appearance provides promising evidence of a new comic talent. (p. 437)

> *Paul Edward Gray, in a review of "Bad Debts," in* The Yale Review, *Vol. LIX, No. 3, March, 1970, pp. 436-37.*

MICHAEL MEWSHAW

Buried in the corpulence of Geoffrey Wolff's second novel [*The Sightseer*], several fine short stories—perhaps even whole novellas—scream desperately to be set free. Wolff often writes exceptionally well. . . . But the best passages of prose, bristling with lean, vivid imagery, lie cheek by flabby jowl with maundering essays on Beauty, Art and Truth, and the narrative is so shapeless that it is all but impossible to synopsize.

Generally, the story wanders in the wake of a young film maker, Caleb Sharrow, who travels from Vienna to Turkey, Bolex ready, finger on the trigger every inch of the way. Having finished a highly praised documentary which dealt in gruesome detail with his father's death, he is now searching for a new project and wondering whether he has used his father's agony callously or has made art of it. His brother, Noel, presses the issue, reiterating questions about the morality or immorality, the truth or illusion, of art.

A big theme, and Wolff knows it and tries to cover the territory with boom shots, wide-angle lenses and lots of tricks with mirrors. But frequently at crucial points the picture drifts out of focus, the characters separate into a mass of dots and the plot grows fuzzy. While episode trips after episode, people meet, talk, make deals, maim and murder with little discernible motivation.

One has to admire Mr. Wolff's energy, however, if not his technique, and admit that certain scenes and characters in *The Sightseer* have an adamant life of their own. The chapters in Istanbul, for instance, capture the essence of an Asian city as one sensitive American might perceive it, and the *yalt,* or oriental palace, where Caleb Sharrow passes a summer, might stand as an example of the structure Wolff aimed for in his book—arabesque, lush, exotic, rambling, infuriating and fascinating. But what Wolff wound up with was confusion, a house falling apart, because, despite touches of elegance, taste and talent, it was built on a foundation far wider than it was deep. (pp. 4-5)

> Michael Mewshaw, "Friends, Movies and Women, Made and Unmade," in The New York Times Book Review, *March 3, 1974, pp. 4-5.*

SAUL MALOFF

The protagonist-narrator of Geoffrey Wolff's novel [*The Sightseer*] is a sightseer in the trick sense of traveler and gawker, the clown with the camera round his neck; and a sightseer in the more central sense of cameraman and filmmaker. Caleb Sharrow is an artist now past his brilliant apprenticeship and primed for a full work of art, his first feature-length movie. But he is not simply a man with a loaded camera seeking to catch out and frame the world. A highly self-conscious artist, he is also a theorist of art. Moreover, as the seer-speaker of the fastidiously written book—and indeed as the keeper of a journal who discovers that writing is his chief pleasure—Sharrow is the author of this parable of art, the quest for art, the penalties exacted by art.

As such, *The Sightseer* stands within an old tradition that has been filled, not with moviemakers of course, but with alchemists and poets, philosophers and necromancers. And the esthetic that grounds it, gives it its organizing principle, by which it is judged, is put boldly as counterpoint to the narrative, providing a thematic weight.

Sharrow, we are told, has established himself with two documentaries, *Death Watch* and *Strike City.* The site of the latter, so named, is a commune of striking black farmworkers in Mississippi, where his twin brother, and foil, lives for a time in support of the strike. . . . Noel is passionately committed; Caleb, the sightseer, gets pretty pictures out of it, a craftily composed film, clever stuff for the arthouses, answerable only to its own esthetic. The debate between the brothers is as old as art itself: Art vs. Reality, Beauty vs. Truth, Imagination vs. Facts, and so on. If the issue seems a false one, which is to say an academic one fit only for seminarians to try their dialectical skills on and long resolved both in theory and practice, Caleb, the brightest, nastiest seminarian of them all, behaves as if it were invented by his graduating class; by, in fact, himself. On balance, he hasn't much use for "reality," the "poverty of true life," a treacherous, sleazy, shifty doxie; the thing is to "outbid reality, outflank history by finding the metaphor in a ruined dream . . . and raise up a work of art." A posturing affected prig—a *Vermont* esthete!—he is much given to posh palaver. . . . Unlike his brother, a sentimentalist and "amateur humanist," Caleb is, by his own description, a "professional artist."

If this isn't depressing enough a portrait of the artist as son-of-a-bitch, we are enrolled in a complete short course in moviemaking expertly taught, meticulous, finely detailed, imaginatively executed—the subject of *Death Watch* being the auteur's blind old father in the awful, withering throes of irreversible gangrenous rot. . . . "You'd blow up the world to film its end. Wouldn't you?" his outraged brother asks. Caleb replies "gently": "No, but if it were coming to an end, I'd like to spend my last few seconds shooting the event, and imposing some sense and beauty on it."

Thus armed Caleb sets sail for Byzantium with loaded cameras to see what he can film to shoot his way through the confusion of life into the clarity of art and at its heart to find the subject that awaits him there. Prodigal nature does his bidding, providing lovely cinematic, panavision effects. . . . (pp. 29-30)

The cast of characters is equally exotic, shootable, mostly Turkish. Caleb is bewitched by mysterious, sulpherous Veilah, all the more irresistible for the mote in her eye; alarmed by her brother, the sinister, pockmarked Nazim, fatally attracted not only to his requiting sister but even more to criminal psychopaths; their morally leprous mother, no less royal for being a fake princess; and involved against his will with Mr. Bright, whose cover as cultural chargé d'affaires at the American Embassy ill conceals his more lethal functions.

Mr. Bright provides the climactic occasion by hiring Caleb to make a wholesome little film celebrating the American Way for the edification of the Turkish masses—a no-nonsense film grounded in what might be called the esthetics of imperialist realism. Caleb sells out—but only apparently; while shooting Bright's film, he's making his own on the sly—*the* film, a merciless study in depravity, lechery, tyranny, the corruptions of egotism and power, murder and mayhem, chaos and dark night. Or so we are told.

Now, on the surface, all this seems a perverse, rather silly exercise of the imagination, melodramatic invention flogged and run amok. But *The Sightseer* aspires to be better than that. Wolff is a gifted, intelligent, serious writer, an admirable scene-painter usually in command of a supple if excessive prose. *The Sightseer* is an interesting conception which finally victimizes him, propelling the narrative from one outlandish element to the next until it collapses beneath sodden weight. Events are willed to occur, mere notions, conveniences without compelling cause or consequence.... Prose turns slowly, first this way, then that, doting on itself, commanding our admiration. It is as though Caleb Sharrow, not Geoffrey Wolff, the talented author of *Bad Debts,* had usurped and corrupted the novel with his interminable nattering. (p. 30)

> *Saul Maloff, in a review of "The Sightseer," in* The New Republic, *Vol. 170, No. 17, April 27, 1974, pp. 29-30.*

RICHARD TODD

Geoffrey Wolff has written a perplexing novel in *The Sightseer* ..., a meditation on the morality of the observer and the artist. Caleb Sharrow, roving film maker, lives off the proceeds of the tidy estate left by his father, whose death was the subject of Sharrow's first successful documentary, *Death Watch....* [Caleb] is a devotee of the Uncertainty Principle, and explicates it at some length: it is impossible to know anything without altering what you know, but the movie man can use "Heisenberg's principle to defeat uncertainty. He makes everything add up to an interesting sum." Ah: art. This is Physics for Journalists, and fashionable stuff among those of us who are paid to watch our fellow men. The moral course of the book consists of Sharrow's being taught the inadequacies of the principle. Part of the lesson comes from Sharrow's twin brother, who (all too schematically) represents the humanitarian qualities Sharrow lacks, and part comes from an increasingly bizarre set of events.

Summary is unfair to the energy and intelligence and occasional humor at work in this book, which has some wonderfully inventive moments. But something goes awry. Wolff and his hero are trapped inside a first-person narration that can't adequately accommodate moral education. He should have had Sharrow study, along with his Heisenberg, one of the lesser principles of twentieth-century thought: Yvor Winters' Fallacy of Imitative Form, which this novel exemplifies. It's a tale of narcissism narcissistically told. (p. 129)

> *Richard Todd, "Getting Real," in* The Atlantic Monthly, *Vol. 233, No. 5, May, 1974, pp. 127-30, 132.*

J. M. EDELSTEIN

In an advance comment about [*Black Sun: The Brief Transit and Violent Eclipse of Harry Crosby*], Irving Howe described it as "highly readable and troubling." Howe is right, as he often is. It is a good story, with all the elements of a spellbinder: the passionate rich, Paris in the '20s, sex, sometimes kinky, scandal in high society and the foreordained ending of tragedy. Geoffrey Wolff makes the most of these exciting elements, writing in a cool and skillful way.

In what is now a familiar but very effective technique, the story begins with the "violent eclipse" of what had been Harry Crosby's "brief transit." On December 10, 1929, ... Harry Crosby, aged 31, put a bullet through the head of his mistress and then killed himself. She was the former Josephine Noyes Rotch of Boston and had been the bride of Albert Smith Bigelow for about six months. Their bodies were discovered in the New York apartment which Harry Crosby had frequently used for his liaisons with his many lovers, and it was a few days before Harry and his wife Caresse were scheduled to return

together to Paris.... The rest of Wolff's engrossing story is the path through Harry Crosby's life to that final day. (p. 25)

[Harry Crosby] was rich, handsome, educated at St. Mark's and Harvard; had been through the war and had miraculously escaped death at Verdun from a direct artillery hit on the ambulance he was driving. He was in love with everything decadent, sensational and suicidal. He drove himself like the mad man he was. He was a drunk; he drugged himself with opium; he gambled for always higher and higher stakes; he lived a life of hysterical self-indulgence. And all this he did in the name of Art. He believed that art and life were the same thing. He was not the first to succumb to the temptation of believing that madness and genius are kinsmen nor the last, probably, to pay the price of worshipping Art as a religion. (pp. 25-6)

If he is remembered at all, Harry Crosby is known as the founder, together with Caresse, of the Black Sun Press. It was started, certainly, so that he and Caresse could print and publish in deluxe editions their own writings. Soon they began to print the work of their friends and contemporaries, and among the glories of the Black Sun Press is the first edition of Hart Crane's *The Bridge* and a portion of James Joyce's *Work in Progress,* as well as the work of such literary figures as Kay Boyle, Archibald MacLeish and D. H. Lawrence.

This, then, is the eminently readable story Geoffrey Wolff has written. But it is a story which has lost its point in the telling, and for that reason it is troubling. If all Geoffrey Wolff, who is a good novelist, had in mind was a vivid narrative he would have done better to fictionalize it. Harry Crosby's, for all its trappings, was a shallow and wasted life. There is little or nothing to be learned from it, and although Geoffrey Wolff provides, as the English say, a "good read," his book leaves one wondering why he wrote it. Harry Crosby?—really! Why? Apparently the source material for the study of Harry and Caresse Crosby and the archives of the Black Sun Press is enormous and available. Much more fascinating and much more deserving would be a book about Caresse Crosby. Wolff is unnecessarily harsh toward Caresse Crosby, for no apparent reason other than that in her autobiography, *The Passionate Years,* she made a few insignificant errors of fact about Harry and their life together and especially the events surrounding his suicide....

Black Sun is an elegant book, but a pointless and disappointing one. Geoffrey Wolff doesn't claim anything for Harry Crosby; he knows that Harry was not a poet and that his life was neither Art nor artful. As a result, this long and dramatically written book has about as much meaning as most of Harry Crosby's own writing. (p. 26)

> *J. M. Edelstein, in a review of "Black Sun: The Brief Transit and Violent Eclipse of Harry Crosby," in* The New Republic, *Vol. 175, No. 19, November 6, 1976, pp. 25-6.*

MARJORIE SMELSTOR

[In *Black Sun: The Brief Transit and Violent Eclipse of Harry Crosby,* Geoffrey Wolff] attempts a cultural history (or so the book jacket states); he focuses upon Paris in the twenties; he introduces a number of personalities of the decade; he includes a collection of photos. And ... Wolff is conscious of Trotsky's and James's descriptions of the noisy complexity involved in being a modern American. (p. 947)

Wolff's purpose is to compile a biography of the eccentric and bizarre founder of the Black Sun Press.... Wolff begins at the end—Crosby's end—by describing the editor-poet's suicide, together with the murder of his mistress, in 1929. This experience of death ... is really the essence of both Wolff's book and Crosby's life, for, as the author states, "It [death] inspired him, literally; breathed life into him. Death was a goal he ran toward full tilt. He was a poet of final stanzas, or so he liked to believe, and that last shot was no more than a punctuation point, a dot smaller than his smallest fingernail, a hard period, full stop." ... Wolff's biography is an effort to describe the way in which Crosby pursued his death-wish, the way in which he tried "... to make the Last Thing Perfect," as Crosby recorded in his notebook.

It is almost impossible to summarize the thirty-one years of Crosby's life without sounding as if one is writing a Gothic novel, and, indeed, Wolff sometimes seems to assume the novelist's role.... (pp. 947-48)

As literary biography, ... **Black Sun** is clearly informed by Wolff's evaluation of Crosby's art-as-religion-as-death orientation. As cultural history, however, the book's direction is not so clear. While there are a number of references to the experience and the personalities of the twenties, we have to question the book jacket's assertion that this study is "rich with the texture of the twenties." Indeed, it is perhaps unfair to judge a book by its cover (or jacket); in this case, however, we cannot help but wish for one of two things in this volume: either a more carefully delineated consideration of the period or a more detailed account of the Black Sun Press and its contributions to literary history. Because the book is really not a history of the times, the latter omission, the cursory account of the Press, is doubtless more obvious. To be sure, Wolff does itemize the important people who were published by Crosby's Press—Joyce, Lawrence, Crane, Pound, Proust, MacLeish, Boyle—and he even speaks of some of their works published by Crosby. But he fails to consider the Press very carefully, when such a consideration might have made this study something more than merely the examination of an eccentric poet's death-wish. (pp. 948-49)

Marjorie Smelstor, in a review of "Black Sun: The Brief Transit and Violent Eclipse of Harry Crosby," in The Georgia Review, *Vol. XXXI, No. 4, Winter, 1977, pp. 947-49.*

ANATOLE BROYARD

In **Inklings** Geoffrey Wolff raises an interesting question and immediately lowers it. Jupe, his protagonist, is a book critic who has always been a maverick but has now turned rogue and savages everything, good or bad. His rage is double-barreled: He cannot stomach most of the novels he reads, yet he has an irresistible desire, like a secret perversion, to write one.

It is a good theme, and Mr. Wolff would seem to be just the man to write it....

After reading **Inklings,** though, I could only regret all the opportunities it overlooked. There are Dostoyevskian possibilities in a literary critic who feels that unpopular truth is his cross to bear. His is the loneliness of the long-distance writer. His is the voice crying in the wilderness, the handwriting on the wall that cannot be seen for the graffiti. He reminds me of Semmelweis, the doctor who discovered that obstetricians in maternity wards were carrying infection from one woman to

the next and that newborn babies were dying because of a lack of simple precautions. When no one would listen to him, Semmelweis hawked his pamphlets outside the hospital, crying "Wash your hands! Wash your hands!"

Instead of washing his hands, Jupe dirties them with unimaginative invective. He can think of nothing better than to call his colleagues names ... and his satirical attack on the "literary establishment" consists of such uninspired antics as wearing a false nose, a clip-on moustache, a plastic spider in his lapel.

All sorts of possibilities are ignored in favor of silly badmouthing. Jupe never asks, for example, why novelists are praised, and critics condemned, for being negative; why novelists are dismissed if they are not "angry," and critics if they are; why a novel is regarded as a spontaneous gift to the public, and a review of a novel as looking a gift horse in the mouth....

The reluctance to exercise discrimination—a word that has lost its original meaning—may be one of the significant dramas of our age, yet Mr. Wolff turns his back on that drama and settles instead for a hamfisted joke. One of Jupe's former students has written a book as a result of his teacher's encouragement. At one time, it seems, Jupe thought it would be amusing to tell all the students in his creative writing class that they were geniuses. Now this genius kidnaps Jupe and forces him at gunpoint to edit and polish his book, which mixes fiction, verse, philosophy and fact, and whose bulk fills 15 beer cartons.

Jupe is also forced to write a critical appraisal of this work. Experienced readers will have no difficulty in guessing which book is a best seller and which a failure. The irony is so heavy that it sinks **Inklings,** which was already leaking badly.

Anatole Broyard, "Make Out, Put Down," in The New York Times Book Review, *January 8, 1978, p. 14.*

DORIS GRUMBACH

Jupe, Geoffrey Wolff's buttermilk-drinking hero in **Inklings** ..., is a literary critic. Surely, you say, I mean a *writer?* Or a novelist, perhaps? These people are often the subjects of novels, even though most readers (publishers assure us) are supposedly indifferent to the trials and fates of writer-heroes. No, Jupe *reviews* books, calls himself "a cultural buccaneer," and writes what his friend Nick (a serious one-novel man) considers "chatterbox stuff." Jupe teaches at a university, figures in New York's literary life, and spends his summers with his wife, Kate, and son in Maine, writing literary criticism.

This funny, tight-fisted novel begins when Jupe irreverently wrecks a panel discussion on "The Death of the Novel" before a yearly gathering of editors, writers, and critics. Afterward, he goes to a literary party. Such festivities are familiar to fiction, but Wolff's buckshot-accurate prose does wonders for the setting....

At the party, Jupe meets Mouse (yes, I'm afraid that *is* her name), a beautiful girl "devoted to literature." They move on to a literary saloon (another deftly re-created scene), and finally Jupe goes home with her. Their relationship continues, Jupe decides to work on a novel, and they head for Maine.... We are treated to some excellent pages about the usual writer's-block travail to which Jupe is now subject.

So far, *Inklings* is predictable, clever in its correct evocation of detail—especially to those familiar with the milieu. But then a young man who has been shadowing Jupe in New York for some time arrives at the Maine retreat. A would-be novelist who calls himself Mole (Man of Letters), he brings with him his life's work, written in longhand and contained in 15 beer cases. He holds Jupe at pistol point and demands that the critic read his manuscript, three times. We are given some samples of Mole's "salty conundrums," and we sense something of what the enormous novel is about. . . .

Inklings has its own ironic ending. The chapter called "Cleaning Up" contains some fine twists that I will not spoil for the reader by describing here. If I have any quarrel with fellow critic Wolff, whose prose is on the whole entertaining, it is that his plot is overingenious, at points so unbelievable that he made me think he was engaging in fantasy. I thought Mole must be another side of Jupe—a younger, creative self who had captured the critic and of whom the critic violently had to rid himself. But *Inklings*'s strength is in its shower of literary allusions and, yes, conundrums. One forgives the strains of plot. It is a novel for literary people, and for those who like looking at and listening to them.

> *Doris Grumbach, "Jupe, Mouse, and a Mole," in* Saturday Review, *Vol. 5, No. 8, January 21, 1978, p. 51.*

WEBSTER SCHOTT

While Geoffrey Wolff continually shifts from high seriousness to low comedy in *Inklings,* playing with language, identities, and the tactics of self-aggrandizement as if he were a standup comic, he wants us most to know about the pain of brokering defective intellectual goods and the temptation—it's finally irresistible to Jupe—of trying to make the genuine article yourself. "I wanted to come home to myself," Jupe says in a moment of loneliness with his wife, "but I couldn't find my way." . . .

Maybe the anguish the committed literary journalist or critic feels as he recalls himself sinking into the sands of hyperbole or struggling to identify art and celebrate it won't submit to a prolonged examination that leads to revelation. There's no hard news here. The best that Wolff can do is give us the condition of disturbance, which leads in *Inklings* to bizarre behavior and absurd consequences. . . .

Inklings moves like a whip. It cracks with black humor. Wolff knows literary politics and the crooks, charlatans, and accidents that shack up in the house of intellect as if he were the landlord himself. I don't believe he accomplished what he set out to do. In *Inklings* Wolff is more stunt man than soul-searcher. His characters are more fabrication than human. But somewhere Wolff was struck by a lightning bolt of words, and he uses them like a demon. I like his book. It will cut every critic who picks it up and amuse just about everyone else.

> *Webster Schott, "Walking the Literary Plank," in* Book World—The Washington Post, *January 29, 1978, p. L3.*

THOMAS LeCLAIR

[*Inklings*] is narrated by a reviewer named Jupe who wants to write a novel but ends up writing a literary biography and then his autobiography to explain why he didn't finish his novel,

part of which he includes. The autobiography could be a novel. In fact, it is a novel, Geoffrey Wolff's if not Jupe's. Geoffrey Wolff is the book critic for *New Times,* the author of a literary biography of Harry Crosby, and a literary gangster mentioned by Jupe at the end of *Inklings*. This is a review, not fiction.

The holdings of the Library of Infinite Regress include Achilles and the tortoise, the lying Cretan, the man on the old Quaker Oats box, Mobius, certain clothing store mirrors, Borges, Barth, and so on. The best undercut big notions, serious misconceptions such as time, space, truth, and identity. *Inklings* is only a minor addition because its receding frames hold satiric pictures of the contemporary publishing world. Comic turns stop the reader from tumbling through into philosophically disturbing echo and reflection. (p. 33)

Wolff's satire seems sharp enough . . . and the parodies—of a first novel, authorized biography, and master editor—are amusing. Jupe is right: Geoffrey Wolff is a hit man, an effective mocker of popularity and pretension. But *Inklings* is also a frame-up, with Wolff as victim and enforcer. His elaborate framing devices, the trap-doors of fictions within fiction, the Shandyian mixture of footnotes and reality, the word play on Mouse, Mole, and the small details of the novel's first pages that reveal characters as Jupe's inventions—they all remind me of the high-wire art of Borges, Nabokov, and Barth where play, risk, and conceptual assault are one.

Wolff, though, is just playing, and he knows it. Mole says of Jupe's work: "it's arch, self-conscious, two-for-a-penny, smart-ass, and ironical." It's true of Jupe's, mostly true of Wolff's. Despite the self-irony, *Inklings* is a smug book in its witty condescension to high art and its satisfaction with its own entertaining facileness. With more talent or some of Mole's passion, Wolff might have made upsetting art behind the back of his journalistic Jupe. Works like Nabokov's *Pale Fire* and Barth's *Lost in the Funhouse* only pretend that limited narrators and self-consciousness cripple. Wolff pretends they are a joke. One of the refrains of *Inklings* is that "words count." But not enough, not for Wolff. (p. 34)

> *Thomas LeClair, in a review of "Inklings," in* The New Republic, *Vol. 178, No. 10, March 11, 1978, pp. 33-4.*

JOHN IRVING

Geoffrey Wolff's autobiography, *The Duke of Deception*—the harsh but affectionate portrait of his father, whose "sustaining line of work till shortly before he died was as a confidence man"—is a book abundant with the complexities and contradictions of family sympathy. Keenly perceptive of family ties and family shame, Geoffrey Wolff has succeeded in being true to his emotionally complicated subject while also being divinely easy to read. In the words of other family members, Geoffrey's father emerges as difficult in the extreme. "I always trusted him," a cousin said, "and he treated me well. He was a good-looking guy, and good company." Another said simply: "He was my friend." And a third looked straight at Geoffrey and told him that his father was "a gonif, a schnorrer. He was just a bum. That's all he ever was." In the delicate telling of his father's story, the son manages to bring all versions of "Duke" Wolff to light. (p. 1)

Geoffrey Wolff tells a story "of love's shortcut through stuff," of the father who surrounds his children with things instead of his presence, yet when he is present he is fiercely there: "He used justice fearsomely, like a roll of coins in his fist.'' The old Duke's vita is both a sham and source of pride to son Geoffrey. ''I wish my father had done more headlong, more elegant inventing,'' Geoffrey notes. ''He was most naturally a fictioneer.'' Geoffrey seems to admire the con man in his father, but moans his lack of scope. The old man lands job after job with phony credentials and is as frequently fired for the discovery of the same, or fired for his lavish ways. . . .

[However], in this book it is not [Geoffrey Wolff's] judgment of his father that is most noticeable, it is his love. He acknowledges what his father loved in him, recounts with uncritical fondness his father driving him back to school at Princeton—in a stolen car. Most important, the Duke of Deception handles his young son's tendency to lie about himself: ''He told me I was better than I thought, that I didn't need to add to my sum. I had warmth, he said; warmth and energy were the important things. These were a long time paying off sometimes, but they paid off. Honesty was the crucial thing, he said, knowing who I was, being who I was. What he said was so; I knew it was so. I didn't even think to turn his words against him, he was trying so hard to save me from something, to turn me back. I had this from him always: compassion, care, generosity, endurance.''

In the face of so much dishonesty and the constant embarrassment of a father's falsehoods, there is such a sunny quality in this son's memory that we must be convinced that this father's affection was at least bright and true. ''But I was a kid, and I saw what I wished to see,'' Geoffrey confesses, forgiving his father at every turn. (p. 18)

The Duke of Deception is not only first-rate autobiography, conscientious and intimate; it is a wholly instructive and provocative biography of the father and swindler, Arthur S. Wolff III; and it is as lucid and complicated a story as a good novel. (p. 20)

> John Irving, ''Father and Son,'' in The New York Times Book Review, *August 12, 1979, pp. 1, 18, 20.*

TIM O'BRIEN

[*The Duke of Deception: Memories of My Father*] is more than a chronicle of the old man's scams and deceits; it is the story of an intense relationship between father and son. This theme is one of literature's oldest and richest lodes—Geoffrey Wolff himself has mined it before, in a novel titled *Bad Debts*—but in this book, which is part biography and part autobiography, he shows there is plenty more gold down there. *The Duke of Deception* is tender, sad, witty, illuminating, and always moving. (p. 46)

Each of us, of course, must sooner or later whittle down those bigger-than-life images of our parents that are formed in childhood; each of us must match the realities, as perceived through a growing maturity, against the fairy-tale versions of our youth. It is built into the system. In this sense, then, each of us has experienced the feeling of having been deceived by a father or mother or older brother. And this is what gives Geoffrey Wolff's story, with its extreme litany of deception followed by eroding fatherly images, such power and universal truth. *The Duke of Deception* awakens us to our own emotions, enlivens our own memories, and compels us to examine our own familial histories. (p. 47)

The Duke of Deception traces a son's attempt to find his father, to strip away the camouflage that hides not only Duke Wolff but all fathers. At times funny, at times sad, the book avoids false sentiment. It is straight and tough and unrelenting in its pursuit of truth. It is also, finally, a book of love. . . .

Late in life, Duke Wolff lived far from his son—across a continent, in prison, in cheap rooming houses—and the son, unwilling and unable to put up with more, preferred it that way. Geoffrey Wolff was by then, as he is today, a successful novelist and book critic, a married man raising his own family, and he did not so much repudiate his father as try to make space for his own life. Wolff is, perhaps, too hard on himself when he writes, ''I was becoming handy with repudiations of every kind, and learning to nurture anger solicitously. I had felt betrayed by my father, and wanted to betray him.'' True, he did not visit Duke during the final months of disintegration; true, he ignored appeals for help and once refused to bail his father out of jail; true, he was not present—nor was anyone—when Duke died poor and without friends on the last day of July 1970. But this book, in its honesty and lucidity, affirms the son's faithfulness to the father. It does not condescend, nor judge harshly, nor forgive gratuitously; it does not ignore the father's failings but neither does it wallow in them. Indeed, in many instances, Geoffrey Wolff celebrates his father's gutty audacity, his flair, his enormous capacity for the outlandish and outlawish. (p. 48)

> Tim O'Brien, ''Tales His Father Told Him,'' in Saturday Review, *Vol. 6, No. 19, September 29, 1979, pp. 46-8.*

DONALD HALL

Readers of this magazine, if they see many periodicals, will have seen numerous notices of *The Duke of Deception.* Most reviewers have praised it, and it is an excellent book—but if reviewers had not liked it at all, they would have reviewed it anyway. Its subject matter guarantees attention: Duke Wolff is a liar, cheater, braggart, phony, and would-be con-man.

It is easy enough, without psychological pretension, to label Duke narcissistic; it is easy enough, without Christopher Lasch's help, to diagnose the American epidemic of narcissism. Duke Wolff does what we all dream of doing. . . . We live on credit, and Wolff is our surrogate who never pays his bills. We live for weekends—ads on television assure us—and Wolff lived one perpetual weekend.

But of course we do not quite do it because we would get caught—and Wolff does that for us also. Our morality play is complete; first we participate in his frauds, then we sit back and let him do time for us. Our illicit desires, let out for a stroll, are leashed by his punishment. If Lincoln's Doctor's Dog was the old recipe for a best-seller, Duke with his infantile indulgence, followed by his melancholy deserts, provides us with two-thirds of a new never-fail formula.

The third part is provided by authorship, for Duke's biographer is Duke's son, critic and novelist Geoffrey Wolff, who remained with his father when his parents' marriage broke up, who tried his own versions of fraudulence—and eventually refused to repeat what his father had done. We are interested in fathers and sons and in mothers and daughters. The romance between the child and the parent of the same sex, while it has not had the press of the other relationship noted by Sophocles, has a dynamic of growth and replacement, the maturing and the aging of mirrors, dependency changing to dominance. In *The Duke of Deception,* we add the complexity that the father was always an infant. There is a doubleness of viewpoint which is poignant—we see Duke from up close as he appeared to his son back then, and from afar as his grown son sees him now—and we watch as the son's belief in the father, misplaced to our certain knowledge, turns sour. (p. 1371)

The problem in writing this book was a problem of tone. It is essential that we put accurate value on the young son's mind and feelings as well as on the father's. If we see the old man through the mature Geoffrey, we see him through the mature Geoffrey watching the young Geoffrey, necessarily a distorting lens. It is often appalling when an autobiographer criticizes his younger self, because it is self-flattery now to blame the self then. Geoffrey Wolff handles this problem with delicacy, restraint, and intelligence, so that we are able to feel compassion for the old man while the young man rages, at the same time as we feel compassion for the young man saddled with this impossible father.

The partial autobiography is a splendid form, the memoir which pretends not to be about its author, but about some segment of life—an idea, a place, a set of relationships—which the author has been witness to. *The Duke of Deception* appears to be about the man of the title, and it is indeed about the man of the title . . . but the context is this man's son's growth and development. As we step back from the book we understand that we have read a small *Bildungsroman* and a romance: Boy meets father . . . Boy loses father . . . Writing a book after the father's death, boy finds father again. (pp. 1371-72)

> *Donald Hall, "A Wolff in Chic Clothing," in* National Review, *Vol. XXXI, No. 43, October 26, 1979, pp. 1371-72.*

JACK BEATTY

Suppose it fell to you to pick a book to go into a time capsule labeled "Not to be opened until the year 2086"—a book that would preserve for posterity a specimen of contemporary prose at its best. What would you pick?

The criterion, I should stipulate, is not greatness or brilliance but style, and style not in the abstract but understood as capturing something essential about this time. . . . If you wanted to bequeath to the future an example of the possibilities of prose—and especially of American prose—you would do well to pick [*Providence,* the] new book by Geoffrey Wolff. . . . (pp. 85-6)

Sentences like these, an inventory of objects stolen by a Providence hoodlet, are why *I* would make that choice:

> Here were some things Skippy took: copper wire (when copper was trading high), the fiberglass top for a Corvette, chrome wheel lugs from a Z-Car (sad surprise for some driver), Pampers (a truckload), three hundred cans of sardines, barbells, mink pelts, a set of bagpipes, a Denver boot, other things too. He'd steal the paint off your house.

Now, that's just a list. No fancy footwork there at all. Still, note the latent artfulness. A writer less deft would have ended this survey of Skippy's swag with the Denver boot, but Wolff throws that line away with a shrug—"other things too"—so that we have time to get the joke before we move on to the

next one, the hyperbole at the end: "He'd steal the paint off your house." This is writing in the teeth of the video age. No camera could capture these objects with this wit and flavor.

Here's more:

> Skippy and his brother Mike grew up good boys, played football, basketball, and baseball at St. Anselms, graduated. Well, Skippy almost graduated. He figured he got booted for quitting the baseball team. Well, spring term of his senior year he got in some trouble, but he was basically a good boy.

Easy to parody, but try giving information so intrinsically dull as entertainingly, or with as much inflection of tone. The prose takes on some of the attributes that character has in a more old-fashioned novel: it battles truth right before our eyes, and loses.

A final example—this one a little fancier:

> And then he heard above the talk of *Warlock*'s timbers and the complaint of her rigging seanoises he had long imagined: the rusty-hinged creak, a great sound of breathing, the squawky click of whales.

The first clause has a Miltonic sprung rhythm to it. We have to let twelve words after "heard" go by, our expectations building, before we discover *what* was heard. The sensation of delay brings (literary) pleasure. "Rusty-hinged creak," a familiar enough phrase, domesticates the sound, brings it closer to us. But "squawky click," exotic to the point of bafflement, restores the strangeness and then some. The whole passage enacts the action it describes; it becomes an encounter with the uncanny. Wolff has given us a bookful of such touches.

[*Providence*] takes place in the eponymous city well known for harboring Brown University, the Rhode Island School of Design, and a congeries of crime bosses who seem to have been put on the planet solely to prove Oscar Wilde right about the relationship between art and life. The title is also a pun, something like providence (fate, say) being what brings five diverse characters together in a taut novel that is part crime story, part melodrama, part criticism of life, and part tragedy. The book asks, In the 1980s what are the forces that can take over a human life and send it smash against the rocks? It answers, Cancer, psychosis, sex, and crime. (p. 86)

The plot, not to put too fine a point on it, catches you by the throat. The subtlety in *Providence* lies elsewhere—in the asides about fate and freedom, in shrewd bits of observation, dialogue, and description, above all in the writing. It includes multitudes, the writing does: wisps from the old masters, the latest burble from pop culture, media noise, drug talk, Valspeak East—everything is here except political wind. "We may not all have lived this way," I'd write in the note to be put in the time capsule, "but this is how we wrote when we tried to render in words and rhythm the intensely serious low comedy of this age." (p. 87)

> *Jack Beatty, "Writing for the Video Age," in* The Atlantic Monthly, *Vol. 257, No. 2, February, 1986, pp. 85-7.*

JAMES CARROLL

In [*Providence*], Geoffrey Wolff's splendid novel, Providence refers first, of course, to the Rhode Island city in which its story unfolds. A lawyer, a cop and a small-time hood become embroiled in events that make the lawyer's wife the hood's victim, and the hood's girlfriend the cop's downfall. Each of these five characters is up against an inexorable force and losing. In the lawyer's case, it is a fatal disease. For the cop, it is the inevitability of his own corruption. For the hood, it is the Boss, the head of big-time crime. For the wife, it is the way madness takes the place of love. For the girlfriend, it is the discovery that the good times she so desperately pursues are what make her feel so bad.

Readers familiar with Mr. Wolff's three previous novels will not be surprised to find this one wonderfully well written, restrained and exuberant at once. . . . In each of his works Mr. Wolff has dared to treat the most somber subject there is—the inevitability of defeat. Perhaps he has become a connoisseur of it. . . .

But *Providence* is a novel to be read for pleasure, for pure enjoyment, because it brings a supremely light touch to its heavy subject. With unfailing irony and profound affection for all his characters, Mr. Wolff presents their awful story as if he thinks it is funny. *Providence* is, in fact, wickedly funny, partly because the situations Mr. Wolff creates for his characters are masterpieces of comic reversal. . . .

What sets *Providence* apart from other works of black humor, particularly of the mock gangster genre, is the fact that Mr. Wolff goes beyond these nutty situations to language itself as the source of his comic energy. Language itself is the first laugh, of course—that we should ever try to put into mere words the mystery of who we are. Yet there is nothing mere about the words in this novel. They are exactly right. Mr. Wolff has an ear for the way the nuances of English tease one another. His paragraphs sparkle because he is a writer at play. Thus each of the five wildly different characters has a distinct voice that is in its way hilarious. If Mr. Wolff has pushed against the limit of his considerable gift for artfully conveying ordinary human talk, whether of the wheeler-dealer's "street" or the Yankee's "hill," he has done so because he knows that what is funny in life is not what happens, but what we say about it. Humor is not an event but an attitude.

Humor is the attitude that rescues us from the predicament implied in the word "providence." We know that something out there, whether God or history, a city in Rhode Island or only death, is arranging things even now with no reference whatever to what we feel or want or choose. Yet all of us insist innately that our choices and feelings do matter, finally, as much as anyone's—even God's. That insistence is what makes us comic, Mr. Wolff suggests, but also noble.

One of the tales used in Bible school to illustrate the religious idea of providence is that of Jonah and the whale. In fact the Jonah story is a comic masterpiece that depends on the juxtaposition of the puny, frightened man against the largest creature of the earth, symbol of all those forces that swallow him. And swallow him the whale does, but to rescue him, not eat him. What a surprise when Jonah is spit out on the beach alive! It is surprise we want from jokes and from fiction and, as in Jonah's tale, from death.

Geoffrey Wolff's *Providence* is not a fable but a novel. Yet in the end, Adam, whom the reader will come to love above all its great characters, is surprised, as Jonah was, and we rejoice. He had sailed far out into the ocean to kill himself. But then, in the menacing fog, he heard "the squawky click of whales. They were talking to one another, and by the way to him. . . . Adam smelled the brine stink of huge mammals guiding one another through oceans blinder than any night he had known, helping one another."

James Carroll, "Laughing Our Way to Defeat," in The New York Times Book Review, *February 16, 1986, p. 7.*

ROSS THOMAS

Providence is essentially a tale of corruption: civic, moral, mental and even, I suppose, spiritual. To tell it, Wolff has deliberately employed a wacky, loose and often wonderful style that breaks most of the rules of grammar known to man. Yet the style serves the story well, for Wolff is writing largely about civic rot and decay and the various maggots that dwell therein. A cooler, less vernacular style might not have served as well—and the horrible, after all, deserves a bit of hyperbole.

Not only does Wolff manage to crawl far inside his characters' minds, but their dialogue is often a treat. . . .

Leukemia is often such a convenient way for a fictional character to die slowly and not too messily, chapter after chapter, that it's something of a pleasure, or at least a relief, to find Adam Dwyer doing it as well as could be expected:

> When he returned from the hospital that Monday . . . he poured himself a beer. Then he loosened his tie, and didn't lose himself in the front-page story about some erstwhile mobster called the Moron. Then he . . . told her he was going to die, soon, and Clara listened . . . Clara thought she had waited a long time for something consequential to happen to her, and now it had, and it was the wrong thing . . .

Cities are only very large communities where people band together for mutual security, services, social contact and commerce, including crime. Some writers have taken real cities and left their own fictional stamp on them. . . . Wolff has left his own imprint on Providence, a city that has shrunk from a population of 250,000 to approximately 150,000—a "jerkwater that outsiders bombed past on their way to Cape Cod."

After reading *Providence* I had the feeling that I had spent two weeks too long there and got to know its citizens just a shade too well. If the mark of a good novel is that it leaves you with a lingering aftertaste, pleasant or unpleasant, then Geoffrey Wolff has written a very good and witty novel indeed.

Ross Thomas, "Mean Streets and Mobsters," in Book World—The Washington Post, *February 23, 1986, p. 7.*

Appendix

The following is a listing of all sources used in Volume 41 of *Contemporary Literary Criticism*. Included in this list are all copyright and reprint rights and acknowledgments for those essays for which permission was obtained. Every effort has been made to trace copyright, but if omissions have been made, please let us know.

THE EXCERPTS IN CLC, VOLUME 41, WERE REPRINTED FROM THE FOLLOWING PERIODICALS:

Agenda, v. 19 & 20, Winter & Spring, 1982; v. 23, Spring & Summer, 1985. Both reprinted by permission.

The American Book Review, v. 3, January-February, 1981; v. 7, May-June, 1985. © 1981, 1985 by *The American Book Review*. Both reprinted by permission.

The American Scholar, v. 37, Spring, 1968. Copyright © 1968 by the United Chapters of Phi Beta Kappa. By permission of the publishers.

The American Spectator, v. 18, October, 1985. Copyright © *The American Spectator* 1985. Reprinted by permission.

Américas, v. 33, September, 1981; v. 34, January-February, 1982. Both reprinted by permission from *Américas*, a bimonthly magazine published by the General Secretariat of the Organization of American States in English and Spanish.

The Atlantic Monthly, v. 223, May, 1974. Copyright 1974 by The Atlantic Monthly Company, Boston, MA./ v. 224, December, 1969 for "Genius Unobserved" by Evan S. Connell, Jr.; v. 256, November, 1985 for "The Art of Conversation" by Lloyd Rose; v. 257, February, 1986 for "Writing for the Video Age" by Jack Beatty. Copyright 1969, 1985, 1986 by The Atlantic Monthly Company, Boston, MA. All reprinted by permission of the respective authors.

Best Sellers, v. 30, September 1, 1970; v. 33, October 1, 1973. Copyright 1970, 1973, by the University of Scranton. Both reprinted by permission./ v. 35, October, 1975; v. 36, December, 1976; v. 37, August, 1977; v. 37, November, 1977; v. 38, March, 1979; v. 42, October, 1982. Copyright © 1975, 1976, 1977, 1979, 1982 Helen Dwight Reid Educational Foundation. All reprinted by permission.

Book Week—The Sunday Herald Tribune, January 30, 1966. © 1966, *The Washington Post*. Reprinted by permission.

Book World—Chicago Tribune, November 23, 1969 for "A New Star in the Tradition of Memorable Punks" by Sara Blackburn; September 5, 1971 for "A Cuban Romance" by Alan Schwartz. © 1969, 1971 Postrib Corp. Both reprinted by permission of *The Washington Post* and the respective authors.

Book World—The Washington Post, February 4, 1968 for "Sick, Sick" by Robert J. Shea; October 26, 1969 for "The Search for a Sense of Self" by Joyce Carol Oates; May 17, 1970 for "Insider's Near East" by Clara Claiborne Park. © 1968, 1969, 1970 Postrib Corp. All reprinted by permission of *The Washington Post* and the respective authors./ March 15, 1970. © 1970 Postrib Corp. Reprinted by permission./ January 29, 1978; January 27, 1980; February 10, 1980; February 15, 1981; May 3, 1981; March 14, 1982; April 25, 1982; October 3, 1982; November 7, 1982; October 9, 1983; December 18, 1983; May 20, 1984; December 16, 1984; February 3, 1985; April 14, 1985; May 5, 1985; September 1, 1985; September 15, 1985; October 13, 1985; October 27, 1985; December 1, 1985; February 23, 1986; April 6, 1986; June 1, 1986. © 1978, 1980, 1981, 1982, 1983, 1984, 1985, 1986, *The Washington Post*. All reprinted by permission.

1979; v. 97, June 8, 1979; v. 98, July 27, 1979; v. 98, November 2, 1979; v. 99, June 20, 1980; v. 100, August 15, 1980; v. 106, November 11, 1983; v. 107, January 13, 1984; v. 110, August 30, 1985; v. 110, October 11, 1985; v. 110, October 18, 1985. © 1960, 1961, 1962, 1963, 1967, 1968, 1969, 1970, 1971, 1973, 1975, 1976, 1977, 1979, 1980, 1983, 1984, 1985 The Statesman & Nation Publishing Co. Ltd. All reprinted by permission.

New York Herald Tribune Book Review, February 4, 1951; May 4, 1952. Copyright 1951, 1952 I.H.T. Corporation. Both reprinted by permission./ February 23, 1958; November 23, 1958. © 1958 I.H.T. Corporation. Both reprinted by permission.

New York Herald Tribune Books, June 19, 1927; March 18, 1928; April 21, 1929; November 9, 1930; February 22, 1942; January 24, 1943. Copyright 1927, 1928, 1929, 1930, 1942, 1943 I.H.T. Corporation. Ali reprinted by permission.

New York Herald Tribune Weekly Book Review, October 22, 1944; March 30, 1947; September 12, 1948. Copyright 1944, 1947, 1948 I.H.T. Corporation. All reprinted by permission.

New York Magazine, v. 13, February 18, 1980; v. 17, February 20, 1984; v. 18, July 15, 1985; v. 18, November 11, 1985; v. 19, January 20, 1986. Copyright © 1980, 1984, 1985, 1986 by News America Publishing, Inc. All reprinted with the permission of *New York* Magazine.

New York Post, February 10, 1984. © 1984, News America Publishing, Incorporated. Reprinted from the *New York Post* by permission.

The New York Review of Books, v. XXXIII, June 12, 1986 for "A Farewell to Hemingstein" by Wilfrid Sheed. Copyright © 1986 Nyrev, Inc. Reprinted by permission of the author./ v. XIV, February 26, 1970; v. XXII, March 6, 1975; v. XXV, January 25, 1979; v. XXVIII, October 8, 1981; v. XXXI, April 26, 1984; v. XXXII, January 31, 1985; v. XXXII, May 9, 1985; v. XXXIII, March 27, 1986. Copyright © 1970, 1975, 1981, 1984, 1985, 1986 Nyrev, Inc. All reprinted with permission from *The New York Review of Books.*

The New York Times, October 15, 1942. Copyright 1942 by The New York Times Company. Reprinted by permission./ February 3, 1957; April 3, 1969; February 20, 1970; April 1, 1972; January 10, 1975; April 24, 1982; September 9, 1982; September 27, 1982; February 10, 1984; February 23, 1984; April 6, 1984; December 10, 1984; June 1, 1985; October 19, 1985; October 23, 1985; October 29, 1985; December 7, 1985. Copyright © 1967, 1969, 1970, 1972, 1975, 1982, 1984, 1985 by The New York Times Company. All reprinted by permission.

The New York Times Book Review, May 4, 1924; April 28, 1929; October 2, 1932; October 25, 1942; January 24, 1943; October 29, 1944; March 24, 1946; March 23, 1947; September 12, 1948; April 3, 1949; April 8, 1951; August 5, 1951; June 27, 1954; August 1, 1954. Copyright 1924, 1929, 1932, 1942, 1943, 1944, 1946, 1947, 1948, 1949, 1951, 1954 by The New York Times Company. All reprinted by permission./ December 22, 1963; July 5, 1964; January 24, 1965; March 7, 1965; May 16, 1965; January 30, 1966; February 27, 1966; February 19, 1967; January 21, 1968; February 4, 1968; February 25, 1968; March 2, 1969; September 14, 1969; February 1, 1970; May 31, 1970; February 14, 1971; August 29, 1971; March 26, 1972; September 24, 1972; October 1, 1972; December 31, 1972; May 27, 1973; September 23, 1973; October 14, 1973; March 3, 1974; February 9, 1975; August 17, 1975; May 2, 1976; May 16, 1977; August 21, 1977; January 8, 1978; April 2, 1978; November 26, 1978; February 11, 1979; August 12, 1979; October 7, 1979; January 6, 1980; February 17, 1980; May 18, 1980; June 29, 1980; September 28, 1980; January 18, 1981; May 3, 1981; May 17, 1981; August 2, 1981; November 22, 1981; January 17, 1982; March 21, 1982; October 10, 1982; October 24, 1982; February 20, 1983; December 25, 1983; February 26, 1984; March 25, 1984; May 6, 1984; June 14, 1984; June 17, 1984; October 28, 1984; March 17, 1985; May 5, 1985; June 9, 1985; June 23, 1985; July 28, 1985; August 4, 1985; August 18, 1985; September 15, 1985; October 13, 1985; October 20, 1985; October 27, 1985; November 24, 1985; December 29, 1985; February 16, 1986; March 9, 1986; May 18, 1986. Copyright © 1963, 1964, 1965, 1966, 1967, 1968, 1969, 1970, 1971, 1972, 1973, 1974, 1975, 1976, 1977, 1978, 1979, 1980, 1981, 1982, 1983, 1984, 1985, 1986 by The New York Times Company. All reprinted by permission.

The New Yorker, v. XXXIII, November 2, 1957; v. XLIV, February 24, 1968; v. L, January 20, 1975; v. LV, February 11, 1980; v. LVII, July 27, 1981. © 1957, 1968, 1975, 1980, 1981 by The New Yorker Magazine, Inc. All reprinted by permission./ v. LVIII, November 29, 1982 for a review of "True West" by Edith Oliver; v. LX, September 10, 1984 for "Modernist, Postmodernist, What Will They Think of Next?" by John Updike; v. LXI, April 8, 1985 for "Listen" by Whitney Balliett; v. LXI, September 2, 1985 for a review of "The Curse of the Starving Class" by Edith Oliver; v. LXI, January 27, 1986 for "Lasso and Peashooter" by Pauline Kael; v. LXI, January 27, 1986 for "Nil Nisi Bonum" by Brendan Gill; v. LXII, February 24, 1986 for "Latin Strategies" by John Updike. © 1982, 1984, 1985, 1986 by the respective authors. All reprinted by permission.

Newsweek, v. LXXIV, July 28, 1969; v. XCIV, September 24, 1979; v. XCV, February 18, 1980; v. XCVII, January 5, 1981; v. XCVIII, September 7, 1981; v. CVI, November 25, 1985. Copyright 1969, 1979, 1980, 1981, 1985, by Newsweek, Inc. All rights reserved. All reprinted by permission.

North Dakota Quarterly, v. 49, Winter, 1981. Copyright 1981 by The University of North Dakota. Reprinted by permission.

Northwest Review, v. 6, Fall, 1963. Copyright © 1963 by *Northwest Review.* Reprinted by permission.

Notes: The Quarterly Journal of The Music Library Association, v. 25, March, 1969 for a review of "A Year from Monday: New Lectures and Writings" by Ellsworth Snyder. Copyright 1969 by the Music Library Association, Inc. Reprinted by permission of the publisher and the author.

The Observer, December 15, 1985 for "Pleasures of Literature" by Anthony Burgess. Reprinted by permission of the author./ May 16, 1971; July 29, 1973; August 3, 1975; January 2, 1977; March 27, 1977; June 12, 1977; September 4, 1977; September 9, 1979; November

THE EXCERPTS IN CLC, VOLUME 41, WERE REPRINTED FROM THE FOLLOWING BOOKS:

Aaron, Joyce. From "Clues in a Memory," in *American Dreams: The Imagination of Sam Shepard*. Edited by Bonnie Marranca. Performing Arts Journal Publications, 1981. Copyright © 1981 by Performing Arts Journal Publications. All rights reserved. Reprinted by permission.

Bloom, Harold. From an introduction to *Modern Critical Views: T. S. Eliot*. Edited by Harold Bloom. Chelsea House Publishers, 1985. Introduction copyright © 1985 by Harold Bloom. All rights reserved. Reprinted by permission.

Bond, David J. From *The Fiction of André Pieyre de Mandiargues*. Syracuse University Press, 1982. Copyright © 1982 by David J. Bond. All rights reserved. Reprinted by permission of the publisher.

Bradby, David. From *Modern French Drama: 1940-1980*. Cambridge University Press, 1984. © Cambridge University Press 1984. Reprinted by permission of the publisher.

Brophy, James D. From "Richard Murphy: Poet of Nostalgia or 'Pietas'?" in *Contemporary Irish Writing*. Edited by James D. Brophy and Raymond J. Porter. Iona College Press, 1983. Copyright © 1983 by James D. Brophy. All rights reserved. Reprinted by permission of the author.

Bruccoli, Matthew J. From *Ross Macdonald*. Harcourt Brace Jovanovich, 1984. Copyright © 1984 by Matthew Bruccoli. Reprinted by permission of Harcourt Brace Jovanovich, Inc.

Bush, Ronald. From *T. S. Eliot: A Study in Character and Style*. Oxford University Press, 1983. Copyright © 1984 by Ronald Bush. Reprinted by permission of Oxford University Press, Inc.

Butterfield, Herbie. From "Ernest Hemingway," in *American Fiction: New Readings*. Edited by Richard Gray. Barnes & Noble, 1983. © 1983 by Vision Press Ltd. All rights reserved. By permission of Barnes & Noble Books, a Division of Littlefield, Adams & Co., Inc.

Earley, Michael. From "Of Life Immense in Passion, Pulse, and Power: Sam Shepard and the American Literary Tradition," in *American Dreams: The Imagination of Sam Shepard*. Edited by Bonnie Marranca. Performing Arts Journal Publications, 1981. Copyright © 1981 by Performing Arts Journal Publications. All rights reserved. Reprinted by permission.

Esslin, Martin. From "Ionesco and the Fairytale Tradition," in *The Dream and the Play: Ionesco's Theatrical Quest*. Edited by Moshe Lazar. Undena, 1982. © 1982 by Undena Publications. All rights reserved. Reprinted by permission.

Gilman, Richard. From an introduction to *Seven Plays*. By Sam Shepard. Bantam, 1981. Introduction copyright © 1981 by Bantam Books, Inc. All rights reserved. Reprinted by permission of Bantam Books, Inc.

Innes, Christopher. From *Holy Theatre: Ritual and the Avant Garde*. Cambridge University Press, 1981. © Cambridge University Press 1981. Reprinted by permission of the publisher.

Jones, Verina. From "Leonardo Sciascia," in *Writers & Society in Contemporary Italy: A Collection of Essays*. Edited by Michael Caesar and Peter Hainsworth. St. Martin's Press, 1984. © Michael Caesar and Peter Hainsworth 1984. Reprinted by permission of St. Martin's Press Inc.

Kermode, Frank. From an afterword to *The Day of the Owl* [and] *Equal Danger*. By Leonardo Sciascia, translated by Archibald Colquhoun and Arthur Oliver [and] Adrienne Foulke. Godine, 1984. Copyright 1984 by Frank Kermode. All rights reserved. Reprinted by permission of David R. Godine, Publishers, Inc.

Kostelanetz, Richard. From *John Cage*. Edited by Richard Kostelanetz. Praeger Publishers, 1970. © 1968, 1969, 1970 by Richard Kostelanetz. All rights reserved. Reprinted by permission of the author.

Kostelanetz, Richard. From *The Old Poetries and the New*. The University of Michigan Press, 1981. Copyright © by Richard Kostelanetz 1981. All rights reserved. Reprinted by permission of the author.

Leal, Luis. From "History and Myth in the Narrative of Carlos Fuentes," in *Carlos Fuentes: A Critical View*. Edited by Robert Brody and Charles Rossman. University of Texas Press, 1982. Copyright © 1982 by the University of Texas Press. All rights reserved. Reprinted by permission of the publisher and the author.

Lemaitre, Georges. From *Four French Novelists: Marcel Proust, André Gide, Jean Giraudoux, Paul Morand*. Oxford University Press, 1938.

McConnell, Frank. From "Stalking Papa's Ghost: Hemingway's Presence in Contemporary American Writing," in *Ernest Hemingway: New Critical Essays*. Edited by A. Robert Lee. Barnes & Noble, 1983. © 1983 by Vision Press Ltd. All rights reserved. By permission of Barnes & Noble Books, a Division of Littlefield, Adams & Co., Inc.

Literature Criticism Series
Cumulative Author Index

This index lists all author entries in the Gale Literary Criticism Series and includes cross-references to other Gale sources. For the convenience of the reader, references to the *Yearbook* in the *Contemporary Literary Criticism* series include the page number (in parentheses) after the volume number. References in the index are identified as follows:

AITN:	*Authors in the News*, Volumes 1-2
CAAS:	*Contemporary Authors Autobiography Series*, Volumes 1-4
CA:	*Contemporary Authors* (original series), Volumes 1-118
CANR:	*Contemporary Authors New Revision Series*, Volumes 1-18
CAP:	*Contemporary Authors Permanent Series*, Volumes 1-2
CA-R:	*Contemporary Authors* (revised editions), Volumes 1-44
CLC:	*Contemporary Literary Criticism*, Volumes 1-41
CLR:	*Children's Literature Review*, Volumes 1-11
DLB:	*Dictionary of Literary Biography*, Volumes 1-53
DLB-DS:	*Dictionary of Literary Biography Documentary Series*, Volumes 1-4
DLB-Y:	*Dictionary of Literary Biography Yearbook*, Volumes 1980-1985
LC:	*Literature Criticism from 1400 to 1800*, Volumes 1-4
NCLC:	*Nineteenth-Century Literature Criticism*, Volumes 1-13
SAAS:	*Something about the Author Autobiography Series*, Volumes 1-2
SATA:	*Something about the Author*, Volumes 1-44
TCLC:	*Twentieth-Century Literary Criticism*, Volumes 1-22
YABC:	*Yesterday's Authors of Books for Children*, Volumes 1-2

Author Index

Author Index

Author Index

Author Index

Author Index

Author Index

Author Index

Author Index

Author Index

Author Index

Author Index

Author Index

Rimbaud, (Jean Nicolas) Arthur
1854-1891................. NCLC 4

Ritsos, Yannis 1909- .... CLC 6, 13, 31
See also CA 77-80

Rivers, Conrad Kent 1933-1968 ..... CLC 1
See also CA 85-88
See also DLB 41

Robbe-Grillet, Alain
1922-......... CLC 1, 2, 4, 6, 8, 10, 14
See also CA 9-12R

Robbins, Harold 1916- .... CLC 5
See also CA 73-76

Robbins, Thomas Eugene 1936-
See Robbins, Tom
See also CA 81-84

Robbins, Tom 1936- .... CLC 9, 32
See also Robbins, Thomas Eugene
See also DLB-Y 80

Robbins, Trina 1938- .... CLC 21

Roberts, (Sir) Charles G(eorge) D(ouglas)
1860-1943.................. TCLC 8
See also CA 105
See also SATA 29

Roberts, Kate 1891-1985 .... CLC 15
See also CA 107
See also obituary CA 116

Roberts, Keith (John Kingston)
1935-.....................CLC 14
See also CA 25-28R

Robinson, Edwin Arlington
1869-1935................... TCLC 5
See also CA 104

Robinson, Jill 1936-...............CLC 10
See also CA 102

Robinson, Kim Stanley
19??- .... CLC 34 (105)

Robinson, Marilynne 1944- ....CLC 25
See also CA 116

Robinson, Smokey 1940- ....CLC 21

Robinson, William 1940-
See Robinson, Smokey
See also CA 116

Roddenberry, Gene 1921- .... CLC 17

Rodgers, Mary 1931- .... CLC 12
See also CANR 8
See also CA 49-52
See also SATA 8

Rodgers, W(illiam) R(obert)
1909-1969.....................CLC 7
See also CA 85-88
See also DLB 20

Rodriguez, Claudio 1934-..........CLC 10

Roethke, Theodore (Huebner)
1908-1963........ CLC 1, 3, 8, 11, 19
See also CA 81-84
See also DLB 5

Rogers, Sam 1943-
See Shepard, Sam

Rogers, Will(iam Penn Adair)
1879-1935.................. TCLC 8
See also CA 105
See also DLB 11

Rogin, Gilbert 1929-..............CLC 18
See also CANR 15
See also CA 65-68

Rohan, Kōda 1867-1947........ TCLC 22

Rohmer, Eric 1920-...............CLC 16
See also Scherer, Jean-Marie Maurice

Roiphe, Anne (Richardson)
1935-..................... CLC 3, 9
See also CA 89-92
See also DLB-Y 80

**Rolfe, Frederick (William Serafino Austin
Lewis Mary)** 1860-1913..... TCLC 12
See also CA 107
See also DLB 34

Rölvaag, O(le) E(dvart)
1876-1931................ TCLC 17
See also DLB 9

Romains, Jules 1885-1972 ....CLC 7
See also CA 85-88

Romero, José Rubén
1890-1952................ TCLC 14
See also CA 114

Rooke, Leon 1934-....... CLC 25, 34 (250)
See also CA 25-28R

Rosa, João Guimarães
1908-1967....................CLC 23
See also obituary CA 89-92

Rosen, Richard (Dean)
1949-.................. CLC 39 (194)

Rosenberg, Isaac 1890-1918...... TCLC 12
See also CA 107
See also DLB 20

Rosenblatt, Joe 1933- ....CLC 15
See also Rosenblatt, Joseph
See also AITN 2

Rosenblatt, Joseph 1933-
See Rosenblatt, Joe
See also CA 89-92

Rosenthal, M(acha) L(ouis)
1917-.......................CLC 28
See also CANR 4
See also CA 1-4R
See also DLB 5

Ross, (James) Sinclair 1908- ....CLC 13
See also CA 73-76

Rossetti, Christina Georgina
1830-1894................ NCLC 2
See also SATA 20
See also DLB 35

Rossetti, Dante Gabriel
1828-1882.................. NCLC 4
See also DLB 35

Rossetti, Gabriel Charles Dante 1828-1882
See Rossetti, Dante Gabriel

Rossner, Judith (Perelman)
1935-....................CLC 6, 9, 29
See also CANR 18
See also CA 17-20R
See also DLB 6
See also AITN 2

Rostand, Edmond (Eugène Alexis)
1868-1918................... TCLC 6
See also CA 104

Roth, Henry 1906-...........CLC 2, 6, 11
See also CAP 1
See also CA 11-12
See also DLB 28

Roth, Philip (Milton)
1933-......CLC 1, 2, 3, 4, 6, 9, 15, 22,
31
See also CANR 1
See also CA 1-4R
See also DLB 2, 28
See also DLB-Y 82

Rothenberg, Jerome 1931-..........CLC 6
See also CANR 1
See also CA 45-48
See also DLB 5

Roumain, Jacques 1907-1944 .... TCLC 19

Rourke, Constance (Mayfield)
1885-1941.................. TCLC 12
See also CA 107
See also YABC 1

Roussel, Raymond 1877-1933 .... TCLC 20
See also CA 117

Rovit, Earl (Herbert) 1927-.........CLC 7
See also CA 5-8R

Rowson, Susanna Haswell
1762-1824.................. NCLC 5
See also DLB 37

Roy, Gabrielle 1909-1983...... CLC 10, 14
See also CANR 5
See also CA 53-56
See also obituary CA 110

Różewicz, Tadeusz 1921- .... CLC 9, 23
See also CA 108

Ruark, Gibbons 1941-..............CLC 3
See also CANR 14
See also CA 33-36R

Rubens, Bernice 192?- .... CLC 19, 31
See also CA 25-28R
See also DLB 14

Rudkin, (James) David 1936- ......CLC 14
See also CA 89-92
See also DLB 13

Rudnik, Raphael 1933-..............CLC 7
See also CA 29-32R

Ruiz, José Martínez 1874-1967
See Azorín

Rukeyser, Muriel
1913-1980............CLC 6, 10, 15, 27
See also CA 5-8R
See also obituary CA 93-96
See also obituary SATA 22
See also DLB 48

Rule, Jane (Vance) 1931-..........CLC 27
See also CANR 12
See also CA 25-28R

Rulfo, Juan 1918-1986 ....CLC 8
See also CA 85-88
See also obituary CA 118

Runyon, (Alfred) Damon
1880-1946.................. TCLC 10
See also CA 107
See also DLB 11

Rushdie, (Ahmed) Salman
1947-.................... CLC 23, 31
See also CA 108, 111

Rushforth, Peter (Scott) 1945-......CLC 19
See also CA 101

Ruskin, John 1819-1900......... TCLC 20
See also CA 114
See also SATA 24

Author Index

Author Index

Author Index

Author Index

CLC Cumulative Nationality Index

Nationality Index

Nationality Index

Nationality Index

Nationality Index

CLC Cumulative Title Index

Title Index

* * * * **20**:419
‘‘A’’ **1**:385; **2**:487; **4**:599; **11**:581; **18**:558-61
‘‘A la créole’’ **38**:21
Aa Went the Blaydon Races **27**:441, 443
Abaddón, el exterminador **10**:446; **23**:381
See also *Abaddon, the Exterminator*
Abaddon, the Exterminator **23**:381
See also *Abaddón, el exterminador*
‘‘The Abandoned’’ **29**:15, 17-18
‘‘The Abandoned British Cemetery at Balasore, India’’ **33**:284
The Abandoned Men **8**:187
See also *Les hommes abandonnés*
The Abandoned Woman **8**:150
Abba Abba **15**:103-04; **22**:78
L'abbé C **29**:45
The Abbess of Crewe: A Modern Morality Tale **5**:398-400; **8**:493-95; **40**:394-95
Abbey Road **12**:364, 376-77, 380; **35**:278, 281-82, 289-90
‘‘Abbeyforde’’ **8**:164
Abbey's Road **36**:18-19
ABC de Castro Alves **40**:34
The ABC Murders **6**:108; **8**:142; **12**:113-14, 117, 119, 122-23
ABC of Economics **7**:333
ABC of Reading **4**:417
ABC: The Alpha Beth Book **18**:367, 369
ABCD **5**:392
ABCDEFGHIJKLMNOP-QRSTUVWXYZ **36**:126-27
The ABC's of Astronomy **17**:127
The ABC's of Chemistry **17**:128
‘‘The Abduction from the Seraglio’’ **23**:48
Abe Lincoln Grows Up **35**:357
Los abel **11**:363-64
‘‘Abenjacán the Bojari, Dead in His Labyrinth’’ **19**:47
Abenteuer eines Brotbeutels **15**:70; **27**:58

‘‘Abercrombie Station’’ **35**:420
‘‘Aberdarcy: The Chaucer Road’’ **40**:41
Aberration of Starlight **22**:394-96; **40**:385, 391
Abgelegene Gehöfte **15**:204
Abhijan **16**:483
‘‘The Abiding Vision’’ **31**:454
‘‘Abigail Adams: Peper-dulse Seaweed and Fever Talk, 1786’’ **36**:135
‘‘Abiku’’ (Clark) **38**:117, 125, 128-29
‘‘Abiku’’ (Soyinka) **36**:409
‘‘Ablazione de duodeno per ulcera’’ **11**:211
Able Was I Ere I Saw Elba: Selected Poems **13**:286-87
‘‘Abnegation’’ **36**:371
The Abolition **35**:369-70
The Abolition of Man **6**:311; **27**:269
The Abolitionist of Clark Gable Place **7**:516
The Abominable Man **7**:502
See also *Den vedervaerdige mannen fraan saeffle*
‘‘The Abomination’’ **40**:335-36
‘‘The Abortion’’ **27**:448
The Abortion: An Historical Romance, 1966 **3**:86-8; **5**:71; **9**:124; **12**:60-3, 69-70; **34**:314-15, 317, 314-15, 317
‘‘Abortion Cycle Number One’’ **25**:402, 404
‘‘About Atlanta’’ **38**:394
About Centennial: Some Notes on the Novel **5**:289
About Face **32**:176
About Fiction **7**:245, 247; **18**:351
About Harry Towns **5**:126-27
‘‘About Infinity and the Lenesdorf Pools’’ **36**:130
About Looking **19**:40
‘‘About Money’’ **40**:258

‘‘About the House’’ **9**:57
About the House **1**:9; **3**:22, 24, 28; **6**:19
About Three Bricks Shy of a Load: A Highly Irregular Lowdown on the Year the Pittsburgh Steelers Were Super But Missed the Bowl **38**:44-5
About Tilly Beamis **38**:182
‘‘Above Dalton’’ **15**:380
‘‘Above Everything’’ **40**:259
Above Suspicion **27**:278-79; **39**:349-51
Above the Barriers **18**:381-82
See also *Poverkh barierov*
Abra **18**:35
‘‘Abraham and Orpheus’’ **10**:464
‘‘Abraham Darby's Bridge’’ **25**:161
Abraham in the Fire **10**:470
Abraham Lincoln: The Prairie Years **10**:450; **35**:343-44, 350, 357
Abraham Lincoln: The War Years **10**:450; **35**:348-51
Abraham's Knife **3**:192
Abraxas **38**:22, 34
Absalom, Absalom! **3**:149, 153, 155-57; **6**:176-77, 180; **8**:207, 210; **9**:200; **11**:197, 202, 206; **14**:168, 176; **28**:138, 140, 143, 145-46
An Absence **40**:263
Absence of Unicorns, Presence of Lions **15**:380
‘‘Absences’’ (Justice) **19**:234
‘‘Absences’’ (Larkin) **18**:295
Absences **2**:431-32; **25**:429
Absent and Present **2**:221
Absent Friends **5**:35-6; **8**:34; **18**:28; **33**:47-9
Absent in the Spring **12**:114
Absent without Leave **2**:68; **3**:75; **11**:58; **27**:61-2
See also *Entfernung von der Truppe*
‘‘Absentia animi’’ **27**:117
Absolute Beginners **4**:314; **23**:282-87

537

Title Index

Title Index

Title Index

Title Index

Title Index

Title Index

Title Index

Title Index

Title Index

Title Index

Title Index

Title Index

Title Index

Title Index

Title Index

Title Index

Title Index

Title Index

Title Index

Title Index

Title Index

Title Index

Title Index

Title Index

Title Index

Title Index

Title Index

Title Index